Encyclopedia *of* Special Education

FOURTH EDITION

Encyclopedia *of* Special Education

A Reference for the Education of Children, Adolescents, and Adults with Disabilities and Other Exceptional Individuals

FOURTH EDITION

Volume 4: Q–Z

Edited by

Cecil R. Reynolds, Kimberly J. Vannest, and Elaine Fletcher-Janzen

WILEY

Library of Congress Cataloging-in-Publication Data:

Encyclopedia of special education: a reference for the education of children, adolescents, and adults with disabilities and other exceptional individuals / edited by Cecil R. Reynolds, Kimberly J. Vannest, and Elaine Fletcher-Janzen.—Fourth edition.
    pages cm
  Includes bibliographical references.
  ISBN 978-0-470-64216-0 (set); ISBN 978-0-470-94938-2 (v. 1); ISBN 978-0-470-94939-9 (v. 2); ISBN 978-0-470-94940-5 (v. 3); ISBN 978-0-470-94941-2 (v. 4); 978-1-118-62830-0 (ebk.); 978-1-118-62845-4 (ebk.); 978-1-118-66058-4 (ebk.).
  1. Children with disabilities—Education—United States—Encyclopedias. 2. Special education—United States—Encyclopedias. 3. People with disabilities—Education—United States—Encyclopedias. I. Reynolds, Cecil R., 1952– editor of compilation. II. Vannest, Kimberly J., 1967– ; editor of compilation. III. Fletcher-Janzen, Elaine, editor of compilation.
  LC4007.E53 2013
    371.903—dc23   2012048628

Printed in the United States of America

10 9 8 7 6 5 4 3 2 1

ENCYCLOPEDIA OF SPECIAL EDUCATION ENTRIES

EDITORIAL STAFF

Heather Davis
Texas A&M University
Letters A–M

Heather Hatton
Texas A&M University
Letters N–Z

Frank E. Vannest
San Pasqual High School,
Retired
Letters A–Z

Contributing Editors

Heather Peshak George
University of South Florida
Positive Behavior supports

Richard Parker
Texas A&M University
Single Case Research

John Davis
Texas A&M University
Single Case Research

Ben Mason
Juniper Gardens,
University of Kansas
Gifted and Talented

Mary Wagner
Principal Scientist in the
Center for Education and
Human Services
Longitudinal Studies

Stacey Smith
Texas A&M University
Reading

Ron Dumont
Fairleigh Dickinson University
Assessments

John O. Willis
Rivier College
Assessments

Kathleen Viezel
Fairleigh Dickinson University
Assessments

Jamie Zibulsky
Fairleigh Dickinson University
Assessments

Mary Capraro
Texas A&M University
Mathematics

Jennifer Ganz
Texas A&M University
Autism

Dalun Zhang
Texas A&M University
Transition

Mitchell Yell
University of South Carolina
Legal Issues in Special Education

Dave Edyburn
University of Wisconsin
Assistive Technology

Sandra Lewis
Florida State University
Visual Impairments

Pat Scherer
International Center on
Deafness and the Arts
Deaf Education

Amanda Chow
Texas A&M University
Biographies and
   Autobiographies

Lauren Williams
Texas A&M University
Organizations and
   Publications

Rose Mason
Juniper Gardens,
University of Kansas
Intelligence

Nancy Hutchins
Texas A&M University
Behavior

CONTRIBUTORS

Susanne Blough Abbott
Bedford Central School District
Mt. Kisco, New York

Marty Abramson
University of Wisconsin at Stout
Menomonie, Wisconsin

Patricia Ann Abramson
Hudson Public Schools
Hudson, Wisconsin

Salvador Hector Achoa
Texas A&M University
College Station, Texas

William M. Acree
University of Northern Colorado
Greeley, Colorado

Tufan Adiguzel
Bahcesehir Unviersity
Isantbul, Turkey

Theresa T. Aguire
Texas A&M University
College Station, Texas

Patricia A. Alexander
University of Maryland
College Park, Maryland

Vincent C. Alfonso
Fordham University
New York, New York

Nancy Algert
Texas A&M University
College Station, Texas

Bob Algozzine
University of North Carolina
    at Charlotte
Charlotte, North Carolina

Kate Algozzine
University of North Carolina
    at Charlotte
Charlotte, North Carolina

Thomas E. Allen
Gallaudet College
Washington, DC

Marie Almond
The University of Texas of the
    Permian Basin
Odessa, Texas

Anna Pat L. Alpert
Texas A&M University
College Station, Texas

Geri R. Alvis
Memphis State University
Memphis, Tennessee

Daniel G. Amen
University of California
    School of Medicine
Irvine, California

Megan Amidon
Texas State University–
    San Marcos
San Marcos, Texas

C. H. Ammons
*Psychological Reports/
Perceptual and Motor Skills*
Missoula, Montana

Song An
Texas A&M University
College Station, Texas

Carol Anderson
Texas A&M University
College Station, Texas

Cynthia Anderson
University of Oregon
Eugene, Oregon

Kari Anderson
University of North Carolina
    at Wilmington
Wilmington, North Carolina

Peggy L. Anderson
University of New Orleans,
    Lakefront
New Orleans, Louisiana

Candace Andrews
California State University,
    San Bernardino
San Bernardino, California

Karal Anhalt
Texas A&M University
College Station, Texas

Jean Annan
Massey University
New Zealand

Stephanie Anselene
University of North Carolina
    at Wilmington
Wilmington, North Carolina

J. Appelboom-Fondu
UniversitéLibre de Bruxelles
Brussels, Belgium

James M. Applefield
University of North Carolina
    at Wilmington
Wilmington, North Carolina

Pauline F. Applefield
University of North Carolina
    at Wilmington
Wilmington, North Carolina

Kimberly F. Applequist
University of Colorado at Colorado
    Springs
Colorado Springs, Colorado

Anna M. Arena
Academic Therapy Publications
Novato, California

John Arena
Academic Therapy Publications
Novato, California

Martin Argan
University of Wyoming
Laramie, Wyoming

Julie A. Armentrout
University of Colorado at Colorado
    Springs
Colorado Springs, Colorado

Laura Arnstein
State University of New York
Binghamton, New York

Patricia Ann Arramson
Hudson Public Schools
Hudson, Wisconsin

Gustavo Abelardo Arrendondo
Monterrey, Mexico

Bernice Arricale
Hunter College, City University
    of New York
New York, New York

H. Roberta Arrigo
Hunter College, City University
of New York
New York, New York

Alfredo J. Artiles
University of California,
Los Angeles
Los Angeles, California

Maria Arzola
University of Florida
Gainesville, Florida

Michael J. Ash
Texas A&M University
College Station, Texas

Adel E. Ashawal
Ain Shams University
Cairo, Egypt

Michelle S. Athanasiou
University of Northern Colorado
Greeley, Colorado

Shannon Atwater
Branson School Online
Branson, Colorado

William G. Austin
Cape Fear Psychological Services
Wilmington, North Carolina

Anna H. Avant
University of Alabama
Tuscaloosa, Alabama

Dan G. Bachor
University of Victoria
Victoria, British Columbia, Canada

John Baer
Rider University
Lawrenceville, New Jersey

Rebecca Bailey
Texas A&M University
College Station, Texas

Morgan Baker
Texas A&M University
College Station, Texas

Timothy A. Ballard
University of North Carolina
at Wilmington
Wilmington, North Carolina

Melanie Ballatore
University of Texas at Austin
Austin, Texas

Tanya Y. Banda
Texas A&M University Press
College Station, Texas

Monique Banters
Centre d'Etudeet de Reclassement
Brussels, Belgium

Deborah E. Barbour
University of North Carolina
at Wilmington
Wilmington, North Carolina

Russell A. Barkley
University of Massachusetts
Medical Center
Worcester, Massachusetts

Charles P. Barnard
University of Wisconsin at Stout
Menomonie, Wisconsin

David W. Barnett
University of Cincinnati
Cincinnati, Ohio

Ellis I. Barowsky
Hunter College, City University
of New York
New York, New York

Susan B. Barrett
Sheppard Pratt Health System
Towson, Maryland

Amanda L. Barth
The Chicago School of Professional
Psychology
Chicago, IL

Lyle E. Barton
Kent State University
Kent, Ohio

Vicki Bartosik
Stanford University
Stanford, California

Paul Bates
Southern Illinois University
Carbondale, Illinois

Stacey L. Bates
University of Texas at Austin
Austin, Texas

Anne M. Bauer
University of Cincinnati
Cincinnati, Ohio

Elizabeth R. Bauerschmidt
University of North Carolina
at Wilmington
Wilmington, North Carolina

Michael Bauerschmidt
Brunswick Hospital
Wilmington, North Carolina

Emily R. Baxter
University of Colorado
Colorado Springs, Colorado

John R. Beattie
University of North Carolina
at Charlotte
Charlotte, North Carolina

George R. Beauchamp
Cleveland Clinic Foundation
Cleveland, Ohio

Melissa Beckham
The Citadel
Charleston, South Carolina

Pena Bedesem
Kent State University
Kent, Ohio

Ronald A. Beghetto
University of Oregon
Eugene, Oregon

Julie Bell
University of Florida
Gainesville, Florida

Karen Bender
University of Northern Colorado
Greeley, Colorado

Ana Yeraldina Beneke
University of Oklahoma
Norman, Oklahoma

Randy Elliot Bennett
Educational Testing Service
Princeton, New Jersey

Richard A. Berg
West Virginia University
Medical Center
Charleston, West Virginia

John R. Bergan
University of Arizona
Tucson, Arizona

Dianne E. Berkell
C.W. Post Campus, Long Island
University
Greenvale, New York

Gary Berkowitz
Temple University
Philadelphia, Pennsylvania

Shari A. Bevins
Texas A&M University
College Station, Texas

John Bielinski
AGS Publishing
St. Paul, Minnesota

Kristan Biernath
The Hughes Spalding International
Adoption Evaluation Center
Atlanta, Georgia

Erin D. Bigler
Brigham Young University
Provo, Utah

Tia Billy
Texas A&M University
College Station, Texas

Roseann Bisighini
The Salk Institute
La Jolla, California

Kendra J. Bjoraker
University of Northern Colorado
Greeley, Colorado

Jan Blacher
University of California, Riverside
Riverside, California

Jose Blackorby
SRI International
Menlo Park, California

Jamie Bleiweiss
Hunter College, City University
   of New York
New York, New York

Gérard Bless
University of Fribourg
Fribourg, Switzerland

Richard Boada
University of Denver
Denver, Colorado

Margot Boles
Texas A&M University
College Station, Texas

L. Worth Bolton
Cape Fear Substance Abuse
   Center
Wilmington, North Carolina

Andy Bondy
Pyramid Educational Consultants
Newark, Delaware

Gwyneth M. Boodoo
Texas A&M University
College Station, Texas

Nancy Bordier
Hunter College, City University
   of New York
New York, New York

Jeannie Bormans
Center for Developmental Problems
Brussels, Belgium

Morton Botel
University of Pennsylvania
Philadelphia, Pennsylvania

Daniel J. Boudah
Texas A&M University
College Station, Texas

Michael Bourdot
Centre d'Etudeet de Reclassement
Brussels, Belgium

E. Amanda Boutot
Texas State University–San Marcos
San Marcos, Texas

Lisa Bowman-Perrott
Texas A&M University
College Station, Texas

Bruce A. Bracken
University of Memphis
Memphis, Tennessee

Mary Brady
Pennsylvania Special Education
   Assistive Device Center
Elizabethtown, Pennsylvania

Tammy Branan
University of Northern Colorado
Greeley, Colorado

Janet S. Brand
Hunter College, City University
   of New York
New York, New York

Don Braswell
Research Foundation, City
   University of New York
New York, New York

T. Berry Brazelton
Children's Hospital
Boston, Massachusetts

Adam S. Bristol
Yale University
New Haven, Connecticut

Courtney Britt
Texas State University–San Marcos
San Marcos, Texas

Warner H. Britton
Auburn University
Auburn, Alabama

Debra Y. Broadbooks
California School of Professional
   Psychology
San Diego, California

Melanie L. Bromley
California State University,
   San Bernardino
San Bernardino, California

Shannon R. Brooks
University of Minnesota
Minneapolis, Minnesota

Michael G. Brown
Central Wisconsin Center for the
   Developmentally Disabled
Madison, Wisconsin

Robert T. Brown
University of North Carolina
   at Wilmington
Wilmington, North Carolina

Ronald T. Brown
Emory University School of Medicine
Atlanta, Georgia

Tina L. Brown
Memphis State University
Memphis, Tennessee

Robert G. Brubaker
Eastern Kentucky University
Richmond, Kentucky

Catherine O. Bruce
Hunter College, City University
   of New York
New York, New York

Andrew R. Brulle
Wheaton College
Sycamore, Illinois

Virdette L. Brumm
Children's Hospital Los Angeles
Kreck/USC School of Medicine
Los Angeles, California

Laura Kinzie Brutting
University of Wisconsin at Madison
Madison, Wisconsin

Donna M. Bryant
University of North Carolina
   at Chapel Hill
Chapel Hill, North Carolina

Elizabeth A. Bubonic
Texas A&M University
College Station, Texas

Milton Budoff
Research Institute for Educational
   Problems
Cambridge, Massachusetts

Carolyn L. Bullard
Lewis & Clark College
Portland, Oregon

Melissa R. Bunner
Austin Neurological Clinic
Austin, Texas

Thomas R. Burke
Hunter College, City University
   of New York
New York, New York

Leslie Burkholder
Idea Infusion Consulting and
   Contracting
Denver, Colorado

Alois Bürli
Swiss Institute for Special Education
Lucerne, Switzerland

Matthew K. Burns
University of Minnesota
Minneapolis, Minnesota

Jason Burrow-Sanchez
University of Utah
Salt Lake City, Utah

Thomas A. Burton
University of Georgia
Athens, Georgia

Michelle T. Buss
Texas A&M University
College Station, Texas

James Button
United States Department of
Education
Washington, DC

Glenda Byrns
Texas A&M University
College Station, Texas

Catherine M. Caldwell
University of Texas at Austin
Austin, Texas

Siglia Camargo
Texas A&M University
College Station, Texas

Claudia Camarillo-Dievendorf
Pitzer College, Claremont
Claremont, California

Anne Campbell
Purdue University
West Lafayette, Indiana

Frances A. Campbell
University of North Carolina
at Chapel Hill
Chapel Hill, North Carolina

Mary Capraro
Texas A&M University
College Station, Texas

Robert M. Capraro
Texas A&M University
College Station, Texas

Elaine Carlson
Westat, Incorporated
Rockville, Maryland

Steven A. Carlson
Beaverton Schools
Beaverton, Oregon

Douglas Carnine
University of Oregon
Eugene, Oregon

Deborah Birke Caron
St. Lucie County School District
Ft. Pierce, Florida

Janet Carpenter
University of Oklahoma
Norman, Oklahoma

Edward G. Carr
State University of New York
at Stony Brook
Stony Brook, New York

Nicole M. Cassidy
The Chicago School of Professional
Psychology
Chicago, Illinois

Suzanne Carreker
Nehaus
Bellaire, Texas

Jodi M. Cholewicki-Carroll
University of South Carolina
Columbia, South Carolina

Eric Carter
Vanderbilt University
Nashville, Tennessee

Stephanie Caruthers
Texas State University–San Marcos
San Marcos, Texas

Catharina Carvalho
Texas A&M University
College Station, Texas

Tracy Calpin Castle
Eastern Kentucky University
Richmond, Kentucky

John F. Cawley
University of New Orleans
New Orleans, Louisiana

Carla C. de Baca
University of Northern Colorado
Colorado Springs, Colorado

Christine D. C. de Baca
University of Northern Colorado
Greeley, Colorado

Constance Y. Celaya
Irving, Texas

Sandra Chafouleas
University of Connecticut
Storrs, Connecticut

James C. Chalfant
University of Arizona
Tucson, Arizona

Mei-Lin Chang
Emory University
Atlanta, Georgia

Elaine A. Cheesman
University of Colorado at Colorado
Springs
Colorado Springs, Colorado

Nina Cheng
University of Texas at Austin
Austin, Texas

Rebecca Wing-yi Cheng
The University of Hong Kong
Hong Kong, China

Robert A. Chernoff
Harbor—UCLA Medical Center
Los Angeles, California

Chris Cherrington
Lycoming College
Williamsport, Pennsylvania

Karen Elfner Childs
University of South Florida
Tampa, Florida

Robert Chimedza
University of Zimbabwe
Harare, Zimbabwe

Kathleen M. Chinn
New Mexico State University
Las Cruces, New Mexico

Mary M. Chittooran
Saint Louis University
Saint Louis, Missouri

Amanda C. Chow
Texas A&M University
College Station, Texas

Elizabeth Christiansen
University of Utah
Salt Lake City, Utah

Elaine Clark
University of Utah
Salt Lake City, Utah

Gary M. Clark
Kansas State University
Manhattan, Kansas

Deanna Clemens
College Station Independent School
District
College Station, Texas

LeRoy Clinton
Boston University
Boston, Massachusetts

Renato Cocchi
Pesaro, Italy

Cynthia Price Cohen
Child Rights International Research
Institute
New York, New York

Shirley Cohen
Hunter College, City University
of New York
New York, New York

Ginga L. Colcough
University of North Carolina
    at Wilmington
Wilmington, North Carolina

Christine L. Cole
University of Wisconsin at Madison
Madison, Wisconsin

Rhonda Collins
Florida State University
Tallahassee, Florida

Sarah Compton
University of Texas at Austin
Austin, Texas

Jennifer Condon
University of North Carolina
    at Wilmington
Wilmington, North Carolina

Jane Close Conoley
University of Nebraska–Lincoln
Lincoln, Nebraska

Benjamin J. Cook
The Chicago School of Professional
    Psychology
Chicago, Illinois

Bryan Cook
University of Hawaii
Honolulu, Hawaii

Clayton R. Cook
University of California, Riverside
Riverside, California

Krystal T. Cook
Texas A&M University
College Station, Texas

Carey E. Cooper
University of Texas at Austin
Austin, Texas

Mary Corlett
University of Texas at Austin
Austin, Texas

M. Sencer Corlu
Texas A&M University
College Station, Texas

Emily Cornforth
University of Colorado
Colorado Springs, Colorado

Vivian I. Correa
University of Florida
Gainesville, Florida

Barbara Corriveau
Laramie County School District # 1
Cheyenne, Wyoming

Lawrence S. Cote
Pennsylvania State University
University Park, Pennsylvania

Kathleen Cotton
Northwest Regional Educational
    Laboratory
Portland, Oregon

Katherine D. Couturier
Pennsylvania State University
King of Prussia, Pennsylvania

Murray Cox
Southwest Adventist University
Keene, Texas

J. Michael Coxe
University of South Carolina
Columbia, South Carolina

Julia H. Coyne
The Chicago School of Professional
    Psychology
Chicago, Illinois

Anne B. Crabbe
St. Andrews College
Laurinburg, North Carolina

Lindy Crawford
University of Colorado at Colorado
    Springs
Colorado Springs, Colorado

M. Franci Crepeau-Hobson
University of Northern Colorado
Greeley, Colorado

Sergio R. Crisalle
Medical Horizons Unlimited
San Antonio, Texas

Chara Crivelli
Vito de Negrar
Verona, Italy

Jill E. Crowley
Saint Louis University
Saint Louis, Missouri

John Crumlin
University of Colorado at Colorado
    Springs
Colorado Springs, Colorado

Jack A. Cummings
Indiana University
Bloomington, Indiana

Jacqueline Cunningham
University of Texas
Austin, Texas

Susan Curtiss
University of California,
    Los Angeles
Los Angeles, California

Juliette Cutillo
Fountain–Fort Carson School
    District 8
Colorado Springs, Colorado

Rik Carl D'Amato
University of Northern Colorado
Greeley, Colorado

Amy J. Dahlstrom
University of Northern Colorado
Greeley, Colorado

Elizabeth Dane
Hunter College, City University
    of New York
New York, New York

Louis Danielson
American Institutes for Research
Washington, DC

Craig Darch
Auburn University
Auburn, Alabama

Barry Davidson
Ennis, Texas

Andrew S. Davis
University of Northern Colorado
Greeley, Colorado

Barbra L. Davis
University of Texas
Austin, Texas

Heather S. Davis
Texas A&M University
College Station, Texas

Jacqueline E. Davis
Boston University
Boston, Massachusetts

John L. Davis
Purdue University
West Lafayette, Indiana

Trina J. Davis
Texas A&M University
College Station, Texas

Raymond S. Dean
Ball State University
Indiana University School
    of Medicine
Muncie, Indiana

Lori Dekeyzer
University of Utah
Salt Lake City, Utah

Elizabeth Delaune
Texas State University–San Marcos
San Marcos, Texas

Jozi De Leon
New Mexico State University
Las Cruces, New Mexico

Bernadette M. Delgado
University of Nebraska–Lincoln
Lincoln, Nebraska

Kendra De Loach
University of South Carolina
Columbia, South Carolina

Allison G. Dempsey
The University of Health Science
    Center at Houston
Houston, Texas

Jack R. Dempsey
University of Florida
Gainesville, Florida

Randall L. De Pry
Portland State University
Portland, Oregon

Lizanne DeStefano
University of Illinois,
    Urbana-Champaign
Champaign, Illinois

S. De Vriendt
Vrije Universiteit Brussel
Brussels, Belgium

Maria Rae Dewhirst
Illinois PBIS Network
La Grange Park, Illinois

Caroline D'Ippolito
Eastern Pennsylvania Special
    Education Resources
Center King of Prussia, Pennsylvania

Mary D'Ippolito
Montgomery County Intermediate
    Unit
Norristown, Pennsylvania

Roja Dilmore-Rios
California State University,
    San Bernadino
San Bernadino, California

Jeffrey Ditterline
University of Florida
Gainesville, Florida

Marilyn P. Dornbush
Atlanta, Georgia

Amanda Jensen Doss
Texas A&M University
College Station, Texas

Susann Dowling
University of Houston
Houston, Texas

Darrell L. Downs
Mount Sinai Medical Center and
    Miami Heart Institute
Miami, Florida

Jonathan T. Drummond
Princeton University
Princeton, New Jersey

Elizabeth McAdams Ducy
Texas A&M University
College Station, Texas

Sharon Duffy
University of California, Riverside
Riverside, California

Jengjyh Duh
National Taiwan Normal University
Taipei, Taiwan

Ron Dumont
Fairleigh Dickinson University
Teaneck, New Jersey

Glenn Dunlap
University of South Florida
Tampa, Florida

Jamie Duran
Texas A&M University
College Station, Texas

V. Mark Durand
University of South Florida
Saint Petersburg, Florida

Brooke Durbin
Texas A&M University
College Station, Texas

Abbey-Robin Durkin
University of Colorado
Colorado Springs, Colorado

Mary K. Dykes
University of Florida
Gainesville, Florida

Alan Dyson
University of Manchester
Manchester, England

Peg Eagney
School for the Deaf
New York, New York

Theresa Earles-Vollrath
University of Central Missouri
Warrensburg, Missouri

Ronald C. Eaves
Auburn University
Auburn, Alabama

Lucille Eber
Illinois PBIS Network
La Grange Park, Illinois

Lauren K. Eby
The Chicago School of Professional
    Psychology
Chicago, Illinois

Jana Echevarria
California State University,
    Long Beach
Long Beach, California

Danielle Edelston
University of California, Riverside
Riverside, California

Retha M. Edens
Saint Louis University
Saint Louis, Missouri

Heather Edgel
University of Utah
Salt Lake City, Utah

Amita Edran
California State University,
    Long Beach
Long Beach, California

Dave Edyburn
University of Wisconsin–Milwaukee
Milwaukee, Wisconsin

John M. Eells
Souderton Area School District
Souderton, Pennsylvania

Cassie Eiffert
University of Florida
Gainesville, Florida

Stephen N. Elliott
University of Wisconsin at Madison
Madison, Wisconsin

Julie Ellis
University of Florida
Gainesville, Florida

Fara El Zein
Texas State University–San Marcos
San Marcos, Texas

Ingemar Emanuelsson
Goteburg University
Goteburg, Sweden

Petra Engelbrecht
University of Stellenbosch
Stellenbosch, South Africa

Carol Sue Englert
Michigan State University
East Lansing, Michigan

Chaz Esparaza
California State University,
    San Bernardino
San Bernardino, California

Christine A. Espin
University of Minnesota
Minneapolis, Minnesota

Kimberly M. Estep
University of Houston–Clear Lake
Houston, Texas

Carol Anne Evans
University of Utah
Salt Lake City, Utah

Michelle Evans
California State University,
San Bernardino
San Bernardino, California

Rand B. Evans
Texas A&M University
College Station, Texas

Rose Fairbanks
Temecula, California

Sarah Fairbanks
University of Connecticut
Storrs, Connecticut

Katherine Falwell
University of North Carolina
at Wilmington
Wilmington, North Carolina

Jennie L. Farmer
University of South Florida
Tampa, Florida

Judith L. Farmer
New Mexico State University
Las Cruces, New Mexico

Stephen S. Farmer
New Mexico State University
Las Cruces, New Mexico

Peter Farrell
University of Manchester
Manchester, England

MaryAnn C. Farthing
University of North Carolina
at Chapel Hill
Chapel Hill, North Carolina

Sharla Fasko
Rowan County Schools
Morehead, Kentucky

Lisa A. Fasnacht-Hill
Keck/USC School of Medicine
Children's Hospital of Los Angeles
Los Angeles, California

Elizabeth I. Fassig
University of Northern Colorado
Greeley, Colorado

Mary Grace Feely
School for the Deaf
New York, New York

John F. Feldhusen
Purdue University
West Lafayette, Indiana

Laurie L. Ferguson
Wright Institute
Berkeley, California
and The Children's Hospital
Denver, Colorado

John M. Ferron
University of South Florida
Tampa, Florida

Britt-Inger Fex
University of Lund
Lund, Sweden

MaryLynne D. Filaccio
University of Northern Colorado
Greeley, Colorado

Donna Filips
Steger, Illinois

Marni R. Finberg
University of Florida
Gainesville, Florida

Jeffrey Finlayson
The Chicago School of Professional
Psychology
Chicago, Illinois

Krista Finstuen
Texas A&M University
College Station, Texas

Luke W. Fischer
The Chicago School of Professional
Psychology
Chicago, Illinois

Sally L. Flagler
University of Oklahoma
Norman, Oklahoma

Dawn P. Flanagan
St. John's University
Jamaica, New York

Dennis M. Flanagan
Montgomery County Intermediate
Unit
Norristown, Pennsylvania

K. Brigid Flannery
University of Oregon
Eugene, Oregon

Kelly Ann Fletcher
Ohio State University
Columbus, Ohio

David Fletcher-Janzen
Colorado Springs, Colorado

Elaine Fletcher-Janzen
Chicago School of Professional
Psychology
Chicago, Illinois

Wendy L. Flynn
Staffordshire University
Staffordshire, United Kingdom

Cindi Flores
California State University,
San Bernardino
San Bernardino, California

Peter T. Force
International Center for Deafness
and the Arts
Northbrook, Illinois

Stephanie R. Forness
University of Northern Colorado
Greeley, Colorado

Constance J. Fournier
Texas A&M University
College Station, Texas

Rollen C. Fowler
Eugene 4J School District
Eugene, Oregon

Emily Fox
University of Michigan
Ann Arbor, Michigan

Jessica H. Franco
University of Texas at Austin
Austin, Texas

Thomas A. Frank
Pennsylvania State University
University Park, Pennsylvania

Leslie Coyle Franklin
University of Northern Colorado
Greeley, Colorado

Mary M. Frasier
University of Georgia
Athens, Georgia

Brigitte N. Fredrick
Texas A&M University
College Station, Texas

Rachel Freeman
University of Kansas
Lawrence, Kansas

Christine L. French
Texas A&M University
College Station, Texas

Joseph L. French
Pennsylvania State University
University Park, Pennsylvania

Alice G. Friedman
University of Oklahoma Health
Services Center
Norman, Oklahoma

Douglas L. Friedman
Fordham University
Bronx, New York

Douglas Fuchs
Peabody College, Vanderbilt
University
Nashville, Tennessee

Lynn S. Fuchs
Peabody College, Vanderbilt
University
Nashville, Tennessee

Gerald B. Fuller
Central Michigan University
Mt. Pleasant, Michigan

Rosemary Gaffney
Hunter College, City University
of New York
New York, New York

Marie Galan
The Chicago School of Professional
Psychology
Chicago, Illinois

Sherri L. Gallagher
University of Northern Colorado
Greeley, Colorado

Jason Gallant
University of Florida
Gainesville, Florida

Diego Gallegos
Texas A&M University
College Station, Texas

Cynthia A. Gallo
University of Colorado
Colorado Springs, Colorado

Jennifer B. Ganz
Texas A&M University
College Station, Texas

Clarissa I. Garcia
Texas A&M University
College Station, Texas

Shernaz B. Garcia
University of Texas
Austin, Texas

Roman Garcia de Alba
Texas A&M University
College Station, Texas

Katherine Garnett
Hunter College, City University
of New York
New York, New York

Jeff Garrison-Tate
Texas A&M University
College Station, Texas

Carrie George
Texas A&M University
College Station, Texas

Heather Peshak George
University of South Florida
Tampa, Florida

Melissa M. George
Montgomery County Intermediate
Unit
Norristown, Pennsylvania

Phil Bless Gerard
University of Fribourg
Fribourg, Switzerland

Verena Getahun
AGS Publishing
St. Paul, Minnesota

Violeta Gevorgianiene
Vilnius University
Vilnius, Lithuania

Harvey R. Gilbert
Pennsylvania State University
University Park, Pennsylvania

Jennifer M. Gillis
University of California, Irvine
Irvine, California

Theresa M. Gisi
Colorado Neurological Associates, PC
Denver and Colorado Springs,
Colorado

Grazina Gintiliene
Vilnius University
Vilnius, Lithuania

Elizabeth Girshick
Montgomery County Intermediate
Unit
Norristown, Pennsylvania

Joni J. Gleason
University of West Florida
Pensacola, Florida

Sharon L. Glennen
Pennsylvania State University
University Park, Pennsylvania

Dianne Goldsby
Texas A&M University
College Station, Texas

Sam Goldstein
University of Utah
Salt Lake City, Utah

Maricela P. Gonzales
Texas A&M University
College Station, Texas

Rex Gonzales
University of Utah
Salt Lake City, Utah

Rick Gonzales
Texas A&M University
College Station, Texas

Jorge Gonzalez
Texas A&M University
College Station, Texas

Suzanne Gooderham
University of Ottawa
Ottawa, Ontario, Canada

Libby Goodman
Pennsylvania State University
King of Prussia, Pennsylvania

Steve Goodman
Michigan Integrated Behavior and
Learning Support Initiative
Holland, Michigan

Fara D. Goodwyn
Texas A&M University
College Station, Texas

Carole Reiter Gothelf
Hunter College, City University
of New York
New York, New York

Elizabeth Ann Graf
University of Northern Colorado
Greeley, Colorado

Steve Graham
University of Maryland
College Park, Maryland

Shannon A. Grant
Texas A&M University
College Station, Texas

Jeffrey W. Gray
Ball State University
Muncie, Indiana

P. Allen Gray, Jr.
University North Carolina at
Wilmington
Wilmington, North Carolina

Ashley T. Greenan
The Chicago School of Professional
Psychology
Chicago, Illinois

Darielle Greenberg
California School of Professional
Psychology
San Diego, California

Jacques Grégoire
Catholic University of Louvain
Louvain, Belgium

Laurence C. Grimm
University of Illinois
Chicago, Illinois

Lindsay S. Gross
University of Wisconsin
Milwaukee, Wisconsin

Suzanne M. Grundy
California State University,
San Bernardino
San Bernardino, California

Amy R. Guerette
Florida State University
Tallahassee, Florida

Nonna Guerra
Texas A&M University
College Station, Texas

John Guidubaldi
Kent State University
Kent, Ohio

Laura A. Guli
University of Texas at Austin
Austin, Texas

J. C. Guillemard
Dourdan, France

Deborah Guillen
The University of Texas of the
    Permian Basin
Odessa, Texas

Steven Gumerman
Temple University
Philadelphia, Pennsylvania

Thomas Gumpel
The Hebrew University of Jerusalem
Jerusalem, Israel

Rumki Gupta
Indian Statistical Institute
Kolkata, India

Terry B. Gutkin
University of Nebraska–Lincoln
Lincoln, Nebraska

Kathryn L. Guy
University of Texas at Austin
Austin, Texas

Patricia A. Haensly
Texas A&M University
College Station, Texas

George James Hagerty
Stonehill College North
Easton, Massachusetts

Angelroba Hairrell
Texas A&M University
College Station, Texas

Danny B. Hajovsky
University of Kansas
Lawrence, Kansas

Robert Hall
Texas A&M University
College Station, Texas

Winnifred M. Hall
University of West Indies
Kingston, Jamaica

Lindsay Halliday
California State University,
    San Bernardino
San Bernardino, California

Richard E. Halmstad
University of Wisconsin at Stout
Menomonie, Wisconsin

Glennelle Halpin
Auburn University
Auburn, Alabama

Donald D. Hammill
PRO-ED, Incorporated
Austin, Texas

Monika Hannon
University of Northern Colorado
Colorado Springs, Colorado

Harold Hanson
Southern Illinois University
Carbondale, Illinois

Elise Phelps Hanzel
California School of Professional
    Psychology
San Diego, California

Jennifer Hargrave
University of Texas at Austin
Austin, Texas

Jennifer Harman
University of Florida
Gainesville, Florida

Janice Harper
North Carolina Central University
Durham, North Carolina

Gale A. Harr
Maple Heights City Schools
Maple Heights, Ohio

Karen L. Harrell
University of Georgia
Athens, Georgia

Frances T. Harrington
Radford University
Blacksburg, Virginia

Karen R. Harris
University of Maryland
College Park, Maryland

Kathleen Harris
Arizona State University
Tempe, Arizona

Patti L. Harrison
University of Alabama
Tuscaloosa, Alabama

Joshua Harrower
Cal State University
Seaside, California

Beth Harry
University of Miami
Miami, Florida

Stuart N. Hart
University of Victoria
Victoria, British Columbia, Canada

Lawrence C. Hartlage
Evans, Georgia

Patricia Hartlage
Medical College of Georgia
Evans, Georgia

Melissa M. Harvey
University of Colorado
Colorado Springs, Colorado

Dan Hatt
University of Oklahoma
Norman, Oklahoma

Anette Hausotter
Bis Beratungsstelle Fur Die
    Intergration
Germany

Leanne S. Hawken
University of Utah
Salt Lake City, Utah

Krista D. Healy
University of California, Riverside
Riverside, California

Lora Tuesday Heathfield
University of Utah
Salt Lake City, Utah

Kathleen Hebbeler
SRI International
Menlo Park, California

Jeff Heinzen
Indianhead Enterprise
Menomonie, Wisconsin

Floyd Henderson
Texas A&M University
College Station, Texas

Rhonda Hennis
University of North Carolina
    at Wilmington
Wilmington, North Carolina

Latanya Henry
Texas A&M University
College Station, Texas

Arthur Hernandez
Texas A&M University
College Station, Texas

Robyn S. Hess
University of Colorado
Denver, Colorado

E. Valerie Hewitt
Texas A&M University
College Station, Texas

Julia A. Hickman
Bastrop Mental Health Association
Bastrop, Texas

Meme Hieneman
Behavioral Services Program
All Children's Hospital
Tampa, Florida

Craig S. Higgins
Stonehill College
North Easton, Massachusetts

Kellie Higgins
University of Texas at Austin
Austin, Texas

Alan Hilton
Seattle University
Seattle, Washington

Delores J. Hittinger
The University of Texas of the
　Permian Basin
Odessa, Texas

Sarah L. Hoadley
Appalachian State University
Boone, North Carolina

Harold E. Hoff, Jr.
Eastern Pennsylvania Special
　Education Resources Center
King of Prussia, Pennsylvania

Elizabeth Holcomb
*American Journal of Occupational
Therapy*
Bethesda, Maryland

E. Wayne Holden
University of Oklahoma Health
　Sciences Center
Norman, Oklahoma

Andrea Holland
University of Texas at Austin
Austin, Texas

Ivan Z. Holowinsky
Rutgers University
New Brunswick, New Jersey

Kristin T. Holsker
The Chicago School of Professional
　Psychology
Chicago, Illinois

Thomas F. Hopkins
Center for Behavioral Psychotherapy
White Plains, New York

Robert H. Horner
University of Oregon
Eugene, Oregon

Najmeh Hourmanesh
University of Utah
Salt Lake City, Utah

Wayne P. Hresko
Journal of Learning Disabilities
Austin, Texas

Carolyn Hughes
Vanderbilt University
Nashville, Tennessee

Charles A. Hughes
Pennsylvania State University
University Park, Pennsylvania

Jan N. Hughes
Texas A&M University
College Station, Texas

Kay E. Hughes
The Riverside Publishing Company
Itasca, Illinois

Aimee R. Hunter
University of North Carolina
　at Wilmington
Wilmington, North Carolina

Nancy Hutchins
Texas A&M University
College Station, Texas

Nancy L. Hutchinson
Simon Fraser University
Buraby, British Columbia

Beverly J. Irby
Sam Houston State University
Huntsville, Texas

Paul Irvine
Katonah, New York

Cornelia L. Izen
George Mason University
Fairfax, Virginia

Lee Anderson Jackson, Jr.
University of North Carolina
　at Wilmington
Wilmington, North Carolina

Elisabeth Jacobsen
Copenhagen, Denmark

Markku Jahnukainen
University of Helsinki
Helsinki, Finland

Emma Janzen
University of Colorado
Colorado Springs, Colorado

Diane Jarvis
State University of New York
　at Buffalo
Buffalo, New York

Phillip Jenkins
University of Kentucky
Lexington, Kentucky

Helen G. Jenne
Alliant International University
California School of Professional
　Psychology
San Diego, California

Jenise Jensen
University of Utah
Salt Lake City, Utah

Jacqueline Jere
University of Zambia
Lusaka, Zambia

Olga Jerman
University of California, Riverside
Riverside, California

Brian D. Johnson
University of Northern Colorado
Greeley, Colorado

Judy A. Johnson
Goose Creek Consolidated
　Independent School District
Baytown, Texas

Kristine Jolivette
Georgia State University
Atlanta, Georgia

Elizabeth Jones
Texas A&M University
College Station, Texas

Gideon Jones
Florida State University
Tallahassee, Florida

Meredith Jones
Texas A&M University
College Station, Texas

Philip R. Jones
Virginia Polytechnic Institute
　and State University
Blacksburg, Virginia

Shirley A. Jones
Virginia Polytechnic Institute
　and State University
Blacksburg, Virginia

Tarcia Jones
Texas A&M University
College Station, Texas

R. Malatesha Joshi
Texas A&M University
College Station, Texas

Diana Joyce
University of Florida
Gainesville, Florida

Song Ju
Texas A&M University
College Station, Texas

David Kahn
Texas A&M University
College Station, Texas

Araksia Kaladjian
University of California, Riverside
Riverside, California

James W. Kalat
North Carolina State University
Raleigh, North Carolina

Maya Kalyanpur
Towson University
Towson, Maryland

Michele Wilson Kamens
Rider Universtiy
Lawrenceville, New Jersey

Randy W. Kamphaus
Dean, College of Education,
    Georgia State University
Atlanta, Georgia

Harrison Kane
University of Florida
Gainesville, Florida

Stan A. Karcz
University of Wisconsin at Stout
Menomonie, Wisconsin

Dilip Karnik
Children's Hospital of Austin
Austin, Texas

Austin J. Karpola
The Chicago School of Professional
    Psychology
Chicago, Illinois

Maribeth Montgomery Kasik
Governors State University
University Park, Illinois

Allison Katz
Rutgers University
New Brunswick, New Jersey

Jen Katz-Buonincontro
University of Oregon
Eugene, Oregon

Alan S. Kaufman
Yale University School of Medicine
New Haven, Connecticut

James C. Kaufman
California State University,
    San Bernardino
San Bernardino, California

Nancy J. Kaufman
University of Wisconsin at Stevens
    Point
Stevens Point, Wisconsin

Scott Barry Kaufman
Yale University
New Haven, Connecticut

Elizabeth Kaufmann
University of Texas at Austin
Austin, Texas

Kenneth A. Kavale
Regent University
Virginia Beach, Virginia

Hortencia Kayser
New Mexico State University
Las Cruces, New Mexico

Forrest E. Keesbury
Lycoming College
Williamsport, Pennsylvania

Jennifer Keith
University of Northern Colorado
Greeley, Colorado

Kristy K. Kelly
The Chicago School of Professional
    Psychology
Chicago, Illinois

Theresa Kelly
University of Northern Colorado
Greeley, Colorado

Courtney A. Kemp
The Chicago School of Professional
    Psychology
Chicago, Illinois

Barbara Keogh
University of California,
    Los Angeles
Los Angeles, California

Leanne Ketterlin-Gellar
University of Oregon
Eugene, Oregon

Kay E. Ketzenberger
The University of Texas of the
    Permian Basin
Odessa, Texas

Eve Kikas
University of Tartu
Tartu, Estonia

Paula Kilpatrick
University of North Carolina
    at Wilmington
Wilmington, North Carolina

Donald Kincaid
University of South Florida
Tampa, Florida

Peggy Kipping
PRO-ED, Incorporated
Austin, Texas

Gonul Kircaali-Iftar
Anadolu University
Eskişehir, Turkey

Bob Kirchner
University of Northern Colorado
Greeley, Colorado

Donald A. Kirson
Counseling Center, University
    of San Diego
San Diego, California

Margie K. Kitano
New Mexico State University
Las Cruces, New Mexico

Howard M. Knoff
University of South Florida
Tampa, Florida

Tim Knoster
Bloomsburg University
Bloomsburg, Pennsylvania

Brandi Kocian
Texas A&M University
College Station, Texas

Dana R. Konter
University of Wisconsin–Stout
Menomonie, Wisconsin

Peter Kopriva
Fresno Pacific University
Fresno, California

F. J. Koopmans-Van Beinum
Amsterdam, The Netherlands

Mark A. Koorland
Florida State University
Tallahassee, Florida

Peter Kopriva
Fresno Pacific University
Fresno, California

L. Koulischer
Instititut de Morphologie
Pathologique Belgium

Martin Kozloff
University of North Carolina
    at Wilmington
Wilmington, North Carolina

Kathleen S. Krach
Texas A&M University
College Station, Texas

Thomas R. Kratochwill
University of Wisconsin at Madison
Madison, Wisconsin

Bob Krichner
Laramie City School District #1
Cheyenne, Wyoming

James P. Krouse
Clarion University of Pennsylvania
Clarion, Pennsylvania

Louis J. Kruger
Tufts University
Medford, Pennsylvania

Moana Kruschwitz
University of Texas at Austin
Austin, Texas

Miranda Kucera
University of Colorado at Colorado
    Springs
Colorado Springs, Colorado

Loni Kuhn
University of Utah
Salt Lake City, Utah

Alexandra S. Kutz
University of Texas at Austin
Austin, Texas

Paul G. Lacava
Rhode Island College
Providence, Rhode Island

Michael La Conte
District 11 Public Schools
Colorado Springs, Colorado

Timothy D. Lackaye
Hunter College, City University
of New York
New York, New York

Iman Teresa Lahroud
University of Texas at Austin
Austin, Texas

Shui-fong Lam
The University of Hong Kong
Hong Kong, China

C. Sue Lamb
University of North Carolina
at Wilmington
Wilmington, North Carolina

Gordon D. Lamb
Texas A&M University
College Station, Texas

Nadine M. Lambert
University of California, Berkeley
Berkeley, California

Russell Lang
Texas State University–San Marcos
San Marcos, Texas

Louis J. Lanunziata
University of North Carolina
at Wilmington
Wilmington, North Carolina

Rafael Lara-Alecio
Texas A&M University
College Station, Texas

Franco Larocca
The University of Verona
Verona, Italy

Kerry S. Lassiter
The Citadel
Charleston, South Carolina

Jeff Laurent
University of Texas
Austin, Texas

Mark M. Leach
University of Southern Mississippi
Hattiesburg, Mississippi

Samuel LeBaron
University of Texas Health Science
Center
San Antonio, Texas

Yvan Lebrun
School of Medicine
Brussels, Belgium

Jillian N. Lederhouse
Wheaton College
Sycamore, Illinois

Donghyung Lee
Texas A&M University
College Station, Texas

Linda Leeper
New Mexico State University
Las Cruces, New Mexico

Ronald S. Lenkowsky
Hunter College, City University
of New York
New York, New York

Mary Louise Lennon
Educational Testing Service
Princeton, New Jersey

Carmen Léon
Andrés Bello Catholic University
Caracas, Venezuela

Richard Levak
California School of Professional
Psychology
San Diego, California

J. Patrick Leverett
The Citadel
Charleston, South Carolina

Allison Lewis
University of North Carolina
at Wilmington
Wilmington, North Carolina

Lucy Lewis
University of North Carolina
at Wilmington
Wilmington, North Carolina

Sandra Lewis
Florida State University
Tallahassee, Florida

Tim Lewis
University of Missouri
Columbia, Missouri

Collette Leyva
Texas A&M University
College Station, Texas

Elizabeth O. Lichtenberger
The Salk Institute
La Jolla, California

Xiaobao Li
University of Houston
Houston, Texas

Ping Lin
Elmhurst College
Elmhurst, Illinois

Janet A. Lindow
University of Wisconsin at Madison
Madison, Wisconsin

Ken Linfoot
University of Western
Sydney
Sydney, Australia

Daniel D. Lipka
Lincoln Way Special Education
Regional Resources Center
Louisville, Ohio

Brittany Little
The Chigo School of Professional
Psychology
Chicago, IL

Cornelia Lively
University of Illinois,
Urbana-Champaign
Champaign, Illinois

Antolin M. Llorente
Baylor College of Medicine
Houston, Texas

Lisa A. Lockwood
Texas A&M University
College Station, Texas

Jeri Logemann
Northwestern University
Evanston, Illinois

David Lojkovic
George Mason University
Fairfax, Virginia

Charles J. Long
University of Memphis
Memphis, Tennessee

Linda R. Longley
University of North Carolina
at Wilmington
Wilmington, North Carolina

Emilia C. Lopez
Fordham University
New York, New York

Esmerelda Lopez
Texas A&M University
College Station, Texas

Araceli Lopez-Arenas
Texas A&M University
College Station, Texas

Patricia A. Lowe
University of Kansas
Lawrence, Kansas

Michael T. Lucas
California State University,
San Bernardino
San Bernardino, California

Emily L. Lund
Texas A&M University
College Station, Texas

Marsha H. Lupi
Hunter College, City University
   of New York
New York, New York

Ann E. Lupkowski
Texas A&M University
College Station, Texas

Teresa M. Lyle
University of Texas at Austin
Austin, Texas

Patricia S. Lynch
Texas A&M University
College Station, Texas

Loleta Lynch-Gustafson
California State University,
   San Bernardino
San Bernardino, California

Philip E. Lyon
College of St. Rose
Albany, New York

James Lyons
University of California, Riverside
Riverside, California

John W. Maag
University of Nebraska–Lincoln
Lincoln, Nebraska

Charles A. MacArthur
University of Maryland
College Park, Maryland

John MacDonald
Eastern Kentucky University
Richmond, Kentucky

Taddy Maddox
PRO-ED, Incorporated
Austin, Texas

Danielle Madera
University of Florida
Gainesville, Florida

Ghislain Magerotte
Mons State University
Mons, Belgium

Susan Mahanna-Boden
Eastern Kentucky University
Richmond, Kentucky

Charles A. Maher
Rutgers University
New Brunswick, New Jersey

Richard Mahoney
Texas State University–San Marcos
San Marcos, Texas

Kebangsaan Malaysia
Texas A&M University
College Station, Texas

Elba Maldonado-Colon
San Jose State University
San Jose, California

David C. Mann
St. Francis Hospital
Pittsburgh, Pennsylvania

Douglas L. Mann
V. A. Medical Center, Medical
   University of South Carolina
Charleston, South Carolina

Lester Mann
Hunter College, City University
   of New York
New York, New York

Denise E. Maricle
University of Wisconsin–Stout
Menomonie, Wisconsin

Donald S. Marozas
State University of New York
   at Geneseo
Geneseo, New York

Ellen B. Marriott
University of North Carolina
   at Wilmington
Wilmington, North Carolina

James E. Martin
University of Oklahoma
Norman, Oklahoma

Tamara J. Martin
The University of Texas of the
   Permian Basin
Odessa, Texas

Stephanie Martinez
University of South Florida
Tampa, Florida

Benjamin A. Mason
Texas A&M University
College Station, Texas

Patrick Mason
The Hughes Spalding International
   Adoption Evaluation Center
Atlanta, Georgia

Rose Mason
University of Kansas
Lawrence, Kansas

Margo A. Mastropieri
Purdue University
West Lafayette, Indiana

Heidi Mathie
University of Utah
Salt Lake City, Utah

Jill Mathis
Laramie School District #1
Cheyenne, Wyoming

Darin T. Matthews
The Citadel
Charleston, South Carolina

Jon Maxwell
Texas A&M University
College Station, Texas

Deborah C. May
State University of New York
   at Albany
Albany, New York

Joan W. Mayfield
Baylor Pediatric Specialty Services
Dallas, Texas

Liliana Mayo
Centro Ann Sullivan
Lima, Peru

James K. McAfee
Pennsylvania State University
University Park, Pennsylvania

Heidi A. McCallister
University of Texas at Austin
Austin, Texas

Cristina McCarthy
University of Utah
Salt Lake City, Utah

Eileen F. McCarthy
University of Wisconsin at Madison
Madison, Wisconsin

Elizabeth McClellan
Council for Exceptional Children
Reston, Virginia

Dalene M. McCloskey
University of Northern Colorado
Greeley, Colorado

George McCloskey
Philadelphia College of Osteopathic
   Medicine
Philadelphia, Pennsylvania

Laura S. McCorkle
Texas A&M University
College Station, Texas

Linda McCormick
University of Hawaii, Manoa
Honolulu, Hawaii

Ryan E. McDaniel
The Citadel
Charleston, South Carolina

Paul A. McDermott
University of Pennsylvania
Philadelphia, Pennsylvania

Breeda McGrath
The Chicago School of Professional
   Psychology
Chicago, Illinois

Kelly McGraw
The Chicago School of Professional
  Psychology
Chicago, Illinois

Kevin S. McGrew
St. Joseph, Minnesota

Stacy E. McHugh
The Children's Hospital
Denver, Colorado

Kent McIntosh
University of British Columbia
Vancouver, British Columbia,
  Canada

Phillip J. McLaughlin
University of Georgia
Athens, Georgia

James A. McLoughlin
University of Louisville
Louisville, Kentucky

James K. McMee
Pennsylvania State University
King of Prussia, Pennsylvania

Paolo Meazzini
University of Rome
Rome, Italy

Frederic J. Medway
University of South Carolina
Columbia, South Carolina

Brenda Melvin
New Hanover Regional Medical
  Center
Wilmington, North Carolina

Marissa I. Mendoza
Texas A&M University
College Station, Texas

James F. Merritt
University of North Carolina
  at Wilmington
Wilmington, North Carolina

Judith Meyers
San Diego, California

Danielle Michaux
VrijeUniversiteit Brussel
Brussels, Belgium

Jennifer Might
University of North Carolina
  at Wilmington
Wilmington, North Carolina

Stephen E. Miles
Immune Deficiency Foundation
Towson, Maryland

Susie Miles
University of Manchester
Manchester, United Kingdom

James H. Miller
University of New Orleans
New Orleans, Louisiana

Kevin Miller
University of Central Florida
Orlando, Florida

Ted L. Miller
University of Tennessee at
  Chattanooga
Chattanooga, Tennessee

Norris Minick
Center for Psychosocial Studies, The
  Spencer Foundation
Chicago, Illinois

Anjali Misra
State University of New York
Potsdam, New York

Andrew A. Mogaji
University of Lagos
Lagos, Nigeria

Lisa Monda
Florida State University
Tallahassee, Florida

Marcia L. Montague
Texas A&M University
College Station, Texas

Lourdes Montenegro
Andrés Bello Catholic University
Caracas, Venezuela

Judy K. Montgomery
Chapman University
Irvine, California

Linda Montgomery
The University of Texas of the
  Permian Basin
Odessa, Texas

Hadley Moore
University of Massachusetts
Boston, Massachusetts

Melanie Moore
University of North Carolina
  at Wilmington
Wilmington, North Carolina

Luis Benites Morales
Universidad San Martin de Porres
Lima, Peru

Susannah More
University of Texas at Austin
Austin, Texas

Marianela Moreno
Andrés Bello Catholic University
Caracas, Venzuela

Mary E. Morningstar
University of Kansas
Lawrence, Kansas

Richard J. Morris
University of Arizona
Tucson, Arizona

Amy Morrow
University of North Carolina
  at Wilmington
Wilmington, North Carolina

Lonny W. Morrow
Northeast Missouri State University
Kirksville, Missouri

Sue Ann Morrow
EDGE, Incorporated
Bradshaw, Michigan

Elias Mpofu
Pennsylvania State University
Harrisburg, Pennsylvania

Tracy A. Muenz
Alliant International University
San Diego, California

Mary Murray
Journal of Special Education
Ben Salem, Pennsylvania

Gladiola Musabelliu
University of Tirana
Tirana, Albania

Magen M. Mutepfa
Zimbabwe Schools Special Services
  and Special Education
  Department
Zimbabwe

Jack Naglieri
The Ohio State University
Columbus, Ohio

Sigamoney Naicker
Western Cape Educational SI
  Department
South Africa

Michael Nall
Louisville, Kentucky

Nicole Nasewicz
University of Florida
Gainesville, Florida

Robert T. Nash
University of Wisconsin at Oshkosh
Oshkosh, Wisconsin

Bonnie K. Nastasi
Kent State University
Kent, Ohio

Diana L. Nebel
University of Northern Colorado
Greeley, Colorado

Cameron L. Neece
University of California,
  Los Angeles
Los Angeles, California

Leslie C. Neely
Texas A&M University
College Station, Texas

Thomas Neises
California State University,
  San Bernardino
San Bernardino, California

Brett R. Nelson
University of Northern Colorado
Greeley, Colorado

Michael Nelson
University of Kentucky Louisville
Louisville, Kentucky

Joyce E. Ness
Montgomery County Intermediate
  Unit
Norristown, Pennsylvania

Ulrika Nettelbladt
University of Lund
Lund, Sweden

Lori Newcomer
University of Missouri
Columbia, Missouri

Lynn Newman
SRI International
Menlo Park, California

Jennifer Nicholls
Dysart Unified School District
El Mirage, Arizona

Robert C. Nichols
State University of New York
  at Buffalo
Buffalo, New York

Sandra Nite
Texas A&M University
College Station, Texas

Matthew K. Nock
Yale University
New Haven, Connecticut

Nancy L. Nassbaum
Austin Neurological Clinic
Austin, Texas

Etta Lee Nurick
Montgomery County Intermediate
  Unit
Norristown, Pennsylvania

Christopher Oakland
New York, New York

Thomas Oakland
University of Florida
Gainesville, Florida

Festus E. Obiakor
Emporia State University
Nigeria

Hector Salvia Ochoa
Texas A&M University
College Station, Texas

Jessica Oddi
The Chicago School of Professional
  Psychology
Chicago, Illinois

Louise O'Donnell
University of Texas Health Science
  Center
San Antonio, Texas
and University of Texas at Austin
Austin, Texas

Joy O'Grady
University of Memphis
Memphis, Tennessee

Masataka Ohta
Tokyo Gakujei University
Tokyo, Japan

Ed O'Leary
Utah State University
Logan, Utah

Daniel Olympia
University of Utah
Salt Lake City, Utah

John O'Neill
Hunter College, City University
  of New York
New York, New York

Robert O'Neill
University of Utah
Salt Lake City, Utah

Ause Tugba Oner
Texas A&M University
College Station, Texas

Caitlin Onks
Bryan ISD
Bryan, Texas

Alba Ortiz
University of Texas
Austin, Texas

Samuel O. Ortiz
St. John's University
Jamaica, New York

Andrew Oseroff
Florida State University
Tallahassee, Florida

Lawrence J. O'Shea
University of Florida
Gainesville, Florida

Marika Padrik
University of Tartu
Tartu, Estonia

Doris Paez
New Mexico State University
Las Cruces, New Mexico

Ellis B. Page
Duke University
Durham, North Carolina

Kathleen D. Paget
University of South Carolina
Columbia, South Carolina

Douglas J. Palmer
Texas A&M University
College Station, Texas

Hagop S. Pambookian
Elizabeth City, North Carolina

Ernest L. Pancsofar
University of Connecticut
Storrs, Connecticut

Sara Pankaskie
Florida State University
Tallahassee, Florida

Maryann Toni Parrino
Montclair University
Upper Montclair, New Jersey

Linda H. Parrish
Texas A&M University
College Station, Texas

Daniel R. Paulson
University of Wisconsin at Stout
Menomonie, Wisconsin

Nils A. Pearson
PRO-ED, Incorporated
Austin, Texas

Mary Leon Peery
Texas A&M University
College Station, Texas

Kathleen Pelham-Odor
California State University,
  San Bernardino
San Bernardino, California

Shelley L. F. Pelletier
Dysart Unified School District
El Mirage, Arizona

Michelle Perfect
University of Texas at Austin
Austin, Texas

Olivier Périer
Université Libre de Bruxelles Centre
  Comprendreet Parler
Brussels, Belgium

Paula Perrill
University of Northern Colorado
Greeley, Colorado

Joseph D. Perry
Kent State University
Kent, Ohio

Richard G. Peters
Ball State University
Muncie, Indiana

Brooke Pfeiffer
Texas State University–San Marcos
San Marcos, Texas

Faith L. Phillips
University of Oklahoma Health
    Sciences Center
Norman, Oklahoma

Jeffry L. Phillips
University of North Carolina
    at Wilmington
Wilmington, North Carolina

Kathleen M. Phillips
University of California, Riverside
Riverside, California

Lindsey A. Phillips
University of Utah
Salt Lake City, Utah

Yongxin Piao
Beijing Normal University
Beijing, China

Diana Piccolo
Missouri State University
Springfield, Missouri

Sip Jan Pijl
Gion University of Groningen
Groningen, The Netherlands

John J. Pikulski
University of Delaware
Newark, Delaware

Casey Pilgrim
The Chicago School of Professional
    Psychology
Chicago, Illinois

Diana E. Pineda
The Chicago School of Professional
    Psychology
Chicago, Illinois

Sally E. Pisarchick
Cuyahoga Special Education Service
    Center
Maple Heights, Ohio

Anthony J. Plotner
University of South Carolina
Columbia, South Carolina

Cynthia A. Plotts
Southwest Texas State University
San Marcos, Texas

Janiece Pompa
University of Utah
Salt Lake City, Utah

Brenda M. Pope
New Hanover Memorial Hospital
Wilmington, North Carolina

John E. Porcella
Rhinebeck County School
Rhinebeck, New York

James A. Poteet
Ball State University
Muncie, Indiana

Michelle W. Potter
University of California, Riverside
Riverside, California

Shawn Powell
United States Air Force Academy
Colorado Springs, Colorado

Kristiana Powers
California State University,
    San Bernardino
San Bernardino, California

David P. Prasse
University of Wisconsin
Milwaukee, Wisconsin

Jennifer Dawn Pretorius
Vaal University of Technology
South Africa

Marianne Price
Montgomery County Intermediate
    Unit
Norristown, Pennsylvania

Elisabeth A. Prinz
Pennsylvania State University
University Park, Pennsylvania

Philip M. Prinz
Pennsylvania State University
University Park, Pennsylvania

Antonio E. Puente
University of North Carolina
    at Wilmington
Wilmington, North Carolina

Krista L. Puente
University of North Carolina
    at Wilmington
Wilmington, North Carolina

Nuri Puig
University of Oklahoma
Norman, Oklahoma

Adam C. Pullaro
California State University,
    San Bernardino
San Bernardino, CA

Elizabeth P. Pungello
University of North Carolina
    at Chapel Hill
Chapel Hill, North Carolina

Robert F. Putnam
May Institute
Randolph, Massachusetts

Shahid Waheed Qamar
Lahore, Pakistan

Cathy Huaqing Qi
University of New Mexico
Albuquerque, New Mexico

Jennifer M. Raad
University of Kansas
Lawrence, Kansas

Linda Radbill
University of Florida
Gainesville, Florida

Shannon Radcliff-Lee
University of North Carolina
    at Wilmington
Wilmington, North Carolina

William A. Rae
Texas A&M University
College Station, Texas

Paige B. Raetz
Western Michigan University
Kalamazoo, Michigan

Katrina Raia
University of Florida
Gainesville, Florida

Craig T. Ramey
University of North Carolina
    at Chapel Hill
Chapel Hill, North Carolina

Sylvia Z. Ramirez
University of Texas
Austin, Texas

Christine D. Ramos
University of Northern Colorado
Greeley, Colorado

Noe Ramos
Texas A&M University
College Station, Texas

Arlene I. Rattan
Ball State University
Muncie, Indiana

Gurmal Rattan
Indiana University of Pennsylvania
Indiana, Pennsylvania

Nancy Razo
Texas A&M University
College Station, Texas

Anne Reber
Texas A&M University
College Station, Texas

April Regester
University of Missouri
Saint Louis, Missouri

Robert R. Reilley
Texas A&M University
College Station, Texas

Fredricka K. Reisman
Drexel University
Philadelphia, Pennsylvania

Kimberly M. Rennie
Texas A&M University
College Station, Texas

Daniel J. Reschly
Peabody College, Vanderbilt
University
Nashville, Tennessee

Cecil R. Reynolds
Texas A&M University
and Bastrop Mental Health
Associates
College Station, Texas

Robert L. Rhodes
New Mexico State University
Las Cruces, New Mexico

William S. Rholes
Texas A&M University
College Station, Texas

Cynthia A. Riccio
Texas A&M University
College Station, Texas

James R. Ricciuti
United States Office of Management
and Budget
Washington, DC

Teresa K. Rice
Texas A&M University
College Station, Texas

Laura Richards
University of Utah
Salt Lake City, Utah

Paul C. Richardson
Elwyn Institutes
Elwyn, Pennsylvania

Sylvia O. Richardson
University of South Florida
Tampa, Florida

Pamela M. Richman
University of North Carolina
at Wilmington
Wilmington, North Carolina

Bert O. Richmond
University of Georgia
Athens, Georgia

Richard Rider
University of Utah
Salt Lake City, Utah

Michelle Ries
University of Memphis
Memphis, Tennessee

Catherine Hall Rikhye
Hunter College, City University
of New York
New York, New York

T. Chris Riley-Tillman
University of Missouri
Columbia, Missouri

Judy Ripsch
The Chicago School of Professional
Psychology
Chicago, Illinois

Mandi Rispoli
Texas A&M University
College Station, Texas

Selina Rivera-Longoria
Texas A&M University
College Station, Texas

Eric Roberts
Texas A&M University
College Station, Texas

Gary J. Robertson
American Guidance Service Circle
Pines, Minnesota

Kathleen Rodden-Nord
University of Oregon
Eugene, Oregon

Kimberly M. Rodriguez
Texas A&M University
College Station, Texas

Olga L. Rodriguez-Escobar
Texas A&M University
College Station, Texas

Anita M. Roginski
The Chicago School of Professional
Psychology
Chicago, IL

Matthew Roith
University of Colorado
Colorado Springs, Colorado

Dahl A. Rollins
Texas A&M University
College Station, Texas

Cassandra Burns Romine
Texas A&M University
College Station, Texas

Jean A. Rondal
University of Liege
Liege, Belgium

Sheldon Rosenberg
University of Illinois
Chicago, Illinois

Leslie D. Rosenstein
Neuropsychology Clinic, PC
Austin, Texas

Bruce P. Rosenthal
State University of New York
New York, New York

Eve N. Rosenthal
Texas A&M University
College Station, Texas

Rosalinda Rosli
Texas A&M University
College Station, Texas

Michelle Ross
The Chicago School of Professional
Psychology
Chicago, IL

Eric Rossen
University of Florida
Gainesville, Florida

Beth Rous
University of Kentucky Human
Development Institute Lexington,
Kentucky

Amy Loomis Roux
University of Florida
Gainesville, Florida

Kathy L. Ruhl
Pennsylvania State University
University Park, Pennsylvania

Elsa Cantu Ruiz
University of Texas at San Antonio
San Antonio, Texas

Joseph M. Russo
Hunter College, City University
of New York
New York, New York

Robert B. Rutherford, Jr.
Arizona State University
Tempe, Arizona

Kim Ryan-Arredondo
Texas A&M University
College Station, Texas

Daniel J. Rybicki
ForenPsych Services
Agoura Hills, California

Anne Sabatino
Hudson, Wisconsin

David A. Sabatino
West Virginia College of Graduate
Studies
Morgantown, West Virginia

Susan Sage
Dysart Unified School District
El Mirage, Arizona

Monir Saleh
Beheshti University
Tehran, Iran

Lisa J. Sampson
Eastern Kentucky University
Richmond, Kentucky

Alfred Sander
Universitat des Saarlandes
Saarbruecken, Germany

Tiffany D. Sanders
University of Florida
Gainesville, Florida

Polly E. Sanderson
Research Triangle Institute
Research Triangle Park, North
    Carolina

Therese Sandomierski
University of Florida
Tampa, Florida

Derek D. Satre
University of California
San Francisco, California

Scott W. Sautter
Peabody College, Vanderbilt
    University
Nashville, Tennessee

Robert F. Sawicki
Lake Erie Institute of
    Rehabilitation
Lake Erie, Pennsylvania

Nancy K. Scammacca
University of Texas at Austin
Austin, Texas

Walter R. Schamber
University of Northern Colorado
Greeley, Colorado

Patrick J. Schloss
Pennsylvania State University
University Park, Pennsylvania

Ronald V. Schmelzer
Eastern Kentucky University
Richmond, Kentucky

Carol Schmitt
San Diego Unified School District
San Diego, California

Carol S. Schmitt
Eastern Kentucky University
Richmond, Kentucky

Sue A. Schmitt
University of Wisconsin at Stout
Menomonie, Wisconsin

Sarah Schnoebelan
University of Texas at Austin
Austin, Texas

Lyle F. Schoenfeldt
Texas A&M University
College Station, Texas

Jacqueline S. Schon
University of Kansas
Lawrence, Kansas

Eric Schopler
University of North Carolina
    at Chapel Hill
Chapel Hill, North Carolina

Fredrick A. Schrank
Olympia, Washington

Louis Schwartz
Florida State University
Tallahassee, Florida

Adam J. Schwebach
University of Utah
Salt Lake City, Utah

Krista Schwenk
University of Florida
Gainesville, Florida

June Scobee
University of Houston,
    Clear Lake
Houston, Texas

Terrance Scott
University of Louisville
Louisville, Kentucky

Thomas E. Scruggs
Purdue University
West Lafayette, Indiana

Denise M. Sedlak
United Way of Dunn County
Menomonie, Wisconsin

Robert A. Sedlak
University of Wisconsin at Stout
Menomome, Wisconsin

Katherine D. Seelman
University of Pittsburgh
Pittsburgh, Pennsylvania

John D. See
University of Wisconsin at Stout
Menomonie, Wisconsin

Margaret Semrud-Clikeman
University of Texas at Austin
Austin, Texas

Amy Sessoms
University of North Carolina
    at Wilmington
Wilmington, North Carolina

Sandra B. Sexson
Emory University School of Medicine
Atlanta, Georgia

Susan Shandelmier
Eastern Pennsylvania Special
    Education Regional Resources
    Center
King of Prussia, Pennsylvania

Alison Shaner
University of North Carolina
    at Wilmington
Wilmington, North Carolina

Deborah A. Shanley
Medgar Evers College, City
    University of New York
New York, New York

William J. Shaw
University of Oklahoma
Norman, Oklahoma

Patricia Scherer
International Center on Deafness
    and the Arts
Northbrook, Illinois

Kaci Deauquier Sheridan
Texas A&M University
College Station, Texas

Susan M. Sheridan
University of Wisconsin at Madison
Madison, Wisconsin

Vedia Sherman
Austin Neurological Clinic
Austin, Texas

Naoji Shimizu
Tokyo Gakujei University
Tokyo, Japan

Agnes E. Shine
Barry University
Miami Shores, Florida

Erin K. Shinners
The Chicago School of Professional
    Psychology
Chicago, Illinois

Ludmila Shipitsina
Institute of Special Education and
    Psychology
Saint Petersburg, Russia

Edward A. Shirkey
New Mexico State University
Las Cruces, New Mexico

Gerald L. Shook
Behavior Analyst Certification Board
Tallahassee, Florida

Dakum Shown
University of Jos
Jos, Nigeria

Almon Shumba
University of KwaZulu-Natal
South Africa

Lawrence J. Siegel
University of Texas Medical Branch
Galveston, Texas

Jeff Sigafoos
University of Wellington at Victoria
Wellington, New Zealand

Rosanne K. Silberman
Hunter College, City University
of New York
New York, New York

Brandi Simonsen
University of Connecticut
Storrs, Connecticut

Lissen Simonsen
University of North Carolina
at Wilmington
Wilmington, North Carolina

Richard L. Simpson
University of Kansas
Lawrence, Kansas

Paul T. Sindelar
Florida State University
Tallahassee, Florida

Jessica L. Singleton
University of Northern Colorado
Greeley, Colorado

Jaime Slappey
University of North Carolina
at Wilmington
Wilmington, North Carolina

Jerry L. Sloan
Wilmington Psychiatric Associates
Wilmington, North Carolina

Jamie Slowinski
The Chicago School of Professional
Psychology
Chicago, Illinois

Julie E. Smart
Utah State University
Logan, Utah

April M. Smith
Yale University
New Haven, Connecticut

Craig D. Smith
Georgia College
Milledgeville, Georgia

E. S. Smith
University of Dundee
Dundee, Scotland

Maureen A. Smith
Pennsylvania State University
University Park, Pennsylvania

Stacey L. Smith
Texas A&M University
College Station, Texas

Judy Smith-Davis
Counterpoint Communications
Company
Reno, Nevada

Mary Helen Snyder
Devereux Cleo Wallace
Colorado Springs, Colorado

Latha V. Soorya
Binghamton University
The Institute for Child Development
Binghamton, New York

Cesar Merino Soto
University Privada San Juan
Bautista
Lima, Peru

Jane Sparks
University of North Carolina
at Wilmington
Wilmington, North Carolina

Jessica Spata
The Chicago School of Professional
Psychology
Chicago, Illinois

Barbara S. Speer
Shaker Heights City School
District
Shaker Heights, Ohio

Donna Spiker
SRI International
Menlo Park, California

Vicky Y. Spradling
Austin State Hospital
Austin, Texas

Harrison C. Stanton
Las Vegas, Nevada

Shari A. Stanton
Las Vegas, Nevada

Tilly R. Steele
National Center for Leadership in
Visual Impairment
Elkins Park, Pennsylvania

J. Todd Stephens
University of Wisconsin at Madison
Madison, Wisconsin

Bernie Stein
Tel Aviv, Israel

David R. Steinman
Austin Neurological Clinic and
Department of Psychology
University of Texas at Austin
Austin, Texas

Cecelia Steppe-Jones
North Carolina Central University
Durham, North Carolina

Linda J. Stevens
University of Minnesota
Minneapolis, Minnesota

Rachael J. Stevenson
Bedford, Ohio

Mary E. Stinson
University of Alabama
Tuscaloosa, Alabama

Roberta C. Stokes
Texas A&M University
College Station, Texas

Doretha McKnight Stone
University of North Carolina
at Wilmington
Wilmington, North Carolina

Eric A. Storch
University of Florida
Gainesville, Florida

Laura M. Stough
Texas A&M University
College Station, Texas

Michael L. Stowe
Texas A&M University
College Station, Texas

Edythe A. Strand
University of Wisconsin at Madison
Madison, Wisconsin

Elaine Stringer
University of North Carolina
at Wilmington
Wilmington, North Carolina

Dorothy A. Strom
Ball State University Indiana
School of Medicine
Muncie, Indiana

Sheela Stuart
Georgia Washington University
Washington, DC

Sue Stubbs
Save the Children Fund
London, United Kingdom

George Sugai
University of Connecticut
Storrs, Connecticut

Jeremy R. Sullivan
Texas A&M University
College Station, Texas

Kathryn A. Sullivan
Branson School Online
Branson, Colorado

Shelley Suntup
California School of Professional
Psychology
San Diego, California

Emily G. Sutter
University of Houston, Clear Lake
Houston, Texas

Lana Svien-Senne
University of South Dakota
Vermillion, South Dakota

Tricia Swan
University of Colorado
Colorado Springs, Colorado

H. Lee Swanson
University of California, Riverside
Riverside, California

Beth Sweeden
University of Wisconsin
Madison, Wisconsin

David Sweeney
Texas A&M University
College Station, Texas

Mark E. Swerdlik
Illinois State University
Normal, Illinois

Thomas G. Szabo
Western Michigan University
Kalamazoo, Michigan

Henri B. Szliwowski
HôpitalErasme, UniversitéLibre de
    Bruxelles
Brussels, Belgium

Pearl E. Tait
Florida State University
Tallahassee, Florida

Paula Tallal
University of California, San Diego
San Diego, California

Mary K. Tallent
Texas Tech University
Lubbock, Texas

Melody Tankersly
Kent State University
Kent, Ohio

C. Mildred Tashman
College of St. Rose
Albany, New York

James W. Tawney
Pennsylvania State University
University Park, Pennsylvania

Joseph R. Taylor
Fresno Pacific University
Fresno, California

Leslie Taylor
University of South Carolina
Columbia, South Carolina

Therese Tchombe
University of Yaounde
Cameroon

Ellen A. Teelucksingh
University of Minnesota
Minneapolis, Minnesota

Tirussew Teferra
Addis Ababa University
Addis Ababa, Ethiopia

Cathy F. Telzrow
Kent State University
Kent, Ohio

Yolanda Tenorio
California State University,
    San Bernardino
San Bernardino, California

David W. Test
University of North Carolina
    at Charlotte
Charlotte, North Carolina

Coleen Thoma
Virginia Commonwealth University
Richmond, Virginia

Carol Chase Thomas
University of North Carolina
    at Wilmington
Wilmington, North Carolina

Jo Thomason
Council of Administrators of Special
    Education
Fort Valley, Georgia

Bruce Thompson
Texas A&M University
College Station, Texas

Spencer Thompson
The University of Texas of the
    Permian Basin
Odessa, Texas

Sage Thornton
University of California, Riverside
Riverside, California

Eva Tideman
Lund University
Lund, Sweden

Steven R. Timmermans
Mary Free Bed Hospital and
    Rehabilitation Center
Grand Rapids, Michigan

Gerald Tindal
University of Oregon
Eugene, Oregon

Renze M. Tobin
Texas A&M University
College Station, Texas

Anne W. Todd
University of Oregon
Eugene, Oregon

Francine Tomkins
University of Cincinnati
Cincinnati, Ohio

Carol Tomlinson-Keasey
University of California, Riverside
Riverside, California

Rachel M. Toplis
Falcon School District 49
Colorado Springs, Colorado

Keith. J. Topping
University of Dundee
Dundee, Scotland

Raymond Toraille
Public Education
Paris, France

Jose Luis Torres
Texas A&M University
College Station, Texas

Audrey A. Trainor
University of Wisconsin–Madison
Madison, Wisconsin

Stanley O. Trent
University of Virginia
Charlottesville, Virginia

David M. Tucker
Austin Neurological Clinic
and University of Texas at Austin
Austin, Texas

Timothy L. Turco
Louisiana State University
Baton Rouge, Louisiana

Mary Turri
University of British Columbia
Vancouver, British Columbia,
    Canada

Lori E. Unruh
Eastern Kentucky University
Richmond, Kentucky

Susan M. Unruh
University of Kansas
Wichita, Kansas

Marilyn Urquhart
University of South Dakota
Vermillion, South Dakota

Cynthia Vail
Florida State University
Tallahassee, Florida

Greg Valcante
University of Florida
Gainesville, Florida

Hubert B. Vance
East Tennessee State University
Johnson City, Tennessee

Aryan Van Der Leij
Free University
Amsterdam, The Netherlands

Heather S. Vandyke
Falcon School District 49
Colorado Springs, Colorado

Christina E. Van Kraayenoord
The University of Queensland
Brisbane, Australia

K. Sandra Vanta
Cleveland Public Schools
Cleveland, Ohio

Juana Vaquero
Texas A&M University
College Station, Texas

Rebecca Vaurio
Austin Neurological Clinic
and University of Texas
at Austin
Austin, Texas

Kathleen Veizel
Farliegh Dickinson University
Teaneck, New Jersey

Donna Verner
Texas A&M University
College Station, Texas

Don Viglione
California School of Professional
Psychology
San Diego, California

Judith K. Voress
PRO-ED, Incorporated
Austin, Texas

Mary Wagner
SRI International
Menlo Park, California

Emily Wahlen
Hunter College, City University
of New York
New York, New York

Christy M. Walcott
East Carolina University
Greenville, North Carolina

Deborah Klein Walker
Harvard University
Cambridge, Massachusetts

Donna Wallace
The University of Texas of the
Permian Basin
Odessa, Texas

Raoul Wallenberg
International University for Family
and Child
Saint Petersburg, Russia

James E. Walsh
The Chicago School of Professional
Psychology
Chicago, Illinois

Marjorie E. Ward
The Ohio State University
Columbus, Ohio

Nicole R. Warnygora
University of Northern
Colorado
Greeley, Colorado

Sue Allen Warren
Boston University
Boston, Massachusetts

John Wasserman
The Riverside Publishing
Company
Itasca, Illinois

Sharine Webber
Laramie County School
District #1
Cheyenne, Wyoming

Lauren M. Webster
Wake Forest University
Winston-Salem, North Carolina

Danny Wedding
Marshall University
Huntington, Virginia

Paul Wehman
Virginia Commonwealth
University
Richmond, Virginia

Michael Wehmeyer
University of Kansas
Lawrence, Kansas

Frederick F. Weiner
Pennsylvania State University
University Park, Pennsylvania

Marjorie Weintraub
Montgomery County Intermediate
Unit
Norristown, Pennsylvania

Bahr Weiss
University of North Carolina
at Chapel Hill
Chapel Hill, North Carolina

Mark Weist
University of South Carolina
Columbia, South Carolina

Shirley Parker Wells
University of North Carolina
at Wilmington
Wilmington, North Carolina

Louise H. Werth
Florida State University
Tallahassee, Florida

Catherine Wetzburger
Hôpital Erasme, Université Libre de
Bruxelles
Brussels, Belgium

Jessi K. Wheatley
Falcon School District 49
Colorado Springs, Colorado

Larry J. Wheeler
Southwest Texas State University
San Marcos, Texas

Annika White
University of California, Riverside
Riverside, California

Michelle White
University of Florida
Tampa, Florida

Jessica Whitely
University of Ottawa
Ottawa, Ontario, Canada

Susie Whitman
Immune Deficiency Foundation
Odessa, Texas

Thomas M. Whitten
Florida State University
Tallahassee, Florida

J. Lee Wiederholt
PRO-ED, Incorporated
Austin, Texas

Lisa Wildmo
Bryan, Texas

Saul B. Wilen
Medical Horizons Unlimited
San Antonio, Texas

Karen Wiley
Universtiy of Northern Colorado
Colorado Springs, Colorado

Greta N. Wilkening
University of Colorado Health
Sciences Center
Children's Hospital
Denver, Colorado

C. Williams
Falcon School District 49
Colorado Springs, Colorado

L. Williams
Falcon School District 49
Colorado Springs, Colorado

Lauren E. Williams
Texas A&M University
College Station, Texas

Mary Clare Williams
Ramey, Pennsylvania

Meredith Williamson
Texas A&M University
College Station, Texas

Diane J. Willis
University of Oklahoma Health
    Sciences Center
Oklahoma City, Oklahoma

John O. Willis
Rivier College
Nashua, New Hampshire

Melissa T. Willison
The Chicago School of Professional
    Psychology
Chicago, IL

Victor L. Willson
Texas A&M University
College Station, Texas

John D. Wilson
Elwyn Institutes
Elwyn, Pennsylvania

Kimberly D. Wilson
University of Texas
    at Austin
Austin, Texas

Margo E. Wilson
Lexington, Kentucky

Carol Windmill
University of Ottawa
Ottawa, Ontario, Canada

Kelly Winkels
University of Florida
Gainesville, Florida

Anna Winneker
University of South Florida
Tampa, Forida

Britt L. Winter
Western Michigan
    University
Kalamazoo, Michigan

Joseph C. Witt
Louisiana State University
Baton Rouge, Louisiana

Monica E. Wolfe
Texas A&M University
College Station, Texas

Bencie Woll
University of Bristol
Bristol, United Kingdom

Bernice Y. L. Wong
Simon Fraser University
Buraby, British Columbia

Mary M. Wood
University of Georgia
Athens, Georgia

Diane E. Woods
World Rehabilitation Fund
New York, New York

Lee L. Woods
University of Oklahoma
Norman, Oklahoma

Frances F. Worchel
Texas A&M University
College Station, Texas

Patricia Work
University of South Dakota
Vermillion, South Dakota

Eleanor Boyd Wright
University of North Carolina
    at Wilmington
Wilmington, North Carolina

Logan Wright
University of Oklahoma
Norman, Oklahoma

Karen F. Wyche
Hunter College, City University
    of New York
New York, New York

Martha Ellen Wynne
Loyola University, Chicago
Chicago, Illinois

Susan Yarbrough
Florida State University
Tallahassee, Florida

Mitchell Yell
University of South Carolina
Columbia, South Carolina

James E. Yeseldyke
University of Minnesota
Minneapolis, Minnesota

Pui-sze Yeung
The University of Hong Kong
Hong Kong, China

Roland K. Yoshida
Fordham University
New York, New York

Mantak Yuen
The University of Hong Kong
Hong Kong, China

Thomas Zane
Johns Hopkins University
Baltimore, Maryland

Ronald Zellner
Texas A&M University
College Station, Texas

Lonnie K. Zeltzer
University of Texas Health Sciences
    Center
San Antonio, Texas

Paul M. Zeltzer
University of Texas Health Sciences
    Center
San Antonio, Texas

Dulan Zhang
Texas A&M University
College Station, Texas

Xinhua Zheng
University of California, Riverside
Riverside, California

Jamie Zibulsky
Farliegh Dickinson University
Teaneck, New Jersey

Walter A. Zilz
Bloomsburg University
Bloomsburg, Pennsylvania

Elizabeth M. Zorn
The Chicago School of Professional
    Psychology
Chicago, Illinois

Kenneth A. Zych
Walter Reed Army Medical Center
Washington, DC

PREFACE TO THE FOURTH EDITION

Work on the first Encyclopedia of Special Education originated in 1982 and the first edition was published in 1987. In this 4th edition we welcome Editor Dr. Kimberly Vannest to the project team. Since the first edition of nearly 2,000 pages, this current version includes nearly 3,000. This encyclopedia both historically captures the terms, individuals, laws, and societal movements of more than 4 decades of Special Education, it also chronicles the evolution of special education.

We remain well aware of how life, research, and standards have changed for those of us who practice in special education. It is an interesting process to look back and see how the *Encyclopedia* has changed over the years and how it has really provided a mirror of the zeitgeist of the times in which we live and practice.

The first edition was full of new ideas such as profile analysis, direct instruction, and terms such as "trainable" and "educable." The field had license to imagine and try ways to rewire the brain that was having trouble in school. This fourth edition clearly marks the federal and state demands for evidence-based practices in classrooms and methodologically rigorous research, perhaps reflecting the end of imagination and the beginning of an era of proof or accountability. Hence, we see behavioral terms and behavioral-oriented credentials enjoying resurgence because they allow for documentation of behaviors that are easy to observe. Accountability is a force to be noticed as it infiltrates and guides current practice even accountability has evolved from a focus on student activities or opportunities, to student outcomes and performance and now teacher evaluation. It will be fascinating to see where we are in another decade.

The first edition was full of new and somewhat untested laws: We were still trying to interpret Public Law 94-142! Since then, we are in the reauthorization of what has evolved into IDEIA (Individuals with disabilities education Act) as Special Education Law has involved eight presidents over time. And conceptualization of disability for accessing services is under new scrutiny for learning disabilities and expanded definitions for autism to reflect the meteoric rise in prevelance. The advocacy and self-advocacy network that surrounds and includes special education students today is vast, connected, and accessible. The Internet has exponentially changed the individual's abilities to learn about support organizations and to reach out to others who have similar concerns and conditions. This movement is not just on a national level, the World Health Organization is rallying the international community to connect the daily living experiences of individuals with disabilities in the *International Classification of Functioning, Disability, and Health*. This classification system was designed to describe the *individual* with a disability, not just to classify the disability itself. Indeed, we remember that in the first edition of the *Encyclopedia*, it was acceptable to label individuals via the disability; therefore, individuals with Schizophrenia were schizophrenics and individuals with Mental Retardation were the mentally retarded. The disability came first and the individual came second. In the second edition of the *Encyclopedia*, we remember stressing heavily with all of our editors and authors that all language referring to clinical populations would have to reflect the individual first and his or her handicapping condition second. This was a major literary turn at the time! The third edition may best be characterized as disability and ability now living side by side as the 3rd edition marked a time beyond mainstreaming, beyond inclusion but of expectation for a respect of difference, and expectation for accommodation and natural adaptation of the environment or curriculum to meet the needs of people, not of the disabled. Humanness is central and our similarities outweigh our differences, even in special education.

The four editions of the *Encyclopedia* have also reflected the evolution of test construction and interpretation. The level of psychometric design is higher than ever before, providing many benefits to the population such as increased specificity in assessing executive functions, trauma, study skills, and so on. The major broadband assessment batteries that measure cognitive abilities and psychological constructs are excellent, theory-based measures that have imaginative and careful design. Therefore, our ability to include well-designed tools in the assessment process has never been better. The fourth edition of the *Encyclopedia* catalogues many new tests and revisions of old and true instruments.

The demand for "countable" accountability of special education outcomes is upon these days. For the past 20 years, the *Encyclopedia* reflected exploration, and now exploration is passé and counting and demanding results is the zeitgeist of the times. Renegades as we are, we have included more and more neuropsychological principles and terms into the various editions of the *Encyclopedia* as we have paid homage to the vast mystery of the human brain and personality that will most likely never be reduced down to accountable facts. Herein lies the rub for those with interests in brain-behavior relationships, the very thing that we seek is unattainable and therein provides continuous wonder, curiosity, and frustration! We are confident that the most important aspect of future research that seeks to improve the daily lives of children with disabilities lies in the study of the brain and its relationship to learning and daily living skills. This process will always be a study of one, and not given to group statistics. Therefore, regardless of the political zeitgeist, we have expressed our desire to support clinical excellence throughout the third edition of the *Encyclopedia* and minimize old ideas that have been parceled out as new and redesigned to fit ends that are not apolitical. The original *Encyclopedia* was bursting with curiosity and wonder about a new field. We wish to maintain this tribute in the current edition and support the continued innocence of true scientific exploration.

New to the ESE-IV were entries on Positive Behavior Supports. We would like to give many thanks to Heather Peshak George, University of South Florida, as a Contributing Editor and her amazing contribution and coverage of this topic. Areas such as autism were brought up-to-date to reflect the most recent knowledge by Jeni Ganz at Texas A&M University as a Contributing Editor and entries reflecting changes in transition services were updated by Dulan Zhang at Texas A&M University. Last but not least, the Drs. Ron Dumont and John Willis again provided a completely new thread of reviews of standardized assessments throughout the *Encyclopedia*. Joining their expertise in assessment reviews were Drs. Kathleen Viezel and Jamie Zibulsky. We once again are pleased to have them as part of our effort in updating over 100 assessment entries. Without the work of many contributing editors and authors, the Encyclopedia would not have been possible.

Please allow us to apologize to our authors if their affiliations or names have changed over the past 20 years and the most recent changes are not incorporated into the fourth edition. We have tried to keep up with the changes but are sure that we have missed a few and promise to remediate in future editions! We also had to make editorial decisions about giving credit where credit was due for updates of entries. Therefore, the reader will notice that we have taken painstaking efforts to list the authors and to which editions they contributed. Minor edits to update references, change archaic terminology, add web pages or update addresses were completed throughout the volumes. We kept a historical "chronicling of the field" approach in our edits so entries for some entities, journals, educational methods, assessments or instructional strategies were maintained in the Encyclopedia, albeit updated by "this term is no longer in use" or "this organization closed in ..." these types of edits are not attributed to the editors In every instance but we take responsibility for any updates beyond the original contribution of the authors.

There are, as usual, many individuals to thank for assisting with the creating and preparation of this volume of work. First, let us thank the contributing editors to the previous and current editions. These individuals took on the responsibilities of looking at where the field has been and where it is going in their respective areas of expertise. They then shepherded many authors into taking on smaller parts to reflect important aspects of the basics and documenting growth. Without their commitment and dedication, we would be bereft of hope for a renovation of this size of work! We would also like to thank the individual authors for their cheerful attitude and dedication to their contributions: They are representatives of the best the field has to offer and we are very grateful for their efforts.

On a personal note - this edition comes at a time of unique personal challenges for each of us. The types of challenges where an individual may question their role in the greater societal fabric or reorder the time spent on things of value. As the newest member of the Editorial team, KV would like to express her belief that this work is not just work, it is a living contribution and documentation of the countless and untold hours of teachers, parents, students, legislators to improve the educational experiences and outcomes of students with disabilities. For every biography there are thousands who dedicate their lives in service. This encyclopedia represents so much more than the sum of the entries, it represents a commitment of people and our culture to improve the lives of others In a way that makes us unique as living organisms on this planet. This work was and is of great value and I'm privileged to be a part of the project.

Cecil would like to thank Julia, as he does so untiringly, for her support in so many ways, and his long-deceased Dad, who gave him the gift of a model of service. Elaine would like to thank Cecil for the opportunity that he gave her many years ago to be a part of this historical project: Words cannot reflect the depth of appreciation. Elaine would also like to thank Kimberly for taking up the baton and continuing the Encyclopedia of Special Education standard of excellence—it is in the best of hands! Kimberly would like to express deep appreciation for the work of her colleagues Cecil and Elaine, and express enduring thankfulness for her father Frank Vannest, who painstakingly checked references and web links for the 3,000-page manuscript. Thanks also to staff and students Heather Davis, Heather Hatton, Amanda Chow, and Erica Strickland for your excellent work. Finally, a personal thank you to Jack–your cheerful patience shooting baskets while I edited from the bleachers, your piano concerts in the background, and most compelling, learning the Aggie war hymn on the bass. Thank you all for the support.

Lastly, we would like to thank the editors at John Wiley & Sons, Inc., Marquita Flemming, Sherry Wasserman, and Kim Nir. What started as a description of the field of special education became a history of special education and a chronicle of its life and times. We have been honored to witness this process and, as always, look forward to future growth.

Q

Q-SORT

The Q-sort is a technique used to implement Q-methodology, a set of philosophical, psychological, statistical, and psychometric ideas propounded by William Stephenson (1953). The Q-sort was developed as a research tool, in particular a tool for exploring and testing theoretical formulations (e.g., about the existence of different educational philosophies). However, its use has been extended to both clinical assessment and to program evaluation.

The Q-sort is a way of rank-ordering objects. The objects ranked usually take the form of statements written on cards (though real objects, such as works of art, have been subjected to the Q-sort also). The sorter is given a set of cards—usually between 60 and 120—and instructed to distribute them into a fixed number of piles arranged along some continuum (e.g., approval to disapproval). The sorter is required to put a specified number of cards in each pile, resulting in a normal or quasinormal distribution. This distribution permits the use of conventional statistical techniques, including correlation, analysis of variance, and factor analysis, in analyzing the results.

The results of the Q-sort typically are used to draw inferences about people (not the objects they are ranking) for theoretical, clinical, or program evaluation purposes. For example, a preliminary theory about the existence of two opposing educational philosophies can be tested by creating a set of statements reflecting each philosophy, having the combined set sorted on an "approval-disapproval" continuum, and analyzing the results to determine if there are groups of people who rank-order the statements in the same way. In the clinical setting, the patient's sort can be compared with those associated with known pathological syndromes. Finally, in program evaluation, sorts made before and after a program can be compared with one another or with a criterion sort meant to represent the desired outcome of the program.

Q-methodology is not universally accepted in the research community (Kerlinger, 1973). Criticisms of Q are based primarily on the fact that it cannot be used easily with large samples and on its violation of the statistical assumption of independence (i.e., the response to one item should not be affected by the response to any other). However, even with these liabilities, Q is regarded by many as a useful tool for particular research and applied purposes.

REFERENCES

Kerlinger, F. N. (1973). *Foundations of behavioral research* (2nd ed.). New York, NY: Holt, Rinehart, & Winston.

Stephenson, W. (1953). *The study of behavior*. Chicago, IL: University of Chicago Press.

RANDY ELLIOT BENNETT
MARY LOUISE LENNON
Educational Testing Service

See also Factor Analysis; Measurement; Philosophy of Education for Individuals With Disabilities; Research in Special Education

QUADRIPLEGIA

Quadriplegia is often referred to as paralysis from the neck down. Although this definition may be accurate for certain conditions, it is also misleading. A more accurate description of quadriplegia is a nonspecific paralysis or loss of normal function in all four limbs of the body. The condition most often affects motor skills but also may affect sensory awareness. Quadriplegia may result from damage to or dysfunction of the brain (e.g., cerebral palsy, stroke, traumatic head injury), spinal cord (e.g., spinal cord injury, amyotrophic lateral sclerosis), or peripheral structures (e.g., muscular dystrophy, multiple sclerosis). The condition also may occur as a result of tumor, toxic chemicals, congenital abnormalities, or infection. The term sometimes includes quadriparesis, which is considered a weakness or incomplete paralysis of the four extremities. Quadriplegia is not generally associated with the head or neck, but it may involve these structures in some conditions (e.g., cerebral palsy).

The specific skills or functions that are lost or impaired for persons with quadriplegia may vary considerably and depend largely on the individual's primary impairment. For example, a person who experiences quadriplegia as a result of a spinal cord injury experiences a loss of sensation and movement below the level of the injury. When the injury occurs at the level of the third cervical vertebra (C3), the person has essentially no sensation or functional use of the body below the neck. On the other hand, a person with a C5 injury has some active movement available at the elbow (flexion and supination) and shoulder (abduction and external rotation), but most other movements are lost. In the latter stages of the Duchenne's form of muscular dystrophy, a person may be able to use the fingers to write, type, or manipulate other small objects. Because of progressive weakness in the large muscles of the body, people with this type of quadriplegia are unable to move their arms at the shoulder or wrist. Unlike quadriplegia from spinal cord injury, sensation in this type of impairment remains intact. Children with quadriplegia owed to cerebral palsy are almost always able to move the joints in their upper extremities. They usually experience normal tactile sensation, but they may have abnormal kinesthetic sensation. Because of abnormal changes in muscle tone in various groups of muscles, movements are either very rigid and stiff, uncoordinated, or limp and flaccid. Children with quadriplegic cerebral palsy also may experience abnormal muscle tone and movement patterns in their neck or facial muscles in addition to involvement in all four extremities.

The specific treatment, education, or other intervention for persons with quadriplegia also is dependent on the impairment that causes this condition. A team approach using multidisciplinary, transdisciplinary, or interdisciplinary models is essential in the care and management of an individual with quadriplegia. Team members may include physicians, nurses, teachers, physical therapists, occupational therapists, speech pathologists, rehabilitation engineers, family members, attendants, and, as often as possible, the affected individual. Sometimes individuals with quadriplegia need considerable assistance for even the most routine activities (e.g., eating a meal), whereas others are able to live independently, pursue a career, and raise a family.

Although quadriplegia usually results in extensive disability, a variety of electronic and nonelectronic devices may be used to facilitate more normal experiences or abilities. Electrically powered wheelchairs, specially designed passenger vans, adapted eating utensils, augmentative communication systems, and personal hygiene and grooming devices are only a few examples that may be used to compensate for impaired skills. These technologic advances have fostered a more independent lifestyle for many people with quadriplegia, but some advocates for people with disabilities would argue that social changes also are needed to permit the greatest level of independence. Elimination of environmental and attitudinal barriers and affirmative action for employment often are identified as essential components of a productive and satisfying life. References illuminating etiology, definition, and management are cited here for further reading.

REFERENCES

Bobath, B. (1985). *Abnormal postural reflex activity caused by brain lesions* (3rd ed.). Rockville, MD: Aspen Systems.

Bobath, B., & Bobath, K. (1975). *Motor development in the different types of cerebral palsy*. London, England: Heinemann Medical Books.

Ford, J., & Duckworth, B. (1974). *Physical management for the quadriplegic patient*. Philadelphia, PA: Davis.

Miller, B., & Keane, C. (1983). *Encyclopedia and dictionary of medical nursing and allied health* (3rd ed.). Philadelphia, PA: Saunders.

Nagel, D. A. (1975). Traumatic paraplegia and quadriplegia. In E. E. Bleck & D. A. Nagel (Eds.), *Physically handicapped children—A medical atlas for teachers* (pp. 209–214). New York, NY: Grune & Stratton.

Trombly, C. A. (1983). Spinal cord injury. In C. A. Trombly (Ed.), *Occupational therapy for physical dysfunction* (2nd ed., pp. 385–398). Baltimore, MD: Williams & Wilkins.

DANIEL D. LIPKA
*Lincoln Way Special Education
Regional Resources Center*

See also Accessibility of Buildings

QUANTITATIVE NEUROIMAGING

Contemporary neuroimaging began with the introduction of computerized tomography (CT) in the 1970s and magnetic resonance imaging (MRI) in the 1980s. Initially, scans were interpreted solely on a clinical basis by appearance of an abnormality, but now, because of the excellent image resolution and structural detail of gross brain anatomy, any identifiable brain structure can be quantified. For example, Figure 17.1 is an MRI from a child who suffered a severe traumatic brain injury, resulting in hippocampal atrophy. Although the reduction in the hippocampus is obvious on visual inspection, quantitative analysis actually demonstrates that it was less than 35% of normal. Since the hippocampus is a critical structure in short-term-memory processing, knowing about its structural integrity, through quantitative analysis, helps the clinician understand the type and extent of cognitive deficits exhibited by a child like this. Computer programs are now available that permit rapid and automated quantitative analyses of the brain integrated with functional neuroimaging techniques that will likely yield powerful clinical tools in understanding the influences of brain damage and dysfunction in special education (see Kesler et al., 2006).

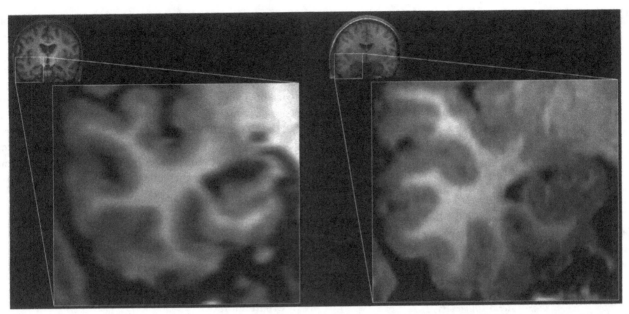

Figure 17.1. A coronal MRI of a 12-year-old child with severe traumatic brain injury is presented on left, with the right temporal area blown-up in the inset, showing severe hippocampal atrophy, as compared to an age-matched control subject on the right. Quantitative analysis indicated the hippocampus to be 2.0 cm in the child with brain injury, whereas the control child had a value consistent with the control mean for this age which is 6.1 cm. Presence of severe hippocampal atrophy is associated with cognitive problems, particularly memory.

REFERENCE

Kesler, S. R., Vohr, B., Schneider, K. C., Katz, K. H., Makuch, R. W., Reiss, A. L., & Ment, L. R. (2006). Increased temporal lobe gyrification in preterm children. *Neuropsychologia, 44,* 445–453.

ERIN D. BIGLER
Brigham Young University

See also **Diffusion Tensor Imaging; Magnetic Resonance Imaging**

QUAY, HERBERT C. (1927–   )

Born in Portland, Maine, Herbert C. Quay received his BS (1951) and MS (1952) in psychology from Florida State University. He later earned his PhD (1958) in clinical psychology from the University of Illinois. During his distinguished career as a teacher and researcher, Quay was chairman of the department of psychology, director of the program in applied sciences, and professor of psychology and pediatrics at the University of Miami. He is currently retired.

Quay questioned the traditional classification system of special education categories, and in 1971 he discovered that the number, rather than type, of behavior symptoms was more effective in identifying psychopathology in a child. This finding acknowledges that most children exhibit most behaviors labeled pathologic at some point in their development without becoming pathological themselves (Werry & Quay, 1971). He also found that an assessor's theory of development and pathology was a factor in how that assessor diagnosed a child (Quay, 1973). That is, if an assessor believed in a theory of process dysfunctions, there would be a different diagnosis than from an assessor who believed in experiential deficits.

His work in the area of psychopathology in children includes the development of the Behavior Problem Checklist, a three-point scale devised using factor analysis to rate traits of problem behaviors in children and adolescents. Quay advocated the checklist to differentiate dimensions of deviance, select treatment programs, and determine systematic differences among children with divergent patterns of deviance (Quay, 1977). Revised procedures for assessment using this tool are delineated in the *Manual for the Revised Behavior Problem Checklist* (Quay & Peterson, 1987).

Since the early 1980s, the vast majority of Quay's work has been in the field of child clinical psychology, including *Handbook of Juvenile Delinquency* (Quay, 1987), part of a Wiley series on personality processes, and *Disruptive Behavior Disorders in Childhood* (Quay & Routh, 1994), a compilation of papers prepared in honor of his retirement (H. C. Quay, personal communication, May 21, 1998). Quay has been recognized in *Who's Who in the World, Who's Who in America, American Men of Science,* and *Leaders in Education.*

REFERENCES

Quay, H. C. (1973). Special education: Assumptions, techniques, and evaluative criteria. *Exceptional Children, 40,* 165–170.

Quay, H. C. (1977). Measuring dimensions of deviant behavior: The Problem Behavior Checklist. *Journal of Abnormal Child Psychology, 5,* 277–287.

Quay, H. C. (1987). *Handbook of juvenile delinquency.* New York, NY: Wiley.

Quay, H. C., & Peterson, D. R. (1987). *Manual for the Revised Behavior Problem Checklist.* Coral Gables, FL: University of Miami.

Quay, H. C., & Routh, D. K. (1994). *Disruptive behavior disorders in childhood.* New York, NY: Plenum Press.

Werry, J. S., & Quay, H. C. (1971). The prevalence of behavior symptoms in younger elementary children. *American Journal of Orthopsychiatry, 41,* 136–143.

E. Valerie Hewitt
Texas A&M University
First edition

Tamara J. Martin
The University of Texas of the Permian Basin
Second edition

QUESTIONNAIRES IN SPECIAL EDUCATION

Questionnaires are often used for gathering research data in special education. They are relatively inexpensive, can assure anonymity, and can be used with relative ease by novice researchers as well as seasoned professionals. Current practice is most typically to use an online form of the survey or questionnaire since online communication or computer-mediated communication is increasingly common. Some example sources include free services such as surveymonkey.com or checkbox.com, sites where participants create their own questionnaire and the system compiles the results automatically. The research on virtual interaction is prolific and likely to continue as social media continues and informal sources of information gathering such as Twitter, Facebook "liking," submitting ratings, and other similar solicitations become expected components of interaction.

In 1979, Pride observed that the mail questionnaire in particular is useful in obtaining data from distant populations. It reaches subjects too busy to be interviewed, enables targeting subgroups of respondents, and is conducive in format to framing responses in a manner suitable for statistical analysis. The mail questionnaire can also "eliminate interviewer bias to questions that are sensitive or embarrassing when posed by an interviewer" (Pride, 1979, p. 59). Even more so, the online survey can reach distinctly targeted as well as inaccessible groups. (Garton, Haythornthwaite, & Wellman, 1999; Wellman, 1997). Online surveys also save time and cost in development, editing or revising, administration, scoring, and data analysis. Online questionnaires also provide a sense of anonymity that mail may not. Sampling issues are not "solved," however, and issues regarding the reliability and validity of online instruments is the subject of much current investigation. Wright (2005) reports on these 20 online companies. He reports costs ranging from free into the thousand dollar-and-up range for licenses and packages.

Active Websurvey
    www.activewebsoftwares.com/activewebsurvey/
Apian Software
    http://www.apian.net/
CreateSurvey
    www.createsurvey.com
EZSurvey
    www.raosoft.com
FormSite
    www.formsite.com
HostedSurvey
    www.hostedsurvey.com
InfoPoll
    www.infopoll.net/
InstantSurvey
    www.netreflector.com
KeySurvey
    www.keysurvey.com
Perseus
    www.perseus.com
PollPro
    www.pollpro.com
Quask
    www.quask.com
Ridgecrest
    www.ridgecrestsurveys.com
SumQuest
    www.sumquest.com/
SuperSurvey
    www.supersurvey.com
SurveyCrafter
    www.surveycrafter.com
SurveyMonkey
    www.surveymonkey.com

SurveySite

    www.surveysite.com

WebSurveyor

    www.websurveyor.com

Zoomerang

    www.zoomerang.com

Popular survey research tools questionnaires (whether online, mailed, completed by telephone, or administered in person) require careful design. The design process includes separate decisions about (a) the kind of information sought (e.g., attitudinal, behavioral), (b) the question structure (e.g., open-ended, close-ended with ordered categories), and (c) the actual choice of words (Dillman, 1978, pp. 79–80). Every investigation presents special requirements and different problems. Oppenheim (1966), Dillman (1978), and Sudman and Bradburn (1982) provide thorough discussions about the many factors to be considered when designing questionnaires and detailed recommendations for writing and presenting questions.

Despite the fact that the mail survey is, in many cases, the most feasible approach for retrieving data from large, widely dispersed samples, many researchers have expressed concern about its methodological rigor and adequacy. This concern is based largely on the grounds of seriously deficient response rates. "The most common flaw is nonresponse of a size or nature which makes the answers nonrepresentative of the total sample and thus the total universe" (Erdos, 1970, p. 142). Returns of less than 40% or 50% are common. Additionally, there are limitations on the nature of data that may be obtained and the quality of responses to many mail questionnaires.

Kanuk and Berenson (1975) confirmed that, despite the proliferation of research studies (well over 200) reporting techniques to reduce nonresponse bias, "there is no strong empirical evidence favoring any techniques other than follow-up and the use of monetary incentives" (p. 451). Research on the topic generally has been narrowly focused, poorly integrated, and contradictory. Erdos (1970) and Dillman (1978) represent the few attempts to improve response rates to mail questionnaires from the perspective of addressing the entire mail survey process.

Dillman's recommendations offer a fully integrated, planned sequence of procedures and techniques that are designed to increase response rates and that are fully adaptable to research problems in special education. His total design method (TDM) attempts to present mail surveys in such a way that respondents develop proprietary attitudes toward the research project in which they are being asked to participate. Based on the tenets of motivational psychology, Dillman has postulated that the process of designing and sending a questionnaire, and getting respondents to complete it in an honest manner and return it, is a special kind of social exchange. His highly prescribed method and related strategies are designed to minimize the costs for responding, maximize the rewards for doing so, and establish trust that those rewards will be delivered. Readily adaptable in its present form, the TDM also provides a useful frame of reference against which the design aspects of each mail survey research problem may be considered.

REFERENCES

Dillman, D. (1978). *Mail and telephone surveys: The total design method.* New York, NY: Wiley.

Erdos, P. L. (1970). *Professional mail surveys.* New York, NY: McGraw-Hill.

Garton, L., Haythornthwaite, C., & Wellman, B. (1999). Studying on-line social networks. In S. Jones (Ed.), *Doing Internet research: Critical issues and methods for examining the net* (pp. 75–105). Thousand Oaks, CA: Sage.

Kanuk, L., & Berenson, C. (1975). Mail survey and response rates: A literature review. *Journal of Marketing Research, 12,* 440–453.

Oppenheim, A. N. (1966). *Questionnaire design and attitudes measurement.* New York, NY: Basic Books.

Pride, C. (1979). Building response to a mail survey. *New Directions for Institutional Advancement, 6,* 59–69.

Sudman, S., & Bradburn, N. M. (1982). *Asking questions.* San Francisco, CA: Jossey-Bass.

Wellman, B. (1997). An electronic group is virtually a social network. In S. Kiesler (Ed.), *Culture of the Internet* (pp. 179–205). Mahwah, NJ: Erlbaum.

Wellman, B., & Haythornthwaite, C. (Eds.) (2002). *The Internet in everyday life.* Oxford, UK: Blackwell.

Wright, K. B. (2005). Researching Internet-based populations: Advantages and disadvantages of online survey research, online questionnaire authoring software packages, and web survey services. *Journal of Computer-Mediated Communication, 10*(3), article 11. http://jcmc.indiana.edu/vol10/issue3/wright.html

Lawrence S. Cote
Pennsylvania State University

Kimberly Vannest
Texas A&M University

See *also* Research in Special Education

QUIGLEY, STEPHEN P. (1927–　)

Born in Belfast, Northern Ireland, Stephen P. Quigley obtained his BA in 1953 in psychology from the University of Denver. He went on to earn both his MA in 1954 in speech and hearing disorders and PhD in 1957 in speech science and psychology at the University of Illinois. Prior to his retirement, Quigley was professor of education, speech, and hearing at the University of Illinois, Urbana–Champaign.

Quigley is best known for his work in the area of communication, language, and the improvement of education for children with hearing impairments (McAnally, Rose, & Quigley, 1999; Paul & Quigley, 1994; Quigley, 1992). His investigations of Noam Chomsky's theory that careful manipulation of stimulus-response could produce more effective insights into language acquisition led to his development of the Test of Syntactical Abilities (Quigley, Steinkamp, Power, & Jones, 1978), a standardized test for the diagnosis and assessment of the syntactical abilities of deaf children.

Quigley has noted the absence of a well-developed first language for deaf children entering school and the manner in which this deficit prevents the examination of language development. He has, thus, conducted important research on the instructional use of American Sign Language and English (Quigley & Paul, 1984a, 1984b). Findings of these investigations suggest the benefits of teaching children with deafness American Sign Language and, as a second language, providing instruction in English.

In addition to his work involving language development, Quigley advocates reading materials for deaf children that recognize their needs while avoiding overspecialization (Quigley, 1982). Among his numerous publications, he has written several books on the topic of reading, including *Reading Practices With Deaf Learners* (McAnally et al., 1999) and *Reading Milestones* (Quigley, 1992).

REFERENCES

McAnally, P. L., Rose, S., & Quigley, S. P. (1999). *Reading practices with deaf learners*. Austin, TX: PRO-ED.

Paul, P. V., & Quigley, S. P. (1994). *Language and deafness*. San Diego, CA: Singular.

Quigley, S. P. (1982). Reading achievement and special reading materials. *Volta Review, 84*(5), 95–106.

Quigley, S. P. (1992). *Reading milestones. Level 6. The orange books*. Beaverton, OR: Dormac.

Quigley, S. P., & Paul, P. V. (1984a). ASL and ESL? *Topics in Early Childhood Education, 3*(4), 17–26.

Quigley, S. P., & Paul, P. V. (1984b). *Language and deafness*. San Diego, CA: College Hill.

Quigley, S. P., Steinkamp, M., Power, D., & Jones, B. (1978). *Test of Syntactical Abilities*. Beaverton, OR: Dormac.

E. Valerie Hewitt
Texas A&M University
First edition

Tamara J. Martin
The University of Texas of the Permian Basin
Second edition

R

RACIAL BIAS IN TESTING (*See Cultural Bias in Testing*)

RACIAL DISCRIMINATION IN SPECIAL EDUCATION

The right to education, nondiscriminatory treatment, equal protection, and due process protection for all children with disabilities was first established by Congress with the Education Amendments of 1974 and the Education for All Handicapped Children Act of 1975 (PL 94-142) and continued in the more recent Individuals with Disabilities Education Act (IDEA). Prior to this national policy, more than 36 court cases throughout the country brought convincing documentation that racially and culturally discriminatory practices existed in special education. Racially and culturally diverse school children continue to be disproportionately represented in special education programs while local and state education officials attempt to improve testing and classification procedures.

Racially and culturally biased identification and placement procedures in special education were initially disputed in *Hobson v. Hansen* (1967). Judge J. Skelly Wright found that the ability-grouping track system in the public schools of the District of Columbia deprived African American disadvantaged students and students with disabilities of "their right to equal educational opportunity with white and more affluent public school children" (p. 401). Relying on factual findings of discrimination, the court ordered the track system abolished in 1969. Subsequently, seven African American children with disabilities labeled as either behavior problems, intellectually disabled, emotionally disturbed, or hyperactive sued the District of Columbia Public Schools for failing to provide them with special education while providing such education to other children (*Mills v. Board of Education, District of Columbia*, 1972). Holding "that Constitutional rights must be afforded citizens despite the greater expense involved" (p. 876), the court's decree established (1) standards and procedures for an "appropriate educational program," (2) a required "comprehensive plan" for identification and notification of students with disabilities and their parents, and (3) in the absence of an "alternative program of education, placement in a regular public school class with appropriate ancillary services [, which] is preferable to placement in a special class" (p. 880).

In California, nine Mexican American students in *Diana v. State Board of Education* (1970) and six African American students in *Larry P. v. Riles* (1972) alleged that they were being misplaced in special classes for the educable intellectually disabled on the basis of inappropriate tests and testing procedures that ignored their cultural and racial learning experiences. Both cases were brought to the Northern California Federal District Court and documented the statistically significant overrepresentation statewide of minorities in special education. *Diana*'s stipulated settlement agreement (1973) established testing procedures in the student's primary language, retesting of Mexican American and Chinese American students currently in classes for the intellectually disabled, and a mandate for a state-developed and appropriate standardized intelligence test.

Judge Peckham in *Larry P.* cited California's historical racial discriminatory use of intelligence quotient (IQ) tests against African Americans and issued a preliminary injunction in 1972 against the San Francisco Unified School District. The injunction prevented the use of intelligence tests for placement purposes and ordered the elimination of the disproportionate placement of African American children in special classes for the educable intellectually disabled. Similarly, a statewide order by the court on December 13, 1974, and a state-imposed moratorium in January 1975 stopped all IQ testing of the educable intellectually disabled for the purposes of placement (1979, p. 931, n.4). The decision was affirmed in 1984.

Mattie T. v. Holladay was a class action suit filed in 1975 on behalf of 26 students with disabilities from seven local school districts in Mississippi against state and local school officials. The suit challenged the policies and practices in special education. The plaintiffs in *Mattie T.* claimed that the schools used racially and culturally discriminatory procedures in the identification, evaluation, and education placement of children with disabilities. Evidence showed that 3 times as many African American children as Anglo-American children were placed in classes for students with intellectual disabilities, and, conversely, twice as many Anglo-American children as African American children were placed in higher-cost and more integrated specific learning disability classes. The court ordered in a consent decree on January 26,

1979, requiring the state to substantially reduce the racial disparity by 1982 by establishing new identification practices and monitoring and enforcement procedures.

Lora v. *Board of Education of the City of New York* was filed in June 1975 on behalf of all African American and Hispanic students assigned to special day schools for the emotionally disturbed in New York City. Citing statistically significant disparities between minorities and Anglo-American students with the same problems, the plaintiffs alleged discriminatory testing and claimed that "the special day schools are intentionally segregated dumping grounds for minorities forced into inadequate facilities without due process" (1978, p. 1214). Following lengthy proceedings, appeals, and recommendations of a national "Lora Advisory Panel," a conciliatory agreement produced nondiscriminatory standards and procedures in 1984.

REFERENCES

Diana v. Board of Education, No. C-70-37 RFP (N.D. Cal. Jan. 7, 1970, June 18, 1973, and Order of May 27, 1974).

Hobson v. Hansen, 269 F. Supp. 401 (D.D.C. 1967), Smuck v. Hobson, 408 F.2d. 175 (D.C. Cir. 1969).

Larry P. v. Riles, 343 F. Supp. 1306 (N.D. Cal. 1972), 502 F.2d. 963 (9th Cir. 1974), 495 F. Supp. 926 (N.D. Cal. 1979), aff'd. 9th Cir., Jan. 23, 1984 (EHLR 555:304, Feb. 3, 1984).

Lora v. Board of Educ. of City of New York, 456 F. Supp. 1211 (E.D.N.Y. 1978), 623 F.2d. 248 (2d Cir. 1980), 587 F. Supp. 1572 (E.D.N.Y. 1984).

Mattie T. v. Holladay, 522 F. Supp. 72 (N.D. Mississippi, 1981).

Mills v. Board of Education of District of Columbia, 348 F. Supp. 866 (D.D.C. 1972).

LOUIS SCHWARTZ
Florida State University
First and Second editions

KIMBERLY APPLEQUIST
University of Colorado at Colorado Springs
Third edition

See also **Diana v. Board of Education; Individuals With Disabilities Education Improvement Act of 2004 (IDEIA); Larry P.; Special Education, Legal Regulations of; Mattie T. v. Holladay; Mills v. Board of Education; PASE v. Hannon**

RAPP-HODGKIN SYNDROME

Rapp-Hodgkin syndrome (RHS) belongs to a group of genetic disorders known as ectodermal dysplasia syndromes. In general, ectodermal dysplasia syndromes are caused by defects in the formation of the ectoderm (the outermost layer of embryonic tissue) during gestation. Ectodermal dysplasia syndromes are multisystem disorders that are characterized by the deficient function or absence of at least two of the following ectodermal structures: skin, teeth, hair, nails, and glands (National Foundation for Ectodermal Dysplasias [NFED], 2001). More than 200 clinically or genetically distinct forms of ectodermal dysplasia have been identified, with classification based on the following considerations: extent, nature, and severity of ectodermal involvement; the presence of associated malformations; and the mode of inheritance (Walpole & Goldblatt, 1991).

Although ectodermal dysplasia syndromes occur in approximately 7 in 10,000 births (NFED, 2001), Rapp-Hodgkin syndrome is an extremely rare condition. Only a few dozen cases have been reported in the medical literature and have included both familial and sporadic cases (National Organization for Rare Disorders [NORD], 1999). Rapp-Hodgkin syndrome, which affects males and females in equal numbers, is inherited as an autosomal dominant genetic trait (NORD, 1999). Features of the disorder may be present at birth in some cases but may not manifest until late infancy in others. The symptoms and physical features of Rapp-Hodgkin syndrome vary widely from case to case (NORD, 1999).

Characteristics

1. Reduced number of sweat glands, pores of the skin, or both, which results in impaired ability (hypohidrosis) or inability (anhidrosis) to sweat. Increased body temperatures (hyperthermia) and heat intolerance may be noted.

2. Cleft palate (incomplete closure of the roof of mouth), cleft lip (abnormal groove in upper lip), or both.

3. Missing or malformed teeth. Teeth may be abnormally small and may have underdeveloped enamel.

4. Abnormally sparse, coarse, and wiry scalp hair in children, with premature hair loss frequently occurring during adulthood.

5. Slow-growing and poorly developed nails on fingers and toes.

6. Other common facial features include abnormally high forehead; narrow nose; high, arched palate; small mouth; and underdeveloped upper jawbone.

Rapp-Hodgkin syndrome has no cure. Treatment is directed toward specific symptoms and is therefore highly individualized. A comprehensive treatment plan requires multidisciplinary coordination across medical specialties (e.g., craniofacial surgeons, dermatologists, dentists). Reconstructive surgery may be warranted to repair cleft palate and cleft lip. Oral surgery, corrective devices, or dentures may be required to provide adequate dentition. During episodes of extended exercise and during summer months (or other periods of high temperatures), monitoring of body temperature is required to avoid hyperthermia.

Intellectual and psychomotor development are typically within normal limits in children with Rapp-Hodgkin syndrome. Special education placement for speech therapy may be required if speech difficulties associated with cleft palate are noted. If the child is susceptible to heat intolerance, air conditioning in the school environment may be necessary, and participation in physical education classes will need to be closely monitored.

Prognosis for children with Rapp-Hodgkin syndrome is good in that general health and life span are within normal expectations (NFED Scientific Advisory Board, 2001). Because Rapp-Hodgkin syndrome is rare, current research is limited primarily to case-study analysis, which serves to document the variability in the clinical expression of this disorder and helps to establish the natural history of the disease.

REFERENCES

National Foundation for Dysplasias. (2001). *What are ectodermal dysplasias?* Retrieved from http://nfed.org/index.php/about_ed/about-ectodermal-dysplasias

National Foundation for Ectodermal Dysplasias Scientific Advisory Board. (2001). *Rapp-Hodgkin syndrome.* Retrieved from http://nfed.org/

National Organization for Rare Disorders. (1999). *Rapp-Hodgkin syndrome.* Retrieved from http://www.rarediseases.org/rare-disease-information/rare-diseases/viewIndex?tab=R

Walpole, I. R., & Goldblatt, J. (1991). Rapp-Hodgkin hypohidrotic ectodermal dysplasia syndrome. *Clinical Genetics, 39,* 14–120.

HEIDI A. MCCALLISTER
University of Texas at Austin

RARE DISEASES (See National Organization of Rare Diseases)

RASE (See Remedial and Special Education)

RASMUSSEN ENCEPHALITIS

Rasmussen encephalitis is a relatively rare disorder defined by chronic inflammation of the brain (unilateral cerebral pathology) that results in progressive deterioration of function in one hemisphere, often followed by gradual partial recovery of function associated with reorganization. Etiology is generally unknown with no indications of viral pathogenesis (e.g., cytomegalovirus) or genetic determination. Rasmussen encephalitis is generally identified following the onset of intractable seizures (Geller et al., 1998; Topçu et al., 1999), but it may not be diagnosed until surgery to address seizure frequency. Actual prevalence of the disorder is unknown.

Characteristics

1. Intractable epilepsy
2. Progressive hemiparesis
3. Progressive cognitive decline
4. Progressive decline of motor abilities on one side of body
5. Difficulty with problem solving in social situations
6. Precocious puberty
7. Impaired academic performance
8. Lack of behavioral inhibition

Source: Caplan, Curtiss, Chugani, & Vinters (1996); Topçu et al. (1999).

Although Rasmussen encephalitis is usually identified in children, cases have been reported in adolescence and adulthood (McLachlan, Girvin, Blume, & Reichman, 1993). With later onset, there appears to be less of an impact on overall cognitive ability. However, later onset has been associated with increased motor and sensory impairment (McLachlan et al., 1993).

Treatment usually involves resective surgery with electrocorticography. Following surgery, prognosis for seizure control is fairly good (Caplan et al., 1996; McLachlan et al., 1993; Topçu et al., 1999). Improvements have been reported in social relations and language in some individuals as well (Caplan et al., 1996). Alternative treatment involves the use of immunoactive drugs (Geller et al., 1998; Topçu et al., 1999).

Due to the presence of both behavioral and academic concerns, children with Rasmussen encephalitis will be eligible for special education services and will require interventions that address multiple areas. Because of the lack of inhibition and precocious puberty associated with progressive deterioration of the frontal cortex, the priorities for intervention (i.e., behavioral control) might suggest identification as severely emotionally disturbed (SED); however, given the underlying cause of the behavioral problems as well as the accompanying cognitive and motor impairments, identification as other health impaired would be most appropriate. The individual educational plan for a child with Rasmussen encephalitis should include goals specific to academic and functional skills, social skills, and increased behavioral control regardless of categorization or placement.

Because of the rarity of the disorder, long-term prognosis in children with Rasmussen chronic encephalitis has not been studied extensively. Multisite studies that control for the extent and location of resection, that control for neuropsychological status prior to and immediately following surgery, and that use long-term follow-up are needed.

REFERENCES

Caplan, R., Curtiss, S., Chugani, H. T., & Vinters, H. V. (1996). Pediatric Rasmussen encephalitis: Social communication, language, PET, and pathology before and after hemispherectomy. *Brain & Cognition, 32,* 45–66.

Geller, E., Faerber, E. N., Legido, A., Melvin, J. J., Hunter, J. V., Wang, Z., & de Chadarevian, J. P. (1998). Rasmussen encephalitis: Complementary role of multitechnique neuroimaging. *American Journal of Neuroradiology, 19,* 445–449.

McLachlan, R. S., Girvin, J. P., Blume, W. T., & Reichman, H. (1993). Rasmussen's chronic encephalitis in adults. *Archives of Neurology, 50,* 269–274.

Topçu, M., Turanli, G., Aynaci, F. M., Yalnizoglu, D., Saatci, I., Yigit, A., & Akalin, N. (1999). Rasmussen encephalitis in childhood. *Child's Nervous System, 15,* 395–402, 403.

CYNTHIA A. RICCIO
Texas A&M University

RATIO IQ

A ratio intelligence quotient or ratio IQ is a score from a test of intelligence (or cognitive or mental ability). Now obsolete as a statistical term, it is still a useful concept for interpreting current levels of mental functioning and, to a limited extent, for predicting future mental development. The ratio IQ has been replaced by most authors of mental ability tests with a standard score such as a deviation IQ.

At the turn of the 20th century, and for the next several decades, tests of mental ability were administered to children of several different chronological ages. The average number of items answered correctly at each age level was recorded. Then the number of items answered correctly by a given child could be compared with the average performance of children of various ages. Such scores were known as a mental age (MA) or age equivalent (AE). Such scores made it possible to say that a particular child of a given age performed on the test as a typical 4-year-old, or another as a typical 6-year-old, or another as an 8-year-old, and so on, but MAs describe only present status.

The concept of a mental quotient to indicate the rate of cognitive development was introduced by William Stern in a paper to the German Congress of Psychology in Berlin in April 1912. With the Stanford Revision and Extension of the Binet-Simon Intelligence Scale in 1916, Lewis Terman introduced the term *intelligence quotient* and its abbreviation, IQ, as a prediction of the rate of future mental development (based on the rate of previous accomplishment). Early IQs were simply the ratio of the mental age to the chronological age, multiplied by 100 to eliminate the decimals (i.e., IQ = MA/CA × 100). However, mental ages represent ordinal, not interval, data, and therefore the distance between two ages (e.g., 4 and 6) is not necessarily the same as between two other ages (e.g., 12 and 14). Also, test authors have not been able to construct tests with equal variability at each age level. As a result, the standard deviation of scores is not the same at each age, and therefore the same ratio IQ obtained at different age levels may not be equal to the same percentile rank. (A ratio IQ that equals or exceeds 3% of the population might be 75 at one age, 68 at another, and 60 at another.) Whereas the statistical properties of a ratio IQ present too many difficulties for its use to be continued except as a concept for interpretation, the simplicity of the concept is still helpful in explaining performance to many consumers. One can say that a 10-year-old child with an IQ of 65 is functioning mentally much like most 6- to 7-year-olds and is exhibiting about two-thirds of a year of mental growth each year. The concept of ratio IQ and mental age seem almost nonsensical when applied to adults. Since ratio IQs represent only ordinal scaling, they can be neither multiplied, divided, added, nor subtracted across ages and are obsolete for most needs in diagnostic settings.

JOSEPH L. FRENCH
Pennsylvania State University

See also **Deviation IQ; Intelligence Quotient**

RATIO SCHEDULES

When teaching new behaviors to children, parents and instructors often begin with a goal of generating high response rates. During house cleaning, for example, chores should be selected, tools assembled, and tasks begun rapidly so that time will be available for more interesting activities when the work is done. In the classroom, hands should be raised so that the teacher can call on many students and rapidly assess what the group has learned and what skills individuals in the group still need to acquire. At work, rapid completion of a set of tasks enables an employee to take a quick break or have an extra few minutes at lunch. Generating such high performance rates from learners involves scheduling reinforcement that can be easily sustained by the instructor or shifted to less intensive schedules as learners' skills become fluent. Effective contingency management requires a basic knowledge of the schedules of reinforcement that make acquiring high rates of desired behavior attainable and sustainable (Mayer, Sulzer-Azaroff, & Wallace, 2011).

Schedules of reinforcement are the conditions under which reinforcers are delivered (Ferster & Skinner, 1957). Under time schedules, reinforcement is provided independent of responses. Interval schedules reinforce on the basis of responses that occur after a given period of time. Ratio schedules are in effect when reinforcement is contingent upon a specified number of responses. Each of these broader schedule categories may be encountered with either fixed or variable requirements. Interval schedules promote lower response rates, whereas ratio schedules encourage higher rates of behavior. Time-based schedules may be useful in reducing unwanted behaviors that have been maintained previously on either of the other schedules.

Fixed-ratio (FR) schedules require a specific number of responses. Factory work involving piecework that pays by the number of products assembled is a good example. When the number of responses required varies at an average rate, reinforcement is said to occur on a variable-ratio (VR) schedule. A teacher assesses that her students on average can complete between 6 and 12 math problems at a time depending on their difficulty level, so she develops a series of worksheets that are completed on a VR 9 schedule, meaning that a student completes each assignment after attempting 9 problems on the average.

Three notable characteristics of ratio schedules have been identified through empirical analysis. Studies on both simple and complex ratio schedules with human participants have indicated that ratio schedules promote high response rates (Alberto & Troutman, 2012; Bijou & Orlando, 1961; Hutchinson & Azrin, 1961; Mayer, Sulzer-Azaroff, & Wallace, 2011). A child permitted extra time at recess upon completion of three classroom cleanup details will hurry to satisfy this requirement. Truckers may rest upon arrival at their destination, so they hasten to deliver their wares as rapidly as possible. If the ratio requirements are abruptly set too high, the worker may give up and not perform on schedule. Individuals who have given up in this manner may become aggressive. This is the result of ratio strain (Hutchinson, Azrin, & Hunt, 1968; Mayer, Sulzer-Azaroff, & Wallace, 2011), which may be remedied by gradually increasing the workload using a progressive ratio schedule. If the rate of responding begins to deteriorate, the instructor may temporarily reduce the response requirement and build back to the previous level more gradually.

A second characteristic of ratio schedules is the probability that after his behavior has been reinforced, an individual will pause before resuming work. Post-reinforcement pause (Reynolds, 1968) is mostly associated with FR schedules; the higher the ratio, the longer the pause. After finishing a lengthy geography exam, William skips his afternoon class and goes to play ball with his friends. Less pronounced pausing is generated on VR schedules and may be seen in the gradually increasing response-rate patterns of fixed-interval schedules. Since the longest pauses are generated by FR schedules, VR schedules are preferred when the goal is high and consistent performance.

The third characteristic of ratio responses is their durability under extinction. Typically, after termination of an FR schedule, a burst of responding is seen. After discontinuing their inadvertent FR reinforcement of Elizabeth's hand-mouthing, staff noted that for a few weeks she initiated hand-mouthing more than ever. VR schedules may be exceptionally persistent under extinction (Mayer, Sulzer-Azaroff, & Wallace, 2011). Tina used to receive phone calls from Jed once every 3 or 4 days. Although Jed has not called in over a month, Tina still races home to sit beside the telephone. In most cases, responding will decrease in frequency over time if the extinction is executed consistently. If a behavior is intermittently reinforced, however, it will resume its previous rate. Tina had begun staying after school to participate in activities and meet new people, but one night Jed called for an assignment; afterward, Tina began racing home again to sit by the phone. Instructors wishing to maintain a behavior over time should consider thinning the schedule of reinforcement as much as possible. Conversely, when the goal is to extinguish a response, great care should be taken to avoid intermittently reinforcing the behavior.

Ratio schedules produce desirable high rates of response. However, because they also promote intense resistance to extinction, it may be beneficial to consider shifting from ratio to interval schedules once a new behavior has been learned in order to thin reinforcement schedules without engendering the kind of emotional responses discussed previously. Fortunately, many studies have demonstrated that the high rates of responding generated under FR schedules can be maintained by VR reinforcement and then continued under interval schedules (Weiner, 1964a, 1964b). Investigators have thinned reinforcement schedules developed when using functional communication training (FCT) to reduce problem behavior by using multiple schedules (Hanley, Iwata, & Thompson, 2001). In this arrangement, three individuals with profound intellectual disabilities who learned alternatives to self-injurious behavior (SIB) for gaining access to food under FR 1 reinforcement were taught to discriminate between periods when reinforcement was and was not available by pairing discriminative stimuli with reinforcement or extinction respectively. Red and white cards distinguished periods when reinforcement was and was not available and succeeded in lowering rates of SIB, maintaining a contingency between the learned behavior and reinforcement, maintaining low levels of alternative responding when reinforcement was unavailable, and decreasing the overall amount of reinforcement that was necessary to maintain the desired behavior.

Another investigation has demonstrated the potential efficacy of using fixed-time (FT) and variable-time (VT) schedules to reduce behaviors previously maintained on VR reinforcement schedules. When an otherwise desirable behavior has been inadvertently shaped up to the point of being maladaptive with ratio-scheduled reinforcement, it may be very difficult to decrease because of the resistance to extinction generated under ratio schedules. Carr, Kellum, and Chong (2001) found that both FT and VT schedules effectively reduced excessive responding to acceptable levels and suggested that this may be useful since it is likely to be easier for caregivers to reinforce behavior at regularly scheduled times. Additionally, the study demonstrated that noncontingent reinforcement could produce durable results even when the time that reinforcement is delivered inadvertently becomes variable.

In summary, ratio schedules are valuable for generating new behaviors at high performance rates. FR schedules may be used when initially training a response; VR schedules are more practical in natural settings. Although ratio schedules support high rates of responding, ratio strain may occur and may be accompanied by emotional behaviors if schedule requirements are increased abruptly. Using an adjusting schedule can remedy the effects of temporary ratio strain. Post-reinforcement pause is a by-product of FR schedules that is often accompanied by unproductive adjunctive behaviors. Ratio schedules produce behaviors that are intensely resistant to extinction. To reduce staff time and costs, it is possible to thin reinforcement rates on a ratio schedule. Care should be taken to avoid intermittently reinforcing unwanted behaviors that have been maintained on ratio schedules. In order to reduce behaviors maintained under ratio schedules, one can consider switching to interval schedules, multiple schedules, or time-based schedules.

REFERENCES

Alberto, P., & Troutman, A. C. (2012). *Applied behavior analysis for teachers*. Upper Saddle River, NJ: Merrill.

Bijou, S. W., & Orlando, R. (1961). Rapid development of multiple-schedule performances with retarded children. *Journal of the Experimental Analysis of Behavior, 4*, 7–16.

Carr, J. E., Kellum, K. K., & Chong, I. M. (2001). The reductive effects of noncontingent reinforcement: Fixed-time versus variable-time schedules. *Journal of Applied Behavior Analysis, 34*, 505–509.

Ferster, C. B., & Skinner, B. F. (1957). *Schedules of reinforcement*. New York, NY: Appleton.

Hanley, G. P., Iwata, B. A., & Thompson, R. H. (2001). Reinforcement schedule thinning following treatment with functional communication training. *Journal of Applied Behavior Analysis, 34*, 17–38.

Hutchinson, R. R., & Azrin, N. H. (1961). Conditioning of mental hospital patients to fixed-ratio schedules of reinforcement. *Journal of the Experimental Analysis of Behavior, 4*, 87–95.

Hutchinson, R. R., Azrin, N. H., & Hunt, G. M. (1968). Attack produced by intermittent reinforcement of a concurrent operant response. *Journal of the Experimental Analysis of Behavior, 11*, 489–495.

Mayer, G. R., Sulzer-Azaroff, B., & Wallace, M. (2011). *Behavior analysis for lasting change*. Cornwall-on-Hudson, NY: Sloan.

Reynolds, G. S. (1968). *A primer of operant conditioning*. Glenview, IL: Scott, Foresman.

Weiner, H. (1964a). Conditioning history and fixed-interval performance. *Journal of the Experimental Analysis of Behavior, 7*, 383–385.

Weiner, H. (1964b). Response cost effects during extinction following fixed-interval reinforcement with humans. *Journal of the Experimental Analysis of Behavior, 7*, 333–335.

THOMAS G. SZABO
Western Michigan University

See also Behavior Assessment; Interval Recording; Interval Schedules

RAVEN'S MATRICES

The Standard Progressive Matrices and the Colored Progressive Matrices (Raven, 1938–1983) are a collection of figures that resemble swatches removed from a wallpaper pattern. The test requires the examinee to locate the swatch that best fits the removed pattern. The test is purportedly an excellent measure of *g* factor intelligence (general intellectual ability; Marshalek, Lohman, & Snow, 1983). The matrices have received wide use around the world because of their easy administration, nonverbal format, and high correlations with traditional measures of intelligence and achievement. The progressive matrices have been used in hundreds of psychological studies internationally.

Since the progressive matrices (developed in the United Kingdom) originated in a psychometric era known for providing examiners with minimal information on standardized sample characteristics, technical adequacy, item construction and use, rationale and theory, and potential uses and misuses of instruments, the progressive matrices manuals provide little information in these areas. Additionally, Levy and Goldstein (1984), editors of *Tests in Education*, the British equivalent of the *Buros Mental Measurements Yearbook*, note that the British have lagged behind the Americans in the care that psychologists have used in the development of psychoeducational assessment measures. However, the large number of studies compiled on the progressive matrices attest to the instruments' use and value.

The matrices are appropriate for individuals ages 5 through adult and are printed in both color (ages 5–11) and standard black-and-white versions (ages 6 and over). The test provides only percentile ranks as an individual's reported score, but even these are not complete; the manual reports performance level only at the 5th, 10th, 25th, 50th, 75th, 90th, and 95th percentiles. Thus, the test only approximates levels of performance. For this reason, the matrices are useful for the rough assessment of the nonverbal reasoning abilities of individuals 5 years and above. Because of the many deficiencies in the test's manuals and standardized samples, it is best used as an assessment tool for research purposes and those occasional clinical instances in which an estimate of an individual's intellectual abilities is needed.

REFERENCES

Levy, P., & Goldstein, H. (Eds.). (1984). *Tests in education: A book of critical reviews*. London, England: Academic Press.

Marshalek, B., Lohman, D. F., & Snow, R. (1983). The complexity continuum in the radex and hierarchical models of intelligence. *Intelligence, 7*, 107–127.

BRUCE A. BRACKEN
University of Memphis

LINDSAY S. GROSS
University of Wisconsin

See also *g* Factor Theory; Intelligence; Intelligence Testing

RAY ADAPTATION OF THE WECHSLER INTELLIGENCE SCALE FOR CHILDREN–REVISED

Ray (1979) adapted the Wechsler Intelligence Scale for Children–Revised (WISC-R) performance scales for an intelligence test designed especially for the hearing impaired. He introduced a set of simplified verbal instructions and added more practice items in an attempt to provide standardized test administration techniques to increase a deaf child's comprehension and performance. Therapists who are unskilled in American Sign Language are able to administer the test. In addition to Ray's version of instructions, several different techniques exist for nonverbal administration (Sullivan, 1982). Seven scores are yielded in the adaptation: Picture Completion, Picture Arrangement, Block Design, Object Assembly,

Coding, Mazes, and Total. Administration time averages about 45 minutes.

The adaptation was normed on 127 hearing-impaired children from 6 to 16 years old. The sample used was not representative of the deaf school-age population, including no low-verbal deaf children and no multiply handicapped children (Sullivan, 1985). Norms provided in Ray's test should be regarded with caution, and thought should be given to other deaf norms developed. The WISC-R performance scales can be a suitable alternative to the Hiskey-Nebraska if the Anderson and Sisco norms are used with a total communication approach for administration (Phelps & Enson, 1986). Genshaft (1985) thinks that the most useful improvement in the adaptation would be separate, representative norms for deaf children.

REFERENCES

Genshaft, J. L. (1985). Review of the WISC-R: For the deaf. In J. V. Mitchell, Jr. (Ed.), *The ninth mental measurements yearbook* (Vol. 2). Lincoln: University of Nebraska Press.

Phelps, L., & Enson, A. (1986). Concurrent validity of the WISC-R using deaf norms and the Hiskey-Nebraska. *Psychology in the Schools, 23*, 138–141.

Ray, S. (1979). *An adaptation of the Wechsler Intelligence Scale for Children–Revised for the deaf*. Natchitoches: Northwestern State University of Louisiana.

Sullivan, R. M. (1982). Modified instructions for administering the WISC-R performance scale subtests to deaf children (Appendix B). In J. M. Sattler (Ed.), *Assessment of children's intelligence and special abilities* (2nd ed.). Boston, MA: Allyn & Bacon.

Sullivan, P. M. (1985). Review of the WISC-R: For the deaf. In J. V. Mitchell, Jr. (Ed.), *The ninth mental measurements yearbook* (Vol. 2). Lincoln: University of Nebraska Press.

LISA J. SAMPSON
Eastern Kentucky University

See also Deaf; Wechsler Intelligence Scale for Children–Fourth Edition

REACTION TIME

Reaction time (RT) tasks are designed to measure the amount of time it takes from presentation of a stimulus to the execution of a designated response. In the classical psychophysics experiment, the examinee is supposed to press a response when a light or auditory signal is presented. The examiner triggers the activation of a timer when presenting the visual or auditory signal (Spreen & Strauss, 1998). Studies have consistently indicated that psychomotor speed accounted for the differences between groups of individuals with brain damage, emotional disorders, and normal controls regardless of modality or hand used in responding. RT tasks have been used to investigate various interactions with cognitive ability (e.g., Deary & Der, 2005; Deary, Der, & Ford, 2001) as well as to measure effects of environmental factors such as sleep deprivation or medication treatment (e.g., Babkoff, Kelly, & Naitoh, 2001).

Simple RT tasks are those tasks that require the individual to respond to each and every stimulus in the same way. In contrast, choice RT tasks require the individual to make choices. For example, the directions may be that if the light is red, the examinee should press the right lever or other specific response, but if the light is blue, the examinee should press the left lever or other specific response. With advances in technology, the study of RT has transitioned to computer-administered tasks with set or random intervals between stimuli and multiple paradigms, including continuous-performance tests (CPTs; see Riccio, Reynolds, & Lowe, 2001 for review).

REFERENCES

Babkoff, H., Kelly, T. L., & Naitoh, P. (2001). Trial to trial variance in choice reaction time as a measure of the effect of stimulants during sleep deprivation. *Military Psychology, 13,* 1–16.

Deary, I. J., & Der, G. (2005). Reaction time explains IQ's association with death. *Psychological Science, 16,* 64–69.

Deary, I. J., Der, G., & Ford, G. (2001). Reaction times and intelligence differences: A population-based cohort study. *Intelligence, 29,* 389–399.

Riccio, C. A., Reynolds, C. R., & Lowe, P. A. (2001). *Clinical applications of continuous performance tests.* New York, NY: Wiley.

Spreen, O., & Strauss, E. (1998). *A compendium of neuropsychological tests* (2nd ed.). Oxford, England: Oxford University Press.

CYNTHIA A. RICCIO
Texas A&M University

See also Intelligence

REACTIVE ATTACHMENT DISORDER

Reactive attachment disorder (RAD) is characterized by a pervasive disturbance in social relatedness and associated with a history of inadequate care, in which a child's physical and emotional needs are often neglected, attachment is disrupted by repeated change in the primary caregiver, or both. Not all children who experience neglect or abuse develop RAD, however; many of the children who are spared have formed stable relationships with other significant adults.

According to the *Diagnostic and Statistical Manual of Mental Disorders–Fourth Edition (DSM-IV)*, there are two subtypes of RAD: inhibited and disinhibited (American Psychiatric Association, 1994). The inhibited child may be withdrawn, hypervigilant, or both and may seek physical proximity to caregivers in an ambivalent or unusual way (e.g., approach caregiver and fall to the ground crying). The disinhibited child may indiscriminately seek proximity to any caregiver, even strangers. For both groups, delays in emotional, language, communication, and cognitive development are often found, but in some cases regression occurs following a period of normal development.

Onset of symptoms must occur before the age of 5 years. The disorder, however, can be diagnosed as early as 1 month. The course is often continuous if interventions are not made early or are inadequate to meet the child's basic needs. There are no reliable prevalence rate data (Zeanah, 2000); however, some researchers estimate the occurrence to be about 1% (Richters & Volkmar, 1994).

Characteristics

1. Marked disturbance and delay in age-appropriate social relatedness must be observed before the age of 5 years.

2. Seen as withdrawn and inhibited or as indiscriminant and disinhibited (e.g., ranging from excessive clinginess to aggressiveness).

3. Emotional delays (e.g., mood lability and low frustration tolerance), as well as delays in language, communication, and cognition not due to MR or PDD.

4. Regression does occur in some cases after a period of normal development.

5. Evidence of pathological care (e.g., persistent neglect of basic needs).

A positive response to therapeutic intervention helps distinguish RAD from other developmental disorders (e.g., pervasive developmental delay, PDD; and mental retardation, MR). Treatment for RAD needs to be multimodal and focus on the interaction between caregiver and child; therefore, parent training and parent education are likely to be key factors in treatment outcome.

Early educational interventions may reduce the negative impact on emotional, cognitive, communication, and language skill development. Interventions that address the marked deficits in social relatedness may in fact help to prevent other difficulties in social and emotional development and later learning. Programs such as Head Start may be of particular benefit for children with RAD. Prognosis, however, is dependent on a number of factors, including the presence of other developmental problems and the ongoing quality of the relationship between the child and significant adults (e.g., parents, relatives, and teachers).

Further research is needed to address problems having to do with the reliability and validity of the diagnostic criteria (Boris, Zeanah, Larrieu, Scheeringa, & Heller, 1998). Not only have the *DSM* criteria changed since the disorder's first inclusion in 1980, but it is also still difficult to differentiate RAD from other pervasive developmental disorders (Mukaddes, Bilge, Alyanak, & Kora, 2000). Developmental researchers also believe there is a need to distinguish between the consequences of so-called pathogenic care and disorders of attachment. To help in this regard, additional criteria have been developed for attachment disorder subtypes, including self-endangering, inhibited, vigilant-hypercompliant, role-reversed, and disrupted attachment disorder (see Zeanah, 2000).

REFERENCES

American Psychiatric Association. (1994). *Diagnostic and statistical manual of mental disorders* (4th ed.). Washington, DC: Author.

Boris, N. W., Zeanah, C. H., Jr., Larrieu, J. A., Scheeringa, M. S., & Heller, S. S. (1998). Attachment disorders in infancy and early childhood: A preliminary investigation of diagnostic criteria. *American Journal of Psychiatry, 155*(2), 295–297.

Mukaddes, N. M., Bilge, S., Alyanak, B., & Kora, M. E. (2000). Clinical characteristics and treatment responses in cases diagnosed as reactive attachment disorder. *Child Psychiatry and Human Development, 30*(4), 273–287.

Richters, M. M., & Volkmar, F. R. (1994). Reactive attachment disorder of infancy or early childhood. *Journal of American Academy of Child and Adolescent Psychiatry, 33*(3), 328–332.

Zeanah, C. H., Jr. (2000). *Handbook of infant mental health* (2nd ed.). New York, NY: Guilford Press.

Lori Dekeyzer
Elaine Clark
University of Utah

READABILITY FORMULAS

Readability formulas are used to measure the difficulty of a text passage and are intended to help match readers with ideal texts. They may be calculated by hand or by computer and may rely on such characteristics as word length, sentence length, syllable length, word frequency, and vocabulary level.

Controversy About and Evolution of Readability Formulas

The first readability formula was published in 1923 (Lively & Pressey), but long before that there were "leveled" readers, like the McGuffy readers, which were developed in 1836 and sold millions of copies before the beginning of the 20th century. After reading formulas came into being, it became possible to "level" any book so instructors would not have to rely on preleveled books. The use of readability formulas has not been without controversy, however. Over the years, researchers have criticized readability formulas for imprecision, inconsistency, and inaccuracy (Britton & Lumpkin, 1977; Fuchs, Fuchs, & Deno, 1984). Some argue for a separation of "readability" from "comprehensibility," because comprehension is more contextual. In the early 1990s another "leveling" movement began, which is not entirely quantitative and takes into account some of the factors that have seemed to be missing in past formulas, such as use of illustrations, required prior knowledge, and topic appropriateness. Newer readability formulas include some of these aspects.

Specific Formulas

There are dozens of readability formulas, some more popular than others. Currently, some of the most prominent are the following.

Fry Readability Graph

The Fry readability graph (Fry, 2002) allows the user to plot the difficulty of a passage based on sentence length and the average number of syllables per word. Because the graph is not under copyright protection, it is available in many publications and at many sites on the Internet.

Bormuth Formula

The Bormuth (1969) formula is calculated according to average number of letters per word, the average number of words per sentence, and the number of words in the passage that are not on the Dale list. The Dale list is a roster of 3,000 words familiar to 80% of fourth graders.

Flesch Reading Ease Score and Flesch-Kinkaid Grade Level Score

These computer-calculated formulas are included in Microsoft Office applications and can be used to calculate the readability of any passage that can be opened in Microsoft Word. The reading ease score and the grade-level score are both computed based on average sentence length (ASL) and average syllables per word (ASW):

Ease score: $206.835 - (1.015 \times \text{ASL}) - (84.6 \times \text{ASW})$
Level: $(.39 \times \text{ASL}) + (11.8 \times \text{ASW}) - 15.59$

New Dale-Chall Readability Formula

The latest revision to the instructions for using the Dale-Chall formula (Chall & Dale, 1995) contains worksheets for assessing necessary prior knowledge, vocabulary and concepts, overall organization, use of headings, questions, illustrations, and physical features, in addition to the standard worksheet for sentence and word length indicators. Scores are given as Cloze scores or grade equivalents. This formula is specifically meant for texts at above the third-grade reading level.

The Lexile Framework

The lexile framework is a two-factor computerized formula that is based on word frequency and sentence length. The range of scores (called lexiles) is from 200 to 1200 and is equated on a table to grade levels 1–12. Lexiles are growing in popularity, partially due to the fact that a database of lexiles for more than 100,000 books and 80 million articles are available at www.lexile.com, which allows the user to enter a lexile level and get a list of appropriate books.

This is a very incomplete list of readability formulas. Further examples can be found in journal articles devoted to describing or critiquing them (Gunning, 2003; Kotula, 2003).

Despite the practical usefulness of readability formulas, it is always important to interpret the scores cautiously. A single passage can have widely varying scores on the differing scales, and formulas alone cannot take into account the meaning and context of a passage.

REFERENCES

Bormuth, J. R. (1969). *Development of readability analysis.* Chicago, IL: University of Chicago Press.

Britton, G. E., & Lumpkin, M. C. (1977). Computerized readability verification of textbook reading levels. *Reading Improvement, 14,* 193–199.

Chall, J. S., & Dale, E. (1995). *Readability revisited: The new Dale-Chall readability formula.* Cambridge, MA: Brookline Books.

Fry, E. (2002). Readability versus leveling. *The Reading Teacher, 56,* 286–291.

Fuchs, L. S., Fuchs, D., & Deno, S. L. (1984). Inaccuracy among readability formulas: Implications for the measurement of reading proficiency and selection of instructional material. *Diagnostique, 9,* 86–97.

Gunning, T. G. (2003). The role of readability in today's classrooms. *Topics in Language Disorders, 23,* 175–189.

Kotula, A. W. (2003). Matching readers to instructional materials: The use of classic readability measures for students with language learning disabilities and dyslexia. *Topics in Language Disorders, 23,* 190–203.

Lively, B. A., & Pressey, S. L. (1923). A method for measuring vocabulary burden of textbooks. *Educational Administration and Supervision, 9,* 389–398.

Michele W. Potter
*University of California,
Riverside*

READING

Reading is the process of deriving meaning from print. While people have been reading as long as language has been written, interest in reading, from both a research and a practical standpoint, has grown markedly in recent years, as evidenced by the demand for such publications as the National Research Council report on preventing reading disabilities in young children, the National Reading Panel (2000) on research-proven methods for teaching children to read, the RAND Reading Study Group (2002) on reading comprehension, and the Carnegie Corporation report (Biancarosa & Snow, 2004) on middle school and high school literacy. In the past 25 years, there has been a concerted effort to understand how the reading process occurs and to translate that knowledge into materials and strategies that more effectively teach reading. Reading educators, long concerned with reading research and its implementation, now work alongside cognitive, educational, and developmental psychologists, linguists, and sociolinguists in the attempt to unravel the mysteries of reading. The stakes in this endeavor became higher with the implementation of the No Child Left Behind Act (NCLB; 2002), which mandates that all students reach proficiency in reading (and other academic subjects) as evidenced by performance on state-administered assessments by the year 2014. Bringing all students to proficiency in reading will require that educators and researchers develop greater understanding both of how the reading process unfolds and of how all students can learn to participate in that process skillfully.

What does it mean to be a proficient reader? Readers can interact with print in a variety of ways; presumably a proficient reader is one who consistently performs these interactions effectively and successfully, carrying out their intended purpose in reading. There are four typical general purposes for reading, corresponding to four basic types of reading. The four types of reading to be discussed are developmental reading, studying, functional reading, and recreational reading.

Developmental reading can be described as the activity undertaken for the purpose of learning how to read. During the colonial period, the Bible, the psalter, and other religious materials were used to teach children to read. A century later, the McGuffey readers were published. These readers were the forerunners of the graded readers often used today, and their appearance paralleled the development of graded schools. Several decades ago, children learned to read with the assistance of the "Dick and Jane" books. With such familiar phrases as "See Dick" and "See Jane," school-aged children across the United States entered the world of formal reading instruction. Today, much of the formal reading instruction in the early elementary grades is still devoted to developmental reading, although children may now encounter in their reading classrooms both commercially produced reading materials created for the purpose of reading instruction and trade books intended for the general public. The appropriate role of each of these types of instructional materials in furthering development in reading remains an issue for reading educators and researchers (Hiebert & Martin, 2004; Morrow & Gambrell, 2000).

As students progress through elementary school, developmental reading remains an integral part of their schooling, with the goal of increasing reading proficiency. Although developmental reading was confined to elementary grades in past years, it has become increasingly common to find developmental reading courses being offered even at the college level. The rationale for this upward trend in developmental reading is the persistent presence of large numbers of college students who have not reached proficiency in reading and who still require some instruction in learning how to read effectively.

In the upper elementary grades and throughout formal schooling, developmental reading is joined by another type of reading: studying. According to Anderson (1979), studying is a special form of reading that is concerned with the accomplishment of some instructional goal. The type of reading engaged in during studying is special for a number of reasons.

While the material used for developmental reading tends to be narrative text (i.e., story-like text), the kind of text students most often study is expository in nature. In its demands on comprehension and recall, expository text appears to possess certain disadvantages compared to narrative text, in that it has no identifiable elements such as plot, character, and setting. In addition, expository text is frequently less colorful, contains more technical language, and can vary in structure. Therefore, the task of studying may be more difficult than other forms of reading because expository text, particularly as presented in textbooks, may be more difficult and less motivational to read. Not only is the text used in studying potentially more difficult to process, but when students study expository texts it is often with the unpleasant expectation of being tested on its content; both of these factors may make studying a less enjoyable reading experience for students.

Because of its nature, studying requires individuals to employ specialized learning and study skills. In addition to the well-known SQ3R method (Robinson, 1970), there are such cognitive strategies as note taking, outlining, paraphrasing, imaging, and rereading that enhance student performance. Some of the other study strategies that have been looked at by researchers in recent years include annotation (Hynd, Simpson, & Chase, 1990), self-testing, and graphic organizers (Robinson & Kiewra, 1995).

While developmental reading and studying are the forms of reading most directly associated with school, there is another form of reading that arises from real-world needs. This form of reading is called functional reading. When we read road signs, find our way on a map, follow a recipe, or order from a menu, we are employing functional reading. Simply stated, functional reading is the reading that is required to accomplish some personal or social as opposed to instructional goal.

It is disheartening to note that there are still many adults in the United States who cannot even read well enough to make sense of the critical print around them. They cannot read the road signs along the road, follow a recipe, fill out a job application, or read the dosage on a medicine bottle. Individuals who lack even this limited reading proficiency are called functionally illiterate. According to government estimates, they number in the tens of millions in the United States.

The final form of reading, recreational, is internally motivated. This form of reading is sometimes described as reading for enjoyment. Recreational reading aims primarily at the reader's entertainment. For example, when you read the comics, a novel, or poetry for pleasure, then you are engaging in recreational reading. There appears to be a strong relation between the amount of recreational reading individuals engage in and their performance on other types of reading tasks such as studying. Because of this relation, programs such as Sustained Silent Reading (SSR), Drop Everything And Read (DEAR), and Accelerated Reader (AR) were developed to encourage children to read more often. The hope of such programs is that students will begin to read more often and, ultimately, more effectively. However, research has not established that encouragement to read does, in fact, improve children's reading achievement or fluency in reading (National Reading Panel, 2000).

Whether developmental, study-oriented, functional, or recreational, reading remains a complex and much-investigated cognitive process. Although most reading researchers and educators would agree that reading is an extremely complex activity involving written language, there is much debate as to which elements of the reading process to foreground in research and instruction. A consensus seems to have been achieved in recent years that some form of balanced instruction is most beneficial for the majority of developmental readers, meaning that they should receive phonics-based instruction aimed at improving their decoding skills, as well as comprehension instruction aimed at improving their grasp of reading as meaning making. The degree of emphasis that each type of instruction should receive for learners at different stages of learning to read and at different levels of proficiency remains controversial, however.

An area of emphasis in the last decade has been a focus on early reading and reading readiness, with the rationale that once children get started on reading successfully, their career as proficient readers is secured. Although attention to the early stages of developmental reading may prevent some reading problems, it appears clear that giving children access to print via decoding is not sufficient for them to develop into proficient readers. Just as learning to read words does not tend to occur naturally without the benefit of targeted instruction, so, too, comprehension of texts, particularly expository or instructional texts, is not a natural by-product of development for many students. Children who can decode competently may still find themselves struggling with comprehension of texts in the higher grade levels, or may experience decreasing motivation to read as they move into adolescence (Guthrie & Alao, 1997). Declining motivation to read in adolescence and adolescents' declining levels of reading achievement have recently moved into the foreground as issues for reading educators, and they will become increasingly important as the provisions of NCLB calling for reading proficiency for all high school students take effect.

Thus, there is growing awareness that a fully developmental model of reading is called for, one that follows the reading process from the earliest stages of gaining access to print all the way through the independent reading of the proficient adult. In aiming at the goal of bringing all students up to proficiency in reading, a full understanding of what the development of proficiency in all types of reading means is warranted. Such an understanding will need to consider the multiple levels and complex interactions involved in reading development, including the delineation of the roles of such varied elements as facilitative reading skills, reading strategies, readers' knowledge and metacognition, and motivation (Alexander, 2002).

Further, it is not enough to consider the internal processing of an individual reader without considering also their reading environment; the importance of understanding situational and contextual aspects of reading is gaining increased recognition. The RAND Reading Study Group (2002) identified three critical elements in reading comprehension: the reader, the text, and the activity, all of which are embedded in a larger sociocultural context. As noted earlier, an individual's purpose for reading is directly linked to the type of reading undertaken (i.e., developmental, for study, functional, or recreational) and influences the nature of the reading process that occurs and also what it means to be a proficient reader in that situation.

Research and instruction in reading are beginning to take these interactive factors into account, but much theoretical and practical groundwork remains to be established. Regardless of the type or view of reading, one fact remains clear: In an information-processing age, the ability to read well is an essential life skill. Further, the investigation of the reading process and of the development of reading ability will continue to reveal new aspects of reading, a complex, dynamic, and fascinating human activity.

REFERENCES

Alexander, P. A. (2002, December). *Profiling the developing reader: The interplay of knowledge, interest, and strategic processing*. The Oscar Causey Research Award Presentation to the National Reading Conference, Miami, FL.

Anderson, T. H. (1979). Study skills and learning strategies. In H. F. O'Neil & C. D. Spielberger (Eds.), *Cognitive and affective learning strategies* (pp. 77–98). New York, NY: Academic Press.

Biancarosa, G., & Snow, C. E. (2004). *Reading next—A vision for action and research in middle and high school literacy: A report to the Carnegie Corporation of New York*. Washington, DC: Alliance for Excellent Education.

Guthrie, J. T., & Alao, S. (1997). Engagement in reading for young adolescents. *Journal of Adolescent & Adult Literacy, 40*(6), 438–447.

Hiebert, E. H., & Martin, L. A. (2004). The texts of beginning reading instruction. In R. B. Ruddell & N. J. Unrau (Eds.), *Theoretical models and processes of reading* (5th ed., pp. 390–411). Newark, DE: International Reading Association.

Hynd, C. R., Simpson, M. L., & Chase, N. D. (1990). Studying narrative text: The effects of annotating vs. journal writing on test performance. *Reading Research & Instruction, 29*(2), 44–54.

Morrow, L. M., & Gambrell, L. B. (2000). Literature-based reading instruction. In M. L. Kamil, P. B. Mosenthal, P. D. Pearson, & R. Barr (Eds.), *Handbook of reading research, Vol. III* (pp. 563–586). Mahwah, NJ: Erlbaum.

National Reading Panel. (2000). *Teaching children to read: An evidence-based assessment of the scientific research literature on reading and its implications for reading success*. Washington, DC: National Institutes of Child Health and Human Development.

No Child Left Behind Act of 2001. (2002). Public Law No. 107-110, Paragraph 115, Stat. 1425.

RAND Reading Study Group. (2002). *Reading for understanding: Toward an R&D program in reading comprehension*. Santa Monica, CA: Science & Technology Policy Institute, RAND Education.

Robinson, D. H., & Kiewra, K. A. (1995). Visual argument: Graphic organizers are superior to outlines in improving learning from text. *Journal of Educational Psychology, 87*, 455–467.

Robinson, E. P. (1970). *Effective study* (2nd ed.). New York, NY: Harper & Row.

PATRICIA A. ALEXANDER
University of Michigan

EMILY FOX
University of Maryland

READING AND EYE MOVEMENTS

Eye-movement research is used to understand the underlying cognitive processes involved in reading. Although it seems as if the eyes move continuously along the text except for some places, in reality it is not so. The eyes make a series of stops and jumps. The periods when the eyes come to rest are called fixations. Visual information is processed only during the fixations. Between the fixations are the periods when eyes move rapidly. These eye movements are called saccades after the French word for "jump." During the saccade the vision is blurred and processing is hindered. When we read, our eyes usually move six to nine character spaces with each saccade. While most saccades in reading move forward, about 10% to 15% move backward, and these are called regressive saccades or regressions. When the eyes move from near the end of one line to near the beginning of the next, this movement is called return sweep.

Recently a number of debates emerged with regard to eye movements. Starr and Rayner (2001) examine three main controversies that exist in the eye-movement research. The first is the extent to which eye-movement behavior is affected by low-level oculomotor factors versus higher-level cognitive processes. The second has to do with the amount of information that can be extracted from the right of fixation. The last one is the question of whether readers process information serially or in parallel.

There are various models of eye-movement control in reading (e.g., Morrison model, EMMA, attention-shift model, SWIFT, minimal control model, and many others). The E-Z Reader model (Reichle, Rayner, & Pollatsek, 2003) is one of the most popular. This model provides a theoretical framework for understanding how word identification, visual processing, attention, and oculomotor control jointly determine where and when the eyes move during reading.

A good reader is expected to have regular, fewer, and shorter fixations, as well as fewer regressions. Examining eye movements is part of studying reading deficits. However, some researchers concluded that eye movements are not the cause of reading disabilities but rather the reflection of them (Rayner, 1985; Starr & Rayner, 2001).

REFERENCES

Rayner, K. (1985). The role of eye movements in learning to read and reading disability. *Remedial & Special Education, 6,* 53–59.

Reichle, E. D., Rayner, K., & Pollatsek, A. (2003). The E-Z Reader model of eye-movement control in reading: Comparison to other models. *Behavioral and Brain Sciences, 26,* 445–526.

Starr, M. S., & Rayner, K. (2001). Eye movements during reading: Some current controversies. *Trends in Cognitive Sciences, 5,* 156–164.

OLGA JERMAN
University of California, Riverside

READING COMPREHENSION

What Is Reading Comprehension?

Although many contending definitions of reading comprehension exit, few dispute that it is the "essence of reading"

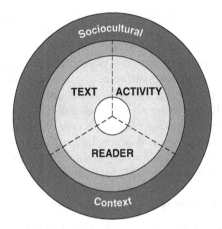

Figure R.1. Four elements of reading comprehension based on RRSG, 2002.

(Durkin, 1993). For reading comprehension to occur, basic skills such as phonemic awareness, fluency, and vocabulary in addition to cognitive processes such as working memory and reasoning must come together. Many different definitions of reading comprehension exist varying on different philosophies. The RAND Reading Study Group (RRSG, 2002) defines reading comprehension as "the process of simultaneously extracting and constructing meaning through interaction and involvement with written language" that occurs through the interaction of four major elements (p. 11). The four fundamental elements of reading comprehension are the reader, the text, the activity, and the sociocultural context (see Figure R.1). Each reader brings unique background experiences and information to the text improving or possibly impairing a reader's comprehension (McCormick, 1987; Pressley & Block, 2002). Texts vary based on readability, structure, and organization that also have an effect on comprehension. The text should match the reader's ability and interest level, but still pose a challenge to the reader (Chall, Jacobs, & Baldwin, 1990). The socioeconomic context for most readers is the classroom; however, organizational grouping, access to technology, or availability of instructional materials can also impact comprehension (RAND, 2002).

Levels of Comprehension

A continuum of depth of understanding exists among readers. Researchers vary on the number and type of levels, however, the two most commonly referenced are the three levels of comprehension (literal, interpretive, and applied) and Bloom's taxonomy (1956): knowledge, comprehension, application, analysis, synthesis, and application.

Three Levels of Comprehension

The least sophisticated level of comprehension is known as *literal*. Questions asked to measure literal comprehension are typically information-seeking or surface level understanding such as: Where did this story take place? What happened to the character in this story? Answers to literal level questions are explicitly stated in the text. The second and more complex level of comprehension is *interpretive*. Questions asked to measure interpretive comprehension require the reader to synthesize information from the text and background knowledge to make inferences such as: What is the author trying to tell us? The third level of comprehension is *applied*. Applied comprehension requires readers to express ideas and opinions based on the text, such as Do you agree with the character's action? How would you have reacted differently?

Bloom's Taxonomy

Bloom (1956) developed a six-tier model that reflects the different levels of comprehension. Bloom's taxonomy subsumes the three levels of comprehension (literal, interpretive, and applied) with the following cognitive levels: knowledge, comprehension, application, analysis, synthesis, and evaluation. These levels, as well as questions that assess the levels, can be found on the following table.

Three Levels of Comprehension		Bloom's Taxonomy	
Levels	Example Questions	Levels	Example Questions
1. Literal	When did this story take place?	1. Knowledge	When did this story take place?
2. Interpretive	What is the author trying to tell us?	2. Comprehension	What was the consequence of the character's action?
3. Applied	Do you agree with the character's action?	3. Application	Why is this significant?
		4. Analysis	What is the evidence to support the character's action?
		5. Synthesis	What might happen if the character had not accepted the bribe?
		6. Evaluation	Do you agree with the character's actions?

Reading Comprehension Strategies

Founded in metacognition, comprehension strategies are specific procedures to help students self-regulate their understanding as they read and write. A strong level of evidence has been found to support direct and explicit comprehension strategy instruction for both young (Shanahan, Callison, Carriere, Duke, Pearson, Schatschneider, & Torgesesn, 2010) and adolescent readers (Kamil, Borman, Dole, Kral, Salinger, & Torgesen, 2008), as well as to confirm the National Reading Panel's (2000) recommendation for multiple-strategy instruction. A common, but not comprehensive, list of reading comprehension strategies are found in the following chart.

Reading Comprehension Strategy	How Proficient Readers Use the Strategy
Monitor comprehension	Proficient readers recognize when they are confused or the text does not make sense.
Bridge text and world knowledge	Proficient readers build world knowledge through a wide reading and make appropriate connections between the text and their personal experiences.
Create graphic or semantic organizers	Proficient readers create graphic representations of the text.
Ask questions	Proficient readers generate questions as they read.
Answer questions	Proficient readers use the text to answer questions asked by the teacher.
Anticipate story structure	Proficient readers identify the organization of the text and use the story structure to recall information from the text.
Summarize	Proficient readers concisely synthesize information from the text.
Build mental images	Proficient readers construct mental images or pictures as they read.
Predict	Proficient readers create expectations of the text, thereby setting a purpose for reading and motivation.

REFERENCES

Bloom, B. S. (Ed.), Engelhart, M. D., Furst, E. J., Hill, W. H., & Krathwohl, D. R. (1956). *Taxonomy of educational objectives: The classification of educational goals. Handbook 1: Cognitive domain*. New York, NY: McKay.

Chall, J. S., Jacobs, V. A., & Baldwin, L. E. (1990). *The reading crisis: Why poor children fall behind*. Cambridge, MA: Harvard University Press.

Durkin, D. (1993). *Teaching them to read* (6th ed.). Boston, MA: Boston University Press.

Kamil, M. L., Borman, G. D., Dole, J., Kral, C. C., Salinger, T., & Torgesen, J. (2008). *Improving adolescent literacy: Effective classroom and intervention practices: A Practice Guide* (NCEE #2008-4027). Washington, DC: National Center for Education Evaluation and Regional Assistance, Institute of

Education Sciences, U.S. Department of Education. Retrieved from http://ies.ed.gov/ncee/wwc

McCormick, S. (1987). *Remedial and clinical reading instruction.* Columbus, OH: Merrill.

National Reading Panel. (2000). *Teaching children to read: An evidence-based assessment of the scientific research literature on reading and its implications for reading instruction.* Washington, D.C.: National Institute of Child Health and Human Development.

Pressley, M., & Block, C. C. (2002). *Summing up: What comprehension instruction could be.* In C. C. Block and M. Pressley (Eds.), *Comprehension instruction: Research-based best practices* (pp. 383–392). New York, NY: Guilford Press.

RAND Reading Study Group. (2002). *Reading for understanding: Towards an R&D program in reading comprehension.* Retrieved from http://www.rand.org/multi/achievementforall/reading/readreport.html

Shanahan, T., Callison, K., Carriere, C., Duke, N. K., Pearson, P. D., Schatschneider, C., & Torgesen, J. (2010). *Improving reading comprehension in kindergarten through 3rd grade: A practice guide* (NCEE 2010-4038). Washington, DC: National Center for Education Evaluation and Regional Assistance, Institute of Education Sciences, U.S. Department of Education. Retrieved from whatworks.ed.gov/publications/practiceguides

STACEY L. SMITH
Texas A&M University
Fourth edition

READING DISORDERS

It is an understatement to say that the process of reading is complex. The variety of models of the reading process that have been created serves as evidence of this complexity. However, it is also true that most individuals will master the demanding skill of reading without much difficulty and in spite of the instructional methods by which they are taught. For many, the acquisition of reading appears to be more or less second nature; yet there are those for whom learning to read is anything but second nature. For these individuals, attempts to acquire even rudimentary reading skills seem destined to fail.

Before we deal specifically with sources of reading difficulties, it is important that this examination of reading disorders be placed into a historical framework. By dealing briefly with the historical perspective, the reader may come to understand some of the issues underlying present thinking in the area of reading disorders.

References to reading difficulties can be traced as far back as the early seventeenth century. The earliest published studies of reading disorders, appearing around the turn of the 20th century, were undertaken by people in the medical profession. In 1896, W. Pringle Morgan, a British ophthalmologist, published what is credited as the first report of a reading disorder. In this report, Morgan presented a detailed account of a young man who could not read despite seemingly adequate intelligence. Morgan speculated that the youth suffered from "congenital word blindness." The explanation of reading problems articulated by Morgan was followed by a series of clinical studies published by Hinshelwood (1917). In his internationally recognized book, Hinshelwood, a Scottish eye surgeon, investigated the role of the brain in congenital word blindness.

The research of British medical professionals like Morgan and Hinshelwood, although generally stimulating little interest among most educators and psychologists at home and abroad, did influence the work of others. Notable among this work were Orton's (1925) studies of hemispheric imbalance. Orton, a neurologist, felt that the principal symptom of reading disorders was strephosymbolia, or severe reversals of language symbols. He felt that this condition was attributable to the lack of cerebral dominance. This pattern of letter reversal, which is often associated with the condition of dyslexia, remains a popular but poor indicator of reading problems.

Two important outcomes of the early medical writings on reading disabilities were rare. First, a medical perspective on reading disorders became evident. As a consequence of this perspective, which is still evident in certain educational circles today, the causes of reading problems were primarily sought among neurological factors. In other words, the focus of reading disorders was believed to lie within the reader (Lipson & Wixson, 1997): a neurological deficit that prevented the reader from successfully completing the reading act.

Even today, those who do not embrace the strongly neurological or psychoneurological view of reading problems (e.g., Spear-Swerdling, 2004) cannot dismiss the lasting impression made by early medical research on the identification and treatment of reading disorders. To illustrate, we need only look at the language of reading remediation. In a clinical setting, in order to provide remediation (improvement) of reading difficulties, the client (reader) is diagnosed (tested), and an instructional treatment (program) is prescribed (developed).

The second outcome of the early medical influence in reading disorders was the development of scientific instruments to isolate the source of reading problems. For example, in 1914, Thorndike developed a group test of reading ability, and in 1915, Gray followed with an oral reading test. As the number of such assessments grew, so did the concern for the improvement of the identified disorder, or remediation. Diagnostic instruments became components of early clinical programs, which were established most often in conjunction with medical schools for the purpose of determining the cause of reading problems (etiology).

Initially, the diagnosis of reading disorders consisted of an extensive battery of physical, neurological, and language assessments that often entailed the individual's admission into a hospital. Today, while these more extensive diagnostic screenings are still administered, particularly in medically related clinics, briefer, more educationally related screenings have become far more prevalent. These school-based assessments focus heavily on reading achievement and aptitude measures and less on the physical characteristics of the reader, such as auditory discrimination and acuity, and even less on potential neurological factors.

Further, at the school level, most initial decisions about students' reading abilities or disabilities are made on the basis of group testing administered by classroom teachers, not by individual tests administered by trained specialists, as is the case in clinical programs. These variations in tests and testing procedures between school-based and medically based reading programs are indicative of fundamental differences between such programs with regard to reading disorders. As noted, the neurological view of reading disorders focuses on functional deficits within the reader. Alternative perspectives in reading disorders center attention elsewhere.

Even from the beginning, with the work of Morgan and others, some preferred to look outside the reader for factors contributing to reading difficulties. Some have sought to blame reading problems on the instruction these readers achieved (Judd, 1918; Uhl, 1916). For example, Judd (1918) contended that the emphasis on phonics instruction in education led to confusion in the reader's eye fixations, thus producing reader disability. C. T. Gray (1922) also put the burden for reading difficulties outside the reader and inside the educational system. Like those holding strongly to neurological views of reading disorders, those holding as strongly to instructional explanations for reading problems, like Judd and Gray, found only limited support.

In contrast to either view, the predominant current approach to reading disorders is an interaction of the two positions, reflecting a position somewhere between the two extremes. Within this more moderate perspective, serious reading problems can be a consequence not only of neurological deficits or misguided instruction but of multiple factors that include physical, emotional, and social conditions. For the remainder of this discussion, we will examine each of these potential contributors to reading failure.

Reading is a complex mental activity that involves the acquisition, manipulation, and retrieval of language symbols by the reader. As discussed, when a failure to read successfully exists, there is the tendency to examine that situation's etiology or cause. Terms such as brain injury, damage, dysfunction, and neuropsychological disorder reflect a neurological etiology. Harris and Sipay (1980) summarized potential indicators of reading-related neurological problems as encompassing (a) a history of

a difficult birth, perhaps involving prolonged labor, an instrumental delivery, or deformity of the head; (b) premature birth; (c) poor balance or general awkwardness; (d) marked language delay; (e) attention deficit; or (f) a history of seizures or brief lapses in consciousness.

There has been a resurgence in emphasis on neurological factors in recent decades (e.g., Shaywitz et al., 2000). This resurgence may be accounted for, in part, by the increased awareness of the brain and brain functioning provided by expanded imaging technology. Among the most common neurologically related reading disorders are alexia (partial or total loss of reading ability), dyslexia, deficit language production, and specific learning disability. Because of the widespread application of the labels of dyslexia and learning disability, we will consider these conditions in more depth.

Dyslexia is certainly one of the most widely applied and perhaps one of the most misused labels for reading problems; the term *dyslexia* has come to be seen as virtually synonymous for reading disability (Lipson & Wixson, 1997). References to dyslexic conditions, which can be traced all the way back to Morgan's writings on congenital word blindness and Orton's research on strephosymbolia, have continued to appear with regularity in the literature. Although many definitions of dyslexia do exist, the root of the word relates to word distortion, and it is frequently and mistakenly associated with letter or word reversals. Dyslexia tends to be considered to be neurological in origin, and thus it is viewed as inherent in the affected individual and not susceptible to cure. A number of typologies of dyslexia have been proposed, with one of the most prominent being the distinction of "deep" and "surface" dyslexia (Balajthy & Lipa-Wade, 2003). "Deep" dyslexia involves decoding difficulties originating in deficient phonological processing, while children with "surface" dyslexia have adequate phonological processing but have difficulties in recognizing words for other reasons.

Despite the popularity of the term, many, principally in the educational community, do not find it useful to label reading-related learning difficulties as dyslexia (Gunning, 2002). While it seems likely that the word dyslexia is too easily and invalidly applied by the general populace, it is equally difficult to discount the number of individuals who display an inability to encode or to manipulate written language; problems in decoding language in written form are central to most current definitions of dyslexia (e.g., Reid, 1998).

Some of the same characteristics that apply to the condition of dyslexia apply as well to the condition of learning disability (LD). According to the Individuals with Disabilities Education Act (IDEA), a specific learning disability is "a disorder in one or more of the basic psychological processes" required to understand language. "The term includes such conditions as perceptual handicaps, brain injury, minimal brain dysfunction, dyslexia, and developmental aphasia" (1997, p. 65083).

Beyond this legal definition, however, there is ample disagreement about the nature, identification, and treatment procedures for learning disabilities. What is most interesting about LD is that in many ways the condition is primarily an educational problem. What frequently unites the vast numbers of students labeled as having LD is that there is a significant gap between perceived potential and demonstrated academic performance. In addition, there is no apparent cause for this gap. It may be related to a combination of affective and cognitive factors, and it may be reflected both in learning and behavioral problems within the learner. Often, teachers and specialists struggle to bring the performance of the student with learning disability up to potential through the application of medical and educational treatments.

While important, neurological factors such as those discussed here account for relatively few of the reading problems encountered in classrooms (Gunning, 2002; Reid, 1998). Other factors, such as physical ones, may also contribute to reading difficulties.

Although reading is a cognitive activity, it also relies heavily on visual and auditory stimuli. There are several sensory deficits that can have an immediate and significant effect on an individual's acquisition and maintenance of reading proficiency. Several of these deficits will be examined in this section.

Although the terms sight and vision are frequently used interchangeably, there are semantic differences in these terms that become important in a discussion of reading disorders. Basically, the word sight refers to the eye's response to light. By comparison, the word vision implies that there is some interpretation of the information transmitted by the eye to the brain. In reading disability research, the term *visual acuity* is employed to represent the state of having good sight. Visual discrimination refers to the individual's ability to detect minute differences between and among visual stimuli. During reading, the learner's eyes must not only see and discriminate among single stimuli but also make saccadic movements or smooth left-to-right progressions and sweeps from line to line of text. The eyes are also required to pause and focus periodically in the reading process. These periodic pauses are called fixations.

Without a doubt, clear and appropriate visual access to the printed page facilitates the individual's ability to process written language. When visual acuity is impaired, the process of reading is diminished, at best, or made extremely difficult, at worst. What precisely is the effect of various visual defects on reading performance? Reviews of the research present inconclusive evidence on the relationship of visual defects to reading performance (Harris & Sipay, 1980), and remediation based on visual training does not appear to be effective (American Academy of Pediatrics, 1998). Several factors that can account for the inconsistent findings of this research include (a) variations in what supposedly similar tests are actually measuring; (b) the brief and unreliable nature of visual tests; (c) the lack of comparability in the ages and visual development of learners; and (d) the adaptability of learners.

There are many visual problems that can impede the learning process. Among the most common visual deficiencies are nearsightedness (myopia), farsightedness (hyperopia), and astigmatism; all are refractive errors or abnormalities in eye shape. When functioning during the reading process, the eyes must make several critical adjustments, and difficulties in performing these adjustments can interfere with the reading process. For example, the muscles of the eye must be operated together in a coordinated fashion, focusing and centering on the visual target in such a way as to produce a single, clear image. At times, there can be a muscular imbalance preventing the eyes from operating in a coordinated way. In certain cases, one eye may assume dominance over the other eye and suppress the vision in the weaker eye, a condition commonly referred to as lazy eye (amblyopia). For the most part, readers with milder cases of muscular imbalance can accommodate well, except when they experience fatigue, tension, or headaches.

While successful reading depends on auditory skills, few severe reading problems can be directly linked to auditory factors. However, in our discussion of reading disorders, several auditory classifications should be considered. These categories are auditory acuity, auditory discrimination, and auditory memory. Auditory acuity refers to the state of having good hearing. Auditory discrimination involves the recognition of minute differences in speech sounds. Phonological awareness, which has been identified as a potential risk factor for the development of reading disability (Blachman, 2000; Snow, Burns, & Griffin, 1998), originates in this ability to discriminate the sounds in spoken words. Students' appropriate production of speech sounds is dependent on their ability to hear such differences as well. Most early reading programs include phonic analysis, which requires students to recognize and reproduce the common sound-symbol patterns in language. Consequently, deficits in auditory acuity or discrimination would place the child at a disadvantage in these early stages of reading acquisition.

Auditory memory comes into play in learning when students encode the sounds in a word to store that word in working memory. Certain students appear to have difficulty in encoding phonological or verbal information completely and accurately, which tends to have negative effects on their comprehension and also on their formation of stable associations between sounds and letters (Torgeson & Hecht, 1996). Also of importance in the reception of auditory stimuli is the individual's ability to mask or eliminate extraneous noises in the environment. As most of us know, the classroom, where so much information is transmitted auditorily, is anything but noise-proof. Focusing on important information in the classroom demands that the learner mask out sounds that would otherwise interfere with the acquisition of salient information.

Beyond the visual and auditory factors presented, there are other physical conditions that may contribute to reading problems. Among these conditions are illness, general awkwardness, glandular problems, and poor nutrition. It must be noted, however, that there is little direct evidence that such conditions significantly affect reading performance. For example, illnesses tend to come into play in reading problems when students suffer from prolonged or chronic ailments. Yet, in most instances, prolonged illnesses prevent the learner from attending school, and it is this lack of school attendance that contributes most to reading difficulties. General awkwardness is not, in itself, a factor in reading problems, but it is of importance in that it is frequently a symptom of minimal brain dysfunction. Further, while glandular abnormalities can result in such physical abnormalities as dwarfism or obesity, there is limited understanding of the effects of endocrine treatments on reading disorders. The effect of malnutrition on reading disorders is also difficult to pinpoint since this condition is also closely tied to socioeconomic status.

To this point, we have been discussing neurological and physical factors that influence reading performance. There are also less easily measured factors within the individual that may influence the reading process. Among these less measurable factors are psychosocial characteristics of the reader. Even from the beginning of work in the area of reading disorders, writers such as Orton (1925) and C. T. Gray (1922) have contended that successful readers are socially and emotionally different from struggling readers. Successful readers have been seen as not only good at reading skills but also psychosocially adjusted. By comparison, disabled readers have been categorized as restless, withdrawn, or introverted (Robinson, 1953).

That certain psychosocial behaviors have been frequently related to poor reading performance is widely accepted. However, the significance of emotional and social factors in causing reading disorders is unclear. Do certain psychosocial behaviors result in reading failure? Does the presence of reading problems have particular emotional or social effects on the reader? Do certain emotional or social behaviors and reading problems develop simultaneously? These questions remain unanswered by the existing literature.

In part, we know little about the relation of psychosocial conditions and reading disorders because the techniques for gathering data in these areas are somewhat unreliable. For example, teacher observation, which may be employed to gather information on a learner's emotional or social behavior, can be biased. Further, teachers generally conduct observations without the benefit of training. Interviews may also be used to collect data on these factors. Yet, even when these interviews are performed by trained specialists, there is little assurance that what the learner says is an accurate reflection of the internal state. Personality measures are another tool for assessing an individual's emotional and social condition. While such measures may provide a better understanding of the condition of the learner than observation and interviews, however, the reliability of these measures is still a point of contention.

Although failing to discern consistent differences on these factors between disabled and able readers, research (Harris, 1971; Harris & Sipay, 1980), has identified various aspects of psychosocial behavior that may contribute to reading problems. For example, Harris and Sipay (1980) delineate the following characteristics as related to reading problems:

- Conscious refusal to learn
- Overt hostility
- Negative conditioning to reading
- Displacement of hostility
- Resistance to pressure
- Clinging to dependency
- Quick discouragement
- Conviction that success is dangerous
- Extreme distractibility or restlessness
- Absorption in a private world

Harris and Sipay's characteristic of extreme distractibility and restlessness as indicative of reading problems relates to the work on attention deficit disorders in the literature on reading disabilities. In particular, attention deficit may be associated specifically with greater risk for a reading disorder (Willcutt & Pennington, 2000). Since the research of Bandura (1969) and Gibson (1969), the importance of attention to learning has been widely accepted. It would appear that students with learning disabilities, for whom there is a gap between potential and academic performance, may suffer from a developmental lag with regard to attention (Reid, 1998; Ross, 1976). Often, students with learning disabilities are unable to sustain attention to task, and the effect is decreased learning. An important element in assisting students with learning disabilities in improving reading performance may be to structure instructional activities to minimize the need for extended attention and to highlight explicitly the features to which students should attend.

Several of the psychosocial characteristics listed by Harris and Sipay (e.g., quick discouragement and negative conditioning) are taken up also in the literature on motivation and engagement (Guthrie & Wigfield, 2000; Wigfield & Eccles, 2001). Byrnes (2001) describes the importance of engagement to learning as follows:

A child who is engaged in a classroom activity is an active, attentive, curious, and willing participant. The opposite would be a disengaged, inattentive, and even resistant student. For

In 1985, the Commission on Reading of the National Academy of Education published *Becoming a Nation of Readers* (Anderson et al., 1985), which synthesized current sociopsycholinguistic theory and research on learning to read and reading to learn. This document provides a theoretical rationale for teachers who would implement the "Essentials" approach.

Reading is not defined as a product or as a set of subskills to be tested but rather as "a process for constructing meaning from written texts…a complex skill requiring the coordination of a number of interrelated sources of information" (p. 7). Those sources lie in the reader, in the text, in fellow students, and in the teacher. Readers bring to the reading task knowledge of the world, of language, of strategies for reading various texts, and of their teachers' purposes and expectations. They also bring their own interests and purposes. Texts present world knowledge in special ways; for example, literary texts have different conventions and structures from informational texts. They vary in purpose, content, and style. Fellow students constitute a community of comprehenders. Through interaction they can share relevant prior knowledge, text knowledge, and reading strategies.

The role of teachers is to orchestrate these interrelated sources, developing productive transactions among readers and texts that lead to more efficient strategies for information processing by students. Information processing involves such active mental searches as drawing on prior knowledge, predicting, questioning, elaborating, transforming, structuring, restating, summarizing, synthesizing, reflecting, and critically evaluating. In practical terms, content teachers can teach reading and study by modeling strategies that incorporate one or more of these searches by having students practice strategies in pairs and in small groups as well as on their own and by having students reflect on and share their experiences with each other in using the strategies.

Two lists of such strategies follow. They were developed by Botel (1984) at the University of Pennsylvania for preparing teachers and reading specialists. The first list includes strategies for reading and comprehending literary texts; the second includes strategies for reading and comprehending expository texts. These strategies are no less vital for the special education student than the regular student. It will be noted that these strategies enable students to experience reading at their own levels.

Strategies for Reading, Writing, and Studying Library Texts Before Reading

Brainstorming

What questions, ideas, or experiences were suggested by the title and opening paragraph(s) or verse?

Write or Talk and Write

Write nonstop about what comes to mind as you think about the title.

Write whatever questions come to mind as you think about the title.

Recall a related remembered experience; share it; write it.

Take notes on the way of life of a character from another culture (categories: family relationships, sources of food, beliefs about nature, housing, community, recreation, education).

While Reading

If you do not understand something, put a mark in the margin and go on.

Picture in your mind's eye what happens in the story.

After Reading

Personal Responding

What stands out for you in the selection?

Retelling

Retell history from the point of view of different characters.

Tell the story to someone in the family, to a friend, to a younger person, etc.

Vocabulary Development

Write key words or expressions and define them in context.

Write words the writer uses to describe a character; then write a brief paragraph about the character using these words.

Write synonyms for key words.

Writing

Prepare questions you would ask if you could interview a character.

Write a journal entry about an important event as if you were the character who experienced it.

Write notes as if you were one of the characters. Write an eyewitness or reporter's account of a scene as it might appear in a newspaper.

Making Tests

Prepare tests on content studied using the same form found in standardized and other tests.

Illustrating

Draw a floor plan of a major setting.

Illustrate a scene.

Make a map or graphic diagram of a key concept or relationship.

Illustrate key words and expressions.

Show the story or episode in a four-frame cartoon.

Dramatizing

Plan a "Reader's Theater"

Plan a panel discussion as if you were characters in the story.

Plan an informal dramatization. Plan a debate.

Compare similarities and differences between your culture and that of a character.

Strategies for Reading, Writing, and Studying Expository Texts Before Reading

Brainstorming

List words and phrases you associate with the title; see if your items can be grouped or chunked. What questions are suggested by the title or opening paragraphs?

What questions would you hope would be answered by the selection?

Previewing

Read the headings and first and last paragraphs; then say or recite briefly what they suggest about the text.

Based on your review, what are the main questions that the author probably set out to answer in the selection?

Making Tests

Prepare tests on content studied using the same form found in standardized and criterion-referenced tests.

While and After Reading

Personal Responding

What stands out for you in the selection?

Taking Notes

Turn headings into questions and answer them.

Underline one or two key words in each paragraph. Write a question for each paragraph or section. Make marginal notes.

Make a map or graphic diagram of a key concept or relationship.

Develop Vocabulary

Write key words and expressions and define them in context.

Reread and Recite

Reread only the key words and write them from memory.

Reread only the key words and write a summary.

As noted earlier, Dupois reported that content teachers know little about teaching reading of their subject.

Adaptation of the two lists of strategies in teaching subject matter should correct that problem. That leaves the problem of students who cannot read texts on their own. These students would benefit greatly from having the material read to them while others in the class read silently. But they can also benefit from involvement with classmates in learning the strategies, in particular when they are practiced and reflected on collaboratively.

Beyond learning the strategies for comprehending texts, students in the content areas should be reading a variety of periodicals and library books independently to broaden their perspectives, deepen their knowledge, and excite their interest in the content. Self-selected independent reading provides another way of accommodating the varying reading levels in a classroom (Anderson et al., 1985; Botel, 1981). Librarians and professional associations of content teachers are excellent sources for such reading. In social studies, the Children's Book Council (1984) produces an excellent list. Earle (1976) prepared a list of high-interest materials for the math classroom.

It is clear that reading in the content areas today deals with how teachers can organize and plan for instruction so as to relate the basic academic competencies (language processes of not only reading but also writing, listening, and speaking) to learning the basic academic subjects. That is true for all students, including special education students in mainstream classrooms as well as in learning centers.

In summary, from the point of view of special education, the proposed ways of teaching content reading would have the effect of providing for more learning and less isolation and fragmentation, less stigmatization and separation from peers, less isolation of teachers, and less fragmentation of language.

REFERENCES

Anderson, R. C., Hiebert, E. H., Scott, J. A., & Wilkinson, I. A. G. (1985). *Becoming a nation of readers: The report of the Commission on Reading*. Washington, DC: National Institute of Education.

Botel, M. (1981). *A Pennsylvania comprehensive reading/communication arts plan*. Harrisburg: Pennsylvania Department of Education.

Botel, M. (1984). *Comprehending texts: Subskills or strategies*. Philadelphia: Graduate School of Education, University of Pennsylvania.

Children's Book Council. (1984). *Notable children's trade books in the field of social studies*. New York, NY: Author.

Dupois, M. M. (Ed.). (1984). *Reading in the content areas: Research for teachers*. Newark, DE: International Reading Association.

Earle, R. A. (1976). *Teaching reading and math*. Newark, DE: International Reading Association.

Goodlad, J. I. (1983). What some schools and classrooms teach. *Educational Leadership, 40*(7), 8–19.

Mercier, L. Y. (Ed.). (1981). *The essentials approach: Rethinking the curriculum for the 80's.* Washington, DC: U.S. Department of Education, Basic Skills Improvement Program.

MORTON BOTEL
University of Pennsylvania

READING MILESTONES–THIRD EDITION

Reading Milestones, a basal reading series developed by Quigley and King (1991) with McAnally, Rose, and Quigley (1999), was designed specifically for individuals with hearing impairment and was originally published in the early 1980s by Dormac, Inc. The series was then acquired by PRO-ED, Inc., in 1995.

Reading Milestones is the most popular reading program of its kind. It is an example of a special text that is recent, extensive, and research based (Power & Leigh, 2000). This successful alternative, language-controlled program is designed to take readers to approximately a fifth-grade reading level. It is especially effective for students with hearing impairments and language delays and is also widely used with others who have special language and reading needs, including individuals with learning disabilities and students learning English as a second language (ESL).

The *Reading Milestones* program includes student readers, student workbooks, spelling books, teachers' guides, and placement tests at each of the six levels. There are 10 student readers included in each level of the program with six stories per book. The stories are representative of the culture of the students using the program. A student workbook accompanies each student reader and includes tasks that emphasize the development of comprehension through the use of procedures such as semantic, story, and word maps; word analogies; and semantic feature analyses. Each level of the program consists of one spelling book that covers books 1 through 5 and one spelling book that covers books 6 through 10, using a number of spelling tasks consisting of words that appear in the story. The teachers' guides provide detailed instructional suggestions that allow educators to create a self-contained program from the reading series (PRO-ED, Inc.). The *Reading Bridge* series includes extension materials for students reading at grade levels 4–5. Additional resources that adhere to the structured approach presented in *Reading Milestones* include the *Simple Language Fairy Tales, Simple English Classics,* and *Most Loved Classics* series.

Extensive revisions were made in the third edition of the program based on recent research, new practices in reading, and feedback from users of the series. Because most students with hearing impairments and/or other special needs lack a basic knowledge base in oral/aural aspects of language, there can be a resulting gap between their language experience and the assumptions inherent in the materials they are given to read. *Reading Milestones* was designed to minimize this gap by beginning with the simplest possible language to ensure initial success in reading and by increasing language acquisition. Students are guided to progress in small increments, accompanied by constant reinforcement and review of concepts, vocabulary, and language constructions, to ensure continuing success and motivation.

This entry has been informed by the sources listed below.

REFERENCES

Brockmiller, P., & Coley, J. (1981). A survey of methods, materials, and teacher preparation among teachers of reading to the hearing-impaired. *The Reading Teacher, 34,* 526–529.

King, C., & Quigley, S. (1985). *Reading and deafness.* Austin, TX: PRO-ED.

Lasso, C. (1987). Survey of reading instruction for hearing-impaired students in the United States. *The Volta Review, 89,* 85–98.

Lasso, C. J., & Mobley, R. T. (1997). National survey of reading instruction for deaf or hard-of-hearing students in the U.S. *The Volta Review, 99,* 31–58.

McAnally, P., Rose, S., & Quigley, S. (1999). *Reading practices with deaf learners.* Austin, TX: PRO-ED.

Power, D., & Leigh, G. R. (2000). Principles and practices of literacy development for deaf learners: A historical overview. *Journal of Deaf Studies and Deaf Education, 5,* 3–8.

PRO-ED, Inc. (n.d.). *Reading milestones: An alternative reading program* (3rd ed.). Retrieved from http://www.proedinc.com

Quigley, S., & King, C. (Eds.). (1991). *Reading milestones* (2nd ed.). Austin, TX: PRO-ED.

PEGGY KIPPING
PRO-ED, Inc.
First and Second editions

ROSE FAIRBANKS
Temecula, California
Third edition

READING REMEDIATION

Reading can be described as a highly complex cognitive activity. As a cognitive task, the reading act requires the successful completion of many simple and complex linguistic skills (Perfetti, 1983). As an illustration, consider the task of reading aloud the word dog. To accomplish this seemingly simple task, a reader must know the letters of the alphabet, must have internalized the sound/symbol patterns common to the English language, and must be able to decode or sound out the word accurately. Decoding alone can be a troublesome venture in the English language, where exceptions appear to outnumber phonetic rules. Further, if an understanding of dog is also required, then the reader must relate the abstract symbols and sounds to the concept of dog stored in long-term memory.

If many skills are required to read and understand a single word, then the skills necessary to make sense of the previous paragraph are far more extensive. It is therefore not surprising that some individuals never acquire reading proficiency. Those individuals who consistently experience difficulties in processing print are part of a population of learners who require special instruction. This special instruction is referred to as reading remediation.

Reading remediation is a branch of language instruction that is concerned with the identification and treatment of reading problems, particularly for students for whom the regular classroom instruction does not prove effective. The successful remediation of reading problems has become of particular importance in recent years due to the enactment of the No Child Left Behind Act (NCLB; 2002), with its requirement that all students be proficient in reading by the year 2014 and its goal of adequate yearly progress toward that goal for students in subgroups, including students in special education and English language learners.

The following text will examine factors that contribute to reading difficulties, consider how the cycle of remediation occurs, discuss levels of reading diagnosis, survey principles that should guide effective diagnosis, and review profiles of readers who may require additional attention in reading instruction.

Even before an individual begins learning to read, there are personal factors that are likely to enhance or inhibit reading performance. Rupley and Blair (1983) identify two broad categories of variables that relate to reading performance: functional and facilitative factors. Functional factors are those personal variables that actually pertain to reading. Sight vocabulary, reading rate, and oral language development are examples of functional factors. In many ways, however, these functional variables are the outcome of other variables that are not directly part of the reading performance but contribute to it. These variables are called facilitative factors, and they are of particular importance in reading remediation. Facilitative factors fall under broad headings such as physical, cognitive, and emotional characteristics. Within each of these broad areas there are conditions that can significantly influence reading performance.

For example, among physical characteristics, we know that gender, visual and auditory ability, and general health influence reading performance; neurological development may have a role as well. Whether owing to genetic or environmental factors, or a combination of both, females have long been thought to have an advantage over males in language acquisition and early language proficiency. Although doubt has been raised as to the existence of such a gender difference in language acquisition and proficiency (Byrnes, 2001), boys do tend to outnumber girls consistently in remedial reading classes.

It is also clear that individuals who suffer from visual or auditory impairments will have more difficulty in acquiring proficiency in written language. Adequate sight and hearing are basic to reading. Among young children, many suspected reading problems can be traced to visual or auditory impairments, many of which are correctable. Once the vision or hearing problem has been corrected, many young children go on to acquire reading proficiency. Consequently, analysis of reading problems frequently begins with vision and hearing screening. In these screenings, visual and auditory acuity and discrimination are tested.

Variations in neurological development or neurological damage during development may be involved in some cases of reading disability. Differences in how the brain is organized and in which areas are active during reading and language processing may result in impaired reading ability, by interfering with the phonological processing involved in learning to read or by more general language processing disturbances (Shaywitz et al., 2000).

Cognitive factors also contribute significantly to the reading process. As we will see in the discussion of reader profiles, the cognitive ability an individual brings to the reading act is a major determinant of the level of proficiency expected. While there is no one-to-one correspondence between intelligence and reading ability, the relationship between the two is strong indeed. Other cognitive factors involved in successful reading performance include memory, attention, and the ability to learn by forming associations. Cognitive factors may be assessed by means of achievement or intelligence test data, or school performance records.

Similarly, an individual's emotional well-being can positively or negatively affect the ability to read. The significant influence of affective factors on learning should not be ignored in the evaluation of reading problems (Gunning, 2002; Richek, Caldwell, Jennings, & Lerner, 1996). Learners who have the cognitive potential may lack the desire or commitment required to do well in reading. Parent/student interviews and self-concept and personality tests may be used to gather information on the emotional condition of a reader.

When a reading problem is suspected, it is prudent to determine whether existing physical, cognitive, and emotional, as well as socioeconomic, cultural, or educational, factors are potential sources of the problem. The systematic assessment of functional and facilitative factors is part of reading diagnosis, which, in turn, is a major component in the remediation cycle.

Much of the language of reading remediation is borrowed from medical science. The medical influence is particularly apparent in the cycle of reading remediation, which comprises three phases: diagnosis, prescription, and treatment.

The diagnosis or data-collection phase of the remediation cycle is devoted to the systematic assessment of existing conditions: a search for evidence that might indicate the source of a reader's problems. It is in this phase that information about the reader and reading performance is gathered and analyzed. Knowledge about the reader may be collected in a spontaneous fashion within the classroom, or it may be amassed through a formal and extensive procedure.

On the basis of careful diagnosis, the second phase of the cycle, the prescription or program-specific phase, is put into place. Prescription is the delineation of the appropriate instructional treatment to be administered. As with the diagnostic procedure, the instructional plan may be informal or formal in nature. An informal prescription might entail little more than the teacher's specification of instructional objectives that seem appropriate for a given reader. A formal prescription, by comparison, may be an elaborate instructional program to be administered by a specialist within a clinic or resource room.

Finally, there is the treatment or program-implementation phase of the cycle. In this phase, the prescribed instructional treatment is carried out and its effectiveness evaluated. From the knowledge gained during instruction and evaluation, additional information gained about the reader and reading performance is gathered. Based on these new data, a revised diagnosis may be rendered, and the remediation cycle begins anew. This remediation cycle forms the basis of reading instruction, whether it occurs in the regular classroom or in the resource room (Barr, Blachowicz, Katz, & Kaufman, 2002).

Diagnosis can take place at several levels of complexity. Those levels, in order of increasing formality, are informal, classroom, and clinical diagnosis (Wilson & Cleland, 1985). In the previous section, the data gathering was apt to be part of the more extensive form of clinical reading diagnosis. Meeting the needs of most readers does not often require that diagnosis reach such a formal level, however. Rather, clinical diagnosis should be the last stage in the diagnostic procedure. For the most part, serving the needs of the reader entails only the first two levels in the sequence of diagnosis, informal and classroom diagnosis.

Informal diagnosis is an ongoing process that takes place continuously in the regular reading classroom. This stage of diagnosis encompasses the teacher's monitoring of reading instruction to determine whether that instruction is appropriate for the learner. If found inappropriate or ineffective, the instruction should be adjusted in some fashion to suit the learner's needs and capabilities more adequately.

If the teacher's minor adjustments in reading instruction are not successful in improving the situation, the teacher moves to the second stage of diagnosis, conducting some testing within the classroom in an attempt to identify the nature of the reading problem. Classroom diagnosis may involve the use of teacher-made or commercial tests that can be administered and interpreted by teachers who have no specialized knowledge of reading or assessment.

Should the classroom teacher's attempts to identify or remediate the reading problem fail, then it is probably time to call in a specialist. It is at this point in the diagnostic sequence that a clinical assessment of the reading problem may be conducted. Following the assessment of facilitative factors, a battery of reading tests may be given. Among the reading skills frequently tested in a clinical diagnosis are sight vocabulary, oral reading, silent reading, listening comprehension, rapid naming, and word analysis skills. The information amassed in diagnosis permits the clinical specialist to prescribe a remediation program for the learner that should improve reading performance. This remediation program may be implemented by the classroom teacher or may require the supplementary services of a reading specialist or resource teacher, which may be provided either in a pull-out program in the resource room or, increasingly in recent years, in the regular classroom, following the mainstreaming or inclusion model of remediation and special education (Gunning, 2002).

The remedial services available for the learner depend on the nature and severity of the diagnosed reading difficulty. School districts vary in the definition of reading difficulty that they use to determine eligibility for remedial reading services, but the most common definitions are based on either functional impairment or discrepancy between assessed ability and achievement. Students with functional impairment fail to meet certain standards of reading achievement and thus are hampered in their functioning in the academic environment. Title 1 and Reading Recovery are programs that use a functional definition of eligibility for the supplemental reading assistance they provide. A discrepancy definition of reading difficulty compares students' assessed level of cognitive ability, typically from an IQ test, with their assessed level of reading achievement. Many states use this standard for eligibility for programs intended to remediate serious reading disabilities (Snow, Burns, & Griffin, 1998). One problem with the use of the discrepancy definition is the likelihood that students with poor reading ability will, for a variety of reasons, perform poorly also on tests of cognitive ability, minimizing the apparent discrepancy and thus rendering them ineligible for additional supportive services.

Because of the major role that diagnosis plays in the remediation cycle, it is imperative that the assessment provide valid and reliable information. Bond and Tinker (1973) outlined some guiding principles for clinical diagnosis that should result in the more effective remediation of reading problems. Many of these principles can still be applied to informal and classroom diagnosis.

1. Diagnosis should be directed toward formulating methods of improvement.
2. Diagnosis should involve more than an appraisal of reading skills and abilities.
3. Diagnosis should be efficient and effective.
4. Diagnosis should be continuous.
5. Diagnosis should seek to identify patterns of behavior.

According to the first of these principles, it is important to remember that diagnosis is not an end in itself. It is conducted to provide accurate information from which effective remediation can be developed. Without the other components of prescription and treatment, diagnosis would be an isolated and meaningless undertaking. Further, for diagnosis to be effective, it must go beyond the assessment of reading alone and examine the learner in a more holistic and multidimensional fashion. That is, the physical, cognitive, emotional, socioeconomic, and educational characteristics of the learner must also be part of the decision-making process.

Another pragmatic concern in the diagnostic procedure is that the amount of testing and the instrumentation be appropriate for the individual case under question. For example, if a physical condition is suspected as the primary cause for existing reading problems, and if visual/auditory screening confirms that hypothesis, then further testing may prove unwarranted. Likewise, it is essential to employ effective (i.e., valid and reliable) measures to test for physical or other factors, and to have those measures administered and evaluated by qualified individuals.

Diagnosis should generally be an ongoing process. Once information has been gathered and an instructional program prescribed, the effects of the prescribed program should be assessed. Even as it pertains to clinical diagnosis, no diagnosis is final, and the treatment prescribed on the basis of formal assessment should be periodically reviewed and revised. It is important to remember that converging evidence is essential for an effective diagnosis. One piece of information is, under most circumstances, insufficient for building a remediation program that will lead to improvement for the learner. Patterns of scores are more likely to convey a more accurate view of the reader's strengths and needs.

Not only do scores produce certain patterns, but the diagnostic data across readers also tend to fall into certain patterns. It is on the basis of these diagnostic patterns that several commonly encountered reader profiles have been generated (Bond & Tinker, 1973; Harris & Sipay, 1980).

Gifted readers are individuals who manifest normal or above normal intelligence and who possess reading skills that are markedly above grade level, where a significant difference is performance at least two years above grade level. It is important to note that the gifted reader may or may not be gifted in other domains; that is, the learner may be advanced in reading skills but average in mathematics or science. Correspondingly, a gifted reader may have intelligence only slightly above average, despite having reading skills that are significantly above grade level. For example, Ruth is a fourth grader with a measured IQ of 125. According to diagnosis, Ruth's sight vocabulary was 6-8 (grade equivalent of sixth grade, eighth month), oral reading 6-3, silent reading 7-1, and listening comprehension 7-5. As these scores indicate, Ruth's overall reading performance is well above the fourth-grade level. We would say that Ruth appears to be a gifted reader.

The needs of the gifted reader may be served within the context of the regular reading class or within a specific gifted program. However, it is expected that these proficient readers will be provided with reading materials and instruction that are commensurate with their demonstrated abilities, whether mainstreamed in the regular reading classroom or grouped with other advanced readers for separate instruction.

Underachievers are similar to gifted learners in that they demonstrate exceptional cognitive potential. However, they may fail to demonstrate reading skills that approach their potential. Dave, for example, is Ruth's fourth-grade classmate. Dave's IQ is estimated to be 140, yet he is performing barely at grade level in reading class. His sight vocabulary is 4-6, silent reading and listening comprehension 4-1, and oral reading 3-8. While Dave's reading scores are not significantly below his grade level, they are significantly below his potential. Although further diagnosis would be appropriate in this case, Dave would be classified as an underachieving reader.

The underachieving reader is often the most difficult case to identify. Primarily because this student's reading performance is near grade level, many classrooms do not recognize or attend to the gap between the underachiever's potential and performance. Further, prescribing and treating the underachiever is a complex undertaking; reading problems may be tied to any number of emotional, physical, neurological, social, or cultural factors that cannot be easily detected or treated.

Sometimes there are learners who do fairly well in reading but who have a problem in one or two skill areas. This type of reader possesses a specific skill deficiency, the most common problem-reader profile. For the most part, these skill-deficient readers remain in the regular classroom with help provided by their classroom reading teacher.

When reading assistance is given in the classroom and is administered by the classroom teacher, it is labeled a corrective reading program. Jake's situation is a case in point. Jake is also in Ruth's fourth-grade class. Although he usually does well in reading, Jake has problems with listening comprehension. As part of his corrective reading program, Jake's teacher works with him on a weekly basis to improve his listening skills. In this way, it is hoped that Jake's listening skills can be brought in line with his other reading skills.

Some readers' problems are not as limited or as easily treated as Jake's. There are those cases in which a learner with normal intelligence performs well below grade level on the majority of reading skills. For example, another fourth grader, Betsy, has an IQ of 101, but her reading grade equivalency scores are as follows: sight vocabulary 1-5; oral reading, preprimer, silent reading, 1-3; listening comprehension, 3-5. Betsy exhibits "unexpected" poor reading (Spear-Swerdling, 2004) and fits into the traditional conception of reading disability as involving a particular difficulty with reading in the absence of other obvious cognitive or sensory impairments. The remediation program required to meet the needs of this type of problem reader is referred to as a remedial reading program. Because of the serious nature of the reading problems being treated, remedial reading programs become the responsibility of a reading specialist or resource teacher. Regular classroom teachers rarely have the training to deal effectively with remedial readers, nor can they provide these individuals the highly individualized attention they need to remediate their reading problems.

The determination to place a learner in a remedial reading program is often the result of a group decision-making process similar to that followed for other categories of special learners. While the primary responsibility for reading remediation falls to the reading specialist, the remediation program can and should involve parents, outside specialists, content-area teachers, and school administrators. Both long- and short-term goals are established for the reader, focusing on cognitive, metacognitive, and affective needs. Progress toward these goals is carefully documented, so that accurate evaluation of the program and the learner is possible.

The last reader profile is that of the garden-variety poor reader. Like the remedial reader, this student demonstrates reading skills that are far below grade level. However, unlike the remedial reader, the garden-variety poor reader's below-average reading performance is not unexpected. Children with garden-variety poor reading exhibit problems with language comprehension in general along with their difficulties with word recognition, hindering their acquisition of reading (Spear-Swerdling, 2004). Victor, who is also in Ruth's class, has reading scores similar to Betsy's. However, his listening comprehension is also well below grade level. Victor's reading scores appear to correspond to his level of language development and cognitive ability. By a discrepancy definition of reading disability, then, he would not be eligible for formal reading remediation. Because of the specialized treatment they require, however, it is often appropriate for garden-variety poor readers to be assigned to a reading specialist or resource teacher for remediation.

In addition to addressing the individual needs and capabilities of students falling under all of these learner profiles, remedial or corrective reading programs must now strive as well toward the goal of having all students score at a proficient level in reading by the year 2014, under NCLB (2002). Increasing awareness of risk factors for reading difficulties and the increasing implementation of effective preventive interventions may reduce the number of students who develop problems in processing print. However, as long as there is the complex process of reading, there will be learners who encounter difficulties and who will require special reading instruction. It is the purpose of effective reading remediation programs to provide appropriate instruction to those learners for whom proficient reading is a goal yet to be achieved.

REFERENCES

Barr, R., Blachowicz, C. L. Z., Katz, C., & Kaufman, B. (2002). *Reading diagnosis for teachers: An instructional approach* (4th ed.). Boston, MA: Allyn & Bacon.

Bond, G. L., & Tinker, M. A. (1973). *Reading difficulties: Their diagnosis and correction* (3rd ed.). Englewood Cliffs, NJ: Prentice Hall.

Byrnes, J. P. (2001). *Cognitive development and learning in instructional contexts* (2nd ed.). Boston, MA: Allyn & Bacon.

Gunning, T. G. (2002). *Assessing and correcting reading and writing difficulties* (2nd ed.). Boston, MA: Allyn & Bacon.

Harris, A. J., & Sipay, E. R. (1980). *How to increase reading ability* (7th ed.). New York, NY: Longman.

No Child Left Behind Act of 2001. (2002). Public Law No. 107-110, Paragraph 115, Stat. 1425.

Perfetti, C. A. (1983). Individual differences in verbal processes. In R. F. Dillon & R. R. Schmeck (Eds.), *Individual differences in cognition* (Vol. 1, pp. 65–104). New York, NY: Amsterdam.

Richek, M. A., Caldwell, J. S., Jennings, J. H., & Lerner, J. W. (1996). *Reading problems: Assessment and teaching strategies*. Boston, MA: Allyn & Bacon.

Rupley, W. H., & Blair, T. R. (1983). *Reading diagnosis and remediation: Classroom and clinic* (2nd ed.). Boston, MA: Houghton Mifflin.

Shaywitz, B. A., Pugh, K. R., Jenner, A. R., Fulbright, R. K., Fletcher, J. M., Gore, J. C., & Shaywitz, S. E. (2000). The neurobiology of reading and reading disability (dyslexia). In M. L. Kamil, P. B. Mosenthal, P. D. Pearson, & R. Barr (Eds.), *Handbook of reading research* (Vol. 3, pp. 229–249). Mahwah, NJ: Erlbaum.

Snow, C. E., Burns, M. S., & Griffin, P. (Eds.). (1998). *Preventing reading difficulties in young children*. Washington, DC: National Academy Press.

Spear-Swerdling, L. (2004). A road map for understanding reading disability and other reading problems: Origins, prevention, and intervention. In R. B. Ruddell & N. J. Unrau (Eds.), *Theoretical models and processes of reading* (5th ed., pp. 517–573). Newark, DE: International Reading Association.

Wilson, R. M., & Cleland, C. S. (1985). *Diagnostic and remedial reading for classroom and clinic* (5th ed.). Columbus, OH: Merrill.

PATRICIA A. ALEXANDER
University of Michigan

EMILY FOX
University of Maryland

REALITY THERAPY

Reality therapy is a recently developed method of psychotherapy that stresses the importance of clients' learning more useful behaviors to deal with their current situations. Reality therapy stresses internal motivation, behavior change, and development of the "success identity." In terms of philosophical or theoretical stance, reality therapy can be described as strongly cognitive or rational in its approach, appealing to the client's reason and emphasizing the possibility of meaningful change, not just in feelings, but in behavior. The therapist takes an active, directive role as teacher, but remains supportive and nonpunitive.

William Glasser, a physician, developed the theory of reality therapy over a period of years beginning with his psychiatric training. Both Glasser's reaction against traditional psychoanalytic psychotherapy and his experiences in working with delinquent youths at a California school for girls probably played major roles in the development of reality therapy (Belkin, 1975).

Glasser (1965) sees the individual as motivated internally by the need to belong, to be loved, and to be a successful, worthwhile person. Control is seen as a major element in the human system: the individual works to control the environment so that internal, personal needs can be met. The individual's interface with the reality of his or her current life situation is the arena of action. Therefore, reality therapy stresses personal commitment, change in behavior, responsibility, and the here and now. The individual's past history is not seen as particularly significant, and the medical model or orthodox concept of mental illness has no place in this approach (Corey, 2012).

The therapist is viewed as a coach or instructor who provides clients with assistance and encouragement in evaluating the usefulness of their current behavior in satisfying their needs. Where the appropriateness of change is recognized, the therapist assists in the development and execution of plans for remediation. Development of the client's strengths and feelings of self-worth leading to a success identity is a key responsibility of the therapist.

Reality therapy is basically a didactic activity, by which the client develops an understanding of reality and learns to act responsibly and effectively in accordance with that reality. A summary of the techniques and procedures of reality therapy is provided by Corey (2012), based on his adaptation and integration of material from several sources. Corey discusses eight steps in therapy: Create a relationship, focus on current behavior, invite clients to evaluate their behavior, help clients develop an action plan, get commitment, refuse to accept excuses, refuse to use punishment, and refuse to give up.

Glasser has promoted the acceptance of his approach by numerous presentations and publications. In *Reality Therapy: A New Approach to Psychiatry* (1965), *Stations of the Mind* (1981), and *Take Effective Control of Your Life* (1984), Glasser develops his theoretical approach to psychotherapy and demonstrates its application to clinical cases. Glasser's *Schools Without Failure* (1969) applies the concepts of reality therapy to the school setting. *Positive Addiction* (1976) treats a different, but related, theme; it also has met with wide public acceptance.

Reality therapy has grown in popularity and influence. It is particularly well received in schools and the criminal justice system, and with counselors who work to rehabilitate handicapped individuals. This psychotherapeutic approach lends itself to short-term, direct, and active therapy.

REFERENCES

Belkin, G. S. (1975). *Practical counseling in the schools*. Dubuque, IA: Brown.

Corey, G. (2012). *Theory and practice of counseling and psychotherapy*. Belmont, CA: Wadsworth.

Glasser, W. (1965). *Reality therapy: A new approach to psychiatry*. New York, NY: Harper & Row.

Glasser, W. (1969). *Schools without failure*. New York, NY: Harper & Row.

Glasser, W. (1976). *Positive addiction*. New York, NY: Harper & Row.

Glasser, W. (1981). *Stations of the mind*. New York, NY: Harper & Row.

Glasser, W. (1984). *Take effective control of your life*. New York, NY: Harper & Row.

ROBERT R. REILLEY
Texas A&M University

See also Psychosocial Adjustment; Psychotherapy With Individuals With Disabilities

RECEPTIVE-EXPRESSIVE EMERGENT LANGUAGE TEST–SECOND EDITION

The Receptive-Expressive Emergent Language Test–Second Edition (REEL-2; Bzoch & League, 1991) is a multidimensional analysis of emergent language. The REEL-2 is specifically designed for use with a broad range of infants and toddlers up to age 3 who are at risk. The instrument is a system of measurement and intervention planning based on neurolinguistic development to identify young children who have specific language problems based on specific language behaviors. Results are obtained from a parent interview and are given in terms of an Expressive Language Age, a Receptive Language Age, and a Combined Language Age.

Bachman (1995) reviewed the instrument and summarized that the REEL-2 covers a wide range of behaviors and could be used with direct observation to elicit information for developing a qualitative description of a child's early language development. Bliss (1995) reported that the advantages of the REEL-2 are in its easy administration and scoring.

REFERENCES

Bachman, L. F. (1995). Review of the Receptive-Expressive Emergent Language Test–Second Edition. In J. C. Conoley & J. C. Impara (Eds.), *The twelfth mental measurements yearbook* (pp. 843–845). Lincoln: University of Nebraska Press.

Bliss, L. S. (1995). Review of the Receptive-Expressive Emergent Language Test–Second Edition. In J. C. Conoley & J. C. Impara (Eds.), *The twelfth mental measurements yearbook* (pp. 845–846). Lincoln: University of Nebraska Press.

Bzoch, K. R., & League, R. (1991). *Receptive-Expressive Emergent Language Scale–Second Edition*. Austin, TX: PRO-ED.

TADDY MADDOX
PRO-ED, Inc.

RECEPTIVE LANGUAGE DISORDERS

The term *receptive language disorder* refers to children who have difficulty understanding input from spoken language relative to expectations for their chronological age. Another term which may also be used to denote this disorder type is language *comprehension deficit*. This difficulty may cause the child problems both in understanding what people say in conversation and in following oral directions within routines and in daily activities. Depending on the child's age and developmental level, he or she may struggle to understand specific words or concepts and or to comprehend meanings conveyed by grammar constructs such as word order, interpreting stories, or making inferences. Comprehension issues may have cascading effects on the child's social interactions with peers and adults.

An estimated 7.4% of children are diagnosed with language impairments (Law, Boyle, Harris, Harkness & Nye, 2000). Receptive language disorders co-exist with difficulties with expressive language or in formulating utterances using language. This dual level of language deficit has been termed a mixed language disorder. It is considered to be more common than an isolated receptive language deficit (Leonard, 2009). Receptive language disorders are also frequently associated with pragmatic language disorders, central auditory processing disorders, and autism spectrum disorders (Lincoln et al., 1992). When receptive language disorders are secondary to a disorder such as autism, they are often identified in the first 5 years of life. In the case of acquired language disorder from traumatic brain injury or other cerebral incident, children may present with receptive language disorder following a significant accident or illness at any age. However, in a majority of children with this diagnosis, there is no known cause for the deficit in understanding spoken language.

Assessment and treatment of receptive language disorders fall within the scope of practice of speech language pathologists (SLPs) in schools and other settings where children are seen for clinical intervention. As a part of initial assessments, children should be seen by an audiologist to rule out hearing loss or difficulty with processing language at a neural level as a cause of their receptive language disorder. Assessment will also include the areas of attention, memory, and sound processing that may affect receptive language abilities. In addition, these children may be referred to neurologists or other medical practitioners to see if a medical cause can be determined and whether medical treatment is appropriate. SLPs work in concert with parents and special educators who see the children in classroom and daily living settings to underscore the goals of clinical intervention. Special educators may also work with children who have associated behavioral and/or academic issues related to their receptive language disorder.

Prognosis for improvement in children with receptive language disorders is considered moderate to poor. Based on an extensive meta-analysis, Law, Garrett, & Nye (2004) asserted that there was insufficient evidence to claim that intervention for children with receptive language difficulties showed positive effects. Present approaches to treatment include structured activities that target a child's overall language or literacy development. Specific receptive targets such as following directions, understanding vocabulary and concepts, and answering questions can be incorporated into activities such as stories or conversation (Paul, 2007). For younger children below age 5, multisensory techniques can be used within play based activities to increase receptive language associated with salient activities. For older children, comprehension may be targeted using a whole language approach which involves simultaneously targeting a variety of language components within meaningful literacy activities.

REFERENCES

Law, J., Boyle, J., Harris, F., Harkness, A., & Nye, C. (2000). Prevalence and natural history of primary speech and language delay: Findings from a systematic review of the literature. *International Journal of Language and Communication Disorders, 35,* 165–188.

Law, J., Garrett, Z., & Nye, C. (2004). The efficacy of treatment for children with developmental speech and language delay/disorder: A meta-analysis. *Journal of Speech, Language, and Hearing Research, 47,* 924–943.

Leonard, L. (2009). Is expressive language disorder an accurate diagnostic category? *American Journal of Speech Language Pathology, 18,* 115–123.

Lincoln, A., Dickstein, P., Courchesne, E., Elmasian, R., & Tallal, P. (1992). Auditory processing abilities in nonretarded adolescents and young adults with developmental receptive language disorder and autism. *Brain and Language, 43,* 613–622.

McLeod, S. & Harrison, L. (2009). Epidemiology of language impairment in a nationally representative sample of 4- to 5-year-old children. *Journal of Speech, Language, and Hearing Research, 52,* 1213–1229.

Paul, R. (2007). *Language disorders from infancy through adolescence: Assessment and intervention.* St. Louis, MO: Mosby Elsevier.

JESSICA H. FRANCO
BARBARA L. DAVIS
Department of Communication Sciences and Disorders, The University of Texas at Austin
Fourth edition

RECIPROCAL DETERMINISM

Reciprocal determinism refers to the interaction between cognition, environmental factors, and behavior, such that behavior is a function of the interaction of the individual with the environment (Bandura, 1986). It is a key component to social learning theory (Bandura) and has been used to explain various maladaptive behaviors exhibited by children and adolescents (e.g., aggression, substance use). It is most consistent with an ecological model in that, when a child is having difficulty in school, the focus is not just on the child but also takes into consideration contextual (i.e., ecological) factors that may be contributing to the child's difficulty. At the same time, reciprocity of interaction is considered in that the child's difficulty in an academic area may affect the feedback he or she is receiving and the teacher's frequency of interaction. In educational domains, this may include assessment of the academic ecology or learning environment. For example, a first grader who is having difficulty in early reading skills may become frustrated because of the lack of success. As a result, the student may exhibit inattention during reading tasks and become reluctant to engage in these tasks. The teacher's response may be to assume that the problem is due to lack of effort, as this is the most obvious behavior.

Only by taking into consideration all information and the potential interactions of task demands, teacher response, and child behavior does it become evident that the child's initial difficulties led to the decreased effort, which in turn is furthering the difficulty and potentially leading to negative relations with the teacher, as well as low academic self-efficacy and decreased effort. Providing both academic supports and positive reinforcement for effort and progress can be implemented to effect change in both the learning and the behavior of the child.

In behavioral domains, this may include functional behavior assessment. By identifying the antecedents and consequences to the behaviors of question, cognitive, behavioral, and environmental factors can be identified. More important, the interactions between these components can be determined so as to effectively bring about change in cognition or behavior by altering the environment. Recent interventions for bullying and aggression have focused on antecedents (e.g., Mattaini et al., 1996). Alternatively, one could impact cognitive processes and behavior in the form of reinforcement or positive behavioral supports (i.e., consequences; Tapper & Boulton, 2005). In this way, understanding of the interaction provides a comprehensive base for case conceptualization and intervention planning.

REFERENCES

Bandura, A. (1986). *Social foundations of thought and action: A social cognitive theory.* Englewood Cliffs, NJ: Prentice Hall.

Mattaini, M. A., Twyman, J. S., Chin, W., & Nam Lee, R. (1996). Youth violence. In M. A. Mattaini & B. A. Thier (Eds.), *Finding solutions to social problems: Behavioral strategies for change* (pp. 75–111). Washington, DC: American Psychological Association.

Tapper, K., & Boulton, M. J. (2005). Victim and peer group responses to different forms of aggression among primary school children. *Aggressive Behavior, 31,* 238–253.

CYNTHIA A. RICCIO
Texas A&M University

See also **Bandura, Albert; Behavioral Modification; Ecological Assessment; Functional Behavior Assessment; Social Learning Theory**

RECLAIMING CHILDREN AND YOUTH: JOURNAL OF EMOTIONAL AND BEHAVIORAL PROBLEMS

Reclaiming Children and Youth: Journal of Emotional and Behavioral Problems is a quarterly journal publishing practical, research-validated strategies for professionals and policy leaders concerned with young people in conflict within school, family, or community. Each issue is topical. The journal was first published in 1992 under the title *Journal of Emotional and Behavioral Problems*. In 1995, the title was changed to the present title to better reflect the journal's emphasis on a positive, reclaiming environment in which changes are made to meet the needs of both youth and society. The journal is owned by Journal of Emotional and Behavioral Problems, Inc. and is published by PRO-ED, Inc.

JUDITH K. VORESS
PRO-ED, Inc.

RECREATION, THERAPEUTIC

Therapeutic recreation is a form of play or physical activity that is used to improve a variety of behaviors that may occur in the cognitive, emotional, social, and physical domains. These activities include games, dancing, horseback riding, and a wide range of other individual and group games and sports.

The intellectual domain may be influenced through gross and fine motor movement activities. There are many theories of cognitive development occurring in sequential order in which motor abilities are the basis for higher thought processes (Kephart, 1960; Piaget, 1950). Theoretically, motor skills help to develop higher skill levels in persons with disabilities by increasing memory, language, and problem solving (Major & Walsh, 1977). Forms of recreation may be used as an alternate to more traditional teaching methods. Humphrey (1976) used games and dancing to aid in reversal difficulties, sequencing difficulties, left and right directionality, and improvement in following direction skills. Physical movement helped to present concepts and skills in a more concrete form. Through imitation and role playing, children were able to use intellectual concepts they had already learned and developed (Yawkey, 1979).

Other forms of learning may be influenced by physical activities and games that have the objective of increasing motivation and attention span. Naville and Blom (1968) stressed educational achievements of concentration, willpower, and self-control through movement.

Emotions can be influenced through recreational activities, which may help individuals improve self-concepts and self-confidence. Being aware of one's body and feeling good about oneself can be associated with the pleasure of recreation. Socially, organized group activities may offer social skill learning through structured interpersonal play. Individuals have opportunities to work together, follow leaders, engage in appropriate behaviors, and develop various forms of self-expression. Recreation can be used not only as a medium for communication but also to help integrate individuals with disabilities with typically developing individuals and teach activities to decrease isolation.

Physically, recreational activities have endless limits. Movement may help individuals increase coordination and range of motion of body movement. For example, water sports, swimming, or water therapy can be extremely valuable to a variety of children and youths with disabilities, as can free motion activities such as creative dance. These activities can increase physical strength and flexibility; having a strong, attractive body correlates with a positive self-image.

Specific programs such as bowling, folk dancing, and even competitive sports have incorporated recreational activities as therapy for different populations; a good example of one of these programs is the Special Olympics for various groups of students with disabilities. Jacques-Dalcroze (1930) first developed eurhythmics for individuals with visual impairments to increase self-confidence and expression through music and rhythm. Gollnitz (1970) developed a rhythmic-psychomotor therapy that combined movement, music, and rhythm for individuals with psychic and developmental disorders. Lefco (1974) followed the idea of the integration of the body and mind when she used dance therapy to promote mental and physical well-being. The Cove Schools in Racine, Wisconsin, and Evanston, Illinois, were designed for students with brain injuries to provide play experiences that may have been missed because of slow rates of development. The Halliwick method deals with the swimming ability of individuals with physical disabilities. Norway has a horseback riding school for individuals with disabilities. Mann, Berger, and Proger (1974) offer a comprehensive review of the research on the influence of physical education on the cognitive, physical, affective, and social domains in which movement was significant in helping individuals with disabilities with different variables in these areas.

In summary, therapeutic recreation includes structured physical and social activities that are designed to have as objectives the enjoyment of leisure time, improved movement, and development of physical strength and social skills. Recreation, adaptive physical education, and physical activities increase or improve social, physical, and mental abilities.

REFERENCES

Gollnitz, G. (1970). Fundamentals of rhythmic-psychomotor music therapy: An objective-oriented therapy for children and adolescents with developmental disturbances. *Acta Paedopsychiatrica: International Journal of Child Psychiatry, 37,* 130–134.

Humphrey, J. H. (1976). *Improving learning ability through compensatory physical education.* Springfield, IL: Thomas.

Jacques-Dalcroze, E. (1930). *Eurhythmics: Art and education.* London, England: Chatto & Windum.

Kephart, N. (1960). *The slower learner in the classroom.* Columbus, OH: Merrill.

Lefco, H. (1974). *Dance therapy.* Chicago, IL: Nelson-Hall.

Major, S., & Walsh, M. (1977). *Learning activities for the learning disabled.* Belmont, CA: Fearon-Pitman.

Mann, L., Berger, R., & Proger, B. (1974). Physical education intervention with the exceptional child. In L. Mann & D. A. Sabatino (Eds.), *The second review of special education.* New York, NY: Grune & Stratton.

Naville, S., & Blom, G. E. (1968). *Psychomotor education: Theory and practice.* Denver: University of Colorado Medical Center.

Piaget, J. (1950). *Psychology of intelligence.* New York, NY: Harcourt & Brace.

Yawkey, T. D. (1979). More on play as intelligence in children. *Journal of Creative Behavior, 13,* 247–256.

DONNA FILIPS
Steger, Illinois

See also Equine Therapy; Recreational Therapy

RECREATIONAL READING FOR INDIVIDUALS WITH DISABILITIES

According to most dictionaries, recreation is an agreeable art, a pastime, or a diversion that affords relaxation and enjoyment. However, most students with disabilities would not link recreation with reading because books symbolize failure and emotional distress (Schanzer, 1973). Therefore, the goal of education should be to encourage students to be independent readers who regularly choose to read. For this to occur, it is necessary for teachers, librarians, and parents to become involved.

Teachers are likely to be the only reading models for many students (Smith, Smith, & Mikulecky, 1978). Therefore, they should be active reading models, talking about what they have been reading and allowing students to see them carrying personal books or magazines. In the classroom, free reading time, when everyone reads without the threat of book reports or lengthy comprehension checks, should be scheduled (Smith et al., 1978). Teachers should be sure to have large classroom libraries of recreational reading materials. However, standard off-the-shelf novels or biographies present frustrating hurdles such as reading level, subject matter, and length (Hallenbeck, 1983). Therefore, such books should be didactic, with important words repeated several times. The themes should relate closely to the lives of the students, and the sentences should be short with simple verb tenses. In addition, pronouns should be placed near the nouns that they modify, and characters should be human beings, not abstract

things or ideas. Finally, the style of writing should be conversational (Slick, 1969). This will help to eliminate the selection of reading material that is too difficult.

To halt deterioration of positive reading attitudes, teachers should talk to students about their reading habits and interests, observe what they read, and get to know their interests so appropriate suggestions can be made (Smith et al., 1978). In addition, reading attitude measures and interest inventories are desirable since there is much intrinsic motivation in reading about something relevant and familiar. When vocabulary and concepts are known, reading rate may increase with excitement, and the likelihood of a successful, pleasurable experience is high (Smith et al., 1978). When reading material is matched to interests, students tend to comprehend from one to two grade levels above tested reading levels (Estes & Vaughn, 1973, cited in Smith et al., 1973). Matching students with reading materials dealing with life interests helps to initiate lifelong reading habits (Smith et al., 1978). To encourage students to read past the school experience, reading must be motivated outside the classroom by curiosity, pleasure and excitement at the new, practicality, prestige and social status with peers, escape and vicarious experiences, expansion and reinforcement of present attitudes and interests, and reflection of personal situations and dilemmas (Smith et al., 1978). Teachers can create this desire to read by conferencing with students about what they have read, by allowing students to conference with one another, and by engaging in motivational activities such as brief oral readings to students and games and gimmicks such as book auctions (Smith et al., 1978).

Librarians can also be helpful in encouraging recreational reading among students with disabilities because they come in contact with all students in an average school week. The librarian should remove all stumbling blocks so that special education students feel free to use the library. For example, the borrowing period may have to be adjusted because these students may need more time to complete a book. In addition, it is important to eliminate the frustration of book selection by establishing a one-to-one relationship with the student and having enough high-interest low-reading-level books available. As special education students begin to frequent the library, praise and commendation should be given. In addition, individual guidance and personal service are needed. It would also be helpful for the librarian to supply the special education class with a list of the new books in the library so that students can request a particular book when visiting the library. Finally, it is helpful to have students act as library aides to assure them that they are needed, are helpful, and are appreciated (Slick, 1969).

For many students, reading takes place at school or not at all. If reading is to become an enjoyable and lifelong experience, it is necessary for reading to occur at home. However, pressure from the parents to read is not the answer since pressure violates the spirit of free reading

(Haimowitz, 1977). As early as the 1940s in Japan, there were two home reading programs. One was a 20-minute mother-child reading process in which parents and children sat for 20 minutes a day and the children read to the mothers. The second was scheduled reading hours once a week in which everyone in the family read (Smith et al., 1978). Programs such as these and others initiated by PTA groups and community groups can be helpful in encouraging recreational reading among students with disabilities.

REFERENCES

Haimowitz, B. (1977, December). Motivating reluctant readers in inner-city classes. *Journal of Reading, 21*, 227–230.

Hallenbeck, M. J. (1983, March). A free reading journal for secondary LD students. *Academic Therapy, 18*, 479–485.

Schanzer, S. S. (1973, Fall). Independent reading for children with learning disabilities. *Academic Therapy, 9*, 109–114.

Slick, M. H. (1969, April 10). Recreational reading materials for special education students. Pittsburgh, PA: University of Pittsburgh, School of Library Science. (ERIC Document Reproduction Service No. ED 046 173)

Smith, C. B., Smith, S. L., & Mikulecky, L. (1978). *Teaching reading in secondary school content subjects: A book-thinking process.* New York, NY: Holt, Rinehart, & Winston.

CAROLINE D'IPPOLITO
Eastern Pennsylvania Special Education

See also **High Interest–Low Vocabulary; Library Services for Individuals With Disabilities; Reading**

assist individuals with disabilities in changing certain physical, emotional, or social characteristics so they may pursue leisure activities and live as independently as possible (National Recreation and Park Association, 1978). Recreational therapy is also concerned with helping individuals with disabilities participate in activities with typically developing peers as much as possible. This integration allows individuals with disabilities to move into the recreational mainstream and become more involved in community recreational activities. In addition to helping individuals with disabilities to engage in recreational activities, recreational therapy also provides other benefits. A second advantage of the program is that appropriate recreational and leisure-time skills can lead to increased physical development, socialization skills, and even cognitive and language development (Schulz & Turnbull, 1984). Therefore, recreational therapy may be recommended to help individuals with disabilities maintain their physical skills, interact socially, and increase academic progress.

REFERENCES

National Recreation and Park Association. (1978). The therapeutic recreator. In W. L. Heward & M. D. Orlansky (1980), *Exceptional children.* Columbus, OH: Merrill.

Schulz, J. B., & Turnbull, A. P. (1984). *Mainstreaming handicapped students: A guide for classroom teachers* (2nd ed.). Boston, MA: Allyn & Bacon.

LARRY J. WHEELER
Southwest Texas State University

See also **Equine Therapy; Occupational Therapy**

RECREATIONAL THERAPY

Recreational activities are necessary for the total well-being of any individual. They provide an important source of pleasure and relaxation. Most individuals learn how to use recreational activities from a lifetime of learning how to play. But as with other skill areas, individuals with disabilities often experience difficulties in using free time appropriately. They may have been sheltered during much of their developmental period, or their disability may have prohibited them from acquiring the skills necessary for participation in recreational activities. Consequently, many individuals with disabilities will require intentional and systematic instruction if they are to acquire those skills. In that regard, recreational therapy is a planned intervention process developed to promote the growth and development of recreational skills and leisure-time activities.

Recreational therapy attempts to eliminate or minimize an individual's disability. It uses recreation to

RECREATION FOR INDIVIDUALS WITH DISABILITIES

Recreation for individuals with disabilities includes individual and group programs of outdoor, social, sports, or educational activities conducted during leisure time. Such programs conducted in medically supervised institutions are identified as therapeutic recreation while those conducted in schools and the community are called community programs (Pomeroy, 1983). The overall goal of recreation programs is to enable each disabled person to participate at the lowest effective care level as independently as abilities and disabilities permit (Stein, 1985).

Recreation services for individuals with disabilities should be distinguished from therapeutic recreation. The latter is a means of intervention to bring about desired changes. In schools, therapeutic recreation is medically prescribed and programmed by recreational therapists. In contrast, the purpose of recreation programs for individuals with disabilities is to provide these students with opportunities to realize their leisure and recreational needs whether on an individual or group basis. Recreation programs in schools or communities for students with disabilities are voluntary in nature and programmed by recreational leaders.

Prior to 1960, most recreation programs for individuals with disabilities were segregated or held in institutions (Robinson & Skinner, 1985). Since 1960 legislative forces and concerned professional organizations have sought to deinstitutionalize and desegregate such programs. With the enactment of PL 94-142, recreation came to be considered as a related service in the schools. During the late 1970s the federal government provided grants to colleges and universities to set up training programs for recreation therapists and adapted physical education teachers and for the development of regional information and resource centers (Robinson & Skinner). Private organizations such as Wheelchair and Ambulatory Sports (http://www.wsusa.org/) and the AHRC (Association for the Help of Retarded Children) have also been active in promoting recreational programs in schools and communities.

Although only 5% to 10% of all persons with disabilities are being reached by existing park and recreation service providers, the prognosis for the future appears to be positive. Statutes to promote barrier-free design, and the changing attitudes of service providers and participants, seem to indicate a trend toward more people with disabilities availing themselves of school or community recreation programs.

Delineated on the basis of the degree of supervision required, there are four types of recreation programs for individuals with disabilities. First, there are special programs limited to persons with specific disabilities (e.g., persons with visual impairments, hearing impairments, or physical disabilities). These programs often revolve around a single activity for the purposes of fun, socialization, and skill development. Second, there are semi-integrated services that allow individuals with disabilities to mix with their typically developing peers in activities that lend themselves to integration. Third, some communities have a buddy system where persons with disabilities participate with typically developing peers in the same activities and programs; scouts and Camp Fire Girls have used the buddy system extensively in their programs. The fourth type of program is one that provides opportunities for total integration in all activities, as is the case in many national parks and recreation areas.

The major categories listed by Russell (1983) of recreational activities for individuals with disabilities are sports and games, hobbies, music, outdoor recreation, mental and literary recreation, arts and crafts, dance, and drama.

Disability programs at the national and international levels are usually of a competitive nature. Examples of these include the Paralympics (http://www.paralympic

.org/), which meets every 4 years in a different part of the world and has four disability groups: deaf, amputee, cerebral palsy, and paraplegic competition. Wheelchair Sports, sponsored by the National Wheelchair Athletic Association, provides competition in track, basketball, and weightlifting. Disabled Sports USA (http://www.dsusa.org/index.html) promotes sports and recreational activities through regional offices across the United States.

Most state and regional programs are part of national structures such as the Special Olympics program (http://www.specialolympics.org/). Some state programs are resident or day camps or outdoor activity centers. There are very few recreation centers that exclusively serve individuals with disabilities. The majority are in large urban areas.

Many schools, colleges, and communities sponsor local recreational programs for individuals with disabilities. Community swim programs seem to be the most popular and widespread.

REFERENCES

Pomeroy, J. (1983). Community recreation for persons with disabilities. In E. Pan, T. Backer, & C. Vosh (Eds.), *Annual review of rehabilitation* (pp. 241–291). St. Louis, MO: Mosby.

Robinson, F., & Skinner, S. (1985). *Community recreation for the handicapped*. Springfield, IL: Thomas.

Russell, R. (1983). *Planning programs in recreation*. St. Louis, MO: Mosby.

Stein, J. (1985). Mainstreaming in recreational settings. *Journal of Physical Education, Recreation & Dance, 5*(56), 25–27.

THOMAS R. BURKE
Hunter College, City University of New York

See also Equine Therapy; Music Therapy; Olympics, Special

REDL, FRITZ (1902–1988)

Fritz Redl was born and educated in Austria and obtained a PhD in philosophy and psychology in 1925 from the University of Vienna. From 1925 to 1936, he trained as an analyst at the Wiener Psychoanalysis Institute and was strongly influenced by the founders of child analytic work, particularly Anna Freud and August Aichhorn.

Redl maintained an interest in group psychology throughout his career. After coming to the United States in 1936, he accepted a teaching position at the University of Michigan and helped establish a guidance program at the Cranbook School, later moving to a position as professor of group work at Wayne State University, where he remained for 12 years. Redl's service to children and the field of mental health included his positions as clinical director of the University of Michigan Fresh Air Camp, chief of the Child Research Branch of the National Institute of Mental Health (1953–1959), and president of the American Orthopsychiatric Association.

Redl's work focused on the exploration of children's behavioral controls, their defenses, and how to prevent or treat the disorganization that results when the behavioral control system is maladaptive (Redl, 1966, 1975). His development of the "life space interview," providing strategies and techniques for immediately dealing with crises in the lives of children, showed his keen awareness of the effects of temporal and spatial arrangements (e.g., the stress of transition) on children's behaviors. Redl also saw how studying the behavior of severely disturbed children helped to illuminate techniques used by the normal child. As an outgrowth of his studies, group work, camp experience, and involvement with social agencies, he established Pioneer House, a residential program for the study and treatment of delinquent children, and the Detroit Group Project, providing clinical group work with children and a summer camp for children from low-income families. Redl's Pioneer House work is summarized in his book *The Aggressive Child* (Redl & Wineman, 1957).

A renowned lecturer and consultant worldwide, Redl was a Pinkerton guest professor in the School of Criminal Justice of New York State University and a visiting professor in the Department of Child Psychiatry of the University of Utrecht in Holland. He died in 1988 in North Adams, Massachusetts, where he had retired in 1973.

REFERENCES

Redl, F. (1966). *When we deal with children: Selected writings.* New York, NY: Free Press.

Redl, F. (1975). Disruptive behavior in the classroom. *School Review, 83*(4), 569–594.

Redl, F., & Wineman, D. (1957). *The aggressive child.* New York, NY: Free Press.

E. Valerie Hewitt
Texas A&M University
First edition

Tamara J. Martin
The University of Texas of the Permian Basin
Second edition

See also Life Space Interviewing

REFERRAL PROCESS

Referral is the process by which students' potential disabilities or gifts are identified for comprehensive individual evaluation by school officials. The identification of students for evaluation is a federally mandated activity for which all school districts and state education departments must have specific policies and procedures (U.S. Office of Education, 1977, sections 121a.128 and 121a.220). The law holds districts and state departments responsible for identifying all children with disabilities within their jurisdictions who require special education or related services, including those in the care of other public and private agencies.

It is reported that some 3% to 5% of the school-age population are referred each year (Algozzine, Christenson, & Ysseldyke, 1982). Of those referred, about three fourths are placed in special education. While these averages may characterize the nation as a whole, individual districts may vary widely in the percentage of students referred, evaluated, and placed.

Students can be referred in one of two major ways (Heller, Holtzman, & Messick, 1982). The first is through the systematic efforts of school districts, community agencies, or government institutions. For example, districts may use very low or very high performance on annually administered achievement tests to refer students. Similarly, hospitals may screen newborns for referral to early intervention programs. Finally, state education departments may conduct print and electronic media campaigns and establish toll-free hotlines aimed at encouraging the referral of students with disabilities or gifts currently not receiving services.

The second major referral mechanism involves the efforts of individuals who know the child. Such individuals include the child's teachers, parents, and physician. Of these individuals, the large majority of referrals appear to emanate from teachers (Heller et al., 1982). The advent of PL 94-142 increased the involvement of others both in and outside the school (Bickel, 1982).

Referrals made by teachers (and other individuals) are generally personal decisions based on subjective criteria. As such, these decisions are open to a variety of influences. The specific factors that influence teacher referrals are difficult to identify with any certainty (Bickel, 1982). However, research suggests that teachers are influenced by several considerations. One consideration is program availability; if no program exists to meet the student's needs, or if no room is available in an existing program, referral is unlikely. Second, teachers seem hesitant to refer if there is a large backlog in assessment. Such backlogs cause teachers to consider referral a meaningless action. Third, parents may influence the process. Teachers may hesitate to refer children whose parents would be likely to react in a hostile manner, or be quick to refer those whose parents exert positive pressure. Finally, eligibility criteria affect the decision. For example, some states and districts require that teachers refer students for placement in a specific program such as one for educable mentally retarded pupils. Hence, teachers may be encouraged to refer only children with particular characteristics.

In addition to these factors, other influences on referral undoubtedly exist (Ysseldyke & Algozzine, 1984). Teachers' decisions likely are affected by their own beliefs about what constitutes normal child development and proper behavior and by the extent to which a given child violates those assumptions. The referral decision is also governed by the teacher's skills in dealing with deviations; those who are less adept in handling learning or behavioral differences may be more likely to refer.

It should be clear, then, that a great amount of personal discretion exists in the referral process (Bickel, 1982). Such discretion allows substantial variation in referral practice within and across districts, suggesting that referral often depends as much on what class or school a child attends as on actual learning capabilities and performance. Because of this personal discretion, there is a tendency to refer children who disrupt school routines and those with more severe, easily verifiable problems.

The subjectivity inherent in the referral process has social and ethical implications. First, there is the possibility that substantial numbers of children are being referred inappropriately. Inappropriate referral is problematic because it wastes valuable resources; creates backlogs in assessment, thereby denying services to those truly in need; and subjects children to the potential stigma of special education placement and to education in an environment that may not meet their needs.

Second, inappropriate referral may disproportionately affect particular social groups. For many years, disproportionate placements of minority children and of males in programs for educable mentally retarded (EMR) students have been documented (Heller et al., 1982). The reasons for these disproportionate placements are many and complex. While these placements are not necessarily inappropriate, their existence raises the question of whether teacher referrals, too, are disproportionate.

Relatively little research has been conducted on the topic of disproportionate referral. Those studies that do exist have used two basic methodologies. Some investigators have analyzed existing referral data to determine whether disproportionate numbers of students from particular groups are referred. Other researchers have presented different groups of teachers with simulated data describing a student and have asked them to make referral decisions. The data received by the groups differed only in the social group membership assigned to the student. While no definitive conclusions can be drawn, the studies have shown a tendency toward higher rates of referral for minorities even though these students presented problems that appeared little different from those of their majority peers (Bickel, 1982).

Concern regarding both the possibility that children are being inappropriately referred and disproportionate placement of minority students in special education has led many school districts to refine their referral processes. These refinements have primarily occurred with respect to teacher referrals. Such referrals were originally passed directly through to the pupil evaluation team. Most refinements have focused on inserting checks and balances into this teacher-to-evaluation team pathway.

The most immediately useful refinement probably has been the introduction of consultation (Zins & Curtis, 1984). Consultation may be provided by a resource teacher, school psychologist, or other specialist. The aim of consultation is to help the teacher deal with the student in the regular classroom. The consultant may work with the teacher to develop, apply, and evaluate the effects of alternative instructional or behavior management strategies (Bennett, 1981).

A second type of referral refinement requires the provision of extensive evidence to support the need for referral. The aim of this evidence is to rule out deficiencies in the learning environment as explanations for failure. Failures of the educational system should be discounted first, lest they be interpreted erroneously as failures of the child (Messick, 1984).

Reporting the findings of the National Research Council Panel on Selection and Placement of Students in Programs for the Mentally Retarded, Messick (1984) suggests the provision of four kinds of evidence. First, evidence should be offered that the school is using effective programs and curricula. This evidence should support the effectiveness of those programs and curricula not just for students in general, but for the ethnic, linguistic, or socioeconomic group from which the referred students actually come. Second, evidence should be presented that the student in question has been adequately exposed to the curriculum. It should be documented that the student was not absent regularly from school and that the teacher implemented the curriculum effectively. Third, objective evidence should be offered that the child has not learned what was taught (e.g., through criterion-referenced tests, systematic behavioral recordings, student work samples). Finally, documentation should be provided to show that systematic efforts were made to correct the problem such as introducing remedial approaches, changing the curriculum materials, or trying a new teacher.

A third refinement is the review of referral requests. Review seems to be conducted most often at the building level. In this system, teacher referrals are reviewed by the principal—or by a committee consisting of the principal, guidance counselor, or other building staff—before being forwarded to the pupil evaluation team. The review is designed to encourage teachers and principals to make greater attempts to deal with problem situations within the regular classroom and local school, and, as a result, to limit the occurrence of inappropriate referrals.

The three refinements described—consultation, evidence, and review—are the major elements of a prereferral intervention model. While many variations on this model exist, prereferral intervention has become an important component in the referral process, helping to ensure that those students referred are truly the ones most in need of special education services.

REFERENCES

Algozzine, B., Christenson, S., & Ysseldyke, J. (1982). Probabilities associated with the referral to placement process. *Teacher Education & Special Education, 5,* 19–23.

Bennett, R. E. (1981). Assessment of exceptional children: Guidelines for practice. *Diagnostique, 7,* 5–13.

Bickel, W. E. (1982). Classifying mentally retarded students: A review of placement practices in special education. In K. A. Heller, W. H. Holtzman, & S. Messick (Eds.), *Placing children in special education: A strategy for equity.* Washington, DC: National Academy Press.

Heller, K. A., Holtzman, W. H., & Messick, S. (Eds.). (1982). *Placing children in special education: A strategy for equity.* Washington, DC: National Academy Press.

Messick, S. (1984). Placing children in special education: Findings of the National Academy of Sciences Panel. *Educational Researcher, 13*(3), 3–8.

U.S. Office of Education. (1977). Education of handicapped children: Implementation of Part B of the Education of the Handicapped Act. *Federal Register, 42*(163), 42474–42518.

Ysseldyke, J. E., & Algozzine, B. (1984). *Introduction to special education.* Boston, MA: Houghton Mifflin.

Zins, J. E., & Curtis, M. (1984). Building consultation into the educational service delivery system. In C. A. Maher, R. J. Illback, & J. E. Zins (Eds.), *Organizational psychology in the schools: A handbook for professionals.* Springfield, IL: Thomas.

RANDY ELLIOT BENNETT
MARY LOUISE LENNON
Educational Testing Service

See also Individuals With Disabilities Education Improvement Act of 2004 (IDEIA); Prereferral Intervention; Response to Intervention; Three-Tier Model

Pavlov and other theorists of learning have used such terms as *conditioned reflex* to imply that even learned behaviors are mechanically determined and that they can be described as stimulus-response connections.

Certain human reflexes can be observed only in infancy (Peiper, 1963). For example, infants reflexively grasp any object placed firmly in the palm of the hand. Newborns grasp an elevated bar tightly enough to support their own weight, at least briefly. If someone strokes the sole of an infant's foot, the infant extends the big toe and fans the others (this is known as the Babinski reflex). If someone touches an infant's cheek, an infant who is awake will often, but not always, turn toward the stroked cheek and begin to suck.

Infant reflexes are suppressed in older children and adults, but the connections responsible for the reflexes are not destroyed. The infant reflexes may return as a result of brain damage, especially damage to the frontal lobes of the cerebral cortex. Neurologists often test for the presence of the Babinski reflex or the grasp reflex as a means of detecting possible dysfunction of the frontal lobes. The infant reflexes may also return temporarily as a result of interference with cerebral activity, such as that caused by an epileptic seizure, excessive levels of carbon dioxide, or certain drugs (Paterson & Richter, 1933).

REFERENCES

Paterson, A. S., & Richter, C. P. (1933). Action of scopolamine and carbon dioxide on catalepsy produced by bulbocapnine. *Archives of Neurology & Psychiatry, 29,* 231–240.

Peiper, A. (1963). *Cerebral function in infancy and childhood.* New York, NY: Consultants Bureau.

Sechenov, I. (1863/1965). *Reflexes of the brain.* Cambridge, MA: MIT Press.

JAMES W. KALAT
North Carolina State University

See also Behaviorism; Behavior Modification; Developmental Milestones

REFLEX

A reflex is an automatic connection between a stimulus and a response. One example is the knee-jerk reflex. Another is the reflexive constriction of the pupil in response to light.

Historically, the concept of the reflex has captured the imagination of many theorists who wished to emphasize the mechanical nature of behavior. René Descartes proposed a hydraulic model to account for the behavior of nonhuman animals. The Russian physiologist Ivan Sechenov (1863/1965) argued that all behavior, including that of humans, is reflexive (meaning that it is determined). Ivan

REGIONAL MEDIA CENTERS FOR THE DEAF

In 1959 the U.S. Office of Education implemented a program, under PL 85-905, to provide captioned films and related media to assist in bringing deaf persons into the mainstream of American life. The program featured the development and dissemination of highly specialized media services and products through four regional media centers. In the 1960s, 13 special education instructional media centers were established in addition to the four regional centers for the deaf. By the end of that decade, those 17 centers had been consolidated into four area learning resource centers (ALRCs). The ALRCs conducted activities related to educational media and technology for all handicapped persons, but specialized centers within the ALRC structure provided educational media and technology services for deaf persons. In 1972 the National Center on Education Media and Materials for the Handicapped replaced the ALRCs.

SHIRLEY A. JONES
Virginia Polytechnic Institute and State University

REGIONAL RESOURCE CENTERS

The Regional Resource Centers (RRCs) were created by the Elementary and Secondary Education Act, Title 6, of 1965. They were intended to assist state educational agencies (SEAs) in the implementation of special education services at a time when special education was just beginning to be recognized as a national concern. The RRCs were intended to help SEAs and local educational agencies (LEAs) in the development of special education services and resources by serving as agents in planning, programming, service delivery, training, and the creation of instructional materials.

The actual operations of the RRCs proceeded through a variety of agencies, including state educational departments, universities, and LEAs. The funding was not as generous as originally intended because the federal government envisioned RRCs as a nationwide enterprise. In the first funding cycle (1970–1974), Pennsylvania established an RRC whose services were directed statewide. Other RRCs, however, had multistate service areas (e.g., the Southwest Regional Resource Center served Arizona, Colorado, Nevada, New Mexico, and the Bureau of Indian Affairs). In multistate agencies, the major modes of service were information, consultation, and in-service training. In state-limited programs such as that of Pennsylvania, it was easier to focus services on specified state needs. For example, Pennsylvania used its funds to create diagnostic-prescriptive programs and to help fund classes to validate them (National Association of State Directors of Special Education, 1976).

A later round of funding of RRCs (1974–1977) resulted in some states being refunded and others funded for the first time. While some states, such as New York and Pennsylvania, maintained statewide services, efforts were being made to move to multistate and regional operations. Thus, the Southeastern Regional Resource Center at Auburn University, in Montgomery, Alabama, was given the responsibility for Alabama, Florida, Georgia, Louisiana, Mississippi, Puerto Rico, South Carolina, and the U.S.

Virgin Islands. Separate agencies were split off from the RRCs to assist in the provision of instructional resources to special educators. These were the Area Learning Resource Centers. By 1983, with legislative amendments to the Education of the Handicapped Act, the RRCs became a matter of discretionary support and funding on the part of states. They were adopted in various forms by state educational agencies or subsumed by the SEAs into other entities.

REFERENCE

National Association of State Directors of Special Education. (1976). *A survey of opinions of state directors of special education on Regional Resource Centers: Report.* Washington, DC: Bureau of Education for the Handicapped.

DON BRASWELL
Research Foundation, City University of New York

See also Special Education, Federal Impact on; Special Education Programs

REGRESSION (STATISTICAL)

Regression is a term widely used in behavioral research. It represents both a statistical technique and a statistical phenomenon. Regression as statistical phenomenon or artifact is addressed here. Simply, it is the effect of imperfect correlation between a predictor and outcome on the mean of the outcome.

The origin of the term dates to Sir Francis Galton's investigations into correlations among human physical characteristics. Galton's (1886) focus was the relationship between the height of adult children and their "midparent" (the average of the mother's height times 1.08 and the father's height), and he collected data on 928 offspring of 205 parents. Galton observed that if a parent grew to be taller than average, the adult offspring's height would tend to be closer to the mean of adult children, and hence smaller than the parent (DiNardo & Tobias, 2001). If one started with the children the same result was found for the parents. Galton used the term *regression* for this finding. He actually observed what occurs when a linear relationship is created for two variables. When both variables are standardized to have a mean of zero and variance of 1.0, the correlation represents the slope of the line representing the linear relationship. As one variable—say, the predictor—increases, the slope shows the increase of the average of the outcome at each predictor score value. Since correlation is in general less than 1.0, this slope predicts that the outcome average score will be less extreme than the predictor. In other words, for an increase of 1 unit of the predictor, the outcome will increase the value of the correlation. If the correlation is .5, then a 1 unit increase in predictor will be associated with an increase of .5 units of outcome, thus the "regression to the mean." If the predictor and outcome are reversed, the same phenomenon is seen.

The importance for special education, gifted education, and other disciplines that routinely deal with populations whose characteristics may often include extreme values is that regression effects occur commonly when another measurement is made and compared to a standard or perhaps to the original characteristics. Assume that students are selected because they are all 2 standard deviations below the mean on a standardized test. Any other measurement made on the students, whether contemporaneous or later, will exhibit a regression effect in that students will be expected to be less extreme on the new variable than the 2 standard deviation below mean that was the basis for their selection. If the new variable correlates .7 with the selection variable, and all the students are exactly 2 standard deviations below the mean on the selection test, they will on average be 1.4 standard deviations ($-2 \times .7$) below average on the new variable. If the group was given a particular treatment, inexperienced researchers might confuse the improvement in the outcome due to regression with a treatment effect.

Hopkins (1968) demonstrated various problems related to special education research following from regression effects. In particular he showed how nonrandom matching creates regression differences in groups that do not have identical population means and standard deviations. Since matched control group designs are common, the problem of misinterpreting regression effects as treatment effects is widespread. He noted that randomization of students into treatment and control groups is the only method that generates comparable regression effects and thus allows estimation of treatment effects without the confounding. In the absence of randomization it is possible under some circumstances to estimate the regression effect and subtract it from outcome scores to obtain an estimate of treatment effect. At best this is a poor substitute for better randomized studies, however.

Another example of the confusion about regression effects occurs with the use of intelligence tests to determine giftedness. Some states define giftedness as high performance on a standardized individual intelligence test, such as 1.25 standard deviations above the mean. When a new test is introduced, some researchers have given the new test to a previously identified gifted group, demonstrated that the mean of the new test is lower than that of the current standard, and concluded that the new test does not select gifted students with equal validity. It is fairly simple to demonstrate that the observed lower mean on the new test corresponds to the regressed estimate.

REFERENCES

DiNardo, J., & Tobias, J. L. (2001). Nonparametric density and regression estimation. *Journal of Economic Perspectives, 15*, 11–28.

Galton, F. (1886). Regression towards mediocrity in hereditary stature. *Journal of Anthropological Institute, 15*, 246–63.

Hopkins, K. D. (1968). Regression and the matching fallacy in quasi-experimental research. *Journal of Special Education, 3*, 329–336.

VICTOR L. WILLSON
Texas A&M University

REGULAR CLASS PLACEMENT (See Inclusion)

REHABILITATION

The term *rehabilitation* refers to any process, procedure, or program that enables an individual with a disability to function at a more independent and personally satisfying level. This functioning should include all aspects—physical, mental, emotional, social, educational, and vocational—of the individual's life. An individual with a disability may be defined as one who has any chronic mental or physical incapacity caused by injury, disease, or congenital defect that interferes with his or her independence, productivity, or goal attainment. The range of disabilities is wide and varied, including such conditions as autism, intellectual disabilities, muscular dystrophy, and a variety of neurological and orthopedic disorders. These disparate conditions may appear singly or in concert. Clearly, the process that is designed to assist persons in obtaining an optimal level of functioning is a complex one.

The complexity of the rehabilitation process necessitates a team approach that involves a range of professionals almost as broad and varied as the types of conditions addressed. Goldenson, Dunham, and Dunham (1978) discuss no fewer than 39 rehabilitation specialists in their handbook. Their list includes such diverse professions as orientation and mobility training, genetic counseling, biomedical engineering, and orthotics and prosthetics, in addition to numerous medical, mental health, therapeutic, and special education fields. In view of the potential involvement of such an array of professionals, it becomes particularly important to remember that the rehabilitation process is not one that is done to or for an individual with a disability, but rather one that is done with the individual and often their families as well. If a person is to become as fully functional as his or her abilities will allow, a process that fosters dependence is a self-defeating one.

It is necessary for the professionals involved in the rehabilitation process to function as a team rather than as separate individuals. McInerney and Karan (1981) have pointed out that without information sharing and cooperative integration, the rehabilitation process will not fit the needs of the client. The client should not be expected to fit the needs of the service delivery system. As rehabilitation is a process, not an isolated treatment, a continuum of services must be provided to give the disabled person assistance in all aspects of life. A program that is cohesive in approach, regardless of the number of professionals involved, is essential. In addition, these services must alter to meet the client's changing needs.

REFERENCES

Goldenson, R. M., Dunham, J. R., & Dunham, C. S. (Eds.). (1978). *Disability and rehabilitation handbook*. New York, NY: McGraw-Hill.

McInerney, M., & Karan, O. C. (1981). Federal legislation and the integration of special education and vocational rehabilitation. *Mental Retardation, 19*, 21–24.

Laura Kinzie Brutting
University of Wisconsin at Madison

See also Rehabilitation; Vocational Education

REHABILITATION ACT OF 1973

The Rehabilitation Act of 1973 authorizes comprehensive vocational rehabilitation services designed to help individuals with physical or mental disabilities become employable. The act also authorizes service projects for persons with special rehabilitation needs. For persons with severe disabilities without apparent employment potential, the act authorizes services to promote independent living. Training programs are provided to help ensure a supply of skilled persons to rehabilitate individuals with disabilities. The act also authorizes a research program, a national council to review federal policy regarding individuals with disabilities, and a compliance board to help enforce accessibility standards for those with disabilities.

The act authorizes state grants for comprehensive services designed to enable individuals with disabilities to become employable. Each state receives an allotment of federal funding that must be matched on a 20% state to 80% federal ratio. Federal funds are allotted on the basis of population and per capita income, with the lower per capita income states receiving a relatively higher allotment on a per capita basis.

Funds are authorized for various service projects for individuals with disabilities. These projects include programs to serve the severely handicapped, migrant workers, Native Americans, and other groups with special needs. Support is provided for training of rehabilitation personnel. State grants and discretionary funds are authorized for independent living services. A client assistance program is required in each state to help clients and applicants obtain services funded under the act.

The National Council on Disability is composed of 15 members appointed by the president. The council establishes general policies for the National Institute on Disability and Rehabilitation Research, advises the president and Congress on the development of programs carried out under the Rehabilitation Act, and reviews and evaluates federal policy regarding programs for individuals with disabilities.

The Architectural and Transportation Barriers Compliance Board was authorized to ensure compliance with the Architectural Barriers Act of 1968 and to promote accessibility for individuals with disabilities. The board is composed of 11 members from the general public (5 of whom must be individuals with disabilities) and 11 representatives of federal agencies.

The National Institute on Disability and Rehabilitation Research administers funds for the rehabilitation research programs. The institute, through a federal interagency committee, is responsible for the coordination of all major federal research related to individuals with disabilities.

James Button
United States Department of Education
First and Second editions

Kimberly F. Applequist
University of Colorado at Colorado Springs
Third edition

REHABILITATION ACT OF 1973, SECTION 504

Section 504 of what is commonly called the Rehabilitation Act is frequently cited as an important precursor to the passage of the Education of All Handicapped Children Act of 1975 (PL 94-142), itself a precursor to the Individuals with Disabilities Education Act. Section 504, among other things, protects the rights of children with disabilities and precludes discrimination in employment and education. The stipulations of the Rehabilitation Act apply to the programs receiving federal financial assistance.

The Rehabilitation Act was cited in the noted *Larry P. v. Riles* decision by Judge Peckham in 1979. This decision cited the state as being in noncompliance with Section 504 in its use of intelligence tests for making placement decisions in special education. Certainly, the Rehabilitation Act of 1973 has had an important impact on special education practice by encouraging more sophisticated and humane treatment of children with disabilities.

REFERENCE

Bersoff, D. N. (1982). The legal regulation of school psychology. In C. R. Reynolds & T. B. Gutkin (Eds.), *The handbook of school psychology*. New York, NY: Wiley.

RANDY W. KAMPHAUS
University of Georgia
First and Second editions

KIMBERLY F. APPLEQUIST
University of Colorado at Colorado Springs
Third edition

REHABILITATION LITERATURE

Rehabilitation Literature is a bimonthly journal published by the National Easter Seal Society. It is principally an educational service journal that abstracts articles published elsewhere and reviews books, journals, films, treatment programs, and so on dealing with the rehabilitation of all types of human disabilities. At least one original feature article appears in each issue. It is written at a level for professional personnel and students training to become professional service providers in all disciplines concerned with the rehabilitation of persons with handicapping conditions.

This abstracting and review journal receives wide circulation among rehabilitation workers and is well regarded in the field. It has been in continuous publication since January 1940; it was taken over by the National Easter Seal Society in 1959. *Rehabilitation Literature* has taken the position that, as an educational service of a large charitable organization, up to 100 reproductions of articles may be made without permission provided they are for free distribution within an organization or classroom. Other rights of reproduction have been reserved. Frequent topics of interest to special educators appear in nearly every issue, bridging such broad areas as stuttering, learning disabilities, aphasias, spina bifida, reading, and general techniques in special education.

CECIL R. REYNOLDS
Texas A&M University

REIFENSTEIN SYNDROME

Reifenstein syndrome (partial androgen insensitivity) is an inherited condition caused by a mutation of the androgen receptor gene in which testes are present but both male and female sexual characteristics exist (Marcelli, Zoppi, Wilson, Griffin, & McPhaul, 1994). In approximately two thirds of the cases, the syndrome is inherited from the mother; in the other third, a mutation occurs. Outward genitalia can range from female (Grade 7), to mixed male and female, to male (Grade 1). Although they possess the chromosomal makeup of males, babies with Reifenstein syndrome may be raised as either males or females, depending on the severity of the syndrome. The approximate prevalence is approximately 1 in every 20,000 births (Gottlieb, Pinsky, Beitel, & Trifiro, 1999). Symptoms of Reifenstein syndrome include sterility, a lack of testosterone, breast development, and the failure of one or both testes to descend into the scrotum. Reifenstein syndrome is present at birth. Other names for Reifenstein syndrome include androgen resistance syndrome, feminizing testes syndrome, Gilbert-Dreyfus syndrome, Goldberg-Maxwell syndrome, incomplete testicular feminization, Lubs syndrome, male pseudohermaphroditism, Morris's syndrome, Rosewater syndrome, testicular feminization syndrome, and Type I familial incomplete male pseudohermaphroditism. A more severe form of Reifenstein syndrome is complete androgen insensitivity (Sinnecker, Nitsche, Holterhus, & Kruse, 1997).

Reifenstein syndrome can be diagnosed prenatally with sequence analysis of the androgen receptor gene (Lumbroso et al., 1994). It is unlikely that specific special education services would be needed for this disorder, other than possible psychological counseling for such issues as gender identity. Although most children with Reifenstein syndrome would have had any needed surgery at a young age, some children may require later surgery; as a result, they may need to miss several days of school.

Characteristics

1. Sterility
2. Failure of one or both testes to descend into scrotum
3. Lack of testosterone development
4. Development of breasts
5. Tubules in testes become hardened
6. Urethra present on underside of penis
7. Gynecomastia upon puberty

Treatment for Reifenstein syndrome depends on the severity and nature of the disorder. If the external genitalia are mostly female, then the usual procedure is removal of the testes and estrogen replacement therapy; the child is then raised as a female. If the external genitalia are less determined, then the decision is left up to the parents and the health care officials as to which gender the child will be. If a child is raised as a male, then androgen replacement therapy will be needed. In both cases, reconstructive surgery and subsequent psychological counseling are usually required (Price et al., 1984).

Future research is continually being conducted on genetic disorders such as Reifenstein syndrome for a wide variety of possible outcomes, including better prenatal screening and more surgical outcomes. This research ranges from the Human Genome Project to more specific genetic studies on all androgen insensitivity disorders.

REFERENCES

Gottlieb, B., Pinsky, L., Beitel, L. K., & Trifiro, M. (1999). Androgen insensitivity. *American Journal of Medical Genetics, 89*(4), 210–217.

Lumbroso, S., Lobaccaro, J. M., Belon, C., Amram, S., Bachelard, B., Garandeau, P., & Sultan, C. (1994). Molecular prenatal exclusion of familial partial androgen insensitivity (Reifenstein syndrome). *European Journal of Endocrinology, 130*(4), 327–332.

Marcelli, M., Zoppi, S., Wilson, C. M., Griffin, J. E., & McPhaul, M. J. (1994). Amino acid substitutions in the hormone-binding domain of the human androgen receptor alter the stability of the hormone receptor complex. *Journal of Clinical Investigation, 94*(4), 1642–1650.

Price, P., Wass, J. A., Griffin, J. E., Leshin, M., Savage, M. O., Large, D. M., ... Besser, G. M. (1984). High dose androgen therapy in male pseudohermaphroditism due to 5 alpha-reductase deficiency and disorders of the androgen receptor. *Journal of Clinical Investigation, 74*, 1496–1508.

Sinnecker, G. H., Nitsche, E. M., Holterhus, P. M., & Kruse, K. (1997). Functional assessment and clinical classification of androgen sensitivity in patients with mutations of the androgen receptor gene: German Collaborative Intersex Study Group. *European Journal of Pediatrics, 156*, 7–14.

JAMES C. KAUFMAN
Educational Testing Service Princeton, New Jersey

REINFORCEMENT, DIFFERENTIAL

Differential reinforcement procedures follow a schedule of reinforcement wherein one response from a response class receives reinforcement and all other responses do not (Alberto & Troutman, 2012; Kazdin, 1980). Four basic types of differential reinforcement exist (Magg, 2004): differential reinforcement of incompatible behavior (DRI), differential reinforcement of alternative behavior (DRA), differential reinforcement of low rates (DRL), and differential reinforcement of other behavior (DRO). These procedures represent positive methods to increase the frequency of a desired behavior or decrease unwanted behavior. Each procedure requires (a) identification of

a target behavior, (b) development of a reinforcement schedule that will provide sufficient opportunities for students to receive rewards, and (c) providing the student a reward contingent upon the target behavior and the set schedule, by the teacher either giving the reward or teaching the student to self-reinforce contingent upon the target behavior and schedule. Two of the differential reinforcement strategies (DRI and DRA) enable educators to focus on the wanted or positive behavior rather than the unwanted or negative behavior. The other two differential reinforcement strategies (DRL and DRO) decrease the occurrence of unwanted behaviors by specifically focusing on the rate or occurrence of the unwanted behavior.

Differential Reinforcement of Incompatible Behavior (DRI)

The teacher and/or student select a behavior that is incompatible with the problematic target behavior. The selected replacement behavior must be topographically incompatible with the unwanted behavior. If students are out of their seat to the point of causing disruption or interrupting learning, for example, sitting in their seat represents an incompatible behavior. Occurrence of the incompatible behavior results in students being rewarded.

Differential Reinforcement of Alternative Behavior (DRA)

Rather than rewarding only actions incompatible to the unwanted behavior, as does DRI, DRA rewards the contingent occurrence of *any* specified functional alternative behavior. Like DRI, DRA procedures reward alternative behavior to replace the function that the unwanted behavior served. If students call out in class consistently without giving others the opportunity to respond, DRA will reward writing answers on response boards and holding the boards up in the air when the teacher asks all students to do this. When implementing DRA teachers either ignore unwanted behavior and reward the performance of the alternative behavior, or interrupt and redirect the unwanted behavior so that the desired alternative behavior occurs, which they then reward.

Differential Reinforcement of Low Rates (DRL)

This procedure gradually decreases the rate of occurrence of unwanted behaviors from an unacceptable level to a rate that can be tolerated. Students receive rewards for scheduled reductions in performance of the target behavior. Rewards can be delivered by the teacher or self-reinforced for either the reduction in the overall occurrence or an increase in the amount of time that occurs between responses. A student, for example, talks 33 times an hour to classmates during lecture or quiet independent work. With the DRL procedure, the student receives a reward for talking 30 times or less for two consecutive days, then

27 times or less for two consecutive days, and so on until the behavior has decreased to only 1 or 2 times per day and maintains at that level. Graphing progress using a changing criterion design provides an excellent means to show progress to students, parents, and educators. The inverse of this procedure, differential reinforcement of higher rates of behavior, can be used in the same way as DRL to increase the occurrence of wanted behavior.

Differential Reinforcement of Other Behavior (DRO)

This procedure delivers a reward, usually after an interval of time, for not engaging in the targeted unwanted behavior. At the end of the time interval whatever the student did, as long as it wasn't the target behavior, receives a reward. If the student has any occurrence of the behavior during the interval, a reward is not delivered. Once the occurrence of the unwanted behavior begins to decrease, the time interval gradually increases. Students, for example, who talk, lightly punch others, or pass papers to classmates during independent seat work an average of four times every 10 minutes may decrease the occurrence of these behaviors when the teacher uses DRO. When students do not talk, punch, or pass papers to classmates during independent seatwork for 3 minutes, they will receive a reward. When this happens for two consecutive days, the interval length may be increased to 5 minutes, then 8, and so on until the students do not perform these behaviors during independent seatwork times.

Differential reinforcement procedures provide useful tools to increase the occurrence of desired behaviors or decrease unwanted behaviors. Their effectiveness depends upon selecting a meaningful primary (e.g., candy), tangible (e.g., chance to pull school spirit or supply item from a reward bag), or social (e.g., lunch with teacher) reward. The delivery of the rewards can occur using a fixed schedule (specific number of times or minutes) or a variable schedule (the number changes from one instance to the next but always in the desired direction and close to a specific average value). Fortunately for teachers, variable schedules generally obtain the best results and facilitate maintenance better than fixed schedules, and these are also the easiest to implement.

REFERENCES

Alberto, P., & Troutman, A. C. (2012). *Applied behavior analysis for teachers*. Upper Saddle River, NJ: Merrill.

Kazdin, A. E. (1980). *Behavior modification in applied settings*. Homewood, IL: Dorsey Press.

Magg, J. W. (2004). *Behavior management from theoretical implications to practical applications* (2nd ed.). Belmont, CA: Wadsworth/Thomson Learning.

JAMES E. MARTIN
University of Oklahoma

See also Negative Reinforcement; Positive Reinforcement

REINFORCEMENT, NEGATIVE (*See* Negative Reinforcement)

REINFORCEMENT, POSITIVE (*See* Positive Reinforcement)

REISMAN, FREDRICKA KAUFFMAN (1930–   )

Fredricka Kauffman Reisman obtained her BA (1952) in psychology, her MS in 1963 in education, and her PhD in 1968 in math education from Syracuse University. Formerly a professor of mathematics education and special education at the University of Georgia in Athens (1979–1983), Reisman began teaching at Drexel University in Philadelphia in 1985, where she became director of the Division of Instruction and Programs and head of teacher preparation in 1991. She currently holds the position of Director of the School of Education at Drexel. Her primary fields of interest include mathematics education, the integration of computing into the assessment and instruction of mathematics, teacher preparation, and diagnostic teaching. Her work has emphasized the prevention of learning difficulties rather than prescription or remediation. Reisman advocates teacher awareness of learner and content characteristics as well as the design of instructional environments that use modern technology.

Reisman has been recognized in *Who's Who in the East* and *Who's Who in America* (1997). Her major publications include *A Guide to the Diagnostic Teaching of Arithmetic* (1982), *Sequential Assessment in Mathematics Inventories* (1986), and *Becoming a Teacher: Grades K–8* (1987).

REFERENCES

Reisman, F. K. (1982). *A guide to the diagnostic teaching of arithmetic* (3rd ed.). Columbus, OH: Merrill.

Reisman, F. K. (1986). *Sequential assessment in mathematics inventories: K–8*. San Antonio, TX: Psychological Corporation.

Reisman, F. K. (1987). *Becoming a teacher: Grades K–8*. Columbus, OH: Merrill.

E. VALERIE HEWITT
Texas A&M University
First edition

TAMARA J. MARTIN
The University of Texas of the Permian Basin
Second and Third editions

REITAN-INDIANA NEUROPSYCHOLOGICAL TEST BATTERY FOR CHILDREN

The Reitan-Indiana Neuropsychological Test Battery for Children (RINTBC; ages 5 through 8), the Halstead Neuropsychological Test Battery for Children (ages 9 through 14), and the Halstead Neuropsychological Test Battery for Adults (ages 15 and older) constitute a global battery commonly referred to as the Halstead-Reitan Neuropsychological Test Battery. Each of these three batteries was devised as a tool for the assessment of brain-behavior relationships. The RINTBC was developed after it became apparent that many of the items on the battery for older children were too difficult for children below the age of 9 (Reitan, 1979).

The developmental research for the RINTBC, conducted at the Neuropsychology Laboratory of the Indiana University Medical Center, began in the mid-1950s. R. M. Reitan, a student of W. C. Halstead, modified several of the tests from Halstead's original adult battery (Halstead, 1947) and also created six new tests to complete this battery for young children. The modified tests include children's versions of the Category Test, Tactual Performance Test, Sensory-Perceptual Disturbances Tests, Finger Oscillation Test, and Aphasia Screening Test. New tests include the Color Form Test, Progressive Figures Test, and Matching Picture Tests; these were designed to measure cognitive flexibility and concept formation. The Target Test and the Individual Performance Test assess reception and expression of visuo-spatial relationships, while the Marching Test measures gross motor coordination (Reitan, 1979). The RINTBC customarily is supplemented by the Reitan-Klove Lateral Dominance Examination, the Reitan-Klove Sensory-Perceptual Examination, Strength of Grip, the Wechsler Preschool and Primary Scale of Intelligence, and the Wide Range Achievement Test (Reitan, 1974).

Reitan and Davison (1974) present a review of research that has demonstrated that the RINTBC effectively differentiates brain-damaged from normal-functioning children, provided the test is administered and interpreted properly by trained professionals. An interpretive guide is available from Reitan (1987).

REFERENCES

Halstead, W. C. (1947). *Brain and intelligence.* Chicago, IL: University of Chicago Press.

Reitan, R. M. (1974). Psychological effects of cerebral lesions in children of early school age. In R. M. Reitan & L. A. Davison (Eds.), *Clinical neuropsychology: Current status and applications* (pp. 53–89). New York, NY: Hemisphere.

Reitan, R. M. (1979). *Manual for the administration of neuropsychological test batteries for adults and children.* Tucson, AZ: Reitan Neuropsychology Laboratories.

Reitan, R. M. (1987). *Neuropsychological evaluation of children.* Tucson, AZ: Reitan Neuropsychology Laboratories.

Reitan, R. M., & Davison, L. A. (1974). *Clinical neuropsychology.* New York, NY: Hemisphere.

GALE A. HARR
Maple Heights City Schools, Maple Heights, Ohio

See also Halstead-Reitan Neuropsychological Test Battery; Neuropsychology

RELATED SERVICES

The Education for All Handicapped Children Act of 1975 (PL 94-142) was the first federal law to hold education agencies responsible not only for the provision of special education services, but for the delivery of related services as well. Related services are defined as "transportation, and such developmental, corrective, and other supportive services … as may be required to assist a handicapped child to benefit from special education" (Section 4a). Subsequent versions of IDEA advance nearly identical language.

Among the services specifically included within the related services definition are speech pathology and audiology, psychological services, medical services (for diagnostic and evaluation purposes only), physical and occupational therapy, recreation, and counseling. However, because the phrase "other supportive services … as may be required" is included in the law, the precise definition of related services remains the subject of debate.

Disputes regarding the type and extent of related services required under PL 94-142 have been the focus of a series of court cases, including the first Supreme Court decision on federal special education law. Litigation has involved questions of eligibility, definition, and financial responsibility. All three issues were addressed in *Hendrick Hudson Board of Education v. Rowley*. In this case, the Supreme Court ruled that a high-achieving deaf student need not be provided a sign language interpreter at the school district's expense, given her demonstrated ability to benefit from the educational program already provided. While the court's decision focused on the narrow issue of one student's right to a particular related service, it suggested that the term *related services* need not be interpreted broadly to mean any service that would improve the quality of a handicapped child's education.

In the subsequent case of *Irving Independent School District v. Tatro*, definition was again at issue, with the focus on medical services required by the law. Medical services are defined in the law as those services provided by a physician for diagnostic and evaluation purposes. The school district argued that catheterizing a student (inserting a tube to drain the bladder) several times daily constituted a nondiagnostic medical service and therefore was not a related service for which the district was responsible. However, the Supreme Court ruled that catheterization is included within the related services definition because it is a simple nonmedical procedure that can be administered by a school nurse. As such, the court felt, catheterization was representative of the other supportive services needed to provide "the meaningful access to education that Congress envisioned" (Court backs catheterization; limits fees in handicap cases 1984).

A major issue underlying both Supreme Court cases is financial responsibility. Related services are expensive to provide, and school districts are struggling to define the limits of their fiscal responsibility. Interpreting the *Rowley* decision, U.S. District Judge John A. Nordberg said, "the Court recognized the unfairness of imposing large financial burdens on states on the basis of broad interpretation of ambiguous language in funding statutes" (Students have no right to free psychiatric care, court rules, 1983). Even with a conservative interpretation of what constitutes related services, state and local education agencies often find themselves in a difficult financial position.

Dealing with the financial ramifications of providing related services is a continuing challenge. In its *Seventh Annual Report to Congress* (1984), the United States Department of Education described effective policies developed to provide related services in cost-efficient ways. One strategy has been to pool resources among local education agencies to make a range of related-service specialists available to students. Another has been to seek third-party funding from public and private insurance providers. A third approach involves establishing joint funding and cooperative programming arrangements among education and human service agencies. For example, a school district and local mental health agency might agree that the mental health agency will provide and assume the related-services costs for the district's seriously emotionally disturbed children (Maher & Bennett, 1984). Each of these arrangements exemplifies efforts to share financial responsibility and work cooperatively to improve the quality of related services available to handicapped children.

REFERENCES

Court backs catheterization; limits fees in handicap cases. (1984). *Education of the Handicapped, 10*(14), 1–3.

Maher, C. A., & Bennett, R. E. (1984). *Planning and evaluating special education services.* Englewood Cliffs, NJ: Prentice Hall.

Students have no right to free psychiatric care, court rules. (1983, Aug. 24). *Education of the Handicapped, 9*(17), 7–8.

U.S. Department of Education. (1984). *Seventh annual report to Congress on the implementation of the Education of the Handicapped Act.* Washington, DC: U.S. Government Printing Office.

MARY LOUISE LENNON
RANDY ELLIOT BENNETT
Educational Testing Service

See also Diagnosis in Special Education; Individuals With Disabilities Education Improvement Act of 2004 (IDEIA); Interpreters for the Deaf; Speech-Language Services

RELIABILITY

Reliability is a core measurement concept in education and the social sciences and is associated with the development and use of psychoeducational tests and direct observation tools. Whether for the purpose of diagnosis or prognosis, reliability provides an index of how much we can depend on an instrument to predictably measure physical, psychological, or educational outcomes of interest. The more dependable an achievement test or observation instrument is, the more confident we are that accurate decisions will be made in special education. The need for measurement confidence is especially important in public education, where educators routinely use test or assessment data to help guide their instructional programming decisions for students. While few measurement tools are perfectly reliable, selecting a commercially available test with a known reputation for being erratic and inconsistent would simply be unethical and unprofessional (American Educational Research Association, American Psychological Association, & National Council on Measurement in Education, 1999).

Reliability is not an all-or-nothing concept; rather, it can be thought of as a sliding scale that ranges from minimal accuracy of measurement to highly dependable measurement of some variable of interest (Gregory, 2004). The degree of a test's reliability is often affected by the number and selected type of items for the test that, in reality, represent a limited and often indirect sampling of the behavioral or cognitive processes of concern. Compounding the issue is that such sampling of human processes is conducted at only one point in time and often in an artificial context. Because of this, test scores can and should be treated only as gross and approximate *indicators* of the construct being measured. For example, when a teacher rates a student on a measure of social competence as having average cooperation skills, the score does not, in itself, tell us all there is to know about the student's true cooperation skills. In this case, it tells us only what the teacher's perception is, as assessed by that instrument and the items responded to. Reliability, in relation to the aforementioned problems of test construction and restricted sampling of complex processes or total content knowledge, should press educators to ask what generalizations are reasonable and appropriate to make from such test or assessment results so that important decisions or conclusions can be made with confidence (Salvia & Ysseldyke, 2004; Thorndike, 2001). When reliability is considered, test scores themselves should be of little inherent interest to educators; educators should ask whether such scores generalize or are reliable over time, whether test items generalize to or are reliable with other test items within the test or assessment instrument itself, and whether there is interscorer generalization, which informs users about the level of scoring agreement between two (or more) examiners. The reliability or generalizability of a test or assessment tool is really about its ability to predict *itself*, thereby demonstrating a high degree of internal quality and structure, which will be needed before external utility (validity) can be expected (Thorndike, 2001).

Perfect internal and time-based consistency is highly desirable in a test or assessment tool, but subtle inconsistencies will inevitably occur in the course of measuring individual or between-group performance. This inconsistency, or variance, in obtained scores is referred to as measurement error and impacts reliability. Charles Spearman (1904) described this problematic issue in relation to measuring human intelligence, thereby laying the foundation for *classical test theory* in the social sciences. Two cornerstone assumptions of this theory are that (1) each person has a stable attribute to measure as captured by the true score on the test, and (2) in the process of measuring such human attributes, measurement error will occur, contributing to the inconsistency or unreliability of an instrument (Gregory, 2004; Kerlinger, 1986). A "true score" is a convenient fiction, because in actuality we can never obtain a pure measure of a person's true traits or abilities on a test. Nevertheless, the theoretical assumption is that a person's underlying true score is stable across successive test administrations (Kaplan, 1964; Thorndike, 2001). In essence, one's true score of a hypothetical trait or skill on a test is the expected value or average score one would receive on an infinite number of repeated measurements of that attribute by the test in use (Lord & Novick, 1968). While an index of reliability contains a hypothetical true score component, it also contains a measurement error component, which consists of random deviations from the true score. In light of this, reliability is defined through error, where the greater the measurement error, the greater the unreliability; less error means greater reliability (Kerlinger, 1986). In the statistical pursuit of estimating the amount of error present between measurement systems and with a person's obtained score on a test, one needs a reliability coefficient and the standard error of measurement (SEM; Salvia & Ysseldyke, 2004). Reliability coefficients are correlations (represented by r) that describe the magnitude or strength of relationship between scores obtained on successive test administrations. Correlations range from 0.0 to +1.0 (the theoretical upper limit) and provide us with information about how stable or accurate measurements are between those successive test administrations (Gregory, 2004). Acceptable magnitudes of reliability range from .70 to more robust correlations of .90 or higher. An acceptable reliability level will depend on what the actual test is being used for (Gregory, 2004). The reliability coefficient helps mathematically explain the proportion or percentage of error variance that exists between the obtained scores of two test administrations. If, for example, the reliability coefficient between two independently obtained IQ scores is $r =$ .80, and is then squared, it tells us that 64% of the variance of the true IQ score can be accounted for or explained between the two test administrations; conversely, 36% of the total test variance is due to error from uncontrolled factors affecting the true measurement of IQ (Kerlinger, 1986; Salvia & Ysseldyke, 2004). There are many good descriptions of what types of variance might occur to affect reliability (i.e., the magnitude of the reliability coefficient; see Cronbach, Gleser, Nanda, & Rajaratnam, 1971; Thorndike, 2001), but generally they come from factors associated with test length, test-retest intervals, constriction or extension of ability range, guessing, and variation within the testing situation (Isaac & Michael, 1981; Salvia & Ysseldyke, 2004).

The other procedure of accounting for reliability error, SEM, is useful for interpreting an *individual's* score on a test and becomes vital in special education when determining eligibility, assessing present level of educational performance, or making appropriate placement decisions. Test administration guides (should) provide SEM data to help users gauge just how much score fluctuation to expect if the test were administered to the individual again. Inextricably linked to SEM is the confidence interval, which conveys the degree of accuracy with which the test identified the underlying true score in relation to the person's obtained score. For example, if a person obtains a full-scale IQ standard score of 100 and that full-scale score is reported to be 90% accurate within a SEM of +/– 10 points, then the examiner would report that, with 90% certainty, the person's *true* IQ is found somewhere between the scores of 90 and 110. If one wants a greater degree of confidence of where that true score falls in relation to the obtained score (e.g., at the 95% level), then the confidence interval will necessarily increase in width to account for more error (Salvia & Ysseldyke, 2004). Again, test manuals or guides should report such information to the consumer.

The purpose of the reliability coefficient, then, is to describe the strength of the test's internal item structure or the stability of test scores over an interval of time. To this end, several reliability methods exist to help achieve this goal (see Gregory, 2004; Isaac & Michael, 1981; Salvia & Ysseldyke, 2004; Thorndike, 2001). In the test-retest reliability method, one test is administered twice to the same group of heterogeneous and representative subjects. Scores are then correlated to see if the second obtained score can be predicted from the first obtained score. The reliability coefficient that is obtained provides an index of temporal stability, which helps us know whether the traits and characteristics being measured between the two time points change a great deal. Shorter time periods between the test-retest points generally produce higher reliability coefficients because there is less chance that true scores have changed. Alternate form (or equivalent form) reliability estimates the extent to which two (or more) different forms of a test are temporally stable from one administration point to the next. For example, if a test developer wants a Form A and a Form B version of an academic achievement test, he or she will have to generate reliability coefficients based on test-retest methodology that informs the user of stability of comparable items over time. In this approach, subjects are not tested twice with identical test items from one test, but with a set of items from Form A at time one and then a set of items from Form B at time two. Fewer and fewer alternate or parallel forms of tests are sold today because it is generally more expensive and difficult to identify equally appropriate and representative items for two forms of a test, and it potentially introduces more error variance from improper content-sampling procedures. Split-half reliability is a substitute for alternate forms whereby items from an existing test are divided into halves. There may be many possible divisible permutations for a test depending on its total item content, but one practical way would be to use an odd-even division of those items. Once properly divided, the two halves are then correlated with each other to estimate the test's internal consistency reliability. This procedure, however, does not provide the best precision for estimating internal consistency. In order to avoid having to correlate all possible divisible permutations to find the best statistical balance between the halves, test developers can now use the coefficient alpha method, which quickly and efficiently indexes the average split-half correlations on all possible divisions of a test into two equally correlated halves. Finally, interscorer reliability supplements the test-retest method, but it is still important because it tells us how much consistency there is in the results when two or more examiners score the same test.

The importance of interscorer or interobserver reliability cannot be understated for applied behavior analysis (ABA) in special education. Although ABA does use correlational methodology, indexing the reliability of instruments is more often accomplished by calculating the percentage of agreement between raters or observers of human behavior. Depending on the recording technique, reliability agreement can be indexed as simple agreement, point-to-point agreement, agreement for occurrence, or kappa index of agreement.

Promoting reliable decisions about special education treatment effectiveness is essential in ABA because of effects such as observer drift, where observer accuracy in recording behavior decays over time; reactivity by those who are aware that they are being observed; observer bias, where assessment errors occur because of observers' expectancies and prejudices; and observer cheating, where in rare cases, observers may purposefully exaggerate reliability agreements (Hartmann, 1984). To enhance proper decisions about treatment effectiveness in ABA, thereby improving an assessment instrument's reliability, Hartmann (1984) suggests that observers should (a) be given enough time to acclimate to the observational setting before reliability data are taken; (b) be separated and made unaware of the purpose of the study as well as when quality control reliability assessment sessions are scheduled; and (c) be reminded about the importance of accuracy and be regularly retrained on observation instruments. It is critically important in ABA that reliability checks be conducted throughout treatment investigation and be calculated by the investigator, not by the observers (Hartmann, 1982).

Reliability is an important measurement concept and standard to consider in special education, especially when numerous commercially available tests or assessment instruments are poorly constructed or possess little or no reliability data attesting to their stability and accuracy. When special educators maintain high standards in their choice of reliable measurement systems, it advertises to the community at large that the profession is concerned about using only the most dependable and accurate decision tools with students with disabilities.

REFERENCES

American Educational Research Association, American Psychological Association, & National Council on Measurement in Education. (1999). *Standards for educational and psychological testing* (2nd ed.). Washington, DC: American Psychological Association.

Cronbach, L. J., Gleser, G. C., Nanda, H., & Rajaratnam, N. (1971). *The dependability of behavioral measurements*. New York, NY: Wiley.

Gregory, R. J. (2004). *Psychological testing: History, principles, and applications* (4th ed.). Wheaton, IL: Allyn & Bacon.

Hartmann, D. P. (1982). Assessing the dependability of observational data. In D. P. Hartmann (Ed.), *Using observers to study behavior: New directions for methodology of social and behavioral science* (pp. 51–65). San Francisco, CA: Jossey-Bass.

Hartmann, D. P. (1984). Assessment strategies. In D. H. Barlow & M. Hersen (Eds.), *Single case experimental designs: Strategies for studying behavior change* (2nd ed., pp. 107–139). Elmsford, NY: Pergamon Press.

Isaac, S., & Michael, W. B. (1981). *Handbook in research and evaluation for education and the behavioral sciences* (2nd ed.). San Diego, CA: EdITS.

Kaplan, A. (1964). *The conduct of inquiry*. San Francisco, CA: Chandler.

Kerlinger, F. N. (1986). *Foundations of behavioral research* (3rd ed.). Orlando, FL: Holt, Rinehart & Winston.

Lord, F., & Novick, M. (1968). *Statistical theories of mental test scores*. Reading, MA: Addison-Wesley.

Salvia, J., & Ysseldyke, J. E. (2004). *Assessment in special and inclusive education* (9th ed.). Boston, MA: Houghton Mifflin.

Spearman, C. (1904). "General intelligence," objectively determined and measured. *American Journal of Psychology, 15*, 201–293.

Thorndike, R. M. (2001). Reliability. In B. F. Bolton (Ed.), *Handbook of measurement and evaluation in rehabilitation* (3rd ed., pp. 29–48). Gaithersburg, MD: Aspen.

ROLLEN C. FOWLER
Eugene 4J School District, Eugene, Oregon

See *also* Research in Special Education

RELIABILITY IN DIRECT OBSERVATION ASSESSMENT

Reliability assessment in direct observation assessment is the measure of the degree of agreement among raters of observed behaviors or events. An appropriate selection in the reliability estimate helps provide an explicit expression of error. There are two fundamental types of interrater agreement that include (1) closeness of association, and (2) exact agreement or reproducibility. To select the most appropriate interrater reliability index, the researcher(s) must determine whether the priority of data collection focuses on *closeness of association* where the raters are given partial credit if their scores are closely recorded or if the data collection focuses on *exact agreement* where there is an absolute occurrence or nonoccurrence of a particular behavior where no partial credit is given, and it is considered an all-or-nothing rating.

To select an interrater reliability index, one must examine the context of the data and how it will be used (see Table R.1). Regarding context, priority may be given to either exact reproducibility or to closeness of association. This choice informs the selection of the index. Indices that emphasize "exact reproducibility" (such as Cohen's Kappa and Percent Agreement) measure the accuracy of recreating identical results using the same measurement tool (e.g., both teachers rated the student's behavior a 5). "Closeness of association" indices (such as Pearson's CC, Kendall's tau-b, and Pearson's *r*) differ from exact reproducibility in that they don't measure whether both observers agree exactly, but rather how closely they agreed on the item (e.g., one teacher rated the student's behavior a 4 and the other a 5).

The next step in reliability index selection is determining the level of scale of the data. Scales with nominal data are most often dichotomous scales (e.g., Yes/No, or 0/1) with no distance between the categories, so exact agreement would be the type of reliability index to use. Nominally scaled categories do exist in education (e.g., three categories of student behavior: internalizing, externalizing, and both internalized/externalizing behaviors). Exact agreement indices also are more appropriate for nominally scaled categories of three or more because there are no degrees of association, order, or equal distance among categories. Data with categories with order or equal distance among categories (ordinal, interval, or ratio) may use either exact agreement or closeness of association depending on the purpose of data collection and context as mentioned earlier.

Once the context, purpose, and level of scale of the data has been used to determine which type of reliability index to calculate, the next step in selecting the most appropriate index is determining the number of categories in the

Table R.1. Determining the Context of the Data and How It Will Be Used

	Closeness of Association	Exact Agreement	Hybrid
What does it measure?	Measures how closely raters agree by allowing credit for "near misses"	Measures how exactly raters agree for perfect agreement or disagreement on the occurrence of a behavior or event	Decreases credit for "near misses" in even increments as the errors are greater distance apart
Some indices to calculate interrater reliability	Pearson *r* (interval scaled) Kendall's tau Kendall's tau-b Spearman's rho (ordinal scaled) Pearson's Contingency Coefficient Cramer's V IntraClass Correlation (equal-interval scales)	Percent Agreement Cohen's Kappa Kappa/Kappa Max Pearson's Phi (dichotomous scales) Scott's Pi	Kappa with Linear Weights Kappa with Quadratic Weights

scale by counting response options. For example, a four-category Likert scale could be Excellent/Good/Fair/Poor. The best selection of interrater reliability index hinges on the number of categories in the scale based on the recent findings from a Monte Carlo study on the reliability of multicategory items by Parker, Vannest, and Davis (2012). They found that not every index is appropriate for every item, and the two most commonly reported indices of reliability (Percent Agreement and Cohen's Kappa; Bryington, Palmer, & Watkins, 2002; Watkins & Pacheco, 2000) may not be the most trustworthy given the type of data and number of categories. Guidelines extracted from their recent study found that two-point items are best assessed by Kappa and Percent Agreement, items with four or more categories are best assessed with Linear Weighted Kappa, and Kendall's tau-b shows the most stability between two and nine category items (Parker et al., 2012).

REFERENCES

Bryington, A. A., Palmer, D. J., & Watkins, M. W. (2002). The estimation of interobserver agreement in behavioral assessment. *The Behavior Analyst Today*, 3(3), 323–328.

Parker, R. I., Vannest, K. J., & Davis, J. L. (2012). *Reliability for multicategory rating scales*. Manuscript submitted for publication.

Suen, H. K., & Lee, P. S. C. (1985). Effects of the use of percentage agreement on behavioral observation reliabilities: Area assessment. *Journal of Psychopathology and Behavioral Assessment*, 7, 221–234.

Watkins, M. W., & Pacheco, M. (2000). Interobserver agreement in behavioral research: Importance and calculation. *Journal of Behavioral Education*, 10(4), 205–212.

Stacey R. Smith
Texas A&M University
Fourth edition

REMEDIAL AND SPECIAL EDUCATION

In 1982, PRO-ED, Inc., purchased the journal *Exceptional Education Quarterly* from Aspen Systems Corporation. In 1984, the name of the journal was changed to *Remedial and Special Education* (RASE), and the journal became a bimonthly. That same year, PRO-ED acquired two additional journals, *Topics in Learning and Learning Disabilities* (from Aspen Press) and *The Journal for Special Educators* (from the American Association of Special Educators); these were also merged into RASE. This journal is devoted to topics involving the education of persons for whom typical instruction is not effective. Emphasis is on

the interpretation of research literature and recommendations for the practice of remedial and special education. RASE thus is alternative to practitioner-oriented teacher journals and pure research journals within the field. All published articles have been peer reviewed.

Judith K. Voress
PRO-ED, Inc.

REMEDIAL INSTRUCTION

The term *remediation* is derived from the word *remedy*, meaning a correction, repair, or cure of something that is awry. Medicines are medical remedies. Remedies in education are called remediations (Ysseldyke & Algozzine, 1984).

Remedial teaching has been distinguished from developmental teaching and from corrective teaching. As usually construed, developmental teaching is the type of instruction given to the majority of students attending regular classes (Otto & McMenemy, 1966; Rupley & Blair, 1983).

Developmental instruction in the modern classroom is likely to be guided by clearly defined instructional objectives. Thus, developmental reading instruction has been described as "a systematic guided series of steps, procedures or actions intended to result in learning or in the reaching of a desired goal" (Harris & Hodges, 1981, p. 157).

Corrective and remedial instruction are both forms of academic assistance provided to students who need special help in various areas of instruction. When that assistance is offered by the classroom teacher within a regular classroom setting to students who are deficient in some particular skills or not achieving up to expectations in particular subject matters, help is identified as corrective instruction. Corrective instruction is given when the type of learning problem, or its degree, is not judged as severe enough to require specific types of remediation. Remedial instruction is usually given to students with more severe or persistent academic difficulties. Usually it is provided by a specialist in a particular skill or content area and in circumstances apart from the child's regular classroom. Remedial instruction often suggests a learning disability; indeed, remedial instructors often act as learning disability specialists.

Arbitrary standards are often set for eligibility for corrective or remedial services: Within 2 years of grade expectation the child may be given corrective instruction, but beyond 2 years the child will receive remedial instruction. Such criteria are often insensitive to growth curves and normal developmental changes and make little sense.

While developmental and corrective as well as remedial instruction attempt to individualize according to students' needs, remedial instruction is most likely to address a student and his or her problems diagnostically and to offer intensive interventions (Reisman, 1982). Thus, remedial instruction is likely to be provided to students whose academic deficiencies or disabilities appear so severe or specialized as to require more precise, intense, or individualized assistance.

In remedial instruction, the distinction may be made between skill remediation and ability or process remediation. The first attempt to correct or strengthen particular academic skills, such as decoding in reading, carrying in two-column addition, and not writing out silent sounds in spelling. In the second, efforts are made to correct presumed deficits in cognitive processes such as perception, memory, and attention. A popular current process approach is that of teaching learning-disabled children to more effectively use cognitive strategies in learning and school performance.

Since special education is based on individualized intensive interventions addressed to students who, because of their handicapping conditions, may not be able to keep up with their nondisabled peers, the notion of remediation, from a special educator's point of view, may be redundant. Indeed, the special education resource room, whether in regular or special education, is likely to be a place where remedial education is offered. Cawley (1984) believes that carefully controlled curricular approaches to the problems of learning-disabled students are likely to be more effective than the traditional diagnostic-prescriptive remedial methods so often emphasized in remediation.

Remedial reading is the most frequently offered form of remedial or corrective help provided in grade school, both elementary and secondary. Remedial mathematics, writing, and so on also go on in regular education settings, but they are less likely to be carried out by remedial specialists. Remedial instruction is often provided at the college level as well as during the lower grades. It is most often required by students who, because of poor earlier preparation, problems in managing English, or specific cognitive deficits, require specialized help to succeed in higher education. Many colleges and other institutions of higher learning provide remedial writing.

REFERENCES

Cawley, J. F. (1984). Preface. In J. F. Cawley (Ed.), *Developmental teaching of mathematics for the learning disabled*. Rockville, MD: Aspen.

Harris, T. L., & Hodges, R. E. (Eds.). (1981). *A dictionary of reading and related terms*. Newark, DE: International Reading Association.

Otto, W., & McMenemy, R. A. (1966). *Corrective and remedial reading*. Boston, MA: Houghton Mifflin.

Reisman, F. (1982). *A guide to the diagnostic teaching of arithmetic*. Columbus, OH: Merrill.

Rupley, W. H., & Blair, T. R. (1983). *Reading diagnosis and remediation: Class & clinic*. Boston, MA: Houghton Mifflin.

Ysseldyke, J. E., & Algozzine, B. (1984). *Introduction to special education*. Boston, MA: Houghton Mifflin.

LESTER MANN
Hunter College, City University of New York

See also **Diagnostic Prescriptive Teaching; Direct Instruction; Remedial Reading**

REMEDIAL READING

According to Smith (1965), the term *remedial reading* first appeared in the professional literature in a 1916 journal article by W. H. Uhl; however, like so many of the terms in the field of reading, the term *remedial reading* has no universally agreed on operational definition. The amount of confusion that exists with respect to the term was expressed well some years ago by Goldberg and Schiffman (1972), who noted:

> Some educators refer to the problem category as remedial, strephosymbolia, associative learning disability, specific reading or language disability, congenital word blindness, primary reading retardation, or developmental dyslexia. One school district may refer to all retarded readers as remedial; another agency, in the same community, may use the term remedial for a small group of children with specific learning disabilities. (pp. 156–157)

Goldberg and Schiffman go on to point out that, because of the widely varying definitions, estimates of the percent of students requiring remedial reading instruction vary from as low as 1% to as high as 20%.

A Dictionary of Reading and Related Terms (T. L. Harris & Hodges, 1981) provides a realistic, though somewhat vague, definition of the term *remedial reading*:

> Any specialized reading instruction adjusted to the needs of a student who does not perform satisfactorily with regular reading instruction. Intensive specialized reading instruction for students reading considerably below expectancy.

Before examining this definition, it might be helpful to quickly introduce two reading terms that are frequently contrasted with the term remedial reading: *developmental reading* and *corrective reading*. Developmental reading refers to instruction that is designed for and offered to the average child who is acquiring reading skills at an average rate. Group instruction, centering around the use of basal readers, is the typical approach to developmental reading instruction.

Corrective reading is a term usually applied to instruction that is offered to children who are essentially average intellectually but who are slower than average in the rate at which they are acquiring reading skills; however, the disparity between where they are expected to be reading, usually based on age, grade placement, and intelligence, is not large. The difficulties that they are encountering are mild enough that, with some adjustments, the responsibility for their reading instruction can be assumed by a regular classroom teacher.

While it seems fairly easy to separate developmental reading from remedial reading, the distinction between corrective and remedial reading is not so clear. The first definition offered by Harris and Hodges would make the two indistinguishable; however, even the second definition offers no clear criteria for separating the two. A. J. Harris and Sipay (1985) list four characteristics that distinguish corrective from remedial programs. The first characteristic is where the treatment takes place. Remedial reading usually takes place in a special classroom or even in a special clinic. The second characteristic is who provides the treatment. Corrective instruction is usually offered by a classroom teacher, while remedial instruction is within the province of a reading or learning disabilities specialist. Third is the number of children treated in a session. Group size is smaller for remedial instruction or is on a one-to-one basis. The final characteristic is the severity of the problem. Otto and McMenemy (1966) sum up this definitional problem when they write:

> In terms of diagnostic and instructional techniques, the distinction between actual corrective and remedial instruction is often one of degree rather than kind. Strictly remedial techniques tend to be more intensive and more highly individualized but usually not intrinsically different from corrective techniques (p. 38–39).

Some authors have tried to bring objectivity to the definition of remedial reading by defining it as referring to children who are reading 2 or more years below grade level. Unfortunately, this simple approach is fraught with problems. To begin with, years with regard to reading skill development are not equal interval units. Reading skills tend to develop rapidly during first through third grade and to develop at a negatively accelerating rate thereafter. A child who at the end of second grade has acquired no reading skills (hence is two years behind) is very different from a grade 8 student who has acquired sixth grade skills. Even Otto and McMenemy (1966), who are among the few professionals who attempt to justify the adoption of a 2-year criterion for defining a remedial reader, are quick to point out that it is "clearly unrealistic" in the early grades and that "slavish application of such an arbitrary criterion would be unfortunate" (p. 37).

A second major problem in adopting a 2-year disparity criterion lies in the method for calculating that disparity. In most cases, the disparity is based on a difference between actual, measured reading achievement of a student and the level he or she should have attained based on some measure of capacity to learn, usually an intelligence test. Unfortunately, there is no agreed-on method for calculating the amount of disparity between expectancy and achievement. Stauffer, Abrams, and Pikulski (1978) have shown that widely different results will be achieved depending on the formula used to calculate the expected level of reading achievement. In addition, tests of intelligence and of reading can yield widely differing results depending on the tests used.

Yet another problem in defining remedial reading lies in the enormous overlap between the concepts of learning disabilities and remedial reading. Given our present level of diagnostic sophistication, distinguishing between these two classifications appears to depend almost totally on arbitrary local definitions or regulations or on funding considerations. Lewis (1983) presents an excellent summary of some of the major considerations that need to be taken into account in providing instruction for the struggling student in reading, regardless of whether that student is labeled as a remedial reader or as a child with a learning disability. The article is also excellent in providing evidence that challenges some widely held misconceptions about students who have severe reading problems.

The confused situation relative to the use of the term *remedial reading* and related terms, described by Goldberg and Schiffman earlier, continues to exist today; in fact, the confusion may be exacerbated by the introduction of even more terms.

While there are apparently no clear-cut ways to diagnostically differentiate among remedial readers, students with learning disabilities, corrective readers, students with dyslexia, and so on, one might wonder if there are any instructional methods or materials that are unique to remedial reading. Textbooks dealing with this topic imply that there are. For example, Bond et al. (1984) indicate that there are four important elements of remedial instruction: It is individualized, it encourages the reader, it uses effective teaching procedures, and it enlists cooperative efforts. While these elements are important to remedial reading, they are also important to all reading instruction. These authors go on to suggest that basal readers, the hallmark of developmental reading instruction, are a primary source of materials for remedial reading.

A careful reading of discussions of remedial reading suggests that the principles of teaching reading are the same regardless of whether we are concerned with remedial or developmental readers. The basic consideration is that remedial reading be based on a careful assessment of what the reader knows and needs to learn in terms of reading skills and that instruction then be at an appropriate level of challenge. Many of the techniques are similar to those used for teaching reading to achieving readers. For example, Rude and Oehlkers (1984) describe how a language experience approach to teaching reading, which centers around the use of reading materials that are dictated by the reader and written by the teacher, can be used for remedial reading; the language experience approach is also a major developmental technique for teaching reading. Nevertheless, there are three approaches that might be considered specifically designed for use in remedial reading.

The first approach is the use of high-interest, low-vocabulary materials. These materials are books, usually designed as a series, that are specifically written to appeal to the interests of older children but that use a limited vocabulary. A. J. Harris and Sipay (1985) include a list of over 90 such series.

The Fernald V-A-K-T approach (V-A-K-T stands for visual, auditory, kinesthetic, and tactile) was devised by Grace Fernald (1943) to treat children with learning problems. In this approach, children learn to read by using all four senses; they see words written by a teacher, they pronounce and hear those same words, and they trace the written copy of the words so as to receive tactile and kinesthetic stimulation. The technique, which is highly prescribed, forces the learner to pay full attention to the word learning process. See Johnson (1966) and Stauffer et al. (1978) for descriptions of this approach.

The Orton-Gillingham approach stresses the importance of learning phonics as the major reading skill. Students learn sounds for letters and are taught to blend the sounds to make words. This, too, is a highly structured and prescribed approach. It also uses multiple sensory stimuli. It is based on the work of an influential neurologist, Samuel T. Orton. The technique is fully described by Orton (1966) and Gillingham and Stillman (1966).

REFERENCES

Bond, G. L., Tinker, M. A., Wasson, B. B., & Wasson, J. B. (1984). *Reading difficulties: Their diagnosis and correction* (5th ed.). Englewood Cliffs, NJ: Prentice Hall.

Fernald, G. M. (1943). *Remedial techniques in basic school subjects.* New York, NY: McGraw-Hill.

Gillingham, A., & Stillman, B. W. (1966). *Remedial training for children with specific difficulty in reading, spelling, and penmanship* (7th ed.). Cambridge, MA: Educators Publishing Service.

Goldberg, H. K., & Schiffman, G. B. (1972). *Dyslexia: Problems of reading disabilities.* New York, NY: Grune & Stratton.

Harris, A. J., & Sipay, E. R. (1985). *How to increase reading ability* (5th ed.). White Plains, NY: Longman.

Harris, T. L., & Hodges, R. E. (Eds.). (1981). *A dictionary of reading and related terms.* Newark, DE: International Reading Association.

Johnson, M. S. (1966). Tracing and kinesthetic techniques. In J. Money (Ed.), *The disabled reader.* Baltimore, MD: Johns Hopkins University Press.

Lewis, R. B. (1983). Learning disabilities and reading: Instructional recommendations from current research. *Exceptional Children, 50*(3), 230–240.

Orton, J. L. (1966). The Orton-Gillingham approach. In J. Money (Ed.), *The disabled reader.* Baltimore, MD: Johns Hopkins University Press.

Otto, W., & McMenemy, R. A. (1966). *Corrective and remedial reading: Principles and practices.* Boston, MA: Houghton Mifflin.

Rude, R. T., & Oehlkers, W. J. (1984). *Helping students with reading problems.* Englewood Cliffs, NJ: Prentice Hall.

Smith, N. B. (1965). *American reading instruction.* Newark, DE: International Reading Association.

Stauffer, R. G., Abrams, J. C., & Pikulski, J. J. (1978). *Diagnosis, correction, and prevention of reading disabilities.* New York, NY: Harper & Row.

JOHN J. PIKULSKI
University of Delaware

See also Basal Readers; Fernald Method; High Interest–Low Vocabulary; Orton-Gillingham Method; Reading; Reading Disorders

REMEDIATION, DEFICIT-CENTERED MODELS OF

Deficit-centered models for the remediation of children's learning problems have been the predominant model, though certainly not the only model, of special education worldwide throughout the 20th century. Deficit-centered remediation focuses on the identification of underlying process deficiencies on the part of the child; it then directs any subsequent intervention at the remediation of these process deficiencies. The assumption of such programs is that once the underlying deficit has been remediated (fixed, removed, or cured), academic learning will occur at a more or less normal pace. Deficit-centered remediation has undergone numerous facelifts since the 1930s, although the strong influence of Samuel T. Orton is felt in most of these programs even today.

One of the most notable examples of deficit-centered remediation is the Illinois Test of Psycholinguistic Abilities (ITPA; Kirk, McCarthy, & Kirk, 1971) and its accompanying curriculum, interventions, and training materials. (Perhaps a more popularly known deficit-centered program, and also one of the most heavily refuted and ineffective, is the Doman and Delacato program at the Institute for the Achievement of Human Potential. This is the approach that calls on the concept of neurological organization and treatment through patterning, among other activities.) The ITPA focuses on the identification and assessment of basic psycholinguistic processes such as auditory reception, auditory sequential memory, visual sequential memory, auditory association, and so on. If a deficit appears in one or more of these areas, a remedial program is then prescribed (Kirk et al., 1971). For example, if a child is referred for a reading program and found to have an auditory reception deficit (determined on the ITPA by the child's inability to respond correctly at an age-appropriate level to such questions as Do bananas fly? Do barometers congratulate? Do chairs sit?), exercises might be prescribed for the child aimed at practicing the hearing and discrimination of similar sounds (e.g., noting the differences between pin and pen, pet and let, then and tin, dot and spot). The child also might be given practice in the following of instructions. Once these activities are mastered, the deficit-centered model argues, learning to read would proceed more or less normally since the cognitive processing (or central process) dysfunction that was the stumbling block to reading has been removed.

Many other assessment techniques and programs exist to identify weaknesses or deficits in cognitive processes for subsequent intervention. Some of the approaches that emphasize treating the child's greatest area of weakness in cognitive processing include those of Ayres (1974), Bannatyne (1980), Ferinden and Jacobson (1969), Frostig and Horne (1964), Kephart (1963), and Vallett (1967). The efficacy of deficit-centered models has been the subject of considerable scrutiny by researchers in psychology and special education for some time. Unfortunately, support for the effectiveness of deficit-centered remediation programs for the remediation of academic deficits is nil, particularly when reading and math are the academic problem areas (Glass & Robbins, 1967; Mann, 1979; Reynolds, 1981a, 1981b; Ysseldyke & Mirkin, 1982). Perceptual and visual-motor functioning can be improved by deficit-centered remediation programs (Myers & Hammill, 1976), but there is, as yet, no documentable generalization for the remediation of the learning problems that trigger the referral.

Other, related areas of research have repeatedly noted potentially major limiting factors in the application of deficit-centered models. Findings from the fields of neurology, genetics, and related areas demonstrate neurological (Adams & Victor, 1977; L. C. Hartlage, 1975; P. L. Hartlage & Givens, 1982; Kolb & Whishaw, 1980; Levine, Brooks, & Shonkoff, 1980) or genetic bases (Adams & Victor, 1977; P. L. Hartlage & Hartlage 1973a, 1973b) for many learning problems in which deficit-centered models or remediation had been thought to be appropriate as the primary method of intervention. From the point of view of many contemporary neuropsychological models, the deficit-centered process approach to remediation is doomed to failure because it takes damaged, dysfunctional, or undeveloped areas of the brain and focuses training specifically on those areas. Not only does our existing knowledge of neurology predict failure for such efforts, but the efforts will not withstand empirical scrutiny.

L. C. Hartlage and Reynolds (1981) have criticized deficit-centered models of remediation as potentially harmful to children. The emotional trauma that may accompany the treatment approach of Doman and Delacato has been widely discussed, and the method has been condemned (Levine et al., 1980). While it is unlikely that other deficit-centered models are as emotionally damaging, it is likely (though unproven) that making children work and practice for lengthy periods (in some cases, years) process skills in which they are deficient without noticeable academic gains is emotionally damaging, particularly to the child's self-esteem, motivation, and likelihood of continuing in school. Glass (1981), in a meta-analysis of the effectiveness of what were deficit-centered models of remediation, reported that a significant number had net negative effects on academic skills—that is, many deficit-centered remediation programs resulted in less academic gains than no special education program at all. In some instances, then, doing nothing is superior to a deficit-centered approach to remediation, when only academic skills are considered.

Recently, cognitive psychologists have become interested in children's information-processing strategies and have made great strides in understanding how children organize, store, and manipulate stimuli. Concomitant with the revival of interest in cognitivism have been attempts to assess "new" cognitive deficits and provide remedial strategies. Haywood and Switzky (1986), among others, propose that through such techniques as Feuerstein's (1979) Learning Potential Assessment Device (known popularly as the LPAD), deficiencies in children's cognitive processes can be identified and targeted for remediation. Conceptually, this new "cognitive science" approach is no different from the approaches of the past—only the names of the processes thought to be deficient are new. The new deficit-centered models have been the subject of debate (Gresham, 1986; Haywood & Switzky, 1986; Reynolds, 1986), and there is evidence that, through the use of a like set of materials, children's scores on tests such as Raven's Matrices (a nonverbal test of intelligence) improve.

However, many of the specific abilities included in the cognitive science models of deficit-centered remediation are covered overtly in prior models and implicitly in many training programs. The cognitive science models do give us some new abilities to train, notably thinking skills and strategies such as metacognition, regrouping, rehearsal and various methods of classification, but merely leave us with new labels for others. The intelligence test score improvement reported by Feuerstein, Haywood, and others (Haywood & Switzky, 1986) likely is due to teaching the test, and generalizability to other tests or to academic skills is not in evidence. As with deficit-centered remediation programs throughout the 20th century, the new cognitive science model is narrow and highly task-specific in its effects. While improvements in these characteristics of children's thinking are desirable, they are not desirable at the neglect of the academic deficiencies that trigger the referral.

There is no evidence that deficit-centered remediation programs aid in such real-world tasks as learning to read, write, or cipher. They remain popular largely on the basis of rational, intuitive appeal and personal testimony or anecdotal data. However, occasional children do improve without treatment and the same percentage or less improve under deficit-centered remediation. As Mann (e.g., 1979) periodically reminds us, we are better off training or teaching for the task at hand, not for the latest process. In assessing the new cognitive science approach to remediation, we are forced to conclude, as has Mann (1979) in his review of process training, "The new scientific pedagogy was going to revitalize education, provide individual prescriptive correctives for learning problems, reclaim the cognitively impaired. Down with models of general intellectual incompetency! Down with medical models of noneducational etiology!... The promised land was at hand. Alas, neither Moses nor we ever crossed to the other side" (Mann, 1979, pp. 529, 538, 539). Process is not a useless variable, however. It is crucial to consider in the diagnosis of learning disabilities as well as certain other disorders; efforts to use process approaches to remediate academic problems seem better built on strength models of remediation than on deficit-centered models.

Strength Models of Remediation

Strength models of remediation also invoke the concept of cognitive or intellectual processes and often measure them in the same way. The resulting approach and techniques differ greatly, however. Strength models argue that the best remedial approach for a child who cannot read is to teach the child reading, not metacognition, rehearsal strategies, auditory reception, or grouping and classification.

In strength models of remediation, direct instruction is encouraged in the area(s) of academic or behavioral difficulty. However, instruction is formatted around the child's best-developed processes, taking advantage of the child's best intellectual abilities and avoiding those processes that are poorly developed, dysfunctional, or inept in this function. As Reynolds (1981b) describes this method, "The strength model is based on processes that are sufficiently intact so as to subserve the successful accomplishment of the steps in the educational program, so that the interface between cognitive strengths [determined from the assessment process] ... and the intervention is the cornerstone of meaningfulness for the entire diagnostic-intervention process" (p. 344). In Lurian terminology, this would denote the need for locating a complex functional system within the brain that operates well enough to be capable of taking control and moderating the learning process necessary to acquire the academic skills in question.

This view is hardly new, though it remains largely untested. Woodrow (1919) suggested teaching to cognitive strengths on the basis of scientific psychology and the interpretation of "laws" of factor analysis, while attempting to reconcile the views of Spearman and of Thurstone (Mann, 1979). Woodrow (1919) observed that "sometimes a high order of intelligence is accompanied by defects which make it imperative to use...the stronger faculties" (p. 293). More directly and in reference to the students with intellectual disabilities, Woodrow (1919) argued that since "Their most valuable asset is rote memory...its training should...form a conspicuous part in their education" (pp. 285–286). Today we hope to use the stronger faculties in developing instructional strategies, as Woodrow also proposed, rather than in training the stronger processes to become even stronger; the latter is not an unlikely side effect of strength models of remediation, however.

Strength models do not tell us specifically what to teach children, as do deficit-centered models, which tell us to teach the specific process that has been found to be deficient. In strength models, the specifics of what to teach come from a detailed task analysis or a diagnostic achievement test that delineates precisely what academic skills are problematic for the child. The strength model of remediation tells us how to teach: how the material best can be organized and presented so that learning has the best opportunity to occur (Reynolds, 1985). The specific techniques of strength models of remediation have been elaborated in a variety of sources, as has validity evidence for the approach (Gunnison & Kaufman, 1982; L. C. Hartlage & Reynolds, 1981; Reynolds, 1981a, 1981b, 1985). Building on strengths has intuitive appeal as well. Deficit models focus on the child's weakest, least developed areas of cognitive processing, the areas in which failures have been experienced most frequently. The stress, anxiety, and self-denigration that may be fostered can be intolerable for many children. Using the child's strengths as building blocks for the acquisition of academic skills or even the remediation of behavioral disorders increases the probability of more positive and successful experiences, reducing stress and alleviating anxiety. Strength models of remediation may have other emotional benefits for children as well.

A strength model of remediation also can serve as a meeting ground for a variety of divergent theoretical models in use in the remediation of a child's problems. One can easily blend cognitive, behavioral, neuropsychological, and psychoeducational models in a strength approach. Behavioral and psychoeducational models that focus on academic skill delineation through task analysis or diagnostic achievement testing are needed to tell us specifically what to teach; cognitive and neuropsychological models that focus on how the child best thinks and processes information tell us how to organize, present, and teach the content and behaviors; behavioral models, particularly positive reinforcement programs using operant techniques, are best at giving the child reason, purpose, and motivation, the why of learning. Of the various processing theories from which to build the how, to implement strength models of remediation, the neuropsychological model seems the most promising (Reynolds, 1981b, 1985), and a blending of this model with others has been proposed on several occasions.

An Illustrative Example

Some authors have advocated the use of behavioral principles in conjunction with neuropsychological techniques for the remediation of academic problems (Horton, 1981; Reynolds, 1981a, 1985). Others have presented exemplary case studies that recommend inclusion of behavior management techniques based on the unique patterns of cognitive strengths within a given child (L. C. Hartlage, 1981; L. C. Hartlage & Telzrow, 1983). The focus in all cases is on assessing as accurately as possible the various dysfunctional or intact neuropsychological processing systems for the child using a variety of assessment devices integrated with data from numerous other sources (e.g., teachers, parents, physicians). The goal is then to design a behavior management program (usually in conjunction with an academic remediation program) that emphasizes the child's particular strengths.

Although this approach seems almost matter of fact in terms of face validity, what actually occurs in schools is usually quite contrary to this model. The following hypothetical case can illustrate how a remediation program might be designed for a given child, based first on a deficit-centered model and second on a strength model.

Tina is an 8-year-old female who is experiencing problems learning to read. The teacher describes her as immature, distractible, and unable to follow classroom instruction. Results of a complete evaluation reveal that Tina possesses average to above average intellectual abilities with significant weakness in her auditory and visual sequencing abilities. She seems to exhibit above average visuo-spatial skills. A classroom observation reveals that she appears to be daydreaming when the teacher gives the morning's assignments and she is frequently reprimanded for talking while she attempts to get information from her peers. Achievement data indicate that she is functioning significantly below her ability in reading, exhibiting almost no knowledge of grapheme-phoneme relationships. Auditory comprehension of material is excellent.

The resultant educational plan based on a traditional deficit-centered model might proceed as follows: Tina would go to a resource room for 45 minutes, 3 days a week, for drill in phonics. This is in addition to the 30 minutes she spends each day in her regular reading program, where phonics is also heavily emphasized. In addition, once a week Tina is provided with training in auditory sequencing skills. A behavior management system is designed whereby she stays in from recess when she has not completed assignments as instructed by the teacher. If this fails, she also stays after school to complete assignments.

On adoption of a strength model perspective, a radically different plan would be designed for Tina. Based on the identical assessment information, the emphasis would shift to capitalizing on Tina's strong visuo-spatial skills while bypassing her weaknesses in auditory sequencing to the maximum extent possible. Therefore, Tina may still benefit from additional reading instruction with a resource teacher, but the emphasis of the techniques would be quite different. It is probable that for a child with deficient auditory sequencing abilities, a strong phonics program to teach reading would prove futile and subsequently frustrating to the child and the teacher. Under the strength model, one would incorporate techniques into the reading program that would allow Tina to use her stronger visuo-spatial abilities. Look-say, rebus, and language experience stories with pictures are all reading programs that have techniques to emphasize visuo-spatial skills and deemphasize sequencing skills. Context would be emphasized. Strength models demand an emphasis on one system not to the exclusion of the other, but rather in preference to it.

Another obvious recommendation would be to have Tina sit as close to the teacher as possible and for the teacher to provide additional visual cues whenever giving oral directions to the class. Writing the directions on the board and having Tina copy them and then illustrate them might be helpful in maintaining her attention. Tina also might benefit from direct instruction in the use of visual imagery for remembering sight words, following direction, and so on.

As for the appropriate behavior management technique, it is possible that simply changing the classroom environment and the demands of the activities would result in an increase in work completed and a reduction in the time spent off task. Strategies that emphasize verbal understanding or memory of specific rules should be avoided. Techniques that provide Tina with visual representation of her behavioral progress (e.g., charting amount of tasks completed) might be the most effective for her. These recommendations may be more difficult to implement only in that they require more creative teachers and support staff. There are, as yet, no purely canned programs or specific techniques for strength models of remediation, since the approach is relatively new and requires great individualization of instruction. It does appear to be worth the effort. Student characteristics should affect the choice of an instructional method. As obvious as this seems, given the tremendous differences observed among children in the depth and breadth of their learning when exposed to a common method, this is clearly not the case in regular or special education at present (Hayes & Jenkins, 1986). Convenience and the needs of administrators all too often dictate the choice of curriculum and methods in special education instruction. Allowing students' characteristics to drive this process under a strength approach to implementing differential instruction offers far greater promise than current practice.

REFERENCES

Adams, R. D., & Victor, M. (1977). *Principles of neurology.* New York, NY: McGraw-Hill.

Ayres, A. J. (1974). *Sensory integration and learning disorders.* Los Angeles, CA: Western Psychological Services.

Bannatyne, A. (1980, September). *Neuropsychological remediation of learning disorders.* Paper presented at the NATO/ASI

International Conference on Neuropsychology and Cognition, Augusta, GA.

Ferinden, W. E., & Jacobson, S. (1969). *Educational interpretation of the Wechsler Intelligence Scale for Children (WISC)*. Linden, NJ: Remediation Associates.

Feuerstein, R. (1979). *The dynamic assessment of retarded performers: The learning potential assessment device, theory, instruments, and techniques*. Baltimore, MD: University Park Press.

Frostig, M., & Horne, D. (1964). *The Frostig program for the development of visual perception*. Chicago, IL: Follett.

Glass, G. V. (1981, September). *Effectiveness of special education*. Paper presented at the Working Conference of Social Policy and Educational Leaders to Develop Strategies for Special Education in the 1980s, Wingspread, Racine, WI.

Glass, G. V., & Robbins, M. P. (1967). A critique of experiments on the role of neurological organization in reading performance. *Reading Research Quarterly, 3*, 5–52.

Gresham, F. (1986). On the malleability of intelligence: Unnecessary assumptions, reifications, and occlusion. *School Psychology Review, 15*, 261–262.

Gunnison, J., & Kaufman, N. L. (1982, August). Cognitive processing styles: Assessment and intervention. In *Assessment and diagnostic-prescriptive intervention: Diversity and perspective*. Symposium conducted at the annual meeting of the American Psychological Association, Washington, DC.

Hartlage, L. C. (1975). Neuropsychological approaches to predicting outcome of remedial educational strategies for learning disabled children. *Pediatric Psychology, 3*, 23–28.

Hartlage, L. C. (1981). Clinical application of neuropsychological test data: A case study. *School Psychology Review, 10*, 362–366.

Hartlage, L. C., & Reynolds, C. R. (1981). Neuropsychological assessment and the individualization of instruction. In G. W. Hynd & J. E. Obrzut (Eds.), *Neuropsychological assessment of the school-aged child: Issues and procedures*. New York, NY: Grune & Stratton.

Hartlage, L. C., & Telzrow, C. F. (1983). Neuropsychological assessment. In K. D. Paget & B. A. Bracken (Eds.), *The psychoeducational assessment of preschool children*. New York, NY: Grune & Stratton.

Hartlage, P. L., & Givens, T. S. (1982). Common neurological problems of school age children. In C. R. Reynolds & T. B. Gutkin (Eds.), *The handbook of school psychology*. New York, NY: Wiley.

Hartlage, P. L., & Hartlage, L. C. (1973a). Comparison of hyperlexic and dyslexic children. *Neurology, 23*, 436–437.

Hartlage, P. L., & Hartlage, L. C. (1973b). *Dermatoglyphic markers in dyslexia*. Paper presented at the annual meeting of the Child Neurology Society, Atlanta, GA.

Hayes, M. C., & Jenkins, J. R. (1986). Reading instruction in special education resource rooms. *American Educational Research Journal, 23*, 161–190.

Haywood, H. C., & Switzky, H. N. (1986). The malleability of intelligence: Cognitive processes as a function of polygenic experiential interaction. *School Psychology Review, 15*(2), 245–255.

Horton, A. M. (1981). Behavioral neuropsychology in the schools. *School Psychology Review, 10*, 367–373.

Kephart, N. C. (1963). *The brain injured child in the classroom*. Chicago, IL: National Society for Crippled Children and Adults.

Kirk, S. A., & Kirk, W. D. (1971). *Psycholinguistic learning disabilities: Diagnosis and remediation*. Urbana: University of Illinois Press.

Kirk, S. A., McCarthy, J., & Kirk, W. D. (1971). *Illinois Test of Psycholinguistic Abilities*. Urbana: University of Illinois Press.

Kolb, B., & Whishaw, I. Q. (1980). *Fundamentals of human neuropsychology*. San Francisco, CA: Freeman.

Levine, M. D., Brooks, R., & Shonkoff, J. P. (1980). *A pediatric approach to learning disorders*. New York, NY: Wiley.

Mann, L. (1979). *On the trail of process*. New York, NY: Grune & Stratton.

Myers, P., & Hammill, D. (1976). *Methods of learning disorders* (2nd ed.). New York, NY: Wiley.

Reynolds, C. R. (1981a). The neuropsychological basis of intelligence. In G. Hynd & J. Obrzut (Eds.), *Neuropsychological assessment of the school-aged child: Issues and procedure*. New York, NY: Grune & Stratton.

Reynolds, C. R. (1981b). Neuropsychological assessment and the habilitation of learning: Considerations in the search for the aptitude × treatment interaction. *School Psychology Review, 10*, 343–349.

Reynolds, C. R. (1985, August). *Putting the individual into the ATI*. Paper presented at the annual meeting of the American Psychological Association, Los Angeles, CA.

Reynolds, C. R. (1986). Transactional models of intellectual development, yes. Deficit models of process remediation, no. *School Psychology Review, 15*, 256–260.

Vallett, R. E. (1967). *The remediation of learning disabilities: A handbook of psychoeducational resource programs*. Palo Alto, CA: Fearon.

Woodrow, H. (1919). *Brightness and dullness in children*. Philadelphia, PA: Lippincott.

Ysseldyke, J., & Mirkin, P. K. (1982). The use of assessment information to plan instructional intervention: A review of research. In C. R. Reynolds & T. B. Gutkin (Eds.), *The handbook of school psychology*. New York, NY: Wiley.

CECIL R. REYNOLDS
Texas A&M University

JULIA A. HICKMAN
Bastrop Mental Health Association

Frostig, Marianne; Illinois Test of Psycholinguistic Abilities; Information Processing; Kaufman Assessment Battery for Children; Learning Potential Assessment Device; Neurological Organization; Orton, Samuel T.; Perceptual Training; Sequential and Simultaneous Cognitive Processing

REMEDIATION, STRENGTH MODELS OF (*See* Remediation, Deficit-Centered Models of)

RENZULLI, JOSEPH S. (1936–   )

Joseph S. Renzulli received his BS in 1958 from Glassboro State College, his MEd in 1962 from Rutgers University, and his EdD in 1966 in educational psychology from the University of Virginia. He is currently the Neag Professor of Gifted Education and Talent Development at the University of Connecticut, where he also serves as the director of the National Research Center on the Gifted and Talented.

Renzulli's research has focused on identification and programming models for both gifted education and general school improvement. In this area, he has developed means of identifying high potential in individuals and creating educational models to maximize giftedness. Developed in the early 1970s, his Three Ring Conception of Giftedness (1978) is considered by many to be the foundation of a more flexible approach to identifying and developing high levels of potential in young people. The Enrichment Triad Model (Renzulli, 1984), a widely used approach for special programs for the gifted and talented, includes general exploratory activities, group training activities, and individual and small-group investigators of real problems. Renzulli is also credited with devising the Revolving Door Identification Model (Renzulli, Reis, & Smith, 1981), a flexible approach to identifying high potential in young people, and the Schoolwide Enrichment Model (Renzulli & Reis, 1997), a plan for general schoolwide enrichment that applies practices developed for the gifted and talented to a system that serves the highly able as well as providing all students a general upgrade of the curriculum.

Renzulli has contributed numerous books and articles to professional literature. His three most recent books are *Enriching Curriculum for All Students* (Renzulli & Gardner, 2000), *Schools for Talented Development: A Practical Plan for Total School Improvement* (Renzulli, 1994), and *Identification of Students for Gifted and Talented Programs* (Renzulli & Reis, 2004).

REFERENCES

Renzulli, J. S. (1978). What makes giftedness? Re-examining a definition. *Phi Delta Kappan*, *60*, 180–184.

Renzulli, J. S. (1984). The triad/revolving door system: A research based approach to identification and programming for the gifted and talented. *Gifted Child Quarterly*, *28*, 163–171.

Renzulli, J. S. (1994). *Schools for talent development: A practical plan for total school improvement*. Mansfield Center, CT: Creative Learning.

Renzulli, J. S., & Gardner, H. (2000). *Enriching curriculum for all students*. Thousand Oaks, CA: Sage.

Renzulli, J. S., & Reis, S. M. (1997). *The schoolwide enrichment model: A how-to guide for educational excellence*. Mansfield Center, CT: Creative Learning.

Renzulli, J. S., & Reis, S. M. (2004). *Identification of students for gifted and talented programs*. Thousand Oaks, CA: Sage.

Renzulli, J. S., Reis, S. M., & Smith, L. H. (1981). *The revolving door identification model*. Mansfield Center, CT: Creative Learning.

TAMARA J. MARTIN
The University of Texas of the Permian Basin

C. WILLIAMS
Falcon School District 49, Colorado Springs, Colorado
Third edition

REPEATED READING

Repeated reading is a remedial reading technique designed to improve fluency and indirectly increase comprehension. The method is based largely on the teaching implications of automatic information processing theory in reading (LaBerge & Samuels, 1974). In automaticity theory, fluent readers are assumed to decode text automatically; attention is therefore free for comprehension. Nonfluent, word-by-word readers, on the other hand, must focus excessive amounts of attention on decoding, making comprehension difficult. The purpose of repeated reading is to make decoding of connected discourse automatic; thus fluency is increased and the reader is able to concentrate on comprehension.

The method involves multiple oral rereadings of connected discourse until a prescribed level of fluency is attained. Samuels's (1979) method, intended as a supplement to developmental reading programs, consists of multiple rereadings of a short passage of from 50 to 200 words, depending on the skill of the student. Reading speed and number of word recognition errors are recorded for each repetition. When the fluency criterion is reached, the student moves on to a new passage.

Chomsky (1976) proposes a similar method. In this variation, students listen to a tape recording of a storybook while following the text. Students read and listen repeatedly to the text until oral reading fluency is achieved. In addition to reported gains in fluency and comprehension, the method of repeated reading is said to promote more positive attitudes toward reading in that it virtually ensures a successful reading experience (Kann, 1983).

Moyer (1982) offers a theoretical rationale for the potential effectiveness of the method with disabled readers. She suggests that for some poor readers the amount of repetition/redundancy offered by traditional reading programs is insufficient to permit the acquisition of reading. Repeated reading of entire passages, however, maximizes redundancy at all levels of written expression. Thus readers are given much practice in using syntactic and semantic cues, as well as in acquiring knowledge of graphophonemic word structure.

REFERENCES

Chomsky, C. (1976). After decoding: What? *Language Arts, 53,* 288–296.

Kann, R. (1983). The method of repeated readings: Expanding the neurological impress method for use with disabled readers. *Journal of Learning Disabilities, 16,* 90–92.

LaBerge, D., & Samuels, S. J. (1974). Toward a theory of automatic information processing in reading. *Cognitive Psychology, 6,* 293–323.

Moyer, S. B. (1982). Repeated reading. *Journal of Learning Disabilities, 15,* 619–623.

Samuels, S. J. (1979). The method of repeated readings. *Reading Teacher, 32,* 403–408.

TIMOTHY D. LACKAYE
Hunter College, City University of New York

RESEARCH IN AUTISM SPECTRUM DISORDERS

Research in Autism Spectrum Disorders (RASD) is a quarterly, high-quality peer-reviewed journal published by Elsevier. RASD publishes empirical studies and literature reviews on topics related to individuals with autism spectrum disorders across the life span. Topics covered include diagnosis, incidence and prevalence, methods of treatment evaluation, education, and pharmacological or psychological interventions. The current editor in chief of RASD is Dr. Johnny Matson, and the editorial board is made up over 40 highly influential international scholars in the field of developmental disabilities. The 2009 impact for RASD is 2.267 and the 5-year impact factor is 2.278. This places RASD among the highest ranked journals in special education, rehabilitation, and psychology.

RUSSELL LANG
RICHARD MAHONEY
Texas State University-San Marcos
Fourth edition

RESEARCH IN SPECIAL EDUCATION

Research in special education is the means through which knowledge and methods of treatment are acquired and verified for application to persons with special needs. Such research encompasses a wide range of methodologies, subjects, issues, and data collection and analysis techniques. Although all special education research contributes to the ever-increasing knowledge base of the field, all types are different to some extent. Research ranges from case studies to single subject and group designs. Each method differs from the others in terms of ease of use, confidence and validity of results obtained, and generality of findings.

Through the process of research, advances are made in what is known about disabilities and how to prevent and treat them through education and training. The importance of research methodology in validating the findings of research must be emphasized. Many hypotheses related to developmental disabilities are advanced in the form of anecdotal reporting and logical analyses. But these hypotheses are speculative, and before being applied to the special education field they must be subjected to verification through research. Only by careful study through controlled research designs can research findings be considered useful and be applied to persons other than those involved in the research study.

Special education research is usually applied research; in other words, it is conducted primarily in the places where individuals with disabilities live, work, and attend school. For example, research has been conducted in group homes, sheltered workshops, resource rooms, and the community. Although less rigorous than research in the experimental laboratory, special education research has the advantage of being relevant to and practical for the subjects involved; that is, the issues studied are usually of high priority for the well-being of the people involved because of their functional relevance. Through rigorously applied research programs, professionals in special education can confirm observations by testing hypotheses on persons with special needs and verifying known effects with different populations. In the long view, research provides a solid foundation of knowledge from which to increase and maintain the intellectual vitality of special education (Drew, Preator, & Buchanan, 1982).

Observation of phenomena is inherent in all research and particularly in special education research. Naturalistic observation is one way to collect information about subjects. With this technique, the researcher observes a person (or group of people) and makes extensive records of the subject's behaviors. The purpose is to be as descriptive as possible to provide a post hoc analysis of possible mediating factors. For example, Currin and Rowland (1985) assessed the communication ability of persons who were labeled profoundly disabled. These researchers videotaped interactions among adult teachers and 15 nonverbal youths and then divided the communication behaviors exhibited by the subjects into eight categories. The researchers provided no training or other intervention. Such a naturalistic account is important because it can provide an accurate description of specific skills in a certain population. This description can, in turn, later be used as a base from which to provide more precise analyses or from which to guide subsequent interventions. Authors of the majority of articles published from 1983 to 1985 in four major special education research journals used naturalistic observation for collecting and reporting their respective information.

Another important characteristic of research is that of systematically manipulating variables and observing the effects of such manipulations on other variables. Typically, a researcher wants to measure accurately how the dependent variable (e.g., subject behaviors targeted for change) is affected when the subject is exposed to the independent variable (one or more factors manipulated by the researcher). Some examples of dependent variables in special education research are number of words read, frequency of correct expressive signs made, number of problems solved, percentage of inappropriate social behaviors exhibited, and frequency of interruptions. Some examples of independent variables in research are teacher praise, repetition of task, removal of child from activity, use of a particular prompting strategy, and administration of drugs.

A third characteristic of most research is use of an experimental method to determine the extent to which independent variables are functionally related to changes in dependent variables. Researchers carefully design how and when their subjects are exposed to independent variables. Experimental designs minimize the possibility that uncontrolled, extraneous factors play a part in changing dependent variables. Research that is not adequately designed to decrease the impact of extraneous factors must be viewed with caution (Sidman, 1960).

A final characteristic of research is analysis of findings. Typically, researchers have used statistical methods to determine whether their results demonstrate a strong (significant) change. Whether the research compares a pre- and postintervention difference, or whether the results obtained from one subject exposed to an independent variable are compared with those of another subject who is not exposed, the intent of the analysis is to assess the degree of difference and make a statement as to whether such a difference could be expected by chance. Statistical methods used in special education research include t-tests, analysis of variance, analysis of covariance, and regression analysis. Numerous authors have addressed the role of statistics and research (e.g., Edwards, 1985; Galfo, 1983). In addition, researchers can determine whether their work has caused an observable practical change in their subjects. This determination is termed functional or clinical significance. For example, assume that a researcher is testing a new method for teaching handicapped students to tell time. For those subjects who learn to use a clock during their daily routine, a definite functional skill has been learned regardless of whether a statistical test indicates statistical significance.

A research design describes the manner in which subjects are exposed to independent variables. Researchers must structure their designs to meet basic criteria that permit confidence in results obtained by the research. All researchers must control for extraneous variables entering into and possibly affecting the research outcome. In other words, the dependent variables measured by the researcher must be affected only by variables manipulated by the researcher. Campbell and Stanley (1963) proposed eight factors that may cause changes in dependent measures regardless of the effect of the independent variables studied. These eight threats to the validity of research follow.

1. *History*: Experiences (in addition to the independent variable) of the subjects. For example, assume that a student is a subject in a research project focusing on peer tutoring to increase appropriate social skills. If the peer tutor becomes ill and misses 3 days of the study, causing the subject to be in training for a fewer number of sessions than the other subjects, this will threaten the validity of the results.

2. *Maturation*: Uncontrolled changes in subjects. For example, infants with disabilities may become fatigued and lose attentiveness over a few hours or late in the day. Behavior changes owed to weariness, hunger, or aging illustrate a maturation threat.

3. *Testing*: The effect of taking a first test on subsequent tests. For example, students who repeatedly take a test improve their test scores over time.

4. *Instrumentation*: Changes in the devices measuring behavior of subjects. For example, mechanical items such as a video camera or cumulative recorder may fail to operate properly. Human observers may become bored or fatigued and as a result unknowingly alter their scoring.

5. *Statistical regression*: Subjects selected for inclusion in a study because of extreme scores on some test or measure. For example, assume some learning-disabled students are selected for a research study on improving reading. These particular students are selected because of their low scores on a reading achievement test given as a pretest measure. The experimental treatment is applied, and then a posttest is given (the same reading achievement assessment). Any increases in posttest scores cannot be assumed to be related to the experimental manipulation because there is a tendency for low scores on a test to rise on subsequent testing.

6. *Selection*: Subjects for experimental and control groups. If a project involves the comparison of two subject groups, the research results may be a function of the subjects' being different initially rather than a function of the experimental manipulation. For example, assume that a school district

receives financial support to hire extra vocational counselors and trainers to work with handicapped students for a year in vocational training. At the end of the year, the superintendent of the district decides to assess whether the extra staff made a positive impact on the vocational success of the students. The administrator arranges for a standard vocational assessment to be given to all of the vocational students who received the assistance and to students in another district who did not. Differences in the assessment scores may be due to a basic difference between the students of the two districts.

7. *Experimental mortality*: Losing subjects from a research study. For example, researchers frequently group subjects along relevant variables such as age, sex, and handicapping condition. If several subjects in one group drop out of the study for any reason, any results of the research showing a difference between the two groups may be due to the loss of the subjects rather than an effect of the independent variable.

8. *Selection-maturation interaction, etc*: A combination of any of the previous factors.

According to Campbell and Stanley, if a researcher arranges the experimental design to minimize the possibility of the mentioned potential alternative explanations, then any changes in the dependent measures can be confidently assumed to be due to the experimental intervention.

A second criterion for all research designs concerns the extent to which results can generalize (be applied directly) to other subjects or conditions. In special education particularly, the results of research need to be relevant to persons similar to those involved in the particular research project. Campbell and Stanley recognized four factors that reduce confidence in generalizing the results of a research study to special needs persons not participating in that study or in settings other than the experimental one:

1. *Effect of testing*: Subjects who are tested may be affected by testing and thus react differently from an untested population. For example, assume that handicapped students are enlisted as subjects in a research project testing the impact of an innovative procedure for increasing spelling accuracy. The subjects are given a preintervention spelling test followed by treatment. Finally, the subjects complete a post test. The subjects may do better than other students simply because they were given a spelling test before the intervention.

2. *Effect of selection of subjects and experimental variable*: Subjects may be more or less sensitive to the experimental intervention than other students. For instance, a special education classroom may be

used extensively by special education researchers for research purposes. If the students in such a classroom are frequently involved as research subjects, and if there are constant visitors and observers in the classroom, then these students may be more or less sensitive to any experimental manipulations than students in other special education classes.

3. *Effect of experimental arrangements*: Conditions of the research itself may affect subjects in a special way. This threat exists, for example, when students from several classes are randomly selected to be in an experimental group and are taken to a new classroom for the study. Subjects who are in an unfamiliar environment with unfamiliar people may react differently to experimental procedures than those in their familiar surroundings.

4. *Multiple treatment/interference of previous treatments*: Previous treatments may have effects on subjects that are unknown, and when working with humans as subjects, locating experimentally naive individuals can be extremely difficult. For example, some researchers study the effect of different variations of a prompting strategy known as stimulus-delay on academic skills. If they were to use the same subjects repeatedly in different experiments, over time these subjects might become familiar with the stimulus-delay method and do better or worse than subjects not initially exposed.

It is important to note that to the greatest extent possible, research in special education must meet these concerns of generalization. The importance of educational research lies with both the improvement of the particular subjects in a research project and the belief that the results and knowledge gained from the research can be applied to other persons with special needs.

All research projects involve either one or more subjects. Single-subject and group designs are labels that describe the primary categories used in special education. The majority of articles published between 1983 and 1985 in four journals devoted exclusively to research on special needs incorporated a group experimental design, either random or matched. A variety of single-subject designs were used as well.

Typically, a single-subject design involves one subject being exposed to all of the experimental conditions involved in the research. One unique characteristic of such designs is that an individual is compared with his or her own performance only. The measurement of behavior takes place before and repeatedly during the intervention. This permits a comparison of an individual's performance at regular points in time. Such within-subject analyses (Sulzer-Azaroff & Mayer, 1977) potentially yield richer information on the performance of individuals than the traditional experimental and control group designs that stress comparing average scores of large groups of subjects. Single-subject designs are particularly useful with both mildly and severely handicapped persons.

The single-subject designs are withdrawal of treatment, alternating treatment, and multiple baseline. Each is relatively easy to use in a classroom, has strong validity, and has been proven useful in many classroom situations. These designs are adaptable for use when targeting academic and social behavior, when attempting to increase or decrease a response, or when working with a single student or group.

The withdrawal-of-treatment evaluation technique typically involves four distinct phases. First, the researcher measures the subject's performance on the target skill prior to a formal attempt at changing the instructional method (baseline). In some cases, the baseline consists of a previous intervention or teaching method other than the intervention of interest. Once this phase is completed, the experimenter intervenes with the independent variable(s) selected. There is frequent measurement of subject performance, usually either per lesson or daily. After the subject's performance stabilizes, the experimenter terminates the intervention and continues to measure the subject's behavior during this second baseline phase. Finally, the researcher reinstates the instruction and continues to measure performance.

Correa, Poulson, and Salzberg (1984) used this design to test the effects of a graduated prompting procedure on the behavior of toy grasping in a 2-year-old with visual impairment and an intellectual disability. The general procedure involved the presentation of a noise-making toy in front of the child and the opportunity for the child to grasp it with no assistance. If the child did so within 10 seconds, he was given praise and the opportunity to manipulate the toy. The experimenters first conducted a series of baseline trials and found that the child touched the toy only when assisted. During the first treatment condition, unassisted touching of the toy increased to a mean of 7% of the trials. Although the following return-to-baseline phase resulted in no unassisted touching of the toy, the subsequent treatment condition increased touching once again to a mean of approximately 18%.

The rationale and strength of this design are apparent. If there is improvement in performance during the times in which the intervention is in effect, and deterioration in performance during the baseline conditions, then the researcher can have confidence that the teaching is the factor resulting in the learning. Such a research design demonstrates experimental control of behavior (Hersen & Barlow, 1976) and minimizes the possibility that uncontrolled factors are responsible for the changes in the subject's performance. On the other hand, there are times when a withdrawal-of-treatment design is not used (Tawney & Gast, 1984). Ethical concerns may contraindicate withdrawing an intervention if the target behavior is very important (e.g., aggression toward peers) or if a

clear, clinically significant change in behavior occurs in the first intervention phase. Methodological concerns may also argue against the use of this design when the target behavior is one that, once learned, is not likely to return to preintervention levels (e.g., learning addition).

The alternating-treatments design involves the exposure of the subject to two or more different treatment strategies for the same behaviors. The treatments are alternated over time. Although obtaining a baseline measure of the behavior is desirable, the researcher need not do this because the primary variable of interest is observed changes in the behavior with respect to the different treatments.

An important characteristic of this design is the use of teacher instructions or cues to signal the student as to which intervention is in effect. Typically, the design is used as follows. The researcher first develops the different strategies and selects a means for notifying the subject of each. The researcher also determines a schedule of when each treatment is to be used. The schedule must allow for each treatment to be used an equal number of times in random order. Once the research begins, the experimenter alternates the conditions, measures the subject's behavior, and records it separately for each treatment.

Barrera and Sulzer-Azaroff (1983) used such a design to compare two different language training programs (oral and total communication) in an attempt to improve expressive labeling of three children with autism. Each day, subjects were exposed to both training programs, but the sequence in which they were used alternated randomly. The experimenter signaled which treatment was in use by providing either vocal cues only (oral communication training) or vocal and gestural cues (total communication).

With this design, a teacher can immediately start to remediate a behavior rather than waiting for the rate of behavior to stabilize during a baseline period. In addition, this design can be used with behaviors irreversible once learned. However, this design is unusual in that it does not reflect the "natural" form of classroom instruction whereby one treatment strategy is used consistently over a period of time. There is also the possibility that the subject might be affected by the sequence of the various treatments. Last, a behavior that changes slowly will not be discovered with this design owing to the frequent switching of independent variables.

The multiple-baseline design involves measurement of multiple target behaviors, subjects, or situations. The targeted responses, for example, may be from one subject, different behaviors of several subjects, or one behavior exhibited by a subject in different situations. After obtaining baseline measures, the researcher applies the intervention to just one behavior while continuing to collect baseline data on the others. The intervention is subsequently applied to the remaining targets in a successive fashion. This design objectively demonstrates the success of intervention if a target response changes only when the intervention is applied to it.

The multiple-baseline design can be used in a variety of different situations. First, it is excellent for use when teaching a student similar behaviors. For example, Haring (1985) used such a design when teaching students with moderate to severe disability to play with different toys. Haring first noted that the children exhibited no appropriate play with any of four different toys. He then trained the children to play correctly with one toy while noting whether spontaneous play occurred with any of the other three toys. Although the children learned to play correctly with the trained toy, there was no generalized play to the other three toys. The children played correctly only after receiving direct training with the other toys.

Such a design is used across individuals and situations in the same manner as with behaviors. Foxx, McMorrow, and Mennemeier (1984) trained two groups of three adults with mild to moderate intellectual disabilities to exhibit appropriate social skills such as being polite and responding to criticism. After obtaining a pre-intervention assessment on all subjects, they taught one group while assessing the other. After several sessions, the subjects in the second group received the training. A multiple baseline across settings is used in a similar fashion. Instead of targeting different behaviors or students, the teacher assesses one behavior of a single student in different situations (e.g., at recess, at lunch, in reading class) and applies the intervention in one setting at a time.

There are limitations associated with the multiple-baseline design (Tawney & Gast, 1984). One concerns repeated testing during the baseline conditions; this could potentially continue for many sessions, especially for the third or fourth behavior (or setting or person). Such a lengthy assessment period precludes training and increases the potential for student frustration. However, this problem is minimized by either providing some type of treatment during baseline—so that the student receives some intervention, albeit not the one of interest—or by collecting baseline assessment infrequently. For example, although a minimum of three assessments is recommended, they could be done at random points throughout the baseline phase. Another disadvantage concerns measuring several behaviors or the behaviors of several different subjects, possibly even in different settings. Such a demanding requirement could be time-consuming and impractical in some situations.

There are several research methodologies incorporating a group design approach, such as random group, matched group, counterbalanced, and norm referenced.

In the random-group design, subjects are randomly selected from a defined population and assigned to two groups. Both groups are given the same pretest. One group is then given the experimental treatment while the other group is given either no treatment or a treatment that will be compared with the experimental treatment. Finally, both groups are given the same posttest. Wang

and Birch (1984) used the random-group design when comparing the instructional effectiveness of two different remedial programs for handicapped students. A total of 179 children were randomly assigned to either a part-day resource room or a full-day class representing an adaptive learning environments model (ALEM). Dependent measures consisted of scores from standardized achievement tests, student attitude surveys, and classroom processes. The results indicated that on the average, students in the ALEM class progressed more than students in the part-day resource room.

Another design, matched group, involves matching subjects in both groups as closely as possible with each other. The matching can occur on variables such as age, sex, learning histories, or intelligence. The variables along which the matching will occur depend on the purposes of the research. For example, Jago, Jago, and Hart (1984) matched subjects in the experimental and control groups along the dimensions of age and etiology of disability. Pretesting, experimental manipulation, and posttesting are done in a manner similar to that in the random-group design.

Counterbalanced design involves exposing subjects to identical experimental interventions but in a different sequence. For example, Carr and Durand (1985) assessed the rate of disruptive behavior exhibited by four children with developmental disabilities in four conditions: (1) an easy task with constant teacher attention, (2) a difficult task with constant teacher attention, (3) an easy task with limited teacher attention, and (4) a difficult task with limited teacher attention. Each child was observed in each of these four situations, but in a varying sequential order. For example, one child was exposed to easy task/limited attention, easy task/constant attention, and difficult task/constant attention. A second child was observed in the order of difficult task/constant attention, easy task/constant attention, and easy task/limited attention.

With the norm-referenced design, only one group of subjects is exposed to the experimental intervention, and standardized tests are used for pretest and posttest assessments. The results are then compared with results obtained by the standardization for that particular test; in other words, the standardization sample serves as the control group. For example, Gersten and Maggs (1982) assessed cognitive and academic changes in a group of children with moderate intellectual disabilities and adolescents over a 5-year period. The dependent measure was the score of the Stanford-Binet Intelligence Test. The independent measure was the DISTAR Language Program. After almost 5 years of language training, the subjects were given the Stanford-Binet, and post-experimental scores were compared with pre-experimental scores on the same test. The researchers found that the subjects were gaining points on their IQ scores faster than the population of children used to standardize the test. The norm-referenced design has serious problems, since seldom will the research sample match a test's standardization sample or all key variables. Standardization samples of tests are just not good control groups.

Group designs are particularly useful when testing the effectiveness of a treatment package or when addressing questions concerning the magnitude of an effect in terms of the number of people positively or negatively affected. They are the design of choice when testing for a general effect. However, giving treatment to one group of subjects and withholding treatment from another group can be ethically questionable. This is a particular concern in the context of educational treatment, but it can be minimized by offering the control group a treatment different from the experimental intervention, or perhaps the treatment in use prior to the experimental intervention. Another limitation concerns the practical difficulty of finding a sufficient number of matched subjects. Individuals with special needs have unique strengths and disabilities, and finding truly matched subjects may be difficult to achieve.

One other disadvantage with some group designs concerns the portrayal of results in statistical means (averages). One can determine a general outcome when experimental and control group averages are compared, but any analysis of the effect the experimental intervention has on individuals is difficult. Reporting averages ignores the number of subjects positively affected, negatively affected, or not affected at all.

A unique problem with a norm-referenced design is that virtually all of the standardized tests developed to date have used persons without disabilities for standardization. Using the results of such a group to assess subjects with disabilities is questionable. However, tests (e.g., the American Association of Mental Deficiency Adaptive Behavior Scales) are being developed using a population with developmental disabilities for standardization purposes. This could make the use of norm-referenced designs more valid.

Meta-analysis is a research approach providing a quantitative analysis of multiple studies, allowing one to address specific research questions across many studies. Kavale and Furness (1999) provide multiple examples of how meta-analysis can be useful in special education, especially in the evaluation of intervention programs.

Research conducted in special education has increased knowledge in the field and at the same time has raised new questions. One important concern is the ethical conduct of the special educator while doing research. Experimenters who use humans as subjects have the responsibility of providing stringent safeguards to protect the health and well-being of their subjects. Professionals in special education must be particularly sensitive to these concerns in that subjects with developmental disabilities may not be capable of understanding the issues involved in the research and thus may not be able to give truly informed consent.

Research safeguards to protect subject rights do exist, and professionals must abide by them. Kelty (1981) summarized several key guidelines for researchers to consider when planning studies using humans. Generally, these involve informed consent on the part of the subject so that the subject truly understands the purpose of the study, any risks or benefits to the subject, and the option to volunteer or to withdraw so that there is maximum possibility for benefit with minimum possibility of harm.

A standard component of research studies is a description of reliability procedures to verify that the primary data collector is accurate in recording the responses of the subjects. Unfortunately, few researchers present a similar case verifying that an experimental treatment is actually applied as proposed. This issue has been termed integrity of treatment (Salend, 1984) and is crucial for confidence in research results. For example, if an experimenter inadvertently implements a different intervention than the one planned, relating the proposed experimental method to the results would be erroneous. Integrity of treatment may be verified with little extra effort on the part of the research designers. As reported in Zane, Handen, Mason, and Geffin (1984), the integrity check can be made part of the traditional reliability check. The reliability scorer notes whether the person implementing the experimental program uses the correct intervention and scores the subject response correctly. By presenting both sets of data, readers can judge to what extent the proposed intervention is actually implemented.

What are some recognized areas of special education in which more research could profitably be done? One area is diagnosis. Techniques that accurately assess the etiology of a person's deficits and discovery of the youngest age at which a true diagnosis can be achieved for various disabilities would have a significant impact. Another area concerns the success of mainstreaming. Ideally, a solid research base should exist to support mainstreaming as well as to delineate ways of making it more successful. Several important questions can be addressed. What is the optimal class ratio of children developing typically and children with developmental disabilities? How does mainstreaming affect the individual student in terms of academic and social success? What effect is there, if any, on the students labeled typically developing? Answers to these questions obtained from systematic research will shed light on the future direction of mainstreaming and lead to even further improvements for individuals with disabilities.

One final research area to pursue is the extent to which practitioners in the field actually apply the findings from special education research (Englert, 1983). The purpose of research is to provide information that can be used to improve the lives of individuals with special needs. To what extent do the techniques and knowledge of special education professionals reflect the most recent research findings? If research findings are not being used by teachers and other special education professionals, the reasons must be sought and corrected. Such a discrepancy may be due to limited access to sources of research findings, a possible lack of skills training, or research that is not useful to practitioners. Whatever the reason(s), research findings must make their way to the people who can use them to enhance the lives of individuals with special needs.

REFERENCES

Barrera, R. D., & Sulzer-Azaroff, B. (1983). An alternating treatment comparison of oral and total communication training programs with echolalic autistic children. *Journal of Applied Behavior Analysis, 16,* 379–394.

Campbell, D. T., & Stanley, J. C. (1963). *Experimental and quasi-experimental designs for research.* Chicago, IL: Rand McNally College.

Carr, E. G., & Durand, V. M. (1985). Reducing behavior problems through functional communication training. *Journal of Applied Behavior Analysis, 18,* 111–126.

Correa, V. I., Poulson, C. L., & Salzberg, C. L. (1984). Training and generalization of reach-grasp behavior in blind, retarded young children. *Journal of Applied Behavior Analysis, 17,* 57–69.

Currin, F. M., & Rowland, C. M. (1985). Communicative assessment of nonverbal youths with severe/profound mental retardation. *Mental Retardation, 2,* 52–62.

Drew, C. J., Preator, K., & Buchanan, M. L. (1982). Research and researchers in special education. *Exceptional Education Quarterly, 2,* 47–56.

Edwards, A. L. (1985). *Multiple regression and the analysis of variance and covariance.* New York, NY: Freeman.

Englert, C. S. (1983). Measuring special education teacher effectiveness. *Exceptional Children, 50,* 247–254.

Foxx, R. M., McMorrow, M. J., & Mennemeier, M. (1984). Teaching social/vocational skills to retarded adults with a modified table game: An analysis of generalization. *Journal of Applied Behavior Analysis, 17,* 343–352.

Galfo, A. J. (1983). *Educational research design and data analysis.* New York, NY: University Press of America.

Gersten, R. M., & Maggs, A. (1982). Teaching the general case to moderately retarded children: Evaluation of a five-year project. *Analysis & Intervention in Developmental Disabilities, 2,* 329–334.

Haring, T. G. (1985). Teaching between class generalization of toy play behavior to handicapped children. *Journal of Applied Behavior Analysis, 18,* 127–139.

Hersen, M., & Barlow, D. H. (1976). *Single-case experimental designs: Strategies for studying behavior change.* New York, NY: Pergamon Press.

Jago, J. L., Jago, A. G., & Hart, M. (1984). An evaluation of the total communication approach for teaching language skills to developmentally delayed preschool children. *Education & Training of the Mentally Retarded, 19,* 175–182.

Kavale, K., & Furness, S. (1999). Effectiveness of special education. In C. R. Reynolds & T. B. Gutkin (Eds.), *The handbook of school psychology* (3rd ed.). New York, NY: Wiley.

Kelty, M. F. (1981). Protection of persons who participate in applied research. In G. T. Hannah, W. P. Christian, & H. B. Clark (Eds.), *Preservation of client rights: A handbook for practitioners providing therapeutic, educational, and rehabilitative services.* New York, NY: Free Press.

Salend, S. J. (1984). Integrity of treatment in special education research. *Mental Retardation, 6,* 309–315.

Sidman, M. (1960). *Tactics of scientific research.* New York, NY: Basic Books.

Sulzer-Azaroff, B., & Mayer, G. R. (1977). *Applying behavior-analysis procedures with children and youth.* New York, NY: Holt, Rinehart, & Winston.

Tawney, J. W., & Gast, D. L. (1984). *Single subject research in special education.* Columbus, OH: Merrill.

Wang, M. C., & Birch, J. W. (1984). Comparison of a full-time mainstreaming program and a resource room approach. *Exceptional Children, 51,* 33–40.

Zane, T., Handen, B. L., Mason, S. A., & Geffin, C. (1984). Teaching symbol identification: A comparison between standard prompting and intervening response procedures. *Analysis & Intervention in Developmental Disabilities, 4,* 367–377.

THOMAS ZANE
Johns Hopkins University

See also **Measurement; Multiple Baseline Design; Multiple Regression; Regression (Statistical)**

RESIDENTIAL FACILITIES

Residential facilities in America have been provided a variety of labels, including school, hospital, colony, prison, and asylum. Both the roles and the labels that institutions for individuals with disabilities have taken on have been reflective of the social and cultural climate of the time (Wolfensberger, 1975). The periods that had major influence on residential institutions have been characterized as follows: early optimism, 1800–1860; disillusionment, 1860–1900; reconsideration, 1920–1930; ebb and flow, 1930–1950; new reconsideration, 1950–1960; and enthusiasm, 1960–1970 (Cegelka & Prehm, 1982).

In the United States no public provisions were made for residential placement and care for individuals with disabilities until the 1800s. Prior to that time individuals with disabilities were placed in a variety of settings. These ranged from poor-houses to charitable centers. Such institutions provided no systematic attempts at rehabilitation or training of individuals with disabilities. Rather, they served as facilities that stored and maintained individuals with and without disabilities. It has been estimated that as late as 1850, 60% of the inhabitants of all institutions in the United States were individuals with hearing impairments, vision impairments, developmental disabilities or intellectual disabilities (National Advisory Committee for the Handicapped, 1976).

The first residential institution designed for individuals with disabilities was established in 1817. That year the

American Asylum for the Education and Institution of the Deaf was established in Hartford, Connecticut. In 1819 a second school, for the blind, was established in Watertown, Massachusetts; it was named the New England Asylum for the Blind. During this period and continuing until the Civil War, a number of eastern states established residential schools for individuals with hearing impairments, vision impairments, or intellectual disabilities, as well as individuals who were orphaned (National Advisory Committee for the Handicapped, 1976).

The development of residential institutions for individuals with intellectual disabilities in the United States began in the 1840s. The growth of such institutions was strongly influenced by the work of Johann Guggenbuhl in Switzerland. In 1848 Samuel Howe convinced the Massachusetts legislature to allocate funds for the establishment of the first public setting for individuals with intellectual disabilities. That same year Harvey Wilbur founded the first private institution for treating individuals with intellectual disabilities. These institutions were designed to provide education and training to children and adolescents with mild to moderate disabilities. After the Civil War, residential institutions fell into disfavor. However, the latter portion of the century was marked by continued growth, in both numbers of facilities and numbers of individuals within those facilities. As the nineteenth century came to a close, it became clear that institutions were not accomplishing training that would lead to the reintegration of individuals with disabilities into the community. By 1900, 7,000 individuals with disabilities were housed in institutions. During this time, the role of residential institutions changed significantly. Their emphasis shifted from training to prevention of intellectual disabilities through systematic segregation of individuals with intellectual disabilities from society (Wolfensberger, 1975).

The view of institutions held by state legislatures and the general public fluctuated until after World War II. By this time institutions were overcrowded and understaffed. The effects of the baby boom in the late 1940s and the early 1950s placed further pressures on these settings. After World War II, a growing acknowledgment of the existence and needs of individuals with special needs was experienced by the nation. This awareness was fostered by parental pressures, returning servicemen's needs, professional enthusiasm, and the availability of public and private funding. These factors led to a reevaluation of procedures, research, and a new understanding of individuals with disabilities and the role of institutions in their treatment, care, and training. By 1969, 190,000 individuals with disabilities were housed in institutions (Cegelka & Prehm, 1982).

By the 1970s a new view of the dangers and inadequacies of institutions was recognized. The courts played a major role in bringing this realization to the fore. *Watt v. Stickney* (1972) affirmed an individual with intellectual disability's right to treatment. *Lessard v. Schmidt* (1972) ensured due process for institutionalized individuals. *Souder v. Brennan* (1973) outlawed involuntary servitude of institutionalized persons. The federal government also caused major reforms with the passage of Title XIX (Medicaid) provisions in 1971. These provisions brought institutions under the same controls and review processes as other service providers for individuals with disabilities. A nationwide push to return individuals with disabilities to the community was experienced. Deinstitutionalization became a social, fiscal, and moral goal within each of the states. Between the late 1960s and the early 1980s, the number of individuals with disabilities being served by public residential institutions declined by over 50,000. At the same time, staff-to-client ratios improved along with the physical quality of many institutions. During the 1980s and 1990s, nearly half of state-operated residential facilities for persons with intellectual disabilities were closed in favor of movement to group homes and other less restrictive environments.

To facilitate the deinstitutionalization process, community-based alternatives were developed and expanded during the 1970s and 1980s. During the same period, a number of small institutions (less than 100 residents) were built. Small group homes, foster placements, semi-independent residences, and nursing homes were heavily relied on to handle individuals leaving institutional placements and as alternatives to initial placement in large residential institutions. Contrary to expectation, few of the older large institutions were closed, and many individuals with disabilities stayed within those larger institutions. Changes in the nation's economic stability during the late 1970s and early 1980s also led to many difficulties in realizing the successful integration of the majority of individuals with disabilities into the community (Cegelka & Prehm, 1982).

Current data concerning residential institutions for individuals with intellectual disabilities reveal a clear picture of institutions in general throughout the United States. In summary, facilities with 15 or fewer residents increased over 500% from 1977 to 1982; they are continuing to increase. Each year in the recent past, 17% of residential facilities have closed or moved, displacing approximately 2.7% of all retarded individuals. The large institutions are far more stable. Within these institutions (generally exceeding 300 clients), individuals with profound intellectual disabilities make up the largest portion of residents. In public institutions, staff-to-client ratio was approximately 1.6 to 1. In these facilities, the direct-care staff ratio is .82 to 1 and the clinical staff ratio is .32 to 1. On the other hand, in community-based residential facilities, the functioning level of the individuals served was notably higher while staff ratios are notably lower (Eplle, Jacobson, & Janicki, 1985; Hill et al., 1985).

Reauthorization of Individuals with Disabilities Education Improvement Act (IDEIA, 2004) and close alignment of the laws with No Child Left Behind (NCLB, 2001), have increased the setting in which students with disabilities are served to over 80% of students in special education being served in the general education setting (U.S. Department of Education, 2011). While large residential facilities continue to provide services to individuals with intellectual disabilities. Institution care has significantly decreased over the past two decades and resulted in a greater inclusion of individuals with significant intellectual disabilities being served in public education and community-based setting programs. Community-based programs often provide services that were previously received in residential institution settings.

REFERENCES

Cegelka, P. T., & Prehm, H. J. (1982). *Mental retardation.* Columbus, OH: Merrill.

Eplle, W. A., Jacobson, J. W., & Janicki, M. R. (1985). Staffing ratios in public institutions for persons with mental retardation. *Mental Retardation, 23,* 115–124.

Giffith, R. G. (1985). Symposium: Residential institutions. *Mental Retardation, 23,* 105–106.

Hill, B. K., Bruininks, R. H., Lakin, K. C., Hauber, F. A., & McGuire, S. P. (1985). Stability of residential facilities for people who are mentally retarded 1977–1982. *Mental Retardation, 23,* 108–114.

National Advisory Committee for the Handicapped. (1976). *The unfinished revolution: Education for the handicapped, 1976 annual report.* Washington, DC: U.S. Government Printing Office.

U.S. Department of Education, National Center for Education Statistics (2011). *Digest of Education Statistics, 2010* (NCES 2011-015), Chapter 2.

Wolfensberger, W. (1975). *The origin and nature of our institutional models.* Syracuse, NY: Human Policy.

ALAN HILTON
Seattle University

See also History of Special Education; Philosophy of Education for Individuals With Disabilities

RESISTANT BEHAVIOR, MANAGEMENT OF

One of the most vexing problems facing educators is managing students' resistance. Serious noncompliant behavior is the most frequent reason young children are referred for psychiatric services (Kuczynski, Kochanska, Radke-Yarrow, & Girnius-Brown, 1987). The comorbidity between emotional/behavioral disorders and defiance has been especially high (Cullinan, 2002). However, students with learning disabilities and those at risk also display serious noncompliant behaviors (McWhirter, McWhirter, McWhirter, & McWhirter, 1998; Smith, 1998).

Walker, Ramsey, and Gresham (2004) state that noncompliance serves as a "gateway behavior" for children developing serious antisocial behavior. It can lead to tantrums, uncooperativeness, aggression, and stealing, and ultimately culminate with delinquency. Walker and colleagues also believe that, in some instances, effectively dealing with noncompliance can prevent children from developing more serious antisocial behavior. The most common approaches for treating noncompliance involve a combination of providing highly contingent positive and negative consequences; providing clear, direct, and specific commands; and having children self-monitor and self-evaluate their behavior (Rhode, Morgan, & Young, 1983; Walker et al., 2004; Zirpoli & Melloy, 1997).

Dimensions of Resistance

Compliance typically has been conceptualized as obedience to adult directives and prohibitions, cooperation with requests and suggestions, or the willingness to accept suggestions in teaching situations (Rocissano, Slade, & Lynch, 1987). From this definition, Zirpoli and Melloy (1997) inferred that noncompliance involves disobedience to directives, uncooperativeness with requests and suggestions, and unwillingness to accept suggestions. Schoen (1986) defined noncompliance in a child as responding to an adult request by refusing to comply, providing no response, or engaging in some unrequested behavior.

Oppositional Defiant Disorder

Severe oppositional behaviors have become so pervasive that they were classified as a psychiatric disorder over 20 years ago in the third edition of the *Diagnostic and Statistical Manual of Mental Disorders* (*DSM-III;* American Psychiatric Association [APA], 1980). However, the term *Oppositional Defiant Disorder* first appeared in the revised version of the third edition (*DSM-III-R*; APA, 1987). The current diagnostic criteria, which can be found in the fourth edition text revision (*DSM-IV-TR*; APA, 2000), require a pattern of negativistic, hostile, and defiant behavior lasting 6 months in which at least four of the following eight symptoms are present: temper outbursts, arguing with adults, refusing to follow adult requests, deliberately annoying people, blaming others for own mistakes, touchy or easily annoyed by others, angry and resentful, and spiteful or vindictive.

Although the inclusion of oppositional defiant disorder in the *DSM* nosology has been questioned (Kazdin, 1989; McMahon & Forehand, 1988), noncompliance represents a practical problem for parents, teachers, and clinicians. As a psychiatric disorder, it is believed to occur in between 2% and 16% of children, depending on the nature of the population sample and methods of estimation (APA, 2000). These estimates should not come as a surprise, because children typically disobey about 20% to 40% of parental requests and commands (Forehand, 1977).

Targets for Intervention

The literature on noncompliance typically has focused on modifying children's behaviors because they are often seen as the source of the problem. However, Walker et al. (2004) insightfully noted that "whether or not a child complies with an adult directive has as much to do with how the command is framed and delivered as it does with the consequences, or lack thereof, that follow the delivery" (p. 309). Walker et al. went on to describe the difference between *alpha* and *beta* commands. Alpha commands are given in a clear, direct, and specific manner, with few verbalizations, and they allow a reasonable time for compliance to occur. Beta commands are vague, overly wordy, and often contain multiple instructions to engage in a behavior. The implication of their discussion is that students' noncompliance may be exacerbated by educators' behaviors.

The modification of educators' behavior has generally focused on maximizing the use of alpha commands (e.g., Forehand & McMahon, 1981; Morgan & Jenson, 1988; Walker & Walker, 1991). However, what is sometimes lost in this discussion is that a plethora of other adult factors can spawn noncompliance in children. In fact, Cormier and Cormier (1985) stated that resistance can arise from any behavior, regardless of the source, that interferes with the likelihood of a successful outcome. This definition provides the impetus for using the term *resistance* instead of the more common words *noncompliance, oppositional,* or *defiant. Resistance* is a more inclusive term because it focuses on the interaction between children's and adults' behaviors. On the other hand, the terms *noncompliance* and *oppositional* suggest that the locus of the problem resides within a child. Consequently, solutions to the problems of noncompliance or opposition will focus solely on changing children's behaviors to the exclusion of also modifying adults' behaviors to obtain a desired outcome.

The Role of Functional Assessment

Functional assessment consists of five processes: (1) describing the problem behavior; (2) identifying events, situations, and times that predict when it will and will not occur; (3) identifying consequences that maintain it; (4) developing hypotheses that describe the behavior, when it occurs, and what reinforcers maintain it; and (5) collecting direct observation data that support the hypotheses. There are two core functions of problem behavior: (1) to obtain something desirable, such as attention from others, tangible objects, or activities (positive reinforcement); and (2) to escape or avoid something aversive, such as a difficult or boring task (negative reinforcement).

This conclusion may be expected because human behavior is complex and subtle. For example, literature from the field of social psychology highlights the influence power/control has on human functioning and interaction. Although power/control does not fit as well into an applied behavior analysis (ABA) paradigm as do attention and escape/avoidance, it nevertheless may be an equally valid function of maladaptive behaviors displayed by some students. Furthermore, it can be functionally analyzed using ABA methodology similar to that used for attention and escape/avoidance (Maag & Kemp, 2003).

Power and Human Functioning

Over 50 years ago, Cartwright (1959), a noted researcher and theorist of group dynamics, believed that few social interactions advance very far before elements of power come into play. Buckley (1967) defined power as "control or influence over the actions of others to promote one's goals without their consent, against their will, or without their knowledge or understanding" (p. 186). In a general sense, power is defined as behaviors producing social influence. It involves one person causing another person to perform a behavior that is contrary to the latter's desire (French & Raven, 1959).

Falbo (1977) described two dimensions of power tactics: (1) rationality versus nonrationality and (2) directness versus indirectness. Rational modes of influence include bargaining techniques. A student who tries to make a deal with the teacher by saying that he will begin his work if he first can finish drawing is an example of direct power behaviors. Nonrational tactics are present in students who try to evade an issue or deceive those who disagree with them. An example of this type of power would be a student who tries to goad a teacher into an argument by saying that she completed her homework but it was taken by a classmate. An example of a direct approach would be ignoring a teacher's direction and continuing to perform the current behavior. Indirect tactics would include hinting or ingratiating oneself. The classic example of this is the "teacher's pet," the student who tries to gain more of the teacher's favor than is given to other students and thus gain more power in the classroom.

Power and Resistance

Many students who show resistance in school do so to obtain power that is absent in other aspects of their lives (Maag, 2001). Being homeless, having parents with mental illnesses, and coming from a family where physical or sexual abuse occurs all contribute to feelings of helplessness (McWhirter et al., 1998). Some children who are depressed often display noncompliant behaviors as a way to combat helplessness, which is characteristic of this disorder (Maag & Forness, 1991). Perceived lack of personal power has resulted in parental discipline styles' contributing to children's delinquency and learning difficulties (Hagan, Simpson, & Gillis, 1987; Leiber & Wacker, 1997; Plax, Kearney, McCroskey, & Richmond, 1986).

Some level of resistance is normal and even desirable. As toddlers and when entering adolescence, children behave in ways to obtain power as a way to assert independence (Richardson, 2000). There is a fine line between refusing to comply with a teacher's request and refusing to yield to peer pressure to take drugs. Nevertheless, to manage students' resistance effectively, teachers must determine if the function of the inappropriate behavior is power/control.

Tactics for Managing Resistance

The process of managing resistance begins by educators ruling out escape/avoidance and attention as the functions of misbehavior (Maag & Kemp, 2003). For example, a student may make animal noises during class. An escape function may be ruled out (or confirmed) by replacing the assigned task with a high-interest activity. If the student makes animal noises to escape a difficult or boring task, then there would be no reason for him to misbehave when given a desirable task because he would not want to escape it. If the student continues to make animal noises when given a high-interest activity, then attention may be tested. An A-B-C analysis would be conducted to determine the antecedents and consequences prompting and maintaining the behavior that, in turn, would be manipulated. The teacher and peers may ignore the student when he makes animal noises, or the student may be removed from class. If animal noises do not decrease, then power may be tested using the techniques described by Maag and Kemp (2003). The following techniques—which are described in greater detail elsewhere (e.g., Maag, 1999; Maag & Kemp, 2005)—are based on the premise that power is the function of a student's misbehavior and focus on changing the context surrounding a behavior.

Changing context can have a profound impact upon reducing resistance. It is based on the assumptions that (a) behaviors derive meaning from context and (b) context serves as a cue that elicits certain behaviors. Therefore, it is axiomatic that when the context surrounding a behavior changes, the meaning, purpose, and desire to engage in the behavior also change (Maag, 1999).

Creating Ordeals

Creating ordeals in order to change context was first described in a systematic way by Haley (1984). The approach is straightforward: A teacher imposes an ordeal appropriate to a student's problem that causes equal or greater distress than the problem. Ordeal therapy shares some similarities with negative practice except that in ordeal therapy the task is something to which the student cannot legitimately object.

Maag (1999) describes a situation in which a teacher who was confronted with a boy who refused to complete his math assignment and instead wrote the name of his school followed by the word "sucks" on the paper. The teacher nonchalantly said that she was sorry his school "sucked" but that he was not being very creative in his writing of the words. She enthusiastically suggested that the boy turn over the paper and write the words repeatedly in various print styles and sizes. The boy, who began in earnest, quickly lost interest and began working on the math assignment.

There are several important qualities in the ordeal described above. First, the teacher did not present the ordeal as a punitive consequence for misbehaving. Instead, she appeared apologetic that the student did not like the school but also pleased that he had the opportunity to practice writing more creatively. Her reaction automatically changed the context: She was not confrontational and consequently was able to avoid a power struggle. Second, the student performed the ordeal because it was congruent with what he wanted to do—write that his school sucked. Third, complying with the teacher's direction to write that his school sucked no longer meant that he was defying a teacher's request and consequently became a bother.

Scrambling Routine

The performance of a series of behaviors can be conceptualized in terms of a stimulus-response chain (Malott, Whaley, & Malott, 1997). A stimulus elicits a response, which in turn becomes a cue to perform another behavior. This approach is sometimes referred to as "sequence confusion" (Lankton, 1985). For example, preparing to take a math quiz may be a cue for a student to feel anxious. Anxiety then becomes a cue for the student to begin crying. Crying, in turn, becomes a cue for the student to run out of the room, and so forth. However, instructing the student to "feel anxious" 15 minutes prior to taking a math quiz scrambles the stimulus-response chain, and the student can no longer perform the behavior as it was performed previously. This example is paradoxical (Simon & Vetter-Zemitzsch, 1985) because if the student brings on anxiety, then he has proof that anxiety is under his control; if he refuses to bring on anxiety, he also has proof that anxiety is under his control because he was able to avoid experiencing it.

Embedding Instructions

Embedding instructions is a technique in which a teacher directs a student to do what she is already doing while interspersing a request for the desired behavior (Maag, 1999). For example, a teacher may embed the following instruction: "Mary, as you shuffle your papers, open your math book to page 18 while talking to Susie." In this situation, Mary is engaging in two undesirable behaviors:

shuffling her papers and talking to Susie. This instruction embeds three separate tasks—two of which Mary is already performing. The part of the instruction with which her teacher is trying to get compliance is opening the math book to page 18. If the instructions were separated, Mary could easily refuse one or all of them. But a refusal when the tasks are combined into a single instruction means what? That Mary will not shuffle her papers? That she will not open her book? That she will not talk to Susie? The effort required to identify what one is refusing in itself is a deterrent to refusal (Bandler & Grinder, 1975). Nor can a refusal of the entire instruction be offered comfortably. To the single tasks she can easily say no. But to the combined task she cannot say no because, if she is shuffling her papers, she must "immediately" open her book and talk to Susie. Hence, Mary may prefer to perform the combined tasks unwillingly rather than put forth the effort to analyze the instruction minutely.

Conclusion

Managing resistance may at first seem to be a massive job because resistant students often do not respond to traditional interventions. However, understanding that adult behavior should be examined and modified as well as the student's is a good first step. The use of functional assessment will help educators determine if noncompliance serves the function of attention, escape, or power. Behaviors controlled by the desire for attention or escape are not truly indicative of resistance, but they are modifiable using traditional ABA techniques, in which most special educators have received training. Techniques for managing resistance are based on the impact of context on behavior. These techniques include, but are not limited to, creating ordeals, scrambling routine, reframing, and embedding instructions. These techniques share the commonality of changing context as a way to facilitate a change in the meaning, purpose, and desire for a student to engage in resistant behaviors.

REFERENCES

American Psychiatric Association. (1980). *Diagnostic and statistical manual of mental disorders* (3rd ed.). Washington, DC: Author.

American Psychiatric Association. (1987). *Diagnostic and statistical manual of mental disorders* (3rd ed., rev.). Washington, DC: Author.

American Psychiatric Association. (2000). *Diagnostic and statistical manual of mental disorders* (4th ed., text rev.). Washington, DC: Author.

Bandler, R., & Grinder, J. (1975). *Patterns of the hypnotic techniques of Milton H. Erickson, M.D.* Capitola, CA: Meta.

Buckley, W. (1967). *Sociology and modern systems theory.* Englewood Cliffs, NJ: Prentice Hall.

Cartwright, D. (1959). A field theoretical conception of power. In D. Cartwright (Ed.), *Studies in social power* (pp. 183–220). Ann Arbor, MI: Institute for Social Research.

Cormier, W. H., & Cormier, L. S. (1985). *Interviewing strategies for helpers: Fundamental skills and cognitive behavioral interventions* (2nd ed.). Monterey, CA: Brooks/Cole.

Cullinan, D. (2002). *Students with emotional and behavior disorders.* Upper Saddle River, NJ: Merrill Prentice Hall.

Falbo, T. (1977). Power strategies in intimate relationships. *Journal of Personality and Social Psychology, 35,* 537–548.

Forehand, R. (1977). Child noncompliance to parental requests: Behavioral analysis and treatment. In M. Hersen, R. M. Eisler, & P. M. Miller (Eds.), *Progress in behavior modification* (Vol. 5, pp. 111–147). New York, NY: Academic Press.

Forehand, R., & McMahon, R. (1981). *Helping the noncompliant child.* New York, NY: Guilford Press.

French, J. R. P., Jr., & Raven, B. (1959). The bases of social power. In D. Cartwright (Ed.), *Studies in social power* (pp. 118–149). Ann Arbor, MI: Institute for Social Research.

Hagan, J., Simpson, J., & Gillis, A. R. (1987). Class in the household: A power-control theory of gender and delinquency. *American Journal of Sociology, 92,* 788–816.

Haley, J. (1984). *Ordeal therapy.* San Francisco, CA: Jossey-Bass.

Kazdin, A. E. (1989). Conduct and oppositional disorders. In C. G. Last & M. Hersen (Eds.), *Handbook of child psychiatric diagnosis* (pp. 129–155). New York, NY: Wiley.

Kuczynski, L., Kochanska, G., Radke-Yarrow, M., & Girnius-Brown, O. (1987). A developmental interpretation of young children's noncompliance. *Developmental Psychology, 23,* 779–806.

Lankton, C. H. (1985). Generative change: Beyond symptomatic relief. In J. K. Zeig (Ed.), *Ericksonian psychotherapy* (Vol. 1, pp. 137–170). New York, NY: Brunner/Mazel.

Leiber, M. J., & Wacker, M. E. (1997). A theoretical and empirical assessment of power-control theory and single-mother families. *Youth and Society, 28,* 317–350.

Maag, J. W. (1999). Managing resistance: Looking beyond the child and into the mirror. In P. Zionts (Ed.), *Inclusion strategies for students with learning and behavior problems* (pp. 229–271). Austin, TX: PRO-ED.

Maag, J. W. (2001). *Powerful struggles: Managing resistance, building rapport.* Longmont, CO: Sopris West.

Maag, J. W., & Forness, S. R. (1991). Depression in children and adolescents: Identification, assessment, and treatment. *Focus on Exceptional Children, 24*(1), 1–19.

Maag, J. W., & Kemp, S. E. (2003). Behavioral intent of power and affiliation: Implications for functional analysis. *Remedial and Special Education, 24,* 57–64.

Maag, J. W., & Kemp, S. E. (2005). I can't make you: Attitude shifts and techniques for managing resistance. In P. Zionts (Ed.), *Inclusion strategies for students with learning and behavior problems* (2nd ed., pp. 247–281). Austin, TX: PRO-ED.

Malott, R. W., Whaley, D. L., & Malott, M. E. (1997). *Elementary principles of behavior* (3rd ed.). Upper Saddle River, NJ: Prentice Hall.

McMahon, R. J., & Forehand, R. (1988). Conduct disorders. In E. J. Mash & L. G. Terdal (Eds.), *Behavioral assessment of childhood disorders* (2nd ed., pp. 105–153). New York, NY: Guilford Press.

McWhirter, J. J., McWhirter, B. T., McWhirter, A. M., & McWhirter, E. H. (1998). *At-risk youth: A comprehensive response* (2nd ed.). Pacific Grove, CA: Brooks/Cole.

Morgan, D. P., & Jenson, W. R. (1988). *Teaching behaviorally disordered students: Preferred practices.* Columbus, OH: Merrill.

Plax, T. G., Kearney, P., McCroskey, J. C., & Richmond, V. P. (1986). Power in the classroom VI: Verbal control strategies, nonverbal immediacy and affective learning. *Communication Education, 35,* 43–55.

Rhode, G., Morgan, D. P., & Young, K. R. (1983). Generalization and maintenance of treatment gains of behaviorally handicapped students from resource rooms to regular classrooms using self-evaluation procedures. *Journal of Applied Behavior Analysis, 16,* 171–188.

Richardson, K. (2000). *Developmental psychology: How nature and nurture interact.* Basingstoke, England: Macmillan.

Rocissano, L., Slade, A., & Lynch, V. (1987). Dyadic synchrony and toddler compliance. *Developmental Psychology, 23,* 698–704.

Schoen, S. (1986). Decreasing noncompliance in a severely multi-handicapped child. *Psychology in the Schools, 23,* 88–94.

Simon, D. J., & Vetter-Zemitzsch, A. (1985). Paradoxical interventions: Strategies for the resistant adolescent. In M. K. Zabel (Ed.), *Teaching: Behaviorally disordered youth* (Vol. 1, pp. 17–22). Reston, VA: Council for Children with Behavioral Disorders.

Smith, C. R. (1998). *Learning disabilities: The interaction of learner, task, and setting* (4th ed.). Boston, MA: Allyn & Bacon.

Walker, H. M., Ramsey, E., & Gresham, F. M. (2004). *Antisocial behavior in school: Evidence-based practices* (2nd ed.). Belmont, CA: Wadsworth/Thomson Learning.

Walker, H. M., & Walker, J. E. (1991). *Coping with noncompliance in the classroom: A positive approach for teachers.* Austin, TX: PRO-ED.

Zirpoli, T. J., & Melloy, K. J. (1997). *Behavior management: Applications for teachers and parents* (2nd ed.). Upper Saddle River, NJ: Prentice Hall.

JOHN W. MAAG
University of Nebraska–Lincoln

See also Behavior Modification; Classroom Management

RESOURCE ROOM

The resource room concept gained popularity following the *Hobsen v. Hansen* litigation, which declared tracking systems illegal and required reevaluation on a regular basis. This litigation was a forerunner for mainstreaming and the concept of least restrictive alternative (environment). This model of service delivery allows a child with a disability to remain in the educational mainstream as much as possible. With the passage of PL 94-142 and further emphasis on the least restrictive alternative, the resource room gained even further popularity. There are over 100,000 resource room teachers in the United States today. Professional special educators have consistently cited the importance of the resource room concept and have noted its viability as a promising alternative to placement in self-contained classes or regular classes without support services (Cartwright, Cartwright, & Ward, 1995; D'Alonzo, 1983; Kasik, 1983; Learner, 1985; Marsh, Price, & Smith, 1983; Meyen, 1982; Reger, 1973; Sabatino, 1972; Sindelar & Deno, 1978; Wiederholdt, 1974).

Usually, students attending resource rooms are identified as individuals with mild disabilities (4% to 6% of the total school population). Resource rooms are a widespread means of service delivery individuals with mild disabilities, and are gaining acceptance for use with children identified as gifted.

There are voluminous data available on the definition of resource rooms (Chaffin, 1974; Deno; 1973; Fox et al. 1972; Hammill & Wiederholdt, 1972; Kasik, 1983; Lilly, 1971; Reger, 1972, 1973; Sabatino, 1972; Wiederholdt, 1974). According to Kasik (1983), a resource room is a place that students receiving special education services attend for less than 50% of their school day for support services. The student remains in the general education classroom for the majority of the academic instruction. The resource room is staffed by a resource room teacher. Attendance in the resource room is determined by a multidisciplinary staff according to the student's individual needs. Students are scheduled into specific time slots to attend the resource room, where they receive remedial instruction from a trained specialist in their deficit areas. A resource room should be well equipped with a wide variety of instructional materials. Individualized instruction may include perceptual training, language development, motor training, social and emotional development, and academic skills development. Resource room class size should be small. A recommended caseload per teacher would be no more than 20 students at any one time. Class sessions are either individual or in small groups of up to five students per session. They are a minimum of 20 minutes and a maximum of 45 minutes in length. The resource room should have the same comfortable characteristics of a regular classroom, such as dimensions of at least 150 square feet, adequate lighting, ventilation, and temperature control. The resource room should be easily accessible to teachers and students and should possess adequate storage space for folders and materials. In general, the resource room should provide a positive learning environment.

Placement in the resource room is intended to be of short duration (Kasik, 1983). As students progress toward specified goals, they are returned to full-time placement in the regular classroom. Return to the regular classroom should progress through a gradual phasing out of support services. The resource room is to be considered as one type of service delivery within the continuum of services available.

REFERENCES

Cartwright, P., Cartwright, C., & Ward, M. (1995). *Educating special learners* (4th ed.). Boston, MA: Wadsworth.

Chaffin, J. D. (1974). Will the real mainstreaming program please stand up! *Focus on Exceptional Children, 5*(6), 1–18.

D'Alonzo, B. (1983). *Educating adolescents with learning and behavior problems*. Rockville, MD: Aspen Systems.

Deno, E. (1973). *Instructional alternatives for exceptional children*. Reston, VA: Council For Exceptional Children.

Fox, W. L., Egnar, A. N., Polucci, P. E., Perelman, P. F., & McKenzie, H. S. (1972). An introduction to regular classroom approaches to special education. In E. Deno (Ed.), *Instructional alternatives for exceptional children*. Reston, VA: Council for Exceptional Children.

Hammill, D. D., & Wiederholdt, L. (1972). *The resource room: Rationale and implementation*. Ft. Washington, PA: Journal of Special Education Press.

Kasik, M. M. (1983). Analysis of the professional preparation of the resource room teacher. *Dissertation Abstracts International*. (University Microfilms International No. DAO 56766)

Learner, J. (1985). *Learning disabilities: Theories, diagnosis, and teaching strategies* (4th ed.). Boston, MA: Houghton Mifflin.

Lilly, M. S. (1971). A training based model for special education. *Exceptional Children, 37*, 747–749.

Marsh, G. E., Price, B. J., & Smith, T. E. C. (1983). *Teaching mildly handicapped children: Methods and materials: A generic approach to comprehensive teaching*. St. Louis, MO: Mosby.

Meyen, E. L. (1982). *Exceptional children and youth* (2nd ed.). Chicago, IL: Love.

Reger, R. (1972). Resource rooms: Change agents or guardians of the status quo? *Journal of Special Education, 6*, 355–360.

Reger, R. (1973). What is a resource room program? *Journal of Learning Disabilities, 6*, 609–614.

Sabatino, D. A. (1972). Resource rooms: The renaissance in special education. *Journal of Special Education, 6*, 235–348.

Sindelar, P. T., & Deno, E. (1978). The effectiveness of resource room programming. *Journal of Special Education, 12*, 17–28.

Wiederholdt, J. L. (1974). Planning resource rooms for the mildly handicapped. *Focus on Exceptional Children, 5*(8), 1–10.

MARIBETH MONTGOMERY KASIK
Governors State University

See also **Cascade Model of Special Education Services; Inclusion; Least Restrictive Environment; Resource Teacher; Self-Contained Class**

RESOURCE TEACHER

Much of the research literature calls for resource rooms to be staffed by highly trained special educators who are personable, demonstrate good human interactional skills, and are prepared professionally in the diagnosis and remediation of single or multiple groups of children with disabilities. Wallace and McLoughlin (1979) identify the resource teacher's main role as including assessment, instructional planning, teacher evaluation, and liaison-consultant duties. Learner (1985) describes the resource teacher as a highly trained professional who is capable of diagnosing the child, planning and implementing the teaching program, assisting the classroom teacher, providing continuous evaluation of the student, and conducting in-service sessions with other educators and the community. Sabatino (1981) states that the role of the resource teacher includes direct service to individuals and small groups of children, consultant services to classroom teachers, and responsibility for assessment and delivery of individualized programs. Kasik (1983) states that the resource teacher needs to be well organized, flexible, self-directed, and effective in time management. Paroz, Siegenthaler, and Tatum (1977) suggest that the resource teacher be actively involved with the total school community, including students and staff members. They add that the "teacher's role is open ended and limited only by time, talent, and acceptance of the teacher by the school administration and staff" (p. 15). The resource teacher is a trained specialist who works with, and acts as a consultant to, other teachers, providing materials and methods to help children who are having difficulties within the regular classroom. Usually, the resource teacher works with a population of students with mild disabilities in a centralized resource room where appropriate materials are housed.

Some of the most common responsibilities a resource teacher will probably be asked to undertake have been identified by Sabatino (1982). The resource teacher will conduct and participate in screening for children with learning disabilities, determine the nature of their learning, and prepare final reports for each referral. Instruction will be provided individually or in small groups. The resource teacher will prepare lessons for use when a child cannot function within the framework of the regular lesson. Students will participate in the resource room until they are integrated full time or until successful transition is complete. Schedules should include six or seven sessions daily, except on Fridays, when the session should be half a day. This allows the teacher to complete reports, observations, parent meetings, consultations, and so on. Consultation with classroom teachers and other pupil services personnel should be consistent. The resource teacher should serve as a resource person and provide supportive assistance for all classroom teachers. Observation in the regular classroom and conferences with regular class teachers and parents about pupil progress should be continuous. In addition to meeting with teachers, the resource teacher may be required to prepare in-service materials and supervise the work of paraprofessionals and volunteers. Despite these suggestions, there is no consistency within the field regarding actual practice.

There are four different types of resource room teachers: (1) categorical, (2) noncategorical, (3) itinerant (or mobile), and (4) teacher-consultant. Categorical programs serve one specific population; noncategorical programs may serve one or more populations. The itinerant resource room teacher travels from one building to another and usually does not have an assigned room from which to work. The teacher-consultant resource room teacher provides consultation to regular class teachers, parents, and other service delivery personnel. Cartwright, Cartwright, and Ward (1995) provide a description of a typical day in the life of a resource teacher in today's schools.

REFERENCES

Cartwright, P., Cartwright, C., & Ward, M. (1995). *Educating special learners* (4th ed.). Boston, MA: Wadsworth.

Kasik, M. M. (1983). Analysis of the professional preparation of the special education resource room teacher. *Dissertation Abstracts International*. (University Microfilms International No. DAO 56766)

Learner, J. (1985). *Learning disabilities: Theories, diagnosis, and teaching strategies* (4th ed.). Boston, MA: Houghton Mifflin.

Paroz, J., Siegenthaler, L., & Tatum, V. (1977). A model for a middle school resource room. *Journal of Learning Disabilities, 8*, 7–15.

Sabatino, D. A. (1981). Overview for the practitioner in learning disabilities. In D. A. Sabatino, T. L. Miller, & C. R. Schmidt (Eds.), *Learning disabilities: Systemizing teaching and service delivery*. Rockville, MD: Aspen.

Sabatino, D. A. (1982). An educational program guide for secondary schools. In D. A. Sabatino & L. Mann (Eds.), *A handbook of diagnostic and prescriptive teaching*. Rockville, MD: Aspen.

Wallace, G., & McLoughlin, J. A. (1979). *Learning disabilities: Concepts and characteristics* (2nd ed.). Columbus, OH: Merrill.

MARIBETH MONTGOMERY KASIK
Governors State University

See also Diagnostic Prescriptive Teaching; Resource Room

RESPIRATORY DISTRESS SYNDROME, ADULT

Adult (or acute) respiratory distress syndrome is an inflammatory disease of the lung characterized by the sudden onset of pulmonary edema and respiratory failure.

The disorder is also known as wet lung, shock lung, stiff lung, and posttraumatic pulmonary insufficiency (O'Toole, 1992).

The incidence of adult respiratory distress syndrome has been difficult to determine, in part because there are a variety of causes. Published estimates range from 1.5–71 cases per 100,000 (American Lung Association, 2001). Early signs of adult respiratory distress syndrome are generally subtle and nonspecific, making an accurate diagnosis difficult (Loeb, 1991). Although adult respiratory distress syndrome is more often observed in adults, it is a well-recognized cause of respiratory failure in children (Walker, 1999) and is associated with a variety of acute diseases in youth who are critically ill (Moloney-Harmon, 1999).

The typical patient with adult respiratory distress syndrome is generally young and otherwise healthy, with no previous lung disease (Loeb, 1991). Adult respiratory distress syndrome occurs as a result of direct injury to the lungs or acute illness (National Organization for Rare Disorders, 1999). The numerous etiological factors associated with adult respiratory distress syndrome include fluid aspiration, septic shock, drug overdose, near drowning, smoke inhalation, pancreatitis, transfusion reaction, and massive trauma or burns (O'Toole, 1992). Adult respiratory distress syndrome usually develops within 24–48 hours after the initial injury or illness. As the disease evolves, a number of respiratory abnormalities develop. These symptoms include hypoxemia (decreased arterial oxygenation), hypoxia (decreased tissue oxygenation), diminished lung compliance, and reduced lung volume (Loeb, 1991).

Characteristics

1. Breathing difficulties
2. Rapid, shallow breathing
3. Hyperventilation
4. Tachycardia (abnormally rapid heart rate)
5. Insufficient levels of oxygen in the circulating blood
6. The appearance of cyanotic (bluish-colored) or mottled skin

The progression of adult respiratory distress syndrome is characterized by four phases. Phase I occurs immediately after the initial injury, infection, or illness. During this phase, the individual is generally alert but may begin to hyperventilate. During Phase II, signs of subclinical respiratory distress, such as tachycardia, and rapid and shallow breathing become apparent. The individual also begins to appear fairly anxious during this phase. It is during the third phase that the person with adult respiratory distress syndrome begins to appear gravely ill, exhibiting numerous and severe symptoms of the disease. Acute respiratory failure occurs during Phase IV, and the individual lapses into a coma. Complications that may result from the late phases of adult respiratory distress syndrome include fatal pulmonary damage, secondary pulmonary infection, and cardiac dysfunction (Loeb, 1991).

Treatment of adult respiratory distress syndrome must begin at the first signs of hyperventilation and decreasing levels of oxygen in the blood if progression of the disease is to be slowed or stopped (O'Toole, 1992). Treatment for adult respiratory distress syndrome typically includes continuous positive airway pressure or mechanical ventilation, fluid management, drug therapy that includes antibiotics for any infection, and nutritional support therapy. Adult respiratory distress syndrome is also frequently treated with steroids (Loeb, 1991).

Special education services may be available to children who have suffered from permanent lung damage related to adult respiratory distress syndrome. Generally, these children will qualify for services with the handicapping conditions of other health impaired or physical disability.

The overall mortality rate of patients, including children, with adult respiratory distress syndrome is greater than 50% (WebMD, 2011). Most survivors of adult respiratory distress syndrome recover normal lung function and lead normal or near-normal lives (Soubani & Pieroni, 1999). However, some individuals may suffer permanent lung damage, which can range from mild to severe (WebMD, 2011).

REFERENCES

American Lung Association. (2001). *Fact sheet: Adult (acute) respiratory distress syndrome.* Retrieved from http://www.lung .org/

Loeb, S. (Ed.). (1991). *Cardiopulmonary emergencies.* Springhouse, PA: Springhouse Corporation.

Moloney-Harmon, P. A. (1999). When the lung fails: Acute respiratory distress syndrome in children. *Critical Care Nursing Clinic of North America, 11*(4), 519–528.

National Organization for Rare Disorders. (1999). *Acute respiratory distress syndrome.* Retrieved from http://www.stepstn .com/cgi-win/nord.exe?proc=Redirect&type=rdbsum&id=611 .htm

O'Toole, M. (Ed.). (1992). *Miller-Keane encyclopedia and dictionary of medicine, nursing, and allied health* (5th ed.). Philadelphia, PA: Saunders.

Soubani, A. O., & Pieroni, R. (1999). Acute respiratory distress syndrome: A clinical update. *Southern Medical Journal, 92*(5), 450–457.

Walker, T. A. (1999). The acute respiratory distress syndrome in children: Recent UMMC experience. *Journal of Mississippi State Medical Association, 40*(11), 371–375.

WebMD. (2011). *Acute respiratory distress syndrome (ARDS)—topic overview.* Retrieved from http://www.webmd.com/lung/tc/acute-respiratory-distress-syndrome-ards-topic-overview

M. FRANCI CREPEAU-HOBSON
University of Northern Colorado

RESPIRATORY DISTRESS SYNDROME, INFANT

Respiratory distress syndrome is a pulmonary disorder that occurs primarily in infants born prematurely. The disorder is a result of incomplete lung development. Respiratory distress syndrome is due to insufficiency of a foamy fluid known as surfactant, a substance essential to expansion of the alveoli, or air sacs of the lungs. Because of their immaturity, premature infants tend to lack surfactant, and their lungs are unable to inflate (American Lung Association, 2000).

Respiratory distress syndrome occurs in 1% of newborns and is the most common lung disease of premature infants (Blackman, 1990). The majority of babies born before 32 weeks of pregnancy will have respiratory distress syndrome (University of Maryland Medicine, 2000). The incidence of the disorder declines with gestational age at birth. Approximately 60% of infants born at less than 28 weeks' gestation, 30% of those born at 28–34 weeks, and less than 5% of those born after 34 weeks will have respiratory distress syndrome (American Lung Association, 2000).

Characteristics

1. Audible grunting noise with each breath
2. Rapid breathing
3. Flaring of the nostrils and retracting of the muscles between the ribs and under the rib cage
4. Cyanosis (bluish coloring) around the lips and nail beds
5. Lethargy
6. Apneic (cessation of breathing) episodes

In anticipation of respiratory distress syndrome in premature infants, neonatal intensive care units routinely monitor the child's pulse and respiration, along with the amount of oxygen in the blood. Treatment is begun at the first clinical sign of respiratory distress syndrome (Blackman, 1990). High oxygen and humidity concentrations are given initially. Intravenous fluids may also be administered. Further treatment depends on the severity of the respiratory distress syndrome. Infants with mild symptoms are given supplementary oxygen whereas those with more severe symptoms may be intubated and managed on a mechanical respirator to prevent the alveoli from collapsing (University of Maryland Medicine, 2000). Special oxygenated liquid may also be instilled in the lungs of infants with severe cases (American Lung Association, 2000). In addition, artificial surfactant may be infused into the lungs of infants who are of high risk for respiratory distress syndrome immediately after birth to prevent or improve the course of the syndrome (University of Maryland Medicine, 2000). Treatment of respiratory distress syndrome without complications generally lasts 5 to 7 days, with the infant gradually needing less added oxygen. The condition usually improves as the infant begins producing adequate amounts of surfactant (Blackman, 1990).

The vast majority of infants with respiratory distress syndrome survive, with recent estimates around 90%. The majority of these infants will develop normally and do well in regular education classes (Blackman, 1990). However, sometimes long-term complications may develop. Complications can be the result of oxygen toxicity, high pressures delivered to the lungs, or the severity of the disease. These complications during the early days of life may affect cognitive development, physical development, and the child's future health status (Blackman, 1990). Longitudinal research has indicated that children with respiratory distress syndrome generally score significantly lower on measures of cognitive and motor functioning than do children without a history of respiratory distress syndrome. It should be noted, however, that in spite of these differences, most of the respiratory distress syndrome samples still scored within the average range by their 1st birthday (see Creasey, Jarvis, Myers, Markowitz, & Kerkering, 1993, for a review). Research has also indicated that school-age children with a history of respiratory distress syndrome—especially when it is severe—are more likely to have poorer memory skills than do children who did not have respiratory distress syndrome (Rose & Feldman, 1996).

Depending on the presence and severity of complications and on any resulting developmental impact, children who had respiratory distress syndrome as infants may qualify for special education services under a number of handicapping conditions. These conditions include infant disability, preschool disability, learning disability, mental retardation, or other health impaired.

The prognosis for infants with respiratory distress syndrome generally is dependent on gestational age and birth weight, which are related to the severity of the disorder (Myers et al., 1992). Complications develop in 10%–20% of infants with respiratory distress syndrome overall, and approximately 10% will die (Blackman, 1990). Potential complications include cardiac arrest while being intubated; hemorrhage into the brain or the lung; respiratory illness, including bronchopulmonary dysplasia; retrolental fibroplasia and blindness; and delayed mental development and mental retardation associated with anoxic brain damage or hemorrhage (University of Maryland Medicine, 2000).

Other, more minor problems may also develop. Children with respiratory distress syndrome are more likely to have severe colds and other respiratory infections and are more likely to be hospitalized during the first 2 years of life. These children are also more likely to have an increased sensitivity to lung irritants such as smoke and pollution and to suffer from wheezing and other asthma-like problems in childhood (University of Maryland Medicine,

2000). Early and effective treatment is critical to preventing and decreasing complications related to respiratory distress syndrome.

REFERENCES

American Lung Association. (2000). *Fact sheet: Respiratory distress syndrome*. Retrieved from http://www.lungusa.org/diseases/RespiratoryDistressSyndromefac.html

Blackman, J. A. (1990). *Medical aspects of developmental disabilities in children birth to three* (2nd ed.). Rockville, MD: Aspen.

Creasey, G. L., Jarvis, P. A., Myers, B. J., Markowitz, P. I., & Kerkering, K. W. (1993). Mental and motor development for three groups of premature infants. *Infant Behavior and Development, 16*, 365–372.

Myers, B. J., Jarvis, P. A., Creasey, G. L., Kerkering, K. W., Markowitz, L., & Best, A. M., III. (1992). Prematurity and respiratory illness: Brazelton Scale (NBAS) performance of preterm infants with broncho-pulmonary dysplasia (BPD), respiratory distress syndrome (RDS) or no respiratory illness. *Infant Behavior and Development, 15*, 27–41.

Rose, S. A., & Feldman, J. F. (1996). Memory and processing speed in preterm children at eleven years: A comparison with full-terms. *Child Development, 67*, 2005–2021.

University of Maryland Medicine. (2000). *Respiratory distress syndrome (infants)*. Retrieved from http://www.healthcentral.com/

M. Franci Crepeau-Hobson
University of Northern Colorado

RESPITE CARE

Respite care complements special education in providing support to families of children with disabilities. Respite care may be defined as temporary care given to an individual with a disability or otherwise dependent for the purpose of providing relief to the primary caregiver (Cohen & Warren, 1985). The concept of respite care is generally associated with intermittent services, although *respite care* is also sometimes used to refer to regularly scheduled services occurring once or twice a week.

Respite care programs first appeared in the mid-1970s in response to the deinstitutionalization movement. Deinstitutionalization meant that many families who would probably have placed their children with disabilities in institutions, either out of choice or as a result of professional advice, no longer had the option to do so. In addition, some children who had been placed in institutions in earlier years were being returned to their families. Thus a substantial number of parents now had to cope with the care needs of their children with severe disabilities each day. The natural breaks that parents of typically developing children experience when their children sleep at a friend's home, visit with relatives, or go to camp were usually not available. It was virtually impossible to obtain paid babysitters, and even relatives were reluctant to assume this responsibility. The primary caregiver, usually the mother, found it impossible to engage in normal activities such as shopping, caring for medical and dental needs, or seeing friends. Parents rarely had time for each other or for their other children. Families experienced severe problems in coping.

Some parents' cries for help were heard by professionals. Other parents, receiving no help from the service field, organized themselves and initiated respite care programs while continuing to bring their plight to the attention of service agencies. It was not until the late 1970s that professionals recognized the importance of respite care services. Parents were the primary advocates for these services prior to that time.

Respite care is a family-support service, designed to improve family functioning and help normalize families of the disabled. This service is of particular importance to families with weak natural support systems, poor coping skills, or strenuous care demands. Difficulty in care provision may reflect the severity of the behavioral problems or the extensiveness of the physical and health care needs of the individual with a disability. Primary caregivers use the relief provided through respite care services to rest, meet their own medical needs, improve relationships with other family members, and engage in some of the common personal or social activities that other adults are able to enjoy (e.g., visiting with a friend, taking a vacation, going shopping).

Models of respite care may vary along several dimensions, such as where the service is provided, what the content/nature of the care is, who provides the care, how the service is administered, and how much time is allotted. The most important variation in models is whether services are provided in the home or in some other setting. In-home services are preferred by a majority of families. In-home services are economical and minimize the adjustments that must be made by the individual with a disability and the family. These services may be of short duration, as when the parents go to a movie, or for a period of a week or two when parents take a vacation. In-home services may be provided by a sitter with only a few hours of training or by a homemaker/home health aide with substantial training.

About 40% of families experience a strong need to have their members with disabilities temporarily out of the home (Cohen & Warren, 1985). Out-of-home services may be provided on evenings, weekends, and holidays, or for continuous periods up to 30 days. These services may be provided in a respite care facility, in a residential facility that reserves some beds for temporary care, or in the home of the respite care provider. Services based on the home of the provider are personalized and economical. They can help expand the social/community experiences of a child with a disability, and they allow for the development of an ongoing relationship between the provider family and the child with a disability.

Babysitting and companionship are the major ingredients of respite care services that are of brief duration. Personal care and nursing care may be required when the client has severe physical or health problems. Social/recreational programming is usually a major component of longer respite care episodes.

Respite care services are often funded through state intellectual/developmental disabilities agencies, with families obtaining services either directly through local offices of these agencies or through community programs supported by funds from these state sources. The provision of respite care services is uneven from state to state and from region to region within states. States that have made strong efforts to provide sufficient respite care services of good quality include Massachusetts, California, Washington, and, most recently, Ohio. Funding problems remain the greatest impediment to the provision of adequate respite care services. In light of funding limitations, parent co-ops and volunteer models of respite care have become popular. Such programs are low in cost and are congruent with the zeitgeist of the 1980s that emphasized self-help and alternatives to government provision.

REFERENCE

Cohen, S., & Warren, R. D. (1985). *Respite care: Principles, programs, and policies.* Austin, TX: PRO-ED.

SHIRLEY COHEN
Hunter College, City University of New York

See also Deinstitutionalization

RESPONSE GENERALIZATION

Often after someone learns a particular behavior, new, untaught responses will emerge in the learner's repertoire. These new behaviors have operant functions similar to the previously learned behavior, but they differ in form or topography and are said to be the result of response generalization. This entry will provide examples that illustrate response generalization, a brief review of the research literature on generalization, and some notes on application.

Examples

Nelson was taught to say "Hello" to his friends in the morning. Subsequent to training, he began saying "Good morning," "What's up?" and "How're you doing?" Similarly,

Paula was trained while walking to look both ways before crossing the street. Recently on her walks, Paula has begun to stop at intersections before crossing.

Problems may ensue if novel responses do not emerge to meet environmental demands. Jasmine has learned to check her pockets for her mittens before leaving for school, but if the mittens are not in her pockets, she does not ask for help and will leave without protection for her hands. Wayne was taught to raise his hand to speak in class. Recently, he began standing and jumping to be called on by his teacher.

Each of these examples illustrates response generalization. The first two scenarios reflect socially relevant results of training that have generalized to new behaviors that are members of the same response class or category as the response initially taught. The third example illustrates a well-learned skill that did not properly shift into a novel behavior with similar behavioral function when warranted. The last scene depicts a learned response that has overgeneralized to a new form that is inappropriate for the setting. As important skills are taught, learners may fail to generate a full repertoire of behaviors to meet the challenges of situations that occur in natural settings. Inversely, a learner may modify strategies to an extent that is inappropriate. An understanding of the process of response generalization is an important tool to assist learners in tasks ranging from developmentally appropriate behaviors to scholastics.

Research

Generalization research began in the early 20th century and focused on continued responding in the presence of novel stimuli. In an early textbook on behavior theory, Clark Hull (1943) hypothesized that behavioral variability occurred after response requirements were altered and previous responses were no longer reinforced. He termed the emergence of novel responses in this manner response generalization, but little empirical research on this behavioral process ensued.

Twenty-five years later, Baer, Wolf, and Risley (1968) encouraged behavior analysts to turn their attention from explorations of basic processes that govern behavior to the development of empirically validated approaches to solving socially relevant problems. These researchers distinguished two predominantly overlooked categories of generalization for applied empirical research, maintenance and response generalization, but again response generalization received little empirical attention.

In recent years, noting the paucity of research in this area, some investigators have asked whether it may be appropriate to soften the criteria for attributing an event to response generalization, which had been defined in the experimental literature as the emergence of novel responses that were neither (a) reinforced during the teaching process nor (b) coached by rules implied during training (Stokes & Baer, 1977). To this end, Ludwig and Geller (1997, 2000) documented the spread of effect of a driving safety training program in which drivers emitted novel desired safe driving responses that had not been trained during the intervention. Even though the untaught safe behaviors may have occurred and been reinforced during the teaching procedure, Ludwig and Geller attributed these novel behaviors to response generalization.

The behavior analytic community has not yet reached consensus over what to include in the classification of response generalization. Some researchers caution that the data have not supported the view that all extensions of a previously taught behavior constitute response generalization (Houchins & Boyce, 2001). Houchins and Boyce (2001) suggest that overgeneralizing in applying the construct of response generalization may cause us to overlook other processes that more accurately account for learning in a specific context. Precise identification of how a response has been brought under stimulus control will highlight the features necessary for subsequent interventions to be successful. For a teacher in the field, the take-home point is that knowing the exact process involved in a learning task makes training the associated behaviors an empirically driven craft, efficient, predictable, and replicable.

Application

Promoting response generalization initially requires using techniques that increase behavioral variability. Instead of reinforcing precisely repeated behaviors, teachers should reinforce a broad spectrum of responses. This loose training prevents the development of overselected response dimensions and fosters creativity (Mayer, Sulzer-Azaroff, & Wallace, 2011).

When seeking to encourage a learner to expand a repertoire of behaviors, use differential reinforcement and extinction. Offering reinforcement for new forms, shapes, or topographies of a previously taught behavior, while withholding reinforcement for the first taught form of the response, aids in the development of novel characteristics of behavior (Cooper, Heron, & Heward, 2008).

To prevent overgeneralization from occurring, discrimination training should accompany training for response generalization. That is, a learner should be taught to distinguish the boundaries of each addition to a class of responses. Teaching learners to mediate their own responses by watching videos of others, watching videos of themselves, removing pictures from icon books, or checking off items on a self-monitoring checklist enables learners to effectively discriminate the limits of acceptability while trying out novel responses across environments (Mayer, Sulzer-Azaroff & Wallace, 2011).

Conclusions

Generalization is a fundamental behavioral process that often occurs without direct training but should not be expected to occur without instruction. Laboratory experiments with humans and nonhumans have identified several processes associated with generalized responding: stimulus generalization, maintenance, and response generalization. Applied research has emerged bringing the understanding of basic processes to bear on matters of social importance. The precise, technical definition of response generalization may have put constraints on research development that have impeded empirical investigation. Further dialogue and research are needed to identify the exact process involved in the development of novel behaviors. This knowledge is vital for constructing sound, empirically validated intervention strategies. Specific strategies such as loose training and differential instruction with extinction have been identified and empirically verified in the teaching and remediation of generalized responding. Such socially relevant outcomes have been the direct result of behavior analytic investigations.

REFERENCES

Baer, D. M., Wolf, M. M., & Risley, T. R. (1968). Some current dimensions of applied behavior analysis. *Journal of Applied Behavior Analysis*, *1*, 91–97.

Cooper, J. O., Heron, T. E., & Heward, W. L. (2008). *Applied behavior analysis*. Upper Saddle River, NJ: Pearson/Merrill-Prentice Hall.

Houchins, N., & Boyce, T. E. (2001). Response generalization in behavioral safety: Fact or fiction? *Journal of Organizational Behavior Management*, *21*(4), 3–11.

Hull, C. L. (1943). *Principles of behavior: An introduction to behavior theory*. Oxford, England: Appleton-Century.

Ludwig, T. D., & Geller, E. S. (1997). Managing injury control among professional pizza deliverers: Effects of goal setting and response generalization. *Journal of Applied Psychology*, *82*, 253–261.

Ludwig, T. D., & Geller, E. S. (2000). Intervening to improve the safety of occupational driving: A behavior-change model and review of empirical evidence [Special issue]. *Journal of Organizational Behavior Management*, *19*(4).

Mayer, G. R., Sulzer-Azaroff, B., & Wallace, M. (2011). *Behavior analysis for lasting change*. Cornwall-on-Hudson, NY: Sloan/Thomas G. Szabo.

Stokes, T. F., & Baer, D. M. (1977). An implicit technology of generalization. *Journal of Applied Behavior Analysis*, *10*, 349–367.

PAIGE B. RAETZ
BRITT L. WINTER
Western Michigan University

See also **Behavior Modification; Generalization**

RESPONSE TO INTERVENTION

Response to Intervention (RTI) is a system that is based on two basic principles. First, all children are able to learn if they are provided high-quality instruction. Second, for students who are struggling learners, the school personnel who bear primary responsibility for their instruction and academic progress are professionals in general education. This is in sharp contrast to traditional instructional approaches, which have placed primary responsibility for struggling learners on professionals in special education. The intended result of RTI is to improve the quality of instruction and educational outcomes for all students.

Models for incorporating RTI typically involve early identification of students who are at-risk of academic or behavioral difficulties based on a mass screening of all students and repeated assessments of students in the same core area, such as reading, mathematics, or social skills. RTI is a dynamic system where the identification of students requiring intervention services is determined based on the assessment of change across time (Fuchs & Fuchs, 1998; Gresham, 2002b). There are a variety of programs available to assist with the implementation of RTI, and almost all of them were developed initially from public health models of disease prevention (Vaughn, Wanzek, Woodruff, & Linan-Thompson, 2007). These models were first used in school-wide applications designed to address and prevent behavior problems in children (Donovan & Cross, 2002).

Most RTI programs are based on a three-tier model of service delivery (Brown-Chidsey & Steege, 2005; Reschly & Ysseldyke, 2002). Tier 1 involves the delivery of high-quality instruction to all students and the screening and monitoring of all students in meeting specific educational outcomes (Gresham, 1999, 2002a, 2002b; Ikeda, Tilly, Stumme, Volmer, & Allison, 1996; Lane, O'Shaughnessy, Lambros, Gresham, & Beebe-Frankenberger, 2001; O'Shaughnessy, Lane, Gresham, & Beebe-Frankenberger, 2003). Tier 1 services are able to meet the learning needs of approximately 75%–80% of the students in a local community (Ogonosky, 2008). Those students needing additional assistance are identified based on the monitoring procedures included in Tier 1. These students are then served at Tier 2, where supplemental instruction and assessment are provided.

The criteria used for identifying students as eligible for Tier 2 services will vary depending on the local community, but students are identified based on data collected at either the screening or progress-monitoring phase of data collection. If high-quality instruction is being delivered at Tier 1, a school campus can expect approximately 15%–20% of its students to be receiving supplemental instruction at the Tier 2 level (Ogonosky, 2008). For the majority of students who are identified as at-risk, the supplemental instruction provided at Tier 2 will be sufficient for them to continue to demonstrate adequate progress within the general curriculum (Tilly, Reschly, & Grimes, 1999). A small percentage of students will require services at Tier 3. On any given campus, only 5%–10% of the student body will move up to the Tier 3 level (Ogonosky, 2008).

Tier 3 involves a rigorous, data-driven, intervention effort. By this time in the process, the child's parent should be involved and decision making should occur through a collaborative process involving a team of school personnel and instructional specialists (Rosenfield, 2000; Rosenfield & Gravois, 1996; Tilly et al., 1999). At Tier 3, the team may determine that the student needs special education services based on documentation that there is a discrepancy between the child's performance and the average level of performance demonstrated by his/her peers, that this discrepancy has not been resolved by high-quality interventions implemented in general education, that the programming elements or instructional intensity required to remedy this discrepancy are beyond the resources that can be reasonably provided in general education, and that there is a clear need for the type of services provided in special education (Reschly & Ysseldyke, 2002). The critical eligibility criterion is resistance to intervention when rigorous standards have been established to ensure quality of interventions (Gresham, 1999). Services at the Tier 3 level are offered as a collaborative effort between general and special education teachers.

Response to Intervention is a system of instruction designed to improve educational outcomes for all students. It starts with the universal screening of all students to identify those students at-risk of academic or behavioral problems. Based on the results of the universal screening, students receive instructional services using a three-tier model, and progress is monitored on a regular basis allowing adjustments to be made to a student's academic program based on his/her response to intervention. By using data for making instructional decisions, Response to Intervention ensures that all students receive high-quality instruction and that additional supports and services are provided to students at the earliest opportunity. Referrals to special education are made after attempts to intervene within general education have proven unsuccessful and once a referral has been made and a student is receiving special education services, the process of monitoring progress continues so that teachers are constantly adjusting their instruction to meet the needs of their students.

REFERENCES

Brown-Chidsey, R., & Steege, M. W. (2005). *Response to Intervention: Principles and strategies for effective practice.* New York, NY: Guilford Press.

Donovan, M. S., & Cross, C. T. (2002). *Minority students in special and gifted education.* Washington, DC: National Academy Press.

Fuchs, L. S., & Fuchs, D. (1998). Treatment validity: A simplifying concept for reconceptualizing the identification of learning disabilities. *Learning Disabilities Research and Practice, 4,* 204–219.

Gresham, F. M. (1999). Noncategorical approaches to K-12 emotional and behavioral difficulties. In D. J. Reschly, W. D. Tilly III, & J. P. Grimes (Eds.), *Special education in transition: Functional assessment and noncategorical programming* (pp. 107–138). Longmont, CO: Sopris West.

Gresham, F. M. (2002a). Resonsiveness to intervention: An alternative approach to the identification of learning disabilities. In R. Bradley, L. Danielson, & D. P. Hallahan (Eds.), *Identification of learning disabilities: Research to practice* (pp. 467–547). Mahwah, NJ: Erlbaum.

Gresham, F. M. (2002b). Response to treatment. In R. Bradley, L. Danielson & D. Hallahan (Eds.), *Identification of learning disabilities: Research to practice* (pp. 467–519). Mahwah, NJ: Erlbaum.

Ikeda, M. J., Tilly, W. D. I., Stumme, J., Volmer, L., & Allison, R. (1996). Agency-wide implementation of problem-solving consultation: Foundations, current implementation, and future directions. *School Psychology Quarterly, 11,* 228–243.

Lane, K. L., O'Shaughnessy, T. E., Lambros, K. M., Gresham, F. M., & Beebe-Frankenberger, M. E. (2001). The efficacy of phonological awareness training with first grade students who have behavior problems and reading difficulties. *Journal of Emotional and Behavioral Disorders, 9,* 219–231.

Ogonosky, A. (2008). *The response to intervention handbook: Moving from theory to practice.* Austin, TX: Park Place.

O'Shaughnessy, T. E., Lane, K. L., Gresham, F. M., & Beebe-Frankenberger, M. E. (2003). Children placed at risk for learning and behavioral difficulties: Implementing a school-wide system of early identification and intervention. *Remedial and Special Education, 24,* 27–35.

Reschly, D. J., & Ysseldyke, J. E. (2002). Paradigm shift: The past is not the future. In A. Thomas & J. Grimes (Eds.), *Best practices in school psychology IV* (Vol. 1, pp. 3–20). Bethesda, MD: National Association of School Psychologists.

Rosenfield, S. A. (2000). Creating usable knowledge. *American Psychologist, 55,* 1347–1355.

Rosenfield, S. A., & Gravois, T. A. (1996). Instructional consultation teams: Collaborating for change. New York, NY: Guilford Press.

Tilly, W. D. I., Reschly, D. J., & Grimes, J. P. (1999). Disability determination in problem-solving systems: Conceptual foundations and critical components. In D. J. Reschly, W. D. Tilly III & J. P. Grimes (Eds.), *Special education in transition: Functional assessment and noncategorical programming* (pp. 285–321). Longmont, CO: Sopris West.

Vaughn, S., Wanzek, J., Woodruff, A. L., & Linan-Thompson, S. (2007). Prevention and early identification of students with reading disabilities. In D. Haager, J. Klingner, & S. Vaughn (Eds.), *Evidence-based reading practices for response to intervention.* Baltimore, MD: Paul H. Brookes.

DAVID KAHN
Texas A&M University
Fourth edition

See also **Empirically Supported Treatment; Learning Disabilities; Learning Disabilities, Problems in Definition of**

RESTRAINT (See Physical Restraint)

RESTRICTIVE DERMOPATHY

Restrictive dermopathy is a rare, fatal skin disease. The skin of infants with restrictive dermopathy is bright red, tight, and inflexible. In infants who survive for more than 2 weeks, the skin becomes progressively more rigid. These infants are generally born with opened mouths and fixed joints. These infants have few creases and furrows on their skin. Most of these infants are born prematurely at about 31 weeks of gestation, and premature rupture of membranes are characteristic. These infants typically have underdeveloped lungs and generally die from respiratory failure or septicemia.

This condition is rare and is inherited in an autosomal recessive pattern. There have been multiple cases of recurrence with siblings.

Characteristics

1. Tight, rigid shiny red skin
2. Scaling and erosion of the skin
3. Minimal crease and skin furrows
4. Small open mouth at birth
5. Small pinched nose
6. Crumpled, flattened, or low-set ears
7. 50% of the infants are born with natal teeth
8. Fixed joints
9. Small jaw

There is no known effective treatment for this condition, and to date there have been no long-term survivors.

Because there have been no long-term survivors of this condition, there are no implications for special education at this time.

Current research focuses on trying to determine what the primary genetic defect may be. Another area of research is examining the biochemistry involved with the keratin proteins and with the failure of the keratinocytes.

This entry has been informed by the sources listed next.

REFERENCES

Sybert, V. (1997). *Genetic skin disorders*. New York, NY: Oxford University Press.

Urdang, L., & Swallow, H. (1983). *Mosby's medical and nursing dictionary*. St. Louis, MO: Mosby.

Witt, D., & Hayden, M. (1986). Restrictive dermopathy: A newly recognized autosomal recessive skin dysplasia. *American Journal of Medical Genetics, 24*, 631–648.

TAMMY BRANAN
University of Northern Colorado

RETARDATION (See Cultural-Familial Retardation; Mental Retardation)

RETENTION IN GRADE

Retention in grade is the practice of having a child stay in or repeat an entire grade after he/she has already completed an entire school year at that grade level (Jackson, 1975). Grade retention is typically implemented as an intervention for improving skills and remains controversial in the field of education. A current increase in retention practice may in part be attributable to both President Clinton, whose educational goals included the ending of social promotion (i.e., promoting children to the next grade who have not met grade-level requirements; Clinton, 1999), and the No Child Left Behind Act (2002), which emphasizes accountability and standards in school.

Many studies have been conducted on retained children and have been compiled in several meta-analyses (Holmes, 1989; Holmes & Matthews, 1984; Jimerson, 2001). Overall, these meta-analyses showed that nonretained students performed around one third of a standard deviation unit better than retained students in both academic and behavioral measures. Because Jimerson's (2001) is the most current meta-analysis, including the most recent studies on retention, his results are further reviewed.

Jimerson's (2001) meta-analysis shows that promotion leads to better outcomes than does retention. Although some effect sizes showed retained students to have more favorable outcomes the year after they had been retained, most of the longitudinal effect sizes showed better outcomes for those students who had been promoted. More specifically, students who had been retained were on average .3 standard deviation units below students who had been promoted in both academic and socioemotional outcomes. Attendance rates were also significantly greater for promoted students (Jimerson). It has also been found that retained students are more likely to drop out of high school and to have lower-paying jobs as adults than students who had been promoted.

It can be concluded that the evidence is in favor of promoting students over retaining students. Promoted students have better long-term outcomes than their matched retained counterparts.

REFERENCES

Clinton, W. J. (1999, January 19). *State of the union.* Retrieved from http://www.cnn.com/ALLPOLITICS/stories/1999/01/19/sotu.transcript/

Holmes, C. T. (1989). Grade-level retention effects: A meta-analysis of research studies. In L. A. Shepard & M. L. Smith (Eds.), *Flunking grades: Research and policies on retention* (pp. 16–32). London, England: Falmer.

Holmes, C. T., & Matthews, K. M. (1984). The effects of non-promotion in elementary and junior high school pupils: A meta-analysis. *Review of Educational Research, 54,* 225–236.

Jackson, G. B. (1975). The research evidence in the effect of grade retention. *Review of Educational Research, 45,* 438–460.

Jimerson, S. R. (2001). Meta-analysis of grade retention research: Implications for practice in the 21st century. *School Psychology Review, 30,* 420–437.

No Child Left Behind Act of 2001. (2002). Public Law No. 107-110, Paragraph 115, Stat. 1425.

KRISTA D. HEALY
University of California, Riverside

RETICULAR ACTIVATING SYSTEM

The reticular activating system is the mass of cells in the brain stem associated with arousal, wakefulness, attention, and habituation. Its dysfunction may be associated with the hyperactivity and attention deficits often observed in children with brain damage.

The major function of the reticular system is to provide for cortical activation via its connections through the diffuse thalamic projection system. If the reticular system is significantly impaired, as in severe head trauma, coma results. However, even with less severe impairment, wakefulness, perception (Livingston, 1967), or cognitive functions are attenuated. The second major function is through the posterior hypothalamus, an area that provides a similar activating influence on the limbic system (Feldman & Waller, 1962; Iwamura & Kawamura, 1962; Routtenberg, 1968).

Specific investigations of the dual arousal systems have revealed different functions of each. Damage to the reticular system attenuates its cortical activation effects but does not impair behavioral arousal. In contrast, damage to the posterior hypothalamus impairs arousal, but cortical activation remains (Feldman & Waller, 1962; Kawamura, Nakamura, & Tokizane, 1961; Kawamura & Oshima, 1962). Because of their anatomical proximity and the neuronal interconnections between the posterior hypothalamus and the reticular system, it is likely that both systems will become impaired by injury or disease, although one system may be affected to a greater extent. This may account for some of the variability observed in brain-impaired children.

REFERENCES

Feldman, S., & Waller, H. (1962). Dissociation of electrocortical activation and behavioral arousal. *Nature, 196,* 1320.

Iwamura, G., & Kawamura, H. (1962). Activation pattern in lower level in the neo-, paleo-, archicortices. *Japanese Journal of Physiology, 11,* 494–505.

Kawamura, H., Nakamura, Y., & Tokizane, T. (1961). Effect of acute brain stem lesions on the electrical activities of the limbic system and neocortex. *Japanese Journal of Physiology, 11,* 564–575.

Kawamura, H., & Oshima, K. (1962). Effect of adrenaline on the hypothalamic activating system. *Japanese Journal of Physiology, 12,* 225–233.

Livingston, R. (1967). Brain in circuitry relating to complex behavior. In G. Quarton, T. Melnechuk, & Schmitt, F. (Eds.), *The neurosciences: A study program.* New York, NY: Rockefeller University Press.

Routtenberg, A. (1968). The two arousal hypothesis: Reticular formation and limbic system. *Psychological Review, 75,* 51–80.

CHARLES J. LONG
Memphis State University

GERI R. ALVIS
University of Tennessee

See also **Attention-Deficit/Hyperactivity Disorder; Brain Damage/Injury; Hyperkinesis**

RETINITIS PIGMENTOSA

Retinitis pigmentosa (RP), "more appropriately named rod-cone generalized dystrophy, is a varied group of disorders characterized by... [progressive] retinal rod and cone degeneration" (Reynolds, 2001, p. 1). No single classification system has been generally accepted; one version is the following: "(1) Congenital RP or Leber's Congenital Amaurosis. (2) Autosomal Recessive RP. (3) Autosomal Dominant RP. (4) X-linked or Sex-linked Recessive RP. (5) Sporadic RP. (6) RP Associated with Systemic Diseases" (Reynolds, 2001, p. 1). Types 1 and 6 are rare; Type 5 is not familial. About 22% and 9% of RP cases are autosomal dominant and sex-linked, respectively. Most of the remaining cases appear to have an autosomal recessive basis, but RP cases do not always follow Mendelian patterns of inheritance, leading to uncertainty about their genetic basis (Baumgartner, 2000). Overall incidence is about 1 in 4,000. Generally, rods are affected first and more severely, leading initially to loss of night and peripheral vision, although cones may become involved in advanced cases (MedlinePlus Health Information, 2001).

The type of RP influences severity, time of onset, speed of progression, and order of appearance of symptoms. Congenital RP is present at birth and associated with persistent visual loss. Recessive RP (Types 2 and 4) usually have childhood or early adolescent onset and poor prognosis. Dominant RP (Type 3) tends to be milder. Sporadic RP has variable outcome. The systemic illnesses with which Type 6 is associated are rare and often fatal; severe RP symptoms often occur early and involve central vision loss (Reynolds, 2001).

Characteristics

1. Night blindness
2. Tunnel vision
3. Vision loss
4. Splotchy pigmentation on the retina

Frequently, RP is not diagnosed until an affected individual begins to lose night or peripheral vision. An ophthalmologist's exam will show splotchy pigmentation on the retina. Vision continues to decline, although total blindness is rare. Because RP is associated with a number of other conditions and disorders, differential diagnosis is important (Beauchamp, 2000).

The symptoms of RP are progressive and often follow a predictable course in which the first symptom is night blindness. Some RP patients may not realize that they have night blindness, although they have noticed difficulty seeing at dusk or nighttime. The next symptom of RP is tunnel vision: The RP patient loses peripheral vision, but central vision is still intact. When RP is in the advanced stages, central vision is compromised and blindness is a possibility. Rate of progression is highly variable from patient to patient and may be correlated with type of RP (Baumgartner, 2000).

No effective treatment to stop the progression of RP is available. Sunglasses may help preserve sight by protecting the retina from ultraviolet light. Some recent but controversial studies suggest that treatment with antioxidant agents such as vitamin A palmitate may delay progression. Treatment consists of vision aids such as corrective glasses or contact lenses, although prescriptions need to be updated in order to keep up with the disorder's progression. More sophisticated aids to vision may be needed depending on the disorder's progression. Counseling is also recommended to help the patient deal with the psychological aspects of vision loss, and a low-vision specialist may help to maintain patient independence (MedlinePlus Health Information, 2001).

REFERENCES

Baumgartner, W. (2000). Etiology, pathogenesis, and experimental treatment of retinitis pigmentosa. *Medical Hypotheses, 54*, 814–824.

Beauchamp, G. R. (2000). Retinitis pigmentosa (RP). In C. R. Reynolds & E. Fletcher-Janzen (Eds.), *Encyclopedia of special education* (2nd ed., Vol. 3, pp. 1546–1547). New York, NY: Wiley.

MedlinePlus Health Information. (2001). *Retinitis pigmentosa.* Retrieved from http://www.nlm.nih.gov/medlineplus/ency/article/001029.htm

Reynolds, J. D. (2001). *Retinitis pigmentosa: Med Help International.* Retrieved from http://medhlp.netusa.net/lib/retinit.htm

MELANIE MOORE
ROBERT T. BROWN
University of North Carolina at Wilmington

RETINOBLASTOMA

Retinoblastoma is a rare form of childhood cancer in which malignant tumor(s) originate in the retina of the eye. The majority (75%) of cases are unilateral retinoblastoma, in which tumors develop in one eye. Tumors that are found in both eyes are referred to as bilateral retinoblastoma (Abramson & Servodidio, 1997).

Retinoblastoma affects 1 in every 15,000–30,000 children who are born in the United States (Abramson & Servodidio, 1997). There are approximately 300 newly diagnosed cases each year in this country (Abramson & Servodidio, 1997; Demirci, Finger, Cocker, & McCormick 1999). It affects children of both genders and of all races equally (Abramson & Servodidio, 1997; Margo, Harman, & Mulla, 1998).

Although there are still many unanswered questions as to why retinoblastoma occurs, it is known that in all cases there is an abnormality in Chromosome 13, the chromosome responsible for controlling retinal cell division. In retinoblastoma, a piece of the chromosome is either deleted or mutated, causing retinal cell division to proceed and the tumor(s) to develop (Abramson & Servodidio, 1997; Finger, 2000; Margo et al., 1998). Most patients (90%) have no family history of the disease. However, when it is inherited, the prevalence rate of retinoblastoma is more common in children whose parents have the bilateral form of the disease (45%) than in children whose parents have the unilateral form (7%–15%; Abramson & Servodidio, 1997).

Characteristics

1. Initial signs of retinoblastoma usually include pupils that have an abnormal white appearance (leukocoria) or crossed eyes (strabismus).

2. Possible redness in eye, pain, poor vision, or inflammation of tissue surrounding the eye.

3. Small tumors appear as translucent, off-white patches, or well-defined nodular lesions of retinal vessels.

4. Large tumors often produce retinal detachment; some portions of the detached retina appear creamy-white, with newly formed blood vessels extending over the surface and dividing into the substance of a tumor.

5. Other indications include failure to thrive (trouble eating or drinking), extra fingers or toes, malformed ears, or mental retardation.

Retinoblastoma can be diagnosed through retinal dilation. An ultrasound examination and a CAT scan may also be performed. Treatment of retinoblastoma varies according to the extent of the disease within and outside of the eye. The current methods for treating retinoblastoma include enucleation, external beam radiation, radioactive plaques, laser therapy, cryotherapy, and chemoreduction. Enucleation involves the surgical removal of the eye and fitting the socket with a synthetic implant at the time of surgery (Abramson & Servodidio, 1997).

Retinoblastoma is a progressive disease. Therefore, most children have vision through at least their first year of life (Warren, 1994). In fact, the majority of children retain vision in at least one eye (Abramson & Servodidio, 1997). Because children with this disorder usually are able to adapt quite well, they are able to lead a normal life and to attend a regular education classroom (Heller, Alberto, Forney, & Schwartzman, 1996). However, it is very important that they wear protective eyewear when engaging in sports and other hazardous activities. There are some instances in which normal vision is impaired sufficiently to necessitate the assistance of visual aids and support systems in order for these children to attend mainstream classes. Some educational components might include using assistive technology, adapting written material, coordinating orientation and mobility services, fostering the development of appropriate play with toys, and promoting peer interactions (Heller et al., 1996). In cases of more serious loss of vision, it may be necessary for some children to attend programs for individuals who are visually impaired or blind. There also seems to be a bimodal distribution of intelligence scores among children with retinoblastoma: Some children's performance falls in the low-average range, whereas other children perform in the well-above-average range (Warren, 1994).

Prognosis is generally successful, especially if the diagnosis occurs early. However, children who inherit retinoblastoma from a parent who has had the bilateral form of the disease may also be at risk for developing other cancers, such as bone tumors (osteogenic sarcoma), skin cancers (cutaneous melanoma), muscle and connective tissue tumors (soft tissue sarcoma), and brain tumors (pineoblastomas; Finger, 2000). Thus, those with a genetic form of the disorder have a less favorable prognosis (Margo et al., 1998). Current research is focused on genetic testing as well as on combating secondary cancers (Rosser & Kingston, 1997).

REFERENCES

Abramson, D. H., & Servodidio, C. (1997). *A parent's guide to understanding retinoblastoma*. Retrieved from www.retino blastoma.com

Demirci, H., Finger, P. T., Cocker, R., & McCormick, S. A. (1999). Interactive case challenge: A 7-week-old female with a "White Pupil" in the left eye. *Medscape Oncology, 2*(5).

Finger, P. T. (2000). *Retinoblastoma*. Retrieved from http://www .eyecancer.com/conditions/Retinalpercent20Tumors/retino .html

Heller, K. W., Alberto, P. A., Forney, P. E., & Schwartzman, M. N. (1996). *Understanding physical, sensory, and health impairments: Characteristics and educational implications*. Pacific Grove, CA: Brooks/Cole.

Margo, C. E., Harman, L. E., & Mulla, Z. D. (1998). Retinoblastoma. *Cancer Control: Journal of the Moffitt Cancer Center, 5*(4), 310–316.

Rosser, E., & Kingston, J. (1997). *Retinoblastoma: Fighting eye cancer in children*.

Warren, D. H. (1994). *Blindness and children: An individual differences approach*. New York, NY: Cambridge University Press.

MICHELLE PERFECT
University of Texas at Austin

RETINOPATHY OF PREMATURITY

Retinopathy of prematurity (ROP) is the most common cause of retinal damage in infancy. ROP is a potentially blinding eye disorder that primarily affects premature infants less than 1,250 grams that are born before 31 weeks of gestation (National Eye Institute, 2011). Incidence has recently been stable, but prevalence is increasing because of the increased survival of infants with very low birth weight—about 67% of infants who weigh less than 3 pounds (1,251 g) and about 80% of infants who weigh less than 2.2 pounds (1,000 g) at birth will manifest some degree of ROP (Menacker & Batshaw, 1997; Merck Manual of Diagnosis and Therapy [Merck], 2001). About 90% of all infants with ROP are in the milder category of the condition and do not need treatment (National Eye Institute, 2011).

Exposure to excessive or prolonged oxygen is the major risk for ROP, but presence of other medical complications also increases risk. Unfortunately, threshold safe levels or durations of oxygen are not known (Merck, 2001). Although it has been suggested as a factor in the development of ROP, the research has determined that lighting levels in hospital nurseries has no effect on the development of ROP (National Eye Institute, 2011).

Characteristics

1. Abnormal proliferation of blood vessels in the retina.
2. Progressively, the vascular tissue invades the vitreous and sometimes engorges the entire vasculature of the eye.
3. Abnormal vessels stop growing and may subside spontaneously.
4. In severe cases, scarring from abnormal vessels contract, leading to retinal detachments and vision loss in early infancy.

Development of the inner retinal blood vessels occurs across the second half of pregnancy. Thus, their growth is incomplete in premature infants. If they continue growth abnormally, ROP results. Incidence and severity of ROP vary with the proportion of retina that is avascular at birth (Merck, 2001).

Vision loss ranges from myopia (correctible with glasses) to strabismus, glaucoma, and blindness (Menacker & Batshaw, 1997). Children with moderate, healed ROP but who have cicatrices (dragged retina or retinal folds) have increased risk for retinal detachments later in life (National Eye Institute, 2011).

Diagnosis is through ophthalmological examination by a specialist in examination of premature infants. Premature infants should have regular examinations over the first year of life because early detection can often lead to effective treatment. ROP is defined by both the stage or degree of the disorder and the area in which it occurs. The American Academy of Pediatrics Section on Ophthalmology (2001) has recently provided detailed recommendations for screening for and intervening in cases of ROP. Appropriately managed premature infants with

birth weights of more than 1,500 grams (3 lb 5 oz) rarely develop ROP, so differential diagnosis of other disorders such as familial exudative retinopathy or Norrie disease should be considered.

Prevention of premature birth when possible is the best approach to avoiding ROP (Menacker & Batshaw, 1997; Merck, 2001). Where prematurity does occur, levels of oxygen should be at the lowest safe levels, and surfactant should be provided to reduce respiratory distress. Recent developments in treatment of ROP with cryotherapy and laser therapy have reduced the incidence of posterior retinal traction folds or detachments by more than 40% and of blindness by about 24% (American Academy of Pediatrics Section on Ophthalmology, 2001; National Eye Institute, 2011). Affected individuals with residual scarring should be examined at least annually for life. Later retinal detachments resulting from such scarring can often be treated effectively if they are detected early. For cases with residual visual loss, special education and adaptive technology may be needed.

REFERENCES

American Academy of Pediatrics Section on Ophthalmology. (2001). Screening examination of premature infants for retinopathy of prematurity. *Pediatrics*, *108*, 809–811.

Menacker, S. J., & Batshaw, M. L. (1997). Vision: Our window to the world. In M. L. Batshaw (Ed.), *Children with disabilities* (4th ed., pp. 211–239). Baltimore, MD: Paul H. Brookes.

Merck Manual of Diagnosis and Therapy. (2001). *Retinopathy of prematurity (retrolental fibroplasia)*. Retrieved from http://www.merck.com/pubs/mmanual/section19/chapter260/2601.htm

National Eye Institute (2011). *Retinopathy of prematurity*. Retrieved from http://www.nei.nih.gov/health/rop/

ROBERT T. BROWN
University of North Carolina at Wilmington

BRENDA MELVIN
New Hanover Regional Medical Center

ELAINE FLETCHER-JANZEN
The Chicago School of Professional Psychology
Fourth edition

RETROLENTAL FIBROPLASIA

Retrolental fibroplasia (RLF) was first recognized in the early 1940s, with the first literature description published in 1942. Over the ensuing decade, many unrelated and sometimes conflicting etiologies for the disease were considered. Among these were water miscible vitamins, iron, oxygen, cow's milk, and abnormal electrolytes, all of which have been shown in positive association to the incidence of RLF. Experimental evidence implicated vitamin E deficiency as a possible cause. Other factors that have been associated with RLF are viral infections, hormonal imbalances, premature exposure of infant eyes to light, and vitamin A deficiency in the mother. The observation that the incidence of the disease increases in direct relation to the duration and exposure of premature infants to oxygen was reported first in 1952. A controlled study was completed in 1954; it established oxygen as the most likely etiologic agent for the condition. The rise of this disease, called by some an epidemic, closely parallels the development of the ability to effectively concentrate oxygen administration to infants in incubators (Silverman, 1980).

The importance of oxygen concentration monitoring became apparent as experimental evidence of the early 1950s accumulated. Ambient oxygen levels were limited whenever possible to 40%, and measurements of oxygen concentration in the blood were made. This did not entirely resolve the issue for several reasons: The disease occurred in the absence of supplemental oxygen therapy; it occurred when 40% oxygen was administered "appropriately"; and this level of supplemental oxygen often was not sufficient to relieve the respiratory distress syndrome that often accompanies prematurity. The important relationship between arterial blood oxygen (PO^2), the respiratory distress syndrome, and retrolental fibroplasia is now well established. However, numerous attempts to monitor and control arterial blood oxygen (PO^2) have been fraught with great difficulties, both technical and physiologic.

Approximately 10% of infants under 2,500 g birth weight are afflicted with respiratory distress syndrome, accounting for approximately 40,000 infants per year in the United States; the incidence of RLF blindness following oxygen administration is a small percentage of the group, perhaps 2%. Recognizing this, many authors now designate this disease retinopathy of prematurity (ROP).

An appreciation of the clinical stages of the disease accompanied experimental evidence concerning its pathophysiology. Evidence suggests that high arterial oxygen levels cause vasospastic constriction of developing peripheral retinal vasculature, inciting the elaboration of vasoproliferative factors. New vessels grow in a moundlike elevation, typically in the temporal peripheral retina (Tasman, 1971). Such neovascularization either may proceed or spontaneously regress. With resolution of the active process, cicatrization (scarring) occurs, which on contraction may drag the retina temporally. If traction is sufficient, peripheral retinal detachment occurs. When the entire retina becomes detached and drawn into a fibrous cicatrix (scar) behind the lens, the disease has reached its most advanced stage, representing the clinical picture for which the disease was named. Additional ocular sequelae include myopia; vitreous opacification; and

a variety of retinal changes, including chorioretinal atrophy, pigmentary retinopathy, and retinal folds. Based on these observations, clinical characterization of the disease recently has been reviewed and a proposed international classification published.

The relationship of oxygen therapy to neurological outcome also was studied. In general, neurologic outcome is inversely related to ocular outcome; that is, spastic diplegia incidence falls and retrolental fibroplasia rises with increased duration of oxygen treatment. Thus, there is a desire to prevent neurologic events following cyanotic attacks (secondary to cardiorespiratory insufficiency) by extending treatment with oxygen; this then increases the risk of RLF.

The full spectrum of consequences of RLF blindness to the child, family, social agencies, school, and community is beginning to be fully considered. Affected individuals tend not to see loss of sight as a major burden. Preconceptions, paternalism, and insensitivity of authorities in the visually oriented world often constrict the lives of those who wish to see this same world nonvisually. A number of factors—medical, legal, and societal—tend to perpetuate the stereotype that the blind wish to shed in their desire to move toward independence. Thus, the complexity of this disease at several levels—visual, neurological, personal, and social—is only now being appreciated.

The visually disabling forms of RLF may affect school performance by limiting sensory input; the degree of disability reflects the severity of disease. Teachers may observe "blindness" where disability is severe. When bilateral retinal blindness is present, braille instruction is required. The educator should be aware of the complexity of problems for individuals with this condition.

REFERENCES

Silverman, W. A. (1980). *Retrolental fibroplasia: A modern parable*. New York, NY: Grune & Stratton.

Tasman, W. (Ed.). (1971). *Retinal diseases in children*. New York, NY: Harper & Row.

GEORGE R. BEAUCHAMP
Cleveland Clinic Foundation

RETT SYNDROME

Rett syndrome (RS) is a disorder that initially appears as a deterioration from apparently normal development in infancy or early childhood. It involves a slowdown in normal development, deceleration of head growth, uninterest in the environment, deterioration of motor functioning, loss of hand use and subsequently locomotion, hand stereotypies (typically hand wringing or clapping), loss of expressive language, autistic and self-abusive behavior, and eventual severe/profound mental retardation. Prevalence estimates vary. Hagberg (1995b) revised the estimate of prevalence of classic RS from 1:10,000 females to closer to 1:15,000. Cases have been reported in all parts of the world and in all ethnic groups (e.g., Moser & Naidu, 1991; Naidu, 1997). First described by Andreas Rett (1966), it initially came to the world's attention largely through the work of Hagberg and his associates (Hagberg, Aicardi, Dias, & Ramos, 1983).

Unique to RS is apparently normal initial development followed by rapid mental and physical deterioration followed by stabilization or even reduction in some symptoms (e.g., Budden, 1997; Hagberg, 1995b). RS is also unusual in that it (a) apparently affects only women, whereas most gender-specific disorders affect only men; (b) is manifested in part through loss of acquired function, but is apparently neurodevelopmental and not neurogenerative; (c) presents in a fairly striking set of behavioral symptoms that have consistent developmental trends; and (d) is almost undoubtedly genetically based, but no marker has been identified. Although the subject of hundreds of articles, it is still relatively unknown in comparison to many other developmental disorders of comparable prevalence. As would be expected, research on the genetic basis focuses on an X-chromosome abnormality. RS is associated with numerous neuroanatomical and neurochemical disturbances, summaries of which can be found in Brown and Hoadley (1999), Budden (1997), Hagberg (1996), or Percy (1996).

Diagnostic Symptoms: Classic RS and RS Variant

Necessary for diagnosis of classic RS is apparently normal pre-, peri-, and early postnatal development followed in infancy or early childhood by sudden deceleration of head growth and loss of acquired skills, including hand use and language (Rett Syndrome Diagnostic Criteria Work Group, 1988). Also required is evidence of mental retardation and the appearance of intense and persistent hand stereotypies: "The almost continuous repetitive wringing, twisting, or clapping hand automatisms during wakefulness constitute the hallmark of the condition" (Hagberg, 1995b, p. 973). Girls who had developed walking must show gait abnormalities; some never develop walking. EEG abnormalities, seizure disorder, spasticity, marked scoliosis, and overall growth retardation are also typical. A number of other behaviors may also be shown, including episodic hyperventilation and breath holding, bloating owing to air swallowing, bruxism, hypoplastic cold red-blue feet, scoliosis, and night laughing (Hagberg, 1995a).

The RS variant model was developed owing to the realization that females with RS are much more heterogeneous than originally thought (Hagberg, 1995a, 1995b).

Diagnosis of RS variant should be made only in girls of 10 years or older age when a subset of the symptoms for classic RS has been met. These behaviors may appear throughout childhood. Typically, girls who meet the criteria for RS variant show less severe symptoms than those associated with classic RS. Both gross and fine motor control may be spared, and mental retardation is less severe. RS variant girls may retain some language, although it tends to be abnormal and telegraphic. Those with language tend to have had a later and milder regression period.

For both parents and therapists, diagnosis should be made as early as possible. Some physicians may be reluctant to diagnose RS early owing to the eventual severity of the disorder, but many parents are frustrated by the lack of a diagnosis that fits their children's behaviors or has implications for treatment and care (Brown & Hoadley, 1999). For that reason, the term *potential RS* (Hagberg, 1995b) has been suggested for use with young cases. RS may be confused with a number of other disorders, particularly autism, so careful diagnosis is necessary.

Developmental Trend

Most girls with classic RS develop through a fairly reliable four-stage sequence of behavioral and physical changes first described by Hagberg and Witt-Engerström (1986). Age of onset, duration of transition from one stage to another, and duration of each is highly variable, however. Except as specifically referenced, information in this section comes from Budden (1997), Hagberg (1995b), Hagberg and Witt-Engerström (1986), and Naidu (1997).

Pre-Stage 1: Early Development

Much pre-Stage 1 development appears normal until at least 5–6 months of age. Early motor skills appear, including reaching for objects. Self-feeding commonly develops, with infants weaning onto solid foods. Many children develop walking, but often with an unusual gait. However, appearance of many infant developmental milestones is delayed or absent. Some slowing of brain growth may be seen in unusually low occipito-frontal circumference as early as 2 months of age. Many girls develop single-word communication, and a few use short phrases.

Stage 1: Early Onset Stagnation

The first stage begins at from 6 to 18 months of age and may last from weeks to months. In many ways the infant appears to hit a developmental wall. Many aspects of cognitive development cease. A deceleration of head growth leads to head circumference generally below average by the end of the second year of life. Hypotonia, uninterest in play and the environment, loss of acquired hand functions, and random hand movements are typical. No obvious pattern of abnormalities is apparent, however.

Stage 2: Rapid Developmental Regression

At between 1 and 3 or 4 years of age, functioning begins to deteriorate so generally and rapidly that the onset may be taken for a toxic or encephalitic state (Hagberg & Witt-Engerström, 1986). Further, Budden (1997, p. 2) reports that the onset "may be so acute that parents can sometimes give a specific date after which their child was no longer 'normal.'" General cognitive functioning, purposeful hand use, and expressive language deteriorate. The classic hand stereotypies, including hand wringing, washing, and mouthing, typically appear and may be continuous during waking hours. Walking may deteriorate or not develop. Gait abnormalities, particularly a spread-legged stance, are generally evident in girls who can walk. Hyperventilation and breath holding are common, as are behaviors characteristic of autism. Seizures and vacant spells resembling seizures may occur, and virtually all RS girls have abnormal EEGs.

Stage 3: Pseudostationary

Stage 3 has a highly variable age of onset, occurring at the end of the rapid deterioration, and lasts until about 10 years of age. Hand stereotypies continue, and mobility may further deteriorate. Mental retardation in the severe/profound range is characteristic. On the other hand, autistic symptoms may diminish, and social interactions, hand use, communication, alertness, and self-initiated behavior may increase. Tremulousness, ataxia, teeth grinding (bruxism), hyperventilation or breath holding, and seizures are common. Overall rigidity is likely to increase and scoliosis to appear. Nonverbal communication through eye pointing may improve.

Stage 4: Late Motor Deterioration

After about age 10 years, motor function decreases further, with increased rigidity, scoliosis, and muscle wasting. Mobility continues to decrease; many girls will be wheelchair-bound. Hands may be held in mouth for long periods. Expressive language, if previously present, generally disappears, and receptive language is decreased. Eye pointing as communication may continue. Chewing and swallowing may be lost, necessitating artificial feeding. However, the final phenotypic characteristics of classic RS cases vary widely. Life span varies, but overall longevity is shorter than normal (Naidu, 1997).

Overall Intellectual Characteristics

Formal assessments indicate that RS girls function at a severe/profound level of mental retardation, but their actual cognitive functioning may be difficult to assess owing to motor and language impairments. For a group of RS girls with a mean age of 9.4 years, Perry, Sarlo-McGarvey, and Haddad (1991) reported these Vineland

Adaptive Behavior Scale (VABS) scores, based on potentially biased interviews with parents: Communication, mean 17.4 months; Daily living skills, mean 16.9; and Socialization, mean 25.9 months. Mean mental age on the Cattell Infant Intelligence was 3.0 months. Most girls attended to visual and auditory stimuli, were interested in toys, and anticipated being fed. Only one appeared to have object permanence, and none succeeded on items requiring language or fine motor skills. The girls attended when spoken to and showed some understanding, but most did not speak or have any other communication system. Most could feed themselves, some with their fingers, and some could use a cup. Most were in diapers and did not perform other self-care tasks. They showed some interest in other people and could discriminate among them, but they showed virtually no play behaviors.

Overall Emotional Characteristics

RS girls show a variety of emotional and behavioral problems. The following information is from a survey of parents by Sansom, Krishnan, Corbett, and Kerr (1993) when the girls' mean age was 10.6 years. Over 75% showed anxiety, particularly in response to external situations. Most episodes were brief and consisted of screaming, hyperventilation, self-injury, frightened expression, and general distress. Precipitating events included novel situations and people, sudden noises, some music, change of routine, and high activity by others close to the child. Low mood, reflected partly in crying, occurred in 70%, but for extended periods in only a few. Almost 50% showed self-injurious behaviors (SIBs). Most were relatively mild, such as biting fingers or hands, but more serious chewing of fingers, head banging, and hair pulling also occurred. Epilepsy was reported in 63%. Although most slept well, early wakening and nighttime laughing, crying, and screaming were common.

Treatment and Management

No completely effective treatment regime is available, and the symptoms appear to follow an inexorable course. However, active intervention may delay the appearance of some symptoms and alleviate others. RS girls typically have very long latencies to respond to directions, an important consideration in all aspects of therapy. Delay to respond may be as long as a minute. Accurate diagnosis is important both to ensure appropriate treatment and to avoid ineffective treatment. For example, three RS girls who had initially been diagnosed with autism were inadvertent participants in Lovaas's intensive behavior modification program, which has been demonstrably effective with autistic children (Smith, Klevstrand, & Lovaas, 1995). Overall, the girls showed few if any changes that might not have occurred without treatment. Individual differences in the degree of various impairments and responsiveness to, as well as tolerance of, various interventions necessitate individualized treatment programs (e.g., Van Acker, 1991). Owing to the multiplicity and diversity of problems associated with RS, a team approach is indicated.

Specialized behavior modification programs have been successful on a variety of behaviors in RS girls of different ages. Techniques such as shaping, graduated guidance, and hand regulation have increased self-feeding and ambulation in RS girls (e.g., Bat-Haee, 1994). Use of mechanical and computer-based adaptive devices may also modify RS girls' behavior, enabling them to communicate and discriminate between such things as favored and non-favored foods (e.g., Van Acker & Grant, 1995). One caution must be expressed, however, about the routine implementation of some of these programs, particularly by parents. Much effort, persistence, and tolerance for frustration are required, since improvement can be slow and even difficult to see. Indeed, Piazza et al. (1993) suggest that parents be warned about the effort involved and the need to keep careful response records in order to see progress.

As apraxia is one of the main effects of RS, physical therapy is critical. It helps RS girls to maintain or reacquire ambulation and to develop or maintain transitional behaviors needed to stand up from sitting or lying positions. The stereotypic hand movements are involuntary, so behavior modification techniques designed to reduce them not only will likely be ineffective but may actually increase the movements by increasing anxiety. Several techniques, including restraints that prevent hand-to-mouth movements or simply holding the girl's hand, may be effective. Generally, whirlpool baths may be helpful. Some of the stereotyped hand clasping and other movements may be reduced by allowing the girl to hold a favored toy (Hanks, 1990).

Most RS girls begin to develop scoliosis before age 8, and many also show kyphosis (hunchback; Huang, Lubicky, & Hammerberg, 1994). The disorders are basically neurogenic but are exacerbated by other factors such as loss of transitional motor skills and spatial perceptual orientation, postural misalignment, and rigidity (Budden, 1997). Physical therapy and careful positioning in seated positions may help slow the development of scoliosis, but corrective surgery is often required.

Although showing strong appetites, most RS girls show serious growth retardation to the point of meeting criteria for moderate to severe malnutrition. Chewing and swallowing problems, as well as gastroesophageal reflux and digestive problems, contribute to the retardation. Speech therapy may be helpful not so much for retaining language as for facilitating chewing and swallowing. Supplementary tube feedings may be necessary to help increase growth (Glaze & Schultz, 1997). Further complicating feeding issues, constipation is common in RS. Although it is generally controllable through diet, laxatives or enemas may be necessary in some cases.

Seizures occur in most RS girls, and their control "is perhaps the most common problem facing the primary care provider or the treating neurologist" (Budden, 1997, p. 7). Seizures occur most commonly in Stage 3 (Glaze & Schultz, 1997). Most seizures can be controlled with antiseizure medication, most frequently carbamazepine and/or valproic acid. Occasionally, in otherwise intractable cases, the ketogenic diet may be used (Budden, 1997), although it presents its own management problems.

Agitation, screaming, and tantrums are frequently reported. The rapid neurologic and physical changes associated with the onset of the disease may understandably provoke emotional outbursts. RS girls frequently respond negatively to stimulus or routine change, so transitions from one setting or pattern to another should be gradual and accompanied by a parent if possible. Agitation or screaming may also reflect pain or irritation from a physical condition that in the absence of language or gestures RS individuals may have no other way to signal. Since the girls go through puberty, caretakers need to be sensitive to their menstrual cycles. Some agitation in older individuals may reflect menstrual discomfort or some other gynecologic disorder that may be easily treatable (Budden, 1997). A variety of treatment approaches have been used; behavior modification may be helpful.

Owing to the lifelong impact of the disorder on parents and other family members, ranging from home care issues to decisions about educational and other placement, counseling for the family will be particularly important (Lieb-Lundell, 1988). Training of the parents in behavior modification may be helpful in managing some aspects of their RS daughter's behavior, including tantrums. Of importance, given the degree of care that RS adults may require and their relative longevity, parents will eventually need to face the issue of lifelong care and make financial arrangements for care of the woman after their death.

REFERENCES

Bat-Haee, M. A. (1994). Behavioral training of a young woman with Rett syndrome. *Perceptual and Motor Skills, 78,* 314.

Brown, R. T., & Hoadley, S. L. (1999). Rett syndrome. In S. Goldstein & C. R. Reynolds (Eds.), *Handbook of neurodevelopmental and genetic disorders of children* (pp. 459–477). New York, NY: Guilford Press.

Budden, S. S. (1997). Understanding, recognizing, and treating Rett syndrome. *Medscape Women's Health, 2*(3), 1–11. Retrieved from http://www.medscape.com/

Glaze, D. G., & Schultz, R. J. (1997). Rett syndrome: Meeting the challenge of this gender-specific neurodevelopmental disorder. *Medscape Women's Health, 2*(1), 1–9. Retrieved from http://www.medscape.com/

Hagberg, B. (1995a). Clinical delineation of Rett syndrome variants. *Neuropediatrics, 26,* 62.

Hagberg, B. (1995b). Rett syndrome: Clinical peculiarities and biological mysteries. *Acta Paediatrica, 84,* 971–976.

Hagberg, B. (1996). Rett syndrome: Recent clinical and biological aspects. In A. Arzimanoglou & F. Goutières (Eds.), *Trends in child neurology* (pp. 143–146). Paris, France: John Libby Eurotext.

Hagberg, B., Aicardi, J., Dias, K., & Ramos, O. (1983). A progressive syndrome of autism, dementia, ataxia, and loss of purposeful hand use in girls: Rett's syndrome: Report of 35 cases. *Annals of Neurology, 14,* 471–479.

Hagberg, B., & Witt-Engerström, I. (1986). Rett syndrome: A suggested staging system for describing impairment profile with increasing age toward adolescence. *American Journal of Medical Genetics, 24*(Suppl. 1), 47–59.

Hanks, S. (1990). Motor disabilities in the Rett syndrome and physical therapy strategies. *Brain and Development, 12,* 157–161.

Huang, T. J., Lubicky, J. P., & Hammerberg, K. W. (1994). Scoliosis in Rett syndrome. *Orthopaedic Review, 23,* 931–937.

Lieb-Lundell, C. (1988). The therapist's role in the management of girls with Rett syndrome. *Journal of Child Neurology, 3*(Suppl.), S31–S34.

Moser, H. W., & Naidu, S. (1991). The discovery and study of Rett syndrome. In A. J. Capute & P. J. Accardo (Eds.), *Developmental disabilities in infancy and childhood* (pp. 325–333). Baltimore, MD: Paul H. Brookes.

Naidu, S. (1997). Rett syndrome: A disorder affecting early brain growth. *Annals of Neurology, 42,* 3–10.

Percy, A. K. (1996). Rett syndrome: The evolving picture of a disorder of brain development. *Developmental Brain Dysfunction, 9,* 180–196.

Perry, A. K., Sarlo-McGarvey, N. & Haddad, C. (1991). Brief reports: Cognitive and adaptive functioning in 28 girls with Rett syndrome. *Journal of Autism and Developmental Disabilities, 21,* 551–556.

Piazza, C. C., Anderson, C., & Fisher, W. (1993). Teaching self-feeding skills to patients with Rett syndrome. *Developmental Medicine and Child Neurology, 35,* 991–996.

Rett, A. (1966). Uber ein eigenartiges Hirnatrophisches Syndrom bei Hyperammonamie im Kindes alter. [On an unusual brain atropic syndrome with hyperammonia in childhood] *Wiener Medizinische Wochenschrift, 116,* 425–428. (As cited in Moser & Naidu, 1991, and Rett Syndrome Diagnostic Criteria Work Group, 1988.)

Rett Syndrome Diagnostic Criteria Work Group. (1988). Diagnostic criteria for Rett syndrome. *Annals of Neurology, 23,* 425–428.

Sansom, D., Krishnan, V. H. R., Corbett, J., & Kerr, A. (1993). Emotional and behavioural aspects of Rett syndrome. *Developmental Medicine and Child Neurology, 35,* 340–345.

Smith, T., Klevstrand, M., & Lovaas, O. I. (1995). Behavioral treatment of Rett's disorder: Ineffectiveness in three cases. *American Journal of Mental Retardation, 100,* 317–322.

Van Acker, R. (1991). Rett syndrome: A review of current knowledge. *Journal of Autism and Developmental Disabilities, 21,* 381–406.

Van Acker, R., & Grant, S. H. (1995). An effective computer-based requesting system for persons with Rett syndrome. *Journal of Childhood Communication Disorders, 16,* 31–38.

ROBERT T. BROWN
University of North Carolina at Wilmington

REVERSALS IN READING AND WRITING

The term *reversals* is usually associated with reading or writing disabilities. Reversals are difficulties characterized in either reading or writing by reversing letters, numbers, words, or phrases (e.g., *saw* for *was, p* for *q*), or what some have referred to as mirror reading or writing.

In Orton's first theoretical papers on reading disabilities (1925, 1928), he suggested that such reversal problems were due to poorly established hemispheric dominance. Orton (1928) cited the following examples of strephosymbolia (literally, "twisted symbols"): (a) difficulty discriminating *b* and *d*; (b) confusion with words like *ton* and *not*; (c) ability to read from mirror images; and (d) facility at writing mirrorlike images. Orton further stipulated that these reversal problems were not caused by mental retardation. Other investigators have since promoted the concept of developmental lag in perceptual abilities as causally related to reading disorders (Bender, 1957; Fernald, 1943).

As a result of this initial work, a variety of programs were developed that attempted to remediate reading disabilities by treating perceptual problems (Forness, 1981). For example, Kephart (1960) focused on the use of motor activities for developing perceptual skills. Additionally, programs such as Barsch's (1965) movigenic curriculum and Delacato's (1966) patterning techniques promoted the evolutionary progression that was seen as a necessary prerequisite for complete perceptual development. Frostig and Horne (1964) developed a visual perceptual program to remediate these difficulties, while Gillingham and Stillman (1960) prescribed the language triangle approach of combining the visual, auditory, and kinesthetic modes for teaching reading and writing.

Empirical support that reversals are due to perceptual deficits has been equivocal. It has been seen that many beginning readers reverse letters and words (Gibson & Levin, 1980). In fact, more than one half of all kindergarten students typically reverse letters (Gibson & Levin, 1980). This is considered a part of the normal component of discrimination learning when children first acquire reading skills. Gibson and Levin (1980) cite research that indicates that normal children continue to make reversal errors until the age of 8 or 9. It was also found that single-letter reversals account for only a small percent of total reading errors exhibited by poor readers. In addition, it has been questioned whether such reversals in learning-disabled students indicate underlying perceptual problems rather than, for example, linguistic problems (Gupta, Ceci, & Slater, 1978).

Remedial programs based on visual-motor perceptual training generally have not resulted in reading improvement (Keogh, 1974). Later research efforts have suggested that reversal problems can be remediated with the use of behavioral techniques. Hasazi and Hasazi (1972) reported an instance in which digit reversals (e.g., 12 for 21) of an 8-year-old boy were remediated by means of contingent teacher attention. With respect to letter reversals, Carnine (1981) provided evidence that discriminations that reflect differences in spatial orientation only (e.g., *b, d*) are best taught singly. In other words, a student should be taught to discriminate *b* from nonreversible letters first, followed by the separate introduction of the letter *d*. Some specific instructional techniques are provided by Hallahan, Kauffman, and Lloyd (1985).

REFERENCES

Barsch, R. H. (1965). *A movigenic curriculum* (Publication No. 25). Madison: Wisconsin State Department of Instruction.

Bender, L. A. (1957). Specific reading disability as a maturational lag. *Bulletin of the Orton Society, 7*, 9–18.

Carnine, D. W. (1981). Reducing training problems associated with visually and auditorily similar correspondences. *Journal of Learning Disabilities, 14*, 276–279.

Delacato, C. H. (1966). *Neurological organization and reading*. Springfield, IL: Thomas.

Fernald, G. (1943). *Remedial techniques in basic school subjects*. New York, NY: McGraw-Hill.

Forness, S. R. (1981). *Recent concepts in dyslexia: Implications for diagnosis and remediation*. Reston, VA: Council for Exceptional Children.

Frostig, M., & Horne, D. (1964). *The Frostig program for the development of visual perception: Teacher's guide*. Chicago, IL: Follett.

Gibson, E. J., & Levin, H. (1980). *The psychology of reading*. Cambridge, MA: MIT Press.

Gillingham, A., & Stillman, B. W. (1960). *Remedial training for children with specific disability in reading, spelling, and penmanship*. Cambridge, MA: Educator's.

Gupta, R., Ceci, S. J., & Slater, A. M. (1978). Visual discrimination in good and poor readers. *Journal of Special Education, 12*, 409–416.

Hallahan, D. P., Kauffman, J. M., & Lloyd, J. W. (1985). *Introduction to learning disabilities* (2nd ed.). Englewood Cliffs, NJ: Prentice Hall.

Hasazi, J. E., & Hasazi, S. E. (1972). Effects of teacher attention on digit-reversal behavior in an elementary school child. *Journal of Applied Behavior Analysis, 5*, 157–162.

Keogh, B. K. (1974). Optometric vision training programs for children with learning disabilities: Review of issues and research. *Journal of Learning Disabilities, 7*, 219–231.

Kephart, N. C. (1960). *The slow learner in the classroom*. Columbus, OH: Merrill.

Orton, S. T. (1925). Word-blindness in school children. *Archives of Neurology and Psychiatry, 14*, 581–615.

Orton, S. T. (1928). Specific reading disability—strephosymbolia. *Journal of the American Medical Association, 90*, 1095–1099.

THOMAS E. SCRUGGS
MARGO A. MASTROPIERI
Purdue University

See also Agraphia; Dysgraphia; Remediation, Deficit-Centered Models of

REVERSE MAINSTREAMING

Reverse mainstreaming is a procedure that introduces typically developing students into special classrooms to work with students with severe disabilities. The purpose is to maximize integration of students. Mainstreaming, a more familiar concept, refers to the integration of individuals with disabilities into the general education classroom to enable each individual to participate in patterns of everyday life that are close to the mainstream. Reverse mainstreaming is, as the name suggests, a procedure carried out in reverse of mainstreaming but striving for the same goals. Reverse mainstreaming can be used for students with any severe disability.

The primary use of reverse mainstreaming has been with individuals with severe and profound intellectual disabilities and individuals with autism. Until the early 1970s these students were educated in segregated environments that had only individuals with disabilities. These environments included institutions and special education schools. Students with mild intellectual disabilities, on the other hand, were more likely to be educated in closer proximity to typically developing peers.

There has been widespread acceptance in the past 25 years of the philosophy of normalization. This philosophy holds that individuals with disabilities should be able to live as similarly as possible to their typically developing peers. Public Law 94-142, adopted in 1978, required that individuals with disabilities be educated as similarly as possible to their typically developing peers. For the individuals with mild intellectual disabilities, this has resulted in considerable integration into general education classrooms. For the individuals with severe intellectual disabilities, this has meant placement in buildings occupied by their typically developing peers. It is frequently unrealistic to expect individuals with severe intellectual disabilities to participate in general education classrooms because of their low-functioning levels and special needs. In these cases, in order to maximize interactions, special educators arrange for typically developing students to participate in the special education classrooms as volunteers, or "peers"; hence, mainstreaming in reverse.

The implementation of reverse mainstreaming requires cooperation and communication between teachers. They must work together to prepare the typically developing peers who will participate. Poorman (1980), who started Project Special Friend in a central Pennsylvania community, recommends using images of children with disabilities followed by discussions about their characteristics and behaviors and about the role of the peers. Topics include communication skills, disabilities, realistic expectations, and dealing with inappropriate behaviors. Opportunities should be provided for the typically developing students to interact in a social way with their friends with special needs.

Poorman (1980) outlines a sequential program, moving from introductions through free play activities to instructional activities in the reverse mainstreaming setting. Almond, Rodgers, and Krug (1979) provide a detailed presentation of techniques for training peer volunteers to work with students with severe autism spectrum disorders. The volunteers initiate individualized educational programs on a one-to-one basis under the supervision of special educators. They participate in the classroom with students with disabilities on a weekly schedule. Donder and Nietupski (1981) describe how reverse mainstreaming can be implemented to maximize social integration on the playground.

In all these instances, typically developing students are introduced into the classroom and playground environment of individuals with severe disabilities in order to maximize interactions. This procedure has been shown to lead to increased learning of preacademic skills and socially appropriate behavior by individuals with disabilities. It also contributes to greater acceptance by their typically developing peers. While sharing goals and accomplishments with mainstreaming, the procedure is still mainstreaming in reverse—bringing the mainstream into the classrooms and the lives of individuals with severe disabilities.

REFERENCES

Almond, P., Rodgers, S., & Krug, D. (1979). A model for including elementary students in the severely handicapped classroom. *Teaching Exceptional Children, 11*, 135–139.

Donder, D., & Nietupski, J. (1981). Nonhandicapped adolescents teaching playground skills to their mentally retarded peers: Toward a less restrictive middle school environment. *Education & Training of the Mentally Retarded, 16*, 270–276.

Poorman, C. (1980). Mainstreaming in reverse with a special friend. *Teaching Exceptional Children, 12*, 136–142.

NANCY L. HUTCHINSON
BERNICE Y. L. WONG
Simon Fraser University

See *also* **Inclusion; Least Restrictive Environment; Mainstreaming; Peer Relationships**

REVISED CHILDREN'S MANIFEST ANXIETY SCALE (See Children's Manifest Anxiety Scale)

REVISUALIZATION

Revisualization has been defined as the active recall of the visual image of words, letters, and numbers (Johnson & Myklebust, 1967). Deficiencies in revisualization prevent students from picturing the visual form of printed material and are related to difficulty in spelling and writing. By contrast, good spellers are able to compare their productions against an auditory or visual image when checking their spelling.

In terms of memory functioning, recall tends to be the area most substantially impaired for children with revisualization deficits, while recognition is somewhat less affected. Therefore, activities such as dictated spelling tests, number sequencing, and drawing from memory are often extremely difficult for students with revisualization deficits. Such deficits will be less apparent when matching and multiple-choice activities are employed.

Johnson and Myklebust (1967) have listed closure and visual sequential memory as two component subprocesses that are deficient in children who cannot revisualize printed material. Closure is the extrapolation of a whole from an incomplete gestalt. Children who have problems with closure are unable to supply missing details and thus are less able to code visual information for later retrieval. Deficiencies in visual sequential memory, the recall of images in order, impairs children's ability to remember the order and position of letters within words and words within sentences.

Instructional materials and techniques have been designed to help children compensate for deficits in closure and sequencing by capitalizing on their intact perceptual processes (Johnson & Myklebust, 1967). Training materials that use well-formed, heavily outlined letters have been recommended for circumventing closure problems. Sequencing deficits have been remediated by using different print sizes or colors. Multisensory techniques have also been suggested for remediating revisualization deficits. Other methods specify the use of initial-consonant cues, verbal labels, verbal mediators, and categorization strategies (Peters & Cripps, 1980).

McIntyre (1982), reporting on research focusing on children with learning disabilities, criticizes the reliance on visual memory in Johnson and Myklebust's approach and contends that reading is a verbal skill. On the other hand, Dodd (1980) has reported that deaf children, relying strictly on visual coding, are able to recognize regular spelling patterns. Peters and Cripps (1980), consolidating the two positions, state that words that have regular sound-letter associations can be coded verbally but that irregular words must be revisualized.

REFERENCES

Dodd, B. (1980). The spelling abilities of profoundly prelingually deaf children. In U. Firth (Ed.), *Cognitive processes in spelling*. London, England: Academic Press.

Johnson, D. J., & Myklebust, H. R. (1967). *Learning disabilities*. New York, NY: Grune & Stratton.

McIntyre, T. C. (1982). *Dyslexia: The effects of visual memory and serial recall*. (ERIC Document Reproduction Service No. ED 227 603)

Peters, M. L., & Cripps, C. (1980). *Catchwords: Ideas for teaching spelling*. New South Wales, Australia: Harcourt Brace Jovanovich.

GARY BERKOWITZ
Temple University

See also Imagery

REYE SYNDROME

Reye syndrome is a condition of unknown origin that is characterized by encephalopathy and fatty degeneration of the liver (National Reye's Syndrome Foundation, 2001). Reye syndrome is acute, rapidly progressive, and typically occurs following a viral illness in children and adolescents treated with aspirin, but rare cases have been found in adults (Ward, 1997). Just as the child appears to be recovering from the viral infection (frequently influenza), protracted, recurring vomiting occurs, followed by neurological and behavioral changes such as listlessness or aggression (National Reye's Syndrome Foundation, 2001; Ward, 1997).

At its peak in 1980, 555 cases of Reye syndrome were reported in the United States. After its association with aspirin was reported in the early 1980s, no more than 36 cases per year have been reported since 1987 (Belay et al., 1999).

Characteristics

1. Prodromal viral-like illnesses
2. Protracted, recurrent vomiting (in infants, vomiting is replaced by diarrhea)
3. Altered mental status such as lethargy, confusion, agitation, and irrational behavior
4. Coma and death likely in undiagnosed cases
5. Biopsy of the liver needed to truly detect the syndrome

Source: National Reye's Syndrome Foundation (2001); University of Michigan Health Systems (2001).

Chances of recovery from Reye syndrome are excellent when the condition is diagnosed and treated in the early stages. However, the degree of recovery is related to damage incurred from brain swelling. There is no cure for Reye syndrome; it should be treated as a medical emergency because of its rapid progression. Treatment is typically directed at reducing brain swelling and returning the body chemistry to normal (University of Michigan Health Systems, 2001).

Because a range from slight to severe brain damage may occur subsequent to recovery from Reye syndrome, psychological and neuropsychological evaluations should be conducted to determine level of functioning. Children who are affected by Reye syndrome may qualify for special education services under a number of categories, including mental retardation and other health impaired. In addition, mandates such as the Individuals with Disabilities Education Act and Section 504 should be consulted as resources to better understand services available to the Reye syndrome survivor in the public education system.

Progress has been made in differentiating Reye syndrome from other metabolic disorders. Reye syndrome is not contagious, and incidence has been greatly reduced by public awareness campaigns regarding the dangers associated with medicating children with aspirin (National Reye's Syndrome Foundation, 2001; Ward, 1997). In addition, increased health providers' awareness of symptoms can aid in early detection and greatly reduce the effects of the progression of Reye syndrome.

REFERENCES

Belay, E. D., Bresee, J. S., Holman, R. C., Khan, A. S., Shahriari, A., & Schonberger, L. B. (1999). Reye's syndrome in the United

States from 1981 through 1997. *New England Journal of Medicine, 340*(18), 1423–1424.

National Reye's Syndrome Foundation. (2001). Retrieved from http://reyessyndrome.org

University of Michigan Health Systems. (2001). Retrieved from http://med.umich.edu/1libr/child/child46.htm

Ward, M. R. (1997). Reye's syndrome: An update. *Nurse Practitioner, 22*, 45–46.

KIMBERLY D. WILSON
University of Texas at Austin

DILIP KARNIK
'Specially for Children Children's Hospital, Austin, Texas

REYNOLDS, CECIL R. (1952–   )

Reynolds was born on February 7, 1952, at the U.S. Naval Hospital in Camp Lejeune, North Carolina. His father, Cecil C. Reynolds, was a career marine, enlisting in 1929 and retiring in 1960. His mother, Daphne, owned and taught at a private preschool and kindergarten for 25 years, later becoming a published poet and author of children's books. Reynolds attended New Hanover High School, graduating in 1969, and turned down a presidential appointment to the United States Naval Academy by Richard Nixon, after being drafted by the New York Mets. He played on various minor league teams within the Mets organization. He made three all-star teams in different leagues prior to a career-ending injury in spring training in 1974, the year of his first major league contract.

Higher Education

Reynolds then returned to his education, earning his BA in psychology in 1975 from University of North Carolina at Wilmington. He then attended the University of Georgia (UGA), earning a MEd in psychometrics in 1976, an EdS in school psychology in 1977, and a PhD in educational psychology in 1978 while studying under Alan S. Kaufman and Ellis Paul Torrance (he was inducted into the UGA Hall of Fame for lifetime achievement in 2006). He completed his internship at the Medical College of Georgia, being mentored there by Lawrence Hartlage as his interests turned more staunchly to neuropsychology.

Academic Career

In the summer of 1978 he took his first academic position at the University of Nebraska, where he remained for 3 years and where he wrote the grants to obtain the Buros Institute for the University, and became the first director of the Buros Institute after its founder, Oscar Krisen Buros (Reynolds was Acting Director during the search for a permanent new director in 1979–1980 and worked as Associate Director in 1980–1981), prior to being driven south to Texas A&M University (TAMU) by the bitter Nebraska winters. In 2006, he was named the Buros Institute Distinguished Reviewer of the Year. Reynolds taught courses primarily in the areas of psychological testing and diagnosis and in neuropsychology, in addition to supervising clinical practica in testing and assessment. He remained at TAMU from the summer of 1981, where he was a professor of educational psychology, a professor of neuroscience, and a Distinguished Research Scholar, until his retirement from the university on July 31, 2008. In September 2008, he was honored by the Texas A&M University Board of Regents with the title Emeritus.

Reynolds holds a diplomate in clinical neuropsychology from the American Board of Professional Neuropsychology, of which he is also a past president; a diplomate in pediatric neuropsychology from the American Board of Pediatric Neuropsychology; and a diplomate in school psychology from the American Board of Professional Psychology, prior to retiring his diplomate in 2004. He is a past president of the National Academy of Neuropsychology, APA Division 5 (Evaluation, Measurement, and Statistics), APA Division 40 (Clinical Neuropsychology), and APA Div. 16 (School Psychology). He is a Fellow of APA Divisions 1, 5, 15, 16, 40, and 53. He maintained a clinical practice for more than 25 years, primarily treating children who had been sexually assaulted as well as individuals with traumatic brain injury. His current consulting work is restricted to his forensic neuroscience practice.

Professional Honors

The American Psychological Association (APA) honored Reynolds with Early Career Awards from the Division of Educational Psychology and separately from the Division of Evaluation, Measurement, and Statistics. He received the Lightner Witmer Award from the APA's Division of School Psychology as the outstanding young school psychologist in the association as well. In 1999, he received the APA Division of School Psychology's Senior Scientist Award. He is past president of three APA divisions, School Psychology (16), Clinical Neuropsychology (40), and Evaluation, Measurement, and Statistics (5). He is editor-in-chief of the APA journal *Psychological Assessment* with a 6-year term, beginning January 1, 2009. He was editor-in-chief of *Applied Neuropsychology* from 2004 to 2008 and serves (or has served) on the editorial boards of 16 scientific journals. He served 12 years as editor and editor-elect of the *Archives of Clinical Neuropsychology*, the official journal of the National Academy of Neuropsychology. Reynolds has served as associate editor of the *Journal of Special Education* and *School Psychology Quarterly* and currently is an associate editor of the American Psychological Association's open journal, *Archives of Scientific*

Psychology. He is a past president of the National Academy of Neuropsychology as well and has received the Academy's Distinguished Clinical Neuropsychologist Award, the Distinguished Service Award, and the President's Gold Medal for service to the Academy. In 1987, the American Library Association declared his *Encyclopedia of Special Education* to be one of the top 25 reference works published in all fields that year. He received the 50th Anniversary Razor Walker Award from the University of North Carolina at Wilmington for his service to the youth of America. He has been named a Distinguished Alumnus of the Year by both of his alma maters, the University of North Carolina at Wilmington and the University of Georgia, the latter also electing him to their academic Hall of Fame. In 2002 he served as a Distinguished Visiting Professor at Wilford Hall, the USAF showcase hospital and training facility at Lackland AF Base in San Antonio, Texas, where he also conducted grand rounds. Reynolds also conducted grand rounds at the Mayo Clinic in Rochester, Minnesota, on the issue of diagnosing learning disorders, and has served as an invited discussant at pediatric grand rounds on several occasions at the annual meeting of the National Academy of Neuropsychology. He has received multiple other national awards for research accomplishments and service as well, including, in 2010, the American Psychological Association's Division of School Psychology Jack I. Bardon Award for a Lifetime of Distinguished Service. In 2011 he was elected a Distinguished Fellow of the National Academies of Practice.

Chronological Listing of Professional Awards Received

2011   Elected Distinguished Fellow of the National Academies of Practice

2010   Jack Bardon Distinguished Service Award, Division of School Psychology of the American Psychological Association

2007   Distinguished Achievement Award for Research, Texas A&M University Former Students Association

2007   Lifetime Achievement Award for Distinguished Contributions, American Board of School Neuropsychology

2006   Distinguished Reviewer of 2006, Buros Institute of Mental Measurements

2005   University of Georgia, Distinguished Alumnus Award for Lifetime Achievement. Also inducted into the College of Education's Hall of Fame

2003   National Association of School Psychologists, Neuropsychology Interest Group, Lifetime Achievement Award in Neuropsychology

2002   Distinguished Visiting Professor, Wilford Hall, U.S. Air Force showcase hospital and training facility, Lackland AF Base, San Antonio, Texas

2001   National Academy of Neuropsychology, Distinguished Service Award

2000   National Academy of Neuropsychology, Distinguished Clinical Neuropsychologist Award

1999   American Psychological Association, Division 16, Senior Scientist Award

1998   Razor Walker Award for service to the youth of America, The University of North Carolina at Wilmington and CAPE (50th Anniversary Award)

1997   President's Gold Medal for service to the National Academy of Neuropsychology

1995   Distinguished Research Scholar Award, Texas A&M University, COE

1995   Faculty co-author of National Academy of Neuropsychology, Student Research Award, winning paper, 1995 NAN Annual Convention

1994   Society for the Psychological Study of Social Issues (APA Division 9), Robert Chin Award for Distinguished Contributions (co-recipient)

1994   Faculty co-author of National Academy of Neuropsychology, Student Research Award, winning paper, 1994 NAN Annual Convention

1988   Paper of the Year, Mid-South Educational Research Association, with A. Kaufman and J. McLean

1987   Interviewed as an "Eminent School Psychologist" in *Communiqué*, the official newsletter of the 30,000+ member National Association of School Psychologists

1987   *Encyclopedia of Special Education* named by American Library Association as one of the top 25 reference works in all fields (Reynolds is senior editor of this work)

1986   Distinguished Achievement in Research, award from the Texas A&M University Former Students Association (university-wide award)

1984   Outstanding Alumnus of the Year, University of North Carolina at Wilmington (one chosen each year)

1984   Outstanding New Faculty Award, College of Education Development Council, Texas A&M University

1983   American Psychological Association, Division of Educational Psychology (15), Early Career Award, with accompanying invited address to the annual meeting of the APA

1983   Awarded Fellow status, American Psychological Association (first year of eligibility)

1983   Awarded Fellow status, National Academy of Neuropsychology (first year of eligibility)

1983   Certificate of Research Achievement, Instructional Research Laboratory, College of Education, Texas A&M University

1981   Invited by the Division of Evaluation and Measurement (5) of the American Psychological Association to deliver a special invited address as an Outstanding Contributor in First Ten Postdoctoral Years to the annual meeting of the APA

1980   American Psychological Association, Division of School Psychology (16) Lightner Witmer Award (awarded annually to the outstanding young school psychologist in the Association)

1979   Awarded Fellow status on the graduate faculty of the University of Nebraska

1978   Kappa Delta Pi Award of Excellence for Outstanding Contributions to Education (awarded annually to the individual judged the most outstanding graduate student in a school of education in the state of Georgia)

1978   Paper of the Year, *Gifted Child Quarterly* (awarded annually by the National Association for Gifted Children) with E. Paul Torrance

Scientific Writings and Impact on Psychology

Reynolds' early work, principally in the 1980s, on empirical evaluation of the cultural test bias hypothesis in clinical assessment was not only prolific but at the cutting edge of psychological science at the time and led to resolution of many of the polemic debates over the use of clinical assessment devices with native-born American ethnic minorities and moved the remaining arguments from emotion to reasoned scientific dialogue (see, e.g., his 1983 *Journal of Special Education* article, "Test Bias: In God We Trust, All Others Must Have Data"). At the same time, he was establishing important research programs in the areas of assessment of anxiety in children and youth and tackling the measurement issues surrounding the field of learning disabilities. The extent of his contributions to psychological science in these areas is easily seen by the fact that, remarkably, two of his papers have been noted as the most-cited articles published in the history of their respective journals: his 1978 article on assessing anxiety published in the *Journal of Abnormal Child Psychology*, and his 1984 *Journal of Special Education* article describing and resolving many of the critical measurement issues in assessment of learning disabilities. His subsequent work in the development of interpretive methods for clinical assessment instruments and debunking of the myths of profile analysis of intelligence test performance resulted in abandonment of unsubstantiated but prevalent clinical practices and in substantial changes in how such tests are interpreted today (for example, see his 2003 article, with R. L. Livingston, in *Archives of Clinical Neuropsychology*, and his opening paper of the 2007 special issue of *Applied Neuropsychology*, which he edited, on this topic), as well as having influenced test development practices. For additional examples, see his 1997 paper on assessment of forward and backward memory span, and his two 2000 papers in *School Psychology Quarterly* on configural frequency analysis and modal profile analysis. His work continues to influence many other researchers, and, since 1985, there have been only three issues of the bimonthly *Journal of Clinical Child and Adolescent Psychology* in which his work has not been referenced in one or more research articles.

He is currently the author of 30 commercially published psychological tests, several of which have profoundly altered the practice of clinical assessment of child and adolescent behavioral and emotional disorders, but also have provided researchers in the field with much-needed objective measures of behavior to the improvement of research in childhood psychopathology generally. His Behavioral Assessment System for Children, for example, is probably the most frequently used measure of child and adolescent behavior in the English-speaking world, and its Spanish redevelopment is widely used throughout Spain and South America in both research and practice.

Reynolds' test manuals have notably influenced how such manuals are now written and developed. His 2003 Reynolds Intellectual Assessment Scales Professional Manual, for example, was the first intelligence test manual to incorporate the 1999 conceptualization of validity in the Standards for Educational and Psychological Testing, a conceptualization largely derived from the work and careful thought of Sam Messick. His 2002 manual for the Comprehensive Trailmaking Test accomplished the same feat for the area of neuropsychological testing. His three measurement textbooks also were the first to explain and promote this modern conceptualization of validity as well.

As a journal editor for more than 19 years, across three major journals (*Archives of Clinical Neuropsychology*, the official journal of the National Academy of Neuropsychology—11 years; Applied Neuropsychology, the official journal of the American Board of Professional Neuropsychology—5 years; and currently as editor of the APA journal *Psychological Assessment*), Reynolds has exerted a strong, positive influence on research in many areas of clinical assessment and testing. Each of these journals experienced a rise in their impact factor during his tenure as editor, but more importantly he implemented standards for assessment research that emphasized empirical work and replicability and raised reporting requirements for assessment work to new highs.

In 1983, Reynolds chaired the Special Education Programs Work Group on Critical Measurement Issues in Learning Disabilities of the U.S. Department of Education. The report of this task force and several related works (Reynolds, 1981, 1984) have been instrumental in developing practical, psychometrically sound models of severe discrepancy analysis in learning disabilities diagnosis.

In 1994, he was one of 52 signatories on "Mainstream Science on Intelligence," an editorial written by Linda Gottfredson and published in the *Wall Street Journal*, which presented a scientific consensus regarding (then) current findings on intelligence to assist in clarifying and differentiating mainstream consensus findings on the issue from some of the more scientifically controversial statements in Herrnstein and Murray's volume, *The Bell Curve* (in which he was miscited as "Cyril" Reynolds).

Today, the most commonly used impact index in academia and other scholarly circles is the H-Index. An H-Index of 25, for example, is considered impressive. This value indicates the person has 25 research articles that have each been cited a minimum of 25 times. Reynolds' H-Index is 54, an unusually impressive value. It is useful to compare his value of 54 with that of other important figures in the history of psychological assessment and measurement. Both Lee J. Cronbach and Anne Anastasi have H-Index values of 47. This sort of comparison very usefully places Reynolds' impact into a relevant context and is an informative quantitative summary of his outstanding impact as a psychological scientist who is now one of the most prolific, and most often cited, scientists in the profession.

BOOKS BY CECIL REYNOLDS

Adams, W., & Reynolds, C. R. (2009). *Essentials of WRAML2 and TOMAL-2 assessment*. Hoboken, NJ: Wiley.

Brown, R. T., & Reynolds, C. R. (Eds.). (1986). *Psychological perspectives on childhood exceptionality: A handbook*. New York, NY: Wiley.

D'Amato, R., Fletcher-Janzen, E., & Reynolds, C. R. (Eds.). (2005). *Handbook of school neuropsychology*. Hoboken, NJ: Wiley.

Fletcher-Janzen, E., & Reynolds, C. R. (2003). *Diagnostic reference manual of childhood disorders*. Hoboken, NJ: Wiley.

Fletcher-Janzen, E., & Reynolds, C. R. (Eds.). (2008). *Neuropsychological perspectives on learning disabilities in the era of RTI: Recommendations for diagnosis and intervention*. Hoboken, NJ: Wiley.

Fletcher-Janzen, E., Strickland, T., & Reynolds, C. R. (Eds.). (2000). *Handbook of cross-cultural neuropsychology*. New York, NY: Plenum Press.

Frisby, C., & Reynolds, C. R. (Eds.). (2005). *Comprehensive handbook of multicultural school psychology*. Hoboken, NJ: Wiley.

Glover, J. A., Ronning, R. R., & Reynolds, C. R. (Eds.). (1989). *Handbook of creativity*. New York, NY: Plenum Press.

Goldstein, S., & Reynolds, C. R. (Eds.). (1999). *Handbook of neurodevelopmental and genetic disorders in children*. New York, NY: Guilford Press.

Goldstein, S., & Reynolds, C. R. (Eds.). (2005). *Handbook of neurodevelopmental and genetic disorders in adults*. Hoboken, NJ: Guilford Press.

Goldstein, S., & Reynolds, C. R. (Eds.). (2011). *Handbook of neurodevelopmental and genetic disorders in children* (2nd ed.). New York, NY: Guilford Press.

Gutkin, T. B., & Reynolds, C. R. (Eds.). (1990). *The handbook of school psychology* (2nd ed.). New York, NY: Wiley.

Gutkin, T. B., & Reynolds, C. R. (Eds.). (2009). *The handbook of school psychology* (4th ed.). Hoboken, NJ: Wiley.

Homack, S., & Reynolds, C. R. (2007). *Essentials of assessment with brief intelligence tests*. Hoboken, NJ: Wiley.

Kamphaus, R. W., & Reynolds, C. R. (1987). *Clinical and research applications of the K-ABC*. Circle Pines, MN: American Guidance Service.

Ramsay, M., Reynolds, C. R., & Kamphaus, R. W. (2002). *Essentials of behavioral assessment*. New York, NY: Wiley.

Reynolds, C. R. (Ed.). (1994). *Cognitive assessment: An interdisciplinary perspective*. New York, NY: Plenum Press.

Reynolds, C. R. (Ed.). (1998). *Detection of malingering during head injury litigation*. New York, NY: Plenum Press.

Reynolds, C. R. (Ed.). (1999). Assessment. Volume 4 of M. Hersen & A. Bellack (Eds.), *Comprehensive clinical psychology*. Oxford, UK: Elsevier.

Reynolds, C. R., & Brown, R. T. (1984). *Perspectives on bias in mental testing*. New York, NY: Plenum Press.

Reynolds, C. R., & Fletcher-Janzen, E. (Eds.). (1989). *Handbook of clinical child neuropsychology*. New York, NY: Plenum Press.

Reynolds, C. R., & Fletcher-Janzen, E. (Eds.). (1990). *Concise encyclopedia of special education*. New York, NY: Wiley.

Reynolds, C. R., & Fletcher-Janzen, E. (Eds.). (1997). *Handbook of clinical child neuropsychology* (2nd ed.). New York, NY: Plenum Press.

Reynolds, C. R., & Fletcher-Janzen, E. (Eds.). (2000). *Encyclopedia of special education* (2nd ed.; 3 vols.). New York, NY: Wiley.

Reynolds, C. R., & Fletcher-Janzen, E. (Eds.). (2002). *Concise encyclopedia of special education* (2nd ed.). New York, NY: Wiley.

Reynolds, C. R., & Fletcher-Janzen, E. (Eds.). (2006). *Special education almanac*. Hoboken, NJ: Wiley.

Reynolds, C. R., & Fletcher-Janzen, E. (Eds.). (2007). *Encyclopedia of special education* (3rd ed.; 3 vols.). Hoboken, NJ: Wiley.

Reynolds, C. R., & Fletcher-Janzen, E. (Eds.). (2009). *Handbook of clinical child neuropsychology* (3rd ed.). New York, NY: Plenum Press.

Reynolds, C. R., & Gutkin, T. B. (Eds.). (1982). *The handbook of school psychology*. New York, NY: Wiley.

Reynolds, C. R., & Gutkin, T. B. (Eds.). (1999). *The handbook of school psychology* (3rd ed.). New York, NY: Wiley.

Reynolds, C. R., Gutkin, T. B., Elliott, S. N., & Witt, J. (1986). *School psychology: Essentials of theory and practice*. New York, NY: Wiley.

Reynolds, C. R., & Horton, A. (Eds.). (2012). *Detection of malingering during head injury litigation* (2nd ed.). New York, NY: Springer.

Reynolds, C. R., & Kamphaus, R. W. (Eds.). (1990). *Handbook of psychological and educational assessment of children: Vol. 1. Intelligence and achievement*. New York, NY: Guilford Press.

Reynolds, C. R., & Kamphaus, R. W. (Eds.). (1990). *Handbook of psychological and educational assessment of children: Vol. 2. Personality, behavior, and context*. New York, NY: Guilford Press.

Reynolds, C. R., & Kamphaus, R. W. (2002). *The clinician's guide to the Behavioral Assessment System for Children: BASC*. New York, NY: Guilford Press.

Reynolds, C. R., & Kamphaus, R. W. (2003). *Handbook of psychological and educational assessment of children: Vol. 1. Intelligence and achievement* (2nd ed.). New York, NY: Guilford Press.

Reynolds, C. R., & Kamphaus, R. W. (2003). *Handbook of psychological and educational assessment of children: Vol. 2. Personality, behavior, and context* (2nd ed.). New York, NY: Guilford Press.

Reynolds, C. R., & Livingston, R. A. (2012). *Mastering modern psychological testing: Theory and methods*. Boston, MA: Pearson Higher Education.

Reynolds, C. R., Livingston, R. L., & Willson, V. L. (2006). *Applications of measurement and assessment in the classroom*. Boston, MA: Pearson Education.

Reynolds, C. R, Livingston, R. L., & Willson, V. L. (2009). *Applications of measurement and assessment in the classroom* (2nd ed.). Boston, MA: Pearson Education.

Reynolds, C. R., & Mann, L. (Eds.). (1987). *Encyclopedia of special education* (3 vols.). New York, NY: Wiley.

Reynolds, C. R., Vannest, K., & Fletcher-Janzen, E. (Eds.). (2013). *Encyclopedia of special education* (4th ed.; 3 vols.). Hoboken, NJ: Wiley.

Reynolds, C. R., Vannest, K., & Harrison, J. (2012). *The energetic brain: Understanding and managing ADHD.* San Francisco, CA: Jossey-Bass.

Reynolds, C. R., & Willson, V. L. (Eds.). (1986). *Methodological and statistical advances in the study of individual differences.* New York, NY: Plenum Press.

Riccio, C. A., Reynolds, C. R., & Lowe, P. A. (2001). *Clinical applications of continuous performance tests: Measuring attention and impulsive responding in children and adults.* New York, NY: Wiley.

Saklosfke, D., Reynolds, C. R., & Schwean, V. (Eds.). (2013). *The Oxford Handbook of Psychological Assessment of Children and Adolescents.* New York, NY: Oxford University Press.

Vannest, K. J., Reynolds, C. R., & Kamphaus, R. W. (2009). *Classroom guide to interventions for behavioral and emotional issues* (Vols. 1 and 2). Bloomington, MN: Pearson Assessments.

Vannest, K., Stroud, K., & Reynolds, C. R. (2011). *Strategies for academic success: An instructional handbook for teaching K-12 students how to study, learn, and take tests.* Los Angeles, CA: Western Psychological Services.

Vannest, K. J., Reynolds, C. R., & Kamphaus, R. W. (2008). *Intervention guide for behavioral and emotional issues.* Bloomington, MN: Pearson Assessments.

Commercially Published Psychological and Educational Tests by Cecil Reynolds

Hammill, D. A., Pearson, N., Voress, J., & Reynolds, C. R. (2004). *Full range test of visual motor integration.* Austin, TX: PRO-ED.

Kamphaus, R. W., & Reynolds, C. R. (1998). *BASC Monitor for ADHD.* Circle Pines, MN: American Guidance Service.

Kamphaus, R. W., & Reynolds, C. R. (2003). *Reynolds Intellectual Screening Test: RIST.* Odessa, FL: Psychological Assessment Resources.

Kamphaus, R. W., & Reynolds, C. R. (2006). *Parenting relationship questionnaire.* Bloomington, MN: Pearson Assessments.

Kamphaus, R. W., & Reynolds, C. R. (2007). *BASC-2 Progress Monitor for adaptability problems.* Minneapolis, MN: Pearson Assessment.

Kamphaus, R. W., & Reynolds, C. R. (2007). *BASC-2 Progress Monitor for ADHD.* Minneapolis, MN: Pearson Assessment.

Kamphaus, R. W., & Reynolds, C. R. (2007). *BASC-2 Progress Monitor for internalizing problems.* Minneapolis, MN: Pearson Assessment.

Kamphaus, R. W., & Reynolds, C. R. (2007). *BASC-2 Progress Monitor for social withdrawal problems.* Minneapolis, MN: Pearson Assessment.

Kamphaus, R. W., & Reynolds, C. R. (2007). *Behavioral and emotional screening system.* Minneapolis, MN: Pearson Assessment.

Reynolds, C. R. (2002). *Comprehensive trail-making test.* Austin, TX: PRO-ED.

Reynolds, C. R. (2007). *Koppitz-2: The Koppitz Developmental scoring system for the Bender-Gestalt test, second edition.* Austin, TX: PRO-ED.

Reynolds, C. R., & Bigler, E. D. (1994). *Test of memory and learning.* Austin, TX: PRO-ED.

Reynolds, C. R., & Bigler, E. D. (2001). *Clinical assessment scales for the elderly.* Odessa, FL: Psychological Assessment Resources.

Reynolds, C. R., & Hickman, J. A. (2003). *The DAP: IQ, The Draw-A-Person Intelligence Test for Children, Adolescents, and Adults.* Austin, TX: PRO-ED.

Reynolds, C. R., & Horton, A. M. (2006). *Test of verbal conceptualization and fluency.* Austin, TX: PRO-ED.

Reynolds, C. R., & Kamphaus, R. W. (1992). *Behavior assessment system for children.* Circle Pines, MN: American Guidance Service.

Reynolds, C. R., & Kamphaus, R. W. (2003). *Reynolds intellectual assessment scales: RIAS.* Odessa, FL: Psychological Assessment Resources.

Reynolds, C. R., & Kamphaus, R. W. (2004). *Behavior assessment system for children–2 (BASC-2).* Circle Pines, MN: American Guidance Service.

Reynolds, C. R., & Kamphaus, R. W. (2007). *Test of irregular word reading efficiency (TIWRE).* Lutz, FL: Psychological Assessment Resources.

Reynolds, C. R., & Livingston, R. (2010). *Children's measure of obsessive-compulsive symptoms.* Los Angeles, CA: Western Psychological Services.

Reynolds, C. R., Pearson, N., & Voress, J. (2002). *Developmental test of visual perception: Adolescent and adult (DTVP-A).* Austin, TX: PRO-ED.

Reynolds, C. R., Richmond, B., & Lowe, P. (2003). *Adult manifest anxiety scale.* Los Angeles, CA: Western Psychological Services.

Reynolds, C. R., Richmond, B., & Lowe, P. (2003). *Adult manifest anxiety scale: College* student edition. Los Angeles, CA: Western Psychological Services.

Reynolds, C. R., Richmond, B., & Lowe, P. (2003). *Adult manifest anxiety scale*: Elderly edition. Los Angeles, CA: Western Psychological Services.

Reynolds, C. R., & Richmond, B. O. (1985). *The Revised Children's Manifest Anxiety Scale.* Los Angeles, CA: Western Psychological Services.

Reynolds, C. R., & Richmond, B. O. (2008). *The Revised Children's Manifest Anxiety Scale (RCMAS-2)* (2nd ed.). Los Angeles, CA: Western Psychological Services.

Reynolds, C. R., & Voress, J. A. (2007). *TOMAL-2: Test of memory and learning,* second edition. Austin, TX: PRO-ED.

Reynolds, C. R., & Voress, J. A. (2012). *TOMAL-SE: Test of memory and learning–senior edition.* Austin, TX: PRO-ED.

Reynolds, C. R., Voress, J. A., & Pearson, N. (2008). *Developmental test of auditory perception.* Austin, TX: PRO-ED.

Stroud, K. C., & Reynolds, C. R. (2006). *School motivation and learning strategies inventory.* Los Angeles, CA: Western Psychological.

REFERENCES

Fletcher-Janzen, E., Reynolds, C. R., & Strickland, T. L. (2000). *The handbook of cross-cultural neuropsychology*. Boston, MA: Kluwer Academic/Plenum.

Reynolds, C. R. (1981). The fallacy of "two years below grade level for age" as a diagnostic criterion for reading disorders. *Journal of School Psychology, 19*, 250–258.

Reynolds, C. R. (1983). Test bias: In God we trust, all others must have data. *Journal of Special Education, 17*, 214–268.

Reynolds, C. R. (1984). Critical measurement issues in learning disabilities. *Journal of Special Education, 18*, 451–476.

Reynolds, C. R., & Bigler, E. D. (1994). *Test of memory and learning*. Austin, TX: PRO-ED.

Reynolds, C. R., & Kamphaus, R. W. (1992). *Behavior assessment system for children*. Circle Pines, MN: American Guidance Service.

Reynolds, C. R., & Kamphaus, R. W. (2003). *The handbook of psychological and educational assessment of children: Intelligence, aptitude, and achievement* (2nd ed.). New York, NY: Guilford Press.

Reynolds, C. R., & Richmond, B. O. (1978). What I think and feel: A revised measure of children's manifest anxiety. *Journal of Abnormal Child Psychology, 6*(2),271–280.

Reynolds, C. R., & Richmond, B. O. (1985). *Revised Children's Manifest Anxiety Scale*. Los Angeles, CA: Western Psychological Services.

RAND B. EVANS
Texas A&M University
First edition

TAMARA J. MARTIN
The University of Texas of the Permian Basin
Second edition

C. WILLIAMS
Falcon School District 49, Colorado Springs, Colorado
Third edition

See also Buros Mental Measurements Yearbook; Children's Manifest Anxiety Scale; Kaufman, Alan S.; Learning Disabilities, Severe Discrepancy Analysis; Torrance, Ellis Paul

REYNOLDS INTELLECTUAL ASSESSMENT SCALES

The Reynolds Intellectual Assessment Scales (RIAS, 2003) is an individually administered test of intelligence assessing two primary components of intelligence, verbal (crystallized) and nonverbal (fluid). Verbal intelligence is assessed with two tasks (Guess What and Verbal Reasoning) involving verbal problem solving and verbal reasoning. On the Guess What (GWH) subtest, the examinee attempts to identify an object or concept from verbal clues (e.g., "What is made of wood, plastic, or metal and makes graphite marks on paper?" or "What is circular or semicircular, is marked with degrees, and is used to measure angles?" or "Who discovered the moons of Jupiter, discovered laws of motion, and was imprisoned for one of his publications?"). On the Verbal Reasoning (VRZ) subtest the examinee completes spoken analogies (e.g., "Stroll is to slow as sprint is to ___" or "Circumnavigate is to perimeter as traverse is to ___"). Nonverbal intelligence is assessed by (Odd-Item Out and What's Missing) that utilize visual and spatial ability tasks. On the Odd-Item Out (OIO) subtest the examinee is given 20 seconds to determine which of six objects or abstract designs does not belong with the others. If the examinee chooses incorrectly, there is a second, 10-second chance to earn partial credit. On the What's Missing (WHM) subtest the examinee is given 20 seconds to tell what part has been removed from a drawing. If the examinee chooses incorrectly, there is a second, 10-second chance to earn partial credit. These two scales combine to produce a Composite Intelligence Index (CIX). In contrast to many existing measures of intelligence, the RIAS eliminates dependence on motor coordination, visual-motor speed, and reading skills.

A Composite Memory Index (CMX) can be derived from two supplementary subtests (Verbal Memory and Nonverbal Memory) which assess verbal and nonverbal memory. However, these memory measures do not contain delayed recall components.

The Verbal Memory (VRM) subtest provides a basic, overall measure of short-term memory skills (e.g., working memory, short-term memory, learning) and measures recall in the verbal domain. The examinee attempts to repeat as precisely as possible several sentences or two short stories that have been read aloud by the examiner. The Nonverbal Memory (NVM) subtest measures the ability to recall pictorial stimuli in both concrete and abstract dimensions. The examinee is given 20 seconds to choose one of six pictures that match a model that was exposed for 5 seconds and removed. If the examinee chooses incorrectly, there is a second, 10-second chance to earn partial credit. These short-term memory assessments require approximately 10 minutes of additional testing time.

The makeup of the battery also allows for the completion of the Reynolds Intellectual Screening Test (RIST). The RIST consists of only two RIAS subtests (one verbal and one nonverbal) that were selected on the basis of theoretical, empirical, and practical considerations. The RIST index is highly correlated with the full scale IQ's of both the WISC-III and WAIS-III. The RIST was designed to be used as a measure for reevaluations or in situations where the full RIAS may not be warranted.

A variety of scores, including T-scores, Z-scores, normal curve equivalents (NCE), stanines and age equivalent (age 3 to 14 years only) scores are provided.

The RIAS was standardized on a normative data sample of 2,438 individuals, from 41 states, aged 3 to 94 years. The normative sample was matched to the 2001 U.S. census on age, ethnicity, gender, educational attainment, and geographical region. During standardization an additional 507 individuals, in 15 different clinical groups, were administered the RIAS to supplement validation of RIAS.

Mean reliability coefficients ranged from .94 to .96 for the four RIAS indexes and from .90 to .95 for the six RIAS subtests. Test-retest reliability of the four index scores ranged from .83 to .91.

The RIAS Manual reports high correlations with the Wechsler Intelligence Scale for Children (WISC-III) [$r = .76$], Wechsler Adult Intelligence Scale (WAIS-III) [$r = .79$], and Wechsler Individual Achievement Test (WIAT) [$r = .69$ for total achievement].

The manual is impressive in its organization and breadth and depth of content and is written in a style that makes it appropriate for psychologists.

REFERENCES

Dombrowski, S., & Mrazik, M. (2008). Test Review of RIAS: Reynolds Intellectual Assessment Scales. *Canadian Journal of School Psychology, 23*(2), 223–230.

Dombrowski, S., Watkins, M., & Brogan, M. (2009). An exploratory investigation of the factor structure of the Reynolds Intellectual Assessment Scales (RIAS). *Journal of Psychoeducational Assessment, 27*(6), 494–507.

Spies, R. A., & Plake, B. S. (Eds.). (2005). *The sixteenth mental measurements yearbook*. Lincoln, NE: Buros Institute of Mental Measurements.

RON DUMONT
Fairleigh Dickinson University

JOHN O. WILLIS
Rivier College

KATHLEEN VEIZEL
Fairleigh Dickinson University

JAMIE ZIBULSKY
Fairleigh Dickinson University

REYNOLDS, MAYNARD C. (1922–   )

A native of Doyan, North Dakota, Maynard Reynolds received his BS in education from Moorhead State University in 1942. He obtained his graduate degrees in educational psychology at the University of Minnesota after World War II, receiving his MA in 1947 and his PhD in 1950. After brief teaching assignments at the University of Northern Iowa and Long Beach State University, he returned to the University of Minnesota, first as the director of the Psychoeducational Clinic, then as the chairman of the Department of Special Education, and more recently, as professor of educational psychology and special education.

In the 1950s Reynolds became involved in the development of programs for exceptional students and issues concerning the diagnosis of such children. In the 1960s Reynolds became the international president of the Council of Exceptional Children (CEC). Later, as the first chair of CEC's Policy Commission, he was increasingly active in advancing the concept that every child has a right to an education. Since the passage of PL 94-142, the Education of All Handicapped Children Act, Reynolds has led national programs in technical assistance systems relating to changes in special education programs. From 1978 to 1984, with James Ysseldyke and Richard Weinberg, Reynolds also helped in Network, a technical assistance effort in the field of school psychology. He has also worked closely with organizations concerned with general and special education teacher preparation, editing a volume entitled *Knowledge Base for the Beginning Teacher* (1989) for the American Association of Colleges for Teacher Education.

Since his retirement from the University of Minnesota in 1989, Reynolds has served in endowed professorships at California State University, Los Angeles and the University of San Diego. He also worked part-time, over a period of seven years, at the Research and Development Center on Inner City Education headed by Margaret Wang at Temple University. With Wang and Herbert Walberg, he edited a five-volume compendium on research and practice in special education.

Reynolds has been included in *Who's Who in America* and *American Men and Women of Science*. He has been given the J. E. Wallace Wallin Award by the CEC for service to handicapped children and the Mildred Thomson Award by the American Association on Mental Deficiencies.

Some of his principal publications include a text, *Teaching Exceptional Children in All America's Schools*, and several articles, including "Categories and Variables in Special Education" (1972), "A Framework for Considering Some Issues in Special Education" (1962), and "A Strategy for Research" (1963).

REFERENCES

Reynolds, M. C. (1962). A framework for considering some issues in special education. *Exceptional Children, 28*, 367–370.

Reynolds, M. C. (1963). A strategy for research. *Exceptional Children, 29*(5), 213–219.

Reynolds, M. C., & Balow, B. (1972). Categories and variables in special education. *Exceptional Children, 38*(5), 357–366.

Reynolds, M. C., & Birch, J. W. (1982). *Teaching exceptional children in all America's schools* (2nd ed.). Reston, VA: Council for Exceptional Children.

Wang, M. C., Reynolds, M. C., & Walberg, H. J. (Eds.). (1987–92). *Handbook of special education: Research and practice* (Vols. 1–5). Oxford, England: Pergamon Press.

E. Valerie Hewitt
Texas A&M University
First edition

Tamara J. Martin
The University of Texas of the Permian Basin
Second edition

RH FACTOR INCOMPATIBILITY

Rh factor incompatibility (erythroblastosis fetalis) results from an antigen-antibody reaction with destruction of the fetal red blood cells (Sherwen, Scoloveno, & Weingarten, 1999). The most lethal form of Rh factor incompatibility is erythroblastosis fetalis. Generally defined, erythroblastosis fetalis is a type of hemolytic disorder found in newborns that results from maternal-fetal blood group incompatibility of the Rh factor and blood group). When an Rh-positive fetus begins to grow inside an Rh-negative mother, it is as though the mother's body is being invaded by a foreign agent or antigen (Pillitteri, 2010). The mother's body reacts to this invasion by forming antibodies that cross the placenta and cause hemolysis of fetal red blood cells. The fetus becomes deficient in red blood cells that transport oxygen and develops anemia; enlarged heart, spleen, and liver; and a cardiovascular system that easily decompensates (Lowdermilk, 2012). Without prompt treatment, hypoxia, cardiac failure, respiratory distress, and death may result.

Prenatal diagnosis of erythroblastosis fetalis is confirmed through amniocentesis and analysis of bilirubin levels within the amniotic fluid. The treatment regime may include intrauterine transfusions to combat red blood cell destruction or immediate transfusions after birth (Pillitteri, 2010). Preterm labor may also be induced to remove the fetus from the destructive maternal environment.

In Rh factor incompatibility, the hemolytic reactions take place only when the mother is Rh-negative and the infant is Rh-positive (Sherwen et al., 1999). This isoimmunization process rarely occurs in the first pregnancy, but risk is great in subsequent pregnancies. A simple injection of a high-titer Rho(D) immune-globulin preparation after delivery or abortion of the Rh-positive fetus can prevent maternal sensitization to the Rh factor (Mosby, Inc., 2010).

Hemolytic diseases of the fetus or newborn are on the decline and occur in only 1.5% of all pregnancies (Sherwen et al., 1999). Since the availability of Rho(D) immune globulin (RhoGAM), the incidence of Rh factor incompatibilities has drastically decreased (Sherwen et al., 1999). Caucasian newborns remain most at risk (15%) for erythroblastosis fetalis; African American newborns have a 6% occurrence rate (Medical College of Wisconsin Physicians and Clinics, 1999).

REFERENCES

Lowdermilk, D. L. (2012). *Maternity and women's health care.* St. Louis, MO: Elsevier Mosby.

Medical College of Wisconsin Physicians and Clinics. (1999). *Erythroblastosis fetalis.* Retrieved from http://chorus.rad.mcw .edu/doc/00889.html

Mosby, Inc. (2010). *Mosby's dictionary of medicine, nursing, and health professions.* St. Louis, MO: Mosby.

Pillitteri, A. (2010). *Maternal & child health nursing: Care of the childbearing and childrearing family.* Philadelphia, PA: Wolters Kluwer/Lippincott William & Wilkins.

Sherwen, L., Scoloveno, M., & Weingarten, C. (1999). *Maternity nursing: Care of the childbearing family* (3rd ed.). Stamford, CT: Appleton & Lange.

Kari Anderson
University of North Carolina at Wilmington

RHYTHMIC MOVEMENT DISORDER

Rhythmic movement disorder (RMD), also known as stereotypic movement disorder (SMD; American Psychiatric Association, 1994), *jactatio captis nocturna*, and *rythmie de sommeil*, refers to a group of stereotypical, rhythmic, repetitive movements or vocalizations (Gillberg, 1995). RMD is diagnosed if it occurs in children—particularly preschool-age children—during drowsy or sleep periods or during the sleep-wake period of the sleep cycle, unlike other types of movement disorders, including SMD.

RMD may include head banging, head rolling, or body rocking, or a combination thereof, involving large muscles of the body. If self-injurious behaviors are included, they usually have poor prognostic outcome.

Characteristics

1. Rhythmic body movements occurring during drowsy or sleep states
2. Stereotyped, repetitive movements involving large muscles

3. Usually involves head and neck
4. Unusual vocalizations
5. Continued humming
6. Head banging
7. Head rolling
8. Body rocking

The prevalence of RMD, or some form of movement disorder associated with the sleep-wake cycle, has been estimated to occur in two thirds of all infants age 9 months and in less than 8% of children 4 years of age or older. The disorder is more common in boys than in girls with an approximate ratio of 3:1. The etiology of these conditions is unknown.

With regard to developmental typology, body rocking appears more common in the first year and other types of RMD tend to be found in older children. A select group of these children go on to develop more serious problems of attention, including attention-deficit/hyperactivity disorder (Gillberg, 1995). Treatment usually involves reassurance of the parents and behavioral interventions (in more severe cases) until RMD disappears as the child matures. Because most children outgrow this condition, special education is usually not necessary.

REFERENCES

American Psychiatric Association. (1994). *Diagnostic and statistical manual of mental disorders* (4th ed.). Washington, DC: Author.

Gillberg, C. (1995). *Clinical child neuropsychiatry*. Cambridge, England: Cambridge University Press.

ANTOLIN M. LLORENTE
Baylor College of Medicine Houston, Texas

RICKETS, HYPOPHOSPHATEMIC

Hypophosphatemic rickets is a disorder that affects the normal growth and repair process of bones. The disorder was previously called *vitamin D resistant* because rickets persisted despite sufficient intake of vitamin D. However, the term was limiting because there also appears to be a disruption in the mineralization of calcium, phosphorus, and alkaline phosphatase. Most forms of hypophosphatemia are X-linked dominant; however, there are also autosomal recessive and sporadic forms of the disease (Carpenter, 1997; Winger, Steeksma, & Jacobson, 2000).

Estimates on the incidence of those born with the disorder have ranged from 1 to 10 out of a million to 1 in 20,000 (Carpenter, 1997). Although most individuals are born with the disorder, symptoms can appear in early infancy (Carpenter, 1997) up through adulthood (Arnold & Bibb, 2000). In the most common form, X-linked hypophosphatemia (XLH), girls are more likely to inherit the disorder than are males because it can never be passed on from a father to a son (Whyte, Schranck, & Armamento-Villareal, 1996). However, there is evidence to suggest that males have more pronounced symptoms than do females (Carpenter, 1997; Whyte et al., 1996).

Although much still remains not understood about this disorder, it is known that symptoms manifest because the body has difficulty converting vitamin D into its active form, which is needed to regulate calcium and phosphate levels in the bloodstream (National Organization for Rare Disorders [NORD], 2000). Moreover, there appears to be a genetic defect on the kidney; this defect interferes with the proximal renal tubular reabsorption of phosphate (Verge et al., 1991). Consequently, the kidneys leak phosphate into the urine (Winger et al., 2000), and there is excess urinary excretion of the mineral. Because phosphorus is needed for calcium metabolism to stimulate bone growth, the weakened bones become thin and bend (NORD, 2000). There can also be problems pertaining to the parathyroid (Carpenter, 1997).

Characteristics

1. Child may experience damage to the skeletal system, such as bowed legs (genu varum), a waddling gait, short stature, narrow head (dolichocephaly), and knees that are too close together (knock-knee or genu valgum).
2. Child may experience pain in his or her bones.
3. Child may have weakened or painful muscles.
4. Child's teeth may also be affected, including tooth decay, abscesses, enlargement of pulp cavity, intraglobular dentin irregularities, occasional enamel defects, or periapical infections.
5. Child may experience frequent vomiting or constipation.
6. Child may experience respiratory or myocardial difficulties.
7. There may be alterations in the child's mental state, in which the child becomes irritable, becomes confused, or lapses into a coma.

Blood samples can be drawn in order to determine a child's level of phosphorus, calcium, and alkaline phosphatase. Urine samples should also be taken in order to determine an individual's renal phosphate handling.

A skeletal examination including radiographic testing is also indicated (Carpenter, 1997).

Currently, there is no cure for the disorder. Individuals with hypophosphatemia are generally treated according to their age as well as the severity of the symptoms (Carpenter, 1997). A common biochemical intervention includes a combination of calcitrol (a form of vitamin D) and phosphate supplements. Because of possible medical complications, it is important to monitor the calcium and phosphate levels in the child's blood and urine (Carpenter, 1997; Verge et al., 1991). Treatment with oral phosphate and vitamin D has been shown to be effective in improving the growth rate and controlling the progression of bowleg deformity (Verge et al., 1991; Winger et al., 2000). However, a child might need surgery to correct severe bone deformities (Verge et al., 1991).

Because phosphate deficiency often causes muscles to be weak, individuals diagnosed with hypophosphatemia should have an examination in order to assess their motor strength. Children may need assistance in developing their gross motor skills and strengthening their muscles. Consequently, it is likely that children with more severe forms of hypophosphatemia will require physical and occupational therapy. Little is known of the cognitive implications; however, just as the physical treatment is contingent upon the presenting symptoms, attention should be given to any manifestations of emotional or cognitive difficulties that call for psychological interventions. The prognosis of hypophosphatemia varies according to the severity of the disease. With the proper medical treatment, most individuals are able to live a normal life span (Verge et al., 1991).

REFERENCES

Arnold, J. L., & Bibb, J. (2000). *Hypophosphatemia.* Retrieved from http://emedicine.medscape.com/

Carpenter, T. O. (1997). New perspectives on the biology and treatment of X-linked hypophosphatemic rickets. *Pediatric Clinics of North America, 44*(2), 443–466.

National Organization for Rare Disorders. (2000). *Familial hypophosphatemia.* Retrieved from http://www.rarediseases.org

Verge, C. F., Lam, A., Simpson, J. M., Cowell, C. T., Neville, J. H., & Silink, M. (1991). Effects of therapy in X-linked hypophosphatemic rickets. *New England Journal of Medicine, 325*(26), 1843–1848.

Whyte, M. P., Schranck, F. W., & Armamento-Villareal, R. (1996). X-Linked hypophosphatemia: A search for gender, race, anticipation, or parent of origin effects on disease expression in children. *Journal of Clinical Endocrinology and Metabolism, 81*(11), 4075–4080.

Winger, L., Steeksma, C., & Jacobson, E. (2000). *XLH network flyer: XLH network.* Retrieved from xlhnetwork.org

MICHELLE PERFECT
University of Texas at Austin

RICKETS, VITAMIN D DEFICIENCY

Vitamin D deficiency rickets is a bone disorder caused by an insufficient intake of vitamin D in a person's diet or inadequate exposure to ultraviolet rays in sunlight. Inadequate phosphorus or calcium in a child's diet can also lead to the development of rickets. The diagnosis of rickets dates back to the mid-17th century, when nearly half of all children born had rickets (Welch, Bergstrom, & Tsang, 2000). Today, incidents of rickets in the United States are extremely low due to the availability of foods that are either naturally rich in vitamin D or fortified with vitamin D. For instance, unless an infant is exposed to a vegetarian diet that does not include milk, most children consume vitamin D in their formulas (Winger, 2000). There are also vitamin D supplements that can be given to children born prematurely or on vegan diets. Nonetheless, in recent years, reports of rickets have increased slightly, especially among African American infants (Kreiter et al., 2000; Welch et al., 2000).

Rickets is most common among children between the ages of 4 months and 2 years. Environmental conditions, such as smog and pollution in cities, can prevent adequate exposure to sunlight. Moreover, rickets may also occur when children wear protective clothing or sunscreen that shields them from the sun's rays (Welch et al., 2000). Additionally, children with dark skin are at an increased risk for rickets because their pigmentation may reduce the production of vitamin D that is derived from exposure to light (Kreiter et al., 2000).

Characteristics

1. Child may have bowlegs, raised bony bumps along the ribs (rachitic rosaries), and other bone deformities.

2. Mild forms may cause only bone and muscle weakness.

3. Enlargement of wrists and ankles is an early sign of rickets.

4. The baby's soft spot may be enlarged, and its closure may be delayed.

5. Shape of the head may become boxlike due to the thickening of skull bones.

6. Delayed formation of teeth, dental deformities, increased sensitivity in the teeth, or damaged tooth enamel may occur.

7. There may be excessive sweating, especially around the head.

8. Child may exhibit restlessness, irritability, restless sleep, muscle weakness, and delays in learning to walk.

Because the body needs vitamin D in order to properly absorb calcium, the bones may become deformed. Initially, the weakened bones begin to bend in response to the child's sitting and progressively become more bowed when the child begins to use the weight-bearing limbs (e.g., the arms and legs; Palfrey, Katz, Schulman, & New, 1995). A physical screening to measure a child's levels of alkaline phosphatase, calcium, and phosphorus can be performed (Winger, 2000). Such tests would include X-rays and blood tests (Palfrey et al., 1995). These tests may not be able to identify the condition if a child has a mild case of rickets; however, in these cases a normal diet should be effective in strengthening bones and muscles (Aronson, 1998).

The severity of rickets depends upon how long a child was deprived of vitamin D either from foods or from exposure to light. Treatment of rickets includes a diet rich in vitamin D, which includes food and beverages such as fish, liver (Palfrey et al., 1995; Winger, 2000), milk, soy products fortified with calcium and vitamin D, and formula that is fortified with vitamin D (Aronson, 1998; Palfrey et al., 1995). Many times these foods are not sufficient, and doctors must prescribe vitamin D supplements. Higher doses of vitamin D may be necessary for children with more severe rickets. Additionally, children also need to be exposed to both natural and artificial light (Aronson, 1998).

Vitamin D deficiency rickets can usually be treated successfully, and its harmful effects can usually be reversed. However, if the disease is not identified and treated immediately or if the case is more severe, symptoms such as bone deformities may not be reversible (Aronson, 1998). Treatment may include wearing supportive shoes or leg braces (Palfrey et al., 1995; Winger, 2000). Children will most likely also need assistance in developing their gross motor skills. In particular, these children may need support with learning to crawl, stand, and walk. Additionally, rickets may result in children having poorly developed or decreased muscle tone. Such children may need support in increasing their muscle strength, flexibility, and stamina. As a result, some children may require services from a physical or occupational therapist.

Prognosis is generally favorable after children are put on a diet nutritionally rich in vitamin D. Therefore, the primary mode of intervention is ensuring that the child receives the proper nutritional supplements. The family may need assistance with monitoring the child's diet, especially if the family is living in poverty. Children who have had rickets may also need to be referred to a dentist because tooth eruption may be delayed or the enamel may be damaged. Future research is focused on preventing the disease in rural or economically disadvantaged areas. In particular, heavy emphasis is being placed on preventing vitamin D deficiency in children in orphanages in China and in Easter European nations, where there continues to be a high occurrence (Aronson, 1998).

REFERENCES

Aronson, J. (1998). *Rickets in Chinese children*. Retrieved from http://members.aol.com/jaronmink/rickets.htm

Kreiter, S. R., Schwartz, R. P., Kirkman, H. N., Charlton, P. A., Calikoglu, A. S., & Davenport, M. L. (2000). Nutritional rickets in African American breast-fed infants. *Journal of Pediatrics*, *137*, 153–157.

Palfrey, J., Katz, A. K., Schulman, I., & New, M. I. (Eds.). (1995). *The Disney encyclopedia of baby and child care*. New York, NY: Hyperion.

Welch, T. R., Bergstrom, W. H., & Tsang, R. C. (2000). Vitamin D-deficient rickets: The reemergence of a once-conquered disease. *The Journal of Pediatrics*, *137*(2), 143–145.

Winger, L. (2000). *Vitamin D metabolism and rickets: XLH network*. Retrieved from http://xlhnetwork.org/larry/website/VitaminD/vitaminD.html

MICHELLE PERFECT
University of Texas at Austin

RIEGER SYNDROME

Rieger syndrome is an autosomal dominant gene disorder characterized by eye anomalies associated with glaucoma, mild craniofacial abnormalities, and absence or malformation of teeth.

This rare disorder of wide expression is estimated to affect fewer than 1 in 200,000 children in the United States (Moody & Moody, 2000).

Characteristics

1. Hypoplasia and malformation of the iris, anterior displacement and thickening of Schwalbe space and adhesion of the iris to Schwalbe space are predominant characteristics.

2. Microdontia, hypodontia, and anodontia are common.

3. Maxillary hypoplasia, cleft palate, and protruding lower lip.

4. Umbilical abnormalities and anal stenosis are occasional.

5. Conducive deafness, blindness, mental retardation, and psychomotor retardation occur in some cases.

Glaucoma develops in 50% of people with Rieger syndrome, making it of primary concern in treatment. Medical therapy is initially implemented. Medications such as beta-blockers, alpha agonists, and carbonic anhydrase inhibitors that decrease aqueous output are more effective than are medications affecting outflow such as pilocarpine (Economou & Simmons, 1999). If medication is no longer effective, surgical interventions such as goniotomy and trabeculectomy are used (Economou & Simmons, 1999). Craniofacial, dental, and orthodontic surgeries are treatments for craniofacial and dental abnormalities. Cleft palate can be surgically corrected as early as 6 months of age, and other procedures may be needed as the face matures and changes (Craniofacial Foundation of Arizona, 1999).

Children with Rieger syndrome may need special education services for their visual impairment. Services may also be required for mental and psychomotor retardation as well as for hearing impairment.

Early glaucoma testing and interventions as well as routine monitoring of intraocular pressure and optic nerve head changes are measures for better prognosis.

REFERENCES

Craniofacial Foundation of Arizona. (1999). *Craniofacial.* Retrieved from http://azcranio.com/

Economou, A., & Simmons, S. T. (1999). Axenfeld-Rieger syndrome. In M. Yanoff & J. S. Duker (Eds.), *Yanoff: Ophthalmology* (1st ed., pp. 12.21.2–12.21.3). London, England: Mosby.

Moody, J., & Moody, K. (2000, November). *Rieger syndrome.* Retrieved from http://rarelinks4parents.homestead.com/RiegSynInfo.html

IMAN TERESA LAHROUD
University of Texas at Austin

RIGHT-HANDEDNESS

Right-handedness is a species-specific characteristic of humans (Hicks & Kinsbourne, 1978). Additionally, right-handedness, also called dextrality, can be considered universal in that 90% of the human population is right-handed (Corballis & Beale, 1983). Since the majority of individuals prefer using their right hands and are also more skilled with their right hands, more positive properties and values have come to be associated with the right than with the left. For example, throughout history the right has represented the side of the gods, strength, life, goodness, light, the state of rest, the limited, the odd, the square, and the singular. The left has been signified by the polar opposites of these characteristics. Maleness also has been traditionally associated with the right, providing symbolic expression of the universality of male dominance (Needham, 1974).

Although people classify themselves as right-handed or left-handed, handedness more accurately spans a continuous range from extreme right-handedness through mixed-handedness or ambidexterity to extreme left-handedness (Corballis & Beale, 1976). Investigators always have been curious about the abundance of right-handedness and the rarity of the various degrees of nonright-handedness. However, studies of historical records and artifacts have revealed enough inconsistencies in incidence to preclude any simple choice between culture or biology to explain the origin of handedness. Consequently, combinations of these various nature and nurture explanations have been invoked. Harris (1980) provides an interesting and detailed account of these various theories.

Corballis and Beale (1983), in an extensive study of the neuropsychology of right and left, have argued that right-handedness is biologically rather than culturally determined. They cite the fact that right-handedness has always has been universal across diverse and seemingly unrelated cultures; moreover, although right-handedness itself is not manifest until late in the first year of life, it is correlated with other asymmetries that are evident at or before birth. They acknowledge that there are environmental pressures to be right-handed and that some naturally left-handed individuals may be compelled to use their right hands for certain tasks, but suggest that these very pressures have their origins in the fundamental right-handedness of most human beings.

Today the relationship between right-handedness and the unilateral representation of language in the left cerebral hemisphere is well documented. Case studies linking the side of brain damage and the incidence of aphasia, or language impairment, have revealed that approximately 98% of right-handers use the left hemisphere of their brain for language. A similar conclusion has been drawn from studies in which linguistic functioning has been impaired in 95% of the right-handers whose left cerebral hemispheres were injected with sodium amobarbitol, a momentarily incapacitating drug.

The hemisphere of the brain used for language in left-handers is more variable. Two thirds of left-handers have demonstrated the use of their left hemisphere. Almost half of the remaining left-handers use their right hemispheres for speech, while the remainder have some capacity for speech in both hemispheres (Rasmussen & Milner, 1975). In view of these data, many investigators suggest that both right-handedness and left cerebral dominance for language are genetically controlled expressions of some underlying biological gradient. This relationship further reveals the significance of right-handedness in the unique cognitive functioning of the human species.

REFERENCES

Corballis, M. C., & Beale, I. L. (1976). *The psychology of left and right.* Hillsdale, NJ: Erlbaum.

Corballis, M. C., & Beale, I. L. (1983). *The ambivalent mind.* Chicago, IL: Nelson-Hall.

Harris, L. J. (1980). Left-handedness: Early theories, facts, and fancies. In J. Herron (Ed.), *Neuropsychology of left-handedness* (pp. 3–78). New York, NY: Academic Press.

Hicks, R. E., & Kinsbourne, M. (1978). Human handedness. In M. Kinsbourne (Ed.), *Asymmetrical function of the brain* (pp. 267–273). New York, NY: Cambridge University Press.

Needham, R. (Ed.). (1974). *Right and left: Essays on dual symbolic classification.* Chicago, IL: University of Chicago Press.

Rasmussen, T., & Milner, B. (1975). Clinical and surgical studies of the cerebral speech areas in man. In K. J. Zulch, O. Creutzfeldt, & G. Galbraith (Eds.), *Otfried Foerster symposium on cerebral localization.* Heidelberg: Springer.

GALE A. HARR
Maple Heights City Schools, Maple Heights, Ohio

See also Cerebral Dominance; Handedness and Exceptionality; Left Brain, Right Brain

RIGHT HEMISPHERE SYNDROME (LINGUISTIC, EXTRALINGUISTIC, AND NONLINGUISTIC)

The role of the right hemisphere in communication was largely unknown 30 years ago (Myers, 1997). Since then an extensive body of research has determined that the right hemisphere handles holistic, gestalt-like stimuli and visual-spatial information and has identified a wide range of communication impairments that can occur subsequent to right hemisphere damage. Three types of right hemisphere syndrome (RHS) deficits are *extralinguistic* (discourse), *nonlinguistic* (perceptual and attentional), and, to a lesser degree, *linguistic* deficits (phonological, semantic, syntactical, and morphological; Hegde, 1998; Myers, 1997; Payne, 1997).

Extralinguistic Deficits

Discourse is the aspect of communication that transcends individual phonemes, words, or sentences. It links "the bits and pieces of language to create representations of events, objects, beliefs, personalities, and experiences" (Brownell & Joanette, 1993, p. vii). Discourse competence is context driven, and context includes a variety of cues—not only words and sentences, but tone of voice, gestures, body positions, facial expressions of the speaker, and the overall purpose and relative formality of the communicative event. Discourse also involves organization, sequencing, and the generation of projections, predictions, and inferences so that sentences are not taken as independent units, but as part of a larger whole (macrostructure) in which central ideas are emphasized and supported. Four major areas make up extralinguistic deficits associated with RHS (Hegde, 1998; Myers, 1997; Payne, 1997):

1. *Macrostructure*: Reduced number and accuracy of core concepts and inferences, reduced specificity or explicitness of information, and reduced efficiency of listening, speaking, reading, writing, and thinking.

2. *Impaired nonliteral language*: Reduced sensitivity to and use of figurative language (similes, metaphors, idioms, proverbs), humor (cartoons, jokes, riddles, puns), teasing, advertisements, slang, verbal aggression, ambiguity, multiple meanings, deception (irony, sarcasm), and capacity to revise original interpretations.

3. *Rhetorical sensitivity/affective components*: Reduced sensitivity to communicative purposes, shared knowledge, emotional tone, partner's communicative state, turn-taking, topic maintenance, gaze; increased impulsivity, excessive talking, shallow responses, and monotonal speech.

4. *Impaired prosody*: Reduced sensitivity to affective prosody (comprehension of others' emotions as reflected in the voice) and use of prosodic features (production of personal emotional states).

Nonlinguistic Deficits

Nonlinguistic deficits associated with RHS include visual perceptual problems, left-side neglect, attentional deficits, and denial of deficits.

Visual perceptual deficits include reduced ability to recognize faces (prosopagnosia) and to construct or reproduce block designs, two-dimensional stick figures, or geometric designs.

Left-side neglect is reduced sensitivity to respond to information on the left, despite the motor and sensory capacity to do so. The definition of *left* may vary according to the type of neglect and the environment. In body-centered neglect, *left* may refer to the left of the body midline. In environment-centered neglect, *left* may refer to the left side of a group of stimuli, regardless of their spatial location, or to the left side of fixed environmental coordinates, such as the left side of a room or book. In other cases, neglect may occur on the left side of a given object, even if that object is located in the right visual field. Thus, neglect may occur in the left or right visual field, depending on the stimulus environment; left may, therefore, be considered relative. Left-side neglect can occur in all modalities (auditory, visual, tactile, smell, taste) but is most often noted and tested in the visual modality. In addition to ignoring the left, individuals with neglect also may demonstrate an orienting bias toward the right: That is, right-sided stimuli "capture" the person's attention.

Attentional deficits include reduced arousal (alertness), vigilance (focusing on relevant pieces of information), and maintained attention to stimuli; selective attention.

Linguistic Deficits

Unlike the communication deficits that occur with left-hemisphere impairment, linguistic deficits are less problematic in RHS. Word retrieval deficits (semantics) occur frequently. Defining categories (e.g., apple, peach, cherry are *fruit*) and identifying collective and single nouns through confrontation naming are characteristic linguistic impairments. Phonological, syntactic, and morphological errors do not characterize the communication patterns of RHS (Hegde, 1998).

Right hemisphere syndrome is associated with strokes, tumors, head trauma, and various neurological diseases in all ethnic groups (Payne, 1997). The syndrome can have significant effects on social and academic aspects of communication learning.

REFERENCES

Brownell, H. H., & Joanette, Y. (Eds.). (1993). *Narrative discourse in neurologically impaired and normal aging adults.* San Diego, CA: Singular.

Hegde, M. N. (1998). *A coursebook on aphasia and other neurogenic language disorders* (2nd ed.). San Diego, CA: Singular.

Myers, P. E. (1997). Right hemisphere syndrome. In L. L. LaPointe (Ed.), *Aphasia and related neurogenic language disorders* (2nd ed.). New York, NY: Thieme.

Payne, J. C. (1997). *Adult neurogenic language disorders: Assessment and treatment—A comprehensive ethnobiological approach.* San Diego, CA: Singular.

STEPHEN S. FARMER
New Mexico State University

See also Nonverbal Language; Pragmatics and Pragmatic Communication Disorders

RIGHT TO EDUCATION

The right to education refers to the legal concept that justifies a school-aged person's freedom to receive educational services. The conceptual and legal development of this right has occurred in conjunction with an increasing societal concern for individuals who exhibit exceptional educational needs. These changing social attitudes have been reflected in judicial decisions and legislative efforts that have substantiated the right of all school-aged children and youths to receive educational services.

The U.S. Constitution, although not explicit in its guarantee of the right to education, has been cited as the fundamental justification for the provision of educational services. Specifically, the right to education has been implied from the Fourteenth Amendment, which states in its equal protection clause, "No State shall...deny to any person within its jurisdiction the equal protection of the laws." Thus, this amendment requires that, where educational services are available, such services must be available to all on an equivalent basis.

Early court cases that addressed the right of the exceptional needs learner to receive educational services did not reflect this interpretation. Generally, litigation in this area prior to the 1950s resulted in exclusionary educational policies (e.g., *Watson v. Cambridge*, 1883; *Beattie v. State Board of Education of Wisconsin*, 1919). However, with the onset of increasing civil rights awareness in the early 1950s, right-to-education court cases evidenced a more positive trend. Some of the more influential court cases that have related to the development of the right-to-education concept for the exceptional needs learner include *Brown v. Board of Education of Topeka* (1954), *Pennsylvania Association for Retarded Citizens v. the Commonwealth of Pennsylvania* (1971), and *Mills v. Board of Education of the District of Columbia* (1972).

The *Brown* case dealt with the rights of a class of citizens (African Americans in the South) to attend public schools in their community on a nonsegregated basis. The major issues in this case were suspect classification (i.e., classification by race) and equal protection. In a unanimous decision for the plaintiff, the Supreme Court emphasized the social importance of education and also ruled that education must be made available on equal terms to all.

The *Pennsylvania Association for Retarded Citizens* (*PARC*) case dealt more specifically with the educational rights of exceptional needs learners. Citing the Fourteenth Amendment rights to due process and equal protection, the judge in this case ruled that Pennsylvania statutes permitting denial or postponement of entry to public schools by mentally retarded children were unconstitutional. The terms of the settlement reached in this case included provision of due process rights to the plaintiffs and identification and placement in public school programs of all previously excluded children.

More general in its plaintiff class, the *Mills* case challenged the exclusion of mentally retarded, epileptic, brain-damaged, hyperactive, and behavior-disordered children from public schools. Finding for the plaintiffs, the court required the defendants to provide full public education or "adequate alternatives." These alternatives could only be provided after notice and a reasonable opportunity to challenge the services that had been given. The progression from *Brown* (1954) to *PARC* (1971) to *Mills* (1972) reflects an increasing sophistication in the awareness of the educational needs of individuals with exceptional learning characteristics. This more complete view of the educational needs and rights of exceptional individuals is also apparent in recent legislation.

Two major legislative efforts that have addressed the educational rights of exceptional needs learners are Section 504 of the Rehabilitation Act of 1973, the Education for All Handicapped Children Act of 1975 (PL 94-142), and its successor, the Individuals with Disabilities Education Act (IDEA). Section 504 of the Rehabilitation Act of 1973 is particularly important because it deals with all programs that receive federal funds. This legislation mandates nondiscrimination on the basis of handicapping conditions if these funds are to continue.

Public Law 94-142 and the IDEA embody the intent of all litigation and legislation that they follow in their highly specific delineation of the educational rights of exceptional needs learners. The law requires that all individuals, regardless of disability or its degree, be offered a free, appropriate education at public expense. The law further specifies that these services must be delivered in the least restrictive environment appropriate for the individual child.

The right to education for children and youths with exceptional learning characteristics has resulted from changing societal views of the needs and rights of these individuals. These attitudes have been reflected in increased litigation questioning the adequacy, availability, and appropriateness of the educational services offered to this group. The outcome of these cases has established a legal basis for a right to education. This litigation has in turn led to legislation developed to ensure that right. For a comprehensive discussion of the right to education for the exceptional needs learner see Wortis (1978) and Sales, Krauss, Sacken, and Overcast (1999).

REFERENCES

Sales, B. D., Krauss, D., Sacken, D., & Overcast, B. (1999). The legal rights of students. In C. R. Reynolds & T. B. Gutkin (Eds.), *The handbook of school psychology* (3rd ed.). New York, NY: Wiley.

Wortis, J. (Ed.). (1978). *Mental retardation and developmental disabilities*. New York, NY: Brunner/Mazel.

J. Todd Stephens
University of Wisconsin at Madison
First and Second editions

Kimberly F. Applequist
University of Colorado at Colorado Springs
Third edition

See also Brown v. Board of Education; Individuals With Disabilities Education Improvement Act of 2004 (IDEIA); Mills v. Board of Education; Pennsylvania Association for Retarded Citizens v. Pennsylvania

RIGHT TO TREATMENT

The term *right to treatment* refers to the legal concept that justifies an individual's freedom to receive therapeutic and/or curative services. Although it was initially developed as an extension of litigation that targeted the availability of medically oriented services for institutionalized individuals, recent legal interpretations of this right have been broadened to include the right to habilitation and the right to education.

The development of the right to treatment reflects a trend of change in societal attitudes about providing services for individuals with exceptional learning or behavioral characteristics. As attitudes have changed, concerned individuals have organized systematic efforts to ensure the availability of these services. These changes have resulted in litigative and legislative efforts that have addressed both the availability and the adequacy of treatment for institutionalized people.

The three major court cases that shaped the legal interpretation of the right to treatment are *Rouse v. Cameron* (1968); *Wyatt v. Stickney* (1970), a class action suit; and *New York Association for Retarded Citizens v. Rockefeller* (1972). In these cases constitutional amendments and state laws were interpreted as requiring treatment services for institutionalized persons. The first court case that dealt with the right of an institutionalized person to receive treatment was *Rouse v. Cameron* (1968). In this case, a man was institutionalized for 4 years after having been found not guilty, by reason of insanity, of a misdemeanor. While institutionalized, Rouse did not receive treatment. Citing constitutional rights (due process, equal protection, freedom from cruel and unusual punishment) and basing the decision on state law, the court ruled that confinement for treatment purposes when treatment was not made available was equivalent to imprisonment. Rouse was subsequently freed.

The *Wyatt v. Stickney* case (1970) was a class action suit filed on behalf of the residents of three residential facilities in Alabama. The case was exhaustive in its pursuit of information and remedies. In the final ruling, standards were delineated with regard to treatment, habilitation, freedom from restraint, and a host of other treatment considerations. The court-ordered remedies included development of appropriate staff ratios, individual habilitation plans, and the delineation of specific procedures for treatment. Thus, according to the rulings of *Wyatt* (1970), treatment must not only be available but also be supported by sufficient staff and planning. Following the initial hearing of *Wyatt*, the New York Association for Retarded Citizens (NYARC) filed a petition against the then governor of the state, Nelson Rockefeller (*NYARC v. Rockefeller*, 1972), requesting relief from the overcrowded and inhumane conditions at the Willowbrook state institution. Citing the constitutional right to due process, the judge in this case ruled for immediate reduction of the resident population and appropriate development of community-based programs. Thus, the *NYARC* case indicated that in addition to having the right to receive adequate services in humane conditions, residents must also be considered as members of a society to which they should be allowed reasonable access.

Each of these cases represents a litigative response to either a complete lack of treatment availability, ineffective delivery of treatment, or use of inappropriate treatment. The decisions in these cases reflect an expanding awareness of the legal right of institutionalized individuals not only to receive treatment but to be allowed access to systematically planned programming that meets the varied needs of the resident.

J. TODD STEPHENS
University of Wisconsin at Madison
First and Second editions

KIMBERLY F. APPLEQUIST
University of Colorado at Colorado Springs
Third edition

See also Right to Education; Wyatt v. Stickney

RILEY-DAY SYNDROME

Riley-Day syndrome, also referred to as Familial Dysautonomia (FD), is a rare, autosomal (non-sex-related chromosome) recessive, genetic disease primarily afflicting Jewish children of Ashkenazi or Eastern European heritage. First described in 1949 by Drs. Riley, Day, Greeley, and Langford, Riley-Day syndrome/FD is a malfunction of the autonomic nervous system and poses severe physical, emotional, and social problems for the afflicted patients.

Individuals affected with FD are incapable of producing overflow tears with emotional crying. Frequent manifestations of FD include inappropriate perception of heat, pain, and taste, as well as labile blood pressures and gastrointestinal difficulties. Other problems experienced by individuals with FD include dysphagia (difficulty in swallowing), vomiting, aspiration and frequent pneumonia, speech and motor incoordination, poor growth, and scoliosis. Other frequent signs are delayed developmental milestones; unsteady gait; corneal anesthesia; marked sweating with excitement, eating, or the first stage of sleep; breath-holding episodes; spinal curvature (in 90% by age 13); red puffy hands; and an absence of fungiform papillae (taste buds) on the tongue (New York University Health System, 1999).

FD is transmitted by a recessive gene provided by both the mother and the father. Although the gene has been localized to the long arm of Chromosome 9 (9q31) with flanking markers, FD carrier detection can only be offered to a family that already has an affected child (McKusick, 1999). Both males and females are equally affected. As yet, there is no screening test for the general population. It is estimated that one in 30 Jews of Eastern European (Ashkenazi) extraction are carriers of the FD gene, with an estimated prevalence of 1 out of every 10,000–20,000 of Ashkenazi heritage. The prognosis of FD is poor, with most patients dying in childhood of chronic pulmonary failure or aspiration (Gandy, 1999); although, FD individuals can survive into their 20s and 30s.

There is no cure for FD, but many of the symptoms can be treated through a variety of interventions and medication. Affected individuals usually are of normal intelligence, and FD patients can be expected to function independently if treatment is begun early and major disabilities avoided. Special education services may be provided under the category of noncategorical early childhood or other health impaired. Early identification and intervention is extremely important for FD children to address developmental delays, gross motor and walking delays, and failure to thrive due to feeding difficulties and excessive vomiting. Upon entering school, speech, physical, and occupational therapies may be beneficial. Specialized feeding techniques may need to be taught. Adapted physical education may be needed to prevent injuries due to insensitivity to pain, and to monitor difficulties with the inability to control body temperature. Individuals affected with FD are prone to depression, anxieties, and even phobias. Families of FD affected children may need psychological support to assist with the emotional demands of caring for a child with a debilitating disease. For additional information contact the Dysautonomia Foundation Inc., 20 East 46th Street, New York, NY 10017. Tel.: (212) 949-6644.

REFERENCES

Gandy, A. (1999). *Pediatric database* (PEDBASE). Retrieved from http://www.icondata.com/health/pedbase/files/LAURENCE .HTM

McKusick, V. A. (1999). *OMIM*™, *Online Mendelian Inheritance in Man*. National Center for Biotechnology Information (NCBI). Retrieved from http://www.ncbi.nlm.nih.gov/

New York University Health System. (1999). Retrieved from http://www.med.nyu.edu/fd/fdcenter.html

KIM RYAN ARREDONDO
Texas A&M University

RIMLAND, BERNARD (1928–2006)

Bernard Rimland earned his BA in 1950 and MA in 1951 at San Diego State University and his PhD in experimental psychology in 1954 from Pennsylvania State University. Upon the diagnosis of his eldest son as autistic, Rimland began extensive research that led to his neural theory of infantile autism. He later founded the National Society for Autistic Children, which later became the Autism Society of America, and established the Autism Research Institute in San Diego in 1967. He served as director of the Autism Research Institute, a nonprofit organization providing parents and professionals worldwide with information on the etiology and treatment of severe behavior disorders in children.

Rimland was an early advocate of the use of behavior modification and a pioneering researcher on the effects of nutrition on behavior and mental health. In his massive review of the literature on autism in the early 1960s, Rimland found no scientific support for the widely held psychoanalytic theories that blamed supposedly unloving families for the child's severe disorder. Discarding the psychoanalytic explanation, Rimland advocated a neurophysiological cause of autism involving, in part, a possible dysfunction of the brain stem reticular formation. The reticular formation is known to play an important role in perception, and children with autism appear to have a perceptual malfunction that results in difficulty distinguishing boundaries between themselves and their surrounding world. Rimland's treatments of choice for the disorder are behavior modification and megavitamin therapy. His research and that of others have shown promising results for megavitamin therapy for treatment of autism and other childhood disorders.

Rimland's major publication contributions included *Infantile Autism: The Syndrome and Its Implications for a Neural Theory of Behavior*, which won him the Appleton-Century-Crofts Award for the 1963 Distinguished Contribution to Psychology. He published and contributed to more than 100 journal articles and served as co-editor of *Modern Therapies*.

In addition to being an honorary board member and founder of the Autism Society of America, Rimland served on 32 advisory boards for publications, research organizations, and schools for children with severe behavior disorders. He was vice president of the Academy of Orthomolecular Psychiatry and the Orthomolecular Medical Society and served as the chief technical advisor on autism for the popular film *Rain Man*.

MARY LEON PEERY
Texas A&M University
First edition

TAMARA J. MARTIN
The University of Texas
of the Permian Basin
Second edition

RISK MANAGEMENT IN SPECIAL EDUCATION

Many times educators are unaware of the relationship between school practices and legal liability. Risk management is a proactive stance that attempts to identify potential areas of liability, evaluate current policy and standards, and provide workable strategies in an attempt to prevent injury and minimize liability (Phillips, 1990). In addition, risk management allows for consistent practices among school personnel covering a wide range of situations and circumstances.

Common risk management strategies in educational settings include appropriate documentation when altering a child's instructional curriculum, specified protocol when a student has expressed suicidal feelings, adherence to state regulations and guidelines in diagnostic assessments, informed consent procedures for parents and children regarding school counseling, and maintaining adequate liability coverage (Wood, 1988). Risk management strategies for school personnel include knowing and following ethical guidelines and keeping current with professional development and standards of practice (Phillips, 1990).

REFERENCES

Phillips, B. N. (1990). Law, psychology, and education. In T. R. Kratochwill (Ed.), *Advances in school psychology* (Vol. 7, pp. 79–130). Hillsdale, NJ: Erlbaum.

Wood, R. H. (1988). *Fifty ways to avoid malpractice*. Sarasota, FL: Professional Resource Exchange.

LINDA M. MONTGOMERY
The University of Texas of the Permian Basin

RITALIN

Ritalin, the trade name for methylphenidate, is a central nervous system stimulant commonly prescribed for children with an abnormally high level of activity or with attention-deficit/hyperactivity disorder (ADHD). Ritalin is also occasionally prescribed for individuals with narcolepsy, mild depression, or withdrawn senile behavior (Shannon, Wilson, & Stang, 1995).

Although all the intricacies of Ritalin are not fully understood, it increases the attention span in ADHD children (Deglin & Vallerand, 1999). Ritalin stimulates the central nervous system with effects similar to weak amphetamines or very strong coffee. Its effects include

(a) increasing attention and reducing activity in hyperactive children, apparently by stimulating inhibitory centers (NIDAInfofax, 1998); (b) diminishing fatigue in individuals with narcolepsy; and (c) increasing motor activity and mental alertness in individuals exhibiting withdrawn senile behavior (Shannon et al., 1995).

All individuals need to be advised to take sustained released Ritalin as a whole tablet and never to crush or chew the pill. Ritalin should be taken at regular intervals during the day and only by the individual for whom it is prescribed (Deglin & Vallerand, 1999). As a stimulant medication, Ritalin may cause sleep disorders if taken late in the day (Skidmore-Roth & McKenry, 1997). To minimize insomnia, the last dose of Ritalin should be taken before 6:00 P.M. Weight loss is another potential side effect of this medication, and individuals should be advised to weigh themselves at least twice weekly (Deglin & Vallerand, 1999). Because of the combined effects of multiple stimulants, all individuals should be informed that they should refrain from drinking any caffeine-containing beverages such as cola or coffee (Skidmore-Roth & McKenry, 1997). As with any continuous medication regime, school personnel should be notified of the medication and any other health-related concerns (Wong, 1995).

Stimulant medications such as Ritalin have strong potential for abuse, and the United States Drug Enforcement Administration (DEA) has placed numerous stringent controls on Ritalin's manufacture, distribution, and prescription. Ritalin is documented to be a strong, effective, and safe medication, but the potential risks in long-term usage need further investigation (NIDAInfofax, 1998).

REFERENCES

Deglin, J., & Vallerand, A. (1999). *Davis's drug guide for nurses* (6th ed.). Philadelphia, PA: F. A. Davis.

NIDAInfofax. (1998, February 27). Retrieved from http://www.nida.nih.gov/Infofax/ritalin.html

Shannon, M., Wilson, B., & Stang, C. (1995). *Govoni & Hayes drugs and nursing implications* (8th ed.). Norwalk, CT: Appleton & Lange.

Skidmore-Roth, L., & McKenry, L. (1997). *Mosby's drug guide for nurses* (2nd ed.). St. Louis, MO: Mosby.

Wong, D. (1995). *Whaley & Wong's nursing care of infants and children* (5th ed.). St. Louis, MO: Mosby.

KARI ANDERSON
University of North Carolina at Wilmington

See also Attention-Deficit/Hyperactivity Disorder; Medical Management

ROBERTS APPERCEPTION TEST FOR CHILDREN

The Roberts Apperception Test for Children (RATC) is a personality assessment technique designed for children ages 6 to 15. The RATC is an attempt to combine the flexibility of a projective technique with the objectivity of a standardized scoring system. Similar to the Thematic Apperception Test and the Children's Apperception Test, the RATC consists of a set of drawings designed to elicit thematic stories. The test consists of 27 cards, 11 of which are parallel forms for males and females. Thus 16 cards are administered during testing, which takes 20 to 30 minutes.

The RATC is said to have significant benefits over similar project measures (McArthur & Roberts, 1982). The test manual is well designed and includes substantial information on psychometric properties of the test, administration, and scoring, as well as several case studies. The picture drawings were designed specifically for children and young adolescents and depict scenes designed to elicit common concerns. For example, specific cards portray parent/child relationships, sibling relationships, aggression, mastery, parental disagreement and affection, observation of nudity, school, and peer relationships. The test has a standardized scoring system, with scores converted to normalized T-scores based on data from a sample of 200 well-adjusted children. Materials for the following four methods may be obtained from the RATC:

1. *Adaptive scales*: Reliance on others, support for others, support for the child, limit setting, problem identification, resolution.
2. *Clinical scales*: Anxiety, aggression, depression, rejection, lack of resolution.
3. *Critical indicators*: Atypical response, maladaptive outcome, refusal.
4. *Supplementary measures*: Ego functioning, aggression, levels of projection.

A review of the RATC in the *Ninth Mental Measurements Yearbook* (Sines, 1985) describes four unpublished validity studies and concludes that the psychometric properties of the test are unimpressive. In perhaps the most substantial of these studies, 200 well-adjusted children were compared with 200 children evaluated at guidance clinics. The normal children scored higher than the children at clinics on all eight adaptive scales; however, the two groups could not be reliably differentiated on the clinical scales for anxiety, aggression, and depression.

Overall, the RATC appears to be a well-designed projective technique for children and young adolescents. The standardized scoring system, while lacking in evidence compared with purely objective measures of personality, appears to be relatively satisfactory compared with similar projective techniques.

REFERENCES

McArthur, D., & Roberts, G. (1982). *Roberts Apperception Test for Children: Test manual*. Los Angeles, CA: Western Psychological Services.

Sines, J. (1985). The Roberts Apperception Test for Children. In J. Mitchell (Ed.), *The ninth mental measurements yearbook*. Lincoln, NE: Buros Institute.

FRANCES F. WORCHEL
Texas A&M University

See also Child Psychology; Personality Assessment

ROBINOW SYNDROME

Robinow syndrome is a genetic disorder that is often called fetal face syndrome due to the characteristic facial appearance resembling that of a fetus of about 8 weeks gestation. Mesomelic dwarfism, hypoplastic genitalia, and dental abnormalities also characterize the disorder.

Robinow syndrome is a rare condition, but exact prevalence is not known. The cases of at least 84 patients have been reported (Aksit et al., 1997). The incidence of the disorder appears to be relatively higher in Turkish populations. One quarter of the reported cases in the literature are Turkish children (Aksit et al., 1997).

Characteristics

1. Craniofacial features—eyes wide apart (hypertelorism), short upturned nose, broad nasal bridge, boxlike forehead (frontal bossing), down-slanting eyes, and wide eye openings (wide palpebral fissures)

2. Dental abnormalities—crowded, crooked, missing teeth

3. Short stature and mesomelic shortening of the forearms

4. Hypoplastic (underdeveloped) genitalia

5. Normal intelligence in most cases, mildly impaired in some

6. Skeletal abnormalities—vertebral anomalies, rib defects, shortening of the ulna and radius, bifid phalanges, and scoliosis

---

The rare combination of anomalies associated with Robinow syndrome has both autosomal dominant and recessive inheritance patterns (Wilcox, Quinn, Ng, Dicks-Mireaux, & Mouriquand, 1997). The recessive type is the rarer of the two and also the more severe. Children born with the recessive version of Robinow syndrome have more marked dwarfism, multiple rib abnormalities, shorter limbs, and shorter fingers and toes (Kantaputra, Gorlin, Ukarapol, Unachak, & Sudasna, 1999).

Reconstructive surgery is often necessary in individuals with Robinow syndrome, particularly in patients with severe scoliosis. Treatment with recombinant human growth hormone has been shown to result in a significant increase in the growth rate of children with Robinow syndrome (Castells, Chakurkar, Qasi, & Bastian, 1999).

There are a number of special educational considerations regarding a child with Robinow syndrome. Developmental delays and mental retardation have been associated with 18% of individuals with the disorder (Butler & Wadlington, 1987). Therefore, psychoeducational testing and the implementation of individualized educational plans may be necessary. Because of the presence of a number of physical deformities, a child with Robinow syndrome is considerably at risk for such psychosocial difficulties as decreased self-esteem, depression, and social maladjustment. However, a child with Robinow syndrome has few physical limitations or health problems and is able to participate in regular activities, including athletics.

The prognosis for children with Robinow syndrome is quite good. Most individuals with the disorder live full lives with normal life expectancy and good health (Butler & Wadlington, 1987). Future research on the disorder will focus on the identification of the gene involved in this disorder and will try to build an understanding of this gene's role in both endocrine function and skeletal development.

REFERENCES

Aksit, S., Aydinlioglu, H., Dizdarer, G., Caglayan, S., Bektaslar, D., & Cin, A. (1997). Is the frequency of Robinow syndrome relatively high in Turkey? Four more case reports. *Clinical Genetics, 52*, 226–230.

Butler, M. G., & Wadlington, W. B. (1987). Robinow syndrome: Report of two patients and review of literature. *Clinical Genetics, 31*, 77–85.

Castells, S., Chakurkar, A., Qazi, Q., & Bastian, W. (1999). Robinow syndrome with growth hormone deficiency: Treatment with growth hormone. *Journal of Pediatric Endocrinology and Metabolism, 12*(4), 565–571.

Kantaputra, P. N., Gorlin, R. J., Ukarapol, N., Unachak, K., & Sudasna, J. (1999). Robinow (fetal face) syndrome: Report of a boy with dominant type and an infant with recessive type. *American Journal of Medical Genetics, 84*, 1–7.

Wilcox, D. T., Quinn, F. M. J., Ng, C. S., Dicks-Mireaux, C., & Mouriquand, P. D. E. (1997). Redefining the genital abnormality in the Robinow syndrome. *Journal of Urology, 157*, 2312–2314.

CASSANDRA BURNS ROMINE
Texas A&M University

ROBINSON, HALBERT B. (1925–1981) AND ROBINSON, NANCY M. (1930–)

Nancy and Hal Robinson performed extensive work in the areas of children with mental retardation, early child care, and gifted children. They coauthored *The Mentally Retarded Child: A Psychological Approach* (1976), an influential text defining the field of mental retardation and emphasizing its research base, and co-edited the *International Monograph Series on Early Child Care* (Robinson, Robinson, Wolins, Bronfenbrenner, & Richmond, 1974), which offers descriptions of early child care options of nine nations, including the United States. *Developmental approaches to giftedness and creativity* (1982) focussed on the UW Early Entrance Program, which admitted middle school-age students to the University, depending on their readiness, prior to entering high school (Robinson & Robinson, 1982).

In 1966, with Ann Peters, Hal Robinson founded the Frank Porter Graham Child Development Center at the University of North Carolina (Robinson & Robinson, 1971), and in 1969 he accepted a position at the University of Washington, Seattle (UW) as a professor of psychology. While at UW, Hal also served as the principal investigator of the Child Development Research Group (CDRG, now the Halbert Robinson Center for the Study of Capable Youth). Child Development Preschool, formerly a CDRG program (later independent of UW), focused on the identification and development of curriculum for children with advanced intellectual and academic skills (Roedell, Jackson, & Robinson, 1980).

Of their many honors, the Robinsons received the Education Award of the American Association on Mental Deficiency in 1982. Additionally, Nancy has served as editor of the *American Journal of Mental Deficiency*, and after Hal's death in 1981, she assumed the directorship of the Hal Robinson Center for the Study of Capable Youth, a position she holds today. She is also a professor of psychiatry and behavioral science at UW and has continued to publish on important topics including the counseling of highly gifted children and mathematically gifted children (Robinson, 1996; Robinson, Abbot, Berninger, Busse, & Mukhopadhyay, 1997).

REFERENCES

Robinson, H. B., & Robinson, N. M. (1971). Longitudinal development of very young children in a comprehensive day care program: The first two years. *Child Development, 42*, 1673–1683.

Robinson, H. B., Robinson, N. M., Wolins, M., Bronfenbrenner, U., & Richmond, J. B. (1974). Early child care in the United States. In H. B. Robinson & N. M. Robinson (Eds.), *International monograph series on early child care*. London, England: Gordon, Breach.

Robinson, N. M. (1996). Counseling agendas for gifted young people: A commentary. *Journal for the Education of the Gifted, 20*(2), 128–137.

Robinson, N. M., Abbot, R. D., Berninger, V. W., Busse, J., & Mukhopadhyay, S. (1997). Developmental changes in mathematically precocious young children: Longitudinal and gender effects. *Gifted Child Quarterly, 41*(4), 145–158.

Robinson, N. M., & Robinson, H. B. (1976). *The mentally retarded child: A psychological approach* (2nd ed.). New York, NY: McGraw-Hill.

Robinson, N. M., & Robinson, H. B. (1982). The optimal match: Devising the best compromise for the highly gifted student. In D. H. Feldman (Ed.), *Developmental approaches to giftedness and creativity*. San Francisco, CA: Jossey-Bass.

Roedell, W. C., Jackson, N. E., & Robinson, H. B. (1980). *Gifted young children*. New York, NY: Columbia University.

ANN E. LUPKOWSKI
Texas A&M University
First edition

TAMARA J. MARTIN
The University of Texas of the Permian Basin
Second edition

ROBOTICS

A robot is a programmable multifunctional device that is capable of performing a variety of tasks, manipulations, and locomotions. Robots come in one of four configurations: rectangular, cylindrical, spherical, and anthropomorphic articulated (Yin & Moore, 1984). These electronic devices have five characteristics that set them apart from other devices: mobility, dexterity, payload capacity, intelligence, and sensory capability. The characteristics are found singly or in combination; however, at present there is no single system that integrates all of the characteristics.

Industrial robots are known for their payload capacity. For example, the large electronic arms used on the automotive assembly lines in Japan are capable of lifting enormous weights and performing the same routines tirelessly. Other robots are recognized for their sensory capability (e.g., to sense temperature or to recognize patterns). Educational robots usually have mobility and dexterity. For example, the Health Company's robot Hero can be told to go forward, backward, left, or right. Hero's arm and hand can manipulate objects. The arm's five axes allow him to wave, gesticulate, lift objects, and drop them. Hero also speaks 64 phonemes, which means the robot can be programmed to speak almost any language. Hero can also respond to light, sound, and objects (Slesnick, 1984).

Turtle Tot is a small robot that can be programmed by young children to count, draw pictures, and move at various angles. A machine that has greater dexterity but less mobility is the Rhino XR II, which is used in college-level engineering classes. The arm is a five-axis manipulator that has a hip, shoulder, elbow, and hand. The hand is capable of pitch, roll, and grip (Shahinpoor & Singer, 1985).

In special education, robots offer the potential to perform two basic functions. First, they can serve as an extension of the teacher by interacting with students and providing instruction in a fascinating area of technology. Second, robots can be controlled by students to meet their personal needs and objectives. For individuals with disabilities, robotics can help alleviate many of the restrictions imposed by limited mobility and dexterity. For the orthopedically disabled in particular, robotics may compensate for missing or impaired human functions (Kimbler, 1984). In the future, robotics may help compensate for visual and auditory disabilities. Scientists are working on robots that will respond to voice commands and have computerized vision.

REFERENCES

Kimbler, D. L. (1984, June). *Robots and special education: The robot as extension of self*. Paper presented at Special Education Technology Research and Development Symposium, Washington, DC.

Shahinpoor, M., & Singer, N. (1985). A new instructional laboratory. *T.H.E. Journal, 13*, 54–56.

Slesnick, T. (1984). Robots and kids. *Classroom Computer Learning, 4*, 54–59.

Yin, R. K., & Moore, G. B. (1984). *Robotics, artificial intelligence, computer simulation: Future applications in special education*. (Contract No. 300-84-0135). Washington, DC: U.S. Department of Education.

ELIZABETH MCCLELLAN
Council for Exceptional Children

See also Computer Use With Students With Disabilities

ROBOTICS IN SPECIAL EDUCATION

Robotics in special education serves two potential functions. First, robotics can operate as an auxiliary to education by providing novel instruction to students, increasing motivation, and acting as an extension of the teacher in an instructional role. These auxiliary educational functions can be found in robots and robotic educational systems available today. They have been put to productive, albeit limited, use in special education. Little research has been conducted to test the efficacy of such uses.

A second, and perhaps potentially more dramatic, use of robotics for the handicapped concerns the robot as an extension of self. The robot is controlled by the individual to meet his or her personal needs and objectives and to control the environment. These functions demand a robot capable of a high level of sophistication in its logic and actions, a level not currently available in a single robotics unit (Kimbler, 1984). Nevertheless, the potential of the robot as an extension of the handicapped individual has prompted speculation concerning relevant applications and preliminary work on requisite performance characteristics.

Speculation on the usefulness of robotics has focused on handicapped conditions that limit mobility, dexterity, and interaction with the environment (Kimbler, 1984). The robot has been conceptualized as providing missing or impaired human functions under the direction of the individual with a disability. Remote control devices have been used in this manner to some extent, and individual robots have been employed in restricted environments to perform limited functions such as serving meals. However, these applications have required modification of the environment. Ideally, the capacity of the robot would be more generalized; it would perform its functions by interacting with existing environments. A second major type of disability for which robotics applications have been conceptualized is sensory impairments, including visual and auditory disabilities. In these cases, the robot would provide sensory interaction as a mobile, dexterous adaptive device, permitting individuals to perceive the environment and then to operate on the setting directly or to control the robot to interact for them.

To support these functions, certain performance characteristics are necessary. For example, mobility under internal control to accomplish external demands is required. This movement needs to be smooth, to vary in speed from very slow to quick, and to react to novel environments through sensory systems. Robotics for these purposes require both payload, or strength and manipulation for that which needs to be carried, and dexterity dimensions to support varied and precise functions. The intelligence of the robot must allow reception and transmission of information through sensory apparatus, coordination of basic motion with its command and sensory input, communication in a conversational mode, and adaptation to new settings and uses. Finally, the robot must combine these characteristics with reasonable size; for acceptable and practical use, the robot must approximate the size of an average adult but maintain adequate bulk, stability, and power.

The robot that meets these requirements is complex and beyond current capabilities. Nevertheless, research on machine intelligence, performance characteristics, and integration proceeds. Work on artificial intelligence, expert systems, real-time computing, sensing capabilities, environmental mapping, conversational input and output, and power sources continues. The present state of technology in each of these areas supports feasibility of the robotic extension but requires packaging into a single working unit (Kimbler, 1984). Additionally, philosophical issues related to the cost of such technology must be addressed before applications of robotics to improve the ability of individuals with disabilities to function in uncontrolled environments can be realized (Blaschke, 1984).

REFERENCES

Blaschke, C. (1984). *Market profile report: Technology and special education*. Falls Church, VA: Project Tech Mark, Education TURNKEY Systems.

Kimbler, D. L. (1984). Robots and special education: The robot as extension of self. *Peabody Journal of Education, 62*, 67–76.

LYNN S. FUCHS
Peabody College, Vanderbilt University

ROCHESTER METHOD

The Rochester method is a multisensory procedure for instructing deaf children in which speech reading is simultaneously supplemented by finger spelling and auditory amplification. The language of signs is wholly excluded from this procedure of instruction (Quigley & Young, 1965).

The Rochester method was established by Zenos Westerfelt at the Rochester School for the Deaf in Rochester, New York, in 1878. Westerfelt was convinced that finger spelling was the best means of teaching deaf children grammatically correct language. He believed that the easy visibility of finger spelling could help in lip reading as well as in speech instruction. (Levine, 1981). The Rochester method is directly related to the method used by Juan Pablo Binet of Spain. He advocated the use of a combination of a one-handed alphabet and speech in his book *The Simplification of Sounds and the Art of Teaching Mutes to Speak*, published in 1620. This method had a resurgence in the Soviet Union in the 1950s under the name neo-oralism, and in the United States in the 1960s (Moores, 1982).

Various studies have assessed the effectiveness of the Rochester method as an educational tool. In reviewing these Quigley (1984) reported that, in general, researchers concluded that children exposed to the Rochester method performed better than comparison groups in finger spelling, speech reading, written language, and reading. They also found that, when good oral techniques are used in conjunction with finger spelling, there are no detrimental effects to the acquisition of oral skills.

The Rochester Method was introduced in an attempt to allow deaf people to participate more fully in general society. It was used in several schools in America and in Europe and continued for approximately 70 years. Because it was a very difficult and required technical skill to execute, both teachers and students began to complain that it was not practical. It was estimated that it took one third of class time to work on lip reading and speech, leaving little time for academics or learning the technical skills of finger spelling. This reduced the time for learning and teachers and students felt that the benefits were not great enough for such a sacrifice in time (Rosenberg-Naparsteck, 2002). The interesting question of whether the method had any long-lasting effect was raised. Some research demonstrated that students using this method acquired better language skills while in 2003 Gunsauls pointed out that American Sign Language contains more finger spelling than any other sign language in the world (Gunsauls, 2003). Since the use of the Rochester Method has greatly decreased in America, today's educators are trying to personalize the child's learning style to the communication method selected instead of trying to fit all children to one model of learning (Musselman, 2000).

REFERENCES

Gunsauls, D. C. (2003). How the alphabet came to be used in a sign language. *Sign Language Studies, 4*, 10–33, 91.

Musselman, C. (2000). How do children who can't hear learn to read an alphabet script? A review of the literature on reading and deafness. *Journal of Deaf Studies and Deaf Education, 5*, 9–31

Levine, E. (1981). *The ecology of early deafness*. New York, NY: Columbia University Press.

Moores, D. (1982). *Educating the deaf: Psychology, principles, and practices*. Boston, MA: Houghton Mifflin.

Quigley, S. (1984). *Language and deafness*. San Diego, CA: College-Hill.

Quigley, S., & Young, J. (Eds.). (1965). *Interpreting for deaf people*. Washington, DC: U.S. Department of Health, Education, and Welfare.

Rosenberg-Naparsteck, R. (2002). The Rochester School for the Deaf. *Rochester History, LXIV*, 1–23.

ROSEMARY GAFNEY
Hunter College, City University of New York

PATRICIA SCHERER
International Center on Deafness and the Arts
Fourth edition

See also **Deaf; Sign Language; Total Communication**

ROEPER REVIEW

The *Roeper Review*, published since 1977 by the Roeper Institute, is a journal on the education of gifted students. It originated as an information periodical for parents whose children attended the Roeper School. The journal has three purposes: (1) presenting philosophical, moral, and academic issues that are related to the lives and experiences of gifted and talented persons; (2) presenting various views on those issues; and (3) translating theory into practice for use at school, at home, and in the general community.

The audience and authors for *Roeper Review* include practicing teachers and administrators, teacher-educators, psychologists, and scientists. They are served by in-depth coverage of important topics in each issue. Some examples of issues discussed in past editions are teacher education for gifted education, social studies education for the gifted, special subpopulations among gifted students, and perceptions of gifted students and their education. The mailing address is *Roeper Review*, 41190 Woodward Avenue, Bloomfield Hills, MI 48304-5020. Website: http://roeper.org/.

ANN E. LUPKOWSKI
Texas A&M University

ROGER, HARRIET B. (1834–1919)

Harriet B. Roger began the first oral school for the instruction of the deaf in the United States in 1863 when she accepted a deaf child as a private pupil in her home. With published accounts of the instruction of the deaf in Germany to guide her, she taught herself how to instruct the child. Her success in this undertaking led to the admission of other deaf children. One of these was Mabel Hubbard, who became Mrs. Alexander Graham Bell and whose father, a prominent lawyer, obtained legislation for the creation of an oral school for the deaf in Massachusetts. Hubbard formed this school by moving Roger's school to Northampton, where, in 1867, they established the Clarke School for the Deaf, the second purely oral school for the deaf in the United States (the Lexington School for the Deaf having opened in New York City earlier that year). Roger, the first teacher and the instructional leader of the Clarke School, remained there until her retirement in 1886.

REFERENCE

Lane, H. (1984). *When the mind hears*. New York, NY: Random House.

PAUL IRVINE
Katonah, New York

ROOS, PHILIP (1930–   )

Born in Brussels, Belgium, Philip Roos obtained his BS in 1949 in biology and psychology with highest distinction from Stanford University and from 1950 to 1951 did postgraduate work there in statistics and clinical and child psychology. He then earned his PhD in 1955 in clinical psychology at the University of Texas, Austin. Roos is currently President of Roos & Associates in Hurst, Texas, a consulting firm providing training to business and industry, and he maintains a private clinical psychology practice as well.

Roos advocates the early use of behavior modification with institutionalized individuals with severe and profound retardation and adolescents with mild retardation who exhibit behavior disorders (Roos & Oliver, 1970). He is the originator of the Developmental Model, used for programming persons with mental retardation, emphasizing the potency of expectations in working with individuals with handicaps, and evaluating the impact of the interpersonal environment in shaping individual development. Roos' model has been the basis for many programs for those with mental retardation and a component of numerous national accreditation standards of agencies working with this population.

Roos has been an active advocate on behalf of children with disabilities and their families, assisting them in dealing with both emotional and practical frustrations, helping to individualize services, and aiding in the establishment of their rights (Roos, 1983). His service to the profession has included the positions of associate commissioner in the Division of Mental Retardation of the New York State Department of Mental Hygiene (1967–1968); national executive director of both the Association of Retarded Citizens (1969–1983) and Mothers Against Drunk Driving (1983–1984); and as a member of the board of directors of the Sunny Von Bulow Victim Advocacy Center (1986–1994). Roos has also been recognized in *Who's Who in America*, *Who's Who in the South and Southwest*, and *Who's Who in Medicine and Healthcare*.

REFERENCES

Roos, P. (1983). Advocate groups of the mentally retarded. In J. L. Matson & J. Mulick (Eds.), *Comprehensive handbook of mental retardation*. New York, NY: Pergamon Press.

Roos, P., & Oliver, M. (1970). Evaluation of operant conditioning with institutionalized retarded children. *American Journal of Mental Deficiency, 74*, 325–330.

E. VALERIE HEWITT
Texas A&M University
First edition

TAMARA J. MARTIN
The University of Texas of the Permian Basin
Second edition

RORSCHACH

The Rorschach, developed by Hermann Rorschach in 1921, is generally regarded as the most widely used projective personality assessment technique (Lubin, Wallis, & Paine, 1971). Five distinct scoring systems developed following Rorschach's death in 1922. Exner's Comprehensive Rorschach System (Exner, 1974, 1978; Exner & Weiner, 1982) has provided the fragmented Rorschach community with a common methodology, language, and literature; it is one of the most frequently used systems.

The Rorschach test stimuli consist of 10 inkblots, half achromatic and half with different degrees of color. Cards are presented individually to subjects, who are allowed to give as many responses as they wish describing "what the cards might be." Determinants that are scored include location, form, color, shading, movement, and quality and quantity of responses. Information obtained from the scored protocol includes personality state and trait characteristics, coping style, extent and quality of self-focus, quality of reality testing, likelihood of suicidal ideation or schizophrenia, depression, maturity, and complexity of psychological operations. Scoring and interpretation of the Rorschach, which is time-consuming and detailed, requires that the examiner be thoroughly trained in Rorschach assessment.

Criticisms of the Rorschach include the length of the time needed for administration, scoring, and interpretation, and the fact that accurate usage is highly dependent on the clinical skills of the administrator. When used to gather descriptive clinical information, the Rorschach is considered to be an empirically valid instrument (Maloney & Glasser, 1982; Parker, 1983). Gittelman-Klein (1978) has presented an in-depth review of the validity of projective techniques, with positive results.

REFERENCES

Exner, J. E. (1974). *The Rorschach: A comprehensive system. Vol. 1: Basic foundations.* New York, NY: Wiley.

Exner, J. E. (1978). *The Rorschach: A comprehensive system. Vol. 2: Current research and advanced interpretation.* New York, NY: Wiley.

Exner, J. E., & Weiner, I. B. (1982). *The Rorschach: A comprehensive system. Vol. 3: Assessment of children and adolescents.* New York, NY: Wiley.

Gittelman-Klein, R. (1978). Validity of projective tests for psychodiagnosis in children. In R. L. Spitzer & D. F. Klein (Eds.), *Critical issues in psychiatric diagnosis.* New York, NY: Raven.

Lubin, B., Wallis, R. R., & Paine, C. (1971). Patterns of psychological test usage in the United States: 1935–1969. *Professional Psychology, 2,* 70–74.

Maloney, M. P., & Glasser, A. (1982). An evaluation of the clinical utility of the Draw-A-Person test. *Journal of Clinical Psychology, 38,* 183–190.

Parker, K. A. (1983). A meta-analysis of the reliability and validity of the Rorschach. *Journal of Personality Assessment, 47,* 227–231.

CONSTANCE Y. CELAYA
Irving, Texas

FRANCES F. WORCHEL
Texas A&M University

RORSCHACH INKBLOT TEST

The Rorschach inkblot test is a widely used projective personality assessment technique. The test is administered in a nondirective fashion (Exner, 1995). Respondents are asked to describe what they can see in a series of 10 inkblots. Administration time with children is approximately 30 minutes, with interpretation taking 30 to 45 minutes. Examiners transcribe the respondent's words and identify the visual percepts, which are then coded and tabulated through an extensively researched, empirically based system. Considerable examiner training is necessary to accomplish the administration, coding, and interpretation tasks.

The Comprehensive System (Exner, 1993) approach makes the Rorschach an objective multiscale performance and personality test. Its administration and coding standards, normative data, and accumulated research provide a sturdy empirical basis to the test. Test-retest reliability for children is as expected given developmental considerations: Some variables demonstrate relatively strong test-retest reliability for a year or two during the primary grade school years (Exner, Thomas, & Mason, 1985; Exner & Weiner, 1995). Test-retest reliability increases gradually, so that almost all measures of trait variables are relatively stable by age 18.

The test yields a large number of variables related to the domains of cognition, affect, interpersonal perception, self-perception, and coping styles, and also various characteristics related to diagnostic categories. Personality, coping, and problem-solving interpretations can be synthesized, along with observations about social, school, family, and problem behaviors, into a description of the psychological functioning of the child.

Criticism of the test has been a popular rallying cry, but empirical reports indicate adequate validity and utility, particularly for issues that are not readily accessible through self-report, brief interview, or observation (Exner, 1993; Viglione, 1999). The fact that all responses are formulated by the subject without prefabrication from test developers allows the test to access personally meaningful information. For example, the Rorschach can shed light on issues that the respondent may be unwilling or unable to express. No other instrument yields such an efficient, yet comprehensive, empirically based understanding of the individual. Criticism about the test may result from a misunderstanding of its so-called projective components. This is not a test of imagination, and it goes far beyond projective processes, despite unfortunate and inaccurate characterizations (e.g., Dawes, 1994).

Rorschach variables have demonstrated concurrent and predictive validity for both academic achievement test scores and classroom performance by young children, even after the effects of intelligence were statistically removed (e.g., Russ, 1980, 1981; Wulach, 1977). These results support the belief that the Rorschach addresses cognitive motivational trends and real-life application of abilities.

As far as the special education evaluation goals of truly understanding a child, the Rorschach can help to identify the psychological factors associated with the expression of observed strengths and weaknesses. For example, the test can help to identify and to understand emotional and psychological disturbances that impede learning, difficulties with peer and authority relationships, inappropriate behaviors that interfere with school performance and socialization, and problem-solving styles that result in poor performance despite intellectual abilities. However, the use of the Rorschach remains controversial, and an opposing view of its reliability and validity is available in Sechrest, Stickle, and Stewart (1998).

REFERENCES

Dawes, R. M. (1994). *House of cards: Psychology and psychotherapy built on myth.* New York, NY: Free Press.

Exner, J. E. (1993). *The Rorschach: A comprehensive system. Vol. 1: Basic foundations* (3rd ed.). New York, NY: Wiley.

Exner, J. E. (1995). *A Rorschach workbook for the comprehensive system* (4th ed.). Asheville, NC: Rorschach Workshops.

Exner, J. E., Thomas, E. A., & Mason, B. J. (1985). Children's Rorschachs: Description and prediction. *Journal of Personality Assessment, 49,* 13–20.

Exner, J. E., & Weiner, I. B. (1995). *The Rorschach: A comprehensive system. Vol. 3: Assessment of children and adolescents* (2nd ed.). New York, NY: Wiley.

Russ, S. W. (1980). Primary process integration on the Rorschach and achievement in children. *Journal of Personality Assessment, 44,* 338–344.

Russ, S. W. (1981). Primary process integration on the Rorschach and achievement in children: A follow-up study. *Journal of Personality Assessment, 45,* 473–477.

Sechrest, L., Stickle, T., & Stewart, M. (1998). The role of assessment in clinical psychology. In C. R. Reynolds (Ed.), Assessment, Vol. 4 of A. Bellack & M. Hersen (Eds.), *Comprehensive clinical psychology* (pp. 1–32). Oxford, England: Elsevier Science.

Viglione, D. J. (1999). A review of recent research addressing the utility of the Rorschach. *Psychological Assessment, 11,* 251–265.

Wulach, J. S. (1977). Piagetian cognitive development and primary process thinking in children. *Journal of Personality Assessment, 41,* 230–237.

DONALD J. VIGLIONE
California School of Professional Psychology

ROSS INFORMATION PROCESSING ASSESSMENT

The Ross Information Processing Assessment–Second Edition (RIPA-2; Ross-Swain, 1996) provides quantifiable data for profiling 10 key areas basic to communicative and cognitive functioning: Immediate Memory, Recent Memory, Temporal Orientation (Recent and Remote Memory), Spatial Orientation, Orientation to Environment, Recall of General Information, Problem Solving and Abstract Reasoning, Organization, and Auditory Processing and Retention. The RIPA-2 enables the examiner to quantify cognitive-linguistic deficits, determine severity levels for specific skill areas, and develop rehabilitation goals and objectives.

The study sample included 126 individuals with traumatic brain injury in 17 states and was representative of TBI demographics for gender, ethnicity, and socioeconomic status. Raw scores are converted to standard scores. Reliability and validity studies performed on individuals with traumatic brain injury (TBI) are reported. Internal consistency reliability was investigated, and the mean reliability coefficient for RIPA-2 subtests was .85, with a range of .67 to .91. Content, construct, and criterion-related validity are reported in the manual.

The earlier edition of RIPA-2 was reviewed in *Eleventh Mental Measurements Yearbook* and *Test Critiques;* references for the newest edition of the instrument are unavailable because of its recent publication date. Franzen (1988) reported that the RIPA appeared to be a good beginning toward producing an instrument capable of profiling the different areas of information processing that might be affected by diffuse or right-hemisphere injury. Ehrlich (1992) felt that the instrument measured selected verbally mediated aspects and could be a useful tool in a clinical setting.

The Ross Information Processing Assessment–Geriatric (RIPA-G; Ross-Swain & Fogle, 1996) is an adaptation that is designed for residents in skilled nursing facilities (SNFs), hospitals, and clinics. In addition to standard questions and stimulus items used for assessing cognitive-linguistic deficits, the RIPA-G incorporates questions from the Minimum Data Set used by nursing staffs in SNFs. These questions provide correlational data with nursing staff's assessments of patients' cognitive-linguistic abilities. Percentile ranks, standard scores, and composite quotients are provided for individual subtests, skill areas, and overall cognitive-linguistic functioning. Periodic retesting provides objective data to assess treatment efficacy and documents progress often required for Medicare and third-party payment. Internal consistency reliability coefficients of the RIPA-G were found to be .80 or greater.

The Ross Information Processing Assessment–Primary (Ross-Swain, 1999) is designed for children ages 5 through 12 who have had a traumatic brain injury, experienced other neuropathologies such as seizure disorders or anoxia, or exhibit learning disabilities or weaknesses that interfere with learning acquisition. The eight subtests measure immediate and recent memory, spatial orientation, temporal orientation, organization, problem solving, abstract reasoning, and recall of general information.

The RIPA-P was standardized on 114 individuals ages 5 through 12 identified as having a traumatic brain injury, learning disability, or other neuropathology affecting information processing. The majority of five reliability coefficients were found to be .80 or above, and more than a third of them were over .90. Validity studies show that the test discriminates between "normal" and LD or neurological problems. Item discrimination coefficients for the RIPA-P range from .36 to .81. Norms include children who have learning disabilities.

REFERENCES

Ehrlich, J. (1992). Review of the Ross Information Processing Assessment. In J. J. Kramer & J. C. Conoley (Eds.), *The eleventh mental measurements yearbook* (pp. 775–776). Lincoln: Buros Institute of Mental Measurements, University of Nebraska Press.

Franzen, M. D. (1988). Review of the Ross Information Processing Assessment. In D. J. Keyser & R. C. Sweetland (Eds.), *Test critiques–Volume VII* (pp. 496–498). Austin, TX: PRO-ED.

Ross-Swain, D. (1996). *Ross Information Processing Assessment–Second edition*. Austin, TX: PRO-ED.

Ross-Swain, D. (1999). *Ross Information Processing Assessment–Primary*. Austin, TX: PRO-ED.

Ross-Swain, D., & Fogle, P. (1996). *Ross Information Processing Assessment–Geriatric*. Austin, TX: PRO-ED.

TADDY MADDOX
PRO-ED, Inc.

ROSWELL-CHALL DIAGNOSTIC READING TEST OF WORD ANALYSIS

The Roswell-Chall Diagnostic Reading Test (Roswell & Chall, 1978) was developed to evaluate the word analysis and word recognition skills of pupils reading at the first-through fourth-grade levels. It may also be used with pupils who are reading at higher levels where there is a suspicion of decoding and word recognition difficulties or for research and program evaluation.

Two comparable forms of the test are available. Each is individually administered. The test has 10 main subtests and four extended evaluation subtests. All of the subtests or only those deemed appropriate may be given. The following skills are measured: high-frequency words, single consonant sounds, consonant diagrams, consonant blends, short vowel words, short and long vowel sounds, rule of silent e's, vowel diagrams, common diphthongs and vowels controlled by *r*, and syllabication (and compound words). The extended evaluation subtests include naming capital letters, naming lower-case letters, encoding single consonants, and encoding phonetically regular words.

The test takes approximately 10 minutes to administer, score, and interpret. Score interpretations are provided in the manual. The test has good reliability and validity. Users should be concerned about the size and somewhat limited nature of the norm sample; therefore, the administrator should be knowledgeable in the kinds of skills needed in most individual testing situations and, in order to interpret the test accurately, be a relatively skilled reading clinician.

REFERENCE

Roswell, F. G., & Chall, J. S. (1978). *Manual of instructions: Roswell-Chall Diagnostic Reading Test of Word Analysis Skills, revised and extended*. LaJolla, CA: Essay Press.

RONALD V. SCHMELZER
Eastern Kentucky University

ROTHMUND-THOMPSON SYNDROME

Rothmund-Thomson syndrome (RTS) is a rare, heritable disorder of the skin and skin derivatives (hair and nails). Approximately 50% of affected individuals will also develop cataracts during the first decade of life. The etiology of RTS is unknown. There are no data regarding its frequency in the general population. The syndrome was first described in 1868 by a German ophthalmologist (Rothmund), who reported several cases in an inbred population near Munich. More than 200 examples of RTS have appeared in the medical literature.

The pattern of inheritance in RTS is autosomal recessive. The disease appears to be far more common in females than it is in males.

Characteristics

1. Wide variation in clinical manifestations of the disorder.

2. Short stature with prenatal growth deficiency.

3. Splotchy redness of the skin, rarely present at birth, that usually begins by 3–12 months of age. Within a few years, these changes progress to *poikiloderma*. This term encompasses a variety of dermal abnormalities, including dilation of blood vessels (telangiectasia), scarring, depigmentation, irregular hyperpigmentation, and atrophy (thinning). These findings give the skin a peculiar and characteristic marbled appearance. Sun-exposed skin is most commonly affected, but the buttocks are also frequently involved. About one third of patients have wart-like lesions; 20% experience blistering prior to the appearance of poikiloderma. Photosensitivity (exaggerated response to sunlight) appears in 35% of patients.

4. Sparse hair that grays early. Thinning of scalp, facial, eyebrow, eyelash, and pubic hair is common. Most patients are bald by age 20–30.

5. Fifty percent of patients develop cataracts in both eyes between 2 and 7 years of age.

6. Small hands and feet, underdeveloped or absent thumbs, syndactyly (webbing or fusion of digits), absent kneecap, clubfoot, and cystic bone changes. Increased incidence of osteoporosis and osteosarcoma (bone cancer).

7. Prominent forehead; small, "saddle" nose.

8. Underdeveloped or absent teeth, dental decay.

9. Small, malformed nails.

10. Skin cancer (basal and squamous cell carcinoma).

11. Five to 13% incidence of mental deficiency.

RTS may engender skin disfigurement severe enough to require plastic surgery. Cataracts causing significant visual impairment should be removed. Hair, nail, and tooth deformities may demand considerable cosmetic attention to improve appearance. Growth deficiency secondary to growth hormone inadequacy may respond to replacement therapy.

Because 5%–13% of children with RTS have some degree of mental deficiency, a neuropsychological evaluation will be helpful to evaluate cognitive strengths and weaknesses. Based on those results, modifications can be implemented if they are needed. Vision support services are available under the special education umbrella for children who develop cataracts and require assistance.

Most patients with RTS have normal mental development and can anticipate normal life expectancy. However, they are at increased risk for developing skin cancer and other types of noncutaneous malignancies. Frequent screening for these problems combined with prompt treatment assures the best prognosis.

For more information, please contact National Institutes of Health/National Arthritis and Musculoskeletal and Skin Diseases Information Clearinghouse, 1 AMS Circle, Bethesda, MD 20892-3675. Tel.: (301) 495-4484.

This entry has been informed by the sources listed below.

REFERENCES

Darmstadt, G. L. (2000). Photosensitivity. In R. E. Behrman, R. M. Kleigman, & H. B. Jenson (Eds.), *Nelson textbook of pediatrics* (16th ed., p. 2001). Philadelphia, PA: Saunders.

Jones, K. (1997). *Smith's recognizable patterns of human malformation* (5th ed.). Philadelphia, PA: Saunders.

National Organization for Rare Disorders. (1997). *Rothmund-Thomson syndrome*. Retrieved from http://www.stepstn.com/cgi-win/nord.exe?proc=GetDocument&rectype=0&recnum=694

BARRY H. DAVISON
Ennis, Texas

JOAN W. MAYFIELD
Baylor Pediatric Specialty Services
Dallas, Texas

ROUSSEAU, JEAN J. (1712–1778)

Jean Jacques Rousseau, French-Swiss philosopher and moralist, revolutionized child-rearing and educational practices with the publication, in 1762, of *Emile*, a treatise on education in the form of a novel. Rousseau contended that childhood is not merely a period of preparation for adulthood to be endured, but a developmental stage to be cherished and enjoyed. He enjoined parents and educators to be guided by the interests and capacities of the child, and was the first writer to propose that the study of the child should be the basis for the child's education. Probably every major educational reform since the 18th century can be traced in some way to Rousseau, and indebtedness to him is clear in the works of Pestalozzi, Froebel, Montessori, and Dewey. An eloquent writer, Rousseau's works on man's relationship with nature, as well as his writings on social, political, and educational matters, were major contributions to the literature of his day.

This entry has been informed by the sources listed below.

REFERENCES

Boyd, W. (1963). *The educational theory of Jean Jacques Rousseau.* New York, NY: Russell & Russell.

Rousseau, J. J. (1969). *Emile.* New York, NY: Dutton.

PAUL IRVINE
Katonah, New York

REFERENCES

Lyon, G., Adams, R. D., & Kolodny, E. H. (1996). *Neurology of hereditary metabolic diseases of children.* New York, NY: McGraw-Hill.

Plante-Bordeneuve, V., Guiochon-Mantel, A., Lacrois, C., Lapresle, J., & Said, G. (1999). The Roussy-Levy family: From the original description to the gene. *Annals of Neurology, 46,* 770–773.

VIRDETTE L. BRUMM
Children's Hospital, Los Angeles Keck / USC School of Medicine

ROUSSY-LEVY SYNDROME

Roussy-Levy syndrome (RSL) is a movement disorder with onset in early childhood. The disorder was first identified in 1926. It is an autosomal dominant inherited degenerative disease of the central nervous system characterized predominantly by ataxia, high arched feet, and areflexia; it is eventually associated with distal muscle atrophy, postural tremor, and minor sensory loss. Slow nerve conduction and demyelination of nerve fibers led to consideration of RLS as a variant of demyelinating Charcot-Marie-Tooth disease (Plante-Bordeneuve, Guiochon-Mantel, Lacrois, Lapresle, & Said, 1999).

Characteristics

1. Onset in early childhood.
2. Slowly progressive, degenerative disease of the central nervous system.
3. Prominent features include delayed motor milestones (i.e., delayed walking and maintaining balance) and an unsteady gait during early childhood, with foot deformities and areflexia.
4. Associated with distal muscle atrophy and weakness, clumsiness, postural tremor, and distal sensory loss.
5. Atrophy of the muscles of the lower extremities, with a pattern of wasting similar to that observed in Charcot-Marie-Tooth disease.

The course of RLS tends to be homogeneous. In most cases, the disease progresses very slowly and remains benign, with only mild to moderate functional handicap and normal life expectancy (Lyon, Adams, & Kolodny, 1996). However, prognosis may be poor due to hypertrophic cardiomyopathy with progression to intractable congestive heart failure, which is the cause of death for many patients. Research is needed to determine the cause of gait ataxia and essential tremor, which distinguish this syndrome from Charcot-Marie-Tooth syndrome.

RUBELLA

Rubella, commonly known as German measles, is a viral infection that primarily affects the skin and lymph glands (March of Dimes, 1999). Although the infection is usually benign in children and adults, it poses a significant threat to pregnant women and their fetuses. Approximately 25% of infants whose mothers contract rubella during the first trimester of pregnancy have one or more birth defects, known collectively as congenital rubella syndrome (CRS); however, infants whose mothers are infected after the 20th week of pregnancy are largely unaffected (Lee & Bowden, 2000). Congenital rubella syndrome has been associated with multiple organ and system malformations, including cardiac, ocular, central nervous system, and skeletal abnormalities (March of Dimes, 1999), and more recently with the onset of schizophrenia in adulthood (Brown et al., 2001).

The pathophysiology of rubella has been confirmed as a single-stranded RNA togavirus that is transmitted through respiratory droplets (Dyne, 2001); replicates in the nasopharyngeal area and lymph nodes; and subsequently spreads to the skin, central nervous system, synovial fluid, and (through the placenta) the developing fetus. Although the specific link between the rubella virus and teratogenecity in the fetus has not been clearly established, it is thought that cell growth inhibition is somehow implicated (Lee & Bowden, 2000). Rubella is known to be highly contagious; about 10% of young adults and 20% of women of childbearing age are susceptible to the virus (National Coalition for Adult Immunization, 2000). The incidence of rubella in the United States was reported to be 20,000 cases in 1964; however, the introduction of large-scale vaccination programs in 1969 has resulted in a significant reduction in the number of new cases. Despite comprehensive efforts by health care professionals, outbreaks of rubella continue to occur in the United States—most recently in upstate New York in 1998 (among young adult Hispanic males; Danovaro-Holliday et al., 2000) and in Nebraska in 1999 (Dyne, 2001). Rubella is endemic throughout the world (Lee & Bowden, 2000) but is more common in countries such as Ethiopia and Greece where a vaccination program is not consistently used (King, 1999).

Characteristics

1. Rubella in childhood may begin with 1 or 2 days of low-grade fever (99–100 °F) and swollen glands in the neck or behind the ears. On the 2nd or 3rd day, a rash appears at the hairline and spreads downward to the rest of the body. The rash does not itch and generally lasts up to 5 days.

2. Other symptoms such as headache, joint pain, loss of appetite, and sore throat are more common in infected adults and teenagers than in children.

3. All symptoms of rubella appear within 12 to 23 days after infection. Rubella is contagious from 7 days before to 5–7 days after the appearance of the rash.

4. Characteristics of CRS may include visual defects, hearing loss (Niedzielska, Katska, & Szymula, 2000), heart defects, mental retardation, and (rarely) cerebral palsy.

5. Infants with CRS may be of low birth weight and may experience temporary problems with feeding, liver and spleen enlargement, diarrhea, pneumonia, meningitis, or anemia. Occasionally, reddish-purple spots that bleed easily may appear on the face or body (March of Dimes, 1999).

Rubella is initially diagnosed upon clinical examination; however, it is confirmed by a positive serological test for rubella immunoglobulin M (IgM) antibody, a substantial increase in titers in serum rubella immunoglobulin G (IgG) antibody levels, or isolation of rubella virus (Dyne, 2001). The most effective approach to eradicating rubella is a three-pronged, preventive regimen that includes (1) vaccination of all children, (2) screening of women of child-bearing age for rubella immunity, and (3) vaccination of those susceptible to rubella. Immunization is successful in 97% of patients, with vaccine-induced antibodies persisting for at least 10 years (King, 1999). The American Academy of Pediatrics (1998) recommends that children be immunized beginning at 12–15 months of age and again at school entry, at 4–6 years of age; however, high coverage with the first dose remains critical (Paulo, Gomes, Casinhas, Horta, & Dominguez, 2000). There is some controversy regarding the relative merits of monovalent (Birchard, 2000) versus multivalent vaccines (Samoilovich et al., 2000); however, the combined measles-mumps-rubella (MMR) vaccine is used most frequently in the United States. Although adverse reactions to the vaccine are uncommon after age 6, mild reactions such as fever (Virtanen, Peltola, Paunio, & Heinonen, 2000) and temporary cerebellar ataxia (Plesner et al., 2000) have been reported in children under the age of 6. Use of the MMR vaccine has recently been linked with autism, which has caused a public outcry (Birchard, 2000); however, extensive studies by Dales, Hammer, and Smith (2001) have failed to corroborate this risk. Overall, the benefits of vaccination far outweigh the risks associated with lack of immunity against rubella.

Treatment of rubella in children and adults is symptomatic, with medications containing acetaminophen, NSAIDS, or antihistamines often prescribed for temporary relief. Children with congenital rubella syndrome may qualify for special educational services under the categories of physical or multiple disabilities and must have their needs addressed through a comprehensive individualized educational program (IEP). Surgical intervention with follow-up care may be necessary for children with cardiac and visual defects, and infants with hearing or vision losses may benefit from special education programs that provide early intervention and build communication and learning skills. Psychoeducational interventions for children with congenital rubella syndrome vary with degree of involvement. Children with cognitive delays will benefit from early intervention and will benefit later from placement in inclusive classrooms, depending on their level of functioning. Children with physical disabilities may need assistance in the school environment; others with multiple disabilities may require early intervention from a team of professionals. Prognosis for rubella in children and adults is positive, with the infection taking a mild, limited course. Prognosis for children with congenital rubella syndrome is variable and depends on severity.

Future research efforts must be directed toward studying the seroepidemiology of rubella, the teratogenecity of the rubella virus, and the links between prenatal exposure to the virus and subsequent problems in adulthood. Additional studies are needed to study the effectiveness of single versus combined vaccines as well as ways to reduce the incidence of rubella in at-risk populations.

REFERENCES

American Academy of Pediatrics. (1998). Policy statement: Age for routine administration of the second dose of measles-mumps-rubella vaccine. (RE9802). *Pediatrics, 101*(1), 129–133.

Birchard, K. (2000). Ireland holds hearing on merits of measles, mumps, and rubella vaccine. *Lancet, 356*(9242), 1665.

Brown, A. S., Cohen, P., Harkavy-Friedman, J., Babulas, V., Malaspina, D., Gorman, J. M., . . . Susser, E. S. (2001). Prenatal rubella, premorbid abnormalities, and adult schizophrenia. *Biological Psychiatry, 49*(6), 473–486.

Dales, L., Hammer, S. J., & Smith, N. J. (2001). Time trends in autism and in MMR immunization coverage in California.

Journal of the American Medical Association, 285(9), 1183–1185.

Danovaro-Holliday, M. C., LeBaron, C. W., Allensworth, C., Raymond, R., Borden, T. G., Murray, A. B., et al. (2000). A large rubella outbreak with spread from the workplace to the community. *Journal of the American Medical Association, 284*(21), 2733–2739.

Dyne, P. (2001). *Rubella.* Retrieved from http://www.emedicine .com/emerg/topic388.htm

King, S. (1999). Vaccination policies: Individual rights (upsilon) community health. *British Medical Journal, 319*(7223), 1448–1449.

Lee, J. Y., & Bowden, D. S. (2000). Rubella virus replication and links to teratogenicity. *Clinical Microbiological Reviews, 13*(4), 571–587.

March of Dimes. (1999). *Rubella: Public health education information sheet.* Retrieved from http://www.marchofdimes.com/ baby/rubella-and-your-baby.aspx

National Coalition for Adult Immunization. (2000). *Facts about rubella for adults.* Retrieved from http://www.n.d.org/ factsheets/rubellaadult.html

Niedzielska, G., Katska, E., & Szymula, D. (2000). Hearing defects in children born of mothers suffering from rubella in the first trimester of pregnancy. *International Journal of Pediatric Otorhinolaryngology, 54*(1), 1–5.

Paulo, A. C., Gomes, M. C., Casinhas, A. C., Horta, A., & Dominguez, T. (2000). Multiple dose vaccination against childhood diseases: High coverage with the first dose remains crucial for eradication. *The IMA Journal of Mathematics Applied in Medicine and Biology, 17*(3), 201–212.

Plesner, A. M., Hansen, F. J., Taudorf, K., Nielsen, L. H., Larsen, C. B., & Pedersen, E. (2000). Gait disturbance interpreted as cerebellar ataxia after MMR vaccination at 15 months of age: A follow-up study. *Acta Paediatrica, 89*(1), 58–63.

Samoilovich, E. O., Kapustik, L. A., Feldman, E. V., Yermolovich, M. A., Svirchevskaya, A. J., Zakharenko, D. E., . . . Titov, L. P. (2000). The immunogenicity and reactogenicity of the trivalent vaccine, Trimovax, indicated for prevention of measles, mumps, and rubella, in 12-month-old children in Belarus. *Central European Journal of Public Health, 8*(3), 160–163.

Virtanen, M., Peltola, H., Paunio, M., & Heinonen, O. P. (2000). Day-to-day reactogenicity and the healthy vaccine effect of measles-mumps-rubella vaccination. *Pediatrics, 106*(5), E62.

MARY M. CHITTOORAN
JILL E. CROWLEY
Saint Louis University

See *also* Cataracts; Congenital Disorders; Mental Retardation

RUBENSTEIN-TAYBI SYNDROME (See National Organization for Rare Disorders)

RUMINATION DISORDER

Rumination disorder is mainly an eating disorder of infancy and childhood. After a period of normal development, an infant or child begins repeatedly and voluntarily to regurgitate and either spit out or (more commonly) rechew food. The food is regurgitated shortly after feeding. Retching or nausea associated with normal regurgitation is not usually seen.

The disorder is uncommon but generally occurs in members of two different groups at different ages. In developmentally normal children, onset is usually at about 3–12 months of age, whereas in those with mental retardation, onset is not until about 5–6 years of age (Kerwin & Berkowitz, 1996). Onset has also been observed in adults. Mortality rate, reported as high as 25% (American Psychiatric Association [APA], 1994), appears to be declining in infants, perhaps because of medical advances (Kerwin & Berkowitz, 1996).

Affected infants and children may adopt a stance with the back arched and head held back while straining and may thrust their tongue or abdomen during regurgitation (Kerwin & Berkowitz, 1996). Children may show some signs of satisfaction or enjoyment after regurgitating but also be irritable between episodes. Malnutrition may occur even in cases in which children eat unusually large amounts of food (APA, 1994).

Characteristics

1. Repeated voluntary regurgitation and spitting out or rechewing of food.
2. Weight loss, malnutrition, dehydration, growth retardation, or failure to meet expected weight gains secondary to regurgitation.

Main criterion for diagnosis of rumination disorder is repeated regurgitation and rechewing of food for at least 1 month following normal functioning. It needs to be differentiated from gastrointestinal or other medical conditions in which regurgitation also occurs and should not be diagnosed if anorexia nervosa, bulimia, or any general medical condition is primarily involved. Differentiation from organic bases for regurgitation may be particularly important in individuals with mental retardation because undiagnosed gastrointestinal and oropharyngeal problems are common in this population (Kerwin & Berkowitz, 1996). If the child has mental retardation or a pervasive developmental disorder, rumination disorder should be separately diagnosed only if it is severe enough to call for clinical attention itself (APA, 1994).

Rumination disorder in developmentally normal infants may go into spontaneous remission (Health

Central, 1998). Several behavioral treatments are available for other cases. The most common treatment is mild aversive training, but oral hygiene, differential reinforcement, or food satiation may also be used (Kerwin & Berkowitz, 1996). Special education is ordinarily not an issue with this disorder, but other services may be available through provisions of the Education of the Handicapped Act Amendment of 1986 (Kerwin & Berkowitz, 1996). Because lack of stimulation, neglect, stress, and problems in parent-child relationships may be predisposing factors (APA, 1994), family therapy and intervention may be useful.

REFERENCES

American Psychiatric Association. (1994). *Diagnostic and statistical manual of mental disorders* (4th ed.). Washington, DC: Author.

Health Central. (1998). *Rumination disorder*. Retrieved from http://www.healthcentral.com/mhc/top/001539.cfm

Kerwin, M. E., & Berkowitz, R. I. (1996). Feeding and eating disorders: Ingestive problems of infancy, childhood, and adolescence. *School Psychology Review, 25,* 316–328.

Robert T. Brown
Paula Kilpatrick
University of North Carolina, Wilmington

RURAL SPECIAL EDUCATION

Approximately 67% of the 16,000 public school districts in the United States are classified as rural because of sparse population or geographic location (Sher, 1978). According to Helge (1984), educational characteristics of rural areas are distinctly different from those of urban areas. Rural areas have higher poverty levels and serve greater percentages of children with disabilities. Populations in rural areas are increasing; however, their tax bases are not. Education costs more in rural areas than in nonrural areas because of transportation requirements and scarce professional resources.

Because of the remoteness of the areas, assessing the effectiveness of special education services to individuals with disabilities has been difficult. One reason for this, according to the director of the National Rural Research Project (Helge, 1984) has been the absence of a consistently applied definition of the term *rural* among federal agencies, educators, and professional organizations. The definition that is most commonly used is the one developed for the 1978 to 1983 research projects funded by the U.S.

Office of Special Education Programs and conducted by the National Rural Research and Personnel Preparation Project. This definition reads:

> A district is considered rural when the number of inhabitants is fewer than 150 per square mile or when located in counties with 60% or more of the population living in communities not larger than 5,000 inhabitants. Districts with more than 10,000 students and those within a Standard Metropolitan Statistical Area (SMSA), as determined by the U.S. Census Bureau, are not considered rural. (p. 296)

The National Rural Research and Personnel Preparation Project was funded (to be conducted in four phases from 1978 to 1981) to investigate state and local educational agencies nationwide in order to determine problems and effective strategies for implementing Public Law 94-142; and to develop profiles of effective special education delivery systems and strategies, given specific rural community and district subcultural characteristics (p. 296).

Phase I, conducted during 1978 and 1979, focused on identifying facilitating and hindering factors that operate to determine the success or failure of rural local educational agency compliance with PL 94-142. Results of this phase showed that problems identified by state educational agencies were grouped in three categories: (1) staffing problems (recruiting and retaining qualified staff); (2) attitudinal variables (resistance to change, suspicions of outside interference, and long distances between schools); and (3) problems based on rural geography (fiscal problems, difficult terrain and economic conditions). Phase II, conducted during 1979 and 1980, was designed to develop profiles interrelating community characteristics and school district characteristics with service delivery options proven viable in other local education agencies with similar characteristics. Phase III (1980) involved using Phase I and II data to develop interdisciplinary models of personnel preparation for effective service delivery to rural subcultures. Phase IV, conducted in 1980 and 1981, was designed to field test and disseminate the modules for use in preservice and in-service training programs (Helge, 1981).

A series of in-service training modules have been developed with topics that range from stress reduction to alternate rural service delivery systems. In addition, several preservice modules are presently being field tested in universities across the country. Topics of the modules include alternate instructional arrangements and delivery systems for students with low-incidence disabilities in rural America; Warren Springs, Mesa: a rural preservice simulation; solving rural parent-professional related dilemmas; working with parents of rural students with disabilities; involving citizens and agencies of rural communities in cooperative programming for students with disabilities; working with peer professionals in rural environments; creative resource identification for providing services to rural students with disabilities; solving educational dilemmas related to school administration; and personal development skills and strategies for effective survival as a rural special educator. These modules are available through the American Council on Rural Special Education.

In a report on the state of the art of rural special education (Helge, 1984), it was noted that major service delivery problems remained basically the same as in the initial study done in 1979. These problems were associated with funding inadequacies, difficulties in recruiting and retaining qualified staff, transportation inadequacies, problems with providing services to low-incidence disabled populations, and inadequacies of preservice training. In addition, many of these inadequacies were seen as future problems.

In an effort to focus on rural special education and the identified service delivery problems, the American Council on Rural Special Education was founded in 1981. This nonprofit national membership organization is an outgrowth of the National Rural Development Institute, headquartered at Western Washington University in Bellingham. The organization is composed of approximately 1,000 rural special educators and administrators, parents of students with disabilities, and university and state department personnel. The specific purposes of the organization are to enhance direct services to rural individuals and agencies serving exceptional students; to increase educational opportunities for rural disabled and gifted students; and to develop a system for forecasting the future for rural special education and planning creative service delivery alternatives.

The American Council on Rural Special Education (ACRES) serves as an advocate for rural special education at the federal, state, regional, and local levels; provides professional development opportunities, and disseminates information on the current needs of rural special education. The ACRES has established a nationwide system to link educators and administrators needing jobs with agencies having vacancies. The ACRES Rural Bulletin Board communicates to interested agencies information regarding rural special education issues and promising practices through SpecialNet, the electronic communication system operated by the National Association of State Directors of Special Education. ACRES publishes a quarterly newsletter and a journal, the *Rural Special Education Quarterly*. These publications include up-to-date information on issues facing students with disabilities in rural America, problem-solving strategies, pertinent legislation and conferences, and articles on rural preservice and in-service strategies. The ACRES also holds a conference each year in the spring, usually at the institute's headquarters. The conferences feature presentations to enhance services to rural disabled and gifted children, media displays of curriculum materials, and hardware and software exhibits.

REFERENCES

Helge, D. I. (1981). Problems in implementing comprehensive special education programming in rural areas. *Exceptional Children, 47*, 514–524.

Helge, D. I. (1984). The state of the art of rural special education. *Exceptional Children, 50*, 294–305.

Sher, J. P. (1978). A proposal to end federal neglect of rural schools. *Phi Delta Kappan, 60*, 280–282.

CECELIA STEPPE-JONES
North Carolina Central University

RUSH, BENJAMIN (1745–1813)

Benjamin Rush, physician, teacher, reformer, and patriot, began medical practice in Philadelphia in 1769. He taught chemistry at the College of Philadelphia and published the first American textbook on that subject. During the Revolutionary War, he served as surgeon-general of the Army and published a textbook on military medicine that was still in use at the time of the Civil War. Following his military service, Rush returned to the practice of medicine in Philadelphia, where he established the first free dispensary in the United States. He is believed to be the first physician to relate smoking to cancer and to advocate temperance and exercise to promote good health. An outspoken advocate of humane treatment for the mentally ill, in 1812 Rush published a work that would influence medical education for generations to come, *Medical Inquiries and Observations Upon the Diseases of the Mind*.

Despite his accomplishments as a physician, political and social issues were Rush's major interests. He was a member of the Continental Congress and a signer of the Declaration of Independence. He was active in the movement to abolish slavery, and was influential in the ratification of the federal Constitution in Pennsylvania. He involved himself in a number of educational causes, advocating improved education for girls and proposing a comprehensive system of public schools that would offer science and practical subjects as well as traditional academics.

REFERENCES

Hawke, D. (1971). *Benjamin Rush*. New York, NY: Bobbs-Merrill.

Rush, B. (1962). *Medical inquiries and observations upon the diseases of the mind*. New York, NY: Hafner. (Original work published 1812)

PAUL IRVINE
Katonah, New York

RUSSELL-SILVER SYNDROME

Russell-Silver syndrome is a rare disorder characterized by retarded growth, asymmetry of the body and face, and a triangular face. There is no known etiology for this disorder; most cases occur from sporadic gene changes. This very rare genetic disorder has a wide variation of characteristics.

Characteristics

1. Low weight and abnormally short length at birth.
2. Delayed closure of anterior fontanel.
3. Face with a triangular shape that decreases with age and downturned corners of mouth.
4. Growth retardation, delayed bone age, weak muscle tone, and poor appetite.
5. Fifth-finger clinodactyly.
6. Asymmetry of the body.
7. Rarer traits include hydrocephalus, frequent ear infections, café au lait spots, high energy, migraine headaches, passing-out spells, and attention-deficit/hyperactivity disorder.

Treatment is symptomatic. A diet high in calories, hypoglycemia treatment, periactin used as an appetite stimulant, a feeding pump, recombinant growth hormone, and gastrostomy may be used to enhance appetite and growth (Cowger, 1998).

Shoe lifts, limb-lengthening surgery, and corrective surgery are methods used to correct asymmetry and other physical abnormalities (Cowger, 1998).

Children with Russell-Silver syndrome may qualify for special education services for physical therapy for the physical disabilities associated with asymmetry and growth retardation. Speech therapy may be needed for speech difficulties due to a hypoplastic mandible. The developmental delays can result in learning disabilities that merit special education services as well. Low self-esteem and emotional problems may arise with appearance, requiring psychological assessment and services.

Prognosis for Russell-Silver syndrome is good because most of the characteristics minimize with time. Research has found some possible locations of a chromosome linked to the syndrome, but none have been confirmed (Cowger, 1998).

REFERENCE

Cowger, M. (1998). *Russell-Silver syndrome*. Retrieved from http://magicfoundation.org/rss.html

IMAN TERESA LAHROUD
University of Texas at Austin

RUSSIA, SPECIAL EDUCATION IN

Special education in Russia first developed from the then-progressive ideas of Vygotsky, Luria, Boskis, Pevzner, Levina, Rau, and other behavioral researchers. They approached the education of a child with special needs while considering his or her complex psychophysiological development, with the most complete possible social rehabilitation of a child as a goal. During the Communist regime these ideas were replaced by a pedagogy that was less child-centered, isolating a child with special needs from society, and establishing several boarding institutions (van Rijswijk et al., 1996).

Recently, Russia has entered a new phase in its thinking and attitudes about special education. A return to the individual child-focus has been augmented by the ideal for full participation or integration in society. Social rehabilitation continues to be valued, but social participation is also highly valued.

The modern phase into which special education has recently entered was necessary because of the absence of protective legislation for the civil rights of children with handicaps or with other special needs. This modern phase of special education in Russia places new emphases on preschool interventions and on staff training of teachers, psychologists, social workers, and others.

Legal Bases for Special Education

During the Soviet period in the republics of the former USSR, the rights of the child (as indicated in the UNO Convention, the UNO Declaration on the rights of the invalids and the rights of the mentally handicapped people) were not well-observed. Within the last decade, Russia's central government has taken firm steps toward ratification and realization of these international documents. Nevertheless, still there is inadequate legislation for special education, although there is some progress in this direction (Aksenova, 1997). The new phase for special education was signaled in part by a landmark Law on Education (1992), which was considered one of the most democratic in the history of Russia. This law was followed four years later by several further insertions and improvements to "About the Education"; these went into effect January 5, 1996.

The Law on Education significantly improved the state guarantee of a free, appropriate public education to people with disabilities. Particularly, Article 50, Point 10 of the Law foresaw the establishment of the special (correctional) educational institutions for children and adolescents with special needs, where they can have treatment, upbringing, education, social adaptation, and integration into society. Note that social rehabilitation is emphasized more than social participation.

A second new law that marks the modern phase of special education in Russia is "On Social Care of Invalids," which went into effect on January 1st, 1996. Article 18 of this Law is dedicated to the upbringing and education of child invalids. According to the law, the educational institutions together with social and health care organizations must provide upbringing and education of children with disabilities, from preschool through secondary school, both within classrooms and outside, according to an individually defined program of rehabilitation. In both mainstream schools and special educational institutions, this education is free.

Another change in the modern phase is that the subjects of the Russian Federation (RF) have received the right to make legislation for solving their local problems, including the field of help and care of children and their families. This is appropriate because the financing of education, health, and other social services is carried out mainly at the expense of local budgets (which also brings about regional differences in type and quality of services). These legislative changes have encouraged public organizations to play a significant role in the improvement of services to children with special needs. In addition, public interest groups are beginning to attempt to influence regional decision making in the field of special education. Newly active public organizations are representing the interests of children with disabilities and their families. However, national networking and sharing of information is still minimal. For example, there is not a uniform data bank on children with disabilities and programs in operation, let alone data on program effectiveness.

Although the recent Russian legislation for the children with special needs is a major step forward, it touches only some aspects of special education. Now Russia must develop a new law specifically for special education; in fact, a draft has been worked out and is under consideration by the State Duma.

Structure of Special Education

In Russia, several ministries are responsible for children with special needs, which causes a number of difficulties. The interdepartmental barriers interfere with creation of an integrated, harmonious, and effective system of social care and support. There is a whole complex of problems: social, scientific, practical. The largest obstacle to progress is the absence of high-grade statistical information about such children; in the Russian Federation there is no uniform state system to account for them.

The system of special education in Russia is based on five age designations and the specific type of disability.

Age Structure

The vertical structure consists of five levels:

1. Early childhood (from 0 to 3 years old)
2. Preschool period (from 3 to 7)
3. Compulsory education (from 7 to 16)
4. Comprehensive education and vocational training (from 15 to 18 and up to 21 for the blind, deaf, and physically handicapped)
5. Adult-invalid training

During the period of early childhood (from birth to 3) children are trained and brought up in home conditions, in establishments for infants, and in homes for children if the child is an orphan. Developmental and remedial work with children with developmental problems is carried out in various centers of early intervention and rehabilitation, in special groups and at psychological-medical-pedagogical consulting centers.

For children of preschool age there are the following establishments:

- Special kindergartens with day and day-night stay
- Remedial homes for children
- Special groups in regular kindergartens
- Special rehabilitation centers
- Preschool groups in special schools (for children with visual, hearing, emotional, and mental disorders)

Special (remedial) educational establishments for children with developmental problems offer programs of elementary regular education, general regular education, and general comprehensive regular education. These establishments must meet special state educational standards. They focus on special remedial work, education, treatment, social adaptation, and integration into society.

Special education is offered within a variety of administrative structures:

- Special (remedial) school (daily or evening)
- Special boarding school
- Rehabilitation centers
- Special class at a regular educational establishment
- Individually in a regular educational establishment
- Home education
- External education
- Education in a stationary medical establishment

Persons with developmental problems may receive both a regular education and vocational training in:

- Special average schools
- Special industrial workshops
- Centers of social-labor rehabilitation
- Special vocational schools

Disability Type (Horizontal) Structure

The horizontal structure of special education in Russia is by eight types of disability:

1. For the deaf (classes for mentally retarded children)
2. For the hard of hearing (classes for mentally retarded children)
3. For the blind (classes for mentally retarded children)
4. For visually impaired (classes for mentally retarded children)

5. With severe speech and language disorders

6. With emotional disabilities (classes for mentally retarded children)

7. With learning disabilities

8. For mentally retarded (special classes for children with severe mental retardation, classes for children with multiple and complex disorders)

For children and teenagers with deviant behavior there exist three kinds of special educational establishments in Russia:

1. Special educational school

2. Special vocational technical school

3. Special (remedial) comprehensive school and special (remedial) professional technical school for children and teenagers with problems in development (learning disabilities, light forms of mental retardation) who commit socially dangerous actions

In Russia, statistics on children with special needs were not available during most of the Communist era. But beginning in 1993 according to the Russian Governmental Decree N 848 (23.08.93), "About the Realization of the UNO Convention on the Rights of a Child" and "International Declaration about the Providing of the Surviving, Care and Development of Children," a governmental statistical report is published every year. Entitled "About the Situation of Children in the Russian Federation," it contains statistics related to demographic and legal mandates for service in Russia as a whole and specific Russian regions.

The number of special schools for children with developmental problems (see Table R.2) is annually increasing. Special (remedial) classes in the mainstream schools have also grown.

In Russia, there are no special schools for children with emotional and behavioral problems. Concerning the education of children with early infant autism, there was no specific approach until recently, when individual groups in special kindergartens and primary schools began to be created for such children. Children with moderate and severe mental retardation usually live in state-financed boarding schools or with families, where education is partial or nonexistent. Until recently such children were labeled incapable of studying. Improvements in the education of these children is slow, but there are increasing numbers of special developmental classes in the schools for children with mild mental retardation.

Russia is still marked by the existence of large numbers of separate special education boarding schools, where the majority of children get psychological, medical, and pedagogical help. Such boarding schools became popular for two reasons. First, because of Russia's large territory, in rural areas the school is usually situated so far from home that daily attendance is impossible. Second, many of these children do not have parents, have been given up for adoption, or have been refused by their parents, becoming wards of the state.

In Russia, approximately 1% to 2% of children from 6 to 16 years old attend special schools (and, more recently, special classes). Until recently in the Russian Federation, a significant number of children who needed special education could not get it because of the scarcity of special schools and personnel, especially in the regions of the far North, Siberia, and rural districts. In remote areas, many children with disabilities received no help.

Integrated Education for Children With Special Needs

In the latter part of this decade, special education in Russia has been improving in two main ways. First, there has been improvement in the existing network of special education programs and their expansion. The second improvement has been in the integrated education of these children (Shipitsina, 1996). The first improvement in the

Table R.2. Schools for children with mental and physical disorders in the Russian Federation (beginning of educational year)[*]

Types of establishments for	Number of schools				Number of students (in thousands)			
	1990	1992	1994	1996	1990	1992	1994	1996
Children with mental or physical handicaps—Total	1817	1835	1848	1889	312.1	277.4	267.4	267.6
Mentally retarded	1452	1459	1443	1440	251.6	217.9	203.9	205.5
The blind	20	19	18	20	3.7	3.3	2.9	3.4
Visually impaired	51	52	56	61	7.8	7.4	8.0	8.5
The deaf (and mute)	82	81	85	84	12.5	11.9	12.0	11.3
The hard of hearing	70	73	73	77	11.2	10.8	10.6	11.0
Children with consequences of poliomyelitis and cerebral palsy	40	40	43	52	6.5	6.0	6.1	6.7
Severe speech and language problems	61	61	61	62	10.8	11.0	11.5	11.9
Learning disabilities	41	50	65	71	8.0	9.1	12.1	13.4
Children with mental or physical disorders set up in regular schools					53.0	119.7	155.5	192.0
Mentally retarded in regular schools					7.1	10.7	10.6	14.7
Learning disabled in regular schools					44.9	103.2	141.9	175.9

[*]Data of the State Statistical Committee of Russian Federation.

type and extent of special services is noted in the table. Note that the number of special schools has increased gradually or has been static. On the other hand, the number of special classes within regular public schools is expanding rapidly (see Table R.2).

Undoubtedly, not all children with problems in development can be integrated into a regular school, but many more can than are presently doing so. The difficult problem is identifying those particular children with developmental problems who can be integrated and when is the best time to start their integrative education.

Generally, in Russia, there are few statistics about the number of children with visual, hearing, and other impairments educated in mainstream schools. We do know that the majority of such children do not get any special help in ordinary schools. In recent years in Moscow, Saint Petersburg, and some other big cities of Russia, research began on the practical psychological and pedagogical guidance of children with sensory and moving problems in the mainstream school.

So far in Russia, the attitude to integrative education is restrained. Parents of children with impairments are commonly advised to place their child in a special boarding home from his or her very early life. The justification is usually that mainstream schools do not have the special staff and that the children cannot receive necessary support in mainstream classes in these schools. Unfortunately, this argument is partly true, as regular schools lack resources, expertise, and philosophies of integration. Usually the nature of integration is not questioned; the majority agree that it is good in the abstract, but that the practical obstacles are too great. Where attitudes are the problem, they usually come from the teachers in the mainstream schools (Makhortova, 1996).

Inclusive Education in the Regular Classroom

Children with different disabilities are included differentially in general education classrooms in Russia. Children with hearing impairments have only recently been included. Today the process of integration of such children into mainstream establishments is steadily expanding (Shmatko, 1996). The integrated education of children with sight impairments in the mainstream school is a rare phenomenon, and most mainstream schools are not yet ready for it. Some of the hesitation is due to concern for the adjustment of the child with disabilities. Some contend that full integration may increase personal problems (Makhortova, 1996).

Special Classes in the Mainstream School

Today in Russia, one of the fastest growing models of integrative education is the organization of special classes in the mainstream school. They are organized:

- For children with intellectual impairments (where there are not any special schools for this category of the children nearby); their number is rather small

- For children with learning difficulties; classes with special educational support or remedial classes
- For children of "risk groups" (with learning difficulties, behavior problems, weak health); classes of compensative education, special educational support, adaptation, and recreation

In rare cases, due to the large distance from the special schools and unwillingness of the parents to refer their children to receive the education in the boarding schools, special classes, or groups for children with sight, hearing, and speech impairments are organized in the mainstream kindergartens and schools.

Despite the positive results of the work of special classes in mainstream schools, serious problems are still not solved.

- Students depend upon the existence of specialists (psychologists, speech therapists, special teachers), which are too few to service the children.
- Frequently, teachers refuse to work in special classes because of difficulties and lack of necessary knowledge about children with problems in development.
- Special classes often have a stigma attached, leading to aggressive social behavior and negative attitudes among peers.
- These classes promote the process of separating out children from the mainstream, permitting general educators to escape from their full responsibilities. Thus, the methods of selecting children for the special classed may be suspect.
- Mainstream education lacks the vocational training that many students with disabilities need in the secondary grades.

Despite all the problems and difficulties, it should be understood that in Russia the process of integration of the children with special needs into the mainstream schools is accelerating. Throughout the country, diverse models and forms of interaction between special and mainstream schools are developing; special schools are being de-emphasized; and conditions for both social adaptation and personal development are being more closely approached than ever before.

REFERENCES

Aksenova, L. I. (1997). Legal bases of special education and social care of children with problems in development. *Journal of Defectology, 1,* 3.

Makhortova, G. H. (1996). Problems of psychological adaptation of children with visual impairments in the mainstream schools. *Journal of Defectology, 4,* 45–50.

Shipitsina, L. M. (1996). *The topical aspects of integrative education of children with problems in development in Russia. Integrative Education: Problems and Prospects.*

Shmatko, N. D. (1996). *Integrative approach to education of children with hearing impairments in Russia. Integrative Education: Problems and Prospects.*

van Rijswijk, K., Foreman, N., & Shipitsina, L. M. (Eds.). (1996). *Special education on the move.* Leuven/Amersfoort, The Netherlands: Acco.

LUDMILLA SHIPITSINA
RAOUL WALLENBERG
International University for Family and Child

See also Luria, Alexander R.; Vygotsky, Lev S.

RUTTER, MICHAEL (1933–   )

On completing his basic medical training at the University of Birmingham, England in 1955, Michael Rutter took residencies in internal medicine, neurology, and pediatrics. His training in general and child psychiatry was done at Maudsley Hospital. Away on fellowship study for a year (1961–1962), Rutter returned to work in the Medical Research Council Special Psychiatry Research Unit. From 1965 to 1994, Rutter served as professor and head of the Department of Child and Adolescent Psychiatry at the University of London's Institute of Psychiatry. His distinguished appointments include honorary director of the Medical Research Council Child Psychiatry Unit (1984–1998); honorary director of the Social, Genetic, and Developmental Psychiatry Research Centre (1994–1998); honorary consultant psychiatrist, Bethlehem and Maudsley Hospitals Trust; and research professor at the Institute of Psychiatry in 1998.

Rutter's major fields of interest indicate a strong interdisciplinary approach, include schools as social institutions, and stress resilience in relation to developmental links between childhood and adult life, psychiatric genetics, neuropsychiatry, psychiatric epidemiology, and infantile autism. As a teacher and researcher, his work centers on building bridges between the areas of child development and clinical child psychiatry.

Rutter's major published contributions include *Child and Adolescent Psychiatry: Modern Approaches* (3rd ed.), *Depression in Young People: Developmental and Clinical Perspectives* (1986), *Antisocial Behavior by Young People* (1998), *Fifteen Thousand Hours: Secondary Schools and Their Effects on Children* (1994), and *Psychosocial Disorders in Young People* (1995). To date, he has written 36 books, 138 chapters, and 300 research articles and associated works.

In 1979 Rutter served as a fellow at the Center for Advanced Study in the Behavioral Sciences at Stanford. He is a Fellow of The Royal Society (FRS), London; Foreign Associate Member of the Institute of Medicine of the National Academy of Sciences, United States; Foreign Honorary Member of the American Academy of Arts and Sciences; Foreign Associate Member of the US National Academy of Education; Founding Member of Academia Europaea; and Fellow of the Academy of Medical Sciences. In addition, he has been a trustee of the Nuffield Foundation since 1992, and became governor of the Wellcome Trust in 1996.

The numerous honorary degrees bestowed upon Rutter include the University of Birmingham in 1990, University of Edinburgh in 1990, University of Chicago in 1991, University of Ghent in 1994, and University of Jyvaskyla, Finland in 1996. He was knighted in January of 1992 and has received many prestigious awards, the most recent being the John P. Hill Award for Excellence in Theory Development and Research on Adolescence from the Society for Research on Adolescence in 1992; the American Psychological Association Distinguished Scientists Award in 1995; the Castilla del Pino Prize for Achievement in Psychiatry, Cordoba, Spain in 1995; and the Helmut Horten Award for research in autism that has made a difference to clinical practice in 1997. He is a member of the editorial boards of some 20 journals.

Rutter is currently Professor of Developmental Psychopathology at the Institute of Psychiatry, Kings College, London. Among his most recent books is the fourth edition of *Child and Adolescent Psychiatry* (2002).

REFERENCES

Rutter, M. (1994). *Fifteen thousand hours: Secondary schools and their effects on children.* London, England: P. Chapman.

Rutter, M., Giller, H., & Hagell, A. (1998). *Antisocial behavior by young people.* New York, NY: Cambridge University Press.

Rutter, M., & Hersov, L. (Eds.). (1985). *Child and adolescent psychiatry: Modern approaches.* Oxford, England: Blackwell.

Rutter, M., Izard, C., & Read, P. (1986). *Depression in young people: Developmental and clinical perspectives.* New York, NY: Guilford Press.

Rutter, M., & Smith, D. J. (1995). *Psychosocial disorders in young people: Time trends and their causes.* New York, NY: Wiley.

Rutter, M., & Taylor, E. E. (2002). *Child and adolescent psychiatry.* (4th ed.). Oxford, England: Blackwell.

MARY LEON PEERY
Texas A&M University
First edition

TAMARA J. MARTIN
The University of Texas of the Permian Basin
Second edition

C. WILLIAMS
Falcon School District 49, Colorado Springs, Colorado
Third edition

S

SABATINO, DAVID A. (1938–)

David A. Sabatino obtained his BA in 1960, MA in 1961, and PhD in 1966 from Ohio State University. He is currently a professor in the department of human development and learning at East Tennessee State University, Johnson City.

Sabatino's interests have focused on gifted children and adolescents, children with disabilities, and psychological assessment (Fuller & Sabatino, 1998; Sabatino, Miller, & Schmidt, 1981; Sabatino, Spangler, & Vance, 1995; Spangler & Sabatino, 1995). He views learning disabilities as complex problems associated with difficulty in information processing. As a complicated problem, Sabatino contends that no one professional, from any single discipline, can meet the needs of all children. Instead, he advocates input from any service provider that can assist a particular child with a disability (Sabatino et al., 1981).

In his work, Sabatino noted that increasing numbers of children with disabilities were being neglected and secondary schools were ill equipped to handle the influx, frequently stressing subject mastery rather than individual growth and learning. Thus, he advocated functional teaching, or teaching the necessary information in order for a child to function at a basic academic level. Teaching a child to read, if he or she does not know how to read, is preferable to labeling that child, according to Sabatino (Sabatino & Lanning-Ventura, 1982).

Sabatino continues his work involving programming for school-age children, investigating demographic and personality characteristics of at-risk high school students. This study indicated a prevalence of six factors, including defensiveness-hopelessness, attention seeking, and family relationship problems, as well as the predominant characteristics of absence of extracurricular activities, a negative attitude toward school, and truancy. This research has important implications for programming for at-risk students (Fuller & Sabatino, 1996).

REFERENCES

Fuller, C. G., & Sabatino, D. A. (1996). Who attends alternative high school? *High School Journal, 79*, 293–297.

Fuller, C. G., & Sabatino, D. A. (1998). Diagnosis and treatment considerations with comorbid developmentally disabled populations. *Journal of Clinical Psychology, 54*, 1–10.

Sabatino, D. A., & Lanning-Ventura, S. (1982). Functional teaching, survival skills and teaching. In D. A. Sabatino & L. Mann (Eds.), *A handbook of diagnostic and prescriptive teaching.* Rockville, MD: Aspen.

Sabatino, D. A., Miller, T. L., & Schmidt, C. R. (1981). *Learning disabilities: Systemizing teaching and service delivery.* Rockville, MD: Aspen.

Sabatino, D. A., Spangler, R. S., & Vance, H. B. (1995). The relationship between the Wechsler Intelligence Scale for Children–Revised and the Wechsler Intelligence Scale for Children–III scales and subtests with gifted children. *Psychology in the Schools, 32*, 18–23.

Spangler, R. S., & Sabatino, D. A. (1995). Temporal stability of gifted children's intelligence. *Roeper Review, 17*, 207–210.

E. Valerie Hewitt
Texas A&M University
First edition

Tamara J. Martin
The University of Texas
of the Permian Basin
Second edition

SAETHRE-CHOTZEN SYNDROME

Saethre-Chotzen syndrome is one variant in a group of rare disorders known as acrocephalosyndactyly. Saethre-Chotzen syndrome is a relatively mild form of acrocephalosyndactyly with a variable pattern of craniofacial, digital, and bone abnormalities. It is also known as acrocephalosyndactyly Type III (ACS III), Chotzen syndrome, and dysostosis craniofacialis with hypertelorism. Saethre-Chotzen syndrome is usually found in several generations of a family (Niemann-Seyde, Eber, & Zoll, 1991). It is an inherited disorder; however, the features can be minor, and the syndrome therefore may remain undiagnosed. It is an autosomal disorder caused by a change or mutation in only one copy of a gene from one biological parent. Therefore, a parent with Saethre-Chotzen syndrome has a 50% chance of passing it on to a child. The altered gene is located on Chromosome 7. Saethre-Chotzen syndrome affects between 1 and 2 people in every 50,000.

Characteristics

1. Due to early closure of the cranial sutures, the infant may have a misshapen head and facial asymmetry (craniofacial asymmetry).

2. Additional malformation of the skull and facial region may also include widely spaced eyes (ocular hypertelorism), shallow eye cavities, drooping of the upper eyelids (ptosis), and abnormal deviation of one eye in relation to another (strabismus).

3. Other symptoms sometimes include a beaked nose, small low-set malformed ears, and an underdeveloped upper jaw (hypoplastic maxilla).

4. This disorder is also associated with malformations of the hands and feet. Certain fingers and toes may be partly fused together (webbed). Short digits (brachydactyly) and great broad toes are also associated with this disorder.

5. Although intelligence is usually normal, some individuals may have mild to moderate mental retardation.

have severe craniofacial, digital, and bone abnormalities. Plastic surgery can help mediate the effects of some of these symptoms. A few individuals may have mild to moderate mental retardation as a result of this disorder. It is likely that these individuals will need some kind of support throughout school and life.

REFERENCES

Clauser, L., Galie, M., Hassanipour, A., & Calabrese, O. (2000). Saethre-Chotzen Syndrome: Review of the literature and report of a case. *Journal of Craniofacial Surgery, 11*(5), 480–486.

Niemann-Seyde, S. C., Eber, S. W., & Zoll, B. (1991). Saethre-Chotzen syndrome (ACS III) in four generations. *Clinical Genetics, 40*(4), 271–276.

Reardon, W., McManus, S. P., Summers, D., & Winter, R. M. (1993). Cytogenetic evidence that the Saethre-Chotzen gene maps to 7p21.2. *American Journal of Medical Genetics, 47*(5), 633–636.

RACHEL TOPLIS
University of Northern Colorado

With Saethre-Chotzen syndrome, the facial appearance tends to improve as the child grows. However, surgery may be necessary in infancy to correct the fusion of cranial structures and the webbing of fingers. Reconstructive surgery may be needed for the eyelids and nose.

Students with Saethre-Chotzen syndrome may not qualify for special services under the Individuals with Disabilities Education Act (1997) if they appear to be benefiting from general education. If mild or moderate mental retardation is present, they may qualify under the mental retardation or significant limited intellectual capacity category. However, students may be able to receive some accommodations under Section 504 of the Rehabilitation Act of 1974. Major plastic surgery should have been carried out during infancy. However, if craniofacial features are a concern to the student, he or she may benefit from individual counseling, especially during identity formation and if the student expresses preadolescent and adolescent concern with body image.

Research investigating Saethre-Chotzen syndrome appears to be making advances in locating the abnormal genetic structure on Chromosome 7 (e.g., Reardon, McManus, Summers, & Winter, 1993). Further research is addressing the possible improvement of physical symptoms. For example, Clauser, Galie, Hassanipour, and Calabrese (2000) had success with surgical remodeling to correct craniofacial deformities in a 13-year-old girl.

The prognosis for someone with Saethre-Chotzen syndrome depends on the severity of the symptoms. Severity runs along a continuum; some individuals have mild symptoms that are never diagnosed, whereas other individuals

SAFETY ISSUES IN SPECIAL EDUCATION

Accountability, malpractice, due process, and liability insurance are all terms familiar to special educators. For teachers to gain protection from legal situations it is critical that children's safety become a high priority. In particular, children with physical impairments and severe disabilities are more prone to accidents, medical emergencies, and injuries. Therefore, teachers must take certain precautions to protect students and staff from unnecessary risks. Specifically, educators must consider many facets of the classroom program in order to create safe environments for children. Four major areas related to safety must be considered: (1) basic first-aid skills, (2) emergency weather and fire drill procedures, (3) safe classroom environments, and (4) parent consent and involvement in classroom activities.

Many states require teachers to obtain certification in first-aid procedures before they are eligible to obtain a teaching certificate. In particular, teachers should be trained in cardiopulmonary resuscitation (CPR) and anti-choking procedures such as the Heimlich maneuver. For teachers working with children who have seizures, a clear understanding of first-aid procedures for managing seizures is critical. Furthermore, basic instruction on poison management, eye injuries, and contusions must be included in first-aid programs. In the same context, children on medication such as Ritalin, Phenobarbital, and

Dilantin, must be carefully monitored for signs of over- or underdosage. Teachers should never be left solely responsible for dispensing any medications to children without the assistance of a physician or school nurse.

Emergency weather and fire drill procedures should be clearly posted in all classrooms. For teachers in certain areas of the country, where tornados and hurricanes are likely, extra efforts must be taken to understand the civil defense procedures for the school. For teachers of individuals with physically disabilities, visual impairments, and severe nonambulatory impairments, procedures should be established with the school principal for added assistance during civil defense drills and fire drills.

Much has been written on designing school facilities and classroom environments for students with disabilities (Abend, Bednor, Froehlinger, & Stenzler, 1979; Birch & Johnstone, 1975; Forness, Guthrie, & MacMillan, 1982; Hutchins & Renzaglia, 1983; Zentall, 1983). Environmental designing of classrooms also involves a safety aspect for children in special education. For example, many classrooms for students with physical disabilities or visual impairments should have adequate storage space for bulky equipment (e.g., wheelchairs, walkers) and materials (e.g., braillers, books, canes). A classroom that is organized and neat ensures safety for children. Cabinets within the classroom holding harmful materials should be inaccessible to students. Rossol (1982) discusses the possible hazards to students in special education using art materials.

Many of the activities developed for students with disabilities involve out-of-school visits such as field trips, community-based training, and recreation/leisure trips. Parental consent would be critical if liability issues arose from one of these activities. Additionally, behavioral intervention programs that might appear intrusive (e.g., time-out, physical restraint, withholding food) must be discussed by the educational team and parents prior to implementation of any such procedures. Each school or district should have policies regarding corporal punishment. Those policies must be understood by all special education teachers and all parents.

In conclusion, safety in special education is a topic that is rarely found in the literature, yet it has enormous implications for teachers working with children with disabilities. Although much of what has been discussed is common sense, it is important to remind teachers of the many safety aspects in special education.

REFERENCES

Abend, A., Bednor, M., Froehlinger, V., & Stenzler, Y. (1979). *Facilities for special education services.* Reston, VA: Council for Exceptional Children.

Birch, J., & Johnstone, B. (1975). *Designing schools and schooling for the handicapped.* Springfield, IL: Thomas.

Forness, S., Guthrie, D., & MacMillan, D. (1982). Classroom environments as they relate to mentally retarded children's

observable behavior. *American Journal of Mental Deficiency,* 3, 259–265.

Hutchins, M., & Renzaglia, A. (1983). Environmental considerations for severely handicapped individuals: The needs and the questions. *Exceptional Education Quarterly,* 4, 67–71.

Rossol, M. (1982). Teaching art to high risk groups. (ERIC Document Reproduction Service No. ED 224 182)

Zentall, S. (1983). Learning environments: A review of physical and temporal factors. *Exceptional Education Quarterly,* 4, 90–115.

VIVIAN I. CORREA
University of Florida

See also Accessibility of Programs; Liability of Teachers in Special Education; Medically Fragile Student; Ritalin

SALVIA, JOHN (1941–　)

John Salvia was born in St. Louis, Missouri. He obtained his BA in 1963 in education and MEd in 1964 in history from the University of Arizona, later earning his EdD in 1968 in special education (with a minor in educational psychology) from Pennsylvania State University. Salvia is currently a professor of special education at Pennsylvania State University.

Early in his professional career, Salvia was a teacher of the educable mentally retarded. His interests have included color blindness in children with mental retardation and assessment in special education (Salvia, 1969; Salvia & Ysseldyke, 1978). His book, coauthored with Ysseldyke, *Assessment in Special and Remedial Education,* provided basic information regarding the assessment process and its resulting data to those who use and need the information but are not involved in the assessment process. His work in this area has also included assessment bias, comparison of test profiles of students with and without disabilities, and assessment strategies for use in instructional decisions (Salvia, 1988, 1990; Salvia & Meisel, 1980).

Salvia has been involved in a children's television workshop and a visiting professor at the University of Victoria, British Columbia, Canada. He was a Fulbright fellow at the University of São Paulo, Brazil, and has been recognized in *Leaders in Education.*

REFERENCES

Salvia, J. (1969). Four tests of color vision: A study of diagnostic accuracy with the mentally retarded. *American Journal of Mental Deficiency,* 74(3), 421–427.

Salvia, J. (1988). A comparison of WAIS-R profiles of nondisabled college freshmen and college students with learning disabilities. *Journal of Learning Disabilities, 21*(10), 632–636.

Salvia, J. (1990). Some criteria for evaluating assessment strategies. *Diagnostique, 16*(1), 61–64.

Salvia, J., & Meisel, C. J. (1980). Observer bias: A methodological consideration in special education research. *Journal of Special Education, 14*(2), 261–270.

Salvia, J., & Ysseldyke, J. E. (1978). *Assessment in special and remedial education*. Boston, MA: Houghton Mifflin.

E. Valerie Hewitt
Texas A&M University
First edition

Tamara J. Martin
The University of Texas
of the Permian Basin
Second edition

SAPIR, SELMA GUSTIN (1916–   )

Born in New York City, Selma Gustin Sapir obtained her BS in 1935 in education and psychology from New York University and her MA in 1956 in psychology from Sarah Lawrence College. She went on to earn her EdD in 1984 in applied clinical psychology from Teachers College, Columbia University. Sapir organized and directed the Learning Disability Laboratory at Bank Street College, New York, a child demonstration center and interdisciplinary training project.

Sapir is the author of the Sapir Dimensions of Learning (1980), Sapir Learning Lab Language Scale (1979), and Sapir Self-Concept Scale, as well as other educational treatment methods combining psychological theory and practices with educational models for children with learning disabilities. Based on child development research, these models emphasize the continual nature of the development process, noting that when a change occurs in one dimension (e.g., social, emotional, or cognitive), growth in other areas takes place as well. Therefore, according to Sapir, recognizing and understanding the norms of development is crucial in this respect (Sapir, 1985).

Sapir advocates a broad theoretical understanding of individual differences, proposes generic training programs, and emphasizes training implications of interdisciplinary collaboration for personnel who work with children with learning disabilities (Sapir, 1986). Additionally, she has examined the concept of "reverse mainstreaming," with nondisabled children, their parents, and teachers visiting the classes of children with disabilities, emphasizing social and physical integration of those

with disabilities (Sapir, 1990). This experimental program increased the probability of successful mainstreaming as well as provided parents and students opportunities for mutual acceptance and perceptions based on experience.

Sapir has made numerous contributions to the field of special education, including the development of graduate programs in learning disabilities and special education in Mayaguez, Puerto Rico and Mons, Belgium. Her service to professional organizations includes United Nations delegate in 1982; member of the board of directors from 1985–1987 and president-elect in 1996 of the International Council of Psychologists; and past president of the Multidisciplinary Academy of Educators.

REFERENCES

Sapir, S. G. (1985). *The clinical teaching model: Clinical insights and strategies for the learning disabled child*. New York, NY: Brunner Mazel.

Sapir, S. G. (1986). Training the helpers. *Journal of Learning Disabilities, 19*(8), 473–476.

Sapir, S. G. (1990). Facilitating mainstreaming: A case study. *Journal of Reading, Writing, & Learning Disabilities International, 6*(4), 413–418.

E. Valerie Hewitt
Texas A&M University
First edition

Tamara J. Martin
The University of Texas
of the Permian Basin
Second edition

SARASON, SEYMOUR B. (1919–2010)

Seymour B. Sarason was born in Brooklyn, New York. He received his BA in 1939 from the University of Newark (now the Newark campus of Rutgers, The State University of New Jersey), later earning both his MA in 1940 and PhD in 1942 in psychology from Clark University. Sarason began his professional career in Connecticut as chief psychologist at the Southbury Training School for the Mentally Retarded and later joined the faculty at Yale University, where he retired in 1989 after two decades of directing the clinical training program.

As one of the first to argue social and cultural influences in the etiology of mental retardation, Sarason is regarded as a major figure in the field (Cherniss, 1991). His advocacy role included broadening society's conceptualization of the needs of those with mental retardation and emphasizing the ability to understand an individual from observation in noncontrived, naturally occurring situations as opposed to test scores obtained in an artificial setting.

As an author and guest lecturer, Sarason was a leader in the field of psychology, writing extensively on school change and school governance (Sarason, 1996, 1997, 1998). A prevailing theme throughout his work was his view that the primary problem confronting our educational system is that schools are uninteresting places for both teachers and children (Cherniss, 1991). Charging the current educational system as incapable of reform, Sarason proposed a system in which adults, both teachers and parents, are responsible for the education of children.

Sarason was the recipient of the Gold Medal Award for Life Contribution by a Psychologist in the Public Interest in 1996 awarded by the American Psychological Foundation. His major publications include *Psychological Problems in Mental Deficiency* (1969) and *Revisiting the Culture of School and the Problem of Change* (1996).

REFERENCES

Cherniss, C. (1991). Biography of Seymour Sarason. *Journal of Applied Behavioral Science, 27*(4), 407–408.

Sarason, S. B. (1969). *Psychological problems in mental deficiency* (4th ed.). New York, NY: Harper & Row.

Sarason, S. B. (1996). *Revisiting the culture of school and the problem of change.* New York, NY: Teachers College.

Sarason, S. B. (1997). *How schools might be governed and why.* New York, NY: Teachers College.

Sarason, S. B. (1998). *Political leadership and educational failure. The Jossey-Bass education series.* San Francisco, CA: Jossey-Bass.

E. Valerie Hewitt
Texas A&M University
First edition

Tamara J. Martin
The University of Texas
of the Permian Basin
Second edition

introductory text, *Assessment of Children* (Third edition), is a standard textbook used in the field of school psychology and clinical psychology, and it remains a classic reference text in the field of special education. He published another assessment text, *Clinical and Forensic Interviewing of Children and Families: Guidelines for the Education, Pediatric, and Child Maltreatment Fields*, in 1998.

Sattler was an expert witness and consultant to the California Attorney General's Office for the case of *Larry P. v. Riles* from September 1977 to April 1978; this was a landmark case in the area of cultural bias in assessment. In addition, he is a coauthor with R. E. Thorndike and E. Hagen of the *Stanford-Binet Intelligence Scale*, Fourth Edition, published in 1986.

Sattler was a Fulbright lecturer at the University of Kebangsaan, Malaysia, from 1972 to 1973, and an exchange professor at the Katholicke Universiteit, Instituut voor Orthopedagogiek, Nijmegen, Netherlands, from 1983 to 1984. He also was an exchange professor at University College Cork, in Cork, Ireland, from 1989 to 1990. In 1979 he was elected a fellow of the American Psychological Association. Sattler has published over 99 articles in the field of psychology and has been a special reviewer for over 70 books, articles, and grant proposals, as well as an editor for such journals as the *Journal of Consulting and Clinical Psychology, Psychology in the Schools, the Journal of Psychoeducational Assessment,* and *Psychological Reports*.

Recently, Jerome Sattler, professor emeritus of psychology was honored by the American Psychological Association's Foundation with its 2005 Gold Medal Award for life achievement in the application of psychology.

REFERENCES

Sattler, J. M. (1992). *Assessment of children* (3rd ed.). San Diego, CA: Sattler.

Sattler, J. M. (1998). *Clinical and forensic interviewing of children and families: Guidelines for the education, pediatric, and child maltreatment fields.* San Diego, CA: Sattler.

L. Williams
Falcon School District 49,
Colorado Springs, Colorado

SATTLER, JEROME M. (1931–   )

Born in New York City, Jerome M. Sattler received his BA from the City College of New York in 1952. He went on to the University of Kansas and earned his MA in psychology in 1953 and PhD in psychology in 1959. As a professor of psychology at San Diego State University, Sattler's research led him to become an authority in the areas of intelligence testing, interviewing, child maltreatment, racial experimenter effects, ethnic minority testing, and racial factors in counseling and psychotherapy. His

SAVANT SYNDROME

Savant syndrome is the ability to reach extraordinary levels of performance often in contrast to the individual's overall intelligence level (Soulieres et al., 2010). Persons with extreme cases of special abilities are considered to be savants. Individuals with savant syndrome have broad intellectual deficits while displaying exceptional behaviors in some normative context (Miller, 1999). The basis of savant syndrome is the significant discrepancy between the individual's general intelligence level and their specific cognitive performance in a particular area (Bolte & Poustka, 2004).

Although a core savant skill has not been identified (Miller, 1999), examples of savant skills include exceptional musical ability, drawing, calculation, learning foreign languages, music, art, mechanical or spatial skills, and calendrical calculation (Neumann et al., 2010; Miller, 1999). Such skills can be grouped into the categories of perceptual, association, or operative skills. Perceptual skills include musical tone labeling and perspective drawing. Association or mapping skills include calendrical calculation and language acquisition. Operative skills include musical composition, the recognition of unknown prime numbers, or the construction of 3-D structures (Soulieres et al., 2010). Savant skills are usually combined with remarkable skills in memory (Neumann et al., 2010). Cognitive models of savant syndrome have also been categorized into skills developed from existing cognitive functions, paradoxical functional facilitation or the interaction between different brain areas, and the enhanced local connectivity of brain regions (Hughes, 2009).

Those with savant syndrome can also be grouped according to skill level. Splinter skills, talented savants, and prodigious savants reflect these different levels. Individuals with splinter skills exhibit intense focus on, and memorization of, extremely narrow areas of personal interest (Treffert, 1999, 2001; Treffert & Wallace, 2004). A talented savant's abilities are generally more extensive and polished (Treffert, 2001). Prodigious savants exhibit significant exceptionalities and are exceedingly rare. To date, there have only been about 100 cases of prodigious savants described in worldwide literature (Bolte & Poustka, 2004). Innate talent is theorized to be a necessity for the development of prodigious savant skill (Heaton & Wallace, 2004). The majority of people with savant syndrome fall within the splinter skill or talented savant category.

Savant syndrome is quite uncommon; however, savant syndrome occurs more often in individuals with autism than in the general population. Approximately 10% of those with an autism diagnosis exhibit savant skills (Neumann et al., 2010). Nearly half of the individuals with savant syndrome have autism and the rest have other forms of developmental disabilities (Hughes, 2009). Similar to autism spectrum disorders, males show signs of savant syndrome 4 times more often than females (Hughes, 2009). Individuals with autism are diagnosed with savant syndrome far more frequently than any other population (Heaton & Wallace, 2004). For this reason, Heaton and Wallace (2004) suggest further research in autism and characteristics of autism to further understand the complexities of savant syndrome. Neumann et al. (2010) suggest that the detailed, focused information

processing style, which is assumed to be a characteristic of autism, associates savant talent with autism spectrum disorders. Superior sensory acuity, enhanced perceptions of patterns and structure, and qualitative differences in perceptions have also been theorized as possible origins of savant skill (Neumann et al., 2010).

Current research has provided some support that motivation distinguishes individuals with disabilities who develop exceptional skill from those who do not (Miller, 1999). Advances in brain imaging allow for a more complete view of the condition and have been used to research the theory of left hemispheric brain damage as a basis for savant talent (Treffert & Wallace, 2004). Some studies suggest a relation between IQ and savant skill level (Miller, 1999). Recent research has yielded findings that indicate most people with savant syndrome fall into the moderate to mild intellectual impairment range, with IQs from 40 to 70 (Treffert & Wallace, 2004). While not as common, savants are also found with normal or greater IQs up to 114 and above (Treffert & Wallace, 2004). Many show language impairments (with and without autism), have extremely narrow areas of interest, and are extremely rule-bound, with little flexibility for creative or cognitive processes. Savant skill can also be acquired later in life after a disease or brain injury is incurred (Treffert & Wallace, 2004). Many theories have been put forth to explain this intriguing syndrome, including eidetic imagery, inherited skills, sensory deprivation with accompanying social isolation, compensation, and reinforcement (Treffert, 1988). While each of these ideas has merit, none can wholly account for the entire sphere of issues surrounding savant syndrome.

The earliest depiction of an individual with savant syndrome appeared in an essay by T. Holliday in 1751 (Treffert, 1988) where Jedediah Buxton is described as having the ability to rapidly multiply nine-digit by nine-digit integers. Then in 1887, J. Langdon Down, thought to be the first person to use the appellation "idiot savant," relayed detailed information on 10 patients exhibiting this dichotomous skill set seen during his 30-year tenure as superintendent of the Earlswood Asylum in England (Treffert & Wallace, 2004). The term "idiot savant" used to describe these individuals is no longer in widespread use due to its negative connotations. With the advent of sophisticated research techniques like fMRIs and the increased use of standardized testing, far more information is available today regarding savant syndrome. As research continues, it is probable that researchers will soon be able to identify the precise neurological features associated with savant syndrome (Treffert & Wallace, 2004).

REFERENCES

Bolte, S. & Poustka, F. (2004). Comparing the intelligence profiles of savant and nonsavant individuals with autistic disorder. *Intelligence, 32,* 121–131.

Heaton, P. & Wallace, G. (2004). Annotation: The savant syndrome. *Journal of Child Psychology and Psychiatry, 45*(5), 899–911.

Hughes, J. R. (2009). Update on autism: A review of 1300 reports published in 2008. *Epilepsy & Behavior, 16*, 569–589.

Miller, L. (1999). The savant syndrome: Intellectual impairment and exceptional skill. *Psychological Bulletin, 125*, 31–46.

Neumann, N., Dubischar-Krivec, A. M., Braun, C., Low, A., Poustka, F., Bölte, S. & Birbaumer, N. (2010). The mind of the mnemonists: An MEG and neuropsychological study of autistic memory savants. *Behavioural Brain Research, 215*, 114–121.

Soulieres, I., Hubert, B., Rouleau, N., Gagnon, L., Tremblay, P., Xavier, S. et al. (2010). Superior estimation abilities in two autistic spectrum children. *Cognitive Neuropsychology, 27*(3), 261–276.

Treffert, D. A. (1988). The idiot savant: A review of the syndrome. *American Journal of Psychiatry, 145*(5), 563–572.

Treffert, D. A. (1999). The savant syndrome and autistic disorder. *CNS Spectrums, 4* (12), 57–60.

Treffert, D. A. (2001). Savant syndrome: "Special faculties" extraordinaire. *Psychiatric Times, 18*(10).

Treffert, D. A., & Wallace, G. L. (2004). Islands of genius. *Scientific American, January Special Edition, 14* (1), 14–23.

NANCY HUTCHINS
Texas A&M University
Fourth edition

SAVE THE CHILDREN FUND AND CHILDREN WITH DISABILITIES

Save the Children began when Eglantyne Jebb, the organization's founder, drew up the *Charter on the Rights of the Child* in 1919. Special mention was made of the disabled child, and this charter has now been enshrined in the UN Convention on the Rights of the Child. Disabled children are children first, and all articles in the convention that refer to children include disabled children.

Save the Children's current policy and practice on disabled children and education has developed from ongoing analytical reflection on a strong body of practical experience in a wide range of countries (in Asia, Africa, the Middle East, and Europe). Disabled children are defined as children with impairments (physical, mental, visual, hearing, speech, or multiple impairments) who are excluded or discriminated against in their local context and culture (Stubbs, 1997).

Beginning in 1960, for 30 years Save the Children supported a pioneering residential school for physically disabled children in Morocco. This was a residential institution that enabled a small group of academically able children to gain access to a high-quality education; many students went on to universities. However, this strategy did nothing for the majority of disabled children, who were still unable to access mainstream education; it did nothing to support parents or to change the negative attitudes of the majority; and it was also unsustainable financially. This concept of "special" and segregated education, while sometimes (not always) providing a quality education to a few, had many limitations.

Learning lessons from this experience, in 1987 Save the Children adopted a clear policy to promote the basic rights of the majority of disabled children, in the context of their family and community, rather than offering a privileged education to a few. Community-based rehabilitation (CBR) was promoted as a strategy to support the disabled child within his or her family and community, and CBR workers would work with the family, the child, and the local school to integrate the disabled child. For more severely disabled children, the focus was on providing daycare, support to parents, and education on activities of daily living in the home. This strategy of integrated education was sustainable, low-cost, and enabled children with disabilities to stay within their families and community. However, the strategy was very dependent on the goodwill of the local school and teachers, and relied largely on changing the child to fit a rigid system (which was not always possible), rather than changing the system to accommodate a variety of children.

In 1990, the Jomtien Conference promoted Education for All. It was followed by the Salamanca Conference in 1994, which drew attention to problems in the school system (methodology, curriculum, teacher skills, attitudes, environment, and so on) that resulted in the exclusion of large numbers of children: disabled children, street children, ethnic minorities, and girls. This was the concept of inclusive education, which differs from special or integrated education in that it places the responsibility on the system, not the child, and is based on a strong belief that children should receive appropriate and relevant education together with their peers in their own communities.

Save the Children's current policy and strategy is "toward inclusion," acknowledging that inclusion is an ideal and that the vast majority of education systems are difficult to change. Interestingly, the increasing number of successful examples of progress towards inclusion are in developing countries in Asia and Africa (Holdsworth & Thepphavongsa, 1996).

In a poor province in China with 56 million people, Save the Children supported a pilot project that integrated two children with mild to moderate mental disabilities into each class. This was achieved through training teachers in child-focused approaches, introducing flexible methodology such as team-teaching and group work, large-scale awareness-raising, promoting parental involvement, and transforming the system from teacher-centered to child-centered. This project is extremely successful in that it not only allowed disabled children access to essential early childhood education, but also improved the system for all children. It has now been scaled up throughout the province with existing resources, as schools support each other.

In Lesotho, Save the Children supported a national inclusive education program, aiming to include all types of disabled children in existing primary schools. The project was piloted in one school in each district by providing in-service training to all teachers in each school, working with the national Disabled People's Organizations to develop knowledge and skills in braille and sign language, and by involving parents and the community. Now it is possible to visit schools where the class sizes are over 100 and to see children signing, visually impaired children sitting next to buddies who offer support, and children with learning difficulties in the front row where the teacher can give them extra support (Stubbs, 1995).

Many of the Western industrialized countries have a legacy of segregated special education provision and professional special educators. In many economically poorer countries, there is more expertise on managing sparse resources, more community solidarity, and a strong tradition and experience of self-reliance. It is Save the Children's experience that pioneers in inclusive education are increasingly found in developing countries and that there are many "lessons from the south" that can inform the international community (Holdsworth & Kay, 1996; Stubbs, 1997).

Through donations to the Global Fund, Save the Children continues to promote school attendance and inclusive education. Targeted mainstreaming has benefited over 300 children with mainstreaming, which includes individual education plans and specially trained teachers with funds provided through Save the Children. For more information please visit: https://secure.savethechildren.org/site/c.8rKLIXMGIpI4E/b.6239401/k.C01C/Global_Action_Fund/apps/ka/sd/donor.asp

REFERENCES

Holdsworth, J., & Kay, J. (Eds.). (1996). *Toward inclusion: SCF UK's experience in integrated education*. Discussion paper, N.I. SEAPRO Documentation Series. Save the Children Fund.

Holdsworth, J., & Thepphavongsa, P. (Eds.). (1996). *Don't use mature wood if you want to bend it; Don't pick old mushrooms if you want to eat them. Experiences of the Lao People's Republic in provision for children with disabilities using the kindergarten sector*. Washington, DC: Save the Children Fund.

Save the Children. (2012). *Mainstream children with disabilities*. Retrieved from: http://www.savethechildren.org/site/c.8rKLI XMGIpI4E/b.6192521/k.42B9/Ensuring_Children_Have_Qual ity_Care.htm#Mainstre

Stubbs, S. (1995). *The Lesotho National Integrated Education Programme: A case study on implementation*. Master's thesis, University of Cambridge, England.

Stubbs, S. (1997). *Education and geopolitical change*. Presented at the Oxford International Conference on Education and Development, Great Britain.

SUE STUBBS
Save the Children Fund

SCALE FOR ASSESSING EMOTIONAL DISTURBANCE

The Scale for Assessing Emotional Disturbance (SAED; Epstein & Sharma) is an individually administered, 52-item measure of emotional and/or behavioral disturbance in children ages 5 through 18. The four-page response form can be completed in approximately 10 minutes by caregivers, counselors, teachers, or other persons knowledgeable about the child. The scale has three sections. The first is Student Competence Characteristics, in which the adult rater compares this child to other students of the same age on a scale of 0 to 4 (0 = far below average, 4 = far above average) in categories such as family support, level of academic achievement, and motivation. The second section is Student Emotional and Behavioral Problems, in which the rater reads a statement (e.g., "makes threats to others") and chooses the number on a scale from 0 to 3 (0 = not at all like the child, 3 = very much like the child) that best represents the child's emotions and behaviors in the past 2 months. The final section is Adversely Affects Education Performance, in which the rater judges the extent to which the student's educational performance is affected by emotional and behavioral problems on a scale of 0 to 5 (0 = not adversely affected, 5 = affected to an extreme extent). The SAED also includes eight open-ended questions that address the child's situational and personal resiliencies and protective factors (e.g., "In what school subject[s] does the child do best?" or "What job[s] or responsibilities has this student held in the community or in the home?"). The scale provides an overall emotional and behavioral functioning SAED Quotient and percentile rank, and seven subscale scores measuring Inability to Learn, Relationship Problems, Inappropriate Behavior, Unhappiness or Depression, Physical Symptoms or Fears, Social Maladjusted, and Overall Competence. Information obtained from the SAED is useful in identifying children with emotional disturbance; in developing Individualized Education Programs (IEPs), treatment, or intervention planning; and in evaluation of a program or treatment plan.

The SAED was normed on students between the ages of 5:0 and 18:11 using data collected from January 1996 to May 1997. Separate norms were produced for 2,266 students without disabilities and 1,371 students with emotional and behavioral disorders. (No explanation whatsoever is given about how these 1,371 children came to be classified as emotionally disturbed.) The manual reports demographics of this standardization sample based on age, gender, geographic location, race, ethnicity, and socioeconomic status.

Scores on the seven subtests are presented in standard scores with a mean of 10 and standard deviation of 3. The overall SAED quotient score has a mean of 100 and a standard deviation of 15.

The interrater reliability of the SAED was tested on six pairs of teachers who were asked to complete the SAED on 44 students previously diagnosed with emotional or behavioral disorders. Correlations between the two raters on the seven subscales and overall SAED scores were around .80. Content sampling revealed that items on the SAED correlate above .75, making it a highly reliable scale. The test-retest reliability was determined by SAED scores for special education children whose teachers rated them twice with about 2 weeks between each rating. Correlations between the two sets of ratings on the seven subscales and overall SAED quotient were between .84 and .94. The SAED was deemed to have criterion validity based on the positive relationships between the SAED and the Teacher Report Form (Achenbach, 1991) and the SAED and the Revised Behavior Problem Checklist (Quay & Peterson, 1996). Construct validity was confirmed through statistically significant differences between the mean scores of the nondisordered and disordered children used to norm the scale.

This entry has been informed by the sources listed below.

REFERENCES

Achenbach, T. M. (1991). *Manual for the Teacher Reports Form and 1991 profile*. Burlington: University of Vermont, Department of Psychiatry.

Cullinan, D., Evans, C., & Epstein, M. H. (2003). Characteristics of emotional disturbance of elementary school students. *Behavioral Disorders, 28*, 94–110.

Dumont, R., & Rauch, M. (2000). Test review: Scale for Assessing Emotional Disturbance by M. Epstein & D. Cullinan (PRO-ED, 1998). *NASP Communiqué, 28*, article 8. Retrieved from http://www.nasponline.org/index.aspx

Epstein, M. H., & Cullinan, D. (1998). *The scale for assessing emotional disturbance*. Austin, TX: PRO-ED.

Epstein, M. H., Cullinan, D., & Ryser, G. (2002). Development of a scale to assess emotional disturbance. *Behavioral Disorders, 28*, 5–22.

Floyd, R. G., & Bose, J. E. (2003) Behavior rating scales for assessment of emotional disturbance: A critical review of measurement characteristics. *Journal of Psychoeducational Assessment, 21*, 43–78.

Quay, H., & Peterson, D. R. (1996). *Revised Behavior Problem Checklist: Professional manual*. Odessa, FL: Psychological Assessment Resources.

RON DUMONT
Fairleigh Dickinson University

JOHN O. WILLIS
Rivier College

SCALES OF INDEPENDENT BEHAVIOR–REVISED

The Scales of Independent Behavior–Revised (SIB-R; Bruininks, Woodcock, Weatherman, & Hill, 1996) is used to assess adaptive behavior and problem behavior. It includes three forms—a Full Scale, Short Form, and Early Development Form. A Short Form for the visually impaired is also available. Administration time ranges from 15 to 20 minutes for either the Short Form or Early Development Form to 45 to 60 minutes for the Full Scale. The SIB-R is norm-referenced and nationally standardized on 2,182 individuals. It is appropriate for use with individuals from birth to 80+ years.

The SIB-R is easier to administer than its predecessor, the original SIB. In addition to the structured interview procedure, a checklist procedure is now available. It is also easier to score. Age-equivalent scoring tables are included in the response booklets for each subscale. A significant feature is the addition of a support score, which predicts the level of support a person will require based on the impact of maladaptive behaviors and adaptive functioning. Another unique feature of the SIB-R is the functional limitations index, which can be used to define the presence and severity of functional limitations in adaptive behaviors.

The test manual contains internal consistency reliabilities (mid to high .90s), test-retest reliabilities for the adaptive behavior scales (.83–.97) and the maladaptive behavior indexes (.69–.90), and interrater reliabilities (most correlations in the .80s). Extensive validity studies reported in the Comprehensive Manual support the developmental nature of the SIB-R adaptive behavior scales. The SIB-R is strongly related to other adaptive behavior measures and highly predictive of placements in different types of service settings.

There is very little independent research on the SIB-R. This is unfortunate, because the comprehensiveness, usefulness, and psychometric qualities of this instrument are truly outstanding.

REFERENCES

Bruininks, R. K., Woodcock, R. W., Weatherman, R. F., & Hill, B. (1996). *Scales of Independent Behavior–Revised (SIB-R)*. Itasca, IL: Riverside.

Maccow, G. (2000). Review of the Scales of Independent Behavior–Revised. *Mental Measurements Yearbook*. Retrieved from http://web.ebscohost.com.lib-ezproxy.tamu.edu:2048/ehost/detail?vid=3&hid=113&sid=357bcb8e-30d2-4345-b63d-a5c75d6ded94%40sessionmgr112&bdata=JnNpdGU9ZWhvvc3QtbGl2ZQ%3d%3d#db=mmt&AN=TIP07002240

Zlomke, L. C. (2000). Review of the Scales of Independent Behavior–Revised. *Mental Measurements Yearbook*. Retrieved from http://web.ebscohost.com.lib-ezproxy.tamu.edu:2048/ehost/detail?vid=3&hid=113&sid=357bcb8e-30d2-4345-b63d-a5c75d6ded94%40sessionmgr112&bdata=JnNpdGU9ZWhvvc3QtbGl2ZQ%3d%3d#db=mmt&AN=TIP07002240

FREDERICK A. SCHRANK
Olympia, Washington

See also Adaptive Behavior

SCALES OF ORDINAL DOMINANCE (See Ordinal Scales of Psychological Development)

SCANDINAVIA, SPECIAL EDUCATION IN

Since the publication of the first edition of the *Encyclopedia of Special Education* (Braswell, 1987), Scandinavian perspectives on special education have changed in some respects. It is true that, in the terms of Braswell, Scandinavian countries "have been in the vanguard with respect to their concern for the social welfare for their citizens" (p. 1381), including those with disabilities. But it is also true that much social policy has been difficult to implement in practice, especially since 1986.

In all Scandinavian countries, special education reform has been dependent on reforms in regular education systems and schools. As part of ongoing globalization patterns, higher priority has been given to values such as competition and education for excellence. These values have been embraced in general education. The guiding perspective of special education policy is an inclusive one, with special education support as much as possible integrated into regular education frameworks. Sweden and Denmark have traditionally been considered leaders in inclusion, and Norway and Finland were seen as following behind (Tuunainen, 1994). This is no longer the case, at least regarding Norway. Decisions on school laws and curricula during the 1990s by Norway's Parliament are more radically inclusive than in the other Scandinavian countries.

As in Sweden, a few general societal policy conditions greatly influence special education. There is ongoing decentralization of decision power and responsibilities

from the national level to local municipalities (less evident in Finland). This process happened concurrently with the effects of an economic recession during most of the 1990s (less evident in Norway). In combination, these two circumstances meant that responsibilities and decision-making power were moved from national and/or central bodies to local municipalities and schools. In Sweden, Denmark, and Norway, there are little or no resources earmarked specifically for special education any longer. School laws and other official guidelines stress that schools shall give high priority to the fulfillment of students' special needs. These resource allocation decisions, made on local levels of the system, had to be made at the same time as severe budget cuts during most of the 1990s. These matters raised sincere questions about what is possible to spend on students with special needs, especially compared to other school and student needs. This is most evident in Sweden and Denmark and, to a lesser extent, in Norway. Norway still has some stipulations for resource allocation for guaranteed support to students with certain severe disabilities. This is a small proportion (only around 2%) of all students, though, and is also a small fraction of all students given special education support in the schools. According to results from an evaluation study (Skårbrevik, 1995), the support given in this way to students with severe disabilities also covers only 20% to 30% of their weekly hours in school. In Sweden and Denmark, this support has to be financed within the frameworks of regular school budgets.

The process of closing down special schools and institutions has continued, and very few special schools are now in use. Most of those are for students who are deaf or hard of hearing, or who have intellectual or multiple disabilities. Again, this closing is going on at a slower rate in Finland than in the other three countries. Many of the former institutions and special schools are in the process of developing into resource centers. Their responsibilities are firsthand competence development and consultant support to schools attended by students with severe disabilities. They also often give shorter, intensive training courses for students, family members, and school teachers. They are still financed by government money, which is seen as necessary in order to guarantee qualified support to children with the greatest need, regardless of where they live or go to school. In most respects these resource centers and their consultant responsibilities are organized on a local basis. At the national level, Sweden has a National Swedish Agency for Special Education, a separate administrative body parallel to the National Agency for Schools. In Norway, the same national administrative body monitors both regular and special education, as well as education for those with more severe disabilities.

In all countries, there is concern about the availability of qualified support given from resource centers to schools, and measures are continuously taken to satisfy necessary competence development. Especially in Norway, where special schools for students with intellectual disabilities have been closed, many resource centers will have to deal with new disability areas, and therefore develop broader and deeper competence. This is a need also in the other Scandinavian countries. In Sweden, this is a responsibility for the National Swedish Agency for Special Education and is financed within regular government budget framework. In Norway, where there is no such monitoring body between the national government ministry and resource centers, the ministry has used some of the financial resources saved by closing institutions toward competence development. A 5-year research and development program (1993–1998) and a 3-year program of resource center development initiatives were both implemented. In comparison to the other Scandinavian countries, this was a massive national government input for increasing the level of competence needed to guarantee the meeting of severe disability special needs, independent of geographic location. The research and development program in special education also meant broadening the competence area through involvement of more academic disciplines and university departments. Over the past 20 to 25 years, it has been important to see special education as a more comprehensive domain than simply medical disability knowledge.

An inclusive education policy means demands on teacher education programs for both special educators and regular education professionals. In all Scandinavian countries, special education objectives are included in regular teaching training programs. This has proved difficult in all the countries, and too little has really been included. This prevents new teachers from being as well prepared as they should be for a job in an inclusive environment. These matters are of current concern, especially in Sweden and Denmark, where preparatory work for teacher training reforms is ongoing. Teacher training is clearly a field of many controversies, and it is not evident that inclusive education needs will be a part of the guidelines for future reforms training for regular education teachers. The continuous changes of special education teacher programs have been more successfully implemented, but this has caused increasing differences between programs at different universities, within Scandinavian countries, and within the region of Scandinavia itself. This may be less the case in Finland, where special education programs are still more centralized, and where there are still specific programs for teaching in special classes or special schools.

Decreasing proportions of students attend special schools or special classes, usually less than 2% or 3% a year. It must be taken into account, though, that such proportion figures do not always give the full picture. This has to do with the decentralized and goal-based educational systems. Partly, this means that differences between local municipalities and schools are increasing, even affecting definitions for special education. There are some statistics from evaluation study reports on what could be a trend toward increasing proportions of students referred to special groups or schools again. For instance, clustering of special education resources sometimes means organization of special classes and schools turning up again on local or regional levels. This is the case in Sweden, according to special schools for students with intellectual disabilities, but corresponding trends are clearly seen in Denmark and, lately, Norway. One factor behind such trends is a lack of sufficient resources, which is related to elite and competitive values and priorities. Also, school officials hear parent worries and complaints that their disabled children are not being adequately supported in the integrated settings. Both circumstances lead to more segregated solutions.

Compulsory schooling is 9 years in all countries, and in some special schools it may be extended to 10. But today there is generally a need for further education in order to meet the demands of employment and society. An increasing number of students have had to continue their educations and go on to upper secondary schools, and the current proportion of each age group doing so is between 95% to 98% in all of the Scandinavian countries. Although this schooling is officially voluntary, from the student point of view it has become obligatory. This is also the case for students with disabilities and learning difficulties. Consequently, special needs have also become important issues in these schools.

Adult education has a long tradition in the Scandinavian countries, and so has special education support within this education area. In Scandinavia, as elsewhere, lifelong learning has become a more commonly used concept in education policy and planning, especially during the 1990s. This meant an expansion of adult education in many respects. Expansion of adult education has also been one of the most important measures taken toward increasing employment, especially in Sweden. Special education support within regular programs, as well as special courses for those with disabilities, have a long tradition. In colleges, universities, and the adult education system at large, support to meet special needs has been further developed in the past 20 years.

From having been nearly culturally homogeneous until the 1960s, Scandinavia has become increasingly multicultural through immigration. During the first decades immigration was mostly a result of labor; more recently, immigrants have moved to Scandinavian countries as refugees for different reasons. This is so especially in Denmark, Sweden, and Norway, while Finland still has a comparatively small immigration rate. In many Danish and Swedish municipalities, the proportion of inhabitants with immigrant background reaches 30% or more, and there are schools in these places where the proportion of immigrant background students are up to 80% to 85%. This multicultural situation creates challenges for special education.

Scandinavian countries are still in the vanguard of special education development in inclusive education.

However, there are many conflicting trends and widening gaps between more privileged students and those who are less well off. The welfare state model, often thought of as guaranteed, has become at risk of being dismantled during the past two decades. These trends also have great influence on education policies, and especially on special education policy and practice. Therefore, Scandinavia will continue to be a very interesting focus for studies of special education.

This entry has been informed by the sources listed below.

REFERENCES

Braswell, D. (1987). Scandinavia, special education in. In C. R. Reynolds & L. Mann (Eds.), *Encyclopedia of special education.* New York, NY: Wiley.

Haug, P. (1997). *Integration and special education research in Norway.* Paper presented at the AERA 1997 Annual Conference, Chicago.

Skårbrevik, K. (1995). Spesialpedagogiske tiltak pa dagsorden. Evaluering av prosjektet "Omstrukturering av spesialundervisning." Volda: Høgskulen og Møreforsking, Forskingsrapport no. 14.

Tuunainen, K. (1994). Finland, Norway, and Sweden. In K. Mazurek & M. Winzer (Eds.), *Comparative studies in special education.* Washington, DC: Gallaudet University Press.

INGEMAR EMANUELSSON
Goteburg University

See also France, Special Education in; Western Europe, Special Education in

SCAPEGOATING

A scapegoat is generally defined as a person or group that bears the blame for the mistakes of others. Typically, this is manifested as a group singling out an individual for unfair attack. In schools such systematic victimization of one child by a group of others can isolate the child from the social life of the class and cause the child to feel unworthy of inclusion in the peer group. At times children with disabilities may be scapegoats, particularly those with low self-esteem, which is usual with disabled children owing to academic, emotional, or physical problems (Gearheart, 1985).

Allan (1985) has reported that the scapegoating of one child by others is a common problem facing teachers and counselors. The scapegoats suffer from social isolation and poor self-concept. This type of environment can only have

a negative effect on learning. This is especially true for children in classes for the disabled. However, the disruptiveness caused by scapegoating is not only destructive to the scapegoat, but also to children who fear that they may become the next victim. These children may develop coping strategies to avoid that possibility. Such strategies may include ingratiating themselves with class leaders, mistreating scapegoats to prove that they are not scapegoats themselves, and refusing to associate with former friends who are now scapegoats.

Nondisabled children require help with social skills as they interact with disabled peers in mainstreamed classrooms. One problem that may arise is the calling of names, which can be dealt with in a variety of ways. Salend and Schobel (1981) described one strategy that they implemented with a fourth-grade class. Discussion included the meaning of names, how names differ, and the positive and negative consequences of names. The last topic included a discussion of the negative effects of nicknames and the importance of considering another person's reaction to the nickname. It is obvious that educators must seriously consider the effects of scapegoating and must continue to develop strategies to counteract the negative effects of scapegoating on children with disabilities.

REFERENCES

Allan, C. L. (1985). Scapegoating: Help for the whole class. *Elementary School Guidance and Counseling, 18,* 147.

Gearheart, B. R. (1985). *Learning disabilities.* St. Louis, MO: Times Mirror/Mosby College.

Salend, S. J., & Schobel, J. (1981). Coping with namecalling in the mainstream setting. *Education Unlimited, 3*(2), 36–38.

JOSEPH M. RUSSO
Hunter College,
City University of New York

See also Self-Concept

SCATTER PLOT ASSESSMENT

Scatter plot assessment is an observational method used to identify temporal conditions and (in some formats) other stimulus conditions that may reliably predict the occurrence or absence of problem behavior. A scatter plot typically resembles a grid with a specified time interval represented by the ordinate axis and successive dates represented by the abscissa. Time intervals can be divided into hour, half-hour, quarter-hour, or smaller increments, depending on the frequency of the behavior, capabilities of the observer, and what information the observer would like to determine (Martella, Nelson, & Marchand-Martella, 2003). At the end of each time interval in the corresponding grid box, relative or absolute problem behavior occurrences are recorded. For example, an open box might indicate the absence of problem behavior; a slash through the box, between 1 and 5 occurrences of problem behavior; and a filled box, more than 5 occurrences of problem behavior (see Figure S.1). Numbers may also be recorded in each box, indicating the exact number of occurrences of problem behavior (Axelrod, 1987). After collecting data (typically for several days), time-correlated patterns of problem behavior responding may emerge. These patterns can be further analyzed to determine environmental events that may evoke problem behavior occurrences (e.g., engaging in specific activities, caregivers present, or transitions).

The scatter plot has been used as a tool to measure multiple types of problem behaviors across multiple situations (Alberto & Troutman, 2012). Touchette, MacDonald, and Langer (1985) suggest that the scatter plot also provides more specific information than a line graph, which reflects response frequency but not temporal distribution. Additionally, scatter plots are said to be easy to use and require minimal training (Symons, McDonald, & Wehby, 1998). However, Axelrod (1987) states that scatter plots are insensitive to identifying noncyclical patterns of behavioral responding and do not specifically identify antecedent and consequent events that may be maintaining problem behavior. Kahng et al. (1998) state further that when analyzing scatter plot data, patterns of responding may not be discernable without the use of statistical analysis procedures. Despite some reservations about the use of scatter plots, they continue to be employed extensively by clinicians and practitioners (Desrochers, Hile, & Williams-Mosely, 1997).

Research

Though many empirical studies reference scatter plots (Durand & Kishi, 1987; Kennedy & Souza, 1995; Lalli, Browder, Mace, & Brown, 1993), the scatter plot itself has been the focus of relatively few empirical evaluations (Kahng et al., 1998). Touchette et al. (1985) published the first article regarding scatter plot assessment and demonstrated that frequency data collected during 30-minute intervals successfully detected time periods and subsequently other stimulus conditions that reliably predicted problem behavior occurrences for two of three participants. Interventions were designed and implemented based on the scatter plot assessment data and were effective in reducing problem behavior to near-zero levels. However, Touchette and colleagues (1985) stated that one participant's scatter plot was deemed "uninterpretable" (p. 349). An effective intervention was eventually developed for the third participant based on other collected data.

Kahng and others (1998) sought to replicate the study of Touchette et al. (1985) and collected scatter plot data continuously during 30-minute intervals for 20 individuals living in residential facilities. They visually analyzed the data from 15 of the 20 scatter plots (the data for five participants were not used due to poor interobserver agreement), but could not discern any temporal patterns of significance. However, when the data were transformed using statistical process control procedures (SPC) into control charts, one or more 30-minute intervals were identified in which problem behavior was more likely to occur for 12 of the 15 data sets. The authors conclude

Name _____ Behavior _____

Scoring	0 = leave blank	1 to 5 = slash in box	5 + = fill in box

8:00–8:30					
8:30–9:00					
9:00–9:30					
9:30–10:00					
10:00–10:30					
10:30–11:00					
11:00–11:30					
11:30–12:00					
12:00–12:30					
12:30–1:00					
1:00–1:30					
1:30–2:00					
2:00–2:30					
Date	9/1	9/2	9/3	9/4	9/5

Figure S.1. Scatter plot example.

that use of statistical procedures (e.g., SPC) may more precisely and accurately identify temporal patterns of responding.

Guidelines for Practice

The usefulness of scatter plot data can be enhanced by considering a few suggestions. First, to set behavior frequency cutoffs or criteria for each time interval (e.g., 0, 1 to 4, >4), Symons and colleagues (1998) suggest determining the number of disruptive behavior events that may be tolerable to a teacher or caregiver during a given time interval and using that information to identify frequency criteria. Second, consider the frequency with which the problem behavior is occurring when choosing a time interval for observation. For example, high-frequency behavior may need to be recorded during shorter time intervals than low-frequency behavior (unless each behavior is discretely recorded), so as not to underestimate the frequency with which the behavior occurs.

Third, numbering each event in the appropriate grid box is a more precise data collection method and alleviates the need to set behavior frequency criteria. Because each event is recorded, selection of an observational time interval is less important, but it may be difficult to monitor accurately when engaging in simultaneous tasks. Fourth, Kahng et al. (1998, p. 602) recommend "that in some cases it may be necessary to assign a 1:1 staff-to-client ratio while scatter plot data are being collected" due to frequent interruptions that may preclude the observer from collecting reliable data. Last, because scatter plots are not conducive to identifying noncyclical patterns of behavior, making notes of antecedent and consequent events can help to identify functional response patterns, when temporal patterns are not observed. O'Neill et al. (1997) developed the Functional Assessment Observation Form (FAO), which incorporates features of a typical scatter plot but also provides columns in which an observer can denote what behavior occurred and possible predictors to and consequences of the behavior.

Though scatter plots are widely used, the research findings suggest that they may not always assist in identifying patterns of behavioral responding. Using scatter plots as part of a multiple method and multiple source assessment plan will help in developing a clearer understanding of the behavior of concern and conditions that affect the probability of its occurrence.

Case Examples

Example 1. "Virginia" frequently engaged in head hitting throughout the day. To determine possible temporal patterns to Virginia's responding, her caregivers collected scatter plot data. Every 30 minutes caregivers recorded whether 0, 1 to 10, or more than 10 head hits occur during an interval. After collecting data for 2 weeks, caregivers reviewed the data and identified that head-hitting occurrences were highly correlated with the presence of one of Virginia's caregivers and/or when Virginia was asked to practice dressing herself. The scatter plot assessment information then informed the development of a behavior intervention to reduce the number of head hits Virginia engaged in.

Example 2. "Jorge" interrupted his classmates and used profanities during the school day. An instructional assistant, Mrs. Montgomery, collected data regarding Jorge's verbal behavior using the Functional Assessment Observation Form (O'Neill et al., 1997). Mrs. Montgomery recorded the number of interruptions and profanities Jorge produced every 30 minutes and also recorded events that preceded and followed each behavior. After collecting data for 3 weeks, Mrs. Montgomery identified that interruptions and profanities were more likely to occur during whole-class instruction and were usually followed by peer laughter. The assessment information was then used to develop a behavior intervention aimed to reduce Jorge's inappropriate verbal behavior.

REFERENCES

Alberto, P., & Troutman, A. C. (2012). *Applied behavior analysis for teachers.* Upper Saddle River, NJ: Merrill.

Axelrod, S. (1987). Functional and structural analyses of behavior: Approaches leading to reduced use of punishment procedures? *Research in Developmental Disabilities, 8,* 165–178.

Desrochers, M. N., Hile, M. G., & Williams-Mosely, T. L. (1997). Survey of functional assessment procedures used with individuals who display mental retardation and severe problem behaviors. *American Journal on Mental Retardation, 101,* 535–546.

Durand, V. M., & Kishi, G. (1987). Reducing severe behavior problems among persons with dual sensory impairments: An evaluation of a technical assistance model. *Journal of the Association for Persons with Severe Handicaps, 12,* 2–10.

Kahng, S., Iwata, B. A., Fischer, S. M., Page, T. J., Treadwell, K. R. H., Williams, D. E., & Smith, R. G. (1998). Temporal distributions of problem behavior based on scatter plot analysis. *Journal of Applied Behavior Analysis, 31,* 593–604.

Kennedy, C., & Souza, G. (1995). Functional analysis and intervention of breath holding. *Journal of Applied Behavior Analysis, 28,* 339–340.

Lalli, J. S., Browder, D. M., Mace, F. C., & Brown, D. K. (1993). Teacher use of descriptive analysis data to implement interventions to decrease students' problem behaviors. *Journal of Applied Behavior Analysis, 26,* 227–238.

Martella, R. C., Nelson, J. R., & Marchand-Martella, N. E. (2003). *Managing disruptive behavior in the schools: A schoolwide, classroom, and individualized social learning approach.* Boston, MA: Allyn & Bacon.

O'Neill, R. E., Horner, R. H., Albin, R. W., Sprague, J. R., Storey, K., & Newton, J. S. (1997). *Functional assessment and program development for problem behavior: A practical handbook* (2nd ed.). Pacific Grove, CA: Brooks/Cole.

Symons, F., McDonald, L., & Wehby, J. (1998). Functional assessment and teacher collected data. *Education and Treatment of Children, 21*, 135–159.

Touchette, P., MacDonald, R., & Langer, S. (1985). A scatter plot for identifying stimulus control of problem behavior. *Journal of Applied Behavior Analysis, 18*, 343–351.

Sarah Fairbanks
University of Connecticut

Schaefer, E. S., & Burnett, C. K. (1987). Stability and predictability of women's marital relationships and demoralization. *Journal of Personality and Social Psychology, 53*(6), 1129–1136.

Schaefer, E. S., & Edgerton, M. (1985). Parent and child correlates of parental modernity. In E. Sigel (Ed.), *Parental belief systems*. Hillsdale, NJ: Erlbaum.

E. Valerie Hewitt
Texas A&M University
First edition

Tamara J. Martin
The University of Texas
of the Permian Basin
Second edition

SCHAEFER, EARL S. (1926–)

A native of Adyeville, Indiana, Earl S. Schaefer received his BA (1948) in psychology from Purdue University and later earned both his MA (1951) and PhD (1954) in psychology at the Catholic University of America. He is currently a professor in the department of maternal and child health in the School of Public Health, University of North Carolina, Chapel Hill. He is also senior investigator at the Frank Porter Graham Child Development Center at the University.

Schaefer's early research began with studies of parent attitudes and behavior as related to child development, resulting in the development of the Parental Attitude Research Instrument and an infant education program (Schaefer & Bell, 1958). This research was later extended to parent-child relationships, child social-emotional development, husband-wife relationships, and mental health of parents and children (Schaefer, 1991; Schaefer & Burnett, 1987; Schaefer & Edgerton, 1985). In his investigations, Schaefer has shown correlations between parental beliefs/values and a child's intellectual development, correlations between a parent's behavior and the child's school development, and the effects of a perceived marital relationship on individual adjustment. This research has important implications for the development of parent education programs.

Among his many honors, Schaefer is the recipient of the Research Scientist Award of the National Institute of Mental Health (1975–1979) and has served as consulting editor of the *American Journal of Mental Deficiency* and *Child Development*.

REFERENCES

Schaefer, E. S. (1991). Goals for parent and future-parent education: Research on parental beliefs. *Elementary School Journal, 91*(3), 239–247.

Schaefer, E. S., & Bell, R. Q. (1958). Development of a parental attitude research instrument. *Child Development, 29*, 339–361.

SCHIEFELBUSCH, RICHARD L. (1918–)

Richard Schiefelbusch received his BS (1940) from Kansas State Teachers College and his MA (1947) in speech pathology and psychology from the University of Kansas. He went on to earn his PhD (1951) in speech pathology at Northwestern University. Schiefelbusch was director of the Bureau of Child Research at the University of Kansas from 1955 to 1990, and since 1989 has held the distinction of professor emeritus at that university.

Schiefelbusch has spent his career helping persons with disabilities. As director of the Bureau of Child Research, he conducted research related to language and communications programs for mentally retarded children and he was instrumental in discovering and developing effective applied behavior techniques for those with severe mental retardation. The studies conducted during his time there were designed to alter the range of educational and social activities of institutionalized children, demonstrating that children with no history of educational success could participate in productive instructional programs. This research was instrumental in the development of innovative treatment and training in language and social skills for children with severe and multiple handicaps. Schiefelbusch's work involving the language potential of people with severe mental retardation was a key element in the establishment of the constitutional right to education and the enactment of the Education of the Handicapped Act in 1966.

Among his numerous awards, Schiefelbusch is the recipient of the Distinguished Service award of the National Association for Retarded Citizens (1983) and the Distinguished Accomplishment award of the American Association of University Affiliated Programs (1987). His major publications include *Language Intervention Strategies* (1978) and *Communicative Competence* (1984).

REFERENCES

Schiefelbusch, R. L. (Ed.). (1978). *Language intervention strategies*. Baltimore, MD: University Park Press.

Schiefelbusch, R. L., & Pickar, J. (Eds.). (1984). *Communicative competence: Acquisition and intervention*. Baltimore, MD: University Park Press.

E. Valerie Hewitt
Texas A&M University
First edition

Tamara J. Martin
The University of Texas
of the Permian Basin
Second edition

SCHILDER DISEASE (ADRENOLEUKODYSTROPHY)

Schilder disease is a very serious progressive disorder characterized by the breakdown or loss of the myelin sheath surrounding nerve cells in the brain and nervous system in addition to the dysfunction of the adrenal gland. There are three forms of this rare genetic disorder: childhood adrenoleukodystrophy (ALD) in 35% of cases, adrenomyeloneuropathy (AMN) occurring in adolescent males and adult men in 40%–45% of cases, and Addison's disease in 10% of cases (Moser, Moser, & Boehm, 1999).

Schilder disease is inherited as an X-linked recessive trait, affecting males with females as the carriers. The prevalence approximates between 1 in 20,000 and 1 in 50,000 equally across races and ethnic groups (Moser, Moser, & Boehm, 1999). The childhood form and Addison's disease are discussed as they both pertain to childhood disorders.

Characteristics

1. Onset between 4 and 10 years of age.
2. Initially behavioral and attentional deficits, resulting in ADD diagnosis until underlying problems arise such as memory loss, perceptual difficulties, deterioration of handwriting skills and school performance, visual impairment, reading difficulties, and difficulty understanding speech.
3. Child also develops coordination disturbance and displays aggressive behavior.
4. Seizures may occur.
5. Between 2 years of age and adulthood, adrenal malfunction (Addison's disease) may cause bronze pigmentation of the skin along with unexplained vomiting and weakness or coma (Moser, Moser, & Boehm, 1999).

Treatment for Schilder disease is experimental. Bone marrow transplantation may be effective, especially for boys and adolescents who are early in the course of childhood onset, who show magnetic resonance imaging (MRI) evidence of brain involvement, and who have a performance IQ above 80 (Moser, Moser, & Boehm, 1999). Adrenal impairment can be treated with corticosteroid replacement therapy.

Another possible treatment consists of dietary supplements with glycerol trioleate and glycerol trierucate (Lorenzo's oil diet), which improves the body's composition of fatty acids but fails to stop the progression of neurological impairment (Apatoff, 1997).

Various special education implications arise with this serious disorder. Physical therapy will be needed to help coordination, gross motor skills, and fine motor skills. Services for learning disabilities in reading, spatial ability, and understanding speech as well as services for mental retardation may also be required. Services should also be provided for visual impairment. Psychological therapy or counseling should be sought for alleviating aggression and other behavioral and personality changes that result from the disease as well as for alleviating the psychological impact of a progressive condition. School staff should be able to effectively handle seizures, should the child experience them.

The severe childhood form becomes fatal in 1–10 years. The effectiveness of new therapies such as lovastatin and 4-phenylbutyrate are to be tested in future research.

REFERENCES

Apatoff, B. R. (1997). Adrenoleukodystrophy. In R. Berkow, M. H. Beers, R. M. Bogin, & A. J. Fletcher (Eds.), *The Merck manual of medical information: Home edition* (p. 321). New York, NY: Pocket Books.

Moser, H. W., Moser, A. B., & Boehm, C. D. (1999, March 9). *X-linked adrenoleukodystrophy*. Retrieved from http://www.geneclinics.org/pro.les/x-ald/details.html?

Iman Teresa Lahroud
University of Texas at Austin

SCHIZENCEPHALY

Schizencephaly is a disorder of grossly abnormal neuronal migration patterns with onset during fetal development. It is characterized by clefts in the parasylvian region of the brain along with additional openings in the regions of the pre- and postcentral gyri. These anomalies may or may not be symmetrical (Baron, Fennell, & Voeller, 1995). Other regions of the brain may also be involved in ways that are not predictable solely on the basis of the diagnosis of schizencephaly. The disorder is diagnosable via fetal ultrasound but CT and MRI studies after birth are necessary to view the extent of the abnormalities in brain structure.

Outcomes vary widely and may range from microcephaly and severe or profound levels of intellectual disability to normal intelligence, although at least some neuropsychological impairment will always be present. Children with schizencephaly may have a variety of neurological problems including hydrocephalus, seizure disorders of various types, intellectual disabilities, and coordination disorders of varying degrees of severity (Baron, Fennell, & Voeller, 1995). Special education programming will be necessary in virtually all cases, but only after careful assessment due to the highly variable expressivity of symptoms. As the child develops, the behavioral and mental symptom complex may change significantly and frequent, comprehensive neuropsychological examinations are recommended.

REFERENCE

Baron, I., Fennell, E., & Voeller, K. (1995). *Pediatric neuropsychology in the medical setting.* Oxford, England: Oxford University Press.

CECIL R. REYNOLDS
Texas A&M University

SCHIZOPHRENIA (*See Childhood Schizophrenia*)

SCHMIDT SYNDROME

Schmidt syndrome is an endocrine disorder that is diagnosed when there are several different malfunctions in the endocrine glands, which are responsible for the production of hormones. Hypothyroidism and Addison's disease are the main characteristics of Schmidt syndrome, although problems with the functioning of other endocrine glands such as the gonads, parathyroids, and pancreas; insulin-dependent diabetes; and autoimmune disorders are common in those with Schmidt syndrome.

Addison's disease specifically refers to the malfunction of the adrenal glands and in most cases a diminished amount of cortisol in the body. This deficiency in turn leads to weakness, fatigue, low blood pressure, and weight loss.

Schmidt syndrome is thought to be inherited by some method, and it seems as if relatives of individuals with Schmidt syndrome are more likely to develop serious endocrine disorders (Anderson, Fein, & Frey, 1980).

Characteristics

1. Addison's disease
2. Hypothyroidism
3. Insulin-dependent diabetes
4. Failure of one or more endocrine glands
5. Autoimmune disorders

Children with Schmidt syndrome are at risk for several different health problems. Addison's disease will cause children to be especially weak and fatigued, and they may not have the energy to attend a full day of school or to keep up with peers at play. Hypothyroidism may lead to problems with weight gain and may make the child susceptible to teasing. Diabetes must be monitored closely—including while the child is in school—and proper instructions for care must be available at all times. Other glandular failure may cause a decrease in the production of various hormones, which may lead to delayed development and other associated health risks, depending on the particular hormones that are lacking. Finally, autoimmune disorders make the child more susceptible to catching colds and more serious diseases from his or her peers.

REFERENCE

Anderson, P. B., Fein, S. H., & Frey, W. G., III. (1980). Familial Schmidt's syndrome. *Journal of the American Medical Association, 244,* 2068–2070.

ALLISON KATZ
Rutgers University

SCHOOL ATTENDANCE OF CHILDREN WITH DISABILITIES

School attendance of students with disabilities, and of all children, is affected by the following factors: motivational level, home and community problems, levels of stress, academic underachievement, rate of failure, negative self-concept, social difficulties, external directedness, improper school placement, inconsistent expectations by parents and teachers, employment outside of school, aversive elements in the school environment, and skill deficiencies (Grala & McCauley, 1976; Schloss, Kane, & Miller, 1981; Sing, 1998; Unger, Douds, & Pierce, 1978). Absenteeism is learned; as it becomes habitual, it increases and continues to reinforce itself (Stringer, 1973).

Since it is difficult to develop effective intervention strategies in academic, social, emotional, and vocational areas if children are not in school, attendance becomes a parallel goal to the successful completion of the disabled student's individual educational plan (IEP). Various authors (Bosker & Hofman, 1994; Jones, 1974; Schloss et al., 1981; Unger et al., 1978) have suggested programs for motivating or changing patterns of behavior of special education students to assist in increasing their school attendance.

Jones (1974) described the Diversified Satellite Occupations Program and Career Development, which allows the student to register in a less structured school setting from the one he or she normally attends, provides a curriculum with an emphasis on occupational guidance for all ages, and shortens the school day. The program was successful in decreasing truancy.

Schloss et al. (1981) evaluated factors related to adverse aspects of attending school and pleasant aspects of staying at home. An intervention program was individually developed to assist the student in increasing the amount of satisfaction received from going to school, decreasing the amount of satisfaction gained from staying home, and actively teaching skills that enhance the student's ability to benefit from going to school. Not only did school attendance improve, but test scores also increased. Unger et al. (1978) described a program that taught students the skills necessary to succeed in school. Each student's attendance pattern was examined, reasons for truancy evaluated, and individual lessons devised. Students' attendance and attitudes toward school both improved.

School attendance for disabled children is mandated by the Individuals with Disabilities Education Act (IDEA). It is extremely important that absenteeism be evaluated constantly by the local educational agency and that steps be undertaken to remediate the situation on an individual basis whenever possible.

REFERENCES

Bosker, R. J., & Hofman, W. H. A. (1994). School effects on dropout: A multi-level logistic approach to assessing school-level correlates of dropout of ethnic minorities. *Tijdschrift voor Onderwijsresearch, 19*(1), 50–64.

Grala, R., & McCauley, C. (1976). Counseling truants back to school: Motivation combined with a program for action. *Journal of Counseling Psychology, 23,* 166–169.

Jones, H. B. (1974). *Dropout prevention: Diversified satellite occupations program and career development. Final report.* Washington, DC: Bureau of Adult, Vocational, and Technical Education.

Schloss, P. J., Kane, M. S., & Miller, S. (1981). Truancy intervention with behavior disordered adolescents. *Behavior Disorders, 6*(3), 175–179.

Sing, K. (1998). Part-time employment in high school and its effect on academic achievement. *Journal of Educational Research, 91*(3), 131–139.

Stringer, L. A. (1973). Children at risk 2. The teacher as change agent. *Elementary School Journal, 73*(8), 424–434.

Unger, K. V., Douds, A., & Pierce, R. M. (1978). A truancy prevention project. *Phi Delta Kappan, 60*(4), 317.

SUSANNE BLOUGH ABBOTT
Bedford Central School District,
Mt. Kiseo, New York

See *also* Individuals With Disabilities Education Improvement Act of 2004 (IDEIA)

SCHOOL EFFECTIVENESS

School effectiveness is a term adopted in the late 1970s to refer to a body of research on identifying effective schools and the means for creating more of them. The movement to research effective schools has been driven largely by three principal assumptions. According to Bickel (1983), these are that: (1) it is possible to identify schools that are particularly effective in teaching basic skills to poor and minority children; (2) effective schools exhibit identifiable characteristics that are correlated with the success of their students and these characteristics can be manipulated by educators; and (3) the salient characteristics of effective schools form a basis for the improvement of noneffective schools.

Bickel (1983) has traced the origins of the school effectiveness movement to three factors. The first is the backlash that developed in response to the Coleman studies (and like research) of the 1960s. These studies left the unfortunate impression that differences among schools were irrelevant in the education of poor and minority children. The second basis, according to Bickel, was the general psychological climate of the 1970s. Principals, teachers, parents, and others seemed ready for a more positive, hopeful message, one that said schools could make a difference and that effective schools did exist in the real world. The final factor described by Bickel is the readiness of the educational research community to accept the findings that to date include such intuitively appealing variables as strong instructional leadership, an orderly school climate, high expectations, an emphasis on basic skills, and frequent testing and monitoring of student progress.

MacKenzie (1983) has noted broad, rapid agreement on the dimensions and fundamental elements of what constitutes effective schools. Table S.1, adapted from MacKenzie's (1983) excellent review, lists these various elements; however, as MacKenzie has discussed, the listing of attributes is truly misleading in this instance. The characteristics of effective schools are largely interactive, producing a circumstance that promotes learning that goes far beyond a summation of the parts. The effectiveness of a school cannot be predicted by

Table S.1. Dimensions of Effective School Research and Corresponding Elements of Effective Schools

Leadership dimensions

Core elements

1. Positive overall school and organizational climate
2. Activities focused toward clear, attainable, relevant, and objective goals
3. Teacher-directed classroom management
4. Teacher-directed decision making
5. In-service training designed to develop effective teaching

Facilitating elements

1. Consensus among teachers and administrators on goals and values
2. Long-range planning
3. Stability of key staff
4. District-level support for school improvement

Efficacy dimensions

Core elements

1. Expectations for high achievement
2. Consistent press for excellence
3. Visible rewards for academic excellence
4. Group interaction in the classroom
5. Autonomy and flexibility to implement adaptive practices
6. Total staff involvement in school improvement
7. Teacher empathy, rapport, and interaction with students

Facilitating elements

1. Emphasis on homework and study
2. Acceptance of responsibility for learning outcomes
3. Strategies to avoid nonpromotion of students
4. Deemphasis on ability grouping

Efficiency dimensions

Core elements

1. Amount and intensity of time engaged in learning
2. Orderly school and classroom environments
3. Continuous assessment, evaluation, and feedback
4. Well-structured classroom learning activities
5. Instruction driven by content
6. Schoolwide emphasis on basic and on higher order skills

Facilitating elements

1. Opportunities for individualized work
2. Number and variety of opportunities to learn
3. Reduced class size

determining the mere presence or absence of each of these factors—they must be assessed as they interact within the school under observation.

As can be seen from the elements of school effectiveness given in the table, making schools particularly good learning environments is a total system effort. Elements are listed that affect the district level, building level, and classroom level. It is difficult to point to any one level as being the most crucial, even though schools are hierarchically arranged; however, if there is one level that deserves more emphasis, it is the classroom. The individual classroom is

where instruction takes place; it will always be the key to the educational process. The classroom is affected by many elements that cannot be ignored. MacKenzie (1983) emphasizes:

> The classroom as a learning environment is nested in the larger environment of the school, which is embedded in a political-administrative structure through which it relates to the surrounding community.... It will be difficult if not impossible to provide effective classroom teaching in a disorderly, disorganized, and disoriented school environment, and it may be nearly as difficult to organize good schools in an atmosphere of political and managerial indifference. (p. 9; Also see Purkey & Smith, 1982)

Effective schools may have been thought, intuitively, by some to bring all students to some designated average level of performance. However, instead of causing students to cluster tightly about some central tendency, effective schools expand the differences among students rather than restrict them. Rich, facilitative environments enhance the results of ability differences, allowing the maximum possible levels of growth; deprived, restrictive environments slow and constrain growth. This does not mean that group differences will necessarily increase. If schools and instruction are particularly effective for all groups, as should be the case, then the overall level of achievement should increase for all groups along with the within group dispersion. This, at least in theory, is currently being attempted in terms of school accountability movement, in which expectations for schools now include test results of special education students (Consortium on Inclusive Schooling Practices [CISP], 1998).

As promising as the school effectiveness literature appears to be, and even with the consensus on the core elements of school effectiveness, a variety of valid criticisms have been offered. These have been summarized and reviewed by Rowan, Bossert, and Dwyer (1983). The technical properties of the research have been criticized as (a) using narrow, limited measures of effectiveness that focus only on instructional outcomes; (b) using design that allows an analysis of relational variables from which cause and effect cannot be inferred; and (c) making global comparisons on the basis of aggregate data, without assessing intraschool variations in organizational climate or outcomes across classes within schools. Rowan et al. (1983) also caution that the effect sizes present in this line of research are questionable. They have argued that the traditional methods of research in school effectiveness resemble "fishing expeditions" that spuriously inflate the probability of finding significant results. Despite these and other problems, the school effectiveness movement has rekindled optimism that schools can be organized and restructured to enhance student performance. As yet, the application of the methods and concepts of the school effectiveness literature have not been applied to special education programs. Special education programs are typically excluded from the data in such studies and desperately need to be assessed. It remains to be seen whether special education programs that can be identified as particularly effective in educating the handicapped are affected by the same variables and with the same form of interaction as are regular education programs. The time to apply the concepts and research methods of school effectiveness to special education is past due. It holds much promise for understanding what makes special education effective and how to effect such changes.

REFERENCES

Bickel, W. E. (1983). Effective schools: Knowledge, dissemination, inquiry. *Educational Researcher, 12,* 3–5.

Consortium on Inclusive Schooling Practices (CISP). (1998). *Including students with disabilities in accountability systems.* Issue brief. Pittsburgh, PA: Allegheny University of Health Sciences.

MacKenzie, D. E. (1983). Research for school improvement: An appraisal of some recent trends. *Educational Researcher, 12,* 5–19.

Purkey, S. C., & Smith, M. S. (1982). Too soon to cheer? Synthesis of research on effective schools. *Educational Leadership, 40,* 64–69.

Rowan, B., Bossert, S. T., & Dwyer, D. C. (1983). Research on effective schools: A cautionary note. *Educational Researcher, 12,* 24–32.

CECIL R. REYNOLDS
Texas A&M University

See also **Special Education Programs; Teacher Effectiveness**

SCHOOL FAILURE

There are many reasons why children fail in school. In some cases, failure may be due to circumstances within the child's environment. In other cases, school failure may be the result of a physical problem originating before, during, or after birth. This section identifies and discusses some of the chief causes of failure in school.

Failure in school often occurs when children come from environments characterized by economic hardship, deprivation, neglect, trauma, divorce, death, foster parenting, drug abuse, poor school attendance, or lack of adequate instruction. Indeed, dyspedagogia carries more of a role in school failure simply because of the theoretical paradigm in Western schools of individualism as opposed

to social/interactive paradigms such as those favored in Russian schools for so many years. Some change may be noted in the teacher preparation and involvement in inner-city schools (Yeo, 1997).

Cultural differences also contribute to school failure. When a language other than English is used in the home and children are limited in English proficiency, they do poorly in school. The cultural values held by students also affect how they perceive their school, their teachers, and their peer group. For example, students' values determine how much they will be motivated in class, how they perceive and respond to authority, and whether they will be highly competitive or more responsive to a cooperative approach to learning. When values differ widely from one culture to another, what is valued in one culture may serve as a barrier to learning in another (Saville-Troike, 1978).

Children who exhibit behavior problems in the classroom also experience school failure. Some children have conduct disorders in which they disrupt the class, constantly irritate the teacher, do not follow directions, are easily distracted, are impulsive, or fail to attend. Other students who are fearful, anxious, withdrawn, or immature have difficulty in responding freely in the classroom and fail to learn to the limits of their abilities. Children whose self-esteem is so low that they believe they are of little worth often learn to be helpless. These children stop trying in school because they think they cannot learn. When children with behavior problems do not conform to the standards of the school environment, they may become socially aggressive, reject the values of the school and society, and come into conflict with authorities. A student may openly confront teachers and administrators, begin using drugs or alcohol, join gangs, break laws, steal, and eventually be expelled from or drop out of school (Knoblock, 1983; Long, Morse, & Newman, 1980; Quay & Werry, 1979).

Children who have difficulty in seeing and hearing often fail in school. Although 1 child in 10 enters school with some degree of visual impairment, most of these problems can be corrected and have no effect on educational development. One child out of a thousand, however, has visual impairments so severe they cannot be corrected. Children who are hard of hearing or deaf have difficulty in learning to understand language. This causes difficulty in learning to speak, read, and write the English language (Barraga, 1983).

Intellectual disabilities result in school failure. Intellectual disabilities may range in severity from mild to moderate to severe to profound. Delayed mental development can contribute to failure in language acquisition and use, achievement in academic subjects, social adjustment, and becoming a self-supporting adult (Mittler, 1981).

Specific learning disabilities can result in failure in school. A learning disability is a dysfunction in one or more of the psychological processes that are involved in learning to read, write, spell, compute arithmetic, etc. In some cases, a child may have an attention disability and may not be able to direct attention purposefully, failing to selectively focus attention on the relevant stimuli or responding to too many stimuli at once. A memory disability is the inability to remember what has been seen or heard. Perceptual disabilities cover a wide range of disorders in which a child who has normal vision, hearing, and feeling may experience difficulty in grasping the meaning of what is seen, heard, or touched. An example is a child who has difficulty in seeing the directional differences between a "d" and a "b," or who requires an excessive amount of time to look at a printed word, analyze the word, and say the word. Thinking disabilities involve problems in judgment, making comparisons, forming new concepts, critical thinking, problem solving, and decision making. A disability in oral language refers to difficulties in understanding and using oral language. All of these specific learning disabilities might cause difficulty in learning to read, write, spell, compute arithmetic, or adopt appropriate social-emotional behaviors (Kirk & Chalfant, 1984). Research cites the need for school-family partnerships (Poole, 1997) and intensive case management (Reid, Bailey-Dempsey, Cain, & Cook, 1994).

School failure is associated with poor physical and mental health outcomes in adulthood. It has long been recognized and documented as a significant pathway to downward social mobility, an effect exaggerated in children with disabilities (Reynolds, 2005).

REFERENCES

Barraga, N. (1983). *Visual handicaps and learning* (Rev. ed.). Austin, TX: Exceptional Resources.

Kirk, S. A., & Chalfant, J. C. (1984). *Academic and developmental learning disabilities*. Denver, CO: Love.

Knoblock, P. (1983). *Teaching emotionally disturbed children*. Boston, MA: Houghton Mifflin.

Long, N., Morse, W., & Newman, R. (Eds.). (1980). *Conflict in the classroom: The education of emotionally disturbed children* (4th ed.). Belmont, CA: Wadsworth.

Mittler, P. (Ed.). (1981). *Frontiers of knowledge in mental retardation: Vol. 1. Social educational and behavioral aspects; Vol. 2. Biomedical aspects*. Baltimore, MD: University Park Press.

Poole, D. L. (1997). The SAFE Project. *Health & Social Work, 22*(4), 282–289.

Quay, H., & Werry, J. (Eds.). (1979). *Psychopathological disorders of childhood* (2nd ed.). New York, NY: Wiley.

Reid, W. J., Bailey-Dempsey, C. A., Cain, E., & Cook, T. V. (1994). Case incentives versus case management: Preventing school failure? *Social Work Research, 18*(4), 227–236.

Reynolds, C. R. (2005, August). *School failure and public health outcomes*. Presidential address to the Division of School Psychology at the annual convention of the American Psychological Association, Washington, DC.

Saville-Troike, M. (1978). *A guide to culture in the classroom*. Rosslyn, VA: National Clearinghouse for Bilingual Education.

Yeo, F. (1997). Teacher preparation and inner-city schools: Sustaining educational failure. *Urban Review, 29*(2), 127–143.

JAMES CHALFANT
University of Arizona

See also Emotional Disorders; Learned Helplessness; Learning Disabilities; Mental Retardation

SCHOOL PHOBIA

School phobia has been the subject of hundreds of research studies and dozens of literature reviews over the past several decades. The phenomenon was first described in 1932 when Broadwin distinguished a type of school refusal from truancy by an anxiety component. The term *school phobia* was coined in 1941 (Johnson et al., 1941). A common definition of school phobia cited in some literature includes the following characteristics:

- Severe difficulty in attending school, often amounting to prolonged absence.
- Severe emotional upset shown by such symptoms as excessive fearfulness, undue temper, misery or complaints of feeling ill without obvious organic cause on being faced with the prospect of going to school.
- Staying at home during school hours with the knowledge of the parents at some stage in the course of the disorder.
- Absence of significant antisocial disorder, such as stealing, lying, wandering, destructiveness, or sexual misbehavior. (Berg, Nichols, & Pritchard, 1969, p. 123)

In contrast to school phobia, truancy is characterized by behaviors that are the opposite of the last two behaviors.

Contemporary writers who use the term *school refusal* generally describe it with the same set of characteristics that defines school phobias that lack intensity (Kearney, Eisen, & Silverman, 1995). An exception is the American Psychiatric Association's (1994) classification system (*DSM-IV*), which describes school refusal as one possible concomitant of separation anxiety disorder, while reserving the term *school phobia* for a fear of the school situation even when parents accompany the child.

The occurrence of school phobia is relatively rare when one considers the abundance of literature devoted to it. Estimates of the incidence of school phobia range from 3.2 to 17 per 1,000 schoolchildren (Kennedy, 1965; Yule, 1979). The wide discrepancy may be due in part to the age at which children are sampled. Prevalence is thought to peak at three different ages: 5 to 7, on entry or shortly after entry to school; 11, around the time children change schools; and 14, often concomitant with depression (Hersov, 1977). Many writers consider school phobia to occur in three girls for every two boys (Wright, Schaefer, & Solomons, 1979). However, this ratio has not appeared in several studies of school phobics reported in the literature (Baker & Wills, 1978; Berg et al., 1969; Hersov, 1960; Kennedy, 1965).

The causes of school phobia have been couched in psychoanalytic, psychodynamic, and social learning theory terms. The psychoanalytic focus frames school phobia within a mutually dependent and hostile parent-child relationship. Some psychoanalysts believe that the unconscious conflict resulting from this relationship leads the child to want to protect the mother, and hence, not leave her. Other psychoanalysts indicate that the conflict surrounding the hostile-dependent relationship with mother is displaced onto the school situation, which becomes the manifest phobic object. In any case, both agree that separation anxiety plays a key role in school phobia (Atkinson, Quarrington, & Cyr, 1985; Kelly, 1973).

An alternative theory that was intended to explain the occurrence of school phobia at later ages was postulated by Leventhal and Sills (1964). Kelly (1973) labeled this theoretical approach, which focuses on the school phobic's unrealistic self-image, as "nonanalytic psychodynamic." According to Leventhal and Sills (1964):

> These children commonly overvalue themselves and their achievements and then try to hold onto their unrealistic self-image. When this is threatened in the school situation, they suffer anxiety and retreat to another situation where they can maintain their narcissistic self-image. This retreat may very well be a running to a close contact with mother. (p. 686)

Others have used the term fear of failure in referring to this theory (Atkinson et al., 1985).

Behavioral theories account for school phobia in terms of both classical and operant conditioning. The former model explains school phobia as a conditioned anxiety response elicited by the school situation or some other school-related event. For instance, an often cited case (Garvey & Hegrenes, 1966) involved a boy whose mother repeatedly told him as he was leaving for school that she might die while he was gone. Eventually, the thought of going to school led to fear of his mother's death. The operant model assumes that internal or environmental cues both trigger and maintain the school phobic behavior.

Atkinson et al. (1985) argued that the three perspectives differ more in focus than in substance because all can account for school phobia as a fear of separation, of the school situation, or of failures in school. For example, the child whose unrealistic self-image leads to a fear of failure in the school situation may be reinforced by parents for not attending school. Similarly, separation anxiety may be a component of school phobia triggered by a traumatic school event.

Coolidge, Hahn, and Peck (1957) were the first to describe subtypes of school phobia. Based on differences within a fairly small sample of 27 school phobics, they discussed neurotic and characterological types. The former were characterized by sudden onset after several years of normal school attendance while the latter were described as more severely disturbed, with the fear of school being only one fear among many in a generally fearful personality. Subsequent investigations by Kennedy (1965) and Hersov (1960) confirmed the general distinction between an acute form and a more pervasive disturbance. Kennedy (1965) elaborated 10 criteria that distinguished type 1 (neurotic) from type 2 (characterological) school phobics based on a sample of 50 children aged 4 to 16. Generally, the former was characterized by acute onset, a first episode, intact family relations, and occurrence in younger children. Type 2 was characterized as being chronic, often accompanied by a character disorder, unstable parental relationship, incipient onset, and a history of prior episodes.

Family relations have been investigated as a separate correlate of school phobia. Hersov (1960) described three patterns of parent-child relationships that characterized his sample of 50 school phobic children aged 7 to 16 years:

1. An overindulgent mother and an inadequate, passive father dominated at home by a willful, stubborn, and demanding child who is most often timid and inhibited in social situations.

2. A severe, controlling, and demanding mother who manages her children without much assistance from her passive husband; a timid and fearful child away from home and a passive and obedient child at home, but stubborn and rebellious at puberty.

3. A firm, controlling father who plays a large part in home management and an overindulgent mother closely bound to and dominated by a willful, stubborn, and demanding child, who is alert, friendly, and outgoing away from home. (p. 140)

The first two relationship types have been considered to be subtypes of characterological school phobia while the third seems more characteristic of the neurotic type (Atkinson et al., 1985). It should be noted that categorization based on a sample of 50 children needs further validation before conclusions are drawn about parent-child correlates. The same caution holds for Kennedy's classification system, particularly of type 2 school phobia, which was based on six children.

As Atkinson et al. (1985) noted in their review, the construct of school phobia is too heterogeneous to be described by a simple dichotomy. They examined five variables related to school phobia, some of which overlap more than others—extensiveness of disturbance, source of fear, mode of onset, age, and gender of the child. The extensiveness of fear can be conceptualized along a continuum with the dichotomies of neurotic/characterological or type

1/type 2 at the end points. Generally, acute or sudden onset is characteristic of type 1, and chronic or gradual onset is characteristic of type 2. When researchers have operationalized acute mode of onset as the occurrence of school phobia after 3 or more years of trouble-free attendance, other correlates emerge. For instance, chronic onset tended to be associated more than acute onset with poor premorbid adjustment, dependency on parents, low self-esteem, and a poor prognosis.

Similarly, source of fear, age, and gender do not bear a one-to-one correspondence with the dichotomous classifications. Generally, four sources of fear have been reported that correspond to the etiological approaches—fear of maternal separation, fear of something or someone at school, fear of failure, and a generally fearful disposition. Atkinson et al. (1985) conclude that the fear sources are not mutually exclusive, and that fears surrounding separation may coincide with more general fearfulness. They caution, however, that conclusions relating the extensiveness of disturbance to a specific fear source are premature based on current studies. In contrast, extent of disturbance and age appear to be related, with older children generally exhibiting more severe disturbance. While Kennedy differentiated type 1 from type 2 phobics in part on age differences, there is no consistent finding that type 1 or acute type is more typical of younger children.

Both psychological and pharmacotherapy have been employed for children experiencing school phobia. We focus here on psychological interventions only. The interested reader is referred to Gittelman and Koplewicz (1985) for an overview of pharmacotherapy of childhood anxiety disorders. Early treatments of school phobia stemmed from the psychoanalytic tradition and focused on resolving the mutual hostile-dependent relationship between the school phobic child and his or her parents. Typically, parallel treatment was carried out on mother and child, with one therapist using play therapy with the child and another therapist "treating" the mother. Johnson et al. (1941) describe treatment as "a collaborative dynamic approach...to relieve the guilt and tension in both patients" (p. 706). Treatment of eight cases reported in their seminal study of school phobia lasted from 5 months to over a year. There does not appear to be consensus among the psychoanalytic clinicians on whether gradual or immediate return is preferable.

The treatment that emerged from Leventhal et al.'s (1967) psychodynamic theory involves "outmaneuvering" the child. Unlike the psychoanalytic approach, rapid return rather than insight is the primary goal of treatment. Once parents are helped to see their complicity in maintaining school avoidance, the parent who is likely to stand firm is chosen to carry out the plan, which is essentially immediate, forced return to school. Kennedy (1965) also advocates forced return to school and described successful treatment of 50 cases of type 1 school phobia. He identified the following six components as essential to successful treatment: (1) good professional public relations; (2) avoidance of emphasis on somatic complaints; (3) forced school attendance; (4) structured interview with parents; (5) brief interview with child; and (6) follow-up (p. 287).

During the past 20 years a proliferation of behavioral treatments of school phobia have occurred. Yule (1979) and Trueman (1984) provide critical reviews of the behavioral treatment of school phobia. Trueman (1984) reviewed 19 case studies between 1960 and 1981 that used behavioral treatments based on classical, operant, or a combination of those techniques. Of the eight studies reviewed that used techniques based on classical conditioning, six used reciprocal, one used implosion, and one used emotive imagery. Six of the studies involved boys aged 10 to 17; two studies involved girls aged 8 and 9. Trueman noted considerable variation among the reciprocal inhibition treatments, making conclusions difficult concerning the most efficacious component. Additionally, he noted the difficulty in distinguishing between systematic desensitization and shaping.

Among the 10 case studies reviewed by Trueman that used operant procedures, five involved boys aged 7 to 12 and five involved girls aged 6 to 14. The change agents varied among studies as well as the specific techniques and the criteria for success. Thus comparisons between procedures are hard to make. The procedures included training parents in positive reinforcement methods, contingency contracting, prompting and shaping, and school-based contingencies. It is important that resolution is long-term for these cases, because longitudinal studies indicate lifelong outcomes (Flakierska, Lindstroem, & Gillberg, 1997). Home-school collaboration is essential (Jenni, 1997).

REFERENCES

American Psychiatric Association. (1994). *Diagnostic and statistical manual of mental disorders* (4th ed.). Washington, DC: Author.

Atkinson, L., Quarrington, B., & Cyr, J. J. (1985). School refusal: The heterogeneity of a concept. *American Journal of Orthopsychiatry, 55*, 83–101.

Baker, H., & Wills, U. (1978). School phobia: Classification and treatment. *British Journal of Psychiatry, 132*, 492–499.

Berg, I., Nichols, K., & Pritchard, C. (1969). School phobia—Its classification and relationship to dependency. *Journal of Child Psychology & Psychiatry, 10*, 123–141.

Broadwin, I. T. (1932). A contribution to the study of truancy. *American Journal of Orthopsychiatry, 2*, 252–259.

Coolidge, J., Hahn, P., & Peck, A. (1957). School phobia: Neurotic crisis or way of life. *American Journal of Orthopsychiatry, 27*, 296–306.

Flakierska, P. N., Lindstroem, M., & Gillberg, C. (1997). School phobia with separation-anxiety disorder: A comparative 20- to 29-year follow-up study of 35 school refusers. *Comprehensive Psychiatry, 38*, 17–22.

Garvey, W. P., & Hegrenes, J. R. (1966). Desensitization techniques in the treatment of school phobia. *American Journal of Orthopsychiatry, 36*, 147–152.

Gittelman, R., & Koplewicz, M. S. (1985). Pharmacotherapy of childhood anxiety disorders. In R. Gittelman (Ed.), *Anxiety disorders in children*. New York, NY: Guilford Press.

Hersov, L. A. (1960). Refusal to go to school. *Child Psychology & Psychiatry, 1*, 137–145.

Hersov, L. A. (1977). School refusal. In M. Rutter & L. Hersov (Eds.), *Child psychiatry: Modern approaches* (pp. 455–486). Oxford, England: Blackwell.

Jenni, C. B. (1997). School phobia: How home school collaboration can tame this dragon. *School Counselor, 44*(3), 206–217.

Johnson, A. M., Falstein, E. J., Szurek, S. A., & Svendsen, M. (1941). School phobia. *American Journal of Orthopsychiatry, 11*, 702–711.

Kearney, C. A., Eisen, A. R., & Silverman, W. K. (1995). The legend and myth of school phobia. *School Psychology Quarterly, 10*(1), 65–85.

Kelly, E. W. (1973). School phobia: A review of theory and treatment. *Psychology in the Schools, 10*, 33–42.

Kennedy, W. A. (1965). School phobia: Rapid treatment of fifty cases. *Journal of Abnormal Psychology, 70*, 285–289.

Leventhal, T., & Sills, M. (1964). Self-image in school phobia. *American Journal of Orthopsychiatry, 34*, 685–694.

Leventhal, T., Weinberger, G., Stander, R. J., & Stearns, R. P. (1967). Therapeutic strategies with school phobics. *American Journal of Orthopsychiatry, 37*, 64–70.

Trueman, D. (1984). The behavioral treatment of school phobia: A critical review. *Psychology in the Schools, 21*, 215–223.

Wright, L., Schaefer, A., & Solomons, G. (1979). *Encyclopedia of pediatric psychology*. Baltimore, MD: University Park Press.

Yule, W. (1979). Behavioral approaches to the treatment and prevention of school refusal. *Behavioral Analysis & Modification, 3*, 55–68.

JANET A. LINDOW
THOMAS R. KRATOCHWILL
University of Wisconsin at Madison

RICHARD J. MORRIS
University of Arizona

See also Childhood Neurosis; Phobias and Fears; Separation Anxiety Disorder

SCHOOL PSYCHOLOGY

Psychology is devoted to the goals of describing and explaining human behavior and promoting conditions that foster human development and welfare. School psychologists generally share these goals and strive to apply psychological theories, concepts, and techniques to facilitate growth and development through education and schools. The birth of psychology occurred about 100 years ago in Germany. Psychologists began working in U.S. schools about 20 years later as child study departments and clinics began to form.

The number of school psychology programs and students has increased during the past two decades (Fagan, 1985). An estimated 2,200 students graduate yearly from more than 200 school psychology programs (Brown & Lindstrom, 1978). Students seeking a specialist's degree frequently take 2 years of graduate work plus a full-time, year-long internship. Those seeking a doctoral degree frequently take 3 years of graduate work and devote 1 or more years each to an internship and a dissertation. Thus, with 3 to 5 years of graduate preparation, school psychologists tend to be the most highly educated behavioral scientists employed by the schools.

Some (Brown, 1982) view school psychology as a profession separate and independent from the professions of psychology and education; others (Bardon, 1982) view school psychology as a specialty within the profession of psychology. In fact, most school psychologists straddle the professions of psychology and education. They provide many services that are unique and drawn from psychology as well as education. A comprehensive study of the expertise of school psychologists (Rosenfeld, Shimberg, & Thornton, 1983) found the practice of school psychology to be similar to the practice of clinical and counseling psychology. In fact, school psychologists devote considerable attention to assessment and organizational issues.

School psychological services differ between communities. Their character is influenced by many conditions: federal and state laws and policies; local institutional traditions, policies, and practices; financial resources and practices governing allocation; availability of psychologists and the nature of their professional preparation; and national, state, and local professional standards. Furthermore, the services often differ for elementary and secondary grades. Although the nature of their services differ, many school psychologists are guided by a scientist-practitioner model (Cutts, 1955), which holds that applications of psychology should be supportable empirically or theoretically and derived from a body of literature that is held in high esteem. Professionals are expected to have good command of this literature discussing the theoretical, empirical, and technical components of their specialties. They are also expected to deliver culturally competent services (Rogers & Ponterotto, 1997).

A comprehensive review of the school psychology literature (Ysseldyke, Reynolds, & Weinberg, 1984) identified the following 16 domains as ones in which school psychology has expertise: classroom management; classroom organization and social structure; interpersonal communication and consultation; basic academic skills; basic life skills; affective/social skills; parent involvement; systems development and planning; personnel development; individual differences in development and learning;

school-community relations; instruction; legal, ethical, and professional issues; assessment; multicultural concerns; and research and evaluation.

While school psychology is a dynamic specialty and one not easily categorized or described, its work in five broad areas is described briefly. School psychologists frequently conduct psychoeducational evaluations of pupils needing special attention. The evaluations typically consider a student's cognitive (i.e., intelligence and achievement), affective, social, emotional, and linguistic characteristics, and use behavioral, educational, and psychological (including psychoneurological [D'Amato, Hammons, Terminie, & Dean, 1992] and psychoanalytic) techniques.

School psychologists also participate in planning and evaluating services designed to promote cognitive, social, and affective development. Their services can include teaching, training, counseling, and therapy. While their principal focus frequently is on individual pupils, they also work individually with parents, teachers, principals, and other educators.

School psychologists also offer indirect services to pupils through educators, parents, and other adults. Their indirect services typically involve in-service programs for teachers, parent education programs, counseling, consultation, and collaboration. Their consultative and collaborative activities involve them with groups composed of students, teachers, parents, and others. Their work as members of the education staff enables them to effect important changes in organizations by working on broad and important issues that impact classrooms, school buildings, districts, communities, corporations, or a consortium of districts and agencies.

School psychologists' knowledge of quantitative methods commonly used in research and evaluation often surpasses that of other educational personnel. Thus they frequently are responsible for conceptualizing and designing studies, collecting and analyzing data, and integrating and disseminating findings.

School psychologists also may supervise pupil personnel and psychological services. In this capacity, they are responsible for conceptualizing and promoting a comprehensive plan for these services, for hiring and supervising personnel, for promoting their development, and for coordinating psychological services with other services in the district or community.

School psychology, like other professions, has developed and promulgated a number of standards that exemplify the profession's values and principles and that serve the needs of service providers, clients, educators, society, and legal bodies (Oakland, 1986).

Most school psychologists work in the schools or within other organizational structures (e.g., mental health clinics, juvenile courts, guidance centers, private and public residential care facilities). State certification is important for these school psychologists. Forty-nine states presently certify school psychologists—an increase of 42 since 1946.

Many school psychologists also want the option to practice privately. Although those who have doctoral degrees typically can be licensed by their states as psychologists, those holding subdoctoral degrees typically have been denied a license to practice psychology independently and increasingly are seeking the right to be licensed and to practice privately.

Five professional journals are devoted to advancing the knowledge and practice of school psychology: *Journal of School Psychology, School Psychology Quarterly, Psychology in the Schools, School Psychology International,* and *School Psychology Review.* An additional 16 secondary and 26 tertiary journals add to the literature (Reynolds & Gutkin, 1990). Persons interested in further information about school psychology are encouraged to consult the professional journals, *The Handbook of School Psychology* (Reynolds & Gutkin, 1999), and the websites of the National Association of School Psychologists (www.nasponline.org) and the American Psychological Association (www.apa.org). The APA website contains links not only to the Division of School Psychology website but to the official documents of APA that define school psychology as a distinct field of practice and describe the typical purview of practice for school psychologists.

REFERENCES

American Psychological Association. (1968). *Psychology as a profession.* Washington, DC: Author.

American Psychological Association. (1972). Guidelines for conditions of employment of psychologists. *American Psychologist, 27,* 331–334.

American Psychological Association. (1973). *Ethical principles in the conduct of research with human subjects.* Washington, DC: Author.

American Psychological Association. (1977). *Standards for providers of psychological services* (Rev. ed.). Washington, DC: Author.

American Psychological Association. (1980). *Criteria for accreditation of doctoral training programs and internships in professional psychology.* Washington, DC: Author.

American Psychological Association. (1981a). *Ethical principles of psychologists* (Rev. ed.). Washington, DC: Author.

American Psychological Association. (1981b). Specialty guidelines for the delivery of services by school psychologists. *American Psychologist, 36,* 639, 670–682.

American Psychological Association. (1985). *Standards for educational and psychological testing.* Washington, DC: Author.

Bardon, J. (1982). The psychology of school psychology. In C. R. Reynolds & T. B. Gutkin (Eds.), *The handbook of school psychology* (pp. 1–14). New York, NY: Wiley.

Brown, D. (1982). Issues in the development of professional school psychology. In C. R. Reynolds & T. B. Gutkin (Eds.), *The handbook of school psychology* (pp. 14–23). New York, NY: Wiley.

Brown, D. T., & Lindstrom, J. P. (1978). The training of school psychologists in the United States: An overview. *Psychology in the Schools*, *15*, 37–45.

Cutts, N. E. (Ed.). (1955). *School psychology at mid-century*. Washington, DC: American Psychological Association.

D'Amato, R. C., Hammons, P. F., Terminie, T. J., & Dean, R. S. (1992). Neuropsychological training in American Psychological Association-accredited and nonaccredited school psychology programs. *Journal of School Psychology*, *30*(2), 175–183.

Fagan, T. (1985). Quantitative growth of school psychology in the United States. *School Psychology Review*, *14*, 121–124.

National Association of School Psychologists. (1978). *Standards for credentialing in school psychology*. Washington, DC: Author.

National Association of School Psychologists. (1984a). *Principles for professional ethics*. Washington, DC: Author.

National Association of School Psychologists. (1984b). *Standards for the provision of school psychological services*. Washington, DC: Author.

National Association of School Psychologists. (1984c). *Standards for training and field placement programs in school psychology*. Washington, DC: Author.

Oakland, T. (1986). Professionalism within school psychology. *Professional School Psychology*, *1*, 9–27.

Reynolds, C. R., & Gutkin, T. B. (1999). *The handbook of school psychology* (3rd ed.). New York, NY: Wiley.

Rogers, M. R., & Ponterotto, J. G. (1997). Development of the multicultural school psychology counseling competency scale. *Psychology in the Schools*, *34*, 211–217.

Rosenfeld, M., Shimberg, B., & Thornton, R. (1983). *Job analysis of licensed psychologists in the United States and Canada*. Princeton, NJ: Educational Testing Service.

Ysseldyke, J., Reynolds, M., & Weinberg, M. (1984). *NASP Blueprints for training and practice*.

THOMAS OAKLAND
University of Florida

See *also* Educational Diagnostician; Psychology in the Schools

SCHOOL PSYCHOLOGY DIGEST (See School Psychology Review)

SCHOOL PSYCHOLOGY REVIEW

School Psychology Review, first published in 1972 as *The School Psychology Digest*, is the official journal of the National Association of School Psychologists (NASP). In 1980, the name of the journal was changed to reflect the change from the publication of condensations of previously published articles to the publication of original research, reviews of theoretical and applied topics, case studies, and descriptions of intervention techniques useful to psychologists working in educational settings. Scholarly reviews of books, tests, and other psychological materials are also published occasionally. Portions of two or three issues each year are reserved for guest-edited miniseries on themes relevant to NASP membership, such as program evaluation, testing and measurement issues, psychological theories, and special education practices. These solicited theme issues differentiate the *Review* from other major school psychology journals.

The primary purpose of the *Review* is to impact the delivery of school psychological services by publishing scholarly advances in research, training, and practices. *School Psychology Review* is a quarterly publication with an editor and appointed editorial advisory board. The founding editor was John Guidubaldi of Kent State University.

A content analysis of the *Review* indicates that approximately 10%–20% of the articles concern professional issues in school psychology, 30%–40% relate to interventions for academic and behavior problems of children, and 30%–35% involve testing and measurement issues. The remaining articles cover a wide array of topics, including program evaluation, psychological theories, and special education practices.

The *School Psychology Review* enjoys the largest circulation (over 20,000 subscribers) of any of the journals representing the field of school psychology, and it is the second most widely distributed journal in the entire discipline of psychology. *School Psychology Review* is published by the National Association of School Psychologists and is a benefit of membership; it may also be purchased separately.

STEPHEN N. ELLIOTT
University of Wisconsin
First edition

DONNA WALLACE
The University of Texas
of the Permian Basin
Second edition

SCHOOL RECORDS (See FERPA [Family Educational Rights and Privacy Act])

SCHOOL REFUSAL

School refusal, also incorrectly known as school phobia, refers to excessive absenteeism from school that arises from qualities internal to the child, not from external forces. School refusal often is accompanied by significant anxiety and feelings of distress.

The term *school phobia* has been utilized incorrectly to refer to chronic refusal to attend school. However, this term is too narrow, because not all school refusers display characteristics of a phobia (i.e., an intense and debilitating fear causing significant life impairment). School refusal does not have its own diagnostic category in the *Diagnostic and Statistical Manual for Mental Disorders* (*DSM-IV-TR*; APA, 2000). Moreover, school phobia is not listed among the specific phobias in the *DSM-IV-TR*.

School refusal behavior has four distinct components (Berg, Nichols, & Prichard, 1969): The child remains at home with parental knowledge. There is an absence of severe antisocial disorders (such as juvenile delinquency, disruptiveness, and sexual activity). The parent(s) have taken reasonable measures to solicit school attendance. The child displays unsuitable emotional behaviors at the prospect of attending school (e.g., may involve temper tantrums or hysterical crying). In addition to observable anxiety symptoms such as crying and sleeping difficulties, school-refusing students may also exhibit somatic symptoms as primary or secondary complaints. Gastrointestinal illness (e.g., stomachaches, nausea), autonomic illness (e.g., headaches, dizziness), and muscular symptoms (e.g., back and joint pain) are common indicators (Fremont, 2003).

School refusal is not a unitary syndrome. Students often refuse to attend school for one or more of the following reasons: to avoid school-based stimuli that provoke a general sense of negative affectivity (e.g., playgrounds, buses, bathrooms, fire alarms); to escape aversive school-based social and/or evaluative situations (e.g., interacting with teachers or peers, avoiding bullying, taking tests); to pursue attention from significant others (e.g., parents or primary caregivers); to pursue tangible reinforcers outside of the school setting (e.g., shopping trips, arcade games; Kearney & Silverman, 1990).

The first two conditions are maintained by negative reinforcement: school avoidance reduces unpleasant physical or emotional symptoms. The last two conditions are maintained by positive reinforcement: the behavior is sustained because the child or adolescent is receiving something enjoyable from it. However, children who are positively reinforced for their school refusal may also be experiencing a relatively high level of anxiety (Brandibas, Jeunier, Clanet, & Fouraste, 2004).

Each of these reasons appears to correspond to a particular causality. Children who avoid school-based stimuli that elicit negative affectivity may be displaying a specific phobia. Children who seek to avoid aversive social or evaluative situations at school may be exhibiting social phobia. Children who stay home from school to spend time with significant others may be displaying separation anxiety. Children who pursue tangible reinforcers outside of school are demonstrating truant behavior; this behavior may also be associated with conduct disorder. It is important to consider that school refusal can serve more than one function (Kearney, Lemos, & Silverman, 2004).

School refusal behavior is commonly linked with anxiety disorders. School refusal was thought to always be due to a separation anxiety disorder. However, separation anxiety is now known to account for a small percentage of school refusals. Children who refuse to attend school are most likely to be diagnosed as displaying social phobia, specific phobias, separation anxiety disorder, or major depressive disorder (Elliot, 1999). Chronic forms of school refusal are likely to occur in the presence of other psychopathology.

As noted, some scholars consider truancy to be one form of school refusal behavior. However, other scholars believe truancy should not be considered school refusal. They note that truancy is usually accompanied by antisocial behavior and occurs without the knowledge of the child's parents, thus violating two of the four components of school refusal created by Berg and colleagues and discussed earlier.

Truant behavior is typically seen as a behavioral disorder, while school refusal is typically viewed as an anxiety disorder. Those who want to exclude truancy from school refusal believe truants have self-control of their actions, while anxiety-based school refusers often have little self-control (Heyne, King, Tonge, & Cooper, 2001). Truants are not likely to be excessively fearful about school attendance. Instead, their absences probably reflect a lack of interest in schoolwork, an unwillingness to conform to the school's expectations and code of behavior, and a desire to engage in more attractive activities in lieu of school (Elliot, 1999).

Estimated prevalence rates for school refusal behavior range from 1% (Heyne et al., 2001) to an astonishing 28% (Kearney et al., 2004). Most studies place the prevalence rate somewhere between 1% and 5%. School refusal appears to occur equally as often among males and females and is not prominent in any racial/ethnic group (King & Bernstein 2001; Kearney et al., 2004). However, school refusal associated with separation anxiety disorder may be more common in younger children (Elliot, 1999). Students who exhibit school refusal generally have normal intelligence, and learning disabilities are not overrepresented in the population of school refusers (Heyne et al., 2001; Evans, 2000).

Triggers of school refusal behavior include family conflict or separation, transitions, academic difficulties, illness, bullying and peer conflict, and traumatic experiences (Heyne et al., 2001; McShane, Walter, & Rey, 2001). School refusal is most likely to occur between the ages of 5 to 7, 10 to 11, and 14 to 16. These ages correspond with early schooling, change of school, and nearing the end of compulsory education, respectively (Heyne et al., 2001). The first peak is associated with separation anxiety, the second with social phobia, and the third with social and other phobias and other disorders such as depression (Csoti, 2003).

Biology also appears to play a role in the manifestation of school refusal behavior. Parents of anxiety-based school refusers have a high rate of anxiety and depressive disorders. Parents of school refusers with separation anxiety have a high rate of panic disorder and separation anxiety disorder, and parents of phobic school refusers have higher rates of phobic disorders. These findings suggest that anxiety-based school refusal is heritable (Martin, Cabrol, Bouvard, Lepine, & Maouren-Simeoni, 1999).

School refusal behavior is associated with many negative outcomes. Long-term absence from school interferes with a student's educational development, resulting in lower grades, grade retention, and a decrease in future opportunities. The social impacts of chronic school refusal include poor self-esteem and family conflict. Costs to society include increased educational expenditures, lessened productivity, and increased social support (Evans, 2000). School refusers are at increased risk for employment difficulties and mental health illness later in life (Fremont, 2003). In particular, students with a later onset of school refusal may have more severe disorders and a poorer prognosis (Elliot, 1999). Because of these negative outcomes, an accurate recognition of the behavior and effective treatment programs are needed to ensure the best possible outlook for these students.

Treatment options for school refusal behavior include behavioral methods, cognitive-behavioral therapy, parent/teacher training, educational support therapy, and medication. Behavioral therapy is primarily based on exposure to stimuli that provoke negative affect and may use systematic desensitization, flooding, modeling, shaping, and contingency management. Cognitive-behavioral therapy typically incorporates techniques to help the child manage anxiety by teaching the child to identify inaccurate beliefs and replace them with more accurate statements. Parent/teacher training encompasses behavior management principles to help the adults adjust the reinforcement contingencies and promote school attendance. Educational support therapy combines information presentations and supportive psychotherapy (Fremont, 2003). Although there is mixed evidence for the effectiveness of pharmacological treatments for school refusal, a tricyclic antidepressant, imipramine, has been found to be effective in conjunction with cognitive-behavioral therapy (Bernstein et al., 2000). Selective seratonin reuptake inhibitors have been utilized in children with separation anxiety disorder, social phobia, and generalized anxiety disorder (Heyne et al., 2001), and may be effective for school refusal behavior. Pharmacologic treatment of school refusal should be used in conjunction with other interventions (Fremont, 2003).

REFERENCES

American Psychiatric Association. (2000). *Diagnostic and statistical manual of mental disorders* (4th ed., text rev.). Washington, DC: Author.

Berg, I., Nichols, K., & Prichard, C. (1969). School phobia, its classification and relationship to dependency. *Journal of Child Psychology and Psychiatry, 10*, 123–141.

Bernstein, G. A., Borchardt, C. M., Perwien, A. R., Crosby, R. D., Kushner, M. G., Thuras, P. D., & Last, C. G. (2000). Imipramine plus cognitive-behavioral therapy in the treatment of school refusal. *Journal of the American Academy of Child and Adolescent Psychiatry, 39*, 276–283.

Brandibas, G., Jeunier, B., Clanet, C., & Fouraste, R. (2004). Truancy, school refusal, and anxiety. *School Psychology International, 25*(1), 117–126.

Csoti, M. (2003). *School phobia, panic attacks, and anxiety in children*. New York, NY: Jessica Kingsley.

Elliot, J. G. (1999). School refusal: Issues of conceptualization, assessment, and treatment. *Journal of Child Psychology and Psychiatry, 40*, 1001–1012.

Evans, L. D. (2000). Functional school refusal subtypes: Anxiety, avoidance, and malingering. *Psychology in the Schools, 37*, 183–191.

Fremont, W. P. (2003). School refusal in children and adolescents. *American Family Physician, 68*, 1555–1560.

Heyne, D., King, N. J., Tonge, B. J., & Cooper, H. (2001). School refusal: Epidemiology and management. *Paediatric Drugs, 3*, 719–732.

Kearney, C. A., Lemos, A., & Silverman, J. (2004). The functional assessment of school refusal behavior. *The Behavior Analyst Today, 5*(3), 275–283.

Kearney, C. A., & Silverman, W. K. (1990). A preliminary analysis of a functional model of assessment and treatment for school refusal behavior. *Behavior Modification, 14*, 340–366.

King, N. J., & Bernstein, G. A. (2001). School refusal in children and adolescents: A review of the past 10 years. *Journal of the American Academy of Child and Adolescent Psychiatry, 40*, 197–205.

Martin, C., Cabrol, S., Bouvard, M. P., Lepine, J. P., & Maouren-Simeoni, M. C. (1999). Anxiety and depressive disorders in fathers and mothers of anxious school-refusing children. *Journal of the American Academy of Child and Adolescent Psychiatry, 38*, 916–922.

McShane, G., Walter, G., & Rey, J. M. (2001). Characteristics of adolescents with school refusal. *Australian and New Zealand Journal of Psychiatry, 35*, 822–826.

MARNI R. FINBERG
University of Florida

See also Childhood Neurosis; Phobias and Fears; School Phobia; Separation Anxiety Disorder

SCHOOL STRESS

Stress is the nonspecific response of the human body to a demand. It is not simply nervous tension but a physiological response of the body. Stress occurs in all living organisms and is with us all the time (Selye, 1976). Stress comes from mental, emotional, and physical activity.

School stress results from the impact of the school environment on children. Physical stress is accompanied by feelings of pain and discomfort, but physical stress is seldom a major factor in school stress. In schools the stressors are most often psychological and result in emotional reactions with accompanying physiological changes in the body. Children with disabilities experience more stress, less peer support, and poorer adjustment than peers without disabilities (Wenz-Gross & Siperstein, 1998).

In school stress, the demands usually result from significant others in the school (i.e., teachers and peers), or those who are expectant about school activities (e.g., parents). School stress is dependent on cognitive processes that lead to emotional reactions and a form or style of coping behavior. The coping behavior may or may not be effective, or the coping behavior may only appear to be effective. When this is the case, the body has changed from a state of alarm and is in the resistance stage. When in the resistance stage, one's ability to deal effectively with other stressors is reduced. Resistance can be maintained only so long before physical or psychological problems occur (Selye, 1976). In the stage of resistance, the person is much more susceptible than when not defensive. In reacting to stress, individuals usually try harder with the coping skills they have or search for other techniques, but when stress is prolonged or is particularly frustrating, it may cause distress physically or mentally. If the stimuli continue to be perceived as stressful, the individual's reaction can be as debilitating as prolonged physical stress in other situations.

Some children are bothered much more than others by what appear to be the same stressors. The intensity of the demand as perceived by the individual and whether the individual is able to manage the stress are the most important factors. Teachers and principals often represent authority and generate the stress that goes with reacting to authority figures. They, and/or parents, often press children to achieve more (sometimes much more) than they are able to produce. School stress often comes from a lack of perceived success, but stress may come from any segment of the environment. Stress can come from those things that are novel, intense, rapidly changing, or challenging the limits of a child's tolerance. Some children pressure classmates to keep up (or to not work very hard regardless of what adults say), to speak as they do, to appear as they do, to disclose secret thoughts, and so forth. Sometimes stress comes from crowding, racial imbalance, the opposite sex, or facing separation from one or both parents or certain friends. Whether in school or out, many children are pressured to perform competitively. Some children thrive on pressure, others wilt and withdraw.

School stress can be prevented by intervening in the environment to eliminate or modify stress-producing situations before they have a chance to affect children; by intervening with children to protect them from the impact of stressors by building up their resistance and personal strength (i.e., self-concept); by intervening with children to

increase their tolerance for stress; and by putting children who are adversely affected by stress in an environment that minimizes stress (Phillips, 1978). There are many techniques and strategies that can be used with children suffering from school stress. Most involve a focus on learning and motivational processes.

REFERENCES

Phillips, B. (1978). *School stress and anxiety*. New York, NY: Human Sciences.

Selye, H. (1976). *The stress of life*. New York, NY: McGraw-Hill.

Wenz-Gross, M., & Siperstein, G. N. (1998). Students with learning problems at risk in middle school: Stress social support, and adjustment. *Exceptional Children, 65*(1), 91–100.

JOSEPH L. FRENCH
Pennsylvania State University

See also School Phobia; Stress and Individuals With Disabilities

SCHOOL VIOLENCE

A number of highly publicized incidents of school violence in West Paducah, Kentucky; Jonesboro, Arkansas; Springfield, Oregon; Littleton, Colorado; and Red Lake, Minnesota, occurred, in which guns have been brought into schools and students and teachers have been killed. These incidents have left many parents, teachers, and students feeling vulnerable and concerned about school safety. According to the Office of Juvenile Justice and Delinquency Prevention of the U.S. Department of Justice, 12% of students reported carrying weapons to school for protection, 28% sometimes or never felt safe while at school, and 11% have stayed home from school or cut classes because of the fear of violence (Yell & Rozalski, 2000). Concern about the danger of weapons on school campuses has resulted in establishing zero-tolerance disciplinary policies associated with bringing weapons to school and with acts of violence. These guidelines grew out of the drug enforcement policies of the 1980s (Morrison & D'Incau, 1997).

Critics of zero-tolerance policy recommend the use of a proactive approach to violence prevention instead of the current focus on punishment of offenders. Although advocates who propose the use of proactive approaches recognize a need for zero-tolerance policy for offenders who bring weapons into the schools, they stress the need to adopt other prevention programs simultaneously. Such prevention strategies may involve a three-tiered model (primary, secondary, and tertiary), with the intensity of prevention and intervention strategies increasing at each level (Dwyer, Osher, & Hoffman, 2000).

At the primary prevention level, efforts to decrease violence and aggression should target all students schoolwide and should be implemented beginning in early elementary school. One of the first steps in implementing a primary prevention program is to address the physical condition of the school building (Dwyer et al., 2000). Physical conditions associated with safety can be addressed by supervising access to the building and grounds, minimizing time in hallways, providing supervision during transition times, and working with local law enforcement to ensure that routes to and from school are safe (Dwyer et al., 2000). Effective instruction of academic material is another crucial component to any violence prevention program (Scott, Nelson, & Liaupsin, 2001). Adequate curriculum contributes to a decrease in physical, relational, and verbal aggression. For example, identification and interventions for students with learning difficulties decreases the likelihood that such students will engage in disruptive behaviors.

Teaching social skills to all members of a school community is another primary prevention effort. The creation of a sense of belonging in a school community decreases risks of violence and aggression (Perry, 1999). The creation of a sense of belonging requires teachers to be trained and encouraged to show warmth and support to students, and for students to display cooperation and prosocial values. In addition, teachers should be trained to supplement strategies that decrease disruptive behaviors in the classroom, so that such behaviors do not escalate into classroom and school crises (Skiba & Peterson, 2000). Students should be taught specific social skills that involve the inclusion of others; ethical values such as fairness, respect, caring, responsibility, and citizenship; as well as conflict resolution and peer mediation skills (Perry, 1999).

At the secondary level of violence prevention, programs should be targeted toward students who are at risk for violent and antisocial behavior. At-risk students are identified through the implementation of early screening measures. Multiple gating approaches (i.e., the use of multiple screening techniques to minimize false positives and negatives) may be used to identify at-risk students (Sprague & Walker, 2000). The three gates to be screened are: teacher nominations and referrals of students exhibiting antisocial behaviors; teacher ratings of student academic and behavior skills; and a search of school, public safety, and corrections records. All school faculty members should be taught the early warning signs for violent and antisocial behavior (Dwyer et al., 2000). Students who are troubled often exhibit multiple early warning signs that, if recognized in time, can help school faculty identify maladaptive behaviors and immediately design and implement interventions for them. Some warning signs include social withdrawal, low school interest and academic performance, expression of violence in writing and drawings, bullying, a history of discipline problems, and excessive anger. After a student has been identified as being at risk for violent and antisocial behavior, comprehensive early interventions that involve both school and family need to be immediately implemented. The display of potential antisocial behaviors warrants interventions designed to target them. Professionals need to be knowledgeable of empirically supported interventions for antisocial behavior.

Finally, adequate early response programs should involve a tertiary tier of interventions, which are implemented when students engage in violent and antisocial behavior. All schools should have a program in place that can be implemented quickly and effectively during a time of crisis (Dwyer et al., 2000). Tertiary levels of early response should also include a zero-tolerance policy, especially when violent behavior and the risk for student safety are unable to be prevented or controlled with the aforementioned methods.

REFERENCES

Dwyer, K. P., Osher, D., & Hoffman, C. C. (2000). Creating responsive schools: Contextualizing early warning, timely response. *Exceptional Children, 66*, 347–365.

Morrison, G., & D'Incau, B. (1997). The web of zero tolerance: Characteristics of students who are recommended for expulsion. *Education and Treatment of Children, 20*, 1–17.

Perry, C. M. (1999). Proactive thoughts on creating safe schools. *The School Community Journal, 9*, 9–16.

Scott, T. M., Nelson, C. M., & Liaupsin, C. J. (2001). Effective instruction: The forgotten component in preventing school violence. *Education and Treatment of Children, 24*, 309–322.

Skiba, R. J., & Peterson, R. L. (2000). School discipline at a crossroads: From zero tolerance to early response. *Exceptional Children, 66*, 335–347.

Sprague, J., & Walker, H. (2000). Early identification and intervention for youth with antisocial and violent behavior. *Exceptional Children, 66*, 367–379.

Yell, M., & Rozalski, M. E. (2000). Searching for safe schools: Legal issues in the prevention of school violence. *Journal of Emotional and Behavioral Disorders, 8*, 1–17.

ALLISON G. DEMPSEY
University of Florida

HADLEY MOORE
University of Massachusetts

See also Crime and Individuals With Disabilities; Juvenile Delinquency

SCHOPLER, ERIC (1927–2007)

Eric Schopler, PhD, (1927–2007) is considered a prominent figure in autism research (General Assembly of North Carolina, 2007; Mesibov, 2007). He was born in Furth,

Germany, but moved with his parents to the United States in 1938. He completed high school in Rochester, New York, and served in the U.S. Army prior to attending the University of Chicago. There, he earned a bachelor's degree, a master's degree in social services administration, and eventually a PhD in child clinical psychology, also working as a therapist and research assistant in Rochester, Providence, and Chicago during that time (General Assembly of North Carolina, 2007). After receiving his doctorate in 1964, Schopler became an assistant professor of psychiatry at the University of North Carolina-Chapel Hill School of Medicine. He continued to work at UNC, obtaining the rank of associate professor in 1966 and full professor in 1973, until his retirement in 2005 (General Assembly of North Carolina, 2007). During his career, Schopler served at various times as the Director of the Child Research Project, Chief Psychologist, and Associate Chair for Developmental Disabilities but is best known for founding Division Treatment and Education of Autistic and related Communication-handicapped Children (TEACCH), which serves the state of North Carolina, and where he served as the co-director from 1972 from 1976 and director from 1976 to 1993 (Mesibov, 2006). He authored over 200 books and journal articles on autism spectrum and related disorders and their treatment, served on numerous editorial and organizational boards, and received numerous awards for lifetime achievement and contribution from the American Psychological Association, American Psychiatric Association, American Psychological Foundation, the University of North Carolina, and the Autism Society of North Carolina (General Assembly of North Carolina, 2007). He and his wife, Margaret Schopler, had three children (Mesibov, 2007).

Schopler is particularly well known for his work on treatment and education of individuals with autism through the use of structure in the environment (Mesibov, 2007). Schopler promoted the idea that families should be partners in the treatment of individuals with autism, rather than being blamed for causing the condition, and that treatment should be educational in focus. His work on assessment and treatment of autism and family and systems supports has been recognized broadly and materials he developed continue to be used worldwide (Mesibov, 2006). Further, as editor of the *Journal of Autism and Developmental Disorders*, a high-tier, refereed, interdisciplinary autism journal, for nearly two-and-a-half decades, Schopler shaped the field toward a focus on empirical evidence in autism research (Mesibov, 2006).

REFERENCES

General Assembly of North Carolina (2007). House Joint Resolution 321. Retrieved from http://www.ncleg.net/sessions/2007/bills/house/pdf/h321v1.pdf.

Mesibov, G. B. (2006). A tribute to Eric Schopler. *Journal of Autism and Developmental Disorders, 36,* 967–970.

Mesibov, G. B. (2007). Eric Schopler (1927–2006). *American Psychologist, 62,* 250.

EMILY M. LUND
JENNIFER B. GANZ
Texas A&M University
Fourth edition

SCHWACHMAN SYNDROME (SCHWACHMAN-DIAMOND SYNDROME)

Schwachman syndrome (SS) is a rare, heritable disorder consisting of pancreatic insufficiency (inadequate amounts of pancreatic digestive enzymes), neutropenia (decreased number of neutrophils, a type of white blood cell), defects in neutrophil function, anomalous bone formation, postnatal growth retardation with poor weight gain (failure to thrive), and short stature. Patients are usually normal at birth but soon develop steatorrhea (greasy, foul-smelling stools secondary to fat malabsorption caused by pancreatic enzyme deficiency) and growth failure.

The etiology of SS is unknown. Its incidence is 1 in 20,000 births. The disorder is found more frequently in males than in females (M:F = 1.8:1). The mode of inheritance is autosomal recessive.

Characteristics

1. Normal appearance at birth

2. Streatorrhea and failure to thrive begin in infancy. Average age of onset is 7–9 months.

3. Neutropenia occurs in more than 95% of patients. Symptoms become evident during infancy or early childhood. Neutropenia predisposes these children to recurrent bacterial infections of skin and mucous membranes (ear infections, pneumonia, dermatitis). Osteomyelitis (bone infection) and sepsis (bacteria in the blood) may also occur and can be fatal.

4. Along with neutropenia, 70% of patients have thrombocytopenia (low platelet counts) and 50% are anemic. A decrease in all three cell lines is called pancytopenia. Thrombocytopenia may lead to spontaneous bruising and bleeding from mucous membranes. Anemia can cause lethargy and (in severe cases) congestive heart failure.

5. Metaphyseal dysostosis (malformed ends of long bones). This characteristic occurs in about 40% of patients.

6. Short stature, syndactyly (webbing and fusion of digits).

7. Ptosis (droopy eyelids) and strabismus (incoordination of eye movement).

8. Dry, scaly skin (ichthyosis), increased skin pigmentation.

9. Increased incidence of lymphoreticular malignancy (lymphoma, leukemia).

10. Cleft palate, dental anomalies.

The initial findings in SS (streatorrhea, failure to thrive, recurrent pneumonias) are also seen in infants with cystic fibrosis, which is a far more common disorder. Thus, SS patients may be initially misdiagnosed. However, these two disorders can be differentiated by a relatively simple laboratory test (sweat chloride analysis) and determination of the presence of the cystic fibrosis gene.

Pancreatic insufficiency is managed by giving enzyme replacement orally. Although this strategy results in improved steatorrhea and fat malabsorption, infants with SS may continue to grow poorly. By age 4, pancreatic abnormalities frequently resolve, and replacement therapy is no longer necessary.

Neutropenia is frequently cyclic. It may require antibiotic therapy when it is accompanied by fever. Packed red blood cell infusions are indicated when hemoglobin levels fall below 80g/L. Platelet transfusions are given when counts are less than 30,000 or for clinically significant bleeding secondary to thrombocytopenia. Some cases of pancytopenia may respond to corticosteroids with or without androgen augmentation. The drugs cyclosporin A and G-CSF are presently undergoing clinical trials for the treatment of pancytopenia.

This disorder has a 25% chance of recurrence in subsequent progeny. Therefore, genetic counseling should be provided for affected families.

There are no specific cognitive deficits associated with SS. Therefore, a child would not require special support services as a result of having SS. If, however, the child's ability to function in the classroom is impaired by his or her illness, he or she would meet eligibility criteria to receive support services as other health impaired.

The average life expectancy of a patient with SS is about 35 years. Individuals with pancytopenia live slightly less than 15 years. These grim statistics indicate a rather poor prognosis for this disorder.

This entry has been informed by the sources listed below.

REFERENCES

Gandy, A. (n.d.). *Schwachman-Diamond syndrome*. Retrieved from http://www.pedianet.com/news/illness/disease/.les/shwachman.htm

National Organization for Rare Disorders. (1999). *Schwachman syndrome*. Retrieved from http://www.rarediseases.org/

Werlin, S. L. (2000). Disorders of the exocrine pancreas. In *Nelson textbook of pediatrics* (16th ed., p. 1190). Philadelphia, PA: Saunders.

BARRY H. DAVISON
Ennis, Texas

JOAN W. MAYFIELD
*Baylor Pediatric Specialty Services,
Dallas, Texas*

SCHWARTZ-JAMPEL SYNDROME

Schwartz-Jampel syndrome (SJS) is an autosomal recessive condition. It is characterized by muscle stiffness, mild muscle weakness, and a number of minor morphological abnormalities. This disorder is caused by a genetic abnormality linked to one or more regions of the first chromosome. This disorder is known by several other names: myotonic myopathy, dwarfism, chondrodystrophy, ocular and facial anomalies, Schwartz-Jampel-Aberfeld syndrome (SJA syndrome), and chondrodystrophic myotonia. Generally, authorities now recognize subtypes of Schwartz-Jampel syndrome. Type 1 is the classic type, usually apparent at birth. Type 1A is often not diagnosed until later in childhood and tends to be less severe. Type 1B is apparent at birth and is more clinically severe. Type 2 is noticeable at birth; however, it does not map onto the same chromosome as Type 1 does and is probably a disorder known as Stüve-Wiedemann (Sigaudy et al., 1998; Superti-Furga et al., 1998), which is more often discussed in the rheumatological and orthopedic literature.

In the United States, Schwartz-Jampel is considered a very rare disease; there is no significant information available on its distribution between ethnic groups. It has been described in both males and females; however, gender prevalence information is not available.

Characteristics

1. Depending upon the subtype of the disorder, symptoms are apparent at birth (Types 1, 1B, 2) or in later childhood (Type 1A).

2. Symptoms include abnormalities of the skeletal muscles, including weakness and stiffness (myotonic myopathy); abnormal bone development (bone dysplasia); joint contractures (bending or extension of joint in a fixed position); and growth delay resulting in short stature (dwarfism).

3. Individuals may also have small, fixed facial features characterized by a puckered facial appearance.

4. Abnormalities of the eyes, such as hypertrichosis of the eyelids (excessive hair growth on and pigmentation of the eyelids).

5. A subset of individuals (20%) may also have mental retardation.

In treating this disorder, the aim is to reduce muscle stiffness and cramping. Nonpharmacological methods such as massage, gradual warming up before exercise, and gradual stretching can help. Some medications (e.g., anticonvulsants and antiarrhythmics) have been found to be useful in other myotonic disorders; however, because this disorder is so rare, at present there are no controlled trials assessing the effectiveness of these drugs with Schwartz-Jampel symptoms. Patients with the characteristic physical appearance of Schwartz-Jampel syndrome may need additional psychosocial support.

Students diagnosed with Schwartz-Jampel syndrome may benefit from general education without special services. However, each case needs to be assessed on an individual basis. Some individuals may qualify for services under the Individuals with Disabilities Education Act (IDEA, 1997) if they have some level of mental retardation. Others may qualify for services due to psychological morbidity caused by the physical deformities (e.g., if the student becomes depressed). Services may be allocated either under IDEA within the category of emotional disturbance or under Section 504 of the Rehabilitation Act of 1974. Students with Schwartz-Jampel syndrome may benefit from counseling during their school career, especially if physical abnormalities are present or if physical limitations caused by muscle weakness or stiffness are frustrating. School personnel should be informed of the effects of Schwartz-Jampel syndrome and support and monitor the use of nonpharmacological (and if necessary, pharmacological) interventions used to reduce muscle stiffness, especially before and after physical exercise, but also during the school day if necessary.

Muscle stiffness or weakness may gradually worsen or remain relatively stable. However, except for patients with Stüve-Wiedemann syndrome (Schwartz-Jampel Type 2), which is fundamentally a different disorder, most patients have a reasonably good prognosis. The muscle weakness can be a factor in delayed motor milestones, such as walking. However, in most cases children do learn to walk and become self-sufficient.

Research continues to investigate the differences and similarities between Schwartz-Jampel syndrome and Stüve-Wiedemann syndrome to clarify this issue. Some researchers suspect that a muscle ion-channel abnormality or a muscle enzyme defect (causes underlying other myotonic disorders) may also underlie this condition.

REFERENCES

Sigaudy, S., Moncla, A., Fredouille, C., Bourliere, B., Lampert, J. C., & Philip, N. (1998). Congenital bowing of the long bones in two fetuses presenting features of Stüve-Wiedemann syndrome and Schwartz-Jampel syndrome type 2. *Clinical Dysmorphology, 7*(4), 257–262.

Superti-Furga, A., Tenconi, R., Clementi, M., Eich, G., Steinmann, B., Boltshauser, E., & Giedion, A. (1998). Schwartz-Jampel syndrome type 2 and Stüve-Wiedemann syndrome: A case for "lumping." *American Journal of Medical Genetics, 78*(2), 150–154.

RACHEL TOPLIS
University of Northern Colorado

SCLERODERMA

Scleroderma is an autoimmune disorder that can affect the skin or the internal organs. In individuals with scleroderma, the immune system causes cells to overproduce collagen. The excess collagen causes normal tissue in the skin or internal organs to be replaced with dense, thick tissue (Cleveland Clinic, 1999). Scleroderma that affects only the skin or muscles is known as localized scleroderma. Localized scleroderma is far more common in children than is systemic sclerosis, the type of scleroderma where the internal organs are involved (Scleroderma Foundation, 2000). However, systemic sclerosis is much more serious and life-threatening. Scleroderma is not contagious and does not appear to be inherited (Cleveland Clinic, 1999).

Overall, approximately 300,000 Americans currently have some form of scleroderma (Scleroderma Foundation, 2000). Of these, 5,000 to 7,000 are children (Cleveland Clinic, 1999). Scleroderma affects females twice as often as it does males, but there are no racial or ethnic group differences in prevalence (Cleveland Clinic, 1999).

Characteristics

1. A patch of skin appears lighter or darker in color than normal.

2. Thickened area of skin, ridges, or small pits in skin.

3. Lack of flexibility in skin in affected area.

4. Pain or stiffness due to joint inflammation.

5. Extreme sensitivity to cold, usually in the hands and experienced as tingling, discomfort, or color changes in hands.

6. Heartburn and trouble swallowing.

7. Fatigue and muscle weakness.

8. Itching.

Initially, scleroderma causes little pain; therefore, parents and children may not seek treatment until the disorder has been present for some time. Treatment cannot commence until the type of scleroderma involved is diagnosed. For localized scleroderma, some medications have been shown to slow the spread of the disease, and some physicians recommend oral vitamins D and E as a treatment (Scleroderma Foundation, 1999). Steroids are used to treat inflammation and fatigue (Cleveland Clinic, 1999). Individuals with localized scleroderma are advised to avoid sun exposure and use moisturizing lotions on the affected areas (Scleroderma Foundation, 2000). Physical therapy also is recommended to maintain range of motion and flexibility and to increase muscle strength and blood flow to the affected areas (Cleveland Clinic, 1999). Orthopedic surgery to correct joint contractures in the hand is needed only in very severe cases (Cleveland Clinic, 1999).

The systemic sclerosis form of scleroderma is more difficult to treat effectively. In addition to the treatments mentioned previously for localized scleroderma, some recommend the drugs d-penicillamine, cyclosporine, and methotrexate (Lehman, 2000). However, these drugs have potentially serious side effects, and patients must be closely monitored while taking them.

There are no reported cognitive effects of any type of scleroderma. Children with joint inflammation as a result of localized scleroderma may need modifications in physical education requirements and would qualify under the other health impaired handicapping condition. Those with systemic sclerosis may require at-home study arrangements as their disease progresses.

Localized scleroderma generally is not life threatening and in almost all cases does not progress into systemic sclerosis. With physical therapy, most children with this type of scleroderma can maintain their joint mobility and the effects of the disease on the child's growth can be limited (Scleroderma Foundation, 1999). Systemic sclerosis can cause serious and life-threatening damage to the internal organs, including the heart, lungs, and kidneys (Lehman, 2000). The long-term prognosis for survival in these severe cases is poor.

REFERENCES

Cleveland Clinic. (1999). *Scleroderma in children*. Retrieved from http://www.medicinenet.com/health_and_living/focus.htm

Lehman, T. (2000). *Scleroderma*. Retrieved from http://www.gold scout.com/sclero.html

Scleroderma Foundation. (1999). *Localized scleroderma*. Danvers, MA: Author.

Scleroderma Foundation. (2000). *Scleroderma fact sheet*. Retrieved from http://www.scleroderma.org/fact.html

NANCY K. SCAMMACCA
University of Texas at Austin

SCOLIOSIS

Scoliosis, a lateral curvature of the spine, is the most common type of spinal deformity. Functional scoliosis results from poor posture or a difference in length of the legs. It is not progressive and usually disappears with exercise. Structural scoliosis, however, is a more severe form, involving rotation of the spine and structural changes in the vertebrae (Ziai, 1984).

Most cases of structural scoliosis are idiopathic—of unknown cause (Benson, 1983). Idiopathic scoliosis occurs most frequently in adolescent females during the growth spurt, ages 12 to 16. If untreated, the condition progresses rapidly throughout the spinal growth period (ages 15 to 16 for girls and ages 18 to 19 for boys). Scoliosis can also accompany neuromuscular disorders such as cerebral palsy and muscular dystrophy, or can develop as a result of infection, trauma, or surgery (James, 1976).

Early diagnosis of scoliosis is essential to prevent progression of the curvature. Treatment varies with the type of scoliosis, the age of the child, and severity of deformity. Mild curvatures require only observation, while more pronounced curvatures require bracing and exercise. In severe cases, surgery is required. Treatment approaches have also included electrostimulation (Benson, 1983) and use of biofeedback techniques (Birbaumer, Flor, Cevey & Dworkin, 1994; Ziai, 1984).

REFERENCES

Birbaumer, N., Flor, H., Cevey, B., & Dworkin, B. (1994). Behavioral treatment of scoliosis and kyphosis. *Journal of Psychosomatic Research*, *38*(6), 623–628.

Benson, D. R. (1983). The spine and neck. In M. E. Gershwin & D. L. Robbins (Eds.), *Musculoskeletal diseases of children* (pp. 469–538). New York, NY: Grune & Stratton.

James, J. I. P. (1976). *Scoliosis* (2nd ed.). Edinburgh, Scotland: Churchill Livingstone.

Ziai, M. (Ed.). (1984). *Pediatrics* (3rd ed.). Boston, MA: Little, Brown.

CHRISTINE A. ESPIN
University of Minnesota

See also **Cerebral Palsy; Muscular Dystrophy**

SCOPE AND SEQUENCE

Scope and sequence information play an important role in the special education of exceptional individuals. In academic areas where curriculum is not readily available, the use of scope and sequence information and task analysis provides the special educator with ways of determining a set of skills (Hargrave & Poteet, 1984).

To provide appropriate programs, special educators need a clear understanding, in the form of a sequence of skills, of what each of the academic domains include. This array of skills is referred to as scope and sequence information. Scope and sequence charts provide schemata of an instructional domain. Scope refers to those skills that are taught; sequence refers to the order in which they are taught. Sequences may be determined from the work of others or may be synthesized by the special educator from experience (Wehman & McLaughlin, 1981).

Scope and sequence charts vary in structure and format among special educators and programs. Scope and sequence information provide a link between assessment and the specification of instructional goals and objectives (Wehman & McLaughlin, 1981). It is essential in developing individual educational programs. Knowledge of the scope and sequence of skills provides the teacher with a clearer profile of those skills that the student has acquired and those that he or she still needs to acquire (Mercer & Mercer, 1985).

REFERENCES

Hargrave, L. J., & Poteet, J. A. (1984). *Assessment in special education.* Englewood Cliffs, NJ: Prentice Hall.

Mercer, C. D., & Mercer, A. R. (1985). *Teaching students with learning problems.* Columbus, OH: Merrill.

Wehman, P., & McLaughlin, P. J. (1981). *Program development in special education.* New York, NY: McGraw-Hill.

ANNE M. BAUER
University of Cincinnati

SCOTLAND, SPECIAL EDUCATION IN

In the United Kingdom, special education services began to be offered in a systematic way from 1913, when Cyril Burt began using psychometrics to assess and categorize children. However, Scotland already had a distinguished record—the first school the in UK for the deaf was established in Edinburgh circa 1767 by Thomas Braidwood. From the 1920s, Scotland developed multidisciplinary assessment within a child guidance system, leading to special school or program placement recommendations. Over time, category labels became more sensitive to the feelings of those categorized (e.g., *idiot* and *moron* became *severely learning disabled*).

Special educational provision includes home-visiting or center-based assessment and advisory services; mobile human and/or material resources within normal classes in regular mainstream schools; special units located within schools; special units located outside (but hopefully near) schools; day special schools; residential special schools; and adult training centers.

In 1980, simplistic disability categories, the implicit underpinning medical model, and automatic placement implications were abandoned. They were replaced by a law that required individual statements or records of special educational needs for children and young people who had pronounced, specific, or complex chronic difficulties. These records specified how these needs were to be met and progress evaluated. The term special needs meant "needs not being met." Thus, records were context-dependent (dependent on the availability of resources where the child was currently educated), rather than focused on labeling a child. The earlier focus on school-age children expanded to include ages 0 through 19. More recently, the government espoused a presumption of mainstreaming for all children to promote social inclusion and raise educational attainment (Scottish Executive, 2000). Additionally, the age range expanded further, to age 24.

The 2005 Education (Additional Support for Learning; Scotland) Act (Scottish Executive, 2004; http://www.legislation.gov.uk/asp/2004/4/contents) established a framework for the policies of inclusion and the "presumption of mainstreaming" in Scottish education. It was an attempt to broaden the narrow definition of special educational needs. The term Additional Support Needs replaced that of Special Educational Needs. This broader term referred to any child or young person who, for whatever reason, required additional support for learning. Possible barriers to learning included physical, social, emotional, family, and care circumstances. Every education authority had a duty to provide a free independent mediation service for parents of children and young people with additional support needs (http://www.scotland.gov.uk/Publications/2005/08/15105817/58187). The Act was intended to provide support for children with long- or short-term barriers to learning. Where more than one support service was involved in the provision of support for a child, a Coordinated Support Plan (CSP) would be drawn up by the relevant agencies. An advice guide for parents is at http://enquire.org.uk/20100622/wp-content/uploads/2010/07/parents-guide-to-asl-2010-01.pdf

In Scotland, approximately 6.5% of the population of children and young people are identified as having additional support needs (this had risen from 4% with special educational needs a decade earlier). In the late 1990s, children with special educational needs included 11,000 in primary (elementary) schools, 14,500 in secondary (high) schools and 7,400 in special schools. More students were expected to be mainstreamed at all ages in the future. However, by the 2000s, 6991 children with special needs were in special schools and 22,910 (77%) were in mainstream schools. The number in special schools had decreased somewhat but not greatly, suggesting that more children in mainstream schools were being assessed (http://www.scotland.gov.uk/Publications/2006/01/121211 42/0). By 2009, 44,176 pupils had additional support needs, of which 68% were boys. These were equally divided between students with learning disabilities and those with social or emotional difficulties. Eighty-five percent of them were in mainstream schools (so 6,626 were in special schools—still not much of a reduction; http://www.scotland.gov.uk/Topics/Statistics/Browse/Scho ol-Education/TrendSpecialEducation). Clearly, one effect of the new Additional Support for Learning legislation (which was designed to reduce bureaucracy) had been to greatly increase the numbers of pupils covered, while special school numbers had not significantly reduced.

The needs of young people requiring additional support to make the transition to postschool education, training, or employment were reviewed in the Beattie Report (Scottish Executive, 1999). It recommended the development of a postschool service for ages 16 through 24, that would complement the assessment and advice provided by colleges and training providers, contribute to contextual assessment that was solution-focused and consistent with inclusiveness, support the transition process, contribute to strategic developments at regional or national level, and improve the understanding, skills, and effectiveness of service providers through consultation, training, and action research.

The pattern of special education assessment and other service provision has changed over the decades. Child guidance clinics traditionally offered multidisciplinary assessment by psychiatrists, social workers, and educational psychologists (McKnight, 1978). Assessments of support for learning, program planning, and subsequent evaluation of progress now more usually involve core input from teachers, educational psychologists (similar to the term school psychologists used in other countries), school medical officers, and of course parents and the individual young person, with other professions (e.g., social worker, speech therapist, pediatrician) contributing as relevant. The ideal is an interdisciplinary rather than multidisciplinary assessment, but educational recommendations remain within the purview of the educational specialists. Medically related services (including speech therapy) are provided by central government (federally) funded medical authorities, while educational and social work services are provided by local government authorities funded by a combination of federal grants and local taxes. Unsurprisingly, coordination of services can present organizational challenges, and the principle of integrated services has been the subject of much rhetoric, in some cases connected to the development of community or full-service schools.

Special education in Scotland has developed significantly during the last 100 years and has long been nationally mandated. However, patterns of service provision still show considerable local variation. Some of this represents strategic adaptation to local needs (as in rural versus urban communities), but in other cases reflects historical accident or political choice (which may or may not be currently functional), or temporal variations in the quality of practice in service at the point of delivery.

REFERENCES

McKnight, R. K. (1978). The development of child guidance services. In W. Dockrell, W. Dunn, & A. Milne (Eds.), *Special education in Scotland*. Edinburgh, Scotland: Scottish Council for Research in Education (SCRE).

Scottish Executive (1999). *Implementing inclusiveness: Realising potential*. (The Beattie Report). Edinburgh, Scotland: Scottish Executive.

Scottish Executive (2000). *Standards in Scotland's schools act*. Edinburgh, Scotland: Scottish Executive.

Scottish Executive. (2004). *Education (additional support for learning) (Scotland) act*. Edinburgh, Scotland: Author.

KEITH J. TOPPING
University of Dundee
Fourth edition

See also **England, Special Education in; International School Psychology Association**

SCOTT CRANIODIGITAL SYNDROME WITH MENTAL RETARDATION

Scott craniodigital syndrome with mental retardation is a rare, X-linked recessive genetic disorder. Children with this syndrome have mental retardation and various craniofacial and extremity abnormalities. Craniofacial features include a small, wide head; small, narrow nose; excessively small jaw; and eyes set far apart. Other head and facial characteristics include an extended hairline, thick eyebrows, and long eyelashes. A startled expression on their face is found among some children (National Organization for Rare Disorders [NORD], 2005).

Extremity abnormalities have also been found among these children, including webbing of their hands and feet. The heels of these children's feet are turned inward as well. Excessive hair growth on different parts of their body have also been reported (NORD, 2005).

Mental retardation is present; therefore, it will be important for the child to enter an early childhood intervention program at age 3, with continued special education services as the child progresses through school.

REFERENCE

National Organization for Rare Disorders (NORD). (2005). *Scott craniodigital syndrome*. New Fairfield, CT: Author.

PATRICIA A. LOWE
University of Kansas

JOAN W. MAYFIELD
Baylor Pediatric Specialty Service

SCOUTING AND INDIVIDUALS WITH DISABILITIES

The scouting movement for boys and girls has made a significant effort to involve youths with disabilities. This was not always the case (Stevens, 1995) but currently in America, all levels of scouting have provisions to mainstream scouts in community units and to develop specialized troops for youngsters with severe disabilities or unusual needs. Scouting organizations catering to members with given disabilities are capable of designing adapted activities. For example, Stuckey and Barkus (1986) reported that the Boy Scout Troop of the Perkins School for the Blind went on a special camping trip at the Philmont Scout Ranch in New Mexico.

The national scout offices coordinate their efforts with a variety of organizations serving and advocating for the disabled. Leadership training materials that deal with issues in scouting for members with disabilities and guidelines on adapting scouting activities are available, as are materials such as taped scout handbooks. A number of adapted merit badge programs allow impaired scouts to earn an award while knowing that they have truly met the requirements for a badge.

Scouting offers youths many opportunities for developing motor, cognitive, and social skills, increasing self-esteem and a sense of achievement, and obtaining a feeling of enjoyment. Boy Scout and Girl Scout programs have worked toward making these benefits available to all youths. Many publications and other materials are available to interested persons from the national offices of Girl Scouts and Boy Scouts and from various local scout executives.

REFERENCES

Stevens, A. (1995). Changing attitudes to disabled people in the Scout Association in Britain (1908–62): A contribution to a history of disability. *Disability & Society, 10*(3), 281–293.

Stuckey, K., & Barkus, C. (1986). Visually impaired scouts meet the Philmont challenge. *Journal of Visual Impairment & Blindness, 80,* 750–151.

LEE ANDERSON JACKSON JR.
*University of North Carolina
at Wilmington*

See also Recreation, Therapeutic

SECKEL SYNDROME

Seckel syndrome, also known as nanocephaly, is a genetic disorder. The incidence of Seckel syndrome is higher in females than males and is due to an autosomal recessive gene (Thoene, 1992). The primary characteristics of the disorder include a very small head (microcephaly); intrauterine and postnatal growth failure, resulting in dwarfism; and sharp facial features with an underdeveloped chin (Rudolph, 1991). Prominence of the midface is typical in children with Seckel syndrome. Children with this disorder have a beak-like nose, large, malformed eyes, and low-set ears without lobes. They are short in stature, ranging in height from 3 to $3\frac{1}{2}$ feet as an adult (Jones, 1988). Other physical abnormalities may include permanent fixation of the fifth finger in a bent position, malformation of the hips, and dislocation of the radial bone in the forearm (National Organization for Rare Disorders, 1998).

Children with Seckel syndrome have moderate to severe mental retardation (Jones, 1988). These children often exhibit hyperactive behavior and have attention and concentration difficulties (Jones, 1988). These children would benefit from a small group educational setting that provides one-on-one instruction and allows them to progress at their own speed. A structured, educational setting with expected rewards and consequences would be optimal. The standard treatment of Seckel syndrome is symptomatic and supportive. Parent training with a pediatric psychologist including behavioral management techniques may be beneficial. Genetic counseling may be helpful as well (Thoene, 1992).

REFERENCES

Jones, K. L. (Ed.). (1988). *Smith's recognizable patterns of human malformation* (4th ed.). Philadelphia, PA: W. B. Saunders.

Rudolph, A. M. (1991). *Rudolph's pediatrics–19th edition*. Norwalk, CT: Appleton & Lange.

National Organization for Rare Disorders (NORD). (1998). *Seckel syndrome*. New Fairfield, CT: Author.

Thoene, J. G. (Ed.). (1992). *Physician's guide to rare diseases.* Montvale, NJ: Dowden.

JOAN W. MAYFIELD
Baylor Pediatric Specialty Service

PATRICIA A. LOWE
University of Kansas

SECONDARY SPECIAL EDUCATION

Special education practice at the secondary level must account for different competencies and a different orientation than would be expected at the elementary level. The practitioner at the elementary level is able to communicate easily with regular classroom teachers because they share common training and a similar purpose in the instruction of basic language and math skills. The most common type of service delivery system in the elementary school seems to be the resource room. This arrangement is a natural extension of the regular classroom, with activities integrated with regular school curriculum. The result is a high degree of continuity from one area to another. Several problems are associated with using this approach at the secondary level. Teachers tend to be divided by areas of specialization and do not focus on individual differences of learners as readily as at the elementary level. This often results in the misinterpretation or misunderstanding of the value and nature of special education programming (Ysseldyke & Algozzine, 1984). This approach is not usually successful because it fails to involve many regular education classroom teachers and disregards the realities of the advanced secondary curriculum. The efforts of the special education practitioner should, therefore, be directed toward immediate problems of the learner and provide for close interaction with teachers and the specific course of study for each student.

Because few models for service delivery of secondary special education services exist, and university training programs have traditionally prepared teachers with an elementary emphasis, many secondary systems have relied on the elementary resource room as a model for service delivery. If the school adopts the philosophy of providing assistance only in the acquisition of basic skills in language and mathematics, then the traditional elementary model might be useful. If the school recognizes, however, the special demands and circumstances of the exceptional student as well as the unique problems associated with the onset of adolescence, then different programming is needed (Marsh, Gearheart, & Gearheart, 1978).

Lerner (1976) asserts that a secondary service delivery system in special education must account for several options in programming. For some students it may be desirable to offer a self-contained classroom, while for others a special resource room may be more beneficial because the teacher can act as a liaison between the regular education teacher, counselor, student, and parent. The school also may offer a variety of specially designed courses for students with learning problems. Lerner holds that resource room teachers in high school must be familiar with the entire curriculum of the school to be successful in remediating and programming for exceptional students. This familiarity would enable the teacher to assist the students in a variety of courses rather than in the remediation of specific academic skills. Remediation must be tied closely to what happens in the mainstream classroom.

Goodman and Mann proposed a different model in 1976. They theorized a basic education program at the secondary level that restricts the activities of the teacher to instruction of mathematics and language arts. Enrollment of students would be limited to those who lacked sixth-grade achievement. The goal for the secondary teacher in special education would be to remediate students to a sixth-grade level to allow for mainstreaming into regular education classes.

Program options, in fact, lie somewhere between the two extremes, with decisions regarding the thrust of programming often dictated by local custom and philosophy. The main objective should be to provide a system of instruction that reduces the complexity without sacrificing quality. A carefully balanced program should include the provision for specific remediation as well as assistance in addressing course work through the accommodation of individual needs. Equal opportunity should allow each student to benefit from academic training and career education to the fullest extent possible. Insufficiency in reading should not deny a student the opportunity to participate and learn in an academic class; nor should it limit the student to training that leads to entry-level skills in low-status jobs. The verbal bias evidenced in the instruction of many schools should not limit the pursuits of intelligent but inefficient learners.

REFERENCES

Goodman, L., & Mann, L. (1976). *Learning disabilities in the secondary school.* New York, NY: Grune & Stratton.

Lerner, J. W. (1976). *Children with learning disabilities* (2nd ed.). Boston, MA: Houghton Mifflin.

Marsh, G. E., Gearheart, C., & Gearheart, B. (1978). *The learning disabled adolescent.* St. Louis, MO: Mosby.

Scranton, T., & Downs, M. (1975). Elementary and secondary learning disabilities programs in the U.S.: A survey. *Journal of Learning Disabilities, 8*(6), 394–399.

Ysseldyke, J. E., & Algozzine, B. (1984). *Introduction to special education.* Boston, MA: Houghton Mifflin.

CRAIG D. SMITH
Georgia College

See also **Resource Room; Resource Teacher**

SECOND LANGUAGE LEARNERS IN SPECIAL EDUCATION

Special education is a field addressing many challenges, one of them being working with second language learners. Today, many children across the United States come from countries and homes where English is not spoken or used as a language in which concepts are discussed. If, as projections suggest, 10%–20% of any given population has some or several disabilities, then special education serves a number of these children. For many such students, English is their second language. This condition currently presents challenges to educators and service providers, impacting the outcomes of evaluations and interventions (Ortiz, 1997). Unlike a child brought up in an English-only environment, the learner of English as a second language shows developmental lags in articulation, vocabulary, insights on syntax, and comprehension of complex oral and printed texts. These conditions, coupled with limited understanding of the stages of second language acquisition, tends to promote overreferral to and placement in special education. For example, Ochoa, Robles-Pina, Garcia, and Breunig's (1999) study across eight states with large populations of second language learners revealed that oral language-related factors (acquisition and/or delays) were the third most common reason for referral of second language learners. Further, Ochoa et al. (1999) state that 8 of the top 13 most commonly cited reasons for referral of these learners could be linked to language; in their study, language reasons accounted for 54% of all responses provided. Equally, limited awareness of conditions that suggest a disability promote patterns of underreferral of this population among general educators who consider the students' problems as typical patterns of second language learners (De León & Cole, 1994).

Until recently, special education in general invested modest efforts attending to the specific communication needs of second language learners and their families, and most support focused on attending to their conditions or disabilities. However, literature within the past 20 years reveals a change in this trend, the effects of which will be reviewed perhaps 5 years from now. Consequently, increasing research, training, and publication efforts raises awareness and educates professionals. For example, guidelines and recommendations based on best practices for children without disabilities are advocated for second language learners with disabilities (California Department of Education, 1997; Fernández, 1992; Gersten, Brengelman, & Jimenez, 1994). The literature reflects continuous appeals to special educators and speech clinicians to incorporate modified approaches like English as a second language (ESL) and/or Sheltered English into their practice (De León & Cole, 1994; Garcia & Malkin, 1993; Gersten, Brengelman, & Jimenez, 1994). However, the appropriateness and effectiveness of such practices are yet to be validated. The following sections address critical issues and challenges related to the education of second language learners with disabilities served in special education programs.

Heterogeneity

Diversity effectively describes the linguistic abilities of second language learners (SLLs) served in special education programs. Different disabilities, cultural and socioeconomic backgrounds, communicative abilities, and degrees of exposure to English are interacting variables that easily confound design and outcomes of many studies involving SLLs. Surveys and studies involving teachers and other categories of service providers working in programs serving SLLs reveal limited knowledge of the stages of second language acquisition through which learners advance naturally (De León & Cole, 1994; Ochoa, Rivera & Ford, 1997; Ortiz & Yates, 1988). Common practice approaches this challenge by educating second language learners as if they were native speakers of English, promoting very few, if any, modifications to interventions (Fernández, 1992). For example, use of ESL or equally meaningful approaches for the instruction of SLLs is recommended in literature but seldom is practiced (De León & Cole, 1994). Quite often, focusing on the child's disability excludes other needs the learner might have related to his or her condition of being a second language learner (such a child is usually expected to perform like a native speaker of English). Furthermore, generic prescriptions studied and validated for children without disabilities continue to be proposed (Fueyo, 1997; Gersten et al., 1994) for a population whose specific linguistic characteristics remain undefined.

Assessment

English language learners (ELLs),[1] as they are currently named, pose a challenge to those participating in the identification process. Unless their disability is obvious—orthopedic or visual impairment, or moderate to severe mental retardation—the question most evaluators encounter upon referral to assessment and possible placement is whether the learner has acquired English in all its linguistic and functional dimensions, or if the learner is advancing within the earlier stages of the long-term process of second language acquisition (Cummins & Sayers, 1995). Has the learner received appropriate instruction using methodology appropriate to the condition of learning English as a second language? Such information is critical to establish a distinction between poor performance due to ongoing development of linguistic competence, due to a disability, or a combination

---

[1]The term *ELL* replaces *LEP*, which is the most common in the literature when it deals with students learning English as their second language. The new term is more inclusive of different levels of proficiency, not just beginning levels.

of both. Actually, Ochoa, Galarza, and Gonzalez (1996) found that only 6% of school psychologists conducting bilingual assessments of second language learners referred for special education actually implemented best practices that would enable them to obtain this critical information. Without establishing this distinction clearly, interpretation of current performance, prereferral strategies, assessment results, categorization, progress, and redesignation can be impacted negatively. Reports continue to emerge that question classification and disqualification for services and offer criticism on the interpretation of assessment data (Cheng, Ima, & Lobovitz, 1994; Garcia & Malkin, 1993; Ochoa et al., 1996; Ochoa, Rivera, & Powell, 1997). These matters demand attention at policy, research, and practice levels given the increasing expectations that all children be educated to reach their potential, and barely anything is being done to monitor an appropriate, meaningful, and effective learning opportunity.

Access to the Curriculum

Reviews of policies and practices affecting second language learners in the United States reveals very limited focus on the specific instructional needs of ELLs with disabilities. Instead, most frequently, discussions on ELLs are embedded within references addressing diversity issues. Searches that include articles referring to culturally and linguistically diverse (CLD) learners with disabilities enables access to some of the scant literature on the pedagogy to educate second language learners in special education. Extracting information from reports is complex since, frequently, linguistic diversity is used to refer to second language learners, particularly Spanish speakers, when in reality linguistic diversity is larger than this subcategory. A plethora of articles focus on cross-cultural variations and culturally relevant interventions rather than on the study of the best, or most effective, instructional practices for children with disabilities requiring the support of instruction in English as their second language.

Comprehensible input facilitates access and consequently impacts learning (Fueyo, 1997). Methodologies designed to teach second language learners without disabilities offer a promising potential in facilitating access to the English curriculum for second language learners affected by one or several disabilities. Attending to the provision of comprehensible input is crucial. Instructional approaches such as English as a Second Language (ESL), the purpose of which is to promote effective early English language acquisition, and Sheltered English, which facilitates the development of higher levels of competence in English as a second language focusing on the development of reading and content-area skills (or academic courses) while strengthening emerging English skills, beg validation of their effectiveness for individuals with disabilities. Such approaches constitute common options

recommended for linguistically appropriate individualized education programs (IEPs) for second language learners with limited English proficiency (California Department of Education, 1997; Gersten et al., 1994; Ortiz, 1997; Ortiz & Garcia, 1990; Ortiz & Yates, 1988).

Opportunities to learn through the first language promise a greater degree of comprehension of the instructional content, but the literature reflects a paucity of studies documenting best practices where this approach is implemented (Cloud, 1993; Willig & Swedo, 1987). Ortiz and Wilkinson (1989) found that in only 2% of the 203 IEPs of second language learners they reviewed was the child's first language specified as the language of instruction. Furthermore, research needs to document for which students this is an effective and valid option.

Professional Development

Most of the research efforts involving second language learners in special education throughout the past 20 years have been dedicated to documenting disparity in identification, access to the curriculum, and appropriate services. Documentation reveals that programs are not responding to the individual needs of second language learners and that the number of teachers familiar with pedagogy that supports second language acquisition is extremely reduced, and in most cases, bilingual paraprofessionals are the ones with direct responsibility for the instruction of these students. As appropriate and effective research-based interventions are validated and cross-referenced with each learner's linguistic profiles, a priority needs to be established to support extended and comprehensive professional development related to the education of students with disabilities for whom English is the second, and often weakest language.

Research and Policy Agenda

A research agenda for the future demands attention to the identification of linguistic abilities, matching instruction to developmental stage, and documentation of effective interventions, with particular emphasis on methodology and support mechanisms to enhance the learning opportunity. A research agenda including attention both to the needs of individuals with moderate to severe disabilities, and to the effects of introduction of the second language for nonspeakers or noncomprehenders of English with disabilities is equally crucial. As more is learned about the effects of modulating instructional practices for SLLs in special education, policies and practices need to respond to these research-based interventions. Ultimately, the role of the researcher, teacher, and service provider is to advocate for the study of a pedagogy that encompasses the range of abilities and competence within any classroom where second language learners are present, particularly those with a disability.

Conclusion

Much needs to be learned about effective interventions for children with disabilities who are learning or who have learned English as their second language. A research agenda must evolve from this critical need so that a solid understanding of appropriateness and effectiveness of recommendations can be developed.

REFERENCES

California Department of Education. (1997). *Guidelines for language, academic, and special education services required for limited-English-proficient students in California public schools, K–12*. Sacramento, CA: Special Education Division.

Cheng, L., Ima, K., & Lobovitz, G. (1994). Assessment of Asian and Pacific Islander students for gifted programs. In S. B. Garcia (Ed.), *Addressing cultural and linguistic diversity in special education* (pp. 30–45). Reston, VA: Council for Exceptional Children.

Cloud, N. (1993). Language, culture, and disability: Implications for instruction and teacher preparation. *Teacher Education and Special Education, 16*, 60–72.

Cummins, J., & Sayers, D. (1995). *Brave new schools: Challenging cultural illiteracy through global learning networks*. New York, NY: St. Martin's Press.

De León, J., & Cole, J. (1994). Service delivery to culturally and linguistically diverse exceptional learners in rural school districts. *Rural Special Education Quarterly, 13*, 37–45.

Fernández, A. T. (1992). Legal support for bilingual education and language appropriate related services for limited English proficient students with disabilities. *Bilingual Research Journal, 16*, 117–140.

Fueyo, V. (1997). Below the tip of the iceberg: Teaching language-minority students. *Teaching Exceptional Children, 30*, 61–65.

Garcia, S. B., & Malkin, D. H. (1993). Toward defining programs and services for culturally and linguistically diverse learners in special education. *Teaching Exceptional Children, 26*, 52–58.

Gersten, R., Brengelman, S., & Jiménez, R. (1994). Effective instruction for culturally and linguistically diverse students: A reconceptualization. *Focus on Exceptional Children, 27*, 1–16.

Ochoa, S. H., Galarza, A., & Gonzalez, D. (1996). An investigation of school psychologists' assessment practices of language proficiency with bilingual and limited English proficient students. *Diagnostique, 21*(4), 17–36.

Ochoa, S. H., Rivera, B. D., & Ford, L. (1997). An investigation of school psychology training pertaining to bilingual psychoeducational assessment of primarily Hispanic students: Twenty-five years after Diana v. California. *Journal of School Psychology, 35*, 329–349.

Ochoa, S. H., Rivera, B. D., & Powell, M. P. (1997). Factors used to comply with the exclusionary clauses with bilingual and L.E.P. pupils: Initial guidelines. *Learning Disabilities Research and Practice, 12*, 161–167.

Ochoa, S. H., Robles-Pina, R., Garcia, S. B., & Breunig, N. (1999). School psychologists' perspectives on referrals of language minority students. *Journal of Multiple Voices for Ethnically Diverse Exceptional Learners, 3*(1), 1–14.

Ortiz, A. A. (1997). Learning disabilities occurring concomitantly with linguistic differences. *Journal of Learning Disabilities, 30*, 321–332.

Ortiz, A. A., & Garcia, S. B. (1990). Using language assessment data for language and instructional planning for exceptional bilingual students. In *Teaching the bilingual special education student* (pp. 25–47). Norwood, NJ: Ablex.

Ortiz, A. A., & Wilkinson, C. Y. (1989). Adapting IEPs for limited-English-proficient students. *Academic Therapy, 24*(5), 555–568.

Ortiz, A. A., & Yates, J. R. (1988). Characteristics of learning disabled, mentally retarded, and speech-language handicapped Hispanic students at initial evaluation and reevaluation. In A. A. Ortiz & B. R. Ramirez (Eds.), *Schools and the culturally diverse exceptional student: Promising practices and future directions* (pp. 51–62). Reston, VA: Council for Exceptional Children.

Willig, A. C., & Swedo, J. J. (1987, April). *Improving teaching strategies for exceptional Hispanic limited English proficient students: An exploratory study of task engagement and teaching strategies*. Paper presented at the annual meeting of the American Educational Research Association, Washington, DC.

Elba Maldonado-Colon
San Jose State University

Salvador Hector Ochoa
Texas A&M University

See also Bilingual Special Education; Bilingual Speech Language Pathology

SECTION 504 OF THE 1973 REHABILITATION ACT (*See* Rehabilitation Act of 1973)

SEEING EYE DOGS (*See* Animals for Individuals With Disabilities; Dog Guides for the Blind)

SEGUIN, EDOUARD (1812–1880)

Edouard Seguin, who demonstrated to the world that mentally retarded individuals can be educated, studied medicine under Jean Marc Gaspard Itard in Paris, and applied the training methods of that famous physician and teacher to the education of the mentally retarded. In 1837 Seguin established the first school in France for the mentally retarded, with remarkable success. In 1848 he moved to the United States, where he practiced medicine, served as director of the Pennsylvania Training School, and acted as adviser to numerous state institutions. He was a founder and first president of the Association of Medical Officers of American Institutions for Idiotic and Feeble-Minded Persons, now the American Association on Mental Retardation.

Seguin's methods, which provided the foundation for the movement for the education of the mentally retarded in the United States, were based on a number of principles: that observation of the child is the foundation of the child's education; that education deals with the whole child; that the child learns best from real things; that perceptual training should precede training for concept development; and that even the most defective child has some capacity for learning. Seguin incorporated art, music, and gymnastics into the educational program and emphasized the use of concrete materials in the classroom.

Seguin's influence on the early development of special education services can hardly be overstated. Samuel Gridley Howe, who was responsible for the formation of the first state school for mentally retarded children in the United States, obtained much of his methodology directly from Seguin. Maria Montessori gave credit to Seguin for the principles on which she based her system of education. Today, more than a century after his death, Seguin's influence is evident in the methods being used to instruct children with learning disabilities.

REFERENCES

Kanner, L. (1960). Itard, Seguin, Howe—Three pioneers in the education of retarded children. *American Journal of Mental Deficiency, 65*, 2–10.

Seguin, E. (1907). *Idiocy and its treatment by the physiological method.* New York, NY: Teachers College.

Talbot, E. *Edouard Seguin: A study of an educational approach to the treatment of mentally defective children.* New York, NY: Teachers College.

PAUL IRVINE
Katonah, New York

SEITELBERGER DISEASE (INFANTILE NEUROAXONAL DYSTROPHY)

Seitelberger disease is an inherited central nervous system condition that is characterized by progressive

degeneration of muscular and coordination ability. The disease is inherited as an autosomal recessive trait. The symptoms and physical characteristics of Seitelberger disease occur due to swelling and degeneration of nerve endings (dystrophic axonal swellings) in areas of the brain and in the central and peripheral nerves. This disease may be referred to as prenatal or connatal neuroaxonal dystrophy. There is also some evidence that this disease is an infantile form of Hallervorden-Spatz syndrome.

Although it is extremely rare, Seitelberger disease appears to be slightly more common among females.

Characteristics

1. The onset of Seitelberger disease is usually before 2 years of age. Many children and infants appear to develop normally until approximately 14–18 months.

2. Often, a progressive decrease in walking ability is evident, or children may experience delays or an arrest in the acquisition of other skills requiring coordination.

3. Children may begin to lose previously acquired skills—for example, sitting or standing.

4. General muscle weakness and muscle tone (hypotonia) may be evident.

5. Involuntary movements of the hands and face (e.g., jerking of the head).

6. Spasticity of the lower arms and legs (sudden involuntary muscle spasms).

7. Progressive paralysis of the lower part of the body (paraplegia).

8. Children with Seitelberger disease also experience vision defects such as involuntary rapid side-to-side movement of the eyes, strabismus (crossing of the eyes), and deterioration of the nerves of the eyes.

9. As neurological impairment progresses, children may experience disorientation, loss of intellectual functioning, and progressive brain abnormalities.

10. Susceptibility to respiratory tract infections increases.

11. Progressive mental retardation occurs.

12. Serious, potentially life-threatening complications may develop.

13. Most affected children die before age 6.

At present, there is no cure for this disease. Genetic counseling is available for individuals who carry the abnormal gene and are considering starting a family. The standard treatment for Seitelberger disease is supportive and addresses the symptoms of the disease—for example, respiratory infections can be treated. However, affected individuals and their families may benefit from services for the visually and physically impaired.

The majority of affected children with this disease do not live beyond 6 years of age. If a child with this diagnosis enters school, it is highly likely that the child will be mentally retarded and have physical disabilities. Therefore, such children will qualify for special services under the Individuals with Disabilities Education Act (1997) within the mental retardation or physical disability category. Students with Seitelberger disease will probably need a variety of services, from specialized nonteaching aides and transportation to physical therapist and speech-language therapists. These students may need assistive devices to communicate and participate in school life as fully as possible. Students with Seitelberger disease may require intensive medical interventions. For example, repeated respiratory tract infections and other serious, potentially life-threatening complications may require these students to be away from school for extended periods of time. School personnel need to be informed of the restrictions of this disorder and work closely with medical personnel, the student, and his or her family. Because the disease is degenerative, accommodations and modifications necessary for students with Seitelberger disease will change over time. School personnel need to be conscientious of the terminal nature of this disease and attempt to prepare the student, his or her peers, and others working with the child. Grief counseling may be necessary.

The prognosis for Seitelberger disease is that it is terminal, with the majority of affected children dying before the age of 6. More information is needed to understand this disease. At present, research investigating Seitelberger disease appears to be aimed at understanding the disorder, investigating its etiology, and developing reliable diagnostic criteria (Nardocci et al., 1999). Some studies suggest that this disease may be related to another neuroaxonal diseases (e.g., giant axonal neuropathy; Begeer et al., 1979; Mahadevan et al., 2000).

REFERENCES

Begeer, J. H., Houthoff, H. J., van Weerden, T. W., de Groot, C. J., Blaauw, E. H., & le Coultre, R. (1979). Infantile neuroaxonal dystrophy and giant axonal neuropathy: Are they related? *Annals of Neurology, 6*(6), 540–548.

Mahadevan, A., Santosh, V., Gayatri, N., Ratnavalli, E., NandaGopal, R., Vasanth, A., ...Shankar, S. K. (2000). Infantile neuroaxonal dystrophy and giant axonal neuropathy: Overlap diseases of neuronal cytoskeletal elements in childhood? *Clinical Neuropathology, 19*(5), 221–229.

Nardocci, N., Zorzi, G., Farina, L., Binelli, S., Scaioli, W., Ciano, C., ...Bugiani, O. (1999). Infantile neuroaxonal dystrophy: Clinical spectrum and diagnostic criteria. *Neurology, 52*(7), 1472–1478.

RACHEL TOPLIS
University of Northern Colorado

SEIZURE DISORDERS

Seizures are relatively common in children and are the most common basis for a referral to a pediatric neurologist (Haslam, 1996). A seizure is a "paroxysmal involuntary disturbance of brain function that may manifest in an impairment or loss of consciousness, abnormal motor activity, behavioral abnormalities, sensory disturbances, or autonomic dysfunction" (Haslam, 1996, p. 1686). In many cases, seizures can be directly related to head trauma resulting from brain injury or high fever. Approximately 8% of children can be expected to have at least one seizure before adolescence (Brown, 1997). Epilepsy may be diagnosed only in an individual who has a series of seizures. Although descriptions of childhood seizures by parents and others may be very helpful in diagnosis, some different seizures (for example, absence and complex partial) may present almost identically in different individuals. Thus, EEG records are an important aspect of diagnosis (Haslam, 1996). Seizure disorders frequently occur in association with more severe degrees of mental retardation and cerebral palsy.

Classification of Seizures

The International Classification of Seizures divides seizures into two major categories: partial and generalized. Partial seizures begin in unilateral (focal or local) areas and may or may not spread bilaterally. Generalized seizures begin with immediate involvement of bilateral brain structures and are associated with either bilateral motor movements, changes in consciousness, or both.

Partial Seizures

Partial seizures are divided into: (1) simple partial attacks that arise from a local area and do not impair consciousness and (2) complex partial attacks that begin in a local area but spread bilaterally and therefore impair consciousness. They are the most common type of seizure disorder, accounting for 40%–60% of all childhood seizures (Brown, 1997; Haslam, 1996). In simple partial types, consciousness is unimpaired; in complex partial types, degree of altered awareness or unresponsiveness is involved.

Simple partial seizures often exhibit primary neurologic symptoms that indicate the site of origin. Partial seizures involve motor activity from any portion of the body. They usually involve the limbs, face, or head, and sometimes cause speech arrest. Hallucinations and visual illusions may occur, depending on the site of the seizure. Partial seizures that progress with sequential involvement of parts of the body that are represented in contiguous cortical areas are termed Jacksonian. Benign rolandic epilepsy is common and may result in the child awakening from sleep and showing motor symptoms. Localized paralysis or weakness that may last for minutes or days sometimes occurs and indicates an underlying structural lesion. Partial motor seizures also can be continuous for extended periods of time.

Complex partial seizures, previously called psychomotor or temporal lobe seizures, are the most common shown in older children and adolescents and occur in over 50% of adults with seizure disorders. The seizures characteristically begin with emotional, psychic, illusory, hallucinatory, or special sensory symptoms. Sometimes, consciousness becomes impaired at the onset of the attack. After the aura, the individual becomes completely or partially unresponsive and may perform apparently purposeful activity. The seizure consists of involuntary motor movements such as eye blinking, lip smacking, facial grimaces, groaning, chewing and other automatisms, but more elaborate behavior can occur. In the state of depressed awareness, patients may actively resist efforts to restrain them. A complete attack usually lasts between 1 and 3 minutes; on recovery, there is complete amnesia for the attack except for the aura or partial motor onset. Complex partial seizures usually begin in the temporal lobe but may originate from the frontal, parietal, or occipital regions.

Generalized Seizures

Generalized seizures involve bilateral brain regions and begin with immediate involvement of both hemispheres. Five types are recognized; (1) absence seizures with associated 3-Hz (cycles per second) generalized spike-and-wave discharges in the electroencephalogram (EEG); (2) atypical absence seizures; (3) myoclonic seizures; (4) tonic-clonic seizures; and (5) atonic seizures.

Absence seizures are not as common as other types of seizures and account for only 5% of all seizure disorders. These seizures are short interruptions of consciousness that last from 3 to 15 seconds each. They are not associated with auras or other evidence of focal onset. Absence seizures begin and end abruptly and recur from a few to several hundred times per day. Ongoing behavior stops. While otherwise immobile, the individual may show inconspicuous flickering of the eyelids or eyebrows about three times per second; there may be simple automatic movements, such as rubbing the nose, putting a hand to the face, or chewing and swallowing. Falling does not occur because of the ability to retain muscle tone. Immediately following the short interruption of awareness, the individual is again mentally clear and fully capable of continuing previous activity. Patients with absence seizures of this type show bilaterally synchronous 3 Hz spike-and-wave discharges, usually occurring against an otherwise normal background activity. The age of onset of these short absence seizures is almost always after age 2; they almost never occur for the first time after age 20. Individuals with short absence seizures rarely have other neurological problems, but 40% to 50% of the patients have infrequent,

easily controlled, generalized tonic-clonic seizures. Photic sensitivity is present in some cases.

Generalized tonic-clonic seizures occur at some time in most patients with seizure disorder regardless of the individual's usual pattern. This type of seizure can be triggered by many various events (e.g., fever, CNS infection, brain abnormality, and hereditary tendency) and also is commonly seen in childhood seizure disorders. A tonic-clonic seizure is classified under generalized seizures if the attack itself, the neurological examination, and the EEG all indicate that bilateral cerebral structures are simultaneously involved at the onset. A tonic-clonic seizure is classified as a partial seizure evolving to a secondarily generalized one if the same criteria indicate that the attack began in one hemisphere and then spread to produce a major generalized attack. Tonic-clonic convulsions usually last 3 to 5 minutes and are characterized by a complex loss of consciousness and falling. As the patient falls, the body stiffens because of generalized tonic contraction of the limb and axial muscles. The legs usually extend and the arms flex partially. After the tonic stage, which usually lasts less than 1 minute, jerking or clonic movements occur in all four limbs for about 1 minute. Next, a period of unconsciousness follows (about 1 minute) during which the patient appears more relaxed. Consciousness then is regained and the patient usually is confused, sleepy, and uncooperative for several minutes prior to full recovery.

Atypical absence seizures generally result in blank stares that can last longer than the typical absence seizure. Atypical absence seizures are often associated with various types of seizure patterns including tonic-clonic, myoclonic, and atonic seizures. Atonic seizures usually begin in childhood and are characterized by sudden loss of postural tone, which can cause slumping, a head drop, and even sometimes resulting in abrupt drops to the floor. These episodes occur without warning, are extremely short, and frequently cause injury. Myoclonic seizures are involuntary contractions of the limb and truncal muscles that are sudden, brief, and recurrent. Slight bilateral symmetric myoclonic movements often occur in persons who have absence seizures, but rarely are severe bilaterally symmetric myoclonic jerks the predominant symptoms of individuals with absence seizures.

Treatment

Seizure disorders can typically be treated with antiepileptic drugs (AEDs). In treating seizures, it is initially important to identify and eliminate factors that potentially cause or precipitate the attacks. Different medications are used for various types of seizures. Medications are used until seizure control is achieved or until toxic side effects limit further increments. In more severe cases, when pharmacological treatments prove completely ineffective, surgery is often the only alternative. Removing lesions or tumors from the brain is often risky and later impairs cognitive functioning. The anterior portion of the temporal lobe is the most frequent site of surgical excision in individuals with medically intractable seizures.

General Concerns

People, particularly children, with seizure disorders frequently and understandably are often fearful and feel that they have relatively little control. In addition to medical management, parents and children may need counseling. Rarely are any special restrictions on activity needed except during swimming and bathing, and parents should be encouraged to allow their children to behave as normally as possible.

An excellent source for further information is the Epilepsy Foundation of America, 4351 Garden City Drive, Landover, MD 20785. Tel.: (800) EFA-1000, e-mail: webmaster@efa.org, website: http://www.epilepsyfoundation.org/.

REFERENCES

Brown, L. W. (1997). Seizure disorders. In M. L. Batshaw (Ed.), *Children with disabilities* (4th ed., pp. 553–593). Baltimore, MD: Paul H. Brookes.

Haslam, R. H. A. (1996). Seizures in childhood. In R. E. Behrman, R. M. Kliegman, & A. M. Arvin (Eds.), *Nelson textbook of pediatrics* (15th ed., pp. 1686–1699). Philadelphia: Saunders.

ROBERT T. BROWN
AIMEE R. HUNTER
University of North Carolina at Wilmington

See also Absence Seizures; Chronic Illness in Children

SEIZURES, ABSENCE

An absence seizure, formerly known as a petit mal, is defined as a sudden, involuntary, transient alteration in cerebral function due to abnormal discharge of neurons in the central nervous system (CNS; Thiele, Gonzalez-Heydrich, & Riviello, 1999). Absence seizures fall in the category of generalized seizures, of which there are two types: primary and secondary. Primary generalized seizures are characterized by synchronous bilateral epileptic discharges. The first sign of seizure appears simultaneously in both hemispheres. A secondary generalized seizure is one that begins in one hemisphere and then spreads throughout the brain. In some cases, generalized tonic-clonic seizures develop; in fact, approximately 50% of children with absence seizures have at least one generalized tonic-clonic seizure during their lifetimes (Fenichel, 1997).

Approximately 150,000 children in the United States are diagnosed each year with a seizure disorder, and fewer than 10% of these seizures are reported to be absence (Hauser, 1994; Holmes, 1999). Absence seizures occur more often in females than in males. The onset is between the ages of 3 and 12 but peaks between the ages of 4 and 8 (Fenichel, 1997). These seizures often remit in adolescence but may persist into adulthood.

Most absence seizures are characterized by frequent episodes of staring and brief loss of consciousness (i.e., 5–30 seconds). The episodes often occur 20 or more times a day and have an abrupt onset and cessation. Most absence seizures involve staring without prominent motor features, but some do involve motor phenomena. Atypical absence occurs less frequently but lasts longer. Children with seizure disorders can however go for several days without a seizure. When seizures do occur, the period in which consciousness is altered is also longer, and the onset and cessation are slower. With atypical absence seizures, the child may also have automatisms (i.e., semipurposeful behaviors in which the child is unaware and has no recall), reduced postural tone, and tonic-clonic movements (i.e., symmetrical and rhythmical jerking). The atypical absence seizure tends to occur more often with other syndromes (e.g., see entry on Lennox-Gastaut syndrome) and is more likely caused by a CNS insult. Children with atypical absence seizures are also more likely to have developmental delay (Menkes & Sankar, 2000).

Characteristics

1. Seizures may be mistaken for daydreaming or inattention.
2. Characterized by an abrupt cessation of activity and brief episodes of staring with a blank face, rolling eyes, and fluttering eyelids.
3. Consciousness can be impaired for up to 30 seconds, and amnesia can occur afterward.
4. Onset is abrupt and without aura or postictal fatigue; activity resumes immediately after the seizure.
5. Seizure activity may occur frequently throughout the day (e.g., 20 or more times).
6. In cases of complex absence, rhythmical and symmetrical jerking can occur, along with changes in postural tone and brief automatisms.

Antiepileptic drug therapy is the recommended treatment for absence seizures—in particular, valproate, clonazepam, and ethosuximide. With antiepileptic drug treatment, prognosis for absence seizures is highly favorable, with complete remission in 70%–80% of cases (Holmes, 1999). Although prognosis for absence seizures is good, many children who have this type of seizure will need to be seen for psychological assessments to determine service needs.

Special education services are not necessarily indicated. Regular classroom accommodations and disability services, however, may be needed to ensure that the child has access to the educational environment (e.g., tutoring by a peer or classroom aide to catch up on work that was missed and allowance for extra time to complete assignments). When special education services are needed, they are likely to be provided for associated conditions rather than for the absence seizure itself (e.g., genetic syndromes and CNS insults causing seizure activity). Educators still need to be aware that untreated recurrent seizures put children at risk for cognitive impairments and psychological disturbance. Depression, anxiety, and behavior problems are not that uncommon. These problems may be explained in part by the fact that the child is the recipient of negative reactions from peers as well as from teachers who mistake the seizure for daydreaming or inattention. Educating school staff and peers may be as critical as any other treatment—that is, aside from medication therapy. Information about seizure types and some of the potential side effects of drug treatment (e.g., decreased motor speed and memory impairment) may be particularly important for the child in the classroom.

Research is still needed to investigate ways in which children with absence seizures can be treated most effectively, including nondrug therapies.

REFERENCES

Fenichel, G. M. (1997). *Clinical pediatric neurology: A signs and symptoms approach* (3rd ed.). Philadelphia, PA: Saunders.

Hauser, W. A. (1994). The prevalence and incidence of convulsive disorders in children. *Epilepsia, 35*(2), S1–S6.

Holmes, G. L. (1999). Generalized seizures. In K. Swaimann & L. Ashwall (Eds.), *Pediatric neurology: Principles and practice* (pp. 634–645). St. Louis, MO: Mosby.

Menkes, J. H., & Sankar, R. (2000). Paroxysmal disorders. In J. H. Menkes & H. B. Sarnat (Eds.), *Child neurology* (pp. 919–1026). Philadelphia, PA: Lippincott Williams & Wilkins.

Thiele, E. A., Gonzalez-Heydrich, & Riviello, J. J. (1999). Epilepsy in children and adolescents. *Child and Adolescent Psychiatric Clinics of North America, 8*(4), 671–694.

ELIZABETH CHRISTIANSEN
ELAINE CLARK
University of Utah

See also Absence Seizures

SEIZURES, ATONIC

Atonic seizures are also referred to as drop attacks and epileptic fall. Hughlings Jackson first described "sudden epileptic falls" in 1886. Unlike most epileptic seizures that involve either positive motor behavior (e.g., tonic, clonic, and myoclonic) or the absence of motor behavior (e.g., absence seizures), atonic seizures involve negative motor phenomena (Andermann & Tenembaum, 1995). The primary characteristic of an atonic seizure is a sudden loss of muscle tone that lasts 1 to 2 seconds. In a small number of cases, myoclonic jerks precede the loss of muscle tone; however, in most cases there is no warning (or aura). As a result, falls and injuries are common. The seizure is accompanied by a brief period of unconsciousness lasting 300 milliseconds to 3 seconds and has an electroencephalogram (EEG) pattern of bilateral synchronous polyspike wave and spike wave (Holmes, 1999).

The atonic seizure typically occurs shortly after awakening and continues throughout the day.

Characteristics

1. Onset is between 2 and 5 years of age.
2. Loss of muscle tone and postural control causes falls and limb-jaw drops.
3. Referred to as drop attacks and epileptic fall.
4. Momentary loss of consciousness during the fall (but rapid recovery).
5. Typically start shortly after awakening but occur frequently during the day.
6. The majority of children with atonic seizures also have myoclonic jerks or tonic seizures.
7. Often seen in children with Lennox-Gastaut syndrome.

The seizures begin between the ages of 2 and 5 but are considered rare in children. The prevalence rate is largely unknown because atonic seizures have been associated with a number of seizure types (both generalized and partial, as well as tonic, clonic, and myoclonic). The condition is often associated with Lennox-Gastaut syndrome (LGS) or with a myoclonicastatic seizure type. In LGS, seizures occur at an early age, involve multiple seizure types, and have a generalized slow-spike and wave EEG pattern. Accompanying the syndrome is impairment in developmental skills, including intellectual ability.

Children who have atonic seizures with associated conditions such as LGS will likely receive special education services in the schools (e.g., self-contained classrooms for students with intellectual disabilities). For children without LGS or other similar syndromes (e.g., Doose syndrome), other health impaired services may be needed—in particular, services provided by the school nurse (e.g., medication management and consultation with treating physicians) and therapists (e.g., occupational or physical therapists if falls have resulted in injuries that prevent the child from accessing an education). Given the frequency of atonic seizures (i.e., sometimes 100 or more episodes a day) and the attentional problems that some of these children have, the resource teaching staff may be needed to ensure adequate exposure to learning material and adequate help completing assignments. Tutoring may also help; such tutoring could be provided by peer tutors or by paraprofessionals in the classroom. Children with atonic seizures should also be provided with counseling to help them to develop mechanisms to cope with their condition. The unexpected nature of the seizures and the safety risks seriously limit some of the activities in which these children can engage, including recreational and social activities.

Unfortunately, antiepileptic drugs have not been found to be particularly helpful in treating atonic seizures. Some of the drugs that are effective in treating associated seizures have in fact been shown to exacerbate atonic seizures (e.g., valproate and clonazepam, both of which have been shown to improve myoclonic seizures). Other drugs have also been found to increase falling, including carbamazepine (Bourgeois, 1995). Felbamate has shown some promise with children who have LGS; however, the drug is indicated more for partial or generalized seizures associated with LGS, not the atonic seizure.

Treatment of atonic seizures remains a challenge and further research is needed to determine what will provide the best control, including both drugs and alternative treatment methods (e.g., the ketogenic diet).

REFERENCES

Andermann, F., & Tenembaum, S. (1995). Negative motor phenomena in generalized epilepsies: A study of atonic seizures. In S. Fahn, M. Hallett, H. Luders, & C. Marsden (Eds.), *Advances in neurology* (Vol. 67, pp. 9–28). Philadelphia, PA: Lippincott-Raven.

Bourgeois, B. (1995). Clinical use of drugs useful in the treatment of atonic seizures. In S. Fahn, M. Hallett, H. Luders, & C. Marsden (Eds.), *Advances in neurology* (Vol. 67, pp. 361–367). Philadelphia, PA: Lippincott-Raven.

Holmes, G. L. (1999). Generalized seizures. In K. Swaimann & L. Ashwall (Eds.), *Pediatric neurology: Principles and practice* (pp. 634–645). St. Louis, MO: Mosby.

ELIZABETH CHRISTIANSEN
ELAINE CLARK
University of Utah

SEIZURES, GENERALIZED TONIC-CLONIC

Generalized tonic-clonic seizures are one of the most common childhood neurological disorders. The seizure involves synchronous bilateral electrical epileptical discharges; therefore, the first signs reflect involvement of both hemispheres of the brain. The seizure, however, can begin in a focal area of the brain (or one hemisphere) as a partial seizure and spread to other areas and become a generalized seizure. Seizures are defined as a sudden, involuntary, transient alteration in neurological function resulting from excessive electrical discharge of neurons. Generalized tonic-clonic seizures, formerly known as grand mal seizures, are the most common and dramatic of childhood seizure manifestations.

Characteristic features include loss of consciousness followed by repetitive rapid (but rhythmic) jerking of the limbs. These movements are followed by slower irregular movements, eyes rolling back, rapid breathing causing saliva to froth, and sometimes incontinence (urinary and bowel). Following the seizure is a postictal sleep phase in which the individual is difficult to awaken. These seizures are often considered to be idiopathic; however, fever, central nervous system infections, and genetic transmission are possible causes. According to Fenichel (1997), the seizure typically occurs during adolescence if there are no associated absence seizures. If absence seizures, however, accompany the generalized seizure, onset tends to be earlier—that is, in the first decade.

The incidence of epilepsy (recurrent unprovoked seizures) in children between birth and 16 years of age is approximately 40 in 100,000 annually. The highest incidence occurs in the first year of life, with 120 in 100,000 cases (Hauser, 1994).

Characteristics

Tonic phase (10–30 seconds in length)

1. Eyes roll upward or deviate to one side
2. Immediate loss of consciousness
3. Falls to ground
4. Stiffens
5. Symmetrical tonic contraction of entire body musculature
6. Rigid extension of arms and legs
7. Mouth forcibly closed
8. May utter cry sound as abdomen and vocal chords contract
9. Increased salivation
10. Arrest of ventilation or apnea
11. Pallor or cyanosis is common

Clonic phase (generally 30–60 seconds but can last up to 30 minutes)

1. Rigidity replaced by violent jerking movements
2. Rhythmic contraction and relaxation of trunk and extremities

3. Movements rapid and rhythmic initially, then become slower and more irregular as seizure ends (decrescendo in frequency but not strength of movements)

4. Urinary or bowel incontinence

Postictal phase (immediately follows clonic phase and varies in duration)

1. Sleep or sleepiness, difficulty in arousal
2. Confusion or agitation
3. Headache, nausea, vomiting
4. Slurred speech
5. Visual disturbances

Anticonvulsant drug therapy is the recommended form of treatment for children with generalized tonic-clonic seizures. Drugs used for tonic-clonic seizures include phenobarbital, phenytoin, carbamazepine, and primidone, to name a few. Treatment of generalized seizures with partial onset is the same as that for primary generalized seizures. If the child does not respond to antiepileptic drug therapy, however, surgery may be used to remove damaged tissue.

Approximately 70%–90% of children with epilepsy of unknown causes become seizure free. Prognosis for continued remission is particularly good if the onset of seizure occurred after 2 years of age, the seizures were a primary generalized type, and the child has normal intelligence. Children who require polydrug treatment for seizure management, however, are more likely to relapse following discontinuance of treatment. Children with recurrent seizures tend to have a greater risk of developing psychological problems than do healthy children or children with other chronic illnesses (Austin, Risinger, & Beckett, 1992).

Depression and anxiety as well as behavior problems are common among children with tonic-clonic seizures. These children are subject to peer rejection and teasing, and some even receive negative reactions from adults. These situations serve only to exacerbate the problems these children have adjusting to their seizure condition and functioning in daily life (e.g., academically and socially). School nurses can help to educate peers and teachers alike about seizures. The child may also need this information as well as information as to how best handle others' reactions. In some cases, it will be necessary to provide psychological therapy for the child. Such therapy may include supportive-insight-oriented treatments, as well as assertiveness training and social skills tips. Including parents is critical, not only to keep them and the child's physician informed about the response to treatment, but also to ensure ample social opportunities outside of school and adequate assistance with homework. Special education services are probably not needed; however, in some cases services for students with other health impairments will be necessary to ensure adequate learning. Section 504 plans are likely to suffice in providing adequate accommodations in the classroom, including reduced workload and peer tutoring to help the child catch up on material missed (e.g., school absences or postictal sleep).

REFERENCES

Austin, J. K., Risinger, M. W., & Beckett, L. A. (1992) Correlates of behavior problems in children with epilepsy. *Epilepsia, 33,* 1115–1122.

Fenichel, G. M. (1997). *Clinical pediatric neurology: A signs and symptoms approach* (3rd ed.). Philadelphia, PA: Saunders.

Hauser, W. A. (1994). The prevalence and incidence of convulsive disorders in children. *Epilepsia, 35*(2), S1–S6.

ELIZABETH CHRISTIANSEN
ELAINE CLARK
University of Utah

SEIZURES, MYOCLONIC

Myoclonic seizures, formerly called minor motor seizures, are characterized by brief, involuntary muscle contractions and may affect one or many muscles bilaterally, although not necessarily symmetrically. A hand may suddenly fling out, a shoulder may shrug, a foot may kick, or the entire body may jerk. It can occur as a single event or as a series of jerks. The abrupt jerking may affect the legs, causing the child to fall, or it may cause the child to drop or spill what he or she is holding. Myoclonic seizures should not be confused with tics, tremors, chorea, or startle responses. Tics can usually be suppressed—at least temporarily—by an effort of will, whereas myoclonus cannot; and myoclonus does not have the characteristic continuous flow of movements as in chorea or the smooth to-and-from movements of tremors.

Characteristics

1. Sudden, brief, involuntary contractures of a muscle or group of muscles
2. Sudden onset without aura or postictal state
3. May or may not experience loss of consciousness
4. May or may not be symmetrical
5. Often occurs early in the morning
6. May occur in association with other seizure forms
7. Often associated with severe central nervous system (CNS) disorders

The multiple seizure types of Lennox-Gastaut syndrome often include myoclonic seizures (see entry on Lennox-Gastaut); however, they are a minor part of the syndrome.

The most common types of myoclonic seizure syndromes in children include the syndromes of infantile spasms (see West syndrome) and juvenile myoclonic epilepsy. Benign myoclonic epilepsy and severe myoclonic epilepsy are the rarest types of myoclonic seizures.

Benign myoclonic epilepsy, which has an onset between 4 months and 2 years of age, is characterized by brief myoclonic attacks, which may include merely nodding of the head or may be severe enough to throw the child to the floor (Fenichel, 1997). Symptoms include head dropped to the chest, eyes rolled back, arms thrown outward, and legs flexed. Affected infants remain neurologically normal but may develop tonic-clonic seizures in adolescence. Complete seizure control can be obtained through the use of valproate.

On the other hand, a healthy infant who develops severe myoclonic epilepsy will experience progressive neurological deterioration that often results in severe brain damage. Onset is usually around 1 year of age and often occurs in conjunction with other seizure types such as generalized tonic-clonic or partial complex seizures. These seizures are resistant to anticonvulsant drugs, and following the onset of these myoclonic seizures, development slows while ataxia and hyperreflexia gradually become evident (Fenichel, 1997).

Juvenile myoclonic epilepsy (JME), also known as Janz syndrome, often occurs upon awakening and is often mistaken for nervousness (Baram, 1999). Onset, which typically occurs at the time of puberty, ranges from 12 to 18 years of age. Juvenile myoclonic epilepsy accounts for between 5.4% and 10.2% of epilepsy types (Grunewald, Chroni, & Panayiotopoulos, 1992). Many children (up to 90%) who experience Janz syndrome also have generalized tonic-clonic seizures and one third experience absence seizures (Fenichel, 1997; Holmes & Stafstrom, 1998). Tonic-clonic seizures may precede myoclonic seizures, or they may be the culminating effect following a series of myoclonic seizures.

Myoclonic seizures are often precipitated by sleep deprivation, alcohol ingestion, or awakening from nocturnal or daytime sleep. Hormonal changes due to menstruation are also a significant precipitant in adolescent females. The drugs of choice in treating juvenile myoclonic epilepsy (JME) include benzodiazepines and valproate. Although valproate has been used more for absence seizures, it has been shown to be effective in 85%–90% of cases of JME, and lamotrigine and clonazepam have been considered as potential alternative drug treatments (Baram, 1999). Adrenal steroids and adrenocorticotropic hormone (ACTH) have been used to treat myoclonic seizures that are refractory to other drugs. Relapse occurs in 75%–100% of individuals with juvenile myoclonic epilepsy when medication is withdrawn. Medication is generally needed for life to maintain seizure control.

Special education services or classroom accommodations may be needed for children whose seizures are concomitant with CNS disorders or whose cognitive functioning has been diminished as a result of the seizures (e.g., severe myoclonic epilepsy). Educators need to be aware that untreated seizures put children at risk for cognitive impairments and psychosocial or psychological maladjustment. Social isolation and poor peer relationships are particularly problematic for school-aged children and adolescents with epilepsy. Depression and anxiety as well as behavior problems are common. Social skills and assertiveness training may be helpful for some children and adolescents (Mitchell, 1999). Peer relations may also be improved by providing information about seizures to the child and to his or her classmates. School staff need to be educated about the seizure type, how to respond if a seizure occurs at school, and the potential side effects of drug treatment (e.g., confusion). This training will allow them to communicate more effectively with parents about seizure activity occurring at school and about the child's progress in school, as well as to provide physicians with critical feedback regarding drug effectiveness.

REFERENCES

Baram, T. Z. (1999). Myoclonus and myoclonic seizures. In K. Swaimann & L. Ashwall (Eds.), *Pediatric neurology: Principles and practice* (pp. 668–675). St. Louis, MO: Mosby.

Fenichel, G. M. (1997). *Clinical pediatric neurology: A signs and symptoms approach* (3rd ed.). Philadelphia, PA: Saunders.

Grunewald, R. A., Chroni, E., & Panayiotopoulos, C. P. (1992). Delayed diagnosis of juvenile myoclonic epilepsy. *Journal of Neurology, Neurosurgery, and Psychiatry, 55*(6), 497–479.

Holmes, G. L., & Stafstrom, C. E. (1998). The epilepsies. In R. B. David (Ed.), *Child and adolescent neurology* (pp. 183–234). St. Louis, MO: Mosby-Year Book.

Mitchell, W. G. (1999). Behavioral, cognitive, and social difficulties in childhood epilepsy. In K. Swaimann & L. Ashwall (Eds.), *Pediatric neurology: Principles and practice* (pp. 742–746). St. Louis, MO: Mosby.

ELIZABETH CHRISTIANSEN
ELAINE CLARK
University of Utah

SEIZURES, PARTIAL

Partial seizures, like all other seizures, result from excessive synchronous discharge of neuronal activity. This activity denotes abnormal cortical functioning. Seizures are fairly common—in fact, 1% of the population have chronic, recurrent episodes, or what is referred to as epilepsy (Thiele, Gonzalez-Heydrich, & Riviello, 1999). Individuals who are predisposed to epilepsy experience seizures when their basal level of neuronal excitability exceeds a critical level or threshold. In 70%–80% of children with epilepsy, however, remission eventually occurs (Wolf, Ochoa, & Conway, 1998). Among children with epilepsy, 40% have partial seizures, which include temporal lobe seizures and seizures that have specific foci of abnormal electrical discharge (e.g., focal motor seizures).

The etiology of partial seizures varies, but they are often associated with an underlying disease or trauma. Possible causes include cerebral scars, central nervous system infection (i.e., meningitis), vascular lesions, porencephalic cysts, neoplasms, developmental cerebral anomalies, and traumatic brain injury. Clinical manifestations of a partial seizure vary depending on the foci of the abnormal electrical activity (e.g., posturing and jerky movements with motor strip foci), including the degree to which the seizure spread and affects other areas of the brain. As a result, partial seizures are classified as one of three categories: simple partial, complex partial, and partial seizure with secondary generalization.

Children who have simple partial seizures will not have impairment of consciousness or an aura. The seizure is more likely to manifest as a motor and sensory response. For example, the child may complain of numbness and tingling, have a bad taste sensation, and experience changes in auditory and visual perception (e.g., distortions of sound and seeing objects as being larger or smaller than they actually are). With complex partial seizures, there is an impairment of consciousness as well as an aura that precedes the seizure. This aura can include fear, déjà vu, abdominal pain, and unusual taste or odor. Automatisms, or repeated purposeless activities, often occur after a brief period of staring (e.g., playing with buttons on clothing, facial grimacing, lip smacking, and making irregular hand movements). Mental confusion and lethargy are also common, as is temporary aphasia (or difficulty communicating). In some cases, partial seizures develop into generalized seizures, in which the electrical activity spreads throughout the brain, causing tonic-clonic and myoclonic movements and brief episodes of staring and loss of consciousness (see entries on generalized tonic-clonic, myoclonic, and absence seizures).

Characteristics

Simple partial seizures

1. No impairment of consciousness or aura
2. Motor responses involving one side of body (e.g., jerking, posturing, and hypertonia)
3. Sensations such as parasthesias, numbness, tingling, auditory experiences, or visual experiences

4. Macropsia or micropsia (i.e., perceiving objects to be larger or smaller than real)

Complex partial seizures

1. Impairment of consciousness
2. Aura that includes complex sensory experiences (e.g., anxiety, fear, déjà vu, unreal feelings, abdominal pain, and unusual taste or odor)
3. Staring into space followed by automatisms (i.e., repeated purposeless activities such as facial grimacing, hand fumbling, lip smacking and chewing, sucking, and walking)
4. Posturing, stiffness, and flaccidity
5. Mental confusion (or disorientation) and transitory aphasia
6. Lethargy

Partial seizures with secondary generalization

1. Begins as a partial seizure and then spreads throughout the brain, resulting in generalized tonic-clonic, myoclonic, and absence seizure

Treatment of choice for seizures is drug therapy. Anticonvulsant drugs are used to keep the level of neuronal excitability below seizure threshold. Although it is preferred, single-drug use is often ineffective, resulting in polydrug use. Drug treatment for partial seizures includes carbamazepine, phenytoin, and primidone, to name a few. Felbamate is also used for children who have partial seizures associated with Lennox-Gaustaut syndrome. Complete control of partial seizures is achieved only 75% of the time (Wong, 1999), and in some cases surgery is needed to remove abnormal tissue or treat the underlying cause (e.g., a brain tumor).

Many of the medications used to prevent seizures can negatively affect learning. Phenobarbital, for example, depresses psychomotor speed and diminishes cognitive speed in memory tasks. Often children treated with this drug develop hyperactivity, motor slowing, and impairment in memory, concentration, and cognitive processing. As a result of negative side effects of antiepileptic medications, some have tried alternative treatments such as the ketogenic diet. Despite some data showing effectiveness in 70% of children with refractory seizures, the ketogenic diet remains controversial (Thiele et al., 1999).

Many children with seizures are absent from school several days a year, thereby missing instructional opportunities and time to complete assignments. It is difficult for these children to compete with unaffected peers. Given the long-term risk of learning problems (Bailet & Turk, 2000), special education services may be needed to help the child with seizures learn the expected amount of information.

Services for this population are often provided under the category of other health impaired; however, depending on the specific deficits, services may be more appropriately provided under specific learning disabilities or emotional disturbance. Regardless of category, children with partial seizures need to be closely followed to ensure that adequate assistance is provided. School nursing and psychological services will be important to monitor progress and identify areas where services are needed (e.g., speech and language and occupational therapy). Counseling may also be important to help the child cope with this medical problem and deal with the frustration that is often experienced. Working with families, especially educating parents and siblings, will also be important and may be an important area on which school psychologists can focus their attention.

The prognosis for children with seizures depends on several factors; however, some of the best predictors of remission include seizure onset under 12 years of age, no history of neonatal seizures and fewer than 21 seizures before treatment, and normal intelligence (Wong, 1999). Like all other seizures, research is needed to determine the treatment that is most effective and has the fewest side effects.

REFERENCES

Bailet, L. L., & Turk, W. R. (2000). The impact of childhood epilepsy on neurocognitive and behavioral performance: A prospective longitudinal study. *Epilepsia, 41*(4), 426–431.

Thiele, E. A., Gonzalez-Heydrich, D., & Riviello, J. J. (1999). Epilepsy in children and adolescents. *Child and Adolescent Psychiatric Clinics of North America, 8*(4), 671–694.

Wolf, S. M., Ochoa, J. G., & Conway, E. E. (1998). Seizure management in pediatric patients for the nineties. *Pediatric Annals, 27*(10), 653–664.

Wong, D. (1999). *Whaley & Wong's nursing care of infants and children* (6th ed.). St. Louis, MO: Mosby.

ELIZABETH CHRISTIANSEN
ELAINE CLARK
University of Utah

SELECTIVE MUTISM

Selective mutism is a psychological disorder of childhood characterized by total and persistent lack of speech in at least one specific environment (such as the classroom), despite the presence of normal speech in other environments. The child is physically capable of producing normal speech and understands the language being spoken. Further criteria for a diagnosis of selective mutism according to the *Diagnostic and Statistical Manual of Mental Disorders*, fourth edition, text revision (*DSM-IV-TR*; American Psychiatric Association, 2000) are: the interference with social communication or with educational or occupational achievement; the persistence of the disturbance for at least 1 month, not limited to the first month of school; the ability of the child to comfortably understand and produce the language being spoken; and the exclusion of another communication disorder (such as poor articulation), which causes the child embarrassment in speaking, or the presence of a pervasive developmental disorder, schizophrenia, or other psychotic disorder.

In the late 19th century in Germany, Kussmaul coined the term *aphasia voluntaria* to describe a condition in which individuals refused to speak in certain situations, despite the ability to speak normally in others (Dow, Sonies, Scheib, Moss, & Leonard, 1995). Tramer named the disorder "elective mutism" in 1934, with the belief that the child was "electing" when and where to speak. The current term, "selective mutism," is a reflection of new theories of etiology that deemphasize oppositional behaviors (Dow et al., 1995) and emphasize that the behavior is selectively dependent on social context (Dummit et al., 1997). Selective mutism has been found in various countries throughout the world, including Israel, Great Britain, Switzerland, Canada, France, Japan, and the United States (Barowsky, 1999). Selective mutism typically develops during the preschool years and can persist through adolescence, although it is usually more transient (Carlson, Kratochwill, & Johnston, 1994) and lasts only for several months (Kehle, Hintze, & DuPaul, 1997). The longer selective mutism persists, the more debilitating it can become (Kehle et al., 1997). It is more common among girls than boys and is seen across all social strata (Steinhausen & Juzi, 1996) and intellectual ability levels (Kehle et al., 1997). This disorder is relatively rare, although estimates of prevalence have been inconclusive (Carlson et al., 1994; Haeberli & Kratochwill, 2005). Bergman, Piacentini, and McCracken (2002) found the prevalence to be .71% in a public school sample. In a comparison of native-born versus immigrant children, selective mutism was found in less than 1 per 1,000 native-born children and 7.9 per 1,000 immigrant children (Dummit et al., 1997).

The etiology of selective mutism is uncertain. A recent shift in speculation as to its etiology deemphasizes its precipitation by a traumatic event (such as sexual abuse or hospitalization) or its possible expression of oppositional behavior, and instead concentrates on familial history and the presence of an underlying anxiety disorder. Some researchers have suggested that selective mutism be considered a behavioral manifestation of a social anxiety disorder (Black & Uhde, 1995; Dummit et al., 1997; Yeganeh, Beidel, Turner, Pina, & Silverman, 2003). Kristensen (1999) found that selective mutism is associated with developmental delay almost as frequently as with anxiety disorders, suggesting a neurobiological etiology for the disorder. In contrast, the learning-theory approach suggests that selective mutism is a learned behavior maintained by social reinforcement, whereas the psychoanalytic approach suggests that selective mutism functions to reduce a child's fear in anxiety-provoking situations through unresponsiveness (Kehle et al., 1997). The following factors have been found to elevate the risk of selective mutism: a background of migration; early developmental risk factors, including complications during pregnancy and delivery; delayed motor development and toilet training; premorbid speech and language disorders (most commonly articulation and expressive language disorders); behavioral abnormalities during infancy and preschool ages (such as relationship problems, separation anxiety, sleep disorders, and eating disorders); comorbid diagnoses (typically enuresis but also including sleeping and eating disorders); and a pattern of social interactions that include withdrawal, anxiety, depression, and schizoid type behaviors (Steinhausen & Juzi, 1996). In addition, a family history of selective mutism, extreme shyness, and/or anxiety disorders may put the child at risk (Dow et al., 1995).

In order to assess selective mutism, the clinician should conduct a comprehensive assessment in order to rule out other possible explanations for the mutism and to evaluate comorbid conditions. The assessment should include: a structured diagnostic interview with the parent(s) with a review of academic, familial, and medical history; a formal evaluation of speech and language ability; an interview with the child, in which the child has the opportunity to respond nonverbally; a medical examination; auditory testing; standardized psychological testing; and a recorded audiotape of the child speaking at home (Dow et al., 1995).

Possibly because of the low incidence of this disorder, successful treatment protocols have not been extensively studied. Selective mutism has been shown to be highly resistant to treatment (Kehle et al., 1997). Psychotherapy is the most common form of intervention, including cognitive and cognitive-behavioral approaches. However, behavioral approaches have been found to be the most effective strategies to use in the treatment of children with selective mutism (Kehle et al., 1997). Behavioral strategies shown to be effective with these children include contingency management programs, stimulus-fading, shaping, escape-avoidance techniques, and self-modeling (Kehle et al., 1997). Barowsky (1999) has described a systematic desensitization, or stimulus-fading, approach. It consists of four phases: Initially the parent engages the child in conversation within the school setting, with the assumption that the child is most comfortable in talking with the parent. In the second phase, the teacher is included as a passive participant who gradually and unobtrusively increases his or her proximity to the child and parent as they converse. Then, in the third phase, the teacher asks the child questions with the parent as intermediary. Finally, in the fourth phase, the teacher and child interact in the presence of a small number of children.

As selective mutism has been redefined as a biologically influenced social phobia, clinicians have increasingly employed medication to treat it. Selectively mute children have made significant improvement after a 12-week trial of fluoxetine in a placebo-controlled, parallel design study (Black & Uhde, 1994), lending support to the placement of selective mutism as a variant of social anxiety, which is also successfully treated with fluoxetine. A trial of medication should be considered if anxiety is a prominent feature and/or if other treatment attempts have failed. Medication alone or in combination with learning-theory approaches has been found to be effective in the treatment of selective mutism in children (Kehle et al., 1997).

Speech therapy has also been successfully used to treat selective mutism, with a focus on articulation and language training, rather than on the psychological aspects of the mutism (Dow et al., 1995). If a selective mute child is insecure about the sound of his or her voice or pronunciation skills, the speech language pathologist can help him or her perfect pronunciation, learn pragmatic skills, and increase comprehension.

The school psychologist can help implement an individualized, school-based multidisciplinary treatment plan by coordinating efforts of parents, clinicians, and teachers. The goal of such a plan is to decrease the anxiety associated with speaking in the school environment and increasing normal interaction and communication.

REFERENCES

American Psychiatric Association. (2000). *Diagnostic and statistical manual of mental disorders* (4th ed., text rev.). Washington, DC: Author.

Barowsky, E. I. (1999). Elective mutism. In C. R. Reynolds & T. B. Gutkin (Eds.), *Handbook of school psychology* (3rd ed., pp. 674–676). New York, NY: Wiley.

Bergman, R. L., Piacentini, J., & McCracken, J. T. (2002). Prevalence and description of selective mutism in a school-based sample. *Journal of the American Academy of Child and Adolescent Psychiatry, 41*, 938–946.

Black, B., & Uhde, T. W. (1994). Treatment of elective mutism with fluoxetine: A double-blind, placebo-controlled study. *Journal of the American Academy of Child and Adolescent Psychiatry, 33*, 1000–1006.

Black, B., & Uhde, T. W. (1995). Psychiatric characteristics of children with selective mutism: A pilot study. *Journal of the American Academy of Child and Adolescent Psychiatry, 34*, 847–856.

Carlson, J. S., Kratochwill, T. R., & Johnston, H. (1994). Prevalence and treatment of selective mutism in clinical practice: A survey of child and adolescent psychiatrists. *Journal of Child and Adolescent Psychopharmacology, 4*, 281–291.

Dow, S. P., Sonies, B. C., Scheib, D., Moss, S. E., & Leonard, H. L. (1995). Practical guidelines for the assessment and treatment of selective mutism. *Journal of the American Academy of Child and Adolescent Psychiatry, 34*, 836–846.

Dummit, E. S., Klein, R. G., Tancer, N. K., Asche, B., Martin, J., & Fairbanks, J. A. (1997). Systematic assessment of 50 children with selective mutism. *Journal of the American Academy of Child and Adolescent Psychiatry, 36,* 653–660.

Haerberli, F., & Kratochwill, T. R. (2005). Selective mutism. In S. W. Lee & P. A. Lowe (Eds.), *Encyclopedia of school psychology* (pp. 489–490). Thousand Oaks, CA: Sage.

Kehle, T. J., Hintze, J. M., & DuPaul, G. J. (1997). Selective mutism. In G. G. Bear, K. M. Minke, & A. Thomas (Eds.), *Children's needs II: Development, problems and alternatives* (pp. 329–337). Washington, DC: National Association of School Psychologists.

Kristensen, H. (1999). Selective mutism and comorbidity with developmental disorder/delay, anxiety disorder, and elimination disorder. *Journal of the American Academy of Child and Adolescent Psychiatry, 39,* 249–256.

Steinhausen, H., & Juzi, C. (1996). Elective mutism: An analysis of 100 cases. *Journal of the American Academy of Child and Adolescent Psychiatry, 35,* 606–614.

Yeganeh, R., Beidel, D. C., Turner, S. M., Pina, A. A., & Silverman, W. K. (2003). Clinical distinctions between selective mutism and social phobia: An investigation of childhood psychopathology. *Journal of the American Academy of Child and Adolescent Psychiatry, 42,* 1069–1075.

SUSAN M. UNRUH
PATRICIA A. LOWE
University of Kansas

SELF-CARE SKILLS (See Self-Help Training)

SELF-CONCEPT

Self-concept is an individual's evaluation of his or her own abilities and attributes. It includes all aspects of an individual's personality of which he or she is aware. Although some authors have drawn distinctions between self-concept and self-esteem (Damon & Hart, 1982), the terms are frequently used interchangeably. Several theoretical models of self-concept exist in the literature. For example, Coopersmith (1967) has suggested that four factors contribute to an individual's self-concept: significance (feeling of being loved and approved of by important others), competence (ability to perform tasks considered important), virtue (adherence to moral and ethical principles), and power (the degree to which an individual is able to exert control over self and others). Harter (1982) found that self-concept can be broken down into three specific components: cognitive, social, and physical competence, and a general self-worth factor.

Children with a positive self-concept are described as imaginative, confident in their own judgments and abilities, assertive, able to assume leadership roles, less preoccupied with themselves, and able to devote more time to others and to external activities. Children with a negative self-concept are described as quiet, unobtrusive, unoriginal, lacking in initiative, withdrawn, and doubtful about themselves (Coopersmith, 1967). School progress and academic achievement are influenced by self-concept, as is vocational choice. Unfortunately, much of the research on the effects of self-esteem has been subject to methodological and theoretical criticism (Damon & Hart, 1982; Wylie, 1979).

Self-concept begins to develop early in life, with children as young as 18 to 24 months able to discriminate between self and others (Lewis & Brooks-Gunn, 1979). As children's thought processes become less concrete and more abstract, there are corresponding changes in self-concept. Younger children (e.g., 9-year-olds) tend to describe themselves in categorical terms (name, age, gender, physical attributes, etc.), while older children take an increasingly abstract view, describing their personal and interpersonal traits, attitudes, and beliefs (Montemayor & Eisen, 1977). There is not, however, any consistent evidence of age-related changes in the level of self-esteem (how positively or negatively one views oneself). The one exception to this is a temporary decline in self-esteem around the time children enter their teens (Simmons et al., 1979).

A number of factors influence an individual's self-concept. Parents appear to play a particularly important role (Coopersmith, 1967). Children with high self-esteem tend to have parents who themselves have high self-esteem and who are warm, nurturing, and accepting of their children while setting high academic and behavioral standards. They set and enforce strict limits on their children and are fair, reasonable, and consistent in their use of discipline. Parents of low self-esteem children alternate unpredictably between excessive permissiveness and harsh punishment. A close relationship with the same-sex parent is typical among high self-esteem children. Findings of higher self-esteem in only children and first-born children suggest that parental attention is important. Other factors associated with high self-esteem include academic success, the presence of a close friendship, and the perceived opinions of others. Physical attractiveness and height are unrelated to self-esteem (Coopersmith, 1967). It is very important for educators to remember that different ethnic groups perceive self-concept and its measurement in different ways (Obiakor, 1992).

Historically instruments with a singular focus were used to measure self-concept: the Piers-Harris Children's Self-Concept Scale (Piers, 1969), the Coopersmith Self-Esteem Inventory (Coopersmith, 1967), the Perceived Competence Scale for Children (Harter, 1982), and the Preschool and Primary Self-Concept Scale (Stager & Young, 1982). Omnibus scales such as the Behavior

Assessment System for Children, second edition (Reynolds & Kamphaus, 2004) include scales designed to measure self-esteem in the larger context of personality and behavioral development.

REFERENCES

Coopersmith, S. (1967). *Antecedents of self-esteem*. San Francisco, CA: Freeman.

Damon, W., & Hart, D. (1982). The development of self-understanding from infancy through adolescence. *Child Development, 53*, 841–864.

Harter, S. (1982). The perceived competence scale for children. *Child Development, 53*, 87–97.

Lewis, M., & Brooks-Gunn, J. (1979). *Social cognition and the acquisition of self*. New York, NY: Plenum Press.

Montemayor, R., & Eisen, M. (1977). The development of self-conceptions from childhood to adolescence. *Developmental Psychology, 13*, 314–319.

Obiakor, F. E. (1992). Self-concept of African-American students: An operational model for special education. *Exceptional Children, 59*(2), 160–167.

Piers, E. V. (1969). *The Piers Harris Children's Self-Concept Scale*. Nashville, TN: Counselor Recordings and Tests.

Reynolds, C. R., & Kamphaus, R. W. (2004). *Behavior assessment system for children* (2nd ed.). Circle Pines, MN: American Guidance Service.

Simmons, R. G., Blyth, D. A., Van Cleave, E. F., & Bush, D. M. (1979). Entry into early adolescence: The impact of school structure, puberty, and early dating on self-esteem. *American Sociological Review, 44*, 948–967.

Stager, S., & Young, R. D. (1982). A self-concept measure for preschool and early primary grade children. *Journal of Personality Assessment, 46*, 536–543.

Wylie, R. C. (1979). *The self-concept: Theory and research on selected topics* (Vol. 2, Rev. ed.). Lincoln: University of Nebraska Press.

ROBERT G. BRUBAKER
Eastern Kentucky University

See also Depression, Childhood and Adolescence; Emotional Lability; Self-Management

SELF-CONTAINED CLASS

The first self-contained special classes were established in the late 1800s and early 1900s as public school classes for the students with moderate intellectual disabilities, hearing impairments, visual impairments, emotionally disabilities, and physical disabilities. Esten (1900) states that special classes for individuals with intellectual disabilities were established to provide students with disabilities with more appropriate class placement. A self-contained classroom for students with disabilities can be defined as one that homogeneously segregates children with disabilities from typically developing peers. Children are usually segregated along categorical groupings. As a result of Dunn's (1968) article on the detrimental aspects of self-contained placements for the mildly disabled, students receiving special education in self-contained classes today are usually "low-incidence," exhibiting more severe problems. Dunn was later refuted by Walker and McLaughlin (1992). However, Kirk and Gallagher (1983) report gifted students are also grouped into special classes according to interests and abilities.

A self-contained class is a place where students receiving special education services spend more than 60% of their school day and receive most of their academic instruction. Typically, caseloads are small, ranging from 5 to 10 students in a class. A wide variety of instructional materials are available to the students. The self-contained class provides the opportunity for highly individualized, closely supervised, specialized instruction. The self-contained classroom is usually taught by one trained teacher who is certified according to the categories served. The self-contained classroom may be categorically specific (serving one population) or cross-categorically grouped (serving multicategorical populations).

Major purposes of a self-contained class as outlined by Sabatino, Miller, and Schmidt (1981) include providing the student with the social and personal adjustment skills necessary to promote school success, and maintaining a constant structure within the instructional environment to reduce distractibility, hyperactivity, restlessness, poor attention span, and control over the rate of information flowing to the learner. Additionally, the purposes include teaching the basic academic and social skills necessary for success in life and making cooperative arrangements based on adequate communication with parents (p. 321). It is possible that a student may be assigned to a self-contained classroom and receive additional resource room assistance or partake in inclusive programming. Placement depends on what is best for the students in terms of least restriction. Usually, students are mainstreamed into regular education for nonacademic subjects such as music, physical education, and art, or academic areas of proficiency. Federal special education laws, especially IDEIA, require that children with disabilities be educated in the least restrictive environment.

REFERENCES

Dunn, L. M. (1968). Special education for the mildly handicapped: Is much of it justifiable? *Exceptional Children, 35*, 5–22.

Esten, R. A. (1900). Backward children in the public schools. *Journal of Psychoaesthenics, 5*, 10–16.

Kirk, S. A., & Gallagher, J. J. (1983). *Educating exceptional children* (4th ed.). Boston, MA: Houghton Mifflin.

Sabatino, D. A., Miller, T. L., & Schmidt, C. R. (1981). *Learning disabilities: Systemizing teaching and service delivery.* Rockville, MD: Aspen.

Walker, J. G., & McLaughlin, T. F. (1992). Self-contained versus resource room classroom placement: A review. *Journal of Instructional Psychology, 19*(3), 214–225.

MARIBETH MONTGOMERY Kasik
Governors State University

See also Least Restrictive Environment; Resource Room; Special Class

SELF-CONTROL CURRICULUM

The self-control curriculum was a product of the work of Fagen, Long, and Stevens (1975). They contended that emotional and cognitive development are closely related and therefore both need to be addressed simultaneously in the instructional process. They held that learning is impaired when learners have negative feelings about themselves. Fagen et al. believed that in many cases of behavior disorders there was an inability on the part of the individual to exert self-control. The self-control curriculum had as its goals the development of self-control and positive feelings.

There were eight enabling skills in the self-control model. Four of these were in the cognitive area and four in the affective area. The eight skills are:

1. *Selecting.* Paying attention to directions/instruction.
2. *Storing.* Remembering directions/instructions.
3. *Sequencing and ordering.* Organizing materials/work areas to perform work.
4. *Anticipating consequences.* Realizing that behavior has consequences and predicting those consequences.
5. *Appreciating feelings.* Expressing feelings by words and actions.
6. *Managing frustrations.* Behaviorally maintaining control in stressful situations.
7. *Inhibiting and delaying.* Delaying actions and reflecting on consequences of possible actions even when excited.
8. *Relaxing.* Consciously relieving bodily tension.

The curriculum has pupil activities and guidelines for teachers for developing more lessons in each unit. The activities involve games, discussions, and role-playing activities. The position taken in the curriculum was that self-control must be taught just as any other subject. General recommendations throughout the curriculum were to proceed from easy to difficult, to proceed in small steps, to use repetition and provide practice, to make activities enjoyable, reinforce efforts, and provide opportunities to practice skills in new situations and settings. Little research has been conducted in the past to validate the curriculum.

REFERENCE

Fagen, S. A., Long, N. J., & Stevens, D. (1975). *Teaching children self-control.* Columbus, OH: Merrill.

ROBERT A. SEDLAK
University of Wisconsin at Stout

See also Self-Monitoring; Social Behavior of Individuals With Disabilities; Social Skills Instruction

SELF-DETERMINATION

The concept of self-determination has had a long history in political science, religion, philosophy, and more recently in psychology and special education. Mencius, a Confucian scholar in 371–289 BCE, believed that common people were equal to kings and that the state should express the will of the people (Simpkins & Simpkins, 2000). The philosopher John Locke believed that men direct their own lives (Locke, 1715). African slaves in America viewed self-determination as the control that people have over their own destiny (Franklin, 1984). Mithaug, Martin, and Agran (1987), with their Adaptability Model, began the conversation about self-determination in special education. They suggested that students with disabilities learn self-regulatory skills to adjust to change as a means of being successful in school and to make a meaningful transition to life after graduation from school. Ward (1988) formalized the introduction of the term self-determination into special education when he claimed that self-determination is the ability for students with disabilities to choose and attain their own goals. This history produced today's macro and micro view of self-determination (Martin, Marshall, & De Pry, 2005). Macro self-determination involves groups of people joining together to self-govern rather than being dominated by a dictator or ruthless ruler. Micro self-determination refers to individuals learning to direct their own lives by choosing and attaining their goals. Special education focuses upon micro-level self-determination issues and instructional strategies.

Self-determined students define and achieve their goals from knowing and valuing themselves (Field & Hoffman,

1994). The Self-Determined Learning Model believes that once students choose a goal, self-determined students will use self-management strategies to help attain their goals and make adjustments in their environment, strategies, or supports to attain their goals (Wehmeyer, Palmer, Agran, Mithaug, & Martin, 2000). Self-determined learning theory (Mithaug, Mithaug, Agran, Martin, & Wehmeyer, 2003) postulates that learning is adjustment and that students learn when an impediment blocks their goal attainment attempts and they need to make adjustments to attain their goals. Martin and Marshall (1995) believe that self-determined students set goals for themselves based on an understanding of their interests, skills, and limits. They then develop a plan to accomplish their goals, implement the plan, self-evaluate their performance, and make needed adjustments to their goals, strategies, or support. To enable students to do this Martin and Marshall (1995) identified seven self-determination constructs that students need to learn: (1) self-awareness, (2) self-advocacy, (3) self-efficacy, (4) decision making, (5) independent performance, (6) self-evaluation, and (7) adjustment.

Wehmeyer and Palmer (2003) found that former high school students with higher levels of self-determination skills had more positive postschool outcomes. Martin et al. (2003) demonstrated that increased use of self-determination skills resulted in improved class behavior, goal attainment, and academic performance. Janzen (2005) discovered that college freshmen that returned to school after their first semester had significantly higher self-determination levels than those who dropped out.

Several self-determination research-based instructional programs and strategies provide teachers the tools needed to increase the opportunities for students to become more self-determined (Trainor, 2005). These include *Steps to Self-Determination* (Hoffman & Field, 2005), the ChoiceMaker lesson packages (Martin et al., 2005), which include the *Self-Directed IEP* (Martin, Marshall, Maxson, & Jerman, 1996), and *Take Action: Making Goals Happen* (Marshall et al., 1999). The *Self-Directed IEP*, for example, increased student participation in their secondary IEP meetings and increased students' level of self-determination (Martin et al., in press). *Take Action* taught students the skills needed to attain their own goals (German, Martin, Marshall, & Sale, 2000). Self-determination contracts enable students with disabilities to attain academic goals (Martin et al., 2003; Mithaug & Mithaug, 2003), and improve vocational performance (Woods & Martin, 2004). Self-determined individuals will use a variety of self-directed instructional strategies to attain self-selected goals, including self-instruction and self-evaluation (Agran, King-Sears, Wehmeyer, & Copeland, 2003).

Students' cultural decision-making identity may impact the viability of self-determination practices such as student-directed transition planning (Trainor, 2005; Valenzuela & Martin, 2005). Student-directed planning and goal attainment that emphasizes individualization may negatively impact collaborative planning with students and their families who view decision making from a collectivist perspective. This issue seems especially relevant to students and families from culturally and linguistically diverse backgrounds, where student goal attainment may reflect family or community needs and interests. Educators need to understand student and family decision-making orientation to successfully collaborate with educational planning and student goal attainment (Valenzuela & Martin).

Since the introduction of the Adaptability Model in 1997, much progress has been made in understanding self-determination. Self-determination powers secondary transition models and practice (Field, Martin, Miller, Ward, & Wehmeyer, 1998); its influence is starting to impact instruction for younger students as well (Palmer & Wehmeyer, 2003), and recommendations for building-level reforms that promote self-determination are emerging (Field & Hoffman, 2002). Yet, much remains to be done to fully understand the effectiveness of self-determination methodology and how to reach widespread implementation.

REFERENCES

Agran, M., King-Sears, M. E., Wehmeyer, M. L., & Copeland, S. R. (2003). *Student-directed learning*. Baltimore, MD: Paul H. Brookes.

Field, S., & Hoffman, A. (1994). Development of a model for self-determination. *Career Development for Exceptional Individuals, 17*, 159–169.

Field, S., & Hoffman, A. (2002). Preparing youth to exercise self-determination: Quality indicators of school environments that promote acquisition of knowledge, skills, and beliefs related to self-determination. *Journal of Disability Policy Studies, 13*, 113–118.

Field, S. S., Martin, J. E., Miller, R. J., Ward, M., & Wehmeyer, M. (1998). Self-determination for persons with disabilities: A position statement of the Division on Career Development and Transition. *Career Development for Exceptional Individuals, 21*, 113–128.

Franklin, V. P. (1984). *Black self-determination: A cultural history of the faith of the fathers*. Brooklyn, NY: Lawrence Hill.

German, S. L., Martin, J. E., Marshall, L., & Sale, R. P. (2000). Promoting self-determination: Using Take Action to teach goal attainment. *Career Development for Exceptional Individuals, 23*, 27–38.

Hoffman, A., & Field, S. (2005). *Steps to self-determination: A curriculum to help adolescents learn to achieve their goals* (2nd ed.). Austin, TX: PRO-ED.

Janzen, A. (2005). *The relationship between self-determination and retention of college freshmen*. Unpublished master's thesis, University of Oklahoma, Norman.

Locke, J. (1715). *An essay concerning human understanding*. Retrieved from http://oregonstate.edu/instruct/phl302/texts/locke/locke1/Book4b.html

Marshall, L. H., Martin, J. E., Maxson, L. M., Miller, T. L., McGill, T., Hughes, W. M., & Jerman, P. A. (1999). *Take Action*. Longmont, CO: Sopris West.

Martin, J. E., & Marshall, L. H. (1995). ChoiceMaker: A comprehensive self-determination transition program. *Intervention in School and Clinic, 30*, 147–156.

Martin, J. E., Marshall, L. H., & DePry, R. L. (2005). Participatory decision-making: Innovative practices that increase student self-determination. In R. W. Flexer, T. J. Simmons, P. Luft, & R. M. Baer (Eds.), *Transition planning for secondary students with disabilities* (2nd ed., pp. 304–332). Columbus, OH: Merrill Prentice Hall.

Martin, J. E., Marshall, L. H., Maxson, L. M., & Jerman, P. L. (1996). *The self-directed IEP*. Longmont, CO: Sopris West.

Martin, J. E., Mithaug, D. E., Cox, P., Peterson, L. Y., Van Dycke, J. L., & Cash, M. E. (2003). Increasing self-determination: Teaching students to plan, work, evaluate, and adjust. *Exceptional Children, 69*, 431–447.

Martin, J. E., Van Dycke, J. L., Christensen, W. R., Greene, B. A., Gardner, J. E., & Lovett, D. L. (in press). Increasing student participation in their transition IEP meetings: Establishing the self-directed IEP as an evidence-based practice. *Exceptional Children*.

Mithaug, D. E., Martin, J. E., & Agran, M. (1987). Adaptability instruction: The goal of transitional programs. *Exceptional Children, 53*, 500–505.

Mithaug, D. E., Mithaug, D., Agran, M., Martin, J. E., & Wehmeyer, M. (2003). *Self-determined learning theory: Predictions, prescriptions, and practice*. Mahwah, NJ: Erlbaum.

Mithaug, D. K., & Mithaug, D. E. (2003). The effects of choice opportunities and self-regulation training on the self-engagement and learning of young children with disabilities. In D. E. Mithaug, D. Mithaug, M. Agran, J. E. Martin, & M. Wehmeyer (Eds.), *Self-determined learning theory: Predictions, prescriptions, and practice* (pp. 141–157). Mahwah, NJ: Erlbaum.

Palmer, S. B., & Wehmeyer, M. L. (2003). Promoting self-determination in early elementary school. *Remedial and Special Education, 24*, 115–126.

Simpkins, C. R., & Simpkins, A. (2000). *Simple Confucianism: A guide to living virtuously*. Boston, MA: Tuttle.

Trainor, A. A. (2005). Self-determination perceptions and behaviors of diverse students with LD during the transition planning process. *Journal of Learning Disabilities, 38*, 233–249.

Valenzuela, R. L., & Martin, J. E. (2005). The Self-Directed IEP: Bridging values of diverse cultures and secondary education. *Career Development for Exceptional Individuals, 28*, 4–14.

Ward, M. J. (1988). The many facets of self-determination. *National Information Center for Children and Youth with Handicaps: Transition Summary, 5*, 2–3.

Wehmeyer, M. L., & Palmer, S. B. (2003). Adult outcomes for students with cognitive disabilities three years after high school: The impact of self-determination. *Education and Training in Developmental Disabilities, 38*, 131–144.

Wehmeyer, M. L., Palmer, S. B., Agran, M., Mithaug, D. E., & Martin, J. E. (2000). Promoting casual agency: The self-determined learning model of instruction. *Exceptional Children, 66*, 439–453.

Woods, L. L., & Martin, J. E. (2004). Improving supervisor evaluation through the use of self-determination contracts. *Career Development for Exceptional Individuals, 27*, 207–220.

JAMES E. MARTIN
University of Oklahoma

See also Adaptive Behavior; Self-Help Training

SELF-DETERMINATION PRACTICES

Over the past two decades, promoting the self-determination of students with disabilities has become a best practice in secondary education and transition services (Wehmeyer, Abery, Mithaug, & Stancliffe, 2003; Wehmeyer, Agran, Hughes, Martin, Mithaug, & Palmer, 2007). Self-determination refers to self- (vs. other-) caused action—to people acting volitionally, based on their own will. Volition is the capability of conscious choice, decision, and intention. Self-determined behavior is volitional, self-caused or self-initiated action.

Models of self-determination. There are several theoretical models of self-determination that have emerged from research and practice in special education. Wehmeyer and colleagues (Wehmeyer et al., 2003; Wehmeyer et al., 2007) proposed a *functional model of self-determination* in which self-determination is conceptualized as a dispositional characteristic (enduring tendencies used to characterize and describe differences between people) based on the *function* a behavior serves for an individual. Self-determined behavior refers to "volitional actions that enable one to act as the primary causal agent in one's life and to maintain or improve one's quality of life" (Wehmeyer, 2005, p. 117). *Causal agency* implies that it is the individual who makes or causes things to happen in his or her life and that the individual acts with an eye toward causing *an effect* to *accomplish* a *specific end* or to *cause* or *create change.*

Self-determination emerges across the life span as children and adolescents learn skills and develop attitudes and beliefs that enable them to be causal agents in their lives. These skills and attitudes are the *component elements* of self-determined behavior, and include choice making, problem solving, decision making, goal setting and attainment, self-advocacy, and self-management skills. The model has been empirically validated (Shogren et al., 2008; Wehmeyer, Kelchner, & Richards, 1996); operationalized by the development of an assessment linked to the theory (Wehmeyer, 1996); served as the foundation for intervention development and provided impetus for a variety of research activities (see Wehmeyer et al., 2007).

Field and colleagues (Field & Hoffman, 2002; Hoffman & Field, 2005) proposed a *five-step model for promoting self-determination* in which self-determination is either promoted or discouraged by factors within the individual's control (e.g., values, knowledge, skills) and variables that are environmental in nature (e.g., opportunities for choice making, attitudes of others). The model has five major components: *Know Yourself and Your Environment, Value Yourself, Plan, Act, and Experience Outcomes and Learn.*

The five-step model was developed over a 3-year effort (Field & Hoffman, 2002) that included over 1,500 student observations and interviews with more than 200 individuals. The model has provided the framework for intervention development, particularly the *Steps to Self-Determination* curriculum (Hoffman & Field, 2005) and its related assessment tools (Field, Hoffman, & Sawilowsky, 2004).

Abery and colleagues (Abery & Stancliffe, 1996; Stancliffe, Abery, & Smith, 2000) proposed an *ecological model of self-determination* that defines the self-determination construct as "a complex process, the ultimate goal of which is to achieve the level of personal control over one's life that an individual desires within those areas the individual perceives as important" (p. 27). The ecological model views self-determination as driven by the intrinsic motivation of all people to be the primary determiner of their thoughts, feelings, and behavior. Self-determination, accordingly, is the product of both the person and the environment—of the person using the skills, knowledge, and beliefs at his or her disposal to act on the environment with the goal of obtaining valued and desired outcomes. The ecological model within which people develop and lead their lives is viewed as consisting of four levels: the *microsystem, mesosystem, exosystem,* and *macrosystem* (See Wehmeyer et al., 2003 for more detail). The ecological model has been empirically evaluated (Stancliffe, Abery, & Smith, 2000), operationalized in the development of assessments (Abery, Stancliffe, Smith, McGrew, & Eggebeen, 1995a, 1995b), and has also provided a foundation for intervention (Abery, Arndt, Greger, Tetu, Eggebeen, Barosko et al., 1994) and research (Stancliffe et al., 2000).

Mithaug (Wehmeyer et al., 2003) hypothesized that self-determination is an unusually effective form of *self-regulation* markedly free of external influence in which people who are self-determined regulate their choices and actions more successfully than others. Mithaug suggested that individuals are often in flux between existing *states* and *goal* or desired states. When a discrepancy between what one has and wants exists, an incentive for self-regulation and action becomes operative. The ability to set appropriate expectations is based on the person's success in matching his or her *capacity* with present *opportunity*. Capacity is the person's assessment of existing resources

(e.g., skills, interests, motivation), and opportunity refers to aspects of the situation that allow the individual to achieve the desired gain. The experience generated during self-regulation is a function of repeated interaction between capacity and opportunity. Mithaug (1998) suggested that "self-determination always occurs in a social context" (p. 42) and that the social nature of the construct is worth reviewing because the distinction between self-determination and other-determination is nearly always in play when assessing an individual's prospects for controlling their life in a particular situation" (p. 42).

The Importance of Self-Determination in Transition

Research has documented that if provided instruction to promote self-determination, students with disabilities can acquire knowledge and skills pertaining to self-determination and its component elements (Algozzine, Browder, Karvonen, Test, & Wood, 2001; Cobb, Lehmann, Newman-Gonchar, & Morgen, 2009; Wehmeyer, Palmer, et al., 2013; Wehmeyer, Shogren, et al., 2013). Also, self-determination status has been linked to the attainment of more positive academic outcomes (Fowler, Konrad, Walker, Test, & Wood, 2007; Konrad, Fowler, Walker, Test, & Wood, 2007), greater access to the general education curriculum (Lee, Wehmeyer, Soukup, & Palmer, 2010; Shogren, Palmer, Wehmeyer, Williams-Diehm, & Little, 2010), and more positive transition outcomes, including better employment and independent living outcomes (Wehmeyer & Palmer, 2003; Wehmeyer & Schwartz, 1997), and more positive quality of life and life satisfaction (Lachapelle et al., 2005; Nota, Ferrari, Soresi, & Wehmeyer, 2007; Shogren, Lopez, Wehmeyer, Little, & Pressgrove, 2006; Wehmeyer & Schwartz, 1998).

Interventions and Assessments to Promote Self-Determination

The National Secondary Transition Technical Assistance Center (Test, Fowler, Kohler, & Kortering, 2010) established a moderate level of evidence for teaching skills related to self-determination and identified self-determination as one of 16 evidence-based predictors of postschool employment, education, and independent living success (Test, Mazzotti, Mustian, Fowler, Kortering, & Kohler, 2009). More recently, Wehmeyer, Palmer et al. (2013) conducted a randomized trial, placebo control group study showing that students who receive interventions to promote self-determination showed significantly greater growth, indicating the efficacy of such interventions.

Specific curricula and instructional models have been validated as well. [It should be noted that a number of programs to promote student involvement in transition planning have been shown to enhance self-determination, and those are covered in a separate entry.] Curricular programs with evidence of their efficacy include *The*

ChoiceMaker Curriculum (with *The Self-Directed IEP* materials; Martin, Marshall, Maxson, & Jerman, 1993), which includes modules on *Choosing Goals* and *Taking Actions*, and the *Steps to Self-Determination Curriculum* (2nd ed.; Hoffman & Field, 2005), which involves lessons using modeling, cooperative and experiential learning, lecture, and discussions to focus on content related to self-determination.

Both of these programs have assessment tools included. There are two widely used norm-referenced measures of self-determination: *The Arc's Self-Determination Scale* (Wehmeyer & Kelchner, 1995), a 72-item self-report measure based on the functional theory of self-determination, and the *AIR Self-Determination Scale* (Wolman, Campeau, Dubois, Mithaug, & Stolarski, 1994), which assesses student capacity and opportunity for self-determination. Both have extensive psychometric data and have been used in research and model development (see Wehmeyer et al. 2003).

The *Self-Determined Learning Model of Instruction* (Wehmeyer et al., 2007) is a model of teaching based on the component elements of self-determination, the process of self-regulated problem solving, and research on student-directed learning. Teachers use the model to teach students to self-regulate problem solving, leading to students setting educational goals, creating action plans to achieve those goals, and monitoring and evaluating their progress toward those goals, modifying their plan or goal as needed. There are more than a dozen studies investigating the efficacy of the SDLMI (see Wehmeyer et al., 2007). Recently, Wehmeyer, Shogren et al. (2013) and Shogren et al. (2010) conducted a group-randomized, modified equivalent control group design study of the efficacy of the SDLMI, establishing the causal impact of the model on student self-determination, transition and academic goal attainment, and access to the general education curriculum.

Infusing Instruction on Component Elements into the Curriculum

The 2004 Amendments to the Individuals with Disabilities Education Act (IDEA) require the individualized education programs (IEPs) of all students with disabilities to contain statements regarding how the student will access the general curriculum. Wehmeyer, Field, Doren, Jones, & Mason (2004) identified two ways in which promoting self-determination will promote such access. First, school standards frequently include goals pertaining to component elements of self-determined behavior. Second, teaching students the skills, like goal setting or problem solving, that enable them to be more self-determined will also enable them to more effectively interact with the general curriculum.

So, more than ever, addressing issues pertaining to self-determination across multiple content domains is important. In addition to curricular materials and teaching models, educators can infuse instruction to promote component elements of self-determined behavior across content areas and across the student's day. The following document some of the critical content areas to achieve this.

Goal Setting

Having the skills to set and attain goals is central to one's ability to act in a self-determined manner. The process of promoting goal-setting skills involves working with students to help them learn to: (a) identify and define a goal clearly and concretely, (b) develop a series of objectives or tasks to achieve the goal, and (c) specify the actions necessary to achieve the desired outcome. At each step, students must make choices and decisions about what goals they wish to pursue and what actions they wish to take to achieve their goals. Goal-setting activities can be easily incorporated into a variety of educational activities and instructional domains, as well as in educational planning, as discussed subsequently. Research has suggested some strategies to follow to make goals both meaningful and attainable for students with disabilities. First, goals should be challenging. If they are too easy, there is no motivation to do the work to attain them, nor is there a feeling of accomplishment after achieving them. Second, while it is preferable for students to set their own goals, if this is not possible and goals need to be set by teachers, then the student's preferences and interests should be incorporated into the goal to increase the student's motivation to pursue the goal. Goals with personal meaning are more likely to be attained.

Choice-Making

Choice-making (e.g., the expression of a preference between two or more options) has received considerable attention in the literature, particularly pertaining to students with intellectual disabilities (Wehmeyer & Bolding, 1999, 2001). Opportunities to make choices should be infused throughout a students' day, as experiences with making choices "teach" students that they can exert control over their environment. Further, choices can be made more meaningful for students by involving them in decisions about what, how, and why they learn (Mithaug, Mithaug, Agran, Martin, & Wehmeyer, 2003).

Problem Solving

A *problem* is an activity or task for which a solution is not known or readily apparent. The process of solving a problem involves: (a) identifying and defining the problem, (b) listing possible solutions, (c) identifying the impact of each solution, (d) making a judgment about a preferred solution, and (e) evaluating the efficacy of the judgment (Wehmeyer et al., 2003). Developing the skills associated with problem solving may be particularly important for students with autism, given their characteristic difficulties with social-emotional understanding. Research suggests that students with autism may have difficulty understanding social and emotional cues, which limit their ability to interact with others (Wehmeyer & Smith, 2012).

Decision Making

Decision making involves coming to a judgment about which of a number of potential options is best at a given time. Making effective decisions involves: (a) identifying alternative courses of action, (b) identifying the possible consequences of each action, (c) assessing the probability of each consequence occurring, (d) choosing the best alternative, and (e) implementing the decision (Furby & Beyth Marom, 1992). Working to promote systematic decision-making skills is best addressed at the secondary level, while at the elementary level a focus on choice-making and problem solving can support the development of effective decision-making skills later in life (Wehmeyer et al., 2003).

When teaching decision-making skills, opportunities to make decisions should be imbedded in the curriculum. By supporting students to make decisions in 'real-world' situations, they will better develop their ability to conceptualize and generalize the decision-making process. The process of evaluating alternatives is an area in which direct instruction should occur; students can be provided support to develop lists of decision options, to evaluate the risk and benefit associated with a given alternative, and to evaluate biases in their decision-making (Furby & Beyth Marom, 1992). Students often evaluate risk somewhat different than adults, perhaps because they see the excitement of risk as positive, rather than negative. However, by teaching students how to evaluate and conceptualize risk, both in terms of short-term and long-term consequences, these biases can be reduced.

Self-Regulation and Student-Directed Learning Skills

Each of the aforementioned areas, goal-setting, choice-making, problem solving, and decision making, are important to enable students to self-regulate their behavior and their lives. *Self-regulation* is the process of setting goals, developing action plans to achieve those goals, implementing and following the action plans, evaluating the outcomes of the action plan, and changing actions plans, if the goal was not achieved (Mithaug et al., 2003). The skills associated with self-regulation enable students to examine their environments, evaluate their repertoire of possible responses and implement and evaluate a response. Student-directed learning strategies involve teaching students strategies that enable them to modify and regulate their own behavior (Agran, King-Sears, Wehmeyer, &

Copeland, 2003). A variety of strategies have been used to teach students with disabilities how to manage their own behavior or direct learning. Among the most commonly used strategies are picture cues and antecedent cue regulation strategies, self-instruction, self-monitoring, self-evaluation, and self-reinforcement. *Picture cues and antecedent cue regulation strategies* involve the use of visual or audio cues that students use to guide their behavior. Visual cues typically involve photographs, illustrations, or line drawings of steps in a task that support students to complete an activity that consists of a sequence of tasks. Audio cues include pre-recorded, taped directions or instructions that the student can listen to as they perform a task. Emerging technologies, like handheld computers, provide new and potentially powerful vehicles to deliver visual or auditory cues to learners. *Self-instruction* involves teaching students to provide their own verbal cues prior to the execution of target behaviors. *Self-monitoring* involves teaching students to observe whether they have performed a targeted behavior and whether the response met whatever existing criteria present. *Self-evaluation* involves teaching the student to compare his or her performance (as tracked through self-monitoring) and to compare that performance with a desired goal or outcome. *Self-reinforcement* involves teaching students to administer consequences to themselves (e.g., verbally telling themselves they did a good job). Self-reinforcement allows students to provide themselves with reinforcers that are accessible and immediate.

Self-Advocacy

Students with disabilities need to learn to advocate on their own behalf. To be an effective self-advocate, students have to learn both how to advocate and what to advocate for. There are ample opportunities for students to practice and learn self-advocacy skills within the context of the educational planning process. When teaching students how to advocate for themselves, the focus should be on teaching students how to be assertive, how to effectively communicate their perspective (either verbally or in written or pictorial form), how to negotiate, how to compromise, and how to deal with systems and bureaucracies. Students need to be provided real-world opportunities to practice these skills. This can be done by embedding opportunities for self-advocacy within the school day, by allowing students to set up a class schedule, work out their supports with a resource room teacher or other support provider, or participate in IEP and transition meetings.

Perceptions of Efficacy and Control

Students need to develop perceptions of efficacy and control, along with self-awareness and self-knowledge, to give them the motivation and confidence to practice the skills discussed above. Research has shown that students with developmental disabilities tend to have less adaptive perceptions of efficacy and outcome expectations than do students without disabilities (Wehmeyer et al., 2003). The same has been found concerning the perceptions of students with disabilities about their ability to exert control over their environment. Students should be provided opportunities to develop adaptive perceptions of their efficacy in performing given behaviors and their ability to exert control over their lives. One of the simplest ways to do this is to provide students with developmental disabilities opportunities to engage in problem solving, goal setting, and to make choices and decisions that are meaningful for them.

Self-Awareness and Self-Knowledge

For students to become more self-determined, they must possess a reasonably accurate understanding of their strengths, abilities, unique learning and support needs, and limitations. Further, they must know how to utilize this understanding to maximize success and progress.

Conclusion

Promoting self-determination and student involvement in educational planning has become best practice in the education of students with disabilities, particularly with relation to transition planning and services. Students with disabilities who leave school as self-determined young people achieve more positive adult outcomes. Moreover, promoting student self-determination provides, as it were, a gateway to the general curriculum for students with disabilities and can result in enhanced leadership skills. If educators are to achieve the outcomes envisioned by the transition mandates in IDEA, they will need to ensure that students with disabilities are provided sufficient opportunities to learn these skills and strategies, and to use them to play a meaningful role in their educational program, from planning to implementation.

REFERENCES

Abery, B. H., Arndt, K., Greger, P., Tetu, L., Eggebeen, A., Barosko, J., ... Rudrud, L. (1994). *Self-determination for youth with disabilities: A family education curriculum*. Minneapolis: University of Minnesota, Institute on Community Integration.

Abery, B. H., & Stancliffe, R. J. (1996). The ecology of self-determination. In D. J. Sands & M. L. Wehmeyer (Eds.), *Self-determination across the life span: Independence and choice for people with disabilities* (pp. 111–145). Baltimore, MD: Paul H. Brookes.

Abery, B. H., Stancliffe, R. J., Smith, J., McGrew, K., & Eggebeen, A. (1995a). *Minnesota Opportunities and Exercise of Self-Determination Scale–Adult Edition*. Minneapolis: University of Minnesota, Institute on Community Integration, Research and Training Center on Community Living.

Abery, B. H., Stancliffe, R. J., Smith, J., McGrew, K., & Eggebeen, A. (1995b). *Minnesota Self-Determination Skills, Attitudes, and Knowledge Evaluation Scale–Adult Edition*. Minneapolis: University of Minnesota, Institute on Community Integration, Research and Training Center on Community Living.

Agran, M., King-Sears, M., Wehmeyer, M., & Copeland, S. (2003). *Teachers guides to inclusive practices: Student-directed learning*. Baltimore, MD: Paul H. Brookes.

Algozzine, B., Browder, D., Karvonen, M., Test, D. W., & Wood, W. M. (2001). Effects of interventions to promote self-determination for individuals with disabilities, *Review of Educational Research, 71*, 219–277.

Cobb, B., Lehmann, J., Newman-Gonchar, R., & Morgen, A. (2009). Self-determination for students with disabilities: A narrative metasynthesis. *Career Development for Exceptional Individuals, 32* (2), 108–114.

Field, S., & Hoffman, A. (2002). Lessons learned from implementing the *Steps to Self-Determination* curriculum. *Remedial and Special Education 23*(2), 90–98.

Field, S., Hoffman, A., Sawilowsky, S. (2004). *Self-Determination Assessment Battery*. Detroit, MI: Wayne State University.

Fowler, C. H., Konrad, M., Walker, A. R., Test, D. W., & Wood, W. M. (2007). Self-determination interventions' effects on the academic performance of students with developmental disabilities. *Education and Training in Developmental Disabilities, 42*(3), 270–285.

Furby, L., & Beyth Marom, R. (1992). Risk taking in adolescence: A decision-making perspective. *Developmental Review, 12*(1), 1–44.

Hoffman, A. & Field, S. (2005). *Steps to Self-Determination* (2nd ed.). Austin, TX: PRO-ED.

Konrad, M., Fowler, C. H., Walker, A. R., Test, D. W., & Wood, W. M. (2007). Effects of self-determination interventions on the academic skills of students with learning disabilities. *Learning Disabilities Quarterly, 30*(2), 89–113.

Lachapelle, Y., Wehmeyer, M. L., Haelewyck, M. C., Courbois, Y., Keith, K. D., Schalock, R., ... Walsh, P. N. (2005). The relationship between quality of life and self-determination: An international study. *Journal of Intellectual Disability Research, 49*, 740–744.

Lee, S. H., Wehmeyer, M. L., Soukup, J. H., & Palmer, S. B. (2010). Impact of curriculum modifications on access to the general education curriculum for students with disabilities. *Exceptional Children, 76*(2), 213–233.

Martin, J. E., Marshall, L. H., Maxson, L. M., & Jerman, P. L. (1996). *The Self-Directed IEP*. Longmont, CO: Sopris West.

Mithaug, D. (1998). Your right, my obligation? *Journal of the Association for Persons with Severe Disabilities, 23*, 41–43.

Mithaug, D. E., Mithaug, D., Agran, M., Martin, J., & Wehmeyer, M. L. (Eds.). (2003). *Self-Determined Learning Theory: Construction, verification, and evaluation*. Mahwah, NJ: Erlbaum.

Nota, L., Ferrrari, L., Soresi, S., & Wehmeyer, M. L. (2007). Self-determination, social abilities, and the quality of life of people with intellectual disabilities. *Journal of Intellectual Disability Research, 51*, 850–865.

Shogren, K. A., Lopez, S. J., Wehmeyer, M. L., Little, T. D., & Pressgrove, C. L. (2006). The role of positive psychology constructs in predicting life satisfaction in adolescents with and without cognitive disabilities: An exploratory study. *The Journal of Positive Psychology*, *1*, 37–52.

Shogren, K., Palmer, S., Wehmeyer, M. L., Williams-Diehm, K., & Little, T. (2010). Effect of intervention with the *Self-Determined Learning Model of Instruction* on access and goal attainment. Manuscript submitted for publication.

Shogren, K. A., Wehmeyer, M. L., Palmer, S. B., Soukup, J. H., Little, T., Garner, N., ...Lawrence, M. (2008). Understanding the construct of self-determination: Examining the relationship between The Arc's Self-Determination Scale and the American Institute for Research Self-Determination Scale. *Assessment for Effective Instruction*, *33*, 94–107.

Stancliffe, R. J., Abery B. H., & Smith, J. (2000). Personal control and the ecology of community living settings: Beyond living-unit size and type. *American Journal on Mental Retardation*, *105*, 431–454.

Test, D. W., Fowler, C., Kohler, P., & Kortering, L. (2010). *Evidence-based practices and predictors in secondary transition: What we know and what we still need to know.* Charlotte, NC: University of North Carolina-Charlotte, National Secondary Transition Technical Assistance Center.

Test, D. W., Mazzotti, V. L., Mustian, A. L., Fowler, C. H., Kortering, L. J., & Kohler, P. H. (2009). Evidence-based secondary transition predictors for improving post-school outcomes for students with disabilities. *Career Development for Exceptional Individuals*, *32*, 160–181.

Wehmeyer, M. L. (1996). A self-report measure of self-determination for adolescents with cognitive disabilities. *Education and Training in Mental Retardation and Developmental Disabilities*, *31*, 282–293.

Wehmeyer, M. L. (2005). Self-determination and individuals with severe disabilities: Reexamining meanings and misinterpretations. *Research and Practice for Persons with Severe Disabilities*, *30*, 113–120.

Wehmeyer, M. L., Abery, B., Mithaug, D. E., & Stancliffe, R. J. (2003). *Theory in self-determination: Foundations for educational practice.* Springfield, IL: Thomas.

Wehmeyer, M. L., Agran, M., Hughes, C., Martin, J., Mithaug, D. E., & Palmer, S. (2007). *Promoting self-determination in students with intellectual and developmental disabilities.* New York, NY: Guilford Press.

Wehmeyer, M. L., & Bolding, N. (1999). Self-determination across living and working environments: A matched-samples study of adults with mental retardation. *Mental Retardation*, *37*, 353–363.

Wehmeyer, M. L., & Bolding, N. (2001). Enhanced self-determination of adults with intellectual disability as an outcome of moving to community-based work or living environments. *Journal of Intellectual Disability Research*, *45*(5), 371–383.

Wehmeyer, M. L., Field, S., Doren, B., Jones, B., & Mason, C. (2004). Self-determination and student involvement in standards-based reform. *Exceptional Children*, *70*, 413–425.

Wehmeyer, M. L., & Kelchner, K. (1995). *The Arc's Self-Determination Scale.* Arlington, TX: The Arc National Headquarters.

Wehmeyer, M. L., Kelchner, K., & Richards, S. (1996). Essential characteristics of self-determined behavior of individuals with mental retardation. *American Journal on Mental Retardation*, *100*(6), 632–642.

Wehmeyer, M. L., & Palmer, S. B. (2003). Adult outcomes from students with cognitive disabilities three years after high school: The impact of self-determination. *Education and Training in Developmental Disabilities*, *38*, 131–144.

Wehmeyer, M. L., Palmer, S., Shogren, K., Williams-Diehm, K., & Soukup, J. (2013). Establishing a causal relationship between interventions to promote self-determination and enhanced student self-determination. *Journal of Special Education*, *46*(4), 195–210.

Wehmeyer, M. L., & Schwartz, M. (1997). Self-determination and positive adult outcomes: A follow up study of youth with mental retardation or learning disabilities. *Exceptional Children*, *63*, 245–255.

Wehmeyer, M. L., & Schwartz, M. (1998). The relationship between self-determination and quality of life for adults with mental retardation. *Education and Training in Mental Retardation and Developmental Disabilities*, *33*, 3–12.

Wehmeyer, M. L., Shogren, K., Palmer, S., Williams-Diehm, K., Little, T., & Boulton, A. (2013). Impact of the *Self-Determined Learning Model of Instruction* on student self-determination: A randomized-trial placebo control group study. *Exceptional Children*, *78*(2), 135–153.

Wehmeyer, M. L., & Smith, T. E. C. (2012). Promoting self-determination and social inclusion: A review of research-based practices. In D. Zagar, M. L. Wehmeyer, & R. Simpson (Eds.), *Educating students with autism spectrum disorders: Research-based principles and practices* (pp. 247–261). New York, NY: Taylor & Francis.

Wolman, J., Campeau, P., Dubois, P., Mithaug, D., & Stolarski, V. (1994). *AIR Self-Determination Scale and user guide.* Palo Alto, CA: American Institute for Research.

MICHAEL WEHMEYER
University of Kansas
Fourth edition

SELF-HELP TRAINING

The skill areas typically included under the domain of self-help are toileting, eating, dressing, and personal hygiene. An obvious reason for training individuals with developmental disabilities in these skills is that there are widespread self-help skill deficits among this population. Another reason is that the acquisition of these skills represents a critical step in the developmental process and can increase self-esteem, promote positive social interaction, and maintain physical health and well-being (Kimm, Falvey, Bishop, & Rosenberg, 1995). Once the skills are acquired, the caregiver's time devoted to the routine maintenance of the individual with developmental disabilities is reduced. The acquisition of self-help skills can have meaningful social consequences. It can increase the possibility of gaining access to valued places and activities.

Probably the most significant development in the training of self-help skills is the application of behavior modification procedures. This has been referred to as one of the most influential factors in improving the care and training of individuals with developmental disabilities in the past 30 years (Whitman, Sciback, & Reid, 1983).

Research in each of the self-help skill training areas has undergone a similar developmental sequence (Reid, Wilson, & Faw, 1980). Early research demonstrated that caregivers, after receiving in-service training, could train a number of developmentally disabled individuals in self-help skills. Even though this research lacked experimental rigor, it did show the usefulness of behavior modification and stimulated further research. Contemporary research has focused on individual skills and has been more methodologically rigorous. There has also been an effort by Azrin et al. (Azrin & Fox, 1971; Azrin & Armstrong, 1973; Azrin, Schaeffer, & Wesolowski, 1976) to develop an intensive training approach that is more comprehensive than previous approaches. Intensive training is intended to produce rapid learning that is resistant to extinction.

Each self-help skill area has some unique characteristics that have affected the direction of research and training in that particular area (Reid et al., 1980). Training in independent toileting has become more complex and focuses on a more naturally occurring sequence of toilet behaviors. Automatic devices are being used to signal trainers when a trainee is about to have a toileting accident or has eliminated into the toilet. Nighttime toileting skills have also been trained to reduce the frequency of enuresis (bed wetting).

It is believed that training independent eating through behavior modification procedures has been relatively successful because food is an inherent reinforcer. In addition to focusing on the acquisition of independent eating skills, researchers and practitioners have attempted to eliminate or reduce inappropriate mealtime behaviors (e.g., eating too quickly and stealing food).

As in training eating skills, dressing has focused on acquisition of appropriate skills and the reduction of inappropriate behaviors (e.g., public disrobing). The generalization of dressing skills to other contexts has been an issue when developing training programs because training typically occurs when dressing is not naturally required. Maintenance over time has also been an important training issue because dressing is less inherently reinforcing than toileting and eating.

It is unusual that little research has been conducted on personal hygiene skills considering their importance in improving independent functioning and helping individuals with developmental disabilities to gain community acceptance. A development in training personal hygiene skills is a packaged approach called independence training (Matson, DiLorenzo, & Esveldt-Dawson, 1981). This approach expands on the typical behavioral training strategy by having trainees evaluate their own progress (self-monitor) and give each other feedback.

There are several areas of concern for future research and practice (Whitman et al., 1983). Often there is a discrepancy between the development of an effective training technology and its day-to-day application by caregivers. Consequently, it is important to understand what factors contribute to caregivers' willingness to carry out training. A component analysis of the multifaceted training strategies, like the intensive training package, could assist practitioners in selecting the most effective and efficient training. As increasing numbers of individuals with developmental disabilities live and work in the community, it will be necessary to train more advanced and complex skills in community contexts. It will also be necessary to determine the social validity of certain self-help skills, particularly in the areas of dressing and personal hygiene. By assessing social validity, practitioners will know what to teach in order to bring a skill into a socially acceptable range. Finally, effective and practical self-help training procedures need to be developed for individuals with physical disabilities.

REFERENCES

Azrin, N. H., & Armstrong, P. M. (1973). The "mini-meal." A method for teaching eating skills to the profoundly retarded. *Mental Retardation, 11*, 9–13.

Azrin, N. H., & Fox, R. M. (1971). A rapid method of toilet training the institutionalized retarded. *Journal of Applied Behavior Analysis, 4*, 89–99.

Azrin, N. H., Schaeffer, R. M., & Wesolowski, M. D. (1976). A rapid method of teaching profoundly retarded persons to dress by a reinforcement guidance method. *Mental Retardation, 14*, 29–33.

Kimm, C. H., Falvey, M. A., Bishop, K. D., & Rosenberg, R. L. (1995). Motor and personal care skills. In M. A. Falvey (Ed.), *Inclusive and heterogeneous schooling: Assessment, curriculum, and instruction* (pp. 187–227). Baltimore, MD: Paul H. Brookes.

Matson, J. L., DiLorenzo, T. M., & Esveldt-Dawson, K. (1981). Independence training as a method of enhancing self-help skills acquisition of the mentally retarded. *Behavior Research Therapy, 19*, 399–405.

Reid, D. H., Wilson, P. G., & Faw, G. D. (1980). Teaching self-help skills. In J. L. Matson & J. A. Mulick (Eds.), *Handbook of mental retardation* (pp. 429–442). New York, NY: Pergamon Press.

Whitman, T. L., Sciback, J. W., & Reid, D. H. (1983). *Behavior modification with the severely and profoundly retarded: Research and application.* New York, NY: Academic Press.

JOHN O'NEILL
Hunter College,
City University of New York

See also Daily Living Skills; Functional Skills Training; Habilitation of Individuals With Disabilities; Rehabilitation

SELF-INJURIOUS BEHAVIOR

Self-injury is one of the most unusual and probably least understood form of aberrant behavior. It may take a variety of forms, including biting, head banging, face slapping, pinching, or slapping. Such behavior has been reported to affect approximately 4% to 5% of psychiatric populations. Approximately 9%–17% of normal young children (9–36 months of age) also exhibit self-injurious behavior (Carr, 1977).

Carr (1977) has reviewed the hypothetical causes of self-injurious behavior. These include positive reinforcement (seeking of attention), negative reinforcement (attempting to escape), sensory input (gaining stimulation), and psychogenic (psychosis) and organic (genetic and biological) factors. Carr was able to support each of the hypotheses, except for the psychogenic and the organic, by retrospectively applying research to each of the causal explanations. Since then, Evans and Meyer (1985) have proposed one additional hypothesis, an absence of appropriate skills, which research appears to substantiate. Each of these hypotheses warrants examination because of the effect they have on the selection of interventions.

Prior to the mid-1960s, self-injurious behavior was thought to be a product of insane persons with deranged or psychotic minds (Lovaas, 1982). This thinking shaped the model mental health professionals used to intervene with persons who exhibited self-injurious behavior. This dictated the extensive reliance on psychotherapy, drugs, and physical restraint for control.

Through a series of unrelated, yet complementary, studies, researchers were able to demonstrate that self-injurious behavior is regulated by the same laws that affect other human behaviors. The data from these early studies clearly point to the validity of applying the learning theory model to the treatment of self-injurious behavior (Lovaas, 1982).

The etiology of self-injurious behavior has been in debate for some time. There appears to be an organic basis for some self-injurious behavior. There are data to support the contention that self-injurious behaviors are seen in the Lesch-Nyhan and de Langhe syndromes, which are both genetically caused. In Lesch-Nyhan syndrome, a rare form of X-linked cerebral palsy found in only males, there is repetitive biting of the tongue, lips, and fingers. It is thought that this behavior is biochemically related. Considerable research has gone into finding a chemical cure for these characteristics. In de Lange syndrome, which is also genetic in origin, a broad variety of self-injurious behaviors have been reported. A biochemical association has not been presented. Other organic origins of self-injurious behavior have been identified. These include elevated pain thresholds and painful and prolonged infections of the middle ear. The data on organic causes of self-injurious behavior are contradictory, and limited chemical and medical mediations have been found. Although there is limited substantiation of organic causes of self-injurious behavior, awareness that there is a possibility of such causal factors, even in a small percentage of the handicapped population, is important. Those who deal directly with disabled individuals should recognize that medical screening is necessary at the onset of any treatment program, and in some cases medical intervention may be appropriate (Carr, 1977; Evans & Meyer, 1985).

The positive reinforcement hypothesis can be easily explained as the individual seeking attention through the use of self-injurious behavior. The caregivers, in turn, reinforce such behavior and allow it to continue or progress in intensity. Under such conditions, behavioral interventions that remove reinforcement (e.g., extinction or time out) from the individual would possess a high probability of being successful (Carr, 1977).

The negative reinforcement hypothesis is explained by the use of self-injurious behavior to escape demands being placed on the individual. By exhibiting this form of aberrant behavior, the disabled person is often allowed by the caregiver or teacher to refrain from participating in a required activity. Appropriate treatment for self-injurious behavior exhibited under these conditions should include interventions that focus on continued demand. In so doing the individual is not allowed to escape the demand (Carr, 1977).

The sensory input hypothesis is based on finding behaviors that provide the disabled person with input into sensory receptors that under average conditions receive limited amounts of stimulation. An example might be found in a visually impaired student who eye gouges. Self-injurious behavior becomes self-reinforcing and in turn self-maintaining. Interventions for behavior motivated in this manner have taken several different directions, including limiting the input that the self-injurious behavior provides the individual. This is done by modifying the environment (e.g., by using padding or placing adaptive devices on the individual). Another intervention that has been successful is the provision of increased amounts of stimulation from other sources (e.g., a vibrator; Carr, 1977).

The absence of alternative skills hypothesis rests on the concept that the disabled person has extremely limited skills. Self-injurious behavior is part of a behavior system of an individual who lacks appropriate behavior to meet functional needs. This hypothesis is probably a subset of one or more of the preceding explanations of self-injurious behavior; however, it implies a somewhat different treatment. Part of the intervention strategy for self-injurious behavior caused by lack of skills would include teaching appropriate skills to replace the self-injurious ones (Evans & Meyer, 1985; Gerra, Dorfman, Plaue & Schlachman, 1995; LeBlanc, 1993).

Iwata et al. (1982) have provided the practitioner with a method for functionally analyzing self-injurious behavior. Using this method it is possible to identify the specific motivational factors causing self-injury in many persons with disabilities. Employing this approach requires observing the individual in four situations: under negative reinforcement, social attention, play, and alone. Mean levels of self-injurious behavior across each situation are determined. Specific patterns of behavior are manifested in a specific setting that often clearly reflects a specific motivational cause for the behavior.

As previously noted, medical interventions are occasionally appropriate and successful in reducing or eliminating self-injurious behavior. Psychotherapy and other psychological methods have also been used to treat self-injurious behavior. Clearly, the most successful and effective interventions have been behaviorally based. Such interventions should be selected on a least-restrictive model and monitored by systematic data collection procedures. Behaviorally based intervention strategies include the use of punishment. Punishment has been shown to be highly successful, at least on a short-term basis, for the treatment of self-injurious behavior. In cases of chronic self-injurious behavior, where life or irreversible damage is threatened, steps as drastic as electrical shock have been used (Lovaas, 1982). These procedures are generally used to suppress serious self-injurious behavior until other approaches can replace them.

Self-injurious behavior poses many problems to the practitioner in its treatment. Although often misunderstood, recent work has provided both a theoretical explanation and a new direction for finding practical, effective, treatment methods for self-injurious behavior (Symons, 1997).

REFERENCES

Carr, E. (1977). The motivation of self-injurious behavior: A review of some hypothesis. *Psychological Bulletin, 84*, 800–816.

Evans, I. M., & Meyer, L. H. (1985). *An educative approach to behavior problems.* Baltimore, MD: Paul H. Brookes.

Gerra, L. L., Dorfman, S., Plaue, E., & Schlachman, S. (1995). Functional communication as a means of decreasing

self-injurious behavior. *Journal of Visual Impairment & Blindness, 89*(4), 343–348.

Iwata, B. A., Dorsey, M. F., Slifer, K. J., Bauman, K. E., & Richman, G. S. (1982). Toward a functional analysis of self-injury. *Analysis and Intervention in Developmental Disabilities, 2*, 3–20.

LeBlanc, R. (1993). Educational management of self-injurious behavior. *International Journal of Child & Adolescent Psychiatry, 56*(2), 91–98.

Lovaas, O. I. (1982). Comments on self-destructive behaviors. *Analysis and Intervention in Developmental Disabilities, 2*, 115–124.

Symons, F. J. (1997). Self-injurious behavior. *Developmental Disabilities Bulletin, 23*(1), 90–104.

ALAN HILTON
Seattle University

See also Applied Behavior Analysis; Self-Stimulation; Stereotypic Behaviors

SELF-MANAGEMENT

Self-management, also termed *self-control, self-regulation,* and *self-direction,* refers to actions intended to influence one's own behavior. Individuals are taught techniques that can be used in a deliberate manner to change their thoughts, feelings, or actions. Students who engage in self-management may, for example, work longer, complete more problems, make fewer errors, engage in fewer aggressive outbursts, or behave appropriately when an adult is not present.

The traditional approach in education has emphasized external management of programming by the teacher. As noted by Lovitt (1973). "Self-management behaviors are not systematically programmed [in the schools] which appears to be an educational paradox, for one of the expressed objectives of the educational system is to create individuals who are self-reliant and independent" (p. 139). Although frequently effective, use of external management procedures has several potential disadvantages (Kazdin, 1980). Implementation of procedures may be inconsistent as teachers may miss instances of behavior, or there may be problems with communication between change agents in different settings. A teacher may become a cue for particular behaviors, resulting in limited generalization to other situations in which that teacher is not present. Other potential disadvantages of external procedures include limited maintenance of behavior change, excessive time demands placed on educators, and the philosophic concern that the student has minimal involvement in the behavior change process.

Self-management procedures offset the concerns associated with external control and offer the possibility of improved maintenance and generalization of behavior change. The focus of self-management in special education is on teaching students to become effective modifiers of their own behaviors through use of such procedures as self-monitoring, self-evaluation, self-consequation, and self-instruction. Although each of these is discussed separately, in practice they frequently have been combined in self-management packages.

Self-monitoring refers to the observation, discrimination, and recording of one's own behavior. A child in the classroom, for example, may record on an index card each math problem completed. Self-monitoring has been demonstrated to have both assessment and therapeutic use with exceptional students who present a wide range of social and academic behaviors. Common problems associated with using self-monitoring as an assessment procedure include the inaccuracy and reactivity (spontaneous behavior change) of self-monitoring, both of which may result in a distorted picture of the initial levels of behavior. When self-monitoring is used as a treatment strategy, however, reactive effects are desired and inaccuracy may not interfere with obtaining this desired reactivity.

Self-evaluation, or self-assessment, is the comparison of one's own behavior against a preset standard to determine whether performance meets this criterion. Standards may be self-imposed or externally determined. In one study, special education students were asked to rate their behavior as "good," "okay," or "not good" when a timer rang at the end of 10-minute intervals. As is typical, self-evaluation was used as one component of a more comprehensive package; this resulted in reductions in disruptive behavior and increases in academic performance in these students (Robertson, Simon, Pachman, & Drabman, 1979).

Self-consequation refers to the self-delivery of positive consequences (self-reinforcement) or aversive consequences (self-punishment) following behavior. Self-reinforcement is preferred over self-punishment when possible and frequently is used in combination with other procedures. As an example, continued low levels of disruptive behavior or increased on-task behavior have been observed in special education students when self-reinforcement procedures were added to multicomponent programs (Shapiro & Klein, 1980).

Self-instruction is a process of talking to oneself to initiate, direct, or maintain one's own behavior. Children with attention deficit disorder, for example, may be taught specific coping self-statements that compete with such classroom problems as distractibility, overactivity, and off-task behavior. Typical training components include cognitive modeling, overt and covert rehearsal, graded practice on training tasks, and performance feedback (Meichenbaum, 1977).

Self-management training frequently combines these and other procedures in multicomponent self-management packages. In one example, disruptive developmentally disabled individuals were taught skills of self-monitoring, self-evaluation, self-consequation, and self-instruction that successfully reduced their chronic and severe conduct difficulties in a vocational training setting (Cole, Gardner, & Karan, 1985; Cole, Pflugrad, Gardner, & Karan, 1985).

Although total self-management is not possible for many special education students, most can be taught to be more self-reliant. Further, evidence suggests that self-management procedures are at least as effective as similar externally managed procedures in facilitating positive behavior change and in ensuring maintenance of this behavior change. Thus, in addition to its therapeutic effects, self-management offers economic, philosophic, legal, and professional benefits for use in special education.

REFERENCES

Cole, C. L., Gardner, W. I., & Karan, O. C. (1985). Self-management training of mentally retarded adults presenting severe conduct difficulties. *Applied Research in Mental Retardation, 6,* 337–347.

Cole, C. L., Pflugrad, D., Gardner, W. I., & Karan, O. C. (1985). *The self-management training program: Teaching developmentally disabled individuals to manage their disruptive behavior.* Champaign, IL: Research.

Kazdin, A. E. (1980). *Behavior modification in applied settings* (Rev. ed.). Homewood, IL: Dorsey.

Lovitt, T. C. (1973). Self-management projects with children with behavioral disabilities. *Journal of Learning Disabilities, 6,* 15–28.

Meichenbaum, D. (1977). *Cognitive-behavior modification: An integrative approach.* New York, NY: Plenum Press.

Robertson, S. J., Simon, S. J., Pachman, J. S., & Drabman, R. S. (1979). Self-control and generalization procedures in a classroom of disruptive retarded children. *Child Behavior Therapy, 1,* 347–362.

Shapiro, E. S., & Klein, R. D. (1980). Self-management of classroom behavior with retarded/disturbed children. *Behavior Modification, 4,* 83–97.

CHRISTINE L. COLE
University of Wisconsin at Madison

See also **Attention-Deficit/Hyperactivity Disorder; Cognitive Behavior Therapy; Self-Control Curriculum; Self-Monitoring**

SELF-MONITORING

Self-monitoring is one component of a more general process variously known as self-management, self-regulation, or self-control. The process of self-monitoring first involves a person's recognizing that a need exists to regulate his or her behavior. To recognize this need, the person must be observing his or her behavior and comparing it with some preset standard. This self-observation and assessment then combines with recording the behavior to create the self-monitoring component (Shapiro, 1981). Other components in the self-management process can include self-reinforcement, standard setting, self-evaluation, and self-instruction. These components have been used in various combinations with self-monitoring to modify many different types of behaviors (e.g., overeating, temper outbursts, negative statements, attending to task) in the developmentally disabled (Cole, Gardner, & Karan, 1983; Marion, 1994).

It has been shown that many different types of developmentally disabled individuals are capable of self-monitoring a range of behaviors in various settings. However, at least some of these individuals, particularly the mentally retarded, need training to acquire self-monitoring skills (Litrownik, Freitas, & Franzini, 1978; Shapiro McGonigle and Ollendick, 1980).

Self-monitoring among nondevelopmentally disabled people has a reactive or therapeutic effect: Those behaviors being monitored tend to change in a desirable direction (McFall, 1977; Nelson & Hayes, 1981). The studies that have assessed the use of self-monitoring in developmentally disabled populations have also found therapeutic effects. For example, mentally retarded individuals have shown increases in the percent of housekeeping chores completed (Bauman & Iwata, 1977), the frequency of appropriate classroom verbalizations (Nelson, Lipinski, & Boykin, 1978), and the productivity of work (Zohn & Bornstein, 1980). Therapeutic decreases have also occurred in face-picking, head-shaking (Zegiob, Klukas, & Junginger, 1978), and tongue-protrusion behaviors (Rudrud, Ziarnik, & Colman, 1984). However, some studies conducted with the developmentally disabled (Horner & Brigham, 1979; Shapiro & Ackerman, 1983) have found the desirable effects of self-monitoring to be short-term or nonexistent, which is consistent with some research conducted on the nondisabled (Kazdin, 1974).

The variable results obtained with self-monitoring are probably due to several intervening factors that can impact on the reactivity or therapeutic value of self-monitoring (Nelson, 1977). The following comments are only suggestive, because the empirical evidence is limited and most of the supporting research has been done with nondevelopmentally disabled people. First, a behavior's valence or a person's desire to change the behavior can affect reactivity. Positively valenced behaviors tend to increase and negatively valenced behaviors to decrease. Generally, reactivity is enhanced by the frequency of self-monitoring; however, there are situations where the act of monitoring can interfere with reactivity, particularly with positively valenced behaviors. Reactivity also tends to be augmented when the recording device is visible and apparent to the person doing the self-monitoring. In addition, if several behaviors are monitored concurrently, the likelihood of change in any of them is suppressed. Finally, training in self-monitoring seems to enhance reactivity, particularly if the behavior is negatively valenced.

REFERENCES

Bauman, K. E., & Iwata, B. A. (1977). Maintenance of independent housekeeping skills using scheduling plus self-recording procedures. *Behavior Therapy, 8,* 554–560.

Cole, C. L., Gardner, W. I., & Karan, O. C. (1983). *Self-management training of mentally retarded adults with chronic conduct difficulties.* Madison: University of Wisconsin, Rehabilitation Research and Training Center, Waisman Center on Mental Retardation and Human Development.

Horner, R. H., & Brigham, T. A. (1979). The effects of self-management procedures on the study behavior of two retarded children. *Education & Training of the Mentally Retarded, 14,* 18–24.

Kazdin, A. E. (1974). Self-monitoring and behavior change. In M. J. Mahoney & C. E. Thoresen (Eds.), *Self-control: Power to the person.* Monterey, CA: Brooks/Cole.

Litrownik, A. J., Freitas, J. L., & Franzini, L. R. (1978). Self-regulation in mentally retarded children: Assessment and training of self-monitoring skills. *American Journal of Mental Deficiency, 82,* 499–506.

Marion, M. (1994). Encouraging the development of responsible anger management in young children. *Early Child Development & Care, 97,* 155–163.

McFall, R. M. (1977). Parameters of self-monitoring. In R. B. Stuart (Ed.), *Behavioral self-management.* New York, NY: Brunner/Mazel.

Nelson, R. O. (1977). Methodological issues in assessment via self-monitoring. In J. D. Cone & R. P. Hawkins (Eds.), *Behavioral assessment: New directions in clinical psychology.* New York, NY: Brunner/Mazel.

Nelson, R. O., & Hayes, S. C. (1981). Theoretical explanations for reactivity in self-monitoring. *Behavior Modification, 5,* 3–14.

Nelson, R. O., Lipinski, D. P., & Boykin, R. A. (1978). The effects of self-recorders' training and the obtrusiveness of the self-recording device on the accuracy and reactivity of self-monitoring. *Behavior Therapy, 9,* 200–208.

Rudrud, E. H., Ziarnik, J. P., & Colman, G. (1984). Reduction of tongue protrusion of a 24-year-old woman with Down syndrome through self-monitoring. *American Journal of Mental Deficiency, 88,* 647–652.

Shapiro, E. S. (1981). Self-control procedures with the mentally retarded. In M. Hersen, R. M. Eisler, & P. M. Miller (Eds.), *Progress in behavior modification.* New York, NY: Academic Press.

Shapiro, E. S., & Ackerman, A. (1983). Increasing productivity rates in adult mentally retarded clients: The failure of self-monitoring. *Applied Research in Mental Retardation, 4,* 163–181.

Shapiro, E. S., McGonigle, J. J., & Ollendick, T. H. (1980). An analysis of self-assessment and self-reinforcement in a self-managed token economy with mentally retarded children. *Applied Research in Mental Retardation, 1,* 227–240.

Zegiob, L., Klukas, N., & Junginger, J. (1978). Reactivity of self-monitoring procedures with retarded adolescents. *American Journal of Mental Deficiency, 83,* 156–163.

Zohn, C. J., & Bornstein, P. H. (1980). Self-monitoring of work performance with mentally retarded adults: Effects upon work productivity, work quality, and on-task behavior. *Mental Retardation, 18,* 19–25.

JOHN O'NEILL
Hunter College,
City University of New York

See also Impulse Control; Self-Control Curriculum; Self-Help Training; Self-Management

SELF-REINFORCEMENT

Self-reinforcement is a self-management strategy in which the performance of a certain behavior to a predetermined standard receives a self-chosen and self-administered reward (Bandura, 1976; Marston, 1964; Shapiro, 1981; Wehman, 1975). With this strategy, individuals are taught to monitor their behavior and administer a reward to themselves rather than receiving it from their teachers (Kazdin, 1978). True self-reinforcement occurs in the absence of externally controlling influences, such as a teacher deciding the type of reward and when it should be given. In applied practice teachers typically provide a menu of rewards students can choose from and teachers establish the reinforcement schedule. Self-reinforcement is usually used in conjunction with self-monitoring or as an extension of self-evaluation (Browder & Shapiro, 1985; Agran, King-Sears, Wehmeyer, & Copeland, 2003). When individuals recognize that they have met a goal or completed a task, they give themselves a reward. Reliance on an external agent such as the teacher to administer the reward may result in missed reinforcement opportunities. With self-reinforcement, students administer the reward, which decreases the possibility of missing a reinforcement opportunity (Wehmeyer, Agran, & Hughes, 1998).

Self-reinforcement has been used to increase a wide variety of behaviors. Early studies demonstrated effectiveness of the strategy in increasing worker productivity (Helland, Paluck, & Klein, 1976), and social skills in the workplace (Matson & Andrasik, 1982). Self-reinforcement often accompanies a token economy system where tokens are distributed, collected, and redeemed at a predetermined time. For example, Novak and Hammond (1983) used self-reinforcement in a token economy to increase reading problem completion in a classroom setting. A meta-analysis of self-reinforcement research found that self-reinforcement had little to no effect on decreasing inappropriate behavior, had a small to moderate effect on increasing on-task behavior, and had a strong positive effect on academic accuracy and productivity (Reid, Trout, & Schartz, 2005).

REFERENCES

Agran, M., King-Sears, M. E., Wehmeyer, M. L., & Copeland, S. R. (2003). *Student-directed learning.* Baltimore, MD: Paul H. Brookes.

Agran, M., & Martin, J. E. (1987). Applying a technology of self-control in community environments for individuals who are mentally retarded. In M. Hersen, R. M. Eisler, & P. M. Miller (Eds.), *Progress in behavior modification* (Vol. 21). Newbury Park, CA: Sage.

Bandura, A. (1976). *Principles of behavior modification.* New York, NY: Holt.

Browder, D. M., & Shapiro, E. S. (1985). Applications of self-management to individuals with severe handicaps: A review. *Journal of the Association for Persons with Severe Handicaps, 10,* 200–208.

Helland, C. D., Paluck, R. J., & Klein, M. (1976). A comparison of self and external reinforcement with the trainable mentally retarded. *Mental Retardation, 14,* 22–23.

Kazdin, A. E. (1978). *History of behavior modification.* Baltimore, MD: University Park.

Marston, A. R. (1964). Variables affecting incidence of self-reinforcement. *Psychological Reports, 14,* 879–884.

Matson, J. L., & Andrasik, F. (1982). Training leisure-time social-interaction skills to mentally retarded adults. *American Journal of Mental Deficiency, 86,* 533–542.

Novak, G., & Hammond, J. M. (1983). Self-reinforcement and descriptive praise in maintaining token economy reading performance. *Journal of Educational Research, 76,* 186–189.

Reid, R., Trout, A. L., & Schartz, M. (2005). Self-regulation interventions for children with attention deficit/hyperactivity disorder. *Exceptional Children 71,* 361–377.

Shapiro, E. S. (1981). Self-control procedures with the mentally retarded. In M. Hersen, R. M. Eisler, & P. M. Miller (Eds.), *Progress in behavior modification* (Vol. 12). New York, NY: Academic Press.

Wehman, P. (1975). Behavioral self-control with the mentally retarded. *Journal of Applied Rehabilitation Counseling, 6,* 27–34.

Wehmeyer, M. L., Agran, M., & Hughes, C. (1998). *Teaching self-determination to students with disabilities.* Baltimore, MD: Paul H. Brookes.

LEE L. WOODS
University of Oklahoma

See also Behavior Modification; Metacognition

SELF-SELECTION OF REINFORCEMENT

When the student involved in a contingency management program is permitted to choose a reinforcer or determine the cost of a reinforcer relative to a target behavior, the technique of self-selection of reinforcement is being used. It is one of several self-management methods. It may be used in isolation or in combination with self-recording or self-evaluation (Hughes & Ruhl, 1985). However, a recording and evaluation system (controlled by either the teacher or the student) must be in operation prior to implementing self-selection of reinforcement.

As with other self-management techniques, self-selection of reinforcement appears to be more effective with students previously exposed to a systematic, externally controlled reinforcement system. Consequently, it may function as a helpful transition step for students being weaned from externally controlled systems. Studies (Cosden, Gannon, & Haring, 1995; Dickerson & Creedon, 1981; Rosenbaum & Drabman, 1979) have indicated that student-selected reinforcers are more effective than those selected by the teacher. This may be true because students are more capable of identifying what is of value to them and what they are willing to work for.

According to Hughes and Ruhl (1985), the following considerations and steps are helpful when teaching students to use self-selection of reinforcement:

1. Begin with a system of externally controlled contingencies.
2. Verify student understanding of ongoing recording and evaluation procedures and directly reteach if student understanding is in doubt.
3. List available reinforcers and have the student identify one for which he or she is willing to work.
4. Determine stringent performance standards for obtaining reinforcement with the student.
5. Establish a time or signal for administration of the reinforcer.

Stringent performance standards for reinforcement (i.e., those requiring a high rating or frequency for all, or almost all, evaluation periods) are important because they result in significantly better performance results than do lax standards (Alberto & Troutman, 1982). Because students tend to set performance standards that are more lenient than those established by teachers (Flexibrod & O'Leary, 1973, 1974; Frederiksen & Frederiksen, 1975), students should be prompted to set vigorous criteria. Verbal prompts, providing examples and rationales and praising acceptable performance standards, will assist the student in determining appropriate criteria. Examples of criteria for reinforcement include obtaining a specified number of tokens or time intervals with low rates of occurrence of an inappropriate behavior.

Regardless of who is recording or evaluating the behavior, a method for communicating the time for reinforcement should be established. For example, the self-selected reinforcement might come at the end of an academic period, after reading five pages of a text, or at the end of the school day when the school bell rings.

REFERENCES

Alberto, P. A., & Troutman, A. C. (1982). *Applied behavior analysis for teachers: Influencing student performance.* Columbus, OH: Merrill.

Cosden, M., Gannon, G., & Haring, T. G. (1995). Teacher-control versus student-control over chance of task and reinforcement for students with severe behavior problems. *Journal of Behavioral Education, 5*(1), 11–27.

Dickerson, A. E., & Creedon, C. F. (1981). Self-selection of standards by children: The relative effectiveness of pupil-selected and teacher-selected standards of performance. *Journal of Applied Behavior Analysis, 141,* 425–433.

Flexibrod, J. J., & O'Leary, K. D. (1973). Effects of reinforcement on children's academic behavior as a function of self-determined and externally imposed contingencies. *Journal of Applied Behavior Analysis, 6,* 241–250.

Flexibrod, J. J., & O'Leary, K. D. (1974). Self-determination of academic standards by children: Toward freedom from external control. *Journal of Educational Psychology, 66,* 845–850.

Frederiksen, L. W., & Frederiksen, C. B. (1975). Teacher-determined and self-determined token reinforcement in a special education classroom. *Behavior Therapy, 6,* 310–314.

Hughes, C. A., & Ruhl, K. L. (1985). Learning activities for improving self-management skills. In B. Algozzine (Ed.), *Educators' resource manual for management of problem behaviors in students.* Rockville, MD: Aspen.

Rosenbaum, M. S., & Drabman, R. S. (1979). Self-control training in the classroom. *Journal of Behavior Analysis, 12,* 467–485.

KATHY L. RUHL
Pennsylvania State University

See also **Applied Behavior Analysis; Behavior Modification; Contingency Contracting; Positive Reinforcement**

SELF-STIMULATION

Self-stimulatory behaviors refer to idiosyncratic behaviors that are repetitive, restrictive, and stereotyped (Koegel, Firestone, Kramme, & Dunlap, 1974). Examples include spinning objects, rhythmic whole-body-rocking, hand flapping, and extended staring (Koegel & Covert, 1972). The behavioral function (i.e., purpose of the behavior or reinforcing its consequence) is thought to serve to obtain automatic reinforcement in the form of a pleasant internal consequence or sensory feedback (Rapp and Vollmer, 2005). However, the term self-stimulation is often applied to behaviors without determining the behavioral function and, it is not uncommon for a behavior that appears to be self-stimulatory to actually serve a social function (e.g., to obtain attention or escape from demands; Cunningham, & Schreibman, 2008). This can be problematic because treatment for self-stimulatory behavior differs from treatment for behaviors that are reinforced by other people (e.g., attention seeking behavior; Rapp & Vollmer, 2005).

The term self-stimulation is occasionally used interchangeably with the term stereotypic behaviors (Cunningham, & Schreibman, 2008). Although self-stimulatory behavior occurs in individuals of all ages and abilities, it appears to occur more often and more intensely in individuals with intellectual and developmental disabilities (Rapp & Vollmer, 2005). Self-stimulatory behaviors are often repetitive motor behaviors (e.g., body rocking, hand flapping, and spinning in circles) and are part of the diagnostic criteria for autistic disorder (American Psychiatric Association, 2000). When a child with an intellectual or developmental disability is engaging in these behaviors, it might be said that the child is "stimming" (i.e., selfstimming). However, the term "stimming" may have a somewhat negative or degrading meaning and is avoided in most professional writing and dialog.

Unfortunately, self-stimulatory behaviors may not always be benign. Some individuals engage in selfstimulatory behaviors that cause injury to themselves. Common self-injurious behaviors (SIB) include head banging, skin picking, and bruxism (i.e., teeth grinding; Lang et al., 2009; Lang, Didden, et al., 2010; Oliver, Murphy, & Corbett, 1987). Treatment for self-stimulatory behavior includes physical exercise (Lang, Koegel, et al., 2010), teaching novel functional play behaviors (Lang, O'Reilly, et al., 2010), environmental enrichment (Rapp & Vollmer, 2005), and matched stimulation procedures in which alternative means of obtaining sensory input or additional forms of reinforcement are provided (Rapp, 2006; 2007).

REFERENCES

American Psychiatric Association (2000). *Diagnostic and statistical manual of mental disorders* (4th ed., text rev.). Washington, DC: Author.

Cunningham, A. B., & Schreibman, L. (2008). Stereotypy in autism: The importance of function. *Research in Autism Spectrum Disorders, 2,* 469–479.

Koegel, R., & Covert, A. (1972). The relationship of selfstimulation to learning in autistic children. *Journal of Applied Behavior Analysis, 5,* 381–387.

Koegel, R., Firestone, P., Kramme, K., & Dunlap, G. (1974). Increasing spontaneous play by suppressing self-stimulation in autistic children. *Journal of Applied Behavior Analysis, 7,* 521–528.

Lang, R., White, P. J., Machalicek, W., Rispoli, M., Kang, S., Aguilar, J., . . . Didden, R. (2009). Treatment of bruxism in individuals with developmental disabilities: A systematic review. *Research in Developmental Disabilities, 30,* 809–818.

Lang, R., Didden, R., Machalicek, W., Rispoli, M., Sigafoos, J., Lancioni, . . . Kang, S. (2010). Behavioral treatment of chronic skin-picking in individuals with developmental disabilities: A systematic review. *Research in Developmental Disabilities, 31,* 304–315.

Lang, R., Koegel, L., Ashbaugh, K., Regester, A., Ence, W., & Smith, W. (2010). Physical exercise and individuals with autism spectrum disorders: A systematic review. *Research in Autism Spectrum Disorders, 4,* 565–576.

Lang, R., O'Reilly, M. Sigafoos, J., Machalicek, W., Rispoli, M., Lancioni, G., . . . Fragale, C. (2010). The effects of an abolishing operation intervention component on play skills, challenging behavior, and stereotypy. *Behavior Modification, 34,* 267–289.

Oliver, C., Murphy, G. H., & Corbett, J. A. (1987). Self-injurious behaviour in people with mental handicap: A total population study. *Journal of Mental Deficiency Research, 31,* 147–162.

Rapp, J. T. (2006). Toward an empirical method for identifying matched stimulation for automatically reinforced behavior: A preliminary investigation. *Journal of Applied Behavior Analysis, 39,* 137–140.

Rapp, J. T. (2007). Further evaluation of methods to identify matched stimulation. *Journal of Applied Behavior Analysis, 40,* 73–88.

Rapp, J. T., & Vollmer, T. R. (2005). Stereotypy I: A review of behavioral assessment and treatment. *Research in Developmental Disabilities, 26,* 527–547.

Courtney Britt
Brooke Pfeiffer
Russell Lang
Stephanie Caruthers
Texas State University-San Marcos
Fourth Edition

See also Autism; Self-Injurious Behavior Stereotypism

SEMMEL, MELVYN I. (1931–　)

Melvyn I. Semmel was born and educated in New York City, receiving his BS (1955) and MS (1957) in special education from City College, City University of New York. He later earned his EdD (1963) in special education with a minor in psychology from George Peabody College. He is currently a professor of special education and director of the Special Education Research Laboratory in the Graduate School of Education, University of California, Santa Barbara.

Semmel's early teacher training led to his involvement with teacher preparation and research on special education methods. In 1968, he pioneered the development of the Computer-Assisted Teacher Training System (CATTS), and later directed the Center for Innovation in Teaching the Handicapped (CITH), a research and development center for alternative teacher training methods and instructional materials. During his tenure at CITH, the center was recognized as the outstanding organization of the year by the National Society for Performance and Instruction. Semmel's research work at the University of California has focused on issues such as use of computers for learners with disabilities, development of new models for research teaching, and devising cognitively oriented interventions for individuals with severe emotional disturbance. He and his colleagues have examined the effectiveness of special education for students with mild disabilities, finding that, based on student performance, no single factor (e.g., structure or organization of school environment) consistently indicated its relative effectiveness (Larrivee, Semmel, & Gerber, 1997).

Semmel has written over 100 books, research papers, articles, and chapters related to special education and educational psychology. He has been recognized in *Who's Who in American Education* and has been elected a life member and fellow of the American Association on Mental Retardation for 30 years of continuous service to the field.

REFERENCE

Larivee, B., Semmel, M. I., & Gerber, M. M. (1997). Case studies of six schools varying in effectiveness for students with learning disabilities. *Elementary School Journal, 98*(1), 27–50.

E. Valerie Hewitt
Texas A&M University
First edition

Tamara J. Martin
The University of Texas of the Permian Basin
Second edition

SENF, GERALD (1942–   )

Gerald M. Senf graduated with honors from Yale University with a BA (1964) in psychology. He went on to earn his MA (1966) in experimental psychology and his doctorate in 1968 in experimental and clinical psychology from the University of California, Los Angeles. During his career, Senf has held the positions of professor of psychology at University of Iowa, associate professor of psychology at University of Illinois, evaluation research director of the Leadership Training Institute in Learning Disabilities, and associate professor of special education at the University of Arizona.

Senf has written extensively on the topics of cognitive functioning and research methodology associated with the study of learning disabilities, with his principal focus on information-processing skills and memory of those with learning disabilities (Senf, 1969, 1972, 1976, 1981, 1986). He has continued to study in the area of cognitive functioning, investigating the comparison of electrical brain activity in normal individuals to individuals with various cognitive impairments to assist the clinician in diagnosing and treating the patient (Senf, 1988).

Senf is coauthor of a screening test, has coedited several books, and has devised computer programs to assist the learning disabled.

REFERENCES

Senf, G. M. (1969). Development of immediate memory for bisensory stimuli in normal children and children with learning disorders. *Developmental Psychology Monograph, 1* (Pt. 2).

Senf, G. M. (1972). An information integration theory and its application to normal reading acquisition and reading disability. In N. D. Bryant & C. E. Kass (Eds.), *Leadership Training Institute on Learning Disabilities* (Vol. 2). Tucson: University of Arizona Press.

Senf, G. M. (1976). Some methodological considerations in the study of abnormal conditions. In R. Walsh & W. T. Greenough (Eds.), *Environment as therapy for brain dysfunction*. New York, NY: Plenum Press.

Senf, G. M. (1981). Issues surrounding the diagnosis of learning disabilities: Child handicap versus failure of the child-school interaction. In T. R. Kratochwill (Ed.), *Advances in school psychology* (Vol. 1, pp. 83–131). Hillsdale, NJ: Erlbaum.

Senf, G. M. (1986). LD research in sociological and scientific perspective. In J. K. Torgesen & B. Wong (Eds.), *Psychological and educational perspectives on learning disabilities*. San Diego, CA: Academic Press.

Senf, G. M. (1988). Neurometric brainmapping in the diagnosis and rehabilitation of cognitive dysfunction. *Cognitive Rehabilitation, 6*(6), 20–37.

Roberta C. Stokes
Texas A&M University
First edition

Tamara J. Martin
The University of Texas of the Permian Basin
Second edition

See also Journal of Learning Disabilities

SENSORINEURAL HEARING LOSS

A sensorineural hearing loss is a hearing impairment resulting from a pathological condition in the inner ear or along the auditory nerve (VIII cranial nerve) pathway from the inner ear to the brain stem. If the pathological condition or site of lesion is confined to the inner ear or cochlea, it is known as an inner ear or cochlea hearing loss. If the site of lesion is along the auditory nerve (as is the case with an acoustic nerve tumor), it is known as a retrocochlear hearing loss. Several audiological, medical, and radiological special tests have been developed to assist in the diagnosis of whether a sensorineural hearing loss is due to a cochlear or retrocochlear site of lesion.

An individual with a sensorineural hearing loss has reduced hearing sensitivity and lacks the ability to discriminate speech sounds, especially when listening in a noisy environment. Tinnitus is a common symptom of a sensorineural hearing loss. Tinnitus is any sensation of sound in the head heard in one or both ears. It may be described as a hissing, whistling, buzzing, roaring, or a high-pitched tone or noise. Dizziness is also a symptom of sensorineural hearing loss; it can range from lightheadedness to a severe whirling sensation, known as vertigo, that leads to nausea.

A sensorineural hearing loss can occur in varying degrees ranging from mild-moderate to severe-profound. The degree of sensorineural hearing loss is determined by averaging the decibel amount of hearing loss across the frequencies needed to hear and understand speech or the speech frequencies (500, 1000, and 2000 Hz). Individuals with a mild to severe hearing loss are usually classified as being hard of hearing, while individuals with a profound hearing impairment are classified as deaf. A sensorineural hearing loss can occur in just one ear (unilateral) or in each ear (bilateral). If the hearing loss occurs in each ear, one ear may be more affected than the other.

A sensorineural hearing loss can be caused by many factors, including genetic diseases (dominant, recessive, or sex-linked), diseases acquired during pre-, peri-, and postnatal periods, and childhood diseases. Adults can obtain sensorineural hearing loss from noise exposure, diseases, medication, and the aging process. Many sensorineural hearing losses are due to unknown etiology. A sensorineural hearing loss also may be part of a syndrome that affects the individual in other ways. A congenital sensorineural hearing loss is one that has existed or has an etiology from birth; an adventitious hearing loss is one that occurred after birth and in most cases is due to injury or disease. If the sensorineural hearing loss occurred prior to the development of speech and language skills, it is known as prelingual; if it occurred after the development of speech and language skills, it is known as postlingual. Standardized batteries of cognitive abilities and memory are being used to assess concurrent learning disabilities and skill strengths and weaknesses (Plapinger & Sikora, 1995; Sikora & Plapinger, 1994).

In children having sensorineural hearing losses, about half the cases are due to genetic causes and half to acquired causes. Meningitis and prematurity are the leading acquired causes of sensorineural hearing loss in children. For adults, the leading cause of sensorineural hearing loss is the aging process, known as presbyacusis, and excessive exposure to noise. Typically, the sensorineural hearing loss from presbyacusis or noise exposure is a progressive reduction of high frequency (1,000 to 8,000 Hz) hearing sensitivity that causes problems in understanding speech.

It is important that individuals with a sensorineural hearing loss have audiological and otological diagnosis and management. In almost all cases, there is no medical treatment for sensorineural hearing loss from a cochlear site of lesion. However, a retrocochlear lesion from a tumor, or some other growth along the auditory nerve may benefit from an operation. Cochlear implants are now available, but their use is controversial (Carver, 1997).

Children and adults with cochlear sensorineural hearing loss can benefit through the use of hearing aids. Most children are fitted with a hearing aid for each ear (binaural amplification) and require auditory and speech reading training, speech and language therapy, and academic tutoring. Adults are usually fitted with either a hearing aid on one ear (monaural) or with binaural amplification. Generally, adults do not need specialized training; however, many adults benefit from speech-reading therapy.

This entry has been informed by the sources listed below.

REFERENCES

Carver, R. (1997). *Questions parents should ask about cochlear implants*. British Columbia, Canada: DCSD.

Gerber, S. E., & Mencher, G. T. (1980). *Auditory dysfunction*. San Diego, CA: College-Hill.

Jerger, J. (1984). *Hearing disorders in adults*. San Diego, CA: College-Hill.

Plapinger, D. S., & Sikora, D. M. (1995). The use of standardized test batteries in assessing skill development of children with mild to moderate sensorineural hearing loss. *Language, Speech & Hearing in Schools*, 26(1), 39–44.

Schubert, E. D. (1980). *Hearing: Its function and dysfunction*. New York, NY: Springer-Verlag.

Schuknecht, H. F. (1974). *Pathology of the ear*. Cambridge, MA: Harvard University Press.

Sikora, D. M., & Plapinger, D. S. (1994). Using standardized psychometric tests to identify learning disabilities in students with learning disabilities. *Journal of Learning Disabilities*, 27(6), 352–359.

Wolstenholmer, G. E. W., & Knight, J. (1970). *Sensorineural hearing loss*. London, England: J. & A. Churchill.

Thomas A. Frank
Pennsylvania State University

See also **Deaf; Deaf Education**

SENSORY EXTINCTION

Sensory extinction is a procedure developed by Rincover (1978) for reducing various pathological behaviors in children with developmental disabilities. It has been used to suppress self-stimulation (Maag, Wolchik, Rutherford, & Parks, 1986; Rincover, 1978), compulsive behaviors (Rincover, Newsom, & Carr, 1979), and self-injury (Rincover & Devaney, 1981). In a sensory extinction paradigm, stereotypy is considered operant behavior maintained by its sensory consequences. For example, repetitive finger flapping might be conceptualized as being maintained by the specific proprioceptive feedback it produces, while persistent delayed echolalia may be maintained by auditory feedback.

Sensory extinction involves masking, changing, or removing certain sensory consequences of behavior. If the sensory reinforcement received is removed, the behavior will be extinguished. For example, if a child continuously spins a plate on a table, a piece of carpet could be placed on the table to remove the auditory feedback resulting from this behavior. Similarly, the stereotypic behavior of a child who ritualistically switches a light on and off could be extinguished by either removing the visual feedback (if seeing the light were reinforcing) or removing the auditory feedback (if hearing the light switch click were reinforcing).

When sensory extinction is used to suppress stereotypy, the preferred sensory consequences of the behavior can be used to teach appropriate behaviors. For example, the child who spins plates could be taught to spin a top instead, since this would provide the same sensory consequences as the maladaptive behavior. Rincover, Cook, Peoples, and Packard (1979) found that children preferred to play with toys that provided sensory reinforcement similar to the sensory reinforcement previously found in the stereotypy.

While sensory extinction is a procedure in which multiple components are altered at the same time (Maag et al., 1986), it remains unclear as to the extent to which stimulus modality is an important factor (Murphy, 1982). Maag et al. found that isolating the sensory consequences for some forms of behavior can be impractical and/or time-consuming. In addition, Maag et al. point out that a cumbersome apparatus is sometimes necessary to mask some types of sensory feedback. This apparatus may restrict the child's ability to participate in activities and also be socially stigmatizing. Therefore, although sensory extinction may represent a viable set of procedures for reducing stereotypy, it should be assessed thoroughly to determine the appropriateness of this intervention for particular children.

REFERENCES

Maag, J. W., Wolchik, S. A., Rutherford, R. B., & Parks, B. T. (1986). Response covariation of self-stimulatory behaviors during sensory extinction procedures. *Journal of Autism & Developmental Disorders, 16,* 119–132.

Murphy, G. (1982). Sensory reinforcement in the mentally handicapped and autistic child: A review. *Journal of Autism & Developmental Disorders, 12,* 265–278.

Rincover, A. (1978). Sensory extinction: A procedure for eliminating self-stimulatory behavior in developmentally disabled children. *Journal of Abnormal Child Psychology, 6,* 299–310.

Rincover, A., Cook, R., Peoples, A., & Packard, D. (1979). Sensory extinction and sensory reinforcement principles for programming multiple adaptive behavior change. *Journal of Applied Behavior Analysis, 12,* 221–233.

Rincover, A., & Devaney, J. (1981). The application of sensory extinction principles to self-injury in developmentally disabled children. *Analysis & Intervention in Developmental Disabilities, 4,* 67–69.

Rincover, A., Newsom, C. D., & Carr, E. G. (1979). Using sensory extinction procedures in the treatment of compulsive-like behavior of developmentally disabled children. *Journal of Consulting and Clinical Psychology, 47,* 695–701.

ROBERT B. RUTHERFORD JR.
Arizona State University

See also Behavior Modification; Self-Stimulation

SENSORY INTEGRATION INVENTORY–REVISED

The Sensory Integration Inventory–Revised for Individuals with Developmental Disabilities (SII-R), developed in 1992 (Reisman & Hanschu), is a screening instrument primarily utilized by occupational therapists (OT) as an initial evaluation to rule in the presence of sensory integration difficulties (Green et al., 2003; Reisman & Hanschu, 1992) in individuals with developmental disabilities. Additionally, the inventory facilitates decision making regarding the appropriateness of treatment utilizing sensory integration techniques for occupational therapists (Smith, Press, Koenig, & Kinnealey, 2005). The profile is appropriate for all ages and can be completed in approximately 30 minutes (Myles et al., 2001).

The questionnaire contains over one hundred behavior-related items which are categorized by four sensory areas including tactile, vestibular, proprioception, and general reactions (Smith et al., 2005). The responses, provided by a respondent familiar with the client, yield a profile comprised of the client's sensory assets and deficits as well as any challenging sensory-related behaviors (Smith et al., 2005). The tool is a checklist, in which the respondent chooses either *typical, not typical,* or *don't know* for each item (Myles, Cook, Miller, Rinner, & Robbins, 2001). The results merely indicate the presence or absence of the behaviors and not the rate or magnitude (Green et al., 2003). Utilization of the SII-R as a formal interview is an additional option for this tool, allowing the practitioner to further query responses, particularly in regards to the pervasiveness of the behavior in question (Myles et al., 2001). The inventory does not yield standard scores; thus, the OT assimilates the responses to ascertain the behaviors and sensory issues or concerns and guide treatment decisions (Myles et al., 2001).

Although the inventory offers a means for determining the presence or absence of the included behaviors, the inventory fails to specify when the behaviors in question began occurring, where they occur, or rate of occurrence (Green et al., 2003), substantially limiting progress monitoring and evaluation of treatment efficacy. Additionally, reliability and validity data for the SII-R is not available, further limiting the confidence one can place in the results (Verdi, 2001).

REFERENCES

Green, D., Beaton, L., Moore, D., Warren, L., Wick, V., Sanford, J. E., & Santosh, P. (2003). Clinical incidence of sensory integration difficulties in adults with learning disabilities and illustration of management. *The British Journal of Occupational Therapy, 66*, 454–463.

Myles, B., Cook, K., Miller, N., Rinner, L., & Robbins, L. (2001). *Asperger syndrome and sensory issues: Practical solutions for making sense of the world.* Shawnee Mission, KS: Autism Asperger.

Reisman, J., & Hanschu, B. (1992). *Sensory Integration Inventory–Revised for Individuals With Developmental Disabilities.* Hugo, MN: PDP Press.

Smith, S., Press, B., Koenig, K., & Kinnealey, M. (2005). Effects of sensory integration intervention on self-stimulating and self-injurious behaviors. *The American Journal of Occupational Therapy, 59*, 418–425.

Verdi, W. (2001). Review of the Sensory Integration Inventory–Revised for Individuals With Developmental Disabilities. In Plake, B and Impara, J. (Eds.), *The Fourteenth Mental Measurement Yearbook* (p. 346). Lincoln, NE: PDP Press.

Rose Mason
Texas A&M University
Fourth edition

SENSORY INTEGRATIVE THERAPY

Sensory integrative therapy is a technique for the remediation of sensory integrative dysfunction developed by A. Jean Ayres (Ayres, 1972). Sensory integrative dysfunction is believed by Ayres and others (Quiros, 1976; Silberzahn, 1982) to be at the root of many learning disorders. Ayres uses the term sensory integrative dysfunction to describe children whose learning problems are due to the failure of the lower levels of the brain (particularly the midbrain, brain stem, and vestibular system) to use and organize information effectively. The principal objective of sensory integrative therapy is to promote the development and the organization of subcortical brain mechanisms as a foundation for perception and learning. Treatment procedures consist of the use of gross motor activities and physical exercise to achieve this goal. Sensory integrative therapy has gained its greatest popularity among occupational therapists.

The five key features of sensory integrative dysfunction follow (Silberzahn, 1982):

1. *Developmental Apraxia.* This is a problem in motor planning and is part of a complex that includes deficits in tactile functions. According to Ayres (1972), the fundamental problem lies in the difficulty in recognizing the time and space aspects of sensation and the relationships among body parts that are necessary for cortical planning of events.

2. *Tactile Defensiveness.* This represents a defensive or hostile reaction to tactile stimuli and is part of a complex believed, in sensory integrative therapy, to include hyperactivity, distractibility, and discrimination problems in most major sensory modalities.

3. *Deficits in Interhemispheric Integration.* These deficits are manifest in problems integrating the two sides of the body. Ayres (1972) believes these deficits are common in children with reading problems and that they can be shown clinically as the child tends to use each side of the body independently and avoids crossing the midline.

4. *Visual and Space Perception Deficits.* These problems are typically associated with a more extensive problem that involves inadequate integration of vestibular, proprioceptive, tactile, and visual stimuli at the level of the brain stem. Developmental apraxia may also result.

5. *Auditory-Language Deficits.* These deficits are a result of problems in areas 3 and 4 and disrupt written and spoken language.

Sensory integrative therapy attempts to remediate these problems through the development of perception and learning via the enhancement of organizations and sensations at the brain stem level. Motor activities are the principal therapeutic media and center around activities that require the child to adapt and organize a variety of sensory motor experiences while taking an active role in each process. Coordinated use of the two sides of the body is promoted.

Carefully controlled studies of the outcome of sensory integrative therapy are lacking, particularly in regard to improvements in academic skills. The therapy is a deficit-centered approach to remediation, though not strictly a process approach. However, it seems unlikely that learning disabilities can be corrected through the use of gross motor activities and physical exercise.

REFERENCES

Ayres, A. J. (1972). *Sensory integration and learning disorders.* Los Angeles, CA: Western Psychological Services.

Quiros, J. B. de. (1976). Diagnosis of vestibular disorders in the learning disabled. *Journal of Learning Disabilities, 9,* 39–47.

Silberzahn, M. (1982). Sensory integrative therapy. In C. R. Reynolds & T. B. Gutkin (Eds.), *The handbook of school psychology.* New York, NY: Wiley.

CECIL R. REYNOLDS
Texas A&M University

See also Ayres, A. Jean; Remediation, Deficit-Centered Models of

SEPARATION ANXIETY DISORDER

Separation anxiety disorder refers to excessive anxiety and fear in response to separation from the home or those with whom a child is attached. The anxiety is displayed before age 18, lasts for at least 4 weeks, and is greater than that normally displayed by others of the same age. Separation anxiety disorder results in significant distress or impairment in social, academic, or other important areas of functioning (American Psychiatric Association [APA], 2000).

Separation anxiety is common in infants and young children. Its symptomology includes an acute and early onset and may occur following a major stressful event in a child's life (e.g., start of school, illness, or death of a parent, a move to a new home or city; APA, 2000). Children with separation anxiety disorder may display persistent and excessive worry about loss or danger occurring to a loved one, reluctance to go to school, impaired functioning in some areas (e.g., reluctant to engage in sports, clubs, or other social events), fear of being alone, reluctance to sleep alone, reoccurring nightmares, and somatic complaints (APA, 2000).

Children who display anxious-resistant attachment, lack of social support, or diminished coping and problem-solving skills are at risk for this disorder. Risk factors for separation anxiety disorder also include parent behaviors (e.g., depression, inhibition, anxiety, obsessive-compulsive, overprotective, or abnormal attachment to the child; Donavan & Spence, 2000; Kearney, Sims, Pursell, & Tillotson, 2003; Manicavasagar, Silove, Wagner, & Hadzi-Pavlovic, 1999). A genetic basis for separation anxiety has been identified (Donovan & Spence, 2000; Feigon, Waldman, Levy, & Hay, 2001). Intervention methods to help overcome separation anxiety disorder may focus on the child, the family, or both. Child-focused interventions have found cognitive behavioral therapy generally provides the most effective treatment method (Barrett, Dadds, & Rapee, 1996). This treatment includes identifying anxious thoughts and replacing them with more adaptive coping self-statements, using small rewards, and promoting parental involvement (Kendall, 1994). Other treatment options include behavioral therapy that focuses strictly on the child's overt behavior, interventions designed to promote social and coping skills, and pharmacological treatments for anxiety (e.g., Fluoxetine and Fluvoxamine; Birmaher et al., 2003; Elliot, 1999; Pine, 2001; Shortt, Barrett, & Fox, 2001).

Family-focused interventions may include helping a parent replace excessive attachment with more healthy forms of attachment, promoting child-parent communication styles, assisting parents in providing social support, and promoting the child's independence (Donavan & Spence, 2000).

Many children display signs of separation anxiety without meeting the criteria for a separation anxiety disorder. For example, separation anxiety is somewhat common during early childhood at the start of school or if a parent must leave the home for a few days or weeks to attend to personal or business responsibilities. Under these conditions, the anxiety associated with separation is normal, often dissipates within a few days or weeks, and does not result in significant distress or impairment in life activities (Bernstein & Borchardt, 1991).

Separation anxiety disorder impacts many areas of a child's life, not only one (e.g., schooling). A diagnosis of school phobia, not separation anxiety disorder, is suitable when the behaviors are limited to school resistance. Additionally, one needs to distinguish separation anxiety from other anxiety disorders, including panic disorder, agoraphobia generalized anxiety disorder, social phobia, specific phobia, obsessive-compulsive disorder, posttraumatic stress disorder, and acute stress disorder. Anxiety is common in them and expressed through cognitive, physiological, and behavioral manifestations (Mash & Barkley, 2003).

Some cultures value childhood independence while others highly value interdependence. Young children in families that value and promote interdependence may be more inclined to display separation anxiety, given their fear to leave their loved ones. Thus, cultural influences should be considered when evaluating the causes of separation anxiety, forming a diagnosis, and planning treatment methods (APA, 2000).

REFERENCES

American Psychiatric Association. (2000). *Diagnostic and statistical manual of mental disorders* (4th ed., text rev.). Washington, DC: Author.

Barrett, P. M., Dadds, M. R., & Rapee, R. M. (1996). Family treatment of childhood anxiety: A controlled trial. *Journal of Consulting and Clinical Psychology, 64*(2), 333–342.

Bernstein, G. A., & Borchardt, C. M. (1991). Anxiety disorders of childhood and adolescence: A critical review. *Journal of the American Academy of Child and Adolescent Psychiatry, 30*, 519–532.

Birmaher, B., Axelson, D. A., Monk, K., Kalas, C., Clark, D. B., Ehmann, M., . . . Brent, D. A. (2003). Fluoxetine for the treatment of childhood anxiety disorders. *Journal of the American Academy of Child and Adolescent Psychiatry, 42*(4), 415–423.

Donavon, C. L., & Spence, S. H. (2000). Prevention of childhood anxiety disorders. *Clinical Psychology Review, 20*(4) 509–531.

Elliott, J. G. (1999). Practitioner review: School refusal: Issues of conceptualization, assessment, and treatment. *Journal of Child Psychology and Psychiatry, 40*(7), 1001–1012.

Feigon, S. A., Waldman, I. D., Levy, F., & Hay, D. A. (2001). Genetic and environmental influences on separation anxiety disorder symptoms and their moderation by age and sex. *Behavior Genetics, 31*(5), 403–411.

Kearney, C. A., Sims, K. E., Pursell, C. R., & Tillotson, C. A. (2003). Separation anxiety disorder in young children: A longitudinal and family analysis. *Journal of Clinical Child and Adolescent Psychology, 32*(4), 593–598.

Kendall, P. C. (1994). Treating anxiety disorders in children: Results of a randomized clinical trial. *Journal of Consulting and Clinical Psychology, 62*(1), 100–110.

Manicavasagar, V., Silove, D., Wagner, R., & Hadzi-Pavlovic, D. (1999). Parental representations associated with adult separation anxiety and panic disorder-agoraphobia. *Australian and New Zealand Journal of Psychiatry, 33*, 422–428.

Mash, E. J., & Barkley, R. A. (2003). *Child psychopathology* (2nd ed.). New York, NY: Guilford Press.

Pine, D. S. (2001). Fluvoxamine for the treatment of anxiety disorders in children and adolescents. *New England Journal of Medicine, 344*(17), 1279–1285.

Shortt, A. L., Barrett, P. M., & Fox, T. L. (2001). Evaluating the FRIENDS program: A cognitive-behavioral group treatment for anxious children and their parents. *Journal of Clinical Child Psychology, 30*(4), 525–535.

JULIE BELL
KELLY WINKELS
University of Florida

SEPTO-OPTIC DYSPLASIA

Septo-optic dysplasia, also known as De Morsier syndrome, is a rare disorder characterized by visual impairments and pituitary deficiencies. The etiology of Septo-optic dysplasia is not known; however, this birth defect is found in a higher percentage of infants who are the first-born children of young mothers. Both genders are affected equally by this rare disorder.

Visual impairments include dimness in sight, especially in one eye (often referred to as lazy eye), and dizziness. These symptoms result from small, not-fully-developed optic disks associated with the visual system. In this disorder, the pupil (the opening in the eyeball through which light enters) does not respond appropriately. Instead of a consistent response, the pupil's response to light of the same intensity varies from one occasion to another. Occasional field dependence has also been noted. Besides visual impairments, an underactive pituitary gland is present either at birth or later in development. If left untreated, a child's growth is stunted. Jaundice may also be present at birth.

Standard treatment for Septo-optic dysplasia is symptomatic and supportive. Hormone replacement therapy is used to treat the pituitary hormone deficiencies. Children with Septo-optic dysplasia are usually of normal intelligence; however, mental retardation or learning disabilities may occur (Thoene, 1992). Occasional sexual precocity has been reported (Jones, 1988).

If a child experiences learning problems or developmental delays, a comprehensive neuropsychological evaluation is recommended to determine cognitive strengths and weaknesses. Based on those results, recommendations can be made, and an individualized educational plan can be developed and implemented in the schools.

REFERENCES

Jones, K. L. (Ed.). (1988). *Smith's recognizable patterns of human malformation* (4th ed.). Philadelphia, PA: Saunders.

Thoene, J. G. (Ed.). (1992). *Physician's guide to rare diseases.* Montvale, NJ: Dowden.

JOAN W. MAYFIELD
Baylor Pediatric Specialty Service

PATRICIA A. LOWE
University of Kansas

SEQUENCED INVENTORY OF COMMUNICATION DEVELOPMENT, REVISED

The Sequenced Inventory of Communication Development, Revised Edition (SICD-R; Hendrick, Prather, & Tobin, 1984) is a diagnostic assessment tool to evaluate the communication abilities of typically developing children and children with intellectual disabilities, ages 4 months to 4 years. The SICD-R utilizes both parental report and observation of communication behaviors. The inventory includes 100 items which are broken into Receptive and Expressive Scales. Responses may also be recorded on the Behavioral Profile that examines awareness, discrimination, understanding, imitation, initiation, response, motor, vocal, and verbal areas. There is also a Process Profile that examines semantics, syntax, pragmatics, perceptual, and phonological areas.

The normative data are from a sample of 252 children, all Caucasian from monolingual homes, who were believed to have normal hearing, language, physical, and mental development. Additional data from a field study in Detroit are also reported; however, Pearson (1989) notes that these additional data do not provide answers to questions about reliability or validity of the SICD-R. Only 10 subjects are reported as a sample providing test-retest data and the reliability value reported was .93. Interrater reliability (based on 21 children) was reported to be 96% agreement between two raters. The reliability data must be viewed with caution because of the small number of subjects in the reliability studies (Mardell-Czudnowski, 1989; Pearson, 1989). Validity data are not complete enough to warrant the SICD-R's use for determining delays (Pearson, 1989).

In 1989, a version of the SICD-R was developed for adults and adolescents who do not possess any speech skills or who have only minimal skills. This version is titled the Adapted Sequenced Inventory of Communication Development (A-SICD; McClennen, 1989). The A-SICD allows examinees to respond through gestures, signing, picture board communication, or voice communication. Like the SICD-R, the A-SICD has both a Receptive and Expressive Scale.

Validation studies for the A-SICD were conducted with 40 subjects between the ages of 16 and 55. Interrater reliability was reported ($N = 10$) to be 88 to 100% on the Receptive Scale and 90 to 100% on the Expressive Scale. Internal consistency was .78 for the Receptive Scale and .91 for the Expressive Scale. Because of the small sample size, the generalizability of these results is questionable. The A-SICD is not norm-referenced; thus, the examiner must use clinical judgement to interpret the inventory. Carey (1995) notes that much of the same information collected on the A-SICD could be obtained through structured observations of the examinee in educational, vocational, or home settings.

REFERENCES

Carey, K. T. (1995). Review of the Adapted Sequenced Inventory of Communication Development. In J. J. Kramer & J. C. Conoley (Eds.), *The twelfth mental measurements yearbook* (pp. 32–33). Lincoln, NE: Buros Institute of Mental Measurements.

Hendrick, D. L., Prather, E. M., & Tobin, A. R. (1984). *Sequenced Inventory of Communication Development*. Seattle: University of Washington Press.

Mardell-Czudnowksi, C. (1989). Review of the Sequenced Inventory of Communication Development. In J. J. Kramer & J. C. Conoley (Eds.), *The eleventh mental measurements yearbook* (pp. 740–742). Lincoln, NE: Buros Institute of Mental Measurements.

McClennen, S. E. (1989). *Adapted Sequenced Inventory of Communication Development*. Seattle: University of Washington Press.

Pearson, M. E. (1989). Review of the Sequenced Inventory of Communication Development. In J. J. Kramer & J. C. Conoley (Eds.), *The eleventh mental measurements yearbook* (pp. 742–744). Lincoln, NE: Buros Institute of Mental Measurements.

ELIZABETH O. LICHTENBERGER
The Salk Institute

See also **Verbal Scale IQ**

SEQUENTIAL AND SIMULTANEOUS COGNITIVE PROCESSING

Sequential and simultaneous are two of many labels used to denote two primary forms of information coding processes in the brain. These coding processes are the primary functions of Luria's (1973) Block II of the brain (the parietal, occipital, and temporal lobes, also known as the association areas of the brain). They have been proposed as fundamental integration processes in Das, Kirby, and Jarman's (1979) model of Luria's fundamental approach to human information processing. Other labels commonly used to distinguish these forms of processing include successive versus simultaneous (Das et al., 1979), propositional versus appositional (Bogen, 1969), serial versus multiple or parallel (Neisser, 1967), and analytic versus gestalt/holistic (Levy, 1972).

No matter what label is applied, the descriptions of the processes corresponding to each label appear to be defining similar processes though some minor distinctions may exist. Thus sequential processing is defined as the processing of information in a temporal or serial order. Using this coding process, analysis of information proceeds in successive steps in which each step provides cues for the processing of later steps. This type of processing is generally employed (e.g., when an individual repeats a series of numbers that have been orally presented). Each stage of processing is dependent on the completion of the immediately preceding stage.

Simultaneous coding processes are used when all the pieces of information or all the stimuli are surveyable at one time and are thus available for processing at one time; that is, the analysis of parts of information can take place without dependence on the parts' relationship to the whole. When an individual discerns the whole object

Figure S.2. An example of a task that might be used to assess an individual's simultaneous cognitive processing skills; what do you think is pictured here? (The answer is in the text.)

with only parts of the picture available, this is usually accomplished using simultaneous processing. Figure S.2 presents an example of a strongly simultaneous processing task. See if you can determine what is pictured. Even with many of the parts missing and the pictured figure only in silhouette form, most individuals beyond the age of 10 to 12 years will recognize the figure to be a man on horseback. Some will have great difficulty or take a long time to recognize the figure; this is true especially if one takes a step-by-step approach to determining the identity of the picture, looking at individual pieces and trying to add them as a simple sum of the separate parts. While not impossible, such an approach is more difficult.

In the literature, several assumptions regarding these two forms of processing are presented. First, sequential and simultaneous processing are not hierarchical. That is, one form of processing does not appear to be more complex than the other. Both appear to require the transformation of stimulus material before synthesis of the information can occur (Das et al., 1979).

Second, determining whether to process information sequentially or simultaneously is not solely dependent on the presentation mode of the stimuli to be processed (e.g., visual or auditory). Rather, the form of processing used appears to be more dependent on the cognitive demands of the task and the unique sociocultural history and genetic predisposition of the individual performing the task (Das et al., 1979; Kaufman & Kaufman, 1983). This may become habitual and individuals do develop preferred styles of information processing.

Third, sequential and simultaneous processing have been indirectly linked to various areas of the brain, but psychologists do not agree on the exact location of each of these functions. Some contend that processing abilities

are best associated with the two hemispheres of the brain (Gazzaniga, 1975; Reynolds, 1981), with sequential processing being a left hemisphere function and simultaneous processing being a right hemisphere function. Luria (1973), on the other hand, located successive or sequential processing as a function of the frontal regions of the brain, with simultaneous processing carried out in the occipital-parietal or rear sections of the brain.

These forms of processing have traditionally been measured in individuals without brain damage with a battery of standardized tests, the components of which are certainly less than pure measures of process. Evidence of simultaneous processing abilities has been inferred from individuals' performance on such instruments as Raven's Progressive Matrices (Raven, 1956), Memory-for-Designs (Graham & Kendall, 1960), and Figure Copying (Ilg & Ames, 1964). Each of these tasks places a premium on visuo-spatial skills and the synthesis of information for successful performance.

Sequential processing abilities have typically been inferred from observing an individual's performance on such tasks as Digit Span (a purely auditory task), Visual Short-Term Memory, and Serial or Free Recall. It is apparent that it is not the mode of presentation but rather the cognitive demands of the task that are the major determining factors in what cognitive processing style is used.

In 1983, the Kaufman Assessment Battery for Children (K-ABC; Kaufman & Kaufman, 1983) was introduced into psychological and educational circles. This instrument was designed as an individually administered intelligence test for children ages $2\frac{1}{2}$ and $12\frac{1}{2}$; it is composed of several subtests that according to factor analytic data, measure sequential and simultaneous processing abilities. Focused on process rather than content as the major distinction of how children solve unfamiliar problems, this instrument has resulted in more controversy and discussion than any intelligence test in recent history (Reynolds, 1985).

Controversy has arisen over the Kaufmans' assertion that knowledge about a child's information-processing abilities, as measured on the K-ABC, in conjunction with other sources of data, can more easily translate into educational programming for children with learning or behavioral problems than traditionally had been possible from data gathered on other, content-based intelligence tests. Primarily employing an aptitude-treatment interaction (ATI) paradigm (Cronbach, 1975) and the habilitation philosophy of neuropsychology (Reynolds, 1981), the Kaufmans propose using knowledge regarding a child's individual strengths in information processing (e.g., simultaneous processing) as the foundation for any remedial plans thus developed. The notion of a strength model of remediation is in direct contrast to the deficit-centered training models that have dominated special education remedial plans for years, but that have proven largely ineffective in improving academic abilities (Ysseldyke & Mirkin, 1982).

Although preliminary data seem encouraging regarding the efficacy of using knowledge of a child's individual processing style to remediate learning or behavioral difficulties (Gunnison, Kaufman, & Kaufman, 1983), the data are not sufficient to support this assumption unequivocably. Much research remains to be done in this area.

REFERENCES

Bogen, J. E. (1969). The other side of the brain: Parts I, II, & III. *Bulletin of the Los Angeles Neurological Society, 34,* 73–203.

Cronbach, L. J. (1975). Beyond the two disciplines of scientific psychology. *American Psychologist, 30,* 116–125.

Das, J. P., Kirby, J. R., & Jarman, R. F. (1979). *Simultaneous and successive cognitive processes.* New York, NY: Academic Press.

Gazzaniga, M. S. (1975). Recent research on hemispheric lateralization of the human brain: Review of the split brain. *UCLA Educator, 17,* 9–12.

Graham, F. K., & Kendall, B. S. (1960). Memory-for-Designs Test: Revised general manual. *Perceptual & Motor Skills, 43,* 1051–1058.

Gunnison, J., Kaufman, N. L., & Kaufman, A. S. (1983). Reading remediation based on sequential and simultaneous processing. *Academic Therapy, 17,* 297–307.

Ilg, F. L., & Ames, L. B. (1964). *School readiness: Behavior tests used at the Gesell Institute.* New York, NY: Harper & Row.

Kaufman, A. S., & Kaufman, N. (1983). *The Kaufman Assessment Battery for Children.* Circle Pines, MN: American Guidance Service.

Levy, J. (1972). Lateral specification of the human brain: Behavioral manifestations and possible evolutionary basis. In J. A. Kiger (Ed.), *Biology of behavior.* Cornallis, OR: Oregon State University Press.

Luria, A. R. (1973). *The working brain: An introduction to neuropsychology.* London, England: Penguin.

Neisser, W. (1967). *Cognitive psychology.* New York, NY: Appleton-Century-Crofts.

Raven, J. C. (1956). *Coloured progressive matrices: Sets A, Ab, B.* London, England: H. K. Lewis.

Reynolds, C. R. (1981). Neuropsychological assessment and the habilitation of learning: Considerations in the search for the aptitude ¥ treatment interaction. *School Psychology Review, 10,* 343–349.

Reynolds, C. R. (Ed.). (1985). K-ABC and controversy [Special issue]. *Journal of Special Education, 18*(3).

Ysseldyke, J., & Mirkin, P. (1982). The use of assessment information to plan instructional interventions: A review of the research. In C. R. Reynolds & T. B. Gutkin (Eds.), *The handbook of school psychology.* New York, NY: Wiley.

JULIA A. HICKMAN
Bastrop Mental Health Association

See also **Information Processing; Kaufman Assessment Battery for Children– Second Edition; Perceptual Training; Remediation, Deficit-Centered Models of**

SEQUENTIAL ASSESSMENT OF MATHEMATICS INVENTORIES: STANDARDIZED INVENTORY

The Sequential Assessment of Mathematics Inventories: Standardized Inventory (SAMI; Reisman & Hutchinson, 1985) is designed to measure the achievement of specific mathematics content objectives and to compare students' performance to national norms. It may be used to assess children in kindergarten through the eighth grade.

The SAMI is presented to students in an easel format, with the questions read aloud by the examiner. Students respond by pointing, writing, or verbally responding. Nine scores are obtained on the SAMI: Mathematical Language (grades K–3 only), Ordinality (grades K–3 only), Number/Notation, Computation, Measurement, Geometric Concepts, Mathematical Applications (grades 4–8 only), Word Problems, and Total. Subtest standard scores have a mean of 10 and a standard deviation of 3.

The SAMI was normed on a sample of about 1,400 students in kindergarten through eighth grade. Test-retest reliability values over a 6-week interval ranged from .43 to .89 with a median of .66. However, five of the subtests have reliability values below .50. Internal consistency values range from .72 to .97 with a median of .93. Validity evidence is limited to one study comparing the SAMI and two standardized achievement tests, as well as the reported intercorrelation of subtests. Fleenor (1992) states that the SAMI has promise as a measure of mathematics performance, but needs more data supporting its reliability and validity.

REFERENCES

Fleenor, J. W. (1992). Review of the Sequential Assessment of Mathematics Inventories: Standardized Inventory. In J. J. Kramer & J. C. Conoley (Eds.), *The eleventh mental measurements yearbook* (pp. 817–819). Lincoln, NE: Buros Institute of Mental Measurements.

Reisman, F. K., & Hutchinson, T. A. (1985). *Sequential Assessment of Mathematics Inventories: Standardized Inventory.* San Antonio, TX: Psychological Corporation.

ELIZABETH O. LICHTENBERGER
The Salk Institute

See also **Mathematics, Learning Disabilities in**

SERIOUSLY EMOTIONALLY DISTURBED

The term seriously emotionally disturbed (SED) has been defined by federal legislation (IDEA) as a condition with one or more of the following characteristics occurring to a marked degree and over a long period of time: (1) inability to learn not explainable by health, intellectual, or sensory factors; (2) inability to develop or maintain appropriate interpersonal relationships with students and teachers; (3) inappropriate behaviors or feelings in normal circumstances; (4) a pervasive mood of depression; (5) a tendency to develop physical symptoms or fears in response to personal or school difficulties [Code of Federal Regulations, Title 34, Section 300. 7(b)(9)]. According to the legislative definition, the term specifically includes childhood schizophrenia but specifically excludes children who are socially maladjusted except when the maladjustment is accompanied by serious emotional disturbance. Although autism was originally included as a form of serious emotional disturbance, in the *Diagnostic and Statistical Manual of Mental Disorders* (*DSM-III*; American Psychiatric Association, 1980), autism was removed from classification as a psychosis and defined as a pervasive developmental disorder. This reclassification of autism was based on research that has established clear differences between autism and the childhood psychoses on a variety of dimensions, including symptomatology, age of onset, family history of psychopathology, language ability, intellectual functioning, and socioeconomic status.

The U.S. Department of Education (1997) reports that the incidence of emotional disturbance in children and youth served in the public schools for the 1995–96 school year was 438,217. The causes of emotional disturbance are varied and include factors such as genetics, trauma, diet, stress, social skills deficits, and family dysfunction. Children and youth exhibit psychiatric disorders in different ways than adults. Therefore, emotional disturbance may be seen in behaviors such as immaturity, hyperactivity, self-monitoring deficits, social skill deficits, learning difficulties, and aggression or self-injurious behavior. Children with the most serious emotional disturbances may exhibit distorted thinking, extreme anxiety, abnormal mood swings, and other symptoms indicative of psychoses (National Information Center for Children and Youth with Disabilities [NICHCY], 1998).

Children and youth with emotional disturbance are identified and referred to special education much in the same way as learning disabled or other exceptional students. Usually, the behaviors that are interfering with the student's ability to succeed in school have been longstanding and have not been responsive to preservice referral interventions by the teacher or school team. The student is assessed usually by the school psychologist who, through a process of inclusion and exclusion, assesses eligibility for services in special education. The assessment must have examined how the student is functioning across settings; have ruled out medical, neurological, and neuropsychological conditions; and have assessed the student across modalities and in an objective and comprehensive manner.

The entrance to special education for SED students has changed over the years to reflect the least restrictive environment (LRE) principle of IDEA and similar legislation. Placement of these students in psychiatric residential facilities has declined in recent years due to LRE and to financial constraints; however, the need for comprehensive treatment is still present. The inclusion movement has advocates that suggest that SED students are best served in the regular classroom with special education support. However, again, the least restrictive environment for SED students should be determined on a case-by-case method. What is least restrictive for one SED student may be a dangerous or nonadvantageous placement for another.

The difficulty of placement, treatment, and education for SED students has probably steered the field to look towards the identification of at-risk students and culturally competent intervention. Lago-Delello (1996) did a study of the differences between kindergarten and first-grade children identified as "at-risk" or "not-at-risk" for the development of severe emotional disturbance on selected factors of classroom dynamics. The comparison focused on teacher factors, classroom interactions, student factors, and instructional factors. Results indicated that at-risk students experienced a markedly different reality in the classroom than their not-at-risk peers. Four major findings emerged: (1) At-risk students were generally rejected by their teachers and not-at-risk peers were not; (2) At-risk students received significantly more negative or neutral teacher feedback statements than not-at-risk peers; (3) At-risk students spent significantly less time academically engaged than not-at-risk peers; and (4) teachers made few accommodations for these students and were generally resistant to making adjustments in tasks, materials, or teaching methods to meet the individual needs of at-risk students. Others (e.g., McKinney, Montague, & Hocutt, 1998) are developing screening instruments and procedures to identify students at risk for emotional disturbance.

Ongoing teacher training for regular and special educators has been identified on many levels; and much of it has targeted multicultural competencies (Singh, 1997). The more that SED students are included in regular education, the more competencies are essential for all personnel involved in the regular education process.

Outcomes for SED students are not as good as they are for students with some other disabilities. Greenbaum (1996) has found that serious problems in these students tend to be present even 7 years after the initial identification. These problems many times become lifelong adjustment issues and are highly correlated with adult high-risk behaviors in crime and substance abuse. The magnitude of the problem with the SED population is supported by data on these students concerning academic outcomes, graduation rates, school placement, school absenteeism, dropout rates, encounters with the juvenile justice system, and identification rates of students of varying socioeconomic backgrounds. Seven interdependent strategic targets have been identified by the Chesapeake Institute (1994) to address the future of policy, funding, and treatment of

SED by federal, state, and local agencies: (1) expand positive learning opportunities and results; (2) strengthen school and community capacity; (3) value and address diversity; (4) collaborate with families; (5) promote appropriate assessment; (6) provide ongoing skill development and support; and (7) create comprehensive collaborative systems. Three universal themes are also stressed: first, collaborative efforts must extend to initiatives that prevent emotional and behavioral problems from developing or escalating; second, services must be provided in a culturally sensitive and respectful manner; and third, services must empower all stakeholders and maintain a climate of possibility and accountability.

The federal government is revising the definition of SED (NICHCY, 1998). Hopefully, more emphasis will be placed on prevention. The identification of at-risk children is the key to preventing serious adjustment problems for many children and youth. The field is moving towards being able to identify, in an objective and a culturally competent manner, young students who are having problems meeting the demands of everyday living. Once identified, this population can receive sensitive programming that includes family participation. Together, the school and family can help those young children who have not yet developed serious emotional difficulties to adjust and to meet the demands of their age group. The alternative is the present situation, where hundreds of thousands of children and youth are already suffering and in serious jeopardy of losing their ability to receive the benefits of an appropriate education.

REFERENCES

American Psychiatric Association. (1980). *Diagnostic and statistical manual of mental disorders* (3rd ed.). Washington, DC: Author.

Chesapeake Institute. (1994). *National agenda for achieving better results for children and youth with serious emotional disturbance.* Washington, DC: Author.

Greenbaum, P. E. (1996). *National adolescent and child treatment study: Outcomes for children with serious emotional and behavioral disturbance.* (ERIC Clearinghouse No. EJ53063)

Lago-Delello, E. (1996, April 1–5). *Classroom dynamics and young children identified as at-risk for the development of serious emotional disturbance.* Paper presented at the Annual International Convention of the Council for Exceptional Children, Orlando, FL.

McKinney, J. D., Montague, M., & Hocutt, A. M. (1998, April 16). *A two year follow-up study of children at risk for developing SED: Implications for designing prevention programs.* Paper presented at the Annual Convention of the Council for Exceptional Children, Minneapolis, MN.

National Information Center for Children and Youth with Disabilities (NICHCY). (1998). *General information about emotional disturbance.* Fact Sheet Number 5 (FS5). Washington, DC: Author.

Singh, N. N. (1997). Value and address diversity. *Journal of Emotional & Behavioral Disorders, 5*(1), 24–35.

U.S. Department of Education. (1997). *Nineteenth annual report to Congress on the implementation of the Individuals with Disabilities Education Act.* Washington, DC: Author.

STAFF

See also Childhood Psychosis; Childhood Schizophrenia; Emotional Disorders

SERVICE DELIVERY MODELS

Service delivery models are programs, processes, and safeguards established to ensure a free, appropriate public education for children and youths with disabilities. The models that have been developed for the delivery of services to school-aged children with disabilities generally reflect in their form and operation the influence of at least three factors: (1) the statutory requirements and congressional intent of Individuals with Disabilities Education Act (IDEA); (2) the nature of the particular state or local education agency providing the services in terms of physical size, population distribution, and, to some extent, the available fiscal and human resources; and (3) the specific needs of the children being served. IDEA requires that children with disabilities to the degree possible be educated with typically developing children and that removal from the regular education environment occur "only when the nature or severity of the handicap is such that education in regular classes with the use of supplementary aids and services cannot be achieved satisfactorily" (U.S.C. 1412(5)(B)). The regulations for the Act elaborate on this condition and refer to a continuum of alternate placements that must include instruction in regular classes with access to resource room services or itinerant instruction if necessary, special classes, special schools, home instruction, and instruction in hospitals and institutions. The regulations also require assurance that the various alternative placements are available to the extent necessary to implement the individualized education program for each child with disabilities. The congressional intent clearly was to ensure the design of models for the delivery of services to meet the instructional needs of each child with disabilities rather than to allow assignment of a child with disabilities to whatever special education services happen to be available at the time, unless those services also happen to meet the needs of the particular child as detailed in that child's individual education plan (IEP).

The continuum of alternative placements as listed in the U.S. Department of Education regulations together with the language of IDEA suggest the basic models for the delivery of special education and related services. The percentage of children placed in different educational settings are reported every year as seen in Table S.2 for

Table S.2. Percentage of Children Ages 3–21 Served in Different Educational Environments Under IDEA, Part B, During the 1994–1995 School Year

State	All disabilities (%)							
	Regular class	Resource room	Separ class	Public separ facil	Private separ facil	Public resid facil	Private resid facil	Home hosp envir
Alabama	44.36	37.73	15.28	1.23	0.17	0.61	0.20	0.41
Alaska	60.71	25.57	13.24	0.03	0.21	0.06	0.13	0.05
Arizona	40.67	36.35	19.82	1.64	0.92	0.19	0.21	0.20
Arkansas	41.13	38.84	14.19	0.29	2.90	0.01	1.11	1.52
California	51.54	19.40	25.09	1.38	1.58	0.20	0.31	0.50
Colorado	69.75	16.48	10.11	1.25	0.19	0.70	0.90	0.62
Connecticut	56.49	18.80	19.53	1.55	2.29	0.05	0.93	0.36
Delaware	26.93	60.21	7.66	4.58	0.01	0.05	0.09	0.47
District of Columbia	13.57	18.82	43.35	13.43	8.87	0.00	1.58	0.38
Florida	40.73	22.31	32.67	2.29	0.30	0.43	0.00	1.27
Georgia	42.38	31.03	25.46	0.67	0.14	0.01	0.10	0.20
Hawaii	43.49	32.24	22.97	0.38	0.06	0.04	0.10	0.72
Idaho	64.97	23.83	9.54	1.03	0.11	0.02	0.24	0.26
Illinois	27.46	33.96	31.17	4.18	2.00	0.42	0.30	0.51
Indiana	61.23	12.09	23.96	1.65	0.10	0.47	0.14	0.35
Iowa	60.77	26.01	10.14	1.65	—	0.90	0.19	0.33
Kansas	50.07	31.38	14.81	1.84	0.75	0.77	0.12	0.26
Kentucky	52.64	32.67	12.56	0.66	0.17	0.76	0.04	0.49
Louisiana	35.53	18.10	42.99	1.30	0.07	1.28	0.06	0.66
Maine	50.51	33.17	10.66	0.83	2.72	0.05	0.82	1.24
Maryland	49.09	19.40	24.36	3.77	1.93	0.65	0.42	0.38
Massachusetts	66.40	13.29	14.24	1.57	3.02	—	0.68	0.79
Michigan	45.10	24.89	22.36	5.50	—	0.20	0.10	1.86
Minnesota	60.06	22.75	10.30	4.70	0.39	0.83	0.26	0.72
Mississippi	34.39	37.25	25.81	0.88	0.18	0.67	0.05	0.76
Missouri	46.29	30.14	20.83	1.54	0.60	0.22	0.17	0.21
Montana	55.90	29.96	11.44	0.80	0.28	0.62	0.55	0.45
Nebraska	58.25	23.64	12.40	3.66	0.27	0.29	0.09	1.40
Nevada	42.18	36.88	17.39	3.28	0.00	0.00	0.03	0.25
New Hampshire	51.97	22.16	19.33	2.88	1.27	0.26	1.51	0.62
New Jersey	45.38	15.59	29.21	3.13	5.27	0.80	0.07	0.56
New Mexico	31.99	28.82	37.65	0.04	0.01	0.94	0.05	0.51
New York	38.82	14.62	35.02	7.42	2.18	0.64	0.52	0.80
North Carolina	58.63	20.75	17.45	1.55	0.46	0.67	0.01	0.47
North Dakota	75.10	12.56	8.98	1.78	0.22	0.52	0.46	0.38
Ohio	57.68	23.12	15.68	2.18	0.00	0.35	0.00	0.99
Oklahoma	49.39	32.96	15.60	0.93	0.09	0.53	0.09	0.40
Oregon	68.79	18.75	8.42	1.33	1.34	0.37	0.28	0.72
Pennsylvania	37.84	28.07	28.98	1.75	1.57	0.61	0.28	0.90
Puerto Rico	7.14	52.90	29.44	4.23	2.09	0.43	0.10	3.68
Rhode Island	51.03	18.76	24.63	0.79	2.67	0.00	1.38	0.73
South Carolina	36.80	36.47	24.26	1.59	0.04	0.48	0.03	0.34
South Dakota	60.81	23.70	11.67	0.58	0.76	0.69	1.63	0.15
Tennessee	49.70	28.79	17.75	0.93	0.80	0.47	0.43	1.13
Texas	27.40	46.78	23.88	0.52	0.03	0.13	0.01	1.26
Utah	40.20	34.98	20.04	2.79	0.00	1.67	—	0.34
Vermont	83.76	4.39	4.96	1.20	1.39	0.12	1.71	2.46
Virginia	38.36	31.14	26.65	1.10	0.73	0.67	0.25	1.09
Washington	50.14	29.22	18.57	1.03	0.32	0.20	0.01	0.51
West Virginia	9.98	70.10	18.32	0.43	0.08	0.57	0.03	0.49
Wisconsin	38.06	37.58	22.59	1.18	0.05	0.35	0.02	0.16
Wyoming	57.05	32.35	8.19	0.38	0.43	0.89	0.55	0.16
American Samoa	62.84	23.65	13.51	0.00	0.00	0.00	0.00	0.00
Guam	35.89	52.79	10.65	0.62	0.00	0.00	0.06	0.00
Northern Marianas	83.57	11.19	3.50	0.00	0.00	0.00	0.00	1.75
Palau	54.95	23.42	17.12	0.00	0.00	0.00	0.00	4.50
Virgin Islands	—	—	—	—	—	—	—	—
Bur. of Indian Affairs	24.49	58.75	14.90	0.22	0.24	0.90	0.40	0.09
U.S. and outlying areas	45.04	27.01	23.26	2.22	1.04	0.43	0.24	0.76
50 states, D.C., & P.R.	45.07	26.96	23.28	2.23	1.04	0.43	0.24	0.76

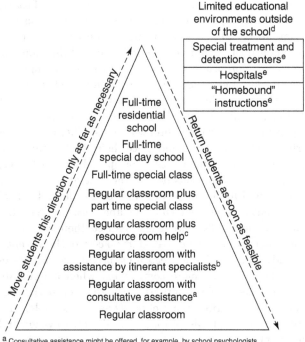

Figure S.3. The original special education cascade.

Source: Reynolds, M.C., and Birch, J.W. (1992). *Teaching exceptional children in all America's schools*. Reston, VA: Council for Exceptional Children. Adapted by E. Fletcher-Jazen.

[a] Consultative assistance might be offered, for example, by school psychologists, consulting teachers, resource room teachers, supervisors or others. The term *consultative* denotes only *indirect* services such as prereferral interventions and no *direct* service or instruction to the child by the consultant.

[b] Direct instruction is provided by the regular and special education teacher in a variety of collaborative or consultative arrangements.

[c] Itinerant specialists commonly include speech and hearing therapists and mobility instructors for the blind, for example. They offer some *direct* instruction to the students involved.

[d] A resource classroom is a special station in a school building that is manned by a resource teacher who usually offers some direct instruction to select students but also usually offers consulting services to regular teacher. Sometimes resource teachers are categorical (such as resource teacher for the blind) but increasingly resource teachers are employed for a more generic, noncategorical role.

[e] This special set of environments is included here in set-aside fashion because usually students are placed in this setting for reasons other than educational. For example, they go to detention centers on court orders for reasons of conviction for some criminal offense; or they go to hospitals or are held at home because of health problems. Special educators often work in these limited environments and some degree of specialization in education is required. But, in the main, there is strong preference, from an educational point of view, for return of the students to regular school environments as soon as feasible.

the 1994–1995 school year. Reynolds (1992) originally laid out a chart showing various organizational patterns for instruction. His work was later modified by Deno and illustrates a cascade of services for children with disabilities (Reynolds & Birch, 1992). The placements as shown in Figure S.3 can be classified according to the amount of direct intervention provided by someone other than the regular classroom teacher; the more direct services necessary, the more a child moves away from the first level placement, the regular classroom. As the triangular shape of the illustration might suggest, more children with special needs should be found in regular classrooms with access to consultant or itinerant support or resource room assistance and fewer in the special classes, special schools, residential schools, or placements outside the school setting. The figure has been adapted to include collaborative/consultative teaching arrangements that allow the special education student to remain in the regular education classroom with direct instruction from the regular and special education teachers.

IDEA and its regulations intend for regular class placement to be the goal for students with disabilities. There will always be some students whose educational needs cannot be met in the regular class, however, without some adaptations, special equipment and/or materials, or extra help (Cartwright, Cartwright, & Ward, 1985). Because the regular class teacher may not be adequately trained to make those adaptations, secure the special equipment or materials, or provide the specialized instruction, full-time regular class placement for some children may be enhanced by the provision of consulting teachers who collaborate with regular class teachers and provide up to and including direct instruction.

Educators, parents, advocates, and others who promote appropriate inclusion of students with disabilities in general education classes believe that doing so will provide those students with greater access to the general education curriculum, appropriate education with their nondisabled peers, raise expectations for student performance, and improve coordination between regular and special educators. They also believe that greater inclusion will result in increased school-level accountability for educational results (U.S. Department of Education, 1998).

In 1994–1995, 2.2 million of the total 4.9 million students with disabilities ages 6 through 21 spent at least 80% of their school day in general education classes (see Table S.2), and more than 95% of all students with disabilities attended regular schools. The environments in which students receive services vary according to the individual needs of the child. Although 87% of students with speech and language impairments were served in regular classes for 80% or more of the school day, only 9.7% of those with intellectual disabilities were served in regular class placements. Students ages 6–11 were more likely to receive services in regular class placements than students ages 12–17 or 18–21 (U.S. Department of Education, 1998).

A resource room program can enable some children who need more intensive instruction in some or all of the basic skills, or whose behavior at times goes beyond what is appropriate or tolerable in the regular class, to remain in the regular class except for limited periods of time each day or week. The resource room model has been particularly popular for students with learning disabilities, although students with other disabilities also profit from additional help provided by resource room teachers. Some resource room programs are organized by disability area while others, particularly in more recent years, accommodate children with a variety of disabilities but whose instructional needs are similar.

Placement in a special class for all or part of the school day is considered necessary for some children. Frequently, the deciding factors for inclusive programming, resource room, part-time special class, or full-time special class placement are the amount of time the child with a disability can benefit from time in the regular class and the severity of the needs of that child. Interestingly, there seems to be considerable overlap in the types of students, the amount of time spent in the regular class, and the ways teachers actually use their time in resource room classes, self-contained special classes, and even residential classes, at least for students with emotional disabilities (Peterson, Zabel, Smith, & White, 1983). This suggests some inconsistencies in determining appropriate placement for children and in defining responsibilities for special and regular education personnel.

Some children with disabilities are placed in special schools for their daily instructional programs. Such children, by the nature of their placement, have limited access to participation in social, academic, extracurricular, or spontaneous activities with typically developing children. These children are, therefore, to be placed in special schools and residential settings only when the severity of their conditions warrants such placement and only for so long as that placement is necessary. The same holds true for those students in settings such as hospitals, treatment centers, and detention facilities that are outside the educational system.

The overriding principle in selecting appropriate placement for a child with disabilities who needs special education and related services is that of the least restrictive environment. No one placement or service delivery system described here can be cited as the best for all children with disabilities, and that includes the regular classroom, although some proponents of full inclusion would argue this point. Rather, selection must be made on the basis of what setting permits the implementation of the IEP designed for a given child and allows for meaningful involvement with typically developing children, if possible in the same community where the child with a disability would attend school if there were no disability necessitating a special education program.

While the service delivery models described represent the typical programs available for children with disabilities, or those that should be available by law and regulation, the specific character of any particular program will be determined in part by the nature of the geography, size, population distribution, and resources available in the child's district of residence. Rural areas have special challenges to face, among which are transportation, length of time en route to programs, recruitment and retention of qualified personnel to serve children with low-incidence disabilities, smaller tax base, and in some communities, the power of tradition (Helge, 1984). Urban areas face another set of challenges that typically include transportation in densely populated areas, desegregation issues, and the problems that develop when large numbers of people with little in common must interact under crowded conditions.

In addition to these special urban and rural factors, there is the impact that access to special education programs in private schools can have. The laws and regulations are clear that children with disabilities must be provided appropriate free public education in approved private day and residential schools only, and in accord with the principle of the least restrictive environment (Grumet & Inkpen, 1982; U.S. Office of Education, 1977). If parents wish for their child with a disability to attend a private school program and place their child in that program themselves, then except for special circumstances, the parents are responsible for the cost of their child's education. But if the private day or residential school placement is recommended as the appropriate one for the child by the child's local school district, then the education program must be provided at no cost to the parents. Already complex issues regarding private school placement become even more complicated when out-of-state private schools offer programs considered appropriate for children with certain types of needs as, for example, children with multiple disabilities or children with vision and hearing impairments.

In summary, the cascade of service delivery models emphasizes the place where children with special needs might be assigned for instruction. These models have collected criticism because of their focus on placement more than program content. Inherent in the instructional cascade is the goal of equipping the regular classroom to be a learning environment where the diverse needs of many children, including disabled, gifted, and disabled gifted learners, can be accommodated (Reynolds & Birch, 1992).

Service delivery models in the context of special education have changed over the years as laws, the inclusion movement, court decisions, local needs, parental pressures, fiscal and human resources, and community concerns have made their influence felt. Ysseldyke and Algozzine (1982) have suggested that change will continue but primarily in response to economic needs. More recently, Crowner (1985) has presented a taxonomy of special education finance and an analysis of funding bases, formulas and types and sources of funds for special education. The balance between congressional intent and legal necessity, local control, fiscal reality, and administrative expediency is delicate at best. For the benefit of all children currently in school and those to come, efforts must continue to be directed at designing and operating service delivery systems that meet the needs of all children, those who have conditions requiring special education and those who do not.

This entry has been informed by the sources listed below.

REFERENCES

Cartwright, G. P., Cartwright, C. A., & Ward, M. E. (1985). *Educating special learners* (2nd ed.). Belmont, CA: Wadsworth.

Crowner, T. T. (1985). A taxonomy of special education finance. *Exceptional Children, 51*(6), 503–508.

Fox, W. L., Egner, A. N., Paolucci, P. E., Perelman, P. F., McKenzie, H. S., & Garvin, J. S. (1973). An introduction to a regular classroom approach to special education. In E. Deno (Ed.), *Instructional alternatives for exceptional children.* Reston, VA: Council for Exceptional Children.

Grumet, L., & Inkpen, T. (1982). The education of children in private schools: A state agency's perspective. *Exceptional Children, 49*(3), 200–206.

Haight, S. L. (1984). Special education teacher consultant: Idealism versus realism. *Exceptional Children, 50*(6), 507–515.

Helge, D. (1984). The state of the art of rural special education. *Exceptional Children, 50*(4), 294–305.

Peterson, R. L., Zabel, R. H., Smith, C. R., & White, M. A. (1983). Cascade of services model and emotionally disabled students. *Exceptional Children, 49*(5), 404–408.

Reynolds, M. C., & Birch, J. W. (1992). *Teaching exceptional children in all America's schools.* Reston, VA: Council for Exceptional Children.

Salund, S. J. (1984). Factors contributing to the development of successful mainstreaming programs. *Exceptional Children, 50*(5), 409–416.

U.S. Office of Education. (1977, August 23). Education of handicapped children: Implementation of Part B of the Education of the Handicapped Act. *Federal Register, 42*(163), 42474–42518.

U.S. Department of Education. (1998). *Nineteenth Annual Report to Congress.* Washington, DC: Author.

Ysseldyke, J., & Algozzine, B. (1982). *Critical issues in special and remedial education.* Boston, MA: Houghton Mifflin.

MARJORIE E. WARD
The Ohio State University

See also Cascade Model of Special Education Services; Individuals With Disabilities Education Improvement Act of 2004 (IDEIA); Least Restrictive Environment; Resource Room; Self-Contained Class

SETTING EVENT

Setting event is a term that is used to describe antecedent events, operations, or conditions that may influence student responding (Chandler & Dahlquist, 2006). The field of Applied Behavior Analysis also refers to setting events as establishing operations (Michael, 1993). Horner, Vaughn, Day, and Ard (1996) write that "the term *setting events* is used to indicate events that alter the likelihood of a behavior by momentarily altering the value of reinforcers or punishers" (p. 382). Generally, setting events are organized around three distinct contexts: (1) biological setting events, (2) environmental setting events, and (3) social or contextual setting events (Chandler & Dahlquist, 2006). Examples of setting events can include the presence or absence of medications, existing medical conditions or illnesses, unusual patterns of sleep, changes in diet, increases in classroom noise or other disruptions, difficult interactions with adults or peers, and alteration of an existing schedule (O'Neill, Horner, Albin, Sprague, Storey, & Newton, 1997).

Horner et al. (1996) emphasizes that setting events do not occasion a problem behavior; instead, they change the conditions that previously existed by altering what was reinforcing or punishing. For example, if a student comes to school and he or she did not have access to dinner the night before or breakfast that morning (biological setting event), the value of food and the desire to access it would be very different than if the student was satiated upon arriving at school. Additionally, if a student had a difficult interaction with a peer during passing period (social setting event), it might increase the likelihood that when presented with a request by the teacher to join a cooperative learning group that the student would refuse to follow that direction, even after prompting and encouragement was attempted, which had been a successful strategy in the past.

Setting events are best understood when examined as part of the three-term contingency (Maag, 1999). The three-term contingency allows teachers to look at behavior in relation to the antecedents that preceded the behavior and the consequences that followed the behavior. The three-term contingency uses the following notation: A–B–C, where A stands for "antecedent," B stands for "behavior," and C for "consequence." Using our definition, setting events are antecedent events, operations, or conditions that can be either proximal or distal to the actual behavior. Therefore, when added to the three-term contingency, you have the following notation: SE–A–B–C. In other words, when Maria misses her medications (setting event), and she is presented with a difficult academic task (antecedent), she runs out of the classroom (behavior), in order to escape or avoid the academic task (consequence).

As teachers and researchers learn to gather information on setting events and their relationship to changes in student behavior, positive behavior interventions and supports can be put in place that may diminish or eliminate the negative effect of the setting event for the person of concern and bring increasing understanding to the role that antecedents play in occasioning both appropriate and challenging behavior (Chandler & Dahlquist, 2006).

REFERENCES

Chandler, L. K., & Dahlquist, C. M. (2006). *Functional assessment: Strategies to prevent and remediate challenging behavior in school settings* (2nd ed.). Upper Saddle River, NJ: Pearson Merrill Prentice Hall.

Horner, R. H., Vaughn, B. J., Day, H. M., & Ard, W. R., Jr. (1996). The relationship between setting events and problem behavior: Expanding our understanding of behavioral support. In L. K. Koegel, R. L. Koegel, & G. Dunlap (Eds.), *Positive behavioral support: Including people with difficult behavior in the community* (pp. 381–402). Baltimore, MD: Paul H. Brookes.

Maag, J. W. (1999). *Behavior management: From theoretical implications to practical applications.* San Diego, CA: Singular.

Michael, J. L. (1993). *Concepts and principles of behavior analysis.* Kalamazoo, MI: Association for Behavior Analysis.

O'Neill, R. E., Horner, R. H., Albin, R. W., Sprague, J. R., Storey, K., & Newton, J. S. (1997). *Functional assessment and program development for problem behavior: A practical handbook* (2nd ed.). Pacific Grove, CA: Brooks/Cole.

RANDALL L. DE PRY
University of Colorado at Colorado Springs

See also **Behavioral Assessment**

SEX DIFFERENCES IN LEARNING ABILITIES

Popular stereotypes and epidemiological research both suggest that boys have more learning and adjustment problems than girls. Boys are more readily referred for psychological services than girls with similar problems (Caplan, 1977). In addition, boys of all ages are more likely than girls to be evaluated or treated for learning problems (Eme, 1979). The reasons for apparent gender differences are widely debated. Some suggest that (a) boys are at some biological or developmental disadvantage that affects learning and adjustment (Ullian, 1981); (b) classrooms, teachers, or professionals are less tolerant of boys than girls (Pleck, 1981); and (c) the problems manifested by girls are perceived differently or considered to be less important. This debate leads one to question whether recognizable gender differences exist in children's learning abilities.

Many persons believe the cognitive abilities of boys and girls differ. The common notion is that boys have better developed quantitative abilities while girls are better in verbal areas. After reviewing literature on psychological gender differences, Maccoby and Jacklin (1974) conclude that three cognitive gender differences are well established: girls have greater verbal ability than boys, while boys have better visual-spatial and mathematical ability than girls. The authors further conclude that gender differences in verbal ability emerge after age 11, gender differences in quantitative (i.e., mathematical) abilities emerge at around 12, and gender differences in spatial ability emerge in adolescence.

Other investigations report gender differences in verbal and spatial abilities at earlier ages than those reported by Maccoby and Jacklin. A number of researchers have found that females as early as age 1 month and throughout the preschool years show some slight verbal advancement over males, an advancement that appears stronger and more reliable after age 10 or 11 (McGuinness & Pribram, 1979; Oetzel, 1966; Petersen & Wittig, 1979). While sex differences are seen more clearly during and after adolescence, male superiority in spatial performance may appear as early as age 6 (Harris, 1978; McGuinness & Pribram, 1979). The magnitude of differences between males and females depends in part on the type of spatial skill. Maccoby and Jacklin (1974) distinguish visual nonanalytic spatial skills (i.e., those solved without the use of verbal mediation) from visual analytic spatial skills (i.e., those solvable with verbal mediation). Postpubescent males score consistently higher than females on most spatial abilities, particularly nonanalytic visualization abilities (Maccoby & Jacklin, 1974; Petersen & Wittig, 1979).

Generalizations regarding gender differences in verbal, spatial, and quantitative areas do not go unchallenged. After reviewing the evidence on cognitive gender differences used by Maccoby and Jacklin (1974), Sherman (1978) reported the magnitude of the gender differences to be very small. Hyde (1981) also concludes from a meta-analysis of the data used by Maccoby and Jacklin (1974) that the gender differences in verbal ability, quantitative ability, visual-spatial ability, and field articulation are small. Sex differences appear to account for no more than 5% of the population variance. In general, gender differences in verbal ability are smaller and gender differences in spatial ability are larger. Hyde questions whether statistically significant sex differences in cognitive abilities are practically significant. In other words, the common notion that girls are better at verbal tasks while boys excel in spatial or mathematical areas largely is meaningless in terms of educational implications. Moreover, a close review of literature examining gender differences is likely to lead readers to conclude that boys and girls exhibit similarities more frequently than differences.

Do sex differences exist in school achievement? The evidence is contradictory. Few gender differences in learning were found in a 5-year longitudinal study of students ages 5 through 9 (Anastas & Reinherz, 1984). However, a review of the cross-national data on gender differences in achievement found that boys' mathematics achievement is higher than that of girls at both the elementary and secondary levels, that boys score higher in all areas of science, and that girls have higher achievement in verbal areas involving reading comprehension and literature (Fennema, 1982; McGuinness, 1993).

Assuming achievement is affected by opportunities to learn (e.g., participation in courses, amount of instruction), and that boys generally have more opportunities to learn mathematics and science than girls (Finn, Dulberg, &

Reis, 1979), we may conclude that girls perform lower in math and science because of fewer opportunities in these areas rather than intrinsic factors. While research infrequently has considered the extent to which differences in socialization and educational experiences may account for differential performance and attainment, many social scientists believe most or even all sex differences in ability and achievement are due to differing cultural and social opportunities and expectations for boys and girls (Levine & Ornstein, 1983). Still, we know little about the origins of sex differences. When gender differences appear, we should be cautious in speculating about their etiologies.

REFERENCES

Anastas, J. W., & Reinherz, H. (1984). Gender differences in learning and adjustment problems in school: Results of a longitudinal study. *American Journal of Orthopsychiatry, 54,* 110–122.

Caplan, P. (1977). Sex, age, behavior and school subject as determinants of report of learning problems. *Journal of Learning Disabilities, 10,* 314–316.

Eme, R. (1979). Sex differences in childhood psychopathology. A review. *Psychological Bulletin, 86,* 574–593.

Fennema, E. (1982, March). *Overview of sex-related differences in mathematics.* Paper presented at the annual meeting of the American Educational Research Association, New York.

Finn, J. D., Dulberg, L., & Reis, J. (1979). Sex differences in educational attainment: A cross-national perspective. *Harvard Educational Review, 49,* 477–503.

Harris, L. J. (1978). Sex differences in spatial ability: Possible environmental, genetic, and neurological factors. In M. Kinsbourne (Ed.), *Asymmetrical function of the brain.* London, England: Cambridge University Press.

Hyde, J. S. (1981). How large are cognitive gender differences? A meta-analysis using w^2 and d. *American Psychologist, 36,* 892–901.

Levine, D. U., & Ornstein, A. C. (1983). Sex differences in ability and achievement. *Journal of Research & Development in Education, 16,* 66–72.

Maccoby, E. E., & Jacklin, C. N. (1974). *Psychology of sex differences.* Stanford, CA: Stanford University Press.

McGuinness, D. (1993). Gender differences in cognitive style: Implications for mathematics performance and achievement. In L. A. Penner & G. M. Batsche (Eds.), *The challenge in mathematics and science education. Psychology's response* (pp. 251–274). Washington, DC: APA.

McGuinness, D., & Pribram, K. H. (1979). The origins of sensory bias in the development of gender differences in perception and cognition. In M. Bortner (Ed.), *Cognitive growth and development.* New York, NY: Brunner/Mazel.

Oetzel, R. (1966). Classified summary of research on sex differences. In E. E. Maccoby (Ed.), *The development of sex differences.* Stanford, CA: Stanford University Press.

Petersen, A. C., & Wittig, M. A. (1979). Sex differences in cognitive functioning: An overview. In M. A. Wittig & A. C. Petersen (Eds.), *Sex-related differences in cognitive functioning: Developmental issues.* New York, NY: Academic Press.

Pleck, J. (1981). *The myth of masculinity.* Cambridge, MA: MIT Press.

Sherman, J. (1978). *Sex-related cognitive differences: An essay on theory and evidence.* Springfield, IL: Thomas.

Ullian, D. (1981). Why boys will be boys: A structural perspective. *American Journal of Orthopsychiatry, 51,* 493–501.

THOMAS OAKLAND
University of Florida

JEFF LAURENT
University of Texas

SEX EDUCATION OF INDIVIDUALS WITH DISABILITIES

Many professionals and parents believe the sexual needs of individuals with disabilities should be met (Craft & Craft, 1981; Fitz-Gerald & Fitz-Gerald, 1979; Love, 1983). The principle of normalization promoted in the United Nations Declaration of Rights of the Mentally Handicapped (United Nations, 1971) underscores this belief. The declaration states that people with disabilities have the same basic rights as other citizens of the same country and the same age. In the United States, normalization is espoused in the Rehabilitation Act of 1973 (PL 93-380) and the Individuals with Disabilities Act (IDEA), which provide for the individualized education of the disabled in accordance with the requirement of the least restrictive environment.

The advocacy of inclusion in school and the movement away from custodial institutional care and toward community living supply the impetus for focusing on the sexual rights of individuals with disabilities (Bass, 1974; Jacobs, 1978; Shindell, 1975; Thornton, 1979). In conjunction with the philosophy of protecting basic human rights, sex education is advocated to achieve the same ends for individuals with disabilities as for their typically developing peers: to develop sexually fulfilled persons who understand themselves, their values, and resulting behaviors (Harris, 1974; Reich & Harshman, 1971). Moreover, many persons agree with Kempton (1977) that sex education is bound to the practical tasks of improving the social and sexual functions of individuals with disabilities. The need to moderate educational goals on the bases of age, gender, type of disability, and severity of the disability is inherent in the nature of sex education of individuals with disabilities.

Alongside the demands for individualization of instruction is a humanistic approach that advocates meeting the needs of persons while deemphasizing labels (Johnson, 1981). In contradiction to the rationale given in the past, this outlook maintains that sex education should not only respond to critical sexual problems as they arise, or to conditioning that seeks to prevent all sexual experiences (Craft & Craft, 1978, 1980; Edmonson & Wish, 1975; Gordon, 1971a, 1971b; Kempton, 1977, 1978). Implied in the normalization philosophy is the goal of working for the good of all by securing individual freedom since, with teaching, training, and the availability of specific support services, individuals with disabilities are more likely to blend into society.

Notwithstanding the fact that the philosophy of normalization has impacted the literature, the topic of sex education for individuals with disabilities is fraught with controversy. Issues and concerns presently being raised include improvement of curricula and resources, training and preparation of teachers, assessment of the effects of teaching, and involvement of the parents in sex education.

Great strides have been made in the individualization of sex education (Johnson & Kempton, 1981). A wealth of curriculum guides exists that identifies programs to meet the varied needs of individuals with disabilities (see Edmonson, 1980, for a 30-reference list of programs and materials available for individuals with visual impairments, auditory impairments, intellectual impairments, and emotional disturbances). Adapted sex education enables even individuals with severe intellectual disabilities to improve their sexual knowledge (Edmonson, 1980). However, outdated sex laws and repressive social attitudes often prevent the optimal development and employment of instructional resources (Sherwin, 1981). Teaching materials aimed at compensating for specific disabilities (e.g., genital models for use with individuals with blindness) can run afoul of obscenity laws. Also, few legal principles protect sex educators, counselors, or therapists (Sherwin, 1981). Audiotactual sex education programs for children with visual impairments have been implemented successfully with the use of models, but touching the human body is seen as problematic (Knappett & Wagner, 1976; Tait & Kessler, 1976). Sex education programs for children with visual impairments should take into account the sexual taboos of our culture (Torbett, 1974). Fortunately, according to Johnson (1981), this negativism is lifting somewhat as judged by a shift from a position of elimination regarding the acceptance of the sexuality of the disabled to a position of toleration. The evolution toward a more permissive attitude regarding sexual expression for recreational rather than procreational purposes has been conducive to this change. Still, sodomy laws in many states condemn all sexual activity as illegal except vaginal intercourse within marriage. These laws deny nonprocreative sex as a legitimate right. For a given person with a disability, this form of sexual expression may be the only one possible. In light of such social taboos and legal

restraints, the development of appropriate programming to suit the individual needs of individuals with disabilities is constrained.

Minimal attention is paid to sex education during the preparation of teachers for students with disabilities. A survey indicated that, while 61% of student teachers in special education courses received some preparation in sex education, this preparation was either an elective option or a few hours of coverage subsumed under a different topic such as methods of teaching (May, 1980). This is regrettable because sex education courses in special education could help teachers overcome their discomfort in dealing with this subject (Blom, 1971). Professionals can increase their comfort with sexual matters as well as improve attitude and knowledge levels as a result of systematic training in sexuality and disability (Chubon, 1981). Kempton (1978) has proposed training professionals to provide services, as well as develop policies, regarding the sexual rights of individuals with disabilities. She advises (1977) that successful programs be broadly conceived to prepare for skills for living in society.

A major obstacle to sex education of individuals with disabilities has been the denial of their sexuality by parents and teachers, who are concerned that education could trigger sexual experimentation and appetite (Craft, 1983). However, experts in this field (Gordon, 1975; Kempton, 1978) have argued that sex education results in improved social behavior, increased self-respect, more openness, and fewer guilt feelings. On the other hand, withholding information fails to deter sexual activity, causes confusion, needless fears, inappropriate behaviors, and unwanted consequences such as pregnancy.

In spite of this authoritative stance, advocates for sex education have provided little evidence that sex education has changed sexual behavior patterns or identified the valid expectations and limitations of their procedures (Balester, 1971). The literature that examines specific sex education programs for individuals with disabilities mainly presents theorizations rather than scientific data (Vockell & Mattick, 1972). Teaching individuals with disabilities is a complex task owing to such factors as low cognitive abilities and academic skill, short attention span, and secondary disabilities of a sensory, physical, emotional, or behavioral nature. Therefore, restraints in setting educational goals have been recommended (Watson & Rogers, 1980). However, programs that facilitate specific abilities (e.g., contraceptive use or knowledge of sexually transmitted diseases) seem to represent too modest a first step toward devising an educational technology of sexual instruction that will empirically appraise the limits of sexual development and social awareness in this diverse population.

While many parents are interested in sex education for their youngsters with disabilities, their sexual conservatism may severely limit the nature of the curriculum. For example, parents of students with sensory impairments give the highest rating to teaching less controversial topics such as cleanliness, knowledge of one's own body, venereal disease, dating, reproduction, pregnancy, marriage, and feelings about self and others. They frequently resist instruction regarding contraceptives, sexual intercourse, sexual deviancy, incest, divorce, masturbation, abortion, sterilization, and pornography (Love, 1983). Parental cooperation and support are crucial to program development and to the transfer of skills from school to home and community settings. Thus it remains essential to involve the parents in cooperative educational efforts by securing their agreement with expectations of instruction (Hamre-Nietupski & Ford, 1981; Kempton, 1975).

Normalization frequently entails the sexual development of individuals with disabilities to enable them to assume more normal lives. While there has been progress in designing and offering sex education programs for individuals with disabilities, several areas of concern have hampered their acceptance. These include (a) constraints imposed on the design and implementation of curricula owing to legal and social restraints that pertain to sexual taboos; (b) neglect by teacher training institutes in the preparation of professionals in special education who are trained in sex education; (c) problems in assessing the effects of teaching because of the nature of affective instructional goals interacting with a diversity of abilities in this population; and (d) conservatism on the part of parents that tends to place limitations on expectations of instruction. These problems hinder but do not preclude change. Models for the successful institutionalization of sex education for individuals with disabilities exist elsewhere, as in Sweden (Grunewald & Linner, 1979). Public policy regarding sex education for the person with disabilities is desirable given the obvious needs in this area (Craft, 1983). The person with disabilities should understand their sexuality, should be safe from sexual exploitation, and should become responsible in their sexual behavior (Cole & Cole, 1993; Craft, 1983).

REFERENCES

Balester, R. J. (1971). Sex education: Fact and fancy. *Journal of Special Education, 5,* 355–357.

Bass, M. S. (1974). Sex education for the handicapped. *Family Coordinator, 23,* 27–33.

Blom, G. E. (1971). Some considerations about the neglect of sex education in special education. *Journal of Special Education, 5,* 359–361.

Chubon, R. A. (1981). Development and evaluation of a sexuality and disability course for the helping professions. *Sexuality & Disability, 4,* 3–14.

Cole, S. S., & Cole, T. M. (1993). Sexuality, disability, and reproductive issues through the lifespan. *Sexuality & Disability, 11*(3), 189–205.

Craft, A. (1983). Sexuality and mental retardation: A review of the literature. In A. Craft & M. Craft (Eds.), *Sex education and counseling for mentally handicapped people.* Baltimore, MD: University Park Press.

Craft, A., & Craft, M. (1980). Sexuality and the mentally handicapped. In G. B. Simon (Ed.), *Modern management of mental handicap: A manual of practice.* Lancaster, England: MTP Press.

Craft, A., & Craft, M. (1981). Sexuality and mental handicap: A review. *British Journal of Psychiatry, 139,* 494–505.

Craft, M., & Craft, A. (1978). *Sex and the mentally handicapped.* London, England: Routledge & Kegan Paul.

Edmonson, B. (1980). Sociosexual education for the handicapped. *Exceptional Education Quarterly, 1,* 67–76.

Edmonson, B., & Wish, J. (1975). Sex knowledge and attitudes of moderately retarded males. *American Journal of Mental Deficiency, 80,* 172–179.

Fitz-Gerald, D., & Fitz-Gerald, M. (1979). Sexual implications of deaf-blindness. *Sexuality & Disability, 2*(3), 212–215.

Gordon, S. (1971a). Missing in special education. Sex. *Journal of Special Education, 5,* 351–354.

Gordon, S. (1971b). Okay, let's tell it like it is (instead of just making it look good). *Journal of Special Education, 5,* 379–381.

Gordon, S. (1975). Workshop: Sex education for the handicapped. In M. S. Bass & M. Gelof (Eds.), *Sexual rights and responsibilities of the mentally retarded.* Proceedings of the Conference of the American Association on Mental Deficiency, Washington, DC.

Grunewald, K., & Linner, B. (1979). Mentally retarded: Sexuality and normalization. *Current Sweden, 237–239.*

Hamre-Nietupski, S., & Ford, A. (1981). Sex education and related skills: A series of programs implemented with severely handicapped students. *Sexuality & Disability, 4,* 179–193.

Harris, A. (1974). What does "sex education" mean? In R. Rogers (Ed.), *Sex education: Rationale and reaction.* Cambridge, England: Cambridge University Press.

Jacobs, J. H. (1978). The mentally retarded and their need for sexuality education. *Psychiatric Opinion, 15,* 32–34.

Johnson, W. R. (1981). Sex education for special populations. In L. Brown (Ed.), *Sex education in the eighties.* New York, NY: Plenum Press.

Johnson, W. R., & Kempton, W. (1981). *Sex education and counseling of special groups.* Springfield, IL: Thomas.

Kempton, W. (1975). Sex education: A cooperative effort of parent and teacher. *Exceptional Children, 41,* 531–535.

Kempton, W. (1977). The mentally retarded person. In H. Gochros & J. Gochros (Eds.), *The sexually oppressed.* New York, NY: Association Press.

Kempton, W. (1978). The rights of the mentally ill and mentally retarded: Are sexual rights included? *Devereux Forum, 13,* 45–49.

Knappett, K., & Wagner, N. N. (1976). Sex education and the blind. *Education of the Visually Handicapped, 8,* 1–5.

Love, E. (1983). Parental and staff attitudes toward instruction in human sexuality for sensorially impaired students at the Alabama Institute for Deaf and Blind. *American Annals of the Deaf, 128,* 45–47.

May, D. C. (1980). Survey of sex education coursework in special education programs. *Journal of Special Education, 14,* 107–112.

Reich, M., & Harshman, H. (1971). Sex education for the handicapped youngsters, reality or repression? *Journal of Special Education, 5,* 373–377.

Sherwin, R. (1981). Sex and the law on a collision course. In W. R. Johnson (Ed.), *Sex in life.* Dubuque, IA: Brown.

Shindell, P. E. (1975). Sex education programs and the mentally retarded. *Journal of School Health, 45,* 88–90.

Tait, P. E., & Kessler, C. (1976). The way we get babies: A tactual sex education program. *New Outlook for the Blind, 70,* 116–120.

Thornton, C. E. (1979). A nurse-educator in sex and disability. *Sexuality & Disability, 2,* 28–32.

Torbett, D. S. (1974). A humanistic and futuristic approach to sex education for blind children. *New Outlook for the Blind, 68,* 210–215.

United Nations. (1971). *Declaration of general and special rights of the mentally handicapped.* New York, NY: U.N. Department of Social Affairs.

Vockell, E. L., & Mattick, P. (1972). Sex education for the mentally retarded: An analysis of problems, programs, and research. *Education & Training of the Mentally Retarded, 7,* 129–134.

Watson, G., & Rogers, R. S. (1980). Sexual instruction for the mildly retarded and normal adolescent. A comparison of educational approaches, parental expectations and pupil knowledge and attitude. *Health Education Journal, 39,* 88–95.

JACQUELINE
CUNNINGHAM
University of Florida

THOMAS OAKLAND
University of Florida

See also **Pediatric Aids; Social Isolation; Social Skills Instruction**

SEX INFORMATION AND EDUCATION COUNCIL OF THE UNITED STATES

The Sex Information and Education Council of the United States (SIECUS) is a nonprofit, voluntary health organization dedicated to the establishment and exchange of information about human sexual behavior. The council is funded primarily by foundation grants and individual contributions. The SIECUS provides information and responds to requests for consultation from churches, communities, school boards, and any other national or international health or educational organizations interested in establishing or improving their sex education programs. As a part of this concern, SIECUS developed a policy and resource guide concerning sex education for the mentally retarded individual (SIECUS, 1971).

The guide begins by observing that the mentally retarded individual has sexual feelings similar to those of all humans, but that because of possible confusion and misunderstanding, the mentally retarded student may need sexual guidance and education to understand sex and his or her own sexuality. The SIECUS provides instructional, curricular, and counseling information in the guide that will be useful in helping the mentally retarded individual to achieve this understanding. Finally, information is provided regarding printed materials, films and filmstrips, tapes, and other teaching aids that may be useful in sex education for the mentally retarded individual.

REFERENCE

SIECUS. (1971). *A resource guide in sex education for the mentally retarded.* New York, NY: Author.

JOHN R. BEATTIE
University of North Carolina at Charlotte

SEX RATIOS IN SPECIAL EDUCATION

As concern grows about sexual bias in society and its effect on children, attention is focusing on the classroom. Sex bias in education is of particular concern to the field of special education. Research indicates that more males than females are served in special education programs, and that the sex label has been recognized as having a profound impact on the education of children with disabilities. Gillespie and Fink (1974) report that the mere identification of children with disabilities as either male or female results in arbitrary practice and discriminatory judgments, and in intervention decisions that limit opportunities for personal and vocational development of those children and youths.

There is a belief among educators that boys are more in need of special services than girls; consequently, more male students are provided with special education services. Boys are much more likely to be referred and treated in all the major categories of disabilities; they are more likely to be identified as exhibiting reading problems, learning disabilities, and intellectual disabilities (Gillespie & Fink, 1974). However, female students are shown to be more in need of special education assistance on the basis of standardized test data (Sadker, Sadker, & Thomas, 1981).

Caplan (1977) suggests that girls with learning disabilities are less likely than boys with learning disabilities to be identified as learning disabled or to participate in special education programs. It is generally accepted among special educators that the male to female ratio in special education is about 3:1. Norman and Zigmond (1980) confirm that learning disabilities usually are identified as a male disorder; they find a ratio of 3.7:1. The authors report that the ratio is similar to the 3:1 ratio suggested by Kirk and Elkins (1975) and the 4.6:1 ratio reported by Lerner (1976). This has not been supported by research on reading disorders (Flynn & Rahbar, 1994).

Rubin and Balow (1971), in a longitudinal study of 967 kindergarten through third grade students, discovered that educationally defined behavior problems were exhibited by 41% of the children participating in their study. When results were reported by sex, the number of boys far exceeded the number of girls; boys were reported to have more attitude and behavior problems, to be receiving more special services, and to be repeating more grades. The authors suggested that teachers accept only a narrow range of behaviors, and that deviations outside this range are viewed as cause for intervention. This is supported by later research (Callahan, 1994).

Further evidence for the disproportionate number of males in special education comes from a study reported in Young, Algozzine, and Schmid (1979) examined behavior patterns of typically developing children, children emotional disturbance, and children with learning-disabilities, and found that boys outnumbered girls 8:1 in the emotionally disturbed sample and 9:1 in the learning-disabled sample.

Mirkin, Marston, and Deno (1982) investigated the referral-placement process and discovered that males were referred far in excess of females; however, this was true only for teacher judgment referrals. For referrals based on academic screening using curriculum-based tasks, no significant differences were found in the number of males versus females referred for special education. Furthermore, females who had been referred by teachers were rated as more problematic than the females referred by the screening tests.

A variety of theories have been proposed to account for the sex ratio discrepancy in special education. Caplan (1977) suggested that the boy/girl learning problem report ratio is aggravated by behavioral differences. Caplan and Kinsbourne (1974) discovered that girls who fail in school tend to behave in socially acceptable ways, but their male counterparts tend to react punitively and aggressively. On the basis of this discovery, the authors suggested that because teachers view aggression as the most disturbing type of behavior, they would be more likely to notice boys who are failing in school than their well-behaved, silent female counterparts. Consequently, boys would be more likely to be recognized as needing special attention, if only to get them out of the classroom.

Physiological explanations for the higher incidence of males in special education also have been offered; several categories of exceptionality such as that of learning disabilities have been explained on the basis of sex-linked genetic traits (Rossi, 1972). However, according to Singer and Osborn (1970), there are no known physiological causes to explain the higher number of males treated for intellectual disability. Singer and Osborn explain the high ratio of males to females receiving treatment as stemming from sociocultural expectations such as behavior differences and less societal tolerance for boys with academic problems.

Whatever the cause of the unbalanced ratio of males to females in special education, it is apparent that a bias exists. Special educators must recognize this discrepancy, establish its causes, and make the delivery of special education services more equitable.

REFERENCES

Callahan, K. (1994). Causes and implications of the male dominated sex ratio in programs for students with emotional and behavioral disorders. *Education and Treatment of Children, 17*(3), 228–243.

Caplan, P. J. (1977). Sex, age, behavior and school subject as determinants of report of learning problems. *Journal of Learning Disabilities, 5,* 314–316.

Caplan, P. J., & Kinsbourne, M. (1974). Sex differences in response to school failure. *Journal of Learning Disabilities, 4,* 232–235.

Flynn, J. M., & Rahbar, M. H. (1994). Prevalence of reading failure in boys compared with girls. *Psychology in the Schools, 3*(1), 66–71.

Gillespie, P. H., & Fink, A. H. (1974). The influence of sexism on the education of handicapped children. *Exceptional Children, 41,* 155–161.

Kirk, S. A., & Elkins, J. (1975). Characteristics of children enrolled in child service demonstration centres. *Journal of Learning Disabilities, 8,* 630–637.

Mirkin, P., Marston, D., & Deno, S. L. (1982). Direct and repeated measurement of academic skills: An alternative to traditional screening, referral, and identification of learning disabled students (Research Report No. 75). Minneapolis: University of Minnesota, Institute for Research on Learning Disabilities.

Norman, C. A., & Zigmond, N. (1980). Characteristics of children labeled and served as learning disabled in school systems affiliated with child service demonstration centers. *Journal of Learning Disabilities, 13*(9), 16–21.

Rossi, A. O. (1972). Genetics of learning disabilities. *Journal of Learning Disabilities, 5,* 489–496.

Rubin, R., & Balow, B. (1971). Learning and behavior disorders: A longitudinal study. *Exceptional Children, 38,* 293–299.

Sadker, D., Sadker, M., & Thomas, D. (1981). Sex equity and special education. *Pointer, 26*(1), 33–37.

Schlosser, L., & Algozzine, B. (1979). The disturbing child: He or she? *Alberta Journal of Educational Research, 25*(1), 30–36.

Singer, B. D., & Osborn, R. W. (1970). Special class and sex differences in admission patterns of the mentally retarded. *American Journal of Mental Deficiency, 75,* 162–190.

Young, S., Algozzine, B., & Schmid, R. (1979). The effects of assigned attributes and labels on children's peer accepted ratings. *Education & Training of the Mentally Retarded, 12,* 257–261.

KATHLEEN RODDEN-NORD
GERALD TINDAL
University of Oregon

See also Prereferral Intervention; Sex Differences in Learning Abilities

SEXUAL ALLEGATIONS IN DIVORCE (SAID) SYNDROME

As the name suggests, the SAID diagnosis applies to false allegations of sexual abuse in the context of contested divorces (Blush & Ross, 1987). Divorce cases that have been prolonged in the court system or have unresolved custody and visitation issues are more likely to generate false accusations. The critical element in diagnosis is considering the contextual issues indicating ulterior motives for the accusing parent.

There are no known data concerning prevalence rates, although some estimates suggest that 20%–55% of custody disputes may require investigation for allegations of sexual abuse. Estimates suggest that nearly 1 million children annually are involved with the divorce of their parents.

Characteristics

1. Child is typically female, under age of 8, and has been involved with contentious divorce proceedings.
2. Child is with custodial parent with histrionic or borderline personality.
3. Allegations of child's abuse surface through custodial parent.

Treatment begins with investigations by the child protective service workers, who generally have little training in recognizing the contextual factors that would define SAID and may hold unfounded beliefs about children (e.g., children don't lie, children cannot talk about things they haven't experienced). The remedy requires a properly trained multidisciplinary team to better evaluate the context of the allegations, including critiquing the

failings in the initial investigation and seeking a more comprehensive study. Contextual issues and personality of the accuser are as important to study as the alleged perpetrator and the alleged victim. The child must be interviewed in a fashion that decreases bias and suggestibility. Multiple data sources and contextual factors are given high priority in evaluating the allegations prior to taking legal actions that may have unintended effects (e.g., Daly, 1992).

Because teachers are mandated reporters of alleged abuse, they may have occasion to initialize the protective service investigation. It is critical that they maintain objectivity and create clear records of their observations and sources of information for any subsequent review of the case. There are no customary special education issues, although children with special needs are more likely to be involved in divorce situations due to added family stress. The added demands for special services and more costly care with such children may also increase the likelihood that SAID allegations will surface in this population. Prognosis improves with early detection and intervention by the courts, with continued court supervision over the first year of treatment. Additional empirical research on detection and treatment outcome is needed.

REFERENCES

Blush, G. J., & Ross, K. L. (1987). Sexual allegations in divorce: The SAID syndrome. *Conciliation Courts Review, 25*(1), 1–12.

Daly, L. W. (1992). Child sexual abuse allegations: Investigative approaches and identifying alternative hypotheses. *Issues in Child Abuse Accusations, 4*(3), 111–117.

DANIEL J. RYBICKI
ForenPsych Services

SEXUAL DISTURBANCES IN CHILDREN WITH DISABILITIES

Most of the research and study concerning sexual disturbances in individuals with disabilities has focused on those persons with physical disabilities and/or intellectual disabilities in institutional settings. Sexual problems also exist in other special populations but they are less well documented.

Monat (1982) outlines a number of problems found in the population of individuals with intellectual disabilities, including excessive and harmful masturbation, same-sex mutual masturbation, opposite-sex mutual masturbation, bestiality (especially in rural areas), sodomy, indecent exposure, child sexual abuse, lewd and lascivious behavior, and statutory rape. Undesired pregnancy is also a problem with individuals with intellectual disabilities, though not necessarily a sexual disturbance.

The approaches recommended today for dealing with sexual disturbances in individuals with intellectual disabilities ask that professionals who attempt to intervene be both knowledgeable about sex and sexuality and comfortable with this knowledge and their own sexuality. Recognition must be given to differing levels of cognitive ability within the population of individuals with intellectual disabilities that lead to variable levels of conceptual understanding and to the likelihood of different sexual behaviors and problems at different levels of functioning. In the past, especially in residential facilities, excessive reliance on moralization, punishment, and sterilization (Haavik & Menninger, 1981) colored attempts to deal with sexual matters. Current approaches generally focus on staff training for desensitization, concrete sex education (including on birth control, marriage, and parenthood), the dispelling of sexual myths, the importance of personal choice and responsibility, the appropriateness of personal social behavior, and the concept of privacy. The staff needs to follow through and review to be certain learning has occurred and the information has been retained. Sex counseling, which is designed to deal with the values and feelings surrounding sexuality, is now more readily available to complement sex education (which is more concerned with the transfer of relevant information).

In examining sexual disturbances, the type of living environment involved is important. With the present preference for community living and independence for individuals with disabilities, greater emphasis must be placed on appropriate community behavior, the legality of different sexual behaviors, personal choices, and the acceptance of responsibility. Adolescents with disabilities or an adult moving to a less restrictive setting must be aware of the dangers of venereal disease, acquired immune deficiency syndrome (AIDS), and prostitution (Monat, 1982). For some, especially those leaving certain residential facilities or protected home settings, community living arrangements, community-based training centers, or job sites of any type may offer the first true coeducational experiences. It has been shown that the knowledge of even noninstitutionalized young men and women with intellectual disabilities is often severely limited (Brantlinger, 1985). West (1979) characterized the observed sexual behavior of institutionalized adolescents and adults with severe intellectual disabilities as essentially normal and appropriate, though sometimes socially improper. He noted that the residents' "sexual activity was very often the only spontaneous cooperative mutual behavior observed and the only interresident interaction apart from aggression."

Attitudes have always played a large part in viewing the sexuality of individuals with disabilities. Sexual disturbances or problems in individuals with physical disabilities, especially those with essentially normal intelligence whose physical disability resulted from postnatal accident, injury, or trauma, have been something of an exception among the general population of individuals with disabilities. Professionals, and probably society in general, seem more willing to recognize the sexual rights of this group and to provide the understanding, support, and even the aids or prostheses to help them regain normal sexuality (Thorn-Gray & Kern, 1983). This view is markedly different from that found when dealing with individuals with intellectual disabilities.

Where education has been unsuccessful in preventing sexual disturbances or counseling has been ineffective in eliminating inappropriate sexual behaviors, a variety of behavioral approaches have been found to be successful in individual cases. Hurley and Sovner (1983) describe case reports on the effective use of response cost procedures, aversive conditioning, overcorrection, in vivo desensitization, and positive reinforcement in dealing with problems such as exhibitionism, public masturbation, public disrobing, and fetishism. Assaultive and inappropriate interpersonal sexual behaviors were successfully eliminated in an adolescent male with Down syndrome through a combination of differential reinforcement of other behaviors and naturalistic social restitution. The control of this behavior was able to be generalized to the student's teachers (Polvinale & Lutzker, 1980).

Sexual problems noted populations of individuals with learning disabilities have often been attributed to conceptual difficulties, disinhibition, or inadequate impulse control. Insights into sex-related difficulties in individuals with visual impairments can be found in Mangold and Mangold (1983) and in Welbourne et al. (1983). Information on sex and deafness can be found in *Sexuality and Deafness* (Gallaudet College, 1979).

REFERENCES

Brantlinger, E. A. (1985). Mildly mentally retarded secondary students' information and attitudes toward sexuality and sex education. *Education & Training of the Mentally Retarded, 20*, 99–108.

Gallaudet College. (1979). *Sexuality and deafness*. Washington, DC: Outreach Services.

Haavik, S. F., & Menninger, K. A. (1981). *Sexuality, law, and the developmentally disabled person: Legal and clinical aspects of marriage, parenthood and sterilization*. Baltimore, MD: Paul H. Brookes.

Hurley, A. D., & Sovner, R. (1983). Treatment of sexual deviation in mentally retarded persons. *Psychiatric Aspects of Mental Retardation Newsletter, 2*(4), 13–16.

Mangold, S. S., & Mangold, P. N. (1983). The adolescent visually impaired female. *Journal of Blindness & Visual Impairment, 77*(6), 250–255.

Monat, R. K. (1982). *Sexuality and the mentally retarded*. San Diego, CA: College-Hill.

Polvinale, R. A., & Lutzker, J. R. (1980). Elimination of an inappropriate sexual behavior by reinforcement and social restitution. *Mental Retardation, 18*(1), 27–30.

Thorn-Gray, B. E., & Kern, L. H. (1983). Sexual dysfunction associated with physical disability: A treatment guide for the rehabilitation practitioner. *Rehabilitation Literature, 44*(5–6), 138–144.

Welbourne, A., Lifschitz, S., Selvin, H., & Green, R. (1983). A comparison of the sexual learning experiences of visually impaired and sighted women. *Journal of Blindness & Visual Impairment, 77*(6), 256–261.

West, R. R. (1979). The sexual behaviour of the institutionalised severely retarded. *Australian Journal of Mental Retardation, 5*, II–L3.

JOHN D. WILSON
Elwyn Institutes

See also Masturbation, Compulsive; Mental Retardation; Self-Stimulation

SHAKEN BABY SYNDROME

Shaken baby syndrome (SBS) is a type of child abuse in which a child is violently shaken while being held by the extremities or shoulders (National Center on Shaken Baby Syndrome [NCSBS], 2000; Wyszynski, 1999). The shaking, which results in a whiplash-like acceleration and deceleration of the head, causes the brain to strike the inner surface of the skull and may have severe—even fatal—consequences. The trauma may lead to the classic triad of SBS: subdural hematoma, brain swelling, and retinal hemorrhages. Bruises of the part of the body held during shaking and fractures of the long bones and of the ribs may also be seen. Crying often triggers the caretaker or guardian's severe shaking (NCSBS, 2000).

Difficult to diagnose because symptoms are often internal, SBS is the leading cause of infant mortality and morbidity in the United States (NCSBS, 2000). Number of deaths and serious injuries has fluctuated in recent years between 750 and 3,750, and many cases remain undiagnosed, so incidence is unknown (Wyszynski, 1999).

Both presenting and outcome characteristics are highly variable, depending on the number and severity of shaking incidents and on the length of time between incidents. According to NCSBS (2000, paragraph 2): "Approximately 20% of cases are fatal in the first few days after injury and the survivors suffer from handicaps ranging from mild—learning disorders, behavioral changes—to moderate and severe, such as profound mental and developmental retardation, paralysis, blindness, inability to eat, or a permanent vegetative state."

Parents or caretakers may call for assistance or bring the infant to the emergency room claiming that it has accidentally fallen from a sofa, bed, or other relatively low object. However, although falls are common in young children, damage of the degree seen in SBS is virtually unknown in such falls. Some presenting characteristics—particularly intraocular hemorrhage—may be symptomatic and helpful in initiating evaluation (NCSBS, 2000). In many states, suspicion of child abuse mandates notification of appropriate authorities. Outcome characteristics of survivors are highly variable and may be seen in virtually any combination (Wyszynski, 1999).

Characteristics

Presenting

1. Range from minor to severe: irritability, lethargy, tremors, vomiting, bradycardia, hypothermia, poor feeding, failure to thrive, seizures, bulging or full fontanels, stupor, or coma

2. Highly symptomatic: subdural hematoma, brain swelling, or retinal hemorrhages

Outcome

1. Mental retardation

2. Motor disorders, including seizure disorders, paralysis, spasticity, and inability to eat

3. Visual and auditory impairments

4. Learning disabilities, behavior disorders, and personality change

---

Treatment of a child with SBS obviously depends on the type and degree of neurological damage and the length of time since the shaking occurred. Often a team approach following a protocol calling for the same interventions used in other types of traumatic brain injuries should immediately follow diagnosis (Wyszynski, 1999). Social service agencies are invariably called to assess the risk to the child in the home. Immediate action should be taken to stabilize the victim's condition. Because brain damage cannot be reversed, much treatment is supportive. According to the Shaken Baby Alliance (1999), a child may need up to seven different therapies, including cognitive rehabilitation and occupational, physical, and speech therapies. Adaptive technology may help reduce the impact of sensory and motor impairments. In some instances the child will need full-time assistance. Appropriate classroom setting will need to be individually determined.

Clearly the best approach to SBS is prevention through education or perhaps direct training of parents, guardians, and other child-care providers. Parents should inform all who care for their infant of the dangers of shaking (NCSBS,

2000). Stress management classes may be helpful in some situations. Clearly, at least hypothetically, SBS is 100% preventable.

REFERENCES

National Center on Shaken Baby Syndrome. (2000). SBS questions. Retrieved from http://www.dontshake.com

The Shaken Baby Alliance. (1999). Impact on the family. Retrieved from http://www.shakenbaby.com

Wyszynski, M. E. (1999). Shaken baby syndrome: Identification, intervention, and prevention. *Clinical Excellence for Nurse Practitioners, 3*, 262–267.

PAULA KILPATRICK
ROBERT T. BROWN
*University of North Carolina,
Wilmington*

SHELTERED WORKSHOPS

The concept of the sheltered workshop was introduced in the United States in 1838 by the Perkins Institute for the Blind. The early workshop programs that followed provided sheltered employment for those whose handicapping conditions precluded competitive employment.

Federal involvement with sheltered workshops came about 100 years later. In an effort to help sheltered workshops compete with other businesses for contracts, the 1938 amendments to the Vocational Rehabilitation Act (PL 75-497) allowed workshops to pay below-minimum wages to employees.

With the passage of the Vocational Rehabilitation Act of 1943 (PL 78-113), persons with intellectual disabilities were considered eligible for rehabilitation services. This initiated a change in rehabilitation programs in the United States. For the first time, there was recognition of persons who had never been employed.

The Vocational Rehabilitation Act amendments of 1965 (PL 89-333) expanded the definition of "gainful employment" to include not only competitive but also sheltered employment. There was an emphasis on the provision of services that would lead toward gainful sheltered employment for more severely disabled individuals. According to Snell (1983):

> Sheltered employment is when an individual is receiving subsidized wages or working for less than minimum wage, with handicapped co-workers at a job that provides limited advancement to competitive work settings and that is organized primarily for therapeutic habilitation or sheltered production. (p. 504)

The Rehabilitation Act of 1973 (PL 93-112) and the continuation amendments up to 1992 emphasized the provision of services that would lead toward gainful sheltered employment for persons with severe disabilities and the transition from school work.

Special education programs help prepare young adults with disabilities to work in sheltered workshops. According to Bigge (1982), the special education curriculum should include transition skills, work evaluation, work adjustment, work experience, vocational skills, and on-the-job training programs.

The sheltered workshop is the most widely used type of vocational training facility for adults with disabilities. Sheltered workshops can be classified into three general types: regular program workshops; work activities centers; and adult day programs. Regular program workshops (or transitional workshops) provide therapies and work intended to foster readiness for competitive employment. The Department of Labor requires that workers earn no less than 50% of minimum wages. Work activities centers (WACs) provide training, support, and extended employment in a sheltered environment to more severely disabled adults. A wage ceiling of 50% of minimum wage has been set for WACs clients. The Fair Labor Standards Act, as amended in 1966, defines regular program workshops and work activities centers. Both are monitored by the Department of Labor. Adult day programs, managed by state developmental disabilities agencies, provide nonvocational services such as socialization, communication skills, and basic work orientation. The primary goal of adult day programs is the acquisition of basic living skills, leading to a decrease in maladaptive behavior and movement toward more vocationally oriented programs.

A sheltered workshop operates as a business. It generally engages in one of three types of business activities: contracting, prime manufacturing, or reclamation. In contracting, there is an agreement that a sheltered workshop will complete a specified job within a specified time for a given price. Workshops bid competitively for each job. Prime manufacturing is the designing, producing, marketing, and shipping of a complete product. A reclamation operation is one in which a workshop purchases or collects salvageable material, performs a reclamation operation, and then sells the reclaimed product. Recently, sheltered workshops have been closing and competitive employment (supported employment, for example) has been substituted. The closure of some workshops has created a division in scholars as to what the best interests are for employment of persons with disabilities (Block, 1997).

This entry has been informed by the sources listed below.

REFERENCES

Bigge, J. L. (1982). *Teaching individuals with physical and multiple disabilities* (2nd ed.). Columbus, OH: Merrill.

Block, S. R. (1997). Closing the sheltered workshop. Toward competitive employment opportunities for persons with developmental disabilities. *Journal of Vocational Rehabilitation, 9*(3), 267–275.

Heward, W. L., & Orlansky, M. D. (1984). *Exceptional children* (2nd ed.). Columbus, OH: Merrill.

Lynch, K. P., Kiernan, J. A., & Stark, J. A. (1982). *Prevocational and vocational education for special needs youth*. Baltimore, MD: Paul H. Brookes.

Mori, A. A., & Masters, L. F. (1983). *Teaching the severely mentally retarded*. Germantown, MD: Aspen.

Schreerenberger, R. C. (1983). *A history of mental retardation*. Baltimore, MD: Paul H. Brookes.

Snell, M. A. (1983). *Systematic instruction of the moderately and severely handicapped* (2nd ed.). Columbus, OH: Merrill.

CAROLE REITER GOTHELF
Hunter College,
City University of New York

See also Vocational Rehabilitation Counseling; Vocational Education

SHENJING SHUAIRUO

Shenjing shuairuo, or neurasthenia, is a culture-bound syndrome found predominately in China, and other East Asian cultures, such as Hong Kong and Korea. In many cases, this syndrome meets the criteria for *Diagnostic and Statistical Manual of Mental Disorders–Fourth Edition* (*DMS-IV*) mood or anxiety disorder and is commonly referred to as "weakness of nerves" (American Psychiatric Association, 1994, p. 849). This disorder is also included in the Chinese Classification of Mental Disorders.

Shenjing shuairuo is the second most common diagnosis in Chinese psychiatric hospitals, and one of the most common neuropsychological diagnoses in general (Weber, 2000). This disorder is also known by a number of indigenous terms: shen-ch'ing, shuai-jo, or huo-ch'ta. According to Chan et al. (2000, p. 2), shenjing shuairuo is closely related to chronic fatigue syndrome in Western cultures such that "clinical similarity...has led to the contention that chronic fatigue syndrome and [shenjing shuairuo] are equivalent disorders cloaked in disparate terminology." According to studies by Chan et al. (2000), pure shenjing shuairuo, or neurasthenia, had a 12-month prevalence rate of 3.66% among Chinese Americans. This rate was higher than the rate of depressive or anxiety disorders. This study thus concluded that "subthreshold anxiety-depression with a symptom profile remarkably similar to that of 'weakness of nerves' has been shown to be the most common form of primary care psychiatric morbidity in the United States" (Chan et al., 2000 p. 2). This disorder apparently has little prevalence among children and affects men and women at similar rates.

Characteristics

1. Physical and mental fatigue
2. Dizziness
3. Headaches
4. Difficulties with concentration
5. Sleep disturbance
6. Memory loss

As stated by Chan et al. (2000, p. 8), "weakness of nerves is flexibly defined by the presence of any three symptoms out of five nonhierarchical groups of fatigue, pain, dysphoria, mental agitation, and sleep symptoms."

This illness is quite prevalent in China and other Asian cultures such that treatment is traditionally referred to medical professionals, especially when the illness presents in somatoform symptoms. It is very important to construct a medical history of the individual with the disorder as well as determine the level of acculturation. Typically, patients take the following assessments to determine levels of acculturation and also to determine whether diagnosis and subsequent medical referral are necessary: Explanatory Interview Catalogue, Structured Clinical Interview for DSM-III-R (SCID), Hamilton Range Scale for Depression, and the Hamilton Rating Scale for Anxiety (Chan et al., 2000).

The likelihood of this disorder's occurring in adolescence or other school-age children is not known and would probably be determined by level of acculturation for high school students. Special education services would probably be unavailable for this condition due to the difficulty of diagnosis and comorbidity with other medical conditions.

REFERENCES

American Psychiatric Association. (1994). *Diagnostic and statistical manual of mental disorders* (4th ed.). Washington, DC: Author.

Chan, C., Chen, C., Lee, D., Lee, S., Weiss, M., & Wing, Y. (2000). *Psychiatric morbidity and illness experience of primary care patients with chronic fatigue in Hong Kong*. Retrieved from http://ajp.psychiatryonline.org/cgi/content/full/157/3/380

Weber, C. (2000). *Shenjing shuairuo: The case of neurasthenia*. Retrieved from http://weber.ucsd.edu/~thall/cbs_neu.html

KIELY ANN FLETCHER
Ohio State University

SHORT-CHAIN ACYL COA DEHYDROGENASE (SCAD)

Short-chain acyl coa dehydrogenase (SCAD) deficiency is an extremely rare inherited mitochondrial fatty acid oxidation disorder first reported in 1987. SCAD has been identified in only a few patients with highly variable clinical features, including (a) a lethal neonatal syndrome; (b) psychomotor retardation, muscle weakness, microcephaly, and poor feeding, all appearing during infancy; and (c) a myopathy in adulthood. Diagnosis may be based on the specific metabolite profile in blood and urine.

Characteristics

1. A lethal neonatal syndrome with failure to thrive, developmental delay, microcephaly, feeding difficulties, vomiting, lethargy, hypertonia, chronic acidosis, seizures, and myopathy
2. A myopathy in adulthood

Treatment involves limitation of fasting stress and dietary fat. Many children with mitochondrial disorders might have normal intelligence, static mental retardation, or developmental delay. Children may have long periods with a stable neurological picture simulating a static encephalopathy and later deteriorate either in an acute or in a slowly progressive manner (Nissenkorn et al., 1999). Many of these children will qualify for services under the classification of other health impaired as a result of their medical complications.

This disorder has been reported in two neonates. One patient died in the neonatal period with hepatic disease and brain edema. Another patient survived with apparently normal development to the age of 2 years. Current research is focused on pathogenesis of the variations and natural history of children with SCAD. Clinical studies are necessary to establish the incidence of SCAD deficiency and to define the spectrum of its clinical manifestations (Corydon et al., 2001).

REFERENCES

Corydon, M. J., Vockley, J., Rinaldo, P., Rhead, W. J., Kjeldsen, M., Winter, V., ... Gregersen, N. (2001). Role of common gene variations in the molecular pathogenesis of short-chain acyl coa dehydrogenase (SCAD). *Pediatric Research, 49*, 18–23.

Nissenkorn, A., Zeharia, A., Lev, D., Fatal-Valevski, A., Barash, V., Gutman, A., ... Lerman-Sagie, T. (1999). Multiple presentation of mitochondrial disorders. *Archives of Disease in Childhood, 81*(3), 209–214.

VIRDETTE L. BRUMM
Children's Hospital,
Los Angeles Keck / USC School of Medicine

SIBLINGS OF INDIVIDUALS WITH DISABILITIES

Siblings of individuals with disabilities have received little research attention compared with the literature available on the effects of a child with disabilities on parents (Crnic, Friedrich, & Greenberg, 1983; Drew, Logan, & Hardman, 1984; Trevino, 1979). The available research, however, suggests that typically developing siblings are a population at risk for behavioral problems, the degree to which is influenced by a number of variables and factors (Crnic et al., 1983; Gargiulo, 1984; Trevino, 1979). Specific factors that appear to interact and contribute to sibling adjustment include the number of typically developing siblings in the family (Powell & Ogle, 1985), the age and gender of siblings (Crnic et al., 1983; Grossman, 1972), and parental response and attitude toward the child with a disability (Trevino, 1979). Trevino (1979) reports that prospects for typically developing siblings having difficulty in adjusting increase when (a) there are only two siblings in the family, one with a disability and one without; (b) the typically developing sibling is close in age to or younger than the sibling with a disability or is the oldest female child; (c) the typically developing child and the child with a disability are the same sex; and (d) the parents are unable to accept the disability. Schwirian (1976), Farber (1959), and Cleveland and Miller (1977) found that the female sibling's role demanded more parent-surrogate duties as she was expected to help care for the child with a disability when she was at home. In addition, sibling literature emphasizes healthy and honest parental attitudes and behaviors toward the child with disabilities as essential to the sibling's positive growth and development.

Grossman (1972) found that socioeconomic status (SES) can also affect sibling responses to a child with a disability. Middle-class families and those from higher SES families tended to be more financially secure and better prepared to use outside resources such as respite care services, thus lessening a youngster's responsibility of caring for a sibling with a disability.

The emotional responses of siblings of individuals with disabilities have been reported to include hostility, guilt, fear, shame, embarrassment, and rejection. Crnic et al. (1983) found that the presence of a child with intellectual disabilities has a detrimental effect on a typically developing sibling's (particularly a female's) individual functioning. This involves high degrees of anxiety, conflicts with parents, and problems in social and interpersonal relationships. On the other hand, Farber (1960) reported, after an extensive study, that many siblings adopted life goals toward dedication and sacrifice (Crnic et al., 1983).

Although the concerns of siblings vary according to the nature and degree of severity of their sibling's disability, key concerns, such as how to deal with parents, what to tell friends, and what kind of future they can expect for their sibling with a disability, appear to be similar across categories of disabilities (Murphy, 1979). If the needs and concerns of siblings are not met, they may result in problems and negative feelings.

The psychological and behavioral problems that may result from having a sibling with disabilities is a reality that must be dealt with by parents and professionals. Siblings can benefit from the experience of having a sibling with disabilities if they are introduced to the situation in an understanding and compassionate way. Siblings and parents should seek support from family counselors, religious organizations, nonprofit agencies, and sibling support groups that focus on the individual needs, attitudes, concerns, and feelings of the nondisabled sibling. Teachers should be alerted to the child's family situation to provide additional support and information.

REFERENCES

Cleveland, D. W., & Miller, N. (1977). Attitudes and life commitments of older siblings of mentally retarded adults: An exploratory study. *Mental Retardation, 15,* 38–41.

Crnic, K. A., Friedrich, W. N., & Greenberg, M. T. (1983). Adaptation of families with mentally retarded children: A model of stress, coping and family ecology. *American Journal of Mental Deficiency, 88,* 125–139.

Drew, C. J., Logan, D. R., & Hardman, M. L. (Eds.). (1984). *Mental retardation: A life cycle approach* (3rd ed.). St. Louis, MO: Times/Mirror Mosby.

Farber, B. (1959). Effects of a severely mentally retarded child on family integration. *Monographs of the Society for Research in Child Development, 24* (whole No. 71).

Farber, B. (1960). Family organization and crisis: Maintenance of integration in families with a severely retarded child. *Monographs of the Society for Research in Child Development, 25,* 1–95.

Gargiulo, R. M. (1984). Understanding family dynamics. In R. M. Gargiulo (Ed.), *Working with parents of exceptional children* (pp. 41–64). Boston, MA: Houghton Mifflin.

Grossman, F. K. (1972). *Brothers and sisters of retarded children: An exploratory study.* Syracuse, NY: Syracuse University Press.

Murphy, A. T. (1979). Members of the family: Sisters and brothers of the handicapped. *Volta Review, 81,* 352–354.

Powell, T. H., & Ogle, P. A. (1985). *Brothers and sisters in the family system.* Baltimore, MD: Paul H. Brookes.

Schwirian, P. M. (1976). Effects of the presence of a hearing impaired preschool child in the family on behavior patterns of older "normal" siblings. *American Annals of the Deaf, 121,* 373–380.

Trevino, F. (1979). Siblings of handicapped children: Identifying those at risk. *Social Casework: Journal of Contemporary Social Work, 62,* 488–493.

MARSHA H. LUPI
Hunter College,
City University of New York

See also **Family Response to a Child With Disabilities; Respite Care**

SICARD, ABBÉ ROCHE AMBROISE CUCURRON (1742–1822)

Abbé Roche Ambroise Cucurron Sicard, educator of the deaf, studied with Abbé Epée at the National Institution for Deaf-Mutes in Paris and, in 1782, opened a school for the deaf at Bordeaux. Sicard succeeded Epée at the National Institution and, except for a few years during the French Revolution, served as its director until his death in 1822. Sicard made many improvements in Epée's educational methods. His most important publication was a dictionary of signs, a work begun by Epée.

The beginning of education for the deaf in the United States was greatly influenced by Sicard. He invited Thomas Gallaudet, who was planning the first school for the deaf in the United States, to observe the methods employed at the National Institute in Paris, with the result that Gallaudet became proficient in Sicard's methods. In addition, Sicard provided Gallaudet with his first teacher, Laurent Clerc.

This entry has been informed by the sources listed below.

REFERENCES

Bender, R. E. (1970). *The conquest of deafness.* Cleveland, OH: Case Western Reserve University Press.

Lane, H. (1984). *When the mind hears.* New York, NY: Random House.

PAUL IRVINE
Katonah, New York

SICKLE-CELL DISEASE

Sickle-cell disease is an inherited blood disorder that occurs as two conditions, sickle-cell anemia (SCA) and sickle-cell trait (SCT). Sickle-cell anemia is the more serious of the two conditions; it can be defined as an abnormality of the hemoglobin molecule, the oxygen-carrying protein in the red blood cells. Oxygen-carrying red blood cells are usually round and flexible. Under certain conditions, the red blood cells of a person with sickle-cell anemia may change into a crescent or sickle cell. This unusual shape causes the cells to adhere in the spleen and other areas, leading to their destruction. This results in a shortage of red blood cells, which has serious consequences for the individual with SCA (Haslam & Valletutti, 1975; March of Dimes, 1985). These consequences include fever, abdominal discomfort, bone pain, damage to the brain, lungs, and kidneys, and, for some, death in childhood or early adulthood (Haslam & Valletutti, 1975; March of Dimes, 1985; National Association for Sickle Cell Disease [NASCD], (1978). Individuals with SCA will experience episodes of pain known as sickle-cell crisis. During these periods, the sickled cells become trapped in tiny blood vessels. This blocks other red blood cells behind them, which lose oxygen and become sickle-shaped, totally blocking the vessels. When the bone marrow inadequately produces red blood cells, the child experiences an aplastic crisis and requires blood transfusion (Weiner, 1973). These crises and their effects vary greatly from person to person. Most people with SCA enjoy reasonably good health much of the time (March of Dimes, 1985; NASCD, 1978).

Sickle-cell anemia occurs when a sickle-cell gene is inherited from each parent. A person with sickle-cell anemia has sickle cells in the bloodstream and has sickle-cell disease. The second condition, sickle-cell trait (SCT), occurs when a sickle-cell gene is inherited from one parent and a normal gene from the other. A person with sickle-cell trait does not have sickle cells in the bloodstream and does not have sickle-cell disease. Persons with SCT may pass the sickle-cell gene on to their offspring (March of Dimes, 1985; NASCD, 1978; Whitten, 1974). As an autosomal recessive disorder, children of parents who both carry the sickle-cell gene have a 50% chance of inheriting SCT, a 25% chance of being a carrier, and a 25% chance of having SCA (Whitten, 1974).

In the United States, sickle-cell disease occurs most frequently among Blacks and Hispanics of Caribbean ancestry. About 1 in every 400 to 600 Blacks and 1 in every 1,000 to 1,500 Hispanics inherit sickle-cell disease (March of Dimes, 1985). Approximately 1 in 12 Black Americans carry a gene for sickle-cell trait (NASCD, 1978). Less commonly affected peoples include those whose ancestors lived in countries bordering on the Mediterranean Sea (Greeks, Maltese, Portuguese, Arabians; NASCD, 1978).

There is no known cure for sickle-cell anemia. However, a number of therapies for reducing the severity and frequency of crises are being tried (March of Dimes, 1985; Weiner, 1973). A blood test for sickle-cell anemia and its trait is readily available; it is called hemoglobin electrophoresis. There is also a prenatal test to determine whether the fetus will develop sickle anemia or be a carrier.

The child with SCA may need to be placed in an educational program that is geared to his or her physical capabilities. Services may assist the child and family in many areas such as adaptation to chronic illness and pain management (Conner-Warren, 1996). Since many individuals with SCA tire easily, children should be encouraged to participate in most school activities of other children their age with the understanding that they may rest more frequently. If communication between the child and family has been open and honest concerning SCA, then the child can develop healthy social attitudes and self-reliance (NASCD, 1978).

REFERENCES

Conner-Warren, R. L. (1996). Pain intensity and home pain management of children with sickle-cell disease. *Issues in Comprehensive Pediatric Nursing, 19*(3), 183–195.

Haslam, R. M. A., & Valletutti, P. J. (1975). *Medical problems in the classroom*. Baltimore, MD: University Park Press.

March of Dimes. (1985). *Genetics series: Sickle cell anemia*. White Plains, NY: Author.

National Association for Sickle Cell Disease (NASCD). (1978). *Sickle cell disease: Tell the facts, quell the fables*. Los Angeles, CA: Author.

Weiner, F. (1973). *Help for the handicapped child*. New York, NY: McGraw-Hill.

Whitten, C. F. (1974). *Fact sheet on sickle cell trait and anemia*. Los Angeles, CA: National Association for Sickle-Cell Disease.

MARSHA H. LUPI
Hunter College,
City University of New York

SIDIS, WILLIAM JAMES (1898–1944)

William James Sidis was a famous child prodigy of the early 20th century who came to a tragic end after leading a short, largely unfulfilled life. Sidis's history and early demise are often cited in early literature opposing acceleration and other aspects of special education for the intellectually gifted. Much of Sidis's life has been distorted in various informal accounts. Montour (1977) has characterized the use of Sidis's story to deny acceleration to intellectually advanced children as the Sidis fallacy. Simply stated, the Sidis fallacy denotes "early ripe, early rot."

In 1909, at the age of 11, Sidis entered Harvard College. A year later he lectured on higher mathematics at the Harvard Mathematical Club. Sidis had performed remarkably in intellectual endeavors throughout his life. By Montour's (1977) account, by the age of 3 he read fluently with good comprehension; he was writing with a pencil 6 months later. By age 4, Sidis was a fluent typist. When he was 6, Sidis could read English, Russian, French, German, and Hebrew; he learned Latin and Greek shortly thereafter. At the age of 8, Sidis passed the entrance exam at the Massachusetts Institute of Technology, developed a new table of logarithms employing base 12 instead of base 10, and passed the Harvard Medical School exam in anatomy. He was well qualified to enter Harvard at that time but was denied entrance based on his age. Sidis earned his BA in 1914, although it has been reported that he completed his work for the degree 2 years earlier. Sidis pursued some graduate study in several fields, including a year in law school, but never earned an advanced degree. He spurned academia after an unsuccessful year as a professor at Rice University at age 20. He became sullen, cynical, and withdrawn from society (Montour, 1977). Sidis chose to live as a loner, working at low-level clerical jobs until his death in 1944, at the age of 46, from a stroke.

Sidis's academic contributions were limited to two books. In 1926 he published *Notes on the Collection of Transfers*. A more serious volume, published in 1925 (but written in 1919 and 1920), *The Animate and Inanimate*, was devoted to a proof of James's theory of reserve energy.

Sidis's turn against academia and his choice to drop out of society seems related to his intellectual talent and precocity only in the most indirect fashion; it was certainly not a result of his academic acceleration. Montour (1977) argues credibly that it was the result of a rebellion against an overbearing, domineering, but emotionally barren father who rejected Sidis at the first sign of any weakness. Although the Sidis case is often cited in opposition to academic acceleration, there is little to support such a position on the basis of Sidis's history. In fact, far more cases of successful acceleration are present with outcomes strongly supportive of acceleration programs. Norbert Wiener (a classmate of Sidis), John Stuart Mill, Merrill Kenneth Wolf, David Noel Freedman, and John Raden Platt are but a few of many such successes (Montour, 1977). Indeed, educational acceleration will be the method of choice for the education of many intellectually precocious youths.

"It was not extreme educational acceleration that destroyed William James Sidis emotionally and mentally, but instead an interaction of paternal exploitation and emotional starvation" (Montour, 1977, p. 276). The events of Sidis's life are often exaggerated and misstated. The Sidis fallacy has restricted the education of the gifted and persists in some educational programs even today; it is yet another myth that afflicts programs for the gifted.

REFERENCES

Montour, K. (1977). William James Sidis, the broken twig. *American Psychologist, 32*, 265–279.

Sidis, W. J. (1925). *The animate and inanimate*. Boston, MA: Badger.

Sidis, W. J. (1926). *Notes on the collection of transfer*. Philadelphia, PA: Dorrance.

CECIL R. REYNOLDS
Texas A&M University

See also Acceleration of Gifted Children; Study of
    Mathematically Precocious Youth

SIDIS FALLACY (*See* Sidis, William James)

SIGHT-SAVING CLASSES

For much of the 20th century it was common to educate children with low vision in "sight-saving classes." This was done in public schools as well as in residential facilities. Such classes for partially sighted children were begun in public schools as far back as 1913 (Livingston, 1986).

The notion behind these sight-saving classes was that a low-vision child's residual vision would be damaged by overuse. The emphasis, thus, was on conserving the child's vision as far as possible. This meant that children whose vision was impaired but still usable were removed from presumably visually stressful situations by reducing visual demands made on them. Some were even educated in dark rooms or blindfolded. The situation today is dramatically altered. It is now believed that all children, including visually impaired ones, benefit from using their visual abilities as much as possible.

REFERENCE

Livingston, R. (1986). Visual impairments. In N. G. Haring & L. McCormick (Eds.), *Exceptional children and youth* (4th ed., pp. 398–429). Columbus, OH: Merrill.

MARY MURRAY
Journal of Special Education

See also Low Vision; Partially Sighted

SIGN LANGUAGE

Sign language is a general term that refers to any gestural/visual language that makes use of specific shapes and movements of the fingers, hands, and arms, as well as movements of the eyes, face, head, and body. There is no international system that is comprehensible to all deaf people. There exists a British Sign Language, a Spanish Sign Language, and Israeli Sign Language and probably a sing language in every country where deaf people have needed to communicate among themselves rapidly, efficiently, and visually without the use of pad and pencil.

American Sign Language, sometimes called Ameslan or ASL, was created over the years by the deaf community in the United States. In ASL, one hand shape frequently denotes a concept. American Sign Language must be differentiated from finger spelling or dactylology, which is the use of hand configurations to denote the letters of the alphabet. In finger spelling, one hand shape stands for one letter. Sometimes finger spelling is used to spell out the English equivalent for a sign (especially proper nouns) when ASL is used. In ASL, interpreters frequently finger spell the word for a technical or uncommon sign for the first time it is used during a conference. Finger spelling with speech and speech reading for additional visual and acoustic cues is called the Rochester method (Quigley & Paul, 1984).

Total communication is the use of signs, finger spelling, speech, speech reading, and, in reality, any and all modes of communication with hearing-impaired people. Although it is possible for ASL to be used as the manual component of total communication, the two terms are not synonymous.

Signed English, developed in the 1960s under the direction of Harry Bornstein of Gallaudet College, is a manually coded system of English used in conjunction with speech. It was devised to facilitate the acquisition of English by young deaf children. It incorporates special signs to indicate affixes (prefixes like *un-*, and suffixes like *-s* and *-ment*) and verb tense.

Signed English is basically an educational tool used in some schools for deaf students. Its use of the specific tense and affix markers slows down the communication process considerably (Schlessinger & Namir, 1978).

Research into the linguistic nature of American Sign Language has shown that the grammar of ASL, like the grammar of all languages, consists of a finite set of rules with which an infinite number of sentences can be created or generated. Deaf children and hearing children of deaf parents who use ASL acquire these rules in much the same way that hearing children abstract linguistic rules from the spoken language to which they are exposed (Bellugi and Klima, 1985). Courses in sign language are offered in many colleges, schools for deaf students, centers for continuing education, and some public libraries. Courses in sign language for hearing learners may also enhance language acquisition because of the multimodal advantage. (Daniels, 1994). For this reason many parents attend sign language classes before the birth of their baby and use it as a communication system during the early life of their child. Parents report that the use of sign language reduces the frustration of both the child and parent when the baby can use a gesture or sign to communicate their wants and needs.

Since the advent of cochlear implants there has been a movement by some educators to limit the use of sign language for any child utilizing a cochlear implant. This has reestablished the conflict between oral and manual (visual) methods of communication which have been present since the onset of education for the deaf. In today's deaf community there is a great deal of respect for American Sign Language. People who are deaf feel that sign language is their basic biological system of communication and they therefore resent suggestions that a deaf child cannot be exposed to sign language as it will harm them. Individuals who are in strong support of American Sign Language are referred to as Deaf (utilizing the capital *D*). Those who prefer speech and do not belong to the deaf cultural community are referred to as deaf (utilizing the lowercase *d*). To date there has been no research which has conclusively indicated that the use of visual cues such as that provided in American Sign Language combined with oral/auditory cues is harmful (Zapien, 1998).

REFERENCES

Bellugi, U., & Klima, E. (1985). The acquisition of three morphological systems in American Sign Language. In F. Powell (Ed.), *Education of the hearing-impaired child*. San Diego, CA: College Hill.

Daniels, M. (1994). The effect of sign language on hearing children's language development. *Communication Education*, *43*(4), 291–298.

Quigley, S. & Paul, P. (1984). *Language and deafness*. San Diego, CA: College Hill.

Schlessinger, I., & Namir, L.(1978). *Sign language of the deaf*. New York, NY: Academic Press.

Zapien, C. (1998, July 15). Options in deaf education—History, methodologies, and strategies for surviving the system. Excerpted by *Exceptional Parent Magazine*.

ROSEMARY GAFFNEY
Hunter College, City University of New York

PATRICIA SCHERER
International Center on Deafness and the Arts
Fourth edition

See also Lipreading/Speech reading; Rochester Method; Total Communication

SIMULTANEOUS COGNITIVE PROCESSING (*See* Sequential and Simultaneous Cognitive Processing)

SINGLE-SUBJECT RESEARCH DESIGN

Education has become more scientific over the past several decades through the use of educational technologies such as formative assessment, evidence-based interventions, and school-wide problem-solving models (e.g., response to intervention and positive behavior supports). However, an applied experimental methodology is also needed because without true experimental designs, one can never defensibly know if any of the aforementioned technologies have been effective. The purpose of this entry is to provide a brief overview of single-case design (SCD) as the ideal candidate for the applied experimental methodology for education (for a more complete overview, see Riley-Tillman & Burns, 2009 or Kennedy, 2005).

SCD is a category of experimental methodology with an extensive history of use in a variety of disciplines (Kazdin, 1982). Interestingly, SCD may be generally unknown to most educational professionals. The limited use of SCD in day-to-day educational practice is unfortunate because

SCD allows for educational professionals to defensibly document the effect of interventions, assess the role of interventions in observed changes, and decide whether or not gathered information has general programming utility (Riley-Tillman & Burns, 2009). This level of understanding of intervention effectiveness is ideal in modern educational systems that embrace a problem-solving orientation requiring defensible statements about intervention effectiveness.

An overview of SCD should start with baseline logic. Baseline logic is the experimental framework for the development of single-case (e.g., a subject, small group or other) experiments (Cooper, Heron, & Heward, 2007; Riley-Tillman & Burns, 2009; Sidman, 1960). Specifically, baseline logic applied setting is comprised of four steps: (1) Prediction, (2) Affirmation of the Consequent (AoC), (3) Verification, and (4) Replication by Affirmation of the Consequent. Each of these is now briefly reviewed.

The goal of the prediction phase (often called baseline) is to document what the preintervention behavior looks like. The collection of a stream of outcome data (a minimum of 3 to 5 data points) provides a comparison for the next stage. One of the best ways to think about the predication statement is "this is what the child's behavior would look like if we don't change anything." As such, it is critical that enough data are collected so that one can be confident in such a statement.

Affirmation of the consequent is the process of conducting an intervention that is expected to change the target behavior in a positive manner. If the intervention works then the data in the intervention phase should alter in the predicted direction away from the data in the prediction phase. If this occurs (e.g., a child's on-task behavior or reading fluency increases after an intervention is applied as predicted) then one has the first piece of evidence that the intervention is working. While it would be simple at this stage to suggest that the intervention caused the change, there is a chance that some other alteration was made at the same time the intervention was applied. For example, perhaps the parents concurrently started having the child tutored outside of the school environment that results in the increase in reading fluency. Because it is possible that some other variable (other than the intervention) caused the positive change, the next phase of verification may be conducted in order to strengthen the interventionist's confidence that the intervention is responsible for the change in the target behavior.

In the verification phase the interventionist will go back to baseline by removing the intervention (in an ABAB design) or by concurrently extending a baseline in a similar setting where the intervention has not been implemented (in a multiple baseline design). In the case of a removed intervention the change observed in the AoC/intervention phase to be stopped (e.g., a positive reading fluency trend observed in the intervention phase decreasing) or reversed (e.g., increase in on-task behavior)

to baseline levels. When observed, this phase increases the confidence that the intervention was responsible for the observed positive effect. To extend confidence that the intervention is responsible for an observed change in the target behavior, the intervention is reapplied in the replication phase.

The goal of this final phase is to again observe if the data changes in the predicted manner. If so, then the interventionists' confidence that the intervention is effective continues to increase. This process documents experimental control, which is required to prove that the target behavior does change (AoC/intervention and replication) when the intervention is present and does not change when the intervention is absent (prediction and verification). Using these four steps of baseline logic several single case designs can be constructed with varying potentials for documenting experimental control.

There are several classic designs including A-B, A-B-A-B, and Multiple Baseline that will now be briefly reviewed. The most basic SCD is the A-B, or Baseline-Intervention design. In an A-B design two phases of baseline logic are present, Prediction and AoC/Intervention. This combination can be observed in Figure S.4. In this example a child's on-task behavior as rated with Direct Behavior Ratings (DBR) was in the 1–2 range in baseline. After the intervention was applied ratings in the 5–7 range with an increasing trend suggested the intervention is effective. The use of a baseline (Prediction) and intervention (AoC) phase allows applied professionals to document if there was a change when the intervention is present. Note that this design does not permit for experimental control as we do not verify the prediction statement or replicate the interventions. Thus, while an A-B design can document that a behavior changed when an intervention was presented, it is not sufficient to say defensibly that the intervention caused the observed change.

If there is a need to be sure that an intervention is responsible for a change in the target behavior then an A-B-A-B design is a better option than an A-B design. The A-B-A-B design builds on the baseline (Prediction) and intervention (AoC) by adding a return to baseline (Verification) phase and a second intervention (Replication) phase. See Figure S.5 for an example of an A-B-A-B design. Building on the example in Figure S.4, the design in Figure S.5 demonstrates a return to baseline (verification) and replication of the intervention. This design not only documents a change in the target behavior when the intervention is conducted, but also fully demonstrates experimental control, increasing our certainty that it was the intervention and only the intervention that was responsible for the change. While this is a very attractive design, in many situations it is not possible or ethical to remove an intervention. In such cases, if experimental control is desired, one should consider a Multiple Baseline design.

The final design that we will discuss is the Multiple Baseline (MB) design. In order to establish experimental

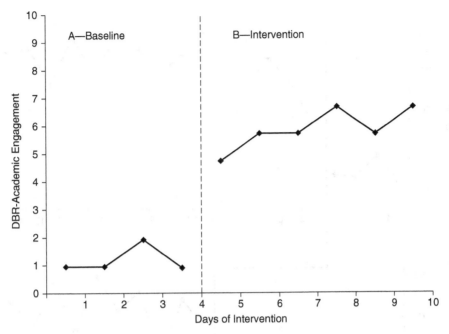

Figure S.4. Sample A-B design.

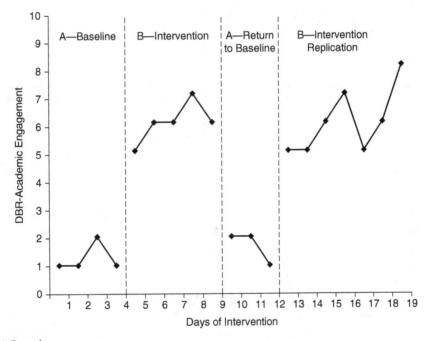

Figure S.5. Sample A-B-A-B graph.

control in a MB design, replication is accomplished by extending the baseline across condition. As such, MB designs can be thought of as a series of A-B designs, using the same treatment and target behavior, with a staggered implementation of the intervention across conditions. The options for a MB condition are typically participants (e.g., Shannon, Chris, and Matt), settings (e.g., morning and afternoon or math, reading and language arts classes), or stimuli (e.g., probes one, two and three). See Figure S.6

for an example of a MB across setting design. In the MB design the lag between each A-B design allows for experimental control. When the intervention is implemented in the first A-B condition, it is essential for the outcome data to change only for that condition. The intervention was not applied in conditions two and three, so there should be no change in the outcome data for those conditions. Thus, the extended baseline phases (A) for conditions two and three are verification of the baseline (A) in condition one. After

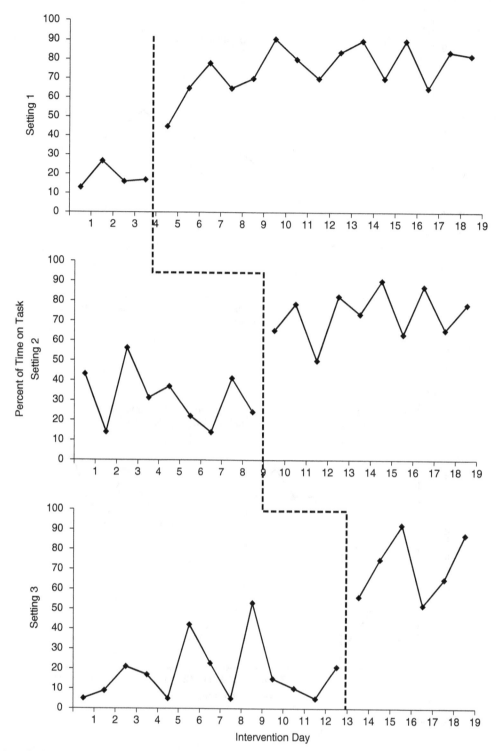

Figure S.6. Sample multiple baseline across setting graph.

the intervention effect has stabilized in condition one, the intervention is applied to condition two. This process is repeated for any additional conditions. For experimental control to be demonstrated, we expect a change in only the outcome data of the second condition. This pattern is replicated for all conditions. Any alteration to this pattern (e.g., a change in the outcome data for conditions one and two when the intervention is implemented for JUST condition one) is a threat to internal validity. Figure S.6 provides an example where the intervention is applied in three settings in a MB design. In this example experimental control is documented as the outcome data changes in each setting only when the intervention is applied and data remains stable otherwise.

Several critical issues when developing an MB design should be noted. First, when selecting the condition (e.g., participants or setting) the goal is that they are as analogous as possible in relation to the intervention so that they will respond to the intervention in the similar manner. At the same time, it is important that each condition is independent enough so that when the intervention is applied to the first condition it does not "bleed" over to the other conditions. In applied settings, if someone wants to document a functional relationship between an intervention and a student's problem behavior and not be forced to remove the intervention, they should choose a MB across setting or stimuli design.

We present these designs as best practice ideals but understand that in an applied setting it is often impossible to implement these designs as intended. As such, it is critical that educational professionals be familiar with baseline logic so they can understand the impact of design changes made in practice. This is particularly important in the case when it is important to make accurate statements about a child's response to an intervention. As noted, this entry was written to be a very brief introduction to the topic of SCD for applied educational professionals. For a more in depth review of SCD in relation to educational topics please refer to Riley-Tillman and Burns (2009) or Kennedy (2005).

REFERENCES

Cooper, J. O., Heron, T. E., & Heward, W. L. (2007). *Applied behavior analysis* (2nd ed.). Boston, MA: Pearson.

Kazdin, A. E. (1982). *Single-case research designs: Methods for clinical and applied settings*. New York, NY: Oxford University Press.

Kennedy, C. H. (2005). *Single case designs for educational research*. Boston, MA: Pearson.

Riley-Tillman, T. C., & Burns, M. K. (2009). *Evaluating educational interventions: Single case design for measuring response to intervention*. New York, NY: Guilford Press.

Sidman, M. (1960). *Tactics of scientific research: Evaluating experimental data in psychology*. New York, NY: Basic Books.

TIMOTHY C. RILEY-TILLMAN
East Carolina University

MATTHEW K. BURNS
University of Minnesota

SHANNON R. BROOKS
East Carolina University
Fourth edition

See also **Applied Behavior Analysis; Research in Special Education**

SINGLETON-MERTON SYNDROME

Singleton-Merton syndrome is a rare disorder of unknown etiology. The primary features of this syndrome include aortic calcification, dental abnormalities, and osteoporosis. Children with Singleton-Merton syndrome have abnormal accumulations of calcium deposits in their aorta, the major artery in the human body, and valves of their heart. Progressive calcification of the aorta and heart valves is life-threatening, as heart block or heart failure may result. In contrast, progressive loss of protein of the bones, resulting in osteoporosis, occurs in individuals with this disorder. Dental abnormalities in the form of poorly developed teeth and/or premature loss of primary teeth are seen in children with this syndrome as well (National Organization for Rare Disorders [NORD], 1997).

Other features of the disorder include generalized muscular weakness and hip and foot abnormalities. Motor delays are not uncommon. These children tend to be relatively short in stature due to growth retardation. Skin lesions, especially on their fingers, are also common among these children (Gay & Kuhn, 1976; NORD, 1997).

Physical therapy and occupational therapy may help motor development and increase muscle strength. Children may receive these support services through the school based on an other health impaired diagnosis.

REFERENCES

Gay, B. B., Jr., & Kuhn, J. P. (1976). A syndrome of widened medullary cavities of bone, aortic calcification, abnormal dentition, and muscular weakness (the Singleton-Merton syndrome). *Radiology, 118*(2), 389–395.

National Organization for Rare Disorders (NORD). (1997). *Singleton-Merton syndrome*. New Fairfield, CT: Author.

PATRICIA A. LOWE
University of Kansas

JOAN W. MAYFIELD
Baylor Pediatric Specialty Service

SIX-HOUR RETARDED CHILD

The term *6-hour retardate* first appeared in the report of the Conference on Problems of Education of Children in the Inner City (President's Committee on Mental Retardation, 1969). The conference was charged with developing a new set of recommendations regarding the problems of children with intellectual disabilities living within the ghettos of U.S. cities. After reviewing the papers of the 92 participants, seven major recommendations were developed: (1) provide early childhood stimulation education as part of the public education program; (2) conduct a study of histories of successful inner-city families who have learned to cope effectively; (3) restructure education of teachers, administrators, and counselors; (4) reexamine present systems of intelligence testing and classification; (5) commit substantial additional funding for research and development in educational improvement for the disadvantaged; (6) delineate what constitutes accountability and hold the school accountable for providing quality education for all children; and (7) involve parents, citizens, citizen groups, students, and general and special educators in a total educational effort. However, one outcome overshadowed all of these recommendations. It was the conclusion that "we now have what may be called a 6-hour retarded child—retarded from 9 to 3, 5 days a week, solely on the basis of an IQ, without regard to his adaptive behavior, which may be exceptionally adaptive to the situation and community in which he lives."

The concept of the 6-hour retarded child survived into the mid-1980s. Today many psychologists and educators have accepted as a given that children identified with mild intellectual disabilities during the school-age years manifest difficulties functioning only in the school setting, and that outside of school, during childhood and in their work lives as adults, they function successfully. Often their intellectual disability is invisible to their employers, families, neighbors, and friends.

The conclusion of the conference participants was not inconsistent with case studies and some published reports of the adult lives of individuals with mild intellectual disabilities. Although observations of children with mild intellectual disabilities led many to believe that as adults they would fail in community adaptation, many investigators observed a high proportion of the adults with intellectual disabilities who achieved satisfactory adjustment, even when a variety of criteria were used.

The results of these early conclusions were confounded by subsequent reports showing that success in adult adaptation was equivocal, at best. The challenge of a more definitive portrayal of the adult lives of individuals with mild intellectual disabilities was undertaken by the Socio-Behavioral Research Group at UCLA, who produced several informative studies of children with mild intellectual disabilities as adults. Edgerton (1984) and Koegel and Edgerton (1984) used a holistic natural approach rather than measures of discrete adult outcomes. They conducted extensive ethnographic participant research studies of several aspects of the adult behavior of individuals who had been children with mild intellectual disabilities.

One of their studies centered on the functioning of Blacks who had been classified as educable mentally retarded (EMR) as children, an adult sample of those who were the object of concern in the 1969 Conference on

Problems of Education of Children of the Inner City. They identified 45 residents in a Black community who had attended EMR classes and who represented the broad range of competencies and lifestyles found among mildly retarded adults in the Black community. The 12 subjects who were selected for their study satisfied one criterion: field researchers, during the course of their first visits, expressed serious doubt that they were, in fact, intellectually disabled. These 12 individuals, when compared with the remainder of the sample, clearly led more normal lives. They had mean IQ scores of 62, 33% were married, and 42% were competitively employed. For 1 year a staff of Black ethnographic field researchers maintained regular contact with the 12 participants, visiting them for 1 to 4 hours a day on an average of 12 separate occasions. The visits took place in homes, at work sites, and schools, during leisure activities, shopping expeditions, and job searches. Both parents and subjects were interviewed regarding any limitations they perceived, as well as their experiences in various aspects of their adult lives.

Although the adult lives of the participants were varied, none of them had "disappeared" into his or her community as a typically developing person. All 12 were seen by others close to them as limited or impaired and most of the 12 participants acknowledged their own limitations. The participants continued to be troubled by the same problems that characterized them during their formal schooling—problems with reading, numerical concepts, and everyday tasks such as shopping, applying for jobs, traveling around the city, eating out in restaurants, making ends meet, and so forth.

Their problems transcended those associated with academic or intellectual pursuits. Their case histories included difficulties arising from poor judgment, vulnerability to exploitation and victimization, need for help in rearing their children, and an inability to comprehend satisfactorily their everyday experiences.

This study and several others of the adult lives of children with mild intellectual disabilities raise serious doubts regarding the efficacy and use of the concept of the 6-hour retarded child. The lives of these participants sometimes paralleled those of the typically developing individuals in the community, but never completely. Even though they were no longer receiving services as adults, they continued to face the same kinds of problems they did as children.

The contrast between the expectancies of the conference participants in 1969 and some of the recent studies such as the work by Edgerton (1984) suggests that regular and special education programs should attend to preparing children with limited potential for the roles they will engage in as adults. Moreover, no one concerned about the future of the pupil with mild intellectual disabilities can be content in the belief that their problems exist only in school and that outside of this setting they function as capably as their age mates.

REFERENCES

Edgerton, R. B. (Ed.). (1984). *Lives in process: Mildly retarded adults in a large city.* Washington, DC: American Association on Mental Deficiency.

Koegel, P., & Edgerton, R. B. (1984). Black "six-hour retarded" children as young adults. In R. B. Edgerton (Ed.), *Lives in process: Mildly retarded adults in a large city.* Washington, DC: American Association on Mental Deficiency.

President's Committee on Mental Retardation. (1969). *The six-hour retarded child.* Washington, DC: Bureau of Education for the Handicapped, Office of Education, U.S. Department of Health, Education, and Welfare.

NADINE M. LAMBERT
University of California, Berkeley

See also Mental Retardation

SKEELS, HAROLD M. (1901–1970)

Harold M. Skeels, pioneer researcher in the field of mental retardation, was responsible for a large number of studies of institutional populations during the 1930s and early 1940s. These studies showed that children placed in unstimulating institutional environments failed to develop normally and that the longer they remained, the greater their deficits became. Skeels reached the conclusion that it is possible to improve intellectual functioning through early stimulation, and he advocated early adoption as an alternative to institutionalization. His findings set off a nature-nurture controversy, and Skeels and his associates were the targets of vehement attacks.

Following service in the armed forces during World War II, and subsequent employment with the U.S. Public Health Service and the National Institute of Mental Health, Skeels made a follow-up study of some of the subjects of his earlier research. The results showed dramatically the long-term effects of differences in childhood environments. By the time his report was published, many of Skeels's concepts from the 1930s had become commonplace: adoption at an early age had become routine, institutional placements were decreasing, and a variety of early childhood services had been developed, including some programs, like Head Start, aimed specifically at early stimulation of disadvantaged and disabled children.

REFERENCES

Crissey, M. S. (1970). Harold Manville Skeels. *American Journal of Mental Deficiency, 75,* 1–3.

Skeels, H. M. (1966). Adult status of children with contrasting early life experiences. *Monograph of the Society for Research in Child Development, 33,* 1–65.

Skeels, H. M., & Dye, H. B. (1939). A study of the effects of differential stimulation. *Proceedings of the American Association on Mental Deficiency, 44,* 114–136.

PAUL IRVINE
Katona, New York

See also Head Start; Nature versus Nurture

SKILL TRAINING

The skill training model rests on the premise that assessment of a student's performance should focus on classroom tasks. Such assessment is usually tied to some hierarchy of skills. Instruction, then, follows directly from the results of the hierarchical assessment and often uses direct instruction skills (Mercer, 1983).

Skill training is a commonly used approach in special education. It provides the teacher with an opportunity to evaluate specific skills, skills that are of immediate and direct concern to classroom instruction. The skill training process usually begins with the administration of a criterion-referenced or teacher-made assessment device. The analysis of the results of the assessment provides the teacher with additional information that is specifically related to classroom interventions. That is, the analysis, focusing on a hierarchy of skills, helps to pinpoint the specific error the student is making, allowing a more precise instructional decision to be made. This instructional decision will usually result in the teacher using some direct instructional technique, concentrating the teaching efforts on a specific academic skill (Gable & Warren, 1993). Pupil progress is continuously measured to ensure that instruction continues to focus on appropriate skills. On mastery of one skill, the teacher and student progress to the next hierarchical skill.

REFERENCES

Gable, R. A., & Warren, S. F. (Eds.). (1993). *Strategies for teaching students with mild to severe mental retardation.* Baltimore, MD: Paul H. Brookes.

Mercer, C. D. (1983). *Students with learning disabilities* (2nd ed.). Columbus, OH: Merrill.

JOHN R. BEATTIE
University of North Carolina at Charlotte

See also Mastery Learning and Special Education

SKINNER, BURRHUS FREDERICK (1904–1990)

B. F. Skinner was born in northeastern Pennsylvania in 1904. He continued to write and work until his death on August 18, 1990. Skinner studied English and classics at Hamilton College, where he received his AB (1926) in literature. After his aspirations of becoming a writer were discouraged, he entered the graduate program in psychology at Harvard, earning his MA in 1930 and his PhD under E. G. Boring in 1931. Regarded as a classic, his dissertation reflected his theory that a reflex arc, a then widely debated concept, was nothing more than the relationship between a stimulus and a response. He argued that all behavior, in fact, could be explained by looking at the stimuli that result in its occurrence. These themes were the root of his theoretical orientation throughout his distinguished and remarkable career.

Skinner completed several postdoctoral fellowships after leaving graduate school, subsequently accepting the position of assistant professor at the University of Minnesota (1936–1945). He was a Junior Fellow in the Society of Fellows of Harvard University from 1933 to 1936. After spending a short time at Indiana University as chairman of the department of psychology (1945–1947), he returned to Harvard as William James Lecturer, where he remained as professor and, ultimately, professor emeritus of psychology until his death in 1990.

Skinner is considered by many to be the most important figure in 20th-century psychology. In the field of education, he is perhaps best known for the development of programmed instruction and teaching machines as well as his behavior modification techniques. These areas allow the special educator to analyze and develop a systematic and situation-specific plan of instruction for learning or behavior. He denounced theoretical explanations of psychology, viewing the discipline as scientific and empirically driven, concerned with the observation of behaviors and the stimuli that bring them about. This Radical Behaviorism, as it has been termed, involves strict adherence to behavioral principles.

Skinner's concept of behaviorism, known as operant conditioning, as well as the results of numerous experiments, were outlined in his first major publication, *The Behavior of Organisms* (1938). The term *operant* refers to the identification of behavior which is traceable to reinforcing contingencies rather then to eliciting stimuli. Skinner believed speculation about what intervenes between stimulus and response or between response and reward to be superfluous.

The idea of creating a utopian community using his principles of conditioning, controlling all aspects of life using positive reinforcement, continued to interest him throughout his life. The notion of this ideal community was delineated in his 1948 novel, *Walden Two*. Another of his major books, *Science and Human Behavior* (1952), dealt with the application of behavioral principles to real-life situations including social issues, law, education, and psychotherapy. In this work, he postulated that the human organism is a machine like any other, thus behaving in lawful, predictable ways in response to external stimuli.

His notorious *Verbal Behavior* was published in 1957. This analysis of human language behavior was roundly criticized, most notably by linguist Noam Chomsky in a devastating review published in 1959. It is generally believed that neither Skinner nor his advocates ever responded successfully to the criticisms raised in this review, often noted as the beginning of the decline in influence of behavioral psychology.

Skinner advanced behaviorism by distinguishing between two types of behavior, respondent and operant, and showing how varying contingencies of reinforcement can be employed to modify or control any type of behavior. Controversy was raised once again by his publication of *Beyond Freedom and Dignity*, a 1971 book in which he dealt with the application of these principles. In this book, he interprets concepts of freedom, value, and dignity in objective terms, suggesting a society designed by shaping and controlling the behavior of citizens with a planned system of rewards (reinforcements). Among his numerous publications, *The Technology of Teaching* (1968) and his autobiographical trilogy (the last part, *A Matter of Consequences*, published in 1983) are of particular interest.

Skinner's contributions to psychology were recognized in 1958 by the American Psychological Association's (APA) Distinguished Scientific Award and again, just before his death, with a Lifetime Achievement Award. Other honors include the National Medal of Science (1968), the gold medal from the APA (1971), and his portrayal on the cover of *Time* magazine (1971).

In later years, Skinner extended his studies to psychotic behavior, instructional devices, and the analysis of cultures. Despite the criticisms and his unwavering position on a broad range of issues, his significant influence and impact on contemporary psychology assures him a place in its history.

This entry has been informed by the sources listed below.

REFERENCES

Skinner, B. F. (1938). *The behavior of organisms: An experimental analysis*. New York, NY: Appleton-Century.

Skinner, B. F. (1948). *Walden two*. New York, NY: Macmillan.

Skinner, B. F. (1953). *Science and human behavior*. New York, NY: Macmillan.

Skinner, B. F. (1957). *Verbal behavior*. New York, NY: Appleton-Century-Crofts.

Skinner, B. F. (1968). *The technology of teaching*. New York, NY: Appleton-Century-Crofts.

Skinner, B. F. (1971). *Beyond freedom and dignity*. New York, NY: Bantam.

Skinner, B. F. (1984). *A matter of consequences*. Washington Square, NY: New York University.

ELAINE FLETCHER-JANZEN
Chicago School of Professional Psychology
First edition

TAMARA J. MARTIN
The University of Texas of the Permian Basin
Second edition

See also Behavior Modification; Operant Conditioning

SKINNER'S FUNCTIONAL LEARNING MODEL

B. F. Skinner's functional learning model, known as operant conditioning, describes the relationship between behavior and the environmental events that influence it. The basic principles of operant conditioning include reinforcement, punishment, extinction, and stimulus control. These principles describe the functionality of events that precede or follow behavior. Reinforcement, for example, serves the function of increasing the strength of behavior. Skinner (1953) described two types of reinforcement. Positive reinforcement refers to the presentation of an event, commonly called a reward, following behavior. For example, a teacher smiles and says, "Good work" following completion of a child's assignment. Negative reinforcement refers to the removal of an event presumed to be unpleasant following behavior. For example, a child's aggressive behavior may cause a teacher to remove an unpleasant request. In both cases, the effect of reinforcement is the same—the child is more likely to engage in the behavior (assignment completion or aggressive behavior) under similar conditions in the future.

The application of operant conditioning to special education involves the arrangement of contingencies of reinforcement to ensure effective learning. Skinner (1968) noted that although students obviously learn outside the classroom without such systematic procedures, "teachers arrange special contingencies which expedite learning, hastening the appearance of behavior which would otherwise be acquired slowly or making sure of the appearance of behavior which might otherwise never occur" (p. 65). Operant techniques have been applied in classrooms more than in any other setting and have been extremely successful in improving a variety of academic and social behaviors in diverse student populations (Kazdin, 1978).

REFERENCES

Kazdin, A. E. (1978). *History of behavior modification: Experimental foundations of contemporary research*. Baltimore, MD: University Park Press.

Skinner, B. F. (1953). *Science and human behavior*. New York, NY: Free Press.

Skinner, B. F. (1968). *The technology of teaching*. Englewood Cliffs, NJ: Prentice Hall.

CHRISTINE L. COLE
University of Wisconsin at Madison

See also Behavior Modification; Conditioning; Operant Conditioning; Skinner, Burrhus Frederick (1904–1990)

SLATE AND STYLUS

The slate and stylus are literacy tools used together to create braille. Slates are produced in metal or plastic and consist of a back with the impressions of a full braille cell, a matrix of two columns of three dots each. The front of the slate has rows and columns of braille cells that serve as a guide to the writer who is blind. Slates are available in various sizes from full pages to single lines. The stylus is the awl-like tool used to create the braille dots. The stylus has a wooden or plastic handle and a long, thin metal tip with a blunted end. Also available for use with the slate and stylus is a wooden eraser that can be used to remove unwanted dots.

When writing on a slate with a stylus, the writer uses the stylus to impress the braille dots onto the page, which then must be turned over to be read. Therefore, a person writing with a slate and stylus will write from the right side of the page to the left. The dots are written using the same spatial relationships among the dots that are created on the braillewriter (Wormsley, 2004), though instead of producing each cell in its entirety, the user writes the dots on the left side of the braille cell first, then the dots on the right side. The slate and stylus takes longer to use; though proficient users can write at an efficient rate. Together, the slate and stylus are useful tools because they are light and easy to carry, and they are especially helpful when the use of a Perkins brailler is impractical because of its size and weight or for writing quick notes to be read by oneself or another braille user.

REFERENCE

Wormsley, D. P. (2004). *Braille literacy: A functional approach*. New York, NY: AFB Press.

SUSAN YARBROUGH
Florida State University
Fourth edition

SLEEP APNEA

Sleep apnea is characterized by recurrent apneas (breathing cessations) during sleep, which can result in a temporary cessation or reduced flow of oxygen to the brain, as well as regular interruptions of the normal sleep pattern (Bedard, Montplaisir, Malo, Richer, & Rouleau, 1993). At the termination of this apneic event, the patient will awaken and then resume breathing. For children with this disorder, this process is often repeated hundreds of times each night (Valencia-Flores, Bliwise, Guilleminault, Cilveti, & Clark, 1996). Individuals with this disorder usually present with complaints of snoring, restlessness, lethargy, and headaches. Symptoms may be transient or more permanent, depending upon the degree of oxygen reduction and the chronicity (Kelly, Claypoole, & Coppel, 1990). The incidence of sleep apnea in children can be estimated to be at between .5% and 3% of the population.

Characteristics

1. Characterized by a temporary cessation of oxygen flow to the brain, resulting in an interruption of the regular sleeping pattern.
2. Common nighttime symptoms include snoring, restlessness, sleepwalking, and enuresis.
3. Daytime symptoms include noisy breathing, morning headaches, and a chronic runny nose.
4. Children with this disorder may exhibit signs and symptoms of diffuse neurological impairment, including a decrease in the ability to learn new information, impaired motor ability, concentration and attention problems, and visual-spatial deficits.
5. Neuropsychological problems may include difficulties with memory, abstract reasoning, cognitive flexibility, and executive tasks (Bedard et al., 1993).
6. Daytime sleepiness can be seen in children with sleep apnea. This can result in vigilance impairments, behavior problems, agitation, and mood disturbance.

The most successful treatment in children is the removal of the child's tonsils and adenoids. Continuous positive airway pressure (CPAP) can also be used with children, especially if children are symptomatic after an adenotonsillectomy. CPAP consists of small (5–20 cm H20) positive pressure, which is introduced through the use of a lightweight mask that the patient wears while he or she sleeps. This treatment does not involve the administration of nocturnal oxygen; rather, CPAP is effective because it splints open the airway and prevents occlusion from occurring (Valencia-Flores et al., 1996). This treatment can be a cumbersome procedure that involves sleeping with a mask over one's face. Compliance from children for this treatment may be problematic. Another surgical technique that has been found to be effective is called a tracheostomy. During this procedure the trachea is entered by vertical incision of the second and third tracheal rings. A tracheostomy tube is used to keep the airway open.

Children who are suffering from sleep apnea can have many special education issues. In addition to the behavior problems that may arise from sleepiness, children with sleep apnea may exhibit difficulty with concentration, attention, and memory; impaired motor ability; impaired planning and reasoning ability; and emotional and behavioral problems.

The symptoms of sleep apnea may be mistaken for attention deficit disorder or an attention-deficit/hyperactivity disorder. Teachers will need to be aware that the child may have trouble attending to or following simple directions. The child may have trouble differentiating between relevant and irrelevant stimuli. The regular education or special education teacher will have to make adjustments such as frequently reviewing the daily schedule with the child or employing multiple teaching modalities such as auditory, tactile, and visual techniques. It is likely that children with sleep apnea who are exhibiting severe symptomology may be served as children classified as other health impaired. If the child's problems are mostly focused in the academic areas, they may be served with children who are diagnosed with learning disabilities.

Children with sleep apnea may also demonstrate difficulty with executive functions. These problems could manifest in limited planning, shifting, and abstraction abilities. These problems may be further complicated by visual-spatial difficulties. Examples of these problems include having difficulty finding their way around the school, difficulty learning and understanding abstract concepts such as units of measurements, and problems learning how to read and do math. It is important for regular and special education teachers to employ patience and target the individual symptoms of sleep apnea and not just focus on the child's troubled behavior.

The prognosis for children with sleep apnea is varied. Factors that affect recovery include the child's weight and comorbidity with other psychological and physiological disorders. In some cases, irreversible anoxic brain damage may have occurred, which can significantly lower the chances of recovery. Because research is currently being conducted about childhood brain impairment, we can expect to see continuing improvements in our ability to treat and understand sleep apnea.

REFERENCES

Bedard, M., Montplaisir, J., Malo, J., Richer, F., & Rouleau, I. (1993). Persistent neuropsychological deficits and vigilance impairment in sleep apnea syndrome after treatment with continuous positive airway pressure (CPAP). *Journal of Clinical and Experimental Neuropsychology, 15*, 330–341.

Kelly, D., Claypoole, K., & Coppel, D. (1990). Sleep apnea syndrome: Symptomology, associated features, and neurocognitive correlates. *Neuropsychology Review, 1*, 323–341.

Valencia-Flores, M., Bliwise, D., Guilleminault, C., Cilveti, R., & Clark, A. (1996). Cognitive function in patients with sleep apnea after acute nocturnal nasal continuous positive airway pressure (CPAP) treatment: Sleepiness and hypoxia effects. *Journal of Clinical and Experimental Neuropsychology, 18*, 197–210.

Andrew S. Davis
University of Northern Colorado

SLEEP TERROR

Sleep terror, also referred to as night terror, is an episode of sudden extreme fright and panic during the night. The individual is abruptly awakened from sleep and emits a piercing scream. Yelling and incoherent verbalizations are common, but the individual is amnestic for the event. Sleep terrors usually occur during the first hour of sleep—that is, during the first non-REM stage of sleep. The longer into the non-REM phase, however, the more severe the episode. The episodes last for no more than 10 or 15 minutes, at which time heart rate is in excess of 160 beats per minute (Murray, 1991).

Sleep terror occurs in about 1%–5% of children under the age of 10. The problem is sometimes difficult to distinguish from nightmares; however, in the case of nightmares, there is less vocalization and panic. Sleep terrors, unlike nightmares, are also more common in children than in adults, and about half of the cases resolve spontaneously by the age of 8. Although adolescents experience sleep terrors, it is quite rare to find these persist into adulthood. When sleep terrors do persist, however, or begin at a later stage than normal (i.e., after age 10), the problem occurs more frequently and appears related to stress. Most cases of sleep terror, however, do not even meet the *Diagnostic and Statistical Manual of Mental Disorders–Fourth Edition (DSM-IV)* criteria for sleep terror disorder (American Psychiatric Association, 2000) because the diagnosis requires that a person's functioning be impaired in a relevant area of daily life (e.g., school, work, and social interactions).

Characteristics

1. Sudden arousal from sleep with intense panic and terror
2. Episode occurs about an hour into sleep and lasts only a few minutes
3. Autonomic arousal, including rapid heartbeat and breathing, and sweating

---

4. Person remains asleep despite appearance of being awake
5. Frequency is about once a week (in children)
6. Typically begins before age 10 and is outgrown by adolescence

---

Sleep terrors are rarely dangerous; however, objects from around the bed that pose a safety risk should be removed. Some individuals do attempt to leave the bed, and when the sleep terror is accompanied by sleepwalking, they will get up. These episodes are extremely frightening for the observer; however, efforts to awaken the person should be avoided (the observer should instead talk to the person in a reassuring voice). Other interventions are rarely needed. In cases in which sleep terror occurs frequently or is associated with other problems (e.g., sleepwalking and daytime functional problems), a physician should be consulted. In some cases, medical conditions may be contributing to the problem (e.g., seizures), and with treatment, the sleep terrors could be resolved. Furthermore, in cases in which individuals are using certain substances or taking medications that exacerbate the problem, this too can be evaluated (e.g., sedatives, including hypnagogic drugs and alcohol). Certain medications are useful to reduce sleep terrors; these medications include diazepam and imipramine, drugs that suppress slow-wave sleep (Murray, 1991). Adults may also benefit from a psychological consult to help identify potential stressors that might be triggering the problem and ways to manage stress more effectively (e.g., stress management training and relaxation therapy). Medical consults may also be important in order to rule out conditions that share certain characteristics, especially those that are treatable (e.g., epilepsy).

Rarely would a child with sleep terror require treatment or even come to the attention of a psychologist. If counseling or any special services (i.e., special education services and classroom accommodations) were needed, they would more likely be unrelated to sleep terror (e.g., learning disabilities).

REFERENCES

American Psychiatric Association. (2000). *Diagnostic and statistical manual of mental disorders* (4th ed., text rev.). Washington, DC: Author.

Murray, J. (1991). Psychophysiological aspects of nightmares, night terrors, and sleepwalking. *Journal of General Psychology, 118*(2), 113–128.

Wendy Wolfe
Elaine Clark
University of Utah

SLEEPWALKING

Sleepwalking, also referred to as somnambulism, is a fairly common problem among children. It involves sitting, walking, or performing other routine behaviors while asleep. Although the individual who sleepwalks typically has his or her eyes open and avoids bumping into objects, there is no indication of awareness. Sleepwalking episodes, which last from 5 to 30 minutes, typically occur 2 hours after the onset of sleep (i.e., during slow-wave, non-REM sleep). It is estimated to occur in 10%–30% of children, most often between the ages of 4 and 8 (American Psychiatric Association [APA], 2000). Sleepwalking typically occurs over several years, but more often than not it remits spontaneously by the age of 15.

Sleepwalkers usually have their eyes open, but they show no recognition except avoidance of objects at times. Sleep talking can be observed; however, communications are often unintelligible (e.g., words and phrases are mumbled). Other behaviors that can occur during sleepwalking include eating and urinating, most often in the bathroom. Individuals may also engage in more complex behaviors, including unlocking doors and using appliances. At times, sleep terror is observed, and individuals may appear to be fleeing harm. Awakening someone during a sleepwalking episode is ill advised because it can lead to disorientation.

Confusion does, however, clear in minutes, and the sleepwalker has no recollection of the sleepwalking event.

Conditions that have been associated with sleepwalking include respiratory-related sleep disorders (e.g., obstructive sleep apnea), a family history of sleepwalking, and psychological stress. Children who are anxious, have experienced traumas, or are under a great deal of stress may be particularly vulnerable to sleepwalking behaviors (DeFrancesco, 1998; Laberge, Tremblay, Vitaro, & Montplaisir, 2000). Furthermore, taking certain drugs, including drugs that reduce REM sleep, are likely to increase sleepwalking.

Characteristics

1. Repeated episodes of walking in sleep, usually starting 2 hours into sleep.

2. Episodes typically last between 5 and 30 minutes.

3. Eyes are open and the person may talk, but he or she is unresponsive to others and difficult to awaken (forced awakening during sleepwalking is ill advised).

4. Amnesia for the event upon awakening.

5. Functional status quickly returns to normal after the person is awake.

6. Drugs that reduce REM sleep and stress can increase sleepwalking.

Treatments that have been found to be effective in reducing sleepwalking behavior include relaxation therapies, biofeedback, and hypnosis (DeFrancesco, 1998). In most cases, however, treatment consists of preventing injury during the sleepwalking episode. This treatment may be done using an alarm that alerts parents that the child is out of his or her bedroom or is in certain areas of the house. Other safety measures include removing dangerous objects and protecting the child from falling down stairs or leaving the house. When sleepwalkers are found wandering around, they should be assisted to bed rather than awakened suddenly. In cases in which sleepwalking cannot be reduced or eliminated so that safety is ensured, medications may be necessary (e.g., benzodiazepines, diazepam, and alprazolom). Children and adolescents who take certain medications (e.g., antidepressants and antipsychotic drugs) may also be more prone to walk in their sleep. A physician consult will therefore be critical to determine whether prescribed drugs are reducing the child's REM sleep and increasing sleepwalking.

Educators need to be aware of sleepwalking primarily for the purpose of accommodating the often-sleepy child in the classroom. When special services are needed, they are usually intended to treat contributing factors, not the sleepwalking behavior itself. For example, counseling may be necessary to help the child learn better coping strategies (e.g., stress management techniques and relaxation exercises). In cases in which sleepwalking causes significant distress or impairment in learning and social functioning, a *Diagnostic and Statistical Manual of Mental Disorders–Fourth Edition* (*DSM-IV*) diagnosis of sleepwalking disorder (APA, 2000) may be warranted and appropriate services should be provided. If learning is significantly impaired, children may be eligible to receive special education service under the category of emotional disorder. Services from the school psychologist may be in order in these cases to not only evaluate the child but also consult with parents and teachers to ensure that everything possible is being done to reduce the child's stress and increase learning and opportunities. A referral to a sleep clinic also needs to be considered in extreme cases.

The prognosis for sleepwalking is good. In fact, it frequently remits spontaneously during adolescence, typically by age 15 (APA, 2000). In some cases episodes may recur, but when the onset is during childhood, this is uncommon. If sleepwalking disorders begin in adults or recur at that time, symptoms are more persistent and the course is one of repeated episodes.

Further research that examines the effectiveness of various treatments is needed—in particular, therapies that are intended to improve REM sleep and consequently prevent sleepwalking (e.g., relaxation therapies and biofeedback). Drug studies are also critical to evaluate new-line drugs that are being prescribed to children and adolescents (e.g., anxiolytic drugs). Finally, research that examines the relationship between sleepwalking and night terrors is needed, given the features that are shared by these two conditions. It is hoped that this research will provide further insights into successful treatment of both.

REFERENCES

American Psychiatric Association. (2000). *Diagnostic and statistical manual of mental disorders* (4th ed., text rev.). Washington, DC: Author.

DeFrancesco, J. (1998). Sleepwalking in children. In A. S. Canter & S. A. Carroll (Eds.), *Helping children at home and school: Handouts from your school psychologist*. Bethesda, MD: National Association of School Psychologists.

Laberge, L., Tremblay, R. E., Vitaro, F., & Montplaisir, J. (2000). Development of parasomnias from childhood to early adolescence. *Pediatrics, 106*(1), 67–74.

CRISTINA MCCARTHY
ELAINE CLARK
University of Utah

SLINGERLAND SCREENING TESTS

The Slingerland screening tests are comprised of four forms with designated grade levels (Form A, grades 1 and 2; Form B, grades 2 and 3; Form C, grades 3 and 4; Form D, grades 5 and 6); (Slingerland & Ansara, 1974; Slingerland, 1974). There are eight subtests for Forms A, B, and C that may be either group or individually administered. These subtests require the students to copy letters and words from a board, copy from a page, perform visual matching exercises by selecting a stimulus word from an array of distractor words with various letter reversals, copy words presented in flashcard fashion, write dictated words, and detect initial and final sounds. For children who exhibit difficulties with portions of the eight subtests, there are individually administered auditory tests designed to assess auditory perception and memory. The student is asked to repeat individual words and phrases, to complete sentences with a missing word, and to retell a story. With the exception of additional subtests assessing personal orientation, Form D is comparable to the other three forms of the test. As noted by Fujiki (1985) and Sean and Keough (1993), the purpose of the Slingerland is not to identify children with linguistic disabilities, but to assess auditory, visual, and motor skills associated with learning to read and write.

Local norms are advocated to interpret the results of students' test performance. This recommendation is necessary because of the notable omission of adequate normative data. Also absent in the manuals is an adequate discussion of reliability, stability, or validity.

REFERENCES

Fujiki, M. (1985). Review of Slingerland Screening Tests for identifying children with specific language disabilities. In J. V. Mitchell (Ed.), *The ninth mental measurements yearbook* (Vol. 2, pp. 1398–1399). Lincoln: University of Nebraska Press.

Sean, S., & Keough, B. (1993). Predicting reading performance using the Slingerland procedures. *Annals of Dyslexia, 43,* 78–79.

Slingerland, B. H. (1974). *Teacher's manual to accompany Slingerland Screening Tests for Identifying Children with Specific Language Disability–Revised Edition* (Form D). Cambridge, MA: Educators.

Slingerland, B. H., & Ansara, A. S. (1974). *Teacher's manual to accompany Slingerland Screening Tests for Identifying Children with Specific Language Disability–Revised Edition* (Forms A, B, and C). Cambridge, MA: Educators.

JACK A. CUMMINGS
Indiana University

See also Language Disorders

SLOSSON INTELLIGENCE TEST REVISED–THIRD EDITION FOR CHILDREN AND ADULTS

The Slosson Intelligence Test Revised–Third Edition for Children and Adults (SIT-R3, 2002, with 1998 calibrated norms) provides a quick and reliable individual screening test of Crystallized Verbal Intelligence. This revision has adapted score sheets for scannable/electronic readers and offers a supplementary manual for the blind or visually impaired. The SIT-R3 has minimal performance items and features embossed materials, allowing for one of the only measures of intelligence for the visually challenged population of both children and adults.

The SIT-3 test items are derived from the following subtests: Vocabulary (33 items), General Information (29 items), Similarities and Differences (30 items), Comprehension (33 items), Quantitative (34 items), and Auditory Memory (28 items).

The test has been nationally restandardized and developed with the American Psychological Association criteria clearly in mind. Multiple statistical procedures were used to assure no significant gender or racial bias. Every item on the test was reevaluated using classical item analysis to choose "good" statistical items and new differential item functioning analysis to find and eliminate biased items. SIT-R3 users may continue to administer and score the SIT-R3 with the 1998 Calibrated Norms Tables as usual and order the supplementary manual when testing persons with low visual acuity.

Administration time for the SIT-R3 takes about 10 to 20 minutes. The assessment measures Vocabulary, General Information, Similarities and Differences, Comprehension, and Quantitative and Auditory Memory. The SIT-R3 correlated .827 with the WISC-R, Verbal Intelligence Quotient, even though the SIT-R3 does not cover Fluid Reasoning performance. The Calibrated Norms reflect a high .828 correlation between the SIT-R3 TSS and the WISC-III Full Scale Intelligence Quotient.

Computer Report aids educators in determining expected achievement and finding levels of ability or weakness. It scores and prints an individual three-page report using the Total Standard Score and computes the Severe Discrepancy Level to determine learning disabilities under federal guidelines. Computer Report is noncompliant with Windows XP.

This entry has been informed by the sources listed below.

REFERENCES

Blackwell, T., & Madere, L. (2005). Test Review of Slosson Intelligence Test–Revised. *Rehabilitation Counseling Bulletin, 48*(3), 183–184.

Erford, B., & Pauletta, D. (2005). Psychometric Analysis of Young Children's Responses to the Slosson Intelligence Test–Primary (SIT-P). *Measurement and Evaluation in Counseling and Development, 38*(3), 130–140.

Plake, B. S., & Impara, J. C. (Eds.). (2001). *The fourteenth mental measurements yearbook*. Lincoln, NE: Buros Institute of Mental Measurements.

Williams, T., Eaves, R., Woods-Groves, S., & Mariano, G. (2007). Stability of scores for the Slosson Full-Range Intelligence Test. *Psychological Reports, 101*(1), 135—140.

RON DUMONT
Fairleigh Dickinson University

JOHN O. WILLIS
Rivier College

KATHLEEN VEIZEL
Fairleigh Dickinson University

JAMIE ZIBULSKY
Fairleigh Dickinson University
Fourth edition

SLOW LEARNERS

Historically, the slow learning child has been described in numerous ways. Ingram's (1960) book, the *Education of the Slow-Learning Child*, discussed the education of the educable children with intellectual disabilities. Johnson (1963) noted that "slow learners compose the largest group of mentally retarded persons" (p. 9). Today, however, the term slow learner most accurately describes children and adolescents who learn or underachieve, in one or more academic areas, at a rate that is below average yet not at the level considered comparable to that of an educable student with intellectual disabilities. Intellectually, slow learners score most often between a 75 and a 90 IQ—between the borderline and low-average classifications of intelligence.

It is unusual to find the slow learner discussed in the standard special education textbook. Indeed, slow learners are not special education students. There is no Individuals With Disabilities Education Act (IDEA) label or definition of slow learner, and these students are not eligible for any monies or services associated with that law. When slow learners receive additional supportive services, it is typically in the regular classroom or in remedial classes that may be supported by federal title funds or programs. These remedial classes are not conceptualized as alternative educational programs; they are used to reinforce regular classroom curricula and learning. Some slow learners are inappropriately labeled as individuals with learning disabled to maintain the enrollment (and funding) of some special education classrooms, or because they would otherwise fail in the regular classroom, despite not having special education needs.

There is no consensus on a diagnostic or descriptive profile that characterizes the slow learner. Indeed, there is very little contemporary research with samples specifically labeled as slow learners. Many slow learners are now described by their specific academic weaknesses; research and/or remedial programs are applied to these academic areas—not to the slow learner labels. Because of this shift in emphasis, earlier research describing slow learners as being from low socioeconomic and minority family backgrounds, academically and socially frustrated, and devalued by teachers and peers, and as having low self-concepts, does not apply (Cawley, Goodstein, & Burrow, 1972).

REFERENCES

Cawley, J. F., Goodstein, H. A., & Burrow, W. H. (1972). *The slow learner and the reading problem*. Springfield, IL: Thomas.

Ingram, C. P. (1960). *Education of the slow-learning child* (3rd ed.). New York, NY: Ronald.

Johnson, G. O. (1963). *Education for slow learners*. Englewood Cliffs, NJ: Prentice Hall.

HOWARD M. KNOFF
University of South Florida

See also Learning Disabilities; Response to Intervention

SLY SYNDROME

Sly syndrome (mucopolysaccharidosis Type VII [MPS VII]), is the rarest mucopolysaccharidoses lysosomal storage diseases (National Organization for Rare Disorders [NORD], 2000), but has the widest effects. Types I (neonatal) and II (early onset) have severe effects, whereas Type III (late onset) has milder ones. In all types, deficiency of the enzyme beta-glucuronidase leads to an accumulation of complex carbohydrates in the brain. Type I is one of the few mucopolysaccharidoses that is present at birth (Pediatric Database, 1994).

Sly syndrome is a very rare (about 20 known cases have been reported worldwide) inherited autosomal recessive metabolic disorder (Pediatric Database, 1994). Characteristics are highly variable across type (Online Mendelian Inheritance in Man [OMIM], 2000).

Characteristics

1. Postnatal growth deficiency and short stature
2. Macrocephaly, skull deformities, hydrocephaly, coarse facies, hearing loss, and corneal opacities
3. Mental retardation and neurodegeneration
4. Multiple skeletal deformities
5. Hirsutism
6. Cardiovascular and other internal organ abnormalities
7. Hydrops fetalis

Because no cure or remedial treatment for the underlying disease is available, treatment is usually supportive. The variety of symptoms call for a team approach involving pediatric, neurological, orthopedic, and ophthalmological specialists and perhaps genetic counseling for the parents (Pediatric Database, 1994). The severity of the early forms necessitate extensive support. Children with the later form will probably be able to attend either special or normal classrooms.

Research on several species of animal models—particularly mice—may lead to experimental treatments. Gene therapy has successfully prevented the disease, and transplants of healthy cells have led to production of beta-glucuronidase in affected mice. The gene for Sly syndrome is now known, and its discovery may lead to further treatments (OMIM, 2000).

REFERENCES

National Organization for Rare Disorders. (2000). *Sly syndrome*. Retrieved from http://www.stepstn.com/cgi-win/nord .exe?proc=Redirect&type=rdb_sum&id=291.htm

Online Mendelian Inheritance in Man (OMIM). (2000). *Mucopolysaccharidosis type VII*. Retrieved from http://www.ncbi .nlm.nih.gov/htbin-post/Omim/dispmim?253220#TEXT

Pediatric Database. (1994). *Sly syndrome*. Retrieved from http:// www.icondata.com/health/pedbase/.les/SLYSYNDR.HTM

PAULA KILPATRICK
ROBERT T. BROWN
University of North Carolina, Wilmington

SMITH-LEMLI-OPITZ SYNDROME

Smith-Lemli-Opitz syndrome is a genetic disorder due to an autosomal recessive gene. A larger number of males are affected by the syndrome than females (Jones, 1988). Smith-Lemli-Opitz syndrome is characterized by facial, limb, and genital abnormalities. Children with Smith-Lemli-Opitz syndrome have small heads; long, narrow faces; slanted or low-set ears; heavy or thick upper eyelids; anteverted nostrils; and small jaws. Squinting of the eyes is also a common characteristic found among these children. These children tend to be short in stature as well. On the palms of their hands and soles of their feet, simian creases are present and webbing often appears between their toes (Jones, 1988; Thoene, 1992). Some children with Smith-Lemli-Opitz syndrome experience seizures and have cardiac anomalies, abnormal EEGs, kidney defects, and cataracts (Jones, 1988).

There are two forms of Smith-Lemli-Opitz syndrome: types I and II. Type II, also known as Lowry-Miller-Maclean syndrome, is a more severe form of the disorder. Stillbirth is a common characteristic of the type II form. Those who do survive have a low birth weight and failure to thrive. A shrill cry, vomiting, and feeding problems are typical in early infancy.

Moderate to severe mental retardation is evident among these children (Thoene, 1992). Special education programs focusing on life-skill training would be beneficial.

REFERENCES

Jones, K. L. (Ed.). (1988). *Smith's recognizable patterns of human malformation* (4th ed.). Philadelphia, PA: Saunders.

Rudolph, A. M. (1991). *Rudolph's pediatrics—19th edition*. Norwalk, CT: Appleton & Lange.

Thoene, J. G. (Ed.). (1992). *Physician's guide to rare diseases*. Montvale, NJ: Dowden.

JOAN W. MAYFIELD
Baylor Pediatric Specialty Service

PATRICIA A. LOWE
University of Kansas

SMITH-MAGENIS SYNDROME

Smith-Magenis Syndrome (SMS; Greenberg et al., 1991; Magenis, Brown, Allen, & Reiss, 1986; Smith et al., 1986) is a multiple congenital anomaly chromosomal disorder associated with deletion in the proximal arm of Chromosome 17 [(17)(p11.2)]. Albeit underdiagnosed, SMS is considered a rare genetic disorder when compared to other genetic abnormalities with an approximate incidence of 1 in 25,000. The clinical phenotype of SMS is marked by brachycephaly, midface hypoplesia, prognatism, hoarse voice, speech delay with or without hearing loss, sleep disturbances, psychomotor and growth retardation, intellectual impairment, and behavior problems including hyperactivity, aggression, onychotillomania, self-hugging, and inappropriate insertion of foreign objects into body orifices. In some cases, children with a complete deletion of arm 17p11.2 are more severely afflicted with facial malformations, cleft palate, and major congenital malformations of the heart, skeletal, and genitourinary systems (Potocki, 2000; Smith et al., 1986). The overall intellectual level of these children has been reported to be within the deficient range. Within this range, most investigations have revealed intellectual skills in the moderate range of mental deficiency (Dykens, Finucane, & Gayley, 1997; Llorente, Voigt, Potocki, & Lupski, 2001; Smith et al., 1986). With regard to adaptation, the adaptive level of children with SMS is usually in the impaired range (low) across all domains (communicative, daily living skills, and social; Dykens et al., 1997; Llorente et al., 2001).

Characteristics

1. Mental retardation
2. Developmental and speech delay with or without hearing loss
3. Behavioral difficulties
4. Dysmorphic head and facial features possible (brachycephaly, midface hypoplesia, prognatism, cleft palate)
5. Possible congenital malformations of the heart, skeletal, and genitourinary systems
6. Hoarse voice and psychomotor and growth retardation
7. Insertion of foreign objects in body orifices

Based on the broad spectrum of clinical severity that children with SMS may experience, and despite the fact that there is no current cure for this genetic disorder, it is important to be flexible in designing any treatment regimen including medication and behavior analytic interventions targeting the behavioral alterations observed in these children. Because there is significant variability of symptom prevalence and manifestation, children diagnosed with SMS may be eligible for special education services under several categories of the Individuals with Disabilities Education Act. Depending on the level of intellectual functioning, a child with SMS may meet the criteria as a student with mental retardation. In addition, if a child has significant speech delays, he or she would be eligible for services under the speech or language impairment category. A child with SMS, particularly one suffering from a congenital abnormality or other severe medical condition (e.g., congenital heart disease), may be eligible for services also under the other health impairment category. Therefore, it is essential that doctors, parents, teachers, and others involved in the care of the child participate in devising the most appropriate educational plan and goals for the child.

Future research should continue to emphasize the determination of more exact cognitive and adaptive profiles, further genetic delineation of the syndrome through genetic research, and potential genetic therapies.

REFERENCES

Dykens, E. M., Finucane, B. M., & Gayley, C. (1997). Brief report: Cognitive and behavioral profiles of persons with Smith-Magenis syndrome. *Journal of Autism and Developmental Disorders, 27*, 203–210.

Greenberg, F., Guzzetta, V., Oca-Luna, R. M., Magenis, R. E., Smith, A. C. M., Richter, S. F.,…Lupski, J. R. (1991). Molecular analysis of the Smith-Magenis syndrome: A possible contiguous-gene syndrome associated with del(17)(p11.2). *American Journal of Human Genetics, 49*, 1207–1218.

Llorente, A. M., Voigt, R. G., Potocki, L., & Lupski, J. R. (2001, May). Cognitive and adaptive profiles of children with Smith-Magenis syndrome. *Proceedings from the 2001 Pediatric Academic Societies Annual Meeting*, 184A (Abstract 1043).

Magenis, R. E., Brown, M. G., Allen, L., & Reiss, J. (1986). De novo partial duplication of 17p[dup(17)(p12 B>p11.2]: Clinical report. *American Journal of Medical Genetics, 24*, 415–420.

Potocki, L. (2000). Circadian rhythm abnormalities of melatonin in Smith-Magenis syndrome. *Journal of Medical Genetics, 37*, 428–433.

Smith, A. C. M., McGavran, L., Robinson, J., Waldstein, G., Macfarlane, J., Zonona, J.,…Magenis, E. (1986). Interstitial deletion of (17)(p11.2p11.2) in nine patients. *American Journal of Medical Genetics, 24*, 393–414.

ANTOLIN M. LLORENTE
Baylor College of Medicine Houston, Texas

SMITH-OPTIZ SYNDROME

Smith-Opitz syndrome, better known as Smith-Lemli-Opitz syndrome (SLOS), is an autosomal recessive syndrome characterized by multiple congenital anomalies, mental retardation, behavioral difficulties, and characteristic dysmorphic facial features (Irons et al., 1997). SLOS is a relatively common inborn error of metabolism caused by deficient activity of the enzyme needed to catalyze cholesterol (Nowaczyk, Whelan, Heshka, & Hill, 1999).

Following phenylketonuria (PKU), SLOS is the second most common recessive hereditary syndrome that causes mental retardation (Nowaczyk et al., 1999). The gene for the enzyme in which individuals with SLOS are deficient has recently been found on Chromosome 11 (Nowaczyk et al., 1999). Incidence information seems to suggest that individuals of Northern European ancestry are more likely to have SLOS in comparison with very low incidence or nonexistent findings of SLOS in individuals of African or Asian descent. Current estimates of the incidence of SLOS state that it occurs in approximately 1 in 20,000 to 40,000 births, although this might be an underestimate considering the lack of research regarding diagnostic issues (Kelley, 1997; Nowaczyk et al., 1999). Furthermore, specific prevalence data regarding SLOS in the general population are as yet unknown.

Based on the wide spectrum of clinical severity that children with SLOS may experience, it is important to be flexible in designing any treatment regimen. Successful outcomes in the areas of growth, behavior, and overall health have been found by implementing dietary therapy with high cholesterol intake (Kelley, 1997; Nowaczyk et al., 1999), although a feeding tube is often necessitated for infants and very young children with feeding problems.

Characteristics

1. Microcephaly
2. Mental retardation
3. Developmental and speech delay
4. Feeding difficulties
5. Behavioral difficulties
6. Genital malformations
7. Dysmorphic facial features
8. Syndactyly (webbing) of second and third toes
9. Failure to thrive

For women who are carrying a SLOS-affected fetus, cholesterol supplementation has been suggested as well (Nowaczyk et al., 1999). Similarly, bile acid supplementation has been successful with some children (Irons et al., 1997; Nwokoro & Mulvihill, 1997).

Because there is a wide variability of symptom prevalence and manifestation, children diagnosed with SLOS may be eligible for special education services under several categories of the Individuals with Disabilities Education Act. Depending on the level of intellectual functioning, children with SLOS may meet criteria for mental retardation or speech or language impairment, or the other health impairment category. As noted, children with SLOS may be affected in many ways. Therefore, it is essential that doctors, parents, teachers, and others participate in providing care and devising the educational plan and goals for the child (Nowaczyk et al., 1999).

The prognosis for children with SLOS is variable. Severe cases have a very high neonatal mortality rate (Kelley, 1997; Nowaczyk et al., 1999). Children with SLOS have benefited from cholesterol replacement therapy. The dietary therapy has restored normal growth patterns and reduced behavioral difficulties in many children and adults with SLOS (Nowaczyk et al., 1999). With this in mind, future research should continue to measure the effect of current treatments and determine more exact prevalence and incidence data.

REFERENCES

Irons, M., Elias, E. R., Abuelo, D., Bull, M. J., Greene, C. L., Johnson, V. P., . . . Salen, G. (1997). Treatment of Smith-Lemli-Opitz syndrome: Results of a multicenter trial. *American Journal of Medical Genetics, 68,* 311–314.

Kelley, R. I. (1997). Editorial: A new face for an old syndrome. *American Journal of Medical Genetics, 65,* 251–256.

Nowaczyk, M. J. M., Whelan, D. T., Heshka, T. W., & Hill, R. E. (1999). Smith-Lemli-Opitz syndrome: A treatable inherited error of metabolism causing mental retardation. *Canadian Medical Association Journal, 161,* 165–170.

Nwokoro, N. A., & Mulvihill, J. J. (1997). Cholesterol and bile acid replacement therapy in children and adults with Smith-Lemli-Opitz (SLO/RSH) syndrome. *American Journal of Medical Ge-netics, 68,* 315–321.

CHRISTINE L. FRENCH
Texas A&M University

SNELLEN CHART

The Snellen chart is a common tool used to determine distance visual acuity. It is made up of rows of letters that get smaller from the top to the bottom of the page. A patient stands 20 feet away from the chart and reads the rows of letters until a row that cannot be read accurately is reached. The size of letters in the last row read correctly indicates the patient's visual acuity at a given distance.

The results of an eye examination that includes a Snellen chart are reported by listing two compared numbers. Most people have an acuity of 20/20, meaning that at 20 feet away, they can see the line that most other people can see from 20 feet away. A person with a visual impairment might have an acuity of 20/200, which means that what a person with typical vision can see at 200 feet, a person who sees 20/200 would have to be 20 feet away from to see. Despite its wide use, the Snellen chart has limitations for use on people with low vision. Since the Snellen chart is administered at a standard distance and has few test items at 20/70, 20/100, and 20/200, the chart is best used as a screening tool in combination with other tools that yield more precise measures at lower acuities (Wilkinson, 2010).

REFERENCE

Wilkinson, M. E. (2010). Clinical low vision services. In A. L. Corn & J. N. Erin (Eds.), *Foundations of low vision: Clinical and functional perspectives* (2nd ed., pp. 238–283). New York, NY: AFB Press.

SUSAN YARBROUGH
Florida State University
Fourth edition

See also Visual Acuity; Visual Impairment

SOCIAL BEHAVIOR OF INDIVIDUALS WITH DISABILITIES

Evidence from Lerner (1985) and Stephens, Hartman, and Lucas (1983) has clearly documented that many children with disabilities experience difficulty in the area of social skills. This difficulty could range from mild problems to severe disorders. Minskoff (1980) considers social perceptual difficulties as among the more serious problems of children with learning disabilities. Drew, Logan, and Hardman (1984) indicate that students with intellectual disabilities often have a higher incidence of emotional problems than typically developing students. Lerner (1985) identified six characteristics of social behavior that are common among children and youths with disabilities: (1) lack of judgment, (2) difficulties in perceiving others, (3) problems in making friends, (4) poor self-concept, (5) problems involving family relationships, and (6) social difficulties in the school setting.

In most instances, children who are receiving special education services have more than one problem and disabilities produce different behaviors in different children (Cartwright, Cartwright, & Ward, 1984). Bloom (1956) proposes a system whereby all education-related activities would fall into three major domains—affective, psychomotor, and cognitive. Cartwright et al. (1984) define the affective domain as the social domain; this deals with an individual's social abilities, such as establishing and maintaining satisfactory interpersonal skills, displaying behavior within reasonable social expectations, and making personal adjustments. Social skills and the ability to get along with others are just as important to the student with disabilities as they are to the typically developing student. In fact, these social skills are even more critical to the person with a disability because the individuals with disabilities are often compared with the norm and must compete for grades, social status, and employment.

Wallace and Kauffman (1986) indicate that social behavior development is inseparable from the student's acquisition of academic skills and that "inappropriate behavior limits the student's chances for success in school: conversely, school failure often prompts undesirable behavior" (p. 165). Wallace and Kauffman (1986) strongly suggest that the remediation of students' social behavior problems is just as important as the remediation of their academic problems.

Social skills have been hard to define and even more difficult to measure according to Wallace and Kauffman (1986), and Strain, Odom, and McConnell (1984). Direct observation is perhaps one of the most reliable methods used in assessment of social skills problems. Other procedures used to assess competence in social behavior are self-reporting and screening instruments, clinical judgment, analysis of antecedent events, interviews, sociometric procedures, behavior and rating scales. However, when assessing an individual's social skills, one must be aware of the situations and circumstances in which the behavior occurs. Social and emotional problems may not be the primary difficulties facing most exceptional children; nevertheless, except for students with behavior disorders of serious emotional disturbance, these problems are present.

Eleas and Maher (1983) suggest that well-adjusted children have certain social and academic skills that many students with mild disabilities do not possess. Such skills as sensitivity to others' feelings, goal-setting persistence, and an adequate behavior repertoire are just a few mentioned. Many more social skills deficits that often plague students with disabilities such as poor self-concept, withdrawal, rejection, attention problems, compound the academic problems. School personnel need to address social skill problems of the student with disabilities. Mercer and Mercer (1985) indicate that teachers can "help foster the student's emotional development as well as the acquisition of social skills" (p. 132). Wallace and Kauffman (1986) and Mercer and Mercer (1985) believe that direct instruction may be the best method for remediating problems associated with social skills deficits. In addition to direct instruction, there are instructional materials and kits available commercially that are designed for teaching social skills. However, many of these kits have little validity data and vary widely in terms of the populations with which they have been used.

Perhaps social competence might be a better term to describe the skills necessary to get along with others. Schulman (1980) defines social competence as "getting along with people, communicating with them and coping with the frustrations of social living" (p. 285). Girls tend to achieve social competence more frequently than boys (Merrell, Merz, Johnson, & Ring, 1992). Nearly all of us need to feel accepted and socially competent. However, many students and adults with disabilities have difficulty, to some degree, in developing those skills necessary for adequate social acceptance.

REFERENCES

Bellach, A. S. (1983). Recurrent problems in the behavior assessment of social skills. *Behavior Research & Therapy, 21*, 29–41.

Bloom, B. (1956). *Taxonomy of educational objectives: The classification of educational goals.* New York, NY: Longman.

Cartwright, C. P., Cartwright, C. A., & Ward, M. E. (1984). *Educating special learners.* Belmont, CA: Wadsworth.

Drew, C. J., Logan, D. R., & Hardman, M. L. (1984). *Mental retardation: A life cycle approach* (3rd ed.). St. Louis, MO: Mosby.

Eleas, M. J., & Maher, C. A. (1983). Social and effective development of children: A programmatic perspective. *Exceptional Children, 4*, 339–346.

Lerner, J. (1985). *Learning disabilities: Theories, diagnosis, and teaching strategies* (4th ed.). Boston, MA: Houghton Mifflin.

Mercer, D. D., & Mercer, A. R. (1985). *Teaching students with learning problems* (2nd ed.). Columbus, OH: Merrill.

Merrell, K. W., Merz, J. M., Johnson, E. R., & Ring, E. N. (1992). Social competence of students with mild handicaps and low achievement: A comparative study. *School Psychology Review, 21*(1), 125–137.

Minskoff, E. H. (1980). Teaching approach for developing nonverbal communication skills in students with social perception deficits. *Journal of Learning Disabilities, 13*, 118–126.

Schulman, E. D. (1980). *Focus on retarded adults: Programs and services.* St. Louis, MO: Mosby.

Stephens, T. M., Hartman, A. C., & Lucas, V. H. (1983). *Teaching children basic skills: A curriculum handbook* (2nd ed.). Columbus, OH: Merrill.

Strain, P. S., Odom, S. L., & McConnell, S. (1984). Promoting social reciprocity of exceptional children: Identification, target behaviors selection, and intervention. *Remedial & Special Education, 1*, 21–28.

Wallace, G., & Kauffman, J. M. (1986). *Teaching students with learning and behavior problems* (3rd ed.). Columbus, OH: Merrill.

HUBERT B. VANCE
East Tennessee State University

See also Adaptive Behavior; Social Skills Instruction; Sociogram

SOCIAL COMMUNICATION QUESTIONNAIRE

The Social Communication Questionnaire (SCQ; Rutter, Bailey, & Lord, 2003), previously the Autism Spectrum Questionnaire (Berument, Rutter, Lord, Pickles, & Bailey, 1999), is designed as a screening tool for autism and autism spectrum disorders (ASD; Rutter et al., 2003). It was developed as a shorter version of the Autism Diagnostic Interview–Revised (Lord, Rutter, & LeCouteur, 1994) and is available in both "Lifetime" and "Current" versions (Rutter et al., 2003). The Current version focuses on the child's social communication skills over the past 3 months whereas the Lifetime version focuses on the child's social communication skills from infancy to present. Both versions are designed as parent-report scales and consist of 40 questions with dichotomous (yes/no) answer choices regarding their child's verbal and social development and behaviors (e.g., "Do you have a to and fro conversation with him/her that involves taking turns or building on what you have said?"). Scores on the SCQ range from 0–40 and have a publisher-recommended cutoff of 15, with scores of 15 or higher indicating the need for clinical follow-up regarding possible diagnosis of ASD (Berument et al., 1999). However, cutoffs as low 11 and 12 have been used in research studies (Norris & Lecavalier, 2010).

The specificity and sensitivity of the SCQ has been examined in multiple populations across multiple settings (Norris & Lecavalier, 2010). Although the measure is officially recommended for children ages 4.0 and above with a mental age of 2.0 and above (Rutter et al., 2003), research has examined its use as a screening tool with children as young as 2 or 3 years (Allen, Silove, Williams, & Hutchins, 2007; Lee, David, Rusnyiak, Landa, & Newschaffer, 2007). Initial data from the publisher reported high specificity (.85) and sensitivity (.75) but was limited to a sample of parents whose children had already received diagnoses of and were receiving services for ASD (Berument et al., 1999; Eaves, Wingert, & Ho, 2006).

Independent evaluation of the SCQ has recently examined its sensitivity and specificity as a screening tool included in pre-evaluation packets for parents whose children had been referred for autism evaluations (e.g., Allen et al., 2007; Eaves et al., 2006; Corsello et al., 2007; Lee et al., 2007). These studies have frequently found lower specificity and sensitivity than originally reported. A recent review of 11 published studies on the SCQ (Norris & Lecavalier, 2010) found sensitivity estimates for ASD versus non-ASD differentiation ranging from .47 to .92 and specificity estimates ranging from .52 to .89 for the same differentiation; sensitivity was generally higher than specificity, meaning that the cut-off scores on the SCQ typically produced more false positives than false negatives when compared with actual ASD diagnoses via clinical evaluation.

One study (Corsello et al., 2007) examined sensitivity and specificity across different age groups and found that the sensitivity and specificity of the SCQ tends to increase with the child's age. Norris and Lecavalier (2010) came to the same conclusion following their review of the literature. Some research has recommended that lower cut-off scores, such as 12, be used in populations where the expected rates of ASD are high, such as in special education or clinical samples, to increase specificity (Lee et al., 2007).

REFERENCES

Allen, C. W., Silove, N., Williams, K., & Hutchins, P. (2007). Validity of the Social Communication Questionnaire in assessing risk of autism in preschool children with developmental problems. *Journal of Autism and Developmental Disorders*, 37, 1272–1278.

Berument, S. L., Rutter, M., Lord, C., Pickles, A., & Bailey, A. (1999). Autism screening questionnaire: Diagnostic validity. *British Journal of Psychiatry*, 175, 444–445.

Corsello, C., Hus, V., Pickles, A., Risi, S., Cook, Jr., E. H., Leventhal, B. L., & Lord, C. (2007). Between a ROC and a hard place: Decision making and making decisions about using the SCQ. *Journal of Child Psychology and Psychiatry*, 48, 932–940.

Eaves, L. C., Wingert, H., & Ho, H. H. (2006). Screening for autism: Agreement with diagnosis. *Autism*, 10, 229–242.

Lee, L., David, A. B., Rusyniak, J., Landa, R., & Newschaffer, C. J. (2007). Performance of the Social Communication Questionnaire in children receiving preschool special education services. *Research in Autism Spectrum Disorders*, 1, 126–138.

Lord, C., Rutter, M., & LeCouteur, A. (1994). Autism Diagnostic Interview-Revised: A revised version of a diagnostic interview for caregivers of individuals with possible pervasive developmental disorders. *Journal of Autism and Developmental Disorders*, 24, 659–685.

Norris, M., & Lecavalier, L. (2010). Screening accuracy of level 2 autism spectrum disorder rating scales: A review of selected instruments. *Autism*, 14, 263–286.

Rutter, M., Bailey, A., & Lord, C. (2003). *Manual for the Social Communication Questionnaire*. Los Angeles, CA: Western Psychological Services.

EMILY LUND
Texas A&M University
Fourth edition

SOCIAL COMPETENCE (*See Adaptive Behavior*)

SOCIAL DARWINISM

Social Darwinism, a social philosophy that was developed in the latter half of the 19th century, was based on the application of Darwin's principles of natural selection and survival of the fittest to the problems of society. Intellectual disabilities, insanity, epilepsy, alcoholism, and other disorders were explained in terms of heredity, genetics, and Darwinian principles. Adams (1971) describes social Darwinism as follows: "the people of above average intelligence by previous standards become the norm in the next evolutionary phase, and the slow ones drop back to become the social casualties of the new order." Social Darwinism was also associated with attempts to interpret intellectual disabilities as deviance rather than incompetence (Farber, 1968).

When Western Europe and North America became industrialized, environmental conditions that hindered the intellectual development of children resulted. Industrialization also led to health hazards that were responsible for the birth of children with biological deficiencies. At the same time, correlations were found between intellectual and social deficits that stimulated a variety of explanatory efforts. According to the principle of social Darwinism, human deficiencies were caused by evolutionary obstacles or the degeneration of genetic matter. The historical perspective of social Darwinism and its relation to the eugenics movement are central to understanding the treatment of individuals with disabilities from the 1850s to the 1950s.

In the 1850s, even before Darwin published his findings and theories, Morel speculated that all varieties of mental illnesses were related and were due to hereditary factors. Noting an association between intellectual disability and sterility, he further postulated that these illnesses became more profound with each succeeding generation, leading ultimately to, sterility and extinction. Morel suggested that mental illnesses were caused by physical diseases, alcoholism, and social environments, and called for more adequate food, housing, and working conditions as preventive measures. Concurrently, with evidence of a genetic inheritable component of intelligence mounting, mental health professionals were becoming convinced that institutional segregation of individuals with disabilities was necessary, thus abandoning their efforts to return individuals with disabilities to the community. Darwinism reached a height of popularity in England in the 14-year period from 1858 to 1872, but its effects were felt until the turn of the century. In the United States, Darwinian doctrine provided justification for the existing status structure prior to and during the Civil War. Darwinian proponents contended that foreigners and members of lower socioeconomic levels were distinct races that were inferior and might justifiably be subjugated. However, the North's victory strengthened the position of the anti-Darwinian proponents (Farber, 1968).

The optimism that characterized the treatment and care of the disabled in the early portion of the 19th century began to disappear in the latter half of the century. Institutions began moving away from treatment programs, replacing them with basic care and maintenance services. The emphasis on rehabilitation and education degenerated into support for terminal institutional placement

(Hardman, Drew, & Egan, 1984). In the early portion of the 20th century, with the introduction of mental tests, researchers found that a large proportion of prison inmates could be classified as individuals with intellectual disabilities. Women with intellectual disabilities were believed to be promiscuous, burdening society with many illegitimate offspring. It was estimated that criminals and unmarried mothers constituted 40% to 45% of the population of individuals with intellectual disabilities. Furthermore, Tredgold and his followers contended that 90% of mental deficiency was due to hereditary factors. Individuals with intellectual disabilities were regarded as unable to sustain gainful employment and a danger to the community and the "race." The solutions that were proposed most often were segregation and sterilization (Farber, 1968).

The "eugenic scare" of the early 1900s has been described as a shift in focus from the protection of individuals with intellectual disabilities from a cruel and exploitative society to the protection of society from contamination by inferior mental stock (Adams, 1971). With social Darwinism setting the stage, the eugenic movement was fed by the alarming increase in pauperism, vagrancy, alcoholism, and delinquency in society, and the association of low mentality and sociopathic behavior within identified families (e.g., the Jukes and the Kallikaks) whose genetic lines had been traced. The eugenic position was manifested in legislation for sterilization and the proposal to extend custodial care to all individuals with intellectual disabilities in the United States during their childbearing years. The first sterilization law was passed in Indiana in 1907, followed by similar legislation in seven other states soon thereafter. (Adams, 1971).

By the 1920s, pessimistic forecasts appeared to have been vindicated in England, where the incidence of intellectual disabilities was sharply increasing. Although eugenicists strove to win the debate on intellectual disabilities during the period from 1900 to 1940, their efforts were hindered by their inability to identify the unfit, to prove causation, and to limit fertility (Macnicol, 1983). In reality, the concept of total social control over individuals with intellectual disabilities was never much more than an idea, and neither wholesale institutional commitment nor sterilization was implemented. Providing institutional care to segregate a large portion of society at public expense proved to be highly impractical. Nevertheless, by associating mental defects with genetic factors, the social forces that were causing pathological living conditions among the poor were neglected and the economic causes for social maladjustment were ignored (Adams, 1971). The negative side effects of involuntary sterilization of individuals with intellectual disabilities have now been documented. Low self-esteem, feelings of failure, a sense of helplessness, and social isolation have all been associated with forced sterilization (Roos, 1975).

Social Darwinism and related social movements have had a profound impact on the treatment of individuals with intellectual disabilities and other individuals with disabilities. However, not all of the effects of the social Darwinism movement were negative. Its popularity, along with the development of special educational services, has been credited with providing an impetus for the systematic study of the prevalence of intellectual disability (Farber, 1968).

REFERENCES

Adams, M. (1971). *Mental retardation and its social dimensions.* New York, NY: Columbia University Press.

Farber, B. (1968). *Mental retardation: Its social context and social consequences.* Boston, MA: Houghton Mifflin.

Hardman, M. L., Drew, C. I., & Egan, M. W. (1984). *Human exceptionality: School, society, and family.* Boston, MA: Allyn & Bacon.

Macnicol, J. (1983). Eugenics, medicine and mental deficiency: An introduction. *Oxford Review of Education, 3,* 177–180.

Roos, P. (1975). Psychological impact of sterilization on the individual. *Law & Psychology Review, 1,* 45–56.

GREG VALCANTE
University of Florida

See also Eugenics; The Jukes and the Kallikaks

SOCIAL INTEGRATION OF CHILDREN WITH DISABILITIES IN SCHOOLS (See Inclusion; Mainstreaming)

SOCIAL ISOLATION

Social isolation has been subsumed under the rubric of social skills or social competence. The problem of defining social isolation in children, specifically, is consonant with the problem of defining social skills or social competence in general. Children labeled as social isolates do not appear to constitute a homogeneous or clearly defined group, and several descriptors have been used in the literature as labels (e.g., shy, isolated, withdrawn, anxious-withdrawn). Social isolation is a behavior pattern that occurs across various categories of children such as autistic, intellectually disabled, schizophrenic, severe visual impaired (Gourgey, 1998), and typically developing.

There is a lack of agreement among investigators regarding the specific behaviors that need to be performed to indicate social skillfulness or competence, and the appropriate behaviors that are not performed, or the inappropriate behaviors that are performed, that indicate a lack of social skillfulness or competence. The contribution of several variables such as age, gender, social status, and situationally specific factors, in determining the presence or absence of social competence is poorly understood. Also, the criterion measures used to assess social isolation (behavioral observations, peer sociometric ratings, teacher ratings) may affect what is labeled as social isolate behavior (Conger & Keane, 1981). These criterion measures may not tap the same dimensions of behavior and may identify different subtypes of children (Gottman, 1977). The behaviors that have been selected as indicators of social isolate behavior have not been empirically determined. They have been chosen on the basis of the face validity of their relationship to the behavior pattern of social isolation, and single measures of social isolation typically have been employed (Conger & Keane, 1981). Additionally, little or no relationship has been found between the two main types of criterion measures used to assess social isolate behavior when they have been compared (i.e., global peer sociometric ratings of acceptance or rejection and behavioral observations of rate of discrete social interactions; Gottman, 1977).

The principal approaches in the conceptualization of social isolation in childhood have been in terms of withdrawal indicated by low rates of social interaction relative to other children and rejection or lack of acceptance by peers (Gottman, 1977). These two groups of social isolates may represent different populations; however, the infrequent use of both methods of assessment with the same groups of children does not allow for a determination of how well these measures agree on or discriminate among different subtypes of children. Also, given the lack of agreement on what behaviors or lack of behaviors are related to social isolation, it is unclear whether low rates of social interaction imply a lack of social skills or a lack of exhibiting social skills that the child possesses. In terms of peer acceptance or rejection, it is not clear whether this is based on a lack of social skills or on behaviors perceived as negative by peers, such as aggressiveness. The grouping together of various behaviors within the category of social isolate behavior obscures assessment and intervention efforts and reduces the likelihood of heterogeneous grouping.

The development of positive social relationships with peers is an important developmental achievement. Typically, social interaction increases and relationships become more stable as children grow older (Asher, Oden, & Gottman, 1977). Thus social isolation may represent a significant deviation in social development. Gronlund (1959) reports that 6% of a sample of grades 3 to 6 had no classroom friends, and 12% had only one friend. A study of elementary age children with problem behavior identified 13.95% of the children referred by teachers for psychological services as withdrawn (Woods, 1964, as cited in Woods, 1969). Strain, Cook, and Apolloni (1976) estimate that 15% or more of children referred for psychological services exhibit social withdrawal as a major presenting symptom. Once a pattern of withdrawal behavior is established, it may persist through childhood and adolescence (Bronson, 1968). The evidence for the carryover of social isolation into adulthood is beset with methodological problems and conflicting results that limit generalizations. It does appear, however, that adults with certain psychiatric disabilities were children with social isolation, but that not all children with social isolation develop psychiatric disabilities as adults (Strain et al., 1976). Hops, Walker, and Greenwood (1979) note that children referred for psychological services because of social isolate behavior appear to lead quiet, retiring lives, with some restriction in social contacts.

Intervention approaches used with children with social withdrawal increasingly emphasize the training of social skills. Social learning procedures (Coombs & Slaby, 1977) have constituted major treatment methods for teaching social skills to children with social isolation (Conger & Keane, 1981; Hops, 1983). The use of instructional packages with multiple components appears to be the best method for teaching social skills. The packages may include a combination of shaping, modeling, coaching, and reinforcement. Cognitively oriented interpersonal problem-solving interventions have also been employed; they emphasize the training of cognitive processes to mediate performance across a range of situations rather than discrete behavioral responses to various situations (Urbain & Kendall, 1980). The cognitive-behavioral approach uses many of the same instructional methods as the social learning approach, but it focuses on teaching problem-solving strategies and verbally mediated self-control (e.g., self-instruction). Music therapy has also been used successfully (Gourgey, 1998).

The evidence to date suggests that interventions have demonstrated modest to moderate effects in teaching social skills to children with social isolation. Also, there are problems in establishing training effects that generalize beyond the treatment setting and maintain over time. Given the importance of positive social relationships with peers, efforts need to be continued to overcome conceptual, methodological, and assessment problems. Advances in these areas may further improve intervention efforts with children for whom peer relationships are problematic.

REFERENCES

Asher, S. R., Oden, S. C., & Gottman, J. M. (1977). Children's friendship in the school setting. In L. G. Katz (Ed.), *Current topics in early education* (Vol. 1). Norwood, NJ: Ablex.

Bronson, W. C. (1968). Stable patterns of behaviors: The significance of enduring orientations for personality development. In J. P. Hill (Ed.), *Minnesota symposia on child psychology* (Vol. 2). Minneapolis: University of Minnesota Press.

Conger, J. C., & Keane, P. (1981). Social skills intervention in the treatment of isolated or withdrawn children. *Psychological Bulletin, 90*(3), 478–495.

Coombs, M. L., & Slaby, D. (1977). Social skills training with children. In B. B. Lahey & A. E. Kazdin (Eds.), *Advances in *clinical child psychology* (Vol. 1). New York, NY: Academic Press.

Gottman, J. M. (1977). Toward a definition of social isolation in children. *Child Development, 48*, 513–517.

Gourgey, C. (1998). Music therapy in the treatment of social isolation in visually impaired children. *RE: View, 29*(4), 157–162.

Gronlund, N. E. (1959). *Sociometry in the classroom.* New York, NY: Harper.

Hops, H. (1983). Social skills training for socially withdrawn/isolate children. In P. Karoly & J. J. Steffen (Eds.), *Improving children's competence.* Lexington, MA: Lexington.

Hops, H., Walker, H. M., & Greenwood, C. R. (1979). PEERS: A program for remediating withdrawal in school. In L. A. Hamerlynck (Ed.), *Behavioral systems for the developmentally disabled: In school and family environments.* New York, NY: Brunner/Mazel.

Strain, P. S., Cooke, T. P., & Apolloni, T. (1976). *Teaching exceptional children: Assessing and modifying social behavior.* New York, NY: Academic Press.

Urbain, E. S., & Kendall, P. C. (1980). Review of social-cognitive problem-solving interventions with children. *Psychological Bulletin, 88*(1), 109–143.

Harold Hanson
Paul Bates
Southern Illinois University

See also **Social Behavior of Individuals With Disabilities; Sociogram**

SOCIAL LEARNING THEORY

Social learning theory is one of the most well-known and most influential models for understanding human behavior. In explaining this theory, it is helpful to describe what it is not, because social learning theory grew out of a reaction to other theoretical orientations. First, social learning theory does not view human behavior as purely a result of internal cognitive thoughts or feelings. Freud, for example, viewed human behavior as mediated by thoughts, wishes, self-concepts, impulses, and so forth. Neither does social learning theory view behavior as strictly a function of environmental events. Thus social learning theory is not a model of human behavior based strictly on the principles of operant conditioning developed by B. F. Skinner. Skinner and others believe that behavior is purely a function of environmental events.

Social learning theory does, however, provide an integration of previous theories such as Freud's and Skinner's. Although social learning theory is closely related to Skinner's principles of operant conditioning, the major difference is the incorporation of internal events as controlling stimuli. Social learning theorists recognize that an individual's thoughts and feelings have a significant impact on behavior.

Social learning theory is a term that has been applied to the views of a relatively wide range of theorists and researchers. Without question, the theorist who has done the most to conceptualize and advance the ideas of social learning theory is Albert Bandura of Stanford University. His more recent work has moved away from the early environmental determinism that characterized behavioristic social learning theory. His most comprehensive presentation is in his 1986 book in which he extensively details his social cognitive theory. No socialization theory has as much careful empirical support as social cognitive theory. Bandura has added significant arguments for why internal evaluative processes must be included in any behavioral theory. At the core of Bandura's theory is the concept of reciprocal determinism. Similar to but more limited than Bronfenbrenner's ecological model, reciprocal determinism conceptualizes behavior as a continuous reciprocal interaction between an individual's thoughts, behaviors, and environmental factors.

This triadic model views human functioning as a three-way interaction among behavior (B), cognitions and other internal events that affect perceptions and actions (P), and a person's external environment (E). An interesting aspect of this view is that each element of the triad affects the other two elements. Thus, not only do internal and environmental events affect behavior, but behavior also affects internal events and the environment in reciprocal fashion.

Bandura's (1986) emphasis on internal mediators can be seen in work on observational learning, enactive learning, predictive knowledge and forethought, interpretations of incentives, vicarious motivators, self-regulatory mechanisms, self-efficacy, and cognitive regulators. Bandura demonstrates how cognitive factors determine what we observe, how we evaluate our observations, and how we use this information in the future. For example when students take tests, they read the questions, answer according to their interpretations of what the teacher wants, receive feedback in the form of grades, and then adjust depending on how successfully they believe they answered the questions graded by the teacher. No behavior occurs in a vacuum without prior internal processes and external effects.

A key component in most social learning theories is observational learning, which is based on the process of modeling. Through modeling, children learn a wide array of complicated skills, such as language and social interaction. Moreover, these skills are learned without reinforcement. This is in stark contrast to radical behavioral theory, which posits that complex behaviors are learned through the reinforcement of gradual changes in molecular response patterns. Teachers make use of observational learning many times a day. For example, some teachers will verbally reinforce a child who is behaving appropriately just so other children will be encouraged to imitate the modeled behavior. Most socialization is the result of observational learning, because it is much more efficient and realistic than the step-by-step shaping advocated by radical behaviorists.

Another key component that has received considerable research attention is the concept of self-efficacy. Self-efficacy is a complex process in which persons assess the likelihood of successfully performing a task based upon their previous mastery (e.g., training), vicarious experience (e.g., modeling of others), verbal persuasion (e.g., encouragement), physiological condition (e.g., health), and affective state (e.g., happy). Persons high in self-efficacy will make realistic judgments of their abilities to perform tasks, will tend to seek appropriately difficult tasks, and will persist in them until completed (Bandura, 1997). Teachers with high teacher self-efficacy will be more likely to believe they can teach a classroom of difficult children. In special education classes, high teacher self-efficacy will result in greater progress and competence in the students.

Social learning theory has also emphasized the concept of internal dialogues. These dialogues, or internal speeches, are used by people to learn information (e.g., to rehearse a phone number), for self-instruction (e.g., "Now what do I do next?"), and for self-reinforcement (e.g., "Way to go!"). These internal dialogues fit in nicely with Vygotsky's developmental theory postulating a cognitive self-guidance system in which these dialogues eventually become silent or inner speech. Teaching internal dialogues to children with learning disabilities may help them become better problem solvers (Berk, 1992).

Because social learning theory has incorporated internal variables (e.g., thoughts and feelings) that are not directly observable, it has been criticized by radical behaviorists. Similarly, the emphasis within social learning theory on environmental factors and the lack of emphasis on cognitive development has caused it to be questioned by developmentalists. Freudian psychologists are dissatisfied with the lack of strong emotional components. Despite these detractors, social learning theory has enormous appeal to a wide variety of professionals. The reason for this appeal is the testability of the theory and the broad coverage of internal and external factors. Social learning theory is seen by many as being very comprehensive in its ability to handle a diverse range of human experiences and problems.

REFERENCES

Bandura, A. (1986). *Social foundations of thought and action: A social cognitive theory*. Englewood Cliffs, NJ: Prentice Hall.

Bandura, A. (1997). *Self-efficacy: The exercise of control*. New York, NY: Freeman.

Berk, L. E. (1992). Children's private speech: An overview of theory and the status of research. In R. M. Diaz & L. E.

Berk (Eds.), *Private speech: From social interaction to self-regulation*. Hillsdale, NJ: Erlbaum.

SPENCER THOMPSON
The University of Texas of the Permian Basin

See also Bandura, Albert; Impulse Control; Mediational Deficiency; Mediation; Observational Learning; Reciprocal Determinism

SOCIAL MALADJUSTMENT

Social Maladjustment (SM) is, at best, a vaguely defined and intensely debated construct. It emerged approximately 30 years ago in an exclusionary clause to the federal definition of students with emotional disturbance (ED): "The term [ED] does not apply to children who are socially maladjusted, unless it is determined that they have an emotional disturbance" (34 CFR Part 300.7(c)(4); OSERS, Office of Special Education and Rehabilitative Services, OSERS, 1997). Although the definition of ED was based on Eli Bower's research in the 1960s, the exclusionary clause for students considered SM seemed to appear with no basis in the empirical literature (Merrell & Walker, 2004). Since that time, researchers and practitioners have struggled to (a) define social maladjustment, (b) identify students who are SM and differentiate them from students who are ED, and (c) serve students who are SM.

Definition and Etiology

Attempts to define social maladjustment range from liberal, or inclusive, to more conservative, or exclusive, definitions. Each interpretation suggests a different etiology.

Liberal interpretation. Some researchers equate SM to a *DSM-IV-TR* (American Psychiatric Association, 2000) diagnosis of conduct disorder, antisocial personality disorder, or oppositional defiant disorder (e.g., Cullinan, 2004), which are assumed to be the product of a constellation of environmental and biological/dispositional risk factors (e.g., Frick, 2004). The range of students who meet criteria for one of the three diagnoses impedes the differentiation of students with SM from students with ED (Merrell & Walker, 2004), leading researchers and practitioners to employ more conservative criteria.

Conservative interpretations. Gacono and Hughes (2004) assert that the distinguishing factor of students with SM is psychopathy, which they describe as a "distinct personality syndrome" (p. 849). According to their definition, students with SM (a) demonstrate traits and behaviors considered "paranoid, borderline, narcissistic, histrionic, and antisocial" (p. 851), resulting from an interplay between physiological (e.g., biochemical abnormalities) and environmental (e.g., family dynamics) factors, and (b) present a greater risk for re-offending and violence.

Perhaps of more use to educators is a specific operational definition, based on an assumption that students with SM "engage in antisocial problem behavior in a willful manner, in the company of other antisocial youths, as a way to maintain or enhance their social status with in the antisocial subgroup, and in a manner that is unlawful" (Merrell & Walker, 2004, p. 902). Students with SM are defined as those who manifest "severe antisocial behavior" (Theodore, Akin-Little, & Little, 2004); that is, those who have been formally adjudicated for delinquent behavior that is purposeful in nature (Merrell & Walker, 2004).

A working definition. Merrell and Walker (2004) summarize that, regardless of interpretation, social maladjustment can best be described as "a pattern of engagement in purposive antisocial, destructive, and delinquent behavior" (p. 901).

Identification

Although a great deal of attention has been given to differentially diagnosing SM from ED, the focus has shifted to using assessment information to guide appropriate intervention (e.g., Hughes & Bray, 2004). Students with SM should be identified, as early as possible, through a comprehensive and intensive screening process in the context of a problem-solving model. Information should be gathered using multiple methods from multiple informants across settings and time.

Evidence-Based Strategies for Intervention

Walker, Ramsey, and Gresham (2004) summarize proven strategies for preventing, intervening with, and de-escalating antisocial behavior. In general, students with SM benefit from assertive communication and function-based supports in a positive environment. Traditional forms of discipline, which may include punishment-based procedures (e.g., the "teacher look," verbal reprimand), typically result in power struggles that may escalate the situation. Because students with SM, by definition, may have a history of engaging in serious aggressive and unlawful behaviors, it is important to know a student's history; this understanding assists in determining the level at which outside support may be required.

A particularly promising approach to supporting students with SM emphasizes the determination of the function, or resulting consequences, of the emitted behavior, and the use of this information to develop behavior intervention plans (Crone & Horner, 2003). For example, one student who engages in intimidating stares may learn that this behavior successfully results in access to peer attention. Hypothesizing this function, an intervention might focus on teaching the student more prosocial behaviors that enable access to the same peer attention. In contrast, another student who engages in the same intimidating stares has learned that the same behavior effectively keeps peers away. The procedure that was used with the first student would be ineffective for this second student, who instead might need to learn how to disengage from peers in more socially acceptable ways (or how to engage peers in ways that are less aversive to him or her). The use of this type of function-based behavior intervention planning fits easily with the working definition of SM.

REFERENCES

American Psychiatric Association. (2000). *The diagnostic and statistical manual of mental disorders* (4th ed., text rev.). Washington, DC: Author.

Crone, D. A., & Horner, R. H. (2003). *Building positive behavior support systems in schools: Functional behavioral assessment.* New York, NY: Guilford Press.

Cullinan, D. (2004). Classification and definition of emotional and behavioral disorders. In $. G. Rutherford, M. M. Quinn, & S. R. Mathur, (Eds.), *Handbook of research in emotional and behavioral disorders.* New York, NY: Guilford Press.

Frick, P. J. (2004). Developmental pathways to conduct disorder: Implications for serving youth who show severe aggressive and antisocial behavior. *Psychology in the Schools, 41,* 823–834.

Gacono, C. B., & Hughes, T. L. (2004). Differentiating emotional disturbance from social maladjustment: Assessing psychopathy in aggressive youth. *Psychology in the Schools, 41,* 849–860.

Hughes, T. L., & Bray, M. A. (2004). Differentiation of emotional disturbance and social maladjustment: Introduction to the special issue. *Psychology in the Schools, 41,* 819–821.

Merrell, K. W., & Walker, H. W. (2004). Deconstructing a definition: Social maladjustment versus emotional disturbance and moving the EBD field forward. *Psychology in the Schools, 41,* 899–910.

Office of Special Education and Rehabilitative Services (OSERS). (1997). IDEA '97 Final Regulations: 34 CFR Part 300, Assistance to States for the Education of Children with Disabilities: Part B of the Individuals with Disabilities Education Act. Retrieved from http://www.cec.sped.org/

Theodore, L. A., Akin-Little, A., & Little, S. G. (2004). Evaluating the differential treatment of emotional disturbance and social maladjustment. *Psychology in the Schools, 41,* 879–886.

Walker, H. M., Ramsey, E., & Gresham, F. M. (2004). *Antisocial behavior in school: Evidence-based practices.* Belmont, CA: Thomson.

BRANDI SIMONSEN
University of Connecticut

SOCIAL MATURITY (*See Adaptive Behavior*)

SOCIAL PHOBIA

Social phobia is a class of anxiety disorder characterized by a persistent fear of situations in which the person is exposed to possible scrutiny by others. The individual fears that he or she may act in a way that will be humiliating and embarrassing. The key feature of social phobia is the fear of being judged by others. In a school setting, this might occur in situations where a child avoids giving speeches in class or entering the school cafeteria or fears asking questions in a classroom. In other settings the child might refuse to eat, drink, or write in public or to attend social activities such as birthday or graduation parties, scout meetings, or church activities. Social phobias can be very selective in that a child may have an intense fear of a single situation, such as speaking in front of a class, but be perfectly comfortable in other situations (Rabian & Silverman, 2000). In applying the criteria to children, it must be demonstrated that the individual has the capacity to engage in socially appropriate behavior with familiar people and that the difficulties are not due to impaired social skills. The social anxiety must also occur in peer settings, not just with adults. Clinical presentation of symptoms may vary across cultures subject to unique social demands. For example, in Japanese and Korean cultures, social phobias may be expressed in terms of fears of giving offense (via excessive blushing, eye contact, or body odor) to others in social situations rather than personal behavior.

Social phobia is estimated to occur in 1% of children and adolescents. Age of onset typically occurs around puberty and peaks after the age of 30. It can occur at younger ages but is rarely diagnosed in children under age 10. The lifetime prevalence rates for social phobia ranges from 3% to 13%. Although a general fear of public speaking is estimated to be as high as 20% in the general population, only 2% experience an intense fear sufficient to warrant the diagnosis.

Characteristics

1. Constant fear of social-performance situations and feedback during these times.

2. Must demonstrate age-appropriate social relationships with familiar people, and the anxiety must also occur in peer settings.

3. Under age 18, symptoms must be present for at least 6 months.

4. Unrecognized fears are addressed.

5. Exposure to the feared situation evokes social phobic behavior.

6. Anxiety must interfere with behavior in both school and social settings and presentation of the trigger evokes fear about the situation.

(Adapted from American Psychiatric Association, 2000)

Although anxiety disorders comprise the most common disorder in childhood, very little research is available supporting the effectiveness of traditional psychotherapy or psychodynamic approaches (Kendall et al., 1997; Rabian & Silverman, 2000). For the management and treatment of childhood phobias, contingency management has been the only treatment considered to be well established (Ollendick & King, 1998). Using criteria established by the American Psychological Association, the following treatments are also considered probably efficacious for treating phobias: systematic desensitization, modeling using the observational learning approach, and several cognitive-behavioral therapy (CBT) approaches. CBT has four major components: recognizing anxious feelings, clarifying cognitions in anxiety-provoking situations, identifying a plan for coping with those situations, and evaluating the success of the coping strategies. In vivo graduated exposure coupled with CBT treatments has also proven effective. Pharmacological interventions for anxiety-based disorders include the use of selective serotonin reuptake inhibitors (SSRIs) such as Prozac, Paxil, Zoloft, Luvox, or Celexa with initial dosages lower than recommended and slowly adjusted for maximum therapeutic effect. Benzodiazepines such as Xanax and Ativan as well as trycyclic antidepressants have shown minimal to modest benefit and in some cases have been no more effective than placebo in children. These treatments are usually provided as an adjunct to psychological treatments.

Children with social phobia may experience declines in classroom performance, school refusal, or avoidance of age-appropriate activities such as going out on dates or socializing with peers. Special education support services may be available to children diagnosed with social phobia under specific categories of other health impairment or severe emotional disturbance or behavior disorder if an impact on the child's education can be established. This may be particularly important if the disorder is chronic in nature. Accommodations may also be requested and provided under Section 504 of the Rehabilitation Act of 1973. Families can benefit from additional counseling and support to implement effectively a treatment plan across both school and home settings.

Social phobia tends to fluctuate throughout the life span, subject to life stressors and situational demands experienced in different settings. Children and adults may experience a remission or decrease in the severity of the symptoms when life circumstances change. The disorder tends to occur in families where there is evidence of anxiety or phobic-based disorders. Rather than a specific anxiety disorder, there tends to be a predisposition in families to some variant within the range of anxiety disorders.

REFERENCES

American Psychiatric Association. (2000). *Diagnostic and statistical manual of mental disorders* (4th ed. text rev.). Washington, DC: Author.

Kendall, P. C., Flannery-Schroeder, E., Panicelli-Mindel, S. M., Southam-Gerow, M., Henin, A., & Warman, M. (1997). Therapy for youths with anxiety disorders: A second randomized clinical trial. *Journal of Consulting and Clinical Psychology*, 65, 366–380.

Ollendick, T. H., & King, N. J. (1998). Empirically supported treatments for children with phobic and anxiety disorders: Current status. *Journal of Clinical Child Psychology*, 27, 156–167.

Rabian, B., & Silverman, W. (2000). Anxiety disorders. In M. Hersen & R. Ammerman (Eds.), *Advanced abnormal child psychology* (pp. 271–289) Mahwah, NJ: Erlbaum.

DANIEL OLYMPIA
University of Utah

SOCIAL SECURITY

Social Security is based on the concept of providing income and health maintenance programs for families in such instances as retirement, disability, poor health, or death. In general, to be eligible for Social Security a person must first pay into Social Security by working and allowing a certain amount of income to be deducted from earnings. Sixteen percent (over 3 million people) of the population in the United States receive Social Security checks. Individuals over 65 (about 25 million) are covered under health insurance called Medicare. In the category of disability, the number receiving benefits are about 3 million.

The Social Security Act of 1935 consisted of three broad areas: (1) Social Security insurance, which included old age, survivors, disability, and hospital insurance (DAS-DHI), unemployment insurance, workman's compensation, compulsory temporary disability insurance, and railroad retirement system and railroad unemployment and temporary disability insurance; (2) government sponsorship of government or farm workers under civil service retirement, national service life insurance, federal crop insurance, public assistance (which is based on need), and veterans benefits; and (3) social assistance (welfare), which includes public assistance, national assistance, old-age assistance, unemployment assistance, and social pension programs that provide cash payments and other benefits to individuals based on need. Owing to the many changes in our society since 1935 such as demographic shifts, changes in values and attitudes, and inflation the Social Security system has been revised.

To be considered disabled under Social Security law a person must have a physical or mental condition that prevents that person from doing any substantial gainful work. The condition must be expected to last for at least 12 months, or expected to result in death. Examples of such conditions include diseases of the heart, lungs, or blood vessels that have resulted in serious loss of heart or lung reserves or serious loss of function of the kidneys; diseases of the digestive system that result in severe malnutrition, weakness, and anemia; and damage to the brain that has resulted in severe loss of judgment, intellect, orientation, or memory. The World Health Organization revised the mental health aspects of the International Classification of Impairments, Disabilities, and Handicaps (ICIDH) in 1995 to assist in the planning of care (Uestuen, van Duuren-Kristen, & Kennedy, 1995). Children of individuals who are eligible disabled persons can receive benefits if they are under 18 or 19, still in high school full time, or disabled before age 22, unmarried, and living at home. If an individual is blind, there are special considerations such as a disability freeze on income averaging for retirement purposes. Work situations for all individuals must require skills and abilities that are comparable to those of the individual's previous work history. If, however, the person is disabled before 22 and the parents are paying into Social Security, they can receive disability benefits. In order to qualify, the person must be unable to work in gainful employment and the person under whose credits they are applying must be retired, disabled, deceased, or fully insured under Social Security.

Another federal program administered by the Social Security Administration for low-income individuals is Supplemental Security Income (SSI). Supplemental security income is not based on work credits. Eligibility is based on age (over 65), income guidelines, and disability at any age for persons who earn below a specific income. In general, individuals living in institutions are not eligible for SSI unless they are classified under the four exceptions listed by the Social Security Administration (1986):

1. A person who lives in a publicly operated community residence that serves no more than 16 people may be eligible for SSI payments.

2. A person who lives in a public institution primarily to attend approved educational or vocational training provided in the institution may be eligible if the training is designed to prepare the person for gainful employment.

3. If a person is in a public or private medical treatment facility and Medicaid is paying more than half the cost of his or her care, the person may be eligible, but the SSI payments limited to no more than $25 per month.

4. A person who is a resident of a public emergency shelter throughout a month can receive SSI payments for up to 3 months during any 12-month period. (pp. 9–10)

In the early 1990s the eligibility for SSI based on childhood disability was expanded because of a Supreme Court decision in *Zebley* v. *Sullivan* (Ford & Schwann, 1992).

To receive SSI under a disability option, the individual must have a physical or mental disability that prevents him or her from gainful employment. The disability must be one that will last at least 12 months or be expected to end in death. For individuals under age 18, the decision is based on whether the disability would not allow the person to work if he or she were an adult.

REFERENCES

Ford, M. E., & Schwann, J. B. (1992). Expanding eligibility for SSI based on childhood disability: The Zebley decision. *Child Welfare, 71*(4), 307–318.

Uestuen, C., van Duuren-Kristen, S., & Kennedy, C. (1995). Revision of the ICIDH: Mental health aspects. *Disability & Rehabilitation: An International Multidisciplinary Journal, 17*, 3–4.

JANICE HARPER
North Carolina Central University

See also Disability; Rehabilitation; Socioeconomic Status

SOCIAL SKILLS INSTRUCTION

Social skills instruction is a method for establishing important social behaviors in our schools. Research suggests that students with disabilities may have an increased likelihood of either exhibiting a social skills deficit (when the student does not know how to perform the targeted social skills) or a performance deficit (when the student does not perform the previously taught social skill at an acceptable level), thus supporting the need for the direct teaching of specific social skills as part of special education support and services (Fletcher-Janzen & De Pry, 2003). Social skills can be taught as part of a universal intervention or as a method of supporting students who need both targeted and intensive/individualized behavioral support (see Sugai et al., 2000). When taught as part of a universal intervention, social skills are also known as school-wide behavioral expectations or character traits.

Social skills are "the individual skills and actions students must master...that allow them to initiate, sustain, adapt, alter, and discontinue interactions as conditions dictate" (Knapczyk & Rodes, 1996, p. 4). Social skills are specific behaviors (instead of feelings) that direct attention toward the development and maintenance of adult and peer relationships (Sugai & Lewis, 1996). Social competence, on the other hand, relates to the judgments that adults make about the student's use of targeted social skills within and across school environments (Fletcher-Janzen & De Pry, 2003). A student is said to be "socially competent" when she or he demonstrates fluency with a variety of socially important skills and uses these skills as conditions dictate. Common social skills include listening to others, taking turns, greeting, joining activities or groups, expressing feelings appropriately, and helping peers.

Colvin and Sugai (1988) argued that in many educational settings academic instruction is approached very differently than social skills instruction. In the former, academic skills are directly *taught* to students with an emphasis on guided and independent practice, instructionally based error correction, and positive reinforcement. Colvin and Sugai noted that social skills instruction is often predicated on the faulty assumption that students already know how to perform socially important skills prior to entering our schools, that when social skills lessons are provided that strategic practice is not required, and that punishment-oriented approaches are typically used to try to shape social behavior. The central thesis of this research is that social skills instruction should be *taught* in a manner that is similar to how we teach academic content; that is, providing explicit social skills instruction with the provision of guided practice, independent practice, and positive reinforcement.

Several assumptions underlie the use of social skills instruction in our schools, including that most social skills are learned behaviors, most social skills problems are learning errors, that instructional methods for teaching social skills are similar to methods for teaching academic skills, and that a reciprocal relationship exists between academic and social competence (Sugai & Lewis, 1996). Social skills assessment should include formative strategies such as systematic direct observation methods (see Alberto & Troutman, 2006) and summative strategies that provide both identification and evaluation of social skills (see Gresham & Elliott, 1990; Walker & McConnell, 1988).

Lesson planning and implementation are often different dependent on whether the student has a performance deficit or a skill deficit. For a performance deficit, the teacher should take advantage of teachable moments, embedded instruction, antecedent-based approaches such as precorrection (see De Pry & Sugai, 2002) and adjusting the current schedule of reinforcement (Elliott & Gresham, 1991). For students who have a social skills deficit, a more direct or active form of instruction is needed (see Social Skills Lesson Plan Outline), including paying attention to three lesson planning features: before instruction, during instruction, and after instruction phases (Darch & Kame'enui, 2004). Before instruction planning includes defining the instructional goal, the learning objectives, and other features that need to be in place that will support the lesson; for example, materials, personnel, monitoring, and evaluation strategies. During instruction features include providing a review set, verbal presentation of the skill, and both guided and independent practice of the skill by the students. During this phase, students are asked to demonstrate the skill using role-plays or simulations (see Guidelines for Conducting Role Plays and Simulations) in the settings where the skill will be required, such as classroom, playground, or cafeteria (Stokes & Baer, 1977). After instruction strategies include the strategic use of teacher prompting to set the occasion for the use of the skill and positive reinforcement contingent upon the correct demonstration of the social skill. In addition, methods for evaluating the effect of the instruction as it relates to use of the skill over time and across settings is an important part of this phase.

In conclusion, students with disabilities may exhibit skill or performance deficits and may need ongoing support to learn and demonstrate socially important social skills in our schools. Social skills instruction is predicated on the belief that social skills are learned behaviors, social skills problems are learning errors, methods for teaching social skills are similar to academic instruction, and a reciprocal relationship exists between social competence and academic competence. As part of lesson planning, emphasis should be placed on before, during, and after instructional phases, as well as including multiple opportunities to practice the social skill in targeted settings. Specific social skills lesson planning features and guidelines for conducting role-plays and simulations are provided in the following (adapted from De Pry, 2005).

Social Skills Lesson Plan Outline

Skill Name_____

BEFORE THE LESSON

Lesson Planning

1. Establish need through assessment and data analysis goal.
2. Establish criteria for student mastery objectives:

   Write instructional objectives across the following learning stages: acquisition, fluency, generalization, maintenance, and adaptation
3. Procedures: Before the lesson review instructional strategies and prepare materials, personnel, room, and monitoring and evaluation procedures

DURING THE LESSON

Learning / Review Set

1. Create interest and motivation as you review prerequisite information and skills
2. Link previous lessons with current lesson
3. State instructional objective

Verbal Presentation of the Skill

1. Name the skill
2. Define the critical rule

3. Provide sufficient examples and nonexamples for students to reach 80% mastery
4. Provide multiple opportunities for student responding (four to six responses per minute)
5. Provide immediate feedback and error correction

Doing the Skill—Guided Practice

1. Demonstrate the skill in the natural environment— MODEL
2. Practice the skill (teacher/student) using preplanned role-plays and simulations—LEAD
3. Evaluate role-plays
4. Provide immediate feedback and error correction
5. Initiate independent practice when at least 80% of the students reach mastery

Doing the Skill—Independent Practice

1. Provide students with clear instructions and expectations
2. Provide multiple practice opportunities using untrained role-plays and simulations—TEST
3. Actively monitor student progress and provide immediate feedback and error correction as needed
4. Assign homework that is school-based and/or home-based

AFTER THE LESSON

Prompting and Reinforcement

1. Provide student(s) with prompts prior to predictable errors in responding
2. Reinforce on a FR schedule during acquisition and VR schedule during maintenance and generalization

Evaluation

1. Collect and graph data on student progress over time and across settings
2. Evaluate student progress (formative and summative) and adjust teaching
3. Plan for additional teaching if needed

Guidelines for Conducting Role Plays and Simulations

- Have all materials ready before each role-play
- Remember, NEVER let participants practice nonexamples of the skill
- Conduct role-plays in target settings
- Pick students who are willing to participate
- Give each participant a script and/or background information of the situation they will role-play
- Remind each participant that it is very important that they try to do a good job
- Teach audience members expectations for watching and evaluating role-plays
- After each role-play (a) reinforce students for participating, (b) reinforce the audience for listening, and

(c) ask the audience and participants behavior-specific questions about the role-play; for example, *Was this an example of* _____ *(name of skill)* _____? *How do you know? What would you do differently to better show* _____ *(name of skill)* _____?

- Provide multiple opportunities to practice the skill to mastery and generalization
- Limit lessons to 15 to 20 minutes
- Have fun!

REFERENCES

Alberto, P. A., & Troutman, A. C. (2006). *Applied behavior analysis for teachers* (7th ed.). Upper Saddle River, NJ: Pearson Merrill Prentice Hall.

Colvin, G., & Sugai, G. (1988). Proactive strategies for managing social behavior problems: An instructional approach. *Education and Treatment of Children, 11*, 341–348.

Darch, C. B., & Kame'enui, E. J. (2004). *Instructional classroom management: A proactive approach to behavior management* (2nd ed.). Upper Saddle River, NJ: Pearson Merrill Prentice Hall.

De Pry, R. L. (2005). *Teaching social competence and character lesson plan template.* Unpublished manuscript.

De Pry, R. L., & Sugai, G. (2002). The effect of active supervision and precorrection on minor behavioral incidents in a sixth grade general education classroom. *Journal of Behavioral Education, 11*, 255–267.

Elliott, S. N., & Gresham, F. M. (1991). *Social skills intervention guide: Practical strategies for social skills training.* Circle Pines, MN: American Guidance Service.

Fletcher-Janzen, E., & De Pry, R. L. (2003). *Social competence and character: Developing IEP goals, objectives, and interventions.* Longmont, CO: Sopris West Educational Services.

Gresham, F. M., & Elliott, S. N. (1990). *Social skills rating system.* Circle Pines, MN: American Guidance Service.

Knapczyk, D. R., & Rodes, P. G. (1996). *Teaching social competence: A practical approach for improving social skills in students at-risk.* Pacific Grove, CA: Brooks/Cole.

Stokes, T. F., & Baer, D. M. (1977). An implicit technology of generalization. *Journal of Applied Behavior Analysis, 10*, 349–367.

Sugai, G., Horner, R. H., Dunlap, G. Hieneman, M., Lewis, T. J., Nelson, C. M., ... Ruef, M. B. (2000). Applying positive behavioral support and functional behavioral assessment in schools. *Journal of Positive Behavioral Interventions, 2*(3), 131–143.

Sugai, G., & Lewis, T. J. (1996). Preferred and promising practices for social skills instruction. *Focus on Exceptional Children, 29*(4), 1–16.

Walker, H. M., & McConnell, S. R., (1988). *The Walker-McConnell scale of social competence and school adjustment: A social skills rating scale for teachers.* Austin, TX: PRO-ED.

RANDALL L. DE PRY
University of Colorado at Colorado Springs

SOCIAL SKILLS INTERVENTIONS FOR HIGH SCHOOL STUDENTS WITH AUTISM AND INTELLECTUAL DISABILITIES

Successful classroom and everyday performance in high school is largely dependent on effective communication and social interaction with teachers and peers across a variety of classes and educational environments. Social skills limitations are exacerbated at the high school level where conversation with teachers and peers becomes the primary medium for social interaction and class participation, and expectations for appropriate communication and requisites to gain social acceptance are raised (Alwell & Cobb, 2009; Wang & Spillane, 2009). However, many students identified with autism and intellectual disabilities lack skills to communicate effectively with teachers and peers and respond appropriately to social stimuli (Hendricks & Wehman, 2009; Reichow & Volkmar, 2010). Opportunities to learn expected social skills are further limited by the fact that 44% of students with autism and 52% of students with intellectual disabilities spend 60% or more of their day outside the general education setting (U.S. Department of Education, 2009), apart from peers who could model expected social behavior.

Unless efforts are made to (a) teach students identified with autism and intellectual disabilities how to communicate effectively, participate socially with their teachers and peers, and engage actively in their classes and (b) provide support and opportunities to practice newly acquired skills, it is unlikely these students will learn to perform behaviors critical to success in school and postschool adult life (Muller, Schuler, Burton, & Yates, 2003). However, although communication and social interaction limitations are hallmark characteristics of individuals with autism and intellectual disabilities, minimal research has addressed these skills with high school students versus young children (e.g., Bellini, Peters, Benner, & Hopf, 2007). For example, Reichow and Volkmar's (2010) extensive review of social skills interventions with students with autism identified *no* studies in high school with students identified with autism and intellectual disabilities (those toward the lower end of the autism spectrum).

Peer-Mediated Social Skills Instruction in High School

Because of the lack of high school studies cited in recent reviews of social skills interventions with students with autism and intellectual disabilities, we sought to identify published studies that included high school participants. In addition, because we were interested in how students interacted with their general education peers, we specifically sought studies that included peers as an intervention component. Involving peers in social skills instruction and support of classroom participation removes the stigma of having adults assist students in general education settings (Carter & Kennedy, 2006). Including multiple peers as supports in students' everyday school settings increases the likelihood that skills will generalize across people, settings, and time (Stokes & Baer, 1977).

Our recent review of the literature (Hughes et al., 2011) identified seven published studies in which incorporating general education peers into social skills instructional programs was effective at increasing social interaction of high school students with autism and intellectual disabilities with their classmates. Published studies were included only if (a) at least one participant was identified with autism, (b) the study was conducted in a general education high school, and (c) general education peers were involved. We briefly describe the identified studies as categorized by salient intervention features, followed by a discussion of implications for research and practice.

Social interaction training and recreational item use. Gaylord-Ross, Haring, Breen, and Pitts-Conway (1984) taught three high school students with autism and intellectual disabilities to initiate interaction by introducing a recreational item (e.g., hand-held videogame) to an array of general education peers during training. Students first were taught to use the recreational item followed by instruction to appropriately engage a peer in social interaction with the item. Following instruction, opportunities to interact with peers were provided in a school courtyard setting. Social interactive behaviors generalized to novel peers after instruction was withdrawn and maintained during a four-month follow-up observation.

Conversational training and Power Cards. Davis, Boon, Cihak, and Fore (2010) taught three high school students with autism—one of whom had an intellectual disability—to ask general education peers questions about their individual interests and to listen to peers' responses while maintaining eye contact. Conversational skills training (e.g., asking questions) was first taught in a group format by a teacher in the absence of peers. Students were then taught to use "Power Cards" (Gagnon, 2001) to prompt interaction with peers. Each student chose a "hero" figure, such as a celebrity sports star, whose picture was printed on a small card alongside a conversational script that focused on a conversational partner's interests. Students were told that their hero had learned to have conversations that focused on a partner's interests. The teacher then instructed students to use their Power Cards and scripts to follow their hero's example when conversing with a peer. Conversational social skills generalized to a novel setting and peer for two of the three students during a teacher-arranged social interaction opportunity.

Conversational training and social problem solving. Plienis et al. (1987) introduced therapist-led group instruction to teach conversational skills and social problem solving to three students, two with emotional disturbance and one with autism. Therapists modeled conversational skills, such as asking questions and expressing interest, and provided opportunities for students to practice skills with each other. In addition, therapists instructed students to use

a problem-solving model for identifying social problems and potential solutions in response to hypothetical scenarios. Finally, students were prompted to use the social problem-solving strategies in social situations at school. Two of three students used their conversational skills with novel peers during generalization probes; limited use of problem-solving steps in response to novel scenarios was observed across students.

Social interaction training and self-management. The remaining four studies were conducted by one research group (Hughes & colleagues), which introduced combinations of social interaction training and self-management. In each of two studies (Hughes, Harmer, Killian, & Niahros, 1995; Hughes, Killian, & Fischer, 1996), a variety of general education peers taught four students with intellectual disabilities or autism to use self-instructional statements (i.e., "I want to talk," "I need to look and talk," "I did it, I talked," "I did a good job") to prompt and reinforce themselves for initiating and responding during conversational interactions with novel peers. A variation of this instructional strategy was used by Hughes et al. (2000) in which an array of general education peers taught five students with intellectual disabilities or autism to prompt themselves to use communication books to initiate conversational topics to novel peers. An additional self-management component of the three studies was that students were asked to set social goals for peer interaction prior to intervention and queried postintervention regarding goal achievement. Further, the array of peer trainers served as multiple exemplars of interaction partners to promote generalization of social behaviors across peers.

In the final study, Hughes et al. (2011) introduced an adult trainer to teach three students with intellectual disabilities or autism to use self-monitoring to prompt a range of social behavior when interacting with peers during training sessions (i.e., holding head up and attending, saying "thank you," initiating conversation). Students were taught to perform the expected social behavior in response to a naturally occurring environmental cue or a picture prompt when interacting with a peer. As in the previous studies conducted by this research group, social behaviors generalized to novel peers and occurrence of self-management behaviors corresponded with performance of expected social behaviors.

Implications for Research and Practice

It is critical that high school students with autism and intellectual disabilities learn expected social interaction skills while they are still in high school. Not only are these skills requisite to developing social relationships with peers; postschool follow-up studies also indicate that the primary reason people with disabilities lose their job is because of difficulty fitting in socially in the workplace versus failing to perform required tasks (e.g., Butterworth & Strauch, 1994; Chadsey, 2007). Fortunately, researchers and practitioners can learn much about effective social skills interventions from the seven identified studies.

First, recreational items, Power Cards, communication books, and similar objects may serve as a "social 'prosthetic' to facilitate interaction among peers who ordinarily had no common language or cultural base on which to build interactions" (Gaylord-Ross et al., 1984, p. 246). Because baseline observations across studies showed that participants rarely interacted with peers even when in proximity, they likely did not share common experiences to serve as a springboard to prompt interaction. A recreational item or list of suggested conversational topics could provide a common ground between two potential partners on which to develop and maintain interaction. Second, involving a variety of peers in social skills training—even as actual trainers—appears to be effective in promoting generalization of social behavior across peers and school settings after instructional assistance is withdrawn. This finding is important because it is critical that students perform expected social behaviors in everyday social situations when teaching staff are not in proximity—such as eating lunch in the cafeteria, walking in the hallways, or going to sports events—as well as in the community or at work. Third, teaching students to prompt and reinforce their newly acquired social skills by self-instructing, self-monitoring, or using a permanent prompt (e.g., picture or script) provides students with a tool to use to apply their skills in new settings and with new interaction partners.

Fourth, in light of the limited opportunity for interaction and few common experiences that typically exist between students with and without autism or intellectual disabilities, both social skills instruction and opportunities for social interaction must be provided simultaneously in order for interaction to occur. Researchers in all seven studies provided opportunities for students to interact with peers both during and following training. Because inclusion and membership in general education settings remain limited for students with autism and intellectual disabilities (U.S. Department of Education, 2009), instructional staff must assume responsibility for ensuring frequent, ongoing interaction between these students and their peers.

Future Directions

Our findings suggest future directions for the field. First, an obvious limitation to the social skills intervention literature base is that only seven published studies were found in which high school students with autism and intellectual disabilities and their general education peers participated. Further, only three studies were conducted in 2000 or later. Perhaps this trend reflects limited federal funding of education research related to social versus academic goals. At the same time, the value of social skills in relation to success in career and college is undisputed. Second, the U.S. school population is becoming increasing diverse; by 2020, the majority of public school students are expected to be low-income and from racially and ethnically diverse groups (National Center for Education Statistics, 2007; Suitts, 2010). However, of the seven studies, only four (Hughes & colleagues') identified participants' race or ethnicity—of the 16 students in these studies, 9 were Black and 7 were White and most attended low-income schools. It is important to know if interventions are effective across diverse cultural backgrounds. Therefore, future researchers should provide salient information about participants' cultural affiliations as well as personal characteristics, such as language and cognition, which may affect social skills intervention outcomes. Continued efforts to address studies' limitations will provide needed information to expand the application and adoption of social skills interventions in high schools.

REFERENCES

Alwell, M., & Cobb, B. (2009). Social and communicative interventions and transition outcomes for youth with disabilities: A systematic review. *Career Development for Exceptional Individuals, 32,* 94–107. doi:10.1177/0885728809336657

Bellini, S., Peters, J. K., Benner, L., & Hopf, A. (2007). A meta-analysis of school-based social skills interventions for children with autism spectrum disorders. *Remedial and Special Education, 28,* 153–162.

Butterworth, J., & Strauch, J. D. (1994). The relationship between social competence and success in the competitive workplace for persons with mental retardation. *Education and Training in Mental Retardation and Developmental Disabilities, 29,* 118–133.

Carter, E. W., & Kennedy, C. H. (2006). Promoting access to the general curriculum using peer support strategies. *Research and Practice for Persons with Severe Disabilities, 31,* 284–292.

Chadsey, J. (2007). Adult social relationships. In S. L. Odom, R. H. Horner, M. E. Snell, & J. Blacher (Eds.), *Handbook of developmental disabilities* (pp. 449–466). New York, NY: Guilford Press.

Davis, K. M., Boon, R. T., Cihak, D. F., & Fore III, C. (2010). Power cards to improve conversational skills in adolescents with Asperger syndrome. *Focus on Autism and Other Developmental Disabilities, 25,* 12–22. doi:10.1177/1088357609354299

Gagnon, E. (2001). *Power cards: Using special interests to motivate children and youth with Asperger syndrome and autism.* Shawnee Mission, KS: Autism Asperger.

Gaylord-Ross, R. J., Haring, T. G., Breen, C., & Pitts-Conway, V. (1984). The training and generalization of social interaction skills with autistic youth. *Journal of Applied Behavior Analysis, 17,* 229–247. doi:10.1901/jaba.1984.17-229

Hendricks, D. R., & Wehman, P. (2009). Transition from school to adulthood for youth with autism spectrum disorder: Review and recommendations. *Focus on Autism and Other Developmental Disabilities, 24,* 77–88. doi:10.1177/1088357608329827

Hughes, C., Cosgriff, J. C., & Brigham, N. (2011). *Review of social skills interventions: High school students with autism and intellectual disabilities.* Manuscript in preparation.

Hughes, C., Fowler, S. E., Copeland, S. R., Agran, M., Wehmeyer, M. L., & Church-Pupke, P. P. (2004). Supporting high school students to engage in recreational activities with peers. *Behavior Modification*, 28, 3–27.

Hughes, C., Harmer, M. L., Killian, D. J., & Niahros, F. (1995). The effects of multiple exemplar self-instructional training on high school students' generalized conversation interactions. *Journal of Applied Behavior Analysis*, 28, 201–218. doi:10.1901/jaba.1995.28-201

Hughes, C., Killian, D. J., & Fischer, G. M. (1996). Validation and assessment of a conversational interaction intervention. *American Journal on Mental Retardation*, 100, 493–509.

Hughes, C., Rung, L. L., Wehmeyer, M. L., Agran, M., Copeland, S. R., & Hwang, B. (2000). Self-prompted communication book use to increase social interaction among high school students. *The Journal of the Association for Persons with Severe Handicaps*, 25, 153–166.

Muller, E., Schuler, A., Burton, B. A., & Yates, G. B. (2003). Meeting the vocational support needs of individuals with Asperger Syndrome and other autism spectrum disabilities. *Journal of Vocational Rehabilitation*, 18, 163–175.

National Center for Education Statistics. (2007) *Status and trends in the education of racial and ethnic minorities*. Washington DC: U.S. Department of Education. Retrieved from http://nces.ed.gov/pubs2007/minoritytrends/tables/table_7_2.asp?referrer=report

Plienis, A. J., Hansen, D. J., Ford, F., Smith Jr., S., Stark, L. J., & Kelly, J. A. (1987). Behavioral small group training to improve the social skills of emotionally disordered adolescents. *Behavior Therapy*, 18, 17–32. doi:0005-7894/87/0017-0032

Reichow, B., & Volkmar, F. R. (2010). Social skills interventions for individuals with autism: Evaluation for evidence-based practices within a best evidence synthesis framework. *Journal of Autism and Developmental Disorders*, 40, 149–166. doi:10.1007/s10803-009-0842-0

Stokes, T., & Baer, D. (1977). An implicit technology of generalization. *Journal of Applied Behavior Analysis*, 19, 349–367.

Suitts, S. T. (2010). *A new diverse majority: Students of color in the South's public schools*. Atlanta: Southern Education Foundation. Retrieved from www.southerneducation.org

U. S. Department of Education (2009). *28th annual report to Congress on the Implementation of the Individuals with Disabilities Education Act, 2006*. Washington, DC: Author.

Wang, P., & Spillane, A. (2009). Evidence-based social skills interventions for children with autism: A meta-analysis. *Education and Training in Developmental Disabilities*, 44, 318–342.

SOCIAL SKILLS RATING SYSTEM

Social skills are socially acceptable learned behaviors that enable a person to interact effectively with others to avoid socially unacceptable responses (Gresham & Elliot, 1984). Social skills problems are persistent, related to low academic performance, and may result in social adjustment problems, and even serious psychopathology. The Social Skills Rating System (SSRS) is a norm-referenced rating scale, the purpose of which is to assist professionals in screening and classifying children suspected of having significant social behavior problems and aid in the development of appropriate interventions for identified children (Gresham & Elliot, 1990). The SSRS is composed of separate rating forms for teachers, parents, and students, and is intended for use with preschool, elementary, and secondary students.

The SSRS samples behaviors in three domains: social skills, problem behaviors, and academic competence. The Social Skills Scale assesses cooperation, assertion, responsibility, empathy, and self-control. These qualities are rated by teachers, parents, and/or students using a 3-point Likert scale (*Never, Sometimes*, or *Very Often*; or *Not Important, Important*, or *Critical*). The Problem Behaviors domain assesses externalizing problems, internalizing problems, and hyperactivity. These qualities are rated by teachers and parents. Academic competence (i.e., reading, mathematics, motivation, parental support, and general cognitive functioning) assesses a student's performance as rated by a teacher using a 5-point scale (1 = lowest 10% to 5 = highest 10%; Gresham & Elliot, 1990). The SSRS can be administered in about 20 minutes and provides standard scores, percentile ranks, confidence bands, and behavior levels (Demaray & Ruffalo, 1995).

The SSRS was standardized during 1988 on a national sample of 4,170 children using self ratings, 1,027 parent ratings, and 259 teacher ratings (Gresham & Elliot, 1990). The sample includes an equal number of girls and boys. Internal consistency coefficients range from .83 to .94 for social skills, from .73 to .88 for problem behaviors, and are .95 for academic competence. Thus, the scale displays a high degree of internal reliability. Test-retest reliability coefficients generally are in the .70s and .80s for the teacher and parent forms, indicating good stability. Coefficients for the student form are in the .50s and .60s. Although the test authors deem them adequate in view of other supporting evidence of their reliability, caution is needed when relying exclusively on them.

Content validity was demonstrated by the use of similar importance ratings for each skill and by previous research. The SSRS correlated significantly with other measures, including the Social Behavior Assessment, Harter Teacher Rating Scale, and various forms of the Child Behavior Checklist. Thus, criterion-related validity is demonstrated. Evidence supporting the construct validity of the SSRS was demonstrated through several studies evaluating developmental change, sex differences, internal consistency, correlations with other tests, factor analyses, convergent and discriminant correlation analyses, and comparisons of contrasted groups (Gresham & Elliot,

1990). International results show that for seventh- to ninth-grade students in Norway, teacher ratings consistently covaried with ratings of problem behaviors as well as academic competence and performance (Ogden, 2003). Also, students referred for services received significantly lower ratings than peers.

Thus, the SSRS is a reliable and valid instrument for assessing social skills in students. Strengths include ratings by multiple informants and the ability to inform interventions. The SSRS identifies specific skill deficits and contributes to an empirically validated method for designing, implementing, and evaluating a formal social skills intervention for elementary school students (Lane, Menzies, Barton-Arwood, Doukas, & Munton, 2005). Weaknesses include low reliability for the student form and a somewhat outdated standardization sample. Weaknesses of the standardization include an overrepresentation of Whites and Blacks, an underrepresentation of Hispanic Americans and other minorities, and limited numbers of students in the 11th ($N = 44$) and 12th ($N = 80$) grades (Demaray & Ruffalo, 1995). However, data obtained from the SSRS may be helpful when conducting a comprehensive assessment and engaging in intervention planning for students in the preschool through secondary grade levels.

REFERENCES

Demaray, M. K., & Ruffalo, S. L. (1995). Social skills assessment: A comparative evaluation of six published rating scales. *School Psychology Review, 24,* 648–671.

Gresham, F. M., & Elliot, S. N. (1984). Assessment and classification of children's social skills: A review of methods and issues. *School Psychology Review, 13,* 292–301.

Gresham, F. M., & Elliot, S. N. (1990). *Social Skills Rating System.* Circle Pines, MN: American Guidance Service.

Lane, K. L., Menzies, H. M., Barton-Arwood, S. M., Doukas, G. L., & Munton, S. M. (2005). Designing, implementing, and evaluating social skills interventions for elementary students: Step-by-step procedures based on actual school-based investigations. *Preventing School Failure, 49,* 18–26.

Ogden, T. (2003). The validity of teacher ratings of adolescents' social skills. *Scandinavian Journal of Educational Research, 47,* 63–76.

JEFFREY DITTERLINE
University of Florida

SOCIAL VALIDATION

In an educational context, social validation is the philosophy of providing psychological services that emphasize the importance of the student's or teacher's subjective opinions about intervention methods. Social validity differs from the statistical notion of validity in several aspects. Statistical validity refers to how well treatment results correlate with an objective set of criteria or other treatment methods. Social validity is concerned with the subjective opinions of teachers, parents, and/or students and how these subjective opinions affect the overall treatment outcomes. In social validity it is assumed "that if the participants don't like the treatment then they may avoid it, or run away, or complain loudly. And thus, society will be less likely to use our technology, no matter how potentially effective and efficient it might be" (Wolf, 1978, p. 206).

Social validity can be assessed on at least three levels (Wolf, 1978). First, we can evaluate the social significance of the treatment goals. Here we consider whether desired outcomes are of any real value to teachers, students, or society in general. The second level of assessment of social validity questions the social appropriateness of the treatment procedures. At this level, teachers and students are asked how acceptable the treatment methods are (i.e., whether the results of the treatment justify the methods used). "Judgements of acceptability include whether a treatment is appropriate for the problem, whether it is fair, reasonable, or intrusive, and whether it is consistent with conventional notions of what treatment should be" (Kazdin, 1980, p. 330). The treatment acceptability paradigm has been used with students and teachers in clinical settings (Kazdin, French, & Sherick, 1981); university settings (Kazdin, 1980); and primary and secondary school settings (Elliott, Witt, Galvin, & Moe, 1986; Turco, Witt, & Elliott, 1985). In the final level of social validation evaluation, teachers and students report their satisfaction with the methods used (i.e., How important are the effects of the treatment methods? Are the teachers and students satisfied with the results, even the unplanned ones?; Wolf, 1978).

Consumer satisfaction differs from treatment acceptability mainly in the timing of the measurements. Treatment acceptability requires teachers and students to judge treatments before they begin. Consumer satisfaction requires teachers and students to judge treatments during the treatment or after the treatment is over. In applied behavior analysis, it is believed that the outcomes of treatments are easily judged based on behavioral changes from baseline measurements. However, according to the social validity paradigm, the usefulness of school interventions can only be judged by the subjective evaluations of the teachers and students participating in the treatment program.

REFERENCES

Elliott, S. N., Witt, J. C., Galvin, G. A., & Moe, G. L. (1986). Children's involvement in intervention selection: Acceptability of interventions for misbehaving peers. *Professional Psychology: Research and Practice, 17*(3), 235–241.

Kazdin, A. E. (1980). Acceptability of alternative treatments for deviant child behavior. *Journal of Applied Behavior Analysis, 13*, 259–273.

Kazdin, A. E., French, N. H., & Sherick, R. B. (1981). Acceptability of alternative treatments for children: Evaluations by inpatient children, parents, and staff. *Journal of Consulting and Clinical Psychology, 49*, 900–907.

Turco, T. L., Witt, J. C., & Elliott, S. N. (1985). Factors influencing teachers' acceptability of classroom interventions for deviant student behavior. *Monograph on secondary behavioral disorders*. Reston, VA: Council for Exceptional Children.

Wolf, M. M. (1978). Social validity: The case for subjective measurement or how applied behavior analysis is finding its heart. *Journal of Applied Behavior Analysis, 11*, 203–214.

TIMOTHY L. TURCO
Louisiana State University

STEPHEN N. ELLIOTT
University of Wisconsin at Madison

See also Applied Behavior Analysis; Teacher Expectancies

SOCIAL WORK

Social work in special education traditionally falls within the realm of the school social worker. The functions performed by social workers within the school include individual and family casework, individual and group work with students, and community liaison services. School social workers have stated their goals as helping students to maximize their potential, developing relationships between the school and other agencies, and offering a perspective of social improvement in the education of students (Costin, 1981).

In 1975, PL 94-142 and subsequent amendments resulting in IDEA mandated free and appropriate education for all students; social work falls under the section providing for related services (Hancock, 1982). The school social worker often participates as a member of an interdisciplinary team, and in some states assumes a permanent position on a child study team. Local boards of education determine the specific roles of team members (Winters & Easton, 1983). As a team member, the social worker may be responsible for gathering family information, coordinating team meetings, developing individualized educational programs, and monitoring services.

The school social worker often participates in the evaluation of students who are being considered for special education. In this regard, the case history is an extremely important tool that the social worker uses to gain environmental, developmental, social, and economic information about the student.

To work effectively with a special population, the school social worker must have several basic competencies. Dickerson (1981) includes counseling, crisis intervention, knowledge of related services, and understanding of adapted curricula and techniques as required skills. To be effective, the school social worker must also hold the belief that special-needs children are entitled to the same rights and privileges as those afforded to their mainstreamed peers.

Often, family members of the children with disabilities need support from the social worker in their efforts to program for their impaired youngsters. The primary goal of the social worker in providing services to family members of individuals with disabilities is to help them face and accept the limiting condition (Dickerson, 1981). The family is encouraged to follow through on recommendations designed to enhance their child's functioning. The social worker helps the family to recognize that the problem is real and that it can be helped by the development of an accepting, positive attitude about the child.

The school social worker may provide a number of different services to the family. Hancock (1982) writes that one role for the school social worker is to support parents in their efforts to become more active participants in school decisions regarding their children. Social workers may contribute information regarding home versus institutional care for severely impaired children. The social worker may also provide direct counseling services to the family, or act as a link to other supportive services. For example, parents might be encouraged to find a support or advocacy group. Ensuring that families receive the financial support to which they are entitled is another important function.

Pupil services such as counseling, sex education, prevocational development, and child advocacy are often performed by the school social worker. As an advocate, the social worker attempts to create systemic changes that improve the quality of the impaired child's school life. The social worker may assume responsibility for shaping a school system's attitudes to reflect more adaptive, relevant, and socially responsible positions (Lee, 1983).

School social workers may be responsible for developing communication links within the school so that teachers, administrators, and other staff can exchange information necessary for student programming. They may also plan in-service workshops in areas related to student welfare. Future trends in special education social work will continue to expand the systems approach to service delivery. To this end, an increase in coordinator and liaison roles for special education social workers is predicted (Randolph, 1982), and mandated in inclusive programming (Pryor, Kent, McGunn, & LeRoy, 1996).

REFERENCES

Costin, L. B. (1981). School social work as specialized practice. *Social Work, 26*, 36–44.

Dickerson, M. O. (1981). *Social work practice and the mentally retarded.* New York, NY: Free Press.

Hancock, B. L. (1982). *School social work.* Englewood Cliffs, NJ: Prentice Hall.

Lee, L. J. (1983). The social worker in the political environment of a school system. *Social Work, 28*(4), 302–307.

Pryor, C. B., Kent, C., McGunn, C., & LeRoy, B. (1996). Redesigning social work in inclusive schools. *Social Work, 41*(6), 668–676.

Randolph, J. L. (1982). School social work can foster educational growth for students. *Education, 102*, 260–265.

Winters, W. G., & Easton, F. (1983). *The practice of social work in the schools.* New York, NY: Free Press.

GARY BERKOWITZ
Temple University

See also Multidisciplinary Team; Personnel Training in Special Education

SOCIODRAMA

Sociodrama is a group-therapy technique developed by J. L. Moreno (1946) as an extension of a group-therapy technique, also devised by Moreno, known as psychodrama. (Moreno is often credited with having initiated group therapy in Vienna just after the beginning of the 20th century.) Though he developed the technique, Moreno did little with sociodrama, preferring to continue his efforts in the development and application of psychodrama. E. Paul Torrance, a psychodramatist who studied with Moreno, later reconceptualized and refined sociodrama as a group problem-solving technique based on Moreno's early work but also incorporating the creative problem-solving principles of Torrance (1970) and Osborn (1963). Sociodrama can be used with all ages from preschool through adulthood.

The primary uses of sociodrama, largely reflecting Torrance's interests and influence, have been in primary prevention of behavior problems with the disadvantaged and other high-risk populations. Sociodrama has also been used in specific treatment programs with adolescents who engage in socially deviant behaviors and with status offenders. Sociodrama seems particularly helpful in introducing and teaching new social behaviors as well as in improving the problem-solving skills of the youngsters involved, giving them more behavioral options.

During sociodrama, a problem or conflict situation that is likely to be common to the group is derived from group discussion. Members of the group are cast into roles, which they play as the situation is acted out. Many production techniques are brought into play to facilitate solution of the conflict; these include the double, the soliloquy, direct presentation, mirror, and role reversal.

The director's role is to keep the action moving in the direction of a resolution, or, preferably, multiple resolutions of the conflict. Each session should end with a series of potential resolutions that can be discussed by the group. Appropriate behaviors can also be practiced. By teaching participants to brainstorm alternative behaviors and to rehearse for real-life problem situations, sociodrama has proved a useful method for treatment and prevention of behavior problems in children and adolescents. Torrance (1982) provides a more detailed presentation of the techniques of sociodrama.

REFERENCES

Moreno, J. L. (1946). *Psychodrama.* Beacon, NY: Beacon House.

Osborn, A. F. (1963). *Applied imagination* (3rd ed.). New York, NY: Scribner's.

Torrance, E. P. (1970). *Creative learning and teaching.* New York, NY: Dodd, Mead.

Torrance, E. P. (1982). Sociodrama: Teaching creative problem-solving as a therapeutic technique. In C. R. Reynolds & T. B. Gutkin (Eds.), *The handbook of school psychology.* New York, NY: Wiley.

CECIL R. REYNOLDS
Texas A&M University

See also Group Therapy; Psychodrama

SOCIOECONOMIC IMPACT OF DISABILITIES

There is a well-established relationship between parents' socioeconomic status and children's school performance (Barona & Faykus, 1992). Caldwell (1970) reports that many of the children from lower socioeconomic classes live in restricted and nonstimulating environments. As a result, low socioeconomic profile is one factor that is significantly related to poor cognitive functioning. There are many more children from lower socioeconomic classes with poor cognitive functioning than from higher socioeconomic classes.

An investigation analyzing the extent to which parental social status influences the decisions made in reference to potentially disabled students was conducted by Ysseldyke et al. (1979). Individuals involved in decision making were given identical data on students referred for evaluation. All data were samples of normal or average performance.

The decision makers were told in half of the cases that the child's father was a bank vice president and the mother a real estate agent. The other half were told that the child's father was a janitor at the bank and the mother a clerk at a local supermarket. As a result of knowledge of the parents' socioeconomic status, the decision makers made different placement and classification decisions for the children. This has been supported in later research (Podell & Soodlak, 1993).

There are many factors associated with socioeconomic status that are considered contributing factors to some disabilities. These include poor health care, inadequate pre- and postnatal care, improper diet, and lack of early stimulation. Zachau-Christiansen and Ross (1979) state that infants from lower socioeconomic families are at greater risk for experiencing or being exposed to conditions that may hinder development. These conditions include low birth weight, lead poisoning, malnutrition, and maternal infections during pregnancy. Kagan (1970) discusses other psychological differences between lower class and more privileged children. The differences are evident during the first 3 years of life and tend to remain stable over time. Variables include language, mental set, attachment, inhibition, sense of effectiveness, motivation, and expectancy of failure. All of the factors play a crucial role in influencing school performance. Deficits in any of these areas limit the child's ability in various cognitive skills. Young children raised in an environment lacking in stimulation and healthy interaction with adults will often be retarded in motor, language, cognitive, and social skills.

Lack of proper nutrition can negatively affect the maturation of the brain and central nervous system. Malnutrition affects brain weight and tends to have lasting effects on learning and behavior. It has a very damaging effect during the first 6 months of life owing to the rate of brain cell development during this period. In the area of mental retardation and learning disabilities, the majority of the students tend to be from lower socioeconomic status homes and racial and cultural minorities. In many cases, the poor achievement of the socioculturally different individual is related to lack of proper nutrition and medical care. Kavale (1980) reports that almost all complications of prenatal life, pregnancy, labor and delivery, and postnatal diseases that are potentially damaging to the infant's brain development are disproportionately high among low socioeconomic groups.

Many other correlates of low socioeconomic status are associated with poor school learning. Some of these correlates are delayed development of language; greater impulsivity; lower intelligence on standard intelligence tests that predict success in standard curricula; lower parental educational levels; families with over five children; poor home climate; lack of variety in sensory stimuli; minimal encouragement of scholastic success within the home; and less time spent on tasks in the classroom and on homework.

An area that is crucial to academic performance is language development. Jensen (1968) lists several factors associated with language development as sources of social class differences and intellectual achievement. In the lower classes, early vocalization by infants is less likely to be rewarded; the child is less likely to have a single mother-child relationship in the early years; there is less verbal interaction and verbal play in response to early vocalizations; and speech tends to be delayed. In the early stages of speech, there is less shaping of speech sounds, in which parents reinforce approximations of adult speech, and much vocal interaction with slightly older siblings whose own speech is only slightly more advanced and who do not systematically shape behavior.

According to MacMillian (1982), the physical environment of lower class homes tends to be related to cultural familial retardation. When compared with middle-class households, lower class households tend to have the father absent from the home, crowded living conditions, poor nutrition and medical care, large family size, dilapidated living environment, and high ratio of children to adults. These factors have a negative impact on the child and his or her social, emotional, and educational adjustment. In many instances, the lower classes are less likely to vote and participate in political or social activities.

MacMillian (1982) has emphasized the dangers of class stereotyping. Determining socioeconomic status and the relationship between the ratings and developmental outcomes can be misleading; there are some exceptions to every rule. It is very important that special education personnel are trained in cultural awareness programming that includes socioeconomic variables. The major concern should be placed on the overall impact of socioeconomic factors in preventing or enhancing the possibility of physical, social, emotional, and intellectual disabilities.

REFERENCES

Barona, A., & Faykus, S. P. (1992). Differential effects of sociocultural variables on special education eligibility categories. *Psychology in the Schools, 29*(4), 313–320.

Caldwell, B. (1970). The rationale for early intervention. *Exceptional Children, 36*, 717–727.

Jensen, A. R. (1968). Social class, race, and genetics: Implications for education. *American Educational Research Journal, 5*, 1–412.

Kagan, J. (1970). On class differences and early development. In V. Denenberg (Ed.), *Education of the infant and young child.* New York, NY: Academic Press.

Kavale, K. A. (1980). Learning disability and cultural-economic disadvantage: The case for a relationship. *Learning Disability Quarterly, 3*, 97–112.

MacMillian D. L. (1982). *Mental retardation in school and society* (2nd ed.). Boston, MA: Little, Brown.

Podell, D. M., & Soodlak, L. C. (1993). Teacher efficacy and bias in special education referrals. *Journal of Educational Research, 86*(4), 247–253.

Ysseldyke, J. E., Algozzine, B., Regan, R., Potter, M., Richey, L., & Thurlow, M. L. (1979). *Psychoeducational assessment and decision making: A computer-simulated investigation* (Research Report No. 32). Minneapolis: University of Minnesota Institute for Research on Learning Disabilities.

Zachau-Christiansen, B., & Ross, E. M. (1979). *Babies: Human development during the first year*. Chichester, England: Wiley.

JANICE HARPER
North Carolina Central University

See also Culturally/Linguistically Diverse Students; Gifted and Talented Children; Socioeconomic Status

SOCIOECONOMIC STATUS

Davis (1986) defines socioeconomic status (SES) as a person's position in the community. There are many factors involved in determining SES. These factors include income, employment, location and cost of home, and social status of the family. Socioeconomic status influences various behavior patterns. For example, the number of children, the year and model of the family car, and the number of vacations per year will vary according to SES.

Society places a high value on wealth and material possessions. There is a tendency to rank individuals based on their wealth and power within the community. Wealth is highly correlated with education, income, and occupation. Studies of social classes in the United States report five or six classes. Hodges (1964) has developed a system of six social classes. The first is the upper-upper class, which represents 1%–2% of the community. This group includes people with wealth, power, and a family name that is prominent. Individuals can only be born into this class, with the exception of a few marrying into it. The lower-upper class also represents 1%–2% of the community. This class does not have a prominent family name and their money is fairly new. However, they have wealth and power. The upper-middle class represents 10% to 12% of the community. These people have college degrees, are usually professionals and successful merchants. The lower-middle class represents 33% of the community. These people are usually small business people, salespeople, clerks, and forepeople. They tend to have average income and education, with high value placed on family, religion, thrift, and hard work. The upper-lower class also represents 33% of the community. In many cases they are employees rather than employers. The lower-lower class represents 15%–20% of the population. These people are unskilled workers. Many are not high-school graduates and may frequently be unemployed.

Socioeconomic status has a direct relationship to the length and quality of life. The lower-lower classes do not live as long as members of the upper class. The poor are more likely to suffer from chronic and infectious diseases and are less likely to see a physician or a dentist. This may be a result of lack of money to pay for medical expenses. However, it has also been found that minor illnesses such as fevers have a low priority in poverty-stricken homes. Other factors such as child-rearing practices are affected by socioeconomic status of the family. Middle-class parents tend to be more permissive, while lower class parents are more rigid (Bassis, Gelles, & Levine, 1980).

Kohn (1969) states that middle-class mothers value self-control, dependability, and consideration, while lower class mothers value obedience and the ability to defend oneself. The middle-class family raises the child in an environment where achievement and getting ahead are encouraged. The lower class family raises the child in an environment that emphasizes the immediate and the concrete. The child is taught to shy away from the new or unfamiliar. According to Boocock (1972), the family characteristic that is the most powerful predictor of school performance is socioeconomic status. More specifically, the higher the socioeconomic status of the family, the higher the child's academic achievement. Socioeconomic status also predicts the number and type of extracurricular activities the child will be involved in and social and emotional adjustment to school. Other areas highly correlated with socioeconomic status include grades, achievement test scores, retentions at grade level, course failures, truancy, suspensions from school, dropout rates, college plans, and total amount of schooling.

REFERENCES

Bassis, M. S., Gelles, R. J., & Levine, A. (1980). *Sociology: An introduction* (2nd ed.). New York, NY: Random House.

Boocock, S. S. (1972). *An introduction to the sociology of learning*. Dallas, TX: Houghton Mifflin.

Davis, W. E. (1986). *Resource guide to special education* (2nd ed.). Boston, MA: Allyn & Bacon.

Hodges, H. M. (1964). *Social stratification*. Cambridge, MA: Schenkman.

Kohn, M. (1969). *Class and conformity*. Homewood, IL: Dorsey.

JANICE HARPER
North Carolina Central University

See also Socioeconomic Impact of Disabilities

SOCIOGRAM

A sociogram (Moreno, 1953) is a graphic display of interpersonal relationships within a group. It is considered one of the most common sociometric techniques used by teachers. In most instances, a sociometric test is administered to a group of children by asking each child who he or she would like to work with on a particular activity. The sociogram displays a diagram of students with whom other students prefer to study, play, or work. It also displays a diagram of students who are rejected and tend to be isolates. Each child is asked such questions as, With which three students would you prefer to study? Which three students do you like best? Which two students do you prefer to play with at recess? Which three students are your best friends? The students' responses to these types of questions are used to construct the sociogram.

There are two types of sociograms: the graphic and the target diagram. The graphic sociogram assigns initial letters of the alphabet (such as A, B, C) to the most popular students. These students appear in the center of the chart. The isolates are assigned middle letters (such as H, I, J), and appear on the edges of the diagram. Stanley and Hopkins (1972) listed the limitations of this chart as difficulty in reading with 30 or more students and requiring a great deal of practice to learn the most effective placement. The target diagram consists of circles, with the most popular students placed in the center and the isolated students placed on the outer edges. According to Stanley and Hopkins (1972), this diagram is more productive for teachers with large classrooms.

The information obtained from a sociogram can be used for assessing students who may be isolated, socially immature, unhappy, and who have disabilities (Conderman, 1995). Once this information has been obtained from the sociogram, the teacher may begin to ask questions to determine why some students are considered isolates and often rejected. This information can assist the teacher with assigning students to groups for class projects and making changes in classroom relationships. It may also alert the teacher to the possibility of an existing or potential disability. Almost 40% of all teachers use sociometric techniques (Vasa, Maag, Torrey, & Kramer, 1994).

REFERENCES

Conderman, G. (1995). Social status of sixth- and seventh-grade students with learning disabilities. *Learning Disability Quarterly, 18*(1), 13–24.

Moreno, J. L. (1953). *Who shall survive? Foundations of sociometry, group psychotherapy, and sociodrama* (2nd ed.). New York, NY: Beacon House.

Stanley, J. C., & Hopkins, K. D. (1972). *Educational and psychological measurement and evaluation.* Englewood Cliffs, NJ: Prentice Hall.

Vasa, S. F., Maag, J. W., Torrey, G. K., & Kramer, J. J. (1994). Teachers' use of and perceptions of sociometric techniques. *Journal of Psychoeducational Assessment, 12*(2), 135–141.

JANICE HARPER
North Carolina Central University

See also **Social Skills Instruction**

SOCIOMETRIC TECHNIQUES WITH INDIVIDUALS WITH DISABILITIES

Sociometric techniques originated by Moreno (1953) are a set of questions used to determine the social organization of a group. There are various types of sociometric techniques that are used with individuals with disabilities. The two most common forms are peer nomination and roster and rating methods. Most peer nomination techniques ask questions such as, With whom would you most like to study? Who would you most like to sit with at lunch? Who would you most enjoy working with on an art project? Who would you most enjoy being with during break? (Mercer & Mercer, 1981 p. 109).

Other forms of peer nomination techniques may ask students questions relating to attitudes and behavior: Which students are very popular? Which students does the teacher like most? Which students cause a lot of trouble? Which students are selfish? (Mercer & Mercer 1981, p. 110). The rating scales usually lists all students in the class along with the rating scale (e.g., 1 = low and 10 = high) and ask each student to rate each person in the class. A score is determined for each child based on the average of their ratings.

Another common sociometric technique is the use of the sociogram, which is a visual display of the interrelationships within a group. The sociogram clearly shows which child is popular and which child is isolated by their positions on a diagram. There are teacher-made sociometric techniques and commercially produced sociometric techniques. The commercially produced techniques include the Ohio Social Acceptance Scale, which is designed for children in grades three through six. There are six headings: (1) my very best friends; (2) my other friends; (3) not friends, but okay; (4) don't know them; (5) don't care for them; (6) dislike them. The children are asked to write the names of their classmates under each of the headings (Wallace & Larsen 1978).

Another commercial technique is the Peer Acceptance Scale, which is used to obtain social status scores of children. This test uses stick figures of two children playing ball together, which is labeled "friend"; two children at a blackboard, which is labeled "all right"; and two children with their backs to each other, which is labeled "wouldn't like." The students are read a list of names of classmates they are familiar with and asked to circle the figure that best describes how they feel about the student (Goodman, Gottlieb, & Harrison, 1972). The information from these sociometric techniques may be helpful to the teacher for the following activities: (1) assigning instructional groups and peer tutors; (2) planning affective development activities; (3) identifying potential groups; (4) predicting interpersonal difficulties within the group; and (5) measuring change in social adjustment (Marsh, Price, & Smith, 1983, p. 51).

With disabled children social acceptance is considered a very important aspect of school adjustment and educational achievement. Sociometric techniques may help the teacher determine whether the disabled child is accepted by his or her nondisabled peers (Conderman, 1995). If the child is not accepted, the next step is to decide which interventions will help to improve the child's social status.

REFERENCES

Conderman, G. (1995). Social status of sixth-and seventh-grade students with learning disabilities. *Learning Disability Quarterly, 18*(1), 13–24.

Goodman, H., Gottlieb, J., & Harrison, H. (1972). Social acceptance of EMRs integrated into a nongraded elementary school. *American Journal of Mental Deficiency, 76*, 412–417.

Marsh, G. E., Price, B. J., & Smith, T. E. (1983). *Teaching mildly handicapped children: Method and materials*. St. Louis, MO: Mosby.

Mercer, C. D., & Mercer, A. R. (1981). *Teaching students with learning problems*. Columbus, OH: Merrill.

Moreno, J. L. (1953). *Who shall survive? Foundations of sociometry, group psychotherapy and sociodrama* (2nd ed.). New York, NY: Beacon House.

Wallace, G., & Larsen, S. (1978). *Educational assessment of learning problems: Testing for teaching*. Boston, MA: Allyn & Bacon.

JANICE HARPER
North Carolina Central University

See also Sociogram

SOFT (NEUROLOGICAL) SIGNS

Neurological soft signs are defined by Shaffer, O'Connor, Shafer, and Prupis (1983) as "nonnormative performance on a motor or sensory test identical or akin to a test of the traditional neurological examination, but a performance that is elicited from an individual who shows none of the features of a fixed or transient localizable neurological disorder" (p. 145). Some sources (e.g., Buda, 1981; Gaddes, 1985) suggest soft signs have a strong age-related component, in that many of the behaviors judged to represent soft signs in children of a certain age would be considered within the range of normal behavior for chronologically younger children (Ardilla & Rosselli, 1996). The term is contrasted with hard neurological signs, which are medically documented symptoms of neurologic disease.

The concept of neurological soft signs developed during the 1960s in conjunction with the nondefunct description of the minimal brain dysfunction (MBD) syndrome (Spreen

et al., 1984). Although there were behavioral differences observed in children described as having MBD syndrome, hard neurologic findings were not demonstrated in the population. The vague, inconsistent behaviors that were observed were called soft neurological signs. To be considered a soft sign, Shaffer et al. (1983) state there should be no association between the observed behavior and a positive history of neurologic disease or trauma. Furthermore, clusters of neurological soft signs should not be pathognomonic of neurologic disease or encephalopathy. Soft signs, by definition, are not indicative of specific central nervous system pathology. Soft signs are not additive in the traditional sense: "the presence of more than one soft sign does not make a hard sign" (Spreen et al., 1984, p. 246).

The generalizability of data from studies of neurological soft signs has been complicated by inconsistency across studies in the specific signs tested. Soft signs have been categorized into three different types: those that may suggest immaturity or developmental delay; those that are mild expressions of classic hard neurological signs, which are difficult to elicit and may be inconsistent; and behaviors that may be associated with nonneurologic causes (Spreen et al., 1984). Testing a population of children for soft signs of the type associated with the first category may identify a different subgroup than would testing for signs associated with the others.

Nearly 100 different neurological soft signs have been identified (Spreen et al., 1984). Such signs encompass a wide variety of behaviors, including impulsivity (Vitello, Stoff, Atkins, & Mahoney, 1990) attention, concentration, fine motor speed, activity level, and affect. Gaddes (1985) lists the following as among the most common neurologic soft signs: motor clumsiness, speech and language delays, left-right confusion, perceptual and perceptual-motor deficits, and deficient eye-hand coordination. Soft signs may occur in conjunction with hyperactivity and specific learning disabilities, but the presence should not be considered pathognomonic of these conditions (Gaddes, 1985).

The relationship between neurologic soft signs and learning and behavior disorders in children has been investigated widely. In a comprehensive review of studies of children conducted prior to 1983, Shaffer et al. (1983) reported these investigations demonstrated consistent relationships between neurological soft signs and IQ scores, as well as diagnosed psychiatric disturbances and behavior problems. The authors described a study of 456 children participating in the Collaborative Perinatal Project of the National Institute of Neurological and Communicative Disorders and Stroke (NINCDS). The subjects were examined for the presence or absence of 18 neurological soft signs at age 7. Specific signs included movement disorders (e.g., tics, tremors, mirror movements) and coordination difficulties (e.g., dysmetria, dysdiadochokinesia). Subjects were rated blind on

15 behaviors (e.g., fearfulness, verbal fluency, cooperativeness, attention span). As in previous studies, the authors reported increased incidence of cognitive dysfunction, learning problems, and behavior disorders in children who exhibited neurologic soft signs.

The etiology of neurological soft signs has not been delineated clearly, and it is likely there are multiple causes. Soft signs may constitute one end of a continuum of neurologic signs, and thus may be a result of mild central nervous system impairment. For other individuals, soft signs may represent a genetic variation (Shaffer et al., 1983). The high incidence of neurologic soft signs in the general population suggests that caution should be exercised when interpreting their significance.

REFERENCES

Ardilla, A., & Rosselli, M. (1996). Soft neurological signs in children: A normative study. *Developmental Neuropsychology, 12*(2), 181–200.

Buda, F. B. (1981). *The neurology of developmental disabilities.* Springfield, IL: Thomas.

Gaddes, W. H. (1985). *Learning disabilities and brain function: A neuropsychological approach* (2nd ed.). New York, NY: Springer-Verlag.

Shaffer, D., O'Connor, P. A., Shafer, S. Q., & Prupis, S. (1983). Neurological "soft signs": Their origins and significance for behavior. In M. Rutter (Ed.), *Developmental neuropsychiatry* (pp. 144–163). New York, NY: Guilford Press.

Spreen, O., Tupper, D., Risser, A., Tuokko, H., & Edgell, D. (1984). *Human developmental neuropsychology.* New York, NY: Oxford University Press.

Vitello, B., Stoff, D., Atkins, M., & Mahoney, A. (1990). Soft neurological signs and impulsivity in children. *Journal of Developmental & Behavioral Pediatrics, 11*(3), 112–115.

CATHY F. TELZROW
Kent State University

See also Neuropsychology; Visual-Motor and
Visual-Perceptual Problems

SOMPA (*See* System of Multicultural Pluralistic Assessment)

SONICGUIDE

The Sonicguide is a mobility aid and environmental sensor for the visually impaired. It operates on the principle of reflected high-frequency sound, which, when converted into audible stereophonic signals, provides the user with information about the distance, position, and surface characteristics of objects within the travel path and immediate environment. Users of all ages (Hill, Dodson-Burk, Hill, & Fox, 1995) learn to locate and identify objects up to a distance of approximately 5 meters.

A transmitter in the center of a spectacle frame radiates ultrasound (high-frequency sound inaudible to the human ear) in front of the wearer. When the ultrasound hits an obstruction such as a wall, a person, or a tree, it is reflected to the aid and received by two microphones below the transmitter. The microphones transform the reflected signals into electrical signals, which are shifted to a much lower range of frequency and converted into audible sounds by two small earphones in the arms of the spectacle frame. The sounds are then directed to each ear by small tubes. These tubes do not interfere with normal hearing and the user learns to integrate the sounds of the Sonicguide with natural sounds to enhance a concept of the environment. The microphones are deflected slightly outward so that sounds produced by objects to either side of the user will be louder in the ear nearer to the object. This process of sound localization occurs in normal hearing and therefore is a natural indication of direction. The pitch of the signal indicates the approximate distance of a reflecting object; it is highest at the maximum range of the aid and gradually reduces as the object comes closer. By interpreting the comparative loudness at each ear of the signal and its pitch and tonal characteristics, the user is able to judge the direction, distance, and surface qualities of reflecting objects.

The electronics of the aid are contained in a control box that is attached by a cable to the spectacle frame. The battery that powers the aid is attached under the control box and the complete unit can be carried in a pocket, at the belt, or on a shoulder strap. The aid's sensors are built into a spectacle frame to encourage the user to develop the same head movements and posture as a sighted person. When the skills of the aid are mastered, safer and more confident travel and a heightened awareness of the environment is assured. In outdoor situations, the device is to be used in conjunction with a long cane or guide dog, unless the area of travel is both familiar and free from hazards at ground level, which the Sonicguide may not detect.

REFERENCE

Hill, M. M., Dodson-Burk, B., Hill, E. W., & Fox, J. (1995). An infant sonicguide intervention program for a child with a visual disability. *Journal of Visual Impairments, 89*(4), 329–336.

MONIQUE BANTERS
*Centre d'Etude et de Reclassement,
Brussels, Belgium*

See also Blind; Electronic Travel Aids; Vision Training

SOTOS SYNDROME (CEREBRAL GIGANTISM)

Sotos syndrome is characterized by prenatal onset of excessive size that persists through at least the first 4 years of life with macrocrania, a high forehead (dolichocephalic), hypertelorism, prominent jaw, premature eruption of teeth, and a narrow palate with prominent, lateral palatine ridges.

Sotos syndrome is believed to be a rare condition, but prevalence is unknown and has not been studied in detail. It is suspected to be an autosomal dominant disorder in familial cases but is most often sporadic, with occurrence increasing with the age of the parents; however, true and confirmed etiology remains unknown (Gillberg, 1995).

Characteristics

1. Prenatal onset of excessive growth persisting until at least age 4 and sometimes into puberty.
2. Macrocephaly, dolichoencephaly, hypotonia, hyperreflexia, and delayed development of gross motor function.
3. Variable levels of intellectual development with reported IQs of 18 to 119, with a mean of 72, and 67% of cases with IQs between 50 and 70 and 75% of the remainder between 71 and 90.
4. Behavior problems are common but highly variable ranging from ADHD-like symptoms to full-blown cases of comorbid autism (e.g., Zappella, 1990).
5. Speech problems and delayed language acquisition are common.

Treatment of Sotos syndrome is entirely symptomatic, and in addition to the previous characteristics, there are more than 40 other occasional abnormalities that occur on an occasional basis in Sotos syndrome. These may require special treatment consideration and may include various seizure disorders, complete to partial callosal agenesis, hypoplasia of the septum pellucidum, septum interpositum, and the cerebellar vermin, glucose dysregulation, increased incidence of at least nine cancers, and multiple orthopedic abnormalities.

Special education placement will approach 100% in cases of Sotos syndrome, but learning and academic skills vary greatly. Individual psychoeducational testing and revisions of educational plans should both occur at least annually between the ages of 4 years and 1 year postpuberty. Qualification for special education services is most often as multiply handicapped due to health problems, behavioral problems, and speech and language delays that are often accompanied by mental retardation. (However, as many as 10% of these children may have IQs within the normal range.) Occupational therapy services are often required due to coordination deficits.

Behavior problems evident in Sotos syndrome include very poor overall social adjustment, increased aggressiveness, temper tantrums, and related difficulties with the self-regulatory systems of the brain producing attention, concentration, and impulse control problems. Social adjustment and emotional problems characterized as emotional immaturity persist into adulthood (Jones, 1997). Prognosis is poor, and some form of supervised living throughout the individual's life along with chronic management via psychopharmacotherapy occurs in nearly all cases. Future research is focusing on etiology and prevention of this serious and pervasive disorder.

REFERENCES

Gillberg, C. (1995). *Clinical child neuropsychiatry*. Cambridge, England: Cambridge University Press.

Jones, K. L. (1997). *Smith's recognizable patterns of human malformation* (5th ed.). Philadelphia, PA: Saunders.

Zappella, M. (1990). Autistic features in children affected by cerebral gigantism. *Brain Dysfunction, 3*, 241–244.

CECIL R. REYNOLDS
*Texas A&M University and
Bastrop Mental Health Associates*

SOUTH AFRICA, SPECIAL EDUCATION IN

The history of education for pupils with disabilities dates back to the missionaries in South Africa. In 1863, three Dominican Sisters started a school for deaf children in the Cape under the guidance of the Roman Catholic Church (Schoeman, 2002). However, private institutions, individuals, and churches provided certain services in order to facilitate the education of pupils with disabilities (Cohen, 1935; Miles, 2001). In 1928, the South African government assumed responsibility for special education. The schools were supported by services (e.g., speech therapy) as depicted in the historical reviews by Marais (1973), Chubb (1932), Dunstan (1932), and Moll (1921). The historical review of speech therapy provides a case history of treatment and education of pupils with speech disabilities in 1927. In 1936, a speech clinic was opened at the University of Witwatersrand (Marais, 1973; Penn, 1978; Salomon, 1942).

By 1948, with the introduction of apartheid, education was provided along racial lines. The result was an education system that was fragmented across 15 departments and unequal, with different special education budgets. In 1994, a single national department of education was established. The democratization process has been guided by a bill of rights and the constitution, which have laid the framework for a South African society based on human rights.

The constitution of South Africa (Act 108 of 1996) states in section 29(1) "that everyone has a right to a basic education including adult basic education." Section 9(3) stresses that the state may not unfairly discriminate directly or indirectly against anyone on one or more grounds, including race, gender, sex, disability, and age. The educational reform has been characterized by policy documents and legislation. The White Paper on Education and Training (Department of Education, 1995), the White Paper on an Integrated National Disability Strategy (Ministry in the Office of the Deputy President, 1997), and the South African Schools Act of 1996 stress the goals of educational reform for all South African citizens. The new goal of educational equity is aimed at redressing past inequalities, improving the quality and efficiency of education in South Africa, and practically realizing the right of all learners to equal access to educational opportunities. The National Education Policy Act 27 of 1997 states in section 4(d) that the Department of Education must endeavor to ensure that no person is denied the opportunity to receive an education to the maximum of his or her ability as a result of a physical disability. Two national commissions of inquiry reports in 1997 (Special Needs in Education and Training and Education Support Services) were used as a basis for a discussion document (Department of Education, 1999). This culminated in the White Paper on Special Needs Education published in 2001 (Department of Education, 2001).

The term *education for learners with special needs* refers to educational support services in public specialized, private specialized, and ordinary public schools in which pupils/learners experience severe learning difficulties and usually are placed in special or remedial classes. The majority of educational support services was earmarked for individual learners and includes support for learning difficulties and those pupils/learners regarded as being at risk due to medical, social, or emotional problems.

In the past, learners with special needs often were labeled in accord with a medical (deficiency-centered) model. Only 20% of children with disabilities were accommodated in specialized education (McClain, 2002). Many learners in mainstream schools have not been given any assistance.

Since 2001 there has been a philosophical shift from excluding learners from the mainstream because of a disability to an inclusive approach to assist all learners. This occurs within a systematic and developmental educational framework (Department of Education, 2001). Special needs include physical, mental, sensory, neurological, or developmental impairments; cognitive differences; and psychological disturbances. Inclusion respects differences and supports all learners to overcome personal and system-wide barriers, unlike a medical deficit model (Engelbrecht, 2004). The inclusive model attempts to change prior practices by creating space and possibilities for all learners.

The inclusive approach envisages that a learner's strengths are to be identified, utilized, and assisted in school-based support teams. The approach to inclusive education is through an organized, systematic, and manageable plan that initially focuses on 30 districts that offer service schools, support teams, and special schools or resource centers (Pandor, 2004).

In 2004, special education was assigned a budget of 1.6 billion rand. The immediate deficiencies in special education are being addressed, and access is being expanded to include the compulsory school age of 7 through 15 (Pandor, 2005).

Pandor (2004) emphasizes the need for early identification of learners (ages 0 through 9) who require personal and specialized support. Field tests adapted on curriculum, human, physical, and material resource development are being used to test strengths and limitations and decide on change and modifications of special schools. The 20-year time frame of the inclusive approach (Department of Education, 2001) is structured so that all barriers to learning will be removed, thereby accommodating special needs within an inclusive education system. Special schools for students with specific handicaps (e.g., students who are blind or deaf) would continue to cooperate with and assist mainstream schools. The inclusive approach encompasses a range of institutions including resource centers, special schools, public adult learning centers, and further and higher education institutions. Primary priorities of this approach include quality assurance, curricula improvements, and specialized training of teachers (Ashmal, 2001; Pandor, 2004).

Psychologists, medical practitioners, speech therapists, and other support personnel are needed to play a vital role in making the inclusive approach a reality. At present the ratio of professionals in support services to students is 1:88, and the number of special schools is 380. Plans call for 500 of the 20,000 primary schools to be converted into schools serving learners with disabilities. During the last few years, the provision of special needs in education has grown significantly, including support services to at least 20 schools for the blind, 47 for the deaf, 54 for the physically disabled and cerebral palsied, 2 for the autistic, and a number for intellectually disabled (Schoeman, 2002).

REFERENCES

Ashmal, K. (2001). Address by the minister of education, Professor Kader Ashmal, MP, at the official launch of the South African-Finnish Co-operation—Programme in Education sector. Retrieved from http://www.info.gov.za/speeches/2001/010514124 5p1006.htm

Chubb, E. M. (1932). Some statistics on mental deficiency. *South African Medical Journal, 6*, 649–652.

Cohen, M. J. (1935). The first South African institution for epileptics. *South African Medical Journal, 9*, 299–300.

Department of Education. (1995, March). White Paper on Education and Training. Pretoria, South Africa: Author.

Department of Education. (1996, November 6). South African Schools Act. Pretoria, South Africa: Author.

Department of Education. (1997). Report of the National Commission on Special Needs in Education and Training (NCSNET) and the National Commission on Education Support Services (NCESS). Pretoria, South Africa: Author.

Department of Education. (1999, August). Consultative Paper No. 1 on Special Education: Building an Inclusive Education and Training System. Pretoria, South Africa: Author.

Department of Education. (2001). Education White Paper 6: Special needs education—Building an inclusive education and training system. Pretoria, South Africa: Author.

Dominican Sisters. (1944). Schools for the deaf in South Africa. Volta Review, 46, 148–150.

Dunstan, J. T. (1932). The sterilization of the unfit. South African Medical Journal, 6, 112–117.

Engelbrecht, P. (2004). Changing roles for educational psychologists within inclusive education in South Africa. School Psychology International, 25(1).

Marais, M. J. (1973). An historical review of speech therapy services in the Transvaal, 1917–1973. Education Bulletin, 17, 77–86.

McClain, C. V. (2002). Governance and legislation in South Africa: A contemporary overview. Retrieved from http://www.disabilityworld.org/01-03_02/gov/southafrica.shtml

Miles, M. (2001). History of educational and social responses to disability in anglophone eastern and southern Africa: Introduction and bibliography. Retrieved from http://www.socsci.kun.nl/ped/whp/histeduc/mmiles/aesabib.html

Ministry in the Office of the Deputy President. (1997, November). The White Paper on an Integrated National Disability Strategy. Pretoria, South Africa: Office of the Deputy President.

Moll, J. M. (1921). Report on the mentally-defective children in government schools, 1919–20. [Cited by C. L. Leipolt. (1932). The intelligence of the infant. Review of R. Stutsman, Mental Measurement of Pre-School Children, New York: World Book Co. South African Medical Journal, 6, 339–340.]

Pandor, N. (2004, August 12). Address by the minister of education. Retrieved from http://education.pwv.gov.za/mainMedia.asp?src=mvie&xsrc=667

Pandor, N. (2005, February 28). Address by the minister of education. Retrieved from http://education.pwv.gov.za/mainmedia.asp?src=mvie@xsrc=818

Penn, C. (1978). Speech pathology and audiology in South Africa: Past, present and future prospectives. In L. W. Lanham & K. P. Prinsloo (Eds.), Language and communication studies in South Africa (pp. 233–259). Cape Town, South Africa: Oxford University Press

Salomon, E. (1942). Speech disorders and their treatment. South African Medical Journal, 16, 215–218.

Schoeman, H. (2002). South Africa: Moving from a centralized and segregated education system to a decentralized and inclusive education approach. Retrieved from http://www.icevi.org/publications/ICEVI-WC2002/papers/01-topic/01-schoeman.htm

UNESCO. (1994). The Salamanca World Conference on Special Needs Education: Access and quality. UNESCO and the Ministry of Education, Spain. Paris: Author.

JENNIFER DAWN PRETORIUS
Vaal University of Technology

SOUTH AMERICA (See Argentina, Special Education in; Mexico, Special Education in; Peru, Special Education in)

SOVIET EDUCATION

Soviet Education was a journal of English-language translations that started publication in 1959 and published through 1991. It made Soviet education literature available through English-language translations for the first time. The founding editors of Soviet Education were Myron Sharpe, Murray Yanowitch, and Fred Ablin.

A topical journal, Soviet Education drew material from Russian-language books and works in teacher training texts, educational psychology, sociology, comparative education, and educational administration. The journal focused on educational policy issues. It was published monthly.

ROBERTA C. STOKES
CECIL R. REYNOLDS
Texas A&M University

SPACHE DIAGNOSTIC READING SCALES (See Diagnostic Reading Scale)

SPAN OF APPREHENSION (See Perceptual Span)

SPASTICITY

Spasticity is a type of cerebral palsy involving a lack of muscle control. Spastic children make up the largest group of the cerebral palsied, constituting 40% to 60% of the total.

Another term that has been used to refer to spastic cerebral palsy is pyramidal. This term was coined because the nerves involved are shaped like pyramids. Spastic cerebral palsy is produced by damage sustained to the nerve cell that is found in the motor cortex. The motor cortex is the gray matter of the brain containing nerve cells that initiate motor impulses to the muscles. The nerve cells have tracts that extend from the neuron in the cortex to the spinal cord. These cells eventually connect with nerve tracts that innervate the limb so that muscle movement can be carried out. If these nerve cells or tracts are injured, spasticity results.

Because spasticity can affect one or all four extremities, it is subdivided into several types. Monoplegia involves one extremity only either an arm or leg. This type is extremely rare. Triplegia involves the impairment of three extremities; it is an unusual occurrence. Hemiplegia means that the abnormality is confined to half of the body, either the right or left side with the arm more involved than the leg. This is the most common locus of involvement. Bilateral hemiplegia or double hemiplegia involves weakness or paralysis of both sides of the body with the arms compromised more than the legs. Another type, quadriplegia, occurs in all four extremities with more disability of the legs than the arms. Diplegia means that all four limbs are affected, with minimal involvement of the arms. Paraplegia is neurologic dysfunction of the legs only. Spastic hemiplegias are the most common group, representing approximately 40% of the total cerebral palsied population, while spastic quadriplegias represent 19% of the total (Capute, 1978).

In mild cases, the spastic child has an awkward gait and may extend his or her arms for balance (Kerrigan & Annaswammy, 1997). In moderate cases, the child may bend the arms at the elbow and hold both arms close to the body with the hands bent toward the body. The legs may be rotated inwardly and flexed at the knees; this causes a "scissoring gait." In severe cases, the child may have poor body control and be unable to sit, stand, and walk without the support of braces, crutches, a walking frame, or other support (Kirk & Gallagher, 1979).

REFERENCES

Capute, A. (1978). Cerebral palsy and associated dysfunctions. In R. Haslam & P. Valletutti (Eds.), *Problems in the classroom* (pp. 149–163). Baltimore, MD: University Park Press.

Kerrigan, D. C., & Annaswammy, T. M. (1997). The functional significance of spasticity as assessed by gait analysis. *Journal of Head Trauma Rehabilitation, 12*(6), 29–39.

Kirk, S., & Gallagher, J. (1979). *Educating exceptional children* (3rd ed.). Boston, MA: Houghton Mifflin.

CECELIA STEPPE-JONES
North Carolina Central University

See also Cerebral Palsy; Physical Disabilities

SPEARMAN, C. E. (1863–1945)

C. E. Spearman grew up in an English family of established status and some eminence; he became an officer in the regular army. He remained in the army until the age of 40, attaining the rank of major. He then obtained his PhD in Wundt's laboratory at Leipzig in 1908 at the age of 45. He was appointed to an academic position at University College, London, where he remained for the rest of his career.

Spearman is known for his theory of general intelligence and for a number of contributions to statistical methodology, including factor analysis, the Spearman rank correlation, and the Spearman-Brown prophecy formula. Spearman's primary interest was in the study of general intelligence, which he preferred to call g. His methodological innovations were directed toward the better definition and measurement of g.

Spearman conceived of intelligence as a general capability involved in the performance of almost all mental tasks, although he saw some tasks as more dependent on g than others. Thus the variance of any mental test may be divided into two parts: a part associated with individual differences in g and a part specific to the test in question. Since the correlation coefficient indicates the proportion of shared variation of two variables, Spearman was able to develop methods of analyzing a matrix of correlations among tests to determine the presence of a general factor and to calculate the g loading for a test, its correlation with the underlying general factor. The conception of intelligence as g provided an objective method of defining intelligence and of evaluating the adequacy of any proposed measure of intelligence.

Spearman's original two-factor theory (Spearman, 1904) included only g and a factor specific to each task. Subsequently, he expanded the theory to include group factors, which are factors common to a group of tasks independent of g. However, his major emphasis was always on g (Spearman, 1927). Subsequent development and mathematical refinement of factor analysis by Thurstone and others emphasized the group factors; g became obscured in the correlation among the primary factors. Today g is recognized as a second-order factor accounting for the correlations among the primaries. There is still disagreement concerning its importance.

REFERENCES

Spearman, C. E. (1904). "General intelligence" objectively determined and measured. *American Journal of Psychology, 15*, 201–293.

Spearman, C. E. (1927). *The abilities of man: Their nature and measurement*. London, England: Macmillan.

ROBERT C. NICHOLS
DIANE J. JARVIS
State University of New York at Buffalo

See also g Factor Theory; Intelligence; Reaction Time

SPEARMAN'S HYPOTHESIS

Charles E. Spearman (1863–1945), an early proponent of the use of factor analytic methods to examine the construct of intelligence, proposed a two-factor theory of intelligence, stating that a general factor (g) and one or more specific factors (s) account for performance on intelligence tests (Spearman, 1927). The g factor, an index of general intelligence, is involved in deductive operations. Tests with high g loadings involve complex mental operations, such as those needed for reasoning, comprehension, and hypothesis testing (Sattler, 2001). Tests with low g loadings require less complex thought processes and emphasize recognition, recall, speed, and visual-motor abilities.

In *The Abilities of Man* (1927), Spearman observed that the average standard score difference between samples of Blacks and Whites in the United States differed from one test to another, and the size of the difference is related to the size of the g loading of the tests. Jensen deemed this "Spearman's hypothesis." Formally stated, it posits that "the relative magnitudes of the standardized mean black-white differences on a wide variety of cognitive tests are related predominantly to the relative magnitudes of the tests' g loadings—the higher the test's g loading, the larger the mean black-white difference" (Jensen, 1992).

Jensen (1985) tested Spearman's hypothesis in 11 large-scale studies, each of which included tests of mental abilities that were administered to Blacks and Whites. The g factor correlated with measures of speed of information processing. In agreement with Spearman's hypothesis, the average differences between Blacks and Whites on mental tests could be interpreted as a difference in g rather than a difference in knowledge, skill, or type of test. Results suggested that Black-White differences in the rate of information processing may account for some of the average difference between them on intelligence tests. An investigation of Spearman's hypothesis using test scores of Blacks, Whites, and Indians in South Africa found strong support for Black-White differences but not for Indian-White differences (Lynn & Owen, 2001).

In industrialized nations the statistical importance of Spearman's g is declining as individuals' IQs increase (Kane & Oakland, 2000). As IQs increase, variance from the average score decreases. This reflects Spearman's "law of diminishing returns," which states that g accounts for less variance in high-IQ groups than in low-IQ groups. High-IQ groups may have more specialized abilities and excel in certain areas over others. Meanwhile, low-IQ groups continue to reflect people with general intelligence, who may excel in areas not covered by current intelligence tests.

REFERENCES

Jensen, A. R. (1985). The nature of the black-white differences on various psychometric tests: Spearman's hypothesis. *Behavioral & Brain Sciences, 8,* 193–263.

Jensen, A. R. (1992). Spearman's hypothesis: Methodology and evidence. *Multivariate Behavioral Research, 27,* 225–233.

Lynn, R., & Owen, K. (2001). Spearman's hypothesis and test score differences between whites, Indians, and blacks in South Africa. *Journal of General Psychology, 121,* 27–36.

Sattler, J. M. (2001). *Assessment of children: Cognitive applications* (4th ed.). San Diego, CA: Jerome M. Sattler.

Spearman, C. (1927). *The abilities of man.* London, England: Macmillan.

JEFFREY DITTERLINE
University of Florida

See also g Factor Theory; Intelligence

SPECIAL CLASS

The first special classes were established in the late 1800s and early 1900s as public school classes for the individuals with intellectual disabilities, hearing impairments, vision impairments, emotionally disturbances, and physical disabilities. Esten (1900) stated that special classes for individuals with intellectual disabilities were established to provide children who learned slowly with more appropriate class placement.

A special classroom for the individuals with disabilities can be defined as one that homogeneously segregates children with disabilities from typically developing children. Children are usually segregated along categorical groupings. As a result of Dunn's (1968) article on the detrimental aspects of special class placements for individuals with mild disabilities, students receiving special education in self-contained special classes today are usually those with more severe disabilities. However, Kirk and Gallagher (1983) report that gifted exceptional students are also grouped into special classes according to interests and abilities. As students with low-incidence disabilities demonstrate proficiency in specific skill areas, they are mainstreamed into regular classes.

Other types of service delivery for students receiving special education support (e.g., resource rooms) do not fall under the label "special class." Resource rooms usually provide service for populations with high-incidence disabilities. Special classes, on the other hand, usually service populations with low-incidence disabilities. In addition, there are four different types of resource rooms: categorical, serving one population; noncategorical, serving more than one population; itinerant; and teacher-consultant. There is usually only one type of special class, self-contained.

REFERENCES

Dunn, L. M. (1968). Special education for the mildly handicapped: Is much of it justifiable? *Exceptional Children, 35,* 5–22.

Esten, R. A. (1900). Backward children in the public schools. *Journal of Psychoaesthenics, 5,* 10–16.

Kirk, S. A., & Gallagher, J. J. (1983). *Educating exceptional children* (4th ed.). Boston, MA: Houghton Mifflin.

MARIBETH MONTGOMERY KASIK
Governors State University

See also Cascade Model of Special Education Services; Inclusion; Resource Room; Self-Contained Class; Service Delivery Models

SPECIAL EDUCATION, EFFECTIVENESS OF (*See* Effectiveness of Special Education)

SPECIAL EDUCATION ELEMENTARY LONGITUDINAL STUDY (SEELS)

The Special Education Elementary Longitudinal Study (SEELS) was funded by the U.S. Department of Education's (ED) Office of Special Education Programs (OSEP) to document the characteristics, experiences, and outcomes of elementary- and middle-school students receiving special education services from 2000 to 2004. SEELS brought data to bear on many key issues that were incorporated into the 1997 reauthorization of the Individuals with Disabilities Education Act (IDEA, PL 105-17) and described special education services and students' school experiences after enactment of the No Child Left Behind Act of 2001 (NCLB, PL107-110).

Conceptual Framework

The SEELS conceptual framework (Figure S.7) shows the comprehensive look at students' experiences that SEELS supported. Student and household characteristics were a fundamental first step in a progression of SEELS analyses and reports, which went on to depict the school programs and services of students as they changed over time. SEELS also focused on the experiences of children outside of school, including their participation in friendships and social activities. The achievements of students in and out of school were a significant focus, as was identifying the aspects of students, households, school programs, and nonschool experiences that contributed to more positive results for students over time. SEELS analyses also highlighted the experiences of students in particular disability categories in "special topic reports."

Sample

SEELS included a nationally representative sample of youth with disabilities who were 6 through 12 years old and receiving special education services in first grade or above on December 1, 1999. SEELS findings generalize to students with disabilities nationally and to those in each of the 12 federal special education disability categories. The study collected data on sample members from multiple sources in three waves.

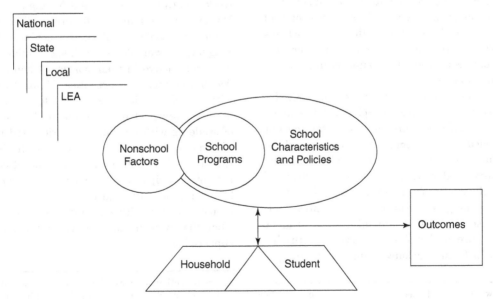

Figure S.7. SEELS Conceptual Framework.

The SEELS two-stage sampling strategy first stratified the universe of school districts serving students in the SEELS age range by region, student enrollment, and community wealth; a random sample of school districts was selected within each stratum and invited to participate in the study. The 77 state-supported "special schools" serving primarily students with sensory impairments and multiple disabilities also were invited to participate. In all, 245 districts and 32 special schools agreed to take part in SEELS and provided rosters of students receiving special education services in the designated age range. These were stratified by primary disability category, as reported by the districts, and students were selected randomly from each disability category. Sampling fractions were calculated that would produce enough students in each category so that, in the final study year, findings would generalize to most disability categories with acceptable precision, accounting for attrition and for response rates to the parent/youth interview. A total of 11,512 students were selected and eligible to participate in SEELS.

Data Sources

Given the breadth of topics addressed in SEELS, data were collected from a variety of sources, including parents/guardians, teachers, principals, school records, and students themselves. Parents were surveyed by telephone and/or mail about students' experiences and outcomes in 2000, 2002, and 2004.[2] Mail surveys were conducted with school staff during the 2000–2001, 2001–2002, and 2003–2004 school years. School staff knowledgeable about the school programs and special education courses of individual sample members were asked to complete a Student's School Program Survey. To understand the experiences of students with disabilities in general education classrooms, the primary language arts teacher of each SEELS student who received language arts instruction completed a Language Arts Teacher Survey. School staff knowledgeable about the characteristics of the schools attended by SEELS students were surveyed to provide a school-level context for the classroom-level information collected in other surveys.

A direct assessment was attempted for each SEELS student for whom parents had completed a telephone interview or mail questionnaire and parental consent had been provided. Assessments were conducted three times, in conjunction with school data collection. The direct assessment used research editions of subtests of the Woodcock-Johnson III (Woodcock, McGrew, & Mather, 2001) that tested language arts and mathematics abilities. The assessment was accompanied by a student interview to measure students' perceptions and attitudes toward school. SEELS also included a functional rating for students for whom the direct assessment was reported to be inappropriate.[3]

Illustrative Findings

Individual and household characteristics (Blackorby et al., 2002; Wagner, 2004; Wagner & Blackorby, 2002; Wagner, Marder, Blackorby, & Cardoso, 2002). Three fourths of elementary and middle school students with disabilities received special education services either for learning disabilities (42%) or speech/language impairments (33%). Males and African American students were larger proportions of students with disabilities than of the general student population, and Hispanic students were a smaller proportion. Students with disabilities were more likely than those in the general population to have parents with lower levels of education, and approximately one quarter lived in poverty, significantly more than of youth in the general population. Overall, 12% of students with disabilities were said to have low functional cognitive skills (e.g., had trouble telling time, counting change), ranging from 7% to 80% across disability categories. More than half of students were reported to speak as well as typically developing children, and about two thirds could converse as well as the general population, although 8% and 10% had a lot of trouble with the two communication skills, respectively, or could not speak or converse at all.

Family support (Wagner, Cadwallader, Newman, Garza, & Blackorby, 2002). Parents had high expectations for their young students with disabilities; 93% expected them to graduate from high school and more than three fourths expected they would go on to postsecondary education. In support of these expectations, more than 90% of students had parents who reported talking to them regularly about school; providing a quiet place for them to do homework; and having household rules about doing homework, limiting television, and having a specific bedtime. However, more than 1 in 10 were never read to at home.

Out-of-school time (Blackorby, Levine, & Wagner, 2007; Wagner, Cadwallader, et al., 2002). Children with disabilities were active in their nonschool hours with personal friends and organized activities. Almost two thirds visited with friends outside of school at least weekly, although 9% were reported never to do so. Almost three fourths of students with disabilities participated in at least one extracurricular group activity, though this is a lower rate of participation than in the general population. The rate of participation in extracurricular groups was stable over time. Although 8 in 10 elementary and middle school students with disabilities had an adult at home when they went home after school, 6% did so to no adult supervision.

---

[2]Parent interviews were conducted by Westat, Inc., under subcontract to SRI.

[3]Data collection for both the direct assessment and functional rating was conducted by Westat Inc. in all three data collection years.

School programs (Blackorby et al., 2004; Levine, 2004; Wagner, 2004a,b). Overall, in 2001, 96% of elementary and middle school students with disabilities attended regular schools that served a wide variety of students. The majority of students with disabilities were instructed in both general education classrooms (74% of their classes) and special education and other settings (26%), although many of those general education classes were nonacademic. Students with disabilities who received their primary language arts instruction in general education classrooms were more likely than those in special education classes to have high levels of self-care, functional cognitive, and social skills and to be in excellent or very good health. They also were more likely to be White and from two-parent and higher-income households.

Although teachers in general and special education classrooms were similar in their education, licensure, and experience, the instruction provided students differed significantly. Relative to peers in special education classes, students with disabilities in general education classes were more likely to read silently, read a variety of kinds of materials, and complete writing assignments frequently, whereas students in special education classes were more likely to practice vocabulary, phonics, and sight word reading and to read aloud frequently. General education classrooms heavily emphasized whole-class instruction compared with special education classes, where small-group and individual instruction provided more opportunity for teacher-student interactions. Classroom activities for students with disabilities in general education classes were more likely to have students work independently and take quizzes or tests, whereas students in special education classes were more likely to respond orally to questions and participate in class discussions frequently.

Virtually all general education teachers teaching students with disabilities received some sort of support in providing instruction to them, most commonly consultation from a special educator. However, 21% of students with disabilities in general education classrooms had teachers who reported they did not receive the support they needed, and 30% had teachers who reported not having adequate training for teaching students with disabilities. However, the large majority of students with disabilities in general education classrooms had teachers who reported that the supports provided directly to students with disabilities in their classrooms were adequate to meet students' needs.

Academic achievement (Blackorby & Cameto, 2004; Blackorby, Chorost, Garza, & Guzman, 2005; Blackorby, Knokey, et al., 2007; Blackorby, Levine, et al., 2007). Although most students with disabilities received passing or even exemplary grades in their classes, more than one fourth had been retained at grade level at some time, and 63% had scores on a standardized achievement test of reading comprehension that were equivalent to the scores

of the bottom one fourth of students in the general population. Mathematics scores were somewhat higher, with 40% of students with disabilities having scores equivalent to the bottom quartile of students in the general population. This pattern of the predominant portion of students with disabilities being in the bottom quartile for the general population of age peers was evident for students in each disability category. Between 2001 and 2004, scores of students with disabilities improved overall, but not enough to close the achievement gap with students in the general population.

Students' social adjustment and behavior (Blackorby & Cameto, 2004; Blackorby, Levine, et al., 2007; Sumi, Marder, & Wagner, 2005). Students with disabilities tended to have lower parent-reported social skills than students in the general population. Nonetheless, teachers' ratings of students' classroom behavior indicated students generally had positive social adjustment in class; on most dimensions of classroom behavior, more than half were reported to behave positively "very often," whereas fewer than 1 in 10 were reported "never" to exhibit most of the positive behaviors assessed. Parents reported that almost two thirds of students with disabilities got along with teachers "very well," and 52% got along "very well" with other students. However, 14% of students with disabilities had been suspended at some time, 8% in the current school year; 1-year rates of suspension were stable over time.

Factors associated with differences in academic achievement (Blackorby, Knokey, et al., 2007; Blackorby, Wagner, et al., 2005). Independent of other differences between them, students with more than one school-identified disability and those with lower functional cognitive skills had both poorer academic outcomes overall and less improvement over time. Although older students had more positive outcomes than younger students, independent of other differences between them, they experienced less improvement in outcomes over time. Both higher household income and parental expectations for students' post–high school education were associated with more positive academic outcomes on several or all measures and with greater improvements over time on some measures. A similar pattern was found regarding students having more positively rated in-class behaviors (e.g., following directions, persisting in completing classroom tasks, and completing homework).

Factors associated with differences social adjustment and behavior (Blackorby, Knokey, et al., 2007; Blackorby, Wagner, et al., 2005). Social adjustment and behavior challenges were more common among students with autism or emotional disturbances than other students, irrespective of other differences between them. Apart from other differences, girls were less likely to be involved in disciplinary incidents at school than boys, and Hispanic students with disabilities were less likely than White students to take part in extracurricular group activities. Higher household income, higher parental involvement at school, and having stronger social skills were related to students' participation in extracurricular groups, apart from other differences between students, and having stronger social skills was associated with a greater increase in participation over time. Higher income also was related to being involved in fewer disciplinary actions at school, as was being rated by teachers as being more cooperative in class and more likely to complete homework on time.

Commentary

Longitudinal analyses enabled SEELS to shed light on how the lives of elementary- and middle-school students with disabilities evolved on many dimensions over 4 years in which they experienced tremendous developmental changes. The perspectives of parents, teachers, and students themselves are represented, as are the experiences of students at a variety of grade levels and in a variety of educational settings. Further, SEELS is unique in documenting longitudinally the wide ranging academic performance of students with disabilities. Reports and data from SEELS are available at www.seels.net

REFERENCES

Blackorby, J., & Cameto, R. (2004). Changes in the school engagement and academic performance of students with disabilities. In J. Blackorby, M. Wagner, P. Levine, L. Newman, C. Marder, R. Cameto, T. Huang, & C. Sanford (Eds.), *Wave 1 Wave 2 overview*. Menlo Park, CA: SRI International.

Blackorby, J., Chorost, M., Garza, N., & Guzman, A. (2005). The academic performance of elementary and middle school students with disabilities. In J. Blackorby, M. Wagner, R. Cameto, E. Davies, P. Levine, L. Newman, C. Marder, & C. Sumi (Eds.), *Engagement, academics, social adjustment, and independence: The achievements of elementary and middle school students with disabilities*. Menlo Park, CA: SRI International.

Blackorby, J., Knokey, A. M., Wagner, M., Levine, P., Schiller, E., & Sumi, C. (2007). *What makes a difference? Influences on outcomes for students with disabilities*. Menlo Park, CA: SRI International.

Blackorby, J., Levine, P., & Wagner, M. (2007). Longitudinal outcomes of students with disabilities. In J. Blackorby, A. Knokey, M. Wagner, P. Levine, E. Schiller, & C. Sumi (Eds.), *What makes a difference? Influences on outcomes for students with disabilities*. Menlo Park, CA: SRI International.

Blackorby, J., Wagner, M., Cadwallader, T., Cameto, R., Levine, P., & Marder, C. (2002). *Behind the label: The functional implications of disability*. Menlo Park, CA: SRI International.

Blackorby, J., Wagner, M., Cameto, R., Davies, E., Levine, P., Newman, L.,...Sumi, C. (Eds.). (2005). *Engagement, academics, social adjustment, and independence: The achievements of elementary and middle school students with disabilities*. Menlo Park, CA: SRI International.

Blackorby, J., Wagner, M., Cameto, R., Marder, C., Levine, P., Chorost, M., & Guzman, A. (2004). *Inside the classroom: The language arts classroom experiences of elementary and middle school students with disabilities*. Menlo Park, CA: SRI International.

Levine, P. (2004). Changes in school enrollment and student services. In J. Blackorby, M. Wagner, P. Levine, L. Newman, C. Marder, R. Cameto, T. Huang, & C. Sanford (Eds.), *Wave 1 Wave 2 overview*. Menlo Park, CA: SRI International.

Sumi, C., Marder, C., & Wagner, M. (2005). The social adjustment of elementary and middle school students with disabilities. In J. Blackorby, M. Wagner, R. Cameto, E. Davies, P. Levine, L. Newman, C. Marder, & C. Sumi (Eds.), *Engagement, academics, social adjustment, and independence: The achievements of elementary and middle school students with disabilities*. Menlo Park, CA: SRI International.

Wagner, M. (2004a). Changes in the characteristics of students with disabilities and their households. In J. Blackorby, M. Wagner, P. Levine, L. Newman, C. Marder, R. Cameto, T. Huang, & C. Sanford (Eds.), *Wave 1 Wave 2 overview*. Menlo Park, CA: SRI International.

Wagner, M. (2004b). Changes in the school programs of students with disabilities. In J. Blackorby, M. Wagner, P. Levine, L. Newman, C. Marder, R. Cameto, T. Huang, & C. Sanford (Eds.), *Wave 1 Wave 2 overview*. Menlo Park, CA: SRI International.

Wagner, M., & Blackorby, J. (2002). *SEELS: Disability profiles of elementary and middle school students with disabilities*. Menlo Park, CA: SRI International.

Wagner, M., Cadwallader, T. W., Newman, L., Garza, N., & Blackorby, J. (2002). *The other 80% of their time: The experiences of elementary and middle school students with disabilities in their nonschool hours*. Menlo Park, CA: SRI International.

Wagner, M., Marder, C., Blackorby, J., & Cardoso, D. (2002). *The children we serve: The demographic characteristics of elementary and middle school students with disabilities and their households*. Menlo Park: SRI International.

Woodcock, R. W., McGrew, K. S., & Mather, N. (2001). *Woodcock-Johnson III*. Itasca, IL: Riverside.

JOSE BLACKORBY
MARY WAGNER
SRI International

SPECIAL EDUCATION, FEDERAL IMPACT ON

The impact of the federal government on special education occurs through two independent, but overlapping, functions: (1) the administration and development of programs, and (2) the compliance monitoring of state education agencies. The administration and development of programs involves the disbursement of discretionary grants and contracts as well as the disbursement of formula grant funds under Part B of the Individuals with Disabilities Education Act (IDEA) and under Part H of the Preschool

Table S.3. State Grant Awards Under IDEA, Part B, Preschool Grant Program and Part H

| State | Appropriation year 1996 Allocation year 1996–1997 | | |
	IDEA Part B	Preschool grant program	Part H
Alabama	40,895,889	5,640,150	4,483,470
Alaska	7,445,561	1,322,423	1,545,710
Arizona	30,926,630	5,149,246	5,306,409
Arkansas	21,767,818	4,947,109	2,549,297
California	228,622,421	36,022,407	41,438,233
Colorado	28,189,964	4,694,437	3,972,753
Connecticut	31,009,767	5,254,252	3,378,163
Delaware	6,415,559	1,273,857	1,545,710
District of Columbia	3,133,152	253,984	1,545,710
Florida	125,183,617	17,772,314	14,722,619
Georgia	54,500,058	8,737,835	8,226,009
Hawaii	6,468,961	857,114	1,569,551
Idaho	9,586,202	2,011,527	1,545,710
Illinois	103,277,776	16,385,574	13,785,909
Indiana	54,064,193	8,046,763	6,065,530
Iowa	26,735,870	3,830,760	2,712,211
Kansas	21,632,619	4,026,335	2,716,195
Kentucky	33,452,225	9,636,295	3,876,538
Louisiana	36,749,462	6,292,502	5,023,051
Maine	12,862,856	2,331,796	1,545,710
Maryland	40,707,760	6,228,185	6,148,806
Massachusetts	64,529,602	9,346,216	8,621,533
Michigan	76,182,721	11,971,373	10,071,913
Minnesota	39,676,213	7,075,455	4,873,116
Mississippi	26,960,663	4,336,103	3,120,649
Missouri	48,997,264	5,509,548	5,422,619
Montana	7,447,163	1,189,852	1,545,710
Nebraska	15,863,867	2,173,630	1,689,626
Nevada	11,381,723	2,077,812	1,783,636
New Hampshire	10,206,502	1,424,148	1,545,710
New Jersey	79,530,001	10,919,997	8,497,315
New Mexico	19,201,461	2,994,648	2,045,597
New York	159,349,369	31,853,656	20,119,188
North Carolina	59,357,530	10,940,998	7,582,020
North Dakota	5,044,365	767,202	1,545,710
Ohio	91,825,830	11,947,090	11,402,583
Oklahoma	29,633,498	3,486,209	3,381,056
Oregon	26,241,486	4,001,396	3,086,097
Pennsylvania	86,078,620	13,510,371	12,702,122
Puerto Rico	18,127,953	2,326,545	4,549,818
Rhode Island	10,118,522	1,531,123	1,568,805
South Carolina	34,921,251	6,775,530	3,852,059
South Dakota	6,432,855	1,428,085	1,545,710
Tennessee	51,036,950	6,661,992	5,414,050
Texas	178,197,295	21,173,206	23,718,333
Utah	21,172,943	3,190,222	2,768,788
Vermont	4,539,452	797,391	1,545,710
Virginia	57,509,947	8,676,144	6,930,714
Washington	43,138,514	8,246,275	5,664,434
West Virginia	18,358,789	3,177,753	1,798,698
Wisconsin	42,946,007	8,889,438	5,553,755
Wyoming	5,064,508	1,021,186	1,545,710
American Samoa	2,546,094	34,783	514,925
Guam	6,151,324	122,726	1,140,327
Northern Marianas	1,570,112	23,626	342,733
Palau	552,502	5,120	78,014
Virgin Islands	4,663,611	87,286	671,647
Bur. of Indian Affairs	28,408,765		3,864,276
U.S. and outlying areas	2,316,593,632	360,409,000	315,754,000
50 states, D.C., and P.R.	2,272,701,224	360,135,459	309,142,078

State grants awards are initial allocations for the 1996 appropriation. October 1, 1996

Grant Program. Discretionary grants are awarded to individuals and organizations in states and territories on a competitive basis. Depending on the specific program for which awards are made, these funds are to be used for research, program/materials development, technical assistance, demonstration, or training. For the most part, these projects do not directly serve handicapped children and youths but rather are intended to support existing programs, demonstrate new or more effective ways of delivering services, train special education and related services personnel, or increase our knowledge of current or promising components of special education (i.e., research efforts). Table S.3 is a list of state grant awards under IDEA Part B, Part H; and preschool grant programs.

In addition to discretionary grant awards and contracts, states also receive annual funds based on the total number of handicapped children and youths receiving special education and related services. The history of funding for the Part B entitlement program under IDEA, state grant program from 1977 to 1996, is shown in Table S.4.

Each state education agency (SEA) must distribute at least 75% of the total funds to local education agencies to be used directly for the education of disabled students. The remaining funds may be used by the SEA, with some portion going toward administrative costs. Thus, federal funds are used to offset some of the additional costs associated with educating students with disabilities.

Until 1994, children and youths with disabilities were also served under the Chapter 1 Handicapped Program. In October 1994, the Improving America's School Act (IASA) was enacted, which reauthorized the Elementary and Secondary Education Act of 1965 (ESEA). However, the Chapter 1 Handicapped Program was not reauthorized. Beginning with the fiscal year (FY) 1995 appropriation, all children with disabilities were served under programs authorized by IDEA. The IASA included a number of amendments to IDEA to provide for a smooth transition to serving all children (U.S. Department of Education, 1997).

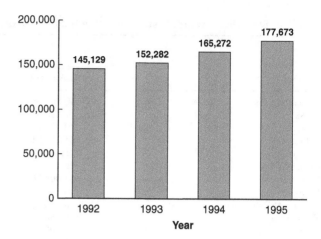

Figure S.8. Number of infants and toddlers with disabilities served under IDEA, Part H. *Source*: U.S. Department of Education, Office of Special Education Programs, Data Analysis Systems (DANS).

Part H of the Individuals with Disabilities Education Act (IDEA) was adopted by Congress in 1986. Part H was designed to address the needs of infants and toddlers with disabilities and their families through a "statewide system of coordinated, comprehensive, multidisciplinary, interagency programs providing appropriate early intervention services to all infants and toddlers with disabilities and their families" (20 U.S.C. §1476 (a)). Figure S.8 shows the number of infants and toddlers with disabilities served under Part H from 1992 to 1995.

The increase in the number of infants and toddlers served under Part H since 1992 (22.4%) has been greater than the growth in the number of children served under Part B. The growth rate is, however, comparable to the number of 3- to 5-year-olds served under Part B (U.S. Department of Education, 1997).

Thus, one of the primary ways special education is impacted by the federal government is through a direct infusion of funds that assist state and local educational agencies in offering special education and related services, or through efforts that further state and local programs (discretionary grants and contracts).

The second major area in which the federal government impacts special education is through compliance monitoring. To accomplish this objective, special education programs engage in program administrative reviews that involve on-site and off-site reviews of information. Where deficiencies are found, corrective actions are requested from the SEA. The corrective actions report includes a description of the steps to be taken by the SEA, timelines for completion, and the documentation to be submitted verifying that deficiencies have been corrected. Should substantial noncompliance be noted, the U.S. Department of Education is authorized to withhold federal funds. Considerable leeway exists within the department's administration of its compliance monitoring efforts to ensure that each state receives funding. Nevertheless, the possibility that a state may not receive federal funds can be

Table S.4. IDEA, Part B State Grant Program: Funds Appropriated, 1977–1996

Appropriation year	IDEA, Part B state grants	Per-child allocation
1977	$251,770,000	$71
1978	566,030,000	156
1979	804,000,000	215
1980	874,190,000	227
1981	874,500,000	219
1982	931,008,000	230
1983	1,017,900,000	248
1984	1,068,875,000	258
1985	1,135,145,000	272
1986	1,163,282,000	279
1987	1,338,000,000	316

persuasive in altering special education programs in that state.

Audette and Algozzine (1997) have suggested that the dearth of legislation monitoring and regulations from the federal level have increased bureaucratic paperwork and procedures to the point of being a major hindrance, asserting that special education is "costly rather than free" (Audette & Algozzine, 1997).

REFERENCES

Audette, B., & Algozzine, B. (1997). Reinventing government? Let's reinvent special education. *Journal of Learning Disabilities, 30*(4), 378–383.

U.S. Department of Education. (1997). *Nineteenth annual report to Congress on the implementation of the Individuals with Disabilities Education Act.* Washington, DC: Author.

MARTY ABRAMSON
University of Wisconsin at Stout

See also Demography of Special Education; Politics and Special Education; Special Education Programs

SPECIAL EDUCATION, GENERIC (*See* Generic Special Education)

SPECIAL EDUCATION, HISTORY OF (*See* History of Special Education)

SPECIAL EDUCATION, HUMANISTIC (*See* Humanistic Special Education)

SPECIAL EDUCATION, PHILOSOPHERS' OPINIONS ABOUT (*See* Philosophy of Education for Individuals With Disabilities)

SPECIAL EDUCATION, PROFESSIONAL STANDARDS FOR (*See* Professional Standards for Special Educators)

SPECIAL EDUCATION, RACIAL DISCRIMINATION IN (*See* Racial Discrimination in Special Education)

SPECIAL EDUCATION, SUPERVISION IN (*See* Supervision in Special Education)

SPECIAL EDUCATION, TEACHER TRAINING IN

The training and practice of special educators have undergone rapid development and change over the past four decades. In recognition of the small number of individuals who were prepared to conduct research and train teachers to educate the retarded, PL 85-926 was passed in 1958. With the passage of this law, funds were allocated to establish doctoral-level university training programs in the area of mental retardation. These training programs, along with a robust postwar economy, resulted in a decade characterized by a proliferation of programs for exceptional children (Tawney & Gest, 1984). The need for trained individuals to run public and private school programs preceded a clear understanding of what and how to teach children with various handicapping conditions. The first special education curricula were watered-down or slowed-down adaptations of regular class programs; they underscored the absence of empirical data in the field. Training, for the most part, focused on how to control children's behavior. The hope was that a child controlled was a child ready to learn.

The 1970s saw a continuance of the optimism of the 1960s and a period of advocacy and activism. Public Law 94-142, a civil rights bill for the disabled, guaranteed a "free and appropriate" education for exceptional children. At the same time, it called on special educators to document, as precisely as possible, children's progress. For the first time in public education, teachers were called on to be accountable. Practically, concerns for accountability meant that the field moved to replace the generalized curricula of the 1960s with more individualized curricula focused on matching instructional strategies to individual learner characteristics. Tawney and Gest (1984) pointed out that "the cumulative effect of the developmental efforts of the 1970s, then, was to set the stage for a new era of intensive programming for handicapped students in the 1980s" (p. 5). Problems with a worsening economy in the late 1970s, however, shifted attention from the problems of the handicapped to more personal priorities.

The reality of the 1990s was essentially economic in character. Given the increase in the number of children being served and the fact that federal, state, and local budgets did not have unlimited resources, the 1990s became a period of retrenchment and uncertainty in special education. There was a clear and pressing need to increase the number of teachers qualified to work with children with disabilities, but at the same time newly trained teachers were being asked to do more with less. Teachers in special education were being called on to be more resourceful, more organized, and more precise in creating, planning, and executing instructional interventions and more directly involved in general or regular education.

In addition to these broad political and economic factors, the quantity and quality of research in human learning and development and pedagogy have had an impact on the preparation of teachers for pupils with disabilities. Out of the massive research and development efforts with disabled and nondisabled children that began in the 1960s, special educators have acquired a substantial base of knowledge concerning effective instructional practices. With this large and growing body of information and the complex roles that special education teachers are currently being asked to assume, effective training of special educators will require greater breadth and depth of preparation than ever before.

While there is a lack of agreement concerning specific knowledge and skills that teachers of individuals with disabilities should possess, there is a growing consensus among regular and special educators concerning the general characteristics of a professional teacher and the framework for teacher preparation programs. The general parameters include the following. First, teachers need a firm foundation in general literacy and in the basic disciplines of the humanities, liberal arts, and sciences as prerequisite to entering the teaching profession (Denemark & Nutter, 1980). Second, special education teachers must be well versed in general education requirements as well as those specific to special education; that is, they must be education generalists as well as education of the disabled specialists (Reynolds, 1979). Their training should include acquiring knowledge of school development; basic academic skill curricula; instructional methods, including the effective use of computer-assisted instruction; and instructional and behavioral management strategies. In return, the inclusion movement has mandated that general educators have the same training in special education. General education teacher license requirements in 22 states include a requirement that teachers have some coursework related to students with disabilities. Eleven states require some practical work with students as well as coursework (U.S. Department of Education, 1997).

Third, as a key to participation in inclusion efforts, special education teachers must function as team members and as consultants, providing interaction with the general education faculty on questions concerning handicapped pupils. Fourth, regardless of the nature and severity of a pupil's disability, all special education teachers must possess effective communication skills to work with parents of children with disabilities. These include a working knowledge of the motivational, cognitive, and social consequences associated with their pupils' handicapping conditions. Special educators should also be able to assess pupils' current levels of functioning, select and implement instructional strategies based on youngsters'

learning characteristics, and evaluate the effectiveness of their instructional procedures.

Last of all, teacher training programs should provide extensive practical experience for their students. This practical experience should be initiated early in the students' training, with greater amounts of professional practice provided as students progress through the program (Scannell & Guenther, 1981). As researchers have recognized that the first year of teaching is critical for the maintenance and development of effective teaching skills, a year-long paid and supervised internship has been recommended as the culminating training experience of a preservice program. For student-teachers to gain the most from these practica, they should be closely monitored and effective models of teaching should be provided. Training that includes the previously noted components cannot be provided in an undergraduate teacher preparation program. The American Association of Colleges of Teacher Education Commission of Education for the Profession argues that the presently constituted teaching profession is, at best, a semiprofession (Howsam, Corrigan, Denemark, & Nash, 1976). The commission recommended a 5-year initial teacher preparation program combining the bachelor's and master's degrees, plus a 6th year of supervised internship to improve the quality of teacher education. Such an effort would enhance the profession of teaching and lead to outstanding pupil achievement. In view of these collective recommendations, it appears that preparation of special education teachers will require the extension of teacher education into graduate training.

Unfortunately, due to declining enrollments in teacher preparation programs and reductions in university budgets, few university faculties have decided to make their programs more rigorous by incorporating the recommendations of leaders in the area of teacher education and special education.

Attrition of special education teachers has been a major concern nationally. Moreover, lack of quality in preservice training has been related to teacher attrition rates. With the extensive and culturally competent (Miller, Miller, & Schroth, 1997) coursework, practica, and internship training required in new programs, graduates will be better prepared to meet the challenges and demands of special education instruction. As a consequence, they may continue to teach youngsters with disabilities for a longer period of time and in a more effective manner.

This entry has been informed by the sources listed below.

REFERENCES

Denemark, G., & Nutter, N. (1980). *The case for extended programs of initial teacher preparation*. Washington, DC: ERIC Clearinghouse on Teacher Education.

Howsam, R. B., Corrigan, D. C., Denemark, G. W., & Nash, R. J. (1976). *Education as a profession: Report of the Bicentennial*

Commission on Education for the Profession of Teaching of the American Association of Colleges for Teacher Education. Washington, DC: American Association of Colleges for Teacher Education.

Keogh, B. K. (1985). *Learning disabilities: Diversity in search of order*. Paper prepared for the Pittsburgh Research Integration Project, University of Pittsburgh.

Miller, S., Miller, K. L., & Schroth, G. (1997). Teacher perceptions of multicultural training in preservice programs. *Journal of Instructional Psychology, 24*(4), 222–232.

Palmer, D. J., Anderson, C., Hall, R., Keuker, J., & Parrish, L. (1985). *Preparation of special educators: Extended generic special education training program* (Report to the U.S. Department of Education, Special Education Programs, Division of Personnel Preparation).

Reynolds, M. (1979). *A common body of practices for teachers: The challenge of Public Law 94-142 to teacher education*. Minneapolis, MN: The National Support System Project.

Scannell, D., & Guenther, J. E. (1981). The development of an extended program. *Journal of Teacher Education, 32*, 7–12.

Tawney, J. W., & Gest, D. L. (1984). *Single subject research in special education*. Columbus, OH: Merrill.

U.S. Department of Education. (1997). *Nineteenth annual report to Congress on the implementation of the Individuals with Disabilities Act* (IDEA). Washington, DC: Author.

Douglas J. Palmer
Robert Hall
Texas A&M University

See also **Human Resource Development; Teacher Burnout; Teacher Effectiveness**

SPECIAL EDUCATION, TELECOMMUNICATION SYSTEMS IN (*See* Telecommunication Systems in Special Education)

SPECIAL EDUCATION INSTRUCTIONAL MATERIALS

More than a decade before the passage of the Education for All Handicapped Children Act, the U.S. Office of Education recognized that one of the main obstacles to education of quality for students with disabilities was the dearth of appropriate instructional materials and services both for the students and for those responsible for their education (Alonso, 1974). The federal government hoped to have established a network of service centers to address this problem by 1980.

The initiation of this effort began in 1963, when two projects were funded—one at the University of Southern California and the other at the University of Wisconsin —to serve as demonstration models for the development and dissemination of effective instructional materials and methods. From this modest beginning were to come 13 regional Special Education Instructional Materials centers (SEIMCs); four regional media centers for the deaf and hearing impaired (RMCs); a Clearinghouse on Handicapped and Gifted Children in the Educational Resources Information Center (ERIC) Network; an Instructional Materials Reference Center at the American Printing House for the Blind; and a National Center on Education Media and Materials for the Handicapped (NCEMMH).

The role of SEIMCs, some of which in various funding periods were also called regional resource centers (RRCs) and area learning resource centers (ALRCs), would change somewhat over the decade of their existence. During the experimental phase, which ran from 1964 to 1966, the two centers were expected to develop appropriate materials and methods for children with disabilities, transform them into workable curricula, and disseminate the results, along with other information, to the field. The early centers were also charged with the exploration of new technologies for instructional purposes as well as for information dissemination (Langstaff & Volkmor, 1974).

The official scope of the centers was not strictly defined by the government. It was acknowledged that needs varied widely from one service area to another, and each program was encouraged to respond to its local situation appropriately and to take full advantage of the special strengths of its staff. In general, however, the activities tended to break down into three categories. The first involved identifying, collecting, evaluating, circulating, and, when necessary, developing or stimulating the development of instructional materials. The second category consisted of field services of various sorts: the training of teachers in the choice, evaluation, and use of instructional media and materials; coordination activities that established or improved the delivery of services to special educators and their students; and technical assistance to state departments of education to ensure the institutionalization of ongoing support services within each state. Finally, the centers were all involved to some extent in the systematic dissemination of information regarding current research, methods, and materials for special education.

REFERENCES

Alonso, L. (1974). *Final technical report of the Great Lakes region special education instructional materials center*. Washington, DC: Bureau of Education for the Handicapped. (ERIC Document Reproduction Service No. ED 094 507)

Langstaff, A. L., & Volkmor, C. B. (1974). *Instructional materials center for special education: Final technical report*.

Washington, DC: Bureau of Education for the Handicapped. (ERIC Document Reproduction Service No. ED 107 086)

JANET S. BRAND
Hunter College,
City University of New York

See also Online Special Education; SpecialNet

SPECIAL EDUCATION PROGRAM

In 1982 Special Education Programs (SEP) succeeded the Office of Special Education as the primary federal agency responsible for overseeing federal initiatives in the education of individuals with disabilities. Although SEP's mission has basically remained the same since the creation of the Bureau of Education for the Handicapped in 1966, its organizational structure has changed. Special Education Programs is divided into five divisions.

The Division of Assistance to States (DAS) has four areas of responsibility. Its primary function is to monitor the extent to which states are implementing the requirements of PL 94-142 and PL 89-313 state-operated programs. The DAS is also SEP's liaison with the Office for Civil Rights when parent complaints are received. The DAS provides technical assistance to states either directly through its program officers or through a national network of regional resource centers. Finally, DAS oversees the awarding of grants to centers that serve the deaf-blind.

The Division of Innovation and Development (DID) carries out SEP's mission for generating new information to help individuals with disabilities. The DID administers several grant competitions. Field-initiated research allows any investigator to suggest a project and student projects are the most widely known. The DID has the U.S. Department of Education's responsibility for conducting the PL 94-142, Section 618, evaluation of the implementation of programs for individuals with disabilities whose results appear in the *Annual Reports to Congress* (U.S. Department of Education, 1986).

The Division of Personnel Preparation administers grant programs to prepare special educators and related services personnel, parents of children with disabilities, and doctoral-level professionals, among others, to serve the needs of students with disabilities.

The Division of Educational Services is responsible for grant projects that develop model programs in the areas of early childhood education, youth employment, services for the severely disabled, transitional services for students changing their least restrictive environment placement, and captioning of films for the hearing impaired.

The Division of Program Analysis and Planning has responsibility for managing the planning and budgetary processes within SEP. It also coordinates the efforts of other divisions when changes are proposed and made to regulations in the administration of PL 94-142, PL 89-313, and the various grant and contract programs.

The current address of SEP is U.S. Department of Education, Special Education Programs, 400 Maryland Avenue, SW, Washington, DC 20202.

REFERENCE

U.S. Department of Education. (1986). *Eighth annual report to Congress on the implementation of Public Law 94-142: The Education for All Handicapped Children Act.* Washington, DC: Author.

ROLAND K. YOSHIDA
Fordham University

SPECIAL EDUCATION AND REHABILITATIVE SERVICES, OFFICE OF

Special Education and the NCTM Standards

One of the primary aims of the reform mathematics movement in the 1980s was to adopt a standards-based system to measure a student's achievement against the concrete standards, instead of measuring how well the student performed compared to others. The standards-based system was a revolutionary step towards a democratic mathematics education as it promoted *equity* between practical and axiomatic mathematics, as well as setting a goal to reach all students.

The standards-based assessment idea was first articulated in the *Agenda for Action*, in which individual differences among students were emphasized and it was suggested that mathematics curriculum should be flexible enough to accommodate the diverse needs of the student population (National Council of Teachers of Mathematics [NCTM], Council, 1980). Special attention was drawn to differentiation of the instruction as a requirement of the equity principle, rather than exclusion of students' with different abilities and needs:

> Differentiated curricula must incorporate the special needs in mathematics of students with handicaps, including physical or learning difficulties. These programs will need to move away from the idea that everyone must learn the same mathematics and develop the same skills. (NCTM, 1980, recommendation 6)

NCTM soon became the focus of the standards-driven reform mathematics movement with the *Curriculum and*

Evaluation Standards (1989), and the equity principle became a part of the new standards, but only as "an economic necessity" (p. 4) to promote mathematics among students from underrepresented ethnicities. The students with learning disabilities in mathematics were absent in the document (Baxter, Woodward, & Olson, 2001). It also became apparent that students in individualized education programs (IEP) were generally provided a less rigorous curriculum that focused on computation (Shriner, Kim, Thurlow, & Ysseldyke, 1993).

The legislation following the 1989 standards (e.g., Goals 2000; Improving America's Schools Act; Individuals with Disabilities Education Act [IDEA]) helped NCTM redefine its definition of the equity principle, which was reflected in the *Principles and Standards for School Mathematics* (PSSM); (NCTM, 2000). Equity was extended to all students who were successful or unsuccessful in mathematics. Although students in special education, including the ones with learning disabilities, or emotional disorders, who composed 72% of the secondary students in special education in 2000 (U.S. Department of Education, 2000, as cited in Maccini & Gagnon, 2002) were still not explicitly mentioned in the PPSM, there was a general understanding that students with IEPs also deserved rigorous mathematics learning opportunities.

Francis Fennel, the past president of NCTM (2006–2008) stated the importance of IEPs for students in special education and suggested special education and mathematics teachers should work in collaboration to adapt the PSSM through intervention assistance (2007). The collaboration seemed to be an appropriate solution to Graham and Fennell (2001), considering the fact that some states did not require a mathematics background for special education teachers and that they needed the expertise of the mathematics teacher for successful implementation of their IEPs.

Today, despite the concerns of researchers that reform-based mathematics require drastic changes to both the form and substance of mathematics instruction (Baxter, Woodward, & Olson, 2001), research has shown that increased emphasis on conceptual understanding in accordance with the NCTM standards has resulted in increased performance in mathematics and enables students in special education to reach a more complex level of mathematics (Maccini, Mulcahy, & Wilson, 2007).

REFERENCES

Baxter, J., Woodward, J., & Olson, D. (2001). Effects of reform-based mathematics instruction in five third-grade classrooms. *Elementary School Journal, 101*(5), 529–548.

Graham, K. J., & Fennell, F. (2001). Principles and standards for school mathematics and teacher education: Preparing and empowering teachers. *School Science and Mathematics, 101*(6), 319–327.

Maccini, P., & Gagnon, J. C. (2002). Perceptions and application of NCTM's standards by special and general education teachers: Implications for practice for secondary students with emotional and learning disabilities. *Exceptional Children, 68*, 325–344.

Maccini, P., Mulcahy, C., & Wilson, M. (2007). A follow-up of mathematics interventions for secondary students with learning disabilities. *Learning Disabilities Research & Practice, 22*, 58–74.

National Council of Teachers of Mathematics. (1980). *An agenda for action: Directions for school mathematics for the 1980s.* Reston, VA: Author.

National Council of Teachers of Mathematics. (1989). *Curriculum and evaluation standards for school mathematics.* Reston, VA: Author.

National Council of Teachers of Mathematics. (2000). *Principles and NCTM standards for school mathematics.* Reston, VA: Author.

Shriner, J. G., Kim, D. Thurlow, M. L., & Ysseldyke, J. E. (1993). *IEPs and standards: What they say for students with disabilities* (Technical Report No. 5). Minneapolis: University of Minnesota, National Center on Educational Outcomes.

M. Sencer Corlu
Texas A&M University
Fourth edition

SPECIALNET

SpecialNet, which was once the largest education-oriented computer-based communication network in the United States, is operated by the National Association of State Directors of Special Education. SpecialNet made it possible for its more than 2,000 subscriber agencies to use the system to send e-mail (messages, forms, reports, questions, and answers) instantaneously to one or many participants. The system also contains electronic bulletin boards, which are topical displays of various information bases, administered by content experts around the country. Nearly 30 such bulletin boards are currently available; they include coverage of personnel development, early childhood education, computers and other technologies, program evaluation, promising practices, federal news, gifted education, parent programs, educational policy, vocational education, and many other topics. The program is no longer in existence but may have spawned the "SpeciaL Ed Connect" program, a similar system.

Judy Smith-Davis
Counterpoint Communications Company

Staff
Fourth edition

See also **Online Special Education; Special Education Instructional Materials**

SPECIAL SERVICES IN THE SCHOOLS

Published by Haworth Press (New York City), *Special Services in the Schools* (SSS) is a quarterly, refereed journal with an applied focus. It is now in its seventh volume. The *SSS* is intended to be read by multidisciplinary professional audiences who provide special services in schools and related educational settings, including school psychologists, guidance counselors, consulting teachers, social workers, and speech and language clinicians. It is the journal's policy to disseminate available information of direct relevance to these professionals. Thus, information published in *SSS* includes reviews of relevant research and literature, descriptions and evaluations of programs, viewpoints on latest trends in policy development, and guidelines for designing, implementing, and evaluating special service programs.

The issues of the journal are organized in a sequence whereby thematic and general issues alternate. Thematic issues have focused on topics such as computers and exceptional children, health promotion strategies, new directions in assessment of special learners, and international perspectives on facilitating cognitive development of children. Articles in general issues have included topics such as evaluation of programs of children of divorce, staff stress and burnout, curricula and programs for pregnant and parenting adolescents, and involving parents in the education of their children with disabilities.

Articles are aimed at being informative and instructive to special educators, psychologists, counselors, nurses, social workers, speech and language clinicians, physical and occupational therapists, and school supervisors and administrators. The material is intended to assist these professionals in performing a wide range of service delivery tasks. These include:

- Assessing individual pupils and groups to determine their special educational needs
- Designing individualized and group programs
- Assisting regular and special classroom teachers in fostering academic achievement and functional living for special students
- Enhancing the social and emotional development of pupils through preventive and remedial approaches
- Helping school administrators to develop smoothly functioning organizational systems
- Fostering the physical well-being of special students
- Involving parents and families in special programs
- Educating and training school staff to more effectively educate special needs students

Manuscripts that focus on the topical areas and service delivery tasks noted are routinely considered for publication. All manuscripts undergo blind review by editorial consultants.

CHARLES A. MAHER
Rutgers University

LOUIS J. KRUGER
Tufts University

SPECIFIC LEARNING DISABILITIES (See Learning Disabilities)

SPECT (SINGLE PHOTON EMISSION COMPUTED TOMOGRAPHY)

Brain SPECT imaging is a nuclear medicine procedure that directly measures relative cerebral blood flow and indirectly evaluates brain metabolism. It is a procedure similar to positron emission tomography (PET) scan. SPECT and PET scans are both nuclear medicine scans and have been conducted in research and clinical settings for more than two decades. SPECT and PET technology offers unique opportunities to examine cerebral metabolism and physiology. New binding isotopes are also allowing researchers and clinicians to track specific neurotransmitters in the brain, including chemicals in the dopaminergic, opiate, benzodiazepine, serotonin, and cholinergic systems. SPECT and PET are considered noninvasive procedures. As nuclear medicine studies, they require the injection of a small amount of radioactive material. SPECT is about half the cost of PET, and both methods allow for specific in vitro measures not offered by other techniques. The isotopes find their way into the working brain, providing a picture of specific parts of the brain while it is engaged in specific tasks. The level of radiation for a single SPECT scan is considered safe. A normal SPECT study demonstrates full, even, symmetrical activity in the brain. Ongoing research continues to generate data defining patterns and meanings of abnormal SPECT studies for specific medical and developmental conditions.

The procedure guidelines of the Society of Nuclear Medicine list the evaluation of suspected brain trauma, dementia, presurgical location of seizures, and the detection and evaluation of cerebral vascular disease as common indications for brain SPECT. The guidelines also note that many additional indications for use of this imaging appear promising.

There is not yet consensus on the usefulness of SPECT in clinical practice in the field of psychiatry and special education. However, an increasing number of clinics around the world are using brain SPECT to evaluate individuals with complex neuropsychological illnesses, such as treatment-resistant depression and attention-deficit/hyperactivity disorder (ADHD) with significant comorbidity, violence, and psychosis. The procedure has yet to be used extensively for children with learning disabilities.

The following is a case example on the potential utility of brain SPECT. A 12-year-old child was admitted to the hospital for episodes of explosive rage. He had been treated for 7 years with six different medications, as well as receiving counseling for ADHD and depression, without benefit. A brain SPECT was ordered by his examining physician and was found to demonstrate marked decreased temporal lobe activity, a common finding in temporal lobe epilepsy. The child was placed on an antiepileptic drug, carbomazepine, and responded well.

This entry has been informed by the sources listed below.

REFERENCES

Amen, D. (2001). Why don't psychiatrists look at the brain: The case for the greater use of SPECT imaging in neuropsychiatry. *Neuropsychiatry Reviews, 2*(1), 1, 19–21.

Devous, M. D. (2002). SPECT functional brain imaging. In *Brain mapping: The method* (pp. 513–533). San Diego, CA: Academic Press.

Holman, B. L., & Devous, M. D. Sr. (1992). Functional brain SPECT: The emergence of a powerful clinical method. *Journal of Nuclear Medicine, 33*, 1888–1904.

Juni, J. E., Waxman, A. D., Devous, M. D., Tikofsky, R. S., Ichise, M., Van Heertum, R. L., . . . Chen, C. C. (2002). Brain perfusion single photon emission computed tomography (SPECT) using Tc-99m radiopharmaceuticals 2.0. Approved 1999. In *Society of Nuclear Medicine procedure guidelines manual*. Washington, DC: Society of Nuclear Medicine.

DANIEL G. AMEN
University of California School of Medicine

SPEECH

In the context of special education, the word *speech* may have two different meanings. Sometimes, it is used to refer to the whole of linguistic skills. Such is the case in compounds such as *speech pathologist* and *speech therapy*. In other cases, the meaning is narrower, with the word referring to spoken language. The use of the word *speech* to denote the whole of verbal abilities is indicative of the cardinal importance of spoken language. Oral language is by far the most frequently used form of verbal communication. It is also the first linguistic ability to be acquired by the child.

Speech (i.e., spoken language) is produced by means of the speech organs. These organs make up parts of the respiratory system and the digestive tract. Usually, expiratory air is used to generate audible speech sounds. If air from the lungs activates the larynx, voiced sounds such as vowels or voiced consonants are produced. If the vocal cords are kept apart and consequently do not vibrate during exhalation, egressive air is turned into voiceless consonants (such as /s/ or /f/). Speech movements are rapid, complex, and finely timed sequences of gestures. Therefore, it takes the child several years to learn to perform them.

Since speech is ordinarily produced on exhalation, air is taken in just prior to starting to speak. Inspiration is caused by a contraction of the diaphragm and of the external intercostal muscles. When it contracts, the diaphragm flattens out and goes down. When the external intercostals contract, they lift up the rib cage. A membrane called parietal pleura is attached to both the diaphragm and the rib cage. When the diaphragm goes down and the rib cage goes up, the parietal membrane follows them. This enlarges the interpleural space, which is the closed space between the parietal membrane and the visceral membrane. The latter membrane enwraps each of the two lungs. Because the interpleural space becomes larger, the pressure in this space drops. Residual air (even after the most forcible expiration possible, some air remains in the lungs; this air is called residual) forces the expansible lungs to dilate so that the visceral pleura can follow the parietal pleura and annihilate the negative pressure in the interpleural space. In the expanded lungs the pressure is now negative, and external air flows in via the nose (or mouth), larynx, and trachea to annihilate it (Kaplan, 1971).

Once the diaphragm starts to relax, the lower part of the parietal pleura is sucked upward by the retractile lungs. Similarly, the upper part of the pleura is sucked downward once the external intercostals start to relax. The retraction of the lungs increases the air pressure in them and air escapes via the upper respiratory tract. If, at some point, the relaxation pressure becomes insufficient to produce audible speech, expiratory muscles, mainly the internal intercostals, are used to draw the rib cage further in (Perkins & Kent, 1985).

On its way out, egressive air passes the larynx. This organ comprises a vertical tube in which a V-shaped horizontal narrowing, called the glottis, is found. The sides of the glottis are formed by two ligaments, which together with the muscle fibers behind them constitute the vocal folds. If the vocal folds are approximated during expiration, the glottis is closed and the air can no longer flow out of the trachea. As a result, the air pressure in the trachea increases. At some point, the pressure is such that it blows the vocal folds apart. Some air escapes through the glottis. As a consequence, the pressure in the trachea diminishes. Moreover, a Bernoulli effect is created in the glottis. The Bernoulli effect is the negative pressure on the sides of a bottleneck when a gas or a liquid flows through it. The glottis forms a bottleneck between the trachea and the pharynx. As a consequence, when air escapes through the glottis, the vocal folds are sucked toward one another. The Bernoulli effect and the temporary decrease in tracheal air pressure enable the elastic vocal folds to come together again. Since the glottis is now closed again, pressure builds up in the trachea until it blows the vocal cords apart, and so on. In this way, the column of pulmonary air is divided into a quick succession of puffs that are fired into the supraglottal cavities (pharynx, mouth, and nasal cavity). The puffs of air hit the air mass present in the supraglottal cavities, causing it to vibrate. These vibrations, leaving the mouth of the speaker, propagate themselves in the air until they reach the ears of a listener, who perceives them as voice. The form of the individual vocal waves varies with the form of the supraglottal cavities (Zemlin, 1968). In this way, it is possible to produce vocal waves that sound like /a/, /u/, or any other vowel.

The puffs of air from the larynx not only hit the mass of air in the supraglottal cavities, but also move it forward. This forward movement can be used to form consonants. These consonants are voiced since their generation is synchronous with voice production. If, on the contrary, the vocal folds are kept in an abducted position and consequently do not vibrate, air from the lungs flows directly into the supraglottal cavities, where it can be molded into voiceless consonants. The shaping of the vocal waves and the molding of egressive air into speech sounds is performed by the articulators. The main articulators are the tongue and the velum. The latter moves upward and shuts off the nasal cavity from the oropharyngeal cavity during articulation of oral sounds. In English, most speech sounds are articulated with the velum in a raised position. Failure of the velum to occlude the passage of air to the nose results in hyperrhinolalia (i.e., nasalized speech).

REFERENCES

Kaplan, H. (1971). *Anatomy and physiology of speech*. New York, NY: McGraw-Hill.

Perkins, W., & Kent, R. (1985). *Textbook of functional anatomy of speech, language, and hearing*. Philadelphia, PA: Taylor & Francis.

Zemlin, R. (1968). *Speech and hearing science: Anatomy and physiology*. Englewood Cliffs, NJ: Prentice Hall.

YVAN LEBRUN
*School of Medicine,
Brussels, Belgium*

See also Language Disorders; Speech Disorders

SPEECH, ABSENCE OF

Many children speak their first recognizable word at age 1 and by 2 are using some type of sentence. When a child has not started speaking by age 2, parents often become concerned about the child's development. However, it is not unusual for the normally developing child not to use his or her first word until some time after the second birthday. However, if a child has no speech by age 5, it is likely that a serious difficulty exists (Bloodstein, 1984).

The most common cause of a lack of speech is an intellectual disability. While many children exhibiting severe intellectual disabilities have the potential to develop some language, those with a profound disability are likely to have no speech throughout their lives (Robinson & Robinson, 1976). Intellectual disabilities may sometimes be due to genetic factors. In other instances, traumatic brain injuries are the known cause of intellectual difficulty. Children with intellectual disabilities who do develop language typically do so in much the same manner as typically developing children but more slowly (Naremore & Dever, 1975; Van Riper & Erickson, 1996). They do, however, tend to exhibit limitations in their vocabulary and syntax usage.

Congenital deafness is another possible cause of a child exhibiting no speech. When a child is born with a profound hearing loss, he or she does not generally develop speech without special intervention. A number of children are born with some degree of hearing loss, but the impairment is not so severe that they cannot use hearing for the development of speech and language. However, a child with profound deafness typically experiences severe problems in developing speech because they have no way of monitoring their own speech production. Surprisingly, a profoundly deaf child's difficulty with hearing is often not noticed until the child is about age 2 and has not spoken his or her first word. This is due in part to the fact that many children with hearing impairments appear to go through the babbling stage in much the same way that children with hearing do.

Once a hearing loss is identified, most children with hearing impairments are fitted with a hearing aid. If the child has more than a 90 dB loss, he or she will probably not learn speech and language through hearing alone. The speech and language training of some children begins with the oral method, where language instruction is carried out primarily by requiring the child to lip read and speak. During the past 30 to 35 years, however, language instruction for children who are deaf has changed. Now most children are exposed to a sign language system once they are identified as deaf. Of children who are born with a profound hearing loss, only a small percentage attain speech that is intelligible to a stranger. However, many do attain a fairly high level of intelligibility to those who are familiar with the speech patterns of individuals who are deaf. It is important to make a distinction between speech and language when referring to children with hearing impairments because many children with profound deafness acquire language without having usable speech.

Another cause of absence of speech is cerebral palsy (Cruickshank, 1976; Pausewang Gelfer, 1996). Cerebral palsy is caused by brain damage occurring at or near the time of birth. Cerebral palsy can be of the type and of such severity that the child will not have sufficient control of the speech mechanism to produce intelligible speech. Some children, as their speech mechanism matures, can learn to produce intelligible speech with the help of specialists. However, other children can communicate only through other means such as communication boards and computers. Because of the physical disability and difficulty in communicating, the intelligence of children with cerebral palsy is often considerably underestimated.

An additional problem that can cause an absence of speech is the presence of social/emotional disturbances, specifically childhood schizophrenia and early infantile autism (Van Riper & Erickson, 1996). Typically, a child with schizophrenia appears to develop normally for the first few years of life and then begins to regress, possibly losing all language and speech. Schizophrenia, characterized by periods of remission, has been found to be resistant to treatment. Unlike schizophrenia, autism seems to be present in a child from birth. Infants with autism often withdraw from social contact, not looking into the eyes of adults and not leaning on the person carrying them. As they grow, their behavior may be characterized by obsessive actions, with play appearing to be stereotyped. Many children with autism fail to develop language. Language usage that does develop can be quite deviant. Some children with autism have been known to speak fully formed sentences, but only once or twice in their lifetimes. Others develop what is known as echolalic speech, where they parrot back what is spoken to them. These utterances do not appear to be used meaningfully. Other children do use some sentences meaningfully, but these seem to be memorized strings of words and are often simple demands. A smaller percentage of children with autism eventually attain a fair degree of speech and language.

Social deprivation can also be a cause of language acquisition problems. However, deprivation must be extremely severe for the child to acquire no speech whatsoever. Human beings appear to have a strong predisposition for learning language. Only minimal conditions of exposure to language need be present for the child to learn to speak. However, there are a few isolated cases of children who apparently have had no exposure to language and therefore do not develop language (e.g., Fuller, 1975). In some cases where a child is consistently deprived of attention, severe language delay may occur. For example, some children who were institutionalized received no attention except for being fed and kept clean. In such situations, many children experienced severe delays in the acquisition of language.

Occasionally, a clinician will see a child who understands language but does not speak at all. No cause can be found. Previously, it was thought that these children were suffering from maternal overprotection: Because the mother anticipated the child's needs, the child did not learn to speak. Over time, however, clinicians expressed doubt about attributing the lack of language usage to the behavior of the mother. While it was true that the mother often responded to the nonverbal cues of the child, it was generally recognized that the mother did this to alleviate severe frustration on both their parts. The mother's behavior is now seen as a response rather than as a cause. Children exhibiting this disorder frequently develop normal language over a period of time.

In the past, many children who did not acquire speech were institutionalized, receiving little or no educational services. With the advent of PL 94-142, many of these children were able to live at home and were provided schooling on a regular basis. Continued refinement of public educational laws (e.g., Individual with Disabilities Education Act Revisions of 1997) and a broader base of services have resulted in marked improvement in the communication skills of a number of children who have difficulty in this area.

REFERENCES

Bloodstein, O. (1984). *Speech pathology: An introduction*. Boston, MA: Houghton Mifflin.

Cruickshank, W. M. (1976). *Cerebral palsy: A developmental disability* (3rd ed.). Syracuse, NY: Syracuse University Press.

Fuller, C. W. (1975). Maternal deprivation and developmental language disorders. *Speech & Hearing Review: A Journal of New York State Speech & Hearing Association, 7,* 9–23.

Naremore, R. C., & Dever, R. B. (1975). Language performance of educable mentally retarded and normal children at five age levels. *Journal of Speech & Hearing Research, 18,* 92.

Pausewang Gelfer, M. (1996). *Survey of communication disorders: A social and behavioral perspective*. New York, NY: McGraw-Hill.

Robinson, N. M., & Robinson, H. B. (1976). *The mentally retarded child* (2nd ed.). New York, NY: McGraw-Hill.

Van Riper, C., & Erickson, R. L. (1996). *Speech correction: An introduction to speech pathology and audiology* (9th ed.). Boston, MA: Allyn & Bacon.

CAROLYN L. BULLARD
Lewis & Clark College
First edition

ROBERT L. RHODES
New Mexico State University
Second and Third editions

See also Autism; Elective Mutism; Mutism; Speech Therapy

SPEECH AND LANGUAGE DISABILITIES (*See* Communication Disorders; Language Disorders)

SPEECH-LANGUAGE PATHOLOGIST

Speech-language pathologist is the recognized title of a professional who evaluates and treats persons with speech and/or language disorders. There is some confusion about this title because there are other equivalent titles for speech-language pathologist, including speech (-language) therapist, speech pathologist, and speech (-language) clinician. In addition, speech-language pathologists sometimes use the informal abbreviated title of SLP. Different titles are used depending on the preferences of speech-language pathologists as well as the particular work settings (schools vs. hospitals, etc.). Different titles do *not* necessarily reflect any differences in educational or skill levels.

Speech-language pathologist is the title officially recognized by the American Speech-Language-Hearing Association (ASHA), a professional organization whose members include speech-language pathologists and audiologists (Van Riper & Erickson, 1996). Although not all speech-language pathologists and audiologists are members of ASHA, many of its members earn ASHA's Certificate of Clinical Competence (CCC), given to persons who hold a master's degree in speech-language pathology.

Speech-language pathologists must also sometimes be licensed by individual jurisdictions (e.g., states or provinces) before being permitted to do speech or language therapy in those jurisdictions. Speech-language pathologists work in schools, universities, hospitals, rehabilitation centers, and other institutions that serve the communicatively disabled.

REFERENCE

Van Riper, C., & Erickson, R. L. (1996). *Speech correction: An introduction to speech pathology and audiology* (9th ed.). Boston, MA: Allyn & Bacon.

Edward A. Shirkey
New Mexico State University

See also Communication Disorders; Speech Therapy

SPEECH-LANGUAGE SERVICES

The provision of services to children and adults who have speech and/or language disorders is a complex problem. According to Cleland and Swartz (1982), delivery of services includes such factors as funding, transportation, and consumer resistance, in addition to problems of keeping service providers up to date in the latest techniques and tools. Speech and language services are provided in a variety of settings (Van Riper & Erickson, 1996) but always by professionals trained as speech pathologists having appropriate certification or a state license. All clinically certified speech-language pathologists are capable of providing a complete range of services. Some choose to specialize, but all have knowledge across a variety of speech and language disorders. The greatest number of speech pathologists are employed in school settings, ranging from preschool through high school. Services provided include screening for speech and hearing disorders, diagnosis, treatment, and referral for more complex disorders. Since children make up the caseload in public schools, the majority of disorders treated are those concerning speech, language, voice, and stuttering. Many hospitals provide speech and language services. Speech clinics are usually established in rehabilitation departments. Speech-language pathologists work with occupational and physical therapists to treat people with physical disorders. Sometimes hospitals also provide services for children, thus offering an alternative to the free services of public schools.

There are speech-language clinics in many large metropolitan areas. Some of these clinics are private; others are associated with hospitals or universities. These clinics usually provide a wide range of services while at the same time being used as a training base for future speech language professionals. Privately funded or publicly funded health service agencies may also provide speech-language services. These agencies provide speech-language services to people from less privileged socioeconomic backgrounds. Speech clinicians employed by these agencies usually are itinerant: They go to the home of the client to provide the speech-language service. Clinics run by these agencies also provide a wide range of clinical services. There is a trend for speech-language pathologists to establish their own speech-language services rather than work for a school, hospital, clinic, or public agency. These individuals set up offices and see clients there. Occasionally, they hire other speech pathologists and enlarge their caseloads to the point where they can call their practice a clinic. Again, services are provided across the full range of speech and hearing disorders. Occasionally, speech-language pathologists are employed by industry. In these settings, the pathologists usually serve a diagnostic function only. In summary, speech-language services cover a wide range of diagnostic and therapeutic treatments in a variety of settings. These settings include public schools, hospitals, private speech clinics, university speech clinics, health service agencies, and private practices.

REFERENCES

Cleland, C. C., & Swartz, J. E. (1982). *Exceptionalities through the lifespan.* New York, NY: Macmillan.

Van Riper, C., & Erickson, R. L. (1996). *Speech correction: An introduction to speech pathology and audiology* (9th ed.). Boston, MA: Allyn & Bacon.

EDWARD A. SHIRKEY
New Mexico State University

See also Speech-Language Pathologists; Speech Therapy

Venkatagiri, H. S. (1994). Effect of sentence length and exposure on the intelligibility of synthesized speech. *American Journal of Speech-Language Pathology, 4,* 4, 36–45.

FREDERICK F. WEINER
Pennsylvania State University

See also Augmentative Communication Systems; Computer Use With Individuals With Disabilities

SPEECH SYNTHESIZERS

A speech synthesizer is an electronic device that attempts to duplicate the human voice. Essentially, it allows a machine to talk to a human being. Of course, a human being must program the synthesizer and tell it what to say.

There are two different techniques for producing speech output that account for almost all the current synthesizer designs. The first is called linear predictive coding (LPC), which attempts to make an electronic model of the human voice. It creates tones much like those of the human vocal folds. These tones are passed through a set of filters that shape the tones into sounds the way that the articulators (tongue, lips, teeth, etc.) shape tones into sounds. This is a popular technique because it requires only enough computer memory to store the filter configurations and therefore is relatively inexpensive to make. Sound quality is acceptable but not realistic because the modeling of the voice is not exact enough to duplicate all the subtle vocal characteristics of human speech. The result is a machinelike speech quality.

The second method of producing speech is referred to as digitized speech. Actually, digitized speech is not synthesized speech. In digitized speech, the sound waves of the speech signal rather than the throat positions are recorded. These waves are then digitized—converted to digital codes and played back when needed. The advantage to this method is that the speech quality is good, sounding like a high-quality tape recorder. Nonetheless, it still takes time for the average listener to adjust to and understand synthesized speech (Venkatagiri, 1994). The disadvantage is that great amounts of memory are required to store the speech waves.

Aside from the industrial application of speech synthesizers, the synthesizers are being used as communication devices for nonspeaking individuals with disabilities and to prompt individuals with disabilities using remediation software (Lundberg, 1995).

REFERENCES

Lundberg, I. (1995). The computer as a tool of remediation in the education of students with reading disabilities. *Learning Disability Quarterly, 18*(2), 89–99.

SPEECH THERAPY

Speech therapy includes all efforts to ameliorate disordered speech. Treatment activities include attempts to improve the speech of persons who have never spoken normally (habilitation) as well as to improve the speech of persons who formerly had normal speech (rehabilitation). A variety of treatment approaches are used, depending on the speaker's age, speech disorder, and the professional training and experience of the speech pathologist. Speech therapy usually includes teaching a person with a speech disorder to speak differently. Concerning adults and older children, however, therapy may consist of play activities during which treatment is indirect.

Although many research investigations have been conducted into the nature and treatment of speech (and language) disorders, much remains unknown. Therapy remains, therefore, often more of an art than a science. The speech pathologist must often rely more on intuition and experience than on research results. Often, no attempt is made to determine the cause of the speech disorder because, in most cases, the cause(s) cannot be found (e.g., Van Riper & Erickson, 1996). Although some speech disorders can be completely cured so that no traces of the original behavior remain, some speech disorders cannot be completely eradicated. For instance, some children and adults who stutter will continue to have vestiges of stuttering despite successful speech therapy.

Clients receive therapy in group and/or individual sessions, and therapy may be short-term (a few sessions) or long-term (several years), depending on the nature and severity of the disorder. The length and frequency of therapy sessions also depend on a variety of factors. (The terms *client, patient*, and *student* are all variously used to refer to the person being treated for a speech disorder, depending on the treatment setting.)

Speech-language pathologists typically assess clients before therapy actually begins, although a period of diagnostic therapy may also be used to help determine the nature of the disorder. Sometimes clients are referred to other professionals by the speech-language pathologist (e.g., audiologists, dentists, physicians).

REFERENCE

Van Riper, C., & Erickson, R. L. (1996). *Speech correction: An introduction to speech pathology and audiology.* Boston, MA: Allyn & Bacon.

EDWARD A. SHIRKEY
New Mexico State University

See also Augmentative Communication Systems; Communication Disorders; Speech-Language Pathologist

SPELLING DISABILITIES

Spelling is a traditional element of the elementary school curriculum and an integral part of the writing process. The primary goal of spelling instruction for both disabled and nondisabled students is to make the act of correctly spelling words so automatic that it requires only a minimal amount of conscious attention. If students master the ability to spell words with maximum efficiency and minimum effort, it is assumed that they will be able to devote more of their attention, and consequently more of their effort, to higher order writing processes such as purpose, content, and organization (Graham, 1982).

It is commonly believed that the majority of students who are labeled disabled exhibit spelling problems. This is particularly the case for students with reading disabilities (Lennox & Siegal, 1993). For instance, MacArthur and Graham (1986) found that students with learning disabilities made spelling errors in approximately 1 out of every 10 words that they used when writing a short story. Although similar spelling difficulties have been reported for other disability categories (Graham & Miller, 1979), it is important to note that our present understanding of spelling difficulties and students with disabilities' development of spelling skills is incomplete.

One development of particular interest in the area of spelling disabilities is the formulation of various systems for classifying spelling problems. Poor spellers who are also poor readers have frequently been classified as dyslexic, while poor spellers who possess normal reading skills have been labeled dysgraphic. In addition, many of the classification schemes presently available represent an attempt to interpret various spelling errors and difficulties as evidence of neurological dysfunction.

Spelling instruction for the individuals with disabilities has, in large part, been based on the use or modification of traditional spelling procedures and techniques. Although students with disabilities may not progress as rapidly through the spelling curriculum or master all of the skills taught to typically developing students, their spelling programs commonly emphasize the traditional skills of (a) mastering a basic spelling vocabulary; (b) determining the spelling of unknown words through the use of phonics and spelling rules; (c) developing a desire to spell words correctly; (d) identifying and correcting spelling errors; and (e) using the dictionary to locate the spelling of words. There is considerable controversy, however, surrounding the issue of which skills should receive primary emphasis. Some experts, for example, recommend that a basic spelling vocabulary should form the core of the spelling program, while others have argued that spelling instruction should take advantage of the systematic properties of English orthography and stress the application of phonics and spelling rules (Graham, 1983).

Although spelling instruction for students with disabilities has received little attention in the research literature, experts generally agree that these students should be taught a systematic procedure of studying unknown spelling words. Effective word study procedures usually emphasize careful pronunciation of the word, visual imagery, auditory and/or kinesthetic reinforcement, and systematic recall (Graham & Miller, 1979). Additional instructional procedures that are considered desirable for use with students with disabilities include using a pretest to determine which words a student should study; presenting and testing a few words on a daily basis; interspersing known and unknown words in each spelling test; requiring students to correct their spelling tests under the guidance of a teacher; periodically reviewing to determine whether spelling skills have been maintained; and using spelling games to promote interest and motivation.

A final point concerns the use of behavioral and cognitive procedures. Although the evidence is not yet conclusive, spelling procedures based on behavioral and/or cognitive principles appear to be particularly effective for students with disabilities. McLaughlin (1982) found, for example, that the spelling accuracy of students in a special class improved as a result of group contingencies. In terms of cognitive procedures, Harris, Graham, and Freeman (1986) found that strategy training improved students with learning disabilities' spelling performance and, in one study condition, improved their ability to predict how many words would be spelled correctly on a subsequent test. Others have found that computers assist in spelling skill acquisition in a meaningful way (Gordon, Vaughn, & Schumm, 1993; Van Daal & Van der Leij, 1992).

REFERENCES

Gordon, J., Vaughn, S., & Schumm, J. S. (1993). Spelling instruction: A review of literature and implications for instruction for student with learning disabilities. *Learning Disabilities Research and Practice, 8*(3), 175–181.

Graham, S. (1982). Composition research and practice: A unified approach. *Focus on Exceptional Children, 14*, 1–16.

Graham, S. (1983). Effective spelling instruction. *Elementary School Journal, 83*, 560–568.

Graham, S., & Miller, L. (1979). Spelling research and practice: A unified approach. *Focus on Exceptional Children, 12*, 1–16.

Harris, K., Graham, S., & Freeman, S. (1986). *The effects of strategy training and study conditions on metamemory and achievement.* Paper presented at the American Educational Research Association, San Francisco.

Lennox, C., & Siegal, L. S. (1993). Visual and phonological spelling errors in subtypes of children with learning disabilities. *Applied Psycholinguistics, 14*(4), 473–488.

MacArthur, C., & Graham, S. (1986). *LD students' writing under three conditions: Word processing, dictation, and handwriting.* Paper presented at the American Educational Research Association, San Francisco.

McLaughlin, T. (1982). A comparison of individual and group contingencies on spelling performance with special education students. *Child and Family Behavior Therapy, 4*, 1–10.

Van Daal, V. H., & Van der Leij, A. (1992). Computer-based reading and spelling practice for children with learning disabilities. *Journal of Learning Disabilities, 25*(3), 186–195.

STEVE GRAHAM
University of Maryland

See also **Writing Remediation**

SPELLING: FOUNDATION OF READING AND THE GREATEST ORNAMENT OF WRITING[*]

Principles of English spelling, spelling assessment, and suggestions for spelling instruction will be outlined in this monograph. The title of the monograph was stated by lexicographer Noah Webster in 1773. Appropriately, Webster called the early reading books he developed "spellers." However, spelling has not received as much attention as reading, both in terms of research studies and classroom instruction. Contrary to the belief that English spelling is irregular and chaotic, nearly 50% of the words are predictable based on sound letter correspondences and another 34% are predictable except for the spelling of one sound. As Chomsky and Halle (1968) noticed, English is a "near optimal system for lexical representation" (p. 49). Spelling is a linguistic task and is closely related to reading, writing, and vocabulary development, as they all rely on the same linguistic abilities. Hence, linguistically explicit spelling instruction improves spelling. Even

[*]Some of the information presented in this article was previously published in Joshi, R. M., Treiman, R., Carreker, S., & Moats, L. (2008). How words cast their spell: Spelling instruction focused on language, not memory, improves reading and writing. *American Educator, 32*(4), 6–16, 42–43.

though spelling instruction needs practice and time, there are three important principles that make learning spelling easy. The principles are (a) letter neighborhoods and patterns, (b) word origin and history, and (c) syllable patterns and meaningful parts of words. We will look at these principles in more detail below.

Principles

Letter Neighborhoods and Patterns

English has certain regularities for spelling words. For instance, *q* is almost always followed by *u* and then another vowel as in *quiet* and *quail*. Most of the exceptions are proper names, such as *Qatar* and *Iraq*. Another example of a letter pattern is English words do not end in *v*; that is why we spell *have, give,* and *love*, exception being *kiev* because it is a borrowed word from Russian. The /k/ sound or hard *c* sound in the initial or medial position can be spelled with *c* or *k*. Before *a, o, u,* or a consonant, /k/ is spelled with *c*, as in *cat, cot, cut,* or *crow*; however, before *e, i,* or *y,* /k/ is spelled with *k,* as in *kettle, kite,* and *sky.* Similar to the exception of some words where *u* does not follow *q,* there are exceptions when /k/ is spelled *k* but followed by *a, o,* or *u,* as in *kangaroo, koala,* and *skunk.* Again, these are words borrowed from other languages. Fortunately, there are more words that follow the letter patterns than words that are exceptions. A good source of information on letter neighborhoods and patterns can be found in Carreker (2011).

Word Origins and History

Approximately 20% to 25% of English words are of Anglo-Saxon/Old English origin and about 10%–15% of words are of Greek origin. About 60% of words are of Latin origin, of which 50% are directly from Latin and another 10% are from Latin through French. English spelling is influenced by its rich and varied history. For example, the sound /sh/ is spelled *sh*, as in *sheep* and *shell*, in Old English or Anglo-Saxon words; the same sound is spelled *ch* in French words of Latin origin, as in *chef* and *chandelier*. In Latin-derived words, /sh/ can be spelled *ti* as in *nation, ci* as in *special,* and *sci* as in *conscious.* In Greek based words, /sh/ may be spelled with different combination, such as *ce* as in *ocean.* Of note, /f/ is always spelled *ph* in words of Greek origin, which tend to be scientific in nature (*photosynthesis, chlorophyll*).

The spelling of some words is unusual because the words are eponyms; that is, derived from a person's name. For instance, *caesarean* is associated with *Julius Caesar,* who is said to have been delivered through surgery and *silhouette* can be traced to Etienne de *Silhouette,* a French finance minister known for his shady deals. An excellent source for the word origins and the history of English can be found in Henry (2010, 2011).

Syllable Patterns and Meaning-Carrying Parts of Words

Orthography deals with the explicit and implicit rules that govern how words are spelled. Two common types of syllables in English are closed and open syllables. These syllables types are helpful in understanding the orthography of English. A closed syllable ends in one vowel followed by at least one consonant; the vowel sound is short, as in *cat, dog,* and *lump.* An open syllable ends in one vowel; the vowel sound is long as in *go, she,* and *hi.*

Knowing about open and closed syllables elucidates why medial consonants are doubled or not in the spellings of two-syllable words. If the first syllable has one medial consonant sound after a short vowel sound, then the medial consonant is doubled, as in *rabbit, muffin,* and *tennis.* When these words are divided into syllables (*rab|bit, muf|fin, ten|nis*), the first syllable in each word is closed, and the vowel is short. However, if the first syllable has one medial consonant sound after a long vowel sound, then the medial consonant is not doubled, as in *tiger, hotel* and *lilac.* When these words are divided into syllables (*ti|ger, ho|tel, li|lac*), the first syllable in each word is open, and the vowel is long. Further knowledge of English orthography includes the convention that some consonants—*y, v, x, h, k*—do not or rarely double; hence, we spell *river* with one *v,* even though /v/ is after a short vowel. Also, because *k* never or rarely doubles, medial /k/ is not spelled with doubled *k* in *ticket* or *rocket* even though there is one medial consonant sound after a short vowel.

Knowing the meaning-carrying parts of words, such a prefix, suffix, or root, is valuable in spelling. For instance, the words *disease* and *decease,* sound similar, however, spelled differently. Knowing the prefix in the first word is *dis-* and the prefix in the second word is *de-,* can help to spell the two words correctly. Similarly, for the suffixes, *-er* and *-or,* knowing that Old English words are basic survival words, the suffix to use would be *-er,* as in *carpenter, baker,* and *butcher.* The suffix *-or* should be added to roots of Latin origin, as in *professor, director,* and *aviator.* Similarly, *-able* is added to Old English base words, such as *readable, passable,* and *breakable,* although the suffix *-ible* is used for Latin roots, such as *visible, audible,* and *edible.* Similarly, /st/ can be spelled with *-est* or *-ist,* but knowing the parts of speech helps in spelling the words correctly; nouns with /st/ are spelled with *-ist,* as in *chemist* and *pharmacist,* although /st/ is spelled with *-est* in adjectives, such as *fastest* and *sharpest.*

Assessment

When assessing spelling, evaluating errors in a qualitative manner rather than just scoring them as right or wrong informs instruction. For example, one student spells *cat* as KAT and another student spells the word *cat* as MB; both spellings are scored as wrong. However, the first student has better knowledge of how to spell than the second student. These students need different instruction. The first student needs instruction about letter neighborhoods (i.e., when to use *c* vs. *k* to spell /k/). The second student needs instruction in phonemic awareness (i.e., how many sounds are in words) and letter-sound correspondences (i.e., which letters spell which sounds).

Researchers (e.g., Apel, Masterson, & Niessen, 2004; Bear, Invernizzi, Templeton, & Johnston, 2008; Tangel & Blachman, 1992; Treiman, & Bourassa, 2000) have used various rubrics to score the spelling errors. For instance, Tangel and Blachman developed a seven-point system to score spelling errors, a score of zero for just some random letters that do not correspond to the sounds of the word although scores from 1 to 5 for varying degrees of accuracy and 6 points for correct spelling. Apel et al. (2004) classified errors into *phonetic, phonological, morphological, orthographic,* and *etymological.* These types of scoring helps the teachers guide the instruction that should be provided for students with spelling difficulties.

Instruction

Explicit and systematic spelling instruction benefits development of good spelling skills. Here, we outline some of the basic concepts to be taught at each grade level. At the Kindergarten level activities that heighten students' awareness of sounds in spoken language, also referred to as phonological awareness, and letter-name and letter-sound knowledge provide a foundation for spelling. By the end of Kindergarten, students should be able to quickly name letters on a chart as the teacher points to each letter and give the sounds of letters with one frequent sound (*b, d, f*) and recognize which letters frequently spell a dictated sound.

In first grade, students should be able to spell one syllable words with one-to-one letter-sound correspondences and should be able to learn a few common patterns such as /k/ before *a, o, u,* or any consonant is spelled with *c* (*cap, color, cut, class*) and before *e, i,* or *y,* is spelled with *k* (*kept, kite, sky*). Similarly, /j/ is spelled *j* before *a, o,* or *u* (*jam, jot, jump*) and spelled *g* before *e, i,* or *y* (*gem, ginger, gym*). Common exceptions are *jet* and *jingle,* yet students can still appreciate knowing the generalizations of letter neighborhoods. Another common pattern that could be introduced is the "floss rule"; after a short vowel in a one-syllable base word, final /f/ is spelled *ff,* final /l/ is spelled *ll,* and final /s/ is spelled *ss* (*puff, bell, miss*).

By second grade, students should be ready for more complex Anglo-Saxon letter patterns and common inflectional endings, such as *-s, -ed,* and *-ing.* The doubling rule helps students know that if a base word ends in one vowel, one consonant, and one accent (all one-syllable words are accented) and a vowel suffix (i.e., one that begins with a vowel) is being added, the final consonant in the base word is doubled (*swimmer, beginning* but *looked, camping,* *opening, redness*). Other common patterns include: final /k/ after a short vowel in a one-syllable word is spelled *ck* (*back, sick, duck*) and final /k/ after a consonant or two vowels is spelled with *k* (*milk, desk, book, peek*). Similarly, final /ch/ after a short vowel in a one-syllable word is spelled *tch* (*catch, pitch*) and after a consonant or two vowels is spelled *ch* (*bench, pouch*); the words *which, such, rich,* and *much* are exceptions. Final /j/ after a short vowel in a one-syllable word is spelled *dge* and after a long vowel, a consonant, or two vowels is spelled *ge* (*badge, fudge* but *age, hinge, scrooge*). With last few patterns, one can see the principle that there are often unique spellings of final consonant sounds after a short vowel in one-syllable words.

By third grade, students are spelling multisyllabic words with the unstressed vowel schwa (*sofa, alone, ribbon*). Common prefixes and suffixes are introduced. For example, they learn to change *y* to *i* as a suffix, such as in *happy-happiness, baby-babies*. Latin based prefixes and suffixes, and roots, such as *port* (*export, import, transport*) and *spect* (*spectacle, spectator, inspect*) are introduced in fourth grade. Greek combining forms, such as *photo* (*photography, photosynthesis*), *philo* (*philosophy, philodendron*) are introduced in grades 5 to 7. Detailed information about teaching spelling can be obtained by referring to Carreker (2011), Henry (2010), Moats (2010), and Joshi, et al. (2008).These instructional strategies are recommendations and depend on other aspects such as student's oral language development, previous exposure to literacy activities, and parental support.

Conclusion

We have outlined important concepts about principles involved in spelling English words, meaningful assessment of spelling errors, and guidelines for spelling instruction. We have emphasized that English spelling is not facilitated by rote memorization but more by understanding linguistic concepts such as speech sounds, letter-sound correspondences, word origins, history of English language, and meaningful word patterns. As Joshi et al. (2008) suggested, "The primary mechanism for word memory is not a photographic memory, as many believe; it is insight into why the word is spelled the way it is" (p. 16). They further recognized that "Spelling, therefore, is a window on what a person knows about words. Learning about words and about the language will improve spelling skills" (p. 42).

REFERENCES

Apel, K., Masterson, J. J., & Niessen, N. L. (2004). Spelling assessment frameworks. In Stone, A., Silliman, E. R., Ehren, B. J., & Apel, K. (Eds.), The *Handbook of language and literacy: Development and disorders.* (pp. 644–660), New York, NY: Guilford Press.

Bear, D. R., Invernizzi, M., Templeton, S., & Johnston, F. (2008). *Words their way: Word study for phonics, vocabulary, and spelling instruction.* Upper Saddle River, NJ: Pearson Prentice Hall.

Carreker, S. (2011). Teaching spelling. In J. R. Birsh (Ed.), *Multisensory teaching of basic language skills* (3rd ed.). Baltimore, MD: Paul H. Brookes.

Chomsky, N., & Halle, M. (1968). *The sound pattern of English.* New York, NY: Harper & Row.

Henry, M. K. (2010). *Unlocking literacy: Effective decoding and spelling instruction* (2nd ed.). Baltimore, MD: Paul H. Brookes.

Henry, M. K. (2011). The history and structure of written English. In J. R. Birsh (Ed.), *Multisensory teaching of basic language skills* (3rd ed.). Baltimore, MD: Paul H. Brookes.

Joshi, R. M., Treiman, R., Carreker, S., & Moats, L. (2008). How words cast their spell: Spelling instruction focused on language, not memory, improves reading and writing. *American Educator, 32 (4)*, 6–16, 42–43.

Moats, L. C. (2010). *Speech to print* (2nd ed.). Baltimore, MD: Paul H. Brookes.

Tangel, D. M., & Blachman, B. A. (1992). Effect of phoneme awareness instruction on kindergarten children's invented spelling. *Journal of Reading Behavior, 24*, 233–261.

Treiman, R. & Bourassa, D. C. (2000). Children's written and oral spelling. *Applied Psycholinguistics, 21*, 83–204.

R. Malatesha Joshi
Texas A&M University

Suzanne Carreker
*Deputy Director of Program Development,
Neuhaus Education Center
Fourth edition*

SPERRY, ROGER W. (1913–1994)

Fifty years of systematic and ingenious research resulted in Roger Sperry's development of novel ideas about the nervous system and mind. Born to a middle-class family in Hartford, Connecticut on August 20, 1913, Sperry dedicated his professional life to understanding two basic questions in psychology: (1) What is consciousness? and (2) What roles do nature and nurture play in the regulation of behavior? Educated at Oberlin College in Ohio (BS in English and MS in psychology), Chicago (PhD in Zoology), and Harvard (postdoctoral fellowship in psychology), Sperry always went against the conventional wisdom of his day, tending to question established fact through simple but brilliant studies. Most of his important studies were completed as Hixson Professor of Psychobiology at the California Institute of Technology.

He indicated that his work could be divided into phases. The first phase, developed at Oberlin and continued through his Chicago years, focused on determining whether the nervous system was malleable or amenable to change through learning. After interchanging nerve fibers in rats, initially motor ones and later sensory ones also, he concluded that the nervous system was more hard-wired than we had previously thought. These experiments were later replicated in a variety of amphibians and mammals, using both motor and sensory fibers. It was during this time that he developed the theory of chemoaffinity of nerve fibers. He proposed that if nerve fibers were cut, they would grow back to their original site using chemically induced growth.

During the 1950s, Sperry began to question whether this hard-wired concept was also found inside the brain (since he had previously worked with fibers in the peripheral nervous system). Initially working with cats and later with monkeys, Sperry began cutting the largest nerve tract in the brain, the corpus callosum. It had been previously thought that this fiber tract's role was essentially to hold the two sides of the brain together. His initial studies reflected that the two sides appeared to have different functions. However, he believed that humans could provide more accurate information regarding the perceived differences.

Together with surgeons Joseph Bogen and Phillip Voegl, Sperry designed a series of studies aimed at discovering the functions of the two sides of the brain and if the brain was as hard-wired as the peripheral nervous system. About a dozen patients with intractable epilepsy had their corpus callosum severed in what is now called "split-brain" preparation. Over numerous studies, some of which are still being carried out, it was discovered that the brain was indeed hard-wired, much like the peripheral nervous system. Further, it was found that the left hemisphere was primarily responsible for verbal information while the right hemisphere controlled visual information.

Additional studies revealed that the patients had two separate minds. Hence, their behavior was not integrated. After further study, Sperry concluded that consciousness was a function of the integration of both sides of the brain simultaneously. Also, he believed that the consciousness emerged from brain function and, in turn, had a downward control on the brain function from which it had been produced.

In his later years, Sperry became interested in the notion that specific value systems, as found in conscious thought, had an effect on the global situation. Specifically, he believed that appropriate values (reduction in overpopulation and pollution) were the solution to the modern problems facing society.

For his scientific work, Sperry shared the 1981 Nobel Prize in Medicine and received the highest awards in the disciplines he worked in, including psychology, neuroscience, and philosophy. With over 300 publications and close to 100 students doing research in nine different continents, Sperry's contributions extend far beyond his half century of research and modern-day psychology. He died at the age of 80 in Pasadena, California from complications of ALS. He is survived by his wife and two children.

This entry has been informed by the sources listed below.

REFERENCES

Puente, A. E. (1995). Roger Wolcott Sperry (1913–1994). *American Psychologist, 50*(11), 940–941.

Sperry, R. W. (1952). Neurology and the mind-brain problem. *American Scientist, 40*, 291–312.

Sperry, R. W. (1982). Some effects of disconnecting the cerebral hemispheres. *Science, 217*, 1223–1226.

ANTONIO E. PUENTE
University of North Carolina at Wilmington

SPIELMEYER-VOGT DISEASE

Spielmeyer-Vogt disease is the juvenile form of a group of progressive neurological diseases known as neuronal ceroid lipofuscinoses (NCL). Also known as Speilmeyer-Vogt-Sjogren-Batten disease or Batten disease after a British pediatrician who first described it in 1903, Spielmeyer-Vogt disease is an autosomal recessive disorder. Therefore, when both parents carry the gene, their children have a 25% chance of developing the disease. Symptoms of Spielmeyer-Vogt disease are linked to the buildup of lipopigments in the body's tissues. These lipopigments are made up of fats and proteins and build up in the cells of the brain and eyes as well as the skin, muscles, and other tissues.

Spielmeyer-Vogt disease is relatively rare, occurring in an estimated 2 to 4 out of every 100,000 births in the United States. This disorder appears to be more common in Northern Europe, Scandinavia, and Newfoundland, Canada. This disease often strikes more than one person in families who carry the defective gene.

Characteristics

1. Vision loss (optic atrophy) is often an early sign, so Spielmeyer-Vogt disease may first be suspected during an eye exam.
2. It is usually diagnosed between 5 and 8 years of age.
3. Individuals may suffer from seizures, ataxia, or clumsiness.
4. This form of NCL progresses less rapidly than do other forms.

5. Although some individuals may live into their 30s, this disease usually ends in death in the late teens or early 20s.

As yet no treatment is known that can halt or reverse the symptoms of Spielmeyer-Vogt disease or other NCLs. However, some of the symptoms can be controlled. Seizures may respond well to anticonvulsant drugs, and other medical problems can be treated as they arise. Some research has reported a slowing of the disease when patients are treated with vitamins C and E and diets low in vitamin A. However, these treatments did not prevent the fatal outcome of the disease. Children diagnosed with Spielmeyer-Vogt disease will be eligible for special services under the Individuals With Disabilities Education Act of 1997 within the physical disability category. The accommodations and modifications necessary will change with the progression of the illness. Psychosocial support will be necessary for the child and his or her family as they come to terms and live with this illness, but also in preparation for death. Teachers and those working with the student need to be well informed about the illness and its symptoms. School staff will need to be able to deal with the manifestation of the illness as it presents itself in class. For example, the student may be able to complete work one day and find it hard to complete any assignments the next day. Additionally, the student may need time away from the classroom to talk about feelings and express anger and concerns. Depending on their medical and psychological needs, students may miss long periods of school.

Research appears to be focusing on identifying the genetic cause of Spielmeyer-Vogt disease. The genes involved may be located on Chromosomes 13 and 15. Identification of specific genes can lead to the development of DNA diagnostics and carrier and prenatal tests. Other research is investigating the theory that Spielmeyer-Vogt disease may be related to a shortage of a key body enzyme called phospholipase A1. Identifying the faulty enzyme may make it possible to treat affected children with natural or synthetic enzymes to counteract the effect and clear away the storage of lipopigments. Other investigators are working to understand the role that lipopigments play in Spielmeyer-Vogt disease and other NCLs. Recently, scientists have identified large portions of the built-up material characteristic to Spielmeyer-Vogt disease as a protein called subunit C. This protein is usually found inside a cell's mitochondria. Scientists are now working to understand why this protein ends up in the wrong location and accumulates inside diseased cells. Another approach taken by researchers has been to test the usefulness of bone marrow transplantations in sheep and mice with NCLs. Using an animal model such as this

will make it easier for scientists to study the genetics of these diseases and improve the overall understanding and treatment of these disorders.

This entry has been informed by the sources listed below.

REFERENCES

DeStefano, N., Lubke, U., Martin, J. J., Guazzi, G. C., & Federico, A. (1999). Detection of beta-A4 amyloid and its precursor protein in the muscle of a patient with juvenile neuronal ceroid lipofuscinosis (Spielmeyer-Vogt-Sjogren). *Acta Neuropathology*, *98*(1), 78–84.

Eksandh, L. B., Ponjavic, V. B., Eiberg, H. E., Uvebrant, P. E., Ehinger, B. E., Mole, S. E., & Andreasson, S. (2000). Full-field ERG in patients with Batten/Spielmeyer-Vogt disease caused by mutations in the CLN3 gene. *Ophthalmic Genetics*, *21*(2), 69–77.

RACHEL TOPLIS
University of Northern Colorado

SPINA BIFIDA

Spina bifida (myelomeningocele) is a congenital abnormality present at birth. The defect begins early in embryogenesis (the first 30 days of gestation), as the central nervous system is developing with a failure of the spinal cord to close over the lower end (Haslam & Valletutti, 1975). Without such closure, normal development of the spinal column cannot occur; the spinal cord and covering membranes bulge out and block further development.

It is a fairly common developmental anomaly, present in .2 to .4 per 1,000 live births (Haslam & Valletutti, 1975). The risks increase dramatically to 1/20 to 1/40 following the birth of one affected infant. It is possible to test for spina bifida through amniocentesis. The amniotic fluid is analyzed by testing for abnormally high alpha fetal protein and acetyl cholinesterase levels. Both are normally present in the fetal cerebrospinal fluid, which, in myelomeningocele, leaks into the amniotic fluid (Behrman & Vaughn, 1983).

Detection at birth is due to the presence of a large bulging lesion or swelling, with or without a skin covering, at the lower part of the back (lumbosacral region). It is the damage to or the defect of the spinal cord that results in a variety of handicapping conditions. Eighty percent of children with spina bifida have hydrocephalus, a condition caused by the accumulation of fluid in the ventricles of the brain (Haslam & Valletutti, 1975). If left untreated, hydrocephalus can result in severe mental retardation.

Treatment consists of diverting the cerebrospinal fluid to some other area of the body, usually the atria of the heart or the abdominal cavity (Wolraich, 1983).

Paraplegia resulting from the disruption of the motor tracts from the brain to the muscles at the spinal cord level leads to weakness and paralysis of muscles. The degree of paralysis depends on the location and extent of spinal cord damage. Bladder and bowel control is often absent and may present one of the biggest obstacles to a child's participation in a regular school program.

Children with spina bifida will require extensive medical, orthopedic, and educational services. This is often expensive and time consuming, creating frustration and financial hardship for the family. Educational programming for these children must consider the need for personnel trained in toileting techniques and physical therapy. While some children with spina bifida may require a self-contained special education class setting, others who are less severely impaired cognitively may be able to perform successfully in a mainstream classroom with support services.

Incidence of spina bifida can be significantly reduced owing to the discovery of a strong link between neural tube defects in general and folic acid deficiency. Folic acid is now known to protect against such defects, although the mode of action is not clear. Women who have had one child with spina bifida who take folic acid supplements during subsequent pregnancies have a 70% reduction in recurrence. Further, folic acid supplements can reduce incidence of new cases of spina bifida by 50%. Thus, all women who may become pregnant are advised to take daily folic acid supplements both before and during the first 12 weeks of pregnancy. Such supplements are in common foods such as bread, flour, and rice (Liptak, 1997).

REFERENCES

Behrman, R. E., & Vaughn, V. C. (1983). Defects of closure tube. In W. B. Nelson (Ed.), *Nelson's textbook of pediatrics* (pp. 1560–1561). Philadelphia, PA: Saunders.

Haslam, R. A., & Valletutti, P. J. (1975). *Medical problems in the classroom: The teacher's role in diagnosis and management.* Baltimore, MD: University Park Press.

Liptak, G. S. (1997). Neural tube defects. In M. L. Batshaw (Ed.), *Children with disabilities* (4th ed., pp. 529–552). Baltimore, MD: Paul H. Brookes.

Wolraich, M. (1983). Myelomeningocele. In J. A. Blackman (Ed.), *Medical aspects of developmental disabilities in children birth to three: A resource for special service providers in the educational setting.* Iowa City: University of Iowa.

MARSHA H. LUPI
Hunter College,
City University of New York

See also Hydrocephalus

SPINAL CORD INJURY

Damage to the spinal cord frequently, but not always, results in paralysis or paresis to the extremities. The specific impairment or dysfunction that occurs in the extremities depends on the corresponding spinal level and the severity of the injury. In some situations, the injury may be only temporary and the individual may not experience any permanent effects. More often, the injury results in permanent damage and loss of function in the involved extremities.

The most common causes of spinal cord injury are accidents in or about the home, falls, bullet wounds, sports injuries, or motor vehicle accidents. The injury is often associated with fractured bones of the spinal column but also may occur from dislocation of one or more of these bones on the other. When the spinal cord is damaged, the nervous pathways between the body and the brain are interrupted. All forms of sensation (e.g., proprioception, touch, temperature, pain) and muscular control are typically lost below the level of the damage. Although nerves outside the spinal cord may be repaired or heal spontaneously, damaged nerves within the spinal cord will not regenerate. If the injury is low on the spinal cord (usually below the first thoracic vertebra), only the lower extremities are involved. This type of injury is called paraplegia. If the injury is higher on the spinal cord (cervical level), all four extremities and the trunk may be involved; this condition is referred to as quadriplegia. Injury to the highest levels of the cervical spine may cause death because of the loss of innervation to the diaphragm. Occasionally, only one side of the cord is damaged. This type of condition is called Brown-Sequard syndrome. Loss of proprioception and motor paralysis occur on the same side as the injury, while loss of pain, temperature, and touch sensations occur on the opposite side.

Immediate treatment after a spinal injury or suspected injury is immobilization. Immobilization prevents further shearing of the spinal column, which may result in further or more permanent damage to the spinal cord. If there is any possibility of spinal cord injury, the injured person should not be moved until trained assistance arrives. Once the injured person has been transported to an appropriate medical facility, the course of treatment varies, depending on the nature of the injury.

During the initial stage of spinal cord trauma, autonomic and motor reflexes below the level of the injury are suppressed. This flaccid paralysis is called spinal shock and may last from several hours to 3 months. As the spinal shock recedes, spinal reflexes return in a hyperactive state. This spasticity or muscular hypertonicity may vary initially at different times of the day or in response to different stimuli, but it becomes more consistent within one year of the injury. The most common form of acute treatment is traction to the spinal column to bring about a realignment and healing of the fractured or displaced vertebrae. Special beds may be used to permit people in traction to be turned from their back to their abdomen, thereby reducing the chance of pressure sores (decubitus).

Artificial ventilation usually is necessary for persons with injuries at or above the level of the third cervical vertebra (C3). Decreased respiratory capacity is present in injuries from C4 through T7 (the seventh thoracic vertebra), making coughing difficult and often necessitating suctioning when the patient gets a respiratory infection. Dizziness or blackout may occur from pooling of blood in the abdomen and lower extremities when a person is first brought to an upright position following a period of immobilization. This is a normal reaction and is avoided through the aid of a reclining wheelchair or a tilt table that allows gradual adjustment to a full upright position. Numerous other secondary conditions or complications may occur for several months or years following a spinal cord injury. These include muscle contracture or shortening, loss of sexual functioning in males, impaired bowel or bladder control, kidney or urinary tract infections, or psychological reactions, to name but a few.

Rehabilitation procedures begin within a few days of the injury and usually continue for several weeks or months after the healing process is complete. The general goal of rehabilitation is to improve the physical capacities and develop adapted techniques to promote as independent a lifestyle as possible. Unfortunately, rehabilitation's goals all too often focus on participation rather than performance (Dudgeon, Massagli, & Ross, 1997). Educational performance for a person with a spinal cord injury is hampered only by the individual's physical limitations. However, the individual may have problems with self-image, coping strategies, accessibility support, and unresolved feelings, all of which may affect educational performance (Mulcahey, 1992). Persons with high-level injuries may require numerous assistive devices such as an electronic typewriter with mouthstick or mechanical page turner. Persons with low-level injuries may not require any specialized assistance to benefit from education. Counseling to help a person adjust to new physical impairments and to develop future vocational pursuits may also be in order.

REFERENCES

Dudgeon, B. J., Massagli, T. L., & Ross, B. W. (1997). Educational participation of children with spinal cord injury. *American Journal of Occupational Therapy, 51*(7), 553–561.

Hanak, M., & Scott, A. (1983). *Spinal cord injury: An illustrated guide for health care professionals.* New York, NY: Springer-Verlag.

Long, C. (1971). Congenital and traumatic lesions of the spinal cord. In T. H. Krusen, F. H. Kottke, & P. M. Ellwood (Eds.), *Handbook of physical medicine and rehabilitation* (2nd ed., pp. 475–516). Philadelphia, PA: Saunders.

Mulcahey, M. J. (1992). Returning to school after spinal cord injury: Perspectives from four adolescents. *American Journal of Occupational Therapy, 46*(4), 305–312.

Trombly, C. A. (1984). Spinal cord injury. In C. A. Trombly (Ed.), *Occupational therapy for physical dysfunction* (3rd ed.). Baltimore, MD: Williams & Wilkins.

Wilson, D. J., McKenzie, M. W., Barber, L. M., & Watson, K. L. (1984). *Spinal cord injury: A treatment guide for occupational therapists.* Thorofare, NJ: Slack.

DANIEL D. LIPKA
*Lincoln Way Special Education
Regional Resources Center*

See also Quadriplegia

SPINOCEREBELLAR DEGENERATION (See Friedreich's Ataxia)

SPITZ, HERMAN (1925–)

Herman Spitz was born on March 2, 1925, in Paterson, New Jersey. He is a noted psychologist and researcher in the field of mental retardation. Spitz obtained his BA at Lafayette College (1948) and PhD at New York University (1955). He was an assistant psychologist (1951–1955) and chief psychologist (1955–1957) at Trenton State Hospital. From 1957 to 1989, Spitz was affiliated with the E. R. Johnstone Training and Research Center, initially as a research associate, and beginning in 1962, as the director of research.

As an author of over 90 publications, Spitz has written extensively on the subject of mental retardation, particularly as related to assessment, intervention (both cognitive and behavioral), and causes (Spitz, 1986a, 1986b, 1994). He has also shown an interest in the unconscious and has authored a book on the topic, exploring how nonconscious movements can influence our expression of ideas, inner conflicts, and wishful thinking, and particularly serving to facilitate communication of individuals who are severely and profoundly retarded or autistic (Spitz, 1997).

Spitz has served as a consulting editor for several professional journals, including the *American Journal of Mental Deficiency* and *Memory and Cognition*. He is a fellow of the American Psychological Association and the American Psychological Society and member of the American Academy on Mental Retardation. In recognition of his research contributions, Spitz has served as an invited lecturer and consultant to numerous institutions, including Alabama University, Columbia University, George Peabody College for Teachers, and the Medical Research Council, London.

This entry has been informed by the sources listed below.

REFERENCES

American Men of Science. (1962). (10th ed.). Tempe, AZ: Jaques Cattell.

Spitz, H. H. (1986a). Disparities in mentally retarded persons' IQ derived from different intelligence tests. *American Journal of Mental Deficiency, 90*(5), 588–591.

Spitz, H. H. (1986b). Preventing and curing mental retardation by behavioral intervention: An evaluation of some claims. *Intelligence, 10*(3), 197–207.

Spitz, H. H. (1994). Fragile X syndrome is not the second leading cause of mental retardation. *Mental Retardation, 32*(2), 156.

Spitz, H. H. (1997). *Nonconscious movement: From mystical messages to facilitated communication.* Mahwah, NJ: Erlbaum.

IVAN Z. HOLOWINSKY
Rutgers University
First edition

TAMARA J. MARTIN
The University of Texas of the Permian Basin
Second and Third editions

SPITZ, RENE ARPAD (1887–1974)

Rene Arpad Spitz, educated in his native Hungary and in the United States, was a leading representative of psychoanalysis in the United States. He served on the faculty of the New York Psychoanalytic Institute, was professor of psychiatry at City College, City University of New York, and the University of Colorado, and was clinical professor of psychiatry at Lenox Hill Hospital in New York City. The author of some 60 monographs and papers, Spitz is best known for his extensive studies of infant development.

REFERENCES

Spitz, R. A. (1962). *A genetic field theory of ego formation.* New York, NY: International Universities Press.

Spitz, R. A., & Cobliner, W. G. (1966). *The first year of life.* New York, NY: International Universities Press.

PAUL IRVINE
Katonah, New York

SPLINTER SKILL (See Savant Syndrome)

SPLIT-BRAIN RESEARCH

The technique of cerebral commissurotomy (split-brain surgery) was first introduced by Van Wagenen in 1940 as a surgical solution for severe and intractable forms of epilepsy. Van Wagenen performed the operation on approximately 2 dozen cases, hoping to be able to restrict the abnormal electrical activation characteristic of epilepsy to a single hemisphere. Unfortunately, the early operations were not successful and the procedure was largely abandoned until the early 1960s, when it was taken up by Roger Sperry working in collaboration with Joseph Bogen and Philip Vogel (Beaumont, 1983). The refined operation proved to be effective in many cases and, more important from scientific perspective, the procedure allowed a unique opportunity to study cerebral organization. Sperry's work with split-brain patients was deemed so important that he shared the Nobel Prize in Medicine in 1981. This award appropriately reflects the tremendous advances that were made in the neurosciences following this seminal work.

The technique of cerebral commissurotomy involves the complete section of the corpus callosum, including the anterior and hippocampal commissures in the massa intermedia. This technique effectively isolates each half of the cortex and prevents transfer of information from one side of the brain to the other. Despite the operation's dramatic nature, postsurgical patients appear to function quite well. Fairly sophisticated testing procedures are necessary to isolate and identify the effects of surgery.

Detailed study of postsurgical split-brain patients reveals that, in fact, a number of problems do exist for these patients (Springer & Deutsch, 1981). The patients frequently report trouble with associating names and faces. This may be due to the differential loci for naming and facial recognition, with the assignment of names occurring in the left hemisphere and the recognition of faces more intimately linked to the right hemisphere. Patients also report difficulty with geometry, and many complain of memory loss. Finally, many postsurgical patients report cessation of dreaming; however, this has not been supported empirically, and these patients continue to show REM sleep postsurgically.

Sperry has consistently maintained that the operation produces two separate minds within one body, each with its own will, perception, and memories. This is supported by numerous anecdotes of conflict between the hemispheres or between the body parts controlled by the respective hemispheres. These reports, albeit fascinating, are largely anecdotal and appear to be somewhat exaggerated. In general, while early studies and writers emphasized the division and uniqueness of the two hemispheres, recent research has been devoted to how the brain works as a whole and how the hemispheres cooperate in transferring information back and forth. Zaidel (1979) has compared performance of each hemisphere operating singly with performance of the brain operating as a whole. He has found that much better results are evident when the brain is working as a whole with the hemispheres serving in tandem. In addition, it is important not to forget that both cortical structures are intimately linked to an integrated subcortical substrate with a number of linked bilateral structures (Corballis, 1998).

Eccles (1977) has reviewed the split-brain research and has argued that it suggests consciousness is intimately linked to speech and therefore must reside in the dominant left hemisphere. However, all such generalizations from split-brain research are limited by the fact that the brains studied are clearly pathological specimens and may not represent normal cognitive functioning.

One of the interesting findings that has emerged from split-brain research is that rudimentary language perception skills have been associated with the right cerebral hemisphere. Recognition of nouns by the right hemisphere appears to be easier than recognition of verbs (Gazzaniga, 1970). This difference is especially marked when a rapid response is required. If patients are given maximum time to respond, the noun-verb distinction is less apparent.

Levy and her colleagues have completed a number of studies with split-brain patients employing chimeric stimulae (Levy, Trevarthen, & Sperry, 1972). These are stimulus items that are composed by joining two half-stimuli. The stimuli are presented in such a way that each half goes to the isolated contralateral hemisphere. On the basis of these studies, Levy has argued that the left hemisphere is best described as analytic while the right is best described as holistic.

Split-brain patients make ideal subjects for dichotic listening experiments in which different stimuli are presented simultaneously in each ear. In addition, for those patients who receive a commissurotomy, divided visual field studies can be employed with less concern for saccadic eye movements. However, considerable experimental skill is necessary to avoid the phenomenon of cross-cuing. This occurs when a patient deliberately or inadvertently develops strategies for delivering information to both hemispheres simultaneously. For example, a subject who is palpating a comb may rub the teeth of the comb with the left hand. Although the tactile information will reach only the right hemisphere in the split-brain patient, the associated sound goes to both ears and may reach the left hemisphere and allow for linguistic identification.

Increasingly, neurosurgeons are performing partial commissurotomies with good success. These procedures allow still more detailed information about the localization of transference fibers in the corpus callosum. For example, it has become clear that somatosensory information is transmitted via the anterior corpus callosum while the rear portion, the splenium, transfers visual information. In addition, there is an indication that some perceptual judgements may be made subcortically (Corballis, 1994).

The work done to date on split-brain patients may offer important clues to help the teacher better understand and educate the child with special needs. Levy (1982) has used split-brain data to develop a model of handwriting posture; Obrzut and Hynd (1981) have applied these findings on cerebral lateralization to children with learning disabilities; and Hartlage (1975) has developed a plan for predicting the outcome of remedial educational strategies based on a model of cerebral lateralization. Perhaps it is only through understanding how each half of the brain works that we will ever approach an understanding of how it works as a whole—a concept supported fully by Sperry (Corballis, 1998).

REFERENCES

Beaumont, J. G. (1983). *Introduction to neuropsychology*. New York, NY: Guilford Press.

Corballis, M. C. (1994). Split decisions: Problems in the interpretation of results from commissurotomized subjects. *Behavioral Brain Research, 64*(1), 163–172.

Corballis, M. C. (1998). Sperry and the age of Aquarius: Science values and the split brain. *Neuropsychologies, 36*(10), 1083–1087.

Eccles, J. C. (1977). *The understanding of the brain* (2nd ed.). New York, NY: McGraw-Hill.

Gazzaniga, M. S. (1970). *The bisected brain*. Englewood Cliffs, NJ: Prentice Hall.

Hartlage, L. C. (1975). Neuropsychological approaches to predicting outcome of remedial educational strategies for learning disabled children. *Pediatric Psychology, 3*, 23–28.

Levy, J. (1982). Handwriting posture and cerebral organization: How are they related? *Psychological Bulletin, 91*, 589–608.

Levy, J., Trevarthen, C., & Sperry, R. W. (1972). Perception of bilateral chimeric figures following hemispheric disconnection. *Brain, 95*, 61–78.

Obrzut, J. E., & Hynd, G. W. (1981). Cognitive development and cerebral lateralization in children with learning disabilities. *International Journal of Neuroscience, 14*, 139–145.

Springer, S. P., & Deutsch, G. (1981). *Left brain, right brain*. San Francisco, CA: Freeman.

Zaidel, E. (1979). Performance on the ITPA following cerebral commissurotomy and hemispherectomy. *Neuropsychologia, 17*, 259–280.

DANNY WEDDING
Marshall University

See also Cerebral Dominance; Left Brain/Right Brain

SPONDYLOEPIPHYSEAL DYSPLASIA

Congenital spondyloepiphyseal dysplasia (SED) is a rare inherited disorder transmitted in an autosomal dominant manner. This disorder is typified by a growth deficiency before birth; it is associated with spinal malformations and abnormalities of the eyes. As the individual ages, the growth deficiency usually results in short stature (dwarfism). SED congenita may also be referred to as pseudo-achondroplasia.

SED occurs approximately once in every 100,000 births, making it one of the most common forms of dwarfism along with achondroplasia and diastophic dysplasia. This disorder affects males and females in equal numbers.

Characteristics

1. This disorder is apparent at birth.

2. Symptoms include curved spine, cervical spinal compression, and short neck. Instability of the spine at C1 and C2 may be present.

3. Individuals may have clubfoot and poorly formed femur heads.

4. Cleft palate is present.

5. Myopia (nearsightedness) is present in 40% of cases. Retinal detachment can occur.

6. As the individual ages, a characteristic appearance develops: The chest is often broad and barrel-like, and the neck is short and gives the appearance of the head resting directly on the shoulders. The extremities are short but long in proportion to the trunk. Hands and feet are normal.

7. A waddling, wide-based gait is evident in early childhood.

8. Motor development may be delayed in infants and children.

9. SED children are susceptible to ear infections.

10. In late childhood, the lumbar spine becomes lordotic (swaybacked). Kyphoscoliosis (spinal deformity) can also occur.

11. Intelligence is usually normal.

12. Adult height ranges from 36″ to 67″ (90 cm to 167.5 cm).

At present there is no cure for this disorder. Although the gene for SED has been located, there is variability in the location of the gene among persons with SED. Prenatal tests are available, but expensive. Medical care focuses on management of complications and orthopedic issues. An evaluation of the cervical spine at C1 and C2 may be performed to assess whether a spinal fusion is needed. Lax ligaments in the neck could lead to spinal injury during contact sports and car accidents. This disorder may result in chest constriction, which can decrease lung capacity.

Due to risks related to lung capacity, small airways, and spine instability, caution should be taken during anesthesia. It is important for individuals with SED to have their cervical or neck vertebrae monitored with careful neurological exams, X rays of the neck flexion and extension, and magnetic resonance images if needed. Orthopedic care may be needed to evaluate hip, spinal, and knee complications. Hip replacements are sometimes warranted in adults. Regular eye exams should be done to evaluate for nearsightedness and detached retinas. Hearing should be checked, and ear infections should be closely monitored. Tubes may need to be placed in the ear. Symptoms such as clubfoot or cleft palate may need to be surgically corrected.

As individuals with SED usually have normal intelligence, it is quite likely that they will benefit academically from regular education and may not need special services under the Individuals With Disabilities Education Act (IDEA) of 1997. This will depend on the psychosocial effects of the disorder on the individual. If students are found to be struggling academically because of social-emotional issues, they may be eligible for services under the emotional disturbance category of IDEA 1997. Additionally, these individuals may be able to access services under Section 504 of the Rehabilitation Act of 1974 if it is deemed necessary. Students with SED may benefit from counseling to address the social-emotional components of this disorder. For example, they may need support to build self-esteem and confidence and to accept (or accommodate) their bodily image within their self-concept and identity. School personnel should be cognizant of the limitations of this disorder. For example, SED students may require time away from school for a variety of medical reasons. Additionally, due to neck instability, individuals with SED should exercise caution and avoid activities and sports that could result in trauma to the neck or head.

The prognosis for this disorder is that it is nonlethal but associated with many complications. Research continues to assess ways to remediate some of the complications of SED, such as correcting the instability of the spine (LeDoux, Naftalis, & Aronin, 1991) and retinal detachments (Ikegawa, Iwaya, Taniguchi, & Kimizuka, 1993). Additionally, research is attempting to investigate possible ways to identify SED prenatally (Kirk & Comstock, 1990).

REFERENCES

Ikegawa, S., Iwaya, T., Taniguchi, K., & Kimizuka, M. (1993). Retinal detachment in spondyloepiphyseal dysplasia congenita. *Journal of Pediatric Orthopedics, 13*(6), 791–792.

Kirk, J. S., & Comstock, C. H. (1990). Antenatal sonographic appearance of spondyloepiphyseal dysplasia congenita. *Journal of Ultrasound Medicine, 9*(3), 173–175.

LeDoux, M. S., Naftalis, R. C., & Aronin, P. A. (1991). Stabilization of the cervical spine in spondyloepiphyseal dysplasia congenita. *Neurosurgery, 28*(4), 580–583.

RACHEL TOPLIS
University of Northern Colorado

SPORTS FOR INDIVIDUALS WITH DISABILITIES

The origin of sports adapted to the needs of individuals with disabilities can be traced to the end of World War II, when thousands of veterans with physical disabilities joined already existing groups of people with congenital and traumatic disabilities. In 1948 Stoke Mandeville Hospital in Aylsburg, England, first introduced an organized wheelchair sports program for patients; the first international games were held there in 1952 (Wehman & Schleien, 1981). This use of sports in rehabilitation was the stimulus for the growth of the international sports for the disabled movement that is prevalent today (DePauw, 1984).

From the beginning it was apparent that adaptations of rules and equipment were going to be necessary for sports programs, and many of the adaptations were the result of the imaginative efforts of the participants themselves. In addition, the participants joined together with others who needed the same adaptations and, through their activities, were able to participate within the wider community. For some persons with disabilities, a sports program means competition; in other situations, the aim of sports is to meet therapeutic needs; for others the objective of sports involvement is to fulfill leisure-time pursuits (R. C. Adams et al., 1982).

Currently, federal mandates regulate physical education services and sports opportunities for individuals with disabilities. IDEA requires a free appropriate public school education, which includes instruction in physical education, in the least restrictive environment. Section 504 of the Rehabilitation Act specifies nondiscrimination on the basis of handicap, and states that equal opportunity and equal access must be provided for handicapped persons, specifically including physical education services, intramurals, and athletics. The most direct mandate for sports opportunities is the Amateur Sports Act of 1978 (PL 95-606; DePauw, 1984).

As a result of this law, the U.S. Olympic Committee initiated a Handicapped in Sports Committee, which changed its name to the Committee on Sports for the Disabled (COSD) in 1983 (DePauw, 1984). Committee membership consists of two representatives from each major national organization in the United States offering sports opportunities for individuals with disabilities. At least 20% of COSD members must be, or must have been, actively participating athletes with disabilities.

There are seven organizations designated as members of COSD. The National Association of Sports for Cerebral Palsy is a program of United Cerebral Palsy providing competitive sports opportunities for individuals with cerebral palsy and similar physically disabling conditions (C. Adams, 1984). The American Association for the Deaf sanctions and promotes state, regional, and national basketball, softball, and volleyball tournaments, the World Games for the Deaf, the AAD Hall of Fame, and the Deaf Athlete of the Year (Ammons, 1984). The National Handicapped Sports and Recreation Association is unique in the world of sports groups in that its members possess a variety of physical and mental disabilities (Hernley, 1984). The National Wheelchair Athletic Association organizes and conducts competition in seven different Olympic sports, and also in wheelchair slalom, involving a race against time over a series of obstacles to challenge a competitor's wheelchair handling and speed skills (Fleming, 1984). The United States Amputee Athletic Association has grown from a small group of competitors in 1981 to a national organization which sponsors annual games (Bryant, 1984). The major purpose of the U.S. Association for Blind Athletes is to develop individual independence through athletic competition without unnecessary restrictions (Beaver, 1984).

Founded in 1968 by Eunice Kennedy Shriver, the first International Special Olympics was a single track and field event with about a thousand participants. Today over one million children and adults with intellectual disabilities from around the world take part in Special Olympics; it is the biggest sports event in which children with disabilities are likely to be involved. Sports activities range from events in swimming, gymnastics, and bowling, to basketball, track and field, and soccer. Racewalking has been adopted as a new sport, and equestrian sporting events are now being offered as demonstration sports.

Sports activities for individuals with disabilities are sponsored by many nonschool groups, however, guarantees of equal opportunities for students with disabilities require that educators and psychologists give more attention to school-sponsored sports programs (Ashen, 1991). Unique and innovative approaches are needed so that these individuals can participate in sports within the schools. One possibility is to have special sections for individuals with disabilities as part of regular track, swimming, and gymnastic meets. It also may be possible to mix people with different disabilities with typically developing individuals in some sports programs. One promising program is the paralympic movement. The Paralympic Games is one of the largest sporting events in the world (Steadward, 1996).

REFERENCES

Adams, C. (1984). The National Association of Sports for Cerebral Palsy. *Journal of Physical Education, Recreation & Dance, 55,* 34–35.

Adams, R. C., David, A. N., McCubbin, J. A., & Rullman, L. (1982). *Games, sports and exercises for the physically handicapped* (3rd ed.). Philadelphia, PA: Lea & Febiger.

Ammons, D. C. (1984). American Athletic Association for the Deaf. *Journal of Physical Education, Recreation & Dance, 55,* 36–37.

Ashen, M. J. (1991). The challenge of the physically challenged: Delivering sport psychology services to physically disabled athletes. *Sport Psychologist, 5*(4), 370–381.

Beaver, D. P. (1984). The United States Association for Blind Athletes. *Journal of Physical Education, Recreation & Dance, 55,* 40–41.

Bryant, D. C. (1984). United States Amputee Athletic Association. *Journal of Physical Education, Recreation & Dance, 55,* 40–41.

DePauw, K. P. (1984). Commitment and challenges, sport opportunities for athletes with disabilities. *Journal of Physical Education, Recreation & Dance, 55,* 34–35.

Fleming, A. (1984). The National Wheelchair Association. *Journal of Physical Education, Recreation & Dance, 55,* 38–39.

Hernley, R. (1984). National Handicapped Sports and Recreation Association. *Journal of Physical Education, Recreation & Dance, 55,* 38–39.

Steadward, R. D. (1996). Integration and sport in the paralympic movement. *Sport Science Review, 5*(1), 26–41.

Wehman, P., & Schleien, S. (1981). *Leisure programs for handicapped persons: Adaptations, techniques and curriculum.* Baltimore, MD: University Park Press.

CATHERINE O. BRUCE
Hunter College,
City University of New York

See also Olympics, Special; Recreational Therapy

STABILITY OF BASELINE DATA IN SINGLE CASE RESEARCH

Within single case research, stability of the baseline data is an important consideration. Stable data in the baseline phase renders a more accurate depiction of participant behavior. In addition, stable data arrays are suggestive of reliable measurement that allow for stronger inferential judgments of intervention effects. Kazdin (2010) recommended stability of baseline data as a prerequisite to the initiation of an intervention. Stable data can be evaluated as consistent, with little slope, and low variability. In applied settings, stable baselines may not be feasible due to the selection of measured outcomes that by are by nature highly variable. Baseline stability may

also be compromised by unreliable measurement and/or change in participant outcomes for reasons unrelated to the study (e.g., maturation). Traditionally, intervention researchers have recommended against implementing an intervention if baseline data are not stable. However, in an examination of baseline data from 165 published single case research studies, Parker, Cryer & Burns (2006) found that 41% of studies showed positive (improvement) trend in the baseline. Positive baseline trend may compromise accurate evaluation of intervention effects. Statistical methods that are sensitive to baseline trend have been developed that allow for more precise appraisals of study effects. Faith, Allison, & Gorman (1996) proposed a regression-based technique to correct baseline trend. More recently, Parker, Vannest, and Davis (2012) recommended a technique that allows for flexibility in choice of trend correction method. Although stability in baseline is preferable, these methods may be used to adjust baseline data when positive trend is present.

REFERENCES

Faith, M. S., Allison, D. B., & Gorman, B. S. (1996). Meta-analysis of single-case research. In R. D. Franklin, D. B. Allison, & B. S. Gorman (Eds.), *Design and analysis of single-case research* (pp. 245–277). Mahwah, NJ: Erlbaum.

Kazdin, A. E. (2010). *Single-case research designs: Methods for clinical and applied settings* (2nd ed.). New York, NY: Oxford University Press.

Parker, R. I., Cryer, J. & Burns, G. (2006). Controlling trend in single case research. *School Psychology Quarterly, 21*(3), 418–440.

Parker, R. I., Vannest, K. J., Davis, J. L. (2012). A simple graph rotation method to control baseline trend within data nonoverlap: GROT. Manuscript submitted for publication.

JOHN L. DAVIS
Texas A&M University
Fourth edition

STAFF DEVELOPMENT

Staff development represents the professional growth of persons toward observable and measurable objectives that benefit an organization and its members. Professional and personal growth are necessary if an organization is to maintain its performance standards, develop a feeling of pride, stimulate its membership, and generate a creative work environment, all of which contribute to personal and corporate well-being.

Staff development is necessary to improve the product of an organization by raising the skill level and awareness of the human resources of that organization. In public schools, the product is education. Teachers design and deliver the product; students consume; and the public evaluates the product based on their observations of its effects on the consumers (children). Education must be accepted as meaningful and pertinent to the children before they learn. The motivating and technical skills of teachers, as salespersons, are vital to the success of the enterprise. The delivery of the product—instruction—requires teacher performance, materials, physical plant, technology, and student motivation. These variables determine the amount of the product the consumers buy or, in some cases, refuse. The teachers' skills, as those of the producer and delivering agent, are the key input in the process. Because of the importance of those skills, development of the staff as a key resource should be continuous and planned, as with any of the other resources of an organization. Development must be perceived as required, meaningful, and attainable by the staff.

Initial planning may begin by determining the needs of the organization and its membership. Needs surveying instruments are designed for that purpose. A staff development plan will fulfill those preferred needs that have been identified. The staff may contribute by assembling a list of requirements that can be collectively prioritized with regard to an organization's needs. This allows for all staff to feel a part of the planning process. Communication of the results of the needs survey should follow.

Another component of basic staff development is the creation of a supportive environment. To establish this environment there are several desirable elements that an administrator should provide, including teaching assignments, scheduling, released time, and special instructional supplies. Administrators must also be sensitive to personal needs and personalities of the staff, supporting them with concern, sincerity, and other humanizing factors. Developing support groups among teachers, organizing functional committees, and being a public relations agent for the school are indicative of a supportive environment. Praising and supporting teachers in the community when adversarial situations are apparent is also important in providing a supportive environment.

The administration should develop a plan for the enhancement of the school's staff resource. The plan may encompass several areas: curriculum; instruction; personal skills; licensure; advanced education; stress management; work environment; administrative support; school, home, community relations; student management; and school organization. Once the needs of the organization have been identified, each staffer's part in the scheme is drawn up and agreed to. The individual's role is contracted for and evaluated in the routine teacher evaluation process. Methods for enhancing the skill level of the organization may include professional in-service training, team teaching, internships, remedial plans of development, individual guided education units, school visitations, outside instruction, and role modeling.

Once needs are identified, a positive environment established, and a plan designed and implemented, monitoring of the professional staff is recommended. Positive feedback to personnel regarding their teaching performance is essential for it identifies the organizational expectations. Monitoring/supervising can be the same activity. Being visible, asking curriculum-directed questions, acknowledging instructional changes, encouraging staff reviews and faculty support groups, organizing creative instructional changes, providing evaluative feedback, and holding teacher conferences are all supervisory techniques under the heading of monitoring. Classroom visitations are important to monitoring. These activities deliver a clear message of administrative interest. When these components are addressed, an environment of trust develops. The teaching staff becomes more accepting of staff development programs once positive staff development has occurred in the school among the staff.

Need identification, planning and implementation, support and monitoring are basic staff development and personal growth activities. Before the typical staff development plans are initiated, these components should be communicated to and experienced by the staff. Teaching personnel need to know their needs have been identified by the administration as part of the organization's requirements. They should realize that the administration wants to provide a supportive, positive, professional working environment and that a system of consistent, fair, sincere supervision/monitoring is in place. Before outside resources are brought to the organization, in-house staff development should be established on a continuing basis. Staff development strategies can fall on deaf ears unless teachers are in an accepting, creative, and productive atmosphere cultivated by involvement in the building's own program.

The administrator is the key person in preparing the staff for a resourceful plan, but only after the staff has been provided the opportunity for in-house planning and leadership. The assets of an organization, human and physical, must be known. A development system can allow for a committee of teachers to help decide in-service and other needs. As the human resources are assessed, staff should be placed in positions where personal/professional talents are best used. An extension of the effort can complete the plan for achievement of the overall objective of the organization.

ANN SABATINO
Hudson, Wisconsin

See *also* Personnel Training in Special Education; Supervision in Special Education

STANDARD DEVIATION

The standard deviation is a measure of the dispersion of sample or population scores around the mean score. It is the most important and most widely used measure of dispersion for quantitative variables when the distribution is symmetric. We compute the standard deviation for a population of n scores by first averaging squared deviations of scores (X) from the mean population (m) using Equation 1:

$$\sigma^2 = \frac{\sum_{i=1}^{m}(X_i - \mu)^2}{n} \qquad (1)$$

This yields the variance of the scores, s^2. The square root of this value, s, is the population standard deviation. For a sample of n scores, the variance is computed using Equation 2:

$$s^2 = \frac{\sum_{i=1}^{m}(X_i - \overline{X})^2}{n-1}, \qquad (2)$$

where $\overline{X}$ is the mean sample score. Here we use $(n - 1)$ as the divisor instead of n because this produces an unbiased sample estimate of s^2. Dividing by n produces a biased estimate. The square root of this value, s, is the standard deviation of the scores in the sample (i.e., the average dispersion of the scores around the mean score).

This measure of dispersion is widely used in the behavioral sciences to describe the spread of scores around the mean score when the distribution of scores is normal. Then we can state the proportion of scores that fall above or below any given value or between any two values by first converting the value(s) to z-score units using

$$z_i = \frac{X_i - \overline{X}}{s} \quad \text{or} \quad z_i = \frac{X_i - \mu}{\sigma} \qquad (3)$$

for a sample or population. For example, for a sample of scores with computed statistics $\overline{X} = 40$ and $s = 5$, the value $X_i = 50$ is two standard deviations above the mean. Thus, from a normal table, we find that 97.72% of the scores fall below 50 while 0.28% are larger than 50.

The size of the standard deviation also indicates the relative spread of two comparable distributions. For example, given that $s = 3$ for males and $s = 5$ for females on a given test, where the mean score, 15, is the same for either group, we can tell that the female scores span a wider range than the male scores, with 16% of the females scoring at least 20 while only 5% of the males obtain this score or higher.

In addition to describing a distribution of scores, the standard deviation is used widely in inferential statistics for describing the spread of the sampling distribution. For example, the standard deviation of the sampling distribution of the sample mean, $\overline{X}$, is given by $(\sigma/\sqrt{n})$ where s is defined in Equation 2, may also obtain the standard deviation of the sample proportion, variance, correlation coefficient, or any other statistic. When so used, the standard deviation is called the standard error of estimate of the statistic. Further, in regression estimation procedures, the standard deviation of the errors of prediction is used to judge the precision of the predicted values. This measure is called the standard error of estimate of prediction. In measurement, we define the standard deviation of the errors of measurement, the standard error of measurement and use it to infer the value of true scores (Hopkins & Stanley, 1981).

This entry has been informed by sources listed below.

REFERENCES

Glass, G. V., & Hopkins, K. D. (1984). *Statistical methods in education and psychology* (2nd ed.). Englewood Cliffs, NJ: Prentice Hall.

Hays, W. L. (1981). *Statistics* (3rd ed.). New York, NY: Holt, Rinehart, & Winston.

Hopkins, K. D., & Stanley, J. C. (1981). *Educational and psychological measurement and evaluation* (6th ed.). Englewood Cliffs, NJ: Prentice Hall.

Kirk, R. E. (1984). *Elementary statistics* (2nd ed.). Monterey, CA: Brooks/Cole.

GWYNETH M. BOODOO
Texas A&M University

See *also* Central Tendency; Normal Curve Equivalent

STANDARDS FOR EDUCATIONAL AND PSYCHOLOGICAL TESTING (See Code of Fair Testing Practices in Education)

STANFORD-BINET INTELLIGENCE SCALE, FIFTH EDITION

The Stanford-Binet, Fifth Edition (SB5, 2003), is an individually administered test of cognitive abilities for ages 2 to 85+. The Full Scale IQ (FSIQ) is derived from the administration of 10 subtests (five Verbal and five Nonverbal). Subtests, including the two routing subtests, are designed to measure 5 factors: Fluid Reasoning, Knowledge, Quantitative Reasoning, Visual-Spatial Processing, and Working Memory. The first two subtests (contained in Item book 1) are routing subtests and are used to determine start points for the remaining Nonverbal (Item book 2) and Verbal (Item book 3) subtests. The two routing subtests contained in book 1 may also be used as a brief measure of intellectual ability. The SB5 also provides examiners the option of calculating Change-Sensitive Scores (CSS)—a method of criteria-referenced scoring rather than normative-referenced, which avoids truncation at high and low ends, as well as an EXIQ (extended IQ)—a special-case application for evaluating subjects with extremely high (or low) IQs.

SB5 subtests are comprised of testlets—brief mini-tests at each level (1 through 6) of difficulty. Testlets typically have either six items or a total of six points at each of the six ability levels for a given subtest.

The SB5 has a mean of 100 and a standard deviation of 15 (in contrast to the prior edition standard deviation of 16). Individual subtests are now scaled with a mean of 10 and a standard deviation of 3.

The SB5 was standardized on a sample of 4,800 individuals. Each of the early years (ages 2 through 4) was divided into half-year groupings (doubling the sample size at that age period) to account for the instability and rapid cognitive change of the very youngest age group. Using variables identified in the U.S. Census (2001) Bureau publications, norm group individuals were stratified according to race/ethnicity, sex, parental education level, and geographic region.

The Technical manual provides strong evidence for reliability and validity. Average internal consistency reliabilities were in the .90s for all scales and indexes, while the individual subtest reliabilities were all in the 80s. Concurrent validity evidence is strong.

The SB5 has an initially steep administration learning curve. While the materials at the lower levels are very child friendly, examiners may consider some difficult to manipulate and administer. Test administration sequence follows the examinee's ability level across all subtests. Testlets, starting at a particular ability level, are administered individual subtests. If an examinee does not obtain a specified basal for any subtest, the examiner immediately drops back one ability level and administers the specific testlet until a basal is reached.

Scoring of the SB 5 test items is relatively easy and consistent with the scoring criteria of other standardized intelligence measures.

This entry has been informed by the sources listed below.

REFERENCES

Alfonso, V., & Flanagan, D. (2007). Best practices in the use of the Stanford-Binet Intelligence Scales, Fifth Edition (SB5), with preschoolers. *Psychoeducational assessment of preschool children* (4th ed., pp. 267–296). Mahwah, NJ: Erlbaum.

Bain, S., & Allin, J. (2005). Review of Stanford-Binet Intelligence Scales, Fifth Edition. *Journal of Psychoeducational Assessment*, 23(1), 87–95.

Canivez, G. L. (2008). Orthogonal higher-order factor structure of the Stanford-Binet Intelligence Scales for children and adolescents. *School Psychology Quarterly*, 23, 533–541.

DiStefano, C., & Dombrowski, S. C. (2006). Investigating the theoretical structure of the Stanford-Binet, Fifth Edition. *Journal of Psychoeducational Assessment*, 24, 123–136

Geisinger, K. F., Spies, R. A., Carlson, J. F., & Plake, B. S. (Eds.). (2007). *The seventeenth mental measurements yearbook.* Lincoln, NE: Buros Institute of Mental Measurements.

Janzen, H., Obrzut, J., & Marusiak, C. (2004). Review of Stanford-Binet Intelligence Scales, fifth edition. *Canadian Journal of School Psychology*, 19(1–2), 235–244.

SB5 Assessment Service Bulletin #2: Accommodations on the Stanford-Binet Intelligence Scales, Fifth Edition.

SB5 Assessment Service Bulletin #3: Use of the Stanford-Binet Intelligence Scales, Fifth Edition in the Assessment of High Abilities.

SB5 Assessment Service Bulletin #4: Special Composite Scores for the Stanford-Binet Intelligence Scales, Fifth Edition. Retrieved from http://alpha.fdu.edu/psychology/SB5_index.htm

Ron Dumont
Fairleigh Dickinson University

John Willis
Rivier College

Kathleen Veizel
Fairleigh Dickinson University

Jamie Zibulsky
Fairleigh Dickinson University
Fourth edition

STANFORD DIAGNOSTIC MATHEMATICS TEST, FOURTH EDITION (SDMT4)

The Stanford Diagnostic Mathematics Test, Fourth Edition (SDMT4; 1996), is designed to measure which areas of mathematics are of specific difficulty to a student. The test is intended to be used for diagnostic purposes as well as to help create appropriate intervention. The test may be administered from grade 1 through community college. Two response formats are provided: multiple choice and free response. A group or individual format may be used in administration.

The content of the items varies across the various age levels. For example, for grades 6 and 7, numeration, graphs and tables, statistics and probability, and geometry are included in the Concepts section. For the Computation section at this level, addition and subtraction of whole numbers, multiplication facts and operations, and division facts and operations are included. Norm-referenced (scaled scores and percentile ranks) and criterion-referenced scores (cut scores) are provided.

The standardization sample of the SDMT4 involved over 40,000 students that were representative of the U.S. school population. Internal reliability coefficients were generally above .80, and interrater reliability for the free-response items is very good (above .95). Evidence for validity was provided by correlations with the Otis-Lennon School Ability test, with correlations among the two instruments in the .60s and .70s.

Generally, the SDMT4 has been favorably reviewed (e.g., Lehmann, 1998; Poteat, 1998). It provides much detail in terms of diagnostic information. The psychometric qualities are strong and lead to obtained scores that are reliable and valid. The SDMT4 is not useful for simply obtaining achievement test norms. It also does not provide information about algebraic operations. It is best used for assessing students that are below average, rather than those that are at or above average functioning.

REFERENCES

Lehmann, I. J. (1998). Review of the Stanford Diagnostic Mathematics Test, Fourth Edition. In J. C. Impara & B. S. Plake (Eds.), *The thirteenth mental measurements yearbook* (pp. 932–936). Lincoln, NE: Buros Institute of Mental Measurements.

Poteat, G. M. (1998). Review of the Stanford Diagnostic Mathematics Test, Fourth Edition. In J. C. Impara & B. S. Plake (Eds.), *The thirteenth mental measurements yearbook* (pp. 937–938). Lincoln, NE: Buros Institute of Mental Measurements.

Stanford Diagnostic Mathematics Test, Fourth Edition. (1996). *Cleveland*, OH: Harcourt Brace Jovanovich.

ELIZABETH O. LICHTENBERGER
The Salk Institute

See also **Mathematics, Learning Disabilities**

STANFORD DIAGNOSTIC READING TEST, FOURTH EDITION

The Stanford Diagnostic Reading Test, Fourth Edition (SDRT4; Karlsen & Gardner, 1996) is intended to diagnose students' strengths and weaknesses in the major components of the reading process. There are several components that are specifically assessed: Phonetic Analysis, Vocabulary, Comprehension, and Scanning. The SDRT4 may be administered in a group or individual format. Students may be assessed with the SDRT4 from the end of grade 1 through the first semester of college. In addition to assessment of reading, the SDRT4 may be used to develop

strategies for teaching reading or may be used to challenge students who are doing well.

The SDRT4 is a diagnostic test, not an achievement test, and as such it provides more detailed coverage of reading skills and places a greater emphasis on measuring the skills of low achieving students. Both norm-referenced and criterion-referenced information is available on reading skills. The normative sample was based on data collected from approximately 53,000 examinees from 1994 to 1995. The sample was found to closely match the total U.S. school enrollment statistics. The criterion-referenced scores include raw scores and Progress Indicator Cut scores. Process Indicator Cut Scores are used to classify students that have demonstrated their competence in specific areas of reading. However, Engelhard (1998) notes that these scores should be used with great caution because insufficient detail is provided on how the cut scores were set and by whom. Engelhard (1998) evaluated the reliability statistics in the SDRT4 manual and found that the use of the shorter subtests for the diagnosis of an individual's strengths and weaknesses is not recommended. No evidence for stability of scores over time is provided.

Overall, the SDRT4 is found to be a sound measure of reading. It provides adequate traditional psychometric information, clear administration directions, and scoring strategies. Teaching suggestions are also described, but the base of the interventions is not clear. Interpretation and intervention based on the SDRT4 should be done by those with specialized knowledge in clinical practices in reading.

REFERENCES

Engelhard, G. (1998). Review of the Stanford Diagnostic Reading Test, Fourth Edition. In J. C. Impara & B. S. Plake (Eds.), *The thirteenth mental measurements yearbook* (pp. 939–941). Lincoln, NE: Buros Institute of Mental Measurements.

Karlsen, B., & Gardner, E. F. (1996). *Stanford Diagnostic Reading Test–Fourth Edition.* Cleveland, OH: Harcourt Brace Jovanovich.

ELIZABETH O. LICHTENBERGER
The Salk Institute

See also **Reading**

STANLEY, JULIAN C. (1918–2005)

Julian C. Stanley received his BS (1937) from what is now Georgia State University and his EdM (1946) and EdD (1950) in experimental educational psychology from Harvard University. Stanley was widely known for his work in test theory, experimental design (Campbell & Stanley,

1963), and statistics, but he was perhaps best known for his study of gifted students. From 1971, he was the director of the Study of Mathematically Precocious Youth (SMPY) and professor of psychology at Johns Hopkins University.

Stanley's interest in the intellectually talented began in 1938, a year after he became a high school science teacher while enrolled in a tests and measurements course at the University of Georgia. He pursued his career as a research methodologist in education and psychology until a grant from the Spencer Foundation enabled him to create SMPY at Johns Hopkins in 1974 (Benbow & Stanley, 1983; Stanley, Keating, & Fox, 1974; Stanley, 1997).

The goals of SMPY include identifying mathematically able youngsters and enabling them to learn mathematics and related subjects faster and better than they might in the usual school curriculum. Some young people who participate in SMPY score a minimum of 700 before the age of 13 on the mathematics portion of the Scholastic Aptitude Test, a score achieved by only about 1 in 10,000 youngsters of their age group. The talent-search concept, covering the entire United States, is conducted at the Institute for the Academic Advancement of Youth (IAAY) at Johns Hopkins and in programs at Duke University, the University of Denver, and the University of Washington.

Known nationally and internationally, Stanley was a Fulbright research scholar at the University of Louvain (1958–1959) and a Fulbright-Hays lecturer in Australia and New Zealand (1974). He served as president of the American Educational Research Association (AERA) from 1965 to 1966, and was the recipient of numerous awards, including the AERA Award for Distinguished Contributions to Research in Education (1980).

REFERENCES

Benbow, C. P., & Stanley, J. C. (1983). *Academic precocity: Aspects of its development.* Baltimore, MD: Johns Hopkins University.

Campbell, D. T., & Stanley, J. C. (1963). Experimental and quasi-experimental designs for research on teaching. In N. L. Gage (Ed.), *Handbook of research on teaching* (pp. 171–246). Chicago, IL: Rand McNally.

Stanley, J. C. (1997). Varieties of intellectual talent. *Journal of Creative Behavior, 31,* 93–130.

Stanley, J. C., Keating, D. P., & Fox, L. H. (1974). *Mathematical talent: Discovery, description, and development.* Baltimore, MD: Johns Hopkins University.

ANN E. LUPKOWSKI
Texas A&M University
First edition

TAMARA J. MARTIN
The University of Texas of the Permian Basin
Second and Third editions

See also Study of Mathematically Precocious Youth

STEINART'S DISEASE (MYOTONIC DYSTROPHY)

Steinart's disease (myotonic dystrophy) appears to be caused by an autosomal dominant characteristic that results in varying degrees of mental retardation, poor muscle development, bilateral facial paralysis, and general muscular wasting. Overt myotonic dystrophy does not usually occur in early infancy. Most often, it manifests itself in late childhood or adolescence. Many children display behavioral characteristics of suspiciousness and moroseness and are asocial and submissive in treatment needs. Mental retardation is often present; although it may vary from mild to severe, it tends to be severe, particularly with early onset of the disease (Carter, 1978).

The older toddler or young child with myotonic dystrophy may have muscular weakness and wasting with psychomotor delay, drooping eyelids, and an open, drooling mouth. Cataracts are present in most individuals. High-arched palates and weak tongues are seen, as is an open, drooling mouth, even in older children. Children often have difficulty in feeding and swallowing. Abnormal curvature of the neck and back is seen. Atrophy of the extremities is often seen and clubfoot may be present. Premature baldness is also seen. Hypogonadism causes premature loss of libido or impotence in affected males. Nasal speech and articulation problems are common, as are vision problems associated with cataracts. Diabetes, heart arrhythmias, and cardiac abnormalities may be present, as well as increased incidence of diabetes mellitus (Lemeshaw, 1982).

Educational planning will often include categorical placement in classes for students with mild mental retardation; however, this disorder may not manifest itself until much later in life but then will remain constant (Tuikka, Laaksonen, & Somer, 1993). For this reason, educational placement will vary with the individual. Health problems may affect education and physical education programs. Speech services will commonly be needed, as will vision services. Orthopedic defects will often necessitate physical and occupational therapy as well as specialized adaptive educational materials. With young children having swallowing and feeding problems, an aide may be required.

This entry has been informed by the sources listed below.

REFERENCES

Carter, C. (Ed.). (1978). *Medical aspects of mental retardation* (2nd ed.). Springfield, IL: Thomas.

Lemeshaw, S. (1982). *The handbook of clinical types in mental retardation.* Boston, MA: Houghton Mifflin.

Menolascino, F., & Egger, M. (1978). *Medical dimensions of mental retardation.* Lincoln: University of Nebraska Press.

Tuikka, R. A., Laaksonen, R. K., & Somer, H. V. K. (1993). Cognitive function in myotonic dystrophy: A follow-up study. *European Neurology, 33*(6), 436–441.

SALLY L. FLAGLER
University of Oklahoma

See also Diabetes; Mental Retardation; Muscular Dystrophy

STEREOTYPISM

People generally are classified and fit into molds or groups that have certain attributable characteristics. With individuals with disabilities, the characteristics especially focused on are disabilities rather than abilities. Labeling an individual or fitting a person into a specific handicapped group or category according to certain characteristics has a few advantages and many disadvantages. The traditional handicapping labels are basically used to explain a medical problem or to aid in educational intervention, but the result generally is stereotyping of individuals, which may lead to misleading and inhumane side effects.

Throughout history, we can see that the treatment and attitudes toward those persons classified as different or abnormal have slowly changed (Kirk, 1972). Frampton and Gall (1955) recognized three stages: pre-Christianity, when individuals with disabilities were mistreated, neglected, or killed; the Christian era, when they were pitied and protected; and the present era. In recent years, individuals with disabilities are being accepted, educated, and integrated more and more into society.

During the early years (before present enlightenment), terms such as *idiot, mad, crazy, moron*, and *imbecile* were used to describe people who differed from the norm (Snell, 1978). These terms carried negative connotations and caused great misconceptions of what disabled individuals are really like. People were actually afraid of these individuals because of the mystery surrounding their disabilities. The fear was due partly to lack of knowledge about the causes of these deviations and partly to lack of exposure to individuals with these characteristics. At first, the disabled were put away in institutions, basements, or closets. Later, they were allowed to be kept in homes but away from schools. Even when education programs became prominent, the special education classrooms were in environments different from other children's. The first special education classrooms in regular schools were in the basement or away from the regular students.

Today, misconceptions arise from stereotyping individuals with disabilities. Although many visually handicapped individuals have no mental retardation, the term *visually handicapped* often carries the connotation that these individuals are physically disabled and severely mentally deficient (Hollinger & Jones, 1970). Goffman (1963) and Edgerton (1967) write extensively of the negative stereotypes and stigmata associated with the mentally retarded. People with cerebral palsy may have an IQ of average or above average, but their physical rigidity and slurred speech often make people talk to them as if they were unable to understand. The hearing impaired have fought against the stereotype of being deaf and dumb. People interacting with blind individuals believe they have to talk loudly in order to be heard. Learning-disabled students and students with attentional problems (Cornett-Ruiz & Hendricks, 1993) are frequently associated with the retarded even though their mental capacities are generally average or above. The emotionally disturbed are thought to be crazy or mad.

The misconceptions have caused many sociological, economic, and other types of barricades for the disabled. These individuals have been denied access to a life that is as normal as possible, not only in the physical environment but also in the social environment. Many individuals with disabilities are still isolated, laughed at, and criticized. Their problems may be increased because of added emotional stress.

We have come a long way toward bringing positive images of individuals with disabilities to the fore. The Special Olympics, media reports of accomplishments of individuals physically or mentally disabled, and improved school programs have helped to eliminate some barriers. Making the public more knowledgeable about definitions of handicapping terminology has improved public opinion. Movies or television shows about deformed or retarded individuals have switched to positive and inspiring messages. As the exceptional person becomes more prevalent in restaurants, stores, schools, and so on, the public becomes educated.

A reversal of roles would be an ideal way for the general public to learn about and relate to individuals with handicapping conditions. Spending a few hours in a wheelchair, with a blindfold on, or with mittens on, would help one to see what it is like to be disabled. It would be important for one to experience the difficulties of having the disability and to feel the stares and other negative attitudes of those more fortunate.

School intervention has changed greatly for the better. Education programs are now a great source for informing the public. Mainstreaming has helped regular classroom students to better understand special education students; mainstreaming has also helped special education students to develop feelings of belonging and self-worth. Exposure to the regular classroom student has given the special education student a model from which to learn.

If less negative labels were used, and if the educational programs were fit to the disabled individual's needs, there would be less stereotyping (Reger, Schroeder, & Uschold, 1968). It is hoped that as the positive trends continue to grow, the stigma will be replaced with understanding and acceptance.

REFERENCES

Cornett-Ruiz, S., & Hendricks, B. (1993). Effects of labeling and ADHD behaviors on peer and teacher judgments. *Journal of Educational Research, 86*(6), 349–355.

Frampton, M. E., & Gall E. D. (1955). *Special education for the exceptional*. Boston, MA: Porter Sargent.

Goffman, E. (1963). *Notes on the measurement of spoiled identity*. Englewood Cliffs, NJ: Prentice Hall.

Hollinger, C. S., & Jones, R. L. (1970). Community attitudes toward slow learners and mental retardates: What's in a name? *Mental Retardation, 8*, 19–13.

Kirk, S. A. (1972). *Educating exceptional children*. Boston, MA: Houghton-Mifflin.

Reger, R., Schroeder, W., & Uschold, K. (1968). *Special education children with learning problems*. New York, NY: Oxford University Press.

Snell, M. E. (1978). *Systematic instruction of the moderately and severely handicapped*. Columbus, OH: Merrill.

DONNA FILIPS
Steger, Illinois

See also History of Special Education

STERN, WILLIAM (1871–1938)

William Stern, German psychologist and pioneer in the psychology of individual differences, introduced the concept of the intelligence quotient in 1912. This quotient, used to express performance on intelligence tests, is found by dividing the subject's mental age as determined by the test performance by the chronological age and multiplying by 100. In the United States, the intelligence quotient, or IQ, was used by Lewis M. Terman in his 1916 Stanford Revision of the Binet Scales.

This entry has been informed by the sources listed below.

REFERENCES

Murchison, C. (Ed.). (1961). *A history of psychology in autobiography*. New York, NY: Russell & Russell.

Stern, W. (1914). *The psychological methods of intelligence testing*. Baltimore, MD: Warwick & York.

PAUL IRVINE
Katonah, New York

STEROID ABUSE

Anabolic-androgenic steroids, better known as simply anabolic steroids, are artificial or synthetic drugs that mimic the effects of testosterone, the male sex hormone. Anabolic steroids are used medicinally to help rebuild tissues that have become weak because of serious injury, illness, or continuing infections. They are also used to treat some types of anemia, to treat certain kinds of breast cancer, and to treat hereditary angiodema, a disorder that causes swelling in the arms, legs, face, windpipe, or sexual organs (WebMD Health, 2000).

In addition to medicinal uses, anabolic steroids have been taken by athletes to build muscle size and boost athletic performance since the 1950s. Increasingly, other segments of the population, including adolescents, have also begun using anabolic steroids (National Institute on Drug Abuse, 2001b). Some youths use steroids in an attempt to reduce body fat or build muscles, whereas others abuse them as part of a pattern of high-risk behaviors (National Institute on Drug Abuse, 2001a).

Steroids are used in several ways. Some are taken orally; others are injected intramuscularly; and a few are contained in creams and gels that are rubbed into the skin (National Institute on Drug Abuse, 2001a). Most users use a combination of oral and injectable forms, a practice known as stacking. Users stack the drugs because it is widely believed that this practice results in a greater effect than when the drugs are used individually, a theory without scientific support. Another common practice is pyramiding. This involves taking the drugs in 6- to 12-week cycles and slowly increasing doses over the course of the cycle. Drugs are taken in this fashion in an effort to allow the body to adjust to the drug and to decrease toxic side effects. As with stacking, these benefits have not been substantiated scientifically (American Academy of Pediatrics, 1997).

Anabolic steroid abuse is increasing among adolescents, and most rapidly among females, although use is still much more common in males. Rate of lifetime use among high school students in this country varies between 4% and 12% for males and 0.5% and 2% for females, depending on grade level (Bahrke, Yesalis, & Brower, 1998). Since 1991, steroid use has increased by 50% among 8th and 10th graders and by 38% among 12th graders (National Institute on Drug Abuse, 2001b).

Research indicates that there are generally few significant side effects associated with the low-dose, intermittent-use patterns typical of most adolescents (Rogol & Tesalis, 1992). However, there are a number of adverse side effects that result from higher doses and more prolonged use of anabolic steroids.

Characteristics

Short-Term Effects

1. Euphoria
2. Acne and other skin changes
3. Increased energy and diminished fatigue
4. Irritability
5. Increased aggressiveness
6. Changes in libido
7. Impotence
8. Distractibility and confusion
9. Mood swings

Long-Term Effects

1. Liver damage and dysfunction
2. Potentially permanent damage to the heart and kidneys
3. Premature closing of the epiphyseal growth plate in children and adolescents, resulting in shorter adult height
4. Hypertension
5. Extremely aggressive and violent behavior known as "roid rage"
6. Male pattern baldness in both sexes
7. Reduced sperm production, shrinking of the testicles, and irreversible breast enlargement in males
8. Masculine characteristics such as deepening of the voice and excessive body hair, as well as decreased breast size and menstrual irregularities in females

---

In addition to the adverse effects associated with steroid use, there are also a number of deleterious consequences that can result when anabolic steroid use is discontinued. These include fatigue, restlessness, mood swings, insomnia, headache, muscle and joint pain, and depressed mood and suicidal ideation (National Institute on Drug Abuse, 2001b).

Research evaluating the effectiveness of anabolic steroids in producing desired effects such as increases in muscle mass and strength have yielded mixed results. Factors such as previous strength training, continued strength training, and adequate dietary protein intake appear to impact steroid efficacy (see Hough, 1990, for a review).

Very few studies examining treatment for anabolic steroid abuse have been conducted. Thus, much of the current knowledge in this area is based on anecdotal evidence from physicians working with individual abusers experiencing withdrawal. For many users, medications designed to restore the hormonal system can be helpful, as can medications that target specific withdrawal symptoms, such as antidepressants and analgesics. In some cases, supportive therapy is sufficient. For severe or prolonged withdrawal symptoms, medications or hospitalization may be necessary (National Institute on Drug Abuse, 2001a).

The key to addressing steroid use and abuse lies in preventive efforts. Historically, efforts have focused on drug testing and educating students about the adverse effects of taking steroids. Research suggests that simply teaching youth about the negative side effects does not result in the internalization of the information, nor does it discourage future use. Presenting both the risks and benefits of steroid use to young people tends to be perceived as more credible, but still does not discourage use. More comprehensive approaches to prevention show greater promise. Effective programs include information related to potential effects of steroids, training on how to refuse offers of drugs, instruction regarding building muscle with strength training and proper nutrition, and proper weight training (National Institute on Drug Abuse, 2001b). Future research efforts are focusing on developing more effective treatment and intervention programs.

REFERENCES

American Academy of Pediatrics. (1997). *Adolescents and anabolic steroids: A subjective review*. Retrieved from www.medem.com/MedLB/article_detaillb.cfm?article_ID=ZZZPJP4M08C&sub_cat=23

Bahrke, M. S., Yesalis, C. E., & Brower, K. J. (1998). Anabolic-androgenic steroid abuse and performance enhancing drugs among adolescents. *Child and Adolescent Clinics of North America, 7*, 821–838.

Hough, D. O. (1990). Anabolic steroids andergogenic aids. *American Family Physician, 41*(4), 1157–1164.

National Institute on Drug Abuse. (2001a). *Anabolic steroid abuse*. Retrieved from http://www.nida.nih.gov/ResearchReports/Steroids/anabolicsteroids3.html#why

National Institute on Drug Abuse. (2001b). *Anabolic steroids: Community drug alert bulletin*. Retrieved from http://www.nida.nih.gov/SteroidAlert/SteroidAlert.html

Rogol, A. D., & Tesalis, C. E., III. (1992). Anabolic-androgenic steroids and the adolescent. *Pediatric Annals, 21*(3), 175–188.

WebMD Health. (2000). *Anabolic steroids (systemic)*. Retrieved from http://www.webmd.com/search/search_results/default.aspx?query=anabolic%20steroids

M. Franci Crepeau-Hobson
University of Northern Colorado

STICKLER (HEREDITARY ARTHRO-OPHTHALMOPATHY)

Stickler syndrome is a connective tissue disorder that affects vision, hearing, joints, craniofacies, and the heart. This progressive condition is inherited as an autosomal dominant trait and is estimated to affect 1 in 10,000 people, although it is one of the rarest to be diagnosed (B. Houchin, 1994).

Characteristics

1. Sight problems including retinal detachment, myopia, cataracts, and glaucoma
2. Hearing loss and deafness in extreme cases
3. Bone and joint problems such as early-onset arthritis, joint pain and hyperextensibility, spine curvature, and abnormality to the ends of long bones
4. Flat face, cleft palate, submucous or high arched palate, and micrognathia
5. Occasional mitral valve prolapse (MVP)

Treatment of Stickler syndrome involves a multidisciplinary approach. Eye examinations should be held regularly with an eye doctor familiar with the syndrome because treatment for cataracts, detached retinas, and glaucoma is more effective with early identification (B. Houchin, 1994). Baseline hearing should also be assessed regularly to monitor hearing loss.

Rheumatological assessment and follow-up is advised for older patients who may benefit from physiotherapy for arthropathy. Presently, no prophylactic therapies exist to lessen joint damage. Treatment for mild spondyloepiphyseal dysplasia includes over-the-counter anti-inflammatory medications both before and after physical activity (Robin & Warman, 2000). Support of the joints is also recommended.

For cleft palate and craniofacial abnormality, otolaryngology, plastic surgery, oral and maxillofacial surgery, pediatric dentistry, and orthodontics are possible treatments (Robin & Warman, 2000).

Screenings for mitral valve prolapse should also be implemented, especially with complaints of chest pain or episodic tachycardia.

Although children with Stickler syndrome are typically of normal intelligence, hearing and visual impairments may lead to learning disabilities (Stickler Syndrome Support Group, 2000). Special education services under learning disabled or other health impairment may be needed for the child. Another educational consideration is the removal of the child from contact sports or rigorous physical activity that may displace the retina or damage the joints (Robin & Warman, 2000).

The diagnostic criteria for Stickler syndrome are soon to be published. Longevity is not affected, and prognosis depends on which gene is mutated and on preventative medical care that can properly diagnose this syndrome (P. Houchin, 2000).

REFERENCES

Houchin, B. (1994). *Stickler syndrome*. Retrieved from http://www.stickler.org/sip/def.html

Houchin, P. (2000). *Stickler syndrome*. Retrieved from http://www.stickler.org/sip/def.html

Robin, N. H., & Warman, M. L. (2000, June 8). *Stickler syndrome*. Retrieved from http://www.geneclinics.org/pro.les/stickler/details.html

Stickler Syndrome Support Group. (2000). *About Stickler syndrome*. Retrieved from http://www.stickler.org.uk/info.htm

TERESA M. LYLE
University of Texas at Austin

STIGMATIZATION (See Labeling)

STIMULANT ABUSE

Stimulant abuse can include a broad category of substances from amphetamines to caffeine that are taken to increase mental activity, offset drowsiness and fatigue, improve athletic performance, curb appetite, and reduce symptoms of depression (A. M. Pagliaro & Pagliaro, 1996). Amphetamines and their derivatives are chemically produced central nervous system (CNS) stimulants that are also commonly used for the treatment of ADHD (e.g., Ritalin; L. A. Pagliaro, 1992). Other forms of stimulants include cocaine, crack (a chemically produced form of cocaine), and crystal meth or "ice," as well as legal substances such as caffeine and nicotine (for persons 18 and older). Of recent concern is the increase among adolescents abusing Ritalin (street named Vitamin R, R-ball, or smart drug). Stimulants can be ingested in tablet or liquid form, smoked, inhaled (snorted), or injected into the blood stream.

As with many other illicit drugs, amphetamines made a comeback in the early 1990s. Use peaked for 8th- and 10th-grade students by 1996 and has gradually continued to decline in these two age groups (Johnston, O'Malley, & Bachman, 1999). The lifetime prevalence use of amphetamines for 12th-grade students continues to hover around 16%. The rates for other forms of stimulants such as cocaine and crack has continued to rise slightly, with a 1999 lifetime prevalence rate for 12th-grade students at 9.8% and 4.6%, respectively. These data do not include nicotine or prescribed drugs such as Ritalin. The

Monitoring the Future study (Johnston et al., 1999) suggests that Ritalin abuse has risen from 1% to 2.8% in the past 5 years. Approximately 3 million children and adolescents in the United States regularly use nicotine (Accessibility of cigarettes, 1992).

Characteristics

Listed in order from low to high doses.

1. Dilation of pupils; decreased appetite; increased blood pressure, heart rate, and respiratory rate

2. Increased mood, sociability, and initiative; improved concentration and "clearer" thinking; increased wakefulness and alertness; decreased boredom

3. Heart palpitation, chest pain, tremor, nausea, headache, dizziness, insomnia, blurred vision, constipation or diarrhea, urinary retention

4. Depersonalization, restlessness, anxiety, confusion, irritation, inability to concentrate

5. Automatic jerking movements; stereotyped, repetitive acts

6. Severe paranoid psychosis, fear, hallucinations, delusions, self-consciousness

Adapted from A. M. Pagliaro & Pagliaro, 1996.

Prevention programs that address social influences and teach children and adolescents to resist societal pressures have demonstrated the most effectiveness in preventing or decreasing use of selected substances, although no program has demonstrated widespread, long-lasting effectiveness (A. M. Pagliaro & Pagliaro, 1996). Cognitive therapy directed at modifying irrational belief systems and deficient coping skills is the most commonly used form of psychotherapy in the treatment of problematic patterns of substance abuse among children and adolescents (A. M. Pagliaro & Pagliaro, 1996). Recovery support groups also appear to be effective adjuncts to behavioral interventions that can lead to long-term recovery. Unfortunately, the rate of relapse following successful treatment is quite high (A. M. Pagliaro & Pagliaro, 1996).

Other than the transdermal nicotine patches and chewing gum widely used as adjuncts to smoking cessation programs (A. M. Pagliaro & Pagliaro, 1996), there are currently no pharmacological treatments for dependence on stimulants. However, medications are sometimes used to treat the side effects of overdose or withdrawal (e.g., antidepressants to combat depressive symptoms sometimes found in those who stop using). The research literature consistently supports the need to use a variety of treatment approaches that are tailored to meet the individual needs of young substance abusers (A. M. Pagliaro & Pagliaro, 1996).

From an educational perspective, substance abuse is clearly associated with decreased academic performance, higher absenteeism, and lower school completion rates (A. M. Pagliaro & Pagliaro, 1996). In addition to these concerns, studies have reported significant residual memory impairment among former cocaine users (e.g., Mittenberg & Motta, 1993). Furthermore, learning among students with ADHD may be adversely affected by the medication commonly prescribed for the treatment of the disorder (Swanson, Cantwell, Lerner, McBurnett, & Hanna, 1991).

To develop the most effective treatment strategies for treating substance abuse in younger populations, further research outlining those approaches that have succeeded with particular groups as well as those that have failed is needed (A. M. Pagliaro & Pagliaro, 1996). Given recent trends in Ritalin abuse, it is important for teachers and schools to be on alert for students selling their medication to others, and it is recommended that schools adopt and enforce policies regarding the use and dispensing of medication (Musser et al., 1998).

REFERENCES

Accessibility of cigarettes to youths aged 12–17 years—U.S., 1989. (1992). *Annals of Pharmacotherapy, 26,* 133–148.

Johnston, L. D., O'Malley, P. M., & Bachman, J. G. (1999). *National survey results on drug use from the Monitoring the Future study, 1975–1998: Vol. 1. Secondary school students* (NIH Publication No. 99-4660). Bethesda, MD: National Institute on Drug Abuse.

Mittenburg, W., & Motta, S. (1993). Effects of chronic cocaine abuse on memory and learning. *Archives of Clinical Neuropsychology, 8,* 477–483.

Musser, C. J., Ahman, P. A., Theye, F. W., Mundt, P., Broste, S. K., & Mueller-Rizner, N. (1998). Stimulant use and the potential for abuse in Wisconsin as reported by school administrators and longitudinally followed children. *Journal of Developmental and Behavioral Pediatrics, 19*(3), 187–192.

Pagliaro, A. M., & Pagliaro, L. B. (1996). *Substance use among children and adolescents.* New York, NY: Wiley.

Pagliaro, L. A. (1992). The straight dope: Focus on learning—Interpreting the interpretations. *Psychopsis, 14*(2), 8.

Swanson, J., Cantwell, D., Lerner, M., McBurnett, K., & Hanna, G. (1991). Effects of stimulant medication on learning in children with ADHD. *Journal of Learning Disabilities, 24,* 219–230.

ROBYN S. HESS
University of Colorado at Denver

STIMULANT DRUGS

Stimulant drugs are a commonly used class of medications for the treatment of inattention, impulsivity, and restlessness in school-age children and adolescents, and, less often, for the treatment of narcolepsy and drowsiness or disorders of arousal in the elderly. Children and adolescents having an attention deficit disorder (American Psychiatric Association, 1994) are the ones most often given these medications because of the significant effects of the drugs on sustained attention. In fact, stimulants are the most commonly prescribed psychotropic medications in child psychiatry (Wilens & Biederman, 1992). The drugs are so named because of their stimulation of increased central nervous system activity, presumably by way of their effects on dopamine and norepinephrine production, and reuptake at the synaptic level of neuronal functioning (Cantwell & Carlson, 1978). The drugs may also have effects on other central neurotransmitters as well as on peripheral nervous system activity. The changes in central neurotransmitter activity result in increased alertness, arousal, concentration, and vigilance or sustained attention, as well as reductions in impulsive behavior and activity or restlessness that is irrelevant to particular tasks (Barkley, 1977, 1981). While a number of substances such as caffeine fall into this class of medications, those most typically used with children and adolescents are methylphenidate (Ritalin), d-amphetamine (Dexedrine), a mixture of dextroamphetamine and racemic amphetamine salts (Adderall; Popper, 1994) and pemoline (Cylert). Despite similar behavioral effects and side effects, the mechanism of action of each of these stimulants is somewhat different, and that for pemoline is not well specified.

The stimulants are relatively rapid in their initiation of behavioral changes and in the time course over which such changes are maintained. Most stimulant drugs, taken orally, are quickly absorbed into the bloodstream through the stomach and small intestine and pass readily across the blood-brain barrier to affect neuronal activity. Behavioral changes can be detected within 30 to 60 minutes after ingestion and may last between 3 and 8 hours, depending on the type of stimulant and preparation (regular or sustained release) employed. Traces of medication and their metabolites in blood and urine can be detected up to 24 hours after ingestion, perhaps corresponding to the clinical observation of persisting side effects after the desired behavioral effects are no longer noticeable.

Approximately 70 percent or more of children over 5 years of age, adolescents, and young adults display a positive behavioral response to the stimulants. Children below age 3 are much less likely to respond well to medication, and the drugs have not been approved by the Food and Drug Administration for children younger than 6 years. The best predictor of a positive response is the degree of inattention before treatment, while that for a poor response is the presence and severity of pretreatment anxiety and emotional disturbance (Barkley, 1976; Loney, 1986; Taylor, 1983).

The medications are taken one to three times per day, with some children taking them only on school days while others remain on medication throughout the week.

Medication is often discontinued during summer vacations from school to permit a rebound in appetite and growth, which may have been mildly suppressed during treatment. Children having more severe, pervasive developmental disorders such as autism or severe behavioral disorders, however, may remain on medication throughout the year (Aman, 1996). The average length of treatment with stimulants is typically 3 to 5 years, but this may increase in the future because of reports of equally positive effects with adolescents and young adults having significant inattention, impulsivity, and restlessness (Woods, 1986).

The most commonly experienced side effects are diminished appetite, particularly for the noon meal, and insomnia, although these are often mild, diminish within several weeks of treatment onset, and are easily managed by reductions in dose where problematic. Increases in blood pressure, heart rate, and respiration may occur, but they are typically of little consequence (Hastings & Barkley, 1978). Other side effects of lesser frequency are sleeplessness (Day & Abmayr, 1998); irritability, sadness, or dysphoria; and proneness to crying, especially during late afternoons, when the medication is "washing out" of the body (Cantwell & Carlson, 1978). Some children experience heightened activity levels during this washout phase. Headaches and stomachaches are infrequently noted and, like all side effects, appear to be dose related. Temporary suppression of growth in height and weight may be noted in some children during the first 1 to 2 years of treatment with stimulants, but there appear to be few lasting effects on eventual adult stature. Between 1 and 2 percent of children and adolescents may experience nervous tics while on stimulant medication, but these diminish in the majority of cases with reduction in dose or discontinuation of medication. A few cases of Tourette syndrome (multiple motor tics, vocal tics, and, in some cases, increased utterance of profanities) have been reported after initiation of stimulant medication (Barkley, 1987). Children with a personal or family history of motor/vocal tics should use these drugs only with caution because of the possible emergence or exacerbation of their tic conditions, observed in more than 50 percent of such children.

The medications appear to improve fine motor agility, planning, and execution, as well as reaction time, speech articulation (in children having mild delays in fine motor control of speech), and handwriting, in some children. Increases in academic productivity, short-term memory, simple verbal learning, and drawing and copying skills frequently are noted, but little, if any, change is seen on tests of intelligence, academic achievement, or other complex cognitive processes (Barkley, 1977). Despite generally positive behavioral improvements in most children with attention-deficit/hyperactivity disorder taking stimulants, these drugs have shown little, if any, significant, lasting effect on the long-term outcome of such children in late adolescence or young adulthood once medication has been discontinued.

REFERENCES

Aman, M. G. (1996). Stimulant drugs in the developmental disabilities revisited. *Journal of Developmental & Physical Disabilities, 8*(4), 347–365.

American Psychiatric Association. (1994). *Diagnostic and statistical manual of mental disorders* (4th ed.). Washington, DC: Author.

Barkley, R. (1976). Predicting the response of hyperactive children to stimulant drugs: A review. *Journal of Abnormal Child Psychology, 4,* 327–348.

Barkley, R. (1977). A review of stimulant drug research with hyperactive children. *Journal of Child Psychology & Psychiatry, 18,* 137–165.

Barkley, R. A. (1981). *Hyperactive children: A handbook for diagnosis and treatment.* New York, NY: Guilford Press.

Barkley, R. A. (1987). Tic disorders and Tourette's syndrome. In E. Mash & L. Terdal (Eds.), *Behavioral assessment of childhood disorders* (2nd ed.). New York, NY: Guilford Press.

Cantwell, D., & Carlson, G. (1978). Stimulants. In J. Werry (Ed.), *Pediatric psychopharmacology.* New York, NY: Brunner/Mazel.

Day, H. D., & Abmayr, S. B. (1998). Parent reports of sleep disturbances in stimulant-medicated children with attention-deficit/hyperactivity disorder. *Journal of Clinical Psychology, 54*(5), 701–716.

Hastings, J., & Barkley, R. (1978). A review of psychophysiological research with hyperactive children. *Journal of Abnormal Child Psychology, 7,* 413–447.

Loney, J. (1986). Predicting stimulant drug response among hyperactive children. *Psychiatric Annals, 16,* 16–22.

Popper, C. W. (1994). The story of four salts. *Journal of Child & Adolescent Psychopharmacology, 4*(4), 217–223.

Taylor, E. (1983). Drug response and diagnostic validation. In M. Rutter (Ed.), *Developmental neuropsychiatry* (pp. 348–368). New York, NY: Guilford Press.

Wilens, T. E., & Biederman, J. (1992). The stimulants. *Psychiatric Clinics of North America, 15*(1), 191–222.

Woods, D. (1986). The diagnosis and treatment of attention deficit disorder, residual type. *Psychiatric Annals, 16,* 23–28.

RUSSELL A. BARKLEY
University of Massachusetts Medical Center

See also Attention-Deficit/Hyperactivity Disorder; Dopamine; Ritalin; Tourette Syndrome

STIMULUS CONTROL

When an event, such as the ring of an alarm clock or the smell of smoke, is observed to increase the probability of a behavior—rising from bed or checking the stovetop—the response is said to be under stimulus control of the antecedent stimulus. Such responsiveness to subtle cues in the environment is imperative for survival. Stopping at red lights, selecting clothing appropriate to the weather, and entering the correct restroom in public buildings require that behavior be sensitive to the surrounding environment. Many of the responses critical to personal and social success are learned by observing parents or other students in school, but when relevant behaviors have not yet been learned, they cannot be effectively influenced by cues in the environment. Teaching such behaviors involves manipulating social and physical contexts to increase successful behavior and make unwanted behavior less likely.

B. F. Skinner suggested that stimuli that immediately precede a response and are present during reinforcement acquire control over the future occurrence of the response. His laboratory experiments demonstrated that specific physical properties of the environment, such as the intensity of light or the pitch of sound, became predictive of certain outcomes for responding, and responding then followed the presentation of those particular stimuli. Skinner highlighted two processes through which stimuli acquire control over behavior: induction and discrimination (Skinner, 1953). When induction occurs, other stimuli present during the reinforcement acquire control over behavior. This is frequently referred to as stimulus generalization, and it is important to survival. Stopping should occur, for example, at street lights that are bright red, dull red, attached to a yellow signpost, or attached to a chrome installment. Discrimination may be said to be the opposite process, where a learner's behavior comes under the control of sharply defined gradients. A child learns to call his father, who has a beard, "Daddy," but soon learns that not all men with beards should be addressed in the same manner.

Generalization and discrimination work together in the formation of concepts, or stimulus classes (Keller & Schoenfeld, 1950). A child learns that apples are red and later that a red ball is not an apple. To teach the concept of redness, a teacher may position a red and a green apple beside one another and ask the child to point to the red apple. The teacher would reinforce only the correct response. Several examples, followed by trials in which yellow and red apples are presented side by side, lead to discrimination. Next, the teacher may show the child many dissimilar objects that are red, such as fire trucks, pillows, and stoplights. The different stimulus properties of these items help to generalize the concept of redness and form a stimulus class for the set of stimuli with common characteristics.

Behavior may be influenced by stimuli that immediately precede reinforced responses, or by contextual variables that alter the value of reinforcers. Changes in the environment that alter the momentary effectiveness of a reinforcer and simultaneously alter the probable frequency of behavior that has preceded the reinforcement are referred to as motivating operations (MOs; Laraway, Snycerski, Michael, & Poling, 2003). When a child has not seen his schoolmates all weekend, the consequence of having time to chat with friends reinforces getting to school early. Not seeing friends all weekend is an MO that has an establishing effect on the reinforcing value of promptly getting to school. Correspondingly, having a headache has an abolishing effect on the reinforcing qualities of social interaction. An effective arrangement of MOs to facilitate learning in the classroom could, for example, involve teaching a child with autism new words 1 hour before lunch with carrot slices offered to reinforce appropriate responses. Skillful assessment of MOs that are present in a learner's life, such as not having gotten enough sleep or having eaten too much lunch, makes acquiring stimulus control by the arrangement of social and physical characteristics of the environment a matter of practice based on evidence rather than routine.

Several strategies for presenting cues and contexts to increase learning have been empirically validated. Presenting or removing environmental prompts that have stimulus control over desired behavior is one noted strategy. O'Neill, Blanck, and Joyner (1980) altered the physical appearance of trash cans at a university stadium to increase their use by fans. A lid resembling a baseball cap placed over the cans that, when lifted, exposed the word "Thanks" was demonstrated to be twice as effective as the unmodified cans. Motivating operations can be arranged so that desirable behaviors are more reinforcing. Researchers who found that hard academic tasks were an MO for aggressive behavior during the following recess period broke academic tasks into smaller chunks and interspersed easier tasks with more difficult ones to decrease problem behaviors (Horner, Day, Sprague, O'Brien, & Heathfield, 1991). Altering the effort required for engaging in targeted activities is another noted strategy. Vollmer, Marcus, and Ringdahl (1995) discussed two boys whose self-injurious behaviors resulted in escape from demanding tasks. When the boys were given the opportunity to take frequent breaks they were more cooperative during activities than when they were asked to remain on task. Inversely, a person with disabilities who engaged in disruptive behaviors while working at a supermarket was given a magazine to look at. The magazine diverted the worker's attention from stimuli that had previously occasioned disruptive behavior, and because it occupied his hands, disruptive behavior became more difficult to engage in (Kemp & Carr, 1995).

Stimulus control is a central aspect of learning that can be facilitated by careful attention to physical and social aspects of the environment. Arranging antecedents that augment generalization, discrimination, and concept formation sets the occasion for a learner to use relevant social behaviors. Making use of MOs such as meal schedules and socialization patterns creates the context in which learning is most likely to occur. Assessing situations that cannot be altered and making environmental accommodations makes engaging in maladaptive behaviors unnecessary. Such procedures for presenting cues and contexts that acquire stimulus control over behavior are well established and empirically validated practices that aid learners in developing skills crucial for success.

REFERENCES

Horner, R. H., Day, H. M., Sprague, J. R., O'Brien, M., & Heathfield, L. T. (1991). Interspersed requests: A nonaversive procedure for reducing aggression and self-injury during instruction. *Journal of Applied Behavior Analysis, 24,* 265–278.

Keller, F. S., & Schoenfeld, W. N. (1950). *Principles of psychology.* New York, NY: Appleton-Century-Crofts.

Kemp, D. C., & Carr, E. G. (1995). Reduction of severe problem behavior in community employment using an hypothesis-driven multicomponent intervention approach. *Journal of the Association for Persons with Severe Handicaps, 20,* 229–247.

Laraway, S., Snycerski, S., Michael, J., & Poling, A. (2003). Motivating operations and terms to describe them: Some further refinements. *Journal of Applied Behavior Analysis, 36,* 407–414.

O'Neill, G. W., Blanck, L. S., & Joyner, M. A. (1980). The use of stimulus control over littering in a natural setting. *Journal of Applied Behavior Analysis, 13,* 370–381.

Skinner, B. F. (1953). *Science and human behavior.* New York, NY: Free Press.

Vollmer, T. R., Marcus, B. A., & Ringdahl, J. E. (1995). Noncontingent escape as treatment for self-injurious behavior maintained by negative reinforcement. *Journal of Applied Behavior Analysis, 28,* 15–26.

THOMAS G. SZABO
Western Michigan University

STIMULUS DEPRIVATION

Stimulus deprivation refers to an increase in reinforcer effectiveness that occurs following a reduction in the availability of or access to that reinforcing event. The effectiveness of reinforcers, especially of primary reinforcers such as food, depends greatly on the deprivation state of the individual. Using edible reinforcers with a student who has just returned from lunch probably will not be as effective as using the same reinforcers immediately prior to lunch, when the student is more likely to be in a state of deprivation for food. Most stimulus events serve as effective reinforcers only if the individual has been deprived of them for a period of time prior to their use.

In general, the longer the deprivation period, the more effective the reinforcer (Martin & Pear, 1983).

The magnitude or amount of a reinforcer required to change behavior is less when the individual is partially deprived of the event (Kazdin, 1980). For example, students who are temporarily deprived of teacher attention may require less attention to maintain behavior than students who have frequent access to teacher attention. If a potential reinforcer is provided in limited quantities, thus creating a partial state of deprivation, that event is more likely to maintain its effectiveness as a reinforcer.

A state of deprivation may be created intentionally by the educator to increase the value of reinforcing events. This procedure is especially valuable with events that previously were effective reinforcers but temporarily show a satiation effect. Using the principle of deprivation, the reinforcer is withheld or reduced in availability for a period of time as a means of increasing the state of deprivation. If free time, listening to music, or a particular edible item shows satiation effects, the teacher may wish to reduce or remove it for a period of time. As students become deprived, the reinforcer can once again be introduced with increased effectiveness.

Ethical and legal issues should be considered prior to use of a deprivation procedure. Major objections typically focus on deprivation of essential primary reinforcers (e.g., food, water, shelter, human contact) on the basis that it constitutes a violation of basic human rights. As noted by Kazdin (1980), however, deprivation is a natural part of human existence. All people are, in some ways, deprived by society of self-expression in such areas as free speech and sexual behavior. Certainly, students receiving special education services who demonstrate academic and behavioral difficulties frequently are deprived of access to employment or other economic opportunities as a result of their characteristics. Thus the negative effects of social deprivation that special education students normally experience as a result of their deficits must be weighed against any temporary negative effects associated with stimulus deprivation used as a treatment strategy (Baer, 1970). A decision to use deprivation, or any other aversive technique, requires careful consideration of the kind of deprivation, the duration of the program, the availability of alternative treatment strategies, and the demonstrable benefits resulting from its use (Kazdin, 1980). As a precautionary measure when using a deprivation procedure, an individual should never be completely deprived of the reinforcing event for a lengthy period of time.

Fortunately, intentional deprivation of reinforcers usually is not necessary, as the natural deprivation that occurs in the course of an individual's daily activities often is sufficient to increase reinforcer effectiveness. Since children in the classroom, for example, do not have unlimited access to free time, they normally experience a mild form of deprivation during the course of a school day. As another example, when using small amounts of edible reinforcers to increase appropriate responding, the only deprivation required may be the natural deprivation that occurs between meals. Thus a variety of events may serve as effective reinforcers simply as a result of natural deprivation without the introduction of more formal deprivation procedures.

REFERENCES

Baer, D. M. (1970). A case for the selective reinforcement of punishment. In C. Neuringer & J. L. Michael (Eds.), *Behavior modification in clinical psychology*. New York, NY: Appleton-Century-Crofts.

Kazdin, A. E. (1980). *Behavior modification in applied settings* (Rev. ed.). Homewood, IL: Dorsey.

Martin, G., & Pear, J. (1983). *Behavior modification: What it is and how to do it* (2nd ed.). Englewood Cliffs, NJ: Prentice Hall.

CHRISTINE L. COLE
University of Wisconsin at Madison

See also Behavior Modification; Operant Conditioning; Stimulus Satiation

STIMULUS GENERALIZATION

Stimulus generalization can be defined as a set of conditions with similar properties that all begin to occasion a specific response. Stimulus generalization is often thought of as the opposite of stimulus discrimination. If tight stimulus control is achieved, then little stimulus generalization can occur. B. F. Skinner discussed stimulus generalization and stimulus control in the following manner: When a response is reinforced under certain conditions the response will most likely occur under very similar conditions. However, due to generalization, other conditions with only some similar properties can also begin to occasion the response (Skinner, 1974). Stimulus generalization was often thought of as a passive process, resulting from poor discrimination training. However, therapeutic behavior change is often dependent on stimulus generalization and needs to be understood as more than a passive process (Stokes & Baer, 1977). Often when training new responses it will be necessary for those responses to generalize to other stimuli, such as settings and individuals.

In 1977, Stokes and Baer summarized the research on stimulus generalization and found that almost half of the applied literature used a method of examining generalization through "train and hope." This method consisted of training on a specific response and then noting any other generalization that co-occurred. The method was labeled "train and hope" because researchers using this method would train one response and then hope that it would generalize to other untrained conditions. In this method no specific training for generalization occurred. Stokes and Baer suggest that behavior analysts should *not* assume that generalization will occur without direct teaching. Furthermore, the authors state that there needs to be more research on generalization and how to specifically train for generalization.

Stokes and Osnes (1989) continued the research of Stokes and Baer (1977) by discussing stimulus generalization as it relates to function. Stokes and Osnes state that there are two important questions that must be asked when assessing stimulus generalization: Did the behavior occur in generalized situations, and what are the functional variables that account for the generalization? In their paper, the authors reformulated the original tactics proposed by Stokes and Baer to offer 12 strategies for programming generalization. All 12 strategies were organized into three general principles: Exploit current functional contingencies, train diversely, and incorporate functional mediators. The first category, exploit current functional contingencies, refers to teaching behaviors that are likely to come into contact with natural contingencies. These contingencies can occur without the direct presence of a change agent (i.e., an adult). The next category, training for diversity, refers to training in a less rigid format. Typical discrimination training consists of rigid training with tight stimulus control. In order to program for generalization, a less rigid format may be beneficial, such as training with multiple exemplars as well as nonexemplars. Multiple-exemplar training consists of teaching the individual multiple examples of correct responding. For example, when teaching a child to make social initiations, training should take place in multiple settings (e.g., school, the park). An additional way to train to diversity is to make antecedents and consequences less discriminable. This can be achieved by delaying the consequences and changing reinforcers. The final category, incorporating functional mediators, refers to incorporating a mediating stimulus that occurs between training and the behavior. There are several different ways that mediators can be incorporated into the training session. One example of incorporating mediating stimuli is the use of self-monitoring materials, such as schedules or self-monitoring forms.

In recent years behavior analytic approaches to treatment for developmental disabilities and autism spectrum disorders have begun to assess and program for generalization using the recommendations described by Stokes and Osnes. For example, Taylor (2001) suggests that when teaching children with autism social skills, generalization will need to be specifically programmed. Taylor recommends using multiple peers and conducting training in several different settings. Training should also involve multiple-exemplar training and teaching the children skills that will contact naturally occurring reinforcers.

Several other professionals in the field have also acknowledged the need for programming for generalization (Anderson, Taras, & Cannon, 1996; Maurice, Green, & Taylor, 2001). For example, Heflin and Alberto (2001) make several recommendations for programming generalization and maintenance when teaching children with autism. The authors suggest that the use of multiple cues, people, settings, and materials can lead to increased generalization skills, especially when teaching in the classroom context.

In summary, stimulus generalization takes place when a response begins to occur in the presence of an untrained stimulus. Generalization has emerged as an important behavioral process that needs to be considered as an independent principle. The view of stimulus generalization as a passive process is no longer an extensive enough account for behavior change. Within teaching and training situations it is now common practice to account for, as well as specifically program for, stimulus generalization.

REFERENCES

Anderson, S., Taras, M., & Cannon, B. (1996). Teaching new skills to young children with autism. In C. Maurice, G. Green, & S. Luce (Eds.), *Behavioral interventions for young children with autism: A manual for parents and peers* (pp. 181–193). Austin, TX: PRO-ED.

Heflin, J. L., & Alberto, P. A. (2001). Establishing a behavioral context for learning for students with autism. *Focus on Autism and Other Developmental Disabilities, 16,* 93–101.

Maurice, C., Green, G., & Luce, S. (2001). *Behavioral interventions for young children with autism: A manual for parents and peers.* Austin, TX: PRO-ED.

Stokes, T., & Baer, D. (1977). An implicit technology of generalization. *Journal of Applied Behavior Analysis, 10,* 349–367.

Stokes, T., & Osnes, P. (1989). An operant pursuit of generalization. *Behavior Therapy, 20,* 337–355.

Taylor, B. (2001). Teaching peer social skills to children with autism. In C. Maurice, G. Green, & R. Foxx (Eds.), *Making a difference: Behavioral interventions for autism* (pp. 83–161). Austin, TX: PRO-ED.

PAIGE B. RAETZ
THOMAS SZABO
BRITT L. WINTER
Western Michigan University

STIMULUS SATIATION

Stimulus satiation refers to the reduction in reinforcer effectiveness that occurs after a large amount of that reinforcer has been obtained (usually within a short period of time). Thus an event that initially shows reinforcing qualities may become ineffective or even aversive for a period of time if experienced too frequently or excessively. Teacher praise may be effective the first few times if it is provided in the morning, but may gradually diminish in value with additional use during the day. Treats and certain activities may be highly reinforcing if used sparingly but may lose their effectiveness if used frequently. The special educator should be sensitive to the principle of satiation and provide alternative reinforcing events when loss of effectiveness is noted (Gardner, 1978).

Satiation is especially common with primary reinforcers such as food. These reinforcers, when provided in excessive amounts within a short period, may lose their reinforcing properties relatively quickly. To prevent or delay satiation, only a small amount of the reinforcer should be provided at any one time. Satiation of primary reinforcers is usually temporary, as these events regain their reinforcing value as deprivation increases.

Secondary reinforcers such as praise, attention, and recognition are less likely than primary reinforcers to be influenced by satiation effects. The category of secondary reinforcers called generalized reinforcers is least-susceptible to satiation. This is due to the fact that the reinforcers themselves (e.g., tokens, grades, money) can be exchanged for a variety of other reinforcing events called back-up reinforcers. Thus satiation of generalized reinforcers is not likely to occur unless the individual becomes satiated with the items or events offered as back-up reinforcers. The greater the number and range of back-up reinforcers available, the less likelihood that satiation will occur (Kazdin, 1980). This would suggest that teachers consider the use of tokens, exchangeable for a wide variety of back-up reinforcers, when tangible events are required to ensure effective learning and behavior (Gardner, 1978).

The principle of satiation may also be used as an intervention tactic to reduce the value of events that appear to serve as reinforcers for maladaptive behavior. In a stimulus satiation procedure, the individual is provided with a reinforcing event with such frequency or in such large quantities that the event loses its reinforcing qualities for a period of time; the result is that the behavior maintained by that reinforcer is weakened. In a frequently cited example, Ayllon (1963) used a stimulus satiation procedure with a hospitalized psychiatric patient who hoarded a large number of towels in her room. Although many efforts had been made to discourage hoarding, these had proved to be unsuccessful, and the staff had resorted to simply removing on a regular basis the towels she had collected. With the stimulus satiation procedure, the staff provided her with large numbers of towels without comment. After a few weeks, when the number of towels in her room reached 625, she began to remove a few, and no more were given to her. The patient engaged in no towel hoarding during the subsequent year.

The purpose of such a stimulus satiation procedure is to reduce or remove the reinforcing qualities of the event serving to maintain the maladaptive behavior. In the Ayllon study (1963) this loss of reinforcer effectiveness was reflected in the patient's comments: "Don't give me no more towels. I've got enough. . . . Take them towels away. . . . Get these dirty towels out of here" (p. 57). Apparently, as the number of towels increased to an excessive level, they were no longer reinforcing and even became aversive to her.

Although long-term maintenance of behavior change was obtained in this case, the effects of stimulus satiation procedures typically are temporary. This is especially true if the reinforcer is highly valuable to the individual. Educators can enhance the effects of a satiation procedure by ensuring that, during the interim period in which the maladaptive behavior is absent or of low strength, other more appropriate replacement behaviors are taught and strengthened (Gardner, 1978).

REFERENCES

Ayllon, T. (1963). Intensive treatment of psychotic behaviour by stimulus satiation and food reinforcement. *Behaviour Research & Therapy, 1,* 53–61.

Gardner, W. I. (1978). *Children with learning and behavior problems: A behavior management approach* (2nd ed.). Boston, MA: Allyn & Bacon.

Kazdin, A. E. (1980). *Behavior modification in applied settings* (Rev. ed.). Homewood, IL: Dorsey.

CHRISTINE L. COLE
University of Wisconsin at Madison

See also **Applied Behavior Analysis; Behavior Modification; Stimulus Deprivation**

STRABISMUS, EFFECT ON LEARNING OF

Strabismus, also called heteropia, is a visual condition in which the two eyes are not parallel when viewing an object. While one eye is fixed on an object, the other eye will be directed elsewhere. Strabismus can be classified in two ways. The first concerns the angle of separation. In concomitant strabismus, the angle of separation is fixed; in noncomitant strabismus the angle between the eye that is fixed and the deviant eye varies. Strabismus also can be classified by whether the visual paths of the two eyes converge or diverge (Harley & Lawrence, 1977).

The effect of strabismus on learning is closely tied to its age of onset. If it occurs later in childhood (Flax, 1993), after other visual reflexes have developed, it can result in double vision (diplopia), which can be stressful and lead to learning disabilities. Lipton (1971) noted significant correlations between strabismus and neurotic traits, character disorders, and learning problems. Haskell (1972), on the other hand, showed no relationship between strabismus and academic achievement.

If the onset of strabismus occurs before the age of 2, the effects are not as severe because other visual reflexes are not as developed. However, early onset of strabismus can lead to the development of ambliopia, a condition in which the brain suppresses the signals coming from the deviant eye. If not corrected, the brain can permanently lose the ability to process a 20/20 image from this eye.

Some form of strabismus occurs in approximately 5% of all children. The percentage increases to 40%–50% for children with cerebral palsy; it is noted in as many as 60% of the children who are visually impaired at birth as a result of their mother's having contracted rubella during pregnancy.

Strabismus can be corrected through lenses if it is detected early in a child's life. Freeman, Nguyen, and Jolly (1996) suggest that amblyopia and strabismus deviation are the major components of visual acuity loss and should be reduced by whatever means are available. Additionally, some doctors recommend eye exercises as a way to correct the condition. This recommendation is controversial. Eden (1978) notes that strabismus often starts early in life, before the child is capable of following any rigorous exercise schedule. Once the child is capable of following such a schedule, permanent visual damage may already have occurred. In school, close work should be limited for students with strabismus, and these students should be given frequent rest periods.

REFERENCES

Eden, J. (1978). *The eye book*. New York, NY: Viking Press.

Flax, N. (1993). The treatment of strabismus in the four- to ten-year-old child. *Child and Adolescent Social Work Journal, 10*(5), 411–416.

Freeman, A. W., Nguyen, V. A., & Jolly, N. (1996). Components of visual acuity loss in strabismus. *Vision Research, 36*(5), 765–774.

Harley, R. K., & Lawrence, G. A. (1977). *Visual impairment in the schools*. Springfield, IL: Thomas.

Haskell, S. H. (1972). Visuoperceptual, visuomotor, and scholastic skills of alternating and uniocular squinting children. *Journal of Special Education, 6*, 3–8.

Lipton, E. L. (1971). Remarks on the psychological aspects of strabismus. *Sight-Saving Review, 4*, 129–138.

THOMAS E. ALLEN
Gallaudet College

See also Ambliyopia; Blind; Cataracts

STRAUSS, ALFRED A. (1897–1957)

Alfred A. Strauss was born in Germany and received his medical degree and subsequent training in psychiatry and neurology there. He left Germany in 1933, became a visiting professor at the University of Barcelona, and helped to establish Barcelona's first child guidance clinics. In 1937 Strauss joined the staff of the Wayne County (Michigan) School, where he served as research psychiatrist and director of child care. In 1947 Strauss founded the Cove School in Racine, Wisconsin, a residential institution that gained an international reputation for its pioneering work with brain-injured children. Strauss served as president of the school until his death.

Strauss made major contributions in the areas of diagnosis and education of brain-injured children. He developed tests for diagnosing brain injury. His studies of children without intellectual deficit who showed characteristics of brain injury in learning and behavior resulted in the first systematic description of a new clinical entity, minimal brain dysfunction. His 1947 book, *Psychopathology and Education of the Brain-Injured Child*, written with Laura Lehtinen, was the major guide for many of the numerous school programs that came into existence for minimally brain-injured children during the 1950s and 1960s.

This entry has been informed by the sources listed below.

REFERENCES

Gardiner, R. A. (1958). Alfred A. Strauss, 1897–1957. *Exceptional Children, 24*, 373.

Lewis, R. S., Strauss, A. A., & Lehtinen, L. E. (1960). *The other child*. New York, NY: Grune & Stratton.

Strauss, A. A., & Kephart, N. C. (1955). *Psychopathology and education of the brain-injured child* (Vol. 2). New York, NY: Grune & Stratton.

Strauss, A. A., & Lehtinen, L. E. (1947). *Psychopathology and education of the brain-injured child* (Vol. 1). New York, NY: Grune & Stratton.

PAUL IRVINE
Katonah, New York

See also Birth Injuries

STRAUSS SYNDROME

The term *Strauss syndrome* was coined by Stevens and Birch (1957) to describe an expanded set of behavioral characteristics of children who could not learn and did not easily fit into other classification systems. It also extended the work of a leading pioneer in the field,

Alfred Strauss. Strauss's ideas regarding the education of brain-injured, perceptually handicapped children were presented in works coauthored first with Laura Lehtinen (1947) and later with Newell Kephart (1955).

The term *Strauss syndrome* was introduced to describe the brain-injured child who evidenced (1) erratic and inappropriate behavior on mild provocation; (2) increased motor activity disproportionate to the stimulus; (3) poor organization of behavior; (4) distractibility of more than an ordinary degree under ordinary conditions; (5) persistent hyperactivity; and (6) awkwardness and consistently poor motor performance (Stevens & Birch, 1957).

Despite the importance of the works of Strauss et al., it became apparent that their description of the brain-injured child pertained only to a certain portion of the total group having neurogenic disorders of learning. Major objections to the term *brain-injured child* were presented by Stevens and Birch (1957). They concluded that:

1. The term is an etiological concept and does not appropriately describe the symptom complex. This is important because the condition that prevails is viewed in terms of symptoms rather than etiology.

2. The term is associated with other conditions, some of which have no relation to the symptom complex commonly referred to as brain injury.

3. The term does not help in the development of a sound therapeutic approach.

4. The term is not suited for use as a descriptive one because it is essentially a generic expression, the use of which results in oversimplification. (p. 349)

It is now considered archaic.

REFERENCES

Stevens, G., & Birch, J. (1957). A proposal for clarification of the terminology used to describe brain-injured children. *Exceptional Children, 23,* 346–349.

Strauss, A., & Kephart, N. (1955). *Psychopathology and education of the brain-injured child* (Vol. 2). New York, NY: Grune & Stratton.

Strauss, A., & Lehtinen, L. (1947). *Psychopathology and education of the brain-injured child* (Vol. 1). New York, NY: Grune & Stratton.

CECILIA STEPPE-JONES
North Carolina Central University

See also Brain Damage/Injury; Etiology; Learning Disabilities; Lesions; MBD Syndrome

STRENGTH MODELS OF REMEDIATION (*See* Remediation, Deficit-Centered Models of)

STREPHOSYMBOLIA

Strephosymbolia is a Greek term that literally means "twisted symbol." Originally used by Samuel T. Orton, strephosymbolia is most commonly used in discussions regarding dyslexia. Orton and others noticed that when certain children read, they often reverse letters, syllables, or words. These children see all parts of a word, but not in the accepted order. So, instead of "pebbles," a strephosymbolic child might see "pelbbse" (Johnson, 1981). This twisting of reading material is viewed as a primary symptom of dyslexia (Clarke, 1973).

Orton believed that strephosymbolia resulted from a failure to establish cerebral dominance in the left hemisphere of the brain (Lerner, 1985). The reversals that resulted from the lack of cerebral dominance were due to failure to erase memory images from the nondominant side of the brain (Kessler, 1980). These memory images were projected to the dominant side of the brain as mirror images, resulting in the reversals of letters and/or words (Kessler, 1980).

Currently, Orton's theory has little credibility, as there has been no substantiation that mirror images are projected onto the brain (Kessler, 1980). Mercer (1983) notes that these difficulties are referred to as severe reading disabilities and are treated according to the specific difficulty.

REFERENCES

Clarke, L. (1973). *Can't read, can't write, can't talk too good either*. New York, NY: Walker.

Johnson, C. (1981). *The diagnosis of learning disabilities*. Boulder, CO: Pruett.

Kessler, J. W. (1980). History of minimal brain dysfunction. In H. E. Rice & E. D. Rice (Eds.), *Handbook of minimal brain dysfunction: A critical review*. New York, NY: Wiley.

Lerner, T. (1985). *Learning disabilities: Theories, diagnosis and teaching strategies* (4th ed.). Boston, MA: Houghton Mifflin.

Mercer, C. D. (1983). *Students with learning disabilities* (2nd ed.). Columbus, OH: Merrill.

JOHN R. BEATTIE
University of North Carolina at Charlotte

See also Dyslexia; Reading Disorders

STRESS AND INDIVIDUALS WITH DISABILITIES

Stress results when physical and psychological demands on an individual exceed personal coping skills. Stress is activated when a threat to security, self-esteem, or safety is perceived. Schultz (1980) suggests that stress is often triggered by environmental interactions, which may be more problematic for children with disabilities than for typically developing children. Children with disabilities may also develop stress reactions to personal thoughts.

In regard to the development of stress, Schultz has suggested a pattern of (1) occurrence of an event, (2) internal assignment of the meaning of the event, and (3) occurrence of internal and external responses to the event depending on the assigned meaning.

Rutter (1981) suggests that resilience is demonstrated by young people who succeed despite stress, but that children with disabilities may be constitutionally less resilient. Particularly stressful periods for children with disabilities include school entry, change of school, and last years of school. The uncertainties present during these periods are exacerbated because of the child's lack of resilience (Kershaw, 1973).

Low-achieving individuals demonstrate more stress than their better-achieving peers. Lower-functioning students with disabilities are subject to more stress in childhood than higher-functioning individuals (Westling, 1986). This increased stress may be due to social rejection and parental overprotection concurrent with the children's reduced capacity for coping with various situations.

Mainstreaming and inclusive practices may produce increased social stress in the student with disabilities. Tymitz-Wolf (1984) analyzed the worries of students with mild intellectual disabilities about mainstreaming as related to academic performance, social interactions, and the transitions inherent in split placement. A range of worries were reported in all three areas, with worries concerning transitions being the most prevalent.

Schultz (1980) contends that stress-management programs for students with disabilities should emphasize instruction in adaptive coping skills, including relaxation training. Relaxation training has been used to decrease stress in students with learning disabilities (Hegarty & Last, 1997; Omizo, 1981).

In addition, it has been found that parental support is very important and can be enhanced by the school providing parent support and parent support training for students (Volenski, 1995).

REFERENCES

Hegarty, J. R., & Last, A. (1997). Relaxation training for people who have severe/profound and multiple learning disabilities. *British Journal of Developmental Disabilities*, *43*(85), 122–139.

Kershaw, J. D. (1973). *Handicapped children in the ordinary school: Stresses in children*. New York, NY: Crane & Russak.

Omizo, M. M. (1981). Relaxation training and biofeedback with hyperactive elementary school children. *Elementary School Guidance & Counseling*, *15*(4), 329–332.

Rutter, M. (1981). Stress, coping, and development: Some issues and some questions. *Journal of Child Psychology & Psychiatry*, *22*, 323–356.

Schultz, E. (1980). Teaching coping skills for stress and anxiety. *Teaching Exceptional Children*, *13*(3), 12–15.

Tymitz-Wolf, B. (1984). An analysis of EMR children's worries about mainstreaming. *Education & Training of the Mentally Retarded*, *19*, 157–168.

Volenski, L. T. (1995). Building support systems for parents of handicapped children: The parent education and guidance program. *Psychology in the Schools*, *32*(2), 124–129.

Westling, D. L. (1986). *Introduction to mental retardation*. Englewood Cliffs, NJ: Prentice Hall.

ANNE M. BAUER
University of Cincinnati

See also Self-Concept

STRONG INTEREST INVENTORY

The Strong Interest Inventory (SVIB-SCII, Fourth Edition; Hansen & Campbell, 1985) assesses an individual's interests in occupations, hobbies, leisure activities, and school subjects. The test has a long history, with its first edition, the Strong Vocational Interest Blank (SVIB), being published over 70 years ago. There have been major changes since the SVIB, most notably a gender equity process that began in 1971. Also, a theoretical framework, Holland's hexagonal model of career types was incorporated into the test. The most recent revision occurred in 1985, and with it came 17 new vocational-technical occupational groups, six newly emerging professional occupations, and updated norms.

The SVIB-SCII is a paper-and-pencil measure in which the respondent is asked to indicate "Like," "Dislike," or "Indifferent" to the items. The test takes an average of 30 minutes to complete and was designed for use with adults and 16- to 18-year-olds with a sixth-grade reading ability. The SVIB-SCII is machine scored, and responses are compared to the interests of people in a wide variety of jobs. The test yields five types of information: scores on 6 General Occupational Themes, 23 Basic Interest Scales, and 207 Occupational Scales. Additionally, there are 2 Special Scales (Academic Comfort and Introversion-Extroversion), and Administrative Indexes (validity scales). Interpretive information includes a profile with an optional interpretive report.

The psychometric properties of the SVIB-SCII are excellent. Over 48,000 people taken from 202 occupational samples were used to construct the Occupational Scales. The fourth edition of the *Manual for the SVIB-SCII* describes the reliability, validity, and sampling procedures for all the scales in detail.

The SVIB-SCII is easy to administer and provides easily understood interpretive results. Critiques of the inventory praise its outstanding interpretive information and excellent psychometric properties (Busch, 1995). One issue with the test is the authors' failure to report response rates for the occupational samples; response rates can affect the representativeness of the sample and thus the predictive validity of the scales (Busch, 1995; Worthen & Sailor, 1995). However, despite the concern, the SVIB-SCII has been described as "by far the best available interest inventory" (Worthen & Sailor, 1995).

REFERENCES

Busch, J. C. (1995). In J. C. Conoley & J. C. Impara (Eds.), *The twelfth mental measurements yearbook*. Lincoln, NE: Buros Institute of Mental Measurements.

Hansen, J. C., & Campbell, D. P. (1985). *Manual for the Strong Interest Inventory* (4th ed.). Stanford, CA: Stanford University Press.

Worthen, B. R., & Sailor, P. (1995). In J. C. Conoley & J. C. Impara (Eds.), *The twelfth mental measurements yearbook*. Lincoln, NE: Buros Institute of Mental Measurements.

DEBRA Y. BROADBOOKS
California School of Professional Psychology

See also **Habilitation; Vocational Rehabilitation Counseling**

STRUCTURE OF INTELLECT

J. P. Guilford (1967), in his work *The Nature of Human Intelligence*, developed a model of intelligence based on his factor analysis of human intellect. The structure of intellect theory (SI) grew out of experimental applications of the multivariate method of multiple-factor analysis. The basic research was carried out on a population of young adults but successive investigations have substantiated Guilford's initial findings with subject samples ranging in age from 5 to 15 years. Implications from this theory and its concepts have led to many new interpretations of already known facts of general significance in psychology.

The major aim of the structure of intellect theory is to give the concept of intelligence a firm, comprehensive, and systematic theoretical foundation. A second aim is to put intelligence within the mainstream of general psychological theory. For his frame of reference, Guilford has chosen what he terms a morphological, as opposed to hierarchical, model. His model, which he also refers to as the "three faces of intellect," includes three categories along with their subclassifications. The three dimensions are content,

referring to types of information that are discriminable by the individual; products, the outcomes of intellectual operations; and operations, referring to the primary kinds of intellectual activities or processes.

The model or cube is a three-dimensional diagram. The operations dimension is broken down into five subclassifications: evaluation, convergent production, divergent production, memory, and cognition. The six types of products are units, classes, relations, systems, transformations, and implications. The four types of content are figural, symbolic, semantic, and behavioral. The complete schema is diagrammed as an array of 120 ($5 \times 4 \times 6$) predicted cells of intellectual abilities. The 120 types of abilities are derived from the intersection of the three-way classification system. Of the 120 discrete factors, at least 82 have been demonstrated; others are still under investigation.

Although Guilford's model has not been widely used, it has pointed to a theory that has been lacking from the beginning of the era of mental testing—to give the concept of intelligence a firm, comprehensive, and systematic theoretical foundation. Guilford maintains that a firm foundation must be based on detailed observation; that the theory itself should include all aspects of intelligence; and that the result must be systematic, embracing numerous phenomena within a logically ordered structure. The outcome is his structure of intellect.

REFERENCE

Guilford, J. P. (1967). *The nature of human intelligence*. New York, NY: McGraw-Hill.

CECELIA STEPPE-JONES
North Carolina Central University

See also **Intelligence; Intelligence Testing**

STUDENT STYLES QUESTIONNAIRE

The Student Styles Questionnaire (SSQ; Oakland, Horton, and Glutting, 1996), a 69-item self-report measure of temperament, assesses four bipolar temperament styles displayed by children ages 8 through 17: extroversion-introversion, practical-imaginative, thinking-feeling, organized-flexible. Its theoretical structure is based on Jung's typology theory of personality (Jung, 1921, 1946) and is consistent with the dimensions on the Myers-Briggs Type Indicator (Myers & McCaulley, 1985).

Extroversion-introversion styles address sources from which people derive energy. Those with an extroverted preference generally draw energy from others and their environments, while those with introverted preferences generally draw energy from themselves through reliance on solitude and personal time. Practical-imaginative styles address qualities on which people rely to acquire and store information. Those with practical styles generally rely on their five senses and what worked previously, while those with imaginative styles generally rely on theory and broader generalizations. Thinking-feeling styles address preferences for forming judgments. Those with thinking preferences generally rely on their thoughts and value logic over sentiment, while those with feeling preferences generally rely on their feelings and subjective judgments. Organized-flexible styles address when one makes decisions. Those with organized styles generally make decisions as early as possible, while those with flexible styles often prefer to postpone decisions as long as possible.

The purposes of the SSQ are to identify talent, adjust for possible personal weaknesses, enhance personal and social understanding, identify preferred learning styles, promote educational development (Horton & Oakland, 1997), identify students with special needs, explore prevocational interests, and facilitate research and evaluation.

The SSQ was normed on 7,902 children and youths ages 8 through 17 nationally stratified by age, gender, race/ethnicity, geographic area, and school type. Test-retest reliability coefficients, examined over 7 months, ranged from .67 (practical-imaginative) to .80 (extroverted-introverted) for the four dimensions, with a mean of .74. Estimates of internal consistency are in the high .90s.

Factor analyses support the four-factor model (Oakland et al., 1996; Stafford & Oakland, 1996a,b). Approximately 40 studies examined the construct validity of the SSQ (Oakland et al., 1996). Additional studies provide support for the equivalence of SSQ constructs for children of various ages, three racial-ethnic groups (African American, Anglo-Americans, and Hispanic-Americans), and gender (Stafford & Oakland, 1996a,b). The temperament patterns of youths as measured by the SSQ and Myers-Briggs Type Indicator are consistent (Oakland et al., 1996). Studies have examined temperament patterns exhibited by children who are gifted academically (Oakland, Joyce, Horton, & Glutting, 2000), are blind (Oakland, Banner, & Livingston, 2000), and display conduct and oppositional defiant disorders (Joyce & Oakland, 2005); relationships between children's temperament and vocational interests (Oakland, Stafford, Horton, & Glutting, 2001); and differences in achievement associated with learning and teaching styles (Horton & Oakland, 1997).

Oakland and international colleagues are conducting various cross-national studies that examine the development of temperament in children and youths. Current published studies focus on Australia (Oakland, Faulkner, & Bassett, 2005), Hungary (Katona & Oakland, 2000), People's Republic of China (Oakland & Lu, 2006), and Costa Rica (Oakland & Mata, in press). SSQ data on children in Brazil, Gaza, Greece, Iran, Israel, Nigeria, Romania, South Africa, South Korea, and Zimbabwe have been acquired and are being prepared for publication.

REFERENCES

Horton, C., & Oakland, T. (1996). *Classroom applications booklet.* San Antonio, TX: Psychological Corporation.

Horton, C., & Oakland, T. (1997). Temperament-based learning styles as moderators of academic achievement. *Adolescence, 32,* 131–141.

Joyce, D., & Oakland, T. (2005). Temperament differences among children with conduct disorders and oppositional defiant disorders. *The California School Psychologist, 10,* 125–136.

Jung, C. G. (1921). *Psychological type.* New York, NY: Harcourt, Brace, & Co.

Jung, C. G. (1946). *Psychological type.* (H. G. Baynes, Trans.). New York, NY: Harcourt. (Original work published 1921)

Katona, N., & Oakland, T. (2000). The development of temperament in Hungarian children. *Hungarian Journal of Psychology, 1,* 17–29.

Myers, I. B., & McCaulley, M. (1985). *Manual: A guide to the development and use of the Myers-Briggs type indicator.* Palo Alto, CA: Consulting Psychological Press.

Oakland, T., Banner, D., & Livingston, R. (2000). Temperament-based learning styles of visually impaired children. *Journal of Visual Impairment and Blindness,* January, 26–33.

Oakland, T., Faulkner, M., & Bassett, K. (2005). Temperament styles of children from Australia and the United States. *Australian Educational and Developmental Psychologist, 19,* 35–51.

Oakland, T., Horton, C., & Glutting, J. (1996). *Student styles questionnaire.* San Antonio, TX: Psychological Corporation.

Oakland, T., Joyce, D., Horton, C., & Glutting, J. (2000). Temperament-based learning styles of identified gifted and nongifted students. *Gifted Child Quarterly, 44,* 183–189.

Oakland, T., & Lu, L. (2006). Temperament styles of children from the People's Republic of China and the United States. *School Psychology International, 27*(2), 192–208.

Oakland, T., & Mata, A. (in press). Temperament styles of children from Costa Rica and the United States. *Journal of Psychological Types.*

Oakland, T., Stafford, M., Horton, C., & Glutting, J. (2001). Temperament and vocational preferences: Age, gender and racial-ethnic comparisons using the Student Styles Questionnaire. *Journal of Career Assessment, 9*(3), 297–314.

Stafford, M., & Oakland, T. (1996a). Racial-ethnic comparisons of temperament constructs for three age groups using the Student Styles Questionnaire. *Measurement and Evaluation in Counseling and Development, 19*(2), 100–110.

Stafford, M., & Oakland, T. (1996b). Validity of temperament constructs using the Student Styles Questionnaire: Comparisons for three racial-ethnic groups. *Journal of Psychoeducational Assessment, 14,* 109–120.

JACK R. DEMPSEY
University of Florida

STUDY OF MATHEMATICALLY PRECOCIOUS YOUTH

The Study of Mathematically Precocious Youth (SMPY) was officially begun on September 1, 1971, by Julian Stanley. Stanley had become intrigued by a 13½-year-old boy who scored extremely well on several standardized mathematics tests. A fear that students such as this one might fail to be identified and appropriately served led Stanley to devise the SMPY at Johns Hopkins University.

The SMPY is geared to the top 1%–3% of mathematics students in U.S. junior high schools (Johnson, 1983). These students often display swift and comprehensive reasoning, an inclination to analyze mathematical structure, a tendency to deal in the abstract, and an untiring approach to working on mathematics (Heid, 1983). Indeed, students accepted into SMPY are so mathematically advanced that they must score at least 700 on the math portion of the Scholastic Aptitude Test (SAT-M) before their 13th birthday (Stanley & Benbow, 1983). Allowances are made for those students who are over 13 years of age. They must score an additional 10 points on the SAT-M for each month of age over 13 years. For example, a student who is 13 years, 2 months, must score at least 720 on the SAT-M before being considered for the SMPY (Stanley & Benbow, 1983).

Once the students have been selected, the goal of the program is to accelerate learning in mathematics. Stanley and Benbow (1982) note that there is no sense in allowing precocious students to languish in slow-paced math classes. Math classes, they feel, should be taught according to individual students' abilities and achievements. Consequently, precocious students should spend less time in math classes, allowing for potential concentration on related topics such as physics (Tursman, 1983). Additionally, by spending less time in math class, mathematically precocious students would spend less time in school. This would allow them to take college courses while still in high school and to enter college at an earlier age (Stanley & Benbow, 1982). This is a goal of SMPY and is strongly emphasized by Stanley as a way to get these students quickly into the workforce (Stanley, 1997).

The SMPY is essentially a summer program. Students are identified, evaluated, and selected for the program throughout the year. Once selected, students participate in an 8-week program, meeting 1 day a week for slightly less than 5 hours per day. Throughout the instruction, the student-teacher ratio never exceeds 1:5 (Stanley, 1980). All instructors are former SMPY graduates and usually range in age from 13 to 20. During this approximately 35-hour program, students will typically demonstrate mastery of material 2 school years beyond where they began (Stanley, 1980).

To achieve such dramatic results, SMPY uses a "diagnostic testing followed by prescriptive instruction" method of instruction (Stanley, 1980; Stanley & Benbow, 1983).

An evaluation determines what the student does not know. The instructors then help the student learn the information without taking an entire course (Stanley & Benbow, 1982).

REFERENCES

Heid, M. K. (1983). Characteristics and special needs of the gifted students in mathematics. *Mathematics Teacher, 76*, 221–226.

Johnson, M. L. (1983). Identifying and teaching mathematically gifted elementary school children. *Arithmetic Teacher, 30*, 55–56.

Stanley, J. C. (1980). On educating the gifted. *Educational Researcher, 9*, 8–12.

Stanley, J. C. (1997). Varieties of intellectual talent. *Journal of Creative Behavior, 31*(2), 93–119.

Stanley, J. C., & Benbow, C. P. (1982). Educating mathematically precocious youth: Twelve policy recommendations. *Educational Researcher, 11*, 4–9.

Stanley, J. C., & Benbow, C. P. (1983). SMPY's first decade: Ten years of posing problems and solving them. *Journal of Special Education, 17*, 11–25.

Tursman, C. (1983). Challenging gifted students. *School Administrator, 40*, cover, 9–10, 12.

JOHN R. BEATTIE
University of North Carolina at Charlotte

See also Acceleration of Gifted Children; Advanced Placement Program; Gifted and Talented Children

STURGE-WEBER SYNDROME

Sturge-Weber syndrome is a rare, congenital, and progressive condition that affects the blood vessels in the skin and the brain. Characteristically, a large pink to purple hemangioma (a birthmark caused by abnormal distribution of blood vessels) extends over one side of the face, including the eye and neck, and is often disfiguring when there is a growth of connective tissue. The facial angioma is usually unilateral but may extend to the other side and conforms largely but not strictly to trigeminal nerve subdivisions (Wyngaarden & Smith, 1988). A similar malformation of blood vessels in the brain may cause some degree of weakness on the opposite side of the body, glaucoma, and epilepsy. This condition develops during embryonic development.

The cause of Sturge-Weber syndrome is unknown, and risk factors have not yet been recognized. The incidence is about 5 in 100,000 births (Wyngaarden & Smith, 1988), and it occurs equally in both sexes. The incidence of Sturge-Weber syndrome is thought to be 8%–15% in live births with an associated portwine stain. Neurologic disorders are also prominent in patients with Sturge-Weber syndrome, and up to 89% of these patients will have seizures that are controllable with medical therapy in only 50% of cases. A smaller proportion of children with Sturge-Weber syndrome (6%) will develop hemiparesis and hemiplegia.

Characteristics

1. Facial port-wine stain
2. Convulsions (seizure disorder) beginning during the first year and worsening with age
3. Visual problems (hemianopsia)
4. Paralysis (hemiparesis-paralysis on one side)
5. Learning disabilities
6. Developmental delays of motor skills

Treatment for Sturge-Weber syndrome is symptomatic. Laser treatment is available to lighten or remove portwine stains. Anticonvulsant medications may be used to control seizures. Paralysis or weakness is treated with appropriate physical therapy. Surgery or eyedrops may be prescribed to control glaucoma. Regular ophthalmologic examinations at 6- to 12-month intervals are recommended. Skull X rays taken after the first 2 years of life usually reveal gyriform ("tramline") intracranial calcification, especially in the occipitoparietal region, due to mineral deposition in the cortex beneath the intracranial angioma (Tierney, McPhee, Papadakis, 1998). Surgical treatment of the intracranial lesion is sometimes successful in reducing seizures.

Special education services, genetic counseling, and physical therapy may benefit patients and their families because progressive mental retardation occurs in 50% of cases, along with learning disabilities—both of which require appropriate school intervention.

Although Sturge-Weber-related seizures can sometimes place patients in potentially life-threatening situations, the disease itself is not fatal. Most cases of Sturge-Weber are mild, and life expectancy is normal.

REFERENCES

Tierney, L. M., Jr., McPhee, S. J., & Papadakis, M. A. (1998). *Current medical diagnosis and treatment* (37th ed.). Stamford, CT: Appleton & Lange.

Wyngaarden, J. B., & Smith, L. H., Jr. (1988). *Cecil textbook of medicine* (18th ed.). Philadelphia, PA: Saunders.

KAREN WILEY
University of Northern Colorado

STUTTERING

Fluency disorders typically are characterized by atypical rates and rhythms of speech, repetitions, and excessive tension and struggle when speaking. The best known and probably least understood fluency disorder is stuttering. Stuttering is somewhat paradoxical in that, while it is relatively easy to identify when listening to speech, it is somewhat difficult to define (Hartman, 1994). Stuttering typically is characterized as an abnormally high occurrence of involuntary stoppages, repetitions, or prolongations in the utterance of short speech.

Stuttering occurs universally and among individuals who differ by age, race, culture, socioeconomic status, occupation, and intelligence. Research has examined neurophysiological, psychological, social, and linguistic influences on stuttering. Stuttering is more common in males than females and often runs in families, implying biological and genetic predispositions (Guitar, 1998). Further, children who are overly dependent, have an excessive need for approval, and have low tolerance for frustration are more likely to stutter. However, the exact cause of stuttering remains unknown and is likely to differ from person to person.

When referred for a stuttering evaluation, the person often is seen by a speech/language pathologist. This professional conducts an evaluation of speech and language development and considers age of onset, family history, and diagnostic criteria for this disorder. No single measure is used to accurately diagnose stuttering. Most often a speech pathologist will include a battery to assess qualities of speech including repetitions, prolongations, blocks, interjections, and restrictions in spontaneous speech and oral reading. Speech/language pathologists also may identify a need for intervention through information obtained from teachers and parents and nonverbal signs of struggle such as eye, head, and body movements.

Individuals often encounter secondary behaviors resulting from stuttering. These behaviors may include undue physical strain and effort while speaking, and avoidance of particular situations, words, sounds, or other situations that may elicit stuttering. These secondary behaviors may become more problematic than the stuttering itself.

Stuttering can affect an individual at any age. However, the onset of stuttering occurs before age 10 in 98% of cases, is most likely to occur between ages 2 and 7, and is rarely retained after puberty. Accordingly, this onset coincides with a period of rapid acquisition and expansion of speech and language skills.

Approximately 5% of North Americans have stuttered at one time in their lives, whereas only 1% stutter at any given time (Mansson, 2000; Yairi & Ambrose, 1999). Normal development and growth account for many cases of recovery without any professional treatment.

Stuttering modification therapy is a popular speech-language technique in treating this population. This approach focuses on the person's attitudes and feelings about stuttering while concurrently helping the person stutter in a more relaxed way in an attempt to make their speech sound more normal. Stuttering modification therapy is based on the idea that feelings of anticipation, anxiety, and expectation contribute to stuttering.

Fluency shaping therapy is a behavioral therapy that focuses on developing fluency. The goal of fluency shaping therapy is to slow the pace of speech, which may result in controlled fluency or spontaneous recovery. Other forms of therapy focus on eliminating avoidances or utilize group therapy with other children who stutter to provide a comfortable environment for speech practice. Approaches also may focus on coping, relaxation techniques, and/or handling teasing from other students. However, no single treatment has emerged as the most effective.

REFERENCES

Guitar, B. (1998). *Stuttering: An integrated approach to its nature and treatment* (2nd ed.). Baltimore, MD: Williams & Wilkins.

Hartman, B. T. (1994). *The neuropsychology of developmental stuttering*. San Diego, CA: Singular.

Mansson, H. (2000). Childhood stuttering: Incidence and development. *Journal of Fluency Disorders, 25,* 47–57.

Yairi, E., & Ambrose, N. G. (1999). Early childhood stuttering I: Persistency and recovery rates. *Journal of Speech, Language, and Hearing Research, 42,* 1097–1112.

Eric Rossen
University of Florida

See also Speech Therapy

ST. VITUS DANCE

St. Vitus Dance, also referred to as Sydenham's chorea, is a transitory movement disorder of childhood that is characterized by purposeless, arrhythmic, involuntary movements of the arms, legs, and face; muscle weakness; and emotional lability (May & Koch, 1999). Movement difficulties may occur on one side of the body (hemichorea) or may be generalized (Goldenberg, Ferraz, Fonseca, Hilario, Bastos, & Sachetti, 1992).

The term chorea was first used in 1686 by British physician Thomas Sydenham to refer to the frenzied movements of religious fanatics who traveled to the shrine of St. Vitus during the Middle Ages. Although its etiology and pathophysiology are unconfirmed, Sydenham's chorea appears to be a delayed complication of Lancefild Group A betahemolytic streptococcal infections (Merck Manual, 2001). It also occurs in about 10% of children following an episode of acute rheumatic fever, with reduced incidence over the last 50 years (Merck Manual, 2001). Sydenham's chorea is thought to be associated with excessive dopamine activity in the basal ganglia (Shannon & Fenichel, 1990) and with immunological response factors, such as the production of antineuronal antibodies (Swedo et al., 1993). Sydenham's chorea may serve as a precursor to other choreas in adulthood; for example, Cardoso et al. (1999), studied 129 adults with chorea gravidarum, many of whom had a history of Syndenham chorea or rheumatic fever during childhood. Sydenham's chorea has also been linked with other disorders, such as obsessive-compulsive behaviors (Mercadante et al., 2000; Swedo et al., 1993) and attention deficit/hyperactivity disorder (ADHD); in fact, Mercadante et al. (2000) concluded that ADHD appears to be a risk factor for Sydenham's chorea in children with rheumatic fever.

Initial suspicions of Sydenham's chorea may occur following parent reports of unusual clumsiness in their children or teacher reports of suddenly illegible handwriting. There is some controversy in the literature regarding its onset, with some sources claiming that symptoms appear gradually and others describing a more abrupt onset. At present, Sydenham's chorea is diagnosed primarily on clinical presentation, as laboratory tests may be negative for infection and the electrocardiogram and neurological exam may be normal. Differential diagnosis must consider familial chorea, mass lesion in the central nervous system, effects of other drugs or toxins, collagen vascular diseases, repetitive spasms, and uncontrolled movements associated with cerebral palsy and attention-deficit/hyperactivity disorder (Merck Manual, 2001).

Characteristics

1. Sydenham's chorea often follows streptococcal infection or rheumatic fever, with up to a 12-month delay before the first symptoms appear. It occurs most often in temperate climates during the summer and early fall.

2. It occurs primarily in prepubescent girls, with peak incidence between 7 and 14 years; occurrence after age 20 is rare.

3. Generally, onset is gradual, and the course is variable, beginning with nervousness, fine motor difficulties, and occasional grimacing. Speech may become indistinct, and characteristic choreic movements may develop.

4. Choreic movements are often aggravated by stress or efforts at control but disappear during sleep.

5. Other signs include a clucking sound during speech production due to tongue contractions, difficulty with tongue control when it is protruded, flexion of the wrists and hyperextension of the joints in the hands and arms when the arms are extended, and spasmodic contractions of the hands during intentional grasping of objects.

6. Associated problems may include hypotonia, emotional lability, obsessive-compulsive behaviors, hyperactivity, and distractibility (Swedo et al., 1993).

Treatment of Sydenham's chorea is symptomatic and may include mild sedatives, tranquilizers, or muscle relaxants to control involuntary movements and to prevent self-injury from flailing arms and legs. Antibiotics such as penicillin and erythromycin are often prescribed until adulthood to minimize complications and prevent recurrence of symptoms (National Institute of Neurological Disorders and Stroke [NINDS], 2000). Drug treatment has been attempted with varying degrees of success as well as risk. For example, antipsychotics such as haloperidol and risperidone have been found effective, but the former is associated with side effects such as tardive dyskinesia, and the latter is not approved for use in children. Anecdotal evidence suggests that severe forms of Sydenham's chorea that do not respond to antipsychotics may be treated effectively with corticosteroids. In addition, neuroleptics such as pimozide have been found successful in some cases (e.g., Shannon & Fenichel, 1990) but unsuccessful in others (e.g., May & Koch, 1999). Finally, the presence of neuronal antibodies in more than 90% of affected children (Swedo et al., 1993) has suggested the use of intravenous immunoglobulin therapy as an alternative to other forms of treatment; in fact, May and Koch (1999) reported rapid improvement in two young girls who had not responded to more conventional therapies. The prognosis for Sydenham's chorea is generally favorable, with spontaneous recovery in 3 to 6 months without lasting effects on muscle control, intelligence, personality, or emotions. However, relapses are not uncommon, and mild signs of chorea may appear intermittently during the year following an acute episode.

Children with Sydenham's chorea may not qualify for special educational services, primarily because of the brief duration of symptoms. They may, however, be eligible for temporary accommodations, depending on the severity of symptoms and the degree to which they interfere with normal functioning in the classroom. Children may need help with handwriting, managing school items, dressing, and feeding. Instruction in self-care skills may allow the child to maintain independence, and an emphasis on safety skills may minimize the possibility of harm to self and others. Older children with Sydenham's chorea may be particularly susceptible to feelings of embarrassment and shame about their inability to control their movements and the reaction that their behaviors elicit from uninformed peers and adults. Such children will need education about their condition, emotional support, and, if necessary, psychotherapy or counseling, both for themselves and their families. Many individuals who come into contact with affected children may be frightened by the nature of Sydenham's chorea; it is essential that they be educated about its possible manifestations, reminded about its temporary nature, and reassured that it is not contagious. Finally, although affected children may need to stay home during the acute phase of the condition, they should be encouraged to return to school as soon as possible.

Additional research that confirms the etiology and pathophysiology of Sydenham's chorea may lead to improved efforts at prevention and treatment. Preferred drug therapies with minimal side effects must be identified. Finally, controlled research studies that focus on the issue of differential diagnosis may help improve management of this condition.

REFERENCES

Cardoso, F., Vargas, A. P., Cunningham, M. C. Q., Amaral, S. V., Guerra, A. A., & Horizonte, A. (1999). Chorea gravidarum: New lessons from an old disease. *Neurology, 52*(Suppl. 2), A121.

Goldenberg, J., Ferraz, M. B., Fonseca, A. S., Hilario, M. O., Bastos, W., & Sachetti, S. (1992). Sydenham's chorea: Clinical and laboratory findings: Analysis of 187 cases (abstract only). *Revista de Paulista Medicina, 110*(4), 152–157.

May, A. C., & Koch, T. (1999). Successful treatment of Sydenham's chorea with intravenous immunoglobulin: Two cases. *Neurology, 52*(Suppl. 2), A42.

Mercadante, M. G. T., Busatto, G. F., Lombroso, P. J., Prado, L., Rosario-Campos, M. C., do Valle, R., . . . Miguel, E. C. (2000). The psychiatric symptoms of rheumatic fever. *American Journal of Psychiatry, 157*(12), 2036–2038.

Merck Manual. (2001). *Sydenham's chorea.* Whitehouse Station, NJ: Merck.

National Institute of Neurological Disorders and Stroke. (2000). NINDS Sydenham chorea information page. Retrieved from http://www.ninds.nih.gov/

Shannon, K. M., & Fenichel, G. M. (1990). Pimozide treatment of Sydenham's chorea. *Neurology, 40*(1), 186.

Swedo, S. E., Leonard, H. L., Schapiro, M. B., Casey, B. J., Mannheim, G. B., Lenane, M. C., & Rettew, D. C. (1993). Sydenham's chorea: Physical and psychological symptoms of St. Vitus Dance. *Pediatrics, 91*(4), 706–713.

MARY M. CHITTOORAN
Saint Louis University

See *also* Sydenham's Chorea

2502   SUBACUTE SCLEROSING PANENCEPHALITIS

SUBACUTE SCLEROSING PANENCEPHALITIS

Subacute sclerosing panencephalitis (SSPE), or Dawson encephalitis, is a progressive, usually fatal neurological disorder typically affecting only children and adolescents. SSPE causes intellectual deterioration, convulsive seizures, and motor abnormalities.

SSPE tends to occur several years after contracting the measles (rubella) virus. Often, the victims and their families are unaware of the dangers of SSPE, as the child has the appearance of completely recovering from the measles infection. Initial symptoms are subtle and insidious (Pedatric Database, 2000). Parents often will not recognize that a child is suffering from this neurological disorder because the physical symptoms of SSPE are few until the disease is advanced.

Characteristics

Initial Stage

1. Diminished performance in schoolwork (often due to forgetfulness, distractibility, and sleeplessness)
2. Bizarre behavior (aggression, changes in speech, hallucinations)
3. Myoclonic jerking (muscle spasms)

Intermediate Stage

1. Seizures
2. Dementia
3. Difficulty swallowing
4. Optic changes including papilledema (swelling of the optic nerve), cortical atrophy, and retinopathy (blindness)
5. Rigidity of body musculature

Final Phase

1. Hypothalamic complications such as hyperthermia (elevated temperature), diaphoresis (excessive sweating), and irregular pulse
2. Coma
3. Death

The diagnosis of SSPE is confirmed by electroencephalogram (EEG), elevated globulin levels, and excessive quantity of measles virus antibody in the serum and spinal fluid (Beers & Berkow, 1999). Brain imaging studies have been conducted of patients with SSPE through computerized tomography (CT) and magnetic resonance imaging (MRI). These studies have revealed cortical atrophy and ventricular enlargement in the brain as a result of SSPE (Pediatric Database, 2000; Sawaishi, Abe, Yano, Ishikawa, & Takada, 1999).

SSPE occurs worldwide, and especially in impoverished regions where immunizations are not readily available. However, the incidence of this disease has dramatically decreased in the United States and Western Europe following the implementation of widespread measles immunization programs. It is estimated that SSPE occurs in about 6–22 per million cases of measles infections and is lower in vaccinated individuals, at about one case per million (Beers & Berkow, 1999). SSPE tends to affect more males than females (2:1) and generally occurs in children and adolescents.

A risk factor for developing SSPE is the contraction of the measles infection before 1 year of age. The risk of SSPE is 16 times greater for children who are 1 year or younger than for children over 5 years old due to increased susceptibility to viral infection, immaturity of the brain, and increased danger of contracting another concurrent viral infection (Sawaishi et al., 1999).

Fatality is usually the end result of SSPE, often because of terminal bronchial pneumonia that is contracted due to the patient's weakened immune system. Affected individuals generally succumb 1 to 3 years after diagnosis, but some may survive for longer periods. There have been rare incidents of some patients having remission of SSPE (Beers & Berkow, 1999).

No specific therapy currently exists for SSPE. Supportive therapy is indicated as symptoms appear. Treatment with inosiplex (an antiviral drug) has been tried, but results are pending. Generally, only symptomatic treatment with anticonvulsants and supportive measures can be offered (Beers & Berkow, 1999).

Immunization against measles is the only known prevention for SSPE. Children are recommended to have received immunization for measles, mumps, and rubella by 15 months of age (Harrington, 1998). Caretakers are urged to contact their healthcare provider or local health clinic if their child has not completed his or her scheduled immunizations. Children who are experiencing symptoms of SSPE and who have been infected with measles or who have not been immunized against measles should be brought to medical attention immediately due to the danger of contracting SSPE.

REFERENCES

Beers, M. H., & Berkow, R. (Eds.). (1999). *Merck manual of diagnosis and therapy* (17th ed.). Whitehouse Station, NJ: Merck.

Harrington, R. G. (1998). Communicable disease in childhood: A guide for parents. In A. Canter & S. A. Carroll (Eds.), *Helping children at home and school: Handouts from your school psychologist*. Bethesda, MD: National Association of School Psychologists.

Pediatric Database. (2000, December 21). Subacute sclerosing panencephalitis. Retrieved from http://www.icondata.com/health/pedbase/.les/subacute.htm

Sawaishi, Y., Abe, T., Yano, T., Ishikawa, K., & Takada, G. (1999). SSPE following neonatal measles infection. *Pediatric Neurology, 20*(1), 63–65.

ANDREA HOLLAND
University of Texas at Austin

SUBSTANCE ABUSE

Substance abuse is often said to be one of the major public health concerns in this country. The term *substance abuse* describes abusive or harmful use of any substance. A drug is any substance that crosses from the bloodstream into the brain and that somehow changes the way the brain is functioning. By this definition, some common substances such as alcohol, nicotine, and even caffeine are considered "drugs." Although caffeine, nicotine, and alcohol are by far the most common drugs in the United States, some other drugs of abuse include marijuana, cocaine, amphetamines ("speed"), heroin and other opiates, hallucinogens (LSD, psilocybin mushrooms, peyote), depressants (barbiturates, benzodiazepines, or "downers"), and prescription drugs. In recent years, the development of "designer" drugs and newer chemical compounds has gotten a good deal of media attention. Such substances as the "date rape drugs," including Rohypnol and GHB, have been gaining in popularity in recent years. Although the use and abuse of these drugs are not nearly as prevalent as some other substances, they are causing some alarm within the community of substance-abuse treatment professionals.

Many drugs are synthesized in a laboratory. Some of the synthetic, or man-made, drugs include prescription drugs such as tranquilizers, barbiturates, sedatives, narcotics, pain medications, and some hallucinogens (LSD). Although some of these drugs are indeed chemical substances, others—such as marijuana, opium, peyote, psilocybin mushrooms, and coca leaves—are natural, organic compounds. Further, some organic plants may be chemically processed to make them more usable to the human body. For example, opium and coca leaves can be processed into heroin and cocaine, respectively (Maisto, Galizio, & Connors, 1995).

Substance abuse is not a recent phenomenon. Evidence indicates that the production of beer began in ancient Egypt as early as 5,000 BCE. Within this country alone, the use and abuse of various substances has reached epidemic proportions at a number of different periods. Tobacco use by Native Americans was apparent long before the arrival of Europeans in the Americas. In the 19th century, morphine and opium were commonly available without a prescription. With the invention of the hypodermic needle in 1840, morphine became even more common for use as a pain medication, fueling a higher prevalence of morphine addiction. Amphetamine, inhalant, hallucinogen, and marijuana use have all been prevalent at different times during our history. Alcohol was prohibited at one time in the United States because of its detrimental effects, only to be legalized and taxed several years later. Although many people consider alcohol prohibition to have been a failure in terms of an overall method of drug control, it did lead to a marked decrease in alcohol use. Lawsuits against the major tobacco companies and efforts to curb tobacco use in the United States may lead to decreases in tobacco use (Maisto et al., 1995).

The effects of different substances depend on a number of biological and psychological factors. Of course, the type of drug that is being used will affect people's experience. Individuals' biological characteristics, such as weight, gender, and initial sensitivity to a substance, may affect their reaction to a particular substance (Maisto et al., 1995). The setting in which the substance is used also affects how an individual will experience the effect of the substance (Maisto et al., 1995). Finally, people's expectations or beliefs about how the substance will affect them play a role in their reaction to a particular substance (Goldman, Brown, Christiansen, & Smith, 1991).

Although neither necessary nor sufficient for a diagnosis of substance abuse or dependence, tolerance and withdrawal symptoms are key indicators of problematic use or addiction. Tolerance and withdrawal symptoms may indicate that the individual's body has become dependent on the drug. Tolerance basically means that the individual's body has become accustomed to the substance, such that larger and larger amounts of the substance are required to produce the same effect. Tolerance is generally developed through repeated exposure to a particular substance. However, some substances with similar actions may have what is known as cross-tolerance, in which an individual who has developed a high tolerance for a particular substance may also have a high tolerance for other, similar substances, even if the substance has not actually been used. Regular use of most substances results in tolerance, at least to some degree.

Depending on the particular substance, abrupt cessation of the substance after a high tolerance has developed may result in withdrawal symptoms. Withdrawal symptoms from any particular drug are experienced most commonly as the direct opposite of the initial effect of the substance and can be psychological, physiological, or both, depending on the substance. Substances such as marijuana and hallucinogens cause no marked physical withdrawal symptoms, but abrupt cessation of use may result in psychological distress that may be severe. Other substances, especially compounds like alcohol, barbiturates, tranquilizers, and some pain medications, cause severe physical pain as well as psychological distress. Although withdrawal from some substances leads to serious enough consequences, such as severe distress, pain, and impairment in functioning, withdrawal from other substances may lead to seizures, coma, and even death.

In addition to experiencing tolerance and withdrawal, many users may become preoccupied with a substance, focusing much of their time and attention on finding, purchasing, and using it. Many people experience craving, or an intense desire to use the substance, when they stop using. Furthermore, some users become so preoccupied with using a substance that they are unable to function in their normal everyday lives.

A number of variations of substance abuse are included in the *Diagnostic and Statistical Manual of Mental Disorders*, fourth edition (*DSM-IV;* American Psychiatric Association, 1994). Criteria are specified in *DSM-IV* for substance intoxication, withdrawal, abuse, and dependence. The major criterion for diagnosis of substance abuse according to the *DSM-IV* is "a maladaptive pattern of substance use manifested by recurrent and significant adverse consequences related to the repeated use of substances." A child or adolescent who is abusing a substance may show a number of behavior changes, including failure to complete school work, marked decreases in academic performance, behavior problems at school and home, problems with the legal system, fighting, arguing, and problems with peers. Substance dependence, by contrast, is more severe than substance abuse. According to the *DSM-IV*, substance dependence is indicated by at least three of the following symptoms: marked tolerance, withdrawal symptoms, using more of the substance than was intended, inability to control or stop using, a desire to stop using, disruption in normal everyday functioning and activities, and continuing to use the substance even after knowing that the use is causing physical or psychological problems. Note that while tolerance and withdrawal are typical hallmarks of addiction, these criteria are neither necessary nor sufficient to indicate substance dependence. One of the reasons that these criteria are not necessary for a diagnosis of substance dependence is the fact that some substances, such as marijuana and most hallucinogens, cause few marked physiological withdrawal symptoms. Thus, substance dependence may be indicated by a disruption in functioning in a number of areas of an individual's life (American Psychiatric Association, 1994).

Although many people assume that the highest rates of substance abuse are in adults, the highest rates of heavy alcohol use and of marijuana use are in those aged 18–25 years (American Psychiatric Association, 1994; U.S. Department of Health and Human Services, 1993). The initial substance use that may eventually lead to abuse or dependence generally begins in adolescence. Adolescents who show symptoms of abuse or dependence are less likely to complete school than those who do not (American Psychiatric Association, 1994). Therefore, and obviously, educators and health professionals need to pay particular attention to the problem of substance abuse in adolescence and young adulthood.

Apparently, little research is available on substance abuse in children enrolled in special education programs. One study on the possible association between special education status and substance abuse yielded alarming results. Gress and Boss (1996) surveyed students from grades 4–12 and found differences in substance use between students in special education and noncategorical classes, especially for students in intermediate (4–6) and junior high (7–8) grades. Some of the most striking differences were found between students in the intermediate grades. For instance, 20% of severely behaviorally disabled but only 2.3% of noncategorical students used marijuana. Interestingly, whereas a high percentage of students with severe behavioral disabilities and specific learning disabilities used alcohol, amphetamines, and inhalants, a lower percentage of students with developmental disabilities used these substances than did noncategorical students. The authors suggest that substance abuse among students in special education programs is related to several factors, including unmet needs for attachment and close relationships, difficulty establishing a "self-identity," a need to have a certain image within the eyes of their peers, and a need for immediate gratification. Common to all children, these factors may be especially important to students in special education who want to fit in. Gress and Boss (1996) suggest that students with serious disabilities may lack some of the necessary internal skills to deal with unmet needs. Risk of substance abuse may increase as a result of psychological, emotional, and social problems related to their specific disabilities (Gress & Boss, 1996).

Since substance use begins to be a problem for many people when they are children and adolescents, many educators and substance abuse professionals focus on prevention of substance use and abuse in this population. A number of different models are in place for prevention of substance use with children and teenagers. One that has gained recent popularity is a social norms approach, in which prevention campaigns are designed to change people's attitudes about social norms regarding substance use. Other methods of substance abuse prevention efforts geared toward children and adolescents include restricting the availability of particular substances, drink/drug refusal training, providing substance-free activities, mentoring programs, values clarification, and the development of appropriate stress management and social skills (Maisto et al., 1995).

Many different treatment methods exist to help people with substance abuse problems. Formal counseling or psychological treatment is available for individuals with substance abuse problems in inpatient, outpatient, and day treatment facilities, depending on the needs of the individual. Many people choose to attend self-help groups, such as Alcoholics Anonymous, Narcotics Anonymous, Women for Sobriety, or Rational Recovery.

Important to note is that although many people in the United States experience substance abuse problems, many others are affected by another person's substance abuse. Many children are affected by the substance abuse of their parents, siblings, extended family members, or friends. Educators should be familiar with issues related to substance abuse and be able to listen nonjudgmentally to the concerns of their students. When a child is experiencing difficulty as a result of either his or her own substance abuse or that of another person, the child should have access to a school counselor, psychologist, or social worker who can provide counseling and resources for the student.

REFERENCES

American Psychiatric Association. (1994). *Diagnostic and statistical manual of mental disorders* (4th ed.). Washington, DC: Author.

Goldman, M., Brown, S., Christiansen, B., & Smith, G. (1991). Alcoholism and memory: Broadening the scope of alcohol-expectancy research. *Psychological Bulletin, 110*, 137–146.

Gress, J., & Boss, M. (1996). Substance abuse differences among students receiving special education services. *Child Psychiatry and Human Development, 26*, 235–236.

Maisto, S., Galizio, M., & Connors, G. (1995). *Drug use and abuse.* Orlando, FL: Harcourt Brace College Publishers.

U.S. Department of Health and Human Services (USDHHS). (1993). *Alcohol and health.* Rockville, MD: Author.

PAMELA M. RICHMAN
ALISON SHANER
University of North Carolina at Wilmington

See *also* **Chemically Dependent Youth; Drug Abuse**

SUBSTANTIA NIGRA

The substantia nigra houses the cell bodies of dopamine containing neurons that project to the striatum (putamen and caudate nucleus). This so-called nigrostriatal pathway is the major dopamine pathway in the brain. The substantia nigra is a midbrain structure and is darkly pigmented, hence its name (i.e., black substance or black body). The nigrostriatal pathway is an important pathway in the extrapyramidal motor system, which controls background movement. Because of the importance of dopamine in the regulatory control of motor as well as emotional functioning, the nigrostriatal system has been implicated in a variety of neurobehavioral disorders (Andreasen, 1984). In particular, a breakdown of normal functioning of the dopaminergic system has been strongly implicated in schizophrenia (Andreasen, 1984). Also, other lines of investigation have suggested that

dopamine plays a role in hyperactivity and attention deficit disorder (Shaywitz, Shaywitz, Cohen, & Young, 1983) and Rett syndrome (Segawa, 1997). The motor maladroitness frequently seen in learning-disabled children may be related in some fashion to basal ganglia/nigrostriatal irregularities (Duane, 1985; Rudel, 1985). The prototype neurologic disorder with primary substantia nigra involvement, and hence dopamine loss, is Parkinson's disease (Kolb & Whishaw, 1985).

REFERENCES

Andreasen, N. C. (1984). *The broken brain.* Cambridge, England: Harper & Row.

Duane, D. (1985). Written language underachievement: An overview of the theoretical and practical issues. In F. H. Duffy & N. Geschwind (Eds.), *Dyslexia: A neuroscientific approach to clinical evaluation.* Boston, MA: Little, Brown.

Kolb, B., & Whishaw, I. Q. (1985). *Fundamentals of human neuropsychology.* New York, NY: Freeman.

Rudel, R. G. (1985). The definition of dyslexia: Language and motor deficits. In F. H. Duffy & N. Geschwind (Eds.), *Dyslexia: A neuroscientific approach to clinical evaluation.* Boston, MA: Little, Brown.

Segawa, M. (1997). Pathophysiology of Rett syndrome from the standpoint of early catecholamine disturbance. *European Child & Adolescent Psychiatry, 6*(1), 56–60.

Shaywitz, S. E., Shaywitz, B. A., Cohen, D. J., & Young, J. G. (1983). Monoaminergic mechanisms in hyperactivity. In M. Rutter (Ed.), *Developmental neuropsychiatry.* New York, NY: Guilford Press.

ERIN D. BIGLER
Brigham Young University

See *also* **Dopamine; Putamen**

SUBTEST SCATTER

Subtest scatter refers to the variability of an individual's subtest scores. The highs and lows of the profile indicate strengths and weaknesses on specific subtests. Differences between composite scores for an individual also are termed scatter. While the term *subtest scatter* may be aptly applied to any multiple subtest battery of basic skills, reading achievement, adaptive behavior, or other tests, the term has been popularized by its association with intellectual assessment. Exactly what role scatter has in diagnosing and differentiating among populations has not been determined. Is scatter a valid indicator for diagnostic purposes, or is it limited to identifying a subject's abilities and achievements in various areas? The believers in the significance of scatter have developed several diagnostic schemes that can be used to differentiate among populations.

Kaufman (1994) points out that scatter, significant differences in abilities measured by the Wechsler Intelligence Scale for Children (WISC-III), occurs frequently in the normal population. On the basis of this finding, he emphasizes the importance of being certain that the intersubtest variability is indeed rare in comparison with that of typically developing children before associating the scatter with abnormality. However, certain characteristic scatter has been consistently found for specific groups. Low scores on arithmetic, coding, information, and digit span subtests of the WISC-III have been shown to characterize the performance of many groups of children with learning disabilities. This has been refuted (Dumont & Willis, 1995). It has been concluded, however, that learning disabilities are more likely to be indicated by intraindividual differences than by set profiles.

Scatter has been applied to problems other than learning disabilities. Different types of intellectual disabilities have been described in terms of scatter (Roszkowski & Spreat, 1982). Organically caused intellectual disabilities exhibited more scatter in Wechsler Adult Intelligence Scale (WAIS) scores than environmentally caused deficiency, but not to a significant degree. Greater scatter may be linked to lower-functioning individuals. Large amounts of scatter on intelligence tests can also be associated with high degrees of maladaptive behaviors (Roszkowski & Spreat, 1983) and social-emotional problems (Greenwald, Harder, & Fisher, 1982). Thus scatter can be associated with behavioral, emotional, and organic disorders, as well as with the more commonly thought of learning disabilities.

There may be evidence linking scatter to various disorders, but it is questionable whether it is strong enough to warrant its use as a diagnostic tool. The greatest portion of the evidence says no (Kavale & Forness, 1984). Subtest scatter may be useful in specifying particular strengths and weaknesses of an individual's performance and in educational intervention planning. Caution is needed with interpretation of scatter and profile analysis, and flexibility is recommended when selecting tests for a particular population (Kamphaus, 1985). Recently developed tests of intelligence argue against interpreting subtest-level scatter and instead focus on various composite indexes (e.g., Reynolds & Kamphaus, 2003).

This entry has been informed by the sources listed below.

REFERENCES

Bannatyne, H. (1971). *Language, reading, and learning disabilities*. Springfield, IL: Thomas.

Decker, S. A., & Corley, R. P. (1984). Bannatyne's "genetic dyslexic" subtype: A validation study. *Psychology in the Schools, 21*, 300–304.

Dumont, R., & Willis, J. O. (1995). Intrasubtest scatter on the WISC-III for various clinical samples vs. the standardization sample: An examination of the WISC folklore. *Journal of Psychoeducational Assessment, 13*(3), 271–285.

Greenwald, D. F., Harder, D. W., & Fisher, L. (1982). WISC scatter and behavioral competence in high-risk children. *Journal of Clinical Psychology, 38*, 397–401.

Kamphaus, R. W. (1985). Perils of profile analysis. *Information/Edge: Cognitive Assessment & Remediation, 1*, 1–4.

Kaufman, A. S. (1994). *Intelligence testing with the WISC-III*. New York, NY: Wiley.

Kavale, K. A., & Forness, S. (1984). A meta-analysis of the validity of Wechsler scale profiles and recategorizations: Patterns or parodies? *Learning Disability Quarterly, 7*, 136–156.

Reynolds, C. R., & Kamphaus, R. W. (2003). *Reynolds intellectual assessment scales*. Odessa, FL: Psychological Assessment Resources.

Roszkowski, M., & Spreat, S. (1982). Scatter as an index of organicity: A comparison of mentally retarded individuals experiencing and not experiencing concomitant convulsive disorders. *Journal of Behavioral Assessment, 4*, 311–315.

Roszkowski, M., & Spreat, S. (1983). Assessment of effective intelligence: Does scatter matter? *Journal of Special Education, 17*, 453–459.

LISA J. SAMPSON
Eastern Kentucky University

See also Factor Analysis; Intelligence; Intelligent Testing

SUDDEN INFANT DEATH SYNDROME

Sudden infant death syndrome (SIDS) is defined as the sudden death of an infant under 1 year of age that remains unexplained after a thorough investigation, which includes performance of an autopsy, examination of the death scene, and a review of the victim and family case history (National Institute of Child Health and Human Development [NICHD], 1997).

SIDS is the leading cause of death in infants between 1 month and 1 year of age. The majority of deaths due to SIDS occur by the end of the 6th month, with a peak incidence between 2 and 4 months of age (SIDS Network, 1993). The prevalence of SIDS in the United States has progressively declined from 1.2 per 1,000 live births in 1992 to 0.74 in 1,000 live births in 1996 (Burnett, 2000). SIDS occurs in all ethnicities and at all socioeconomic levels. However, Native American infants are approximately three times more likely to die of SIDS than are Caucasian infants, and African American infants are two to three times more susceptible to SIDS than Caucasian infants (NICHD, 1997). There also is a higher incidence of SIDS for low birth weight and premature infants (NICHD, 1997). Additionally, 60%–70% of SIDS victims are males, and 65% of SIDS deaths occur in autumn and winter (Burnett, 2000).

Characteristics

1. Occurs between 1 month and 1 year of age
2. Has no known cause and is currently unpredictable
3. Infant appears to be healthy prior to death
4. Death occurs very quickly, usually during sleep and with no signs of suffering
5. Causes intense grief for parents and families

(Based on information cited in SIDS Network, 1993)

Because of the currently unpredictable and unpreventable nature of SIDS, the focus has turned to risk-factor intervention. Numerous environmental and behavioral influences appear to place an infant at higher risk of dying from SIDS. For example, studies have revealed that infants who were placed to sleep on their stomachs were at a greater risk for SIDS. Therefore, caregivers can eliminate this risk factor by placing infants on their backs or sides when they go to sleep (NICHD, 1997). Other recommendations include good prenatal care; avoiding exposure of the baby to smoke, drugs, or alcohol both during pregnancy and after the birth; using firm bedding materials; avoiding overdressing the baby; taking the infant to regular well baby checkups; and breast-feeding the baby (NICHD, 1997). However, following these recommendations does not necessarily prevent death from SIDS.

When an infant dies from SIDS, this can elicit intense emotional reactions from the parents and family. The inability to explain the infant's death may provoke self-questioning and self-blaming by parents and other caregivers (Carroll & Siska, 1998). Normal reactions include guilt, anger, and grief. In addition, high rates of anxiety and depression have been found in mothers of SIDS victims (Boyle, 1997), and low income and less education have been linked to more prolonged distress (Murray & Terry, 1999). Given the detrimental effects of losing a child or a family member to SIDS, it is imperative that emphasis be placed on providing these families with information, counseling, and support. To illustrate, parent support groups are widely available, and early participation may help promote effective communication and decrease the isolation that these families feel (DeFrain, Taylor, & Ernst, 1982). Additionally, the family may benefit from individual, marital, or family counseling.

The siblings of the SIDS victim also will be significantly affected by the death of the infant. Care should be taken when informing children of the baby's death. It is recommended that parents explain the death as a result of a physical failure in the infant's body and reassure their children that this will not happen to them (DeFrain et al., 1982). Children may feel guilty and upset about their sibling's death but may not show their feelings in obvious ways (NICHD, 1997). If the child is disturbed by the death, he or she may have academic or social difficulties in school. Early identification of the child's maladjustment may be aided by considering other signs, such as bed wetting, nightmares, misbehaving, and clinging to parents (NICHD, 1997).

Future research should explore the effects of support groups and counseling on the recovery of families who have lost a baby to SIDS. Additionally, subsequent studies should examine how families of SIDS victims might be affected when they do not seek social support. Future research should focus also on the etiology and prevention of SIDS.

REFERENCES

Boyle, F. M. (1997). *Mothers bereaved by stillbirth, neonatal death or sudden infant death syndrome*. Aldershot, England: Ashgate.

Burnett, L. B. (2000, September 8). *Pediatrics, sudden infant death syndrome*. Retrieved from http://www.emedicine.com/emerg/topic407.htm

Carroll, J. L., & Siska, E. S. (1998, April 1). *SIDS: Counseling parents to reduce the risk*. Retrieved from http://www.aafp.org/afp/980401ap/carroll.html

DeFrain, J., Taylor, J., & Ernst, L. (1982). *Coping with sudden infant death*. Lexington, MA: Lexington Books.

Murray, J. A., & Terry, D. J. (1999). Parental reactions to infant death: The effects of resources and coping strategies. *Journal of Social and Clinical Psychology, 18,* 341–369.

National Institute of Child Health and Human Development (NICHD). (1997, April). Fact sheet: Sudden infant death syndrome. Retrieved from http://www.nichd.nih.gov/sids/sids_fact.htm

SIDS Network. (1993). *What is SIDS?* Retrieved from http://www.sids-network.org/sidsfact.htm

Eve N. Rosenthal
Karla Anhalt
Texas A&M University

SUGAI, GEORGE M. (1951–   )

Like many special educators, George M. Sugai came to the profession through an indirect path. While studying botany at the University of California, Santa Barbara, Sugai worked summers at Camp Harmon in Santa Cruz, California, where his interest began in working with children and youth with disabilities. After receiving his bachelor's degree in biological science, Sugai enrolled and received his master's degree and teaching certification in special education with a specialization in educating students with behavioral disorders (BD) from the University of Washington, Seattle, in 1974. Sugai taught in a special education classroom in Colorado, one of the first under the new special education law (PL 94-142).

Sugai returned to the University of Washington as a doctoral student, and further developed his interest in working with severe social behavior challenges, specifically among students with BD. Following the completion of his PhD in 1980, Sugai worked as an assistant professor at the University of Kentucky (1979–1983) and as Treatment Director at Spaulding Youth Center in Tilton, New Hampshire (1983–1984), then returned to higher education at the University of Oregon to codirect the resource consultation program with Dr. Gerald Tindal. He was promoted to professor in 1997. In 2005, Sugai accepted the Carole J. Neag Endowed Chair as professor at the University of Connecticut, where he currently works.

Sugai's research and outreach service primarily focus on building school-wide systems of positive behavior support (SWPBS). SWPBS provides a problem-solving process for teams of educators within schools to address the social behavioral needs of all students across a continuum of intensified related supports. Sugai, along with colleagues at the University of Oregon, was awarded one of the first federal grants to examine school-wide systems of support for children with disabilities, "Project PREPARE: Promoting Responsible, Empirical, and Proactive Alternatives in Regular Education for Students with Behavior Disorders." Subsequent to this initial work, Sugai has served as codirector of the "Office of Special Education Programs Center for Positive Behavioral Interventions and Supports," first funded in 1998. Sugai has also pursued several related lines of research in the areas of functional behavioral assessment, social skills, and effective academic instruction. To date, Sugai has been awarded over $25 million in extramural funding to support his research and demonstration activities along with training grants to prepare the next generation of leaders in the fields of BD and SWPBS.

In 2005, Sugai was awarded the Midwest Symposium for Leadership in Behavioral Disorders "Outstanding Leader in Behavioral Disorders." Sugai was also the 2009 recipient of the Ernie Wing Award for "Excellence in Evidence-Based Education," and has received recognition through an additional three nominations and six awards.

He serves on 12 journal editorial boards and has served as guest reviewer on many others. To date he has written 115 peer-refereed journal articles, 25 chapters, five books, and dozens of technical reports and implementation guidelines. Among his many publications are included seminal works such as his 1993 article, "School-wide and Classroom Management: Reconceptualizing the Integration and Management of Students with Behavior Problems in General Education," which lays the foundation of SWPBS; his 1996 articles with colleagues at the University of Oregon, "Integrated Approaches to Preventing Antisocial Behavior Patterns Among School-Age Children and Youth," appearing in the *Journal of Emotional and Behavioral Disorders*; "Reducing Problem Behavior Through a School-Wide System of Effective Behavioral Support: Investigation of a School-Wide Social Skills Training Program and Contextual Interventions," appearing in *School Psychology Review* in 1998; and his 1999 article, "Effective Behavior Support: A Systems Approach to Proactive School-Wide Management" appearing in *Focus on Exceptional Children*, and his 2000 article, "Applying Positive Behavioral Support and Functional Behavioral Assessment in Schools," appearing in the *Journal of Positive Behavioral Interventions*, which provides the first complete descriptions of the SWPBS process. Recently, Sugai coedited a compendium of best practices related to supporting children and youth with significant challenging behaviors in the "Handbook of Positive Behavior Support" and has extended his school-wide behavior support work into the area of Response to Intervention (Fairbanks, Simonsen, & Sugai, 2008).

In addition to his impressive track record as one of the leading scholars in BD and SWPBS, Sugai has continued to provide service and outreach to educators, families, advocacy groups, and state and federal policymakers. Sugai has given over 500 professional conference presentations, has served on federal blue ribbon panels, provides ongoing technical assistance to school districts and state departments of education, and was invited by President George W. Bush to participate in a White House–sponsored summit on behavioral and mental health challenges among children and youth. Sugai also remains an active teacher and mentor chairing 28 doctoral dissertations and providing state of the art training for thousands of preservice special education teachers.

This entry has been informed by the sources listed below.

REFERENCES

Colvin, G., Kameenui, E. J., & Sugai, G. (1993). School-wide and classroom management: Reconceptualizing the integration and management of students with behavior problems in general education. *Education and Treatment of Children, 16,* 361–381.

Fairbanks, S., Simonsen, B., & Sugai, G. (2008). Classwide secondary and tertiary tier practices and systems. *Teaching Exceptional Children, 40*(6), 44–54.

Lewis, T. J., & Sugai, G. (1999). Effective behavior support: A systems approach to proactive school-wide management. *Focus on Exceptional Children, 31*(6), 1–24.

Lewis, T. J., Sugai, G., & Colvin, G. (1998). Reducing problem behavior through a school-wide system of effective behavioral support: Investigation of a school-wide social skills training program and contextual interventions. *School Psychology Review, 27*, 446–459.

Sailor, W., Dunlap, G., Horner, R. H., & Sugai, G. (Eds.). (2009). *Handbook of positive behavior support*. New York, NY: Springer.

Sugai, G., Horner, R. H., Dunlap, G. Hieneman, M., Lewis, T. J., Nelson, C. M.,...Wilcox, B. (2000). Applying positive behavioral support and functional behavioral assessment in schools. *Journal of Positive Behavioral Interventions, 2*, 131–143.

Walker, H. M., Horner, R. H., Sugai, G., Bullis, M., Sprague, J. R., Bricker, D., & Kaufman, M. J. (1996). Integrated approaches to preventing antisocial behavior patterns among school-age children and youth. *Journal of Emotional and Behavioral Disorders, 4*, 193–256.

TIM LEWIS, PHD
University of Missouri

SUICIDAL IDEATION

Suicidal ideation describes destructive thoughts and plans about dying. All people may occasionally experience such thoughts, but in a suicidal person they are uncontrollable and chronic. Suicide can be seen as the final step on a path that begins with suicide ideation and proceeds to planning, threatening, attempting, and completing suicide (Barrios, Everett, Simon, & Brener, 2000). Some young people make suicide attempts impulsively but more initially have suicidal thoughts. Although many more youth engage in suicide ideation than actually commit suicide, suicide is a leading cause of death in that age group. The 1999 national Youth Risk Behavior Surveillance System (YRBSS) survey (Kann et al., 2000) found that in the United States, approximately 75% of all deaths among those 10–24 years of age are caused by motor-vehicle accidents, other accidents, homicide, and suicide. Of the respondents, 7.8% reported at least one suicide attempt during the 12 preceding months.

Characteristics

1. Chronic feelings of sadness and hopelessness that interfere with daily activities
2. Chronic and uncontrollable thoughts about one's own death
3. Has made specific suicide plan

Overall, during the 12 months preceding the YRBSS survey, (a) 28.3% of students felt so sad or hopeless for 2 or more consecutive weeks that they stopped some usual activities; (b) 19.3% seriously considered suicide; (c) 14.5% made a specific suicide plan; (d) 8.3% attempted suicide at least once; and (e) 2.6% made a suicide attempt that had to be treated medically. Generally, incidence in all categories except for the last was higher in female students than in male students across racial-ethnic and grade subpopulations. Racial-ethnic differences also appeared, with incidence higher in Hispanic students than in Blacks, and higher in Black students than Whites (Kann et al., 2000).

Suicidal ideation predicts not only suicide attempts in both high school and college students but also other risk-taking behaviors including not using seat belts as driver or passenger, driving after drinking alcohol, carrying weapons, and engaging in physical fights. Additionally, suggestive relationships exist between suicide ideation and playing with firecrackers, pointing a gun at someone, accepting dares, and behaving in a way that leads police to shoot at them. Suicide ideation may also be related to using drugs (tobacco, alcohol, and others) and engaging in unprotected sex (Barrios et al., 2000).

Across age, risk conditions for suicide attempts include depression (particularly with signs of hopelessness), substance abuse (particularly alcohol), schizophrenia, panic disorder, and borderline personality disorder. Additional risk conditions in adolescents are impulsive, aggressive, and antisocial behavior and history of family violence and disruption. Probability of an attempt increases with the number of conditions shown and with occurrence of a stressful event (Gliatto & Rai, 1999).

Treatment for individuals either directly manifesting suicidal ideology or a number of the above conditions initially involves detailed interviews, initially directed toward determining whether suicidal ideology has occurred, and if so, in what detail. The following is summarized from Gliatto and Rai (1999), who presented detailed information on steps in diagnosis and treatment options for potentially suicidal patients. A patient who has a specific plan, has access to the means to carry out the plan, and has suffered recent stressors should be hospitalized immediately—involuntarily if necessary. Confidentiality can be legally breached if a patient at serious risk for harming himself or herself refuses permission for the therapist to contact anyone, and family members should be informed of hospitalization. The patient should not be left alone until placed in a secure environment. Depending on the seriousness of the suicidal ideation and the number of accompanying conditions, either inpatient or outpatient treatment may be appropriate. For patients who show minimal levels of ideation, have no specific plan, are not intoxicated or showing pathological behavior, and have not previously attempted suicide, signing a "no-harm contract" may be sufficient. In the contract, the patient agrees not to harm himself or herself for a specific and brief time, generally 1 or 2 days, and to contact the therapist if anything changes. Frequent direct or telephone follow-up is necessary, as is renewal of the contract as it expires.

The National Center for Injury Prevention and Control is focusing on science-based prevention strategies to reduce injuries and deaths from suicide. Suicide prevention programs are available for adolescents and young adults (Centers for Disease Control and Prevention, 1994). School and community gatekeeper training helps school staff, community members, and clinical health care providers to identify and refer students at risk for suicide. Suicide education teaches students about suicide, warning signs, and how to seek help. Screening programs use questionnaires to identify those at high risk. Crisis centers and hotlines provide telephone counseling for suicidal persons. Intervention after a suicide focuses on friends and relatives of persons who have committed suicide in part to help to prevent suicide contagion.

REFERENCES

Barrios, L. C., Everett, S. A., Simon, T. R., & Brener, N. D. (2000). Suicide ideation among US college students. *Journal of American College Health, 48*, 229–234.

Centers for Disease Control and Prevention. (1994). Programs for the prevention of suicide among adolescents and young adults; and suicide contagion and the reporting of suicide: Recommendations from a national workshop. *Morbidity and Mortality Weekly Report (MMWR), 43*(No. RR-6), 1–23.

Gliatto, M. F., & Rai, A. K. (1999). Evaluation and treatment of patients with suicidal ideation. *American Family Physician, 59*, 1500–1507.

Kann, L., Kinchen, S. A., Williams, B. I., Ross, J. G., Lowry, R., Grunbaum, J. A., ... State and Local YRBSS Coordinators. (2000, June 9). Youth Risk Behavior Surveillance—United States, 1999. *Morbidity and Mortality Weekly Report, 49*/SS05, 1–96. Retrieved from http://www.cdc.gov

AMY SESSOMS
ROBERT T. BROWN
University of North Carolina

SUICIDE

Suicide describes the act of intentionally killing oneself, whereas the term *parasuicide* refers to an unsuccessful or uncompleted suicide attempt (Kauffman, 2005). Suicide is the third leading cause of death for persons aged 15–24, with only accidents and homicides resulting in more deaths for this age group (Jensen, 2005). Data from 1992 indicated that children, youths, and young adults in this age group accounted for approximately 16% of all recorded suicides (Centers for Disease Control and Prevention, 1995). Cimbolic and Jobes (1990) write that adolescent males have a higher suicide rate than adolescent females; however, adolescent females have a higher parasuicide rate. The difference between parasuicide rates for females and suicides in males is a function of the method used, with males typically using more lethal means (e.g., firearms, hanging). Due to the stigmatizing effect of suicide, it is believed that the actual rate of suicide may be 2 to 3 times higher than what is officially reported (Guetzloe, 1991).

Suicide is a result of a complex interaction between environmental, social, psychological, and biological factors. Kauffman (2005) writes:

> The many complex factors that contribute to children's and adolescents' suicidal behavior include major psychiatric problems, feelings of hopelessness, impulsivity, naïve concepts of death, substance abuse, social isolation, abuse and neglect by parents, family conflict and disorganization, a family history of suicide and parasuicide, and cultural factors, including stress caused by the educational system and attention to suicide in the mass media. Youth with emotional and behavioral disorders, especially those who use alcohol or illicit drugs, are a particularly high risk of suicidal behavior. (p. 400)

Information on the rate of suicidal behavior in children and youths who receive special education services is sparse. Guetzloe (1989, 1991) writes that evidence of a specific psychiatric disorder (e.g., mood disorder, depression, bipolar disorder, conduct disorder, psychosis) and other disabilities (e.g., developmental disabilities, deafness, physical and/or orthopedic disabilities, cerebral palsy) may contribute to suicidal ideation and possibly be overlooked by educators and care providers. For example, Peck (1985) reviewed all suicides of children and youths under the age of 15 that occurred in Los Angles County over a 3-year period ($n = 14$). Fifty percent of the sample had a documented learning or behavioral disability (i.e., hyperactivity, perceptual disorders, or dyslexia). In one particular case, Peck wrote that a student who committed suicide had received adequate educational support for his learning disability, but very little attention was given to his general feelings of unhappiness and frustration, which, in retrospect, placed him in a category of needing immediate mental health support.

McBride and Siegel (1997) investigated the role that learning disabilities played in adolescent suicides by researching spelling and handwriting errors found on suicide notes. Data from this study suggested that nearly 90% of the 27 suicide notes reviewed showed significant spelling and handwriting deficits. The spelling and handwriting errors were judged to be similar to those of students who have identified learning disabilities. The authors concluded that "there is evidence that children and adolescents with unrecognized, poorly treated, or untreated learning disabilities are at a higher risk of developing secondary behavior problems and psychiatric disorders than those who received adequate intervention. In the present study... none of the adolescents who committed suicide had been identified as learning disabled or were receiving special education help" (pp. 657–658). Interestingly, Kauffman (2005) writes that performance in school can be a factor in adolescent suicide, with an increase in suicides and parasuicide occurring in the spring term, when performance indicators, such as grades and graduation, receive greater attention.

Awareness, prevention, and intervention are critical features of successful suicide intervention programs. Jensen (2005) describes a prevention strategy that includes four steps: (1) focusing on improving services for students who are depressed and/or feeling hopeless (i.e., observation, identification, and intervention services); (2) elimination of access to lethal means of killing oneself (e.g., guns, knives, ropes, medication); (3) provision of comprehensive adult support for at-risk individuals; and (4) limiting access to media coverage that glamorizes or publicizes suicide. Educators should familiarize themselves with local resources (policies, curricula, assessments, counseling, and mental health support) that might be needed if a student is considered a risk for suicide. Specific guidelines for working with a person who has expressed suicidal feelings or thoughts include (1) taking all suicide threats seriously, (2) focusing on establishing communication with the person of concern, (3) providing emotional support, and (4) seeking immediate assistance from trained professionals (Kauffman, 2005).

In summary, suicide is the third leading cause of death in children and youths. A review of the literature suggests that students with disabilities may be at higher risk for suicidal ideation, especially students with depression, mood disorders, or undiagnosed disabilities. Educators have the responsibility to increase awareness, prevention, and intervention activities at their schools and should know how to access local resources and expertise should they encounter a student who has expressed suicidal thoughts or feelings. Guidelines for working with students who have expressed suicidal ideations include taking all threats seriously, establishing communication, providing emotional support, and seeking immediate assistance from a trained professional.

REFERENCES

Centers for Disease Control and Prevention. (1995). Suicide among children, adolescents, and young adults—United States, 1980–1992. *Morbidity and Mortality Weekly Report*, *44*(15), 289–308.

Cimbolic, P., & Jobes, D. A. (1990). Youth suicide: The scope of the problem. In P. Cimbolic & D. A. Jobes (Eds.), *Youth suicide: Issues, assessment, and intervention* (pp. 3–8). Springfield, IL: Charles C. Thomas.

Guetzloe, E. C. (1989). *A special educator's perspective on youth suicide: What the educator should know.* ERIC Clearinghouse on Handicapped and Gifted Children, Council for Exceptional Children.

Guetzloe, E. C. (1991). *Suicide and the exceptional child* (Report No. E508). Reston, VI: ERIC Clearinghouse on Disabilities and Gifted Education. (ERIC Document Reproduction Service No. ED340152)

Jensen, M. M. (2005). *Introduction to emotional and behavioral disorders: Recognizing and managing problems in the classroom.* Upper Saddle River, NJ: Pearson Merrill Prentice Hall.

Kauffman, J. M. (2005). *Characteristics of emotional and behavioral disorders of children and youth* (8th ed.). Upper Saddle River, NJ: Pearson Merrill Prentice Hall.

McBride, H. E. A., & Siegel, L. S. (1997). Learning disabilities and adolescent suicide. *Journal of Learning Disabilities*, *30*, 652–659.

Peck, M. L. (1985). Crisis intervention treatment with chronically and acutely suicidal adolescents. In M. L. Peck, N. L. Farberow, & R. E. Litman (Eds.), *Youth suicide* (pp. 112–122). New York, NY: Springer.

RANDALL L. DE PRY
University of Colorado at Colorado Springs

SULLIVAN, ANN (*See Macy, Ann Sullivan*)

SULLIVAN PROGRAMMED READING

The Sullivan Programmed Reading system comprises an individualized programmed workbook approach to teaching reading to students in first through third grade. The sequence of the 3-year system extends from Reading Readiness through Series III, with diagnostic prescriptive teaching aids and student activities that are designed to optimize individual pacing. Pupils systematically progress from letter discrimination to word recognition or to reading sentences and stories. The first 10 weeks of the program are spent in the development of basic vocabulary and the acquisition of skills that are necessary for the use of programmed material. This part of the series is teacher-directed or oriented and must be done as a class or group. Afterward, the program allows each pupil to progress according to his or her own rate of learning. The pupil is provided with a minimal amount of information, a problem is posed, a response is solicited, and the response is corrected or reinforced. The child makes the response, then checks his or her answer against the correct response that is revealed as a slider moves down the page to reveal the next frame (Hafner & Jolly, 1972; Moyle & Moyle, 1971; Scheiner, 1969; Sullivan Associates, 1968).

The Reading Readiness and Programmed Readers Series I, II, and III provide sequential instruction in consonants, vowels, sight words, punctuation, suffixes, contractions, possessives, capitals, and comprehension. Placement tests indicate at which point in the series to enter a pupil who begins in the system after first grade. The Programmed Reading Program comprises 23 levels, with one book per level. Pupils progress through each book and are expected to pass an end-of-book test before proceeding to the next book. A total of 3,266 words are introduced in the complete program (Hafner & Jolly, 1972; Sullivan Associates, 1968).

The following components of the Sullivan Associates system may be ordered as kits or separately. Reading Readiness consists of two kits, each of which contains two full-color, 72-page Big Books, two comprehensive teacher guides, 2-hour-long tape cassettes, a set of Webstermasters, and a wire easel and alphabet strips. On completion of the prereading stage, the child should master (1) the names of letters; (2) how to write letters; (3) the sounds that represent letters; (4) left-to-right sequencing; (5) the concept that words are formed from groups of letters; and (6) the ability to read the words yes or no in sentences. Series I, II, and III Programmed Readers Books 1 to 23 provide logical linguistic progression, constant reinforcement, colorful art, and stimulating story content. By the end of the eighth book in Series I, 14 vowels and 23 consonant classes will have been mastered; in addition, children will know approximately 450 words phonetically and 10 sight words. On completion of Series III, 25 more vowels and consonant classes, a total of 3,200 new words, and 40 more sight words will have been mastered.

Two sets of seven filmstrips that are primarily designed to introduce the readers to new words supplement Books 1 to 14. Each filmstrip reviews material from the previous level and presents new vocabulary and characters. Three sets of Activity Books reinforce ideas provided by the programmed series through cutout patterns for characters, puppets, and games. Webstermasters allow duplications to supplement each series of programmed readers. Read and Think Series are provided for Series I and II and are to be read after completion of the programmed text to motivate children to read for enjoyment. Achievement tests (criterion-referenced) measure student progress in terms of predetermined behavioral objectives for each series. There is an item-by-item analysis of the skills tested and specific remediation for each item that is missed. Word cards and response booklets allow pupils to write their answers using a wax pencil or crayon, making the tests reusable. Teachers' guides are organized by book, skill, and unit. An overview of decoding and comprehension information, and a listing of the sound-symbol and vocabulary progression and content summary, are outlined. Each grade also contains a reading aloud, dictation, creative writing, and test section for each book level, and specific item-by-item instructions for both with remediative recycling options (Sullivan & Associates, 1968). For uses with exceptional children, see Lerner (1985).

REFERENCES

Hafner, L., & Jolly, H. (1972). *Patterns of teaching reading in the elementary school*. New York, NY: Macmillan.

Lerner, J. (1985). *Learning disabilities: Theories, diagnosis and teaching strategies* (4th ed.). Dallas, TX: Houghton Mifflin.

Moyle, D., & Moyle, L. (1971). *Modern innovations in the teaching of reading*. London, England: University of London Press.

Scheiner, L. (1969). An evaluation of the Sullivan Reading Program (1967–1969) Rhoads Elementary School. Washington, DC: U.S. Department of Health, Education and Welfare. (ERIC Document Reproduction Service ED 002 362)

Sullivan Associates. (1968). *Sullivan Associates programmed reading, Sullivan Press*. New York, NY: McGraw-Hill.

FRANCES T. HARRINGTON
Radford University

SUMMARY OF PERFORMANCE

In the 2004 reauthorization of the Individuals with Disabilities Education Improvement Act (IDEA), Congress required that young adults with disabilities be provided with a summary of performance (SOP) as they prepare to exit high school by graduating, completing a certificate program, or aging out of eligibility. Although this relatively new requirement is not considered to be a specific transition component, it is conceptually linked to the transition to adulthood because the purpose of the document is to provide information that will be useful in the contexts of employment, postsecondary education, and independent living. The SOP functions as a bridge between the entitlement provisions of IDEA and the eligibility provisions of Section 504 of the Rehabilitation Act and the Americans with Disabilities Act (Kochhar-Bryant & Izzo, 2006).

The defining characteristics of the document, its purpose, and guidelines for its development are, congruent with other IDEA mandates, loosely described in the legislation (Dukes, Shaw, & Madaus, 2007). Because SOP is a relatively new component of IDEA, definitive information is limited. Based on the contents of the legislation, scholarship, and examples from the field, each of these components is discussed below.

The IDEA provides this definition of an SOP, "A summary of the child's academic achievement and functional performance, which shall include recommendations on how to assist the child in meeting the child's postsecondary goals" (§ 1414, c, 5, B, ii). At a minimum the SOP, according to IDEA, must include an articulation of measurable postsecondary goals, a description of the present levels of academic and functional performance, and recommendations for future goal attainment. The SOP should be designed when the timing of the student's exit from school is known. For example, designing an SOP during a student's senior year, or during the last year of special education eligibility (usually at age 21) are appropriate junctures at which to work on the document. Members of the group charged with designing the SOP are similar to those who design students' individual education programs (IEPs). The student with a disability, his parents, educators, and other key personnel should all be involved in designing the document based on assessment data and students' school, employment, and life experiences. The SOP is intended to be a document with real-world value, bridging school-based disability related information with the contexts of adulthood where this information is needed. The young adult with a disability, chiefly responsible for articulating this information about himself at work, college or technical school, and in daily life, must play an integral role in its creation (Field & Hoffman, 2007).

If the SOP is to be a useful document it must be comprehensive and go beyond the minimum requirements documented in IDEA; its content should address short-term and long-term goals and it should contain information that individuals with disabilities need and use during the transition to adulthood (Patton, Clark, & Trainor, 2009). Firstly, the SOPS should contain personal information such as address, date of birth, etc. Having one document that contains this type of factual information is useful when completing applications for employment and housing, registering to vote, registering for postsecondary courses, and completing questionnaires prior to medical and other social services appointments. Secondly, the SOP should contain present levels of academic, cognitive, and functional performance (Madaus, Bigaj, Chafouleas, &

Simonsen, 2006). While most IEPs contain similar information, the SOP should focus on employment, further education, and daily living. Thirdly, the document should state the current postsecondary goals that have been identified and articulated by the young adult with a disability.

In addition to future goals, the SOP should also contain a list of accommodations and modifications that the individual with the disability has tried, and a description of their efficacy (Patton et al., 2009). For example, a youth with attention deficits may have been given testing accommodations, such as extended time and a separate setting during high school, with varied success rates. If this information is noted on the SOP, the young adult transitioning to community college or other postsecondary educational settings can use this document to inform her meetings with disability service coordinator at her postsecondary institution. Unfortunately, the process for sharing this documentation has not been clearly delineated in education policy, potentially compromising its routine acceptance and use in the employment and educational contexts of adulthood (Shaw, 2006).

Two additional types of information that Patton and colleagues (2009) have identified as essential components to the SOP include a functional impact statement and recommendations. The functional impact statement highlights how areas of need may affect the transition process. For instance, if a young adult with a significant cognitive disability has difficulty sequencing steps to complete a task, the functional impact statement would address how this will likely impact employment. In this example a functional impact statement might include the following: *Tony has difficulty following a multistep process in the correct order of steps*. Then, for the same individual a recommendation might include: *Tony should continue to utilize a checklist to follow the correct sequence of steps in multistep tasks*.

The SOP provides an additional opportunity for educators to augment the transition to adulthood for youth with disabilities. If SOPs maintain a clear focus on information that is gathered and articulated by youth with disabilities, with guidance from educators and parents, these documents have the potential to be practical and informative in the contexts of employment, postsecondary education, and daily life.

REFERENCES

Dukes, L., Shaw, S., & Madaus, J. (2007). How to complete a summary of performance for students exiting to postsecondary education. *Assessment for Effective Intervention*, *32*(3), 143–159.

Field, S., & Hoffman, A. (2007). Self-determination in secondary transition assessment. *Assessment for Effective Intervention*, *32*(3), 181–190.

Individuals with Disabilities Education Improvement Act of 2004, 20 U.S.C. § 1400 et seq. (2004).

Kochhar-Bryant, C., & Izzo, M. V. (2006). Access to post-high school services: Transition assessment and the summary of performance. *Career Development of Exceptional Individuals*, *29*, 70–89.

Madaus, J., Bigaj, S., Chafouleas, S., & Simonsen, B. (2006). What key information can be included in a comprehensive summary of performance? *Career Development for Exceptional Individuals*, *29*, 90–99.

Patton, J. R., Clark, G. M., & Trainor, A. A. (2009). *Summary of performance system* [Computer software and manual]. Austin, TX: PRO-ED.

Shaw, S. (2006). Legal and policy perspectives on transition assessment and documentation. *Career Development for Exceptional Individuals*, *29*, 108–113.

AUDREY A. TRAINOR
JAMES R. PATTON
Fourth edition

SUMMER SCHOOL FOR INDIVIDUALS WITH DISABILITIES

Extended-year programs for individuals with disabilities have been a highly debated issue for many years. The position of many individuals is that extended school year programs are needed for students with disabilities to prevent the loss of existing skills, accelerate the acquisition of new skills, and provide recreational programming and respite care for the parents. There are nine main questions for which there are no appropriate answers: (1) Do extended school year programs accomplish instructional objectives, and, if so, how much? (2) If students do learn something, is it additive to what is learned during the school year? (3) Do students without extended school years lose skills, or do they increase maladaptive (i.e., irritant) responding? (4) Do students without extended school years catch up to students who do experience extended school year programming and thus negate the effect of the extended year? (5) If students with extended school years do have additive learning, is the cost effectiveness of that learning acceptable? (6) What types of extended school years (e.g., school, school plus recreational, recreational, short programs, long programs) have what types of effects, and what are the desired effects (e.g., retention, gain, degree of gain)? (7) What are the "do-ability" variables? (e.g., What teachers and aides will be involved? Is burnout an issue? Who will supervise?) (8) How will documentation be provided? (9) Is there student burnout?

There are some other questions that do have answers. First, do students with disabilities have a right to a public education? Public Law 94-142 and Section 504 of the Rehabilitation Act of 1973, have defined the right of children with disabilities to a free appropriate public education. Second, do specific classes of students with disabilities have a right to an extended school year? The courts have substantiated the right of specific classes of children with disabilities to extended (over 180-day) school year programs in a number of court cases (e.g., *Armstrong v. Kline*, 1979). Additional cases are currently pending throughout the United States. Therefore, while there is growing educational and legal support for extended-year programming, many questions still need to be addressed.

Empirical support for the current policy on extended-year programs for individuals with disabilities is difficult to find in the literature. Browder, Lentz, Knoster, and Wilansky (1984) found that the primary methodology for determining both eligibility for and effectiveness of extended-year programs was the subjective judgments of teachers and parents (Bahling, 1980; McMahon, 1983). This information, while not surprising, does not provide empirical support for extended school year programming. Ellis (1975a) studied the effects of a summer program on possible regression of 16 children with multiple handicaps and blindness and found that none of the students had regressed in eight target skill areas (e.g., communication skills). In a second study, Ellis (1975b) examined the skill levels of 145 students with physical and neurological disabilities and found a significant improvement in skill areas for the summer program participants. In contrast, Edgar, Spence, and Kenowitz (1977), in a study that examined the findings of 18 summer programs, found that the data (e.g., teacher observations, rating scales) did not strongly support the premise that such programs facilitated the maintenance of skills. However, these results are possible when there is not a coherence between the school year objectives and those of the summer program. Therefore, there are conflicting data concerning the effectiveness of extended-year programming in either maintaining or extending the learning repertoire of students with disabilities.

Zdunich (1984) reported on data gathered on extended-year programs in Canada. This study examined the effects of four types of summer programming (short programs, high-structure, low-structure, and medium-structure programs). A control group that received no summer programming was also used in the study. While the study's sample size was relatively small (overall $n = 186$), its results were interesting. First, the study found that maladaptive behaviors had been significantly reduced only in the high- and medium-structure programs and that students in the other conditions increased maladaptive responding. Second, skill development (e.g., communication, self-help, fine motor skills) was significantly greater in high- and medium-structure programs. Other types of summer experiences showed relative maintenance of skills with some small amount of skill regression. In addition, the skill acquisition data held constant over the following academic year. The study also examined many variables related to each of these two major concerns. It should provide a substantial increase in our database on the educational and social impact of extended school year programming.

REFERENCES

Bahling, E. (1980). *Extended school year program, Intermediate Unit #5, June–August, 1980.* Paper presented at the annual international convention of Council for Exceptional Children, Philadelphia, PA. (ERIC Document Reproduction Service No. 208 609)

Browder, D. M., Lentz, F. E., Knosten, T., & Wilansky, C. (1984). *A record-based evaluation of extended school year eligibility practice.* Unpublished manuscript.

Edgar, E., Spence, W., & Kenowitz, L. (1977). Extended school year for the handicapped: Is it working? *Journal of Special Education, 11,* 441–447.

Ellis, R. S. (1975a). Summer preplacement program for severely multihandicapped blind children. *Summer 1975, Evaluation Report.* New York City Board of Education. (ERIC Document Reproduction Service No. ED136489)

Ellis, R. S. (1975b). Summer education program for neurologically and physically handicapped children. *Summer 1975, Evaluation Report.* New York City Board of Education. (ERIC Document Reproduction Service No. ED136489)

McMahon, J. (1983). Extended school year programs. *Exceptional Children, 49,* 457–460.

Zdunich, L. (1984). *Summer programs for the severely handicapped.* Edmonton, Alberta, Canada: Alberta Education.

LYLE E. BARTON
Kent State University

See also Tutoring

SUPERVISION IN SPECIAL EDUCATION

Current emphasis in special education is on the employment of a program administrator specifically for exceptional children. Other titles used are special education director and supervisor of exceptional children's programs. For most states, the administrator or director of special education must have an academic degree at the master's level in the education of exceptional children or a related field. Owing to the nature of the position, it is also helpful if this person completes the requirements for a supervisor's or administrator's certificate in addition to the master's degree in special education. The educational program for the preparation of exceptional children's program administrators is basically the same as for preparing general school administrators. The major difference in their preparation is in the specific exceptional children's program content requirement.

The exceptional children's program administrator has been identified by the North Carolina Division for Exceptional Children as

> one who plans, develops, coordinates, supervises, administers, and evaluates the effectiveness of local educational agency's educational programs. The program administrator provides guidance and leadership to all exceptional children program personnel. The role is performed under the general supervision of the superintendent or designee. The program administrator maintains a cooperative relationship with principals, other school personnel, other related service agencies, and parents. The administrator is responsible for maintaining the program within local, state, and federal guidelines, rules, regulations, and laws which govern exceptional children.

Program administrators should have competencies in the administration of exceptional children's programs, including assessment; planning and implementing programs; budgeting; communicating with parents, central office staff, principals, other service providers, and state and local agencies; staff development; and program evaluation. Another area of expertise necessary for program administrators is the application of school law administration of exceptional children's programs. This includes knowledge of legislation about the handicapped as it relates to IDEA other state and federal statutes; confidentiality guidelines; due process procedures; procedures for auditing and evaluating compliance; authority of the hearing officer; and schools' responsibility for various placements, transportation, suspension and expulsion, related services, competency tests, and evaluations.

Program administrators should be well versed in supervision of instruction centered around personnel management. They should be able to interview and select qualified exceptional children's teachers, observe and evaluate teachers to identify teaching strengths and weaknesses, and develop professional growth plans for teachers and support staff. The administrator should be able to design instructional units that specify performance objectives, instructional sequences, learning activities, and materials and evaluation processes, and prepare an educational plan that includes curriculum content and level, activities, alternative teaching strategies, and evaluation of learning outcomes (Sage & Burrello, 1994). The program administrator should also be able to evaluate the quality, utility, and availability of learning resource materials.

This entry has been informed by the sources listed below.

REFERENCES

Competencies and guidelines for approved teacher education programs. (1983, September). Raleigh: Division for Exceptional Children, North Carolina Department of Public Instruction.

Comprehensive system of personnel development report. (1984, August). Raleigh: Division for Exceptional Children, North Carolina Department of Public Instruction.

Sage, D. D., & Burrello, L. C. (1994). *Leadership in educational reform: An administrator's guide to changes in special education.* Baltimore, MD: Paul H. Brookes.

CECELIA STEPPE-JONES
*North Carolina Central University,
Administration of Special Education*

See also **Politics and Special Education**

SUPPORTED EMPLOYMENT

The term *supported employment* emerged in the 1980s and is based on the belief that all people, regardless of disability, can work (Wehman, 2006). Supported employment is a method of providing supports for a person with a significant disability to perform work in an employment site. The Individuals with Disabilities Education Improvement Act of 2004 (IDEIA; 2004) mandates local education agencies (LEAs) to measure transition services and outcomes for youth with disabilities using State Performance Plan (SPP) Indicators 13 and 14. Supported employment is one transition service that is measured by Indicators 13 and 14.

School personnel are encouraged to follow the Fair Labor Standards Act (FLSA) when providing community-based employment supports (Johnson, Sword, & Habhegger, 2005). The FLSA describes which work activities are acceptable for student workers and information to be included in an Individualized Education Program (IEP).

Supported employment consists of the following steps:

- Prior to placement on an employment site the prospective employee participates in an evaluation to determine strengths, preferences, interests and needs. Based on that evaluation, a variety of employment opportunities are identified.

- The next phase surrounds an analysis of an employment site to identify tasks and the environment in which employment tasks occur. During this phase the supported employee might visit an employment site where a situational assessment is administered. This assessment provides information about how the supported employee responded to the environment and how well she or he completed basic tasks.

- After the employment site is agreed upon by all parties (employee, management, and employment specialist), training commences. The supported employee then typically works with assistance from a trained specialist to develop skills in the workplace.

- As the supported employee's work skills increase, the employment specialist eventually fades support. Typically a plan for long-term follow-up is developed with the supported employee's on-site supervisor or manager. The employee maintains regular contact with the specialist while developing relationships with co workers (www.worksupport.com/resources).

REFERENCES

Individuals with Disabilities Education Improvement Act of 2004, 20 U.S.C. § 1400 et seq. (2004).

Johnson, D. R., Sword, D. F., & Habhegger, B. (2005). *Handbook for implementing an comprehensive work-based learning program according to the Fair Labor Standards Act* (3rd ed.). Retrieved from http://www.ncset.org/publications/essentialtools/flsa

Wehman, P. (2006). *Life beyond the classroom: Transition strategies for young people with disabilities* (4th ed.). Baltimore, MD: Paul H. Brookes.

WEHMAN WITTIG
Fourth edition

See also **Transition; Vocational Rehabilitation Counseling**

SUPPORTED LIVING

Supported living is a model of living arrangement for individuals with disabilities who choose to live in the community. It was developed in the latter part of 20th century as an alternative to the more restrictive living arrangements such as institutions or supervised living. As an outcome of the self-advocacy movement, supported living is based on the philosophy of person centered planning and focuses on supporting individuals' living based on the needs and preferences of the individual. It supports the belief that people, regardless of their disabilities, should live in the community where they want, with whom they want, for as long as they want, with whatever supports they need to make that happen (Ferguson, Hibbard, Leinen, & Schaff, 1990).

Supported living provides individuals with disabilities access to community housing options that are typical residences generally considered by adults without disabilities, are not owned by the same agency that provides supports and services to individuals who live there, and are chosen by the resident with a disability (Test, Aspel, & Everson, 2006). If shared with others, the decision about whether to share or with whom to share must be at the discretion of the person with a disability. Research has found that costs associated with supported living are no more than costs for more restrictive living arrangements; yet those living in the community have achieved significantly better outcomes than those living in more restrictive environments (Lucyshyn, Olson, & Horner, 1995; Stancliffe & Keane, 2000).

Advantages to supported living include individual choice and the availability of supports to assist individuals to access and participate in typical activities and functions of community life. The individual can choose to live in a setting of their choice including, but not limited to, family home or home of their own. They may own or lease homes or apartments in their own names, or in the name of their parents, relatives, or housing organizations (Test, Aspel, & Everson, 2006). Individuals are not required to have certain skills before accessing a particular living option. Supports can include an array of services tailored to individual needs for the purpose of assisting individuals being as independent as possible. Example of services and supports include personal assistance services, professional services, dental services, day habilitation services, supported employment services, prevocational services, transportation, behavioral services, vision/hearing services, supported living consultation, and recreational and social integration supports.

REFERENCES

Ferguson, P. M., Hibbard, M., Leinen, J., & Schaff, S. (1990). Supported community life: Disability policy and renewal of mediating structures. *Journal of Disability Policy Studies, 1,* 9–35.

Lucyshyn, J., Olson, D., & Horner, R. H. (1995). Building an ecology of support: A case study of one young woman with severe problem behaviors living in the community. *Journal of the Association for Persons with Severe Handicaps, 20,* 16–30.

Stancliffe, R. J., & Keane, S. (2000). Outcomes and costs of community living: A matched comparison of group homes and semi-independent living. *Journal of Intellectual and Developmental Disability, 25,* 281–305.

Test, D. W., Aspel, N. P., & Everson, J. M. (2006). *Transition methods for youth with disabilities.* Upper Saddle River, NJ: Merrill.

DULAN ZHANG
Texas A&M University
Fourth edition

SURROGATE PARENTS

The Individuals with Disabilities Education Act (IDEA) included parental participation as a major component in the educational planning for children with disabilities. The purpose of including parents was to ensure that the rights of the child and the parents are protected. This component of IDEA officially recognized the parents as a crucial and viable force in the life of their child and required their input in the educational planning and decision-making process. However, there are instances when the parents of a child with disabilities, for various reasons, are unable to represent him or her in the educational decision-making process. This is when the public agency responsible for educating the child appoints a surrogate parent. According to federal regulations, a surrogate parent is appointed when (1) no parent can be identified; (2) the public agency, after reasonable efforts, cannot discover the whereabouts of a parent; or (3) the child is a ward of the state under the laws of that state (*Federal Register*, 1977, p. 42496).

Surrogate parents are individuals who are responsible for ensuring that the child with disabilities receives a free appropriate education in the least restrictive environment. The surrogate parents' role is limited to the educational needs of the child. However, more and more grandparents are taking on this role (Rothenberg, 1996). Specifically, the role of the surrogate parents, based on the federal regulations, relates to

(1) The identification, evaluation, and educational placement of the child....

(2) The provision of a free appropriate education to the child.... The public agency may select a surrogate parent in any way permitted by state law. The public agencies shall insure that a person selected as surrogate has no interest that conflicts with the interests of the child he or she represents; and has knowledge and skills that ensure adequate representation of the child. The person who is appointed as a surrogate parent cannot be an employee of the public agency that is directly involved in the education and care of the child. (*Federal Register*, 1977, p. 42496)

Shrybman (1982, pp. 267–268) listed the following rights of surrogate parents to:

1. Review all written records regarding the child's education.
2. Take part in the evaluation and development of the individual education plan (IEP).
3. Reject, accept, or recommend changes in the IEP.
4. Request and/or initiate a second evaluation.
5. Initiate mediation, hearing, or appeals procedures.
6. Receive legal help at no cost if such assistance is necessary in the furtherance of the surrogate's responsibilities.
7. Monitor the child's program.

8. Recommend changes in the pupil's placement.

9. Take advantage of all the rights afforded to natural parents in the special education decision-making process.

Each state is required to develop specific requirements for the selection of the surrogate parents. Once the need has been proven by the local agency, the criteria and responsibilities are specifically defined. A surrogate parent does not have to be a professional person; however, it is important that the surrogate have a general knowledge of state and federal laws relating to individuals with disabilities. In addition, knowledge of the rules and regulations of the public school system and specific information about the child's disability and educational needs are crucial areas. The state is responsible for education and training of the surrogate parent to ensure adequate representation of the child.

The surrogate parent has many responsibilities that must be understood and explained by the local agency. Knowledge of these responsibilities are essential if the educational needs of the child are to be met in the least restrictive environment. A surrogate parent may be dismissed from his or her role if the local agency determines that the roles and responsibilities outlined by federal and state regulations have been neglected, or the well-being of the child is at risk. Shrybman (1982) listed the responsibilities of surrogate parents of children with disabilities: to attend any training program the local agency offers; to be sure there are no areas of interest that conflict with their responsibilities to the child; to be involved in identification, evaluation, program development, initial placement, review placement, and reevaluation; to be knowledgeable of the child's educational needs, wishes, and concerns; to maintain confidentiality of all records; to be aware of support provided by human services in the community; and to be sure the child is receiving special education in the least restrictive environment.

REFERENCES

Federal Register. (1977). Washington, DC: U.S. Government Printing Office.

Rothenberg, D. (1996). Grandparents as parents: A primer for schools. (ERIC Digest No. ED401044)

Shrybman, J. A. (1982). Due process in special education. Rockville, MD: Aspen.

JANICE HARPER
North Carolina Central University

See also Individuals With Disabilities Education Improvement Act; Parent Education

SURVIVAL SKILLS

Survival skills are essential components of functional teaching. Many educators use the terms survival skills and functional teaching synonymously. Heward and Orlansky (1984) define functional skills as skills that are "frequently demanded in a student's natural environment" (p. 340). Cassidy and Shanahan (1979) suggest the term survival emphasizes the need to develop skills that will help individuals to attain personal goals and social responsibilities. A few examples of survival skills include balancing a checkbook, riding a bus, completing a job application, reading a menu, and shopping for groceries (Alcantara, 1994). Survival skills have also been extended to self-management skills in the classroom (Synder & Bambara, 1997).

Sabatino (1982) emphasized the importance of the functional curriculum model to prepare the individuals with disabilities for a vocational career. Examples of survival skills from this model include a word list from a driver's manual, social skills training, and using technical terms to understand career information. McDowell (1979) further stressed the need for adolescents with disabilities to exhibit specific behaviors to help them function successfully in today's society and on the job. These behaviors include showing respect for others, demonstrating good manners, knowing when certain behaviors are appropriate, and learning to accept and follow directions.

Sabatino and Lanning-Ventura (1982) state that there is an important question that must be addressed by teachers of students with disabilities at the secondary level. When should the educational program focus on survival skills and not on overcoming educational disabilities? The answer to this question should be based on the individual characteristics of the student. However, functional teaching is most appropriate when the chances for academic gains are limited.

An essential component of survival skills in the area of reading is selection of materials. Cassidy and Shanahan (1979) identified the three basic criteria for selection as relevance, necessity, and frequency. Relevance implies considering the student's age, current level of functioning, and geographical area when selecting materials. In terms of geographical area, using materials such as a phone book or a bus schedule from a student's hometown is more appropriate than using commercial materials. Necessity suggests selecting materials that are representative of tasks required in the real world. Frequency deals with the number of times the student will deal with the materials selected. Activities such as reading menus and container labels occur often in the real world.

Potential strengths of the functional curriculum model identified by Alley and Deshler (1979) include the following: (a) students are equipped to function independently, at least over the short term, in society; (b) students may be better prepared to compete for specific jobs on graduation from high school; and (c) instruction in the functional curriculum may have particular relevance for the high school junior or senior with a severe disability (p. 50).

REFERENCES

Alcantara, P. R. (1994). Effects of videotape instructional package on purchasing skills of children with autism. *Exceptional Children, 61*(1), 40–55.

Alley, G., & Deshler, D. (1979). *Teaching the learning disabled adolescent: Strategies and methods.* Denver, CO: Love.

Cassidy, J., & Shanahan, T. (1979). Survival skills: Some considerations. *Journal of Reading, 23,* 136–140.

Heward, H. L., & Orlansky, M. D. (1984). *Exceptional children.* Columbus, OH: Merrill.

McDowell, R. L. (1979, May). *The emotionally disturbed adolescent* (PRISE Reporter, No. 3). (pp. 1–2). King of Prussia: Pennsylvania Resource and Information Center for Special Education.

Sabatino, D. A. (1982). An educational program guide for secondary schools. In D. A. Sabatino & L. Mann (Eds.), *Diagnostic and prescriptive teaching.* Rockville, MD: Aspen.

Sabatino, D. A., & Lanning-Ventura, S. (1982). Functional teaching: Survival skills and tutoring. In D. A. Sabatino & L. Mann (Eds.), *Diagnostic and prescriptive teaching.* Rockville, MD: Aspen.

Synder, M. C., & Bambara, L. M. (1997). Teaching secondary students with learning disabilities to self-manage classroom survival skills. *Journal of Learning Disabilities, 30*(5), 534–543.

JANICE HARPER
North Carolina Central University

See also Daily Living Skills; Functional Instruction; Functional Skills Training

SUSTO

Susto, or "soul loss," is a folk illness attributed to a frightening or traumatic event. It is said that the event causes the soul to leave the body and results in unhappiness and sickness (American Psychiatric Association [APA], 1994). Other terms for this culture-bound syndrome include *espanteo, pasmo, tripa ida, perida del alma,* and *chilbih* (APA, 1994). This disorder can also be classified as a culture-specific idiom of disease and distress such that symptoms are extremely variable and may occur months or years after the supposedly precipitating event.

Behavioral manifestations of susto are similar to childhood depression and many other simple childhood illnesses. In some cases it has been postulated that susto is "equivalent to ailments characterized by modern medicine such as hypoglycemia" (Castro & Eroza, 1998, p. 204). According to ethnographic case studies, this disorder can be measured in terms of "degree of social stress" present in symptomatic cases and explained as a result of "the lack of adjustment present in relation to social expectations" (Castro & Eroza, 1998, p. 204).

Typically, susto is related to psychological experiences associated with situations involving loss or grief. However, susto in children is more likely related to a frightening or traumatic event (Castro & Eroza, 1998). According to Castro and Eroza (1998), there are two stages to the susto process in children. First, they might simply be frightened, in which they will cry continuously during the night and cannot sleep. Second, if the susto symptoms persist, they begin to exhibit the same characteristics of adults, such as lack of appetite and fatigue. Thus, a child with susto can exhibit the previous characteristics at various stages of the syndrome.

There are no known prevalence or incidence studies with regard to susto, but there are ethnographic case studies of this disorder. Susto is primarily prevalent among Mexican, Central American, and South American populations. According to ethnographic reports, susto impacts high percentages of women and children. Men can also exhibit susto and report similar symptoms but at a lower concentration (Castro & Eroza, 1998).

Characteristics

1. Physical weakness
2. Somnolence
3. Loss of appetite
4. Fever and diarrhea
5. Depression
6. Hesitancy

By most ethnographic accounts, susto is treated by both traditional healers and medical professionals. However, within some Latin cultures there is a correlation between doctors and pain; therefore, many susto sufferers, termed asustados, do not seek medical attention for their ailments. Traditional healers use the basic measure of "sensing the sick person's pulse" to begin treatment. According to ethnographic reports, after finding the pulse, the healer "throws a little red corn into a container of blessed water and then prays, 'Shadow, come back to your center'" (Castro & Eroza, 1998, p. 215). With three complete sessions, the patient is deemed cured of susto. If symptoms persist after traditional treatment, the asustado will be referred to a doctura by the traditional healer (Castro & Eroza, 1998, p. 215).

It is unlikely that instances of susto would be identified in the United States in terms of referral for special education assessment for services. However, if the duration of the symptoms are long-term or chronic, academic achievement may be affected, and personnel may be brought in for child studies.

Differential diagnosis of this syndrome hinges on an acculturation assessment of the child and family. A family history of this condition should be noted as well as an analysis of current cultural practices and beliefs of the immediate and extended family. Differential diagnosis may also be dependent on ruling out common childhood illnesses that present with similar symptoms, and therefore a multidisciplinary approach with medical professionals would be very helpful.

A positive instance of Susto will require a culturally sensitive treatment plan that includes significant educational personnel and support and input from the family. Relevant school personnel and students may need to be educated as to the nature of the student's condition with recommendations for support.

REFERENCES

American Psychiatric Association. (1994). *Diagnostic and statistical manual of mental disorders* (4th ed.). Washington, DC: Author.

Castro, R., & Eroza, E. (1998). Research notes on social order and subjectivity: Individuals' experience of susto and fallen fontanelle in rural community in Central Mexico. *Culture, Medicine, and Psychiatry, 22,* 203–230.

KIELY ANN FLETCHER
Ohio State University

SWEDEN, SPECIAL EDUCATION IN

Access to equivalent education for all is the basic principle guiding Swedish education from child care to young adulthood. In accordance with this principle, pupils in need of special support are not to be treated in a differential manner, and their rights are not explicitly or separately defined. However, an emphasis is placed on the schools' obligation to attend to all pupils' needs. Thus, special education support is integrated as much as possible into the framework of regular education. National goals set up by the government are combined with a remarkably high degree of local responsibility. Municipalities are free to use collected taxes and state funding for whatever services and systems are judged to be best for their respective areas. Many municipalities delegate budgets directly to individual schools. The municipalities, schools, individual staff, and pupils formulate concrete goals that are appropriate for their own environment and make their own plans for the activities necessary in order to attain the national goals.

The current curriculum for compulsory school (grades 1–9) does not use the word or concept *mainstreaming*, but promotes the view that all pupils are to be educated in regular classes. If this is not possible, the school must indicate very clearly why other educational options for a pupil should be considered. This is an important pedagogic guideline governing school organization and operation. Earlier debates focused upon prerequisites for integration. Currently, however, the focus has shifted toward the need for the justification of segregated options, if such options are under consideration. For all pupils in need of special support, an action plan of provision must be worked out by their teachers in consultation with the pupils themselves, their parents, and specialist support teachers. This plan, which identifies needs, and the provisions for meeting them, must be continuously evaluated. All teachers educated in the new teaching training program from 2001 onward are educated in special needs education to better prepare them to meet the needs of all pupils within regular education. The intention is that specialists of special needs education are educated to advise teachers and to cooperate with the managers of schools to ensure that the needs of all pupils are met.

A special program exists for pupils with severe learning disabilities and mental retardation. This was previously the responsibility of the regional counties, but since 1996 it has been delegated to the local school board in each municipality. The special program is now closely linked to or integrated into regular school activities. A basic principle of governmental policy concerning disability is that children and young people with disabilities must be offered education in their own municipality in order that they may continue to live at home.

By 2001, special schools and institutions had ceased to exist, with the exception of regional schools for deaf children in need of instruction in sign language. The former special schools and institutions have developed into resource centers, financed by government money. Their responsibilities are competence development and consultant support to schools attended by pupils with severe disabilities.

The educational goals decided by the government are expressed in three national curricula, one for preschools, one for compulsory schools, and one for upper secondary schools. The curricula are partly consistent in order to make these activities a homogeneous system. The municipalities and their schools are responsible for finding ways of attaining these goals, evaluating the efforts, and improving the work. The government supports the municipalities and their schools in their strivings to provide and develop the quality of their internal activities. The Swedish National Agency for Education is the central administrative authority for the Swedish public school system as well as for preschool activities. It defines goals in order to administrate, informs in order to influence, and reviews in order to improve. Regardless of the method, however, the focus is always on the assertion of the right of each individual to knowledge and personal development. A government mandate from 2003 states that all activities for which local and independent school authorities are responsible will be reviewed by the agency. The overall goal is "to design and carry out the educational inspection to ensure that every pupil in each school obtains the best possible education." Special guidelines stress that schools shall give high priority to the fulfillment of the pupils' special needs. The Swedish Agency for School Improvement is responsible for general support to schools within nationally prioritized areas and support for the local development of improvement work.

The Swedish Institute for Special Needs Education is a nationwide authority for coordination of state support for special needs education and provides cost-free distribution of information and knowledge about special needs in education. All measures are aimed at enhancing the expertise within the municipal authorities.

In Sweden 73% of women work part time or full time outside their homes. This is the highest figure in Europe and explains why as many as 76% of children aged 1–5 spend 4–10 hours each day in child care at preschool, where parents pay a subsidized fee depending on income. Since 2003, all children aged 4–5 have been offered free schooling for at least 525 hours per year. The provision is mandatory for the municipalities. Most child-care centers are organized in groups of 15–20 children with two to three preschool teachers. All children in need of special support should, as far as possible, receive their daily care within their ordinary child care group by means of special supervision to the regular staff or by extra personnel. There are special groups only for children with deafness or autism.

School is compulsory for children between ages 7 and 16. Children can start school at age 6 voluntarily, which most children have since 1999. According to the national curriculum, all compulsory education is organized in a way such that individual solutions are possible for all pupils, thereby strengthening the pupils' influence and personal responsibility and taking into account all pupils' needs

and individuality. The majority of pupils in need of special educational support are educated in general basic compulsory classes. In order to meet these pupils' special needs, teachers are regularly given consultations by a specialist teacher. An assistant to the teacher may work with a pupil for longer or shorter periods within the framework of the larger group's activities. As an exception, a pupil may leave the larger group for limited periods to work with a specialist teacher within the same organization, either individually or in a group for pupils with similar needs. The underlying principle is that the goals pertaining to any specific subject shall be achieved by each pupil but that the ways to attain these goals and the time utilized may vary. At grades 5 and 9 national compulsory tests are conducted in the subjects of mathematics, English, and Swedish. These tests are the basis for individual evaluations as well as for school plans and national comparisons. The aim is that every child shall pass in these subjects. However, about 10% do not achieve this and are restricted in their choice of further education. Grades or written comments are not allowed to be given to pupils until grade 8 of compulsory school. Until then, developmental talks are held each term by the teacher with each pupil and parents attending.

An increasing number of students (98%) continue their education and go on to upper secondary schools, which are free of charge. Upper secondary education is divided into 17 national 3-year programs, which offer a broad general education and basic eligibility to continue studies at the postsecondary level, even for students with disabilities and learning difficulties. Consequently, special needs have also become important issues at this level, and pupils have the same right to special support as in compulsory schools. Those pupils who have not been able to reach the goals of the compulsory school and hence are not eligible to apply to a national program may attend an individual one. In this all pupils have their own study plan, and it is possible to combine school with employment. The national programs for the severely learning disabled, which are 4 years in length, are especially oriented toward vocational training.

Within 2 years, about 50% of the students continue to study at the postsecondary level. Most universities and postsecondary schools are state-run and free of charge. The Equal Treatment of Students at Universities Act of 2001 aimed at making higher education, both entry and study, more accessible in all respects for people with disabilities. The Service for Students with Disabilities gives support to students with permanent disabilities, including dyslexia, neuropsychological problems, and documented psychiatric disorders. The support can consist of assistance with note taking, mentorship, sign language interpretation, and individual guidance. The Swedish Library of Talking Books and Braille produces course literature at the university level.

The Habilitation Services Department organized within the health services is regulated by two pieces of legislation, the Disabled Persons Support and Service Act and the Health and Medical Services Act, which guarantee free of charge certain forms of support for persons with developmental disabilities (i.e., physical disabilities, mental retardation, autism, or related conditions), persons who have major or chronic disabilities requiring extensive support, and persons with serious learning difficulties or those who have suffered brain damage during growth or adulthood. These acts require habilitation centers to provide counseling and other forms of personal support. However, the intention is not to replace but to supplement the other services provided by the municipality or county health care departments. The services include several experts who make assessments and provide medical treatments as well as educational, social, and psychological support in close consultation with the individual person, the family, and other resources in society.

The Assistive Technology Services incorporate collective and broad medical and technical expertise for children and adults with physical disabilities, speech impairment, and cognitive difficulties. These services are all free of charge and well developed.

The task of the disability ombudsman is to monitor the basic human rights of persons with disabilities. This involves dealing with complaints, providing legal advice, and providing information. There are several very active parents' movements engaged in the promotion of the rights of children with different kinds of special needs.

The identification and investigation of individual needs for special support take place in a variety of ways. From birth to compulsory school there are regular health checks for all children, with an attendance rate of about 99%. A very large proportion of children attend organized child care, and hence the need for special support can in many cases be identified before the child attains school age. Health services and to some extent psychologists are available for consultation with child care and school staff and with pupils and parents. During the last decade Swedish psychologists have shown an increasing interest in endeavoring to understand the possible neuropsychological bases of learning disabilities and behavior problems. This has resulted in an emphasis being placed on a neuropsychological approach to assessment. Although a diagnosis is often necessary in order to allocate resources, it is emphasized that learning disabilities constitute a heterogeneous diagnostic entity. To a varying extent, learning disabilities may accompany other diagnoses, ranging from mental retardation, attention-deficit/hyperactivity disorder (ADHD) and nonlanguage learning disability to primary psychiatric problems such as anxiety, depression, and posttraumatic stress disorder. In some children dyslexia, dyscalculia, or unspecified learning disability constitutes the prevailing problem. Due to the acceptance of the concepts of multifinality and equifinality, a problem is regarded to have very different explanations, backgrounds, and consequences, thus requiring different modes of intervention. In order to gain an understanding of the characteristics that differentiate any given child from other children having the same diagnosis, neuropsychological assessment is considered to be a valuable tool. Such assessment is achieved by the administration of an extensive test battery supplemented with tests of attention, language, memory, perception, visuo-spatial abilities, and learning. An analysis of behavioral and emotional problems is accomplished by interview, observation, and self-rating questionnaires. In addition, parent and teacher ratings of child behavior are obtained. This approach allows an understanding of the individual's array of strengths and weaknesses, thereby enabling the psychologist not only to describe specific deficits but also to perform the essential task of identifying those areas in which the abilities are intact and thus may be used as beneficial compensatory strategies.

As a complement to this description of the state of the art of special education in Sweden, it may be appropriate to mention some current issues that merit attention. Although in some respects it is beneficial, the decentralized educational system also has disadvantages. Insofar as there are no resources earmarked for special education, this must be financed within the frameworks of regular school budgets. It is clearly apparent that in times of economic recession the differences between more and less economically strong local municipalities and schools tend to increase, jeopardizing the fulfillment of some pupils' special needs. It has also been observed that the decentralization process has affected the way in which special education has been defined. Thus, the inclusion of pupils into special programs for those with severe learning disabilities has remarkably increased, which in the long run could create obstacles regarding future studies and working opportunities.

Some pupils do not receive sufficient support. A large group consists of pupils described as shy, quiet, and reluctant to take the initiative. Also, those who act out are sometimes overlooked. In these cases it is not a question of their receiving insufficient support; rather, their unruliness can conceal problems that the school has not been able to identify, which results in their being given the wrong kind of support. Schools seldom have the time or the opportunity to make thorough analysis of the underlying reasons for a pupil's behavior. Measures taken about pupils are often based on vague assumptions and preconceived ideas. The behavior itself must be dealt with, in order to make the pupil behave as normally as possible. Although neuropsychological assessments are in great demand, the number of educational psychologists qualified to meet these demands is very low. In Europe, the number of educational psychologists per 1,000 pupils varies between 0 and 2. In Sweden this figure is 0.3. Swedish psychologists are well educated and licensed, but thus far there is no legislation stipulating the number of educational psychologists that should be available in the schools, because this is the responsibility of each municipality to decide.

In the report it also emerged that second-generation immigrants constitute the largest proportion of pupils in need of more support than they receive. The proportion of inhabitants with immigrant and often refugee backgrounds reaches 30% or more in several Swedish municipalities; in some schools the proportion of immigrant-background pupils can reach 80%–85%. Many of these children have deficits in their mother tongue as well as in their Swedish language skills, sometimes in combination with psychological problems. This situation places challenging demands on special education. Although the policy for immigrant pupils has been to provide free of charge teaching of their mother tongue in addition to Swedish, a critical discussion of whether this is beneficial for children with learning disabilities is ongoing.

Since the 1990s there has been a trend toward the creation of an increasing number of independent schools, a process facilitated by means of a school capitation allowance system. The proportion of pupils attending independent schools has doubled since the year 2000. However, there is a continuing concern that segregation and differences in quality between schools may increase as an effect of school choice, perhaps with negative long-term consequences for scholastic equality.

The tendency to implement new methods without quality assurance and a general negligence as to whether the fundamental changes in the educational system during the last decade have had an effect on the field of special education pose critical concerns.

Although the overall picture in some respects is complicated and problematic, Sweden might still be considered in the vanguard of special education development in inclusive education, thus making the further development of policy and practice intriguing and worthy of attention.

REFERENCE

Swedish Agency for School Improvement. (2005). *Pupils who need support but do not receive enough*. Report No. U04:075. Stockholm, Sweden: Liber Distribution.

Eva Tideman
Lund University

SWITZERLAND, SPECIAL EDUCATION IN

Education in Switzerland

Switzerland is a confederation of 26 cantons, which include 2,929 political municipalities. The cantons are autonomous states. Their population varies from 14,100 to 1,178,800 citizens. For further statistic key data, refer to the Internet (http://www.admin.ch/bfs/).

Switzerland does not have national school/educational legislation. The cantons remain the highest authority in this area, except for certain fields of vocational education. Article 69 of the Swiss Federal Constitution specifies the responsibilities of the 26 cantons for an adequate, sufficient, and free compulsory education. Compulsory education (preschool, primary school, lower secondary school) is subordinate to the Cantonal Departments of Public Education. Each canton is highly independent with regard to school administration and organization, which leads to an extreme decentralization of the school authority in Switzerland. Only a few institutions on the tertiary level (e.g., universities, advanced vocational training, higher vocational schools) are administered and supported by the federal government. The federal government also promotes and supports the cooperation and coordination between the cantons.

Figure S.9 is a diagram of the basic structure of the various cantonal school systems. It reveals the differences in the organization of the primary and the secondary level of compulsory education. In some cantons the decision for secondary school has to be made much earlier than in others, and depending on the canton, education on the lower secondary level lasts for 3, 4, or 5 years. On the lower secondary level, schools in most cantons provide three to four streams for pupils with different abilities and competences.

Common to all 26 educational systems are:

- *The basic structure*: Preschool (kindergarten), primary level, lower secondary level. The possibilities for educational courses on the upper secondary level, as well as on the tertiary level, depend on the size of the respective canton.

- *The compulsory education*: For all children between 6 to 7 years and 15 to 16 years, school attendance is compulsory on the primary and on the lower secondary level. Preschool is mandatory only in some cantons, but on a national level, children attend kindergarten almost without exception. Depending on the canton, preschool lasts 1 to 2 years.

- *The beginning of the school year*: All over Switzerland, the school year begins in late summer.

According to the constitution, the Swiss Conference of Cantonal Directors of Education has to guarantee a minimal intercantonal coordination. Members of the conference are the cantonal directors of education and/or other responsible representatives. The conference employs a few collaborators on a full-time basis, but mostly it mandates numerous commissions to prepare and elaborate different papers and documents. The Conference of Cantonal Directors of Education cannot promulgate any laws, it can only elaborate recommendations on behalf of the cantons.

The cantonal autonomy, mentioned above, has some clear advantages in the field of education. On one hand, it

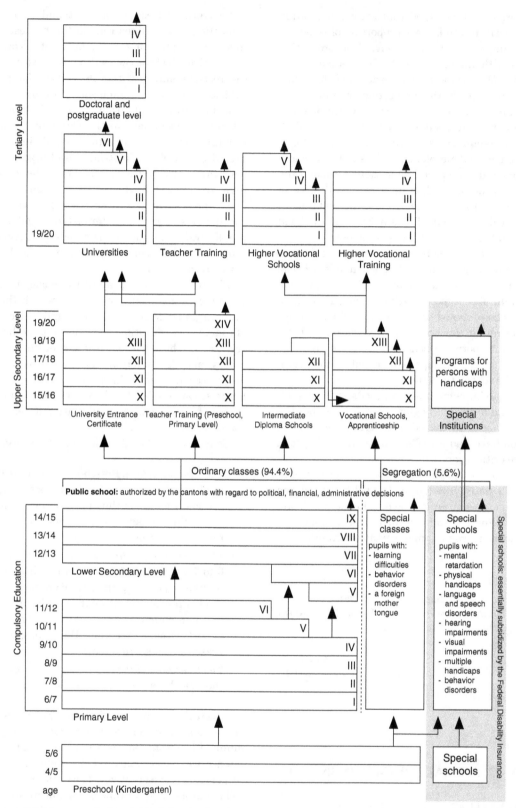

Figure S.9. Diagram of the system of education in Switzerland.

preserves the political and cultural diversity. One example is the Romansch speaking part of Switzerland: In a country with a strictly centralistic government, Romansch would probably not have become one of the official languages at school and it would have died out sooner or later. On the other hand, it is questionable whether this strong decentralization is really necessary and whether it is still appropriate at the start of the 21st century. How is it useful to maintain a special department of education for units that are as small as some of the Swiss cantons? And how can school reforms be effected on a Swiss level if federalism is of such high importance? It often takes years to come to an agreement on a Swiss level, even for simple reforms like the beginning of the school year or the 5-day school week.

Such examples emphasize the difficulty to effect more extensive reforms such as the integration of children with special needs, reforms that can hardly be realized in a federalistic state like Switzerland.

The Education of Children With Special Educational Needs

Preschool Level

Small children with disabilities and/or developmental problems are taken care of by early childhood special education services. Early education of children with special needs can be extended from birth to kindergarten, special kindergarten, or the start of school. The most common kind of early childhood interventions are the mobile education programs: They take place at the child's home where the specialist works with the child and the family in their usual environment once or twice a week. In some cases, early childhood education programs take place in institutions or a clinic where the child lives. Most services are staffed with professionals with a degree in special education; some services also employ other specialists such as speech therapists, physiotherapists, or specialists for the education of children with sensory impairments. Costs for early childhood special education are borne to a great extent by federal disability insurance. Cantons, municipalities, or other public or private responsible bodies contribute according to specific agreements.

Compulsory Education Level

If children need special help, they usually attend a special class (tied to the regular school) or a special school (managed partly by private organizations and partly by the canton, subsidized by federal disability insurance). Thus, children with special educational needs are mostly segregated from the regular school (see Figure S.9). Actually, 5.6% of all school-age children are schooled in classes with a special curriculum (Bundesamt für Statistik, 1997). A good number of children in regular classes,

special classes, and special schools get additional support and assistance from itinerant support services (between 10% to 20%, depending on the area in which they live). These services mostly provide psychological counseling and speech/language and psychomotor therapy. School services also include school medical service, school dental service, vocational counseling, and support teaching for immigrant children with a foreign mother tongue. Over the past 25 years, an increasing trend toward the integration of children with special educational needs into the regular school system can be observed; in some cantons, a restricted kind of integration is already practiced. As mentioned above, special schooling embraces all the school- and education-oriented endeavors for children and youths with special needs. On the compulsory education level, this function is assumed by special classes and special schools.

Special classes are small classes that contain no more than 12 children with relatively minor disabilities (learning difficulties, mild emotional disturbances, and mild sensory and speech/language disorders). Due to the structure and the grouping of these classes, they practice segregation, although they are mostly located in public schools and are under the political and financial authority of the Cantonal Departments of Education. Apart from the special classes for children with learning difficulties, many cantons also provide special classes for pupils with behavior disorders, speech/language impairments, physical handicaps, or a foreign native language. According to their special concept and the group of pupils, such classes should be taught by special teachers with a degree in special education. Unlike the regular classes, special classes are not homogeneous with regard to the age of their pupils. Depending on the number of pupils, they are grouped on four levels, which cover the compulsory education span: introduction classes or lower level, middle level, upper level, and vocational classes on the lower secondary level.

Special schools are open to all children with severe sensory, physical, and/or mental handicaps who benefit from federal disability insurance. They hold their own school facilities, mostly connected to a residential home. Special schools are managed partly by private organizations and funds under cantonal authority and partly by the canton, and they are subsidized by federal disability insurance (IV). Special schools are relatively autonomous. IV-supported special schools are classified as follows: special schools for children and youths with severe emotional and behavior disorders, with mental and multiple handicaps, with physical handicaps, with severe visual and hearing impairments, and with specific speech/language impairments. Not all these types of special schools are run by every canton, but there are contractual agreements for intercantonal cooperation.

Most cantons have their own legal provisions for their special classes and special schools. Due to its high financial commitment, the federal disability insurance has an important influence on the organization and the development of the special schools to which almost 2.5% of all Swiss pupils are referred.

Postschool Level

This level is particularly dominated by vocational training, although part of the vocational education already takes place on the secondary level I. On the lower secondary school level, programs include early vocational exposure/choice, vocational counseling, and vocational preparation courses. Schools on this level maintain close cooperation with vocational guidance services.

After their compulsory education, a good part of those exiting special classes take up vocational training (apprenticeship), or they enter an individualized vocational program that takes into account the trainee's difficulties and problems. The vocational training runs on a dual basis: The young people are trained in practical work in a particular enterprise 3 to 4 days a week, and 1 to 2 days a week they go to a vocational training school, where they attend general education classes as well as specific classes referring to their professional field. The training ends with a federal diploma. Some young persons with minor disabilities do not go through vocational training, but they might work on their parents' farms or carry out some unskilled work.

Young people who have difficulties training for a job in the free market because they suffer from physical handicaps (visual or—rarely—hearing impairments) get their training in specialized institutions. Many of the youths with mental retardation are occupied in sheltered workshops. On their way toward professional life, young persons with disabilities are supported by professionals of the vocational guidance services, run by the federal disability insurance. For further information on special education in Switzerland refer to Bürli (1993).

A Challenge for Educational Policy: The Integration of Children With Special Educational Needs Into Regular Classes

Except for the integration of the increasing number of immigrant children within the Swiss educational system, the integration of children with special educational needs is one of the most difficult and intriguing challenges for school authorities in Switzerland. Looking back on the educational policy of the past years, the Swiss school authorities have made many efforts to establish and develop a highly differentiated network of special schools and special classes. Toward the end of the 1970s, this differentiation reached its high actual standard.

Integration is defined as the common schooling and education of handicapped and nonhandicapped pupils in ordinary classes of the public school system, with an adequate support for the children with special educational needs. This definition does not include the school settings that only practice a more or less close cooperation between special classes and ordinary classes, even if both types of classes are located under the same roof, which may allow regular interactions between handicapped and nonhandicapped pupils. Real integration is characterized by common instruction of all pupils.

How Has Integration Been Implemented up to This Day?

Most of the pupils with special educational needs in regular classes in Switzerland are children with speech and language disorders. The schooling of this category of pupils in ordinary classes should rather be seen as nonsegregation than integration. Despite their special therapeutic needs, these pupils have never been systematically segregated. In Switzerland, pupils with specific, as well as complex, speech and language disorders usually remain in their regular classes, because the Swiss public school system can provide a dense network of special logopedic support. Only about 5% to 10% of the children with speech and language disorders are referred to a special school. Most of them suffer not only from speech/language impairments, but also from behavior disorders and/or learning difficulties.

The most remarkable development toward mainstreaming can be observed in the field of learning difficulties. About 25 years ago, pupils with learning difficulties could remain in their ordinary class for the first time. Besides the instruction based on the regular curriculum they did get special assistance by a support teacher. In 1995, approximately 300 Swiss schools practiced this kind of integration. About 8% to 12% of all pupils with learning difficulties were integrated in ordinary classes. This seems to be quite a low quota, but with regard to Swiss standards it can be considered a rather high proportion (Bless, 1995, pp. 61–64).

Pupils with a foreign native language attend ordinary classes in most Swiss cantons. Usually, they get special support for improving their knowledge of the standard school language. Several cantons with a high population density run special classes for these pupils, but they aim to integrate them in ordinary classes as soon as possible. But despite these integrative tendencies, the statistics plainly show a growing number of pupils with a foreign mother tongue in special classes (Kronig, 1996).

Pupils with physical handicaps or with hearing and visual impairments are integrated on a small scale. Two preconditions are essential for their mainstream placement. On one hand, these pupils have to be able to achieve the academic standard of their class without a differentiation of the regular curriculum. On the other hand, the schools have to be able to make available the necessary therapeutic support on their premises.

Despite the limited attempts to implement integration in Switzerland, several encouraging projects have been initiated lately. Some special schools apply new methods: They provide support for pupils with special educational needs who attend ordinary schools. For example, the staff of a special school support several mentally handicapped children attending the kindergarten of their residential area. One special school for pupils with hearing and language impairments did transform its division for the hearing impaired into a support and advisory center. They closed down their special classes, integrated the pupils in ordinary classes, and granted them systematic regular support. These individual cases should not be overvalued, but they can give signals for further attempts.

A look back on the evolution of mainstreaming in Switzerland proves that two conditions are essential for integration:

1. *Integration must not cause any further expenses.* The federal disability insurance (IV) is of high importance for the development of integration. The IV has an impeding influence on all integrative efforts, as it only subsidizes education of pupils with special educational needs in special schools and classes. As IV contributes largely to school tuition, board, and lodging, the cantons—which are responsible for the schooling and education of mentally handicapped children—are not interested in integrating these pupils. However, some of the enactments of IV make it possible to provide an integrative pedagogic and therapeutic care for pupils who need speech therapy, psychomotor therapy, or training in hearing and lipreading. As long as integrative measures do not cause any further expenditures, the cantons are willing to back them up. If integrative measures exceed regular expenses, the cantons stop such efforts. For example, the integration of pupils with learning difficulties does not cause any problems because the cantons finance both ordinary classes and special classes (see Figure S.9); therefore it does not matter in what classes these pupils are schooled. Pupils with speech and language impairments can be mainstreamed, because IV pays for their special support without having these pupils referred to a special school.

2. *Integration must not disturb the regular teaching in the classroom.* As long as classroom instruction can be accomplished in its regular way, integration is accepted. As soon as teachers have to individualize their lessons beyond a certain degree, integration does not have a good chance. For instance, pupils with hearing impairments and additional severe learning difficulties are rarely taught in ordinary classes, because integrating these children asks for a high degree of differentiation and individualization.

How Can the Actual and the Future Development of Integration Be Assessed?

If we take into consideration the number of integrated pupils, we can observe neither a slowdown nor a standstill. If we consider the categories of pupils who are integrated into mainstream education, integration seems to have come to a standstill, because many groups of children with special educational needs—particularly the mentally handicapped pupils—are excluded from integrative schooling. As long as the financial conditions and structures for the disabled in Switzerland are not fundamentally changed, true and real integration—that means common education and schooling of all children—will never be possible. Only a basic reorganization of the financial system can open the way to school reforms which aim at integration in the true sense of the word.

The following determinants do or may obstruct a further reorganization of the Swiss system of education in favor of true integration:

- A political system with 26 autonomous ministries of education is not very flexible with regard to a reorganization of the educational system within a useful period.
- On an all-Swiss level, there is no strong political will to support integration.
- Financial resources set a limit to integration. The structures of financing the disabled in Switzerland have been drawn up in view of segregation. They corroborate the segregation of the disabled, and they place at a disadvantage all the cantons that strive for an extensive integration.
- Unlike the advocates for integration, the special schools can rely on an efficient lobby. Most of the boards of directors of special schools can count on the honorary support of popular politicians and of other well-known personalities of regional or cantonal importance.
- Generally, the attitude of the majority of teachers towards integration is rather ambivalent. Basically, teachers recommend and support integrative ideas and efforts, but when it comes to realizing such ideas and efforts, they are rather cautious and reserved.
- Compared to Germany, Austria, or other countries, Switzerland does not have any serious parents' movement in favor of the handicapped.

An extensive evaluation of integrative trends and tendencies within the Swiss educational system cannot be restricted to listing and classifying specific cases of realized integration. Such an approach to integration is liable to consider only one specific aspect of the reality. Another important aspect is the constant study of the relevant statistic data (Bundesamt für Statistik, 1997). Contrary to the widespread view of numerous politicians and professionals or specialists in the field of education, the Swiss educational system has become more and more intolerant towards children with specific educational needs. Figure S.10 shows a continuous increase of segregated children since the school year 1983–1984 (4.26%). In 1995–1996, their number equaled 5.63%. It is remarkable that the number of segregated children increases parallel to the beginning and intensifying discussion on integration.

How can this increasing quota of segregated pupils be explained? Up to the mid-1990s no special schools and few special classes had been closed down, despite all integrative efforts. Thus, special institutions remain an option for the education of children with special needs. It is true that more and more of these children are integrated into the regular schools, but, on the other hand, the loss of such children is offset by segregating other groups of pupils, mostly children of immigrant families (see Figure S.11).

Special classes and schools are still used—or misused—to normalize the regular school. But over the past years, the segregation policy has changed. Actually, more immigrant children are referred to special classes, which initially had been set up for children with minor disabilities.

To sum up the latest developments in the field of special education, we notice that the schools have considerable trouble managing the growing diversity of their pupils. Despite the intensified discussion on integration of the past years, our schools are still not apt to more integration.

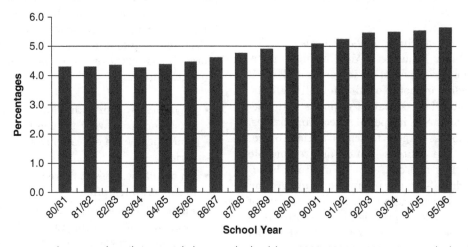

Figure S.10. Percentage quota of segregated pupils in special classes and school from 1980–1981 to 1995–1996, calculated on the basis of the total number of pupils of the primer and the lower secondary level (compulsory education).

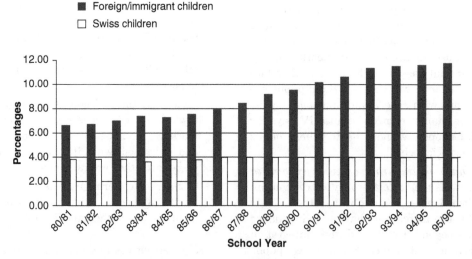

Figure S.11. Percentage quota of Swiss children and children of immigrant families in special education classes and schools from 1980–1981 to 1995–1996, calculated on the basis of the total number of pupils in compulsory education.

On the contrary, they have even become more intolerant of children who do not comply with their standards.

REFERENCES

Bless, G. (1995). *Zur Wirksamkeit der Integration. Forschungsüberblick, praktische Umsetzung einer integrativen Schulform, Untersuchungen zum Lernfortschritt.* BernStuttgart-Wien, Switzerland: Haupt-Verlag.

Bless, G. (1997). Integration in the ordinary school in Switzerland. In *Implementing inclusive education, OECD proceedings* (pp. 97–102). Paris, France: Organisation for Economic Co-operation and Development.

Bundesamt für Statistik. (1997). *Schülerinnen, Schüler und Studierende 1995/96.* Bern, Switzerland: Bundesamt für Statistik (BFS).

Bürli, A. (1993). *Special education in Switzerland. Aspects 50.* Lucerne, Switzerland: Edition SZH, Swiss Institute for Special Education.

Kronig, W. (1996). Besorgniserregende Entwicklungen in der schulischen Zuweisungspraxis bei ausländischen Kindern mit Lernschwierigkeiten. Vierteljahresschrift für Heilpädagogik und ihre Nachbargebiete (VHN).

Organisation for Economic Co-operation and Development (OECD). (1997). *Education at a glance 1997: OECD indicators.* Paris, France: Author.

GÉRARD BLESS
University of Fribourg

See also Western Europe, Special Education in

SYDENHAM'S CHOREA

Sydenham's chorea is more commonly known as St. Vitus Dance, but it also may be called minor chorea, rheumatic chorea, or acute chorea. It is generally regarded as an inflammatory complication of rheumatic fever, tonsillitis, or other infection; it also can be associated with pregnancy (chorea gravidarum). The condition is most prevalent in young girls between the ages of 5 and 15 and more common in temperate climates during summer and early fall. The condition has declined substantially in recent years owing to a similar decline in rheumatic fever. It is characterized by involuntary choreic movements throughout the body and occurs in about 10% of rheumatic attacks.

Choreic movements are rapid, purposeless, short-lasting, and nonrepetitive. The movements usually begin in one limb and flow to many different parts of the body; they may resemble athetoid cerebral palsy. Fidgety behavior, clumsiness, dropping of objects, facial grimacing, awkward gait, and changes in voice or slurred speech are common symptoms that may occur at onset. A month or more may pass before medical attention is sought because these symptoms initially may be mild. Anxiety, irritability, and emotional instability also may occur because of the uncontrolled movements. The involuntary motions disappear during sleep and occasionally are suppressed by rest, sedation, or attempts at voluntary control. Sydenham's chorea is nonfatal, and recovery usually occurs within 2 to 6 months. Recurrence may happen two or three times over a period of years in almost one third of the people affected.

Differential diagnosis depends on ruling out other causes through history and laboratory studies. There are no characteristic laboratory abnormalities, and pathologic studies suggest scattered lesions in the basal ganglia, cerebellum, and brain stem. No deficits in muscle strength or sensory perception are found during neurologic examination. The course of the impairment is variable and difficult to measure because of its gradual diminution.

There is no specific treatment, but some medications (phenobarbital, diazepam, perphenazine, or haloperidol) can be effective in reducing chorea. In most situations, the person with Sydenham's is encouraged to return to school or work, even if residual symptoms continue. In severe cases, protection from self-injury by using restraints may be necessary. The prognosis for recovery is variable but the condition inevitably subsides. Reassurance that the condition is self-limiting and eventually will decline without residual impairment is in order for people with Sydenham's, their families, teachers, and classmates. Behavioral problems, mild motor abnormalities, and poor performance in psychometric testing have been reported after the chorea dissipates. It is important that affected individuals receive therapeutic support (Moore, 1996).

This entry has been informed by the sources listed below.

REFERENCES

Berkow, R. (Ed.). (1982). *Merck manual* (14th ed.). Rahway, NJ: Merck, Sharp, & Dohme Research Laboratories.

Bird, M. T., Palkes, H., & Prensky, A. L. (1976). A follow-up study of Sydenham's chorea. *Neurology, 26,* 601–606.

Fahn, S. (1985). Neurologic and behavioral diseases. In J. Wyngaarden & L. Smith, Jr. (Eds.), *Cecil textbook of medicine* (17th ed., pp. 2074–2075). Philadelphia, PA: Saunders.

Magalini, S., & Scarascia, E. (1981). *Dictionary of medical syndromes* (2nd ed.). Philadelphia, PA: Lippincott.

Merritt, H. H. (1979). *A textbook of neurology* (6th ed.). Philadelphia, PA: Lea & Febiger.

Moore, D. (1996). Neuropsychiatric aspects of Sydenham's chorea: A comprehensive review. *Journal of Clinical Psychiatry, 57*(9), 407–414.

Nuasieda, P. A., Grossman, B. J., Koller, W. C., Weiner, W. J., & Klawans, H. L. (1980). Sydenham's chorea: An update. *Neurology, 30*, 331–334.

DANIEL D. LIPKA
*Lincoln Way Special Education
Regional Resources Center*

See also Chorea; Huntington's Chorea; St. Vitus Dance

SYNAPSES

The synapse is the structure that mediates the effects of a nerve impulse on a target cell, permitting communication among nerve cells, muscles, and glands. It is a synapse that joins the terminal end of an axon of one neuron with the dendrites or cell body of another. The synapse was first described by Sir Charles Sherrington in 1897. The word itself means "connection."

Messages arrive at the synapse in the form of action potentials. Synaptic potentials are triggered by action potentials; they in turn trigger subsequent action potentials, continuing the neural message on to its destination. While action potentials vary in frequency, they do not vary in form or magnitude. It is the synaptic potential that is responsible for variance in the nervous system.

The synaptic terminals on the end tips of axons take on various forms such as ball-like endings (boutons), nobs, spines, and rings. These terminals almost, but not quite, make contact with a part of another neuron (usually a dendrite or occasionally an axon or cell body). The space between the terminal of one neuron and the other neuron is called the synaptic cleft. This cleft is miniscule, typically on the order of about 200 angstroms. Transmission time across the synaptic cleft is approximately .3 to 1.0 msec.

Synaptic transmission can be electrical or chemical, although the former is uncommon in the mammalian brain (Gazzaniga, Steen, & Volpe, 1979). With chemical transmission, one cell, the presynaptic, secretes molecules that cross a synaptic cleft and join with a postsynaptic cell. The presynaptic cell endings contain mitochondria and synaptic vesicles that hold various neurotransmitters. The neurotransmitter substances are released in tiny packettes called quanta. These substances can serve excitatory or inhibitory purposes, and not all are currently identified. However, major excitatory neurotransmitters include acetylcholine, noradrenalin, serotonin, and dopamine. Important inhibitory transmitters include gamma-aminobutric acid (GABA) and glutamate. Specific receptor molecules that receive these neurotransmitters have been identified on the postsynaptic cell.

Synapses generally are classified as axiodendritic or axiosomatic. The typical pattern is axiodendritic; this pattern occurs when an axon meets a dendrite. Somewhat less common is the axiosomatic pattern, in which an axon meets a cell body.

This article has been informed by the sources listed below.

REFERENCES

Barr, M. D. (1979). *The human nervous system: An anatomic viewpoint* (3rd ed.). New York, NY: Harper & Row.

Gazzaniga, M., Steen, D., & Volpe, B. T. (1979). *Functional neuroscience*. New York, NY: Harper & Row.

DANNY WEDDING
Marshall University

See also Dendrites; Dopamine

SYNTACTIC DEFICIENCIES (*See* Childhood Aphasia; Expressive Language Disorders; Language Disorders)

SYPHILIS, CONGENITAL

Congenital syphilis is a form of syphilis diagnosed in children who are born with the disease. It is caused by the same spirochete, Treponema pallidum, that causes syphilis in adults. The disease is passed to the fetus from the infected mother before birth. Children with congenital syphilis may have symptoms immediately upon birth or may have none for several years (Syphilis, congenital, n.d.).

The incidences of syphilis are rising in the United States, from 691 cases diagnosed and reported in infants under 1 year of age in 1988 to 3,209 cases diagnosed and reported for the same age group in 1993. The risk of transmission from an infected mother to her fetus is 70%–100% if the mother is untreated (Bennett, Lynn, Klein, & Balkowiec, 1997). Because it is transmitted to unborn fetuses, males and females are affected equally by the disease.

Characteristics

1. Prenatal characteristics of the disorder include inflammation of the umbilical chord, reduction in the mother's estrogen level, and an increase in serum progesterone levels in the mother.

2. Early symptoms in the infant include high cholesterol levels; anemia; fever; jaundice; shedding of skin or blisters on palms and soles; bloody discharge from nose, called "snuffles"; failure to thrive; rash near the mouth, genitalia, or anus; impaired hearing; and an abnormal nose with no bridge, known as "saddle nose."

3. Later symptoms include enlarged liver and/or spleen; bone pain; lower leg bone abnormality called "saber shins"; joint swelling; Hutchinson teeth, which are notched and peg-shaped; vision loss; gray areas on the anus and vulva; convulsions; and mental retardation.

(Bennett et al., 1997; Congenital syphilis, n.d.; Syphilis, congenital, n.d.)

The treatment for congenital syphilis is penicillin. If the mother is diagnosed with syphilis while pregnant, she may also take penicillin, which can prevent the child from being born with the infection (Syphilis, congenital, n.d.). Blood tests or analysis of cerebrospinal fluid can be used to diagnose the mother or newborn child with syphilis. However, serum tests at times give false negatives and make it more difficult to diagnose infants with syphilis when it may be present (Bennett et al., 1997).

Some children born with congenital syphilis may be in need of special education services due to mental retardation and hearing loss. Speech therapy may be indicated in some cases. Other issues facing education professionals are related to diagnosis of the disorder in young children and reporting of possible sexual abuse. If symptoms of syphilis are not visible or reported until the child is older, it is then difficult to determine whether the child actually has congenital syphilis or syphilis secondary to sexual abuse. Medical and education professionals may be in the difficult position of determining whether a report of possible child sexual abuse should be made (Christian, Lavelle, & Bell, 1999).

The best prognosis for congenital syphilis can be given if the mother is diagnosed and treated during her pregnancy, thus not passing the disease on to her fetus. There is a high infant mortality rate (30%–40%) of children born with syphilis. For those who live, if syphilis is suspected, the child should be tested and treated as soon as possible. The child should also continue to be tested for syphilis, in case another round of treatment is necessary. Although syphilis can be treated, the effects cannot be reversed. Some (i.e., Glasser, 1996) argue that infants with no symptoms at birth, but whose mothers had syphilis while the child was in utero, should be treated with penicillin. The Centers for Disease Control have also established guidelines for medical professionals to follow when an infant is at risk for having syphilis (Glasser, 1996).

REFERENCES

Bennett, M. L., Lynn, A. W., Klein, L. E., & Balkowiec, K. S. (1997). Congenital syphilis: Subtle presentation of fulminant disease. *Journal of the American Academy of Dermatology, 36,* 351–354.

Christian, C. W., Lavelle, J., & Bell, L. M. (1999). Preschoolers with syphilis. *Pediatrics, 103,* e4.

Congenital syphilis. (n.d.). Retrieved August 1, 2001, from http://www.nlm.nih.gov/

Glasser, J. H. (1996). Centers for Disease Control and Prevention guidelines for congenital syphilis. *Journal of Pediatrics, 129,* 488–490.

Syphilis, congenital. (n.d.). Retrieved August 1, 2001 from http://www.stepstn.com/cgi-win/nord.exe

MARY HELEN SNIDER
Devereux Cleo Wallace

SYRINGOBULBIA

Syringobulbia is closely associated with syringomyelia. Both are forms of brain stem neurological disorders that are characterized by a cavity or cyst (syrinx) in the spinal cord. Syringomyelia, which is the more common form, is characterized by cavitation of the central spinal cord and often extends downward along the entire length of the spinal cord. Syringobulbia is characterized by cavitation that appears in the brain stem. These disorders are slowly progressive disorders that are congenital, although there is evidence that syringomyelia and syringobulbia may also be a result of trauma (Kettaneh, Biousse, & Bousser, 2000; Thoene, 1995). These disorders are often associated with craniovertebral anomalies (e.g., Arnold-Chiari syndrome).

Syringobulbia is very rare (fewer than 1 in 100,000 births) and can affect either gender, although there appears to be a slight predilection towards males.

Characteristics

1. Although the defect may be congenital, for unknown reasons the cavity does not increase in size until teenage years or young adulthood. Therefore, symptoms may not be present until this time

2. Symptoms often begin with loss of peripheral sensory functioning. For example, the deficit often begins with a lack of pain or temperature sensation in the fingers

3. Syringobulbia may include vocal chord paralysis

4. Atrophy and fibrillation of the tongue muscles (muscle twitching involving individual muscle fibers acting without coordination)

5. Difficulty in articulating words (Dysarthria)

6. Vertigo

7. Rapid involuntary oscillation of eyeballs (nystagmus)

8. Abnormal deficiency or absence of sweating

9. Bilateral facial sensory impairment

10. Distal sensory or motor dysfunction due to medullary compression

To treat syringobulbia, possible underlying problems, such as anomalies of the spine or base of the brain, should be corrected. Surgical drainage of the cavity may be necessary, and shunts may be implanted. This type of surgery has been found to be successful in alleviating the symptoms of syringobulbia, but severe neurological deterioration may not be surgically reversible.

Because the disorder does not usually become apparent until the teens or early adulthood, it is likely that students with a diagnosis of syringobulbia will already be in junior high or high school. These students will be eligible for special services under IDEA (1997) within the other physical disability category. The type of services needed will depend on the symptoms and progression of the disorder. If the disorder is diagnosed before severe neurological damage has taken place and the individual responds to surgery well, school-based services may not be as intense and encompassing as for a student who experiences severe neurological impairment.

Students may need speech and language assistance if they have experienced vocal chord paralysis and dysarthria. Services may include counseling to understand and accommodate the necessary changes in their lives due to the disorder. For example, students with spinal cord disorders may have to limit their physical activities to reduce the possibility of damage and trauma to the spine. Syringobulbia may be associated with moderate to severe back pain. Therefore, students may need to be educated in pain management techniques. These students may require close observation and monitoring of medication, so school personnel need to be cognizant of the limitations of the disorder and to work closely with medical personnel. Students with syringobulbia may require extended time away from school for medical reasons. For example, students diagnosed during their school years will probably require spinal surgery, which is often associated with long recovery periods. Therefore, the school will need to make accommodations to help the student keep up with schoolwork and eventually reintegrate the student back into the school.

Present research is addressing the need for a comprehensible differential diagnosis for syringobulbia and syringomyelia (e.g., Penarrocha, Okeson, Penarrocha, & Angeles Cervello, 2001). Additionally, research is addressing the possibility of trauma to the head and neck as a cause for these disorders (e.g., Kettaneh et al., 2000).

REFERENCES

Kettaneh, A., Biousse, V., & Bousser, M. G. (2000). Neurological complications after roller coaster rides: An emerging new risk? *Presse Med, 29*(4), 175–180.

Penarrocha, M., Okeson, J. P., Penarrocha, M. S., & Angeles Cervello, M. (2001). Orofacial pain as the sole manifestation of syringobulbia-syringomyelia associated with Arnold-Chiari malformation. *Journal of Orofacial Pain, 15*(2), 170–173.

Thoene, J. G. (Ed.). (1995). *Physicians guide to rare diseases* (2nd ed.). Montvale, NJ: Dowden.

RACHEL TOPLIS
University of Northern Colorado

SYSTEM OF MULTICULTURAL PLURALISTIC ASSESSMENT

The System of Multicultural Pluralistic Assessment (SOMPA; Mercer & Lewis, 1979) was designed to provide a comprehensive measure of the cognitive abilities, perceptual-motor abilities, sociocultural background, and adaptive behavior of children ages 5 through 11 years. It employs three models of assessment and attempts to integrate them into a comprehensive assessment: (1) the medical model, defined as any abnormal organic condition interfering with physiological functioning; (2) the social system model, determined principally from labeling theory and social deviance perspectives taken from the field of sociology, which attempts to correct the "Anglo conformity" biases of the test developers who have designed IQ tests for the past 90 years; and (3) the pluralistic model, which compares the scores of a child with the performance levels of children of a similar ethclass (that is, the same demographic socioeconomic, and cultural background) correcting for any score discrepancies with the White middle class. English- and Spanish-language versions of the scale are available.

The SOMPA is a complex and somewhat innovative system of assessment designed to ameliorate much of the conflict over assessment in the schools. The senior author, Mercer, a sociologist, conceptualized SOMPA in the late 1960s and early 1970s from her work in sociology's labeling theory and her sociological surveys and studies of intellectual disability, particularly mild intellectual disability, as a sociocultural phenomenon. The SOMPA has been extensively reviewed and debated (Humphreys, 1985; Nuttall, 1979; Reynolds, 1985; Reynolds & Brown, 1984; Sandoval, 1985). Unfortunately, presentation of the SOMPA for clinical application as opposed to pure research appears to have been premature. Major conceptual and technical issues pertaining to the scale have not been resolved adequately, even considering that a complete resolution of most of these issues is not possible. As a result, the SOMPA has contributed to the controversy over assessment practices in the schools rather than moved the field closer to a resolution. Even though controversy frequently can be stimulating to a discipline, in many ways, SOMPA has polarized the assessment community.

One of the major conceptual problems of the SOMPA centers around its primary underlying assumption. Mercer developed the SOMPA in response to her acceptance of the cultural test bias hypothesis. Briefly stated, this hypothesis contends that all racial, ethnic, socioeconomic, or other demographically based group differences on mental tests are due to artifacts of the tests themselves and do not reflect real differences. According to Mercer and Lewis, this is due to the extent of Anglocentrism (degree of adherence to White middle-class values, norms, and culture) apparent in most, if not all, mental measurements. In accepting this hypothesis as fundamentally correct, Mercer relies primarily on the mean differences definition of bias, which states that any differences in mean levels of performance among racial or ethnic groups on any mental scale is prima facie evidence of bias. The principal purpose of the SOMPA is to remove this bias by providing a correct estimate of intellectual abilities, an estimated learning potential (ELP). While adding a "correction factor" to the obtained IQs of disadvantaged children is not a new idea, the SOMPA corrections are unique in their objectivity and in having a clearly articulated, if controversial, basis. The corrections are based on the child's social-cultural characteristics and equate the mean IQs of Blacks, Whites, and Hispanics with varying other cultural characteristics such as family structure and degree of urban acculturation.

Unfortunately for the SOMPA, its underlying assumption that mean differences among sociocultural groups indicate cultural bias in tests is the single most rejected of all definitions of test bias by serious psychometricians researching the cultural test bias hypothesis (Jensen, 1980; Reynolds, 1982). The conceptual basis for the SOMPA is far more controversial than it appears in the test manuals and is indeed open to serious question. If other approaches to the cultural test bias hypothesis had demonstrated the existence of bias, then the need for a resolution to the problem such as proposed by Mercer would remain tenable. However, the large body of evidence regarding the cultural test bias hypothesis, gathered primarily over the past decade, has failed to

substantiate popular claims of bias in the assessment of native-born ethnic minorities. For the most part, the psychometric characteristics of well-designed and carefully standardized tests of intelligence such as the Wechsler scale have been shown to be substantially equivalent across ethnic groups (Jensen, 1980; Reynolds, 1982).

If this argument is dismissed and Mercer's contentions regarding test bias accepted, other serious conceptual issues remain. The ELP, a regression-based transformation of Wechsler IQs, is said to provide a good estimate of the child's innate intelligence or potential to profit from schooling. Such a claim is difficult to support under any circumstances. It is unlikely that we will ever be able to assess innate ability since environment begins to impact the organism at the moment of conception. We are left only with the possibility of observing the phenotypic construct. Furthermore, as of this writing, no evidence exists relating ELP to any other relevant criteria (Reschly, 1982).

Others have noted substantial agreement in criticisms of the SOMPA ELP, particularly regarding its construct validity (Humphreys, 1985; Reschly, 1982). Humphreys (1985) argues that

> Estimated learning potential is a thoroughly undesirable construct. Many people want to hear and believe the misinformation furnished by ethclass norms, but this is dangerous for it solves no real problems. It is conceivable, of course, that several generations from now black and Hispanic performance on standard tests of intelligence and achievement might equal the white majority. In this limited sense, ethclass norms might not misinform, but an inference that requires 50 years or more to validate helps little in dealing with today's children. They need higher scores on measures of reading, listening, writing, computing, mathematics, and science, not ethclass IQs. (p. 1519)

The ELP may in fact be misleading and result in a denial of special education services to children who are seriously at risk of academic failure or already experiencing such failure. As Reschly has stated, "All of the direct uses of ELP at present and in the foreseeable future are questionable" (p. 242). Equally controversial, even in Mercer's home field of sociology, is labeling theory, another important concept in the establishment of the need for a system like SOMPA. If we accept the contention that false negatives are more desirable than false positives in the diagnosis of mental retardation, a check on the utility function tells us that it would most likely be best to diagnose no children as mentally retarded since the incidence in Mercer's model in particular is far less than 3%.

Technical problems are also evident in the development and application of the concept of ELP. As noted, the ELP is a regression-based transformation of Wechsler IQs to a scale with a mean of 100 and standard deviation of 15 independent of a child's sociocultural characteristics. These transformations are made on the basis of the

SOMPA sociocultural scales. Based on data derived during the norming of the SOMPA, regression equations were derived for determining the ELP. The stability of these regression equations and their generalizability to children outside the standardization sample have been called into question. Since the SOMPA was not normed on a stratified random sample of children nationwide, but rather on a sampling restricted to California, generalizability studies received some priority on the measure's publication. Regression equations derived from samples from other states, notably Texas and Arizona, have not been at all similar to the original equations; even the multiple R between the various sociocultural variables and Wechsler IQ varies substantially (i.e., from .30 to .60 in some cases) across states and across ethnic groups (Reschly, 1982). Given the state of contemporary applied psychometrics and the sophisticated normative sampling of such scales as the Wechsler series and the recent Kaufman Assessment Battery for Children, the failure to provide an adequate standardization sample for the SOMPA is inexcusable and not characteristic of the publisher.

The reliability of the ELP will also be dependent to a large extent on the stability of the sociocultural scales from which the corrections to the obtained Wechsler IQs are derived. The stability of these scores has been seriously questioned in at least one study. Over a 4-year period, Wilkinson and Oakland (1983b) report test-retest correlations that range from .39 to the high .90s across scales. Within scales and across demographic groupings such as race, sex, and socioeconomic status, the correlations also vary considerably, pointing up the real possibility of bias in the SOMPA. Apparently the ELP can change dramatically for individual children over a 4-year period (given that half of the stability coefficients reported for the SOMPA sociocultural scales are below .80), a result that seems antithetical to the entire concept of the ELP.

Stability of other SOMPA scales that should be relatively stable has also been questioned. The SOMPA health history inventory shows test-retest reliability coefficients ranging from −.08 (!) to .96. Considerable differences are evident within scales across demographic groupings as well. The trauma scale shows a stability coefficient of .23 for males and .74 for females (Wilkinson & Oakland, 1983a). Prepostnatal scores show a stability of .78 for Whites and .96 for Blacks, a scale that should remain highly stable since the SOMPA begins at age 5 years.

These are but a few of the conceptual and technical issues plaguing the SOMPA. Much work was needed on the SOMPA prior to its presentation for practical application, work that was not done. The conceptual issues in particular needed clarification.

On another level, the SOMPA must be questioned as an assessment system for children especially. The SOMPA is designed primarily as a means of providing a fairer scheme of classifying children into diagnostic categories. It has clearly not been validated adequately for this purpose. However, a more far-reaching concern to the clinician working with children experiencing school failure is the development of programs for the habilitation of learning. The SOMPA provides no real clues to the development of such interventions. This is especially damaging to practical applications of the SOMPA because it requires a substantial investment of professional time to be properly administered. The commitment of so much time and effort to an assessment system that does not provide considerable help with the development of individual educational programs cannot be justified in any kind of cost-benefit analysis. The emphasis on prevention-intervention-habilitation is more in keeping with the needs of the field.

The SOMPA cannot be recommended for use at this time. Its conceptual, technical, and practical problems are simply too great. Nevertheless, it was an innovative, gallant effort at resolving the conflict over assessment practices in the schools. Although widely used in the first several years after publication, the SOMPA quickly disappeared from the repertoire of most school psychologists and is now antiquated.

REFERENCES

Humphreys, L. G. (1985). Review of System of Multicultural Pluralistic Assessment. In J. V. Mitchell (Ed.), *Ninth mental measurements yearbook*. Lincoln, NE: Buros Institute.

Jensen, A. R. (1980). *Bias in mental testing*. New York, NY: Free Press.

Mercer, J., & Lewis, J. (1979). *System of Multicultural Pluralistic Assessment*. New York, NY: Psychological Corporation.

Nuttall, E. V. (1979). Review of System of Multicultural Pluralistic Assessment. *Journal of Educational Measurement, 16*, 285–290.

Reschly, D. J. (1982). Assessing mild mental retardation: The influence of adaptive behavior, sociocultural status, and prospects for nonbiased assessment. In C. R. Reynolds & T. B. Gutkin (Eds.), *The handbook of school psychology*. New York, NY: Wiley.

Reynolds, C. R. (1982). The problem of bias in psychological assessment. In C. R. Reynolds & T. B. Gutkin (Eds.), *The handbook of school psychology*. New York, NY: Wiley.

Reynolds, C. R. (1985). Review of System of Multicultural Pluralistic Assessment. In J. V. Mitchell (Ed.), *Ninth mental measurements yearbook*. Lincoln, NE: Buros Institute.

Reynolds, C. R., & Brown, R. T. (Eds.). (1984). *Perspectives on bias in mental testings*. New York, NY: Plenum Press.

Sandoval, J. (1985). Review of System of Multicultural Pluralistic Assessment. In J. V. Mitchell (Ed.), *Ninth mental measurements yearbook*. Lincoln, NE: Buros Institute.

Wilkinson, C. Y., & Oakland, T. (1983a, August). *Stability of the SOMPA's health history inventory*. Paper presented to the annual meeting of the American Psychological Association, Anaheim, CA.

Wilkinson, C. Y., & Oakland, T. (1983b, August). *Stability of the SOMPA's sociocultural modalities.* Paper presented to the annual meeting of the American Psychological Association, Anaheim, CA.

CECIL R. REYNOLDS
Texas A&M University

See also Adaptive Behavior; Cultural Bias in Testing; Mercer, Jane R.; Vineland Adaptive Behavior Scales—Second Edition

SYSTEMS-LEVEL CHANGE, SCHOOL-WIDE POSITIVE BEHAVIOR SUPPORT

School-Wide Positive Behavior Support (SWPBS) is an application of a behaviorally based systems approach to enhance the capacity of schools, families, and communities to design effective teaching and learning environments. This is accomplished by systematically integrating research-validated behavioral practices into the settings in which teaching and learning occurs. In other words, SWPBS uses evidence-based behavioral practices to change our school systems, our school environments, and ultimately the behavior of our staff and students. Attention is focused on creating and sustaining universal (school-wide), supplemental (classroom and targeted groups), and intensive (individual) systems of support that improve lifestyle results (personal, health, social, family, work, recreation) for all children and youth by making problem behavior less effective, efficient, and relevant and desired behavior more functional.

What Is a Systems Approach in SWPBS?

An organization is a group of individuals who work together to achieve a common goal. Systems are needed to support the collective use of best practices by individuals within the organization. The School-Wide PBS process emphasizes the creation of systems that support the adoption and durable implementation of evidence-based practices and procedures and that fit within ongoing school reform efforts. This application of a positive behavior support system within a school is not easily developed apart from similar support systems changes that occur at a state and district level. Understanding those foundational systems of support that make the actual application of support in schools possible is addressed in the *Implementation Blueprint and Self-Assessment: School-Wide Positive Behavioral Interventions and*

Support (Sugai, et al, 2010). This blueprint provides further elaboration on how to establish systems that support the adoption and durable implementation of evidence-based practices and procedures and that fit with and are a part of ongoing school reform efforts. This approach focuses on the interactive and self-checking process of organizational correction and improvement around four key elements:

1. *Outcomes*: Academic and behavior targets that are endorsed and emphasized by students, families, and educators.
2. *Practices*: Interventions and strategies that are evidence based.
3. *Data*: Information that is used to identify status, need for change, and effects of interventions.
4. *Systems*: Supports that are needed to enable the accurate and durable implementation of the practices of PBS.

The practical experience of implementing SWPBS in hundreds of state and district school systems and in thousands of schools has established an organizational logic for addressing key systems features that impact sustainable SWPBS implementation at a school, district, and state level. As an initial step, a *leadership team* is developed to address multischool (district) or multidistrict (state or regional) leadership and coordination. The leadership *team or structure* is needed to lead the school reform process and increase the system's capacity in four primary areas:

- *Training capacity*: Refers to the system's ability to self-assess for specific programmatic and staff development needs and objectives, develop a training action plan, invest in increasing local training capacity, and implement effective and efficient training activities.
- *Coaching capacity*: Refers to the system's ability to organize personnel and resources for facilitating, assisting, maintaining, and adapting local school training implementation efforts for both initial training and on going implementation support.
- *Evaluation capacity*: Refers to the system's ability to establish measurable outcomes, methods for evaluating progress toward these measurable outcomes, and modified or adapted action plans based on these evaluations.
- *Behavioral expertise*: Refers to the critical behavior content knowledge, as well as the process and organizational strategies, to support the system with implementing a multitiered system of support.

To enable and support the leadership team's efforts, the PBS implementation must have (a) adequate and sustained *funding support*; (b) regular, wide, and meaningful *visibility*; (c) relevant and effective *political support*;

and (d) *policies* and related practices (integrated or collaborative initiatives) that promote or do not inhibit the development of an effective SWPBS system. Finally, exemplars or *demonstrations* of effective and sustainable implementation are necessary at the district and school level to provide evidence of the impact of the four key elements: outcomes, practices, data systems, and support system.

REFERENCE

Sugai, G., Horner, R. H., Algozzine, R., Barrett, S., Lewis, T., Anderson, C.,... Simonsen, B. (2010). *Implementation Blueprint and Self-Assessment: School-Wide Positive Behavioral Interventions and Support.* Eugene: University of Oregon.

DONALD KINCAID
University of South Florida
Fourth edition

SYSTEMS OF CLASSIFICATION

A system of classification can be developed in an effort to identify individuals as members of one of the major disability categories (e.g., learning disabilities), or it may be used to provide a subclassification within a major area of exceptionality (e.g., Down syndrome as a subcategory of intellectual disability). Contemporary special education services rely heavily on the classification of general disabilities and, to a lesser extent, on subclassifications.

The historical origins of the use of classification systems are dominated by two events. First, special education represents a unique educational development derived from the discipline of psychology. As such, it emerged in light of that discipline's intense interest in the measurement and study of individual differences. Subsequent refinements in measurement, including the development of classification systems based on reliable individual differences, were transferred to special education practice in the first part of the 20th century. A second related influence arose from the attempts of early special educators to provide a science of treatment. That is, the study of individual differences led to the acceptance of a nosological orientation in treatment. Long practiced in medicine, the nosological orientation presumes that disorders can be isolated with reference to etiology, that etiology can ultimately be treated, and that subsequent cases can be similarly addressed (i.e., treatment proceeds from symptom to diagnosis of etiology to specification of treatment). In this approach, the development of a precise system of classification and subclassification is essential.

Possibly the most influential classification system now in effect is that provided within the Individuals with Disabilities Education Act. Ysseldyke and Algozzine (1984) indicate that through this legislation, the U.S. Department of Education recognizes 11 categories of exceptionality, although some states recognize more or fewer categories. In most states, the categories represent an effective determinant of service: If an individual is not a member of the specified disability category, services are not mandated. Thus, systems of classification, and related entry procedures, are essential in the selection process that ultimately determines entrance to special education.

A number of subclassification systems exist within the broad categories of exceptionality. Most of these attempt to suggest, if not prescribe, the general course of diagnosis and treatment. Two well-known systems typify this approach. The *Diagnostic and Statistical Manual of Mental Disorders, Fourth Edition* (*DSM-IV*; American Psychiatric Association, 1994) is a psychiatrically derived classification system for use with children and adults with emotional disorders. The *DSM-IV* is the standard classification system within mental health facilities in the United States, though it has far less official influence in public education. In the *DSM-IV*, disorders are grouped into five major divisions (intellectual, behavioral, emotional, physical, and developmental). Each division is further partitioned into specific disorders as defined by rigid diagnostic criteria. Individuals thus receive codes that indicate the diagnosed disabilities. Recent criticisms suggest that this system is archaic and needs to be redefined. Psychiatric classification of personality disorders, for example, could be classified in terms of severity and subtype (Tyrer, 1996).

A second classification system is used in the diagnosis and treatment of intellectual disabilities. The American Association on Mental Deficiency classification system (Grossman, 1983) is based on a number of factors, including intelligence and adaptive behavior. In this system, the degree of intellectual disability is specified as mild, moderate, severe, or profound. The intent of the system is clearly to specify training and structural support needs.

It is erroneous to conclude that these two well-accepted classification systems are acceptable to all agencies, that alternatives are nonexistent, or that particular systems are not revised over time. For example, the *DSM-IV* is in the fourth substantially revised edition and tends not to be used in schools; alternatives such as Quay's (1964) system are often favored. Nor is there a paucity of systems. MacMillan (1982) reports at least 10 systems were used in the 20th century with individuals with intellectual disabilities. Of these, four are now in common use. Clearly, classification systems are modified in response to the influence of social pressures, research bases, and professional opinions.

A number of theoretical and pragmatic pitfalls are evident in current classification systems. Three are particularly germane. First, the fact that multiple classification systems exist and are endorsed by various agencies creates opportunities for classification and service provision irregularities. Second, there is question as to whether behavioral diagnostic techniques possess the necessary reliability and validity to provide precise classification; error in measurement and misassignment to categories is possible (Salvia & Ysseldyke, 1985). Third, the significance of classification systems based on etiology may prove to be less important to the behavioral than the medical sciences. That is, treatment links have generally not been established between etiological diagnosis and behavioral treatment. Such links may prove difficult or impossible to achieve (Neisworth & Green, 1975).

Despite these criticisms, classification systems remain an important consideration for special education. Kauffman (1977) provided a rationale for the continuation of attempts to classify behavior: Classification is a fundamental aspect of any developing science of behavior; classification is of importance in organizing and communicating information; and classification systems, if scientifically investigated, may ultimately assist in the prediction of behavior and offer insights into the preferred method of treatment. As noted by Kauffman (1977), the alternative to continued development of classification systems is "an educational methodology that relies on attempts to fit interventions to disorders by random choice, intuition, or trial and error" (p. 27).

REFERENCES

American Psychiatric Association. (1994). *Diagnostic and statistical manual of mental disorders* (4th ed.). Washington, DC: Author.

Grossman, H. J. (Ed.). (1983). *Manual on terminology and classification in mental retardation* (3rd ed.). Washington, DC: American Association on Mental Deficiency.

Kauffman, J. M. (1977). *Characteristics of children's behavior disorders*. Columbus, OH: Merrill.

MacMillan, D. L. (1982). *Mental retardation in school and society* (2nd ed.). Boston, MA: Little, Brown.

Neisworth, J. T., & Green, J. G. (1975). Functional similarities of learning disabilities and mild retardation. *Exceptional Children, 42*, 17–21.

Quay, H. C. (1964). Dimensions of personality in delinquent boys as inferred from factor analysis of case history data. *Child Development, 35*, 479–484.

Salvia, J., & Ysseldyke, J. E. (1985). *Assessment in special and remedial education* (3rd ed.). Boston, MA: Houghton Mifflin.

Tyrer, P. (1996) New ways of classifying personality disorder. *Psychiatrist, 7*(1), 43–48.

Ysseldyke, J. E., & Algozzine, B. (1984). *Introduction to special education*. Boston, MA: Houghton Mifflin.

TED L. MILLER
University of Tennessee

***See also* Diagnostic and Statistical Manual of Mental Disorders; Learner Taxonomies**

T

TACHISTOSCOPE

The tachistoscope, or t-scope, is an instrument for presenting visual stimuli for very brief times at a controlled level of illumination (Stang & Wrightsman, 1981). The t-scope may be a self-contained unit or mounted on a slide projector.

Often the goal of tachistoscopic presentation is to determine the threshold at which subjects verbally report recognition of a stimulus. Research using the tachistoscope also has been carried out concerning the existence of subliminal perception where stimuli are said to affect behavior below the conscious threshold of perception.

Reading involves very briefly viewing words; the tachistoscopic task was broadly assumed to mimic the requirements faced by skilled readers. Despite questions of the applicability of t-scope research to everyday reading tasks, a variety of components of reading have been examined in the presence of varying speeds of presentation and levels of illumination. The threshold of word recognition can be determined and models of skilled reading can be constructed (Carr & Pollatsek, 1985; Gough, 1984; Mewhort & Campbell, 1981). The performance of skilled and disabled readers can be compared to determine the differences that might be diagnostically significant (Pirozzolo, 1979).

REFERENCES

Carr, T., & Pollatsek, A. (1985). Recognizing printed words: A look at current models. In D. Besner, T. G. Waller, & G. E. Mackinnon (Eds.), *Reading research: Advances in theory and practice* (Vol. 5, pp. 2–82). Orlando, FL: Academic Press.

Gough, P. B. (1984). Word recognition. In P. D. Pearsen (Ed.), *Handbook of reading research* (pp. 225–291). New York, NY: Longman.

Mewhort, D. J. K., & Campbell, A. J. (1981). Toward a model of skilled reading performance: An analysis of performance in tachistoscopic tasks. In G. E. Mackinnon & T. G. Waller (Eds.), *Reading research: Advances in theory and practice* (Vol. 1.3, pp. 39–118). New York, NY: Academic Press.

Pirozzolo, F. J. (1979). *The neuropsychology of developmental reading disorders*. New York, NY: Praeger.

Stang, D., & Wrightsman, L. (1981). *Dictionary of social behavior and social research methods*. Monterey, CA: Brooks-Cole.

LEE ANDERSON JACKSON JR.
University of North Carolina at Wilmington

See also Perceptual Span

TAIJIN KYOFUSHO

Taijin Kyofusho syndrome (TKS) is a culture-bound psychiatric syndrome distinctive to Japan that in some ways resembles social phobia defined in the *DSM-IV* (American Psychiatric Association [APA], 1994). This disorder resembles social anxiety reaction. TKS is a cultural variation of social anxiety and is a function of how given cultures shape the way in which its members define and construe the self as the object of social threat (Dinnel, Kleinknecht, & Kleinknecht, 1997). This syndrome is included in the official Japanese diagnostic system for mental disorders.

There are no known incidence or prevalence studies on TKS, and according to Dinnel et al. (1997) epidemiological data are not available. However, according to APA (1994), this disorder is distinctive to Japan. As with social phobias in Western cultures, "the typical age of TKS onset in Japan is in adolescence and early adulthood" (Dinnel et al., 1997, p. 160). TKS is conceptualized as running a wide range of severity from "the highly prevalent but mild social concerns of adolescence, through social phobia, to inordinate concern with bodily features in which the person obsesses on some imagined or exaggerated physical defect" (Dinnel et al., 1997, p. 161). There are also clinical data that indicate that inversely to Western social phobias, more males than females exhibit the TKS condition (Dinnel et al., 1997).

Taijin Kyofusho literally means symptoms (*sho*) of fear (*kyofu*) experienced when people have face-to-face contact. TKS is described as an "obsession of shame, manifest by morbid fear of embarrassing or offending others by blushing, emitting offensive odors or flatulence, staring inappropriately, improper facial expressions, a blemish or physical deformity" (Dinnel et al., 1997, p. 161). The key factor in this type of social avoidance is the fear of disrupting group cohesiveness by making others uncomfortable. The essential feature of social phobia is marked fear in social or performance situations in which one might be embarrassed or in which others might judge one to be odd or different. The same conceptual fear is present in TKS, except that the fear is not for oneself but for one's familial or social group.

Characteristics

1. Obsession with shame
2. Morbid fear of embarrassment
3. Social avoidance
4. Extreme fear of social interaction

In terms of treatment, it is extremely important to discern the cultural background and level of assimilation of the person exhibiting TKS characteristics. A particular scale is utilized to assess both the characteristics of TKS and the level of acculturation of the afflicted student: the Suinn-Lew Asian Self-Identify Acculturation Scale. This scale was developed by Suinn, Rickland-Figueroa, Lew, and Vigil in 1987 and is available in both the United States and Japan. In East Asian cultures, largely one's familial or social group defines the self, such that the self is an extension of that group. According to Dinnel et al. (1997, p. 161), "individualism, self-aggrandization, or deviation from the group is not tolerated: 'the nail that stands out gets pounded.'" Therefore, determining the level of acculturation to Western standards and perceptions about group-self identification is necessary with these individuals.

It is doubtful that special education services would be available for students exhibiting TKS. However, referrals to culturally appropriate and competent mental health service providers would be essential.

REFERENCES

American Psychiatric Association. (1994). *Diagnostic and statistical manual of mental disorders* (4th ed.). Washington, DC: Author.

Dinnel, D. L., Kleinknecht, E. E., & Kleinknecht, R. A. (1997). Cultural factors in social anxiety: A comparison of social phobia symptoms and taijin kyofusho. *Journal of Anxiety Disorders*, *11*, 157–177.

KIELY ANN FLETCHER
Ohio State University

TAIWAN, SPECIAL EDUCATION IN

The early development of special education in Taiwan has its root in the tenets of Confucianism: "education for all" and "instruction by potential." In this context, efforts are made both by government agencies and private sectors to ensure that all exceptional individuals are entitled to a right to appropriate education. The protocol of educational alternatives for students with disabilities in Taiwan can be traced back to the late years of the 19th century. Interestingly, early attempts to educate the individuals with disabilities were inaugurated by the clergy. To illustrate, the first special day school (built in 1886 for children who are deaf and mute) was funded by English churches and staffed by ministers. This day school served as a catalyst for establishment of similar facilities throughout the island. Public schools did not provide special education programs until 1961, when the Dong-Men elementary school of Taipei developed the first self-contained class of its kind for children with emotional disturbances.

Educational programs for children with mental retardation (MR) have played a major role in the development of special education within the public schools. Actually, special education and classes for students with MR were considered one and the same. The confusion was attributed to overemphasis on developing programs for MR children and the lack of programs for other exceptional children and youth, which in turn was associated with the overrepresentation of students with mental retardation.

Few efforts had been organized before the 1980s to fight for the rights of populations with disabilities. The stimulus for increased public interest in and governmental attention to the welfare of people with disabilities is attributed in part to political parties and academic scholars who had their advanced studies abroad. In the late 1970s as the major opposition political party emerged, the rights movement for people with handicaps became overwhelming. The outcome has been passage of the Special Education Act of 1984 (Ministry of Education, 1984) and similar legislation, plus significant changes in schools and communities.

The Special Education Act of 1984 provides the framework for special education policies and its regulations delineate a broad guideline for criteria for the identification, placement, and delivery of educational services for children with special needs. Specifications of the regulations include classroom organization, instructional objectives, and teaching methods and materials. Much of the impetus for the laws passed in the 1980s stems from issues surrounding education of children with MR, including (a) the assumed negative impact of labels, (b) expansion of special class placement, and (c) excessive reliance on single assessment measures—primarily the intelligence test.

In each locality, the Ministry of Education develops a Special Education Coordination Committee in charge of programming and monitoring of enforcement of laws and regulations associated with special education. The local government designates the Identification, Placement and Consultation Committee (IPC) to deal with special education practices in schools. The revised Special Education Act of 1997 (Ministry of Education, 1997) is characterized by an addition of zero rejects to the array of special services and an extension of children from school-aged to preschool. Specifically, public schools are now open by law to all children and youths with disabilities aged 3 to 18.

Current Status

Currently, each county develops the IPC Committee. Homeroom teachers refer students with special needs. Referral is delivered to the committee, which initiates assessments and makes the final decision. The committee also recommends (based on the least-restrictive principle) the placement options ranging from regular classes to institutions. Children with disabilities are placed in the following categories: mental retardation, visual impairments, hearing impairments, language disorders, physical handicaps, health impairments, behavioral disorders, learning disabilities, and multiple handicaps. The current policy mandates that students with mild disabilities are placed in the regular classes with resource room services; those with moderate impairments are placed in the self-contained classes; and those with severe and profound handicaps are recommended to special schools and institutions respectively.

To reduce stigmatization to the minimum, schools have long adopted terms with educational implications. The *wisdom-developing* designation, for example, is used to refer to education associated with MR, *illumination-developing* designation for visual impairments, and *love-developing* for physical handicaps. Thus, not only do we have *Taipei Wisdom-Developing School* and *Tainan Illumination-Developing School*, but in the regular school there are *audition-developing* classes for students with hearing impairments.

Prospectus

Many educational problems of exceptional children and youth can be prevented or minimized through the provision of comprehensive services. The revised Special Education Act of 1997 applies to handicapped individuals ages 3 to 18. Many more special needs children are eligible for special education services. The role of the public school has been extended both in the nature of services and the ages of students served. Identification of exceptional children and high-risk children as infants or preschoolers has become a widespread practice, and early childhood programs designed to enhance development of the handicapped and prepare them for school have been demonstrated to be effective. Several metropolitan cities have already mandated the provision of preschool programs for children with disabilities. Career programs designed specifically for post–junior-high adolescents are under assessment across the island and the programs are gaining in popularity. Community resources are being applied to help young adults with handicaps establish themselves as active members of the community.

While full inclusion is in practice in the West, it appears that Taiwan has a long way to go yet. Quite against the worldwide trend of normalization, special day schools are recently flourishing in Taiwan. There were only two special day schools here for children with MR in 1980, but in 10 years, eight new schools have been added to the list, at the increase rate of one school each year. A few more are either on blueprints or under construction.

It is hoped that the Office of Special Education will be soon established both in central and local governments to coordinate policies and practices in special education. Many issues in the field of special education in Taiwan remain unresolved, but the prospect is promising, with the government starting to play the key role in setting the stage for further development.

REFERENCES

Ministry of Education. (1984). *Special Education Act*. Taipei City, Taiwan: Author.

Ministry of Education. (1997). *Revised Special Education Act*. Taipei City, Taiwan: Author.

JENGIYH DUH
National Taiwan Normal University

TALKING BOOKS

Talking books, also referred to as *audiobooks*, are audio-recorded books that read the story to the listener. Talking books are beneficial to struggling readers, English language learners, and those with visual impairments. Talking books are widely available online for rental and for download. The National Library of Congress provides free talking book services to those with visual impairments.

STAFF

See also American Printing House for the Blind

TANGIER DISEASE

Tangier disease is an extremely rare autosomal recessive metabolic disorder. The disease is characterized by decreased levels or even a complete absence of high-density lipoproteins (HDL) concentrations in one's plasma and increased cholesteryl esters in the tonsils, spleen, liver, skin, and lymph nodes.

The reported cases of Tangier disease range from 40 to 50 cases worldwide (Smith & Villagomez, 2000). The majority of the cases tend to be localized in one single area of the United States (Tangier Island, Virginia). The original settlers to the island came in 1686, and it is possible that one or two of them were carriers of the disease and passed it down through their bloodline.

Characteristics

1. Very large, orange tonsils that have a characteristic gross and histological appearance, as well as enlarged liver, spleen, and lymph nodes.
2. Hypocholesterolemia, abnormal chylomicron remnants, and markedly reduced HDLs in the plasma also characterize Tangier disease.
3. An increased incidence of atherosclerosis is also common.
4. A small number of patients have also been diagnosed with coronary artery disease and ocular abnormalities (Online Mendelian Inheritance in Man, 2000; Smith & Villagomez, 2000).
5. Patients with the disease have a defect in cellular cholesterol and lipid removal, which results in near-zero plasma levels of HDL and in massive tissue deposition of cholesteryl esters.

Currently, the treatment for Tangier patients is dependent on the various symptoms, ranging from heart surgery to removal of organs. Also, some of the disease's affects may be controlled by some dietary changes, for example, less dietary intake (Smith & Villagomez, 2000). Gene therapy has been proposed as a possible treatment but is difficult because there is nothing specifically wrong with the gene involved in HDL conversion. The problem is in the cellular transportation (Newman, 1997). Many of the specific processes within the cell are still not known, so any extensive treatment is still investigational.

Due to the nature of the symptoms in Tangier disease, it is not likely that special education services would be necessary. The exception would be if the child is experiencing ocular abnormalities, in which case the child may require assistance through vision impairment services.

Prognosis depends mostly on the symptoms exhibited by the patient. If complications such as heart disease and atherosclerosis go undetected, the eventual outcome may be an early death. The recent discovery of the link between the ABC1 transporter and Tangier disease genes and a better understanding of its mechanism might shed new light on a new treatment for this disease (Smith & Villagomez, 2000).

REFERENCES

Newman, J. (1997). *Tangier disease*. Retrieved from http://www-personal.umd.umich.edu/

Online Mendelian Inheritance in Man. (2000). *Tangier disease*. Retrieved from http://www.ncbi.nhm.nih.gov/

Smith, A., & Villagomez, S. (2000). *Tangier disease*. Retrieved from http://endeavor.med.nyu.edu/student-org/ama/docs/mgb 1999–2000/ab14.htm

SARAH COMPTON
University of Texas at Austin

TARDIVE DYSKINESIA

Tardive dyskinesia (TD), which means late abnormal movement, is an iatrogenic effect of long-term use of neuroleptic or antipsychotic medications. Individuals who have been on chronic antipsychotic medications may develop uncontrollable movements, ranging from mild tongue movements to chorea, that impair their daily life. They may have problems with manual dexterity, eating, speaking, and even breathing. Symptoms may (a) increase under stress, during voluntary motor activity, and during attempts to inhibit the movements; (b) decrease under sedation; and (c) disappear during sleep (Alexander & Lund, 1999). After medication is discontinued, TD may gradually diminish in severity or persist and become permanent. Therefore, prevention is crucial (Healthnotes Online, 2000).

Characteristics

1. Orofacial dyskinesia (most characteristic feature): slow onset of mild tongue movements and lip smacking followed by bulging of the cheeks, chewing movements, grimacing, and arching of the eyebrows.
2. Movements of extremities and trunk including choreoathetoid-like movements of fingers, hands, arms, and feet.
3. Rocking and swaying and rotational pelvic movements.

Prevalence estimates for TD vary widely, owing in part to variation across study in type and length of medication, age and gender of patients, and diagnostic criteria used.

One estimate is 14% among all those on neuroleptic medications. The strongest correlate of both incidence and severity of TD is increasing age. Some studies report higher rates in women and those who smoke (Alexander & Lund, 1999).

Early differential diagnosis is important for prevention of TD. L-DOPA, taken by patients with Parkinson's disease, is the only nonneuroleptic drug that consistently produces dyskinesia, but it may actually improve neuroleptic-induced TD. TD-like conditions have occasionally been reported in patients using a variety of medications to treat a variety of disorders. These medications include reserpine, tetrabenazine, metoclopramide, tricyclic antidepressants, benztropine, phenytoin, and amphetamines. Information on the onset of symptoms is important for differential diagnosis. TD may need to be differentiated from Sydenham and Huntington chorea, congenital torsion dystonia, somatoform disorders, and stereotyped behaviors that frequently accompany schizophrenia itself.

No effective treatment is available for TD. Either discontinuing or reducing the dosage of patients' current medication or switching them to an atypical antipsychotic medication such as clozapine or olanzapine may decrease the symptoms. On the theory that TD stems from dopamine hypersensitivity, most pharmacological treatments have used drugs that reduce dopamine activity or enhance CNS cholinergic effect. However, none of the numerous drugs tried have had consistently positive results. Clinicians have reported effectiveness of a variety of vitamin and mineral supplements (Healthnotes Online, 2000), but positive effects in some cases have decreased as quality of evaluation research increased. Perhaps the most and best research has been on vitamin E, but its effects vary widely across study, even among those using double-blind designs (Alexander & Lund, 1999). Much of the research is limited by small samples, variations in subject population, and supplement regimen, making overall interpretation difficult. Other alternative treatments continue to be tried, with mixed results at best (Healthnotes Online, 2000).

Despite the lack of effective treatment, prognosis is better than traditionally thought. Spontaneous recovery occurs much more frequently than early reports suggested, particularly in younger patients. Overall, about 60% of TD patients show decreased symptoms within 2 to 3 years after stopping taking neuroleptics, with an inverse relationship between improvement and patients' age.

REFERENCES

Alexander, B., & Lund, B. C. (1999). Clinical psychopharmacology seminar: Tardive dyskinesia. *Virtual Hospital: The Apprentice's Assistant*, 1–20. Retrieved from http://www.diegori.it/InternetMedico/Farmaci/Psychopharmacology,%20Clinical%20Seminar.htm

Healthnotes Online. (2000). *Tardive dyskinesia*. Retrieved from http://www.pccnaturalmarkets.com/health/health-condition/tardive-dyskinesia/~default

SHANNON RADLIFF-LEE
ROBERT T. BROWN
University of North Carolina, Wilmington

TASH

Formerly the Association for Persons with Severe Handicaps, TASH is an international advocacy association of people with disabilities, their family members, other advocates, and professionals working toward a society in which inclusion of all people in all aspects of community is the norm. The organization is comprised of members concerned with human dignity, civil rights, education, and independence for all individuals with disabilities. Creating, disseminating, and implementing programs useful for the education and independent lifestyles of persons who are severely handicapped is a primary objective of TASH.

Formed in 1975, TASH is a membership-supported, not-for-profit association with chapters in 34 states and members in 35 countries. Current membership includes professionals, paraprofessionals, parents, and medical and legal personnel. The organization's mission is to stretch the boundaries of what is possible through building communities in which no one is segregated and everyone belongs, forging new alliances that embrace diversity, advocating for opportunities and rights, and eradicating injustices and inequities. In addition, TASH strives to actively support research, disseminate knowledge and information, and support progressive legislation and litigation. Promoting excellence in services and inclusive education for all individuals is another aim of the association.

TASH seeks to promote the full participation of people with disabilities in integrated community settings that support the same quality of life available to people with disabilities. This task is accomplished through its facilitation of training in best practices, systems change, Americans with Disabilities Act (ADA), and Individuals with Disabilities Education Act (IDEA). TASH also strives to provide information, linkage with resources, legal expertise, and targeted advocacy. The organization accomplishes its work by disseminating information via a monthly newsletter covering current disability-related issues and a quarterly academic journal containing cutting-edge research. TASH also sponsors an annual conference and topical workshops, and advocates on behalf of people with disabilities and their families through building grassroots coalitions.

TASH'S central office is located at 29 W. Susquehanna Avenue, Suite 210, Baltimore, MD 21204. The association can be reached via telephone. Tel.: (410) 828-8274; fax (410) 828-6706; TDD (410) 828-1306; e-mail info@tash.org; or by visiting TASH's website at www.tash.org.

TAMARA J. MARTIN
The University of Texas of the Permian Basin

TASK ANALYSIS

Task analysis is a teaching strategy that encompasses the breaking down and sequencing of goals into teachable subtasks. Moyer and Dardig (1978) noted it is a critical component of the behavioral approach and it serves a dual role in the instruction of learners with disabilities. First, it serves an effective diagnostic function by helping teachers pinpoint a student's individual functioning levels on a specific skill or task. Second, it provides the basis for sequential instruction, which may be tailored to each child's pace of learning. A thorough task analysis results in a set of subtasks that form the basic steps in an effective program. In essence, task analysis is both an assessment and a teaching tool (Ysseldyke & Elliott, 1999).

Task analysis has been acclaimed to be an effective strategy for the mildly disabled learner (Bateman, 1974; Siegel, 1972; Tawney, 1974). Gold (1976) applied this technique to the education of severely handicapped learners with great success and Williams, Brown, and Certo (1975) stated that task analysis is critical to teachers of severely disabled learners, since programmatic steps must be sequenced with precision and care.

According to Mithaug (1979), the procedures that define task analysis have evolved from Frederick Taylor's work measurement studies and Frank and Lillian Gilbreth's motion studies conducted in the late 1800s. Motion analysis was the precursor of today's task analysis, although many elements critical to motion analysis have not been included in the educational applications of task analysis. The term task analysis came into increasing use during the 1950s, whenever tasks were identified and examined for their essential components within the workplace. This foreshadowed subsequent applications of task analysis to teach individuals with disabilities in the late 1960s.

Guidelines for designing and implementing task analysis programs have been suggested (Moyer & Dardig, 1978; Siegel, 1972). These are:

Limit the scope of the main task.

Write subtasks in observable terms.

Use terminology at a level understandable to potential users.

Write the task in terms of what the learner will do.

Focus attention on the task rather than the learner.

In choosing a method of task analysis, Moyer and Dardig (1978) noted that all tasks, whether from the psychomotor, cognitive, or affective domains, can be broken down into simple units of performance. However, there is no foolproof strategy for selecting the appropriate method of analysis for a given task. It is helpful first to identify the domain of the learning task and then to apply the appropriate task analysis procedure. They suggest five possible methods of task analysis that may be adopted by the special education teacher:

1. Watch a master perform. This requires watching and writing down all the steps that are required to perform the task as it is performed by someone adept at it.

2. In a variation of the first method, have the teacher perform the task, making note of the required steps. Sometimes this is difficult in that performing the task may interfere with recording the steps.

3. Work backward from the terminal objective, making note of the required steps.

4. Brainstorm. This entails writing down all the component steps without regard to order. Then, once all steps have been identified, arrange them into some logical order.

5. Make the conditions under which the task is completed progressively more simple. As the learner gains proficiency, slowly change the simplified conditions (e.g., trace name; gradually remove the model: dark model, light model, dotted model).

The ability to analyze tasks, a skill that can be acquired by any teacher, enables the detection of trends in a student's performance and the modification of task components during an instructional session (Junkala, 1973). Thus it is an extremely effective instructional method and diagnostic tool in special education.

REFERENCES

Bateman, B. D. (1974). Educational implications of minimum brain dysfunction. *Reading Teacher, 27,* 662–668.

Gold, M. C. (1976). Task analysis of a complex assembly task by the retarded blind. *Exceptional Children, 43,* 78–84.

Junkala, J. (1973). Task analysis: The processing dimension. *Academic Therapy, 8*(4), 401–409.

Mithaug, D. E. (1979). The relation between programmed instruction and task analysis in the pre-vocational training of severely and profoundly handicapped persons. *AAESPH Review, 4*(2), 162–178.

Moyer, J. R., & Dardig, J. C. (1978). Practical task analysis for special educators. *Teaching Exceptional Children, 11*(1), 16–18.

Siegel, E. (1972). Task analysis and effective teaching. *Journal of Learning Disabilities, 5*, 519–532.

Tawney, J. W. (1974). *Task analysis.* Unpublished manuscript, University of Kentucky.

Williams, W., Brown, L., & Certo, N. (1975). Basic components of instructional programs for the severely handicapped students. *AAESPH Review, 1*(1), 1–39.

Ysseldyke, J., & Elliott, J. (1999). Effective instructional practices: Implications for assessing educational environments. In C. R. Reynolds & T. B. Gutkin (Eds.), *The handbook of school psychology* (3rd ed.). New York, NY: Wiley.

EILEEN F. MCCARTHY
University of Wisconsin at Madison

See also **Behavior Modification; Behavioral Assessment; Behavioral Objectives**

TAT (*See* Thematic Apperception Test)

TAXONOMIES

Taxonomy is the science of systematics. It incorporates the theory and practice of classification, or sorting and ordering significant similarities and differences among members of a system to facilitate precise communication about members, enhance understanding of the interrelationships among members, and suggest areas where additional relationships might be discovered. Early attempts to design taxonomies date back to the third century BC and Aristotle's efforts to classify animals as warm- or cold-blooded. Theophrastus, Aristotle's pupil, concentrated on a system for sorting plants. In the 18th century in Sweden, Linnaeus designed a classification system for botany that has served as a basis for almost all subsequent systems.

Among the more commonly used taxonomies today are the Library of Congress and Dewey Decimal systems for the classification of books and the taxonomies developed for the classification of plants and animals. The latter contains categories that permit the identification of individual organisms according to species, genus, family, order, class, phylum, and kingdom.

In the late 1940s, members of the American Psychological Association who were concerned about the problems of precise communication among college examiners and researchers involved in testing and curriculum development began work on the classification of educational objectives. The result was the preparation of taxonomies of educational objectives or intended student outcomes in the cognitive, affective, and psychomotor domains (Bloom, 1956; Harrow, 1972; Krathwohl, Bloom, & Masia, 1964). The major classes in these three taxonomies are presented

Cognitive Domain
1. Knowledge
2. Comprehension
3. Application
4. Analysis
5. Synthesis
6. Evaluation

Affective Domain
1. Receiving/attending
2. Responding
3. Valuing
4. Organization
5. Characterization

Psychomotor Domain
1. Reflex movement
2. Basic fundamental movement
3. Perceptual abilities
4. Physical abilities
5. Skilled movements
6. Nondiscursive movements

Figure T.1. Taxonomies of educational objectives for the cognitive, affective, and psychomotor domain. *Source*: Bloom, 1956; Harrow, 1972; Krathwohl, Bloom & Masia, 1964.

in Figure T.1. All three reflect an emphasis on the intended outcomes of instruction and the student behaviors that would demonstrate achievement of each outcome.

Stevens (1962) developed a taxonomy for special education that focuses on physical disorders. He observed that classification systems then in use were typically based on a medical model with an emphasis on disease, etiology, and symptomatology. His intent was to improve communication regarding educationally relevant attributes or somatopsychological or body disorders and the special education procedures students with such disorders might require. Stevens stressed the differences among the terms *impairment, disability,* and *handicap* and provided for attributes that carried significance for planning special education programs. Figure T.2 lists Stevens' classes.

In 1980 the World Health Organization (WHO) published its *International Classification of Impairments, Disabilities, and Handicaps.* This section relates consequences of disease to circumstances in which disabled persons are apt to find themselves as they interact with others and adapt to their physical surroundings. The purpose of WHO's efforts, which are summarized in Figure T.3, was to prepare a taxonomy that would ease the production of statistics regarding the consequences of disease, facilitate the collection of statistics useful in planning services, and permit storage and retrieval of information about impairments, disabilities, and handicaps (WHO, 1980). Diagnosis, a useful precursor to treatment, is a form of taxonomic classification (e.g., see Kamphaus, Reynolds, & McCammon, 1999).

Ultimately, taxonomies should be comprehensive, improve communication, stimulate thought, and be

1. *Somatopsychological variants*
    1.1 Handicap
    1.2 Disability
    1.3 Impairment
2. *Educationally significant attributes of somatopsychological disorders*
    2.1 Nature of condition
    2.2 Nature of therapeutic process
    2.3 Psychological aspects
    2.4 School considerations
    2.5 Cultural considerations
    2.6 Etc.
3. *Special education procedures*
    3.1 Modification of laws
    3.2 Finance
    3.3 Instructional modifications
    3.4 Noninstructional services
    3.5 Administrative modifications
    3.6 Ancillary services
    3.7 Etc.

Figure T.2. Taxonomy in special education for children with body disorder. *Source*: Stevens, 1962.

Impairments
1. Intellectual
2. Other psychological
3. Language
4. Aural
5. Ocular
6. Visceral
7. Skeletal
8. Disfiguring
9. Generalized, sensory, and other

Disabilities
1. Behavior
2. Communication
3. Personal care
4. Locomotor
5. Body diposition
6. Dexterity
7. Situational
8. Particular skill
9. Other activity restrictions

Handicaps
Survival roles
1. Orientation
2. Physical independence
3. Mobility
4. Occupational
5. Social integration
6. Economic self-sufficiency
7. Other handicaps

Figure T.3. WHO classification of impairments, disabilities, and handicaps. *Source*: WHO, 1980.

accepted by professionals in the field for which they were designed (Bloom, 1956). Whether the taxonomies available for special educators lead to the achievement of these goals remains to be seen, but without taxonomies as a guide, communication would be surely impaired (Kamphaus et al., 1999).

REFERENCES

Bloom, B. S. (Ed.). (1956). *Taxonomy of educational objectives: The classification of educational goals: Handbook I. Cognitive domain.* New York, NY: McKay.

Harrow, A. J. (1972). *A taxonomy of the psychomotor domain: A guide for developing behavioral objectives.* New York, NY: McKay.

Kamphaus, R. W., Reynolds, C. R., & McCammon, C. (1999). Roles of diagnosis and classification in school psychology. In C. R. Reynolds & T. B. Gutkin (Eds.), *The handbook of school psychology* (3rd ed.). New York, NY: Wiley.

Krathwohl, D. R., Bloom, B. S., & Masia, B. B. (1964). *Taxonomy of educational objectives: Classification of educational goals: Handbook II. Affected domain.* New York, NY: McKay.

Stevens, G. D. (1962). *Taxonomy in special education for children with body disorders.* Pittsburgh, PA: Department of Special Education and Rehabilitation, University of Pittsburgh.

World Health Organization (WHO). (1980). *International classification of impairments, disabilities, and handicaps.* Geneva, Switzerland: Author.

MARJORIE E. WARD
The Ohio State University

See *also* Bloom, Benjamin S.; Systems of Classification

TAY-SACHS DISEASE

Tay-Sachs disease is a lysosmal storage disorder that is characterized by the absences of the enzyme Hexosaminidase (Hansis & Grifo, 2001). The deficiency allows harmful quantities of a fatty substance, called GM2 ganglioside, to build up in the tissues and nerve cells of the brain. This buildup results in a progressive deterioration of the central nervous system and in a loss of visual functions (Branda, Tomczak, & Natowicz, 2004; Hansis & Grifo, 2001). This genetic disorder is transmitted by an inherited autosomal recessive gene that is found more frequently among people of Jewish and European origin (Branda et al., 2004; Kaback & Desnick, 2001; Risch, 2001). Approximately 1 in 250 people are carriers of the Tay-Sachs disease; 1 in every 27 people of Jewish ancestry in the United States are carriers (National Institutes of Health, 2005).

Tay-Sachs syndrome manifests itself in infants between the ages of 4 to 8 months. Initial signs include a loss of peripheral vision, an abnormal startle response, cherry red spots on the retinas, a delay in psychomotor development, and a gradual regression in learned abilities (i.e., the loss of the ability to sit up; Filho & Shapiro, 2004; Hansis & Grifo, 2001; National Institutes of Health, 2005). In later stages of the disease children experience recurrent seizures, diminishing mental function, blindness, and eventually paralysis (Filho & Shapiro, 2004; National Institutes of Health, 2005). Death generally occurs before the age of 6 (Gravel et al., 2001). In addition to the infantile form of Tay-Sachs disease there are much rarer late onset forms with similar symptoms that are caused by varying residual enzyme activity (Gravel et al., 2001). Treatment is limited to managing the symptoms of the disease with proper nutrition, anticonvulsant medications used to suppress seizures, and other techniques used to maintain an open airway (National Institutes of Health, 2005). Genetic screening has resulted in a 90% reduction in the annual incidences of Tay-Sachs disease that are reported in North America (Kaback & Desnick, 2001).

REFERENCES

Branda, K., Tomczak, J., & Natowicz, M. (2004). Heterozygosis for Tay-Sachs and Sandhoff diseases in non-Jewish Americans with ancestry from Ireland, Great Britain, or Italy. *Genetic Testing, 8,* 174–180.

Filho, J., & Shapiro, B. (2004). Tay-Sachs disease. *Archaeological Neurological, 61,* 1466–1468.

Gravel, R. A., Kaback, M. M., Proia, R. L., Sandhoff, K., Suzuki, K., & Sukuzi, K. (2001). The Gm2 gangliosides. In C. R. Scriver, A. L. Beaudet, W. S. Sly, & D. Valle (Eds.), *Metabolic and molecular bases of inherited diseases* (8th ed., Vol. 1, pp. 3827–3876). New York, NY: McGraw-Hill.

Hansis, C., & Grifo, J. (2001). Tay-Sachs disease and preimplantation genetic diagnosis. *Advances in Genetics, 44,* 22–28.

Kaback, M., & Desnick, R. (2001). Tay-Sachs disease: From clinical description to molecular defect. *Advances in Genetics, 44.*

National Institutes of Health. (2005). *Tay-Sachs disease.* Retrieved from http://www.ninds.nih.gov/disorders/taysachs/taysachs.htm

Risch, N. (2001). Molecular epidemiology of Tay-Sachs disease. *Advances in Genetics, 44,* 42–51.

BRANDI KOCIAN
Texas A&M University

See also Congenital Disorders; Genetic Counseling; Genetic Testing; Genetic Transmissions

TEACCH

Treatment and Education of Autistic and related Communication-handicapped Children (TEACCH) is a clinical service and professional training program designed to improve educational and behavioral outcomes for children with autism spectrum disorders (ASD). TEACCH is based at the University of North Carolina at Chapel Hill, and now includes nine regional centers in North Carolina. The center directors are all UNC faculty members who offer comprehensive services, professional training, and consultation for individuals with ASD. TEACCH faculty members also engage in autism intervention research (Mesibov & Shea, 2010).

The TEACCH program was founded in 1966 by Eric Schopler and Robert J. Reichler (Mesibov & Shea, 2010). TEACCH began as a research project partially supported by the National Institute of Mental Health. The purpose of the project was to investigate misconceptions about ASD. Research examined whether ASD is primarily an emotional disorder that causes children to withdraw from their hostile and pathological parents, if parents of children with ASD are educationally privileged and from an upper social class, and if children with ASD have potential for normal or better intellectual functioning. The studies demonstrated that ASD is a developmental disability rather than an emotional illness, that parents come from all social strata and do not cause their children's disability, and that intellectual disabilities and ASD can coexist (Panerai et al. 2009).

The theoretical rationale for the TEACCH approach is based on the idea that individuals with autism share similar characteristics, particularly the preference of visual information, a heightened awareness of details, difficulties with social interaction, engagement in repetitive, restricted, and stereotyped behavior, difficulties with the concept of time, and deficits in verbal and non-verbal communication (Mesibov & Shea, 2010). Research on these common characteristics led to the development of the TEACCH program, which is based on four principles. First, parents should be collaborators and co-therapists in the treatment of their children. Second, treatment for individuals with ASD should involve individualized teaching programs that use behavior theory and special education. Next, teaching programs should be developed through individualized diagnosis and assessment. Lastly, program implementation should be by psychoeducational therapists or teachers (Mesibov & Shea, 2010). Those who implement treatments should function as generalists rather than specialists in a technical field such as physical therapy or speech therapy. Treatment outcomes are evaluated according to the interaction between improved skills and environmental adjustments to deficits (Schopler, Mesibov, & Hearsey, 1995).

The TEACCH program integrates education, training, and research efforts with clinical services. Training is provided for various specialists, including teachers, psychologists, psychiatrists, pediatricians, speech pathologists, and social workers (Panerai et al. 2009). TEACCH emphasizes collaboration between parents and professionals.

Educators and parents establish routines and cues at home and in the classroom to create consistency and promote generalization. Community adaptation is facilitated through parent groups. Each center has a parent group affiliated with the Autism Society of North Carolina, a chapter of the Autism Society of America (Schopler et al., 1995). The purpose of this collaboration is to improve community awareness of individuals with ASD and to develop new and cost-effective services. Home adjustment is facilitated at five regional TEACCH centers. Each center is located in a city housing a branch of the state university system to facilitate both research and training (Mesibov & Shea, 2010). The centers' main functions are to provide diagnosis and individualized assessment involving family and school. Parents are trained to function as co-therapists using behavior management and special education techniques. The centers' staff provide professional training and consultation (Mesibov & Shea, 2010). School adjustment is fostered through special education classrooms in the public schools that include four to eight children with a teacher and an assistant teacher. These classrooms are under TEACCH direction. TEACCH functions include hiring teachers, teacher in-service training, diagnosis and placement of children, and ongoing classroom consultation for behavior problems and curriculum issues (Mesibov & Shea, 2010).

TEACCH has been adapted for use in early intervention programs, residential programs, social groups, summer camps, recreational programs, counseling sessions, and in employment settings (Mesibov & Shea, 2010). Studies from TEACCH programs have suggested that individuals with ASD function better in a structured setting (Mesibov & Shea, 2010; Schopler et al., 1995). Structured Teaching, an instructional approach developed by TEACCH, promotes independent functioning through the use of visual supports and organized environments (Mesibov & Shea, 2010; Schopler et al., 1995). Structured Teaching consists of the following components: physical organization of the environment, visual schedules designed to establish order in daily activities, aid in transitions, and to foster communication, work systems that prompt students to complete activities, and visual task organization (Mesibov & Shea, 2010; Panerai et al., 2009).

REFERENCES

Mesibov, G. B., & Shea, V. (2010). The TEACCH program in the era of evidence-based practice. *Journal of Autism and Developmental Disorders, 40,* 570–579.

Panerai, S., Zingale, M., Trubia, G., Finocchiaro, M., Zuccarello, R., & Ferri, R., & Elia, M. (2009). Special education versus inclusive education: The role of the TEACCH program. *Journal of Autism & Developmental Disorders, 39,* 874–882.

Schopler, E., Mesibov, G. B., & Hearsey, K. (1995). Structured teaching in the TEACCH system. In E. Schopler (Ed.), *Learning and cognition in autism* (pp. 243–268). New York, NY: Plenum Press.

NANCY HUTCHINS
Texas A&M University

RICHARD MAHONEY
ELIZABETH DELAUNE
RUSSELL LANG
Texas State University-San Marcos
Fourth edition

See also Autism; Filial Therapy; Journal of Autism and Developmental Disorders

TEACHER BURNOUT

Increased public demands on education have produced additional pressures and stresses on teachers. Needle, Griffin, Svendsen, and Berney (1981) report that teaching ranks third in the hierarchy of stressful professions. Studies conducted by teachers' unions and other educational agencies support the notion that many teachers are currently "burning out" (Cichon & Koff, 1980; Wilson & Hall, 1981). Special educators in particular may be at high risk for burnout and its consequences (Bradfield & Fones, 1985).

Burnout has been defined in a variety of ways in the literature during its nearly 10-year history (Gold, 1985). Weiskopf (1980) defines burnout by its relationship to six categories of stress often found at the teaching workplace. They include work overload, lack of perceived success, amount of direct contact with children, staff-child ratio, program structure, and responsibility for others. Freudenberger (1974) and Maslach (1977) find the general theme of burnout to be "emotional and/or physical exhaustion resulting from the stress of interpersonal contact." It can be viewed as a gradual process with stages ranging from mild to severe (Spaniol & Caputo, 1979).

Burnout seems to affect people working in the human social services professions particularly because of the degree of intimacy that they experience with their clients and the extended period of time that they work with them. Moreover, many of the recipients of human services do not respond to the efforts of professionals, causing disillusionment and frustration (Pines & Maslach, 1977). This may be particularly true for special education teachers because of the unique nature of their teaching responsibilities (Bradfield & Fones, 1985).

Many causes for burnout in the helping professions have been proposed. In education, occupational burnout may arise from the failure of the work environment to provide the teacher with the support and encouragement needed and expected (Needle et al., 1981). Bensky et al. (1980) point out that often teachers are not given clearly defined job descriptions and receive additional job responsibilities for which they are unprepared or to which they are unaccustomed. Role ambiguity, if not clarified as part of the education process, is likely to lead to an increase in job-related stress and dissatisfaction (Coates & Thoresen, 1976; Greenberg & Valletutti, 1980). Many teachers have cited violence, vandalism, disruptive students, inadequate salaries, lack of classroom control, lack of job mobility, and fear of layoffs as reasons for burnout (Gold, 1985).

The effects of burnout vary from individual to individual depending on such variables as personality, age, sex, and family history. Physiological manifestation may include such reactions as migraine headaches, ulcers, diarrhea, muscle tension, and heart disease. Emotional manifestations include such reactions as depression, anxiety, irritability, and nervousness. Behavioral manifestations generally include excessive smoking or overeating (American Academy of Family Physicians, 1979).

The ways in which teachers may manifest specific responses to burnout on the job is cause for concern. Spaniol and Caputo (1979) have formulated a list of symptoms that may indicate that a teacher is experiencing burnout: a high level of absenteeism, lateness for work, a low level of enthusiasm, decline in performance, lack of focus, a high level of complaints, lack of communication, and a lack of openness to new ideas.

The implications of teacher burnout are grave and broadly based. They include the individual's own personal dissatisfaction, his or her family's unhappiness, chronic health problems, problems with colleagues and school administrators, and, ultimately, ineffective teaching. Sparks and Ingram (1979) reported that the teachers from whom students learn the most are reasonable, relaxed, enthusiastic, and interested in their students. Teachers who are consistently feeling stressed have been described as irritable, tense, humorless, depressed, self-involved, and unable to perform their job well. In general, Needle et al. (1981) found that job stress affects the classroom environment, the teaching/learning process, and the attainment of educational goals and objectives.

To reduce the possibility of teacher burnout, teachers must be provided with knowledge and information on effective methods of coping with stress in the environment. One popular method has been involvement in stress management workshops (Betkouski, 1981). These workshops have been effective in providing teachers with strategies for coping with stress such as forming support groups, reviewing exercise and nutrition patterns, developing hobbies and interests outside the work environment, and practicing relaxation techniques (Shannon & Saleeby, 1980). The prevention of burnout in teaching, however, must first and foremost involve a serious commitment to improving the quality and circumstances under which teachers work.

REFERENCES

American Academy of Family Physicians. (1979). *A report on the lifestyles/personal health in different occupations: A study of attitudes and practices.* Kansas City, KS: Research Forecasts.

Bensky, J., Shaw, S. F., Gouse, A. S., Bates, H., Dixon, B., & Beane, W. (1980). Public law 94-142 and stress: A problem for educators. *Exceptional Children, 47*(1), 24–29.

Betkouski, M. (1981, March). On making stress work for you: Strategies for coping. *Science Teacher, 48,* 35–37.

Bradfield, R. H., & Fones, D. M. (1985). Stress and the special teacher: How bad is it? *Academic Therapy, 20*(5), 571–577.

Cichon, D. J., & Koff, R. H. (1980, March). Stress and teaching. *National Association of Secondary School Principals Bulletin,* 91–103.

Coates, T. J., & Thoresen, C. E. (1976). Teacher anxiety: A review with recommendations. *Review of Educational Research, 46,* 159–184.

Freudenberger, H. J. (1974). Staff burn-out. *Journal of Social Issues, 30*(1), 159–165.

Gold, Y. (1985). Burnout: Causes and solutions. *Clearinghouse, 58,* 210–212.

Greenberg, S. F., & Valletutti, P. J. (1980). *Stress and the helping professions.* Baltimore, MD: Paul H. Brookes.

Maslach, C. (1977). Job burnout: How people cope. *Public Welfare, 36,* 61–63.

Needle, R., Griffin, T., Svendsen, R., & Berney, M. (1981). Occupational stress: Coping and health problems of teachers. *Journal of School Health, 51,* 175–181.

Pines, A., & Maslach, C. (1977, April). *Detached concern and burnout in mental health professions.* Paper presented at the 2nd National Conference on Child Abuse and Neglect, Houston, TX.

Shannon, C., & Saleeby, D. (1980). Training child welfare workers to cope with burnout. *Child Welfare, 59*(8), 463–468.

Spaniol, L., & Caputo, J. (1979). *Professional burnout: A personal survival kit.* Boston, MA: Human Services Associates.

Sparks, D., & Ingram, M. J. (1979). Stress prevention and management: A workshop approach. *Personnel & Guidance Journal, 59,* 197–200.

Weiskopf, P. A. (1980). Burn-out among teachers of exceptional children. *Exceptional Children, 47*(1), 18–23.

Wilson, C. F., & Hall, L. L. (1981). *Preventing burnout in education.* La Mesa, CA: Wright.

Marsha H. Lupi
*Hunter College,
City University of New York*

See also Teacher Effectiveness; Teacher Expectancies

TEACHER CENTERS

A teacher center (TC) represents a centralized setting that facilitates teacher development, in-service programs, and the exchange of ideas (Hering, 1983). Initially, TCs were funded directly with federal dollars. The basis for this funding was the passage in 1976 of PL 94-482. Approximately 110 TCs were directly supported by the federal government. However, as noted by Edelfelt in 1982, "The categorical assignment of funds for teacher centers ... [was] terminated in the fiscal year 1982 federal budget" (p. 393). The majority of TCs have continued as a result of their funding from other local and state sources. Their continuation supports the contention that the original concepts that premised their initiation are still valid.

A primary factor that led to the origination of TCs in the United States in the mid-1970s was the interest of teachers in being in charge of their own in-service training and to keep up with new educational trends and curricular concepts. The idea was that TC in-service programs were to depart from the traditional and standard in-service programs; for example, one-time sessions on a given topic such as discipline or learning activities for the talented and gifted. In contrast, the intent of established TC in-service programs was to be innovative and to influence professional development; those goals are still desirable today.

Another of the original precepts was that TCs would have a full-time director who was both an administrator and a teacher. The director would then become the nucleus of a governing board that was to consist of local citizens. Boards with an efficient mix of leadership, inspiration, and idealism were and are in a position to effectively institute needed changes. Weiler (1983) has outlined a blueprint for the establishment of new TCs that make needed changes possible.

Researchers (Commission on Reading, 1984; Committee on Education and Labor, 1984; Kozal, 1984; Tunley, 1985; Zorinsky, 1985) estimate that 12% to 18% of the teenage and adult population groups are functionally illiterate. There are 25 million to 40 million Americans who are disabled with depressed literacy skills in the primary academic areas of reading, writing, and arithmetic. This instructional need is one that active TCs can legitimately embrace through the initiation of planned in-service programs that retrain teachers to be more efficient in their instruction.

Beyond the need for TC to endorse direct instructional intervention to improve the efficiency of classroom instruction, Hering (1983) identified a composite of five major functions that TCs can attend to: (1) assist teachers in their more immediate awareness of changes in instructional knowledge as it appears in educational literature; (2) assist teachers to be more efficient in meeting the social educational goals of students that society expects its nation's schools to attend to; (3) assist teachers to be more effective in their classrooms in attending to their students' developmental and remedial instructional needs; (4) assist teachers in achieving increased social and psychological competence; and (5) assist teachers as a faculty group to be more responsible to the needs of the group.

The history of TCs (Edelfelt, 1982) has had its share of developmental setbacks. However, as Hering (1983) has pointed out, TCs that work toward a quality program of instruction for all students will simultaneously attain from the community and the school board recognition of the worth and the work of teachers. Teacher centers that are influential in achieving quality instruction for any one group or classification of students have the probability of doing the same for any other group or classification of students, including the student receiving special education services.

REFERENCES

Commission on Reading. (1984). *Becoming a nation of readers*. Washington, DC: U.S. Department of Education.

Committee on Education and Labor. (1984). *Illiteracy and the scope of the problem in this country*. Washington, DC: U.S. Government Printing Office.

Edelfelt, R. A. (1982, September). Critical issues in developing teacher centers. *Education Digest, 48,* 28–31.

Hering, W. M. (1983). *Research on teachers' centers: A summary of fourteen research efforts*. Washington, DC: National Institute of Education.

Kozal, J. (1984). *Illiterate America*. Garden City, NY: Doubleday.

Tunley, R. (1985, September). America's secret shame. *Reader's Digest, 104–108.*

Weiler, P. (1983, September). Blueprint for a teacher center. *Instructor, 93,* 146–148.

Zorinsky, E. (1985). The National Commission on Illiteracy Act. *Congressional Record, 131*(41). Washington, DC: U.S. Government Printing Office.

ROBERT T. NASH
University of Wisconsin at Oshkosh

***See also* Inservice Training of Special Education Teachers; Instructional Media/Materials Center**

TEACHER EDUCATION AND SPECIAL EDUCATION

Teacher Education and Special Education is the official journal of the Teacher Education Division (TED) of the Council for Exceptional Children (CEC). The purposes of *Teacher Education and Special Education* are to support goals of the TED, and to stimulate thoughtful consideration of the critical issues that are shaping the future of teacher education.

The journal is published four times a year and the first issue of each volume is a potpourri issue that includes articles dealing with a wide range of topics. The second issue focuses on preservice, in-service, or doctoral preparation. The third issue focuses on a topic of timely interest in personnel preparation. The last issue focuses on research and/or evaluation activities related to personnel preparation.

REBECCA BAILEY
Texas A&M University

See also Council for Exceptional Children

TEACHER EFFECTIVENESS

Over the past several decades, field-based studies have been conducted on the teaching process that related specific teaching behaviors to student achievement outcomes. The results of the early studies (Anderson, Evertson, & Brophy, 1979; Crawford, Gage, Corno, Stayrook, & Mitman, 1978; Fisher, Filby, & Marliave, 1978; Good & Grouws, 1977, 1979; Stallings, Needles, & Strayrook, 1979) were that there is a common set of process variables that can be observed or documented in effective teachers across grade and subject areas. It is further indicated that less effective teachers do not demonstrate these same behaviors to the appropriate degree. Continued research demonstrated clearly that teachers do make a difference in children's lives, especially with regard to classroom learning (see review by Gettinger & Stoiba, 1999).

The body of this research clearly speaks to a technology of teaching, making it increasingly clear that teachers and what they do are important determinants of student achievement. We know that effective teachers (a) optimize academic learning time; (b) reward achievement in appropriate ways; (c) use interactive teaching practices; (d) hold and communicate high expectations for student performance; and (e) select appropriate units of instruction. There are exceptions to these and other principles, and as such, teachers need to be adaptable. The research does not say that there is one best system of teaching but rather that the teacher must constantly be analyzing the feedback from students and performance data and making decisions to modify the instruction. Therefore, the findings from the teacher effectiveness studies and related research should be reviewed as road maps with the teacher constantly making decisions regarding the best route to pursue and sometimes altering the selected route based on new information. In general, the literature strongly addresses the need to train teachers as accurate decision makers. It is not level of effort or the aspiration to teach well that differentiates effective instruction; it is rather knowledge, skill, and confidence (Elmore, Peterson, & McCarthey, 1996).

Changing teachers' behaviors has not been found to be as difficult a task as first believed (Good, 1979). Studies have examined the amount of intervention needed to create a change that will affect teacher effectiveness (Caladarci & Gage, 1984; Good, 1979; Mohlman, Caladarci, & Gage, 1982). Caladarci and Gage (1984) found that there is a lower limit in regard to how little can be done while still achieving a meaningful change in behavior. Periodic direct observation of teachers appears to be one component that facilitates adoption of the practices. An enthusiastic presentation of the information to the teachers and a spirit of support for the practices also appear to be important. Mohlman et al. (1982) found that teacher acceptance of change to the use of effective teaching practices was based on (a) teaching recommendations being stated in explicit, easily understood language; (b) a philosophical acceptance of the suggested practice on the part of the teacher; and (c) teachers' perceived view of the cost in terms of time and effort and a belief that the investment in time and effort was worth the payoff in expected student achievement.

Mohlman et al. (1982) also found that teacher acceptance of the innovations is more important than understanding of the innovations. One other finding from the research is that teachers who were trained in effective teaching practices either by workshop, summaries, or workbooks are much more likely to use these practices in their classrooms than teachers who were not provided with such information.

Various authors have separated the major components of effective teaching practices into different configurations. One possible organization places these practices under the domains of management, decision making, time utilization, and instruction, all of which interact with each other and result in the development of a supportive classroom climate. These domains and their subdomains are based on the experimental and correlational research reported regularly in journals on studies involving instructional strategies.

Effective teachers use effective classroom management. Effective classroom management means (a) organizing the physical classroom to minimize disruptions; (b) establishing teaching rules and procedures and adhering to those rules and procedures; and (c) anticipating problem situations and having action plans to prevent problems or deal with them when they occur. Effective teachers have a strong command of their subject matter and a keen awareness of how children think and learn (Elmore et al., 1996).

Management has repeatedly been demonstrated as a critical element of effective teaching in major studies, including *The First Grade Reading Group Study* (Evertson et al., 1981) and *The Study of a Training Program in Classroom Organization and Management for Secondary School Teachers* (Fitzpatrick, 1981). Management includes the establishment and teaching of rules and procedures, specification of consequences, physical organization of the classroom, and behaviors on the part of the teacher that prevent disruptive behavior. Good room management eliminates potential distractions for students and minimizes opportunities for students to disrupt others. Students' desks are arranged so that students can easily see instructional displays and visuals and so that students can be easily monitored by the teacher. Students are seated so as to eliminate "action zones." These zones are created when students select seating locations. There is a tendency in self-selection for high-ability learners to sit together in the front and low-ability students to sit at the back or side. The more effective teacher will intermingle with these students. When hand raisers are spread throughout the room, it will enable teachers to spread their attention more evenly and become sensitized to low responders.

Rules govern student behaviors such as talking and respect for property. Effective teachers have only three to six rules stated in generic language. These are posted and taught through examples to students at the beginning of the school year. Merely posting rules is less effective than posting and teaching the rules. Established procedures and routines are time-saving mechanisms. When procedures are established, students know when to use the bathroom, how to head papers, how to distribute and collect assignments, how to ask for help, and so on. Without such established procedures, time is lost in explanations, or students disrupt the classroom by not knowing the procedures.

Consistency in enforcing the rules is a hallmark of effective teachers. Effective teachers have a hierarchy of consequences they follow to maintain the rules. Eye contact, moving closer to a student, or a pointed finger might be the first level of intervention. Withholding a privilege, assigning detention, conferencing with a student, or having a student restate a broken rule might be the second level. Contacting parents, behavioral contracting, or outside assistance might constitute the third level. In all cases, the teacher should remain calm when enforcing a rule.

Prevention of problems is largely brought about by advanced planning. A teacher can help prevent behavior problems by staying in close proximity to students while frequently teaching and monitoring them. A teacher should plan positive comments that can be used with students to establish a positive mood. Finally, a teacher should formulate plans to handle hypothetical disciplinary situations.

One major reason why management is such a critical variable in the teaching process is because of its relationship to instructional time. Instructional time is highly related to academic achievement. Walberg's (1982) review of studies involving time and achievement found correlation ranges from .13 to .71 with a median of .41. Ninety-five percent of the 25 studies reviewed as "time-on-learning" reported positive effects. Instructional time is lost for members of a class where students are disruptive, procedures are not readily available for teaching, and students do not understand the teacher's behavioral expectations.

Decision making is generally an unobservable phenomenon, but the products of the decision are observable. Teachers regularly make decisions on content, time allocations, pacing, grouping, and class activities. If the content is not taught, then students generally do not learn. The literature uses the term "opportunity to learn" when describing this phenomenon. According to Berliner (1984), teachers make content decisions based on (a) the amount of effort required to teach the subject, (b) the perceived difficulty for the students, and (c) the teacher's personal feelings of enjoyment. In making content decisions, knowledge of the subject discipline appears to be of importance. The teacher's philosophy also enters into content decisions. Research from teacher effectiveness studies shows wide variability between the subject matter content covered by teachers of the same subject and grade.

Time allocation decisions involve time allotted across the school day and within a curriculum area. Observational studies on teacher behavior indicate that less than 1% of the time available in reading classes focuses on the teaching of reading comprehension (Pearson & Gallagher, 1983). Fisher et al. (1978) found some teachers of the same grade level allocated 16 minutes of instruction in math each day while others were allocated 51 minutes. The basic principle that evolves from this data is that teachers' time allocation decisions can affect students' opportunity to learn.

Pacing involves the rate at which a teacher covers the course or subject material. The more material that is covered, the more opportunity to learn is given; hence, each student attains a higher achievement level. The corollary to the pacing principle is that students need to be learning the material at the pace that is followed. More effective teachers solicit regular feedback from students by frequent tests and questioning; they use that information to gauge the pace of the instruction. Sometimes the textbooks impose a pace. Why do students learn to spell 20 new words each week? Because the textbooks are set up to teach 20 words a week. Some students could learn 40, others only 10. Teachers need to be aware of how materials may put limitations on pacing.

If grouping is to be done, the teacher must base the grouping on objective criteria related to a valid achievement measure and must frequently reassess the value of the grouping. A problem inherent in grouping is the possible increased gap that can be created among different groups based on a difference in pacing. Grouping decisions cannot be taken lightly, and alternatives to grouping and differential pacing might be explored by teachers prior to a grouping decision. Teachers need to understand the consequences of grouping decisions as reflected in subsequent student achievement.

Appropriate use of time is a third component in a teaching effectiveness model. Research by Stallings et al. (1979), and Walberg (1979), and many others has revealed that time use is more important than time per se. Time can be conceptualized according to the activities being conducted. Berliner (1984) has identified the following components of time: allocated time, engaged time, time related to outcome, and academic learning time. Academic learning time (ALT) is most related to student achievement. The key is to increase the amount of ALT within the time allocated for instruction. Strategies related to room arrangement, minimizing transition time, and teaching material at the conceptual level of students all need to be addressed to increase ALT. Research on effective teachers reveals that they plan the use of their school day, allocate a greater percent of the school day to the basic subjects, and teach in groups so that students can get more instructional time. They spend 50% of their reading periods actually engaged in reading instruction. They use short periods of time (not over 30 seconds) to assist individual students with problems in seat work. They circulate among the students doing seat work to ensure a high degree of on-task behavior.

Most research on teacher effectiveness has been done with students in the elementary grades; some has been done at the junior high or secondary level. All have come to similar conclusions about effective teaching (Lightfoot, 1981; Stallings, 1981). MacKinzie (1983) has noted, however, that while the core principles are the same, their expression in actual practice are different. High school faculties are content specialists who hold little investment in basic skills.

Teaching strategies are the final component of the model. They represent a wide variety of specific procedures. These strategies are based on basic principles of learning and the interaction of those principles with student characteristics. Teaching requires knowledge, explanation, elaboration, and clarification. Sequence, order, modeling, appropriate practice, goal setting, basic concept development, feedback, questioning, and a host of procedures and learning principles can be collapsed under this heading. The critical feature is to train teachers in the effective use of these procedures and in making decisions on when to best use each.

Effective teachers practice effective instruction a large percentage of the day. Instruction requires explanation, demonstration, and clarification. Effective instruction requires that material be explained and reviewed so that new material can be linked to old. Using demonstration and practice while focusing attention on the relevant dimension of a concept is a teaching art. The science of instruction followed by effective teachers is comprised of modeling, questioning, providing prompts and cues, providing feedback, and providing opportunities to practice newly learned skills. Students in classes taught by effective teachers know the goals and the expectations of the teachers for meeting those goals. Finally, research substantiates that effective teachers are people who believe they can make a difference in student achievement.

REFERENCES

Anderson, L. M., Evertson, C. M., & Brophy, J. E. (1979). An experimental study of effective teaching in first-grade reading groups. *Elementary School Journal, 79,* 193–222.

Berliner, D. C. (1984). The half-full glass: A review of research in teaching. In P. L. Hosford (Ed.), *Using what we know about teaching.* Alexandria, VA: Association for Supervision and Curriculum Development.

Caladarci, T., & Gage, N. L. (1984). Effects of minimal intervention on teacher behavior and student achievement. *American Educational Research Journal, 21*(3), 539–555.

Crawford, J., Gage, N., Corno, L., Stayrook, N., & Mitman, A. (1978). *An experiment on teacher effectiveness and parent assisted instruction in the third grade* (3 vols.). Stanford, CA: Center for Educational Research at Stanford.

Elmore, R., Peterson, P., & McCarthey, S. (1996). *Restructuring in the classroom: Teaching, learning, and school organization.* San Francisco, CA: Jossey-Bass.

Evertson, C., Emmer, E., Clements, B., Sanford, J., Worsham, M., & Williams, E. (1981). *Organizing and managing the elementary school classroom.* Austin: Research and Development Center for Teacher Education, University of Texas.

Fisher, C. W., Filby, N. N., & Marliave, R. (1978). *Teaching behaviors, academic learning time, and student achievement: Final report of Phase III-B, beginning teacher evaluation study (technical report V-1).* San Francisco, CA: Far West Regional Laboratory for Educational Research and Development.

Fitzpatrick, K. (1981). *Successful management strategies for the secondary classroom.* Downers Grove, IL.

Gettinger, M., & Stoiba, K. (1999). Excellence in teaching: Review of instructional and environmental variables. In C. R. Reynolds & T. B. Gutkin (Eds.), *The handbook of school psychology* (3rd ed.). New York, NY: Wiley.

Good, T., & Grouws, D. (1977). Teaching effects: A process-product study in fourth-grade mathematics classrooms. *Journal of Teacher Education, 28,* 49–54.

Good, T. L. (1979). Teacher effectiveness in the elementary school: What we know about it. *Journal of Teacher Education, 30,* 52–64.

Good, T. L., & Grouws, D. A. (1979). The Missouri mathematics effectiveness project. *Journal of Educational Psychology, 71,* 355–382.

Lightfoot, S. L. (1981). Portraits of exemplary secondary schools: Highland Park. *Daedalus, 110*(4), 59–80.

MacKinzie, D. E. (1983). Research for school improvement: An appraisal of some recent trends. *Educational Researcher, 12*(4), 5–17.

Mohlman, G., Caladarci, T., & Gage, N. L. (1982). Comprehension and attitude as predictors of implementation of teacher training. *Journal of Teacher Education, 33,* 31, 36.

Pearson, P. D., & Gallagher, M. C. (1983). The instruction of reading comprehension. *Contemporary Educational Psychology, 8,* 317–344.

Stallings, J. A. (1981). *What research has to say to administrators of secondary schools about effective teaching and staff development.* Paper presented at the Conference Creating the Conditions for Effective Teaching, Center for Educational Policy and Management, Eugene, OR.

Stallings, J., Needles, M., & Strayrook, N. (1979). *The teaching of basic reading skills in secondary schools, Phase I and Phase II.* Menlo Park, CA: Stanford Research Institute.

Walberg, H. J. (1979). *Educational environments and effects: Evolution, policy, and productivity.* Berkeley, CA: McCutchon.

Walberg, H. J. (1982). What makes schooling effective? A synthesis and a critique of three national studies. *Contemporary Education: A Journal of Reviews, 1*(1), 22–34.

ROBERT A. SEDLAK
University of Wisconsin at Stout

See also **Teacher Burnout; Teacher Expectancies; Teaching Strategies**

TEACHER EXPECTANCIES

The general area of teacher expectancies involves investigating the effects of teachers' perceptions, beliefs, or attitudes about their students. Rosenthal and Jacobson (1968) tested kindergarten through fifth-grade children and then randomly identified some of them by telling their teachers that they had the greatest potential to show significant academic achievement over the school year. Results demonstrating that these children made significantly greater IQ gains than the control groups were interpreted to suggest that the teachers' expectations for the higher potential children influenced their teaching interactions with them, positively affecting the children's learning, as manifested in the higher scores. These results and interpretations were rejected by some owing to methodological flaws (e.g., the failure to measure the teachers' changed expectations and their teaching interactions). Later studies (Hall & Merkel, 1985) failed to replicate these results and indicated that teachers base their expectations for the most part on criteria relevant to academic performance and that they do not bias children's education.

With respect to the disabled student, teacher expectations have been discussed mostly in conjunction with the effects of labeling. Within this field, there is a fear that children's special education labels will cause teachers, parents, and others to lower their expectations for these children's academic and social development. The term *self-fulfilling prophecy* has been used to describe teachers' expectations and resulting instructional interactions that reinforce disabled children to act in a manner consistent with the stereotypical characteristics of their handicap. There is the possibility that these children will have difficulty in learning because "they are disabled," and may master skills only up to a level popularly ascribed to their disability. This self-fulfilling prophecy, then, might lower teachers' and others' expectations for disabled children, lower the children's expectations for themselves, and significantly limit the educational opportunities for them because they are not exposed to more advanced work or complex learning situations.

The research investigating teacher expectancies with individuals with disabilities has been inconclusive. While some studies have demonstrated that labels do affect teacher perceptions and expectations of exceptional children, others have shown no significant negative effects. MacMillan (1977) appropriately concludes:

> Although it [the evidence] does not demonstrate convincingly that calling attention to people with [for example] intellectual deficiencies by giving them special attention is always a bad thing, the controversy over labeling should make us all more sensitive to its potential hazards. (p. 245)

Hobbs (1975), who coordinated a national study on the effect of labels and their resulting expectancy effects, similarly noted no simple solution to the issues as long as labels are required for entrance into special education programs and for the reimbursement of federal and state funds to finance these programs. What appears necessary are ways to minimize the potential expectancy effect of labels while permitting their continued use in the field.

REFERENCES

Hall, V. C., & Merkel, S. P. (1985). Teacher expectancy effects and educational psychology. In J. B. Dusek (Ed.), *Teacher expectancies* (pp. 67–92). Hillsdale, NJ: Erlbaum.

Hobbs, N. (1975). *The future of children.* San Francisco, CA: Jossey-Bass.

MacMillan, D. L. (1977). *Mental retardation in school and society.* Boston, MA: Little, Brown.

Rosenthal, R., & Jacobson, L. (1968). *Pygmalion in the classroom.* New York, NY: Holt, Rinehart, & Winston.

HOWARD M. KNOFF
University of South Florida

TEACHING AND CONSULTATION

Consultation as one of the methods of delivering services to exceptional children was recognized by Reynolds (1962) in his Hierarchy of Services for Special Education Services. In this hierarchy, it was recognized that the majority of students classified as exceptional should and could be served in general education classrooms with consultation being one of the support services. Deno (1970) also recognized the teacher consultant as part of a "cascade of services." Kirk and Gallagher (1979) indicated that to facilitate mainstreaming, school systems might provide consultation services to regular teachers in the form of special education teachers, psychologists, social workers, and medical personnel. They go on to indicate that consultants are available to regular teachers when they have questions about a child or when they need advice concerning special materials and methods of instruction. Thomas, Correa, and Morsink (1995) provide an extensive look at the historical and legal foundations of consultation, collaboration, and teaming in special education beginning with the Deno model.

A number of definitions of and terms for consultation have been formulated. The terms include triadic process (Tharp, 1975), developmental and problem-centered consultation (Bergan, 1977), and collaborative problem solving (Medway, 1979). In special education, Idol, Paolucci-Whitcomb, and Nevin (1986) defined collaborative consultation as "an interactive process that enables people with diverse expertise to generate creative solutions to mutually defined problems." Dettmer, Thurston, and Dyck (1995) defined school consultation and the role of the consultant as an "activity in which professional educators and parents collaborate within the school context by communicating, cooperating, and coordinating their efforts as a team to serve the learning and behavioral needs of students." It also is important to note what consultation is not. Pryzwansky (1974) pointed out that consultation should not be an "expert" providing some type of prescription. Other cautions include one for a distinction between a medical model and a behavioral approach and one for the differences between consultation and counseling and consultation and collaboration.

Three of the most popular models of consultation in special education are triadic, organizational, and behavioral. In the triadic model there is a target (person with problem), a mediator (person with means to influence change), and a consultant (person with knowledge to mobilize mediator's influence.) Thomas et al. (1995) describe the collaborative consultation model of Idol, Paolucci-Whitcomb, and Nevin (1986) as an extension of the triadic model in which the target is the student with a problem, the mediator is the general education teacher, and the consultant is the special educator or other professional. Organizational consultation focuses on interactions, interrelationships, shared decision making, and communication

skills. The emphasis is on change with an organization or group. The consultant's role is primarily that of facilitator. Behavioral consultation emphasizes student behavior change. This model uses direct observation, identification of target behavior for change, and data-based interventions and assessment. Gutkin and Curtis (1982) identified characteristics present in the majority of consultation models they reviewed. These include indirect service delivery, consultant-consultee relationship, coordinate status, involvement of consultee in the consultation process, consultee's right to reject consultant suggestions, voluntary nature of consultation, and confidentiality.

The process of consultation is summarized by Thomas et al. (1995) in eight steps:

1. Establishing the relationship.
2. Gathering information.
3. Identifying the problem.
4. Stating the target behavior.
5. Generating interventions.
6. Implementing interventions.
7. Evaluating the interventions.
8. Withdrawing from the consultative relationship.

A concept closely related to consultation is teaming. Teams within special education are generally thought of as organized groups of professionals from different disciplines. Their common goal is cooperative problem solving. Combining collaboration and teamwork builds on the strengths of both approaches. Teaming models include the multidisciplinary team, the interdisciplinary team, and the transdisciplinary team. The multidisciplinary team concept evolved from the medical model, in which experts in various fields shared their observations and generally reported them to one person. The interdisciplinary team is similar to the multidisciplinary team, but generally the team members evaluate a child and meet to share their observations. The transdisciplinary team model is a combination of the two previously mentioned and attempts to reduce fragmentation. It is viewed as an education/treatment model that integrates assessment, program goals, and objectives from various disciplines. Its characteristics, according to S. Lyon and Lyon (1980), are a joint team and professional development approach and implementation of role release. Orelove and Sobsey (1991) identify other characteristics as an indirect therapy approach, multiple lines of communication, and integration of services.

Consultation, collaboration, teaming, and family involvement have been stressed in special education (especially since the passage of PL 94-142), and these concepts have been strengthened with each amended or reauthorized version of this law. Teachers and other school personnel are recognizing the importance of shared decision making as the needs of children become increasingly complex. The emphases on effective schools, total quality management, site-based management, comprehensive schools, and inclusion are providing the impetus for a model combining the salient features of previously identified consultation, collaboration, and teaming approaches. Thomas et al. (1985) proposed such a model, which they describe as interactive teaming. Interactive teaming is defined as a mutual or reciprocal effort among and between members of a team to provide the best possible educational program for a student. This model has 10 elements drawn from previous research of models and programs with interactive teaming components. These are the elements that must be present for the model to be effective.

Legitimacy and autonomy.

Purpose and objectives.

Competencies of team members and clarity of roles.

Role release and role transitions.

Awareness of the individuality of team members.

Process of team building.

Attention to factors that affect team functioning.

Leadership styles.

Implementation procedures.

Commitment to common goals.

Consultation in special education has evolved from the concept of a professional sharing expertise with a regular classroom teacher to one of the special educator being a member of a team in which all individuals have critical roles.

REFERENCES

Bergan, J. R. (1977). *Behavioral consultation.* Columbus, OH: Merrill.

Deno, E. (1970). Special education as developmental capital. *Exceptional Children, 37,* 229–237.

Dettmer, P., Thurston, L. P., & Dyck, N. (1995). *Consultation, collaboration, and teamwork for students with special needs.* Boston, MA: Allyn & Bacon.

Gutkin, T. B., & Curtis, M. J. (1982). School-based consultation. In C. R. Reynolds & T. B. Gutkin (Eds.), *The handbook of school psychology.* New York, NY: Wiley.

Idol, L., Paolucci-Whitcomb, P., & Nevin, A. (1986). *Collaborative consultation.* Rockville, MD: Aspen.

Kirk, S. A., & Gallagher, J. J. (1972). *Educating exceptional children* (2nd ed.). Boston, MA: Houghton Mifflin.

Kirk, S. A., & Gallagher, J. J. (1979). *Educating exceptional children* (3rd ed.). Boston, MA: Houghton Mifflin.

Lyon, S., & Lyon, G. (1980). Team functioning and staff development: A role release approach to providing integrated educational services for severely handicapped students. *Journal of the Association for the Severely Handicapped, 5,* 250–263.

Medway, F. J. (1979). How effective is school consultation? A review of recent research. *Journal of School Psychology, 17,* 285–292.

Orelove, F. P., & Sobsey, D. (1991). *Educating children with multiple disabilities: A transdisciplinary approach* (2nd ed.). Baltimore, MD: Paul H. Brookes.

Pryzwansky, W. W. (1974). A reconsideration of the consultation model for delivery of school-based psychological services. *Journal of Orthopsychiatry, 44,* 579–583.

Reynolds, M. C. (1962). A framework for considering some issues in special education. *Exceptional Children, 29,* 147–169.

Tharp, R. G. (1975). The triadic model of consultation: Current considerations. In C. A. Parker (Ed.), *Psychological consultation: Helping teachers meet special needs.* Reston, VA: Council for Exceptional Children.

Thomas, C. C., Correa, V. I., & Morsink, C. V. (1995). *Interactive teaming: Consultation and collaboration in special programs* (2nd ed.). Englewood Cliffs, NJ: Merrill.

ELEANOR BOYD WRIGHT
CAROL CHASE THOMAS
University of North Carolina at Wilmington

TEACHING EXCEPTIONAL CHILDREN

Teaching Exceptional Children (*TEC*) is an official publication of the Council for Exceptional Children (CEC). *TEC* is specifically for teachers, administrators, and other special education professionals of children with disabilities, as well as children who are gifted. The journal was first published in 1968, currently has an average circulation of more than 35,000, and is disseminated 6 times annually.

TEC features timely, practical, peer-reviewed articles that present methods and materials for classroom use. The publication also presents current issues in special education teaching and learning. Further, *TEC* brings its readers the latest information on technology, assistive technology, and procedures and techniques with applications to students with exceptionalities. Each issue is themed to correspond to leading issues in the field, with a focus on immediate application. The journal also offers regular columns and learning guides to help users earn Continuing Education Units (CEUs) for their participation.

TEC is printed in full color. A subscription to *TEC* also allows users access to *TEC Plus*, the online companion to *TEC*, which contains more content for special educators as well as new features such as case studies, case stories, and book reviews. *TEC Plus* is available on the Internet each month readers receive *TEC*.

Inquiries regarding subscriptions or manuscript submissions should be referred to the CEC Headquarters located at 1110 North Glebe Road, Suite 300, Arlington,

VA 22201. Information can also be found online under the *Publications* tab of the CEC website: www.cec.sped.org/ Tel.: (888) 232–7733. E-mail: service@cec.sped.org

RICK GONZALEZ
Texas A&M University
Third edition

BENJAMIN J. COOK B. A.
Chicago School of Professional Psychology
Fourth edition

See also Council for Exceptional Children

TEACHING: INCLUSION AND CO-TEACHING

Co-teaching is a form of instruction in which a general education teacher and special education teacher work together in an inclusive classroom consisting of students with and without disabilities. Typically, the types of students with disabilities found in a co-teaching environment are students considered to have mild disabilities (i.e., learning, behavioral, and speech/language disabilities). Because students with mild disabilities bring a number of general and specific weaknesses to classrooms that may be structurally rigid and where information may be poorly organized, too abstract, uninteresting, and assumes a great deal of prior knowledge, a teacher who specializes in learning processes is a critical support.

Two issues emerge, however: (1) How do teachers teach together to facilitate more successful learning by students with and without disabilities? and (2) What kinds of teacher and student outcomes can be expected?

What Does Research Say About Co-Teaching?

The literature on co-teaching or collaborative instruction has primarily described barriers to collaboration (e.g., Johnson, Pugach, & Hammittee, 1988; Phillips & McCullough, 1990), types of collaborative relationships (e.g., Bauwens, Hourcade, & Friend, 1989; Dettmer, Thurston, & Dyck, 1993), and a variety of collaborative skills and roles (e.g., Friend & Cook, 1992; Knackendoffel, Robinson, Deshler, & Schumaker, 1992), and provided little data on the instructional dynamics of two teachers teaching students with and without disabilities or the performance of the students in inclusive classes (e.g., Idol, Nevin, & Paolucci-Whitcomb, 1994; Reeve & Hallahan, 1994).

In one of the few existing data-based reports on co-teaching, Hudson (1990) described gains for one group of elementary children with and without mild disabilities in grade-point average, achievement test scores, number of academic objectives mastered, adaptive behavior

ratings, peer status, and school attendance when they were enrolled in two classrooms employing the Class-Within-a-Class Model for collaborative teaching. Schulte, Osborne, and McKinney (1990) discovered that students with mild disabilities who received some instruction from the special education teacher in general education settings made greater overall gains on a standardized achievement test as compared to students receiving resource room support for one period per day, and as compared to students in the general education classroom where consultation was only provided by the general education teacher. There were no significant differences on a criterion-referenced test, however.

Another study on collaborative instruction in an elementary setting provided negative results. Zigmond and Baker (1990) observed teachers and students with learning disabilities in inclusive classrooms where a combination of collaborative instruction and consultation took place. They concluded that the types of support and kinds of instruction by teachers were essentially "business as usual." Students did not make significant gains on a standardized achievement test, they earned lower grades, and curriculum-based measures showed only minimal progress. Boudah, Schumaker, and Deshler (1997) found that teachers could learn to teach together but that teacher change translated to only minimal change in student engagement and use of learning strategies. Students also continued to perform poorly on unit tests and quizzes.

Descriptions from these and other studies indicate several other characteristics of co-teaching. Many co-teaching relationships are arranged by building administrators (Boudah et al., 1997). Perhaps because of such arrangements and little training, the special education teacher also typically functions in one of two roles: (1) provider of indirect services to students through consultation with the general education teacher (e.g., Peck, Killen, & Baumgart, 1989; Tindal, Shinn, Walz, & Germann, 1987) or (2) provider of at least some direct services within general education classrooms, but primarily or exclusively to students with disabilities and with apparently few interactions between the two teachers (e.g., Givens-Olge, Christ, & Idol, 1991; Hudson, 1990). Thus, in the second role, the special education teacher functions more like an instructional aide than a specialist or teacher of at least equivalent instructional status. In addition, many collaboratively taught classes may include a large number of students with disabilities and thus operate like "low-track" classes (Boudah & Knight, 1999). Such efforts then may lead to ceiling effects on teacher instructional change and student performance (Boudah et al., 1997).

What Might Co-Teaching Look Like?

The keys to two teachers working in the same classroom are the interactions between the teachers as well as the interactions between the teachers and students (Boudah et al., 1997). Thus, there are several possible models for co-teaching (e.g., Bauwens & Hourcade, 1997; Burrello, Burrello, & Friend, 1996). Some of the models may be called (a) teach and circulate or observe, (b) station teaching, (c) alternative teaching, and (d) team teaching.

In the first model (*teach and circulate or observe*), one teacher would present the content material (e.g., a lesson on the geography of France), and the other teacher would circulate among the students to assist as needed, or collect observation data on student behavior and performance. Teachers might use *station teaching* in order to individualize support for groups of students. For instance, one teacher may need to reteach material to one group of students who were absent the previous day, the other teacher may need to review material for a group with learning disabilities, and another group of students may work independently on an assignment. In *alternative teaching*, a small group of students might sit with one teacher in a corner of the room for additional review, reteaching, enrichment, or help completing an assignment or test.

Team teaching is more dynamic. During class instruction, teachers function in two primary roles: presenter and enhancer. During whole group instruction, the *presenter* presents content information such as facts, rules, concepts, and themes in a subject area such as social studies, math, science, or English. Meanwhile, the *enhancer* arbitrates between students and the content material being presented in class. For instance, in one instructional sequence, a science teacher might talk about a specific concept while the special education teacher simultaneously summarizes the most important points by writing bulleted statements on the chalkboard; later, the special education teacher might talk about another part of the science concept while the science teacher elaborates by providing some specific examples or an analogy. The sequence may finish with both teachers functioning as enhancers, one prompting students to summarize a chronology of facts or events while the other interjects by prompting students to predict what would happen if a different order of events had occurred. Therefore, while the presenter teaches *what* to learn, the enhancer, in essence, teaches *how* to learn the material (Boudah et al., 1997).

At least initially, the general education teacher may function in the presenter role more often, and the special education teacher commonly may function in the enhancer role. This is for obvious reasons: The general education teacher is likely to be more knowledgeable about the content being presented, and the special education teacher's strength is usually related to teaching skills or strategies for learning. Eventually, however, the general education teacher and the special education teacher may function equally as presenter and enhancer, and both teachers may function as presenter or enhancer at any given time during a lesson. Thus, through this kind of instructional process, the special education teacher and general education

teacher can complement and support each other, like partners who are dancing together (Adams, Cessna, & Friend, 1992).

In summary, in co-teaching, both teachers should be actively engaged in teaching students. Both teachers should monitor and enhance student understanding of information and concepts presented in class. Teachers can help each other expand and clarify information and concepts, teach strategies, and enhance, rather than "water down," content. Either teacher can provide whole group or individualized instruction, and both teachers are responsible for managing student behavior and evaluating performance.

Where Do Teachers Start?

As with any method for delivering instructional services to students with disabilities, it is important to focus first on the needs of individual students and decide which students would benefit from co-teaching in inclusive classes. This may not include every student or even every student with a particular disability classification. Once those decisions have been made, clustering a small number of students with disabilities in an inclusive class may not only be instructionally effective, but also may be a more efficient way for special education teachers to serve students.

In addition, co-teaching is often a change in the typical operations of a school. Therefore, co-teachers need to build their plans and schedules with the principal. In order to set up successful experiences, teachers also should be allowed to decide who will teach together. Special education teachers who are trying to facilitate inclusion may need to target general education teachers who may have some special education experience, background, and/or exposure. These teachers are most likely to understand the needs of students with disabilities and be adaptable to instructional change.

Next, co-teachers may want to conduct observations in each others' classes so that they become familiar with their partner's teaching styles and routines. Observations can provide opportunities to think about appropriate co-teaching models and ways to modify and adapt instructional methods. Co-teachers also may find that it is worthwhile to pilot one class for a period of time, develop a relationship, plan as a team, teach as a team, and evaluate team performance before committing to co-teaching for a longer period of time.

Co-teachers should seek out training experiences on specific collaborative skills as well as ways of building shared expectations. Committing to a regular team planning time can also help clarify expectations. Team planning and organization also should lead to more dynamic teaching in the classroom.

School restructuring efforts often highlight coordination and collaboration as important dimensions of the delivery of educational services for children in a broad array of programs including gifted education, English as a Second Language (ESL), Chapter 1 (Association for Supervision and Curriculum Development, 1991), as well as special education. Such integration of services necessarily requires the collaboration of those assigned to work with such a diversity of students. Co-teaching is one way for teachers to collaborate in order to provide a free and appropriate education to some students with disabilities in general education classrooms.

REFERENCES

Adams, L., Cessna, K., & Friend, M. (1992, October). *Co-teaching: Honoring uniqueness and creating unity*. Presentation made at the Annual Conference of the Council for Learning Disabilities, Kansas City, MO.

Association for Supervision and Curriculum Development. (1991). *Resolutions 1991*. Washington, DC.

Bauwens, J., & Hourcade, J. J. (1997). Cooperative teaching: Pictures of possibilities. *Intervention in School and Clinic, 33*(2), 81–85, 89.

Bauwens, J., Hourcade, J. J., & Friend, M. (1989). Cooperative teaching: A model for general and special education integration. *Remedial and Special Education, 10*, 17–22.

Boudah, D. & Knight, S. (1999). Creating learning communities of research and practice; Participatory research and development. In D. M. Byrd & D. J. McIntyre (Eds.), *Research on professional development schools: Teacher education yearbook VII* (pp. 97–114). Thousand Oaks, CA: Corwin Press.

Boudah, D. J., Schumaker, J. B., & Deshler, D. D. (1997). Collaborative instruction: Is it an effective option for inclusion in secondary classrooms? *Learning Disability Quarterly, 20*(4), 293–316.

Burrello, L. C., Burrello, J. M., & Friend, M. (Producers). (1996). The power of 2: Making a difference through co-teaching *[Film]*. Indiana University Television Services and Elephant Rock Productions. (Available from CEC Resources, Association Drive, Reston, VA)

Dettmer, P., Thurston, L. P., & Dyck, N. (1993). *Consultation, collaboration, and teamwork for students with special needs*. Boston, MA: Allyn & Bacon.

Friend, M., & Cook, L. (1992). *Interactions: Collaboration skills for school professionals*. New York, NY: Longman.

Givens-Olge, L., Christ, B. A., & Idol, L. (1991). Collaborative consultation: The San Juan Unified School District project. *Journal of Educational and Psychological Consultation, 2*(3), 267–284.

Hudson, F. (1990). *Research reports for Kansas City, Kansas public schools division of special education on CTM-collaborative teaching model at Stony Point South Elementary School, 1989–90*. Kansas City: University of Kansas Medical Center, Department of Special Education.

Idol, L., Nevin, A., & Paolucci-Whitcomb, P. (1994). *Collaborative consultation* (2nd ed.). Austin, TX: PRO-ED.

Johnson, L. J., Pugach, M. C., & Hammittee, D. J. (1988). Barriers to effective special education consultation. *Remedial and Special Education, 9*, 41–47.

Knackendoffel, E. A., Robinson, S. M., Deshler, D. D., & Schumaker, J. B. (1992). *Collaborative problem solving: Team teaching series*. Lawrence, KS: Edge.

Peck, C. A., Killen, C. C., & Baumgart, D. (1989). Increasing implementation of special education instruction in mainstream preschools: Direct and generalized effects of nondirective consultation. *Journal of Applied Behavior Analysis, 2*(2), 197–210.

Phillips, V., & McCullough, L. (1990). Consultation-based programming: Instituting the collaborative ethic in schools. *Exceptional Children, 56*, 291–304.

Reeve, P. T., & Hallahan, D. P. (1994). Practical questions about collaboration between general and special educators. *Focus on Exceptional Children, 26*(7), 1–12.

Schulte, A. C., Osborne, S. S., & McKinney, J. D. (1990). Academic outcomes for students with learning disabilities in consultation and resource programs. *Exceptional Children, 57*(2), 162–171.

Tindal, G., Shinn, M. R., Walz, L., & Germann, G. (1987). Mainstream consultation in secondary settings: The Pine County model. *Journal of Special Education, 21*, 94–106.

Zigmond, N., & Baker, J. (1990). Mainstream experiences for learning disabled students (Project MELD): Preliminary report. *Exceptional Children, 57*(2), 176–185.

DANIEL J. BOUDAH
Texas A&M University

See also Inclusion

TEACHING STRATEGIES

Teaching strategies are those activities that are conducted by a teacher to enhance the academic achievement of students. A teaching strategy is based on a philosophical approach that is used in conjunction with a learning strategy. Teachers generally choose a particular approach based on their educational background and training, their personal beliefs, the subject being taught, the characteristics of the learner, and the degree of learning required.

Training backgrounds of special educators can range from the behavioral to the process-oriented. Teachers with behavioral backgrounds will use approaches that are task specific and focus on observable behaviors. Those coming from a process background are more inclined to follow approaches that focus on underlying processes. They try to treat the hypothesized cause of the problem or deficit rather than the observable behavior. Approaches such as perceptual-motor training or cognitive training may be followed by teachers with process orientations. Perceptual-motor training approaches are controversial and have questionable effectiveness in regard to academic achievement (Arter & Jenkins, 1979; Kavale &

Forness, 1999; Sedlak & Weener, 1973). Cognitive training approaches focus on thinking skills and learning how to learn rather than specific content skills. The research on this approach is promising. Examples of behavioral approaches are direct instruction and applied behavior analysis. These approaches focus on identifying the specific content to be taught and teaching that content in a systematic fashion using a prescribed system of learning strategies. There are also subject-specific approaches. For example, in reading, some of the different approaches available are the linguistics approach, phonics, sight word, Fernald, multisensory, language experience, and the neurological impress method. These approaches focus on the organization of the materials needed for instruction and also prescribe, in some cases, specific strategies to be used.

In addition to an approach, the application of a learning strategy to a situation is needed to create a teaching strategy. A learning strategy becomes a teaching strategy when the teacher systematically plans, organizes, and uses a learning strategy with a student to achieve a specific outcome. In many texts, these learning strategies are referred to as generic strategies or principles of instruction. These strategies generally are used in conjunction with a particular phase of learning (e.g., acquisition, retention, or transfer), or for a particular type of learning (e.g., discrimination, concept, rule, problem solving). Generic strategies used for the acquisition phase include giving instruction (verbal, picture, modeling or demonstration, reading), revealing objectives to the learner, providing appropriate practice on a skill, providing feedback to the learner, organizing material into small steps and in sequential order, checking on student comprehension through questions, and offering positive and negative examples of concepts. However, it is also important for students to learn to teach others through the development of their own strategic and skillful processing of information (Alexander & Murphy, 1999).

The generic strategies that can be used to maintain skills already acquired are overlearning, reminiscence, and spaced review. To teach for transfer, multiple examples of the application of the skill or concept are needed, along with teaching the skill with the appropriate cues in the setting in which it is to be practiced. Gradually fading artificial cues and relying on natural cues in the environment is another strategy used by teachers to facilitate transfer. Some other examples of teaching strategies are the use of mnemonics, peer teaching, assigned homework, graded homework, cooperative learning, mediated instruction, and computer-assisted instruction. In strategies such as these, a variety of learning strategies are organized and used.

REFERENCES

Alexander, P., & Murphy, P. (1999). What cognitive psychology has to say to school psychology. In C. R. Reynolds & T. B.

Gutkin (Eds.), *The handbook of school psychology* (3rd ed.). New York, NY: Wiley.

Arter, J. A., & Jenkins, J. R. (1979). Differential diagnosis—Prescriptive teaching: A critical appraisal. *Review of Educational Research, 49*, 517–555.

Kavale, K., & Forness, S. (1999). The effectiveness of special education. In C. R. Reynolds & T. B. Gutkin (Eds.), *The handbook of school psychology* (3rd ed.). New York, NY: Wiley.

Sedlak, R. A., & Weener, P. (1973). Review of research on the Illinois test of psycholinguistics abilities. In L. Mann & D. Sabatino (Eds.), *The first review of special education*. Philadelphia, PA: JSE.

ROBERT A. SEDLAK
University of Wisconsin at Stout

See also Ability Training, Early Efforts in Applied Behavior Analysis; Direct Instruction; Mnemonics; Teacher Effectiveness

TECHNIQUES: A JOURNAL FOR REMEDIAL EDUCATION AND COUNSELING

Techniques was published from 1984 to 1987 with Gerald B. Fuller and Hubert Vance as coeditors. The journal provides multidisciplinary articles that serve as an avenue for communication and interaction among the various disciplines concerned with the treatment and education of the exceptional individual and others encountering special problems in living. The orientation is primarily clinical and educational and reflects the various types of counseling, therapy, remediation, and interventions currently employed. The journal does not mirror the opinion of any one school or authority but serves as a forum for open discussion and exchange of ideas and experiences.

The specific sections in *Techniques* represent the following six content areas:

1. *Educational and psychological materials.* This section helps the professional to keep current by evaluating, critiquing, comparing, and reviewing educational, counseling, and psychological materials (e.g., programs, kits) that are being proposed or used in applied settings.

2. *Research studies.* This section offers empirical research, case studies, and discussion papers that focus on specific counseling, therapy, and remediation techniques that cut across various disciplines.

3. *Practical approaches in the field.* This section provides a description of hands-on techniques or approaches that the author(s) have used and found to be successful within their field.

4. *Parent education.* This section provides comprehensive treatment of such topics as disruptive children and youths, single-parent families, reconstituted families, and prevention and treatment of child abuse and neglect.

5. *Bibliotherapy.* This is a compilation of books that are useful for the child and parent as well as the practitioner. The topics are practical and address such issues as divorce, self-concept, and drug abuse.

6. *What's new in the field.* This section provides current information in the areas of remedial programs and counseling techniques, and includes reviews of current software programs.

GERALD B. FULLER
Central Michigan University

TECHNOLOGY FOR INDIVIDUALS WITH DISABILITIES

If there is one word that summarizes the impact of technology in the past 25 years, it is zeitgeist, the spirit of the time. The inculcation of silicon chips and microprocessors into our everyday lives irrevocably changed us from an industrial society to an informational society (Toffler, 1982). If disabled persons are to function fully in this society, they must have access to the myriad technologies that can improve communication, information processing, and learning. While technological advances are making inroads in the reduction of the impact of motoric, sensory, and cognitive disabilities, the real potential is yet to be met. The following section is an introduction to some of the technologies that are currently affecting the lives of disabled persons. It also offers an overview of some of the technologies that have yet to fulfill their promise.

The computer is second only to the printing press in its impact on the way in which humans acquire and distribute information. As computers are reduced in size and cost, their impact is multiplied geometrically. The computer has two characteristics that are particularly significant for disabled individuals: (1) as hardware decreases in size, it generally increases in capacity; and (2) the more sophisticated computers become, the easier they are to use. These characteristics are very important for individuals with disabilities in several respects. First, as computers become smaller, they also become more portable. For example, hand-held computers can be attached to wheelchairs to improve mobility. Second, as computers become easier to use, they are more accessible to the disabled. For example, reducing the number of keystrokes required to perform certain computer functions has greatly facilitated their use.

Microprocessor-based technology facilitates communication in two ways: as a compensatory device for sensory disabilities and as an assistive device for individuals whose physical impairments make communication difficult. Examples of compensatory devices include talking computer terminals that can translate text into speech (Stoffel, 1982); special adaptive devices for computers that can provide visual displays of auditory information by translating sound into text (Vanderheiden, 1982); and Cognivox, an adaptive device for Apple personal computers that combines the capabilities of voice recognition and voice output (Murray, 1982).

For individuals with motoric disabilities, communication aids have been developed that allow them to operate computers with single-switch input devices. These devices may be as simple as game paddles and joysticks or as sophisticated as screen-based optical headpointing systems. Keyboard enhancers and emulators help individuals with restricted movement by reducing the number of actuations necessary for communication. For example, Minispeak is a semantic compaction system that can produce thousands of clear, spoken sentences with as few as seven keystrokes (Baker, 1982). Adaptive communication devices can also be linked with computers to help the disabled control their living environments (e.g., by running appliances, answering the telephone, or adjusting the thermostat).

The term telecommunication means communication across distance. It is a means of storing text and pictures as electronic impulses and transmitting them via telephone line, satellite, coaxial and fiber optic cables, or broadcast transmission. Telecommunication offers several advantages over traditional means of communication. First, telecommunication is relatively inexpensive when spread across time and users. Also, telecommunicating helps alleviate the problems associated with geographic remoteness or the isolation imposed by limited mobility. Information-gathering and dissemination need not be limited to schools. It can occur in the home or office; a local area network (LAN) can link several computers or terminals to a computer with expanded memory. Such a system permits several operators to use the same software and data simultaneously. A wide-area network links computers from distant geographic regions. Examples of this networking capability can be found in several states where all of the local agencies are linked to the state agency. Statewide systems greatly reduce the time and paperwork necessary for compliance with special education legislation.

SpecialNet is another example of a wide-area network. Subscribers use it primarily to access electronic bulletin boards and to send messages through electronic mail. Electronic bulletin boards function much the same as traditional corkboards found in most schools. Users can post messages to obtain information, or they can read messages to find out the latest information about a given topic. For example, the employment bulletin board on SpecialNet posts vacancies in special education and related services. The Request for Proposals (RFP) bulletin board has information on the availability of upcoming grants and contracts. The exchange bulletin board is for users to post requests for information. Electronic mail, as the name implies, is a system whereby computer users can send and receive messages through their computers. On the SpecialNet system, each subscriber is given a special name that identifies his or her mailbox; with the aid of word processing and telecommunication software, users can send short or long documents in a matter of seconds.

In addition to capabilities offered by electronic bulletin boards and electronic mail, individuals with telecommunication hookups have access to information from large electronic libraries that store, sort, and retrieve bibliographic information. For example, the Educational Resources Information Center (ERIC), operated by the Council for Exceptional Children, is the largest source of information on handicapped and gifted children. Other important sources of information are the Handicapped Exchange (HEX), which contains information on handicapped individuals, and ABLEDATA, which is a catalog of computer hardware, software, and assistive devices for individuals with disabilities.

Another important form of telecommunication is teletext, a one-way transmission to television viewers. Teletext uses the vertical blanking interval (VBI), the unused portion of a television signal, to print information on television screens. Applications of teletext include news headlines, weather forecasts, and information on school closings. Closed captioning is a form of teletext that allows hearing-impaired individuals to see dialogue (JWK International, 1983). Experiments are now under way to use teletext to transmit instructional material. Broadcasters can transmit public domain software into homes and schools that have computers and special transmission decoding devices.

A videodisk is a tabletop device that is interfaced with a monitor to play video programs stored on 12-inch disks. When interfaced with a computer, the videodisk becomes interactive, and thus becomes a powerful instructional tool. Part of the videodisk's power comes from its storage capacity; it can hold 54,000 frames of information, including movies, filmstrips, slides, and sound. When combined with the computer's branching capacity, videodisks allow students to move ahead or go back according to the learner's needs. Information can also be shown in slow motion or freeze frame. One of the earliest educational videodisks was the First National Kidisc, a collection of games and activities for children. The California School for the Deaf in Riverside also developed a system to use the videodisk to teach language development and reading. With this system, students use light pens to write their responses on the screen (Wollman, 1981). In the past,

videodisk technology has been very expensive because of the cost in developing the disks. Now, however, educators and other service providers can have customized disks made at relatively low cost.

Artificial intelligence refers to the use of the computer to solve the same types of problems and to make the same kinds of decisions faced by humans (Yin & Moore, 1984). Because scientists do not fully understand how humans solve problems and make decisions, they have debated whether true artificial intelligence is possible. So far, the closest they have come is the development of expert systems, natural systems, and machine vision. Expert systems are computer programs that use knowledge and inference strategies to solve problems. The systems rely on three kinds of information: facts, relations between the facts, and methods for using the facts to solve problems (D'Ambrosio, 1985). An example of an expert system is Internist, which makes medical diagnoses. Natural language processing is the use of natural speech to communicate with computers and to translate foreign language texts. Machine vision takes advantage of sensory devices to reproduce objects on the computer screen. These technological applications, like many others, offer potential benefits to disabled individuals, but their use for physical or cognitive prostheses hinges on the commitment of vast resources for their development.

A robot is a device that can be programmed to move in specified directions and to manipulate objects. What distinguishes a robot from other technologies and prosthetic devices is its capacity for locomotion. Robotic arms can pick up and move objects, assemble parts, and even spray paint. Robots of the future will not only be able to move, they will also be able to sense the environment by touch, sight, or sound. More important, the robot will be able to acquire information, understand it, and plan and implement appropriate actions (Yin & Moore, 1984). While robots offer great potential as prosthetic devices for the disabled, their current use is limited primarily to research and manufacturing. To some extent, robots are being used in classrooms to teach computer logic.

Specific technologies are in use today in special education classrooms for nearly all categories of disabling conditions, including communication disorders, health impairments, hearing impairments, visual impairments, and students with learning disabilities in particular (e.g., see Cartwright, Cartwright, & Ward, 1995). Technology is growing most rapidly in areas where it was first used and seems to have the greatest impact on quality of life issues in the sensory impairments and communication disorders. Computer-aided instruction is on the rise as well, especially with children with learning disabilities, but is a latecomer. As recently as 1990, the major textbook in learning disabilities (Myers & Hammill, 1990) makes no mention of technology for learning disability interventions.

REFERENCES

Baker, B. (1982). Minispeak: A semantic compaction system that makes self-expression easier for communicatively disabled individuals. *Byte, 7,* 186–202.

Cartwright, P., Cartwright, C., & Ward, M. (1995). *Educating special learners* (4th ed.). Boston, MA: Wadsworth.

D'Ambrosio, B. (1985). Expert systems—Myth or reality? *Byte, 10,* 275–282.

JWK International. (1983). *Teletext and videotex* (Contract No. 300-81-0424). Washington, DC: Special Education Programs Office.

Murray, W. (1982). The Cognivox V10-1003: Voice recognition and output for the Apple II. *Byte, 7,* 231–235.

Myers, P., & Hammill, D. (1990). *Methods for learning disorders* (4th ed.). Austin, TX: PRO-ED.

Stoffel, D. (1982). Talking terminals. *Byte, 7,* 218–227.

Toffler, A. (1982). *The third wave.* New York, NY: Bantam.

Vanderheiden, G. (1982). Computers can play a dual role for disabled individuals. *Byte, 7,* 136–162.

Wollman, J. (1981). The videodisc: A new educational technology takes off. *Electronic Learning, 1,* 39–40.

Yin, R. K., & Moore, G. B. (1984). *Robotics, artificial intelligence, computer simulation: Future applications in special education.* Washington, DC: U.S. Department of Education.

ELIZABETH MCCLELLAN
Council for Exceptional Children

See also Computer Use With Students With Disabilities; Robotics; Robotics in Special Education; SpecialNet

TECSE (*See* Topics in Early Childhood Special Education)

TEGRETOL

Tegretol (carbamazepine) is an anticonvulsant medication indicated for the treatment of various types of seizure disorders. In addition, Tegretol may also be prescribed for the treatment of manic-depressive disorders, resistant schizophrenia, rage outburst, or alcohol withdrawal management (Shannon, Wilson, & Stang, 1995).

Tegretol should be taken with food to minimize gastric irritation. All individuals need to be advised to take sustained released Tegretol as a whole tablet and never crush or chew the pill. Tegretol must be taken at regular intervals during the day and exactly as ordered by the physician (Deglin & Vallerand, 1999). Abrupt discontinuation may result in severe seizure activity and is not recommended (Shannon et al., 1995). Possible side effects include dizziness or drowsiness, and those starting treatment should take great care to avoid operating any machinery or driving a vehicle until their response to Tegretol is analyzed (Deglin & Vallerand, 1999). Since photosensitivity reactions also may occur, excessive sunlight should be avoided and sunscreen protection routinely used (Shannon et al., 1995).

Tegretol may cause breakthrough bleeding in women taking oral contraceptives (McKenry & Salerno, 1998). Women should be instructed to use other birth control methods as Tegretol may interfere with the effectiveness of their oral contraceptives. Tegretol is also excreted in breast milk and is not recommended in nursing mothers (McKenry & Solerno, 1998). Tegretol, along with other anticonvulsant medications such as phenytoin, (Dilantin), valproic acid (Depakene/Depakote), primidone (Mysoline), and phenobarbitol, appears to have teratogenic effects, and prenatal exposure to multiple ones appears to increase risk to the fetus (Jones, 1997). Women with seizure disorders who are at risk for pregnancy should be tested to determine if medication can be suspended if they have been seizure free for 2 years or at least maintained on a low dose. The conflict between potentially adverse effects of seizures on mother and fetus and medication on the fetus may be difficult to resolve.

An individual taking Tegretol should be advised that a medical alert identification card, bracelet, or necklace should be with the person at all times to alert health care providers of the medications that the person is taking as well as any pertinent medical history (Skidmore-Roth & McKenry, 1997). With any continuous medication regime, school personnel should be notified of this medication and any other health-related concerns (Wong, 1995).

REFERENCES

Deglin, J., & Vallerand, A. (1999). *Davis's drug guide for nurses* (6th ed.). Philadelphia, PA: Davis.

Jones, K. L. (1997). *Smith's recognizable patterns of human malformation* (5th ed.). Philadelphia, PA: Saunders.

McKenry, L., & Salerno, E. (1998). *Pharmacology in nursing* (20th ed.). St. Louis, MO: Mosby-Year Book.

Shannon, M., Wilson, B., & Stang, C. (1995). *Govoni & Hayes drugs and nursing implications* (8th ed.). Norwalk, CT: Appleton & Lange.

Skidmore-Roth, L., & McKenry, L. (1997). *Mosby's drug guide for nurses* (2nd ed.). St. Louis, MO: Mosby-Year Book.

Wong, D. (1995). *Whaley & Wong's nursing care of infants and children* (5th ed.). St. Louis, MO: Mosby-Year Book.

KARI ANDERSON
University of North Carolina at Wilmington

See also Absence Seizures; Anticonvulsants; Grand Mal Seizures

TELECOMMUNICATION DEVICES FOR THE DEAF

Telecommunication devices for the deaf (TDDs or TTYs) make communication available to the hearing-impaired population by providing video or printed modes of communication. Using a modem, or acoustic coupler, a TDD user types out a message to another user. This message either moves across a video display screen or is typed on a roll of paper. In this fashion, conversations can be held and information exchanged.

TDDs use a regular or slightly modified keyboard. Some special terminology is used to facilitate ease of transmission. GA, for go ahead indicates to one user that the other is waiting for a reply. SK, for stop keying, denotes the completion of a conversation. Often a Q is typed to imply a question.

The number of TDDs in public and private use is increasing rapidly. Public service agencies such as libraries, schools, and airlines are using TDDs to enable the hearing-impaired population to use their services (Low, 1985). Police and fire departments use TDDs to ensure the safety of hearing-impaired individuals. The TDD has been hailed as a great contributor to the independence of hearing-impaired persons.

REFERENCE

Low, K. (1985). Telecommunication devices for the deaf. *American Libraries, 16*, 746–747.

Mary Grace Feely
School for the Deaf

See also Electronic Travel Aids

TELECOMMUNICATIONS SYSTEMS IN SPECIAL EDUCATION

The use of telecommunication technology for special education mirrors the explosion of technology in society. In the same way that commercial electronic network services such as CompuServe and the Source have become widely known to the general public, SpecialNet is an e-mail service and information source specifically for special educators. Similarly, transformation of the telephone system from copper to fiber optic wire facilitates rapid data transmission for any use, including perhaps transfer of data on special education students as they move from district to district.

Certain types of telecommunication technologies (e.g., computer-assisted instruction) delivered over telephone lines from a central location, as in the University of Illinois' PLATO system, are being made obsolete as modifications are made for computers, thus reducing the costs of instruction delivery. Other technologies involving electronic memory and telephone transmission are expanding, notably ABLEDATA, a bibliographic source of information on assistive devices for the disabled.

Telecommunications technology, currently in a period of rapid change, may transform special education practice in much the same way that it is transforming communication worldwide. However, in contrast to other technologies developed specifically for the disabled, special education will benefit from technological advances for all citizens. Thus the average modern family may use a computer and modem as a link to specialized news sources, stock quotes and discount brokers, specialized electronic news services, targeted mailboards, or e-mail. Disabled persons, using the same systems, may communicate with other persons with similar interests, scan specialized information sources, work in competitive employment from their homes, and avail themselves of services provided for all citizens. Special educators in public schools and higher education may use telecommunications for much the same purposes, targeting their efforts toward the acquisition of information from rapidly expanding specialized information networks.

James W. Tawney
Pennsylvania State University

See also Electronic Travel Aids

TEMPERAMENT

Individual differences in temperament have been recognized for centuries. The Greeks talked of four basic dispositions, Kretschmer (1925) and Sheldon (1942) related personality to body types, and Eysenck (1967) linked constitutional and personality variables. Yet, the notion of constitutional contributions to behavior received only limited formal attention from U.S. psychologists and educators until relatively recently. Major impetus to the study of temperament has come from the work of psychiatrists Alexander Thomas and Stella Chess and their colleagues (Thomas & Chess, 1977; Thomas, Chess, Birch, Hertzig, & Korn, 1963), but independent support for the notion of temperament may be found in pediatric and psychiatric research (Carey, 1981, 1982, 1985a; Graham, Rutter, & George, 1973; Rutter, 1964; Rutter, Tizard, & Whitmore, 1970), in longitudinal studies of development (J. Lerner & Lerner, 1983; Werner & Smith, 1982), in research on infants (Bates, 1980, 1983; Rothbart & Derryberry, 1981), and on child-family interactions (Dunn & Kendrick, 1982;

Hinde, Easton, Meller, & Tamplin, 1982; Stevenson-Hinde & Simpson, 1982), in twin studies (Goldsmith & Gottesman, 1981; Matheny, Wilson, & Nuss, 1984; Wilson, 1983; Wilson & Matheny, 1983), and in work in behavioral genetics (DeFries & Plomin, 1978; Plomin, 1982; Torgersen, 1982). Temperament is an important area of concern from both research and applied perspectives. Its relevance to special education and the development and adjustment of children with disabilities is increasingly recognized.

Definitions

Although intuitively appealing, temperament has somewhat different definitions, depending on the investigator. Thomas and Chess (1977) view temperament as a stylistic variable. They consider that temperament describes how an individual behaves, not what an individual does or how well he or she does it. Thomas and Chess identified nine dimensions of temperament or behavioral style: activity level, adaptability, approach/withdrawal, attention span and persistence, distractibility, intensity of reaction, quality of mood, rhythmicity (regularity), and threshold of responsiveness. The dimensions were derived in part from Thomas and Chess's clinical observations and were formalized in major longitudinal research, the New York Longitudinal Study (NYLS). In Thomas and Chess's view, these temperamental variations are, in part, constitutional in base.

The constitutional or biological anchoring of temperament is apparent in other definitions. Buss and Plomin (1975, 1984) propose that to be considered a temperament, a behavioral predisposition must meet criteria of developmental stability, presence in adulthood, adaptiveness, and presence in animals, and must have a genetic component. They define four dimensions that, in their view, meet these criteria: emotionality, activity, sociability, and impulsivity. Rothbart and Derryberry (1981), based primarily on their studies of human infants, suggest that temperament is best conceptualized as individual differences in reactivity and regulation that are presumed to be constitutionally based. Their formulation emphasizes arousal (or excitability) and the neural and behavioral processes that regulate or modulate it, a formulation consistent with that of Strelau (1983). Goldsmith and Campos (1986) adopt a somewhat different perspective, defining temperament as individual variation in emotionality, including differences in the primary emotions of fear, anger, sadness, pleasure, and so forth, as well as in a more general arousal; they consider both temperament and intensive parameters. It should be noted that a major definitional issue relates to distinctions between temperament and personality (Goldsmith & Campos, 1982; Rutter, 1982). Many investigators consider temperament a constitutional and genetic component of personality. This view is well reflected in the definition that emerged from the 1980 New Haven Temperament Symposium: "Temperament involves those dimensions of personality that are largely genetic or constitutional in origin, exist in most ages and in most societies, show some consistency across situations, and are relatively stable, at least within major developmental areas" (Plomin, 1983, p. 49). Thus, despite differences in specific components and in emphases, there is some consensus that temperament is an individual difference that has its basis in biological or constitutional makeup, has some stability across setting and time, and is linked to differences in behavioral or expressive styles (Bouchard, 1995).

Measurement

Adequacy of measurement has been a persistent problem for researchers of temperament (Hubert, Wachs, Peters-Martin, & Gandour, 1982; Plomin, 1982; Rothbart, 1981; Rothbart & Goldsmith, 1985; Rutter, 1982). Rothbart and Goldsmith (1985) note that the three most commonly used data-gathering techniques for infant temperament studies are questionnaires, home observations, and laboratory observations. With older children there has been reliance primarily on parent, caretaker, or teacher reports gathered through interviews or questionnaires. Measures designed for use with adults (Burks & Rubenstein, 1979; Guildford & Zimmerman, 1949; Lerner, Palermo, Spiro, & Nesselroade, 1982) are usually self-report formats. In addition to issues of psychometric adequacy of scales, individual investigators have developed measuring instruments and techniques that are consistent with their own conceptualizations of temperament. Thus scales differ in the number of dimensions identified and in the content of those dimensions. As an example, the Thomas and Chess scale taps nine dimensions; the Buss and Plomin (EASI) scale taps four. Similarly, behavior observations in natural and laboratory settings vary according to project and investigator. The consequence has been continuing concern about constructs and measures (Baker & Velicer, 1982; Bates, 1980, 1983; Plomin, 1982; Rothbart, 1981; Thomas, Chess, & Korn, 1982; Vaughn, Deinard, & Egeland, 1980; Vaughn, Taraldson, Crichton, & Egeland, 1981). Given the importance of Thomas and Chess's influence on this field, and the relevance of their work to clinical and educational practice, their questionnaires will be described in more detail.

Thomas and Chess developed a Parent Temperament Survey (PTS) and a Teacher Temperament Survey (TTS). The PTS contains 72 items, 8 for each of the 9 hypothesized dimensions of temperament. The TTS, similar in format, contains 64 items (the dimension of rhythmicity is not included). Items were selected to describe behavioral expressions of the various temperament dimensions (e.g., "When first meeting new children, my child is bashful"; from the TTS: "Child will initially avoid new games and activities, preferring to sit on the side and watch"). Items are rated 1 (hardly ever) to 7 (almost always). Dimensional scores (means of the items in each dimension) are assumed to be independent. Factor studies and qualitative analyses within the NYLS suggested three temperamental constellations that described two thirds of the sample: the easy child, characterized as regular or rhythmic, positive in approach to new stimuli, adaptable to change, and mild or moderately intense and positive in mood; the difficult child, described as irregular, negative in response to new stimuli, low or slow in adaptability, and intense, often negative in mood; and the slow-to-warm-up child, viewed as mildly intense in reactivity, slow to adapt, but given time, positive in involvement.

A number of investigators have modified the PTS and TTS but have maintained Thomas and Chess's conceptual framework. Keogh, Pullis, and Cadwell (1980, 1982) reduced both parent and teacher scales to 23 items each and identified simpler factor structures. The three primary factors in the TTS were task orientation, personal-social flexibility, and reactivity, an essentially negative factor. The PTS yielded two multidimensional factors and two single-dimension factors: social competence and reactivity, and mood and persistence. These factors are generally consistent with those identified by Windle and Lerner (1985) in their life span research and with those defined by Martin and his colleagues (Martin, 1984a; Paget, Nagle, & Martin, 1984) in work with schoolchildren. Also working within the Thomas and Chess framework, Carey, Fox, and McDevitt (1977) have done extensive scale development. Their questionnaires cover infancy through the elementary school years and include the Infant Temperament Questionnaire (ITQ; Carey, 1970; Carey & McDevitt, 1978), the Toddler Temperament Scale (Fullard, McDevitt, & Carey, 1978), the Behavioral Styles Questionnaire (McDevitt & Carey, 1978), and the Middle Childhood Temperament Questionnaire (Hegvik, McDevitt, & Carey, 1982). These instruments are similar in format, describe behaviors that are age and setting appropriate, and have good reliability and internal consistency. Each scale contains approximately 100 items and requires about 30 minutes for a parent to complete. Thus there are a number of instruments designed to capture parents' and teachers' views of children's temperamental characteristics. Despite their clinical appeal and usefulness, many of the questionnaires have been challenged on a number of counts: lack of independence of items and dimensions, item unreliability or bias, unknown factorial organization across developmental periods, or situational specificity of behaviors. Clearly, there are real and continuing uncertainties in the measurement of temperament that mandate caution in interpreting temperament findings. Yet, there is also considerable consistency of findings across studies and approaches, which argues for the robustness of temperament variables.

Clinical Applications

There are increasing numbers of reports of the importance of temperament in pediatric and psychiatric settings. Pediatricians Carey (1981, 1985a, 1985b, 1985c) and Weissbluth (1982, 1984; Weissbluth et al., 1982; Weissbluth, Brouillette, Kiang, & Hunt, 1985; Weissbluth & Green, 1984) emphasize that temperament is an influence on children's development and adjustment, specifically linking infants' temperamental characteristics to a variety of pediatric problems (e.g., colic, sleep difficulties). In recent work, Carey (1985b) suggests that temperament may also be viewed as an outcome or consequence of various clinical conditions, for example, pre-, post-, and perinatal conditions or insults. From psychiatric and psychological perspectives, there has also been a continuing interest in temperament as a predisposing factor for behavioral and emotional or adjustment problems (Barron & Earls, 1984; Cameron, 1977; Chess & Korn, 1970; Earls, 1981; Graham et al., 1973; Rutter, 1964; Thomas & Chess, 1977; Thomas, Chess, & Birch, 1968). Maziade et al. (1985) found difficult temperament predicted psychiatric diagnosis in later childhood, and Kolvin, Nicol, Garside, Day, and Tweddle (1982) reported relationships between temperament and aggression in clinic-referred boys. Although the processes linking temperament and problems in behavior and adjustment are not yet explicit, there appears to be enough evidence to infer a relationship.

Educational Applications

The formal application of temperament constructs to educational practice is relatively recent but is growing. As part of the NYLS, Gordon and Thomas (1967) reported that children's temperament influenced teachers' estimates of their school abilities, and Carey, Fox, and McDevitt (1977) identified relationships between parents' ratings of children and adjustment in school. A number of investigators report relationships between temperamental patterns and academic performance in school (Chess, Thomas, & Cameron, 1976; Hall & Cadwell, 1984; Hegvik, 1984, 1986; Keogh, 1982a; Keogh & Pullis, 1980; Lerner, 1983; Lerner, Lerner, & Zabski, 1985; Martin, 1984b, 1985; Martin, Nagle, & Paget, 1983; Pullis, 1979; Pullis & Cadwell, 1982; Skuy, Snell, & Westaway, 1985). It should be noted that in general, there are nonsignificant or marginally significant relationships between temperament and cognitive ability as indexed by IQ (Keogh, 1982a, 1982c; Pullis, 1983), although Martin (1985) identified moderate and significant relationships between temperament attributes of adaptability, approach/withdrawal, and persistence and IQ in a sample of Grade 1 pupils. Overall, the evidence suggests that temperament and cognitive ability are partially independent contributors to educational achievement.

In addition to achievement in academic content, there is considerable evidence to suggest that temperamental variations are related to children's personal and social adjustment in school. Billman (1984), Carey et al. (1977), Chess et al. (1976), Feuerstein and Martin (1981), Hall and Keogh (1978), Keogh (1982a, 1982b, 1982c), Kolvin et al. (1982), Lerner (1983), Lerner et al. (1985), Martin (1985), Paget et al. (1984), Terestman (1980), and Thomas and Chess (1977) have linked children's temperament and behavior and adjustment problems. The impact of temperament may be particularly powerful where children have other handicapping or problem conditions (Keogh, 1982c), although there are temperamental differences within groups of handicapped children (Hanson, 1979). Field and Greenberg (1982) suggest that temperament patterns may be associated with particular handicapping conditions, and Chess, Korn, and Fernandez (1971) report a high number of behavior disorders related to difficult temperament patterns in a group of young congenital rubella children; the latter findings were consistent with the relationship between temperament and behavior problems in a group of mentally delayed children (Chess & Korn, 1970). In a series of ongoing studies, (Keogh, Bernheimer, Pelland, & Daley, 1985) confirmed links between developmentally delayed children's temperament and their behavior problems and adjustment. Lambert and Windmiller (1977) found strong correlations between selected temperament attributes and hyperactivity in a large group of at-risk elementary school children. There also is some tentative evidence linking temperament to adjustment and achievement problems of learning-disabled pupils (Keogh, 1983; Pullis, 1983; Scholom & Schiff, 1980).

Temperament may contribute to school achievement and adjustment in several ways (Keogh, 1986) and is related to intellectual performance (Brebner & Stough, 1995). It may be a factor in a generalized response set; that is, some temperaments may fit well with the complex and changing demands of school whereas others do not. Temperament may affect a child's specific preparation for learning by allowing activity and attention to be modulated and directed easily and quickly. Temperament may interact with particular subject matter to facilitate or impede learning. Individual differences in temperament are also significant contributors to children's personal-social adjustment in school. Intuitively, at least, interpersonal problems have a strong foundation in child-peer and child-teacher interactions. Thus, personal style, or temperament, may be a major factor in problem behavior. If the relationship between children's temperament and their achievement and behavioral adjustment in school is considered within Thomas and Chess's "goodness of fit" notion, then both child characteristics and setting or task demands and conditions must be taken into account. Goodness of fit has important implications for identification, diagnosis, intervention, and treatment.

REFERENCES

Baker, E. H., & Velicer, W. F. (1982). The structure and reliability of the teacher temperament questionnaire. *Journal of Abnormal Child Psychology, 10*(4), 531–546.

Barron, A. P., & Earls, F. (1984). The relation of temperament and social factors to behavior problems in three-year-old children. *Journal of Child Psychology & Psychiatry, 25*(1), 23–33.

Bates, J. E. (1980). The concept of difficult temperament. *Merrill-Palmer Quarterly, 26*(4), 299–319.

Bates, J. E. (1983). Issues in the assessment of difficult temperament: A reply to Thomas, Chess, and Korn. *Merrill-Palmer Quarterly, 29*(1), 89–97.

Billman, J. (1984, October). *The relationship of temperament traits to classroom behavior in nine year old children: A follow-up study*. Paper presented at the Conference on Temperament in the Educational Process, St. Louis, MO.

Bouchard, T. (1995). Longitudinal studies of personality and intelligence. In D. Saklofske & M. Zeidner (Eds.), *International handbook of personality and intelligence*. New York, NY: Plenum Press.

Burks, J., & Rubenstein, M. (1979). *Temperament styles in adult interaction: Application in psychotherapy*. New York, NY: Brunner/Mazel.

Buss, A. H., & Plomin, R. (1975). *A temperament theory of personality development*. New York, NY: Wiley.

Buss, A. H., & Plomin, R. (1984). *Temperament: Early developing personality traits*. Hillsdale, NJ: Erlbaum.

Cameron, J. R. (1977). Parental treatment, children's temperament, and the risk of childhood behavioral problems: Initial temperament, parental attitudes, and the incidence and form of behavioral problems. *American Journal of Orthopsychiatry, 48*, 140–147.

Carey, W. B. (1970). A simplified method for measuring infant temperament. *Journal of Pediatrics, 77*, 188–194.

Carey, W. B. (1981). The importance of temperament-environment interaction for child health and development. In M. Lewis & L. A. Rosenblum (Eds.), *The uncommon child*. New York, NY: Plenum Press.

Carey, W. B. (1982). Clinical use of temperament data in pediatrics. In R. Porter & G. M. Collins (Eds.), *Temperament differences in infants and young children* (pp. 191–205). London, England: Pitman.

Carey, W. B. (1985a). Clinical use of temperament data in pediatrics. *Developmental & Behavioral Pediatrics, 6*(3), 137–142.

Carey, W. B. (1985b). Interactions of temperament and clinical conditions. In M. Wolraich & D. K. Routh (Eds.), *Advances in developmental and behavioral pediatrics* (Vol. 6, pp. 83–115). Greenwich, CT: JAI.

Carey, W. B. (1985c). Temperament and increased weight gain in infants. *Development & Behavioral Pediatrics, 6*(3), 128–131.

Carey, W. B., Fox, M., & McDevitt, S. C. (1977). Temperament as a factor in early school adjustment. *Pediatrics, 60*(4), 621–624.

Carey, W. B., & McDevitt, S. C. (1978). Revision of the Infant Temperament Questionnaire. *Pediatrics, 61*, 735–739.

Chess, S., & Korn, S. (1970). Temperament and behavior disorders in mentally retarded children. *Archives of General Psychiatry, 23*, 122–130.

Chess, S., Korn, S., & Fernandez, P. (1971). *Psychiatric disorders of children with congenital rubella*. New York, NY: Brunner/Mazel.

Chess, S., Thomas, A., & Cameron, M. (1976). Temperament: Its significance for early schooling. *New York University Education Quarterly*, 7(3), 24–29.

DeFries, J. C., & Plomin, R. (1978). Behavioral genetics. *Annual Review of Psychology*, 29, 473–515.

Dunn, J., & Kendrick, C. (1982). Temperamental differences, family relationships, and young children's responses to change within the family. In R. Porter & G. M. Collins (Eds.), *Temperamental differences in infants and young children* (pp. 87–105). London, England: Pitman.

Earls, F. (1981). Temperament characteristics and behavior problems in three-year-old children. *Journal of Nervous & Mental Disease*, 169, 367–387.

Eysenck, H. J. (1967). *The biological basis of personality*. Springfield, IL: Thomas.

Feuerstein, P., & Martin, R. P. (1981, April). *The relationship between temperament and school adjustment in four-year-old children*. Paper presented at the annual meeting of the American Educational Research Association, Los Angeles.

Field, T., & Greenberg, R. (1982). Temperament ratings by parents and teachers of infants, toddlers, and preschool children. *Child Development*, 53, 160–163.

Fullard, W., McDevitt, S. C., & Carey, W. B. (1978). *The toddler temperament scale*. Unpublished manuscript, Temple University, Philadelphia.

Goldsmith, H. H., & Campos, J. J. (1982). Toward a theory of infant temperament. In R. M. Emde & R. J. Harmon (Eds.), *The development of attachment and affiliative systems* (pp. 161–193). New York, NY: Plenum Press.

Goldsmith, H. H., & Campos, J. J. (1986). Fundamental issues in the study of early temperament: The Denver twin temperament study. In M. E. Lamb & A. L. Brown (Eds.), *Advances in developmental psychology* (pp. 231–283). Hillsdale, NJ: Erlbaum.

Goldsmith, H. H., & Gottesman, I. I. (1981). Origins of variation in behavioral style: A longitudinal study of temperament in young twins. *Child Development*, 52, 91–103.

Graham, P., Rutter, M., & George, S. (1973). Temperamental characteristics as predictors of behavior disorders in children. *American Journal of Orthopsychiatry*, 43(3), 328–339.

Guildford, J. P., & Zimmerman, W. (1949). *The Guildford-Zimmerman Temperament Survey*. Beverly Hills, CA: Sheridan Supply.

Hall, R. J., & Cadwell, J. (1984, April). *Temperament influences on cognition and achievement in children with learning disabilities*. Paper presented at the annual conference of the American Educational Research Association, New Orleans, LA.

Hall, R. J., & Keogh, B. K. (1978). Qualitative characteristics of educationally high-risk children. *Learning Disability Quarterly*, 1(2), 62–68.

Hanson, M. J. (1979). A longitudinal description study of the behaviors of Down's syndrome infants in an early intervention program. *Monographs of the Center on Human Development*. Eugene: University of Oregon.

Hegvik, R. L. (1984, October). *Three year longitudinal study of temperament variables, academic achievement, and sex differences*. Paper presented at the Conference on Temperament in the Educational Process, St. Louis, MO.

Hegvik, R. L. (1986, May). *Temperament and achievement in school*. Paper presented at the sixth occasional Temperament Conference, Pennsylvania State University.

Hegvik, R. L., McDevitt, S. C., & Carey, W. B. (1982). The middle childhood temperament questionnaire. *Developmental & Behavioral Pediatrics*, 3, 197–200.

Hinde, R. A., Easton, D. F., Meller, R. E., & Tamplin, A. M. (1982). Temperamental characteristics of 3–4 year olds and mother-child interactions. In R. Porter & G. M. Collins (Eds.), *Temperamental differences in infants and young children* (pp. 66–86). London, England: Pitman.

Hubert, N. C., Wachs, T. D., Peters-Martin, P., & Gandour, M. J. (1982). The study of early temperament: Measurement and conceptual issues. *Child Development*, 53, 126–132.

Keogh, B. K. (1982a). Children's temperament and teachers' decisions. In R. Porter & G. M. Collins (Eds.), *Temperamental differences in infants and young children* (pp. 269–279). London, England: Pitman.

Keogh, B. K. (1982b). *Temperament and school performance of preschool children* (Technical report, Project REACH). Los Angeles: University of California.

Keogh, B. K. (1982c). Temperament: An individual difference of importance in intervention programs. *Topics in Early Childhood Special Education*, 2(2), 25–31.

Keogh, B. K. (1983). Individual differences in temperament: A contribution to the personal-social and educational competence of learning disabled children. In J. D. McKinney & L. Feagens (Eds.), *Current topics in learning disabilities* (pp. 33–55). Norwood, NJ: Ablex.

Keogh, B. K. (1986). Temperament and schooling: What is the meaning of goodness of fit? In J. V. Lerner & R. M. Lerner (Eds.), *New directions for child development: Temperament and social interaction in infants and children*. San Francisco, CA: Jossey-Bass.

Keogh, B. K., Bernheimer, L., Pelland, M., & Daley, S. (1985). *Behavior and adjustment problems of children with developmental delays* (Technical report). Los Angeles: University of California, Graduate School of Education.

Keogh, B. K., & Pullis, M. E. (1980). Temperamental influences on the development of exceptional children. In B. K. Keogh (Ed.), *Advances in special education: Vol. 1. Basic constructs and theoretical orientations* (pp. 239–276). Greenwich, CT: JAI.

Keogh, B. K., Pullis, M. E., & Cadwell, J. (1980). *Project REACH* (Technical report). Los Angeles, CA: University of California.

Keogh, B. K., Pullis, M. E., & Cadwell, J. (1982). A short form of the Teacher Temperament Questionnaire. *Journal of Educational Measurement*, 29(4), 323–329.

Kolvin, I., Nicol, A. R., Garside, R. F., Day, K. A., & Tweddle, E. G. (1982). Temperamental patterns in aggressive boys. In R. Porter & G. M. Collins (Eds.), *Temperamental differences in infants and young children* (pp. 252–268). London, England: Pitman.

Kretschmer, E. (1925). *Physique and character*. New York, NY: Harcourt.

Lambert, N. M., & Windmiller, M. (1977). An exploratory study of temperament traits in a population of children at risk. *Journal of Special Education, 11*(1), 37–47.

Lerner, J. V. (1983). The role of temperament in psychosocial adaptation in early adolescents: A test of a "goodness of fit" model. *Journal of Genetic Psychology, 143*, 149–157.

Lerner, J. V., & Lerner, R. M. (1983). Temperament and adaptation across life: Theoretical and empirical issues. In P. B. Baltes & O. G. Brim (Eds.), *Lifespan development and behavior* (Vol. 5). New York, NY: Academic Press.

Lerner, J. V., Lerner, R. M., & Zabski, S. (1985). Temperament and elementary school children's actual and rated academic performance: A test of a "goodness of fit" model. *Journal of Child Psychology and Psychiatry, 26*, 125–136.

Lerner, R. M., Palermo, M., Spiro, A., & Nesselroade, J. (1982). Assessing the dimensions of temperamental individuality across the life-span: The dimensions of temperament survey (DOTS). *Child Development, 53*, 149–160.

Martin, R. P. (1984a). *The Temperament Assessment Battery (TAB)*. Athens: University of Georgia, Department of School Psychology.

Martin, R. P. (1984b, October). *A temperament model for education*. Paper presented at the Conference on Temperament in the Educational Process, St. Louis, MO.

Martin, R. P. (1985, July). *Child temperament and educational outcomes: A review of research*. Paper presented at the Symposium on Temperament, Leiden, The Netherlands.

Martin, R. P., Nagle, R., & Paget, K. (1983). Relationships between temperament and classroom behavior, teacher attitudes, and academic achievement. *Journal of Psychoeducational Assessment, 1*, 377–386.

Matheny, A. P. Jr., Wilson, R. S., & Nuss, S. M. (1984). Toddler temperament: Stability across settings and over ages. *Child Development, 55*, 1200–1211.

Maziade, M., Caperaa, P., Laplante, B., Boudreault, M., Thivierge, J., Cote, R., & Boutin, P. (1985). Value of difficult temperament among 7-year-olds in the general population for predicting psychiatric diagnosis at age 12. *American Journal of Psychiatry, 142*(8), 943–946.

McDevitt, S. C., & Carey, W. B. (1978). The measurement of temperament in 3–7 year old children. *Journal of Child Psychiatry & Psychology, 19*(3), 245–253.

Paget, K. D., Nagle, R. J., & Martin, R. P. (1984). Interrelationships between temperament characteristics and first-grade teacher-student interactions. *Journal of Abnormal Child Psychology, 12*(4), 547–560.

Plomin, R. (1982). Behavioral genetics and temperament. In R. Porter & G. M. Collins (Eds.). *Temperamental differences in infants and young children* (pp. 155–167). London, England: Pitman.

Plomin, R. (1983). Childhood temperament. In B. B. Lahey & A. E. Kazdin (Eds.), *Advances in clinical child psychology* (Vol. 6, pp. 45–92). New York, NY: Plenum Press.

Pullis, M. E. (1979). *An investigation of the relationship between children's temperament and school adjustment*. Unpublished doctoral dissertation, University of California, Los Angeles.

Pullis, M. E. (1983). *Temperament influences of teachers' decisions in regular and mainstreamed classes*. Paper presented at the meeting of the American Educational Research Association, New York.

Pullis, M. E., & Cadwell, J. (1982). The influence of children's temperament characteristics on teachers' decision strategies. *American Educational Research Journal, 19*(2), 165–181.

Rothbart, M. K. (1981). Measurement of temperament in infancy. *Child Development, 52*, 569–578.

Rothbart, M. K., & Derryberry, D. (1981). Development of individual differences in temperament. In M. E. Lamb & A. L. Brown (Eds.), *Advances in developmental psychology* (Vol. 1, pp. 37–86). Hillsdale, NJ: Erlbaum.

Rothbart, M. K., & Goldsmith, H. H. (1985). Three approaches to the study of infant temperament. *Developmental Review, 5*, 237–260.

Rutter, M. (1964). Temperament characteristics in infancy and the later development of behavior disorders. *British Journal of Psychiatry, 110*, 651–661.

Rutter, M. (1982). Temperament: Concepts, issues and problems. In R. Porter & G. C. Collins (Eds.), *Temperamental differences in infants and young children* (pp. 1–19). London, England: Pitman.

Rutter, M., Tizard, J., & Whitmore, K. (1970). *Education, health, and behavior: Psychological and medical study of childhood development*. New York, NY: Wiley.

Scholom, A., & Schiff, G. (1980). Relating infant temperament to learning disabilities. *Journal of Abnormal Child Psychology, 8*, 127–132.

Sheldon, W. (1942). *The varieties of temperament: A psychology of constitutional differences*. New York, NY: Harper.

Skuy, M., Snell, D., & Westaway, M. (1985). Temperament and the scholastic achievement and adjustment of black South African children. *South African Journal of Education, 5*(4), 197–202.

Stevenson-Hinde, J., & Simpson, A. E. (1982). Temperament and relationships. In R. Porter & G. M. Collins (Eds.), *Temperamental differences in infants and young children* (pp. 51–65). London, England: Pitman.

Strelau, J. (1983). *Temperament-personality-activity*. New York, NY: Academic Press.

Terestman, N. (1980). Mood quality and intensity in nursery school children as predictors of behavior disorder. *American Journal of Orthopsychiatry, 50*, 125–138.

Thomas, A., & Chess, S. (1977). *Temperament and development*. New York, NY: Brunner/Mazel.

Thomas, A., Chess, S., & Birch, H. G. (1968). *Temperament and behavior disorders in children*. New York, NY: New York University Press.

Thomas, A., Chess, S., Birch, H. G., Hertzig, M., & Korn, S. (1963). *Behavioral individuality in early childhood*. New York, NY: New York University Press.

Thomas, A., Chess, S., & Korn, S. J. (1982). The reality of difficult temperament. *Merrill-Palmer Quarterly, 28*(1), 1–20.

Torgersen, A. M. (1982). Influence of genetic factors on temperament development in early childhood. In R. Porter &

G. M. Collins (Eds.), *Temperamental differences in infants and young children* (pp. 141–154). London, England: Pitman.

Vaughn, B., Deinard, A., & Egeland, B. (1980). Measuring temperament in pediatric practice. *Journal of Pediatrics, 96*, 510–514.

Vaughn, B., Taraldson, B., Crichton, L., & Egeland, B. (1981). The assessment of infant temperament: A critique of the Carey Infant Temperament Questionnaire. *Infant Behavior & Development, 40*, 1–17.

Weissbluth, M. (1982). Plasma progesterone levels, infant temperament, arousals from sleep, and the sudden infant death syndrome. *Medical Hypotheses, 9*, 215–222.

Weissbluth, M. (1984). Sleep duration, temperament, and Conners' ratings of three-year-old children. *Developmental & Behavioral Pediatrics, 5*(3), 120–123.

Weissbluth, M., Brouillette, R. T., Kiang, L., & Hunt, C. E. (1982). Clinical and laboratory observations: Sleep apnea, sleep duration and infant temperament. *Journal of Pediatrics, 101*(2), 307–310.

Weissbluth, M., & Green, O. C. (1984). Plasma progesterone concentrations and infant temperament. *Developmental & Behavioral Pediatrics, 5*(5), 251–253.

Weissbluth, M., Hunt, C. E., Brouillette, R. T., Hanson, D., David, R. J., & Stein, I. (1985). Respiratory patterns during sleep and temperament ratings in normal infants. *Journal of Pediatrics, 106*(4), 688–690.

Werner, E. E., & Smith, R. S. (1982). *Vulnerable, but invincible: A longitudinal study of resilient children and youth.* New York, NY: McGraw-Hill.

Wilson, R. S. (1983). The Louisville twin study: Developmental synchronies in behavior. *Child Development, 54*(2), 298–316.

Wilson, R. S., & Matheny, A. P. (1983). Assessment of temperament in infant twins. *Developmental Psychology, 19*, 172–183.

Windle, M., & Lerner, R. M. (1985). *Reassessing the dimensions of temperamental individuality across the life span: The Revised Dimensions of Temperament Survey* (DOTS-R). Unpublished manuscript, Johnson O'Connor Research Foundation, Chicago.

BARBARA KEOGH
*University of California,
Los Angeles*

See also **Attention-Deficit/Hyperactivity Disorder; Body Image; Learned Helplessness; Personality Assessment; Teacher Expectancies**

or unknown. Environmental agents include drugs and similar agents (e.g., alcohol, anticonvulsants, LSD), hormones, infections (e.g., cytomegalic inclusion disease, influenza, mumps, rubella, syphilis, toxoplasmosis), radiation, mechanical trauma, hypotension (low blood pressure), vitamin deficiency or excess (hypervitaminosis A), and mineral deficiency (zinc). Genetic causes include chromosomal abnormality (e.g., Down syndrome, trisomy 13) and various hereditary patterns—sporadic, dominant, recessive, and polygenetic. Maternal-fetal interactions are exemplified by advanced maternal age and maternal hypothyroidism. Finally, a variety of dysmorphic syndromes are undetermined as to etiology. Many congenital abnormalities may be detected prior to birth. The primary means for such diagnosis has been through amniocentesis. Additionally, imaging systems such as ultrasonography demonstrate relatively gross abnormalities late in development (Spaeth, Nelson, & Beaudoin, 1983).

The timing of development helps to clarify the spectrum of associated malformations. Injuries prior to the 15th day of gestation affect development of primary germ layers; such abnormalities are usually so global that survival of the fetus is unusual. Between weeks 2 and 7, insults cause major abnormalities that affect whole organ systems. Following the first trimester (the period of differentiation of organ detail and organ interrelationship), abnormalities tend to be more limited and specific. While timing of embryonic or fetal insult relates closely to manifest anomaly, certain substances may cause varying malformations, though the time of insult is constant.

REFERENCES

Duke-Elder, S. (1963). *System of ophthalmology: Vol. III, Part 2. Congenital deformities.* St. Louis, MO: Mosby.

Spaeth, G. L., Nelson, L. B., & Beaudoin, A. R. (1983). Ocular teratology. In T. D. Duane & E. A. Jaeger (Eds.), *Biomedical foundations of ophthalmology* (Vol. 1, pp. 6–7). Hagerstown, MD: Harper & Row.

GEORGE R. BEAUCHAMP
Cleveland Clinic Foundation

See also **Central Nervous System; Genetic Variations; Thalidomide**

TERATOGEN

The word teratogen drives from the Greek *teras*, signifying a marvel, prodigy, or monster; thus, by definition, a teratogen is an agent that causes developmental malformations or monstrosities (Duke-Elder, 1963). The causes can be environmental, genetic, multifactorial, maternal-fetal,

TERMAN, LEWIS M. (1877–1956)

Lewis M. Terman received his PhD in education and psychology from Clark University, where he studied under G. Stanley Hall. Experienced as a schoolteacher, principal, and college instructor, in 1910 he joined the faculty of Stanford University, where he served as head of the psychology department from 1922 until his retirement in 1942.

With an interest in mental tests dating from his graduate studies at Clark University, Terman became a leading figure in the newly born testing movement, developing dozens of tests during his career. The best known and most widely used of his tests were the Stanford-Binet tests of intelligence, which he adapted from the Binet-Simon Scale of Intelligence in 1916 and revised in 1937. He also developed the Army Alpha and Beta tests (the first group intelligence tests) for use in classifying servicemen during World War I. With the publication of the Stanford-Binet tests in 1916, Terman introduced the term intelligence quotient (IQ), a term that quickly became a part of the general vocabulary.

In 1921 Terman initiated the first comprehensive study of gifted children. His staff tested more than 250,000 schoolchildren to identify 1,500 with IQs above 140. This sample of boys and girls was studied intensively and followed up periodically in a study that continues today. Terman found that, contrary to the popular belief at the time, children with high IQs tend to be healthier, happier, and more stable than children of average ability. In addition, they are more successful in their personal and professional lives. Terman, who can be credited with founding the gifted child movement, used his findings to promote the provision of special educational programs for able students.

This entry has been informed by the sources listed below.

REFERENCES

Fancher, R. E. (1985). *The intelligence men.* New York, NY: Norton.

Hilgard, E. (1957). Lewis Madison Terman: 1877–1956. *American Journal of Psychology, 70,* 472–479.

Murchison, C. (Ed.). (1961). *A history of psychology in autobiography.* New York, NY: Russell & Russell.

PAUL IRVINE
Katonah, New York

See also **Stanford-Binet Intelligence Scale**

TERMAN'S STUDIES OF THE GIFTED

In 1911, while at Stanford University, Lewis M. Terman began a systematic collection of data on children who achieved exceptionally high scores on the Stanford-Binet Intelligence Test. In the early 1920s, working with Melita Oden, he administered the Stanford-Binet test to students referred to by teachers as being "highly intelligent." Studies of their traits and the extent to which they differed from unselected normal children were begun in 1925.

Terman's subjects were in a 1,500-child sample (800 boys and 700 girls) that was in the top 1% of the school population in measured intelligence; that is, they possessed tested IQs of 140 or higher (Cravens, 1992; Terman & Oden, 1925).

Terman and Oden (1951) summarized the characteristics of the students in their gifted sample as (1) slightly larger, healthier, and more physically attractive; (2) superior in reading, language usage, arithmetical reasoning, science, literature, and the arts; (3) superior in arithmetical computation, spelling, and factual information about history and civics (though not as markedly as in the areas covered in (2); (4) spontaneous, with a variety of interests; (5) able to learn to read easily, and able to read more and better books than average children; (6) less inclined to boast or overstate their knowledge; (7) more emotionally stable; (8) different in the upward direction for nearly all traits.

Follow-up studies in 1947, 1951, and 1959 were completed to obtain a comparison between promise and performance. Follow-up studies by other authors have obtained less "perfect" findings, in that not all of the subjects were found to be geniuses in the sense of transcendent achievement in some field (Feldman, 1984). More recent studies have supported Terman's findings on emotional stability (Schlowinski & Reynolds, 1985), reported happiness (Holahan, Holahan, Velasquez, & North, 2008), spontaneity, and creativity in play (Barnett & Fiscella, 1985), and reading aptitude (Anderson, Tollefson, & Gilbert, 1985).

The entire set of data sources for Terman's original group is maintained in closed files at Stanford University. It is estimated that less than half of the coded responses of this source of data have been transferred to tabulation sheets.

REFERENCES

Anderson, M. A., Tollefson, N. A., & Gilbert, E. C. (1985). Giftedness and reading: A cross sectional view of differences in reading attitudes and behavior. *Gifted Child Quarterly, 29*(4), 86–189.

Barnett, L. A., & Fiscella, J. (1985). A child by any other name. A comparison of the playfulness of gifted and non-gifted children. *Gifted Child Quarterly, 29*(2), 61–66.

Cravens, H. (1992). A scientific project locked in time: The Terman genetic studies of genius, 1920s-1950s. *American Psychologist, 47,* 183–189. doi:10.1037/0003–066X .47.2.183

Feldman, D. H. (1984). A follow-up of subjects scoring about 180 IQ in Terman's "Genetic Studies of Genius." *Exceptional Children, 50*(6), 518–523.

Holahan, C. K., Holahan, C. J., Velasquez, K. E., & North, R. J. (2008). Longitudinal change in happiness during aging: The predictive role of positive expectancies. *International Journal of Aging and Human Development, 66*(3), 229–241.

Schlowinski, E., & Reynolds, C. R. (1985). Dimensions of anxiety among high IQ children. *Gifted Child Quarterly*, *29*(3), 125–130.

Terman, L. M., & Oden, M. H. (1925). *Genetic studies of genius: Mental and physical traits of a thousand gifted children*. Stanford, CA: Stanford University Press.

Terman, L. M., & Oden, M. H. (1951). The Stanford studies of the gifted. In P. A. Witty (Ed.), *The gifted child*. Boston, MA: Heath.

ANNE M. BAUER
University of Cincinnati

See also Gifted Children; Gifted Children and Reading

TEST ANXIETY

Test anxiety is such a universal phenomenon that it hardly requires general definition. In school, on the job, or for various application procedures, tests are required. Performance on a test can impact negatively on the test-taker. Thus an essential component for an anxiety arousal state exists when the individual is placed in a test-taking situation. Test situations are specific and thus present an opportunity to investigate the nature of anxiety.

Test anxiety is usually regarded as a particular kind of general anxiety. Ordinarily, it refers to the variety of responses—physiological, behavioral, and phenomenal (Sieber, 1980)—that accompany an individual's perceptions of failure. The person experiencing test anxiety often has a fear of failure as well as a high need to succeed. Both the fear of failure and the drive for success may be internalized. In some instances, either may seem more of a desire on the part of the test-taker to please a parent or other significant individual. Regardless of the originating causes of test anxiety, it can be a debilitating state of arousal.

One of the major challenges for theorists and researchers on test anxiety is to ascertain why anxiety appears to motivate some persons yet limits seriously the performance of others. Findings from several researchers suggest that the individual's expectations of success or failure on a test are strongly correlated to the development of test anxiety (Heckhausen, 1975; Weiner, 1966). For example, it may be argued that those who are low in motivation to succeed attribute failure to a lack of ability whereas those who are high in motivation to succeed see failure as emanating more from a lack of effort. Heckhausen (1975) cites data showing that those persons with a high fear of failure tend to attribute success more to good luck than those persons with a high expectation of success. Thus, for those who expect to succeed, anxiety may be more of a motivating force than for those who fear

failure. For the latter group, initial anxiety may become a debilitating form of test anxiety.

Another avenue of investigation seeks to understand the affective value of test-taking in the context of its social significance. For some persons, test anxiety is heightened if it occurs where there is an observer of the test-taking performance (Geen, 1979; Geen & Gange, 1977). Test anxiety may then be heightened if there are judges, monitors, or others with whom the test-taker must interact. Some persons may, therefore, find an oral or observed performance type of test more anxiety-producing than a written test. For such persons, it appears that test anxiety is more a response to their need for and perceptions of social approval than it is to an internalized need to demonstrate competence.

In summary, much of the available research and numerous self-reports suggest that test anxiety is a recurring problem for children and adults. Moreover, test anxiety often appears to inhibit the usual maximal level of performance of the individual. Thus if a test situation is to be used as an effective means of assessing human potential, it is important that we understand more fully the origin of test anxiety as well as its impact on individual performance.

REFERENCES

Geen, R. G. (1979). The influence of passive audiences on performance. In P. Paulus (Ed.), *The psychology of group influence*. Hillsdale, NJ: Erlbaum.

Geen, R. G., & Gange, J. J. (1977). Drive theory of social facilitation: Twelve years of theory and research. *Psychological Bulletin*, *84*, 1267–1288.

Heckhausen, H. (1975). Fear of failure as a self-reinforcing motive. In I. G. Sarason & C. D. Spielberger (Eds.), *Stress and anxiety* (Vol. 2). Washington, DC: Hemisphere.

Sieber, J. E. (1980). Defining test anxiety: Problems and approaches. In I. G. Sarason (Ed.), *Test anxiety: Theory, research, and applications*. Hillsdale, NJ: Erlbaum.

Weiner, B. (1966). The role of success and failure in the learning of easy and complex tasks. *Journal of Personality & Social Psychology*, *3*, 339–344.

BERT O. RICHMOND
University of Georgia

See also Anxiety; Stress and Individuals With Disabilities

TEST EQUATING

Test equating is a technique for making the characteristics of two tests similar or identical, if possible, so that an individual's scores on the two tests mean the same thing.

This process is accomplished currently through statistical means. There are two different problems associated with test equating. One is the problem of equating scores on two tests that were designed to be of the same difficulty, for the same kind of student, with the same content. This is called *horizontal equating*. The other problem is how to equate tests that were designed for different populations, often younger and older students, in which the content overlaps. In this case, one test will be hard for the younger students and the other will be quite easy for the older. This is called *vertical equating*.

Horizontal equating, while by no means completely solved as a statistical problem, is the better developed and studied of the two. The problem is best stated as follows: For a students with ability A, the relative placement of their score on Test 1 is identical to the relative score on Test 2 if the two tests have been perfectly equated. Mathematically, the two frequency distributions must be equal in normalized form. This means that a youngster's score on Test 1 is the same number of standard deviations from the mean and exceeds the same percent of other scores as on Test 2. There are three major techniques for achieving horizontal equating.

The first method of horizontal equating is called the *equipercentile method*. It is the most widely used and seems to be the most robust method under a variety of conditions. Simply put, observed score distributions are matched for percentile points. That is, the score at the first percentile point in Test 1 is equated to the score at the first percentile point for Test 2. This is done for all percentile points up to 99 or perhaps 99.9. There is a smoothing of the equated scores so that there are no abrupt jumps in scores from one percentile to the next. This procedure has been shown by Petersen, Marco, and Stewart (1982) to be not as good as linear equating, the next technique covered, in which the tests are similar and linear in relationship to each other. When there is a nonlinear relationship between the tests, the equipercentile technique is superior. This case is not common.

Linear equating is the application of a straight-line equation of the form $Y = aX + b$. The parameters are functions of the means and standard deviations of the two tests (Braun & Holland, 1982). Not surprisingly, it works best when there is just a simple linear relation between true test scores.

The third technique for equating tests horizontally consists of a number of related techniques grouped under the heading item-characteristic curve (ICC) techniques. These techniques generally make somewhat stronger assumptions about the nature of the test and the test-taker than do the other two methods. They are based on a model that allows estimation of a test-taker's ability. $T1$ on Test 1 and $T2$ on Test 2. These two scores then are equated, and the observed score from which they have been estimated can be calculated. Thus we can begin with either test, estimate the student's underlying ability on the test, and use that ability score on the other test to calculate an equivalent observed score. Since the procedure works both ways, it is hoped that the tests give similar results between calculated and actual observed scores. In general, such procedures have proven inferior to linear or equipercentile methods for large-scale standardized tests, which are carefully constructed. The ICC methods may be better for smaller, experimentally oriented tests, but their restriction to large samples makes this a rare usage.

Vertical equating is a more difficult problem, conceptually and statistically. The primary techniques used have been based on ICC models. They have not proven satisfactory to date. If two tests are given to a student, one that is hard for him or her and one that is easy (or easier), the ICC methods tend to overpredict ability score on the easy test and underpredict it on the hard test (Kolen, 1981).

REFERENCES

Braun, H. I., & Holland, P. W. (1982). Observed-score test equating: A mathematical analysis of some ETS equating procedures. In P. W. Holland & D. B. Rubin (Eds.), *Test equating* (pp. 9–49). New York, NY: Academic Press.

Kolen, M. J. (1981). Comparison of traditional and item response theory methods for equating tests. *Journal of Educational Measurement*, 19, 279–293.

Petersen, N. S., Marco, G. L., & Stewart, E. E. (1982). A test of the adequacy of linear score equating models. In P. W. Holland & D. B. Rubin (Eds.), *Test equating* (pp. 71–135). New York, NY: Academic Press.

VICTOR L. WILLSON
Texas A&M University

See also Measurement

TEST FOR AUDITORY COMPREHENSION OF LANGUAGE, THIRD EDITION

The Test for Auditory Comprehension of Language, Third Edition (TACL-3; Carrow-Woolfolk, 1999), appropriate for ages 3 years to 9 years 11 months, is an individually administered measure of receptive spoken language that assesses a subject's ability to understand the following categories of English language forms: Vocabulary, Grammatical Morphemes, and Elaborated Phrases and Sentences.

The TACL-3 consists of 142 items, divided into three subtests.

1. *Vocabulary*: Assessing the literal and common meanings of word classes (nouns, verbs, adjectives, and

adverbs), and of words that represent basic percepts and concepts.

2. *Grammatical Morphemes*: Assessing the meaning of grammatical morphemes (prepositions, noun number and case, verb number and tense, noun-verb agreement, derivational suffixes), and the meaning of pronouns, tested within the context of a simple sentence.

3. *Elaborated Phrases and Sentences*: Assessing the understanding of syntactically based word relations and elaborated phrase and sentence constructions, including the modalities of single and combined constructions (interrogative sentences, negative sentences, active and passive voice, direct and indirect object), embedded sentences, and partially and completely conjoined sentences.

It uses the popular point-to-the-picture-of-the-word-I-say technique. This simple procedure eliminates the external influences that are present in a less structured format. At the beginning of each subtest the phrase "Show me" is used to introduce each stimulus item. The examiner begins at the first item in each of the three subtests and stops when the examinee has three consecutive responses. Each item is composed of a word or sentence and a corresponding picture plate that has three full-color drawings. One of the three pictures for each item illustrates the meaning of the word, morpheme, or syntactic structure being tested. The other two pictures illustrate either two semantic or grammatical contrasts of the stimulus, or one contrast and one decoy. The examiner reads the stimulus aloud and the subject is directed to point to the picture that he or she believes best represents the meaning of the item. No oral response is required on the part of the examinee. The test takes approximately 15 minutes to 30 minutes to administer.

All scoring is dichotomous—1 for correct and 0 for incorrect. Correct responses are noted in the Profile/Examiner's Record Book as either A, B, or C.

Percentile ranks, standard scores, and age equivalents are available for children ages 3 to 0 through 9 to 11. The TACL-3 provides a variety of norm comparisons based on a standardization sample of 1,102 children, relative to socioeconomic factors, ethnicity, gender, and disability that are the same as those estimated for the year 2000 by the U.S. Bureau of the Census. Studies have shown the absence of gender, racial, disability, and ethnic bias. Reliability coefficients are computed for subgroups of the normative sample (e.g., individuals with speech disabilities, African Americans, European Americans, Hispanic Americans, females) as well as for the entire normative group.

Earlier editions of the TACL were reviewed extensively; references for the newest edition of this instrument are unavailable because of its recent publication date. A review of the TACL-R by Schmitt (1987) concluded that

the instrument can be considered both a valid and reliable test for determining an individual's knowledge of the test's constructs. Bankson (1989) reported that the TACL-R could be particularly useful as part of a comprehensive language evaluation of children referred for language disorders. Haynes (1989) felt the test was a well designed and psychometrically sound instrument for evaluating limited aspects of comprehension.

REFERENCES

Bankson, N. W. (1989). Review of the test for auditory comprehension of language-revised. In J. C. Conoley & J. J. Kramer (Eds.), *The tenth mental measurements yearbook* (pp. 822–824). Lincoln: Buros Institute of Mental Measurements, University of Nebraska Press.

Carrow-Woolfolk, E. (1999). *Test for Auditory Comprehension of Language, Third Edition*. Austin, TX: PRO-ED.

Haynes, W. O. (1989). Review of the test for auditory comprehension of language-revised. In J. C. Conoley & J. J. Kramer (Eds.), *The tenth mental measurements yearbook* (pp. 824–826). Lincoln: Buros Institute of Mental Measurements, University of Nebraska Press.

Schmitt, J. F. (1987). *Test critiques*: *Volume VI* (pp. 586–593). Austin, TX: PRO-ED.

Auditory comprehension http://www.med.unc.edu/

RON DUMONT
Fairleigh Dickinson University

JOHN O. WILLIS
Rivier College

KATHLEEN VEIZEL
Fairleigh Dickinson University

JAMIE ZIBULSKY
Fairleigh Dickinson University
Fourth edition

See also Auditory Processing

TEST OF ADOLESCENT AND ADULT LANGUAGE, FOURTH EDITION

The Test of Adolescent and Adult Language, Fourth Edition (TOAL-4; Hammill, Brown, Larsen, & Wiederholt, 1994) is an individually administered, norm-referenced test used to assess spoken and written language in students ages 12 years, 0 months to 24 years, 11 months and is appropriate for use with students enrolled in secondary and postsecondary education programs.

The TOAL-4 is used to assess the linguistic aspects of listening, speaking, reading, and writing of adolescents and adults. The TOAL-4 consists of six subtests, which combine to create the General Language Ability standard score, as well as separate Written and Spoken Language Ability standard scores. These subtests include:

- Spoken language subtests

  Word Opposites requires providing the antonyms of words provided by the examiner.

  Word Derivations requires providing a missing word at the end of the second sentence the examiner says, deriving from a key word.

  Spoken Analogies requires finishing an examiner's partial analogous sentence with a word to complete the analogy.

- Written language subtests

  Word Similarities requires writing the synonyms for printed stimulus words.

  Sentence Combining requires writing one grammatically correct sentence from two or more sentences provided by the examiner.

  Orthographic Usage requires writing down all the correct words and punctuation marks to provided sentences.

The TOAL-4 was standardized on 1,671 individuals ages 12 to 24, and included 65 to 193 individuals per age group. The sample represents the U.S. population with respect to the 2004 census in terms of gender, ethnicity, geographic region, Hispanic status, exceptionality status, family income, and parent education level. However, it is notable that the number of students included in most validity studies of exceptionality status is quite small (Kluppel, 2010). It is also notable that reviewers of earlier versions of this instrument expressed concerns about the old norms used, and that the authors have now renormed the instrument with an updated sample.

The measure has high internal consistency (i.e., alpha coefficients ranging from .94 to .97 for the composite scores and from .83 to .96 for individual subtest scores), and adequate test-retest reliability over a 2-week period. The content, criterion-related, and construct validity of the measure is also sufficient. Analyses were conducted that demonstrate the test differentiates among groups of individuals with and without language disabilities, and that scores on the TOAL-4 are correlated with scores on other measures of spoken and written language.

Several changes were made to this new version of the TOAL, including the reduction of subtests from eight to six, the use of a new normative sample, and enhanced focus on reliability and validity. It is a sound instrument to use for the purpose of assessing these specific spoken and written language skills and will need to be augmented with other measures in order to assess a student's broader skill set in the area of literacy or social communication.

This entry has been informed by the sources listed below.

REFERENCES

Hammill, D. D., Brown, V., Larsen, S. C., & Wiederholt, J. L. (1994). *Test of Adolescent and Adult Language–Fourth Edition*. Austin, TX: PRO-ED.

Kluppel, D. V. (2010). Review of the Test of Adolescent and Adult Language, Fourth Edition. In B. S. Plake & J. C. Impara (Eds.), *The eighteenth mental measurements yearbook*. Lincoln, NE: Buros Institute of Mental Measurements.

Langlois, A. (2010). Review of the Test of Adolescent and Adult Language, Fourth Edition. In B. S. Plake & J. C. Impara (Eds.), *The eighteenth mental measurements yearbook*. Lincoln, NE: Buros Institute of Mental Measurements.

RON DUMONT
Fairleigh Dickinson University

JOHN O. WILLIS
Rivier College

KATHLEEN VEIZEL
Fairleigh Dickinson University

JAMIE ZIBULSKY
Fairleigh Dickinson University
Fourth edition

TEST OF EARLY MATHEMATICAL ABILITY, THIRD EDITION

The Test of Early Mathematical Ability, Third Edition (TEMA-3; Ginsburg & Baroody, 2003) measures the mathematics abilities of children between the ages of 3 and 0 and 8 and 11 years. The test measures informal and formal (school-taught) concepts and skills in the following areas: numbering skills, number-comparison facility, numeral literacy, mastery of number facts, calculation skills, and understanding of concepts. It has two parallel forms, each containing 72 items. The items of the instrument were chosen based on existing research and national norms. Almost every item is linked to an empirical research study. The items are sequenced in order of increasing difficulty.

The TEMA-3 standardization sample was composed of 1,219 children. The characteristics of the sample approximate those in the 2001 U.S. census. The results of the test, which takes approximately 20 minutes to administer, may be reported as standard scores ($M = 100$, $SD = 15$), percentiles, and age- or grade-equivalents. Reliabilities are in the .90s; validity has been experimentally established. Also provided is a book of remedial techniques (*Assessment Probes and Instructional Activities*) for improving skills in the areas assessed by the test. Numerous teaching tasks for skills covered by each TEMA-3 item are included. After giving the test, the examiner decides which items need additional assessment information and uses the book to help the student improve his or her mathematical skills.

A separate Probes guide (Ginsburg, 2003) provides a series of follow-up questions to be used after the standard testing to examine children's methods of solution and their "zone of proximal development" with respect to key items failed during standard administration. For each item, the Probes session begins with reworded questions designed to determine if the child did not understand the original question. A strategy question then follows to identify the child's method of solution (e.g., Tell me what you are thinking about this problem?). Next, a justification question is asked (e.g., Can you prove to me that 2 and 2 is 5?). Finally, the examiner gives a hint (e.g., How about using your fingers to count?) to determine whether the child can solve the problem with some adult assistance. Conducting this sequence of questioning may reveal the source of the child's difficulty, which could directly inform a teacher's instruction or a clinician's intervention.

This entry has been informed by the sources listed below.

REFERENCES

Bliss, S. (2006). Review of "Test of Early Mathematics Ability-Third Edition." *Journal of Psychoeducational Assessment, 24*(1), 85–88.

Ginsburg, H. P. (2003). *Assessment probes and instructional activities for the test of early mathematics ability-3.* Austin, TX: PRO-ED.

Ginsburg, H. P., & Baroody, A. J. (2003). *The test of early mathematics ability: Third edition.* Austin, TX: PRO-ED.

Spies, R. A., & Plake, B. S. (Eds.). (2005). *The sixteenth mental measurements yearbook.* Lincoln, NE: Buros Institute of Mental Measurements.

VanDerHeyden, A., Broussard, C., & Cooley, A. (2006). Further development of measures of early math performance for preschoolers. *Journal of School Psychology, 44*(6), 533–553.

Ron Dumont
Fairleigh Dickinson University

John O. Willis
Rivier College

Kathleen Veizel
Fairleigh Dickinson University

Jamie Zibulsky
Fairleigh Dickinson University
Fourth edition

TEST OF EARLY READING ABILITY, THIRD EDITION

The Test of Early Reading Ability, Third Edition (TERA-3; Reid, Hresko, & Hammill, 2002) measures the actual reading ability of young children. The test consists of three subtests: Alphabet (29 items) measures knowledge of the alphabet and its uses, Conventions (21 items) measures knowledge of the conventions of print, and Meaning (30 items) measures the construction of meaning from print.

There are five identified purposes of the TERA-3: (1) to identify children who are below peers in reading development; (2) to identify strengths and weaknesses of individual children; (3) to document progress as a result of early reading intervention; (4) to serve as a measure in reading research; and (5) to serve as one component of a comprehensive assessment. To their credit, the authors clearly state that the TERA-3 is not to be used as a sole basis for instructional planning.

Each subtest has a mean of 10 and a standard deviation of 3. An overall Reading Quotient is computed using all three subtest scores. Performance is reported as a standard score ($M = 100$; $SD = 15$), percentile rank are provided. Age equivalents and grade equivalents are also given; the authors provide cautionary remarks about their use in the manual. The TERA-3 has two alternate, equivalent forms. Answers receive a score of 1 for correct or 0 for incorrect, and expected answers are clearly indicated in the examiners record booklet.

The TERA-3 was standardized on a relatively small stratified national sample of 875 children. These children were well matched on several critical demographics projected by the U.S. Bureau of the Census for 2000. Normative data are given for every 6-month interval. Both internal consistency and test-retest reliability are reported in the test manual. Reliability is consistently high across all three types of reliability studied. All but 2 of the 32 coefficients reported approach or exceed .90.

This entry has been informed by the sources listed below.

REFERENCES

Harper, S., & Pelletier, J. (2008). Gender and language issues in assessing early literacy: Group differences in children's performance on the test of early reading ability. *Journal of Psychoeducational Assessment, 26*(2), 185–194.

Huff, E., Dancer, J., Evans, S., & Skoch, A. (2006). Validity and reliability of the test of early reading ability-second edition with preschool age children. *Perceptual and Motor Skills, 102*(1), 288–290.

Reid, D. K., Hresko, W. P., & Hammill, D. D. (2002). *Test of Early Reading Ability–third edition (TERA-3).* Austin, TX: PRO-ED.

REVIEWED IN

Plake, B. S., Impara, J. C., & Spies, R. A. (Eds.). (2003). *The fifteenth mental measurements yearbook*. Lincoln, NE: Buros Institute of Mental Measurements.

RON DUMONT
Fairleigh Dickinson University

JOHN O. WILLIS
Rivier College

KATHLEEN VEIZEL
Fairleigh Dickinson University

JAMIE ZIBULSKY
Fairleigh Dickinson University
Fourth edition

TEST OF EARLY WRITTEN LANGUAGE, SECOND EDITION

The Test of Early Written Language, Second Edition (TEWL-2; Hresko, Herron, & Peak, 1996) measures early writing ability in children. The test can be used as a diagnostic device for children ages 4–0 to 10–11 and as a research tool for children 3–0 to 3–11. It consists of 57 untimed items, presented in developmental sequence, which assesses the use of conventions, linguistics, and conceptualization. The Basic Writing subtest requires responses to specific items (spelling, capitalization, punctuation, sentence construction, and metacognitive knowledge) while the Contextual Writing subtest depends on the authentic assessment (story format, cohesion, thematic maturity, ideation, and story construction) of a writing sample. Each subtest may be given independently or combined to provide a Global Writing Quotient.

The *Basic Writing Subtest* requires the administrator to establish a starting point for the child using suggested beginning items provided in the manual. Items for young students, for example, require them to draw a picture of a favorite TV character and tell about it, identify writing "instruments," indicate directionality of printed text, and to write their name. Older students are asked to construct sentences from haphazardly presented words, combine sentences, identify writing conventions, and to complete similar tasks. These items, scored 1 or 0, are recorded in an individual Profile/Record Booklet.

The *Contextual Writing Subtest* requires the child to write a story about a visual stimulus. For younger students a simple scene is used; older students respond to a more complete scenario, for example, a detailed playground scene. With the aid of a key, the student's story is scored on a 0 to 3 scale for 14 specific criteria, for example, sentence structure, ideation, thematic maturity, structure, sequence, use of dialogue, cohesion, elaboration. Unlike many published writing tests, the student has the opportunity to review and edit the story prior to scoring in *TEWL-2*.

Three quotients (Basic Writing, Contextual Writing, and Global Writing) are provided each based on a mean of 100 and a standard deviation of 15. Percentile ranks, age equivalents, standard score quotients, and normal curve equivalents are also provided. The TEWL-2 norms represent more than 1,400 children from 33 states. Normative information generally conforms to population characteristics for gender, race, ethnicity, geographic region, and urban/rural residence relative to the 1990 U.S. Census data. Internal consistency and reliability coefficients all exceed .90. Substantial content-description procedures, criterion-prediction procedures, and construct-identification procedures are presented.

The materials are well prepared; the manual is particularly useful, especially for scoring the *Contextual Writing Subtest*. Administering both tests is relatively time consuming, but as the measure is to be used diagnostically with at-risk students only, large numbers should not be involved. The provision of comparable forms permits the alternate form's use in assessing the impact of any interventions.

The TEWL–2 possesses an excellent conceptual framework and content-appropriate tasks. However, assessing a student's writing abilities from one sample of expressive writing using a single stimulus may impose serious limitations on the scope, and probably the quality and dependability, of the diagnostic information generated by the task.

This entry has been informed by the sources listed below.

REFERENCES

Bryant, B. R., & Bryant, D. P. (2003). Assessing the writing abilities and instructional needs of students. In C. R. Reynolds & R. W. Kamphaus (Eds.), *Handbook of psychological and educational assessment of children* (Ch.18). New York, NY: Guilford Press.

Hresko, W. P., Herron, S. R., & Peak, P. K. (1996). *Test of Early Written Language, Second Edition*. Austin, TX: PRO-ED.

Hurford, D. P. (1998). Review of the test of early written language, second edition. In J. C. Impara & B. S. Plake (Eds.), *The thirteenth mental measurements yearbook* (pp. 1027–1030). Lincoln: The Buros Institute of Mental Measurement, University of Nebraska Press.

Penner-Williams, J., Smith, T. E., & Gartin, B. C. (2008) Written language expression: Assessment instruments and teacher tools. *Assessment for Effective Intervention, 34*(3), 162–169.

Trevisan, M. S. (1998). Review of the test of early written language, second edition. In J. C. Impara & B. S. Plake (Eds.), *The thirteenth mental measurements yearbook* (pp. 1027–1030).

Lincoln: The Buros Institute of Mental Measurement, University of Nebraska Press.

RON DUMONT
Fairleigh Dickinson University

JOHN O. WILLIS
Rivier College

KATHLEEN VEIZEL
Fairleigh Dickinson University

JAMIE ZIBULSKY
Fairleigh Dickinson University
Fourth edition

TEST OF LANGUAGE DEVELOPMENT—INTERMEDIATE, FOURTH EDITION

The Test of Language Development–Intermediate, Fourth Edition (TOLD-I:4; Hammill & Newcomer, 2008) is an individually administered, norm-referenced test used to assess spoken language in children ages 8 years, 0 months to 17 years, 11 months. The battery takes approximately 30 to 60 minutes to administer and includes six subtests that measure different components of spoken language, namely semantics and grammar skills.

Two subtests measure listening abilities; two measure organizing abilities; and two measure speaking abilities. The combination of all six subtests is utilized to derive the examinee's overall Spoken Language score, and composite scores by category (as illustrated below) can be derived as well.

	Semantics	Grammar
Listening	*Picture Vocabulary* requires pointing to a picture that best represents a two-word stimulus.	*Multiple Meanings* requires stating as many different meanings for a stated word as possible.
Speaking	*Morphological Comprehension* requires distinguishing between grammatically correct and incorrect sentences.	*Sentence Combining* requires forming one compound or complex sentence from two or more simple sentences.
Organizing	*Relational Vocabulary* requires stating how three words, spoken by the examiner, are alike.	*Word Ordering* requires forming a complete, correct sentence from a randomly ordered string of words.

The TOLD-I:4 provides scores in the form of scaled subtest scores, standard composite scores, percentile ranks, and age equivalents for interpretation.

All new normative data were collected from a sample of 1,097 students who were representative of the 2005 U.S. population with respect to age, sex, race, geographic region, Hispanic status, exceptionality status, family income, and educational attainment of parents. Internal consistency estimates for all subtests and composites, when averaged across age ranges, were at or above .90 (although the examiner's manual does not provide this information broken down by age range). Test-retest reliability was found to be adequate in a sample of 103 students ($n = 68$ for 8- to 12-year-olds, $n = 35$ for 13- to 17-year-olds). The authors provide detailed information regarding the content-description validity of each subtest and demonstrate that the test correlates well with other measures of spoken language and that students score similarly on this measure and other measures of spoken language. Other indicators of validity are provided as well, and the authors thoughtfully discuss the presented data. Overall, this measure appears to meet a variety of reliability and validity standards.

This most recent version of the TOLD-I has not yet been reviewed in the *Buros Mental Measurements Yearbook*, although the TOLD-3:I has been reviewed and was found to be a well-developed and psychometrically sound instrument. Two notable changes to this newest version of the TOLD-I are that the Organizing subtests are new additions and that the age range for the test has been extended to include children ages 13 years, 0 months through 17 years, 11 months.

REFERENCE

Hammill, D. D., & Newcomer, P. L. (2008). *Test of Language Development–Intermediate*, Fourth Edition. Austin, TX: PRO-ED.

RON DUMONT
Fairleigh Dickinson University

JOHN O. WILLIS
Rivier College

KATHLEEN VEIZEL
Fairleigh Dickinson University

JAMIE ZIBULSKY
Fairleigh Dickinson University
Fourth edition

TEST OF LANGUAGE DEVELOPMENT—PRIMARY, FOURTH EDITION

The Test of Language Development—Primary, Fourth Edition (TOLD-P:4; Hammill & Newcomer, 2008) is an individually administered, norm-referenced test used to assess spoken language in children ages 4 years, 0 months to 8 years, 11 months. The battery takes approximately 30 to 60 minutes to administer and includes nine subtests that measure different components of spoken language, namely semantics, grammar, and phonology skills.

Three subtests measure listening abilities; three measure organizing abilities; and three measure speaking abilities. The results of these subtests can be combined to form composite scores for the major dimensions of language represented below.

	Semantics	Grammar	Phonology
Listening	*Picture Vocabulary* requires pointing to a picture that best represents a stimulus.	*Syntactic Understanding* requires pointing to a picture that best represents the meaning of sentences.	*Word Discrimination* requires recognizing the differences in significant speech sounds.
Speaking	*Oral Vocabulary* requires giving oral directions.	*Morphological Completion* requires recognizing, understanding, and using common English morphological forms.	*Word Articulation* requires correctly uttering important English speech sounds.
Organizing	*Relational Vocabulary* requires stating how two words, spoken by the examiner, are alike.	*Sentence Imitation* requires imitating English sentences.	*Word Analysis* requires segmenting words into smaller phonemic units.

The TOLD-P:4 provides scores in the form of scaled subtest scores, standard composite scores, percentile ranks, and age equivalents for interpretation.

The TOLD-P:4 was standardized on a sample of 1,108 children, representative of the 2005 U.S. population with respect to age, sex, race, geographic region, Hispanic status, exceptionality status, family income, and educational attainment of parents. Internal consistency estimates for all subtests, when averaged across age ranges, were at or above .80, and all composite scores, when averaged across age ranges, were at or above .90 (although the examiner's manual does not provide this information broken down by age range), and test-retest reliability was found to be adequate using a sample of 89 students ($n = 53$ for 4–6 year olds, $n = 36$ for 7- to 8-year-olds). The authors provide detailed information regarding the content-description validity of each subtest and demonstrate that the test correlates well with other measures of spoken language and that students score similarly on

this measure and other measures of spoken language. Other indicators of validity are provided as well, and the authors thoughtfully discuss the presented data. Overall, this measure appears to meet a variety of reliability and validity standards.

This most recent version of the TOLD has not yet been reviewed in the *Buros Mental Measurements Yearbook*, although the TOLD-3:P has been reviewed and was found to be an extremely well-developed and psychometrically sound instrument. Notably, reviewers of that instrument stated that floor and ceiling effects were a concern, and the authors indicate that such effects have been eliminated for core subtests and composites on the TOLD-4:P.

REFERENCE

Hammill, D. D., & Newcomer, P. L. (2008). *Test of Language Development–Primary*, Fourth Edition. Austin, TX: PRO-ED.

RON DUMONT
Fairleigh Dickinson University

JOHN O. WILLIS
Rivier College

KATHLEEN VEIZEL
Fairleigh Dickinson University

JAMIE ZIBULSKY
Fairleigh Dickinson University
Fourth edition

TEST OF MEMORY AND LEARNING

The Test of Memory and Learning (TOMAL; Reynolds & Bigler, 1994) is a comprehensive battery of 14 memory and learning tasks (10 core subtests and 4 supplementary subtests) designed to assess persons ages 5 years, 0 months through 19 years, 11 months. Five subtests form the Verbal Memory Index, while five more form the Nonverbal Memory Index. Additional subtests for each index are available as additions to the core subtests. Four measures of delayed recall, given 30 minutes after the start of testing, permit the comparison of performance across time. Also included with the TOMAL are directions for computing five supplementary indexes (Attention/Concentration, Sequential Recall, Free Recall, Associative Recall, and Learning). Finally, normative tables are provided on the Supplementary Analysis forms so that a person's learning and retention curves can be drawn and compared. To provide greater flexibility to the clinician, a set of four purely empirically derived factor indexes representing Complex Memory, Sequential Recall, Backward Recall, and Spatial Memory have been made available as well.

Subtests include Memory-for-Stories (MFS), Facial Memory (FCM), Word Selective Reminding (WSR), Visual Selective Reminding (VSR), Object Recall (OBR), Abstract Visual Memory (AVM), Digits Forward (DSF), Visual Sequential Memory (VSM), Paired Recall (PRC), Memory-for-Location (MFL), Manual Imitation (MIM), Letters Forward (LSF), Digits Backward (DSB), and Letters Backward (LSB). These subtests systematically vary the mode of presentation and response so as to sample verbal, visual, motoric, and combinations of these modalities in presentation and in response formats. The TOMAL subtests are scaled to the familiar metric of mean equaling 10 and a standard deviation of 3 (range 1 to 20). Composite or summary scores are scaled to a mean of 100 and standard deviation of 15.

Test material includes two booklets containing the stimuli for subtests; Facial Memory chips; Visual Selective Reminding test board; Delayed Recall cue card set; protocols for test including separate Supplementary Analysis forms; and the examiner's manual.

Administration time for the Core Battery (10 subtests) is approximately 45 minutes, while the entire battery (10 core subtests, 4 alternative subtests, and 4 recall subtests) takes approximately 60 to 75 minutes. Directions for each subtest are contained on the protocol pages, so the manual is not needed during administration. The Facial Memory, Paired Recall, Digits Backward, and Letters Backward subtests are the only subtests to provide unscored teaching tasks. Teaching items are also allowable on a number of other subtests, but only after the person has attempted an item and received a score of 0.

The TOMAL was standardized on 1,342 people selected as representative of the U.S. 1990 population estimates. Fifteen different age groups were divided by geographic area (17 states), race, gender, and ethnic group. Socioeconomic status (SES) was determined on the basis of the test site chosen. The sample was also stratified by urban versus rural residence. The size of the 15 sample ages tested ranged from a low of 42 at age 18 to a high of 163 at age 11.

Internal reliabilities for the TOMAL are generally high, ranging from a low of .56 to a high of .98. Of the four core indexes, all but Delayed Recall have reliabilities in the .90s. Delayed Recall averages .85 across all ages. Each of the five supplementary indexes has reliability estimates in the .90s. Of the 14 core subtests, 9 have an average reliability in the .90s, while the remaining 5 are in the .80s. Delayed recall subtests generally had lower reliabilities than did the other subtests.

Test-retest reliability coefficients for the core and supplementary indexes ranged from .81 to .92. The 14 subtest reliabilities averaged .81. Average test-retest reliability for 3 of the 14 subtests was found to be in the .70s.

Two of these subtests, Facial Memory and Abstract Visual Memory, are primary subtests of the Nonverbal Memory Composite.

The TOMAL scores correlate approximately .50 with measures of intelligence and achievement, indicating that the TOMAL is related to but not the same as the measures. Measures of intelligence typically correlated with one another in the .75 to .85 range while correlating with measure of achievement in the .55 to .65 range.

Since publication of the TOMAL, several studies have provided evidence of convergent and divergent validity of the TOMAL subtests as measures of various aspects of memory by examining patterns of correlations among TOMAL subtests and the Rey Auditory Verbal Learning Test and the Wechsler Memory Scale–Revised.

This entry has been informed by the sources listed below.

REFERENCES

Bigler, E. D., & Adams, W. V. (2001). Clinical neuropsychological assessment of child and adolescent memory with the WRAML, TOMAL, and CVLT-C. In A. S. Kaufman & N. L. Kaufman (Eds.), *Specific learning disabilities and difficulties in children and adolescents: Psychological assessment and evaluation* (pp. 387–429). New York, NY: Cambridge University Press.

Dumont, R., Whelley, P., Comtois, R., & Levine, B. (1994). Test of memory and learning (TOMAL): Test review. *Journal of Psychoeducational Assessment, 12,* 414–423.

Lowther, J. L., & Mayfield, J. (2004). Memory functioning in children with traumatic brain injuries: a TOMAL validity study. *Archives of Clinical Neuropsychology, 19,* 89–104.

Reynolds, C. R., & Bigler, E. (1994). *Test of memory and learning.* Austin, TX: PRO-ED.

RON DUMONT
Fairleigh Dickinson University

JOHN O. WILLIS
Rivier College

TEST OF NONVERBAL INTELLIGENCE, FOURTH EDITION

The Test of Nonverbal Intelligence, Fourth Edition (TONI-4; Brown, Sherbenou, & Johnsen, 2010) was created as a language-free measure of intelligence, aptitude, abstract reasoning, and problem solving for persons ages 6–0 through 89–11. It does not require the subject to read, write, or speak, and the examiner's oral directions are very brief and simple. Responding to each item does not involve much more movement than a point, nod, or other symbolic gesture indicating a response decision. The battery takes 15 to 20 minutes to administer. This measure is particularly useful for individuals who are deaf, language disordered (both expressive and receptive), non-English speaking, and those with conditions resulting from mental retardation, developmental disabilities, autism, cerebral palsy, stroke, traumatic brain injury, or other neurological impairment.

The two equivalent forms of the TONI-4 make it ideal for use in situations dependent on pre- and posttesting. Each form contains 60 items arranged to become progressively more difficult. Raw scores are converted to percentile ranks and to deviation quotients that have a mean of 100 and a standard deviation of 15 points.

The abstract/figural subject matter of the test ensures that each item presents a novel problem. There are no words, numbers, familiar pictures, or symbols within the test, reducing the effects of educational, cultural, or experiential backgrounds on performance.

The test was renormed on a sample of 2,272 people, and the examiner's manual indicates that the majority of participants were tested between the fall of 2005 and spring of 2008. The normative group was stratified by age across the variables of geographic region, gender, race and ethnicity, family income, and educational level achieved by the adult participants and parents of minor participants. The sample is representative of the U.S. population with respect to these variables.

The authors report that this measure has high internal consistency and adequate equivalence of the two forms of this measure. Test-retest reliability ranged from .84 for adults sampled to .90 for school-age participants. Scores on this measure are highly correlated with other nonverbal intelligence tests and moderately to strongly associated with scores on school achievement measures. The authors provide much evidence of the measure's reliability and validity.

This most recent version of the TONI has not yet been reviewed in the *Buros Mental Measurements Yearbook*, although the TONI-3 has been reviewed and was found to be a well-developed and psychometrically sound instrument. Notably, reviewers of past versions of this instrument indicate that the authors explore the reliability and validity of the measure extensively and, even prior to the changes made in the TONI-4, herald it as an extremely useful measure for people unable to demonstrate their abilities on an intelligence test requiring intact language and/or motor skills.

REFERENCE

Brown, L., Sherbenou, R. J., & Johnsen, S. K. (2010). *Test of Nonverbal Intelligence–Fourth Edition*. Austin, TX: PRO-ED.

RON DUMONT
Fairleigh Dickinson University

JOHN O. WILLIS
Rivier College

KATHLEEN VEIZEL
Fairleigh Dickinson University

JAMIE ZIBULSKY
Fairleigh Dickinson University
Fourth edition

TEST OF ORTHOGRAPHIC COMPETENCE (TOC)

The Test of Orthographic Competence (TOC; Mather, Roberts, Hammill, & Allen, 2008) is an individually administered battery of tests that can be used to assess recognition of aspects of the English writing system that are essential to reading and writing, such as letter recognition, symbol recognition, and spelling ability. Such orthographic skills are important in the process of early reading development, along with the phonological skills assessed by a variety of other measures. The basic battery is designed to be administered to individuals ages 6 years, 0 months through 17 years, 11 months and takes approximately 30 to 45 minutes to administer. There are three different versions of the TOC, one for 6- to 7-year-olds that includes four subtests, one for 8- to 12-year olds that includes six subtests, and one for 13- to 17-year-olds that includes six subtests.

The version for 6- to 7-year-old students includes the following subtests:

Signs and Symbols requires recognition of a series of graphical and numerical signs and symbols.

Grapheme Matching requires identifying two identical symbols, letters, or groups of letters from a series of five figures.

Homophone Choice requires identifying the correct spelling of a pictured object from several written options.

Punctuation requires adding appropriate punctuation to presented sentences.

Raw scores on all subtests are combined to form an overall Orthographic Ability composite. On versions of the test designed for older students, three additional composite scores can be derived as well.

The version for 8- to 12-year-old students includes the following subtests:

Conventions

> *Punctuation*, as described earlier.
>
> *Abbreviations* requires accurately identifying the meaning of abbreviations such as "Dr."

Spelling Accuracy

> *Sight Spelling* requires completing a partially spelled irregular word when presented with some of its letters and hearing it pronounced.
>
> *Homophone Choice*, as described earlier.

Spelling Speed

> *Letter Choice* requires identifying letters (p, d, b, or q) that are missing from incomplete words and writing in as many missing letters as possible within 2 minutes.
>
> *Word Scramble* requires reorganizing scrambled letters to spell as many real words as possible within 3 minutes.

The version for 13- to 17-year-old students follows the same structure as the version for 8- to 12-year-olds, with the exception of the *Homophone Choice* task, which is substituted with a *Word Choice* task that requires the child to pick which of three phonetically regular spelling choices accurately represents a word spoken by the examiner. Scaled scores and percentile ranks are provided for all subtests, and standard scores and percentile ranks are provided for all composites.

The instrument was normed on 1,477 students; these students were representative of the U.S. population in 2005 with respect to geographic region, gender, ethnicity, Hispanic status, family income, educational level of parents, and exceptionality status. Internal consistency of this measure was found to be adequate, as alpha coefficients for all subtests round to or exceed .8 and alpha coefficients for all composites exceed .9. Test-retest reliability was investigated using a small sample ($n = 74$) of students tested over a 2-week interval, and all subtests and composite scores were moderately to highly correlated over that time point ($r = .70—95$). The examiner's manual provides information regarding the scoring of each subtest, which appears to be fairly simple, and interrater reliability estimates all round to or exceed .9.

The authors provide detailed information regarding the content-description validity of each subtest and demonstrate that the test correlates well with other measures of written language. Other indicators of validity are provided as well, and the authors thoughtfully discuss the presented data. Overall, this measure appears to meet a variety of reliability and validity standards, although the small size of the standardization sample and the test-retest sample should be taken into account. The TOC has not yet been reviewed in the *Buros Mental Measurements Yearbook*, and independent studies examining this measure have yet to be conducted. However, it may provide practitioners with a brief and useful assessment tool for examining a child's orthographic dexterity.

REFERENCE

Mather, N., Roberts, R., Hammill, D., & Allen, E. (2008). *Test of Orthographic Competence*. Austin, TX: PRO-ED.

Ron Dumont
Fairleigh Dickinson University

John O. Willis
Rivier College

Kathleen Veizel
Fairleigh Dickinson University

Jamie Zibulsky
Fairleigh Dickinson University
Fourth edition

TEST OF PHONOLOGICAL AWARENESS, SECOND EDITION: PLUS (TOPA-2+)

The Test of Phonological Awareness, Second Edition: PLUS (TOPA-2+; Torgesen & Bryant, 1994) measures young children's awareness of the individual sounds in words and ability to accurately pair sounds and the letters that represent them. This latter skill was not measured in the earlier version of the TOPA, which tested only phonemic awareness, and the word PLUS in the title of this version of the test signifies the inclusion of a subtest focused on the alphabetic principle. The TOPA-2+ can be group or individually administered to children ages 5 through 8 years, and is most appropriate to administer to children in the second semester of kindergarten through the end of second grade. There are two versions of the instrument; the kindergarten version can be administered in 15 to 30 minutes, and the early elementary version can be administered in 30 to 45 minutes.

The TOPA-2+ kindergarten version can be used to identify children in kindergarten who may profit from instructional activities to enhance their phonological awareness in preparation for reading instruction. This measure can be administered any time during the kindergarten year, but the authors state that it will be more sensitive to individual differences during the second half of the year. To test phonemic awareness, children are administered 10 items requiring them to identify which word of three presented words begins with the same sound as a target word and which word of four presented words begin with a different sound as a target word. The newly added Letter-Sounds subtest includes 15 items that require children to identify which letter, from a set of four, corresponds to a presented phoneme.

The Early Elementary version can be used to determine if first- and second-grade students' difficulties in early reading are associated with delays in development of phonological awareness. This version of the measure is structured similarly to the kindergarten version, but each task is slightly more sophisticated. To measure phonemic awareness, children are required to identify the final sounds in words. Thus, children are administered 10 items requiring them to identify which word of three presented words ends with the same sound as a target word and which word of four presented words ends with a different sound as a target word. The Letter-Sounds test requires children to spell simple, single-syllable pseudowords, which vary from two to five phonemes in length.

Previous to this edition of the test, the kindergarten version was normed on a significantly smaller sample of children than the early elementary version, and the sample was not representative of the U.S. population nationally. The TOPA-2+ was normed on a group of 2,085 students from 26 states (including 1,035 for the kindergarten version and 1,050 for the early elementary version). The sample is representative of the U.S population in 2001 with respect to geographic region, gender, race, ethnicity, family income, and educational attainment of parents.

Internal consistency reliabilities range from .80 to .90, indicating that both subtests have adequate internal consistency across the age range. Test-retest reliability also appears to be adequate. Additionally, item analyses were conducted (and are included in the examiner's manual) to support overall validity and the consistency of the measure for various racial and gender groups. Evidence of content, predictive, and construct validity also is provided in the manual.

The most notable change to this revised edition of the TOPA is the addition of the Letter-Sounds subtest, which allows examiners to assess children's early literacy skills more holistically. It continues to be a psychometrically sound instrument that can be administered with ease, and in a timely manner, in a small group setting.

This entry has been informed by the sources listed below.

REFERENCE

Fenton, R. (2005). Review of the test of phonological awareness-second edition: PLUS. In B. S. Plake & J. C. Impara (Eds.) *The sixteenth mental measurements yearbook.* Lincoln, NE: Buros Institute of Mental Measurements.

Torgesen, J. K., & Bryant, B. R. (1994). *Test of Phonological Awareness–Second Edition: PLUS (TOPA-2+).* Austin, TX: PRO-ED.

RON DUMONT
Fairleigh Dickinson University

JOHN O. WILLIS
Rivier College

KATHLEEN VEIZEL
Fairleigh Dickinson University

JAMIE ZIBULSKY
Fairleigh Dickinson University
Fourth edition

TEST OF READING COMPREHENSION, FOURTH EDITION (TORC-4)

The Test of Reading Comprehension, Fourth Edition (TORC-4; Brown, Wiederholt, & Hammill, 2009) is an individually administered measure of silent reading comprehension. The battery is designed to be administered to individuals ages 7 years through 17 years, 11 months and takes approximately 45 minutes to administer. The third edition of the TORC contained eight subtests; however, this newer version includes only five subtests, which are combined to form a composite called the Reading Comprehension Index (a standard score with a mean of 100 and a standard deviation of 15).

1. *Relational Vocabulary* requires choosing words that are related to one another from a series of words presented in writing.
2. *Sentence Completion* requires reading a list of word pairs and choosing the word pair that best completes a written sentence.
3. *Paragraph Construction* requires rearranging several sentences presented out of order to form a coherent paragraph.
4. *Text Comprehension* requires reading a short passage and then answering multiple-choice questions related to the passage.
5. *Contextual Fluency* requires reading a passage of connected text, with no breaks between words, and drawing a line between as many words as possible within 3 minutes.

The TORC-4 was normed on 1,942 people who were representative of the U.S. population with respect to age, sex, race, geographic region, Hispanic status, exceptionality status, family income, and educational attainment of parents. Internal consistency estimates are consistently high, with .89 being the lowest reported reliability coefficient, indicating that all subtests have adequate internal consistency across the age range. Test-retest reliability was explored with a group of 68 regular class public school students ($n = 32$ for 7- to 12-year-olds, $n = 36$ for 13- to 17-year-olds), tested over a 1- to 2-week period. The examiner's manual states that the coefficients for all subtests in the combined groups equaled or exceeded .80, and the coefficients for the Reading Comprehension index in both groups exceeded .90. Validity was explored through item analysis. It is notable that the *Contextual Fluency* subtest was not included in internal consistency or validity estimates of differential item functioning, due to the speeded nature of the subtest and its inappropriateness for inclusion in item analysis. Thus, little information regarding this subtest's reliability and validity is included. All other subtests appear to function as intended.

This most recent version of the TORC has not yet been reviewed in the *Buros Mental Measurements Yearbook*, although the TORC-3 has been reviewed. Reviewers of this earlier version raised questions about the instrument's use with elementary school-age children, as well as some of its psychometric properties. The authors indicate that the TORC-4 does not have the floor effects that the older version had, thus making this instrument more appropriate for use with younger students.

REFERENCE

Brown, V., Wiederholt, J. L., & Hammill, D. D. (2009). *Test of Reading Comprehension–Fourth Edition*. Austin, TX: PRO-ED.

RON DUMONT
Fairleigh Dickinson University

JOHN O. WILLIS
Rivier College

KATHLEEN VEIZEL
Fairleigh Dickinson University

JAMIE ZIBULSKY
Fairleigh Dickinson University

TEST OF SILENT CONTEXTUAL READING FLUENCY (TOSCRF)

The Test of Silent Contextual Reading Fluency (TOSCRF; Hammill, Wiederholt, & Allen, 2006) is a brief measure of word identification and reading fluency that can be administered individually or to groups of children ages 7 years, 0 months through 17 years, 11 months of age. Students are given 3 minutes to complete the TOSCRF, and the authors estimate that the total administration time is 10 minutes. There are four alternate forms of the measure, and each includes a series of increasingly sophisticated passages adapted from the Gray Oral Reading Tests, Fourth Edition (Wiederholt & Bryant, 2001) and the Gray Silent Reading Tests (Wiederholt & Blalock, 2000). The use of these passages are a notable feature of this instrument, as their use differentiates this measure from the Test of Silent Word Reading Fluency (Mather, Hammill, Allen, & Roberts, 2004), which requires students to complete the same type of task, but with words that are not contextually linked.

On both measures, these passages are displayed in uppercase letters without punctuation or spaces between the words, and the student is prompted to draw lines between each word. The student's raw score on the TOSCRF is the total number of words correctly identified, and this raw score is then translated into a global standard score, along with a corresponding percentile rank, age equivalent, and grade equivalent. Reviewers (Smith, 2007; Soares, 2007) have questioned whether scoring of this measure is as simple as it seems, as extensive instructions regarding how to score words separated by diagonal or misplaced lines are provided, and examiners may need to make somewhat subjective decisions regarding scoring procedures. Although interrater reliability coefficients are reported to be .99, scoring was completed by four staff members who worked for the publisher of this test (rather than practitioners less familiar with the scoring procedures).

The norms are based on a sample of 1,898 students that ranged in age from 7 to 18 years. The sample was representative of U.S. population in 2002 with respect to sex, race, and ethnicity, geographic region, highest education achieved by primary caregiver, and exceptionality status. The authors present detailed information regarding the reliability and validity of this measure in the examiner's manual and do note they are only in the early stages of exploring the test's validity. Although the data presented is adequate in many ways, some concerns have been noted. When conducting test-retest reliability trials over the course of 2 weeks, evidence of practice effects was apparent across forms and age ranges. The authors recommend that, if these effects are replicated, the measure not be readministered until at least 2 months have passed (although they have not yet studied test-retest reliability over this period of time). Additionally, the authors attempt to demonstrate the reliability and validity of this very constrained measure by comparing performance on it to performance on intelligence tests, which reviewers have suggested may be theoretically and practically inappropriate.

Bell, McCallum, Kirk, Fuller, and McCane-Bowling (2007) administered this measure to a small sample ($n = 52$) of students ages 9 to 15 years, along with other measures of academic and reading achievement, and their findings support "the use of the TOSCRF as a quick screener and as a gross measure of reading progress" (p. 46). However, it is notable that they found that the measure did not function well as a progress monitoring tool and was not highly correlated with an administered measure of reading comprehension ($r = .32$). Bell et al. (2007) present evidence demonstrating that the TOSCRF is an adequate and valid measure of broad reading, but caution that it should not be used as a proxy measure of reading comprehension. Other reviewers seem to agree that this brief measure can be a helpful screening tool, or a useful component of a more comprehensive reading battery, but should not be used as a primary indicator of reading difficulties.

REFERENCES

Bell, S., McCallum, R., Kirk, E. R., Fuller, E. J., & McCane-Bowling, S. (2007). Investigation of the psychometric attributes of the test of silent contextual reading fluency. *Assessment for Effective Intervention, 33*(1), 39–46.

Hammill, D. D., Wiederholt, J. L., & Allen, E. A. (2006). *Test of Silent Contextual Reading Fluency.* Austin, TX: PRO-ED.

Mather, N., Hammill, D. D., Allen, E. A., & Roberts, R. (2004). *Test of silent word reading fluency.* Austin, TX: PRO-ED.

Smith, L. F. (2007). Review of the test of silent contextual reading fluency. In B. S. Plake & J. C. Impara (Eds.), *The seventeenth mental measurements yearbook.* Lincoln, NE: Buros Institute of Mental Measurements.

Soares, L. M. (2007). Review of the test of silent contextual reading fluency. In B. S. Plake & J. C. Impara (Eds.), *The seventeenth mental measurements yearbook.* Lincoln, NE: Buros Institute of Mental Measurements.

Wiederholt, J. L., & Blalock, G. (2000). *Gray silent reading tests.* Austin, TX: PRO-ED.

Wiederholt, J. L., & Bryant, B. R. (2001). *Gray oral reading tests–Fourth edition.* Austin, TX: PRO-ED.

RON DUMONT
Fairleigh Dickinson University

JOHN O. WILLIS
Rivier College

KATHLEEN VEIZEL
Fairleigh Dickinson University

JAMIE ZIBULSKY
Fairleigh Dickinson University
Fourth edition

TEST OF SILENT WORD READING FLUENCY

The Test of Silent Word Reading Fluency (TOSWRF; Mather, Hammill, Allen, & Roberts, 2004) is a brief measure of word identification and word reading fluency that can be administered individually or to groups of children ages 6 years, 6 months through 17 years, 11 months of age. Students are given 3 minutes to complete the TOSWRF. There are two alternate forms of the measure, and each includes one page with a series of words displayed without punctuation or spaces between the words. The words presented become increasingly sophisticated, with the first lines of letter strings forming short, high frequency words and the later lines forming longer and less commonly used words. The student is prompted to draw lines between each word to indicate recognition of each individual word. The words presented are not contextually linked in any way, which differentiates this measure from the Test of Silent Contextual Reading Fluency (Hammill, Wiederholt, & Allen, 2006), which requires students to complete the same type of task, but with words that are taken from coherent narrative passages. The student's raw score on the TOSWRF is the total number of words correctly identified, and this raw score is then translated into a global standard score, along with a corresponding percentile rank, age equivalent, and grade equivalent.

This sample was normed using a sample of 3,592 students ranging in age from ages 6 years, 6 months through 17 years, 11 months. The sample was representative of the U.S. population in many ways, but was less ethnically diverse than the country as a whole and fell below the mean in terms of educational achievement (Young, 2005). Furthermore, it is notable that nearly 20% of the sampled participants were members of exceptionality groups and that this figure exceeds the percentage of the U.S. population that falls into these groups (Beck, 2005).

Preliminary reliability and validity data is explored in depth in the examiner's manual. Alternate forms reliability estimates ranged from .73 to .87, when the two versions of the test were administered 2 weeks apart, and test-retest reliability from that same time period was .69. There is some evidence that students do exhibit a practice effect on this instrument, as scores on the second administration were almost .3 of a standard deviation higher than scores from the first administration (Beck, 2005). Interrater reliability estimate was found to be .99, but scoring procedures have been criticized for being less straightforward than they seem (i.e., in reviews of the closely related Test of Silent Contextual Reading Fluency; Smith, 2007; Soares, 2007), and interrater effects were derived from scoring completed by one of the authors and then several other raters who worked for the publisher. The measure does appear to differentiate between good readers and poor readers, indicating adequate construct validity, and is modestly to moderately correlated with measures of word identification and reading comprehension, indicating some degree of criterion-related validity. Bell et al. (2006) found the TOSWRF to have adequate concurrent validity, based on the significant correlations between scores received on this measure and selected subtests from the Woodcock Johnson Tests of Achievement, Third Edition and the Comprehensive Test of Basic Skills. Additionally, author presented reliability and validity data provides support for the assertion that this measure can be used as a screening tool for identifying struggling readers, but reviewers caution that it should not be misconstrued as a measure of reading fluency (Beck, 2005; Young, 2005). In light of its adequate psychometric properties, brevity, and the fact that it can be administered to many students simultaneously, the TOSWRF may be particularly useful in school settings.

REFERENCES

Beck, M. D. (2005). Review of the test of silent word reading fluency. In B. S. Plake & J. C. Impara (Eds.), *The sixteenth mental measurements yearbook*. Lincoln, NE: Buros Institute of Mental Measurements.

Bell, S., McCallum, R., Burton, B., Gray, R., Windingstad, S., & Moore, J. (2006). Concurrent validity of the test of silent word reading fluency. *Assessment for Effective Intervention, 31*(3), 1–9.

Hammill, D. D., Wiederholt, J. L., & Allen, E. A. (2006). *Test of silent contextual reading fluency*. Austin, TX: PRO-ED.

Mather, N., Hammill, D. D., Allen, E. A., & Roberts, R. (2004). *Test of silent word reading fluency*. Austin, TX: PRO-ED.

Smith, L. F. (2007). Review of the test of silent contextual reading fluency. In B. S. Plake & J. C. Impara (Eds.), *The seventeenth mental measurements yearbook*. Lincoln, NE: Buros Institute of Mental Measurements.

Soares, L. M. (2007). Review of the Test of Silent Contextual Reading Fluency. In B. S. Plake & J. C. Impara (Eds.), *The seventeenth mental measurements yearbook*. Lincoln, NE: Buros Institute of Mental Measurements.

Young, J. W. (2005). Review of the test of silent word reading fluency. In B. S. Plake & J. C. Impara (Eds.), *The sixteenth mental measurements yearbook*. Lincoln, NE: Buros Institute of Mental Measurements.

RON DUMONT
Fairleigh Dickinson University

JOHN O. WILLIS
Rivier College

KATHLEEN VEIZEL
Fairleigh Dickinson University

JAMIE ZIBULSKY
Fairleigh Dickinson University
Fourth edition

TEST OF VARIABLES OF ATTENTION

The Test of Variables of Attention (TOVA, 1989/1996) is an individually administered visual continuous performance test designed primarily for diagnosing children with attentional disorders and for monitoring the effectiveness of medication in treating attentional disorders. The TOVA requires neither language skills nor recognition of letters or numbers. The task is relatively simple: one of two easily discriminated visual stimuli (a small square adjacent to the top of a larger square or a small square adjacent to the bottom of a larger square) is presented for 100 milliseconds at 2-second intervals, and the subject is required to click a button whenever the specific target appears but must inhibit responding whenever the nontarget appears. There are two conditions during the test: (1) infrequent presentation of targets that is designed to measure attention; and (2) frequent presentation of targets that is designed to measure impulsivity.

Seven scores are obtained on the TOVA: errors of omission, errors of commission, mean correct response time, variability, anticipatory responses, multiple responses, and postcommission response time. The TOVA kit provides a manual to aid in interpretation of test results and the test itself provides computerized test interpretations. The TOVA kit also provides two videotapes that demonstrate how the TOVA may be used to screen for ADHD, to predict response to medication, and to monitor the psychopharmacological treatment.

The manual provides normative data on 1,590 subjects, at 15 different ages separated by sex. The norms are not stratified and little, if any, information is provided about the makeup of these children and adults. No breakdowns for socioeconomic levels, geographic regions, education levels, or race information are provided. There is no evidence in the manual that the normative sample includes (or for that matter, excludes) special education students or children on stimulant medication. Above age 20, there are very few males in the norming tables. For ages above 19 the numbers in the norming sample age groups drops considerably from an average of 168 subjects per group (age 4 to 19) to 36 subjects per group (age 20 to 80-plus). Still, the norm sample is impressive for a test not published by a major company.

The evidence for test-retest reliability is based on a study (no citation is provided) that report no significant differences between testing for a randomly selected group of normal children, ADHD subjects, and LD normal adults. The validity data are not adequate for the TOVA. There is a question about the content validity of the measure (i.e., whether a small sample of behaviors is a valid estimate of characteristic behavior for the individual), as a very limited research base is provided (Hagin & Dellabella, 1998).

In terms of providing an accurate assessment of the presence or absence of ADHD, the TOVA produces fairly high rates of misclassification (15% false positive rate and 28% false negative rate; Stein, 1998). Overall the technical characteristics of reliability and validity are not adequately provided in the TOVA manual (Hagin & Dellabella, 1998; Stein, 1998). The TOVA can be used as part of a diagnostic battery for purposes of diagnosing attentional disorders.

This entry has been informed by the sources listed below.

REFERENCES

Chae, P. K. (1999). Correlation study between WISC-III scores and TOVA performance. Psychology in the Schools, 36, 179–185.

Chae, P. K., Kim, J-H., & Noh, K-S. (2003). Diagnosis of ADHD among gifted children in relation to KEDI-WISC and T.O.V.A. performance. Gifted Child Quarterly, 47, 192–201.

Forbes, G. B. (1998). Clinical utility of the test of variables of attention (TOVA) in the diagnosis of attention-deficit/hyperactivity disorder. Journal of Clinical Psychology, 54, 461–476.

Hagin, R. A, & Dellabella, F. (1998). Review of the test of variables of attention In J. C. Impara & B. S. Flake (Eds.), The thirteenth mental measurements yearbook (pp. 1058–1060). Lincoln, NE: Buros Institute of Mental Measurements.

Plake, B. S., & Impara, J. C. (Eds.). (2001). The fourteenth mental measurements yearbook. Lincoln, NE: Buros Institute of Mental Measurements.

Stein, M. B. (1998). Review of the test of variables of attention. In J. C. Impara & B. S. Flake (Eds.), The thirteenth mental measurements yearbook (pp. 1060–1062). Lincoln, NE: Buros Institute of Mental Measurements.

Weyandt, L., Mitzlaff, L., & Thomas, L. (2002). The relationship between intelligence and performance on the test of variables of attention (TOVA). Journal of Learning Disabilities, 35(2), 114.

Wu, Y., Huang, Y., Chen, Y., Chen, C., Chang, T., & Chao, C. (2007). Psychometric study of the test of variables of attention: Preliminary findings on Taiwanese children with attention-deficit/hyperactivity disorder. Psychiatry and Clinical Neurosciences, 61(3), 211–218.

WEBSITES

http://www.tovatest.com/

http://alpha.fdu.edu/psychology/tova_comments.htm

http://alpha.fdu.edu/psychology/CPT_comparison.htm

http://alpha.fdu.edu/psychology/cpt_review.htm

RON DUMONT
Fairleigh Dickinson University

JOHN O. WILLIS
Rivier College

KATHLEEN VEIZEL
Fairleigh Dickinson University

JAMIE ZIBULSKY
Fairleigh Dickinson University
Fourth edition

TEST OF WORD FINDING, SECOND EDITION

Test of Word Finding, Second Edition (TWF-2; German, 2000) assesses an important expressive vocabulary skill. An examiner can diagnose word-finding disorders by presenting five naming sections: Picture Naming: Nouns; Picture Naming: Verbs; Sentence Completion Naming; Description Naming; and Category Naming. The TWF includes a special sixth comprehension section that allows the examiner to determine if errors are a result of word-finding problems or are due to poor comprehension. The instrument provides formal and informal analyses of two dimensions of word finding: speed and accuracy. The formal analysis yields standard scores, percentile ranks, and grade standards for item response time. The informal analysis yields secondary characteristics (gestures and extra verbalization) and substitution types. Speed can be measured in actual or estimated item response time.

The TWF-2 was developed to be administered to children ages 4 years through 12 years 11 months. Three forms are provided: a preprimary form for preschool and kindergarten children; a primary form for the first and second grades; and an intermediate form for the third through sixth grades.

The TWF-2 uses four different naming sections to test a student's word finding ability: Picture Naming Nouns assesses a student's accuracy and speed when naming compound and one- to four-syllable target words. Sentence Completion Naming assesses a student's accuracy when naming target words to complete a sentence read by the examiner. Picture Naming Verbs assesses a student's accuracy when naming pictures depicting verbs in the progressive and past tense forms. Picture Naming Categories assesses a student's accuracy and speed when naming objects and the distinct categories to which they belong.

Five supplemental analyses are provided to allow the examiner to gain critical information, enhance the interpretation of a student's test performance, and help formulate a word finding intervention plan. Three of the informal analyses (Phonemic Cueing Procedure, Imitation Procedure, Substitution Analysis) probe the nature of students' word-finding errors. The two other analyses (Delayed Response Procedure and Secondary Characteristics Tally) contribute to interpreting the student's Word Finding Quotient.

Standard scores and percentile ranks are provided. The instrument was nationally standardized on 1,836 individuals from 26 states. Characteristics of the sample matched the national population in 1997. Reliability coefficients for typical performing students and students with word-finding difficulties exceeded .84. Correlations between TWF-2 and other tests of vocabulary showed a considerable relationship.

This entry has been informed by the sources listed below.

REFERENCES

German, D. J. (2000). *Test of Word Finding–Second Edition.* Austin, TX: PRO-ED.

Tafiadis, D., Larentzaki, S., Magioglou, D., Mpourakis, I., Neofotistou, M., Pagoni, A., & Tafiadi, M. (2010). The test of word finding (TWF-2): A pilot study and validation of the test in normal Greek population aged from 4 years till 4 years and 11 months. *Annals of General Psychiatry, 9*(1).

REVIEWED IN:

Plake, B. S., Impara, J. C., & Spies, R. A. (Eds.). (2003). *The fifteenth mental measurements yearbook.* Lincoln, NE: Buros Institute of Mental Measurements.

RON DUMONT
Fairleigh Dickinson University

JOHN O. WILLIS
Rivier College

KATHLEEN VEIZEL
Fairleigh Dickinson University

JAMIE ZIBULSKY
Fairleigh Dickinson University
Fourth edition

TEST OF WORD READING EFFICIENCY

The Test of Word Reading Efficiency (TOWRE; Torgesen, Wagner, & Rashotte, 1999) is an individually administered timed test of word reading efficiency in the English language for children and adults ages 6.0 to 24.11. This test is a measure of an individual's ability to pronounce printed words fluently and accurately. The test focuses on two main abilities: the ability to sound out words with speed and accuracy and the ability to recognize familiar words as whole units or sight words. The goal of the TOWRE is to quantify an individual's level of skill with regard to word identification. Research shows that this is critical for ultimate reading success.

The test consists of two subtests, each with alternate forms. The Sight Word Efficiency (SWE) subtest assesses the number of real printed words that can be identified accurately within 45 seconds. There is a total of 104 words in subtest one; however, not all testees will finish the list within the allotted time. The Phonetic Decoding Efficiency (PDE) subtest measures the number of printed nonwords that can be pronounced accurately within 45 seconds. This test has 63 nonwords. When giving only one test form, the test should take about 5 minutes, including directions and practice items. Implementing both forms can take between 7 to 8 minutes to complete.

Forms A and B for both subtests are of equal difficulty. The tester first administers the practice items to the individual. If both forms are given, directions may be omitted for the second form. After the practice items are completed, the test taker is asked to read the list of words or nonwords printed on the card as quickly as possible. If they cannot read a word, they may skip it and go to the next word. They must stop reading after 45 seconds. Each test taker starts at the first word regardless of age. There are no basals or ceilings for this test.

Test descriptions and history, testing and scoring procedures, and standardizations/statistics can be found in the examiner's manual. Normative tables used for scoring purposes can be found in the appendix of the examiner's manual. Test responses and scores are recorded on profile/examiner record booklets that are included with the test, separate forms for Form A and Form B.

Standardization data for the TOWRE was collected in fall 1997 to spring 1998. The sample consisted of 1,507 individuals from 30 states. The sample was not a complete representation of the current population at the time. The geographic distribution of adults was uneven, there was a lack of representation of Native Americans for children and adults, and the Hispanic population was underrepresented for the school-age child.

The alternate forms reliability coefficients computed from standard scores for the TOWRE (total word reading) ranged from .94 to .98. The alternate-form reliability for subtest one ranged from .86 to .97, and .91 to .97 for subtest two. Test-retest reliability among all forms and age groups for the TOWRE ranged from .82 to .97. Concurrent validity was examined by looking at the correlations between the TOWRE and other reading tests. The correlation between the phonemic decoding efficiency subtest and the work attack subtest of the Woodcock Reading Mastery Tests-Revised was .85, and the correlation between sight word efficiency subtest and the word identification subtest of the WRMT-R was. 89.

Predictive validity was examined by looking at the correlations between the TOWRE and the Gray Oral Reading Tests, Third Edition. The correlation between the sight word efficiency subtest and the GORT ranged from .75 to .87, and the correlation between the phonemic decoding efficiency subtest and the GORT ranged from .47 to .68. These correlations show that the TOWRE can be a strong predictor of reading ability. Its predictive validity is much higher than that of the WRMT-R.

The TOWRE appears to be a reliable and valid test of word reading efficiency. The easy administration and short testing time also adds to its appeal.

This entry has been informed by the sources listed below.

REFERENCE

Torgesen, J. K., Wagner, R. K., & Rashotte, C. A. (1999). *Test of Word Reading Efficiency*. Austin, TX: PRO-ED.

REVIEWED IN:

Hagan-Burke, S., Burke, M., & Crowder, C. (2006). The convergent validity of the dynamic indicators of basic early literacy skills and the test of word reading efficiency for the beginning of first grade. *Assessment for Effective Intervention, 31*(4), 1–15.

Plake, B. S., Impara, J. C., & Spies, R. A. (Eds.). (2003). *The fifteenth mental measurements yearbook*. Lincoln, NE: Buros Institute of Mental Measurements.

Rashotte, C. A., Torgesen, J. K., and Wagner, R. K. (1999). *Examiner's manual for the test of word reading efficiency*. Austin, TX: PRO-ED.

RON DUMONT
Fairleigh Dickinson University

JOHN O. WILLIS
Rivier College

KATHLEEN VEIZEL
Fairleigh Dickinson University

JAMIE ZIBULSKY
Fairleigh Dickinson University
Fourth edition

TEST OF WRITTEN LANGUAGE, FOURTH EDITION

The Test of Written Language–Fourth Edition (TOWL-4; Hammill & Larsen, 2009) was designed to identify students with writing difficulty, determine individual strengths and weaknesses, and monitor written language progress in youth aged 9 years, 0 months to 17 years, 11 months. The authors also note it can be used as a research tool. The TOWL-4 is a revision of the TOWL-3 (Hammill & Larsen, 1996) and contains new normative data, improved evidence of sound psychometrics, new colored stimulus cards, and the inclusion of grade-based as well as age-based norms.

The TOWL-4 contains seven subtests (with two equivalent forms A and B) that measure the student's writing competence through both essay-analysis (spontaneous) formats and traditional test (contrived) formats. With the exception of a 15-minute time allotment in story writing, the TOWL-4 is untimed, and the full battery can be completed in approximately 60 to 90 minutes. Using a pictorial prompt, the student first writes a story that is scored on orthography and grammar (Subtest 6: Contextual Conventions), as well as composition quality (Subtest 7: Story Composition). The contrived subtests are: Vocabulary, Spelling, Punctuation, Logical Sentences and Sentence Combining.

Subtests produce scaled scores and percentile ranks. Additionally, three composites are available: Contrived Writing, Spontaneous Writing, and Overall Writing. Each composite produces index scores and percentile ranks. The manual also provides age and grade equivalents as well as descriptive terms for scaled and index scores. The authors note the difficulties in interpreting age and grade equivalents and report they provide them "reluctantly" due to their mandated use in several systems.

The TOWL-4 was standardized on a 17-state sample of 2,205 individuals aged 9 to 17 years in 2006 and 2007. The sample was representative of the U.S. population in terms of geographic region, gender, race/ethnicity, household income, parental education, and educational disability status.

Average internal consistency coefficients for age and grade-based subtest scores across both forms ranged from .72 to .92. Coefficients for the composites were somewhat higher; and ranged from .82 to .96. Alternate forms reliability was calculated by comparing Form A and Form B scores across the normative sample. Scores were similar, and correlations were generally above .80. The Overall Writing index correlation was .94 and .95 for age and grade-based norms respectively, suggesting Forms A and B can be used relatively interchangeably. Test-retest reliability was measured on a sample of 84 Texan students ranging in age from 9 to 17 years. Both forms were administered with a 2-week intervening time period. Results indicated adequate to good test-retest reliability. An alternate-forms delayed administration procedure was also used, and again, adequate reliability was demonstrated. Finally, interrater reliability coefficients also were good; however, this was based off one study using two PRO-ED raters. More investigation should be completed with usual care providers.

The manual also provides evidence for content, criterion-prediction, and construct validity. Content-description validity was demonstrated by describing the rationale for test content, including the pictures selected for the spontaneous writing demands, as well as conducting conventional item analysis and differential item functioning analysis. The TOWL-4 correlated highly with the Written Language Observation Scale (WLOS; Hammill & Larsen, 2008)), the Reading Observation Scale (ROS; Wiederholt, Hammill, & Brown, 2009) and the Test of Reading Comprehension–Fourth Edition (TORC-4; Brown, Wiederholt, & Hammill, 2009). The authors demonstrated the TOWL-4 has adequate positive predictive power to predict literacy. Lastly, evidence for construct-identification validity was provided by demonstrating performance was related to age and grade as expected, subtests were intercorrelated but not redundant, TOWL-4 scores correlated with overall measures of intelligence, differences between special groups were as expected (i.e., the learning-disabled students scored lower than gifted students), all subtests loaded heavily on the same factor, and finally, through item validity analysis.

Overall, the TOWL-4 seems to provide a good update of the popular TOWL-3. However, further studies of its psychometric properties should be conducted by independent researchers to further bolster evidence for soundness. The manual is easy-to-follow, and even the guidelines for scoring the more subjective components are clear.

As of the time of this writing, no reviews for or studies of the fourth edition of the TOWL were available.

REFERENCES

Brown, V. L., Wiederholt, J. C., & Hammill, D. D. (2009) *Test of Written Composition–Fourth Edition*. Torrance, CA: Western Psychological Services.

Hammill, D. D., & Larsen, S. C. (1996). *Test of Written Language–3 (TOWL-3)*. Austin, TX: PRO-ED.

Hammill, D. D., Larsen, S. C. (2008). *Written Language Observation Scale*. Austin, TX: PRO-ED.

Hammill, D. D., & Larsen, S. C. (2009). *Test of Written Language–Fourth Edition (TOWL-4)*. Austin, TX: PRO-ED.

Wiederholt J. C., Hammill, D. D., & Brown, V. L. (2009). *Reading Observation Scale*. Austin, TX: PRO-ED.

Ron Dumont
Fairleigh Dickinson University

John O. Willis
Rivier College

Kathleen Veizel
Fairleigh Dickinson University

Jamie Zibulsky
Fairleigh Dickinson University
Fourth edition

TESTS IN PRINT

Tests in Print (Buros, 1961, 1974; Mitchell, 1983; Murphy, Conoley, & Impara, 1994) are volumes that provide a comprehensive index of commercially available educational and psychological tests in English-speaking countries.

The volumes contain descriptive information about each test (e.g., the age or grade levels for which the test is designed, author, publishing company, scale scores); literature related to the specific test; an index to all reviews of the test in previous Buros *Mental Measurement Yearbooks;* and references to test descriptions and related literature cited in previous *Test in Print* volumes.

The most current, *Tests in Print VI* (Murphy, Conoley, & Impara, 2002), contains thousands of descriptions of commercially available tests; references for specific tests; an alphabetical listing of test names, a directory of publishers with addresses, and an index to their tests; a title index showing both in print and out-of-print tests since previous listings; a name index for test authors, reviewers, and authors of references; and a classified subject index for quickly locating tests in particular areas.

REFERENCES

Buros, O. K. (1961). *Tests in print*. Highland Park, NJ: Gryphon.

Buros, O. K. (1974). *Tests in print II*. Highland Park, NJ: Gryphon.

Mitchell, J. V. Jr. (1983). *Tests in print III*. Lincoln, NE: Buros Institute of Mental Measurements.

Murphy, L. L., Conoley, J. C., & Impara, J. C. (1994). *Tests in print IV*. Lincoln, NE: Buros Institute of Mental Measurements.

Murphy, L. L., Conoley, J. C., & Impara, J. C. (2002). *Tests in print VI*. Lincoln, NE: Buros Institute of Mental Health Measurements.

Jane Close Conoley
University of Nebraska
First edition

Elizabeth O. Lichtenberger
Salk Institute
Second edition

See also **Buros Mental Measurements Yearbook**

TEST-TAKING BEHAVIOR

Psychoeducational testing is invaluable for identifying students' strengths, limitations, and those conditions under which they learn best. The results of testing assist in describing behaviors, making diagnoses, estimating prognoses, assisting in intervention planning and evaluation, and in other ways. A student's behavior during testing often affects the quality of the test results. Thus, observations as to whether students are cooperative, talkative, attentive, or interested and motivated are important because their test behavior affects the validity of the test data and can have important personal consequences. Several behavior qualities that can influence student performance have been identified (Oakland, Glutting, & Watkins, 2005).

Examiners should provide a comfortable, distraction-free testing environment to promote examinee attention and concentration. Receptive language qualities such as listening and expressive language skills, including oral expression, are important because modifications in test use may be necessary when a child exhibits language deficits or is not fluent in English. Examiners must be aware of physical and motor qualities that may adversely impact test performance. A child's gross muscle control impacts the assessment of adaptive behavior, and fine motor control is important for writing and other test items requiring physical manipulations. Good rapport between the examiner and child is important for establishing trust, cooperation, and promoting more valid results. The examiner should smile frequently, talk with the child before testing, and reinforce the child's efforts. A child's personal readiness for being tested includes sufficient rest, adequate food, alertness, attention, and concentration. A child's motivation to engage in and sustain testing activity over time is important for ensuring personal readiness and maintaining good rapport. A child's temperament (e.g., extroversion or introversion) and learning styles also may impact test performance. These and other factors should be considered when assessing test behavior and judging the quality and validity of testing results.

Although informal observations during testing are important, formal rating scales may be more useful for assessing a student's test session behaviors and test performance. International research results show that among young children aged at least 3.5 years in Finland, refusal to test was associated with compromised neuropsychological and linguistic test scores. Test refusal is thought to reflect a child's underlying skills deficits and attempts to avoid failure rather than the display of non-compliant or oppositional behavior (Mäntynen, Poikkeus, Abonen, Aro, & Korkman, 2001). Other international results show that among 10- to 12-year-old Turkish children, test session behaviors indicating avoidance, inattentiveness, and uncooperativeness were associated with test performances on the Wechsler Intelligence Scale for Children, Revised (Oakland, Gulek, & Glutting, 1996).

Freedom from distractibility and processing speed scores from the Wechsler Intelligence Scales for Children, Third Edition are not lower for children who display inappropriate test-taking behaviors (Oakland, Broom, & Glutting, 2000). Thus, examiners are not advised to rely on test score profiles from intelligence tests when judging test-taking behaviors. Children with attention-deficit/hyperactivity disorder compared to matched controls tend to display more inattentive, avoidant, and uncooperative behaviors, thus depressing the magnitude of children's IQs (Glutting, Robins, & de Lancey, 1997). An understanding of test session behaviors allows an examiner to decide whether testing results accurately reflect a child's cognitive abilities. This information helps educational professionals identify important qualities not measured by the test, understand thought processes used in a child's responses, discuss the child's qualities with teachers and parents, and make necessary interventions and modifications in the type and intensity of instruction.

REFERENCES

Glutting, J. J., Robins, P. M., & de Lancey, E. (1997). Discriminant validity of test observations for children with attention deficit/hyperactivity. *Journal of School Psychology, 35,* 391–401.

Mäntynen, H., Poikkeus, A., Abonen, T., Aro, T., & Korkman, M. (2001). Clinical significance of test refusal among young children. *Child Neuropsychology, 7,* 241–250.

Oakland, T., Broom, J., & Glutting, J. (2000). Use of freedom from distractibility and processing speed to assess children's test-taking behaviors. *Journal of School Psychology, 38,* 469–475.

Oakland, T., Glutting, J., & Watkins, M. W. (2005). Assessment of test behaviors with the WISC-IV. In A. Profitera, D. H. Saklofske, & L. G. Weiss (Eds.), *WISC-IV clinical use and interpretation: Scientist practitioner perspectives* (pp. 435–463). San Diego, CA: Elsevier Academic Press.

Oakland, T., Gulek, C., & Glutting, J. (1996). Children's test-taking behaviors: A review of literature, case study, and research on Turkish children. *European Journal of Psychological Assessment, 12,* 240–246.

JEFFREY DITTERLINE
University of Florida

See also Test Anxiety

TEST-TEACH-TEST PARADIGM

The Test-Teach-Test Paradigm (TTT-P) is representative of an instructional concept that is similar to the concept of teaching students how to read by using the phonics approach. To conceptualize the TTT-P, we need to review some other terms: direct instruction, model-lead and test, criterion assessment, criterion instruction, and appropriate practice.

Fundamentally, the TTT-P represents an instructional sequence. The portrayal that follows (Nash, 1985) is an adaptation of the instructional sequencing suggested by Bateman (1971) and Engelmann and Brunder (1969). In the course of this portrayal, some of the other terms referred to above will be employed. The instructional concept and postures of both Bateman and Engelmann are regarded by many as representing a kind of pioneering methodology of the 1970s that distinguished special educational instruction from regular education.

A. *The initial testing part of the TTT-P.* In a reading test with beginning second-grade students, all of the students misread the word *blew.*

B. *The teaching part of the TTT-P.*

1. The teacher begins by saying, "We are going to learn to read the word *blew* by use of sounds using a simultaneous multisensory instructional procedure."

2. Next, the teacher directs the students to copy down the word that has been written out on the blackboard in front of the students.

3. Then the teacher models for the students what it is that they are to do.

   a. The teacher states that this word has three sounds. The teacher says the sounds, /b/, /l/, and /ew/, and simultaneously underlines each of them while doing so, *b l ew.*

   b. Next, the teacher, using a lead, says, "We, all of us, will now individually underline the three sounds that this word has—simultaneously saying the sound of the letter or letters as we do so." The teacher and the students all together and in an audible voice do so, *b l ew.*

   c. The teacher, using an intervening test, says, "Your turn—reunderline each sound saying each sound out loud as you do so." The students do so, *b l ew.*

   d. Next, the teacher, using another model, says, "I will now loop and say in an audible voice the sounds in this word, *b l ew.*"

   e. Then, using another lead, the teacher says, "We will now all together loop and say the sounds in this word." Students and teacher do so, *b l ew.*

   f. Next, the teacher, using another intervening test, says, "Your turn, now all by yourself you loop and say out loud the sounds in this word." The students do so, *b l ew.*

   g. The teacher, using another lead, says, "We will now underline and say the word rapidly." The teacher and the students do so, *b l ew.*

   h. Then the teacher, using another intervening test, says, "Your turn—now all by yourself, you are to underline and say the word rapidly." The students do so, *b l ew.*

   i. Last, the teacher says, "All of you have just read the word *blew* correctly."

C. *The test part of the TTT-P.* This last phase in the TTT-P is the simplest part to do and can be attended to in a number of ways. Using our example word, a teacher could offer repeated appropriate practice experiences in reading this particular word. The process of the TTT paradigm as exemplified can be replicated across any and all instruction, be it initial or advanced, and across any and all tasks, with spelling as one of the more obvious ones. In the course of doing so, the teacher will automatically be involved with these initial concepts (Nash, 1986):

1. *Direct instruction*: The precise identification of what students are to learn and how they are going to do so.

2. *Model-lead and test*: While carrying out any given bit of instruction, the teacher can model what the student is to do and simultaneously follows this with a lead (i.e., doing the task with the student). At this point, the teacher can employ a simple test of what it is that the student knows.

3. *Criterion assessment (CA)*: Both of the test parts of the TTT-P are examples of CA. The first part tests what it is the teacher is to teach if the student fails the test; the second test of the TTT-P is simply a reaffirmation and check on what the teacher intended to teach.

4. *Criterion instruction (CI)*: The teaching part of the TTT-P represents CI because there is an intended 1:1 correlation between the first test and the subsequent needed instruction.

5. *Appropriate practice*: In the execution of the instruction associated with the TTT-P, the teacher will be implementing the model-lead-test concept automatically and involving the student in the necessary practice.

Instruction that implements the concepts reviewed is instruction that guarantees student success. These patterns can be repeated as often as student errors dictate.

REFERENCES

Bateman, B. D. (1971). *The essentials of teaching.* Sioux Falls, SD: Adapt.

Engelmann, S., & Brunder, E. (1969). *Distar reading.* Chicago, IL: Science Research.

Nash, R. T. (1985). *Remediation courses.* Project Success, University of Wisconsin–Oshkosh. Unpublished raw data.

Nash, R. T. (1986). *Manual for remediating the reading and spelling deficits of elementary, secondary and post-secondary students.* Flossmoor, IL: Language Prescriptions.

ROBERT T. NASH
University of Wisconsin at Oshkosh

See also **Diagnostic-Prescriptive Teaching**

TETHERED SPINAL CORD SYNDROME

Tethered spinal cord syndrome occurs when the spinal cord does not hang freely in the spinal canal but instead is attached at a point in the spine, restricting movement and causing stretching and damage.

Characteristics

External Spinal Physical Manifestations

1. Lipoma or fatty tumors at the base of the spine.
2. Meningocele manque, which is a lesion resembling a cigarette burn.
3. Dermal sinus tract or sacral dimple.
4. Asymmetrical buttock crease.
5. Hemangioma, which is a benign tumor comprised of blood vessels.
6. Skin tags.
7. Hypertrichosis, or the appearance of an excessive growth of hair, in the midline region.

Urological Physical Manifestations

1. In infants an absence of dry periods between diaper changes.
2. A lack of success in toilet training, increased toileting urgency, and/or incontinence.

Orthopedic Physical Manifestations

1. Back pain and/or scoliosis.
2. Foot deformities such as an exaggerated height of the arch or discrepancies in foot or leg length.
3. Muscle atrophy of the lower extremities.

Neurological Physical Manifestations

1. Decreased or absent reflexes.
2. Decreased sensation to touch and temperature in the lower extremities.
3. Lower extremity weakness.

Surgery may be considered to free the spinal cord to prevent further damage, but usually the patient will not regain motor control that has already been lost (Greif & Stalmasek, 1989). If unrepaired, a reported 90% of patients will develop irreversible deficits. There is a 50% chance of returning to baseline mobility. Orthopedic anomalies and bladder dysfunctions have lower probabilities of correction (Cartwright, 2000). Early diagnosis and treatment are important in curbing the permanent effects.

A patient with tethered spinal cord syndrome may have many special needs. With bladder dysfunction, catheterization may be necessary. Because of loss of feeling in the lower extremities, care should be taken in examining for bruising, cuts, and blistering, as the patient may not realize they are present. If scoliosis is present, it may need to be surgically corrected. The muscle atrophy may produce a need for walking assistance through the use of a cane, crutches, or wheelchair in extreme situations. Modifications may need to be made in an educational setting to accommodate children with this syndrome.

This entry has been informed by the sources listed below.

REFERENCES

Cartwright, C. (2000). Primary tethered cord syndrome: Diagnosis and treatment of an insidious defect. *Journal of Neuroscience and Nursing, 32,* 210–215.

Greif, L., & Stalmasek, V. (1989). Tethered cord syndrome: A pediatric case study. *Journal of Neuroscience Nursing, 21,* 86–91.

Nelson, W. E., Behrman, R. E., Kliegman, R. M., & Arvin, A. (1996). *Nelson textbook of pediatrics* (15th ed.). Philadelphia, PA: Saunders.

CAROL SCHMITT
San Diego Unified School District

TETRAHYDROBIOPTERIN DEFICIENCY (BH4)

Deficiency in tetrahydrobiopterin (BH4) is a rare genetic disorder due to a defect in metabolism of amino acids. BH4 impairs the metabolism of enzymes resulting in hyperphenylalanimia and a defect of neurotransmitter synthesis. Clinical manifestations are similar and usually indistinguishable from classic phenylketonuria (PKU). In most cases of BH4, progressive neurological symptoms appear between the ages of 2 and 12 months despite excellent dietary control. The syndrome may involve mental deterioration, intractable seizures, arrest in motor development, microcephaly, and occasionally abnormal movements.

Characteristics

1. Hyperphenylalaninemia.
2. Progressive neurological symptoms between the ages of 2 and 12 months despite excellent dietary control.
3. Neurological and neurocognitive manifestations: mental deterioration, loss of head control, hypertonia, drooling.

4. Swallowing difficulties and myoclonic seizures despite adequate dietary therapy.

5. Plasma phenylalanine levels as high as those in classic PKU or in the range of benign hyperphenylalaninemia.

The incidence of BH4 deficiency is approximately 1 to 2 per million live births, compared to 150 per million in the hyperphenylalaninemias. Incidence is about 2% of infants with hyperphenylalaninemia.

Long-term efficacy of various therapies is unknown and includes:

1. Low phenylalanine diet. If a restricted diet is given early, ideally in the first months of life, the adverse consequences of persistent hyperphenylalanimia are mostly avoided. When such treatment is started later, results are less favorable. Diet in conjunction with additional therapies is recommended for at least the first two years of life.

2. Neurotransmitter precursors. Administration of 1-dopa and 5-hypdroxytryptophan may prevent neurological damage if started early in life. Treatment started after 6 months of age, although resulting in some improvement, has not reversed existing neurological damage.

3. All patients with hyperphenylalanine should be tested for BH4 deficiency as early as possible because it gives rise to devastating neurological illness. BH4 replacement via oral administration of the cofactor in small daily doses is necessary to normalize serum levels of phenylalanine.

The duration of treatment, as well as the development of novel treatments, continues to be a focus of BH4 research.

Children suffering from BH4 should be evaluated for special education services and may be eligible under the classification of other health impairment as a result of their medical condition.

This entry has been informed by the sources listed below.

REFERENCES

Lyon, G., Adams, R. D., & Kolodny, E. H. (1996). *Neurology of hereditary metabolic diseases of children*. New York, NY: McGraw-Hill.

Nelson, W. E., Behrman, R. E., Kliegman, R. M., & Arvin, A. M. (1996). *Nelson textbook of pediatrics* (15th ed.). Bangalore, India: Prism Books.

Scriver, C. R. (Ed.). (1995). *The metabolic and molecular basis of inherited disease* (7th ed.). New York, NY: McGraw-Hill.

VIRDETTE L. BRUMM
Children's Hospital Los Angeles
Keck / USC School of Medicine

TEXT-TO-SPEECH

Text-to-speech refers to a media format generated by a hardware or software system that will render digital textual information (such as text contained in a word processing document or web page) into audio format using a speech synthesis program. Most text-to-speech systems work in conjunction with personal computers. Prior to the advent of internal soundcards on computers, text-to-speech was accomplished by using hardware-based external speech synthesis devices. Such devices have fallen out of favor as increasingly capable and powerful soundcards have become standard equipment on most personal computers. With the exception of specialized text-to-speech devices, such as embedded text-to-speech on braille embossers, refreshable braille, and note-taking devices, most text-to-speech is accomplished using software programs.

Text-to-speech is a media format rather than a specific technology. As such, there are multiple applications. In the disability realm, text-to-speech is commonly used by people with visual and cognitive impairments. For people with visual impairments, software technologies such as screen magnification programs and screen readers frequently combine text-to-speech with other media formats such as screen magnification and refreshable braille displays to produce a powerful multimodal presentation of information. In the area of learning disabilities, text-to-speech is frequently combined with other software utilities such as word prediction, homophone identification, audible spell checking, and sometimes voice recognition to produce a formidable composition suite.

Closely related to text-to-speech technology are scanning and optical character recognition (OCR) technologies. Since text-to-speech can only be rendered from digital textual information, scanners and OCR programs can be used to convert printed documents into digital ones. The documents can then be "read" by text-to-speech technology.

In 2004, AT&T developed a set of high-quality consumer text-to-speech fonts termed AT&T Natural Voice fonts (AT&T, 2005). These 16-bit fonts are compatible with both Microsoft and Macintosh speech operating system interfaces. Commercial examples of text-to-speech are routinely used in voice automation systems like technical and customer support. For example, text-to-speech technology can be used to present a menu to the user while voice recognition technology may be used to navigate the menu.

REFERENCE

AT&T. (2005). *AT&T Natural Voices*. Retrieved from http://www.naturalvoices.att.com/

DAVID SWEENEY
Texas A&M University

***See also* Computer Use With Students With Disabilities; Technology for Individuals With Disabilities**

THALASSEMIA MAJOR

Thalassemia is a blood disorder of genetic origin that results from the interaction of thalassemia genes and those genes associated with abnormal hemoglobins. Heterozygous thalassemia or thalassemia minor is the less serious form of the disorder and is generally without symptoms. Homozygous thalassemia or thalassemia major is the more serious form of the disorder and if untreated can lead to massive splenomegaly and death by 5 years of age. Thalassemia major also is referred to as *Cooley's anemia* or *Mediterranean anemia* due to its high prevalence in Mediterranean and Middle Eastern countries (e.g., Cyprus, Greece, Turkey, and Italy) and descendants from these areas. Other regions where thalassemia major may be found include Southeast Asia and Africa. With increased mobility and marriage between ethnic groups, the prevalence of thalassemia major has decreased considerably over time; with geographic differences in prevalence, no single prevalence rate is cited. Although prevalence of the major form is of increasing rarity, individuals with thalassemia minor are carriers for the major form and should engage in genetic counseling prior to having children.

Characteristics

1. Anemia characterized by slowed production of red blood cells and decreased life of red blood cells.
2. Medical complications associated with iron overload caused by recurrent transfusions.
3. Impaired growth due to the enlargement of the spleen (splenomegaly).
4. Jaundice.
5. Skeletal changes and osteopenia.
6. Growth retardation.
7. Possible cognitive impairment.

If untreated, thalassemia major will result in death prior to school age. Treatment options for thalassemia major include regular blood transfusions, use of iron chelation therapy, splenectomy, and bone marrow transplant (Al-Salem, 1999; Muretto & Angelucci, 1999). Continual follow-up care is needed, and medical complications, including iron overload in the case of transfusions, may arise from the treatment. It is important for communication to be kept open among parents, physicians, and school personnel to ensure that all persons working with the child are kept up to date on the child's medical status.

Cognitive impairment can be associated with thalassemia major (Monastero, Monastero, Ciaccio, Padovani, & Carmarda, 2000). The extent of cognitive decline was found to be associated with the duration of transfusional therapy and the delay between beginning transfusion therapy and the onset of chelation therapy (Monastero et al., 2000). If this is the case, or if the child's progress in school is affected by medical issues, the child may be eligible for special education services, including homebound tutoring during medical crises.

Psychosocial issues for children and adolescents with thalassemia are similar to those for children with chronic illness in general (Nash, 1990; Tsiantis, 1990). Parents often tend to be overprotective, and this can result in child behaviors associated with learned helplessness and dependence. This overprotection can be enhanced by the "delayed" growth (dwarfism) associated with the disorder. At the same time, there is increased stress on the child and the family, including siblings. Psychological interventions need to be ecological in nature and build on the strengths of the family (Nash, 1990). Across cultures, having a child with thalassemia often has a unifying effect on the family (Tsiantis, Dragonas, Richardson, & Anastopoulos, 1996). Factors associated with less positive response to the child's illness include father's educational level and the extent of major medical complications. Because of the genetic component to thalassemia major, the possibility exists for more than one child in a family to have the disorder, and this would further complicate the impact on the family.

Although aggressive medical treatment can offset the major problems associated with thalassemia major, the frequent transfusions and resulting iron overload can bring on additional complications. Combined with other medical treatments including bone marrow transplants and splenectomy, and with the introduction of iron chelation therapy, it is estimated that 80% of individuals with thalassemia major reach a median age between 23 and 31 years. This is a significant increase in life expectancy from 30 years ago; medical advances may increase this even further in the future. With the increased life expectancy, however, additional issues regarding family status, genetic counseling, and employment issues that were not previously of concern are in need of research (DiPalma, Viello, Zani, & Facchini, 1998).

REFERENCES

Al-Salem, A. H. (1999). Is splenectomy for massive splenomegaly safe in children? *American Journal of Surgery, 178,* 42–45.

DiPalma, A., Viello, C., Zani, R., & Facchini, A. (1998). Psychosocial integration of adolescents and young adults with thalassemia major. *Annals of the New York Academy of Sciences, 850,* 355–360.

Monastero, R, Monastero, G., Ciaccio, C., Padovani, A., & Carmarda, R. (2000). Cognitive deficits in beta-thalassemia major. *Acta Neurologica Scandinavia, 102,* 162–168.

Muretto, P., & Angelucci, E. (1999). Successful treatment of severe thalassemia. *New England Journal of Medicine, 341*, 92.

Nash, K. B. (1990). A psychosocial perspective: Growing up with thalassemia, a chronic disorder. *Annals of the New York Academy of Sciences, 612*, 442–449.

Tsiantis, J. (1990). Family reactions and relationships in thalassemia. *Annals of the New York Academy of Sciences, 612*, 451–461.

Tsiantis, J., Dragonas, T., Richardson, C., & Anastopoulos, D. (1996). Psychosocial problems and adjustment of children with beta-thalassemia and their families. *European Child and Adolescent Psychiatry, 5*, 193–203.

CYNTHIA A. RICCIO
Texas A&M University

THALIDOMIDE

Thalidomide was among the first drugs for which teratogenicity was established. A teratogen is a chemical agent that can cross the placenta and cause congenital malformations. Effective as a sedative and a tranquilizer, thalidomide is an example of a teratogen that had positive effects on the mother but devastating consequences for the embryo. Even after decades of study, the mechanism by which thalidomide causes deformities is not understood (T. J., 1999).

Teratogenicity became suspected with the birth of a relatively large number of babies with phocomelia (seal-flipper limbs) and a variety of other deformities in Europe in the late 1950s and early 1960s. Phocomelia is a condition in which arms and/or legs are drastically shortened or absent and fingers/toes extend from the foreshortened limbs or the trunk. Thalidomide was widely distributed in Europe, where it is estimated to have affected more than 7,000 individuals. It was withdrawn from the market in late 1961 before it passed Food and Drug Administration approval in the United States (Moore, 1982). Teratogenicity was unusually high; more than 90% of women who took thalidomide during a particular period in pregnancy had infants with some type of defect (Holmes, 1983).

Thalidomide is the only drug whose timing of harmful effects has been well established, causing defects only if taken by the mother when the embryo was 34 to 50 days old; earlier or later consumption had no adverse effects (Holmes, 1983). Individual defects can be traced to particular days when the mother took the drug. The specificity of the embryo's age for thalidomide effects provides a particularly dramatic example for a critical period.

The particular complex of effects is sometimes termed the thalidomide syndrome (Landau, 1986). Phocomelia is the most common and pronounced sign, but absent or deformed ears and digits are common, and malformations of forehead, heart, and digestive system occasionally occur. Generally, overall intelligence is unaffected, but some language deficits have been reported (Holmes, 1983; Landau, 1986; Moore, 1982). Because thalidomide has teratogenic but not mutagenic qualities, thalidomide-syndrome individuals would be expected to have normal children.

Despite the horrific consequences of prenatal exposure to thalidomide, research on its potential benefits began again shortly after it was withdrawn from the market. In 1964, thalidomide was given to a patient with leprosy because of evidence of the drug's antiinflammatory benefits; within days the patient's symptoms subsided and stayed reduced with continued use of thalidomide (Blakeslee, 1998). It has received FDA approval for use in treatment of leprosy and may be of benefit in treatment of a number of other diseases, including brain and other forms of cancer, inflammatory disease, and autoimmune disorders. Thalidomide is now being used experimentally with AIDS and appears to relieve symptoms such as oral ulcers and severe weight loss. Some research suggests that thalidomide may inhibit HIV replication (Blaney, 1995). Thalidomide has been said to be nontoxic among those taking the drug; researchers have yet to find a lethal dose (Blakeslee, 1998).

However beneficial, thalidomide remains a major human teratogen and therefore its use must be carefully monitored to avoid any recurrence of the severe malformations seen in children whose mothers were some of thalidomide's first users.

REFERENCES

Blakeslee, D. (1998). Thalidomide. *Journal of the American Medical Association* [HIV/AIDS Information Center]. Retrieved from http://www.ama-assn.org/ama

Blaney, C. (1995). Second thoughts about thalidomide. *Medical Sciences Bulletin*. Retrieved from http://www.pharminfo.net/

Holmes, L. B. (1983). Congenital malformations. In R. E. Behrman & V. C. Vaughn (Eds.), *Nelson textbook of pediatrics* (12th ed.). Philadelphia, PA: Saunders.

Landau, S. I. (1986). *International dictionary of medicine and biology*. New York, NY: Wiley.

Moore, K. L. (1982). *The developing human* (3rd ed.). Philadelphia, PA: Saunders.

Travis, J. (1999, February 20). Modus operandi of an infamous drug.. *Science News, 155*(8), 124–126.

ROBERT T. BROWN
AIMEE R. HUNTER
University of North Carolina at Wilmington

See also **Early Experience and Critical Periods; Etiology**

THEIR WORLD

Their World is a former publication of the Foundation for Children with Learning Disabilities (FLCD), now the National Center for Learning Disabilities (NCLD). The FCLD was founded in 1977 and began publication of *Their World* in 1979. The publication was presented each year at FCLD's annual benefit in New York City. *Their World* was a public awareness vehicle, intended to educate the public about learning disabilities generally while emphasizing the accomplishments of individuals with learning disabilities. *Their World* published real-life stories about the way families cope with children with learning disabilities. *Their World* supported after school, summer, athletic, and creativity programs as a support network for individuals with learning disabilities and their families. The publication was distributed to over 75,000 parents, educators, legislators, and professionals each year.

CECIL R. REYNOLDS
Texas A&M University

See *also* Foundation for Children With Learning Disabilities

THEMATIC APPERCEPTION TEST

The Thematic Apperception Test (TAT) is a projective assessment instrument developed by Henry Murray (1938) as a means of investigating his theory of personality. Designed for use with subjects ages 7 and older, TAT has become one of the most widely used assessment techniques. The test materials consist of 31 black and white pictures depicting characters in various settings. Each picture is designed to elicit particular themes or conflicts. Subsets of pictures (typically 8 to 10) are selected for administration depending on the individual's age and sex and the nature of the presenting problem. Subjects are asked to tell a story about each picture as it is presented. Typical instructions stress that subjects use their imagination and include in their response a description of what the characters in the scene are doing, thinking, and feeling, the preceding events, and the outcome. Responses are recorded verbatim by the examiner. An inquiry is usually conducted after all pictures have been presented.

The TAT has also been presented in group form; this requires the subject to provide written responses. Murray and others (Groth-Marnat, 1984) have devised scoring systems for TAT; however, in clinical practice, such systems are rarely used (Klopfer & Taulbee, 1976). Variations on the TAT include the Children's Apperception Test and the Senior Apperception Test (Bellack, 1975), which include stimulus materials believed to be more relevant to children and the elderly, respectively.

REFERENCES

Bellack, L. (1975). *The TAT, CAT and SAT in clinical use* (3rd ed.). New York, NY: Grune & Stratton.

Groth-Marnat, G. (1984). *Handbook of psychological assessment.* New York, NY: Van Nostrand Reinhold.

Klopfer, W. G., & Taulbee, E. S. (1976). Projective tests. In M. R. Rosenzweig & L. W. Porter (Eds.), *Annual review of psychology, 17,* 543–567.

Murray, H. A. (1938). *Explorations in personality.* New York, NY: Oxford University Press.

ROBERT G. BRUBAKER
Eastern Kentucky University

See *also* Emotional Disorders; Personality Assessment

THEORY OF ACTIVITY

The theory of activity is a general theoretical paradigm for psychological and developmental research that has its historical roots in work carried out in the Soviet Union between 1925 and 1945 by L. S. Vygotsky, A. R. Luria, A. N. Leontiev, and their colleagues (Leontiev, 1978, 1981; Minick, 1985; Wertsch, 1981, 1985). Activity theory is among the most important intellectual forces in contemporary Soviet psychology, providing a unifying conceptual framework for a wide range of psychological theory, research, and practice. As a consequence of linguistic, political, and conceptual barriers, however, it was only in the late 1970s that psychologists and social scientists in Western Europe and the United States began to become aware of activity theory.

The theory of activity is the product of an effort by Vygotsky's students and colleagues to extend the theoretical framework Vygotsky had developed between 1925 and his death in 1934. Vygotsky had been concerned with two fundamental limitations in the psychological theories of his time. First, he felt that many psychologists had underestimated or misrepresented the influence of social and cultural factors on human psychological development. He was particularly concerned with the failure to clarify the mechanisms of this influence. Second, Vygotsky felt that the disputes between the traditional psychology of mind and the behaviorist theories that were emerging in the 1920s reflected a widespread tendency in psychology and philosophy to represent mind and behavior in conceptual isolation from one another rather than as connected aspects of an integral whole (Davydov & Radzikhovskii,

1985; Minick, 1987). Vygotsky's work and the subsequent emergence of activity theory were attempts to develop a theoretical paradigm that would overcome these limitations in existing theory.

A central premise of the theory of activity is that human psychological development is dependent on a process in which the individual is drawn into the historically developed systems of social action that constitute both society and the life of the mature adult. Within this framework, psychological development or change is dependent on the individual's progressively more complete participation in social life. Modes of organizing and mediating cognitive activity are mastered and the relationship to the external world of objects and people is defined in this process.

Three additional characteristics of activity theory are also extremely important to any effort to understand it. First, the concepts, constructs, and laws that provide the basic content of psychological theory developed within this framework and that determine how psychological characteristics and their development are conceptualized are represented and defined in such a way that a connection is consistently maintained between psychological characteristics and the organization of social action (Minick, 1985). For example, Leontiev (1978) defines personality as a system of hierarchically related goals and motives that derives its structure from (1) the objective relationships among the actions that constitute the social system; (2) the objective relationships among the actions that constitute the life of the individual; and (3) the subjective relationships among these actions that are defined by the individual's values and beliefs. With this approach to the definition of scientific constructs in psychology, it becomes impossible to conceptualize the psychological characteristics of the individual or the laws of psychological functioning and development apart from the organization of concrete social systems and the individual's place in them (Minick, 1985). This can be contrasted with theoretical frameworks in which key constructs are defined in ways that conceptually isolate the psychological (e.g., reversible operations, traits, or associative networks) and the social (e.g., social roles, social norms, social organization).

Second, the goal-oriented action serves as the central analytic object in activity theory (Davydov & Radzikhovskii, 1985; Leontiev, 1978; Zinchenko, 1985). To analyze psychological characteristics and psychological processes in connection with socially organized action systems, one has to identify an appropriate analytic unit for the development of theory and research. As a basic unit both of the psychological life of the individual and of the organization of society, the goal-oriented action has assumed this role in activity theory.

Third, the theory of activity is based on a schema that emphasizes the importance of considering three levels of analysis in studying the goal-oriented action and the psychological processes that function and develop in connection with it (Leontiev, 1978). At the level of activities,

general yet socially and culturally defined motives are considered. For example, there are important differences in the organization of actions and goals in western systems of formal schooling and in more traditional apprenticeship systems. In formal schooling, education and learning are the motives that provide the general organizing framework for concrete goal-oriented actions. In apprenticeship, these motives are subordinated to the economic motives connected with the production of products for use or sale. At the level of operations, the impact of the object world on the way an action is carried out is considered. Under different conditions, a single set of motives may lead to the emergence of different concrete goals or to different ways of performing actions in order to realize those goals. This system of analytic levels (i.e., activity-motive, action-goal, and operation-condition) has provided activity theory with a useful framework for analyzing psychological functioning and development without losing sight of its connections with the physical and social environment in which it occurs.

As a general perspective on psychology and psychological development, the theory of activity has had an important impact on theory and practice in the broad domain of special education in the Soviet Union. While a detailed discussion of the nature of this impact is impossible in this context, a useful illustration is available in the English translation of a volume by Alexander Meshcheryakov in which he reviews his work with children with hearing and vision impairments (Meshcheryakov, 1979).

REFERENCES

Davydov, V. V., & Radzikhovskii, L. A. (1985). Vygotsky's theory and the activity-oriented approach in psychology. In J. V. Wertsch (Ed.), *Culture, communication, and cognition: Vygotskian perspectives* (pp. 35–65). New York, NY: Cambridge University Press.

Leontiev, A. N. (1978). *Activity, consciousness, and personality.* Englewood Cliffs, NJ: Prentice Hall.

Leontiev, A. N. (1981). *Problems of the development of mind.* Moscow, Russia: Progress.

Meshcheryakov, A. N. (1979). *Awakening to life: Forming behavior and the mind in deaf-blind children.* Moscow, Russia: Progress.

Minick, N. (1985). *L. S. Vygotsky and Soviety activity theory: New perspectives on the relationship between mind and society.* Unpublished doctoral dissertation, Northwestern University, Evanston, IL.

Minick, N. (1987). The development of Vygotsky's thought. Introduction to L. S. Vygotsky, Collected works: *Problems of general psychology* (Vol. 1). New York, NY: Plenum Press.

Vygotsky, L. S. (1987). Thinking and speech. In V. V. Davydov (Ed.), L. S. Vygotsky, *Collected works: General Psychology Vol. 1* (N. Minick, Trans.). New York, NY: Springer.

Wertsch, J. V. (Ed.). (1981). *The concept of activity in Soviet psychology.* New York, NY: Sharpe.

Wertsch, J. V. (1985). *Vygotsky and the social formation of mind.* Cambridge, MA: Harvard University Press.

Zinchenko, V. P. (1985). Vygotsky's ideas about units for the analysis of mind. In J. V. Wertsch (Ed.), *Culture, communication, and cognition: Vygotskian perspectives* (pp. 94–118). New York, NY: Cambridge University Press.

NORRIS MINICK
*Center for Psychosocial Studies,
The Spencer Foundation*

See also Vygotsky, Lev S.; Zone of Proximal Development

THERAPEUTIC COMMUNITY

The therapeutic community as a model for psychosocial rehabilitation was developed following World War II by Maxwell Jones, a psychiatrist, in Great Britain. This approach developed out of Jones's experience in working with soldiers on a psychiatric unit who had suffered emotional trauma and with persons with personality problems. Jones's approach was a reaction to the traditional psychiatric hospital practice that produced dependent patients who needed resocialization in addition to treatment of their illness if they were to be discharged. He believed the hospital could be purposefully employed as a significant therapeutic milieu by facilitating full social participation by the patients (Main, 1946). Providing appropriately organized social environments, rather than just psychotherapeutic or medical approaches, was the method of effecting change in patients. Jones's work was significant for the development of social psychiatry, in which emphasis is placed on the environmental sources of stress that cause persons to learn maladaptive ways of coping rather than on illness or deviancy, the traditional psychiatric emphases.

Jones initially presented the principles and practices of the therapeutic community in *Social Psychiatry: A Study of Therapeutic Communities* (1952), but the book was limited in detail. A clearer explication of the underlying themes that guided and shaped the social interactions in the therapeutic community was provided by R. N. Rapoport, an anthropologist, in *Community as Doctor* (1960). Themes identified by Rapoport were those of (1) democratization—an equal sharing among community members of the power in decision making about community affairs; (2) permissiveness—the toleration of a wide degree of behavior from members of the community; (3) communalism—the free exchange of information and observations among all members of the community, including patients and staff; and (4) reality confrontation—the continuous presentation to the patients of interpretations of their behavior from the perspective of other members of the therapeutic community.

The principal social methods used in the therapeutic community were the discussion of events that occurred within the context of frequent community group meetings by all community members; the facilitation of exchange of information among members of the community; the development of relationships between staff and clients that emphasized their status as peers in learning through interacting with each other; the provision of frequent situations in which patients could learn more adaptive ways to cope with problematic situations by interacting with community members; and the continued examination by community members, especially staff members, of their roles to find more effective ways of functioning.

The ideology of the therapeutic community was never completely operationalized, and some found it extremely difficult to implement (Manning, 1975). Rapoport (1960) offered reasons for the difficulty in implementing Jones's ideology and explanations of why later therapeutic movements used many but not all of the principles. First, there were limits set by the local community on the extremes in democracy or permissiveness that would be tolerated; second, communalism encouraged communication in groups rather than between individuals; third, conflicts arose between ideological themes such as when excessively dominant behavior is permissively tolerated but might be anti-democratic; and fourth, there was an unresolved conflict between the rehabilitation goals that required the hospital to approximate the conditions of life outside the hospital and the treatment goals that required different conditions for the recovery of the patient than those in which the problems developed. About the same time that development of therapeutic communities was taking place, psychotropic medications were introduced into psychiatric practice. This resulted in the obscuring of the effects of the therapeutic community as psychotropic medications were often used with persons who were also in therapeutic communities. In addition, no satisfactory study of the efficacy of the therapeutic community as a treatment approach was ever conducted, though it had wide support among mental health clinicians.

The therapeutic community as developed by Jones declined from the period of the late 1950s (Manning, 1975). Other therapeutic community movements have developed that serve persons with drug, alcohol, and social adjustment problems, and persons in correctional settings. These movements have developed some distinctive characteristics in their approach to treatment but have been greatly influenced by the work of Jones.

REFERENCES

Jones, M. (1952). *Social psychiatry: A study of therapeutic communities.* London, England: Tavistock.

Main, T. F. (1946). The hospital as a therapeutic institution. *Bulletin of the Menniger Clinic, 10,* 66–70.

Manning, N. (1975). What happened to the therapeutic community. In K. Jones & S. Baldwin (Eds.), *The yearbook of social policy in Britain.* London, England: Routledge & Kegan Paul.

Rapoport, R. N. (1960). *Community as doctor.* London, England: Tavistock.

HAROLD HANSON
PAUL BATES
Southern Illinois University

See also **Community Residential Programs; Psychoneurotic Disorders; Social Behavior of Individuals With Disabilities**

THERAPEUTIC RECREATION (See Recreation, Therapeutic)

THINK ALOUD

Think Aloud is a cognitive behavior modification program designed to improve social and cognitive problem-solving skills in young children. Based on the pioneering work of Meichenbaum, Goodman, Shure, and Spevak, and tied to theory regarding development of self-control, Think Aloud was conceived as a training program to decrease impulsivity, encourage consideration of alternatives, and plan courses of action. It emphasizes the use of cognitive modeling as a teaching tool in which teachers model their own strategies for thinking through problems. Students are then encouraged to "think out loud" while systematically approaching each problem through asking and answering four basic questions: What is my problem? How can I solve it? Am I following my plan? How did I do?

The original small group (two to four students) program (Camp & Bash, 1985) was tested on 6- to 8-year-old boys identified as hyperaggressive by teachers. In the hands of trained teachers, improvement in cognitive impulsivity was demonstrated across several trials, as was improvement in prosocial classroom behavior. Although significant decreases in aggressive behavior were also observed, this was not significantly more than observed in attention-control groups. A refresher course 6 to 12 months after the original program supported previously developed skills and led to significant decreases in hyperactivity and increases in friendliness.

With some demonstrated success in altering thinking and behavior patterns in aggressive boys in the small group situation, the authors reasoned that a more "dilute" program such as found in a large classroom should benefit a broader range of children with mild to moderate deficits in social and cognitive problem skills. In addition, availability of a classroom version of the program would help regular classroom teachers to support skills learned in the small group program. Consequently, they began in 1976 to build Think Aloud Classroom Programs spanning grades 1 to 6 (Bash & Camp, 1985a, 1985b; Camp & Bash, 1985).

Development and study of these programs was supported in part by ESEA Title IV grants to the Denver public schools. Few of the classroom program studies could be conducted with random assignment to experimental or traditional teaching programs. However, within limitations imposed by a nonequivalent control group design, children in the Think Aloud classrooms improved on measures of both social and cognitive problem-solving skills more than children in nonprogram classrooms at all grade levels. Cognitive differences between children in the Think Aloud classroom programs and comparison children were most reliable for the program for grades 1 and 2 and the program for grades 5 and 6. Differences in social problem-solving skills were reliable at all grade levels. The classroom programs can easily be adapted for use in an individual or tutorial program to intensify and individualize the experience. The materials now provide challenge to children over a broad range of developmental levels, making them suitable for special education classrooms as well as regular classrooms, for some middle school children, and for children with special needs for social skills training or assistance in curbing impulsivity.

REFERENCES

Bash, M. A. S., & Camp, B. W. (1985a). *The think aloud classroom program for grades 3 and 4.* Champaign, IL: Research.

Bash, M. A. S., & Camp, B. W. (1985b). *The think aloud classroom program for grades 5 and 6.* Champaign, IL: Research.

Camp, B. W., & Bash, M. A. S. (1985). *The think aloud classroom program for grades 1 and 2.* Champaign, IL: Research.

STAFF

See also **Camp, Bonnie; Impulse Control**

THINKING CENTERS (See Creative Studies Program)

THORAZINE

Thorazine is the trade name for the generic antipsychotic agent chlorpromazine. Though Thorazine was among the first synthesized drugs that were found effective in the control of behavioral symptoms associated with psychotic disorders, it is no longer as widely prescribed as it was 30 years ago. However, Thorazine is still used as a benchmark against which new antipsychotic agents are compared in terms of frequency of side effects and efficacy. Thorazine is of the drug class phenothiazine and tends to produce the classic panorama of side effects associated with the phenothiazine group.

In addition to use as a major tranquilizer with psychotic individuals, Thorazine also is used in emergency situations to limit the effects of LSD and to control prolonged behavioral reactions after intoxication with other hallucinogens. One of the major criticisms of Thorazine as a therapeutic agent has been its reported abuse as a chemical restraint (Leavitt, 1982).

In use with children, several cautions must be considered: children are more likely to show side effects; dose-related attentional problems can develop and thus create interference in learning (Seiden & Dykstra, 1977); and seizures may be potentiated in children with a preexisting seizure disorder (Bassuk & Schoonover, 1977).

REFERENCES

Bassuk, E. L., & Schoonover, S. C. (1977). *The practitioner's guide to psychoactive drugs*. New York, NY: Plenum Medical.

Leavitt, F. (1982). *Drugs and behavior*. New York, NY: Wiley.

Seiden, L. S., & Dykstra, L. A. (1977). *Psychopharmacology: A biochemical and behavioral approach*. New York, NY: Van Nostrand Reinhold.

ROBERT F. SAWICKI
Lake Erie Institute of Rehabilitation

THORNDIKE, EDWARD L. (1847–1949)

E. L. Thorndike was an early theorist and writer who applied psychology to education. He was educated at Wesleyan, Harvard, and Columbia universities, with most of his professional career spent at Teachers' College, Columbia University. He is best known for his contributions to learning theory (Thorndike, 1905, 1931, 1932, 1935, 1949) and intellectual assessment (Thorndike, 1901, 1926, 1941).

Thorndike's major contribution to learning theory, termed the Law of Effect, is well known as a basic behavioral principle. The Law of Effect states: "any act which in a given situation produces satisfaction becomes associated with that situation, so that when the situation occurs, the act is more likely to recur also" (Thorndike, 1905, p. 203). His theory of connectionism was cognitively oriented and viewed both physical and mental acts as involving the establishment of neural pathways.

Learning was viewed as taking place when pathways were established through repetition.

Thorndike's measurement interests were diverse, as reflected by his famous dictum, "If anything exists, it exists in some amount. If it exists in some amount, it can be measured" (Thorndike, 1926, p. 38). His multifactored approach to measurement viewed intelligence as comprising abstract, mechanical, and social abilities. Intellectual assessment to Thorndike also involved the dimensions of attitude, breadth, and speed (i.e., level of difficulty, number of tasks, and rate of completion, respectively). This multifactored approach was in contrast to the approach of others of his time, who viewed intelligence as a general or unitary factor. Thorndike developed many tests, especially college entrance and achievement tests.

REFERENCES

Thorndike, E. L. (1901). *Notes on child study*. New York, NY: Macmillan.

Thorndike, E. L. (1905). *The elements of psychology*. New York, NY: Seiler.

Thorndike, E. L. (1926). *The measurement of intelligence*. New York, NY: Teacher's College, Columbia University.

Thorndike, E. L. (1931). *Human learning*. New York, NY: Century.

Thorndike, E. L. (1932). *Fundamentals of learning*. New York, NY: Columbia University.

Thorndike, E. L. (1935). *The psychology of wants, interests and attitudes*. New York, NY: Appleton-Century.

Thorndike, E. L. (1941). Mental abilities. *American Philosophical Society, 84,* 503–513.

Thorndike, E. L. (1949). *Selected writings from a connectionist's psychology*. New York, NY: Appleton-Century-Crofts.

JOSEPH D. PERRY
Kent State University

See also **Measurement**

THOUGHT DISORDERS

In the diagnosis of a psychiatric illness, it is common to evaluate disturbances in the following areas: consciousness, emotion, motor behavior, perception, memory, intelligence, and thinking (Ginsberg, 1985). Disorders in thinking, although most commonly associated with schizophrenia, may also occur in paranoid disorders, affective disorders, organic mental disorders, or organic delusional syndromes such as those owed to amphetamine or phencyclide abuse (*Diagnostic and Statistical Manual of Mental Disorders*, fourth edition [*DSM-IV*]; American

Psychiatric Association, 1994). Schizophrenic patients, however, tend to show more severe and specific forms of thought disorders and may continue to show some degree of idiosyncratic thinking when not in the acute phase of the disease (Ginsberg, 1985). According to *DSM-IV* (1994), at some point, schizophrenia always involves delusions, hallucinations, or certain disturbances in the form of thought most often expressed by the patient in disorganized speech. A thought disorder is but one of the criteria needed for a diagnosis of schizophrenia; the illness is also characterized by disorganization in perceptions, communication, emotions, and motor activity. The term thought disorder encompasses a large array of dysfunctions, including disturbances in the form of thought, structure of associations, progression of thought, and content of thought.

Disturbances in Form of Thought

Thinking in a healthy individual occurs in a rational, orderly way. A thought might be stimulated by unconscious or conscious impulses, affective cues, or biological drives, yet the thinking process itself is directed by reason and results in a reality-oriented conclusion. As characterized by Ginsberg (1985), disturbances in the form of thought result in sequences that are no longer logical. In formal thought disorders, thinking is characterized by loosened associations, neologisms, and illogical constructs. In illogical thinking, thinking contains erroneous conclusions or internal contradictions. In dereism, there is mental activity not concordant with logic or experience. In autistic thinking, thinking gratifies unfilled desires but has no regard for reality (p. 500).

Disturbances in Structure and Progression of Associations

In *DSM-IV*, these disturbances are included under the Form of Thought category. However, as described by both Ginsberg (1985) and Kolb (1968), a division of this category is warranted. In a healthy individual, each separate idea is logically linked with ideas both preceding and following that idea. This progression occurs in a coherent fashion and at a relatively steady, moderate rate of speech. In severe cases of disorder, however, speech becomes so disjointed as to be incomprehensible. It then includes:

1. *Flight of ideas*—An extremely rapid progression of ideas with a shifting from one topic to another so that a coherent whole is not maintained and considerable digression occurs from the beginning to the ending of the story. There is generally some association between thoughts (e.g., a single word in one sentence will lead to a following sentence). Flight of ideas is associated with a lack of goal-directed activity and with heightened distractibility and an accelerated inner drive. A patient might

respond to the question, "What is your name?" with, "My name is David. David was in the *Bible*, which is a religious document written many years ago. I feel that religion leads to persecution for many important citizens as a result of their beliefs which have been well thought out; however, thought is a very abstract concept as might be noted of music and art."

2. *Clang associations*—Similar to flight of ideas. With clang associations, the stimulus that prompts a new thought is a word similar in sound, but not in meaning, to a new word.

3. *Retardation*—Speech becomes slow and labored; often a lowered tone of voice is used. The patient may relate that his or her thoughts come slowly or that it is very difficult to concentrate or think about a topic.

4. *Blocking*—An unconscious interruption in the train of thought to such an extent that progression of thought comes to a complete halt. This is usually temporary, with thought processes resuming after a short time.

5. *Pressure of speech*—An excessive flow of words to such an extent that it becomes difficult to interrupt the speaker.

6. *Preseveration*—An occurrence in which the patient uses the same word, thought, or idea repeatedly, often in response to several different questions. One patient, when being diagnosed with the Rorschach Inkblot Test, responded to all 10 separate cards, "That looks like a man's genitals. Why are you showing me all these pictures of the same thing?"

7. *Circumstantiality*—The patient is eventually able to relate a given thought or story, but only after numerous digressions and unnecessary trivial details. This occurs largely in persons who are not able to distinguish essential from nonessential details. It is often observed in persons of low intelligence, in epileptics, and in cases of advanced senile mental disorder.

8. *Neologism*—When entirely new words are created by the patient.

9. *Word salad*—An incoherent mixture of words and phrases.

10. *Incoherence*—Similar to word salad, the difference being that incoherence is generally marked by illogically connected phrases or ideas. Word salad generally consists of illogically connected single words or short phrases. A patient speaking incoherently may state, "Yes, this is the great reason for truth and validity as you must know and we all must know in times of need all great men who have an interest in greatness, perhaps, yes, cold is a very nice color, but, not inconsequentially as we

have every reason to believe that our President is for better or worse, no, yesterday."

11. *Irrelevant answer*—An answer that has no direct relevance to the question asked.

12. *Derailment*—Gradual or sudden deviation in one's train of thought without blocking.

Disturbances in Content of Thought

The most common disturbance in the content of thought involves a delusion, which is an idea or system of beliefs that is irrational, illogical, and with little or no basis in fact. In normal, healthy individuals, fantasy, daydreaming, rationalization, or projection can be used as effective ways to handle stress. Delusions appear to be an exaggerated form of this type of thinking. Delusions, however, are indicative of severe psychopathology in that they are patently absurd, and patients cannot be argued out of their beliefs despite overwhelming evidence refuting the delusions. There are several different types of delusions, based on the specific thought content:

1. *Delusions of grandeur*—Belief that an individual is special, important, or in some way superior to others. In many instances the patient may actually believe that he or she is someone else (e.g., God).

2. *Delusions of reference*—Belief that innocent remarks or actions of someone else are directed exclusively at the patient. One hospitalized patient explained that whenever carrots were served at dinner, it meant that she was to take two baths that night; whenever ham was served, it meant that she was to avoid speaking to anyone until the following day.

3. *Delusions of persecution*—The belief that others are spying on, plotting against, or in some way planning to harm the patient.

4. *Delusions of being controlled*—The belief that one's thoughts and actions are imposed by someone else. Similar to this are thought broadcasting (the belief that one's ideas are broadcast to others); thought insertion (the belief that ideas are being inserted into one's head); and thought withdrawal (the belief that ideas are being removed from one's head).

Other less common delusions include self-accusation, sin, guilt, somatic illness, nihilism, religiosity, infidelity, and poverty (*DSM-IV*, 1994; Ginsberg, 1985; Kolb, 1968; MacKinnon & Michels, 1971).

Several theories have been advanced to account for the existence of thought disorders. The more psychogenic of these theories point to inadequate ego functioning, such that the patients create their own reality to cope with overwhelming stress and anxiety. Biological theories view thought disorders as being genetically transmitted.

Research in this area has focused on chemical neurotransmitters such as dopamine; it found differing levels of such chemicals in disturbed and healthy individuals. The effectiveness of drug therapy in treating thought disorders lends credence to biological theories. Other theories such as learning, cognitive, and family approaches are more environmentally based, and hold that persons with thought disorders may learn maladaptive ways of thinking or acting in response to live circumstances or unhealthy family situations (Worchel & Shebilske, 1983).

REFERENCES

American Psychiatric Association. (1994). *Diagnostic and statistical manual of mental disorders* (4th ed.). Washington, DC: Author.

Ginsberg, G. (1985). The psychiatric interview. In H. Kaplan & B. Sadock (Eds.), *Comprehensive textbook of psychiatry/IV* (Vol. 1, pp. 500–501). Baltimore, MD: Williams & Wilkins.

Kolb, L. (1968). *Noye's modern clinical psychiatry* (7th ed.). Philadelphia, PA: Saunders.

MacKinnon, R., & Michels, R. (1971). *The psychiatric interview*. Philadelphia, PA: Saunders.

Worchel, S., & Shebilske, W. (1983). *Psychology: Principles and applications*. Englewood Cliffs, NJ: Prentice Hall.

FRANCES F. WORCHEL
Texas A&M University

See also Diagnostic and Statistical Manual of Mental Disorders (DSM IV); Emotional Disorders

THREE-TIER MODEL

The three-tier model is a layered instructional based on primary, secondary, and tertiary intervention principles (Good, Kame'enui, Simmons, & Chard, 2002). As an approach to academic goal attainment (i.e., learning to read), the three-tier model applies these levels of intensity to classrooms and student performance in targeted academic skills (Vaughn, 2002; Vaughn, Linan-Thompson, & Hickman, 2003). The primary level, or Tier 1, is comprised of the core instructional program that is provided to all students with the assumption that this program addresses key components of academic skills. For example, in reading, it would be expected that the core instructional program would address phonemic awareness, phonics, fluency, vocabulary, and comprehension. At key points in the instructional process, data-based decision making or assessment occurs. This involves collection of data on all students with results of the assessment used to identify those students who evidence gaps in instructional areas and need to move into Tier 2. Tier 2 involves the provision of secondary or supplementary instruction to address the deficits of students identified with the large-scale assessment, as well as follow-up and monitoring. Tier 2 may include problem-solving teams (comparable to prereferral teams) with the teams providing ongoing support and consultative services to the classroom teacher (e.g., Kovaleski, 2003) or it may involve small group instruction or tutoring (Texas Reading Organization, n.d.). As students are able to meet benchmark criteria, they are discontinued from the supplemental program and return to Tier 1. Those students who still do not reach appropriate benchmarks as a result of interventions at Tier 2 move into Tier 3 for more intensive and individualized assessment and intervention, possibly through special education (Berninger, 2002; Texas Reading Organization, n.d.). The movement through the three tiers is intended to be dynamic with students moving from Tier to Tier as they do or do not meet established benchmarks (Vaughn, 2002; Vaughn & Fuchs, 2003).

With increased emphasis on group application and delivery of instruction (as opposed to an individualized, special education delivery model), implementation of the three-tier model requires significant changes in service delivery at a systems level (Denton & Fletcher, 2003; Shapiro, 2000). Most of the recent research on the three-tier model has been with reading instruction in the primary grades (e.g., Berninger, 2002; Vaughn et al., 2003). Additional research to determine which instructional programs at Tier 1 and Tier 2 are empirically supported or evidence based not only in reading, but in other academic areas is needed. Some work has been done in math (e.g., Fuchs et al., 2005) and in written expression (Berninger, 2002). Further, the research needs to expand beyond primary grades; the change in developmental level of the child and conceptual level of what is required, as well as the changes in contextual demands as students progress from elementary to middle school to high school, require replication of evidence-based instruction at varying levels for differing instructional goals. Finally, research to demonstrate the generalizability of evidence-based instruction across culturally and linguistically diverse groups is needed (e.g., Vaughn, Mathes, Linan-Thompson, & Francis, 2005).

REFERENCES

Berninger, V. (2002). Best practices in reading, writing, and math assessment intervention links: a systems approach for schools, classrooms, and individuals. In A. Thomas & J. Grimes (Eds.), *Best practices in school psychology IV* (pp. 851–865). Bethesda, MD: National Association of School Psychologists.

Denton, C., & Fletcher, J. (2003). Scaling reading interventions. In B. Foorman (Ed.), *Preventing and remediating reading difficulties: Bringing science to scale* (pp. 445–463). Baltimore, MD: York.

Fuchs, L. S., Compton, D. L., Fuchs, D., Paulsen, K., Bryant, J. D., & Hamlett, C. L. (2005). The prevention, identification, and cognitive determinants of math difficulty. *Journal of Educational Psychology, 97,* 493–513.

Good, R. H., Kame'enui, E. J., Simmons, D. S., & Chard, D. J. (2002). *Focus and nature of primary, secondary, and tertiary prevention: The CIRCUITS model* (Tech. Rep. No. 1). Eugene: University of Oregon, College of Education, Institute for the Development of Educational Achievement.

Kovaleski, J. F. (2003, December). *Secondary interventions in a three tier model: Program features and system issues.* Paper presented at the National Research Center on Learning Disabilities Responsiveness-to-Intervention Symposium, Kansas City, MO.

Shapiro, E. (2000). School psychology from an instructional perspective: Solving big, not little problems. *School Psychology Review, 29,* 560–572.

Texas Reading Organization. (n.d.). *Levels of intervention.* Retrieved from www.texasreading.org/otala

Vaughn, S. (2002). *A 3-tier model for preventing / reducing reading disabilities.* Retrieved from http://utsystem.edu/

Vaughn, S. R., & Fuchs, L. S. (2003). Redefining learning disabilities as inadequate response to instruction: The promise and potential problems. *Learning Disabilities Research & Practice 18,* 137–146.

Vaughn, S., Linan-Thompson, S., & Hickman, P. (2003). Response to instruction as a means of identifying students with reading/learning disabilities. *Exceptional Children, 69,* 391–409.

Vaughn, S., Mathes, P. G., Linan-Thompson, S., & Francis, D. J. (2005). Teaching English language learners at risk for reading disabilities to read: Putting research into practice. *Learning Disabilities Research & Practice, 20,* 58–67.

CYNTHIA A. RICCIO
Texas A&M University

See also Empirically Supported Treatment; Learning Disabilities; Learning Disabilities, Problems in Definition of

TICS

Tics are recurrent, rapid, abrupt movements and vocalizations that represent the contraction of small muscle groups in one or more parts of the body. Motor tics may include eye blinking, shoulder shrugging, neck twisting, head shaking, or arm jerking. Vocal tics frequently take the form of grunting, throat clearing, sniffing, snorting, or squealing. These abnormal movements and sounds occur from once every few seconds to several times a day, with varying degrees of intensity. Although tics are involuntary, they often can be controlled briefly. However, temporary suppression results in a feeling of tension that can be relieved only when the tics are allowed to appear. Tics increase with anxiety and stress and diminish with intense concentration (Shapiro & Shapiro, 1981). The prevalence for tic disorders is 1.6% or about 3.5% individuals in the United States. Boys are affected more frequently than girls (Baron, Shapiro, Shapiro, & Ranier, 1981).

The *Diagnostic and Statistical Manual of Mental Disorders*, fourth edition, delineates three major tic disorders that are based on age of onset, types of symptoms, and duration of the condition: transient tic disorder, chronic motor tic disorder, and Tourette syndrome (American Psychiatric Association, 1994). Familial studies suggest that these classifications may not represent distinct disorders but, rather, reflect a continuum of severity of the same disorder (Golden, 1981). The transient tic disorder or "habit spasm" is the mildest and most common of the disorders. Symptoms develop during childhood or adolescence and usually are observed in the face, head, or shoulders. Vocal tics are uncommon. Tic frequency, as well as intensity, generally fluctuates during the course of the disorder. Such childhood tics are transient and benign, disappearing after several months to 1 year.

Symptoms of the chronic motor tic disorder, which appear either in childhood or after the age of 40, are similar to those associated with the transient tic disorder. Vocalizations develop infrequently. When they are present, they tend to be grunts or other noises caused by contractions of the abdomen or diaphragm. The severity, intensity, and type of involuntary movement persist unchanged for years.

Tourette syndrome, the most severe condition, is differentiated from the other tic disorders by the presence of both motor and vocal tics and a pattern of symptoms that waxes and wanes as the tics slowly move from one part of the body to another. Complex movements such as jumping and dancing are often exhibited. Not always present, but confirmatory of Tourette syndrome, are echolalia (repetition of words or phrases spoken by others), palilalia (repetition of one's own words), coprolalia (involuntary swearing), echopraxia (imitation of the movement of others), and copropraxia (obscene gesturing). Although the nature and severity of these symptoms vary over time, the disorder rarely remits spontaneously and usually remains throughout life (Shapiro, Shapiro, Bruun, & Sweet, 1978).

REFERENCES

American Psychiatric Association. (1994). *Diagnostic and statistical manual of mental disorders* (4th ed.). Washington, DC: Author.

Baron, M., Shapiro, A. K., Shapiro, E. S., & Rainer, T. D. (1981). Genetic analysis of Tourette syndrome suggesting major gene effect. *American Journal of Human Genetics, 33*, 767–775.

Golden, G. S. (1981). Gilles de la Tourette's syndrome. *Texas Medicine, 77*, 6–7.

Shapiro, A. K., & Shapiro, E. S. (1981). The treatment and etiology of tics and Tourette syndrome. *Comprehensive Psychiatry, 22*, 193–205.

Shapiro, A. K., Shapiro, E. S., Bruun, R. D., & Sweet, R. D. (1978). *Gilles de la Tourette's syndrome*. New York, NY: Raven Press.

Marilyn P. Dornbush
Atlanta, Georgia

See also Echolalia; Echopraxia; Tourette Syndrome

TIME ON TASK

The amount of time that students spend on task has been an issue that concerns teachers in all fields, not just those involved with special education. Squires, Huitt, and Segars (1981) have identified three measures of student involvement that may be used to determine time on task. The first, allocated time, is simply the amount of time that is planned for instruction. Obviously, students will probably not be on task for the entire time that has been allocated. The second measure, which addresses this observation, is known as *engagement rate*. It is defined as the percent of allocated time that students actually attend to the tasks they are assigned. The third measure, engaged time, is the number of minutes per day students spend working on specific academic or related tasks; it is an integration of allocated time and engagement rate. Stallings and Kaskowitz (1974) found that, given certain maximum time limits based on a child's age and the subject matter at hand, engaged time is the most important variable that is related to student achievement. Given this finding, many researchers have focused on increasing time on task.

As an example, Bryant and Budd (1982) used self-instruction training with three young children who had difficulties in attending to task in kindergarten or preschool. The researchers trained the children to verbalize five separate types of self-instruction: (1) stop and look; (2) ask questions about the task; (3) find the answers to the questions posed in (2); (4) give instructions that provide guidance; and (5) give self-reinforcement for accomplished tasks. The results indicated an increase in on-task behavior for two of the children and, when used in combination with an unintrusive classroom intervention of reminders and stickers, all three of the children exhibited marked increases in their engaged time.

A somewhat different approach to the study of on-task behaviors was undertaken by Whalen, Henker, Collins, Finck, and Dotemoto (1979), who examined the effects of medication (Ritalin) on the on- and off-task behaviors of children identified as hyperactive. They found clear differences in a maladaptive direction in the behaviors of their subjects who had been diagnosed as hyperactive under placebo conditions when compared with peers who had no diagnoses of hyperactivity. However, while the authors acknowledged that the medication did result in more on-task and prosocial behaviors in many of their subjects, they cautioned against a wholesale reliance on medications since many long-term effects had not yet been studied. Rather, the researchers felt that careful study of all variables in individual situations (e.g., teacher tolerance, cost effectiveness, environmental adaptations) must be undertaken when making treatment decisions.

REFERENCES

Bryant, L. E., & Budd, K. S. (1982). Self-instruction training to increase independent work performance in preschoolers. *Journal of Applied Behavior Analysis, 15*, 259–271.

Squires, D., Huitt, W., & Segars, J. (1981). Improving classrooms and schools: What's important. *Educational Leadership, 39*, 174–179.

Stallings, J. A., & Kaskowitz, D. (1974). *Follow through classroom observation evaluation, 1972–1973*. Menlo Park, CA: Stanford Research Institute.

Whalen, C. K., Henker, B., Collins, B., Finck, D., & Dotemoto, S. (1979). A social ecology of hyperactive boys: Medication effects in structured classroom environments. *Journal of Applied Behavior Analysis, 12*, 65–81.

ANDREW R. BRULLE
Wheaton College

See also Attention-Deficit/Hyperactivity Disorder; Attention Span

TIME-OUT

Time-out has been used in public school settings since the 1970s and has both popular and scientific connotations. The popular use of this term generally refers to the removal of a student from a situation due to noncompliance, disruption, or other types of problem behavior (Maag, 1999). Time-out is also a specific behavioral strategy, grounded in applied behavior analysis, which is more correctly titled *time-out from positive reinforcement* (Alberto & Troutman, 2006). Cooper, Heron, and Heward (1987) define time-out as "the withdrawal of the opportunity to earn positive reinforcement or the loss of access to positive reinforcers for a specified period of time, contingent upon the occurrence of a behavior; the effect is to reduce the future probability of that behavior" (p. 440). This

definition describes a procedure that uses a technique called *extinction*. Extinction is broadly defined as withholding reinforcement. As noted, the intended effect of this procedure is to decrease a problem behavior. Therefore, time-out falls under the category of a punishment-oriented behavior reduction strategy. However, it is notable that specific aversives are not directly applied; only that positive reinforcement is removed for a designated period of time contingent on a problem behavior (Sulzer-Azaroff & Mayer, 1991). Educators and psychologists have several options if they choose to use time-out, including removing the reinforcement from the student or removing the student from access to the reinforcement (Zirpoli, 2005). Three time-out procedures that meet this criterion include (1) nonseclusionary time-out, (2) exclusionary time-out, and (3) seclusionary time-out.

Nonseclusionary time-out is a technique where the student's access to specific reinforcers (or all reinforcement) occurs for a specified period of time in the setting where the problem behavior was demonstrated. A benefit of this procedure is that the student can remain in the instructional or target setting instead of being removed due to the problem behavior. Examples of nonseclusionary time-out include (a) asking a student to put his or her head down on his or her desk; (b) removal of materials, teacher attention, or access to the teacher or other adults for a specified period of time; (c) removal from activities, including use of contingent observation where the student is allowed to watch the activity and observe more appropriate responses by peers, but is not allowed to participate; and (d) visual or facial screening for students with more severe problem behavior, such as stereotypy (Alberto & Troutman, 2006).

Exclusionary time-out is a technique where the student is physically removed from an activity or environment that she or he finds reinforcing for a specified period of time (Zirpoli, 2005). Examples of exclusionary time-out include placing a student in the hallway or in a designated time-out area and/or moving a student to a study carrel or corner of the classroom contingent upon a targeted problem behavior (Maag, 1999).

Seclusionary time-out is the most restrictive method employed and involves placing the student in a seclusion or time-out room for a specified period of time. Cooper et al. (1987) write that "a time-out room is any room outside the individual's normal educational or treatment environment that is devoid of positive reinforcers and in which the individual can be safely placed for a temporary period of time" (p. 445). Seclusionary time-out has been used for behaviors such as verbal and physical aggression and property destruction (Alberto & Troutman, 2006).

Zirpoli (2005) writes that time-out can be misused or applied inappropriately, thereby exposing the student to unintended effects or harm. A common misuse of this procedure is when an educator prolongs the time that the student is in time-out by exceeding the actual amount of time that is necessary to reduce the problem behavior. As a general guideline, time in seclusionary time-out should be calculated as one minute for each year of age, not to exceed 12 minutes total (Colorado Department of Education, 2000). Another common misapplication of this procedure occurs when educators fail to recognize that some students engage in problem behavior with the intent to be removed from an instructional activity that they perceive as aversive, thus putting the teacher in a position of inadvertently reinforcing escape-maintained problem behavior. Finally, removal of the student from instructional tasks may negatively affect current and future educational performance, thus underscoring the importance of using proactive and preventative instructional methods before resorting to the use of punishment-oriented strategies.

Educators that use time-out should always adhere to district, state, and national policies, including receiving training for the correct use of time-out procedures and keeping accurate records for each episode that requires a time-out (Maag, 1999). Moreover, every effort should be made to continually evaluate the effect of the time-out procedure on student behavior and to pair the program with reinforcing activities and verbal reinforcement when the student is meeting previously taught academic and behavioral expectations (Zirpoli, 2005). For students with chronic or persistent problem behavior a functional behavioral assessment should be conducted and a behavior intervention plan developed and implemented.

In conclusion, time-out from positive reinforcement is a behavior reduction technique that is used contingent upon an inappropriate behavior. Time-outs are organized under two categories—techniques that remove reinforcement from the student (nonseclusionary time-out) and techniques that remove the student from access to reinforcement (exclusionary and seclusionary time-outs). Educators should always attempt to match the intensity of the time-out procedure with the intensity of the problem behavior. Because time-out is a behavior reduction technique, educators have the added responsibility of ensuring that this procedure serves a legitimate educational function and meets all district, state, and national guidelines (Alberto & Troutman, 2006). In addition, use of any behavior reduction strategy should always be paired with instructionally based strategies that are both proactive and preventative (see School-wide Positive Behavior Support) by explicitly teaching students appropriate replacement responses as part of an ongoing effort to provide a continuum of positive behavioral interventions and supports. For students who have either targeted or intensive/individualized behavior support needs, a functional behavioral assessment and implementation of a behavior intervention plan is recommended (Sugai et al., 2000).

REFERENCES

Alberto, P. A., & Troutman, a. C. (2006). *Applied behavior analysis for teachers* (7th ed.). Upper Saddle River, NJ: Pearson Merrill Prentice Hall.

Colorado Department of Education. (2000). *Guidelines for the use of non-exclusionary and exclusionary time-out with youth 3–21 years old receiving public education services*. Denver: Author. Retrieved from http://www.cde.state.co.us/

Cooper, J. O., Heron, T. E., & Heward, W. L. (1987). *Applied behavior analysis*. New York, NY: Macmillan.

Maag, J. W. (1999). *Behavior management: From theoretical implications to practical applications*. San Diego, CA: Singular.

Sugai, G., Horner, R. H., Dunlap, G. Hieneman, M., Lewis, T. J., Nelson, C. M.,...Ruef, M. (2000). Applying positive behavioral support and functional behavioral assessment in schools. *Journal of Positive Behavioral Interventions, 2*, 131–143.

Sulzer-Azaroff, B., & Mayer, G. R. (1991). *Behavior analysis for lasting change*. Fort Worth, TX: Harcourt Brace College.

Zirpoli, T. J. (2005). *Behavior management: Applications for teachers* (4th ed.). Upper Saddle River, NJ: Pearson Merrill Prentice Hall.

RANDALL L. DE PRY
University of Colorado at Colorado Springs

***See also* Behavior Modification; Discipline**

TIME SAMPLING

Time sampling is an intermittent means of recording behavior by observing the subject at certain prespecified times and recording his or her behavior in a manner prescribed by the time sampling method in use. According to Arrington (1943), the major impetus to developing various time sampling procedures was provided by the National Research Council between 1920 and 1935. The council, which controlled many research fund allocations, had become concerned because the diary records typically used in research on the behavior of children were neither comparable nor exact. This group began to encourage research that used quantifiable and replicable methods of data collection. One of the first researchers to accept the challenge was F. L. Goodenough (1928), whose technique involved dividing an observation session into a series of short intervals and recording whether or not the target behavior occurred during each of those intervals. Other researchers in child development and psychology (e.g., Arrington, 1932; Bindra & Blond, 1958; Olson, 1929; Parten, 1932) adopted and refined these procedures.

In more recent times, a common terminology has developed that defines the various types of time sampling methods. In a landmark study, Powell et al. (1977) discussed three different types of time sampling procedures: (1) whole interval recording, (2) partial interval recording, and (3) momentary time sampling. In all of these procedures, the observation session is divided into a series of intervals. When the intervals are equal, the procedure is known as fixed interval (e.g., every 30 seconds). When the interval lengths are assigned at random but still average to the desired length (e.g., on the average, every 30 seconds), the procedure is known as variable interval.

In whole interval time sampling, the behavior is scored as having occurred only if it has endured for the entire interval; in partial interval time sampling the behavior is recorded as having occurred if it occurs at all (even for an instant) during the interval. In the technique known as momentary time sampling (MTS), the data collector records what behavior is occurring exactly at the end of each interval.

Repp, Roberts, Slack, Repp, and Berkler (1976) demonstrated conclusively that partial interval time sampling was not an accurate means of recording behaviors when frequency was the dimension of interest. Powell et al. (1977) conducted a study on the accuracy of all of these procedures and concluded that, when used to estimate the duration of a behavior, whole interval time sampling generally provided an underestimate while partial interval recording provided an overestimate. Momentary time sampling procedures both over- and underestimated the true duration of the behavior but, when averaged, provided the most accurate measure. The researchers felt that MTS interval lengths as long as 60 seconds could be used to collect accurate data. In an extension of this study, Brulle and Repp (1984) demonstrated that MTS procedures provide an accurate estimate of the duration of the behavior when averaged, but that each data entry, even when intervals are as short as 30 seconds, is subject to considerable error. They recommended that only very short intervals be used if averages are not acceptable.

The Student Observation Scale (SOS) of the Behavior Assessment System for Children is an example of a standardized time-sampling procedure that uses a fourth approach successfully. The SOS employs brief intervals, and at the end of each, the examiner/observer records all behaviors occurring at any time during the 3-second observation (Reynolds & Kamphaus, 1992). After recording, behavior is again observed, and the process is repeated for a 15-minute total time sample.

REFERENCES

Arrington, R. E. (1932). Interrelations in the behavior of young children. *Child Development Monographs*, No. 8.

Arrington, R. E. (1943). Time sampling in studies of social behavior: a critical review of techniques and results with research suggestions. *Psychological Bulletin*, 40, 81–124.

Bindra, D., & Blond, J. (1958). A time-sample method for measuring general activity and its components. *Canadian Journal of Psychology*, 12, 74–76.

Brulle, A. R., & Repp. A. C. (1984). An investigation of the accuracy of momentary time sampling procedures with time series data. *British Journal of Psychology*, 75, 481–488.

Goodenough, F. L. (1928). Measuring behavior traits by means of repeated short samples. *Journal of Juvenile Research*, 12, 230–235.

Olson, W. C. (1929). A study of classroom behavior. *Journal of Educational Psychology*, 22, 449–454.

Parten, M. B. (1932). Social participation among preschool children. *Journal of Abnormal Social Psychology*, 57, 243–269.

Powell, J., Martindale, B., Kulp, S., Martindale, a., & Bauman, R. (1977). Taking a closer look: Time sampling and measurement error. *Journal of Applied Behavior Analysis*, 10, 325–332.

Repp, A. C., Roberts, D. M., Slack, D. J., Repp, C. F., & Berkler, M. S. (1976). A comparison of frequency, interval, and time-sampling methods of data collection. *Journal of Applied Behavior Analysis*, 9, 501–508.

Reynolds, C. R., & Kamphaus, R. W. (1992). *Behavior assessment system for children*. Circle Pines, MN: American Guidance Service.

ANDREW R. BRULLE
Wheaton College

See also **Behavioral Assessment; Behavior Assessment System for Children; Behavior Charting; Behavior Modification**

TOFRANIL

Tofranil is the proprietary name for the drug Imipramine, which primarily is used in the treatment of major depression and nocturnal enuresis. It has been suggested that Tofranil may be useful in the treatment of school phobia (Hersov, 1985).

Though Tofranil has proved to be an effective treatment for major depression in adults (American Medical Association, 1983), its use with children is questionable. Shaffer (1985) reports that there have been few well-designed studies of the effectiveness of Tofranil and childhood depression. In one reported study in which Tofranil was compared double blind with a placebo, a 60% response rate was reported in both groups. In adults, Tofranil has a mild sedative effect that serves to lessen anxiety, though it is not intended to be used for this symptom. It has been suggested that it is this anxiety effect that may be helpful in a multidisciplinary approach toward school refusal (Hersov, 1985). In the 1990s, use of Tofranil declined in favor of selective serotonin reuptake inhibitors, such as Prozac and Zoloft.

In children, Tofranil is most frequently used to ameliorate nocturnal enuresis. Numerous studies have demonstrated Tofranil's effectiveness in decreasing nighttime enuresis in most children (Shaffer, Costello, & Hill, 1968). The effect is seen rapidly, and almost always within the first week of treatment (Williams & Johnston, 1982). Unfortunately, research also has suggested that once the medication is withdrawn, many of these children begin wetting again. The effects of long-term treatment have not been studied (Shaffer, 1985). The relapse rate following cessation of the drug compares unfavorably with the withdrawal of the pad and bell procedure. The mode of action of Tofranil in decreasing nocturnal enuresis is not understood. An adverse side effect of Tofranil may be increased restlessness, agitation, and confusion.

REFERENCES

American Medical Association (AMA). (1983). *AMA drug evaluations* (5th ed.). Philadelphia, PA: Saunders.

Hersov, L. (1985). School refusal. In M. Rutter & L. Hersov (Eds.). *Child and adolescent psychiatry: Modern approaches* (2nd ed., pp. 382–399). St. Louis, MO: Blackwell.

Shaffer, D. (1985). Enuresis. In M. Rutter & L. Hersov (Eds.), *Child and adolescent psychiatry: Modern approaches* (2nd ed., pp. 465–481). St. Louis, MO: Blackwell.

Shaffer, D., Costello, A. J., & Hill, I. D. (1968). Control of enuresis with Imipramine. *Archives of diseases in childhood, 43,* 665–671.

Williams, D. I., & Johnston, J. H. (1982). *Pediatric urology* (2nd ed.). London, England: Butterworth Scientific.

GRETA N. WILKENING
Children's Hospital

See also **Depression, Childhood and Adolescent; Enuresis**

TOKEN ECONOMY

A token economy refers to a system in which conditioned reinforcers (e.g., token or point) are (a) contingently delivered following engagement in a target behavior and (b) can be exchanged for preferred items/events. A token economy involves the delivery of a stimulus (i.e., token) that can be exchanged for other preferred items (backup reinforcer). Token deliveries acquire the function of a conditioned or secondary reinforcer, meaning they are paired with and effective in accessing a backup reinforcer and thus become associated with an increase in the future probability of a target behavior occurring. The backup reinforcer is either a primary (unconditioned) reinforcer, that is, a reinforcer that is biologically or innately of value to an individual, or it is other conditioned reinforcers (Miller,

1997). Tokens may be considered generalized reinforcers if multiple backup reinforcers are available for exchange.

Token economies are practical because they (a) are generally employed by everyday caregivers and practitioners (Leslie, 1996), (b) provide an alternative to the regular delivery of primary and highly-valued conditioned reinforcers (Miller, 1997), and (c) are effective in increasing a wide range of target behaviors (Alberto & Troutman, 2003). Martella, Nelson, and Marchand-Martella (2003) note, however, that token economies are a contrived system of reinforcement and that skills reinforced through token economies in certain environments may not occur in others. Additionally, gradually fading the use of tokens is necessary to ensure that behavior change is maintained without the regular delivery of reinforcers.

Research

Research spanning multiple domains and content areas has been conducted evaluating the use of token economies. The first and most influential studies regarding token economies were directed by Teodoro Ayllon and Nathan Azrin, who in 1965 empirically evaluated the implementation of a token economy in a hospital psychiatric ward. Tokens were delivered by hospital staff contingent upon client's engaging in a range of work-related behaviors. Results indicated that when tokens were delivered contingently, work-related behavior improved substantially for a majority of clients (Leslie, 1996). In another example, DeLuca and Holborn (1992) rewarded the bicycling behavior of boys with points that could be exchanged for preferred items. The bicycling behavior of the participants doubled in many cases after the point system was implemented.

Fox, Hopkins, and Anger (1987) were successful in reducing work time lost due to injuries and the number of accidents and injuries at two open-pit mine sites, following institution of a token economy. The costs associated with implementing the token economy were much lower than costs associated with injuries and lost work time, and results were maintained over several years. McLaughlin and Malaby (1972) found that a token economy implemented in a general education classroom was effective in increasing the assignment completion rate of students in the classroom.

Token economies have doubtlessly affected myriad areas of behavior research and practice (Alberto & Troutman, 2003; Miller, 1997) and have been successfully employed (a) in special and general education classrooms, homes, clinics, and group home facilities (Alberto & Troutman, 2003); (b) for individuals (Luiselli, 1996) and groups (Adair & Schneider, 1993); and (c) across a wide range of behaviors, including social skills (Rasing, Coninx, Duker, & Van Den Hurk, 1994), self-care skills (Ayllon & Azrin, 1965), and academic skills (McGinnis, Friman, Carlyon, 1999).

Guidelines for Implementation

A token economy can be set up in a number of ways, but involves a few principal steps. Instituting a token economy requires (a) determining the target behavior, (b) selecting tokens, (c) identifying what will be offered as backup reinforcers and the number of tokens required to receive backup reinforcers, and (d) creating a system to record token deliveries (Sulzer-Azaroff & Mayer, 1991). Also, before implementing a token economy, careful instructions to explain and teach the rules, process, and requirements of the system to both implementers and those who will participate in the system are necessary.

Check marks, poker chips, stickers, smiley faces, and stamps are common objects and symbols used as tokens, and may be stored in a receptacle or printed on a sheet of paper and eventually counted (Alberto & Troutman, 2003). In a classroom, teachers or instructional assistants may deliver tokens, prompt students to deliver tokens to themselves, or teach students to evaluate their own behavior or the behavior of others and deliver tokens accordingly. To ensure counterfeiting does not occur, hard-to-obtain objects or marked/initialed tokens should be used.

Back-up reinforcers are likely to be most effective when (a) a variety of choices are available, (b) individuals can choose their own reinforcers, (c) reinforcers are immediately available after earning all tokens, and (d) the reinforcer delivered appropriately corresponds to the amount of effort required to earn tokens. These suggestions are especially important considerations for younger individuals or individuals with disabilities. Additionally, for such populations, tokens may also need to be delivered immediately after a target behavior occurs. Use of tangible tokens may be the best choice for younger children and those with severe disabilities, as they allow individuals to easily see the accumulation or removal of tokens. Finally, tokens may also need to be exchanged on a more frequent basis for younger children and those with disabilities.

A response cost procedure is commonly employed in token economies (Martella et al., 2003). Specifically, when individuals engage in undesired behavior, a specified number of tokens may be removed from their possession. However, Sulzer-Azaroff and Mayer (1991) suggest maintaining a positive balance of tokens to avoid negative side effects associated with "owing" more tokens than have been earned. These side effects might include social withdrawal, aggression, and reduced probability of desired behavior.

The development of a plan to systematically fade token systems is essential. Pairing token deliveries with more naturally occurring rewards, such as praise and other social reinforcers, will ensure sustained behavior change when tokens are gradually faded. Additionally, lengthening the time between occurrences of target behaviors and token deliveries, increasing the number of tokens required to exchange for preferred items, and providing tokens on an intermittent basis will be useful strategies to incorporate when planning to fade token systems (Sulzer-Azaroff & Mayer, 1991).

Case Example 1

"Felix" is a 6-year-old child with difficulties staying in his seat. To address this concern, a timer is placed on Felix's desk. If at the end of a random interval of time Felix has remained in his seat, he can put a marble (token) into a cup on his desk. At the end of class, if Felix earns three or more marbles he can play with designated toys or draw at his desk for 5 minutes (backup reinforcer).

Case Example 2

"Mrs. Garcia" is a ninth-grade teacher who is having trouble keeping her students from talking out in class without raising their hand. Mrs. Garcia implements a point system in which a line (denoting a point) is written on the chalkboard when a student raises his or her hand to speak. At the end of class, if more than 25 points are accumulated, students can either choose to have 10 minutes of computer time, play board games, or contribute the points toward a larger pool of points. When the students earn 200 points, they can have a class popcorn and movie party or a pizza party.

Case Example 3

"Mr. Horace" is concerned that his students are frequently tardy to his class and not in their seats when the bell rings. Mr. Horace decides to give an index card to each student in the class. When a student is on time to class he stamps his or her point card. At the end of the school week, if students have earned four or more stamps they can pick a prize from a prize box.

REFERENCES

Adair, J., & Schneider, J. (1993). Banking on learning: An incentive system for adolescents in the resource room. *Teaching Exceptional Children, 25*(2), 30–34.

Alberto, P. A., & Troutman, A. C. (2003). *Applied behavior analysis for teachers* (6th ed.). Upper Saddle River, NJ: Merrill Prentice Hall.

Ayllon, T., & Azrin, N. H. (1965). The measurement and reinforcement of behavior of psychotics. *Journal of Applied Behavior Analysis, 8,* 357–383.

DeLuca, R. V., & Holborn, S. W. (1992). Effects of a variable-ratio reinforcement schedule with changing criteria on exercise in obese and nonobese boys. *Journal of Applied Behavior Analysis, 25,* 671–679.

Fox, D. K., Hopkins, B. L., & Anger, W. K. (1987). The long-term effects of a token economy on safety performance in open-pit mining. *Journal of Applied Behavior Analysis, 20,* 215–224.

Leslie, J. C. (1996). *Principles of behavioral analysis*. The Netherlands: Harwood Academic Publishers.

Luiselli, J. (1996). Multicomponent intervention for challenging behaviors of a child with pervasive developmental disorder in a public school setting. *Journal of Developmental and Physical Disabilities, 8,* 211–219.

Martella, R. C., Nelson, J. R., & Marchand-Martella, N. E. (2003). *Managing disruptive behavior in the schools: A school-wide, classroom, and individualized social learning approach.* Boston, MA: Allyn & Bacon.

McGinnis, J. C., Friman, P. C., & Carlyon, W. D. (1999). The effect of token rewards on "intrinsic" motivation for doing math. *Journal of Applied Behavior Analysis, 32,* 375–379.

McLaughlin, T. F., & Malaby, J. (1972). Intrinsic reinforcers in a classroom token economy. *Journal of Applied Behavior Analysis, 5,* 263–270.

Miller, L. K. (1997). *Principles of everyday behavior analysis* (3rd ed.). Pacific Grove, CA: Brooks/Cole.

Rasing, E., Coninx, F., Duker, P., & Van Den Hurk, A. (1994). Acquisition and generalization of social behaviors in language-disabled deaf adolescents. *Behavior Modification, 18,* 411–442.

Sulzer-Azaroff, B., & Mayer, G. R. (1991). *Behavior analysis for lasting change.* Fort Worth, TX: Holt, Rinehart, and Winston.

SARAH FAIRBANKS
GEORGE SUGAI
University of Connecticut

See also Applied Behavior Analysis; Behavior Therapy

TONGUE, GEOGRAPHIC

Geographic tongue is a term applied to a map-like appearance of the tongue resulting from irregular bare patches on its surface. This patchy form of glossitis (loss of papillae causing the tongue to appear smooth) changes location and appearance from day to day. It is a benign condition but can be persistent. This disorder is often self-limiting and does not require treatment. The causes of geographic tongue are unknown, although allergies or local irritants such as hot, spicy food may be involved. It is also possible that this condition may be a reaction to stress. Geographic tongue may also be known as benign migratory glossitis.

Geographic tongue is a relatively common tongue problem that affects males and females alike.

Three characteristics:

1. Red, "bald" patches accentuated by white rings found on the upper surface of the tongue (the dorsum).

2. In some cases individuals may feel sore or burning pain.

3. The location changes from day to day (migration).

Once diagnosed, frequently no treatment is applied. This condition is often self-limiting. If treatment is required, it responds well to topical steroids, which can be prescribed by a dentist (e.g., Lidex gel applied four times a day). Treatment may provide significant improvement but does not permanently cure the condition. If the condition is reoccurring and persistent, the affected individual may need to avoid local irritants (e.g., hot and spicy food, alcohol, tobacco), or an allergy assessment may be needed. Alternatively, stress may be involved, and addressing the cause of the stress may be necessary.

A student with this diagnosis may be experiencing mild to moderate discomfort. Therefore, a student experiencing intermittent mouth pain may be seen by the school nurse frequently. In most cases, however, the condition is self-limiting, and no treatment is prescribed. Symptoms should diminish within approximately 10 days. If the condition persists, the student may need further medical consultation and treatment. School personnel may be involved in monitoring the student and administering medication. If it is determined that the condition is due to an allergic reaction to food or another allergen, it may be necessary for the school to provide an alternative diet for this student. In certain cases, stressors may exacerbate the condition. In this case, the student may benefit from counseling to alleviate stress or find ways to deal with the stress more effectively.

The prognosis for geographic tongue is excellent. The condition is often self-limiting. Research continues to explore treatment approaches for geographic tongue (Flaitz & Baker, 2000) and etiological factors (Gonzaga, Torres, Alchorne, & Gerbase-Delima, 1996).

REFERENCES

Flaitz, C. M., & Baker, K. A. (2000). Treatment approaches to common symptomatic oral lesions in children. *Dental Clinics of North America, 44*(3), 671–696.

Gonzaga, H. F., Torres, E. A., Alchorne, M. M., & Gerbase-Delima, M. (1996). Both psoriasis and benign migratory glossitis are associated with HLW-Cw6. *British Journal of Dermatology, 135*(3), 368–370.

RACHEL TOPLIS
University of Northern Colorado

TONIC NECK REFLEX, ASYMMETRICAL
(*See* Asymmetrical Tonic Neck Reflex)

TOPICS IN EARLY CHILDHOOD SPECIAL EDUCATION

Topics in Early Childhood Special Education (TECSE) is a quarterly published, peer-reviewed journal that features timely issues in early childhood special education. Three of the four issues are topical and one is nontopical. The topical issues address an identified problem, trend, or subject of concern and importance to early intervention. The *TECSE* provides information to those interested in services provided to infants, toddlers, and preschoolers who display developmental delays and disabilities and their families. Readers can purchase individual articles on the journal website. The *TECSE* has been published continuously since 1981. PRO-ED, Inc. purchased the journal from Aspen Press in 1983. PRO-ED, Inc. is located at 8700 Shoal Creek Boulevard, Austin, TX 78757.

This entry has been informed by the source listed below.

REFERENCE

Dunlap, G. (Ed.). (2011). *Topics in early childhood special education*. Austin, TX: PRO-ED. Retrieved from http://www.proedinc.com/customer/content.aspx?redid=28

JUDITH K. VORESS
PRO-ED, Inc.
Third edition

KRISTIN T. HOLSKER
Chicago School of Professional Psychology
Fourth edition

TOPICS IN LANGUAGE DISORDERS

Topics in Language Disorders, also known as *TLD*, is a double-blind, peer-reviewed journal published quarterly. Originating in 1980, the journal serves as a scholarly resource to professionals in the field such as speech and language pathologists, neurologists, and physicians. Comprehensive articles, including review articles and reports of original data-based research, provide evidence-based information that connects theory, current research, and practice.

The purpose of the journal is to provide information to clinicians, researchers, and others with an interest in typical development, lifespan functioning, and disorders of spoken and written language and communication with a focus on interdisciplinary and international concerns. Emphasis is placed on providing theoretically and scientifically sound information to support culturally appropriate evidence-based practices in home, school, clinic, and community-based settings. The aim is to promote interdisciplinary collaboration and consideration of differing views.

Each quarterly issue addresses a different topic coordinated by an issue editor. Most peer-reviewed articles are solicited by issue editors, but unsolicited manuscripts are also considered.

The journal is available in paper copies as well as electronically through its dedicated website, and as part of Ovid collections to universities. Continuing education credits (CEUs) are available to members of the American Speech and Hearing Association by completing activities provided in the journal.

ANNE CAMPBELL
Purdue University
Third edition

NICOLE M. CASSIDY
Chicago School of Professional Psychology
Fourth edition

TORCH COMPLEX

TORCH complex is a phrase used by some authors (e.g., Nahmias & Tomeh, 1977; Thompson & O'Quinn, 1979) to group a set of maternal infections whose clinical manifestations in children are so similar that differentiation among them on the basis of those symptoms alone may not be possible. TORCH stands for *TO*xoplasmosis, *R*ubella, *C*ytomegalovirus, and *H*erpes. Generally speaking, with the exception of herpes, the infections have only mild and transitory effects on the mother, but through pre- or perinatal transmission, they may produce severe and irreversible damage to offspring. The major manifestations are visual and auditory defects and brain damage, which may result in mental retardation. The infections generally destroy already formed tissue rather than interfering with development; infants are frequently born asymptomatic but gradually develop symptoms in the early years of life.

Although the major symptoms of the members of the TORCH complex are similar, the detailed symptoms, mechanisms of action, and times of major action differ.

REFERENCES

Nahmias, A. J., & Tomeh, M. O. (1977). Herpes simplex virus infections. In A. M. Rudolph (Ed.), *Pediatrics* (16th ed.). Englewood Cliffs, NJ: Prentice Hall.

Thompson, R. J., & O'Quinn, A. N. (1979). *Developmental disabilities*. New York, NY: Oxford University Press.

ROBERT T. BROWN
University of North Carolina at Wilmington

See also Cytomegalovirus; Herpes Simplex I and II; Rubella; Toxoplasmosis

TORRANCE CENTER FOR CREATIVE STUDIES

The Torrance Center for Creative Studies is a research center dedicated to investigations of the development of creative potential. Its research and development program honors and builds on the legacy of Ellis Paul Torrance, a native Georgian and a University of Georgia Alumni Foundation distinguished professor emeritus. This legacy is best reflected in the following statement:

> In almost every field of human achievement, creativity is usually the distinguishing characteristic of the truly eminent. The possession of high intelligence, special talent, and high technical skills is not enough to produce outstanding achievement.... It is tremendously important to society that our creative talent be identified, developed, and utilized. The future of our civilization—our very survival—depends upon the quality of the creative imagination of our next generation. (Torrance, 1959, p. 1)

Torrance, a pioneer in research on the identification and development of creative potential, is best known for his work in the development and refinement of the Torrance Tests of Creative Thinking (TTCT), the most widely used tests of creativity in the world.

The goals of the research and instructional program of the Torrance Center are to investigate and evaluate techniques and procedures for assessing creative potential and growth; to develop, apply, and evaluate strategies that enhance creative thinking; and to facilitate national and international systems that support creative development.

Four components—assessment, development, education, and evaluation—provide the organizational structure for the research and instructional programs of the center. Each component has been designed to contribute research that verifies and expands our understanding of creativity as a major ingredient in the development of human ability and that carries out the further development of instructional and evaluation technology to enhance the development of that ability.

Research on instruments and procedures to assess creative potential and to evaluate creative growth form the basis of the assessment component. Research on tests developed by Torrance, including validity studies, refinement of administration and scoring procedures, interpretation of test results, and on the effects of strategies to develop creative ability are coordinated through the center in conjunction with Scholastic Testing Service, the publishers of the Torrance tests and the Georgia Studies of Creative Behavior.

Two programs to investigate and evaluate techniques that facilitate or inhibit creative thinking and to determine the nature of systems and activities that support and encourage creative growth form the basis of the development component. The Future Problem Solving Program (FPS), founded in 1974 by E. Paul and J. Pansy Torrance, involves a deliberately interdisciplinary approach to studying and solving problems. It was motivated by a belief that we have reached a point in civilization at which education must devote a considerable part of the curriculum to helping students enlarge, enrich, and make more accurate their images of the future (Torrance, 1980). The FPS program is now international. The Georgia FPS program is coordinated through the Torrance Center.

A major program initiative of the Torrance Center is the Torrance Creative Scholars Program. This program provides educational services to those individuals who score in the top $1\frac{1}{2}\%$ of the national population on the TTCT, verbal and/or figural. The program is consistent with Torrance's assertions (1984) that

> [A] common characteristic of people who have made outstanding social, scientific, and artistic contributions has been their creativity. Since we are living in an age of increasing rates of change, depleted natural resources, interdependence, and destandardization, there are stronger reasons than ever for creatively gifted children and adults to have a fair chance to grow. We must find these "world treasures" and give them support so that they can give society those things it so desperately needs.

A unique aspect of the Torrance Creative Scholars Program is its use of a mentoring component. This component provides a year-round mentoring network for the creative scholars. Individuals selected by Torrance are designated Torrance creative scholar-mentors; they provide mentoring services to the scholars in a variety of ways. These mentors are also eligible to become Torrance creative scholars and to receive the services of the program.

Scoring and validation of scores on the TTCT for the Torrance Creative Scholars Program are coordinated through Scholastic Testing Service. Programs and services are developed and implemented through the Torrance Center.

The third component, education, provides training for educators interested in creativity. This component operates in conjunction with the degree programs (master's, sixth year, and doctoral) offered through the department of educational psychology at the University of Georgia. Training programs offered through the center include the Torrance Center Summer Creativity Institute, the Challenge Program for preschool through fifth graders, and the Visiting Scholars Program for national and international scholars. In addition, there is the annual E. Paul Torrance Lecture and the library and archives donated to the university by Torrance. A future goal of the Torrance Center is to endow an E. Paul Torrance Research Professor Chair. The final component, evaluation, focuses on quantitative and qualitative evaluations of assessment techniques, educational strategies, and support systems for the various programs of the center.

The Torrance Center for Creative Studies was formally established at the University of Georgia in the spring of 1984 by Mary M. Frasier. It is located in the Department of

Educational Psychology, College of Education, University of Georgia, Athens, GA 30602.

REFERENCES

Torrance, E. P. (1959). *Understanding creativity in talented students*. Paper prepared at the Summer Guidance Institute Lecture Series on Understanding the Talented Student, University of Minnesota.

Torrance, E. P. (1980). Creativity and futurism in education. *Retooling Education, 100*, 298–311.

Torrance, E. P. (1984). *The search for a nation's treasure* (Keynote address). St. Louis, MO: National Association for Gifted Children.

MARY F. FRASIER
University of Georgia

See also Creativity; Creativity Tests; Torrance, Ellis Paul

TORRANCE, ELLIS PAUL (1914–2003)

Ellis Paul Torrance earned his AA at Georgia Military College in 1936, his BA at Mercer University in 1940, his MA at the University of Minnesota in 1944, and his PhD at the University of Michigan. He served as professor of educational psychology and as department chairman at the University of Georgia until he retired in 1984.

Torrance was widely recognized for his voluminous contributions to the field of creative, gifted, and future education. At the heart of his philosophy was the impetus to change the goals, needs, and concepts in education. Future educational institutions need to cultivate not only learning, but thinking. As a means of teaching versatility in thinking, Torrance reconceptualized and refined sociodrama as a group creative problem-solving technique. In addition, his efforts to identify gifted people from different cultures and all ages produced the Torrance Tests of Creative Thinking (TTCT). He has also produced Thinking Creatively in Action and Movement (TCAM), Sounds and Images, What Kind of Person are You?, the Creative Motivation Scale, and Style of Learning and Thinking (SOLAT).

Torrance contributed to more than 2,000 publications and more than 40 books, including *Guiding Creative Talent, Education and the Creative Potential, Creative Learning and Teaching, Gifted, and Talented Children in the Regular Classroom*, and *Making the Creative Leap Beyond*. He directed 118 doctoral dissertations and 39 masters' theses.

Torrance and his late wife Pansy were the founders of the Future Problem Solving Program (1974), which teaches problem-solving skills to thousands of children in America and abroad. His many honors and awards include being appointed Alumni Foundation Distinguished Professor in 1973, being awarded a grant by the Japan Society for the Promotion of Science to study creativity and creative instruction within Japanese educational institutions, and receiving the Life Creative Achievement Award from the American Creativity Association in 1994.

This entry has been informed by the sources listed below.

REFERENCES

Torrance, E. P. (1962). *Guiding creative talent*. Englewood Cliffs, NJ: Prentice Hall.

Torrance, E. P. (1963). *Education and the creative potential*. Minneapolis: University of Minnesota.

Torrance, E. P., & Safter, H. T. (1998). *Making the creative leap beyond*. Buffalo, NY: Creative Education Foundation.

Torrance, E. P., & Sisk, D. A. (1965). *Gifted and talented children in the regular classroom*. Buffalo, NY: Creative Education Foundation.

STAFF

See also Creativity Tests; Torrance Center for Creative Studies

TORRANCE TESTS OF CREATIVE THINKING

The Torrance Test of Creative Thinking (TTCT) is composed of two tests designed to examine creativity. The Torrance Test of Creative Thinking–Verbal (TTCT-V) examines a variety of verbal aspects, and the Torrance Test of Creative Thinking–Figural (TTCT-F) explores figural aspects of creative thinking. Both versions were originally developed in 1966 by E. Paul Torrance and associates and were renormed in 1974, 1984, 1990, and 1998. Each has two parallel forms, A and B. To date, the TTCT has been translated into 35 languages. The tests are accompanied by separate technical and norms manuals for both the verbal and figural forms, separate scoring guides for each form, and a review of research on the TTCT.

The TTCT-V may be administered to first graders through adults and requires 40 minutes to administer. The TTCT-F may be administered to kindergartners through adults and requires 30 minutes to administer. The TTCT-V uses six word-based activities to assess mental fluency, flexibility, and originality by asking participants to ask questions, improve products, and "just suppose." The TTCT-F consists of three activities, each of which requires 10 minutes to complete: picture construction, picture completion, and repeated figures of lines or circles. These picture-based activities assess mental fluency, originality, elaboration, abstractness of titles (i.e., titles given to drawings), and resistance to premature closure (i.e., the ability to continually process and consider the variety of information given in responses). In addition to these five norm-referenced measures are

13 criterion-referenced measures, or "creative strengths": emotional expressiveness, storytelling articulateness, movement or action, expressiveness of titles, synthesis of incomplete figures, synthesis of lines or circles, unusual visualization, internal visualization, extending or breaking boundaries, humor, richness of imagery, colorfulness of imagery, and fantasy.

The TTCT-F may be scored using a "streamlined" scoring procedure that provides standardized scores for both the listed mental characteristics and the accompanying creative strengths. The TTCT-V may be scored using the provided norms, standardized scores, and national percentiles provided in the *Manual for Scoring and Interpreting Results* and the *Technical Supplement*. Scoring takes approximately 20 minutes per participant per form, and requires attention to detail, practice, and careful study of the manual; a scoring service is also provided by the publisher.

The TTCT-F was normed on a sample of 88,355 students from 42 states; the streamlined scoring norms were based on a sample of 55,600 from 37 states. (Geographic differences were reported by grouping the states sampled into the four regions used by the U.S. Department of Commerce, the National Assessment of Educational Progress, and the National Education Association.) The TTCT-V was normed on a sample of 37,327 students. In addition, one has the option of choosing age-related norms or grade-related norms for both children and adults.

Extensive information on validity is provided in the TTCT manual. With regard to predictive validity, TTCT scores have been significantly correlated with creative achievement in 9-month, 7-year, 22-year, and 40-year longitudinal studies (Millar, 2002; Torrance & Wu, 1981). The TTCT-F manual of 1998 provides a range between .89 and .94 for the internal reliability of the items in the creative index; the inter-rater reliability for the test is reported to be above .90. Test-retest reliabilities and alternate-form reliabilities range from .59 to .97.

This entry has been informed by the sources listed below.

REFERENCES

Almeida, L., Prieto, L., Ferrando, M., Oliveira, E., & Ferrándiz, C. (2008). Torrance test of creative thinking: The question of its construct validity. *Thinking Skills and Creativity, 3*(1), 53–58.

Chase, C. I. (1985). Review of the Torrance tests of creative thinking. In J. V. Mitchell Jr. (Ed.), *The ninth mental measurements yearbook* (pp. 1631–1632). Lincoln: Buros Institute of Mental Measurements, University of Nebraska.

Clapham, M. M. (1998). Structure of figural forms A and B of the Torrance tests of creative thinking. *Educational & Psychological Measurement, 58,* 275–283.

Cramond, B. (1993). The Torrance tests of creative thinking: From design through establishment of predictive validity. In R. F. Subotnik & K. D. Arnold (Eds.), *Beyond Terman:*

Contemporary longitudinal studies of giftedness and talent (pp. 229–254). Norwood, NJ: Ablex.

Cramond, B., Matthews-Morgan, J., Torrance, E. P., & Zuo, L. (1999). Why should the Torrance tests of creative thinking be used to assess creativity? *Korean Journal of Thinking & Problem Solving, 9,* 77–101.

Heausler, N. L., & Thompson, B. (1988). Structure of the Torrance tests of creative thinking. *Educational and Psychological Measurement, 48,* 463–468.

Kim, K. (2006a). Can we trust creativity tests? A review of the Torrance tests of creative thinking (TTCT). *Creativity Research Journal, 18*(1), 3–14.

Kim, K. (2006b). Is creativity unidimensional or multidimensional? Analyses of the Torrance tests of creative thinking. *Creativity Research Journal, 18*(3), 251–259

Millar, G. W. (2002). *The Torrance kids at mid-life: selected case studies of creative behavior.* Westport, CT: Ablex.

Rosenthal, A., DeMers, S. T., Stilwell, W., Graybeal, S., & Zins, J. (1983). Comparison of interrater reliability on the Torrance test of creative thinking for gifted and non-gifted students. *Psychology in the Schools, 20,* 35–40.

Runco, M. A., & Albert, R. S. (1985). The reliability and validity of ideational originality in the divergent thinking of academically gifted and nongifted children. *Educational and Psychological Measurement, 45,* 483–501.

Swartz, J. D. (1988). Torrance tests of creative thinking. In D. J. Keyser & R. C. Sweetland (Eds.), *Test critique* Vol. 7 (pp. 619–622). Kansas, MS: Test Corporation of America, a Subsidiary of Westport Publisher.

Torrance Center for Creative Studies: http://www.coe.uga.edu/

Torrance, E. P., & Wu, T. (1981). A comparative longitudinal study of the adult creative achievements of elementary school children identified as highly intelligent and as highly creative. *Creative Child and Adult Quarterly, 6,* 71–76.

Treffinger, D. J. (1985). Review of the Torrance tests of creative thinking. In J. V. Mitchell Jr. (Ed.), *The ninth mental measurements yearbook* (pp. 1632–1634). Lincoln, NE: Buros Institute of Mental Measurements, University of Nebraska.

Website for the Torrance Tests of Creative Thinking, including a detailed critique: www.coe.uga.edu/torrance/

Direct link to the critique: www.coe.uga.edu/torrance/

Wechsler, S. (2006). Validity of the Torrance tests of creative thinking to the Brazilian culture. *Creativity Research Journal, 18*(1), 15–25.

RON DUMONT
Fairleigh Dickinson University

JOHN O. WILLIS
Fairleigh Dickinson University

KATHLEEN VEIZEL
Fairleigh Dickinson University

JAMIE ZIBULSKY
Fairleigh Dickinson University

See also Gifted and Talented Children, Insight (in the Gifted); Torrance, Ellis Paul

TORSIONAL DYSTONIA

The term *dystonia* was first used by H. Oppenheim in 1911 to denote the coexistence of muscular hypotonia and hypertonia. Since that time, the term has been used to describe a symptom of abnormal muscle contraction, a syndrome of abnormal involuntary movements, and a disease that has either a genetic or ideopathic origin. Torsional dystonia is commonly referred to as a progressive disorder characterized by slow, twisting movements that ultimately may result in bizarre, twisting postures of the extremities or trunk. Some causes of torsional dystonia are identifiable while other causes remain unknown, making classification of the condition difficult.

The disorder has a gradual onset, beginning between the ages of 5 and 15, and commonly involves the foot or leg. Torsional dystonia may spread to several parts or all of the body, but the condition is not present during sleep. Contractures or permanent muscle shortening and joint deformity ultimately occur. Hereditary forms of torsional dystonia are more common than ideopathic forms; one hereditary form is found most often in Ashkenazic Jews. The diagnosis of dystonia is based on clinical signs because diagnostic laboratory or biopsy findings are not known. The symptoms suggest dysfunction in the extrapyramidal system, since temporary drug-induced symptoms have occurred from medications that have a known effect on the basal ganglia of the extrapyramidal system.

Treatment of torsional dystonia generally has been disappointing. Medications such as diazepam (Valium), car-bamazepine (Tegretol), haloperidol, and, in some cases, levodapa or anticholinergic drugs have been helpful in reducing the severity of the symptoms; but none of these medications has been consistently effective. Various neurosurgical or biofeedback procedures have resulted in isolated improvement but consistent benefits have not been achieved through these approaches. This entry has been informed by the sources listed below.

REFERENCES

Berkow, R. (Ed.). (1982). *The Merck manual* (14th ed., p. 1363). Rahway, NJ: Merck, Sharp, & Dohme.

Fahn, S. (1985). The extrapyramidal disorders. In J. Wyngaarden & L. Smith, Jr. (Eds.), *Cecil textbook of medicine* (17th ed., pp. 2077–2078). Philadelphia, PA: Saunders.

Fahn, S., & Roswell, E. (1976). Definition of dystonia and classification of the dystonic states. In R. Eldridge & S. Fahn (Eds.), *Advances in neurology* (Vol. 14, pp. 1–5). New York, NY: Raven.

Magalini, S., & Scarascia, E. (1981). *Dictionary of medical syndromes* (2nd ed.). Philadelphia, PA: Lippincott.

Marsden, C. D. (1976). Dystonia: The spectrum of the disease. In M. D. Yahr (Ed.), *Basal ganglia* (pp. 351–365). New York, NY: Raven.

Marsden, C. D., Harrison, M. J. G., & Bundey, S. (1976). Natural history of idiopathic torsion dystonia. In R. Eldridge & S. Fahn (Eds.), *Advances in neurology* (Vol. 14, pp. 177–187). New York, NY: Raven.

Zeman, W. (1976). Dystonia: An overview. In R. Eldridge & S. Fahn (Eds.), *Advances in neurology* (Vol. 14, pp. 91–101). New York, NY: Raven.

DANIEL D. LIPKA
*Lincoln Way Special Education
Regional Resources Center*

See also **Physical Anomalies; Physical Disabilities**

TOTAL COMMUNICATION

The expression total communication can be used in the general sense of communication through all possible channels, not only vocal (including verbal) communication, but also communication provided by such other means as mimicry, gestures, and so on. Recently, total communication has been used mainly in a more restricted field, namely the education of deaf children. It presents itself not as a method, but as "a philosophy incorporating the appropriate aural, manual, and oral methods of communication in order to ensure effective communication with and among hearing impaired persons" (Garretson, 1976, p. 300). It advocates the use of various modes of communication, such as speech (which should not be neglected, as the deaf live among a majority of hearing people), written language (reading and writing), sign language, finger spelling, pantomime, and so on.

In recent years, methods of teaching deaf children applying this philosophy have been used in a steadily increasing number of schools in the United States and in Europe. These schools gave up the oral method that had prevailed since the end of the nineteenth century, mainly in Europe, where the resolutions of the International Congress held in Milan in 1880 were accepted and recommended almost unanimously (Lane, 1980).

According to the defenders of total communication, the oral approach, including lip reading, gives unsatisfactory results as far as linguistic and cognitive development are concerned (Conrad, 1979). It is argued that even if the hearing loss is discovered early, poor parent-infant communication delays the acquisition of language considerably and irretrievably, except with children whose residual hearing is sufficient to make communication possible. Ensuing education in specialized institutions is slower and less differentiated than with hearing children and, instead of reducing the gap, increases the retardation of the deaf children.

Total communication advocates the use of signing as the most appropriate mode of early communication between parents and hearing-impaired children. The double exposure to sign and speech (about 9 out of 10 deaf children have hearing parents) should allow partially hearing children equipped with appropriate audiological aids to be educated together with their hearing peers; children whose residual hearing is insufficient should be educated through a wide network of activities, of which "spoken language, finger spelling, signing, and written language constitute the linguistic core. Being capable of consistent transmission and internal symbolization of linguistic signals, these are the media of special relevance to linguistic and cognitive growth" (Evans, 1982, p. 91).

Evans (1982) shows three problematic issues for total communication: (1) the way the linguistic competence in sign language, with its own lexical, morphological, and syntactic characteristics, is to be transferred to linguistic competence in the spoken language of the community in which the deaf person is living; (2) the necessity for a specific training or recycling of teachers in total communication; and (3) the role of the (hearing) parents, who being confronted suddenly with the deafness of their baby, are obliged to learn the sign language in which they are going to communicate with the child in a very short time.

The philosophy of total communication remains unaltered in a variant in which the exposure to speech and sign is replaced by cued speech. The deaf child is taught to perceive the spoken language through a combination of residual hearing, lipreading, and a limited number of disambiguating signs near the speaker's face (Cornett, 1967).

Opponents of total communication think that signing may prove harmful and impede the acquisition of a spoken language and that too much time spent on teaching signs (finger spelling, etc.) could be used more appropriately to teach the spoken language. They stress the fact that some deaf children, albeit a minority, educated through the oral method succeed in obtaining a satisfactory level in spoken language perception and production.

REFERENCES

Conrad, R. (1979). *The deaf schoolchild: Language and cognitive functioning*. London, England: Harper & Row.

Cornett, O. (1967). Cued speech. *American Annals of the Deaf*, *112*, 3–13.

Evans, L. (1982). *Total communication: Structure and strategy*. Washington, DC: Gallaudet College Press.

Garretson, M. D. (1976). Total communication. In R. Frisina (Ed.), A bicentennial monograph on hearing impairment: Trends in the U.S.A. *Volta Review, 78*.

Lane, H. (1980). A chronology of the oppression of sign language in France and the United States. In H. Lane & F. Grosjean (Eds.), *Recent perspectives on American sign language*. Hillsdale, NJ: Erlbaum.

S. De Vriendt
Vrije Universiteit Brussel, Belgium

See *also* American Sign Language; Deaf Education

TOURETTE SYNDROME

Tourette syndrome is a child-onset neurological disorder characterized by involuntary movements or vocalizations, otherwise known as tics and occurs in approximately .04% to .4% of the population (Peterson, Pine, Cohen, & Brook, 2001; Singer & Walkup, 1991). Symptoms are evident before age 18 and are seen most commonly between the ages 2 and 15. Males are 2 to 5 times more likely than females to be diagnosed with this disorder (American Psychiatric Association, 1994). Signs of Tourette syndrome first are seen in frequent, repetitive, meaningless, and rapid tics of the limbs, arms, and/or face (e.g., eye blinking). The tics occur in bouts and generally are seen daily or every other day. Over time, tics can become more complex, resulting in multiple motor movements. Further, the course of the disorder is characterized by symptom waxing and waning, whereby displaying periods of remission that may last from weeks to years.

Verbal tics usually are seen in the form of throat clearing, coughing, grunting, shouting, or barking. Like motor tics, verbal tics may become more complex over time, whereby grunts turn into words, and words turn into phrases. The verbal tics may be characterized by echolalia, palilalia, or coprolalia. Echolalia, most commonly seen in children with autism, is the repetition of words and phrases made by others. Palilalia is the repetition of one's own word. Coprolalia is the involuntary utterance of obscene words or phrases.

Tourette syndrome appears to be genetic (American Psychiatric Association, 1994). Associated features often include attentional problems (e.g., attention deficit disorder, attention-deficit/hyperactivity disorder), behavioral problems (e.g., oppositional defiant disorder), obsessive-compulsive disorder, sleep disorders, and learning disabilities (American Psychiatric Association, 1994). Neuroleptics (e.g., pimozide, haloperidol) have been found to be somewhat effective in the treatment of Tourette syndrome. However, adverse side effects may prompt many patients to cease its use in treatment (Chappell et al., 1995).

REFERENCES

American Psychiatric Association. (1994). *Diagnostic and statistics manual of mental disorders* (4th ed.). Washington, DC: Author.

Chappell P. B., Leckman, J. F., & Riddle, M. A. (1995). The pharmacologic treatment of tic disorders. *Child and Adolescent Psychiatric Clinics of North America, 4,* 197–216.

Peterson, B. S., Pine, D. S., Cohen, P., & Brook, J. S. (2001). Prospective, longitudinal study of tic, obsessive-compulsive, and attention-deficit/hyperactivity disorders in an epidemiological sample. *Journal of the American Academy of Child and Adolescent Psychiatry, 40,* 685–695.

Singer, H. S., & Walkup, J. T. (1991). Tourette syndrome and other tic disorders: Diagnosis, pathophysiology, and treatment. *Medicine, 70,* 15–32.

JASON GALLANT
University of Florida

See also Echolalia; Echopraxia; Tics; Tourette Syndrome Association

TOURETTE SYNDROME ASSOCIATION

The Tourette Syndrome Association, a voluntary nonprofit organization, was founded for the purpose of assisting individuals with Tourette syndrome, their families, friends, and concerned professionals. The primary objectives of the association include disseminating information regarding symptomatology and treatment of Tourette syndrome and raising funds to encourage and support scientific research into the nature and causes of the disorder.

In an effort to promote understanding of Tourette syndrome, the organization publishes quarterly newsletters, pamphlets, medical reprints, and films, and publicizes the disorder in newspapers, magazines, radio, and television. It provides support groups at a regional level for sharing current information about research, treatment, and management of Tourette syndrome. Information may be obtained from the Tourette Syndrome Association, Bell Plaza Building, 42-40 Bell Boulevard, Bayside, NY, 11361.

MARILYN P. DORNBUSH
Atlanta, Georgia

See also Tics; Tourette Syndrome

TOXIC SHOCK SYNDROME

Toxic shock syndrome is a very rare disease that is associated with strains of staphylococcus aureus, which is a bacterium that is a common inhabitant of the skin, oral cavity, and vagina. The staph bacterium can, under certain conditions, produce a toxin that attacks the immune system through the bloodstream (Toxic shock syndrome, 2000). This potentially life-threatening bacterial infection has been most often associated with the use of tampons during a woman's menstrual cycle.

Annual incidence in the United States in 1987, according to the Centers for Disease Control, was 1 to 2 out of 100,000 women ages 15 to 44. During that period, there was a small epidemic of toxic shock syndrome, reportedly caused by use of superabsorbent tampons. Since that time, reported cases have fallen to fewer than 10 per year since 1995. In some cases, use of barrier contraceptive devices has also been associated with toxic shock syndrome. Approximately 5% of all reported cases are fatal.

Characteristics

1. Sudden fever of 102 degrees or higher.
2. Vomiting or diarrhea.
3. Dizziness or feeling of weakness, fainting, or disorientation.
4. Rash resembling a sunburn that appears on palms of hands and soles of feet.
5. Headache.
6. Sore throat.
7. Aching muscles.
8. Bloodshot eyes.

Treatment involves providing blood and urine samples for detection of an infection. Hospitalization for a short period of time is likely, with a flood of antibiotics in order to clear the infection. There is a slight chance that the toxins produced by the staph bacteria could result in kidney failure (Mayo Clinic, n.d.).

It is unlikely that a student who has had toxic shock syndrome would qualify for special education services. Because the syndrome is completely curable with antibiotics and there are no severe or long-term effects in the majority of the cases, it is not a handicapping condition as outlined in IDEA 1997.

Following the outbreak of toxic shock syndrome in the early 1980s that was associated with the use of superabsorbent tampons, manufacturers began to print warning labels on tampon boxes about the possible dangers of prolonged use. Once women became aware of the dangers and began either to use tampons intermittently or to use tampons that were less absorbent, the outbreak subsided. There have been no extensive research studies on toxic shock syndrome since that time.

REFERENCES

Mayo Clinic. (n.d.). *Toxic shock syndrome.* Retrieved from http://mayoclinic.com/.ndinformation/diseasesandconditions

Toxic shock syndrome. (2000). Microsoft Encarta Online Encyclopedia 2000. Retrieved from www.encarta.com

CHRISTINE D. CDE BACA
University of Northern Colorado

See also Toxoplasmosis

TOXOCARIASIS (VISCERAL LARVA MIGRANS)

Toxocariasis is an infection that results from the invasion of parasites found in the intestines of dogs and cats. About 10,000 people are affected annually with toxocariasis in the United States.

Characteristics

1. Child ingests vegetation, dirt, or feces contaminated with the toxocara parasite eggs.
2. The eggs hatch in the child's intestine, and the larvae burrow into the intestinal wall.
3. The larvae migrate to the brain, eye, liver, lung, heart, and other organs, causing inflammation and tissue damage.
4. The child may develop a fever, cough, wheezing, an enlarged liver, and seizures.
5. Rashes and pneumonia may also occur.
6. Ocular larva migrans (larva entering the eye) may cause inflammation and formation of a scar on the retina, decreasing visual acuity and possibly causing crossed eyes.

Usually symptoms are so mild that treatment is not used, however, for more severe symptoms there is no current proven effective treatment. Mebendazole may be the most successful treatment. Diethylcarbamazine may also be beneficial, and prednisone may be taken to alleviate symptoms (Piessens, 1997). Eye treatment is more difficult and may entail measures designed to prevent further eye damage.

Children who experience visual impairment from the ocular larva migrans may need special education services to support their handicap.

The infection usually comprises mild symptoms that go away without treatment in 6 to 18 months (Piessens, 1997). However, each year more than 700 people infected with ocular larva migrans have permanent partial loss of vision (Division of Parasitic Diseases, 1999).

REFERENCES

Division of Parasitic Diseases. (1999, August 15). *Toxocariasis.* Retrieved from http://www.cdc.gov/ncidod/dpd/parasites/toxocara/factsht_toxocara.htm

Piessens, W. F. (1997). *Toxocariasis.* In R. Berkow, M. H. Beers, R. M. Bogin, & A. J. Fletcher (Eds.), *Merck Manual of medical information–Home edition* (pp. 904–905). New York, NY: Pocket Books.

TERESA M. LYLE
University of Texas at Austin

TOXOPLASMOSIS

Toxoplasmosis is caused by an intracellular protozoan, Toxoplasma gondii, which is transmitted via the blood to the prenatal fetus. This congenital infection causes mild to severe mental and motor retardation. The largest number of newborns will be asymptomatic in the neonatal period so they must be observed for ocular and central nervous system disability. The newborn with symptomatic toxoplasmosis will present at birth with one or more of the following: head abnormalities (large or small), cerebral calcifications, brain damage, muscle spasticity, convulsions and seizures, visual and hearing impairments, and eye infections. An enlarged liver and spleen, which cause an extended abdomen, are often present. Rashes and jaundiced skin may be seen in infants. Motor impairment as a result of brain damage may be seen. Prognosis is poor; death occurs in 10% to 15% but a high percentage of children have neuromotor defects, seizure disorders, intellectual disability, and damaged vision (Behrman, 1977; Carter, 1978).

Children often need self-help skills training (including feeding and toileting) from an early age (Hunt & Gibby, 1979). Related services may be required for speech, vision, and hearing deficits. Physical and occupational therapy may also be needed. Since a variety of health problems may be present, a medical consultation will probably be needed. Team placement and management will be necessary for adequate educational programming.

REFERENCES

Behrman, R. (Ed.). (1977). *Neo-natal-perinatal diseases of the fetus and infant* (2nd ed.). St. Louis, MO: Mosby.

Carter, C. (Ed.). (1978). *Medical aspects of mental retardation* (2nd ed.). Springfield, IL: Thomas.

Hunt, M., & Gibby, R. (1979). *The mentally retarded child: Development, training and education* (4th ed.). Boston, MA: Allyn & Bacon.

SALLY L. FLAGLER
University of Oklahoma

See also Functional Skills Training; Mental Retardation

TOY LENDING LIBRARIES

Toy libraries, occasionally named a Toybrary, are lending libraries with a broad range of toys, learning materials, and equipment appropriate for young children. Many traditional public libraries offer a toy section that includes puzzles, games, stuffed animals, blocks, and so on, that can be checked out and taken home by children and adults. However, the real growth in toy lending libraries is a part of the increasing need for child care outside the traditional home setting. Toy lending libraries and resource centers are becoming more common across the country as child-care needs and services grow and as people become more interested and involved in meeting the needs of children and those who care for them. Such libraries allow the various child-care programs in a specific geographic area to pool their resources and share equipment, as well as to exchange ideas and information. These libraries are particularly useful to people in isolated areas or those who work alone. When these libraries limit their use to certified day-care providers, they may also serve as a motivating force that results in a greater pool of licensed and certified day-care providers.

Types of equipment typically found in such libraries include recreational equipment, sand and water play sets, transportation equipment, farm and animal sets, blocks and other manipulatives, housekeeping materials, make believe materials, infant toys, puzzles, perception, alphabet, and math materials, and large and small motor toys. Funding for toy lending libraries comes from a number of sources. The most common would be government (national, state, or local) grants, foundation awards, local United Ways, and dues from members. Special groups such as state groups (Councils for Exceptional Children) have also been known to provide start-up funds for such libraries. For more information, visit http://www.usatla.org/USA_Toy_Library_Association/Welcome.html

DENISE M. SEDLAK
*United Way of Dunn County,
Menomonie, Wisconsin*

See also Day-Care Centers; Play

TRACE MINERALS

Trace minerals are minerals found in very small quantities in the human body but having significant relationships to certain metabolic events necessary for normal function. Severe deficiencies of trace minerals can result in a variety of handicaps, including orthopedic and learning disabilities. Some minerals and their relative levels in the body affect memory and attention as well. An overabundance or improper metabolism of some minerals also may produce problems. Depending on the particular mineral and the chronicity of the deficiency (or oversupply), mineral-related handicaps may or may not be reversible, though all are treatable to a large extent.

STAFF

See also Etiology; Nutritional Disorders

TRAINING FOR EMPLOYMENT IN TRADITIONAL SETTINGS

Students with mild or moderate disabilities can be educated or trained to succeed as adult workers in many vocations. The vocational program that prepares students with disabilities will be similar to regular vocational education; however, unique components should be evidenced.

All vocational preparation programs should begin with an assessment phase. Students' job interests, abilities, and readiness will be evaluated. For many students receiving special education services, this assessment procedure will be their first directed opportunity to examine their own capabilities and limitations as they relate to employment (Weisgerber, 1978).

The assessment phase should be comprehensive to provide information that will help the instructors and students to set appropriate vocational goals. Also, adequate assessment data will ensure that the subsequent training program will be effective. Specific job skills capabilities should be identified, as well as appropriate interpersonal relationship skills. More workers with disabilities are dismissed from their employment because of lack of social skills than lack of job skills (Weisgerber, Dahl, & Appleby, 1981).

The primary goal of the training phase of a vocational program for students with disabilities will be to prepare them for successful employment. To accomplish this goal, several components must be integrated into the total program (Weisgerber et al., 1981).

The faculty responsible for these programs must continually be aware of the limitations and capabilities of the students and the employment community. Job analyses that include data concerning vocational opportunities, employers' attitudes toward individuals with disabilities, and the community's receptivity to accommodating individuals with disabilities should be conducted periodically.

An amicable relationship among special education teachers, vocational education faculty, and community employers will facilitate successful employment of graduates with disabilities. Teachers who are knowledgeable about their students' work abilities can be effective advocates for these students when they are seeking employment.

Vocational training programs should use technology to assist their students in increasing their abilities and reducing the effects of their disabilities. Familiarity with new devices will enable the faculty to share this knowledge with prospective employers to promote employment of students with disabilities in traditional settings.

Securing realistic work sites either at school or in businesses and factories will increase the effectiveness of a special education vocational program. By practicing specific job skills that will be used in a vocation, students will not have to be retrained when they become employed, saving the employers time and money.

Teachers who advocate employment of students with disabilities should have expertise in the area of adaptations for job sites. Alteration of the workplace and occasionally the work routine may enable the worker with disabilities to become more productive. In these instances, it is the environment that is handicapping rather than the physical or mental limitations of the worker (Wade & Gold, 1978).

REFERENCES

Wade, M. G., & Gold, M. W. (1978). Removing some of the limitations of mentally retarded workers by improving job design. *Human Factors, 20,* 339–348.

Weisgerber, R. A. (Ed.). (1978). *Vocational education: Teaching the handicapped in regular classes.* Reston, VA: Council for Exceptional Children.

Weisgerber, R. A., Dahl, P. R., & Appleby, J. A. (1981). *Training the handicapped for productive employment.* Rockville, MD: Aspen.

JONI J. GLEASON
University of West Florida

See also Habilitation; Vocational Education

TRAINING IN THE HOME

Literature relating to child development frequently states that parents and other family members are the primary teachers of infants and young children. A great deal of the teaching and learning of young children in the home occurs during everyday activities such as watching TV and completing daily chores. As a result of the parents' role in teaching and socializing young children, it is essential to include the family and the home environment in any intervention plan for young children at risk (Fallen & Umansky, 1985). According to Cartwright, Cartwright, and Ward (1995) many children with disabilities tend to have problems generalizing from the specific teaching setting to other settings. Therefore, an advantage of home-based training is that many opportunities are available for the parents to apply learning to life activities.

One home-based approach to early education is the Portage project. This project was designed to meet the needs of young children in rural Wisconsin. Emphasis was placed on the skills of parents in teaching their disabled children. A teacher would visit the home and provide the parents with the necessary materials, written instructions, and forms for record keeping. Some of the basic assumptions that this project was developed around are that parents are concerned about their children and want them to develop to their maximum potential; that parents can, with assistance, learn to be effective teachers; that the socioeconomic and educational levels of the parents are no indication of the willingness to help or the amount of gains the children will achieve; and that precision teaching maximizes the chances of success for children and parents. Research has shown that when parents are involved in their children's treatment and education, children do better. The family is considered the most effective system for fostering the development of the child (Shearer, 1974).

On the other hand, there are some educators who strongly suggest that parents should leave teaching of academics to the schools. Lerner (1981) states that when children with learning disabilities are tutored by their parents, it makes the children feel stressed. This is because there is a good chance that the children will feel like failures in front of the most important people in their lives. This stress tends to have a negative effect on the parent-child relationship. Lerner emphasized that parents should concentrate on teaching children domestic tasks and helping them develop a good self-image. Barsch (1969) feels that parents do not have the patience to teach their children. He lists several reasons why parents should not teach academics. They include:

1. Parents lack essential teaching skills.
2. The parent-child instructional session often results in frustration and tension for both members.
3. Most parents and children wish that academics could be accomplished during the school day.
4. Most teachers do not have the time to guide the parents.
5. When both the home and school stress academics, the child finds little rest.

6. Parents differ greatly in their competence as teachers.

7. Parents may feel guilty if they do not find the time to tutor their child regularly.

It has been established that some parents can successfully tutor their children. Therefore, the parents' decision to tutor or not should be made on an individual basis. According to Kronick (1977), a major question that should be addressed in terms of whether to tutor or not is whether tutoring can be accomplished without depriving any family member of resources that assist in maintaining a well-balanced life. If the parents decide to teach their children at home, Lovitt (1977) has suggested four guidelines for parents. They should establish a specific time each day for the tutoring sessions; keep sessions short; keep responses to the child; and keep a record.

REFERENCES

Barsch, R. H. (1969). *The parent teacher partnership*. Reston, VA: Council for Exceptional Children.

Cartwright, G. P., Cartwright, C. A., & Ward, M. E. (1995). *Educating special needs learners* (4th ed.). Boston, MA: Wadsworth.

Fallen, N. H., & Umansky, W. (1985). *Children with special needs* (2nd ed.). Columbus, OH: Merrill.

Kronick, D. (1977). A parent's thoughts for parents and teachers. In N. G. Haring & B. Bateman (Eds.), *Teaching the learning disabled child*. Englewood Cliffs, NJ: Prentice Hall.

Lerner, J. W. (1981). *Learning disabilities: Theories, diagnosis and teaching strategies* (3rd ed.). Boston, MA: Houghton Mifflin.

Lovitt, T. C. (1977). *In spite of my resistance...I've learned from children*. Columbus, OH: Merrill.

Shearer, M. S. (1974). A home based parent training model. In J. Grim (Ed.), *First chance for children: Training parents to teach: Four models* (Vol. 3, pp. 49–62). Chapel Hill: Technical Assistance Development System, North Carolina University.

JANICE HARPER
North Carolina Central University

See *also* Family Response to a Child With Disabilities; Homebound Instruction; Tutoring

TRAINING SCHOOLS

Training schools were an intricate part of the larger multipurpose residential facilities known as the *colony plan* that were established in the late 1800s. These schools served children and adolescents who were not considered eligible for public school education because of their unique educational needs.

The evolvement of the training school concept was based on earlier work by Samuel Gridley Howe (1801–1876). Howe's Perkin School for the Deaf (1848) led to the development of other self-contained schools (e.g., Massachusetts School for Idiots and Feeble-Minded Youth, 1855). Although Howe's 10-bed unit was the first residential facility established, it was not until 1848 that the first large facility, the Syracuse Institution of the Feeble-Minded was developed. Harvey B. Wilbur (1820–1883), a physician, became the first superintendent of this facility. Like Howe, Wilbur was very much influenced by the philosophy and principles of Edward Seguin; he placed a great deal of emphasis on education.

Although institutions for individuals with disabilities were initially viewed as beneficial by many throughout history, their purpose, programs, and administration changed drastically. The small homelike educational establishment was replaced by the larger, overcrowded, and underfinanced multipurpose facility that would typify institutions for generations to come (Kanner, 1964).

Initially, training schools in institutions were intended to serve school-aged exceptional needs children and adolescents. As years passed, it became increasingly clear that individuals who reached the age limit for school programming had few choices for continued educational services. Typically, these adults were sent to almshouses or other similar institutions.

Though educational programs continued in institutions, there was a growing emphasis on vocational training. Most of the basic operations in running these large facilities were the sole responsibility of the individuals who resided at the facility. Therefore, skills that were taught to the residents had a direct application toward the continued function of the institution (Scheerenberger, 1983).

By 1890 the school facilities of the 1850s evolved into larger facilities intended to serve four distinct groups of residents. The colony plan was developed to serve (1) the teachable portion of a school-attending group, (2) the helpless, deformed, epileptic, and unteachable, (3) the male adults who had reached school age but were unable to become self-supportive, and (4) the female adults who at that time needed close supervision. The colony plan included training schools as well as an industrial, custodial, and farm department.

As early as the 1860s, however, advocacy of education in public schools was being heard. Although it is difficult to determine precisely when the first public school special education program was initiated, credit is usually given to the public school system of Providence, Rhode Island. An auxiliary school for 15 students with intellectual disabilities opened in December 1896 (Woodhill, 1920). By 1898 the city of Providence established three more auxiliary schools and one special education classroom in a public school.

Other cities soon followed Providence's example. By the turn of the century, special education provisions for the mentally retarded shifted from total residential training schools to generally accepted, though not always implemented, education in public school systems.

REFERENCES

Kanner, L. (1964). *A history of case and study of the mentally retarded.* Springfield, IL: Thomas.

Scheerenberger, R. C. (1983). *The history of mental retardation.* Baltimore, MD: Paul H. Brookes.

Woodhill, E. (1920). Public school clinics in connection with a state school for the feeble-minded. *Journal of Psycho Asthenics, 25,* 14–103.

MICHAEL G. BROWN
*Central Wisconsin Center for the
Developmentally Disabled*

See also History of Special Education; Humanism and Special Education

TRANQUILIZERS

The term *tranquilizer* is a superordinate that may be applied to two general classes of psychoactive drugs: antipsychotic agents (major tranquilizers) and antianxiety agents (minor tranquilizers). Both major and minor tranquilizers produce sedative effects, though to different degrees. Minor tranquilizers tend to produce fewer neurotoxic side effects, but appear to be more likely candidates for abuse (Blum, 1984). The following table summarizes the two groups of tranquilizers.

The major tranquilizers were developed in an attempt to humanize the treatment of individuals with psychoses, who were being given long-term treatment in psychiatric hospitals. The drugs were developed based on observations of related agents that produced calming effects on wild animals. Unlike the minor tranquilizers, the major tranquilizers have not been found to be physically addictive. Abrupt withdrawal, however, has been reported to induce insomnia, anxiety, and gastrointestinal symptoms (Brooks, 1959; see Table T.1).

In terms of the general public, the minor tranquilizers are more familiar and also show more pervasive, popular use. The benzodiazapines are often used to reduce the effects of chronic stress, tension, and emotional discomfort. Valium was at one time the most prescribed drug in the United States, with 75% of the prescriptions being issued by nonpsychiatrists (Blum, 1984).

In addition to more general stress-reducing effects, Valium is also a drug of abuse. Dosages of 100 to 500 mg

Table T.1. Tranquilizers

Major	Minor
Phenothiazines	*Benzodiazapines*
Thorazine (Chlorpromazine)	Valium (Diazepam)
Stelazine (Trifluoperazine)	Librium (Chlordiazepoxide)
Mellaril (Thioridazine)	Dalmane (Flurazepam)
Prolixin (Fluphenazine)	Tranxene (Chlorazepate)
Thioxanthenes	*Meprobamate*
Navane (Thiothixene)	
Butyrophenones	
Haldol (Haloperidol)	

produce intoxication (Patch, 1974). Valium also is used by substance abusers to deal with the frightening effects of a "bad trip" after hallucinogen (e.g., LSD) ingestion or to diminish the hangover effects after amphetamine intoxication (Blum, 1984). Therapeutically, Valium has been found to produce symptomatic relief for tension and anxiety states, free-floating agitation, mild depressive symptoms, fatigue, and short-term treatments of insomnia (Katzung, 1982). In addition, benzodiazapines have been used as adjuncts in the treatment of seizure disorders, since administration tends to raise the seizure threshold (Katzung, 1982). Valium also has been used to relieve skeletal muscle spasms, whether induced by local reactions or trauma, and spasticity secondary to upper motor neuron disorders (Blum, 1984).

Effects commonly reported owing to drug sensitivity or to intoxication include anticholinergic effects. In addition, lethargy, headache, slurred speech, tremor, and dizziness also have been reported (Blum, 1984). Paradoxical reactions including acute periods of increased excitability, increased anxiety, hallucinations, insomnia, rage, and increased muscle spasticity also have appeared in the literature (Blum, 1984). Though severe overdose of Valium is uncommon, symptoms include somnolence, confusion, coma, and blunted reflexes (Blum, 1984). The minor tranquilizers have not been found to be physically addictive; however, habituation (psychosocial accommodation to the effects of the drugs) has been reported frequently.

REFERENCES

Blum, K. B. (1984). *Handbook of abusable drugs.* New York, NY: Gardner.

Brooks, G. W. (1959). Withdrawal from neuroleptic drugs. *American Journal of Psychiatry, 115,* 931.

Katzung, B. G. (1982). *Basic and clinical pharmacology.* Los Altos, CA: Lange.

Patch, V. D. (1974). The dangers of diazepam: a street drug. *New England Journal of Medicine, 190,* 807.

ROBERT F. SAWICKI
Lake Erie Institute of Rehabilitation

See also Mellaril; Thorazine

TRANSDISCIPLINARY MODEL

Originally conceived by Hutchison (1974), the transdisciplinary model is one of several team approaches for the delivery of educational and related services to students with disabilities. The other team models are the multidisciplinary model and the interdisciplinary model. In a multidisciplinary model, team members maintain their respective discipline boundaries with only minimal, if any, coordination, collaboration, or communication (McCormick, 1984). The interdisciplinary model differs from the multidisciplinary model in that there is some discussion among the involved professionals after their individual assessments have been completed and at least an attempt to develop a coordinated service delivery plan. However, the programming recommendations are often not realistic. The teacher may not have the skills to implement the recommendations or the authority to arrange for their provision (Hart, 1977). Another problem is the lack of provision for follow-up and feedback in the interdisciplinary model.

The transdisciplinary model is the only one of the three models to adequately address the issue of coordinated service delivery. This model suggests specific procedures for sharing information and skills among professionals and across discipline boundaries. It is differentiated from the other models by its emphasis on coordination, collaboration, and communication among the involved discipline representatives and its advocacy of integrated services.

The transdisciplinary model assumes: (a) joint functioning (team members performing assessment, planning, and service delivery functions together); (b) continuous staff development (commitment to expansion of each team member's competencies); and (c) role release (sharing functions across discipline boundaries; Lyon & Lyon, 1980). The professional makeup of a transdisciplinary team varies depending on the needs of the student. It may include few or many professionals, but whenever possible they coordinate their assessment procedures and plan as a group for the student's daily programming.

Transdisciplinary team members are accountable for seeing that the best practices of their respective disciplines are implemented (McCormick & Goldman, 1979). However, their responsibility does not stop there. They are also responsible for monitoring program implementation, training others if necessary, and revising programs when evaluation data indicate that the procedures are not working. The teacher is usually coordinator and manager of team processes so that there is no duplication of efforts or splintering of services.

REFERENCES

Hart, V. (1977). The use of many disciplines with the severely and profoundly handicapped. In E. Sontag, J. Smith, & N. Certo (Eds.), *Educational programming for the severely and profoundly handicapped*. Reston, VA: Council for Exceptional Children, Division of Mental Retardation.

Hutchison, D. (1974). A model for transdisciplinary staff development (United Cerebral Palsy: Technical Report No. 8).

Lyon, S., & Lyon, G. (1980). Team functioning and staff development a role release approach to providing integrated educational services for severely handicapped students. *Journal of the Association for Severely Handicapped*, 5(3), 250–263.

McCormick, L. (1984). Extracurricular roles and relationships. In L. McCormick & R. Schiefelbusch (Eds.), *Early language intervention*. Columbus, OH: Merrill.

McCormick, L., & Goldman, R. (1979). The transdisciplinary model: Implications for service delivery and personnel preparation for the severely handicapped. *AAESPH Review*, 4(2), 152–161.

LINDA McCORMICK
University of Hawaii, Manoa

See also Itinerant Services; Multidisciplinary Teams

TRANSFER OF TRAINING

Transfer of training, also referred to as *stimulus generalization* or *generalization*, takes place when a behavior that has been reinforced in the presence of one stimulus event occurs in the presence of different but similar stimuli. Using the behavior analytic $S > R > C$ paradigm, the emphasis of this learning construct is on (1) the characteristics of the events that precede a behavior, and (2) the relationship of these characteristics to the occurrence of the behavior under similar stimulus conditions.

From this viewpoint, increasing similarities in events that precede a behavior result in an increased likelihood of stimulus generalization. Conversely, there is a decreased likelihood of the trained behavior occurring as these preceding events become more dissimilar. Applied to educational programming, the influence of these similarities might be beneficial or problematic. Thus a student may be trained to respond to questions asked by an adult male teacher by raising his or her hand. If this student responds likewise in other classroom settings to questions asked by female adults, a beneficial transfer of training has occurred. However, if the student responds to his father's inquiry, "Why are you late?" by raising his or her hand, the transfer of training that has taken place might be viewed as potentially problematic.

This example highlights some of the problems that relate to transfer of training and also touches on the fundamental role of this learning explanation in the educational process. Almost without exception, students are exposed to information and material with specific stimulus characteristics or in specific stimulus settings. Traditionally, this stimulus-specific training is assumed to automatically transfer to similar stimulus events. The accuracy of this assumption is highly questionable when teaching the learner with exceptional needs. As the severity of an individual's learning problems increases, so does the need for implementation of more specific interventions that are geared toward systematically promoting transfer of training.

A variety of approaches and procedures have been applied in order to increase the positive transfer of training. These attempts have been effective to varying degrees in achieving this purpose. Specific recommendations for achieving transfer of training have been offered by Martin and Pear (1983) and Stokes and Baer (1977). These recommendations include (a) training the skills in the situation where the behavior is to occur, (b) presenting a variety of stimulus events, (c) programming common stimulus characteristics across settings, and (d) training with sufficient examples.

Training the skill in the situation where it is expected to occur addresses the relationship between the training efforts extended to develop a student's skills in one setting and the implicit desire to have that student perform those skills in another setting. The use of this tactic requires the development of as many similarities as possible between the two settings, or actual skill training in the targeted situation. Therefore, if a student is being taught to locate the correct restroom using international door symbols, as much of the training as possible should take place in similar (analogue) or actual (in vivo) settings.

Another technique for promoting transfer of training is the presentation of a variety of stimulus events. Also referred to as *training loosely*, this tactic involves providing the student with a wide variety of stimuli to allow practicing of the response under different but similar conditions. Accordingly, training situations might involve different trainers, differing verbal requests, and so on, each serving as a stimulus event for the same desired student response.

Programming of common stimuli is another tactic used to promote transfer of training. Alternatively referred to as the "don't teach basketball with a football" technique, this procedure focuses on the establishment of stimulus bridges between the training setting and the goal environment. Thus students are taught to respond to the materials, statements, or other stimulus events that will actually be present in the goal environment.

The final tactic suggested by these authors involves the presentation of representative stimulus events during training. In contrast to teaching a student to respond by presenting all possible stimulus options (e.g., every possible configuration of the word poison), the emphasis of "training sufficient examples" is on the use of stimulus events that encourage responses to example stimuli. Application of this technique in teaching a student to respond

to teacher greetings might involve training the student to say "hi" to one teacher and priming generalization of the response by rewarding the student's response to another teacher.

The effectiveness of education to a large extent relates to the amount of training that is transferred from one stimulus event to another similar event or setting. With the exceptional learner, this transfer must often be directly encouraged. For a comprehensive explanation of transfer of training and related teaching considerations, the reader is referred to texts by Sulzer-Azaroff and Mayer (1977) and Alberto and Troutman (2012).

REFERENCES

Alberto, P., & Troutman, A. C. (2012). *Applied behavior analysis for teachers*. Upper Saddle River, NJ: Merrill.

Martin, G., & Pear, J. (1983). *Behavior modification: What it is and how to do it* (2nd ed.). Englewood Cliffs, NJ: Prentice Hall.

Stokes, T. F., & Baer, D. M. (1977). An implicit technology of generalization. *Journal of Applied Behavior Analysis*, *10*, 349–367.

Sulzer-Azaroff, B., & Mayer, G. R. (1977). *Applying behavior-analysis procedures with children and youth*. New York, NY: Holt, Rinehart, & Winston.

J. Todd Stephens
University of Wisconsin at Madison

See also Generalization

TRANSFORMATIONAL GENERATIVE GRAMMAR

In 1957 Noam Chomsky revolutionized the field of English grammar and research with the publication of the book *Syntactic Structures*. Chomsky, considered the father of the theory of transformational grammar, proposed a finite set of operations (called *transformations*) that produce (or generate) sentences of infinite number and variety without producing nonsentences. These operations are acquired during the first few years of life through exposure to conversation rather than through formal study. They are internalized by the speaker without his or her being aware of or able to state them.

Chomsky's theory describes the language people do use rather than the language they ought to use (Cattell, 1978; Chomsky, 1957). It focuses on competence, the ideal speaker-listener's complete command of language, as opposed to performance, the actual use of language in concrete situations as affected by imperfection and inconsistency. Unlike the traditional grammarian who deals with sentence form, or surface structure, Chomsky distinguishes between surface structure and its underlying meaning or deep structure. This is the level at which grammatical relationships are preserved. By way of example, Quigley, Russell, and Power (1977) present the sentences "John is easy to please" and "John is eager to please." These two sentences are identical to one another in surface structure but completely different in deep structure. Muma (1978) elaborates by pointing out that the sentence "I bes here" (nonstandard dialect) is not inferior to the sentence "I am here" (standard dialect), as both are identical at the deep structure level.

Deep structures are turned into surface structures through transformations that expand, delete, and reorder sentence constituents, or component parts. These operations may be applied to all sentences without changing their meanings. Examples of transformations applied to the sentence "boys like girls" would include question (Do boys like girls?), negation (boys don't like girls), and passive voice (girls are liked by boys; Quigley et al., 1977).

Transformational grammarians view the sentence as a hierarchical organization of constituents. By applying a series of rewriting rules of increasing specificity, it is possible to analyze sentence structure, working backward through the derivation of a sentence to discover the initial transformational rule by which it was generated. These rewriting rules enable linguists to describe sentences pictorially using tree diagrams. Crystal, Fletcher, and Gorman (1977) point out that the easiest and best known of these rules is represented by the formula S Æ NP + VP, or rewrite the sentence as a noun phrase and a verb phrase.

Transformational generative grammar has been applied successfully to research into language function (Dever, 1971), language development and delay, dialectic differences, and ESL studies (Quigley et al., 1977). Its detractors have noted that the distinction between language competence and performance is minimal at best when dealing with individuals with language disorders (Crystal et al., 1977). Akmajian, Demers, and Harnish (1980) note that Chomsky's model has been challenged at every level, resulting in numerous changes since the mid-1960s.

REFERENCES

Akmajian, A., Demers, R. A., & Harnish, R. M. (1980). *Linguistics: An introduction to language and communication*. Cambridge, MA: MIT Press.

Cattell, N. R. (1978). *The new English grammar*. Cambridge, MA: MIT Press.

Chomsky, N. (1957). *Syntactic structures*. The Hague: Mouton.

Chomsky, N. (1965). *Aspects of the theory of syntax*. Cambridge, MA: MIT Press.

Crystal, D., Fletcher, P., & Gorman, M. (1977). *The grammatical analysis of language disability: A procedure for assessment and remediation*. London, England: Arnold.

Dever, R. B. (1971). *The case for data gathering*. Journal of Special Education, 5, 119–126.

Muma, J. R. (1978). *Language handbook: Concepts, assessment, intervention*. Englewood Cliffs, NJ: Prentice Hall.

Quigley, S. P., Russell, W. K., & Power, D. J. (1977). *Linguistics and deaf children*. Washington, DC: Alexander Graham Bell Association.

SUSAN SHANDELMIER
Eastern Pennsylvania Special Education Regional Resources Center

See also Chomsky, Noam; Language Disorders; Linguistic Deviance

TRANSITION

Transition simply means a change in status, situation, or location. Developmental psychologists believe that human development is a continuous process with a connected sequence of stages; at each stage, an individual is confronted with a set of unique problems and related developmental tasks. From this perspective, transition is the process of changing from one developmental stage to another. Examples of transitions include from childhood to adolescence, from adolescence to early adulthood, and from middle to late adulthood. The transition to early adulthood is the most dramatic of all transitions because, during this period of time, an individual forms preliminary adult identity by making major choices that will define his or her place in the adult world. From social and educational perspectives, graduation from high school represents a major milestone for every adolescent because it marks the transition from adolescence to young adulthood. Whether or not a high school student makes a successful transition from adolescence to adulthood directly affects his or her quality of life as an adult. A major developmental task for adolescents is to expand personal independence; prepare for employment, postsecondary education, and community living; and develop new relationships with peers and community members.

Successful completion of the transition from high school to adulthood is a challenge for everyone, but is particularly difficult for those with disabilities because they face additional challenges associated with having a disability. These challenges and difficulties require education to play a more critical role in facilitating task development of adolescents with disabilities and do a better job in preparing them for adulthood. Therefore, in special education, transition commonly refers to the process of facilitating a student's moving from high school to adulthood. This concept was initially proposed by Will (1984), who conceptualized transition as a movement from school to work via one of three bridges: no special services, time-limited services, and ongoing services. Halpern (1985) offered an improved model that expanded transition outcome areas to include three areas of adult living, including employment, residential environment, and social and interpersonal networks. In his view, transition is a change in status from behaving primarily as a student to assuming emergent adult roles in the community. It was not until 1990 when a more widely accepted definition of transition was offered in the Individuals with Disabilities Education Act (IDEA), which defined transition as a coordinated set of activities for a child with a disability that facilitates the child's movement from school to post-school activities.

In the 2004 reauthorization of IDEA, transition services is defined as "a coordinated set of activities for a child with a disability that (a) is designed to be within a results-oriented process, that is focused on improving the academic and functional achievement of the child with a disability to facilitate the child's movement from school to post-school activities, ...; (b) is based on the individual child's needs, taking into account the child's strengths, preferences, and interests; and (c) includes instruction, related services, community experiences, the development of employment and other post-school adult living objectives, and when appropriate, acquisition of daily living skills and functional vocational evaluation." The transition process starts from knowing the student's strengths, preferences, and interests. Based on the student information, the IEP (individualized education program) team collectively identifies postschool activities and goals that are pertinent to the student. To help the student in reaching the postschool goals, transition services need to start no later than age 14. A coordinated set of activities must be planned for each individual student with an IEP and updated annually. When planning a student's transition services, a top-down approach should be taken to identify specific transition skills from the primary adult life domains (Cronin & Patton, 1993). Examples of adult life domains include employment/education, community involvement, physical/emotional health, personal responsibility and relationships, leisure pursuits, and home and family.

A great deal of research has been done to identify value-based and evidence-based practices. As a result, a set of transition practices has been recommended. Some of the value-based practices include paid or unpaid work experience, employment preparation, family involvement, general education inclusion, social skills training, daily living skills training, self-determination skills training, and community or agency collaboration (Landmark, Ju, & Zhang, 2010). Examples of evidence-based transition practices are included in the "Evidence-Based Secondary Transition Practices" entry in this encyclopedia.

REFERENCES

Cronin, M. E., & Patton, J. R. (1993). *Life skills instruction for all students with special needs.* Austin, TX: PRO-ED.

Halpern, A. (1985). Transition: A look at the foundation. *Exceptional Children, 51,* 479–486.

Individuals with Disabilities Education Act (IDEA) of 1990, PL 101-476, 20 U.S.C. § 1400 et seq. (1990).

Individuals with Disabilities Education Improvement Act (IDEIA) of 2004, PL 108-446, 20 U.S.C. § 1400 et seq. (2004).

Landmark, L. J., Ju, S., & Zhang, D. (2010). Substantiated best practices in transition: Fifteen plus years later. *Career Development for Exceptional Individuals, 33,* 165–176.

Will, M. (1984). *OSERS programming for the transition of youth with disabilities: Bridges from school to working life.* Washington, DC: U.S. Department of Education.

DULAN ZHANG
Texas A&M University
Fourth edition

See also Vocational Education; Vocational Rehabilitation Counseling

TRANSITION ASSESSMENT

Transition assessment as a key component of the transition planning process was primarily a recommended practice in transition services literature until the Individuals with Disabilities Education Improvement Act of 2004 and its supporting regulations in 2006. While not defining transition assessment precisely, the Act used language that left no doubt of bipartisan congressional intent. In the definition of transition services, the specific addition of the terms "improving the academic and functional achievement" gave focus to a transition services process that addressed both academic and life-related competencies. The definition of transition services also qualifies the phrase, "a set of coordinated activities," with the caveat that those services "shall be based on the individual child's needs, taking into account the child's strengths, preferences, and interests" (IDEA 2004; 20 U.S.C. § 1414 *et seq.*).

To further emphasize congressional intent, the language of IDEA 2004 specified that the Individual Education Program (IEP) for all students 16 and older (and younger when appropriate) must have appropriate measurable postsecondary goals "based upon age-appropriate transition assessments related to training, education, employment, and, where appropriate, independent living skills." The language in this section gives an assessment target for getting at academic and functional achievement or performance across the areas of education and training, employment, and independent living skills. These three areas may be generalized in terminology as the areas of learning, working, and living—the three primary areas of possible postsecondary outcome goals.

Without a legal definition of transition assessment, professionals are left to try to define it in terms of recommended practice. Sitlington, Neubert, Begun, Lombard, and Leconte (2007) propose this definition:

> Transition assessment is an ongoing process of collecting information on the student's strengths, needs, preferences, and interests as they relate to the demands of current and future living, learning, and working environments. This process should begin in middle school and continue until the student graduates or exits high school. Information from this process should be used to drive the IEP and transition planning process and to develop the SOP [Summary of Performance] document detailing the student's academic and functional performance and postsecondary goals. (pp. 2–3)

If one can agree to Clark's (2007) broad view of assessment as "question-asking," then it follows that transition assessment is a process of asking the important questions that every student and family should ask when planning for current and future learning, working, and living environments. That is, what are the postsecondary goals for continuing on for further education or training, for employment, and/or for living in the community? Once one or more of these dreams for the future translate into tentative postsecondary goal statements, they inform the school on the direction of next steps in question-asking. If the student or family chooses not to use school time or focus on all three of these goal areas, the nature and type of question-asking activities get more targeted in content. These questions can be raised in a variety of both formal and informal activities.

Typically, there are three general types of information needed in the transition planning process: (1) knowledge (information, facts, concepts, etc., related to adult learning, living, and working); (2) skills (performance of skills expected in learning, working, and living environments); and (3) intelligent application of knowledge and skills (functional achievement, including practical and social intelligence, self-determination, maintenance of physical and mental health and fitness, social and interpersonal relationships, community participation). Assessment activities that cut across all three of these general types of information for use in planning would include or be based on questions related to strengths, support needs, preferences, and interests.

Specific areas for question-asking vary with individual students and their postsecondary outcome goals but may include:

- Interests related to learning, living, and working.
- Preferences related to learning, living, and working environments.

- Physical health and fitness status.
- Communication skills.
- Current information on cognitive development and performance.
- Adaptive behavior and skills.
- Social and interpersonal relationship skills.
- Emotional development and mental health.
- Independent and interdependent living skills.
- Recreation and leisure skills.
- Employability and vocational skills.
- Choice-making and self-determination skills.
- Community participation and citizenship skills.
- Needed supports or accommodations.
- Needed linkages with current and future support services.

IEP case managers, transition services personnel, IEP team members, special education support staff, and related services personnel may select from a variety of formal or informal assessment alternatives. Formal transition assessment instruments will have some evidence of validity and reliability and some might also have norms. Informal assessments do not have any demonstrated validity or reliability evidence, nor would they ever have norms.

Formal assessment instruments used in transition planning may include standardized tests or formal inventories or scales. Most of these are paper-and-pencil or computerized assessments that require varying degrees of reading comprehension and response capability. Accommodations may be appropriate for some of these (e.g., reading items to student, manual signing for student, extended time, adaptation of materials for blind students) but for others standardized administrations must be used. Formal transition instruments or scales may include general screening inventories of transition knowledge and skills or specific inventories of transition-related knowledge and skills. Most of the instruments directly pertaining to transition-related strengths, interests, or preferences do not require a highly skilled psychometrist or diagnostician, although those related to cognitive functioning, adaptive behavior, and emotional or behavioral functioning likely will. Administration of formal assessments is a matter of careful reading and administration procedure. Accurate interpretation and communication of results also require users to read and follow the instrument administration and interpretation guidelines in the manuals.

Informal assessment activities include curriculum-based assessments, interviews, surveys or questionnaires, checklists, rating scales, observation logs or observation protocols, commercially available or web-based instruments, environmental/ecological assessments, or person centered planning. Each of these has its own advantages and disadvantages. Each also requires a set of skills for administration or interpretation that not all school personnel have without some training.

A practical issue in the transition assessment process is determining responsibility for coordinating the process. That person is most often the IEP case manager, but in some cases a transition specialist may assume the role of transition assessment coordinator and case manager when a student reaches 16. Whoever does assume the coordination role draws on the assistance and collaboration of a range of possible contributors, starting with the student and his/her family. At school there will be special education personnel, paraprofessionals, general educators, career and technical educators, school administrators, guidance counselors, school psychologists and/or diagnosticians, related services personnel, and school building employees. Outside of school there are employers, work supervisors, extended family, community organizations and agencies, health care professionals, or disability advocates (adults or peers).

The most critical uses of transition assessment information are the IDEA mandates for developing a student's IEP annually and then as the basis for the Summary of Performance (SOP) for all students graduating or exiting after age eligibility expires. Other uses include course of study placement decisions, instructional decisions, guidance and counseling, referrals, curriculum planning, and documentation of procedures under IDEA.

REFERENCES

Clark, G. M. (2007). *Assessment for transitions planning* (2nd ed.). Austin, TX: PRO-ED.

Sitlington, P. L., Neubert, D. A., Begun, W. H., Lombard, R. C., & Leconte, P. J. (2007). *Assess for success: A practitioner's handbook on transition assessment* (2nd ed.). Thousand Oaks, CA: Corwin.

GARY M. CLARK
University of Kansas
Fourth edition

TRANSITION PLANNING (RELATIONSHIP TO THE IEP AND THE PROCESS)

Transition planning is the process of identifying goals and implementing strategies to facilitate postschool success for students with disabilities. Transition planning is a required component of the individualized education program (IEP), and there are timelines that must be met including (a) having transition services in place when the student is 16 years of age, (b) ensuring that the transition services are updated annually, (c) advising the parent and the student that upon the age of majority rights transfer to the student, and (d) providing a summary of performance at the student's dismissal IEP meeting (Individuals with Disabilities Education Improvement Act [IDEIA], 2004). When Congress reauthorized the Individuals with Disabilities Education Act in 2004, it ensured that IDEIA was aligned with the No Child Left Behind Act of 2001. The importance of planning the educational program so that students with disabilities have the greatest opportunity to achieve their postsecondary goals was stressed. As a result, states were required to develop state performance plans that address the five monitoring priorities and 20 performance or compliance indicators as identified by the U.S. Department of Education's Office of Special Education Programs (OSEP, 2007).

One of the monitoring priorities is effective transition. There are three indicators within this priority, but one of the indicators (i.e., Indicator 12) pertains to the transition from Part C early childhood intervention services to Part B early childhood special education services. The other indicators are Indicators 13 and 14. Indicator 13 is the "percent of youth aged 16 and above with an IEP that includes coordinated, measurable, annual IEP goals and transition services that will reasonably enable the student to meet the post-secondary goals" (IDEIA, 2004, 20 USC 1416(a)(3)(B)). Indicator 14 is the "percent of youth who had IEP documents, are no longer in secondary school and who have been competitively employed, enrolled in some type of postsecondary school, or both, within one year of leaving high school" (IDEIA, 2004, 20 U.S.C. 1416(a)(3)(B)). Clearly, transition planning as a part of the IEP process is critical.

Effective transition planning is individualized and directly impacts the development of the remainder of the student's IEP. The IEP process is cyclic (refer to Figure T.4) and consists of several active components: assessment of the student, assembly of the IEP team, statement of the student's present levels of academic achievement and functional performance (PLAAFP), specification of special education and related services and aids needed, development of annual goals and short-term objectives, determination of the least restrictive environment, and implementation of the IEP. When the student reaches transition age, transition planning is infused into the IEP process, as shown in Figure T.5. Although Figure T.5 only adds two additional components to the IEP process (i.e., development of postsecondary goals and the development of the summary of performance [SOP] on exiting high school), the other components in the process are expanded to take into consideration the student's transition desires and needs.

Transition Planning in the IEP Process

Assessment of the Student

Transition assessment is a critical part of transition planning. It provides the IEP team with information regarding

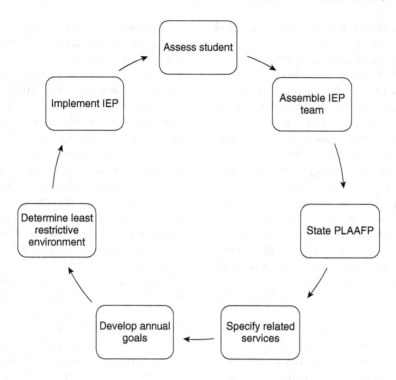

Figure T.4. The IEP process.

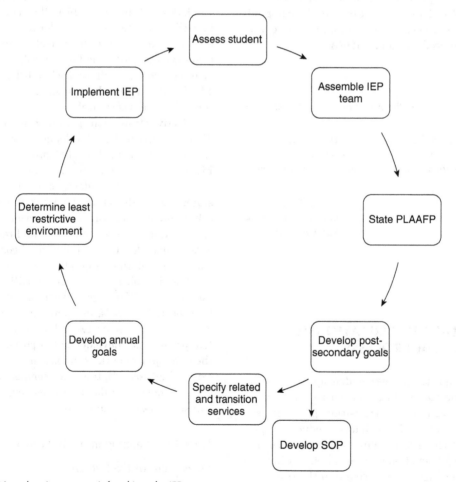

Figure T.5. The transition planning process infused into the IEP process.

the student's "abilities, attitudes, aptitudes, interests, work behaviors, levels of self-determination and self-advocacy skills, interpersonal skills, academic skill level, and independent living skills" (p. 5; Miller, Lombard, & Corbey, 2007). Transition assessment results are used to make decisions regarding the other aspects of the IEP process.

Assembly of the IEP Team

For a student who is transition age, the IEP team consists of the student when appropriate, parent or guardian, at least one regular education teacher, at least one special education teacher, a representative of the local education agency who has the authority to commit resources (usually an administrator), an individual who can interpret evaluation results, and other individuals who have knowledge of expertise regarding the student (IDEIA, 2004). The local education agency needs to seek parental or adult student consent to invite agency representatives if there is a possibility that their services may be needed to assist the student with transitioning, and the local education agency needs to ensure the contribution of any absent IEP team members.

Statement of Present Levels of Academic Achievement and Functional Performance

The statement of the student's PLAAFP should include enough information to help the IEP team understand the student's strengths and weaknesses in academic achievement and functional performance domains. These data are used to determine the student's needs regarding the attainment of the postsecondary goals. Although the IEP typically focuses on remediation of the student's deficits, during transition the IEP team also uses knowledge of the student's strengths to build a foundation for the student to reach his or her postsecondary goals.

Development of Postsecondary Goals

The development of the student's postsecondary goals is one of the most important aspects of transition planning (deFur, 2003; Halpern, 1994). There are a variety of ways to engage the student and family in the development of postsecondary goals, but the end result should be measurable postsecondary goals in education and training, employment, and independent living, if needed.

Specify Related and Transition Services

Special education–related services are those that enable the student to benefit from his or her education. Some examples of related services include transportation, speech-language services, physical and occupational therapies, and rehabilitation counseling. Transition services

are a coordinated set of activities that facilitate the student's transition from school to postschool activities. The transition services that are required to be addressed include instruction, course of study, related services, community experiences, development of employment and other postschool adult living objectives, acquisition of daily living skills, and provision of functional vocational evaluation (IDEIA, 2004). The transition services need to be based on the student's needs, strengths, preferences, or interests. Some of the transition services may not be applicable to some students; however, there should be documentation in the IEP document detailing why a particular transition service is not necessary.

Develop Annual Goals

Academic and functional annual goals need to be measurable, and there needs to be at least one annual goal that supports each of the student's postsecondary goals. The IEP team needs to specify how the student's progress toward meeting the goals will be measured and reported (IDEIA, 2004).

Determine Least Restrictive Environment

Students who receive special education services and aids are required to be instructed in the least restrictive environment as possible. When planning for transition, the IEP team needs to ensure that the instructional setting is appropriate for the student to be able to achieve his or her postsecondary goals. If the student has a goal of attending a postsecondary school, the IEP team needs to ensure that the student will meet the state standardized testing, course of study, and credit requirements for the type of graduation plan that is needed to pursue postsecondary education.

Implement IEP

During this part of the IEP process, all of the planning that has occurred is implemented. If it seems unlikely that the student will be able to achieve his or her post-secondary or annual goals or if any of the participating agencies fail to provide the transition services, then the IEP team will need to reconvene and start the process over (IDEIA, 2004).

Develop Summary of Performance

Finally, when the student has met the criteria for exiting high school, the IEP team will meet to develop the SOP. The SOP includes a summary of academic achievement and functional performance, in addition to recommendations on how to assist the child in meeting his or her postsecondary goals (IDEIA, 2004).

REFERENCES

deFur, S. H. (2003). IEP transition planning—From compliance to quality. *Exceptionality, 11*(2), 115–128.

Halpern, A. S. (1994). The transition of youth with disabilities to adult life a position statement of the division on career development and transition, the council for exceptional children. *Career Development for Exceptional Individuals, 17*(2), 115–124.

Individuals with Disabilities Education Improvement Act (IDEIA) of 2004, PL 108-446, 20 U.S.C. § 1400 *et seq.* (2004).

Miller, R. J., Lombard, R. C., & Corbey, S. A. (2007). *Transition assessment: Planning transition and IEP development for youth with mild to moderate disabilities.* Boston, MA: Pearson.

No Child Left Behind Act (NCLB) of 2001. PL 107-110, 20 U.S.C. § 6301 *et seq.* (2001).

Office of Special Education Programs. (2007). *OSEP Part B and C State Monitoring and Formula Grants.* Retrieved from http://www.ed.gov/policy/speced/guid/idea/monitor/index.html

DULAN ZHANG
Texas A&M University
Fourth edition

TRANSPORTATION OF STUDENTS WITH DISABILITIES

Transportation of students with disabilities is usually viewed as an administrative requirement to ensure access to public education. It is seldom viewed as an opportunity to teach students community mobility skills. However, community mobility is the dynamic concept within the issue of transportation of students with disabilities. The ability of an individual to participate independently or semi-independently in all aspects of community life (e.g., domestic, recreational, vocational) is dependent on community mobility (Wehman, Renzaglia, & Bates, 1985). Community mobility refers to movement from one place to another within a particular setting and travel between two community locations. The concept of community mobility was originally developed in program practice and literature related to working with individuals with visual impairments. In this literature, community mobility is referred to as orientation and mobility training.

For individuals with visual impairments, orientation and mobility training has long been a well-respected component of the curriculum. As the rights of all citizens to participate in the least restrictive environment have been acknowledged, the concept of community mobility has been broadened to include individuals with physical disabilities, intellectual disabilities, emotional disturbances, and other disabilities. Assurances for meeting the basic transportation needs to and from school have been established within PL 94-142 for all special education students. However, the transportation needs of students with disabilities are complex.

The ability of a person to be independently mobile is dependent on several factors. One of the primary factors that influences the degree of mobility attained by individuals with disabilities is the opportunity for travel from one place to another. Opportunity for mobility can be restricted by both physical and attitudinal barriers. In many communities, extensive physical modifications have been made, including construction of ramps, widening of doorways, installment of elevators, cutting out of curbs, and purchase of lift buses. Although these modifications have removed many barriers to independent mobility, obstacles still exist in all communities. Realistically, many of these obstacles are not going to be eliminated. Some of these obstacles are outside of the control of engineers and educators (e.g., weather conditions, natural terrain). Since mobility obstacles are likely to remain in every community, efforts must be directed toward teaching individuals to overcome these problems. By combining environmental changes with specific instruction programs, citizens with disabilities are provided easier access as well as more skills for traveling independently within their communities. Community mobility training programs should reflect this dual concern for improving physical accessibility and training skills that compensate for various environmental barriers.

Attitudinal barriers can severely restrict a person's chances for learning independent mobility skills in an even more devastating way than physical obstacles. These barriers result from a combination of overprotectiveness and lowered expectations. Parents and professionals have contributed to this problem. According to Perske (1972), "such overprotection endangers the client's human dignity, and tends to keep him from experiencing the risk taking of ordinary life which is necessary for normal growth and development" (p. 29).

Overprotectiveness and lowered expectations can combine to present attitudinal barriers that severely limit a person's opportunity to acquire independent living skills. However, the development of responsible and effective community mobility training programs can alleviate fears and concerns regarding safety and consequently raise the expectations of parents and professionals for independent living by handicapped individuals. The development of such programs will significantly increase the opportunity an individual will have to acquire independent living skills (Wehman, Renzaglia, & Bates, 1985).

More community mobility training programs have begun to emphasize the functional relationship between public transportation and access to community services. For example, Sowers, Rusch, and Hudson (1979) used systematic training procedures to teach an adult with severe intellectual disabilities to complete the following 10-behavior sequence to ride the city bus to and from work: (1) cross controlled intersections, (2) cross unmarked intersections, (3) use bus tickets, (4) walk to bus, (5) identify the correct bus, (6) board, (7) ride, (8) depart, (9) transfer, and (10) walk to work. Further, Marholin, O'Toole, Touchette, Berger, and Doyle (1979) taught four adults with moderate to severe intellectual disabilities to use public bus transportation to travel between a public institution and various community locations for shopping and eating in a restaurant.

The responsibility of public schools for transporting students with disabilities to and from school programs must be expanded to include greater sensitivity to the unique community mobility needs of individual students. In meeting these responsibilities, educators should promote the development of a normalized repertoire of transportation skills. At a basic level, this could involve assistance that enables handicapped students to use the same transportation system in association with their nondisabled peers. At a more complex level, this would require a commitment to teaching a variety of mobility skills that would enhance a person's ability to access community activities throughout his or her lifetime.

REFERENCES

Marholin, D., O'Toole, K., Touchette, P., Berger, P., & Doyle, D. (1979). I'll have a big mac, large fries, large coke, and apple pie—Of teaching adaptive community skills. *Behavior Therapy, 10,* 236–248.

Perske, R. (1972). The dignity of risk. In W. Wolfensberger (Ed.), *The principle of normalization in human services.* Toronto, Ontario: National Institute on Mental Retardation.

Sowers, J., Rusch, F. R., & Hudson, C. (1979). Training a severely retarded young adult to ride the city bus to and from work. *AAESPH Review, 4,* 15–22.

Wehman, P., Renzaglia, A., & Bates, P. (1985). *Functional living skills for the moderately and severely handicapped.* Austin, TX: PRO-ED.

PAUL BATES
Southern Illinois University

See also Electronic Travel Aids; Mobility Instruction; Travel Aids for Individuals With Disabilities

TRAUMA, PSYCHOLOGICAL

Traumatic incidents, which are usually unexpected and uncontrollable, create psychological trauma. They are events where the individual's life or another person's life is in danger, or their safety is severely compromised. Examples would include serious injury, natural disaster, school violence, childhood sexual or physical abuse, torture, rape, or watching a parent experience violence. Individuals who experience a traumatic incident tend to feel insecure and vulnerable (Lerner & Shelton, 2001; Volpe, 1996).

Survivors of trauma experience the "imprint of horror": the sights, sounds, and smells recorded in the victim's mind during the traumatic event. Traumatic stress can cause victims to experience emotional, cognitive, behavioral, and physiological effects that overwhelm their coping and problem-solving abilities (Lerner & Shelton, 2001). The longevity and severity of the trauma impact the intensity of the resultant symptoms. For example, a single, short-term event such as a severe beating will typically result in less impact on an individual's level of functioning than chronic victimization, such as ongoing child sexual or physical abuse. However, any traumatic event has the potential to cause psychological damage (Lerner & Shelton, 2001; Volpe, 1996).

Studies of the prevalence of childhood trauma indicate that it is a public health problem (Volpe, 1996). Several hundred thousand cases of child sexual and physical abuse are reported yearly, and this number generally reflects an underestimate. More and more children are at risk for violence as incidents increase in schools. Over half of school-age children in domestic violence shelters show clinical levels of anxiety and posttraumatic stress (Volpe, 1996).

Characteristics

Acute responses to trauma can include shock, denial, dissociation, panic, fear, hopelessness, horror, grief, irritability, confusion, hypervigilance, perseverative thoughts, aimless pacing, erratic behavior, and physiological symptoms such as elevated heart rate, elevated blood pressure, muscle tension, dizziness, headaches, and gastrointestinal upset.

Less Acute Symptoms Include

1. Preschool children (ages 1 to 5): Engaging in behaviors that are immature and that have been abandoned in the past, such as thumb sucking, bed wetting, fear of the dark, loss of bladder control, speech difficulties, decreases or increases in appetite, clinging and whining, and separation difficulties.

2. Childhood (ages 5 to 11): Sadness and crying, school avoidance, poor concentration, physical complaints (e.g., headaches), fear of personal harm, regressive behavior (clinging, whining), nightmares, aggressive behavior at home or school, bed wetting, confusion, eating difficulty, irritability, attention-seeking behavior, anxiety and fears, and withdrawal-social isolation.

3. Early adolescence (ages 11 to 14): Sleep disturbance, increase or decrease in appetite, withdrawal or isolation from peers, loss of interest in activities, rebelliousness, generalized anxiety, school difficulties, including fighting, fear of personal

> harm, physical ailments (e.g., bowel problems), poor school performance, depression, concentration difficulties.

Treatment for psychological trauma can be provided by either school personnel or outside therapists. Counseling techniques would include giving the client a chance to "tell their story" about the event, which would include talking about the facts about the experience, what they were doing at the time of the event, physical reactions, and their thoughts and feelings at the time of the event. Counseling would also help to support clients, educate them about the effects of trauma and what symptoms they can expect, and help them normalize responses to an abnormal situation so that they know they are not alone. Longer term psychological treatment would include individual or group therapy focused on helping the child to understand that their current dysfunctional behaviors and symptoms may have helped them cope with the trauma they experienced. In addition, therapy would help the child develop necessary skills not previously learned because of the arrest in emotional development after a severe trauma. Finally, therapy would help the child to establish boundaries, help them with communication and relationship skills, and help them to feel more empowered and able to advocate for themselves (Harris, 1998).

There are many ways that schools can help children cope with traumatic events that have taken place in both the home and the school. Traumatized children are at risk for delinquency, other acting-out behaviors, and regressive behavior in the classroom. School-based programs can aid these children in their recovery. Children who have experienced violence in the home should be referred to the school psychologist, guidance counselor, or social worker. However, when the school is the location of the trauma, more global measures should be taken. Classrooms can provide curricular materials about traumatizing events, symptoms of stress-related disorders, and healthy responses to stress that can help create discussions in a supportive atmosphere. Other interventions can include small-group activities and projective techniques such as artwork, play, writing in a journal, and storytelling. The school can also teach coping skills, relaxation techniques, and encourage normalization and recovery as well as correcting misperceptions and fears (Pfefferbaum et al., 1996; Volpe, Lerner, & Lindell, 1998). Pfefferbaum et al. (1996) also point out that the school environment is not a place to discuss revenge fantasies and that the school must be sensitive to when it is prudent to refer an at-risk child to an outside clinician for more intensive individual work.

Individuals can respond to a trauma in myriad ways, depending on whether they have a history of trauma, personality variables, severity and proximity of the event, level of social support, genetic predisposition to mental health disorders, and availability of immediate treatment (Volpe et al., 1998).

If treatment for traumatized children is administered promptly and effectively, future problems generally associated with childhood trauma such as increased suicide risk, increased mental health disorders such as depression and PTSD, increased health problems due to higher level of risk-taking behaviors, and substance abuse can be ameliorated (Lerner & Shelton, 2001; Read et al., 2001). However, without treatment, children are at a significant risk for delinquency, substance abuse, school dropout, and problems in their relationships with others (Volpe, 1996).

REFERENCES

Harris, M. (1998). *Trauma recovery and empowerment a clinicians guide for working with women in groups* (pp. xiii–xiv). New York, NY: Free Press.

Lerner, M. D., & Shelton, R. D. (2001). *Acute traumatic stress management (ATSM): Addressing emergent psychological needs during traumatic events.* New York, NY: American Academy of Experts in Traumatic Stress.

Pfefferbaum, B., Jonas, P., Jonas, R., Moore, V. L., Sconzo, G. M., Gurwitch, R. H., & Messenbaugh, A. K. (1996). The Oklahoma City bombing: The Oklahoma City public school response. *Trauma Response, 2,* 15–17.

Read, J., Agar, K., Barker-Collo, S., Davies, E., & Moskowitz, A. (2001). Assessing suicidality in adults: Integrating childhood trauma as a major risk factor. *Professional Psychology: Research and Practice, 32,* 367–372.

Volpe, J. S. (1996). Effects of domestic violence on children and adolescents: An overview. *Trauma Response, 2,* 12–13.

Volpe, J. S., Lerner, M. D., & Lindell, B. (1998). *A practical guide for crisis response in our schools.* Commack, NY: American Academy of Experts in Traumatic Stress.

JENNIE KAUFMAN SINGER
*California Department of Corrections
Parole Outpatient Clinic*

APRIL M. SMITH
Yale University

See also **Panic Disorder; Posttraumatic Stress Disorder**

TRAUMATIC BRAIN INJURY

Traumatic brain injury (TBI) refers to any class of mechanical injury to the brain. Approximately 100,000 children and adolescents are hospitalized annually for TBI (Kraus, Fife, & Conroy, 1987). It is estimated that an additional 100,000 children sustain TBI annually but either do not seek medical treatment or are treated and released by emergency facilities. TBI is one of the leading causes of hospitalization and mortality throughout childhood and adolescence, with the incidence peaking sharply between the ages of 15 and 24 years. Males are 2 to 4 times more likely than females to sustain a head injury, particularly during adolescence (Goldstein & Levin, 1990).

Characteristics

1. Immediate loss of consciousness (LOC) of variable duration may occur from the initial trauma. Later onset LOC may occur secondary to hematoma or other causes of increased intracranial pressure.

2. Posttraumatic amnesia (dense anterograde amnesia of variable duration) may occur following regaining consciousness or following the injury in the absence of LOC. Retrograde amnesia for events preceding the TBI is also common.

3. The pattern of neuropsychological dysfunction can vary widely. Often there is focal neurological injury resulting from contusion, hemorrhage, and laceration, along with more diffuse injury resulting from diffuse axonal injury, excitotoxicity, edema, or other causes of mass effect.

4. The neuropsychological outcome of TBI is largely dependent on the age of the individual at the time of injury and on the nature, location, and severity of the injury involved. Longer-term sequelae often include declines in intellectual-executive functioning, attention, and memory.

5. Personality change following TBI is common, particularly problems with temper modulation, initiation, motivation, and affective lability.

6. The majority of children have Glasgow Coma Scale (GCS) scores less than or equal to 4, and 65% of children with GCS of 5 to 8 have outcomes associated with mortality, persistent vegetative state, or severe neurological disability.

7. The majority of children with GCS of 13 to 15 have good outcomes with little or no neurological deficits.

Head injuries are classified as either closed, in which the skull and dura are not compromised, or open, in which these structures are penetrated. The mechanisms of injury in TBI are multifactorial. First, as the head undergoes rapid acceleration or deceleration, injury occurs as the brain strikes the interior surface of the skull. This can result in focal contusion or laceration. The frontal and temporal poles are particularly vulnerable due to frictional abrasion with bony protuberances of the anterior and middle cranial fossae (Bigler, 1990). In addition, because the

brain and skull are of different densities and accelerate and decelerate at different velocities, repeated oscillations of these collision-abrasive forces occur. Hence, in addition to damage at the point of initial impact (coup), damage at the opposite pole (contracoup) and other sites is common. Angular, or shearing, forces also result in diffuse axonal injury, particularly at the gray-white matter junction, corpus callosum, and brain stem. Biochemical perturbations also contribute to neuronal damage through excitotoxicity. Specifically, mechanical trauma to the brain can cause the indiscriminate release of neurotransmitters (particularly glutamate), eventually leading to necrosis (Povlishock & Christman, 1995). A variety of other secondary factors can cause injury and affect outcome including hemorrhage into the dural spaces, ventricles, or parenchyma, as well as cerebral edema, hydrocephalus, increased intracranial pressure, hypotension, ischemia, and failure of other bodily systems.

The typical etiology of head injury and associated pathological findings vary over the course of childhood (Goldstein & Levin, 1990). Children aged 5 years or younger are most likely to sustain TBI in accidents and falls. Because children's skulls are not fully fused and the physical force in this type of injury is more focal, younger children are more likely to sustain skull fracture and delayed intracranial hematoma than are older children. School-aged children are more likely to be injured in pedestrian-motor vehicle accidents, bicycle accidents, and sports activities. These injuries are most often associated with concussion. Older children and adolescents, aged 10 to 19, most often sustain TBI in motor vehicle accidents.

Neuropsychological assessment is recommended to assist in treatment planning. Speech, occupational, and physical therapies are often necessary early in rehabilitation. Psychotherapy for the child and his or her family is also recommended to assist them in adjusting to the effects of TBI (Telzrow, 1990). Specific behavioral therapy may be necessary to help with problems with temper modulation, frustration tolerance, and task persistence. Formal social skills training may also be indicated. Academic accommodations are usually necessary in cases of moderate to severe TBI. Special education programs for these children should include an environment designed to minimize stress, with a low pupil-to-teacher ratio. Academic programs should utilize intensive, repetitive instruction with an emphasis on integrating classroom instruction with real-life situations by including parents and physicians in the academic process (Telzrow, 1990).

REFERENCES

Bigler, E. D. (1990). Neuropathology of traumatic brain injury. In E. D. Bigler (Ed.), *Traumatic brain injury: Mechanisms of damage, assessment, intervention, and outcome.* Austin, TX: PRO-ED.

Goldstein, F. C., & Levin, H. S. (1990). Epidemiology of traumatic brain injury: Incidence, clinical characteristics, and risk factors. In E. D. Bigler (Ed.), *Traumatic brain injury: Mechanisms of damage, assessment, intervention, and outcome.* Austin, TX: PRO-ED.

Kraus, J. F., Fife, D., & Conroy, C. (1987). Pediatric brain injuries: The nature, clinical course, and early outcomes in a defined United States population. *Pediatrics, 79*(4), 501–507.

Povlishock, J. T., & Christman, C. W. (1995). Diffuse axonal injury. In S. G. Waxman, J. D. Kocsis, & P. K. Stys (Eds.), *The axon: Structure, function and pathophysiology.* New York, NY: Oxford University Press.

Telzrow, C. F. (1990). Management of academic and educational problems in traumatic brain injury. In E. D. Bigler (Ed.), *Traumatic brain injury: Mechanisms of damage, assessment, intervention, and outcome.* Austin, TX: PRO-ED.

REBECCA VAURIO
DAVID M. TUCKER
Austin, Texas

TRAUMATIC BRAIN INJURY AND SCHOOL REENTRY

Traumatic brain injury (TBI) involves a physical injury to the brain caused by an external force, resulting in diminished consciousness or coma (Stratton & Gregory, 1994). There are two types of traumatic brain injuries: open and closed head injuries. Open head injuries occur when an object (e.g., a bullet or shell fragment) penetrates the skull and produces damage to the brain. The damage tends to be localized about the path of the penetrating object (Lezak, 1995). In contrast, closed head injuries are more common than open head injuries and are more likely to produce diffuse damage (Begali, 1992). A blow to the head without penetrating the skull is an example of a closed head injury. In closed head injuries, the direct impact causes the brain, which is floating in cerebrospinal fluid within the skull, to strike the inside of the skull in one or more places. The movement of the brain within the skull causes shearing and tearing of nerve fibers and contusions (i.e., bruising; Lezak, 1995). In addition to the primary effects (e.g., the bruising, shearing, tearing), secondary effects are often present in the form of brain swelling and hemorrhaging. The secondary effects compound the damage, resulting in a wide variety of neural structures being affected (Stratton & Gregory, 1994). As a result, diversity in behavioral sequelae (i.e., consequences) in TBI patients is the norm rather than the exception. Impairments in cognition, language, memory, attention/concentration, conceptual functions, abstract reasoning, judgment, academic achievement or new learning, and perception have been reported in children and adolescents with traumatic brain injury. Motor and sensory deficits have also been noted along with behavioral and socioemotional problems (Begali, 1992). For additional information on the sequelae associated with TBI, see the entry on traumatic brain injury in children.

Head injury is a common occurrence among children and adolescents. It is the leading cause of death and disability in children (Begali, 1992). Approximately 1 million children in the United States experience a head injury each year (Research and Training Center in Rehabilitation and Childhood Trauma, 1993). Of these 1 million, 165,000 children and adolescents are hospitalized with a traumatic brain injury yearly (National Information Center for Children and Youth with Disabilities [NICCYD], 1993). Although most of these children and adolescents will enjoy a substantial recovery, 16,000 to 20,000 of these individuals will have moderate to severe injuries producing long-term effects (Clark & Hostetter, 1995).

Children with TBI are not new to the schools; however, the number of severely injured children surviving and returning to schools has grown. Sophisticated medical technology has resulted in an increased survival rate among children following a traumatic brain injury (Rapp, 1999). Federal law mandates that these children are to be served by the schools; however, educators and parents often lack the knowledge on how to best serve these students (Blosser & DePompei, 1991).

In 1990, traumatic brain injury was added to the list of eligibility categories under the Individuals with Disabilities Education Act (IDEA). IDEA, or Public Law 101-476, is the major special education law in the United States. PL 101-476, now PL 105-17, defines a traumatic brain injury as:

> An acquired injury to the brain caused by an external force, resulting in total or partial functional disability or psychosocial impairment, or both, that adversely affects a child's educational performance. The term applies to open or closed head injuries resulting in impairments in one or more areas, such as cognition; language; memory; attention; reasoning; abstract thinking; judgment; problem-solving; sensory, perceptual and motor abilities; psychosocial behavior; physical functions; information processing; and speech. The term does not apply to brain injuries that are congenital or degenerative, or injuries induced by birth trauma. (*Federal Register*, 1992, p. 44802)

According to the federal law, children and adolescents who experience a brain injury resulting from internal as opposed to external trauma are excluded from this definition and services. In other words, children whose injuries are caused by internal events, such as brain tumors, cerebral vascular accidents, exposure to environmental toxins, or central nervous system infections cannot be served under the TBI category, but may be eligible for services under another special education category (e.g., other health impaired). Some states, however, have opted to identify, classify, and serve a broader range of children whose injuries are the result of either external or internal trauma (Rapp, 1999). State rules and regulations should be consulted to determine whether children whose brain injury is the result of internal trauma are eligible for services under the TBI category.

To be eligible for services under the TBI category of IDEA, children's educational performances must be adversely affected by their injury. For those individuals with TBI who are not eligible for special education and related services under IDEA, Section 504 of the Vocational Rehabilitation Act of 1973, a civil rights law, may provide sufficient services and protections in the general education classroom. Section 504 outlines the school district's responsibility to provide educational accommodations and related services to allow students with disabilities to have equal access to all publicly funded programs available to their typically developing peers. In either case, the federal law is quite clear. Children with TBI who are eligible under IDEA or Section 504 must be served. Thus, plans must be developed and services implemented in order to successfully reintegrate these children into the classroom following their injury.

A number of resources must be mobilized and activities planned and implemented prior to a child's return to school to ensure successful school reentry, including assignment of a case manager, formation of a school or interdisciplinary team, inservice training for school personnel, family education, peer education, notification to the State's Vocational Rehabilitation Office, and collaboration among the systems (home, school, hospital/rehabilitation unit). Successful school reintegration is dependent upon collaboration and open communication among the family, school, and hospital/rehabilitation systems. Open communication is imperative in all stages of recovery. Information exchanged should begin immediately following the injury, when the child is first admitted to the hospital (Clark, 1997); however, controversy exists as to which system is responsible for making the initial contact. Haak and Livingston (1997) suggest the school should take the initiative and contact the parents to obtain permission to contact the medical facility. Opening communication channels helps ensure that the child will be appropriately served.

The school should appoint a representative (i.e., a case manager), who is knowledgeable about TBI, to serve as a liaison among the different systems. The case manager's role should be to establish and maintain communication and coordinate services among the systems on behalf of the child. The case manager should relay information to the school from the hospital regarding the severity of the child's injury, current behavior, medication management (Clark, 1997), progress, and expected discharge and school reentry dates (Haak & Livingston, 1997). Through the case manager, assessment results and the hospital/rehabilitation unit's recommendations can be forwarded to the school. The case manager provides the

medical facility, on the other hand, with information from the school regarding the child's educational history, any preinjury assessment results, classroom assignments, and the school's progress in preparing for the child's reentry (Clark, 1997); for example, removal of architectural barriers, if needed. The case manager also communicates with the parents to obtain information about the child's current status and any problems the child may be experiencing.

Family education is also critical to a child's successful school reentry. The child's family needs to receive general information on TBI and TBI sequelae. They also need to be informed about the child's specific needs (e.g., educational needs) and abilities. Medical professionals and the case manager can help educate the family in these areas. Medical professionals can also provide the family with information on TBI and TBI sequelae, whereas the case manager can provide the family with information on IDEA and Section 504. The child's family needs to know what services are available in a school district, eligibility criteria to receive these services, process to obtain these services, and child and family's rights in relation to these services under the federal law (Ylvisaker, Hartwick, & Stevens, 1991).

Inservice training is another essential activity needed to facilitate a child's successful reentry back into the school setting. Common reactions of school personnel about a child preparing to return to school are either sheer panic or overconfidence. Panic may result because of the school personnel's lack of knowledge on how best to serve the child, whereas the staff's overconfidence may be based on the assumption that the child is fully recovered and educational programming can begin where it had abruptly ended at the time of the accident. These reactions are typical, but unnecessary (Rapp, 1999). Inservice training can inform and address the issues and concerns of the school staff. Inservice training conducted by an individual with expertise on TBI (e.g., a rehabilitation professional) can provide general information about TBI and TBI sequelae. The professional with expertise on TBI should provide information on the specific needs and abilities of the child as well (Ylvisaker et al., 1991). Information about intervention strategies that may be beneficial to the child in and outside the classroom should also be included (Clark, 1997).

Besides inservice training, in-class meetings should be held between the case manager and the child's peers to educate classmates about TBI and discuss the child's condition and possible changes in his/her behavior (e.g., changes in personality). A discussion with the student's classmates about the child with his/her permission (Ylvisaker et al., 1991) may help peers to develop a better understanding of the situation and support for the student.

The state's Office of Vocational Rehabilitation should also be contacted in the likelihood that a child with TBI will need their services in order to obtain employment upon graduation from high school. Many vocational rehabilitation offices have tracking systems. Notification results in the youth's name being entered into the vocational rehabilitation system for future services. In addition, the school counselor and vocational liaison specialist for the school district should be made aware of the need to develop community-based work experiences for the child. On-site training will help the individual with TBI develop work skills needed to succeed in a competitive employment market (Ylvisaker et al., 1991).

Before the child with TBI is discharged from the medical facility, the formation of a school or interdisciplinary team is needed to develop a plan for school reentry. The team is composed of a variety of professionals, the child's parents, and the child. The team usually consists of a general education teacher, special education teacher, case manager, school psychologist, parent, and student. Other team members may include a neuropsychologist, counselor, rehabilitation specialist, speech pathologist, physical therapist, and occupational therapist. The team's composition is dependent upon the child's needs (Clark, 1997). The team develops a tentative plan consisting of accommodations and intervention strategies and addresses the possibility that special education and related services will be needed.

Transitions from the medical facility to home and from home to school, along with the injury and its aftermath, are stressful periods for most children with TBI and their families. Guidelines exist to assist families with these transitions (e.g., Cohen, Joyce, Rhoades, & Welks, 1985). For example, Cohen et al. provide guidelines to help families and school personnel determine when a child is ready to return to school and will benefit from the school experience. According to Cohen and colleagues, a child is ready to return to school when he/she is able to attend for 10–15 minutes at a time, tolerate 20–30 minutes of classroom stimulation, function in a group setting, follow simple directions, engage in meaningful communication, and demonstrate some degree of learning. These guidelines are means of helping families reduce the stress associated with the transitions.

For the child with TBI, the transition and return to school can be very stressful and upsetting. The return to school highlights the losses in cognitive abilities, academic skills, physical functioning, and changes in behavior. These losses and changes can be demoralizing to the child and make the child a target of misperceptions. An increase in risk-taking behavior (Begali, 1992), social isolation, and withdrawal may result. Classmates' understanding and support are essential during these critical periods.

The transition from home to school can result in parental frustration and stress as well. In her review, Begali (1992) reported that common parental frustrations have been found, including lack of teacher understanding about TBI, reduced parental contact with support networks, inappropriate class placements, and social isolation of the child. For the family of a child with TBI,

the injury and recovery process never occur in an interpersonal vacuum. Brain injury affects both the child and his or her family (Haak & Livingston, 1997). The family may have difficulty accepting their child's limitations and possible changes in personality. Moreover, financial difficulties, injury to other family members, and weariness may exist as the result of the accident. Schools can assist the family in the aftermath of TBI by empowering the family to play an active role in their child's education, teaching the family about TBI, and offering support and counsel. Family stress and frustration highlights the importance of developing a school reintegration plan and the value of having a knowledgeable and well-prepared school staff (Begali, 1992).

When a child with TBI returns to school, questions arise concerning the most appropriate placement for the child to receive his or her education. Not all children with TBI will require special education. Some students will need only monitoring in the classroom with slight adjustments made in the curriculum based on teacher observations. Others, on the other hand, will require special education and related services. To receive these services, a student must be "educationally diagnosed" (Begali, 1992). In other words, an evaluation needs to be conducted to determine a child's eligibility for special education.

Assessment plays a prominent role in determining eligibility and treatment of traumatic brain injured children and adolescents (Begali, 1992). Assessment results provide invaluable information and help determine educational placement, related services, and instructional goals. Psychoeducational, ecological, neuropsychological, and neurological evaluations should be conducted and results should be integrated in order to determine appropriate accommodations and modifications needed in the school environment to provide optimal learning experiences for children and adolescents with TBI. Standardized testing supplemented with testing of the limits and process procedures will provide invaluable information for designing appropriate accommodations and interventions (Kaplan, 1988).

A standard psychoeducational evaluation consists of an intelligence test, achievement test, and behavioral rating scales (Rapp, 1999). A psychoeducational evaluation can predict future learning potential and learning disabilities; however, children and adolescents with TBI are more likely to have problems with attention or concentration, memory, new learning, problem solving, and socioemotional behavior, which will not be appropriately assessed using only a standard psychoeducational battery (Rapp, 1999; Reitan & Wolfson, 1992). Therefore, other evaluation procedures are needed.

In contrast, a neuropsychological evaluation assesses a broad range of brain-behavior relationships, current cognitive strengths and weaknesses, and new learning. Educational and vocational program goals can be developed based on these assessment results. Neuropsychological evaluations and neurological evaluations, consisting of physical assessments conducted by medical specialists, should be used to augment standard psychological assessments (Goldstein, 1984). A neuropsychological evaluation should be conducted before the child reenters school and reevaluations should be conducted frequently during the first year (Rapp, 1999). Begali (1992) recommends conducting a reevaluation every 3 to 6 months for the first 2 years postinjury. Following the first or second year postinjury, reevaluations should be conducted before major school transitions, when new problems arise, or when lack of educational progress is reported (Rapp, 1999).

Ecological evaluations consist of observations of children or adolescents in a variety of settings. Students with TBI usually have difficulty monitoring and regulating their own behavior in the real world, generalizing skills and abilities, and cognitive organization. Formal testing cannot assess these skills with any degree of accuracy, nor does formal testing have any resemblance to the real world or classroom environment. Thus, observations complement formal testing. Observations of children and adolescents with TBI provide a means of monitoring these students' progress and evaluating educational programs and interventions (Rapp, 1999). Observations should be conducted on a frequent basis.

Informal testing such as curriculum-based and criterion-based assessment is also recommended. Curriculum-based and criterion-based assessment may be used to guide instructional efforts and provide feedback. Program deficiencies can be identified and revisions of instructional objectives can be made. The main point to remember in the assessment of children with TBI is that frequent formal and informal testing will be needed to monitor these children's progress, as these children can recover substantial cognitive, physical, and behavioral functioning in short periods of time (Clark, 1997).

If a child is found to be eligible for special education based on assessment results and other relevant information, the individualized education program (IEP) team, the members of the school, or interdisciplinary team will develop an IEP. The IEP is a document stating the educational goals and objectives and specific educational and related services that will be provided. The IEP is required to address the child's current level of educational performance in the areas affected by the disability (Clark, 1997). This requirement can be a challenge to the IEP team, as dramatic changes are seen in individuals with TBI during the first 3 months of recovery (Lezak, 1995). Thus, constant review and updating of educational goals and objectives is needed to keep pace with the child's recovery. A review of the IEP within 3 months of its implementation is recommended. After the initial review, the IEP should be reviewed periodically thereafter (Clark, 1997). For those who do not qualify for special education and related services under IDEA, but do qualify for services under Section 504, the school's 504 team will need to develop a plan to ensure that children with TBI are adequately served as well.

Because of the dramatic changes seen in children with TBI during the recovery process and the fact that no two traumatic brain injuries are alike, educational programs for children with TBI must be individualized, flexible, and delivered in a timely manner. Educational programs for children with TBI should ensure that professional training, instructional methods, and program practices parallel the state-of-the-art in head trauma rehabilitation. Quality educational programs should include the following options: environmental control, low student-to-teacher ratio, individualized and intensive instructional techniques (Begali, 1992), flexible class scheduling, and community-based experiences.

Some children with TBI need a more controlled environment in the schools, such as a self-contained placement. Common characteristics found among children with TBI are their limited ability in interpreting environmental cues and responding to these cues in socially appropriate ways (Wood, 1990), hypersensitivity and hyposensitivity to sensory stimuli (Savage & Wolcott, 1994), and difficulty remembering class schedules and organizing their materials. Temporary placement in a self-contained classroom may provide these individuals with the time needed to develop coping strategies to interact appropriately and to handle the less predictable and more demanding general educational environment (Begali, 1992).

Flexible class scheduling is another mark of a quality educational program for children and adolescents with TBI. Children with TBI often lack the stamina needed to attend school on a full-time basis when they first return. Shortened school days and reduction in class load and number of classes may be needed to combat fatigue. Appointments with specialists, such as an occupational or physical therapist, may need to be scheduled into the school day as well. Thus, the actual time spent in the classroom may be very limited upon initial reentry (Begali, 1992).

Small classes where the student-to-teacher ratio is low may be beneficial to some children with TBI, especially those with severe head injuries. In these smaller classes, children with TBI can receive more intensive training, closer supervision, and more frequent feedback. In addition, distractions in these classes are more likely to be held to a minimum in comparison to the larger regular education classes (Begali, 1992).

Individual and intensive instructional opportunities are other key features of quality education programs for children with TBI. Children with TBI may need individual instruction or additional instructional assistance due to cognitive impairments, problems with new learning, loss of specific skills, or behavioral problems. Remediation, compensation, and accommodation strategies may be helpful in addressing these children's difficulties. For learned maladaptive behaviors, changes in the environment and setting clear limits may be beneficial. Accommodation strategies are often the initial intervention methods used when children with TBI return to the classroom. Remediation of specific lost skills is also an appropriate strategy to use with children with TBI. Practice, repetition, and more time to relearn specific lost skills are examples of remediation strategies. Teaching compensatory strategies is another set of intervention methods that may be used to circumvent cognitive impairments. With compensatory strategies, such as the use of mnemonics, new ways of performing and learning tasks are acquired (Rapp, 1999). To maximize instructional time, limits on transitional time and extracurricular classes may be set. Attendance in an extended school program during the summer months, if eligible, may be helpful in preventing regression in learning. Due to the rapid changes in cognitive, physical, and behavioral skills and abilities, dynamic and responsive instructional approaches tailored to the individual will be required (Begali, 1992). For additional information on more specific intervention strategies to use with students with TBI, see the entry on traumatic brain injury in children.

Community-based work experience is another indicator of a quality educational program for children with TBI. In 1990, IDEA required school districts to provide students in special education with transitional services. Children with TBI who are in special education and are 14 years of age or older qualify for these services. Participation in community-based work experiences occurs during the school day. These students go to work sites located in their community to receive on-the-job training. These work experiences are arranged to help students develop good work skills, work habits, and social skills needed in today's competitive employment market. The goal of the school-to-work experience is for students to develop the skills needed to obtain meaningful employment and to have independent living opportunities upon graduation (Haak & Livingston, 1997).

School reentry is a challenging experience for the student, family, and school. At present, limited information exists on school reentry programs for children with TBI. In addition, empirical research demonstrating the effectiveness of school reentry programs for children with TBI is lacking. Collaboration among the systems (home, school, medical, and community) and drawing upon the technical expertise of these resources are needed in order to assist these children on their road to recovery.

REFERENCES

Begali, V. (1992). *Head injury in children and adolescents*. Brandon, VT: Clinical Psychology Publishing Company.

Blosser, J. L., & DePompei, R. (1991). Preparing education professionals for meeting the needs of students with traumatic brain injury. *Journal of Head Trauma Rehabilitation*, 6(1), 73–82.

Clark, E. (1997). Children and adolescents with traumatic brain injury: Reintegration challenges in educational settings. In E. D. Bigler, E. Clark, & J. E. Farmer (Eds.), *Childhood traumatic brain injury: Diagnosis, assessment, and intervention*. Austin, TX: PRO-ED.

Clark, E., & Hostetter, C. (1995). *Traumatic brain injury: Training manual for school personnel*. Longmont, CO: Sopris West.

Cohen, S., Joyce, C., Rhoades, K., & Welks, D. (1985). Educational programming for head injured students. In M. Ylvisaker (Ed.), *Head injury rehabilitation: Children and adolescents* (pp. 383–411). San Diego: College-Hill Press.

Diamond, R. (1987). Children and head injury. In a. Thomas & J. Grimes (Eds.), *Children's needs: Psychological perspectives*. Washington, DC: National Association of School Psychologists.

Federal Register. (1992, September 9). Individual with Disabilities Education Act (IDEA). U.S. Department of Education Regulations. Washington, DC: U.S. Government Printing Office.

Goldstein, G. (1984). Neuropsychological assessment. In G. Goldstein & M. Hersen (Eds.), *Handbook of psychological assessment* (pp. 181–211). New York: Pergamon Press.

Haak, R. A., & Livingston, R. B. (1997). Treating traumatic brain injury in the school: Mandates and methods. In C. R. Reynolds & E. Fletcher-Janzen (Eds.), *Handbook of clinical child neuropsychology* (2nd ed., pp. 482–505). New York, NY: Plenum Press.

Kaplan, E. (1988). A process approach to neuropsychological assessment. In T. Boll & B. K. Bryant (Eds.), *Clinical neuropsychology and brain function: Research, measurement, and practice* (pp. 129–167). Washington, DC: American Psychological Association.

Lezak, M. D. (1995). *Neuropsychological assessment* (3rd ed.). New York, NY: Oxford University Press.

National Information Center for Children and Youth with Disabilities (NICCYD). (1993). *Traumatic brain injury*. Fact sheet number 18 (FS 18). Washington, DC: Author.

Rapp, D. L. (1999). Interventions for integrating children with traumatic brain injuries into their schools. In C. R. Reynolds & T. B. Gutkin (Eds.), *The handbook of school psychology* (3rd ed., pp. 863–884). New York, NY: Wiley.

Reitan, R. M., & Wolfson, D. (1992). *Neuropsychological evaluation of older children*. South Tucson, AZ: Neuropsychology Press.

Research and Training Center in Rehabilitation and Childhood Trauma. (1993). *National Pediatric Trauma Registry*. Boston, MA: Tufts University School of Medicine, New England Medical Center.

Savage, R. C., & Wolcott, G. F. (Eds.). (1994). *Educational dimensions of acquired brain injury*. Austin, TX: PRO-ED.

Stratton, M. C., & Gregory, R. J. (1994). After traumatic brain injury a discussion of consequences. *Brain Injury*, 8(7), 631–645.

Wood, R. L. (1990). Neurobehavioral paradigm for brain injury rehabilitation. In R. Wood (Ed.), *Neurobehavioral sequelae of traumatic brain injury* (pp. 3–17). New York, NY: Taylor & Francis.

Ylvisaker, M., Hartwick, P., & Stevens, M. (1991). School reentry following head injury: Managing the transition from hospital to school. *Journal of Head Trauma Rehabilitation, 6*, 10–22.

PATRICIA A. LOWE
University of Kansas

CECIL R. REYNOLDS
Texas A&M University

TRAUMATIC BRAIN INJURY AND SPECIAL EDUCATION SERVICES

Traumatic brain injury (TBI) involves an insult to the brain, not of a degenerative or congenital nature, but caused by an external physical force of sufficient magnitude producing a diminished or altered state of consciousness and/or associated neurological or neurobehavioral dysfunction (Begali, 1992). Mild to severe structural or physiological changes in the neural tissue of the brain resulting from TBI may cause transient to permanent changes in behavior (Begali, 1992; Savage & Wolcott, 1994). Tissue abnormalities and neural damage resulting from TBI may be due to the direct impact following an accident involving the head or may be due to secondary effects (i.e., secondary damage or metabolic changes) associated with the trauma (Begali, 1992).

TBIs may be classified into two types, open and closed head injuries. Open head injuries involve the penetration of the skull and brain by a foreign object. The agents commonly responsible for open head injuries include bullets, shell fragments, knives, rocks, and blunt instruments. Gunshot wounds account for the majority of open head injuries, although knife and scissor wounds are frequently reported as well (Ward, Chisholm, Prince, Gilmore, & Hawkins, 1994). Open head injuries result in an increased risk of infection, bleeding, and seizures, as bone fragments or shattered pieces of shells or bullets penetrate the brain (Rapp, 1999). Primary damage, however, tends to be localized about the path of the penetrating object. As a result, cognitive losses and changes in behavior due to the localized damage are relatively circumscribed and predictable. Depending on the location of the injury, open head injuries may result in specific intellectual impairments and behavioral changes, memory deficits, slower information processing, attention and concentration difficulties, and changes in the ability to deal with everyday cognitive demands (Begali, 1992).

Closed head injuries, on the other hand, are more common and more diffuse in comparison to open head injuries (Lezak, 1995). Closed head injuries result from a direct impact to the brain, such as a blow to the head, without penetration of the skull. There are three types of closed head injuries (Reynolds, personal communication, June 6, 1997) produced by two mechanical factors, namely, direct contact forces and inertial forces (Begali, 1992; Katz, 1992). An acceleration injury occurs when an individual's head accelerates too quickly (e.g., when a child's head is hit with a baseball bat). In an acceleration injury, the child's skull, which surrounds the brain (a gelatin-like substance supported and floating in cerebrospinal fluid), compresses against the brain and forces the brain to move to the opposite side of the initial point of impact where the brain hits the inside of the skull again. The point of initial impact is called the coup, whereas the secondary point of impact, orthogonal to the plane (i.e., opposite side) of the initial point of impact, is called the counter coup. Damage to the brain in an acceleration injury occurs at both the coup and counter coup, with more severe damage at the coup.

In contrast, a deceleration injury occurs when an individual's head decelerates or stops too quickly (e.g., when an adolescent's head strikes an immovable or stationary object, such as a car's dashboard during a motor vehicle accident). Under these circumstances, the brain moves forward and strikes the inside of the skull (coup) and then moves in the opposite direction (backward) and strikes the inside of the skull again (counter coup). In a deceleration injury, brain damage is more severe at the site of the counter coup than the coup.

A pinball injury is a third type of closed head injury. A pinball injury may also occur during a motor vehicle accident when the individual's head strikes the dashboard and then the individual is thrown from the vehicle and lands on the ground, hitting the side of his/her head. A pinball injury results in multiple points of impact producing damage at a number of coup and counter coup sites.

Coup and counter coup damage is the product of direct contact forces. Inertial forces, on the other hand, generate other types of injuries, such as shearing and tearing of nerve fibers. Shearing and tearing of nerve fibers occur in acceleration, deceleration, and pinball closed head injuries. Shearing and tearing result from brain movement and rotation of the brain within the skull. Tearing injuries are likely to occur when nerve fibers projecting from the base of the brain are stretched to their limit, resulting in their snapping or tearing. In contrast, shearing injuries may occur, for example, when association fibers, which connect different areas of the brain together, scrape against the bony ridges of the inside of the skull. This scraping movement results in the removal of layers of association fibers.

Brain damage typically occurs in two stages, namely, the primary and second injury. The primary injury is the damage that occurs at the time of the injury, whereas the second injury results from the damage incurred from the primary injury (Lezak, 1995). Primary injuries in closed head injuries include skull fractures, concussions, contusions, and shearing and tearing injuries. A skull fracture is a crack in the cranium (i.e., the skull) surrounding the brain. The skull fracture may vary in size or severity. A contusion occurs when the brain strikes the inside of the skull (i.e., a coup or counter coup), resulting in bruising of the brain. Blood vessels may also rupture during the accident or shortly thereafter, causing extensive bleeding. Bleeding within the cranium is dangerous and possibly fatal, as the blood accumulates in this case surrounding the brain with no place to go. As a result, pressure mounts inside the cranium. This pressure can be fatal. In contrast, a concussion occurs when the brain strikes the inside of the skull, resulting in a period of confusion or loss of consciousness. A variety of primary injuries are possible when a closed head injury occurs. Thus, each closed head injury is unique and is dependent upon the physical characteristics of the insult and the movement of the brain within the skull (Begali, 1992).

Secondary damage or the second injury develops after the insult in either an open or closed head injury. Secondary complications include (a) edema (brain swelling due to an increase in fluid content); (b) infarction (loss of brain tissue due to blood deprivation); (c) increased cranial pressure (buildup of pressure in the cranium); (d) hypoxia (oxygen deprivation); (e) hemorrhage (rupture of blood vessels in the brain); (f) hematoma (collection of blood in the brain tissue); and/or (g) infection (Pang, 1985). Secondary damage may also result from metabolic change (North, 1984), damage to the pituitary gland and hypothalamus, electrolyte disturbance (a chemical imbalance in the blood), and/or hyperventilation (excessive breathing; Pang, 1985).

Head injury is a common occurrence among children and adolescents; however, prevalence rates and incidence of TBI have been difficult to ascertain, as incongruities in classification procedures and methodological weaknesses in epidemiological studies have been reported (Lehr, 1990). It has been estimated that more than 1 million children in the United States sustain a mild to severe traumatic brain injury each year (Research and Training Center in Rehabilitation and Childhood Trauma, 1993). Researchers have estimated that 10 out of every 100,000 children die as a result of brain injury yearly (Luerssen, 1991). Pediatric patients account for approximately 40% of the TBI cases reported on an annual basis, which translates, based on different estimates, into 200,000 to 600,000 TBI child and adolescent cases each year that come to the attention of medical professionals (Brandstater, Bontke, Cobble, & Horn, 1991; Crouchman, 1990). The majority of these TBI cases occur in youth between the ages of 15 and 19 years due to automobile accidents (Farmer & Peterson, 1995). Many of these individuals will require educational support once they return to school. Approximately 50% of the children and adolescents who sustain a traumatic brain injury need educational support during the first year following their injury (Donders, 1994). It is estimated that 8% to 20% of the special education population

is believed to have suffered a traumatic brain injury (Savage, 1991).

Gender differences have also been reported. Males are twice as likely as females to sustain a traumatic brain injury at all ages, except in infancy and the senior years of life (Lezak, 1995). This gender differential is found to be the greatest during the peak trauma years, the 15- to 24-year age range (Naugle, 1990), when males are 4 times more likely than females to suffer an injury (Vernon-Levett, 1991). Males also tend to sustain more severe brain injuries than females, with the male to female mortality ratio being 4:1 (Frankowski, Annegers, & Whitman, 1985).

The external forces that produce TBIs tend to vary with the age of the individual (Farmer & Peterson, 1995; Goldstein & Levin, 1990). Infants, toddlers, and preschoolers are more likely to acquire TBIs due to falls, physical abuse, and vehicular accidents (Rapp, 1999). Physical abuse, such as shaken baby or thrown infant syndrome, is the leading cause of traumatic brain injury among infants. Sixty-six percent of the infants who are physically abused sustain a brain injury as a result of the abuse (Bruce & Zimmermann, 1989). Falls, on the other hand, are the major source of TBI among children under age 5 and account for more than 50% of the injuries in the toddler and preschool population (Kraus et al., 1984). After age 5, pedestrian and bicycle injuries increase, with motor vehicle accidents, falls, recreation and sports injuries, and assaults contributing to the rate of injury (Mira, Tucker, & Tyler, 1992). Not surprisingly, adolescents and young adults are at the greatest risk of any age group for acquiring TBIs (Savage & Wolcott, 1994), primarily through motor vehicle accidents but also from sports injuries and assaults (Rapp, 1999). During adolescence, the combination of increased risk-taking behaviors and learning how to drive often lead to an increase in motor vehicle accidents. Automobile accidents account for three deaths and 260 injuries among children and adolescents each day (Brain Injury Association, 1997). Overall, moving vehicle accidents and falls are the major causes of head trauma (Lezak, 1995). Moreover, the risk of sustaining a brain injury increases dramatically with each successive TBI an individual experiences (Brain Injury Association, 1997).

There are many factors that influence the outcomes of traumatic brain injury in children: child, family, medical, school, and community factors (Farmer, 1997). A level of influence within these factors either increases the risk of poor outcomes, or creates a buffer or offers protection, and thus maximizes optimal outcomes. For example, child factors can serve as either risk or protective factors that influence TBI outcomes. Child factors include preinjury characteristics, age/developmental stage at onset, type and persistence of impairments, postinjury adjustment, and severity of injury. Type and persistence of impairments are determined by the nature of the injury, such as a closed versus open head injury, and the location and severity of the injury (Warzak, Mayfield, & McAllister,

1998). Postinjury adjustment, on the other hand, is dependent on the child and family's coping resources and the child's social acceptance by others (Wade, Taylor, Drotar, Stancin, & Yeates, 1996). Preinjury characteristics include genetics and the child's preexisting medical, behavioral, and affective status. Harrington (1990) reported that children with TBI with above-average intelligence, academic skills, and social skills tend to have a better prognosis than those individuals with TBI with below average skills. Students with TBI, however, are more likely to have preexisting academic problems and prior behavioral problems in comparison to their classmates (Farmer, Clippard, Wiemann, Wright, & Owings, 1997).

Another potential differentiating factor that influences TBI outcomes is the age of onset or the child's developmental stage at the time of the injury. The relationship between age of onset and recovery from brain injury, however, is complex and is not well understood (Dalby & Obrzut, 1991). Early research suggested a high degree of plasticity in the brains of young children (i.e., children's brains had the ability to compensate for some injuries by reorganizing neural function). In other words, a young child's brain was thought to be more resilient in response to injury, as other brain structures spared of injury assumed the function of the damaged areas (Farmer & Peterson, 1995). Subsequent studies, however, have indicated young children's superior recovery from head trauma cannot be presumed (Farmer, 1997). In fact, recent studies have found just the opposite (i.e., more unfavorable outcomes) in younger children who have experienced a brain injury in the areas of language development (Ylvisaker, 1993), attention (Kaufmann, Fletcher, Levin, Miner, & Ewing-Cobbs, 1993), intellectual and behavioral functioning (Michaud, Rivara, Jaffe, Fay, & Dailey, 1993), and problem solving (Levin et al., 1994).

Preliminary evidence suggests preschool children may be at greatest risk (Farmer & Peterson, 1995). Disruption of primary skills (e.g., sensory, motor, language, behavioral, social skills) in early childhood may result in changes in learning, such as the order, rate, and level of learning, and development of higher order skills, such as self-regulation of behavior and planning ability (Farmer, 1997). In addition, some research (e.g., Lehr & Savage, 1990) suggests early brain injury may result in delayed, late-onset effects in which a child who appears to be fully recovered shows a marked decline in functioning over time.

Brain injury severity is another factor that influences TBI outcomes. Severity is medically diagnosed using the terms mild, moderate, and severe. Classification of brain injury severity is based on three critical factors. These three critical factors include an individual's level of consciousness, degree of posttraumatic amnesia experienced, and physical findings. In general, severity of head trauma serves as a good prognosticator of behavioral and neuropsychological outcomes (Kreutzer, Devany, Myers, &

Marwitz, 1991), with more long-lasting changes in physical, cognitive, and behavioral functioning occurring with more severe TBI cases (Fay et al., 1993; Jaffe et al., 1993). Although children and adolescents who sustain severe TBIs are more likely to experience chronic effects, individual differences must be taken into account. Some individuals with severe head injuries have not encountered significant disability, whereas some children and adolescents with mild brain injuries have symptoms that cause significant and lasting impairments (Farmer, 1997; Fay et al., 1993).

Diminished or altered level of consciousness is one of the most commonly used indicators of brain trauma. The Glasgow Coma Scale (GCS; Teasdale & Jennett, 1974) is a means of assessing an individual's level of consciousness following a brain injury. The GCS is routinely used to measure the degree and duration of altered consciousness within 24 hours of the trauma and to periodically monitor changes in consciousness during the early stages of recovery (Teasdale & Jennett, 1974). A GCS score is obtained through observing, evaluating, and summarizing the patient's best-rated responses, ranging from 1 to 6 in motor movements, 1 to 5 in verbal functioning, and 1 to 4 in eye movements. Possible scores range from 3 to 15. Coma is diagnosed when there is no eye opening, inability to obey commands, and inability to speak. One critical limitation of the GCS, however, is its development and use almost exclusively with adults and older adolescents. Thus, the clinical utility of the GCS with the younger child population is questionable, as the presentation of coma differs across young children and adults (Lehr, 1990). In response to the limited utility of the GCS, alternative measures for use with comatose pediatric patients have been developed, such as the Children's Coma Scale (CCS; Raimondi & Hirschauer, 1984). The CCS has been used to assess the level of consciousness in infants and toddlers up to age 3. Possible scores range from 3 to 11 and are not interchangeable with the GCS. The CCS, however, has its limitations as well, as the predictive validity of this scale has not been examined due to limited use (Lehr, 1990).

The degree of posttraumatic amnesia (PTA) is another indicator of brain injury severity. Posttraumatic amnesia refers to the period of time when an alert individual who has experienced a brain injury has "persistent difficulties retaining new information" (Farmer & Peterson, 1995, p. 233). Estimates of brain injury severity based on PTA duration vary from less than 5 minutes to more than 4 weeks (Bigler, 1990). PTA duration correlates well with GCS ratings, with the exception of extreme GCS scores (Bigler, 1990), as PTA duration typically lasts 4 times longer than the period of unconsciousness or coma (Lezak, 1995). Children's Orientation and Amnesia Test (Ewing-Cobbs, Levin, Fletcher, Miner, & Eisenberg, 1989) or structured parent interviews (Rutter, Chadwick, Shaffer, & Brown, 1980) have been used to assess PTA in children. PTA is difficult to assess in young children, as children's memories are less reliable and accurate than adults. As a result, PTA is usually not assessed and reported in children under the age of 9 (Lehr, 1990).

A third indicator of injury severity is gauged by examining physical findings through a variety of medical procedures. Physicians conduct neurological examinations to assess sensory deficits, reflexes, and the motor system. Medical professionals also use a variety of technologically advanced medical procedures to assess the degree of damage sustained. Computerized tomography, magnetic resonance imagery, functional magnetic resonance imagery, single-photon emission computer tomography, positron emission tomography, regional cerebral blood flow, and brain electrical activity mapping have proven to be useful, some procedures more than others (Lezak, 1995), in evaluating the severity of injury.

Although assessment of the level of brain injury severity has its limitations, the three critical factors (i.e., level of consciousness, duration of posttraumatic amnesia, and physical findings) offer a means of predicting TBI outcomes. A mild brain injury has been defined as a GCS score of 13 to 15, which suggests little or no impairment in speaking and motor and eye movement. A PTA of less than 1 hour occurs and no known structural damage to the brain is evident (Binder, 1986). Approximately 75% to 90% of all head trauma falls into this category (Alves & James, 1985). Students who sustain a mild brain injury often make good academic recovery but may experience attention and concentration difficulties, fatigue, and deficits in retaining new information. Deficits following a mild TBI tend to be subtle but may have considerable impact on social, familial, academic, and occupational functioning (Lezak, 1995). The term "walking wounded" used to describe these individuals seems appropriate, as the effects of the disability often go unnoticed (Wade et al., 1996). Clusters of symptoms in affective, social, cognitive, somatic, and sensory areas may persist following a mild TBI (Warzak et al., 1998).

Moderate brain injury has been defined as a GCS score of 9 to 12 and a PTA duration of 1 to 24 hours (Bigler, 1990). Eight percent to 10% of all head injuries fall into this category (Lezak, 1995). An individual with a GCS score of 9 to 12 is able to open his or her eyes, flex his or her muscles, and speak intelligibly but is unable to sustain a conversation. Significant residual impairments often result due to the trauma. Persistent headaches, memory deficits, and difficulties with adaptive living skills have been reported (Lezak, 1995; Warzak et al., 1998). If frontal lobe damage is sustained (i.e., damage to the anterior portion of the brain), more impulsive behavior and temper outbursts or affective muting may be exhibited, whereas damage to the temporal lobe, located near the middle to top half of one's ears, may result in a true learning disorder. Planning ability and self-monitoring are frequently compromised as well. Students who have experienced a moderate brain injury may require special education and related services.

A severe head injury has been defined as a GCS score of 3 to 8 and a PTA duration of more than 24 hours (Bigler, 1990). When an individual has a GCS of 3 to 8, the ability to open one's eyes, obey commands, or utter recognizable words may be absent. Fewer than 10% of head trauma victims fall into the severely injured category (Lezak, 1995). Attention deficits, behavioral slowing (i.e., both mental processing and response), memory impairments, diminished awareness of one's deficits, and impaired reasoning and verbal fluency are common (Mitiguy, Thompson, & Wasco, 1990). Insight and empathy may be compromised as well. Perseverative behavior may be displayed. Moreover, planning ability and ability to choose among alternatives may be impaired. Acting-out behavior and apathy may be exhibited and social isolation is common (Lezak, 1995). Students who experience a severe brain injury will require a variety of special services. These individuals are highly unlikely to return to the general education classroom without considerable support (Warzak et al., 1998).

Children and adolescents with TBI represent a heterogeneous group with regard to neurobehavioral characteristics and outcomes. These individuals may display a wide variety of difficulties or deficits. The difficulties or deficits may occur in one or more of the following areas: physical functioning, cognitive functioning, behavioral control, and socioemotional functioning.

Physical sequelae (i.e., consequences) associated with traumatic brain injury in children and adolescents include motor deficits, sensory deficits, speech/language dysfunction, seizure disorders, postconcussive syndrome, and fatigue. Motor deficits vary in degree depending upon the site and extent of the damage to the brain. Deficits range from fine volitional movements to severe paralysis. Motor deficits may include hemiplegia (paralysis on one side of the body), hemiparesis (weakness affecting one side of the body), hypotonicity (low muscle tone of trunk and extremities), rigidity, spasticity, tremors, ataxia (inability to coordinate voluntary muscles), and apraxia (problems in planning and executing sequential movement; Begali, 1992; Savage & Wolcott, 1994). Prognosis for a full motor recovery is relatively good in TBI patients and is better than a prognosis for full cognitive recovery. Recovery of motor functions in TBI accidents follows a predictable course with lower limb functioning returning sooner and more completely than upper limb functioning, and proximal (trunk) movements returning sooner and more completely than distal (extremity) movements. Moreover, children with TBI may lose functional use of their dominant hand and will need to learn how to write and perform various hand activities with their nondominant hand. Recovery and refinement of balance reactions or proper weight shifting and control may not occur, however, until after youngsters are discharged to their homes and schools. Thus, physical rehabilitation may be needed in the school setting (Begali, 1992).

Sensory impairments associated with TBI vary in degree depending on the extent of damage to the brain. Sensory deficits may include visual field deficits (i.e., restriction of an individual's field of vision), squinting, defects in color vision, double vision, and tracking disorders (Begali, 1992). Reduced auditory acuity and impaired ability to taste or smell have also been reported (Savage & Wolcott, 1994). Hypersensitivity and hyposensitivity to sensory stimuli have been noted as well (Begali, 1992; Savage & Wolcott, 1994).

Speech/language dysfunction may occur with TBI. Dysarthia characterized by poor phonation skills, hypernasality, poor articulation, slow rate of speech, and monotonic speech is found in some children and adolescents following TBI. Apraxia and aphasia may also result from brain injury. Apraxia involves the inability to execute preplanned, purposeful sequences for oral communication, whereas aphasia results in partial or complete impairment in language comprehension. Aphasic individuals are able to comprehend one or two words or short phrases rather than lengthy discourse (Begali, 1992).

Epilepsy may also occur following a traumatic brain injury. Penetrating head injuries are more likely to produce epilepsy than closed head injuries (Lezak, 1995). Approximately 5% of children and adolescents who experience a closed head injury will develop epilepsy within 4 years after the injury (Begali, 1992). Seizures are more likely to occur in children under 5 years of age or children who have a severe injury. Seizures usually appear in the first few weeks of recovery after the head trauma. Seizures may have a delayed onset as well and begin approximately 3 months after the injury (Hauser & Hersdorffer, 1990). On the other hand, individuals who experienced a TBI and have had seizures in the past but have been seizure-free for 3 years can be 95% certain that they will not experience another seizure (Parker, 1990). Antileptic drugs, such as phenytoin, phenobarbital, carbamazepine, and valproate have been prescribed; however, these medications do have negative side effects. Negative side effects vary depending on the medication used and the individual. Side effects include sedation, speech disturbances, dizziness, and cognitive impairment (Bagby, 1991).

Besides seizures, a head injury, and specifically a mild head injury, may result in postconcussive syndrome. Approximately 50% of individuals who experience a mild traumatic brain injury report symptoms associated with a postconcussive syndrome 3 or more months after the injury (Rutherford, 1989). Fatigue, dizziness, headache, and memory deficits are the most common symptoms (Edna & Cappelen, 1987). The syndrome tends to remit with time; however, 4% of the individuals who experience this syndrome report persistent memory problems and 20% report persistent headaches 1 year after the injury (Wilberger, 1993). Students with postconcussive syndrome may be viewed as lacking in motivation or being noncompliant or defiant in the school setting, when in reality they have attention, concentration, and memory problems.

Chronic fatigue and hypersensitivity to noise are complications that often occur as a result of head trauma (Lezak, 1995). Chronic fatigue prevents individuals with TBI from functioning at their premorbid pace. Shortened school days and reduced course loads are often implemented to combat fatigue. On the other hand, hypersensitivity to noise may produce stress in children with TBI. Certain times of the school day may be overtaxing to these children, such as lunchtime or recess. Thus, reintegration into the more stimulating or hectic parts of the school day must be done gradually.

Cognitive deficits are among the most common sequelae of TBI (Lezak, 1995); however, the pattern of impairment will vary from individual to individual (Crosson, 1992). Intelligence, attention/concentration, language functions, memory, abstract reasoning and judgment, academic achievement and new learning, visual-motor skills, and perception are highly susceptible to dysfunction (Begali, 1992).

A direct relationship between the severity of TBI and degree of cognitive/intellectual impairment has been reported (Oddy, 1993). Drops of 10 points in mean verbal IQ and 30 points in performance IQ on intelligence tests have been noted in children with severe head injuries (Chadwick, Rutter, Shaffer, & Shrout, 1981). Children and adolescents with TBI show more pronounced and persistent deficits in performance IQ than in verbal IQ. As a result, individuals who have experienced a brain injury are more likely to have difficulties learning new skills and solving problems than performing well-learned skills or retrieving factual information. Viewed another way, visual-perceptual and visual-motor skills are less likely to recover fully in comparison to verbal abilities in children with TBI (Begali, 1992). Location of the injury, however, has an effect, as verbal and academic skills tend to be more impaired following left hemisphere damage, whereas visuospatial skills tend to be more impaired following right hemisphere lesions (Wilkening, 1989).

Attention and concentration difficulties are common problems among children and youth following a traumatic brain injury (Lezak, 1995). A poor attention span is not conducive to school learning and is related to a slower rate of information processing (van Zomeren & Brouwer, 1994). Difficulties with sustained attention, selective attention, switching attention, and divided attention have been reported (Haak & Livingston, 1997). These attention difficulties contribute to a variety of cognitive problems including memory, learning, language problems, and social interactions. Off-task behavior is common among these individuals, especially in unstructured classroom settings (Begali, 1992).

Significant expressive and receptive language deficits may follow a severe closed head injury, with expressive language abilities being more affected than receptive

(Wilkening, 1989). Two thirds of the individuals with language deficits, however, recover fully or at least improve to the point where only word-finding or word-naming ability is impaired (Begali, 1992). Verbal fluency, reading comprehension, and writing may also be affected (Lezak, 1995). The speed and ease of verbal production (fluency) and reading comprehension may be hindered. Moreover, students, especially younger students, may struggle with their writing as they are unable to recall letter-form movements, how to spell words correctly, or put words together to form sentences (Ewing-Cobbs & Fletcher, 1990). Auditory comprehension may be impaired as well in either a global or selective manner. Specifically, comprehension of classes of words may be affected, such as colors or prepositions (Begali, 1992). Moreover, conversational skills, which require the integration and interplay of linguistic, cognitive, and social skills, are highly susceptible to disruption following TBI in children (Russell, 1993).

Memory disorders are the most common and persistent sequelae of traumatic brain injury (Levin, 1985). When memory deficits persist, these deficits interfere with academic progress. Deficits in new learning or recent memory are more likely to be affected than rote memory. During the early stages of recovery, long-term memory or memory for earlier events return first, followed by memory for events occurring closer to the time of the injury (Lezak, 1995). Retrograde amnesia, a loss of memory for events preceding the injury, may also occur if an individual is rendered unconscious by the head trauma (Begali, 1992). Overall, memory following TBI may be less complete and show less improvement than other cognitive skills.

Conceptual functions, abstract reasoning, and judgment may also be impaired as a result of head trauma. Children who have experienced a mild to severe brain injury or have experienced diffuse damage tend to do poorly on measures of abstract thinking (Lezak, 1995). These individuals have difficulty distinguishing relevant from irrelevant material and essential from nonessential detail. Children and adolescents may have difficulty categorizing and generalizing information or applying rules, such as social rules or rules associated with grammar or mathematics. They may misinterpret social cues, make inappropriate remarks, or miscommunicate their intentions (Begali, 1992).

Academic achievement or new learning may also be affected by head injuries. Inconsistency in academic proficiency has been reported (Begali, 1992). Children with TBI may perform new learned skills accurately one day but are unable to perform the skills correctly the next day. For example, the steps learned to perform long division with precision are forgotten when the child is required to perform the task again on another occasion.

Visual-motor and visual-perceptual problems are also common among children and adolescents who have experienced a brain injury. Visual-motor and visual-perceptual difficulties may include problems with directions, misperceptions, and configural distortions (Lezak, 1995). The ability to attend to detail and part-to-whole conceptualization is likely to be poor. Visual-motor dexterity tends to be slow as well.

Behavioral and socioemotional difficulties are common sequelae following TBI in children and adolescents. These difficulties may be the most prominent features associated with the injury (Oddy, 1993). The behavioral and socioemotional disturbances often exist as premorbid characteristics or tendencies that are exacerbated in response to the injury (Lezak, 1995). Although a well-defined pattern of behavioral and socioemotional difficulties does not exist, there are certain constellations of problems that occur more frequently than others (Haak & Livingston, 1997). Begali (1992) and Savage and Wolcott (1994) reported increases in overactive/hyperactive behavior, impulsivity, aggression, agitation/frustration, disinhibition, oppositional behavior, dependency, and lack of motivation among children and adolescents following TBI. Psychological adjustment difficulties have also been noted, including emotional lability (mood swings), anger, anxiety, withdrawal, and depression. Children and adolescents with TBI may experience difficulty in reading social cues and have poor interpersonal skills. Self-esteem issues may arise as these individuals become aware of or recognize the changes and deficits associated with their injury.

As noted, severity of the injury is related to cognitive deficits; however, the relationship between injury severity and behavioral adjustment is more complex and less understood (Ewing-Cobbs & Fletcher, 1990). Besides severity of the injury and premorbid characteristics, type of damage, site and laterality of lesion, age of onset, gender (Begali, 1992), family adaptation (Wade et al., 1996), and environmental factors influence behavioral outcomes (Farmer & Peterson, 1995).

Initial recovery following a traumatic brain injury tends to occur in a predictable series of stages, ranging from a coma to more purposeful and appropriate behavior (Farmer & Peterson, 1995). An eight-stage scale, the Rancho Los Amigos Level of Cognitive Functioning Scale (Hagen, Malkmus, & Durham, 1981), is used in rehabilitation settings to describe an individual's progress during the early stages of recovery. Children with more severe brain injuries are found at the lower levels of this scale and usually progress more slowly than individuals with less severe head injuries. Individual differences in recovery rates, however, must be taken into consideration, with some individuals recovering more rapidly and others remaining indefinitely at earlier stages of recovery. Attainment of the highest level on the Rancho Los Amigos scale does not necessarily indicate a full recovery to premorbid levels of functioning. Thus, students at each stage of recovery will need support and assistance from the schools.

Recovery from a TBI typically occurs most rapidly during the first 6 to 12 months following injury. Many children continue to show improvement in abilities 18 to

36 months postinjury. In some cases, progressive improvement has been observed beyond the 36-month postinjury mark (Boyer & Edwards, 1991).

In 1990, the Individuals with Disabilities Education Act (IDEA), Public Law 101-476 (PL 101-476), the main special education law in the United States, added traumatic brain injury as a separate eligibility category. Under this law, children with TBI whose educational performance is adversely affected by their disability are entitled to receive appropriate special education and related services necessary to meet their individual needs. According to PL 101-476, now PL 105-17, TBI is defined as follows:

"Traumatic brain injury means an acquired injury to the brain caused by an external physical force, resulting in total or partial functional disability or psychosocial impairment, or both, that adversely affects a child's educational performance. The term applies to open or closed head injuries resulting in impairments in one or more areas, such as cognition; language; memory; attention; reasoning; abstract thinking; judgment; problem-solving; sensory, perceptual and motor abilities; psychosocial behavior; physical functions; information processing; and speech. The term does not apply to brain injuries that are congenital or degenerative, or brain injuries induced by birth trauma." (*Federal Register*, 1992, p. 44802)

IDEA requires the child's brain injury to be caused by an external physical force, not internal trauma (e.g., a stroke, a brain tumor), in order for the student to meet eligibility requirements. Professionals continue to debate the appropriateness of excluding children whose brain injuries are the result of internal trauma. Some states, however, have opted to identify and classify a broader range of children and adolescents whose injuries are the result of either an external physical force or internal trauma (Rapp, 1999). Thus, a significant amount of variability exists across states regarding educational policy and eligibility criteria for students with TBI (Katsiyannis & Conderman, 1994). State rules and regulations should be consulted to determine whether children whose brain injuries are the result of internal trauma are eligible for services under the TBI category or the more generic IDEA category of other health impaired (OHI).

Whatever the etiology, children with brain injuries whose educational performance is adversely affected by their injuries are entitled to an evaluation to assess eligibility for special education. If eligible for special education and related services under the TBI or OHI category, an individualized educational program (IEP) must be developed. The purpose of the IEP is to specify the student's short- and long-term educational needs.

For those individuals with TBI who are not eligible for special education and related services under IDEA, Section 504 of the Vocational Rehabilitation Act of 1973, a civil rights law, may provide sufficient services and protections in the school setting. Section 504 outlines the school district's responsibility to provide educational accommodations and related services to enable disabled students to have equal access to all publicly funded programs available to their nondisabled peers. Through a written plan, the school's 504 team outlines the educational accommodations and related services necessary, so a disabled student will be able to access and benefit from his or her educational program.

Assessment plays a prominent role in determining eligibility and in the treatment paradigm of traumatic brain injured children and adolescents (Begali, 1992). Assessment results provide invaluable information and help determine educational placement, related services, and instructional goals. Psychoeducational evaluations, ecological evaluations, neuropsychological evaluations, and neurological evaluations should be conducted and results should be integrated in order to determine appropriate accommodations and modifications needed in the school environment to provide optimal learning experiences for children and adolescents with TBI. Standardized testing supplemented with testing of the limits and process procedures will provide invaluable information for designing appropriate accommodations and interventions (Kaplan, 1988).

A standard psychoeducational evaluation consists of an intelligence test, achievement test, and behavioral rating scales (Rapp, 1999). A psychoeducational evaluation can predict future learning potential and learning disabilities under normal circumstances; however, children and adolescents with TBI are more likely to have deficits in attention and concentration (Kaufmann et al., 1993), retaining and retrieving new learning (Jaffe et al., 1993), organization and problem solving (Levin et al., 1988), and changes in behavior (Deaton, 1994), which will not be appropriately assessed using only a standard psychoeducational battery (Reitan & Wolfson, 1992). A psychoeducational evaluation may be appropriate and useful, however, in determining whether a student has lost any previous learned information (Rapp, 1999).

In contrast, a neuropsychological evaluation assesses a broad range of brain-behavior relationships, current cognitive processes, and new learning. Individual strengths and weaknesses can be identified, and degree of deficits approximated. Educational and vocational program goals can be developed, and practical implications of brain injury upon everyday functioning can be assessed. Neuropsychological evaluations as well as neurological evaluations, consisting of physical assessments conducted by medical specialists, should be used to augment standard psychological assessments (Goldstein, 1984). A neuropsychological evaluation should be conducted before the child reenters school and reevaluations should be conducted frequently during the first 18 to 24 months following the injury (Rapp, 1999). Begali (1992) recommends conducting a reevaluation every 3 to 6 months for the first 2 years postinjury. Following the first or second year postinjury, reevaluations should be conducted before major school transitions, when new or different problems arise, or lack of educational progress is reported (Rapp, 1999).

Ecological evaluations consist of observations of children or adolescents in a variety of settings. Students with TBI usually have difficulty monitoring and regulating their own behavior in the real world, generalizing skills and abilities, and cognitive organization. Formal testing conducted in a structured setting cannot assess with any degree of accuracy any difficulties in the aforementioned areas nor does formal testing have any resemblance to the real world or classroom environment. Thus, real world observational assessments complement formal testing. Observations of children and adolescents with TBI provide a means of monitoring these students' progress and evaluating the appropriateness of educational programs and interventions developed for these individuals (Rapp, 1999). Observations should be conducted on a frequent basis.

Informal testing such as curriculum-based and criterion-based assessment is also recommended. Curriculum-based and criterion-based assessment may be used to guide instructional efforts and provide feedback. Program deficiencies can be identified and revision of instructional objectives may be made based on the results of frequent informal testing in the classroom.

In the classroom, a child or adolescent with TBI can be a real challenge. Educators may feel stymied in their efforts to reintegrate the child or adolescent with TBI into the school setting. Educational success for a child with TBI depends not only on the child but also on the teacher who is knowledgeable about brain injury, has a feeling of self-efficacy or self-competence in the classroom, and fosters a positive teacher-student relationship with the child (Farmer & Peterson, 1995).

Many schools have adopted home-school consultation models to address the educational needs of children with TBI. In home-school consultation (e.g., Conjoint Behavioral Consultation; Sheridan, Kratochwill, & Bergen, 1996), a consultant (i.e., a school psychologist) works with consultees (i.e., teachers and parents) to address the difficulties encountered by the child. Through collaborative consultation, parents and the school engage in a mutual process that leads to a reorganization around the child who has a brain injury. An empowerment model is adopted where parents take an active and central role in the educational programming for their child, including programs to meet their child's academic, social, emotional, behavioral, and vocational needs. Parents and school personnel share equally in the identification and prioritization of issues to be addressed through individual interventions. Parents and teachers along with school specialists develop and implement intervention strategies to address the issues of concern. The child's progress is monitored and modifications are made when needed. Continued dialogue between the school and home is encouraged to ensure the best possible treatment regimen for the child (Conoley & Sheridan, 1997).

Classroom placement is one of the first questions raised when a child with TBI is discharged from the hospital or rehabilitation unit. School placement may range from participation in the regular education classroom with no special supports to residential placement, depending on the child's age and learning needs (Savage, 1991). Initially, a self-contained classroom may be needed to prevent overstimulation and to increase teacher contact. Shorter school days and a reduced workload may also be needed to offset fatigue (Farmer & Peterson, 1995).

Limited research exists on the best instructional methods to use with traumatic brain injured children. Thus, sound teaching practices used with other disabled learners is what is currently recommended for use with this heterogeneous group of learners (Begali, 1992). Systematic and structured programs and compensatory training are recommended. Direct instruction in the students' most intact sensory modality is suggested to optimize children's learning. Tape recording of materials or duplicates of other students' notes may be helpful when poor note-taking skills exist. To monitor progress in learning, assignment notebooks reviewed on a regular basis by teachers and parents may also be helpful. Extended deadlines, breakdown of tasks into smaller units, reduced workload, and alternate means of assessment may need to be implemented. Establishment of routine in the classroom is extremely important and will be required, as TBI children need consistency (D'Amato & Rothlisberg, 1997). For reading recovery, material should be presented initially in a vertical format with a gradual transition to a horizontal presentation. Graph or lined paper turned sideways is suggested for youngsters who are having difficulties with mathematical computations due to visual-spatial or graphomotor difficulties. Multiple-choice formats or matching formats are recommended for students with memory problems, whereas oral exams are suggested for children with problems in written expression (Begali, 1992).

As noted earlier, attention/concentration difficulties affect a number of children with TBI. A variety of intervention strategies have been suggested to address attention/concentration difficulties, including environmental modifications, behavioral approaches, direct retraining approaches, biofeedback training, metacognitive and self-regulatory strategies (Mateer, Kerns, & Eso, 1997) and stimulant medication (Begali, 1992). Perhaps the simplest approach to help children with TBI attend in the classroom is to make environmental modifications. Environmental modifications may be as simple as having preferential seating arrangements, cueing/redirecting a child when off task, or presenting information in smaller units with multiple repetition. Behavioral approaches to increase attending may involve the implementation of a response-cost program in which privileges are taken away for lack of attending. Examples of direct retraining approaches are computer-based activities, pencil and paper exercises, and other manipulatives to allow children to practice and exercise a variety of attention-dependent skills or processes. Self-monitoring, on the other hand, falls under the rubric of self-regulatory strategies where children monitor their own attending behaviors.

A variety of strategies have also been suggested to remedy memory deficits. Memory deficits are one of the major cognitive sequelae associated with traumatic brain injuries. Internal strategies such as mnemonics, verbal strategies, and visual imagery may prove to be beneficial. External aids may also be helpful, as they may be used to extend or supplement the internal storage mechanisms. Examples of external aids include computer-based systems, paging systems, electronic organizers, and memory notebooks (Mateer et al., 1997). Direct instruction that is presented in a logical and unambiguous format using behavioral techniques, such as task analysis, modeling, shaping, reinforcement of appropriate responses, and continuous assessment have proven to be effective with a wide range of learners, including students with TBI (Colvin, 1990).

Motor deficits, sensory deficits, language/speech difficulties, and perceptual problems have also been reported as common sequelae of traumatic brain injured children. Computer-assisted training, paper and pencil cancellation tasks, mazes, visual closure worksheets, and eye-hand retraining techniques may be useful in addressing perceptual problems (Begali, 1992). In contrast, strategies to address language-processing problems may include pairing verbal with written instructions, avoiding figurative language, providing ample time to process information, and varying one's voice and intonation when repeating instructions (Blosser & DePompei, 1989). Direct remediation of specific language/speech deficits or compensatory training may also be needed. Consultation with medical specialists, however, may be the best strategy to use to address sensory deficits. Likewise, consultation with physical and occupational therapists is recommended to address motor deficits.

Social functioning may be impaired when individuals experience a brain injury. TBI can interfere with social functioning for a variety of reasons, including poor communication skills, limited mobility, decreased social cognition, and aggressive behavior. Social skills training and group activities such as cooperative learning activities may be beneficial in helping children with TBI to improve their social competency and acceptance by peers (Farmer & Peterson, 1995).

Behavioral sequelae following TBI are diverse. Both externalizing (e.g., aggression, noncompliance, anger outbursts) and internalizing (e.g., anxiety, depression) behaviors have been reported (Begali, 1992). Intervention strategies to address externalizing behaviors in the classroom environment include public posting of classroom rules and applying appropriate consequences for compliant and noncompliant behavior. Other classroom management strategies that have proven effective in reducing externalizing behaviors include teacher reprimands, precision requests, and time out. Effective use of teacher praise, on the other hand, can increase the frequency of appropriate behaviors (Kehle, Clark, & Jenson, 1997).

The predominant psychological issue faced by children and adolescents with TBI and their families is loss (Begali, 1992). The family may mourn the loss of the individual they once knew (Lezak, 1995). In other words, personality changes often accompany a traumatic brain injury. The child or members of the child's family may display shock, denial, grief, depression, and anxiety as a result of the changes. Thus, education about TBI, individual counseling for the child, family support and advocacy, and/or family therapy for the entire family, including siblings, may be needed to help the child and family cope with the changes that have occurred in the aftermath of the injury (Conoley & Sheridan, 1997).

A traumatic brain injury can be devastating not only to the child but also to the child's family. Following traumatic brain injury, a child's reintegration into the school setting can be a challenging experience. Comprehensive assessment and intervention strategies are needed to enhance the child's outcome in all areas of functioning. Collaboration among parents, educators, hospital/rehabilitation staff, and community members is needed in order to help these children and adolescents achieve independence, reach their academic potential, and lead satisfying and quality lives (Farmer & Peterson, 1995).

REFERENCES

Alves, W. M., & James, J. A. (1985). Mild brain injury: Damage and outcome. In D. P. Beck & J. T. Povlishock (Eds.), *Central nervous system trauma: Status report–1985*, Washington, DC: National Institutes of Health.

Bagby, G. (1991). Advances in anticonvulsant therapy. *Headlines*, *2–5*, 7–8.

Begali, V. (1992). *Head injury in children and adolescents*. Brandon, VT: Clinical Psychology Publishing Company.

Bigler, E. D. (1990). *Traumatic brain injury*. Austin, TX: PRO-ED.

Binder, L. M. (1986). Persisting symptoms after mild head injury: A review of the postconcussive syndrome. *Journal of Clinical and Experimental Neuropsychology*, *8*(4), 323–346.

Blosser, J., & DePompei, R. (1989). The head injured student returns to school: Recognizing and treating deficits. *Topics in Language Disorders*, *9*(2), 67–77.

Boyer, M. G., & Edwards, P. (1991). Outcome 1 to 3 years after severe traumatic brain injury in children and adolescents. *Injury*, *22*(4), 315–320.

Brain Injury Association. (1997). *Pediatric brain injury [fact sheet]*. Alexandria, VA: Author.

Brandstater, M. E., Bontke, C. F., Cobble, N. D., & Horn, L. J. (1991). Rehabilitation in brain disorders: Specific disorders. *Archives of Physical Medicine and Rehabilitation*, *72*, S332–S340.

Bruce, D. A., & Zimmermann, R. A. (1989). Shaken impact syndrome. *Pediatric Annals, 18*, 482–494.

Chadwick, O., Rutter, M., Shaffer, D., & Shrout, P. E. (1981). A prospective study of children with head injuries: IV. Specific cognitive deficits. *Journal of Clinical Neuropsychology, 3*, 101–120.

Colvin, G. (1990). Procedures for preventing serious acting-out behavior in the classroom. *Direct Instruction Newsletter, 9*, 27–30.

Conoley, J. C., & Sheridan, S. M. (1997). Pediatric traumatic brain injury: Challenges and interventions for families. In E. D. Bigler, E. Clark, & J. E. Farmer (Eds.), *Childhood traumatic brain injury: Diagnosis, assessment, and intervention* (pp. 177–189). Austin, TX: PRO-ED.

Crosson, B. A. (1992). *Subcortical functions in language and memory*. New York, NY: Guilford Press.

Crouchman, M. (1990). Head injury: How community pediatricians can help. *Archives of Diseases in Children, 65*, 1286–1287.

Dalby, P. R., & Obrzut, J. E. (1991). Epidemiological characteristics and sequelae of closed head-injured children and adolescents a review. *Developmental Neuropsychology, 7*, 35–68.

D'Amato, R. C., & Rothlisberg, B. A. (1997). How education should respond to students with traumatic brain injury. In E. D. Bigler, E. Clark, & J. E. Farmer (Eds.), *Childhood traumatic brain injury: Diagnosis, assessment, and intervention* (pp. 213–237). Austin, TX: PRO-ED.

Deaton, A. V. (1994). Changing the behaviors of students with acquired brain injuries. In R. C. Savage & G. F. Wolcott (Eds.), *Educational dimensions of acquired brain injury* (pp. 257–275). Austin, TX: PRO-ED.

Donders, J. (1994). Academic placement after traumatic brain injury. *Journal of School Psychology, 32*, 53–65.

Edna, T. H., & Cappelen, J. (1987). Late post-concussional symptoms in traumatic head injury. An analysis of frequency and risk factors. *Acta Neuropsychologica, 86*, 12–17.

Ewing-Cobbs, L., & Fletcher, J. M. (1990). Neuropsychological assessment of traumatic brain injury in children. In E. D. Bigler (Ed.), *Traumatic brain injury* (pp. 107–128). Austin, TX: PRO-ED.

Ewing-Cobbs, L., Levin, H. S., Fletcher, J. M., Miner, M. E., & Eisenberg, H. M. (1989). Posttraumatic amnesia in head-injured children: Assessment and outcome. *Journal of Clinical and Experimental Neuropsychology, 11*, 58.

Farmer, J. E. (1997). Epilogue: An ecological systems approach to childhood traumatic brain injury. In E. D. Bigler, E. Clark, & J. E. Farmer (Eds.), *Childhood traumatic brain injury: Diagnosis, assessment, and intervention* (pp. 261–275). Austin, TX: PRO-ED.

Farmer, J. E., Clippard, D. S., Wiemann, Y. L., Wright, E., & Owings, S. (1997). Assessing children with traumatic brain injury during rehabilitation: Promoting school and community reentry. In E. D. Bigler, E. Clark, & J. E. Farmer (Eds.), *Childhood traumatic brain injury: Diagnosis, assessment, and intervention* (pp. 33–62). Austin, TX: PRO-ED.

Farmer, J. E., & Peterson, L. (1995). Pediatric traumatic brain injury: Promoting successful school reentry. *School Psychology Review, 24*(2), 230–243.

Fay, G. C., Jaffe, K. M., Polissar, N. L., Liao, S., Martin, K. M., Shurtleff, H. A.,... Winn, H. R. (1993). Mild pediatric traumatic brain injury: A cohort study. *Archives of Physical Medicine and Rehabilitation, 74*, 895–901.

Federal Register. (1992, September 9). Individuals with Disabilities Education Act (IDEA), U.S. Department of Education Regulations. Washington, DC: U.S. Government Printing Office.

Frankowski, R. F., Annegers, J. F., & Whitman, S. (1985). Epidemiological and descriptive studies: Part I. In D. Becker & J. T. Povlishock (Eds.), *Central nervous system trauma: Status report* (pp. 33–45). Bethesda, MD: National Institutes of Health, National Institute of Neurological and Communicative Disorders and Stroke.

Goldstein, F. C., & Levin, H. S. (1990). Epidemiology of traumatic brain injury: Incidence, clinical characteristics, and risk factors. In E. D. Bigler (Ed.), *Traumatic brain injury* (pp. 51–67). Austin, TX: PRO-ED.

Goldstein, G. (1984). Neuropsychological assessment. In G. Goldstein & M. Hersen (Eds.), *Handbook of psychological assessment* (pp. 181–211). New York, NY: Pergamon Press.

Haak, R. A., & Livingston, R. B. (1997). Treating traumatic brain injury in the school: Mandates and methods. In C. R. Reynolds & E. Fletcher-Janzen (Eds.), *Handbook of clinical child neuropsychology* (2nd ed., 482–505). New York, NY: Plenum Press.

Hagen, C., Malkmus, D., & Durham, P. (1981). *Rancho los amigos: Levels of cognitive functioning*. Downey, CA: Professional Staff Association.

Harrington, D. (1990). Educational strategies. In M. Rosenthal, E. Griffith, M. Bond, & J. E. Miller (Eds.), *Rehabilitation of the adult and child with traumatic brain injury* (2nd ed., pp. 476–492). Philadelphia, PA: Davis.

Hauser, W. A., & Hesdorffer, D. C. (1990). *Epilepsy: Frequency, causes and consequences*. Landover, MD: Epilepsy Foundation of America.

Jaffe, K. M., Fay, G. C., Polissar, N. L., Martin, K. M., Shurtleff, H., Rivara, J. B., & Winn, H. R. (1993). Severity of pediatric traumatic brain injury and neurobehavioral recovery at one year—a cohort study. *Archives of Physical Medicine and Rehabilitation, 74*, 587–595.

Kaplan, E. (1988). A process approach to neuropsychological assessment. In T. Boll & B. K. Bryant (Eds.), *Clinical neuropsychology and brain function: Research, measurement, and practice* (pp. 129–167). Washington, DC: American Psychological Association.

Katsiyannis, a., & Conderman, G. (1994). Serving students with traumatic brain injury a national survey. *Remedial and Special Education, 15*, 319–325.

Katz, D. I. (1992). Neuropathology and neurobehavioral recovery from closed head injury. *Journal of Head Trauma Rehabilitation, 7*, 1–15.

Kaufmann, P. M., Fletcher, J. M., Levin, H. S., Miner, M. E., & Ewing-Cobbs, L. (1993). Attentional disturbance after pediatric closed head injury. *Journal of Child Neurology, 8*, 348–353.

Kehle, T. J., Clark, E., & Jenson, W. R. (1997). Interventions for students with traumatic brain injury: Managing behavioral disturbances. In E. D. Bigler, E. Clark, & J. E. Farmer (Eds.), *Childhood traumatic brain injury: Diagnosis, assessment, and intervention* (pp. 135–152). Austin, TX: PRO-ED.

Kraus, J. F., Black, M. A., Hessol, N., Ley, P., Rokaw, W., & Sullivan, C. (1984). The incidence of acute brain injury and serious impairments in a defined population. *American Journal of Epidemiology, 119*, 186–201.

Kreutzer, J. S., Devany, C. W., Myers, S. L., & Marwitz, J. H. (1991). Neurobehavioral outcome following brain injury. In J. S. Kreutzer & P. H. Wehman (Eds.), *Cognitive rehabilitation for persons with traumatic brain injury a functional approach.* Baltimore, MD: Paul H. Brookes.

Lehr, E. (1990). Incidence and etiology. In E. Lehr (Ed.), *Psychological management of traumatic brain injuries in children and adolescents* (pp. 1–98). Rockville, MD: Aspen.

Lehr, E., & Savage, R. (1990). Community and school integration from a developmental perspective. In J. Kreutzer & P. Wehman (Eds.), *Community integration following traumatic brain injury* (pp. 301–310). Baltimore, MD: Paul H. Brookes.

Levin, H. S. (1985). Outcome after head injury: Part II. In D. Becker & J. T. Povlishock (Eds.), *Central nervous system trauma: Status report* (pp. 281–303). Bethesda, MD: National Institutes of Health, National Institute of Neurological and Communicative Disorders and Stroke.

Levin, H. S., High, W. M., Ewing-Cobbs, L., Fletcher, J. M., Eisenberg, H. M., Miner, M. E., & Goldstein, F. C. (1988). Memory functioning during the first year after closed head injury in children and adolescents. *Neurosurgery, 22*, 1043–1052.

Levin, H. S., Mendelsohn, D., Lilly, M. A., Fletcher, J. M., Culhane, K. A., Chapman, S. B., Harward, H., Kusnerik, L., Bruce, D., & Eisenberg, H. M. (1994). Tower of London performance in relation to magnetic resonance imaging following closed head injury in children. *Neuropsychology, 8*, 171–179.

Lezak, M. D. (1995). *Neuropsychological assessment* (3rd ed.). New York, NY: Oxford University Press.

Luerssen, T. G. (1991). Head injuries in children. *Neurosurgery Clinics of North America, 2*, 399–410.

Mateer, C. A., Kerns, K. A., & Eso, K. L. (1997). Management of attention and memory disorders following traumatic brain injury. In E. D. Bigler, E. Clark, & J. E. Farmer (Eds.), *Childhood traumatic brain injury: Diagnosis, assessment, and intervention* (pp. 153–175). Austin, TX: PRO-ED.

Michaud, L. J., Rivara, F. P., Jaffe, K. M., Fay, G., & Dailey, J. L. (1993). Traumatic brain injury as a risk factor for behavioral disorders in children. *Archives of Physical Medicine and Rehabilitation, 74*, 368–375.

Mira, M. P., Tucker, B. F., & Tyler, J. S. (1992). *Traumatic brain injury in children and adolescents: A sourcebook for schools.* Austin, TX: PRO-ED.

Mitiguy, J. S., Thompson, G., & Wasco, J. (1990). *Understanding brain injury: Acute hospitalization.* Lynn, MA: New Medico.

Naugle, R. I. (1990). Epidemiology of traumatic brain injury in adults. In E. D. Bigler (Ed.), *Traumatic brain injury.* Austin, TX: PRO-ED.

North, B. (1984). *Jamieson's first notebook of head injury* (3rd ed.). London, England: Butterworths.

Oddy, M. (1993). Head injury during childhood. *Neuropsychological Rehabilitation, 3*, 301–320.

Pang, D. (1985). Pathophysiologic correlations of neurobehavioral syndromes following closed head injury. In M. Ylvisaker (Ed.), *Head injury rehabilitation: Children and adolescents* (pp. 3–71). San Diego, CA: College-Hill Press.

Parker, R. S. (1990). *Traumatic brain injury and neuropsychological impairment: Sensorimotor, cognitive, emotional and adaptive problems of children and adults.* New York, NY: Springer-Verlag.

Raimondi, A. J., & Hirschauer, J. (1984). Head injury in the infant and toddler. *Child's Brain, 11*, 12–35.

Rapp, D. L. (1999). Interventions for integrating children with traumatic brain injuries into their schools. In C. R. Reynolds & T. B. Gutkin (Eds.), *The handbook of school psychology* (3rd ed., pp. 863–884). New York, NY: Wiley.

Reitan, R. M., & Wolfson, D. (1992). *Neuropsychological evaluation of older children.* South Tucson, AZ: Neuropsychology Press.

Research and Training Center in Rehabilitation and Childhood Trauma. (1993). *National pediatric trauma registry.* Boston, MA: Tufts University of Medicine, New England Medical Center.

Russell, N. K. (1993). Educational considerations in traumatic brain injury: The role of the speech-language pathologist. *Language, Speech, and Hearing Services in the Schools, 24*, 267–275.

Rutherford, W. H. (1989). In H. S. Levin, H. M. Eisenberg, & a. L. Benton (Eds.), *Mild head injury.* New York, NY: Oxford University Press.

Rutter, M., Chadwick, O., Shaffer, D., & Brown, G. (1980). A prospective study of children with head injuries: I. Design and methods. *Psychological Medicine, 10*, 633–645.

Savage, R. C. (1991). Identification, classification, and placement issues for students with traumatic brain injuries. *Journal of Head Trauma Rehabilitation, 6*(1), 1–9.

Savage, R. C., & Wolcott, G. F. (Eds.). (1994). *Educational dimensions of acquired brain injury.* Austin, TX: PRO-ED.

Sheridan, S. M., Kratochwill, T. R., & Bergen, J. R. (1996). *Conjoint behavioral consultation a procedural manual.* New York, NY: Plenum Press.

Teasdale, G., & Jennett, B. (1974). Assessment of coma and impaired consciousness: A practical scale. *Lancet, 2*, 81–84.

VanZomeren, A. H., & Brouwer, W. H. (1994). *Clinical neuropsychology of attention.* London, England: Oxford University Press.

Vernon-Levett, P. (1991). Head injuries in children. *Critical Care Nursing Clinics of North America, 3*, 411–421.

Wade, S. L., Taylor, G., Drotar, D., Stancin, T., & Yeates, K. O. (1996). Childhood traumatic brain injury: Initial impact on the family. *Journal of Learning Disabilities, 29*(6), 652–661.

Ward, J. D., Chisholm, a. H., Prince, V. T., Gilman, C. B., & Hawkins, A. M. (1994). Penetrating head injury. *Critical Care Nursing Quarterly, 17*, 79–89.

Warzak, W. J., Mayfield, J., & McAllister, J. (1998). Central nervous system dysfunction: Brain injury, postconcussive syndrome, and seizure disorder. In T. S. Watson & F. Gresham (Eds.), *Handbook of child behavior therapy* (pp. 287–309). New York, NY: Plenum Press.

Wilberger, J. E. (1993). Minor head injuries in American football: Prevention of long term sequelae. *Sports Medicine, 15*, 338–343.

Wilkening, G. N. (1989). Techniques of localization in child neuropsychology. In C. R. Reynolds & E. Fletcher-Janzen (Eds.), *Handbook of clinical child neuropsychology* (pp. 291–310). New York, NY: Plenum Press.

Ylvisaker, M. (1993). Communication outcome in children and adolescents with traumatic brain injury. *Neuropsychological Rehabilitation, 3*, 367–387.

PATRICIA A. LOWE
University of Kansas

CECIL R. REYNOLDS
Texas A&M University

TRAUMATIC BRAIN INJURY IN CHILDREN

Incidence and Problems

Traumatic brain injury (TBI) in children remains a major health problem and has been reported to be the leading cause of death between the ages of 2 to 44 (Hay, 1967). Actual incidence records are only available for those with more severe injuries who sought medical treatment, but it is estimated that approximately 15,000 suffer severe traumatic brain injury in the United States each year (Di Scala, Osberg, Gans, Chin, & Grant, 1991). Severe TBI produces many observable changes, and even more changes in a child's cognitive functions. In less severe TBI, or later in the recovery, the child may appear to be functioning normally, but subtle cognitive deficits may remain that influence behavior in diffuse ways or that remain unnoticed until later stages of development are reached.

Assessment of the nature and extent of the consequences of TBI in children is more difficult and challenging than with adults, yet effective treatment and remediation requires an objective appraisal of cognitive strengths and weaknesses. Underestimating the capacity of recovery may lead to delayed rehabilitation with efforts aimed at the consequences of the injury rather than at preventative therapy (Stover & Zeiger, 1976). On the other hand, underestimating the extent of the impairment may lead to excessive stress or difficulty in emotional adjustment (Taylor et al., 1995). Clearly, even mild head injury can become a significant disruptive event to a child and his or her family unless the consequences are properly evaluated and effective rehabilitation is instituted.

Development and Time to Recovery

For a time it was generally believed that TBI sustained early in life was associated with less deleterious effects (Kennard principle). Children were thought to have a more resilient nervous system because they appear to recover more rapidly than adults, experience less persistent symptoms (Black, Jeffries, Blumer, Wellner, & Walker, 1969), and seldom report postconcussion symptoms (Rutter, Chadwick, & Shaffer, 1983). However, this notion is at best only partially accurate (Bolter & Long, 1985). Recent research has suggested that the likelihood of residual cognitive deficits is greater with early injury (Max et al. 1997; Taylor & Alden, 1997).

Children can "grow out" of some early deficits, but not others. In some cases, dysfunction may only appear later in the course of development (Goldman, 1971, 1972, 1974; Teuber & Rudel, 1962; Wrightson, McGinn, & Gronwall, 1995). For example, damage to the immature frontal lobes of a young child may not produce behavioral manifestations until much later in development when those cortical areas would normally assume functional prominence (Russell, 1959). It is likely that the effects of head injury in children combine with other functions in their development and may have widespread effects (Korkman, 1980). Age is only one variable of importance in determining the extent of recovery. In addition to age, one must consider location, nature, and the extent of the injury in order to determine the effects of the injury upon subsequent behavior.

Severity of Injury

The pathophysiology of brain injury is similar in children and adults. Severity of injury is usually measured by duration of coma and/or posttraumatic amnesia (PTA), although both are difficult to assess in younger children (Leigh, 1979). As a general guide, children experiencing coma of more than 7 days seldom recover to their preinjury level. Even coma of less than 7 days or PTA of less than 3 weeks is usually associated with permanent cognitive impairment (Stover & Zeiger, 1976).

Cognitive Consequences

After severe head injury, obviously impaired physical functions tend to improve rapidly, whereas cognitive dysfunction may resolve less quickly. Head injury frequently affects intelligence, memory, speech, language, and other functions. The effects upon cognitive functions are pervasive during the first 6 months following injury (Levin & Eisenberg, 1979). Later in recovery, the effects are often characterized by slowed information processing, poor problem solving ability, impulsivity, distractibility, and poor stress tolerance with irritability and emotional lability. In addition, researchers have documented memory impairment, decreased visuospatial processing (Lord-Maes & Obrzut, 1996), and decreased attentional shift (Ewing-Cobbs et al., 1998). Common behavioral symptoms also include hyperkinesis (32%), discipline problems (10%), and lethargy (87%; Black et al., 1969), as well as ADHD (Max, Arndt, et al., 1998). These effects are observed in school performance and in neuropsychological testing. More important is the finding that children suffering even mild head trauma, with little or no coma and/or PTA, demonstrate attenuated cognitive abilities.

Children are undergoing significant developmental changes and even mild TBI can cause developmental setbacks leading to immature behaviors. Such damage may cause a loss of previously mastered skills and compromise future ability for the acquisition of new skills.

Emotional and Social Factors

In addition to physical impairment and cognitive dysfunction, the brain-injured child is at risk for the development of emotional problems (Max et al., 1997; Max, Koele, et al., 1998). The risks are greater in those with low premorbid IQ, from a low socioeconomic class, or from broken homes (Rutter et al., 1983). Preinjury family environment has also been shown to affect recovery (Yeates et al., 1997). Survivors of TBI are at a greater risk of developing psychiatric disorders as well, which is positively correlated with injury severity (Max et al., 1997; Max, Koele, et al., 1998).

Assessment Strategies

Proper assessment strategies leading into the development and enactment of an individually tailored intervention plan are critical in facilitating the successful reentry of the brain-injured child into his or her premorbid environment. These assessment strategies focus on cognitive, emotional, and environmental factors that interact and shape subsequent behavior. Initial assessment should focus on the neuropsychological consequences of the injury. This assessment examines the relationship between the functioning of the brain and the cognitive processing abilities exhibited by the child. This assessment of cognitive abilities, coupled with a consideration of the type and severity of injury, developmental factors, and emotional functioning of the child, affords a view of basic strengths and weaknesses in cognitive functioning, which can serve to identify initial intervention strategies.

Repeated neuropsychological assessments are not necessary in most cases. Rather, a psychoeducational assessment should be of greater value later in recovery. Aptitude and achievement tests are not sensitive to the impact of a brain injury on functioning immediately following a TBI. However, they become critical components later in the assessment process for evaluating the impact of the child's processing strengths and weaknesses on school performance. The comparison of performance on aptitude and achievement tests given before and after the injury is valuable in evaluating changes in the child's ability to acquire and retain new information.

The child's emotional functioning and reaction to the environment in daily life is another key component of the assessment process. Observation of the child at home, within class, while interacting with peers, and so on is most likely to add to an understanding of the child's problems within these environments. Other assessment strategies include interviewing and utilizing scales of adaptive and emotional functioning. Evaluation of the appropriateness of the child's environment to his or her level of cognitive ability, emotional functioning, and behavioral control is needed.

Intervention Strategies

Examination of interacting cognitive, emotional, and environmental factors should be considered in the development of treatment plans. Traditional behavior management strategies may be helpful, but not completely adequate, for aiding the recovery of function in children with TBI. Because individuals with TBI often exhibit impaired concentration and memory and also have a low tolerance for frustration, environmental considerations must be made. Children with TBI should be afforded less distracting and more structured environments for study. Allowing children more time to complete their tasks can combat slowed processing. The lowered stamina of a child with TBI can be accommodated by providing frequent breaks and shortening the school day. The child's reentry into the normal school situation should be a gradual process. Care should be taken to insure that he or she is working at a level that will produce some successes. Resources such as special education and speech/language specialists should be utilized as needed. Additionally, consideration of emotional functioning should determine the need for psychological intervention. The reader is referred to a more extensive discussion of an ecological model of assessment and intervention (Farmer & Peterson, 1995; Long & Ross, 1992; Sbordone & Long, 1996).

REFERENCES

Black, P., Jeffries, J. J., Blumer, D., Wellner, A., & Walker, A. E. (1969). The posttraumatic syndrome in children. In a. E. Walker, W. F. Caveness, & M. Critchley (Eds.), *Late effects of head injury* (pp. 142–149). Springfield, IL: Thomas.

Bolter, J. F., & Long, C. J. (1985). Methodological issues in research in developmental neuropsychology. In L. C. Hartlage

& C. F. Telzrow (Eds.), *The neuropsychology of individual differences* (pp. 41–59). New York, NY: Plenum Press.

Di Scala, C., Osberg, J. S., Gans, B. M., Chin, L. J., & Grant, C. C. (1991). Children with traumatic head injury: Morbidity and postacute treatment. *Archives of Physical Medicine and Rehabilitation, 72,* 662–666.

Ewing-Cobbs, L., Prasad, M., Fletcher, J. M., Levin, H. S., Miner, M. E., & Eisenberg, H. M. (1998). Attention after pediatric traumatic brain injury: A multidimensional assessment. *Child Neuropsychology, 4*(1), 35–48.

Farmer, J. E., & Peterson, L. (1995). Pediatric traumatic brain injury: Promoting successful school reentry. *School Psychology Review, 24*(2), 230–243.

Goldman, P. S. (1971). Functional development of the prefrontal cortex in early life and the problem of neuronal plasticity. *Experimental Neurology, 3,* 366–387.

Goldman, P. S. (1972). Developmental determinants of cortical plasticity. *Acta Neurobiologica Experimentalis, 32,* 495–511.

Goldman, P. S. (1974). An alternative to developmental plasticity: Heterology of CNS structures in infants and adults. In D. Stein, J. Rosen, & N. Butters (Eds.), *Plasticity and recovery of function in the central nervous system* (p. 109). New York, NY: Academic Press.

Hay, R. (1967). Head injuries. *Canadian Medical Association Journal, 97,* 1364–1368.

Korkman, M. (1980). An attempt to adapt methods of Luria for diagnosis of cognitive deficits in children. Convention paper INS, San Francisco, CA.

Leigh, D. (1979). Psychiatric aspects of head injury. *Psychiatric Digest, 21–34.*

Levin, H. S., & Eisenberg, H. M. (1979). Neuropsychological impairment after closed head injury in children and adolescents. *Journal of Pediatric Psychology, 4,* 389–402.

Long, C. J., & Ross, L. K. (1992). *Handbook of head trauma: Acute care to recovery.* New York: Plenum Press.

Lord-Maes, J., & Obrzut, J. E. (1996). Neuropsychological consequences of traumatic brain injury in children and adolescents. *Journal of Learning Disabilities, 29*(6), 609–617.

Max, J. E., Arndt, S., Castillo, C. S., Bokura, H., Robin, D., Lindgren,...Mattheis, P. J. (1998). Attention-deficit hyperactivity symptomatology after traumatic brain injury: A prospective study. *Journal of the American Academy of Child and Adolescent Psychiatry, 37*(8), 841–847.

Max, J. E., Koele, S. L., Smith, W. L., Sato, Y., Lindgren, S. D., Robin, D. A., & Arndt, S. (1998). Psychiatric disorders in children and adolescents after severe traumatic brain injury: A controlled study. *Journal of the American Academy of Child and Adolescent Psychiatry, 37*(8), 832–840.

Max, J. E., Lindgren, S. D., Knutson, C., Pearson, C. S., Ihrig, D., & Welborn, A. (1997). Child and adolescent traumatic brain injury: Psychiatric findings from a pediatric outpatient specialty clinic. *Brain Injury, 11*(10), 699–711.

Russell, W. R. (1959). *Brain, memory, learning a neurologist's view.* Oxford, England: Clarendon.

Rutter, M., Chadwick, O., & Shaffer, D. (1983). Head injury. In M. Rutter (Ed.), *Developmental neuropsychiatry* (pp. 83–111). New York, NY: Guilford Press.

Sbordone, R. J., & Long, C. J. (1996). *Ecological validity of neuropsychological testing.* Delray Beach, FL: St. Lucie.

Stover, S. L., & Zeiger, H. E. (1976). Head injury in children and teenagers: Function/recovery correlated with the duration of coma. *Archives of Physical Medicine and Rehabilitation, 57,* 201–205.

Taylor, H. G., & Alden, J. (1997). Age-related differences in outcome following childhood brain insults: An introduction and overview. *Journal of the International Neuropsychological Society, 3,* 555–567.

Taylor, H. G., Drotar, D., Wade, S., Yeates, K., Stancin, T., & Klein, S. (1995). Recovery from traumatic brain injury in children: The importance of the family. In S. H. Broman & M. E. Michel (Eds.), *Traumatic head injury in children* (pp. 188–216). New York, NY: Oxford University Press.

Teuber, H. L., & Rudel, R. G. (1962). Behavior after cerebral lesions in children and adults. *Developmental Medicine and Child Neurology, 4,* 3–20.

Wrightson, P., McGinn, V., & Gronwall, D. (1995). Mild head injury in preschool children: Evidence that it can be associated with a persistent cognitive defect. *Journal of Neurology, Neurosurgery, and Psychiatry, 59*(4), 375–380.

Yeates, K. O., Taylor, H. G., Drotar, D., Wade, S. L., Klein, S., Stancin, T., & Schatschneider, C. (1997). Preinjury family environment as a determinant of recovery from traumatic brain injuries in school-age children. *Journal of the International Neuropsychological Society, 3*(6), 617–630.

CHARLES J. LONG
JOY O'GRADY
MICHELLE RIES
University of Memphis

TRAUMATIC BRAIN INJURY, MILD

A mild traumatic brain injury results from a change in brain functioning due to physical trauma with possible permanent sequelae. There are open head injuries, when the skull is penetrated, and closed head injuries, when the skull is not penetrated. After one head injury, the risk of a second injury is tripled; and after a second head injury, the risk of a third injury is 8 times greater (Brain Injury Association, 1995). The severity of brain injury is determined through the utilization of a number of standardized scales. The most commonly used scale is the 15-point Glasgow Coma Scale (GCS), which evaluates the stimulus required for the child to induce eye opening, motor response, and verbal response. A mild injury is classified as a score of 13 or more. A second means of measuring brain injury severity is the length of posttraumatic amnesia, which is the time between the injury and the return of ongoing memory. A mild injury involves amnesia of 1 hour or less.

The reason for numerous measures lies with the lack of consensus relating to the definition of traumatic head injury and how to measure it. For example, it is common knowledge that a person does not have to lose consciousness to have a head injury (Bigler, 1990). Furthermore, children can sustain a more serious injury than an adult without losing consciousness, which leaves in question the appropriateness of using the same scales for all ages (Ewing-Cobbs et al., 1997). Finally, medical staff do not evaluate all injuries at the time of the accident, so measures required are not recorded at requisite times if at all.

It is estimated that 56,000 Americans die annually from brain injuries (Brain Injury Association, 1995). Further, 373,000 Americans are hospitalized annually as a result of head injuries, and 99,000 of those injuries result in moderate to severe lifelong disabilities (Brain Injury Association, 1995). Males are reported as incurring more head injuries than females. For example, Bigler (1990) reported that the ratio of male to female injuries was 2:1 in his information search. Traumatic brain injury (TBI) has become a major medical issue (Hilton, 1994), and "the economic cost of brain injuries in the United States is estimated to be $48.3 billion annually" (Brain Injury Association, 1995, p. 1).

Characteristics

1. Cognitive deficits.
2. Cognitive profiles are varied; no two head injuries are exactly alike.
3. Fatigue.
4. Language deficits, particularly social language.
5. Behavior problems.
6. Premorbid behavior problems are exacerbated.
7. Behavioral deficits and adaptive skills are found in longitudinal studies to adulthood.
8. The earlier in life the injury, the worse the developmental outcome is.
9. The more severe the injury, the worse the outcome is.
10. Developmental course may be changed. A skill may be delayed or not develop, and the structure of the skill may be changed.
11. Recovery may take up to 5 years for children versus 3 years for adults. Some advocate that for every year younger the child is, the longer is the recovery process.
12. Deficits become more apparent as time goes on. Children often do not keep up with their peers, and developmental skills often are not accomplished or lag behind.

Treatment of mild TBI starts with medical providers in case of a concussion, a hemorrhage, or other physical sequelae. Once the child is medically stable, school and social activities may resume except for contact sports, and care should be taken not to incur another injury (e.g., wearing a helmet for biking). If all symptoms are not resolved by 3 months, an evaluation is recommended. The most thorough assessment is a neuropsychological evaluation, which focuses on brain-behavior relationships. The assessment should include cognitive, academic, emotional, social, adaptive, and behavioral functioning. The assessment will be the basis for further treatment and a baseline so that developmental progress can be monitored. Many interventions require changes in the environment such as a structured routine and a reduced level of stimulation. The child needs to learn to pace him- or herself and recognize limits. If adjustment problems develop, counseling with a therapist knowledgeable about mild TBI is warranted. Unfortunately, mild injuries are often not diagnosed, or once the initial trauma is over, the child is thought to have fully recovered. As development unfolds and later skills are affected, no one connects a previous TBI with deficit.

Traumatic brain injury is recognized as a specific diagnostic category as of the reauthorization of PL 94-142 (now PL 101-476, or IDEA, 1990). Therefore, school staff may complete or participate in the assessment of the child for special education services. Specialized training is required before providing needed services for students with TBI; therefore, a school district may need to consult with providers in the community to successfully fulfill educational obligations for the child (D'Amato, & Rothlisberg, 1996). A positive and collaborative relationship between school staff and parents is particularly important as the family has a moderator effect on the recovery of the child. The higher functioning the family is, the better the prognosis for outcome (Taylor et al., 1999).

Prognosis is positive for the majority of children incurring a mild brain injury. A small portion of children have permanent sequelae that will require special education classes, and compensatory strategies for a lifetime. Researchers are involved with longitudinal studies, deficits and developmental intertwine (Ewing-Cobbs et al., 1997), and moderator factors in recovery (Taylor et al., 1999). These lines of research are needed for a long-term understanding.

REFERENCES

Bigler, E. D. (Ed.). (1990). *Traumatic brain injury*. Austin, TX: PRO-ED.

Brain Injury Association. (1995). *Fact sheet: Traumatic brain injury*. Washington, DC: Author.

D'Amato, R. C., & Rothlisberg, B. A. (1996). How education should respond to students with traumatic brain injury. *Journal of Learning Disabilities, 29*(6), 670–683.

Ewing-Cobbs, L., Fletcher, J. M., Levin, H. S., Francis, D. J., Davidson, K., & Miner, M. E. (1997). Longitudinal neuropsychological outcome in infants and preschoolers with traumatic brain injury. *Journal of the International Neuropsychological Society, 3,* 581–591.

Hilton, G. (1994). Behavioral and cognitive sequelae of head trauma. *Orthopedic Nursing, 13*(4), 25–32.

Taylor, H. G., Yeates, K. O., Wade, S. L., Drotar, D., Klein, S. K., & Stancin, T. (1999). Influences on first-year recovery from traumatic brain injury in children. *Neuropsychology, 13*(1), 76–89.

THERESA M. GISI
*Colorado Neuropsychological Associates,
P.C. Denver and Colorado Springs,
Colorado*

TRAVEL AIDS, ELECTRONIC (See Electronic Travel Aids)

TRAVEL AIDS FOR INDIVIDUALS WITH DISABILITIES

The United States Department of Justice provides a guide to disability rights and laws to ensure equal opportunities for people with disabilities. Encompassed within this document are guidelines for access to public transportation, public accommodation, and air carriers (Disability Rights Section, 1996). The United States adheres to these guidelines and provides disabled travelers with various options for traveling. Numerous opportunities for accessible travel by car, boat, train, or airplane are available to those with handicaps. Airlines have become more accessible by arranging for an aisle seat (many of which have removable arms for easier access), notifying the crew that a special needs traveler will be on board, and meeting special requests such as dietary needs or supplemental oxygen. Wheelchairs may be gate-checked for easier accessibility as they will be the first items offloaded at the traveler's destination or at any change of planes. Travelers with disabilities should ask the airlines or their travel agent to make reservations for the most direct route and to allow ample time to change planes if necessary.

Train travel is another option for the travelers with disabilities. Amtrak provides information and details about station accessibility along its routes. Train aisles are narrow, so wheelchair access may be limited. However, often meals are served at the person's seat. Conductors give hearing-impaired travelers necessary announcements in writing. Guide dogs travel free, and most trains are equipped with signs in braille.

Avis Rent-a-Car and Hertz Car Rental companies offer hand-control cars if reserved well in advance. Other car companies also have vehicles to offer special needs clients, including wheelchair-accessible vans.

If traveling by ship, the travelers with disabilities should check accessibility before making a reservation. Most major cruise lines have accessible cabins and public areas, but some small ships have limited access. The special needs traveler should check with each ship to find out what provisions have been made for the disabled and if specific needs can be met (Reamy, 1978).

Quick travel answers can be found from sources, such as *Fodor's Great American Vacations for Travelers with Disabilities* (1994). The Internet also provides multiple sites providing travel information and answering specific questions. Project Action (1999) has a comprehensive database with city and state listings of accessible travel options. National 800 numbers are listed on the Project Action website with public transportation, airport transportation, hotel shuttles, private bus, and even tour companies' information links. Information can be located online.

Access Amtrak, 60 Massachusetts Avenue, Washington, DC 20002. American Foundation for the Blind, Travel Concessions for Blind Persons, 15 W. 16th Street, New York, NY 10011. Centers for the Handicapped, Inc., 10501 New Hampshire Avenue, Silver Spring, MD 20903, Tel.: (301) 445-3350. Diabetes Travel Service, 349 E. 52nd Street, New York, NY 10022. INTERMEDIC, 777 Third Avenue, New York, NY 10007. International Association for Medical Assistance for Travelers, 350 5th Avenue, Suite 5620, New York, NY 10001. National Easter Seals Society, Information Center, 230 W. Monroe Street, Chicago, IL 60606. Society for the Advancement of Travel for the Handicapped (SATH), "The United States Welcomes Handicapped Visitors" (cassette or braille available), 5014 42nd Street, NW, Washington, DC 20016, Tel.: (202) 966-3900. Travel Tips for the Handicapped, U.S. Travel Service, Department of Commerce, Washington, DC 20230. Wheelchair Wagon Tours, P.O. Box 1270, Kissimmee, FL 32741, Tel.: (305) 846-7175. Whole Person Tours, 137 W. 32nd Street, Bayonne, New Jersey 07002, Tel.: (201) 858-3400.

REFERENCES

Fodor's great American vacations for travelers with disabilities. (1994). New York, NY: Fodor's Travel Publications.

Project Action. (1999). http://www.projectaction.org/

Reamy, L. (1978). *Travel ability.* New York, NY: Macmillan.

U.S. Department of Justice. (1996). Disability rights section. Retrieved from http://publications.usa.gov/

SUE A. SCHMITT
*University of Wisconsin at Stout
First edition*

KARI ANDERSON
*University of North Carolina at Wilmington
Second edition*

TREACHER-COLLINS SYNDROME (See National Organization of Rare Disorders)

TREATMENT ACCEPTABILITY

Treatment acceptability is a form of social validation that asks consumers how they feel about treatment methods prior to treatment. "Judgments of acceptability are likely to embrace evaluation of whether treatment is appropriate for the problem, whether treatment is fair, reasonable, and intrusive, and whether treatment meets with conventional notions about what treatment should be" (Kazdin, 1980, p. 259). The most basic assumption of the acceptability hypothesis is that the acceptability of a treatment method will influence the overall efficacy of the treatment. Methods that consumers feel are the most acceptable will be more effective than methods that are judged to be unacceptable. As Wolf (1978) stated, "If the participants don't like the treatment then they may avoid it, or run away, or complain loudly. And thus, society will be less likely to use our technology, no matter how potentially effective and efficient it might be" (p. 206).

Research efforts in treatment acceptability have followed the same general procedures (Elliott, 1986). Subjects receive written, audio, oral, or audiovisual descriptions of problem behaviors and procedures for treating the problem behaviors. Then the subjects answer a number of questions designed to assess how acceptable the treatment is for improving the problem behavior. A number of scales of similar format have been developed for assessing treatment acceptability in different target populations. The Treatment Evaluation Inventory (TEI; Kazdin, 1980) has 15 questions scored on a 7-point Likert scale used with children and adults. The TEI requires subjects to make judgments about how acceptable an intervention is, how suitable the intervention is, how much the intervention is liked, and so on. The Intervention Rating Profile (IRP; Witt & Martens, 1983) has 20 questions scored on a 6-point Likert scale; the questions were specifically written to assess teachers' acceptability judgments of interventions in classroom situations. The IRP has been used to delineate a number of treatment variables that affect teachers' acceptability ratings (Turco, Witt, & Elliott, 1985; Witt, Elliott, & Martens, 1984). The Children's Intervention Rating Profile (CIRP; Elliott, 1986) has seven questions scored on a 6-point Likert scale. The CIRP has been used by a number of researchers (Elliott, Witt, Galvin, & Moe, 1986; Turco & Elliott, 1986; Turco, Elliott, & Witt, 1985) to assess children's treatment acceptability.

REFERENCES

Elliott, S. N. (1986). Children's ratings of the acceptability of classroom interventions for misbehavior: Findings and methodological considerations. *Journal of School Psychology, 24,* 23–35.

Elliott, S. N., Witt, J. C., Galvin, G. A., & Moe, G. L. (1986). Children's involvement in intervention selection: Acceptability of interventions for misbehaving peers. *Professional Psychology: Research and Practice, 17,* 235–241.

Kazdin, A. E. (1980). Acceptability of alternative treatments for deviant child behavior. *Journal of Applied Behavior Analysis, 13,* 259–273.

Turco, T. L., & Elliott, S. N. (1986). Assessment of students' acceptability of teacher-initiated interventions for classroom misbehaviors. *Journal of School Psychology, 24,* 277–283.

Turco, T. L., Elliott, S. N., & Witt, J. C. (1985). Children's involvement in treatment selection a review of theory and analogue research on treatment acceptability (pp. 54–62). *Monograph on Secondary Behavioral Disorders.* Reston, VA: Council for Exceptional Children.

Turco, T. L., Witt, J. C., & Elliott, S. N. (1985). Factors influencing teachers' acceptability of classroom interventions for deviant student behavior (pp. 46–53). *Monograph on Secondary Behavioral Disorders.* Reston, VA: Council for Exceptional Children.

Witt, J. C., Elliott, S. N., & Martens, B. K. (1984). Factors affecting teachers' judgments of the acceptability of behavioral interventions: Time involvement, behavior problem severity, and type of intervention. *Behavior Therapy, 15,* 204–209.

Witt, J. C., & Martens, B. K. (1983). Assessing the acceptability of behavioral interventions. *Psychology in the Schools, 20,* 570–577.

Wolf, M. M. (1978). Social validity: The case for subjective measurement or how applied behavior analysis is finding its heart. *Journal of Applied Behavior Analysis, 11,* 203–214.

TIMOTHY L. TURCO
Louisiana State University

STEPHEN N. ELLIOTT
University of Wisconsin at Madison

See also **Teacher Effectiveness; Teacher Expectancies**

TRENDS IN REHABILITATION AND DISABILITY

Introduction

The purpose of this article is to introduce and explore four models of disability: the traditional model, medical model, social model, and integrative model (Seelman, 2002). The four models often appear in sequential stages in the history of many industrialized countries. With the exception of the integrative model, the knowledge base for each model tends to exclude that of the other models. Throughout this article, the models are illustrated by corresponding policies, practices, and research, using country-based examples mainly from the United States and, to a lesser extent, Japan. These models have implications for professional education and training of people with disabilities. Conclusions and recommendations will therefore address professional education and training people with disabilities as well as international and country-based policies, practices, research, and collaboration.

Trends

A number of international trends illustrate the importance of reexamining disability models that are operative in countries and international organizations. The first trend involves conflict between health professionals who identify with the medical model and people with disabilities who identify with the social model. Throughout the world, people with disabilities, who have formed a Disability Movement, are criticizing the medical model of disability and demanding greater participation in decision making (Basnett, 2001). The introduction of the World Health Organization's International Classification of Functioning, Disability and Health in 2001 suggests that a more integrative model may be emerging within the international community (WHO, 2001). The integrative model adjusts for some of the criticisms of the other models and is already influential in country-based policy, practice, research, and professional training.

The second trend involves technology. Increasingly, access to technology is associated with human rights as reflected in the Americans with Disabilities Act of 1990, the proposed United Nations Convention on the Rights of People with Disabilities, and the World Summit on the Information Society. Policies, practices, and research in universal design and design for all are examples of this trend. Human rights and technology are associated with demands to make mainstream systems and products, such as communication systems, transportation systems, and cell phones, accessible. However, accessibility features in mainstream systems and products may be regarded as "social add-ons"—not competitive in the global marketplace. Human rights and technology are also associated with policies, practices, and research in special or assistive technology for individuals (e.g., wheelchairs, hearing aids). Interface problems for individuals with disabilities and technology and interfaces between specialized and mainstream technology have generated interest among researchers. The Trace Research and Development Center at the University of Wisconsin is one of a number of centers that conduct research on interfaces.

A third trend involves rehabilitation research itself. To justify payment, rehabilitation researchers across disciplines are called on to show evidence of outcomes, efficacy, and effectiveness of assistive technology (Fuhrer, 2001). A fourth trend involves the struggles of social welfare program administrators to keep benefit programs solvent while serving growing numbers of people with disabilities, especially older people. Countries are adopting a mix of social welfare, civil rights, and other policies to address disability issues (Van Oorscot & Hvinden, 2001; Zeitzer, 2002). Countries are struggling to contain costs of public welfare systems but have often failed to adopt policies that may defer, lessen, or negate the need for expensive institutionalization, such as accessible mainstream systems and products. Finally, the fifth trend is poverty—a barrier to the support of disability programs in developing countries where the majority of people with disabilities live. Many cultures continue to use a traditional model of disability. In the absence of scientific and health infrastructures, disability policy and practices may be based almost exclusively on culture and religion (Barnes & Mercer, 2003; Coleridge, 1993; Ingstad & Whyte, 1995).

Models of Disability

Four models of disability are explored in this section: the traditional model, medical model, social model, and integrative model. The following factors are considered for each model: (a) knowledge base, (b) roles, (c) rules and relationships, (d) temporal and spatial parameters, and (e) bias. Corresponding policies, practices, and research are identified for each model.

The Traditional Model

The traditional model is based on culturally and religiously determined knowledge, views, and practices. Depending on cosmology, social organization, and other factors, cultures show a broad range of perspectives that place people with disabilities on a continuum from human to nonhuman. For example, some cultures practice infanticide, rejecting the humanity of disabled infants. The roles people with disabilities may assume within a given culture range from participant to pariah (Barnes & Mercer, 2003; Ingstad & Whyte, 1995). When persons with disabilities are devalued, they may be perceived as demonic or unfortunate, and often take on the role of an outcast (Coleridge, 1993). The bias of the traditional model is cultural relativity. Objective, scientifically based knowledge is not associated with this model.

Across cultures, people with disabilities have been valued differently. In his presidential address before the American Association of Physical Medicine and Rehabilitation, Thomas E. Strax, MD, made the following observation:

> From the beginning of time, humankind has wrestled with the paradox of what to do with people with disabilities. In ancient times, they were simply put to death. They were a burden on the tribe. In ancient Greece, there were two cities. Sparta removed the weak and the elderly for the good of the rest. In Athens, the warrior class protected the weak. (Strax, 2003, p. 943)

The Medical Model

The medical model is based on scientific views and practice, typically in the medical and health knowledge base. The "problem" is located within the body of the individual with a disability. The context of the medical model is the clinic or institution. Persons with disabilities assume the role of patient, a role that may be of either short-term or long-term duration depending on several factors, including the individuals' condition, policies related to institutionalization and community supports, and professional and social attitudes about disability. Authority lies with professionals. The bias of the model is the biomedical perception of normalcy and the narrow band of legitimate knowledge, usually medical and health related. Explanation of disability is reduced to the impairment level. The perspective of the person with a disability and social factors are not routinely within the knowledge base of the medical model.

Worst and Best Practices

In the West during the 20th century, examples of worst and best medical research practices for people with disabilities can illustrate the strengths and weaknesses of the medical model. Worst practice examples can be drawn from most countries and regions.

- Willowbrook Experiments, United States: This study was designed to follow the natural progression of a disease—in this case viral hepatitis. Children with disabilities were intentionally infected with the virus and then studied during the progression of the disease. A particularly disturbing aspect of the research was that it was reviewed and approved by the New York State Departments of Mental Hygiene, Mental Health, the Armed Forces Epidemiological Board, and the New York University School of Medicine, in addition to the Willowbrook School. Although parental consent was given, the consent was based on the school's declaration that there was room for new students at the school only in the experimental unit.

- The Holocaust and people with disabilities: There evidence to show that people with disabilities were systematically exterminated and were the subjects of medical experiments during the World War II Nazi period in Germany (*Forgotten Crimes: The Holocaust and People with Disabilities*, 2001).

- Most countries and international organizations also have many examples of best practices within the medical model. These include:

  - Breakthroughs in biomedical and technological sciences and clinical applications that have saved lives and extended the lifespan of individuals with disabilities (National Institute on Disability and Rehabilitation Research, 1999).

- Research policy reform (http://www.hhs.gov/ohrp/index.html).

- International Classification of Impairments, Disabilities and Handicaps (ICIDH; WHO, 1980).

After World War II, the international community adopted reforms and provided guidelines for research. These policies include the Nuremberg Code of 1947, the United Nations Universal Declaration of Human Rights of 1948, and the World Medical Association's Declaration of Helsinki of 1964. Later, some countries began to adopt policies such as institutional review boards to protect research subjects.

The influential ICIDH, which identified the cause of disability within the individual, was adopted by many users, including policymakers (social security benefits, employment, occupational health), demographers, epidemiologists and statisticians (surveys), and health planners (utilization, resources). Even before the adoption of the ICIDH, health professionals created policy and designed surveys and utilization practices within the medical model. Throughout the 20th century, countries adopted general social welfare and health policies (which usually included people with disabilities) as the first stage in a series of disability policies that would later include general and specialized education, employment, and accessibility policies for disabled people. Examples of social welfare and health policy include Japan's Social Insurance System developed in 1922 and the Social Security Act adopted in the United States in 1935 (Miyatake, 2000).

Measurement Tools

Development and use of research measurement tools, such as the Functional Independence Measure (FIM), and concepts such as the normal curve reinforced the medical model. These tools were designed to measure impairment at the body level with the goal of curing the cause of the impairment—or at least minimizing performance difficulties. The test sites are usually clinics, rehabilitation centers, or other controlled sites. The distance walked is a key component of the health-related quality of life measure for the FIM. The measure focuses on the independent function of the person without contextual supports.

Professional Training

The knowledge base used to educate health professionals is rigorous and routinely limited to medicine and the health sciences. Therefore, health professionals may develop a view of disability that differs substantially from the reality of many disabled people. The following is a quotation from a medical doctor, before he became disabled and afterward:

[I began] to examine his nervous system... felt a sense of horror come over me. You can't feel anything here on your shoulder? You can't move your legs? I next met this man in a spinal cord unit in 1985 as I was pushed to the computer next to him in occupational therapy. A few months earlier, I had severed my cervical spinal cord playing rugby and I was a quadriplegic—slightly more impaired than was my former patient. Now, 15 years after becoming disabled, I find myself completely at home with the concept of…being me. Now I know that my assessment of the potential quality of life of severely disabled people was clearly flawed. (Basnett, 2001, p. 45)

Disabled people may develop a view of health care that is very different from the one held by professionals. Although professionals may view people with disabilities as patients, people with disabilities often accept their disabilities and move away from the patient role to resume life roles of worker, student, and parent within the community.

Legacy of the Medical Model

The medical model is based on a narrow range of views and practices involving health and welfare. Research and research tools are useful for medical purposes but not as useful for social purposes, such as measuring accessibility and participation. Professional education and training, to the extent that it has not incorporated information about quality of life and accessibility, has resulted in a "dual perspective" situation. Therefore, there is a widening gap of understanding between professionals and patients who are at some stage of transformation and recovery (Gabard & Martin, 2003).

The Social Model

The social model is based on knowledge of the experience and views and practices of people with disabilities. The model locates the problem within society, rather than within the individual with a disability. From the perspective of the social model, disability is conceived more as diversity in function or the result of discrimination in policies, practices, research, training, and education. Individuals with disabilities are the authorities. They assume a range of roles—especially the advocate role—to pursue full expression of educational and employment opportunities and citizenship. Rules are determined within a framework of choice and independent living with strong support from organized disability communities. The biases of the social model include: limiting the causes of disability either exclusively or mainly to social and environmental policies and practices, or advancing perceptions of disability in mainly industrialized countries that emphasize individual rights rather than advancing broader economic rights that may reflect the needs of impoverished developing countries (Albrecht, Seelman, & Bury, 2001; Barnes & Mercer, 2003).

Policies and Practices

While retaining health and welfare policies of the first stage of disability policy, countries are in various stages of transition from the medical model to the social model. International organizations, some industrialized countries, and some developing countries have adopted second and third stage policies and practices of special laws in education, employment, civil rights, and accessibility. The United Nations began adopting disability human rights declarations in the 1970s in support of the principle of normalization of the lives of people with disabilities. Most countries in the second stage of disability policy have adopted special education and employment policies such as Japan's School Education Law of 1947 and the Individuals with Disabilities Education Act of 1975 in the United States, which involved civil rights and mainstreaming of most children with disabilities (Statistical Abstracts, 2003). Japan and the United States are among countries that have adopted special employment-related laws, such as Japan's Human Resources Development Promotion Law of 1969 and the U.S. Rehabilitation Act of 1973, which also involved civil rights (Ministry of Labor, 1999). Most of these laws provided services that were controlled by professionals. In the third stage, some countries began to move from special needs policies to a civil rights policy such as the Americans with Disabilities Act of 1990 in the United States. Others continued with a health, welfare, special education, and special employment approach and often added policies to make buildings and information more accessible (Heyer, 2000).

Measurement Tools

The social model perspective incorporates research that examines problems of quality of life, user satisfaction, participation, and accessibility of various domains of the environment. The perspective also examines problems of participation of people with disabilities in the research process, including survey research. Researchers have explored methods to interview people with disabilities in survey research. Section 508 of the U.S. Rehabilitation Act as amended in 1998 may require federal electronic-based surveys to be accessible to people with disabilities, not only in the collection of survey data, but also in the analysis and reporting stages. New research tools have emerged to measure quality of life and satisfaction, including the Quebec User Evaluation of Satisfaction with Assistive Technology and the Psychosocial Impact of Assistive Devices Scale (Cook & Hussey, 2002; Scherer, 2002). Researcher David Gray has been involved in the development of measures of the environment. Gray changes the outcome measure from capacity to participation, which focuses on the individual's ability to function in his or her own environment. Although people with disabilities may score low in clinical tests of capacity, they may participate in many life activities including work, education, and family and community life.

A number of the Rehabilitation Engineering Research Centers (RERCS) of the National Institute on Disability and Research (NIDRR) have developed assistive technologies and universal design products that have increased participation of people with disabilities. For example, the RERC on Universal Design and the Built Environment has developed a squat toilet and a visitable house.

Research efforts have also worked toward the development of accessible communication devices. Title IV of the Americans with Disabilities Act charged the telephone companies with a provision of interstate and intrastate telephone relay services that will provide deaf, hard-of-hearing, and speech-impaired persons with telephone service functionally equivalent to service for hearing persons. The private sector has competed for contracts to develop and manage relay services. The CapTel System can be used by people with some degree of hearing loss because it works like a telephone but also displays every word the caller says during the conversation.

Researchers have also modeled stages of change in organizations as they move toward accessibility. The Center for Rehabilitation Sciences & Technology at the University of Wisconsin at Milwaukee developed a model called A3. The A3 model conceptualizes stages in which organizations meet the needs of people with disabilities, focusing on the physical and virtual environment, consumer products, services, and systems. The A3 model includes three elements: advocacy, accommodation, and accessibility. The advocacy stage has the following characteristics:

- Minimal anticipation of needs.
- Reactive to "complaints."
- Sometimes the person with the disability advocates.
- Other times someone else advocates for the person with the disability.
- People with disabilities receive a different "product" than people without disabilities.

The next stage is accommodation. Characteristics of accommodation include:

- Anticipation of needs.
- Prepared to meet needs.
- "Complaints" are reduced as there is a system in place.
- People with disabilities still receive a different "product" than people without disabilities.
- Likely requires additional time, money, effort, etc.

The third stage is accessibility. Characteristics of accessibility are:

- Proactive.
- Recognition that better design can reduce the need for individual accommodation.

- Everybody receives the same "product."
- People with disabilities do not require additional time, money, effort, etc.

Education and Training

The social model is based on a knowledge base of experiences of individuals with disabilities living in society. Adoption of the social model has led to demands to educate and train architects, designers, engineers, and lawyers, as well as people with disabilities.

Engineers have begun to receive clinical training. The University of Pittsburgh School of Health and Rehabilitation Sciences provides training in the Center for Assistive Technology and the University of Pittsburgh School of Law has launched a Disability Law curriculum. A number of universities, including the University of Pittsburgh, have added a Disability Studies curriculum.

The Integrative Model

The Integrative Model has a broad knowledge base ranging from medicine to literature that is informed by the experiences of people with disabilities. The Integrative Model is "under construction." From the integrative perspective, individuals with disabilities have many roles, including citizen and patient. There are a number of evolving policies and practices that are representative of this model. Some of them are represented in the World Health Organization International Classification of Functioning, Disability and Health; the U.S. Institute of Medicine's *Enabling America: Assessing the Role of Rehabilitation Science and Engineering;* and the *NIDRR Long-Range Plan* (Brandt & Pope, 1997; National Institute on Disability and Rehabilitation Research, 1999; WHO, 2001).

Policies and Practices

While retaining general health, welfare, special education, and employment policies and practices of the first and second stages, countries are in various stages of transition to a civil rights approach and related universality of design applications in systems and markets. International organizations, such as the World Health Organization, have developed a more universal approach to disability. The following interpretation of the ICF illustrates its universality and integrative characteristics (Schneider, 2001):

Universal model—Not a minority model.

Integrative model—Not merely medical or social.

Interactive model—Not linear progressive.

Parity—Not etiological causality.

Inclusive—Contextual, environment, and person.

Cultural applicability—Not western concepts alone.

Operational—Not theory driven alone.

Life span coverage—Not adult driven (children, elderly).

Human functioning—Not merely disability.

The components of the ICF encourage a broad and integrative classification. The three components of the ICF are body components, activities and participation, and environment. ICF researchers will be challenged to identify the relationships among the components.

The Disability Movement is pressing a number of international organizations for conventions and statements of principle committed to full integration of people with disabilities in society. The United Nations is being pressed to adopt a convention on the rights of people with disabilities.

The World Summit on the Information Society is being pressed to adopt a section on disability within the draft Declaration of Principles. Many of these initiatives have precedent in U.S. law. The Americans with Disabilities Act of 1990 (ADA) recognizes the full civil rights of people with disabilities. The ADA also provides assistive technology and accessibility of communications with important roles in the realization of rights and opportunities. The United States has regulated the communications industry to assure access. The original Communications Act of 1934 recognized universal access for all people in the United States. In 1996, the new Telecommunications Act was amended to include rules requiring telecommunications manufacturers and service providers to make their products and services accessible to people with disabilities, if readily achievable. The United States has also created market incentives to motivate industry to make its systems and products accessible. As Section 508 of the Rehabilitation Act requires, the United States government constitutes a large market for accessible technology and employs the federal procurement system to purchase it. Section 508 requires access to electronic and information technology provided by the federal government. The law applies to all federal agencies when they develop, procure, maintain, or use electronic and information technology. Federal agencies must ensure that technology is accessible to employees and members of the public with disabilities to the extent it does not impose an "undue burden." Section 508 speaks to various means for disseminating information, including computers, software, and electronic office equipment. It applies to, but is not solely focused on, federal pages on the Internet or the World Wide Web. It does not yet apply to web pages of private industry.

Measurement Tools and Principles

Disability is not inherent in measurement tools designed with the integrative model in mind. Psychological, social, and environmental factors must be incorporated into assessments that are based on an integrative model. Assessment measures that are consistent with the integrative model assume a real world context of school, family, and employment. Health service performance measures should be based on consumer outcomes. Some measures of disability may be disability specific in which case they may change the perception of the capability of the individual.

Researchers at the RERC at the University of Buffalo have developed a prototype database on anthropometry of wheelchair users. Researchers at the Department of Rehabilitation Sciences and Technology, School of Health and Rehabilitation Sciences have developed a Virtual Reality Tele-Rehabilitation System for Analyzing the Accessibility of the Physical Environment.

Education and Training

The ICF has become a useful framework on which to base coursework for individuals across a wide number of fields, including the health professions, social work, psychology, and Disability Studies. Over 30 ICF-related courses have been identified in universities in the United States and Canada. For example, the University of Pittsburgh Department of Occupational Therapy has adopted the ICF as the foundation for curriculum design.

Conclusions, Opportunities, and Challenges

In the international area, the following policy, research, and practice opportunities and challenges exist:

- Monitor U.N. Implementation of the Standard Rules and enact a U.N. Disability Human Rights Convention.
- Incorporate a statement on accessibility for people with disabilities into the World Summit on the Information Society draft principles.
- Support developing countries in provision of programs and participation for people with disabilities.
- Develop the ICF measures for social and environmental factors so that assessment measures assume a real world context of school, family, and employment.
- Base health service performance on consumer outcomes.
- Generate global marketplace incentives and standards to support universal design, usability, and accessibility in product design and sale.
- Add disability to surveys of health, income, employment, and education.
- In addition to the aforementioned, the domestic area provides the following opportunities and challenges:
  - Commit public and private research and development funding to technological inclusion of people with disabilities.
  - Promote technological inclusion by linking technology policy to civil rights.

- Monitor research policies to protect people with disabilities in research conducted abroad with domestic research funding.
- Create a government marketplace for usable and accessible systems and products.

In the practice area, the following opportunities and challenges exist:

- Promote science, technology, and education and training opportunities for people with disabilities.
- Integrate the perspective of people with disabilities and social and environmental factors into curricula.
- Broaden the range of disciplines that address disability to include engineers, designers, and lawyers.
- Adopt the ICF as a framework to develop health-related professional education.

In research, the following opportunities and challenges exist:

- Develop measures of social factors and environmental domains.
- Develop accessible survey research process and questions about social behavior and environmental accessibility.
- Develop evidence-based practice.
- Develop assistive technology outcome measures.

Opportunities for collaboration exist: Develop strategies based on the Tokushima Agreement among Japan, the United States, Australia, and Europe.

REFERENCES

Albrecht, G., Seelman K., & Barry M. (2001). *Handbook of disability studies*. Thousand Oaks, CA: Sage.

Barnes, C., & Mercer, G. (2003). *Disability*. Cambridge, UK: Polity Press.

Basnett, I. (2001). Health care professionals and their attitudes toward decisions affecting disabled people. In G. L. Albrecht, K. D. Seelman, & M. Bury (Eds.), *Handbook of disability studies* (pp. 450–467). Thousand Oaks, CA: Sage.

Brandt, E. N., & Pope, A. M. (Eds.). (1997). *Enabling America: Assessing the role of rehabilitation science and engineering*. Washington, DC: National Academy Press.

Coleridge, P. (1993). *Disability, liberation and development*. United Kingdom and Ireland: Oxfam.

Cook, A. M., & Hussey, S. M. (2002). *Assistive technologies: Principles and practices* (2nd ed.). St. Louis, MO: Mosby.

Forgotten crimes: The holocaust and people with disabilities. (2001). Oakland, CA: Disability Rights Advocate.

Fuhrer, M. J. (2001). Assistive technology outcomes research: Challenges met and yet unmet. *American Journal of Physical Medicine & Rehabilitation, 80*(7), 523–535.

Gabard, D. L., & Martin, M. M. (2003). *Physical therapy ethics*. Philadelphia, PA: Davis Co.

Heyer, K. (2000). From welfare to rights: Japanese disability law. *Asia Pacific Law and Public Policy Journal 1*, 6.

Ingstad, B., & Whyte, S. R. (Eds.). (1995). *Disability culture*. Los Angeles: University of California Press.

Ministry of Labor. (1999). *Employment and its promotion of disabled persons in Japan a guide to employment for employers and disabled persons*. Prefectural Governments, Japan Association for Employment of the Disabled.

Miyatake, G. (2000). *Social security in Japan* (Vol. 17). Tokyo, Japan: Foreign Press Center.

National Institute on Disability and Rehabilitation Research. (1999). *NIDRR long-range plan*. Washington, DC: National Institute on Disability and Rehabilitation Research, U.S. Department of Education.

Scherer, M. J. (Ed.). (2002). *Assistive technology: Matching device and consumer for successful rehabilitation*. Washington, DC: American Psychological Association.

Schneider, M. (2001, June). *Participation and environment in the ICF and measurement of disability: Classification, assessment, surveys and terminology*. Paper presented at the World Health Organization United Nations Meeting on Measurement of Disability, New York.

Seelman, K. D. (2002, October 24). *Disability studies and the disciplines: Bridges and chasms*. Paper presented at the Invest in Disability Week, Ann Arbor, Michigan.

Strax, T. E. (2003). Consumer, advocate, provider a paradox requiring a new identity paradigm. *Archives of Physical Medical Rehabilitation, 84*, 943–945.

U.S. Bureau of the Census. (2003). *Statistical abstracts of the United States*. Washington, DC: Author.

Van Oorscot, W., & Hvinden, B. (2001). *Disability policies in European countries*. Dordrecht, The Netherlands: Kluwer Law International.

World Health Organization (WHO). (1980). *International classification of impairments, disabilities, and handicaps*. Geneva, Switzerland: Author.

World Health Organization (WHO). (2001). *International classification of functioning, disability and health*. Geneva, Switzerland: Author.

Zeitzer, I. (2002). The challenges of disability pension policy: Three Western European case studies of the battle against the numbers. In E. Fultz & R. Marcus (Eds.), *Reforming worker protections: Disability pensions in transformation*. Budapest, Hungary: International Labor Organization.

KATHERINE D. SEELMAN
University of Pittsburgh

See also **Annual Report to Congress on the Implementation of the Individuals with Disabilities Education Act, Twenty-Fifth Executive Summary of Demography of Special Education**

TRIARCHIC THEORY OF INTELLIGENCE (See Intelligence, Triarchic Theory of)

TRICHORHINOPHALANGEAL SYNDROME

Trichorhinophalangeal syndrome is a relatively rare hereditary condition that is traced to a defect on Chromosome 8. Children born with this disorder have thin, sparse hair; thick, heavy eyebrows along the bridge of the nose, thinning out toward the distal portions of their faces; a pear-shaped or bulbous nose; large eyes; thin upper lip; small and/or extra teeth; small jaw; and a horizontal groove under their chin. These children are short in stature and have thin fingernails. Abnormalities of the skeletal system, including short, stubby fingers and toes, are common. Problems in bone growth appear around age 3 or 4 years and persist and worsen until adolescent growth is completed. Degenerative hip disease may develop in the young adult and senior years (Jones, 1988; Rudolph, 1991).

Trichorhinophalangeal syndrome comes in two forms: Types I and II, with Type II more severe than Type I. Besides the degree of severity, other distinguishing characteristics of Type II include a smaller head circumference and susceptibility to upper respiratory infections. Moreover, these children have mild to moderate mental retardation and delayed onset of speech. Children with Type I are usually of normal intelligence. Some children with Type II may have a hearing loss. Standard treatment for the syndrome is symptomatic and supportive. Surgery may be performed to correct limb and extremity abnormalities. Genetic counseling may also be helpful (Thoene, 1992).

For children who are mentally retarded or speech delayed, it will be important to begin services through an Early Childhood Intervention (ECI) program. Based on the child's progress and development, he/she may continue to require additional support through special education or speech therapy.

REFERENCES

Jones, K. L. (Ed.). (1988). *Smith's recognizable patterns of human malformation* (4th ed.). Philadelphia, PA: Saunders.

Rudolph, A. M. (1991). *Rudolph's pediatrics—19th edition.* Norwalk, CT: Appleton & Lange.

Thoene, J. G. (Ed.). (1992). *Physician's guide to rare diseases.* Montvale, NJ: Dowden.

JOAN MAYFIELD
Baylor Pediatric Specialty Service

PATRICIA A. LOWE
University of Kansas

TRICHOTILLOMANIA

Trichotillomania is a low-incidence disorder (occurring in less than 1% of pediatric referrals) of self-injurious behavior that consists of pulling out one's hair; it is often accompanied by trichophagia, subsequent eating of the hair. The etiology of trichotillomania is unknown, but it has long been held to be of a psychoanalytic or Freudian nature. It occurs most often in conjunction with a major psychological or psychiatric disorder, particularly schizophrenia and lower levels of mental retardation, though it also occurs with narcissistic personality disorders. In special education programs, it is most often encountered among mentally retarded populations. Incidences of trichotillomania have also been reported in conjunction with episodes of child abuse. Incidence is generally greater in females than males.

A variety of treatment approaches have been attempted with this unusual disorder, including psychoanalysis, traditional psychotherapies, hypnotherapy, and a variety of operant and other behavior modification techniques. Generally, the earlier the age of onset, the greater the likelihood of successful treatment (Sorosky & Sticker, 1980). Behavioral techniques appear to be the most successful methods of treating trichotillomania and trichophagia, particularly when competing responses can be developed, although success has been reported with a variety of techniques and the role of spontaneous remission is not known. Sources of treatment information include Azrin and Nunn (1973), Bayer (1972), and Mannino and Delgado (1969).

Some recent animal research suggests that a variety of self-injurious behaviors, including trichotillomania and trichophagia, may, in some cases, be of neurological origin. Relationships to damage of cells around the substantia nigra have been suggested.

REFERENCES

Azrin, N. H., & Nunn, R. G. (1973). Habit reversal: A method of eliminating nervous habits. *Behavior Research & Therapy, 11,* 619–628.

Bayer, C. A. (1972). Self-monitoring and mild aversion treatment of trichotillomania. *Journal of Behavior Therapy & Experimental Psychiatry, 3,* 139–141.

Mannino, F. C., & Delgado, R. A. (1969). Trichotillomania in children: A review. *American Journal of Psychiatry, 4,* 229–246.

Sorosky, A. D., & Sticker, M. B. (1980). Trichotillomania in adolescence. *Adolescent Psychiatry, 8,* 437–454.

CECIL R. REYNOLDS
Texas A&M University

See also Self-Injurious Behavior

TRISOMY 13: 13+ SYNDROME (PATAU SYNDROME)

Patau syndrome, now more commonly called *Trisomy 13*, is a severe disorder in which the child has an extra Chromosome 13 in every cell. Some 95% of affected individuals die in infancy, most shortly after birth. The few survivors will have severe mental retardation, sensory impairments, and probably seizures and failure to thrive. The disorder has several variants. Trisomy 13 mosaicism leads to mixed chromosomal makeup: Some of the individual's cells have the normal two 13 chromosomes, and others have three. Outcome depends on the number of abnormal cells and may vary from near fully impaired to near normal. Partial trisomies on either the proximal or distal segment of Chromosome 13 lead to craniofacial abnormalities and severe mental retardation. Partial trisomy on the distal segment generally has more severe effects (Jones, 1997).

Incidence is about 1 in 5,000 to 10,000 births and increases with mothers' age. No gender difference is known (Jones, 1997; Pediatric Database, 1993).

Characteristics

1. Severe brain damage, with incomplete development of forebrain and optic and olfactory nerves; spina bifida in many cases.
2. Microcephaly with sloping forehead.
3. Sensory defects, including apparent deafness and visual impairments (microphthalmia, numerous other eye defects).
4. Cleft palate or lip.
5. Numerous skeletal deformities, including polydactyly of hands, flexion of fingers, thin or missing ribs.
6. Cardiac abnormalities.
7. Abnormal genitalia.

Diagnosis is on the basis of chromosomal analysis. Either amniocentesis or chorionic villus sampling may provide prenatal diagnosis. Prognosis for the full trisomy 13 is poor, and provision of extreme measures to prolong life is questionable (Jones, 1997). Treatment is supportive. The few cases of full trisomy 13 that survive infancy will need a wide range of medical services including surgery to repair the most serious physical impairments. The even fewer cases that survive to childhood will need a range of interventions, including separate classroom placement and services for severe visual and auditory impairments. Outcomes of the variants range from near normal to near fully impaired and call for case-by-case determination of needs. Parents may be referred to the Support Organization for trisomy 18, 13, and other related disorders (SOFT) website for assistance: http://www.trisomy.org/.

REFERENCES

Jones, K. L. (1997). *Smith's recognizable patterns of human malformation* (5th ed.). Philadelphia, PA: Saunders.

Pediatric Database. (1993). Trisomy 13 syndrome. Retrieved from http://www.icondata.com/health/pedbase/.les/TRISOMY1.HTM

ROBERT T. BROWN
University of North Carolina, Wilmington

TRISOMY 18

As indicated by its name, trisomy 18 is a congenital disease owed to the presence of three Chromosomes 18 instead of two. Trisomy 18 symptomatology was first described by Edwards, Harnden, Cameron, Crosse, and Wolff (1960); therefore, the term *Edwards syndrome* is sometimes used instead of trisomy 18. As in many autosomal trisomies, severe polymalformations are observed. Moreover, affected patients show many common features, so that trained physicians are able to diagnose the syndrome on clinical inspection. Generally, trisomy 18 newborns are postmature (42 weeks of pregnancy), but nevertheless show a birth weight below 2,500 g (Hamerton, 1971); hydramnios (too much amniotic fluid) is the rule. An elongated skull with prominent occiput is noted, together with microcephaly. Micrognatia (small mandible), low-set ears, short neck, short sternum, prominent abdomen with umbilical hernia, and narrow hips are usual findings. The extremities are also characteristic: fingers are in forced flexion, very difficult to unfold, and deviated so that the third one is recovered by the second and the fourth. Arches are present in most, if not all, fingers. These dermatoglyphic configurations are rare in normal people or in those with other chromosome diseases. Clubfoot is frequent, and the big toe is in dorsiflexion. Internal malformations include severe congenital heart anomalies in more than 95% of all cases, either intraventricular, septal defects or patent ductus arteriosus. Indeed, premature death can be related to these heart defects. Failure to thrive is the rule and, despite palliative treatment, death occurs in a mean time of 70 days (Hamerton, 1971). Developmental retardation is always observed, but accurate testing is difficult.

From a cytogenetic point of view, standard trisomy 18 concerns more than 80% of all cases. Mosaicism trisomy 18/normal cell line occurs in less than 10% of patients; survival may be longer and symptomatology less severe. Trisomy 18 from a transmitted translocation by one of the parents is rare. Incidence is situated around 1 in 10,000 births (Hook & Hamerton, 1977). This is much less than in trisomy 21; the symptoms are more severe, and many affected embryos are spontaneously aborted early in pregnancy. Interestingly, 80% of all newborn cases are female, suggesting a strong lethality in the male. Some authors (Conen & Erkman, 1966) have also reported on a different survival rate depending on whether the baby is a girl (294 days) or a boy (96 days). Maternal age is above average (32 years), but the relationship is not as clear, as in trisomy 21. In the presence of a small fetus showing few movements and severe hydramnios, it may be profitable to have a late prenatal diagnosis, during the seventh or eighth month of pregnancy. This may avoid a caesarean section for the mother.

REFERENCES

Conen, P. E., & Erkman, B. (1966). Frequency and occurrence of chromosomal syndromes. II. E-trisomy. *American Journal of Human Genetics, 18*, 387–398.

Edwards, J. H., Harnden, D. G., Cameron, A. H., Crosse, V. M., & Wolff, O. H. (1960). A new trisomic syndrome. *Lancet, 1*, 787–790.

Hamerton, J. L. (1971). *Human cytogenetics* (Vol. 2). New York, NY: Academic Press.

Hook, E. B., & Hamerton, J. L. (1977). The frequency of chromosome abnormalities detected in consecutive newborn studies—Differences between studies—Results by sex and by severity of phenotypic involvement. In E. B. Hook & I. A. Porter (Eds.), *Population cytogenetics—Studies in human.* New York, NY: Academic Press.

L. KOULISCHER
Institut de Morphologie Pathologique, Belgium

See also **Genetic Counseling**

TRISOMY 21

Trisomy 21 or *Down syndrome* is a combination of birth defects characterized by mental retardation, abnormal facial features, heart defects, and other congenital disorders. Approximately 1 in 800 to 1 in 1,000 infants is born with this disorder (March of Dimes, 1997). Trisomy 21 occurs in all races and economic levels; however, incidence is highest among Caucasians. More than 250,000 individuals with trisomy 21 (March of Dimes, 1997) live in the United States. Life expectancy and quality of life has greatly increased over the past 20 years due to improved treatment of related complications and better developmental educational programs (Ball & Bindler, 1999). Mortality rates for infants with trisomy 21 and

congenital heart defects remain high at 44%. However, overall life expectancy among adults has improved to more than 55 years (March of Dimes, 1997).

The cause of trisomy 21 is unknown. A number of theories including genetic predisposition, radiation exposure, environmental factors, viruses, and even infections have been proposed (Wong, 1995). Trisomy 21 does result from an aberration in Chromosome 21 in which three copies instead of the normal two occur due to faulty meiosis (nondisjunction) of the ovum or, sometimes, the sperm. This results in a karyotype of 47 chromosomes instead of the normal 46. The incidence of nondisjunction increases with maternal age and the extra chromosome originates from the mother about 80% of the time (Wong, 1995). Mothers over the age of 35 years are at the greatest risk for rearrangement of their chromosomes and their risk of having a child with trisomy 21 increases greatly with age. At age 35, the risk is calculated to be 1 in 385 births, at age 40, the risk increases to 1 in 106 births, and at age 49, the risk of having a baby with trisomy 21 is 1 in 11 (Wong, 1995). Prenatal testing through amniocentesis or chorionic villus identifies trisomy 21 (March of Dimes, 1997). Both procedures carry a risk of infection and miscarriage. Genetic counseling is available for couples with a known family history of genetic birth defects and is also indicated for mothers over the age of 35 (March of Dimes, 1997).

The physical signs of trisomy 21 are apparent at birth (Figure T.6). The newborn is lethargic and has difficulty eating. Trisomy 21 newborns have almond-shaped eyes with epicanthal folds, a protruding tongue, a small mouth, a single palmar crease (simian crease), small white spots on the iris of the eye (Brushfield spots), a small skull,

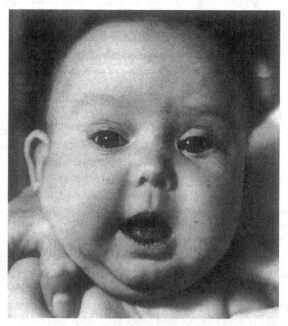

Figure T.6. Characteristic facies of a trisomic 21 child.

a flattened bridge across the nose, a flattened profile, small and low-set ears, and a short neck with excess skin (Wong, 1995). Slowed growth and development are characteristic of this syndrome, especially in speech formation. Other physical abnormalities include dry, sensitive skin with decreased elasticity, short stature, broad hands and feet, abnormal fingerprints, and hypotonic limbs (Ball & Bindler, 1999). Premature dementia similar to Alzheimer's disease usually occurs during the fourth decade of life, and an increase in leukemia, diabetes mellitus, thyroid disorders, and chronic infections are all common in individuals with trisomy 21 (Wong, 1995).

The degree of mental retardation with trisomy 21 varies greatly and ranges from mild to profound. Although children with trisomy 21 can usually do most things that any child can learn to do (walking, talking, dressing, self-feeding, and toileting), they develop at a slower rate and at a later age (March of Dimes, 1997). The exact age of achievement of developmental milestones and skills cannot be predicted. However, early intervention programs beginning in infancy encourage these special children to reach their greatest potential.

Special education programs are available around the country with many children fully integrated into regular classroom situations (March of Dimes, 1997). The future for special children with trisomy 21 is brighter than 20 years ago. Many will learn to read, write, take care of themselves, and hold partially supported employment while living semi-independently in group homes (March of Dimes, 1997).

REFERENCES

Ball, J., & Bindler, R. (1999). *Pediatric nursing: Caring for children* (2nd ed.). Stamford, CT: Appleton & Lange.

March of Dimes. (1997). *Down syndrome: Public education information sheet.* Retrieved from http://www.marchofdimes.com/baby/down-syndrome.aspx

Wong, D. (1995). *Whaley & Wong's nursing care of infants and children* (5th ed.). St. Louis, MO: Mosby-Year Book.

KARI ANDERSON
University of North Carolina at Wilmington

See also Down Syndrome; Genetic Counseling

TRUNCUS ARTERIOSUS, PERSISTENT

Persistent truncus arteriosus is a congenital heart defect associated with a high mortality rate. In normal fetal development the truncus arteriosus divides into the aorta and pulmonary artery. If the truncus arteriosus persists beyond the fetal stage, a single arterial trunk arises from the normally formed ventricles, and blood from both ventricles will mix, affecting the pulmonary and systemic circulation. If the infant survives, pulmonary vascular obstructive disease often develops due to extreme hypertension (high blood pressure) in the lungs. This disorder is also often associated with ventricular septal defects. Persistent truncus arteriosus is also known as *Buchanan syndrome*, and approximately 35% of infants with persistent truncus arteriosus also have DiGeorge syndrome.

Persistent truncus arteriosus appears to affect male and female infants equally. No ethnic predilection is documented. In the United States persistent truncus arteriosus represents 1% to 2% of congenital heart defects in live born infants. Therefore, this disorder is present in approximately 5 to 15 infants per 100,000 live births.

Characteristics

1. Babies born with this condition have difficulty breathing; blood oxygen is low; and the skin has a bluish color (cyanosis).
2. The infant's appetite is adversely affected, resulting in slow weight gain and impeded growth.
3. Increased rate of respiration (tachypnea).
4. Congestive heart failure.
5. Enlarged heart.
6. Without surgery, only 50% of the affected infants will survive beyond 1 month, and 90% of infants will die within 6 months.
7. With surgery, the survival rate at a 10- to 20-year follow-up is above 80%.
8. As the child grows, repeated surgeries are necessary (reinterventions).

Treatment usually consists of surgical repair, with closure of the ventricular septal defect. This consists of consigning the common artery trunk to the left ventricles and reconstructing the right ventricle outflow tract. If surgery takes place in the neonatal period, survival is dramatically increased. Children who have the surgical repair early in life often require further surgical intervention on the right ventricle tract, as this does not grow along with the child. Infants also showing signs of congestive heart failure are commonly treated with standard measures (e.g., digitalis and diuretic medicines).

Most children with a diagnosis of persistent truncus arteriosus can attend regular education classes following successful surgery. In some cases, students may have special education needs, which can be met under IDEA 1997 within the physical disability category. For example, the school may need to limit stair climbing or provide transportation. In some cases, pediatric cardiologists encourage children to do physical activity, within limits, to help keep their hearts fit (e.g., swimming and bicycling). However, in some cases, a pediatric cardiologist may advise a child to avoid strenuous activity. Children with this disorder may need to make regular visits to a cardiologist and possibly have additional surgeries to correct additional problems. As the student may be away from school for medical reasons, school personnel need to be aware of the child's diagnosis and work closely with medical personnel to make appropriate educational accommodations.

Among individuals who survive the postoperative stage, the prognosis for persistent truncus arteriosus is good. Reinterventions, however, are essentially inevitable. Recent research has been exploring whether and when there is an optimum time to perform surgery (e.g., Shrivastava, 2000). More longitudinal research is needed to explore the outcome and effects of heart surgeries on individuals over a long period of time (e.g., Higgins & Reid, 1994).

REFERENCES

Higgins, S. S., & Reid, A. (1994). Common congenital heart defects: Long-term follow-up. *Nursing Clinics of North America, 29*(2), 233–248.

Shrivastava, S. (2000). Timing of surgery/catheter intervention in common congenital cardiac defects. *Indian Journal of Pediatrics, 67*(4), 273–277.

RACHEL TOPLIS
University of Northern Colorado

TUBERCULOSIS

Tuberculosis (TB) is a disease caused by the organism mycobacterium tuberculosis, also called *tubercle bacilli* (Centers for Disease Control and Prevention [CDC], 1994). Microscopic droplets containing tubercle bacilli may be expelled into the air when a person with infectious TB disease coughs or sneezes. Other people may inhale this air and become infected (New Jersey Medical School National Tuberculosis Center [NJMS], 1997). However, prolonged exposure to a person with TB disease is usually necessary for transmission to occur (National Institute of Allergy and Infectious Diseases [NIAID], 1999). Moreover, it is important to distinguish between TB infection and TB disease, as they refer to different presentations

of TB. These terms are not used interchangeably in this text.

People infected with M. tuberculosis do not have symptoms of TB disease and cannot spread TB to others (CDC, 1994). Approximately 10% of people who have TB infection will develop the disease at some point, and the risk is greatest during the first 2 years of infection (NJMS, 1997). Some people who have TB infection have an increased chance of developing TB disease. This includes infants, young children, older adults, people with HIV infection, people who inject illicit drugs, people who are sick with other diseases that weaken the immune system, and people in close contact with a person who has infectious TB disease (CDC, 1994).

To determine whether a person has TB infection, a Mantoux tuberculin skin test (TST) is given. Diagnosis of TB disease is based also on the results of a chest X-ray, a bacteriologic examination, and the individual's medical history (NJMS, 1997). However, these diagnostic measures may be inadequate when determining if a child has TB disease. Specifically, children display nonspecific clinical symptoms, and it may be difficult to interpret the skin tests and chest radiographs of children (Khan & Starke, 1995). Thus, the diagnosis of active TB disease in children typically occurs when the disease is found in an adult. This is of great concern because the adult may be transmitting the disease to others as well.

TB disease is the leading cause of death in the world from a single infectious organism. An estimated one third of the world's population is infected with TB bacterium, and approximately 10 to 15 million people in the United States are among them (NIAID, 1999). A total of 18,371 cases of TB disease in the United States were reported to the Centers for Disease Control and Prevention in 1998 (NIAID, 1999). More than 70% of the TB cases reported in 1993 were ethnic minorities (NJMS, 1997). The number of TB cases in children reported in the United States increased by 36% between 1985 and 1993 (NJMS, 1997).

Characteristics

TB Infection

1. The human body prevents the bacteria from growing.
2. No symptoms.
3. Cannot spread TB to others.
4. Can develop TB disease later in life if not treated.

TB Disease

1. Symptoms depend on part of body where TB bacteria are located.

2. TB in the lungs may cause a bad cough that lasts longer than 2 weeks, pain in the chest, and coughing up blood or sputum.

3. General symptoms include fatigue, weight loss, no appetite, chills, fever, and night sweating.

4. Highly infectious.

Source: Based on information cited in CDC, 1994.

Generally, the same methods are used for treating TB in adults and children. Individuals with TB infection receive preventive therapy, which typically consists of a daily regimen of isomiazid that lasts 6 months. It is recommended that children receive 9 months of preventive therapy (NJMS, 1997). Due to the increased likelihood of TB dissemination in infants and young children, treatment should be started as soon as the diagnosis is suspected (CDC, 1994). The required treatment for TB disease is at least 6 months, and the regimen includes at least two different drugs (NJMS, 1997). It is critical for both TB infection and TB disease patients to complete treatment. One effective strategy to ensure adherence to treatment is directly observed treatment (DOT), in which patients with TB infection or TB disease receive their antibiotic therapy under the supervision of a health service worker (CDC, 1994). This has resulted in high treatment completion rates.

A social stigma is attached to TB in general. For instance, children with TB disease likely would be placed in a hospital setting where they would not have close contact with anyone in order to prevent TB bacteria from spreading while being treated. This could be an anxiety-provoking and potentially traumatic experience for children with TB disease. When such children return to school, they may have a difficult time adjusting. Also, they may fall behind in schoolwork if treatment for TB has compromised school attendance. Ultimately, this experience may result in poor academic performance.

Future research should explore the etiology of TB infection. Improvements in diagnostic methods for children also should be a focus of study. Additionally, preventive measures should be examined.

REFERENCES

Centers for Disease Control and Prevention. (1994). *Questions and answers about TB*. Retrieved from http://www.cdc.gov/nchstp/tb/faqs/qa.htm

Khan, E. A., & Starke, J. R. (1995). Diagnosis of tuberculosis in children: Increased need for better methods. *Emerging Infectious Diseases, 1*, 115–123.

National Institute of Allergy and Infectious Diseases. (1999, July). *Tuberculosis*. Retrieved from http://globaltb.njms.rutgers.edu/

New Jersey Medical School National Tuberculosis Center. (1997, September 26). Tuberculosis. Retrieved from http://www.umdnj.edu/~ntbcweb/q%26aintro.htm

EVE N. ROSENTHAL
KARLA ANHALT
Texas A&M University

See also Chronic Illness in Children

TUBEROUS SCLEROSIS

Tuberous sclerosis is an inherited disorder transmitted as an autosomal dominant trait with variable penetrance affecting the skin, brain, retina, heart, kidneys, and lungs. It belongs to the group of diseases called *phakomatoses*, characterized by malformations, the presence of birthmarks, and the tendency to tumor formation in the central nervous system, skin, and viscera. The estimated frequency of occurrence is 1 per 30,000 live births (Berg, 1982). About 25% of the patients are sporadic owing to new mutations.

Tuberous sclerosis is a protean disorder chiefly manifested by epilepsy, mental deficiency, and cutaneous lesions. Convulsions are the most frequent initial symptom (up to 88%), presenting often in early life as infantile spasms (about 70%), usually between the fourth and sixth months of life. The convulsions later become generalized grand mal epilepsy and focal or akinetic seizures (Gomez, 1979; Hunt, 1983; Jeavons & Bower, 1964; Pampiglione & Moynahan, 1976). Mental retardation, when present, is usually severe; one third of the patients may have normal intelligence (Gomez, 1979). Only 12% to 15% of affected subjects are free of epilepsy and mental retardation. The cutaneous lesions are multiple. Adenoma sebaceum is the characteristic sign of the disease. It appears in the face between 1 and 5 years of age (usually after 4 years), starting as a macular rash over the cheeks in a butterfly appearance, then increasing in size and covering the nose, lips, and chin with a granular aspect. Those adenoma named *Pringle's* are seldom absent but they may grow very slowly. Hypopigmented leaf-shaped spots called white or achromatic spots or depigmented nevi are the most frequent sign in up to 95% of cases (Hunt, 1983); they are disseminated over the trunk and the limbs and are present at birth (Gold & Freeman, 1965), but they increase in number during the first 2 years of life. They appear more numerous under Wood's light and may be demonstrable in clinically asymptomatic parents.

Shagreen patches are thickenings of skin best seen in the lumbosacral region. Periungueal fibroma (Koenen tumors) are more often present on the toes than on the fingers and appear after the first decade and in adults; they may be the only sign in parents of an affected child.

The pathology in the nervous system shows the presence of cortical malformations, variable in size (called *tubers*), that contain neurons, astrocytic nuclei, and giant cells. The tubers also can be located in the subependymal area and contain calcium deposits that can be identified on X-rays or CAT scans. They may grow into the ventricles, interfering with cerebral spinal fluid circulation, blocking the foramen of Monro or the aqueduct of Sylvius, and producing hydrocephalus and signs of raised intracranial pressure. Tumors can also be present in the heart, the lungs, and the kidneys, but they can be discovered easily by ultrasound examination showing angiomyolipoma or even cystic tumors (Avni et al., 1984). The examination of the ocular fundus may reveal tumoral lesions at the nerve head or about the disk, even in the absence of vision complaints.

Diagnosis of the disease is based on the association of epilepsy, mental retardation, and skin lesions. It can be made very early in life on the presence of infantile spasms and achromatic spots in correlation with the cerebral calcifications seen on CAT scans of the brain (Lee & Gawler, 1978).

REFERENCES

Avni, E. F., Szliwowski, H., Spehl, M., Lelong, B., Baudain, P., & Struyven, J. (1984). Renal involvement in tuberous sclerosis. *Annales de Radiologie, 27*, 2–3, 207–214.

Berg, B. O. (1982). Neurocutaneous syndromes. In K. F. Swaiman, & F. S. Wright (Eds.), *The practice of pediatric neurology.* New York, NY: Mosby.

Gold, A. P., & Freeman, J. M. (1965). Depigmented nevi: The earliest sign of tuberous sclerosis. *Pediatrics, 35*, 1003–1005.

Gomez, M. R. (1979). Clinical experience at the Mayo Clinic. In M. R. Gomez (Ed.), *Tuberous sclerosis* (pp. 16–20). New York, NY: Raven.

Hunt, A. (1983). Tuberous sclerosis: A survey of 97 cases. *Developmental Medicine and Child Neurology, 25*, 346–357.

Jeavons, P. M., & Bower, B. D. (1964). Infantile spasms. *Clinics Developmental Medicine, 15*, London, England: Sime/Heinemann.

Lee, B. C., & Gawler, J. (1978). Tuberous sclerosis. Comparison of computed tomography and conventional neuroradiology. *Radiology, 127*(2), 403–407.

Pampiglione, G., & Moynahan, E. I. (1976). The tuberous sclerosis: Clinical and EEG studies in 100 children. *Journal Neurology Neurosurgery & Psychiatry, 39*, 666–673.

Henri B. Szliwowski
Hôpital Erasme,
Université Libre de Bruxelles, Belgium

TURKEY, SPECIAL EDUCATION IN

All special education services are planned and monitored by the Directorate General of Special Education and Guidance Services of the Ministry of National Education in Turkey. These special education services are regulated by the Special Education Law (KHK/573), which replaced the old law in 1997. Basic principles of special education in Turkey, as cited in the Special Education Law, are:

- All special needs individuals should be provided special education services according to their interests, desires, sufficiencies, and abilities.
- Special education should be started as early in one's life as possible.
- Special education services should be planned and administered without segregating the special needs individuals from their social and physical environments to the greatest extent possible.
- Priority should be given to educating special needs individuals with other individuals (i.e., in regular education environments) by considering their educational performances and modifying the instructional goals, contents, and processes.
- Collaboration should be made with other organizations and institutions providing rehabilitation services in order to prevent the interruption of services.
- Individualized education plans should be developed and education programs should be individualized for special needs individuals.
- Families should be encouraged to take part in every process of special education actively.
- Opinions of nongovernmental organizations of special needs individuals should be considered in developing special education policies.
- When planning special education services, elements should be included to facilitate special needs individuals' interactions with and adaptation to society.

There are guidance and research centers affiliated with the Directorate General of Special Education and Guidance Services in every major town to plan and monitor the local special education services. Main responsibilities of the guidance and research centers are:

- To accept referrals from schools and conduct assessments.
- To identify special needs individuals.
- To place identified individuals in regular or special education environments.
- To follow-up the special needs individuals.
- To conduct in-service training to education personnel.

There are 214 guidance and research centers all around Turkey at press time. Personnel of these centers mainly include special education teachers, guidance practitioners, and psychologists.

Regulation of Special Education Services was launched in 2006 to extend the amendments of the Special Education Law. This regulation states that preschool is compulsory for 37- to 72-month-old special needs children. On the other hand, 8-year-long primary education is compulsory for all children in Turkey, including special needs children as well. There are various placement alternatives (i.e., day and night special schools, special classes, vocational schools, and inclusive classes with and without supports) for special needs students. However, as mentioned earlier, special education legislation has described inclusion, either full or partial, as the preferred option for special needs students from preschool on.

In the school year of 2010 to 2011 a total of 173,507 special needs students received special education services, about half in segregated and half in inclusive environments. Total number of students in preschools, primary schools, and secondary schools was about 17 million during the same period. Thus, about 1% of all students in schools were special needs students.

For those who cannot receive formal special education or for those who need additional special education support services, one-to-one or group-support services are provided by private special education and rehabilitation centers. Every special needs individual has a right to claim financing of up to 12 hours of these services per month from the Ministry of National Education. In the school year of 2010 to 2011 a total of 186,634 special needs individuals received special education support services from such centers.

Special education as a professional discipline has progressed considerably during the first decade of the new millennium in Turkey. While special education teacher training programs existed in only three universities a decade ago, special education teachers are trained in 16 universities at this writing. There are 70 professors holding doctoral degrees in special education affiliated with these universities. However, more than 50 of them are members of four universities (i.e., Abant Izzet Baysal, Anadolu, Ankara, and Gazi Universities), leaving one or two professors to each of the remaining universities. Hence, increasing the number of qualified special education teacher trainers is one of the top priorities of Turkey.

The oldest of the above mentioned special education teacher training programs was opened at Anadolu University in early 1980s and started to graduate special education teachers in 1987. Thus, many teachers who have been teaching special needs students for many years were originally trained as regular education teachers with or without special education certificates. However, because most of the above mentioned universities' special education departments are rather young, shortage of special education teachers, especially in the area of developmental disabilities continues to be an important problem nationwide.

In Turkey special education departments may offer 4-year undergraduate programs in three special needs categories: intellectual disabilities, hearing disabilities, and visual disabilities. Teacher training programs for individuals with intellectual disabilities have a behavioral orientation and offer core courses in mild-to-severe intellectual disabilities. Elective courses in autism spectrum disorders are also offered. Teacher training programs for individuals with visual disabilities aim to equip prospective teachers with knowledge and skills necessary for teaching partially sighted and blind students. In teacher training programs for individuals with hearing disabilities, auditory-oral approach is followed. About one third of the above mentioned universities also offer graduate programs in categorical or noncategorical special education.

Nongovernmental organizations have had a vital role in the special education system in Turkey since 1950. There are estimated to be more than 50 foundations and about 400 associations related with various kinds of disabilities. Most of these organizations conduct awareness and fund raising activities whereas a relatively small number of them also provide services such as education of special needs individuals or personnel training.

Regarding special education research in Turkey, in addition to traditional quantitative research methodologies, single-subject experimental research and qualitative research methodologies are also quite reputable. Although these research methodologies differ from each other remarkably in terms of philosophical orientations as well as data collection and analysis procedures, both are perceived to be imperative for the progress of special education knowledge and practices. Accordingly, the number of research studies conducted by qualitative or single-subject designs has been on the rise in the past several years. Category of developmental disabilities is the most researched area in Turkey followed by hearing disabilities. Effects of behavioral interventions such as errorless teaching and functional assessment on developmental, academic, and social growth of individuals with developmental disabilities as well as facilitating behavioral competencies in teachers and caregivers can be claimed to be the predominant research interests.

GONAL KIRCAALI-IFTAR
Anadolu University

See also Eastern Europe, Special Education In; Western Europe, Special Education In

TURNBULL, ANN P. (1937–   )

An Alabama native, Ann P. Turnbull received her BSEd from the University of Georgia, her MEd from Auburn University in 1971, and her EdD from the University of Alabama. Her formal education emphasized special education of children with mental retardation, and early practical experience was gained as a teacher of children with mild mental retardation at schools in La Grange, Georgia (1968–1970). She is currently codirector of the Beach Center on Families and Disability and a professor in the department of special education at the University of Kansas.

Turnbull's research focuses on family systems and family-centered services and includes programmatic implementation of policy requirements associated with PL 94-142. Parental involvement in educational decision making and the development of a conceptual framework for family research and intervention based on family systems theory has been a major interest of Turnbull. Her focus on policy issues includes exploring government-provided services for enhancing the ability of families to provide care for their members with disabilities.

In 1988, Turnbull was a Joseph P. Kennedy Jr. Policy Fellow working with the U.S. House of Representatives Select Committee on Children, Youth, and Families, and in 1990 she was selected as one of three women from the international field of mental retardation to receive the Rose Fitzgerald Kennedy Leadership Award. Among her many leadership roles in professional and family organizations, she has served as chair of the family committee for the International League of Societies for Persons with Mental Handicaps and member of the board of directors of the American Association on Mental Retardation. She is currently a member of the board of directors of Zero to Three of the National Center for Clinical Infant Programs and the Autism National Committee. Turnbull was inducted as a member of the University of Kansas Women's Hall of Fame in 1994.

She is a reviewer for the journal *Exceptional Children* and the *Journal of the Association for Persons with Severe Handicaps*. She is assistant editor of the *Journal of Positive Behavior Interventions*. She was the vice president of the American Association on Mental Retardation for 2001 to 2002, and president of that association from 2003 to 2004. She was a member of the National Advisory Board, National Center on Family Support from 2000 to 2001, and a member of the National Advisory Board, Ready to Learn Initiative, Public Broadcasting System in 2001.

Turnbull has been the principal investigator on more than 20 federally funded research grants, and has authored and coauthored 25 books and many more articles, chapters, and monographs. Her books include *Cognitive Coping, Families, and Disability* (1993); *Exceptional Lives: Special Education in Today's Schools* (1995); and *Families, Professionals, and Exceptionality: Collaborating for Empowerment* (1997).

REFERENCES

Turnbull, A. P., Patterson, J. M., Behr, S. K., Murphy, D. L., Marquis, J. G., & Blue-Banning, M. J. (Eds.). (1993). *Cognitive coping, families, and disability*. Baltimore, MD: Paul H. Brookes.

Turnbull, A. P., & Turnbull, H. R. (1997). *Families, professionals, and exceptionality: Collaborating for empowerment* (3rd ed.). Columbus, OH: Merrill/Prentice Hall.

Turnbull, A. P., Turnbull, H. R., Shank, M., & Leal, D. (1995). *Exceptional lives: Special education in today's schools*. Columbus, OH: Merrill/Prentice Hall.

E. VALERIE HEWITT
Texas A&M University
First edition

TAMARA J. MARTIN
The University of Texas of the Permian Basin
Second edition

RACHEL M. TOPLIS
Falcon School District 49,
  Colorado Springs, Colorado
Third edition

TURNBULL, H. RUTHERFORD (1937–　)

H. Rutherford Turnbull received his BA in political science from Johns Hopkins University in 1959 and his LLB/JD from the University of Maryland Law School in 1964. He later attended Harvard Law School, earning his LLM in the Urban Studies program in 1969. As the father of an adult son with mental retardation and autism, Turnbull has specialized in law and public policy affecting persons with mental and developmental disabilities. He is currently codirector of the Beach Center on Families and Disability and professor of special education and courtesy professor of law at the University of Kansas.

Turnbull concentrates his research and training in four areas: special education law and policy, mental disability law and policy, public policy analysis, and ethics as related to disability policy and service provision. His initial work in the areas of special education law and rights of institutionalized persons led him to concentrate on issues that define and redefine the concepts of consent, least restriction, and parent participation in the education of children with disabilities. His work with policymakers and professional caregivers has focused on issues concerning the treatment of infants with disabilities and the restructuring of Medicaid financing of residential and other services for persons with mental retardation.

Turnbull's service in elected and appointed leadership includes president of the American Association on Mental Retardation (1985–1986), director of the Association for Retarded Citizens of the United States (1981–1983), chairman of the American Bar Association Commission on Mental and Physical Disability Law (1992–1995), and trustee of the Judge David Bazelon Mental Health Law Center (1993–1997). He served as chairman of the Judge David Bazelon Center for Mental Health Law in the years 2001, 2002, and 2003.

Since developing his specialization in the mid-1970s while professor of public law and government at the Institute of Government of the University of North Carolina in Chapel Hill (1969–1980), Turnbull has authored more than 125 articles, book chapters, monographs, technical reports, reviews, and commentaries related to disability issues. His major works include *Consent Handbook* (1978), *Free Appropriate Public Education: Law and the Education of Children with Disabilities* (1997), and *Exceptional Lives: Special Education in Today's Schools* (1998). He has been "of counsel" on amicus briefs in two disability cases heard by the United States Supreme Court as well as author and draftsman of North Carolina's special education law and limited guardianship law and PL 100-407, Assistive Technology for Individuals with Disabilities Act of 1988.

Turnbull was recognized in *Who's Who in America* from 1995 to 2003. His honors include the National Public Service Award of the International Council for Exceptional Children (1996) and the National Leadership Award of the American Association on Mental Retardation (1997).

REFERENCES

Turnbull, A. P., Turnbull, H. R., Shank, M. S., & Leal, D. J. (1998). *Exceptional lives: Special education in today's schools.* Columbus, OH: Merrill/Prentice Hall.

Turnbull, H. R. (1978). *Consent handbook.* Washington, DC: American Association on Mental Retardation.

Turnbull, H. R. (1997). *Free appropriate public education: Law and the education of children with disabilities* (Rev. ed.). Denver, CO: Love.

TAMARA J. MARTIN
The University of Texas of the Permian Basin

RACHEL M. TOPLIS
Falcon School District 49,
Colorado Springs, Colorado

TURNER SYNDROME

Turner syndrome (TS) is a genetic disorder characterized by a complete or partial loss of one of the X chromosomes. TS affects approximately 1 out of 2,500 female live births; however, in rare cases males have been affected and share similar features seen in females (Rovet, 2004). This syndrome is characterized by skeletal, lymphatic, and reproductive abnormalities and recent advances indicate brain structure abnormalities. Improvements in hormone understanding has allowed for treatment of some of the related deficits historically associated with TS.

TS was first described in the early 1800s, but more thoroughly described by Turner in the 1930s as characterized by sexual infantilism, short stature, abnormality of elbow formation, and webbing of the neck (Turner, 1938). Polani, Lessof, and Bishop (1956) first linked TS to the X chromosome due to an increased incidence of colorblindness found in the TS population. Monosomy is accountable for approximately 50% of all cases, followed by mosaicism (30%), and the remaining associated with various deletions, rearrangements, or translocations (Jacobs et al., 1997). The differences in genetic abnormalities account for the variability seen in the physical and cognitive expressions of the syndrome (Rovet, 2004).

In addition to those characteristics initially described by Turner, distinctive physical features associated with TS are short stature and low production of female sex hormones resulting in the lack of estrogen production, lower androgen levels, and the lack of ova (Bishop et al., 2000). TS has been associated with a smaller fourth digit metacarpal and high arched palate that contributes to feeding difficulties (Rovet, 2004). Further cranial deformations contribute to a higher incidence of ear canal infections (Stenberg, Nylen, Windh, & Halcrantz, 1998). Deficits in lymph clearance result in fetal demise and complications. TS has been connected with renal abnormalities, cardiac abnormalities, pigmented nevi, thyroid dysfunction, impaired glucose tolerance, hypertension, and nail dysplasia (Lippe, 1991; Miyabara, Suzumori, Yonemitsu, & Sugihara, 1997).

Brain structure analysis using neuroimaging has recently identified abnormalities in the parietal lobes, reduced volume of the hippocampus, caudate, lenticular, and thalamic nuclei (Murphy et al., 1993). These findings lend support to associated symptoms characterized by deficits in long-term memory, executive processing deficits, and visuospacial deficits. Genetic studies have identified the area of the X chromosome responsible for many of the physical and cognitive deficits seen in TS (Zinn et al., 1998). Verbal ability tends to be normally distributed; however, performance abilities tend to two standard deviations below the mean (Bishop et al., 2000; Garron, 1977). Deficits can also be seen in math associated skills as well as memory (Bishop et al., 2000).

Special education practitioners should be aware of the wide distribution of characteristics associated with TS. Recent hormone replacement therapy has allowed for treatment resulting in normal stature and less obvious physical expressions of the syndrome (Rovet, 2004). Full psychoeducational evaluations and neuropsychological evaluations should take place to determine learning deficits and strengths due to the variability in expression. Not all of those who express mosaic genetic makeup or undergo hormone replacement therapy will be sterile; however, therapy surrounding issues of sterility should be addressed when appropriate.

REFERENCES

Bishop, D., Canning, E., Elgar, K., Morris, E., Jacobs, P., & Skuse, D. (2000). Distinctive patterns of memory function in subgroups of females with Turner syndrome: Evidence for imprinted loci on the X-chromosome affecting neurodevelopment. *Neuropsychologia, 38*, 712–721.

Garron, D. C. (1977). Intelligence among persons with Turner's syndrome. *Behavior Genetics, 7*, 147–152.

Jacobs, P., Dalton, P., James, R., Mosse, K., Power, M., ... Skuse, D. (1997). Turner syndrome: A cytogenetic and molecular study. *Annals of Human Genetics, 61*, 471–483.

Lippe, B. (1991). Turner syndrome. *Endocrinology Metabolism Clinicians of North America, 20*, 121–152.

Miyabara, S., Suzumori, K., Yonemitsu, N., & Sugihara, H. (1997). Developmental analysis of cardiovascular system of 45, X fetuses with cystic hygroma. *American Journal of Medical Genetics, 68*, 135–141.

Murphy, D. G. M., DeCarli, C., Daly, E., Haxby, J. V., Allen, G., ... Schapiro, M. (1993). X-chromosome effects on female brain: A magnetic resonance imaging study of Turner's syndrome. *Lancet, 342*, 1197–2000.

Polani, P. E., Lessof, M. H., & Bishop, P. M. F. (1956). Colour-blindness in "ovarian agenesis" (gonadal dysplasia). *Lancet, 2*, 118–119.

Rovet, J. (2004). Turner syndrome a review of genetic and hormonal influences on neuropsychological functioning. *Child Neuropsychology, 10*(4), 262–269.

Stenberg, A. E., Nylen, O., Windh, M., & Halcrantz, M. (1998). Otological problems in children with Turner's syndrome. *Hearing Research, 124*, 85–90.

Turner, H. (1938). A syndrome of infantilism, congenital webbed neck, and cubitus valgus. *Endocrinology, 23*, 566.

Zinn, A., Tonk, V., Chen, Z., Flejter, W., Gardner, A., Guerra, R., ... Ross, J. L. (1998). Evidence for a Turner syndrome locus or loci at p11.2–p22.1 *American Journal of Human Genetics, 63*, 1757–1766.

MICHELLE T. BUSS
Texas A&M University

See also Genetic Counseling; Genetic Testing; Genetic Transmission; Klinefelter's Syndrome; Mosaicism

TUTORING

Tutoring is a method of instruction in which one or a small group of students (tutees) receive personalized and individualized education from a tutor. Tutoring is widely used with students of all ages and all levels of ability. However, in elementary and secondary schools, it is most often used as an adjunct to traditional classroom instruction: (a) to provide remedial or supplementary instruction to students who have difficulty learning by conventional methods, including mainstreamed, handicapped children; (b) to provide students with increased opportunities to actively participate in the learning process and receive immediate feedback; and (c) to help relieve the classroom teacher of instructional and noninstructional duties.

In most cases, tutoring is provided to students by someone other than the regular teacher. This may be an adult who volunteers or is paid, a college student, a programmed machine or computer, or, in many cases, another student. The term *peer tutoring* is used when children serve as tutors to others close to their age who are functioning at a lower level. The term cross-age tutoring is used when older children or adolescents work with tutees who are several years younger than themselves.

The practices of peer and cross-age tutoring were recorded as early as the first century AD by Quintilian in the *Institutio Oratoria*. However, the practice was not formalized and instituted on a widespread basis until the late-18th century by Andrew Bell in India and later by William Lancaster in England. Tutoring was standard practice in the one-room schoolhouses of America until graded classes helped reduce the heterogeneity of student ability. Renewed interest in children teaching children began in the early 1960s because of shortages in professional teachers. Educators argued that disadvantaged children might learn more from a peer than from an adult. Several large-scale tutoring programs in New York City, Washington, DC, Chicago, Michigan, and California were successful (Allen, 1976).

Since 1970, numerous research studies and anecdotal reports have documented the benefits of tutoring for both the tutee and the tutor. Both have been found to benefit in terms of increases in achievement, school attitudes, peer acceptance, and self-image (Devin-Sheehan, Feldman, & Allen, 1976). Successful outcomes of tutoring have been reported for nondisabled tutees, tutees in special education including the moderately retarded, and those with aggressive behavior disorders (Maher, 1982).

Research further indicates that the effectiveness of tutoring depends greatly on how it is organized and structured and the nature of the relationship between the tutor and tutee. Some guidelines for developing a successful tutoring program follow.

Tutors must be carefully selected, trained, and supervised. Prospective tutor recruits must be dependable, responsible, and knowledgeable in the skill to be taught. They must be trained in tutoring skills (e.g., praising, task analysis, direct instruction, communication) and be provided with specific materials. A designated tutor supervisor must be available. Tutors and tutees should be matched carefully so that they have good rapport and work together conscientiously. Contracts are helpful in spelling out the responsibilities of each. If possible, tutoring should be held twice weekly for at least 30 minutes each session over a minimum of 10 weeks. The program should be continually monitored to determine its effectiveness. Meetings should be scheduled separately with the tutors and tutees to discuss any problems.

Extensive descriptions of tutorial procedures can be found in Allen (1976) and Ehly and Larsen (1980). The use of disabled students as tutors for the nondisabled has been discussed by Osguthorpe (1984).

REFERENCES

Allen, V. L. (1976). *Children as teachers: Theory and research on tutoring*. New York, NY: Academic Press.

Devin-Sheehan, L., Feldman, R. S., & Allen, V. L. (1976). Research on children tutoring children: A critical review. *Review of Educational Research, 46*, 355–385.

Ehly, S. W., & Larsen, S. C. (1980). *Peer tutoring for individualized instruction*. Boston, MA: Allyn & Bacon.

Maher, C. A. (1982). Behavioral effects of using conduct problem adolescents as cross-age tutors. *Psychology in the Schools, 10*, 360–364.

Osguthorpe, R. T. (1984). Handicapped students as tutors for nonhandicapped peers. *Academic Therapy, 19*, 473–483.

FREDERIC J. MEDWAY
University of South Carolina

See also Teaching Strategies

TWINS

Twins may pose a number of educational problems because of their close relationship and their strong attachment to one another. For instance, they often show language delay. Because they are content with each other's company and consequently socialize less with other children and adults than singletons, they tend to be less influenced by the linguistic environment (Luchsinger, 1961). Indeed, they may develop a jargon that enables them to communicate with one another but that is incomprehensible to others. This private idiom is called *cryptophasia*. Cryptophasia is not a language sui generis (as some have thought it was), but a sort of pidgin based on the language of the adults (Lebrun, 1982). Despite reduced vocabulary and absence of grammar, it makes communication possible between the twins; they have so many affinities that they can understand one another with just a few words. To improve the twins' language command, speech therapy may be necessary. Moreover, it may be desirable to separate them part of the day so that they can learn to socialize.

REFERENCES

Lebrun, Y. (1982). Cryptophasie et retard de langage chez les jumeaux. *Enfance (3)*, 101–108.

Luchsinger, R. (1961). Die Sprachentwicklung von ein- und zweiengen Zwillingen und die Vererbung von Sprachstörungen in den ersten drie Lebensjahren. *Folia Phoniatrica (13)*, 66–76.

YVAN LEBRUN
School of Medicine, Brussels, Belgium

See also Zygosity

U

ULCERS

Ulcers are characterized by a persistent, burning pain in the abdomen as a result of a sore or lesion in the lining of the stomach or duodenum. Prevalence rates from the National Digestive Diseases Information Clearinghouse (NDDIC, 1998) indicate that about 4 million people are affected by ulcers and that approximately 40,000 people have surgery for persistent problems, with complications resulting in death for 6,000 of them. Although ulcers can develop at any age, they are rare in teenagers, and even rarer in children.

Characteristics

1. Persistent burning in the abdomen between the breast-bone and naval.
2. Often occurs between meals and in the early morning hours.
3. Less common symptoms include nausea, vomiting, loss of appetite, and weight loss.
4. Bleeding may occur in the stomach, resulting in weakness and fatigue.

Ulcers may be diagnosed with an upper gastrointestinal series and X-rays using a barium trace. In addition, an endoscopy may be performed under light sedation. Once an ulcer's presence and location has been confirmed, various tests may be performed for confirmation of the bacterium Helicobacter pylori. Tests include blood, breath, and stomach tissue. Before proceeding with treatment, it is important to rule out the possibility of nonsteroidal antiinflammatory drugs (NSAIDs) related ulcers as well as nonulcer dyspepsia.

Etiology has historically been attributed to a number of causal factors but is believed to be primarily attributed to H. pylori bacteria that invade the lining of the stomach or duodenum (Ewald, 2000). Lifestyle factors such as smoking, alcohol, caffeine, and emotional stress may contribute to the exacerbation of symptoms through production of acid and the reoccurrence of ulcers. Physical stress, such as a severe injury, greatly increases the chance of ulcers as the immune system is overtaxed, combating a host of infectious agents. NSAIDs, such as aspirin, ibuprofen, and naproxen sodium, can make the stomach vulnerable to the harmful effects of acid and pepsin by impacting the stomach's ability to produce mucus and bicarbonate, which form a protective coating for the stomach lining.

H. pylori, a spiral-shaped bacterium found in the stomach, causes tissue damage by producing the enzyme urease. Urease neutralizes stomach acid, enabling the bacteria to survive. After penetrating the stomach's protective mucus lining, the bacteria make the stomach more susceptible to the harmful effects of hydrochloric acid and pepsin, which are naturally produced to aid in digestion. Local inflammation may occur, which may result in an ulcer. Whereas most people with H. pylori infection develop gastritis, an inflammation of the stomach lining, only a small number will have symptoms or problems related to the infection. It is unclear why some people have symptoms and others do not. H. pylori is more common in older adults, African Americans, Hispanics, and lower socioeconomic groups. H. pylori may be transmitted from person to person through contaminated food and water. Most individuals appear to be infected during childhood, with the infection of H. pylori lasting a lifetime.

Relative to the H. pylori causal hypothesis, Jefferson (1998) found in a meta-analysis of treatment studies that 20% of patients treated with antibiotics had a reoccurrence of ulcers within 6 months, despite a cure of infection and no report of NSAIDs use. This suggests that other factors may contribute to the development of ulcers.

Treatment is related to diagnosis with lifestyle change having little impact, other than stopping smoking, which has been related to reoccurrence. Acid blockers (Cimetidine, Famotidine, Ranitidine) and mucosa protection medications (Sulcralfate and Misoprostol) reduce symptoms. With the presence of H. pylori, antibiotics have the most dramatic effect in eradicating the ulcer. The National Institutes of Health indicate the most effective therapy as a 2-week triple therapy, with a 90% success rate for both duodenal and stomach (not associated with NSAIDs) ulcers. This includes acid reducers, mucosal protectors, and antibiotics. In extreme cases (bleeding, perforation), surgery may be required with laparascopic procedures to be used in the future. This will hopefully prevent peritonitis, an inflammation of the abdominal cavity and wall.

Special education services for children may be warranted in extreme circumstances with services being provided under the umbrella of Other Health Impairment.

However, this is unlikely due to the success of current therapies in treating ulcers, as well as the infrequent occurrence in childhood and adolescence. Services may include a variety of supports focusing on accommodations and modifications in the regular education classroom and standardized test taking. Future research will hopefully determine why some people with H. pylori bacteria do not develop ulcers while others do and explore the hypothesized contribution of emotional stress.

REFERENCES

Ewald, P. (2000). *Plague time*. New York, NY: Free Press.

Jefferson, T. C. (1998). Has the impact of helicobacter pylori therapy on ulcer recurrence in the United States been overstated? *Journal of the American Medical Association, 280*, 1466–1480.

National Digestive Diseases Information Clearinghouse. (1998). *Stomach and duodenal ulcers*. Retrieved from http://www.gastro.com/ulcers.htm

R. Brett Nelson
Diana L. Nebel
University of Northern Colorado

ULCERS AND CHILDREN WITH DISABILITIES

Although little empirical evidence exists to substantiate the relationship between ulcers and disabilities, it appears that children with disabilities may be more predisposed to ulceration than their typically developing peers. Kim, Learman, Nada, and Thompson (1981) found that 5.4% of the residents in a large institution for children with disabilities had peptic ulcers.

Other factors often associated with disabilities also appear to lead to ulceration. For example, ulcers are more likely to occur in children with lower IQs (Christodoulou, Gargoulas, Poploukas, & Marinopoulou, 1977; Kim et al., 1981). Additionally, ulcers occur more often in children who are withdrawn and less likely to express their feelings or frustrations (Chapman & Loeb, 1967; Christodoulou et al., 1977), similar to some emotionally disabled children. Finally, children who come from extended family situations (e.g., divorced or separated parents) are more likely to have ulcers (Ackerman, Manaker, & Cohen, 1981), a factor that has been shown to be more likely to occur in children with disabilities than in their typically developing peers (Beattie & Maniscalco, 1985).

Particular types of ulcers, particularly ulcerative colitis, may result in growth retardation and cosmetic problems

that may lead to eligibility for services under the IDEA (Gillman, 1994; McClung, 1994).

REFERENCES

Ackerman, S. H., Manaker, S., & Cohen, M. I. (1981). Recent separation and the onset of peptic ulcer disease in older children and adolescents. *Psychosomatic Medicine, 43*, 305–310.

Beattie, J., & Maniscalco, G. (1985). Special education and divorce: Is there a link? *Techniques, 1*, 342–345.

Chapman, A. H., & Loeb, D. G. (1967). Psychosomatic gastrointestinal problems. In I. Frank & M. Powell (Eds.), *Psychosomatic ailments in childhood and adolescence*. Springfield, IL: Thomas.

Christodoulou, G. N., Gargoulas, A., Poploukas, A., & Marinopoulou, A. (1977). Primary peptic ulcers in childhood: Psychosocial, psychological and psychiatric aspects. *Acta Psychiatrica Scandinavica, 56*, 215–222.

Gillman, J. (1994). Inflammatory bowel diseases: Psychological issues. In R. Olsen, L. Mullins, J. Gillman, & J. Chaney (Eds.), *Pediatric psychology*. Boston, MA: Longwood.

Kim, M., Learman, L., Nada, N., & Thompson, K. (1981). The prevalence of peptic ulcer in an institution for the mentally retarded. *Journal of Mental Deficiency Research, 25*, 105–111.

McClung, H. (1994). Inflammatory bowel diseases: Medical issues. In R. Olsen, L. Mullins, J. Gillman, & J. Chaney (Eds.), *Pediatric psychology*. Boston, MA: Longwood.

John R. Beattie
University of North Carolina at Charlotte

See also Antisocial Behavior; Divorce and Special Education; Emotional Disorders

ULTIMATE INSTRUCTION FOR THE SEVERE AND PROFOUNDLY RETARDED

The criterion of ultimate functioning (Brown, Nietupski, & Hamre-Nietupski, 1976) refers to a method of prioritization that may be used in developing programs for the learner with severe or profound disabilities. Although the type of disability may vary, this program development philosophy has most often been applied to individuals who have been classified as intellectually disabled.

Use of this type of rationale to develop curricula for such persons extends from three major assumptions (Brown et al., 1976). First, the learner with severe or profound disabilities should be taught skills that increase the student's independence in and access to less restrictive environments. Second, transfer of training, response generalization, and response maintenance cannot be assumed to occur with such learners. Third, programming efforts for the learner with severe or profound disabilities should address the wide variety of individual learning characteristics of this group. Thus application of the criterion of ultimate functioning in developing curricula for these students requires that the skills and behaviors taught to such individuals should relate directly to the behaviors that will be expected of them in nonschool environments.

Brown et al. (1976) developed the concept of the criterion of ultimate functioning in response to inadequacies of educational programs that had been generated based on alternative curriculum philosophies. With the learner with severe and profound disabilities, these philosophies have often been either developmental or nontheoretical in nature (Haring & Bricker, 1976).

The developmental approach to curriculum delineation reflects adherence to a stage or hierarchical explanation of learning. From this perspective, the skills that are taught the learner with severe or profound disabilities are dictated by the pattern of development that often takes place with the typically developing child. Moving from the simple to the complex, the skills that are taught in developmentally oriented curricula might include teaching a student to vocalize before teaching words or teaching visual orientation before teaching word recognition. Proponents of a developmental approach to education feel that the simpler tasks must be mastered before the more complex skills are taught. Actual applications of a developmental orientation to the education of the learner with severe and profound disabilities have often been criticized because of their inflexibility (e.g., "John is stabilized at the preoperational level") and lack of direct relationship to the teaching of immediately relevant skills (e.g., teaching object use through picture matching).

An alternative approach that has been used to develop curricula for the learner with severe or profound disabilities has been referred to as nontheoretical (Haring & Bricker, 1976). This orientation develops curriculum content based on teacher-specified individual needs of the student. The emphasis of these types of programs has been on the use of specific methodologies that effectively teach the student new and increasingly complex skills. These skills do not reflect a particular developmental progression but instead are those skills that are relevant for the student as decided by the teacher. Although the emphasis on methodological consistency apparent in curricula of this type has often led to impressive skill acquisition, these skills have, at times, reflected teacher priorities that are not necessarily consistent with the best interests of the student (e.g., sitting quietly but not necessarily completing a task).

In response to the potential limitations of these curriculum development approaches, the criterion of ultimate functioning (Brown et al., 1976) suggests teaching skills that are (1) relevant to student needs in light of individual learning characteristics; (2) immediately useful in terms of the environment(s) in which the student functions; and

(3) able to increase the independence and ability of the student to attain access to more normative social environments. The teaching methods that are used from this perspective are based on specific analysis of the skills of the student and the requirements of the environment. Differences between these two assessment areas become the teaching objectives.

The criterion of ultimate functioning, used as a rationale for curriculum development with the learner with severe and profound disabilities, breaks with the traditional developmental curriculum orientation. The skills that are taught are directly relevant in terms of the environments in which the student does, or is expected to, function. Building on techniques that emphasize specific analysis of student behaviors and environmental requirements, this approach systematically teaches the student with disabilities skills that increase independence in and access to less restrictive settings. In contrast with the nontheoretical approach mentioned previously, this focus on independence and normative (chronologically age-appropriate) environments reflects a view of the student as an integral part of society. Theoretically, the degree to which the student might access social environments is a direct function of teaching the skills necessary for effective adaptation to those environments. Accordingly, the skills that are taught address not only the immediate relevance of learning experiences but also the long-term relevance of such skills.

REFERENCES

Brown, L., Nietupski, J., & Hamre-Nietupski, S. (1976). The criterion of ultimate functioning. In M. A. Thomas (Ed.), *Hey! Don't forget about me*. Reston, VA: Council for Exceptional Children.

Haring, H., & Bricker, D. (1976). *Overview of comprehensive services for the severely/profoundly handicapped*. New York, NY: Grune & Stratton.

J. Todd Stephens
University of Wisconsin at Madison

See also **Curriculum for Students With Severe Disabilities; Ultimate Instruction for the Severe and Profoundly Retarded**

UNITED CEREBRAL PALSY

United Cerebral Palsy (UCP) is a national voluntary association comprised of state and local affiliates and the national organization, United Cerebral Palsy Associations (UCPA), which is headquartered in New York City. The

UCP's mission is to education, advocate, and provide support services to ensure a life with limits for people with a spectrum of disabilities. Local affiliates provide direct services to individuals with cerebral palsy and their families, including special education, transitional services, and community living facilities. State affiliates coordinate the programs of local affiliates; provide services to areas not covered by locals, and work with agencies at the state level to further UCP goals.

The UCP began as a parent group organized to improve services and educational programming for children with cerebral palsy. One of the first formal units was the Association for Cerebral Palsy, established in 1942, in California. In 1946, a parent group formed the New York State Association for Cerebral Palsy. These groups, along with others like them evolved into a national agency that provides advocacy for legislative efforts, research and training, and direct services to clients. On August 12, 1948, the national organization was established as the National Foundation for Cerebral Palsy, a nonprofit membership corporation located in New York City. On August 12, 1949, the corporate name was changed to United Cerebral Palsy Associations, Inc. By 1952, more than 100 affiliates were linked with the national organization. As of 2007, about a million dollars was being put into each of the following programs: public and private grants, medical research and education, public policy analysis/advocacy, public education, life without limits, and other grants. The goal of the group has broadened from only people with cerebral palsy to any person with a disability. There are more than 100 affiliates, and the UCP is helping more than 167,000 people with disabilities a day.

UCPA works in many ways to generate new programs and services. In representing UCP in national affairs, UCPA cooperates with federal government agencies that administer programs that affect individuals with disabilities. In addition, UCPA articulates UCP's positions on national issues such as national health services and transportation of people with disabilities. The UCPA develops model services for people with disabilities that are designed to be replicated in local communities (Cohen & Warren, 1985). Through the UCP Research and Educational Foundation, UCPA promotes research into the causes of cerebral palsy, means of prevention, training of medical and allied personnel, and biomedical technology to improve mobility and communication. In addition, the UCP, through its affiliates, provides housing, therapy, assistive technology training, early intervention programs, community living, state and local referrals, employment assistance, and advocacy.

As of 2004, the program "Life Without Limits" has been the focus of the UCP. This program helps to create a new vision of the future for individuals with disabilities; increase public awareness about the serious challenges that still remain; and develop strategies, initiatives, programs, and public policy to make this vision a reality. This program has released many articles and writing about how people with disabilities live every day and how the world treats and helps those with disabilities. In order to promote awareness and raise money for the cause, the UCP created the Ride Without Limits, a 2-day, 200-mile bike ride across three communities in the United States. This ride raised nearly $500,000 dollars. With these programs, the UCP is striving for complete inclusion in the community for people with disabilities and providing those services to different states without services. Another program the UCP has is ABLE Young Professionals Network. It allows for young professionals that are committed to supporting UCP to advance UCP's mission of creating a life without limits for people with a spectrum of disabilities. They increase education and awareness of disability issues by volunteering at local affiliates and in the community, attending social events, and participating in fundraising opportunities.

This entry has been informed by the sources listed below.

REFERENCES

Cohen, S., & Warren, R. (1985). *Respite care: Principles, programs, and policies*. Austin, TX: PRO-ED.

Nielsen, C. (1978). *The cerebral palsy movement and the founding of UCPA, Inc.* Unpublished manuscript.

United Cerebral Palsy Associations. (1983). *Annual report 1983*. New York, NY: Author.

United Cerebral Palsy Associations. (2007). *Focus on the future: 2007 annual report*. New York, NY: Author.

United Cerebral Palsy, Inc. (2011). *About United Cerebral Palsy*. Retrieved from http://www.ucp.org/about

CAROLE REITERGOTHELF
Hunter College, City University of New York

AMANDA CHOW
Texas A&M University at College Station
Fourth edition

See also Advocacy for Children With Disabilities; Cerebral Palsy

UNITED KINGDOM, SPECIAL EDUCATION IN THE (*See* England, Special Education in)

UNITED STATES DEPARTMENT OF EDUCATION

The United States Office of Education, a precursor to the current federal Department of Education, was created by an act of Congress in 1867. Its original mission was to collect and disseminate information on the condition of education in the states and U.S. territories. According to Campbell, Cunningham, Nystrand, and Usdan (1990), the Office of Education was responsible for establishing a system to identify and advance promising educational practices in school districts throughout the country. The Department of Education's website also states that the Office of Education was created to help establish effective school systems by collecting information on schools and teaching in ways that would help the States.

During the 19th and early 20th century, the Office of Education was located within the U.S. Department of the Interior. In 1939 the office was transferred to the jurisdiction of the Federal Security Agency. Its final home, prior to achieving Cabinet level (departmental) status, was with the U.S. Department of Health, Education, and Welfare (1953–1980) (HEW).

Public Law 96-88, passed by Congress and signed by President Carter in 1979, created the U.S. Department of Education (ED). The new department assumed all of the functions previously assigned to the Office of Education, and also included education-related programs and functions previously administered by other entities within HEW such as rehabilitation. Soll (1984) suggests that the rapid proliferation of social programs and the political mobilization of various educational constituencies combined to stimulate the creation of a cabinet-level Department of Education.

Although exercising a modest role in American education during its first century of existence, the federal-level education agency has assumed an increasingly important role in administering national education initiatives. Recently (since 2009), the federal Office (now Department) of Education has been charged with (1) the establishment of policies relating to federal financial aid for education and administering and monitoring distribution of said funds; (2) collecting data and overseeing research on schools in the United States, then providing the information to Congress, educators, and the general public; (3) identifying the major issues and problems within education and bringing national attention to the problems; and (4) ensuring equal access to education for all individuals and enforcing federal statutes that prohibit discrimination in programs and activities receiving federal funds.

According to the Department of Education's website, the 2011 fiscal year budget for all activities administered by the ED was approximately $69.9 billion. In addition, for updates on the Department of Education's activities and other resources, individuals may find journals such as the *ED Review* and many others listed on the website. The ED is headquartered in Washington, DC, where about 3,600 staff members work in six different buildings. There are another 1,400 staff members working in 10 regional offices around the United States. To mail something to the ED, individuals should send their concerns to U.S. Department of Education, 400 Maryland Avenue, SW, Washington, D.C. 20202. In addition, individuals may call Tel.: (800)

USA-LEARN (800-872-5327) for more information about the ED.

REFERENCES

Campbell, R. F., Cunningham, L. L., Nystrand, R. O., & Usdan, M. D. (1990). *The organization and control of American schools*. Columbus, OH: Prentice Hall.

Soll, C. D. (1984). The creation of the Department of Education. In R. J. Stillman (Ed.), *Public administration: Concepts and cases* (3rd ed., pp. 370–377). Boston, MA: Houghton Mifflin.

GEORGE JAMES HAGERTY
Stonehill College
Second edition

KIMBERLY APPLEQUIST
University of Colorado at Colorado Springs
Third edition

AMANDA C. CHOW
Texas A&M University at College Station, Texas
Fourth edition

Office of Special Education and Rehabilitative Services; Politics and Special Education

UNITED STATES DEPARTMENT OF EDUCATION'S LONGITUDINAL STUDIES PROGRAM

The 1975 passage of the Education for All Handicapped Children Act (EHA, PL 94-142) required all public schools receiving federal funds to provide access to a free, appropriate public education to children with disabilities and provided funds to states to support that requirement. The legislation also included provisions for identifying children with disabilities, evaluating their abilities and needs, and creating an individualized educational program (IEP) with parent input that would provide education and related services in the least restrictive environment appropriate to the child. Procedural safeguards were specified to protect these rights.

In addition to these provisions, Section 618 of PL 94-142 authorized the Commissioner of Education to "conduct, directly or by grant or contract, such studies, investigations, and evaluations as are necessary to assure effective implementation of this part" (Sec. 618[a]) and required that ED produce an annual report to Congress to document aspects of the law (e.g., the growth in students served under the law as a result of "child find" provisions). In response, the Bureau of Education of the Handicapped (BEH) in the Department of Health and Human Services (which became the Office of Special Education Programs in the Department of Education in 1980) commissioned a number of "special studies," beginning in the late 1970s. Among them was a series of evaluation studies that focused on issues and challenges involved in the early implementation of EHA.

For example, early complaints that the IEPs required under the law were too burdensome led BEH to commission a study of the IEP process. Conducted by the Research Triangle Institute (now RTI International) and drawing on the experiences of a nationally representative sample of schools from across the country, the study found that the average length of an IEP was two pages, although there were some that were 30 pages long. This study assuaged concerns about the burden on schools and school districts and may have stopped early attempts to amend the provisions of the law; some were concerned that critical provision of the law might be modified or even eliminated if the law was opened for amendments. Another early study, which examined evaluation procedures used for the identification of students with disabilities, was initiated to address concerns about overidentification of racial and ethnic minority children. Another study surveyed day and residential facilities that served students with disabilities and described the demographics of the students placed in those facilities and the services provided to them.

One of the special studies, conducted by SRI International, was unique in that it documented the implementation of EHA over time through longitudinal case studies of 22 school districts as they implemented the provisions of the law (Wright, Cooperstein, Renneker, & Padilla, 1982). The study documented the "rapid translation of federal requirements into local level action," the importance of local and state resources in meeting the intent of the law, and the key role of "boundary crossers" in establishing new relationships and procedures in serving students with disabilities (Stearns, Greene, & David, 1980). This became the first national longitudinal study specifically intended to inform special education policy.

These initial studies examined the extent to which the provisions of the statute and corresponding regulations were implemented, reflecting a widespread belief at that time, which was implicit in many OSEP actions, that achieving a goal of precise implementation of procedural requirements would ensure good outcomes for children and youth. By the mid-1980s, the focus on procedural implementation began to change in response to an increasing awareness that even when processes and procedures were well implemented, students might not be achieving the desired outcomes. It was in this context that the first of OSEP's child-based longitudinal studies came about, the National Longitudinal Transition Study (NLTS).

Congress had heard anecdotal reports that the transition from school to postschool life was not going smoothly for many youth with disabilities. Reflecting a concern for the poor transition outcomes of these youth, the 1983 reauthorization of EHA (PL 98-199) required that state and local education agencies report the anticipated transition needs of students with disabilities who were leaving school and established services to facilitate school to work transition through research and demonstration projects. The law also mandated that OSEP commission a study of "a sample of handicapped students, encompassing the full range of handicapping conditions, examining their educational progress while in special education and their occupational, educational, and independent living status after graduating from secondary school or otherwise leaving special education" (PL 98-199, section 618). This study was to document the extent of the transition challenges nationally and help understand how transition outcomes might be improved.

NLTS findings had dramatic and far-reaching impacts both on the investments made through the IDEA discretionary grant programs and, most importantly, on the reauthorization of IDEA in 1997 (PL 105-17). The most important issues addressed with the 1997 amendments involved ensuring that students with disabilities had access to the general education curriculum. The original EHA required that students with disabilities be for clarity served in the least restrictive environment to the maximum extent appropriate but until the 1997 amendments, there were no requirements for IEPs to address the supports and services that students with disabilities would need to truly participate in the general education curriculum. NLTS had made it evident that large numbers of students with disabilities, who were not successful in general education courses, had no supports or services to enable them to succeed there and would subsequently drop out (Hebbeler, 1993; Wagner, 1991). Further, their general education teachers reported not having training or supports to enable them to provide effective instruction to these students (Hebbeler, 1993). These findings led to very critical enhancements to IDEA that have taken on even more importance since the enactment of the No Child Left Behind Act of 2001 (NCLB). That law holds schools accountable for the achievement of students with disabilities based on the same grade-level content standards as used for typically developing students.

The Congressional mandate in the 1983 EHA amendments provides extremely valuable insights about the experiences of secondary school-age students with disabilities as a whole; Congress also mandated that the study report national figures on students in each of the 11 federal special education disability categories in use at the time. Because this requirement increased the cost of the study exponentially, it is unlikely that OSEP would have ensured that there would be adequate samples for each disability category if this had not been required.

NLTS reports depicted particularly discouraging outcomes for youth in some disability categories. For example, 59% of students with emotional disturbances had dropped out of high school and 73% of those youth had been arrested within 3 to 5 years of leaving high school (Wagner, 1992).

Examination of school records for these students typically found that they did not have specific behavior plans in their IEPs nor were they receiving services that might be designed to address their social/behavioral issues. The 1997 reauthorization included provisions to ensure that students with these disorders have behavior plans and receive services that they need to improve both academic and social/behavioral outcomes. In addition to these policy changes, OSEP invested significant research funds to expand the knowledge base regarding effective dropout-prevention programs and behavioral supports for students with emotional disturbances, supported model demonstration projects to advance our implementation knowledge, and funded national technical assistance centers to help take to scale evidence-based practices to improve these outcomes.

A major by-product of the significant impact of NLTS was that it convinced policymakers both within ED and in the Congress of the importance of investing in large-scale studies such as NLTS, and it demonstrated the level of resources that were necessary to undertake national studies. As a result, the 1997 IDEA amendments gave OSEP access to a set-aside amount of up to 1% of the formula grant funds for Part B of IDEA (which provides funds to states for preschool and elementary and secondary school special education programs) to be used for national studies. With access to these resources, OSEP developed a plan for a comprehensive program of national longitudinal studies that would cover the full age range of children and youth with disabilities from birth through 22-plus. The National Early Intervention Longitudinal Study (NEILS) had been funded in 1996 to assess the characteristics, experiences, and outcomes of infants and toddlers with disabilities who received early intervention services under Part C of IDEA (see http://www.sri.com/neils/). With the new set-aside funds, OSEP issued design contracts for the Pre-Elementary Education Longitudinal Study (PEELS, see http://peels.org/); the Special Education Elementary Longitudinal Study (SEELS, see http://www.seels.net/); and the second generation of NLTS, the National Longitudinal Transition Study-2 (NLTS2, see http://www.nlts2.org/). The similar design features of NLTS and NLTS2 enabled important comparisons between the two study cohorts (Wagner, Cameto, & Newman, 2003; Wagner, Newman, & Cameto, 2004; Wagner, Newman, Cameto, & Levine, 2005), which document the "good news and the work ahead" (American Youth Policy Forum, 2002) in educating children and youth with disabilities. In addition to these child-based studies, the funding also enabled OSEP to fund the Special Education Expenditure Study (SEEP), a Study of Personnel Needs in Special Education (SPeNSE), and a study of the State and Local Implementation of IDEA (SLIIDEA).

The 2004 reauthorization of IDEA reassigned the authority to conduct research in special education, including managing these large-scale studies, from OSEP to the newly created National Center for Special Education Research (NCSER) within ED's Institute of Education Sciences (IES) and also eliminated the 1% set aside for funding the large-scale studies. Nonetheless, IES has continued to fund studies of the impacts of IDEA, including commissioning a third national longitudinal study of the outcomes of youth with disabilities in transition to young adulthood.

More information is now available on children and youth with disabilities than was available in 1997 due to requirements that ED collect performance data from states on children and youth with disabilities, including data on some of the key variables that were first demonstrated to be critical though the national studies. Having this alternative source of outcome data may have lessened to some degree the perceived importance of the national studies for policymakers. However, it can be argued that the "bare bones" indicator data collected by OSEP and other agencies, although important, cannot replace the richness of the data produced through the national child-based longitudinal studies. The breadth of data items the databases include enables researchers to examine the relationships between variables (e.g., various patterns of high school course-taking and the likelihood of completing high school and going on to postsecondary education) and to build testable statistical models to help account for differences in the outcomes achieved. In turn, these can lead to important amendments to our laws and serve as the basis for investments in research and new model development, training, and technical assistance. These studies represent one critical element in a continuous process of evaluation and improvement that is desperately needed if we are to ensure that the 35 years of progress that has been achieved for students with disabilities since EHA's passage in 1975 continues for the next 35 years.

REFERENCES

American Youth Policy Forum. (2002). *Twenty-five years of educating children with disabilities. Good news and the work ahead*. Washington, DC: American Youth Policy Forum.

Hebbeler, K. (1993). *Traversing the mainstream: Regular education and students with disabilities in secondary school*. Menlo Park, CA: SRI.

Stearns, M. S., Greene, D., & David, J. L. (1980). *Local implementation of PL 94-142: First-year report of a longitudinal study*. Menlo Park, CA: SRI.

Wagner, M. (1991). *Dropouts with disabilities: What do we know? What can we do? A report from the National Longitudinal Transition Study of Special Education Students*. Menlo Park, CA: SRI.

Wagner, M. (1992). "A little help from my friends": The social involvement of young people with disabilities. In M. Wagner, R. D'Amico, C. Marder, L. Newman & J. Blackorby (Eds.), *What happens next? Trends in postschool outcomes of youth with disabilities*. Menlo Park, CA: SRI.

Wagner, M., Cameto, R., & Newman, L. (2003). *Youth with disabilities: A changing population*. Menlo Park, CA: SRI.

Wagner, M., Newman, L., & Cameto, R. (2004). *Changes over time in the secondary school experiences of students with disabilities. A report of findings from the National Longitudinal Transition Study (NLTS) and the National Longitudinal Transition Study-2 (NLTS2)*. Menlo Park, CA: SRI.

Wagner, M., Newman, L., Cameto, R., & Levine, P. (2005). *Changes over time in the early postschool outcomes of youth with disabilities. A report from the National Longitudinal Transition Study (NLTS) and the National Longitudinal Transition Study-2 (NLTS2)*. Menlo Park, CA: SRI.

Wright, A. R., Cooperstein, R. A., Renneker, E. G., & Padilla, C. (1982). *Local implementation of P.L. 94-142: Final report of a longitudinal study*. Menlo Park, CA: SRI.

LOUIS DANIELSON
American Institutes for Research

UNIVERSAL DESIGN

Universal design has been developed and adopted in an attempt to make all products and environments accessible or usable by the full range of individuals desiring to use them. Universal design was first introduced as an architectural concept associated with providing access to buildings and facilities for individuals having a variety of abilities and disabilities. Initially, private and public facilities had few provisions for individuals with disabilities and, consequently, utilization and access was somewhat limited. Early attempts at providing adequate accessibility usually consisted of efforts such as adding wooden ramps and custom elevators to stairways, adding specialized handrails, widening doorways, and so forth. These efforts obviously involved retrofitting changes to existing structures. Universal design principles, on the other hand, advocate the initial design of facilities to accommodate as many people as possible regardless of age, ability, or situation. Due to the functionality of the design, everyone may benefit from the increased usability factors. For example, while ramps were initially provided for disability access, they have universal benefits and are used every day for the convenience of individuals delivering equipment, pulling wheeled computer bags, or pushing strollers. Similar benefits are experienced by the everyday use of automatic door openers. By designing these features into the initial structures, they are even more useful, less obtrusive, more economical, and more aesthetic. Similar benefits can be experienced in the design of telephones, electronics, utensils, tools, and so on. Today's computer operating systems have similar usability features intended for individuals with disabilities but which offer added features for everyone, such as screen magnification features used in teaching situations.

Consequently, everyone benefits from the awareness and expertise that universal design has brought to the creation of today's products and environments.

Ron Mace is credited with coining the term *universal design* (cited in Pisha & Coyne, 2001). The earliest reference to the term in the literature was found in a bibliography of resources authored by Brown and Vargo (1993), which listed a pamphlet entitled "Universal Design: Housing for the Life Span of All People" (Mace, 1988). Mace became a principal investigator for the Center for Universal Design at the University of North Carolina in 1989, where he continued his work in accessible architecture (Center for Universal Design, 1997a). In 1997, Mace and his group published the most definitive model of UD thus far delineated—"The Seven Principles of Universal Design" (Center for Universal Design, 1997b). Ron Mace died on June 29, 1998 (Center for Universal Design, 1997a), but the Center continues to provide information and leadership in this area (see Center for Universal Design at N.C. State University, IDEA Center at the University at Buffalo, & Universal Design Educator's Network, 2004).

The early definitions of UD are remarkably similar. Brown and Vargo (1993) defined UD as the design of a building, product, or environment so that it can be used by all people. In 1996, Lozada also defined UD in architectural terms: "The idea behind universal design is building a home that is equipped to accommodate someone with special needs but at the same time is not inconvenient for the average person who may not have a disability" (p. 18). It is interesting to note that Lozada used the double negative "not inconvenient" to describe the benefits of UD to people without disabilities. This phrase created emphasis on the benefits of UD to people *with* disabilities. Mace and his colleagues at the Center for Universal Design subtly changed the emphasis in their definition, which stated:

> Universal design is the design of products and environments to be usable by all people, to the greatest extent possible, without the need for adaptation or specialized design.... The intent of universal design is to simplify life for everyone by making products, communications, and the built environment more usable by as many people as possible at little or no extra cost. Universal design benefits people of all ages and abilities. (Center for Universal Design, 1997b, p. 1)

What was striking about this definition was that "disability" had been taken out of it. There was no longer a demarcation between the two populations. Even so, authors would—and still do—continue to associate UD with disability access.

One of the first areas that UD would be applied was technology integration. Early work at the Center for Universal Design had applied the seven principles to industrial and electronic engineering in devices such as kiosks and mobile telephones. Numerous product designers and industrial engineers had embraced UD concepts in the design of their products (see Center for Universal Design, 2004).

However, a schism between *product engineering* intended for people without disabilities and *rehabilitation engineering* intended for those with disabilities would appear in the literature. For the most part, early publications considered UD an extension of assistive technology and rehabilitation engineering (Brown & Vargo, 1993; Burgstahler, Comden, & Fraser, 1997; Lozada, 1996; McGuinness, 1997). This is a theme that continues today (Hitchcock & Stahl, 2003; McGuire, Scott, & Shaw, 2003; Scott, Loewen, Funckes, & Kroeger, 2003), though some theorists (Rose & Meyer, 2002; Stahl, 2004) have more broadly applied UD and question the utility of drawing such a distinction since the stated objective of UD is to design environments that include everyone.

In keeping with the disability theme, much of the research referencing concepts of UD has focused on assistive technology; that is, the application of technology to accommodate people with disabilities. Fichten et al. (2001) completed a fairly large study of assistive technology integration in the higher education environment. They concluded that institutions generally have a poor plan to integrate assistive technology into the campus environment. Faculty often did not have basic knowledge of how assistive technologies worked. Subsequently, faculty inadvertently adopted instructional materials and methods that prevented access to the curriculum. This violated the UD principle of perceptible information in that it prevented effective communication (instruction) regardless of ambient conditions or sensory abilities. Fichten et al. (2001) also concluded that assistive technology had many benefits in the educational environment, but also could create barriers to learning. Their work put the application of UD to assistive technology squarely in the purview of future researchers.

An area receiving special attention with regard to universal design is that of web page accessibility. Like buildings, accessibility features were initially added to existing websites as individuals discovered problems encountered by viewers with sensory or motor disabilities. Various standards and agencies have been established to help ensure that websites are designed to accommodate the widest range of individuals regardless of age, ability, or situation. Examples include the W3C Web Content Accessibility Guidelines (WCAG) 2.0 and the Center for Applied Special Technology's (CAST) Bobby software that examines web pages and "notes technical or design issues that may present barriers to persons with disabilities who access the site" (Cooper, 1999).

Universal design concepts in education have led to concepts such as Universal Design for Learning. CAST has proposed Universal Design for Learning (UDL; Center for Applied Special Technology, 2005), a design feature that provides a blueprint for creating flexible goals, methods, materials, and assessments that accommodate learner differences by creating educational materials that provide multiple approaches to meet the needs of diverse learners. As with architecture and product development, the potential benefits are experienced by all individuals who interact with the materials, not just by those with disabilities.

REFERENCES

Brown, D. S., & Vargo, J. (1993). Bibliography of resources on universal design. *Journal of Rehabilitation, 59*(3), 8–11.

Burgstahler, S., Comden, D., & Fraser, B. (1997). Universal design for universal access: Making the Internet more accessible for people with disabilities. *Alki, 13*(3), 8–9.

Center for Applied Special Technology. (2005). *What is Universal Design for learning?* Retrieved from http://cast.org/udl/

Center for Universal Design. (1997a). *Design pioneer and visionary of universal design.* Retrieved from http://www.ncsu.edu/ncsu/design/cud/about_us/usronmace.htm

Center for Universal Design. (1997b). *What is universal design?* Retrieved from http://www.ncsu.edu/ncsu/design/cud/

Center for Universal Design. (2004). *Resources.* Retrieved from http://www.ncsu.edu/ncsu/design/cud/

Center for Universal Design at N.C. State University, IDEA Center at the University at Buffalo, and Universal Design Educator's Network. (2004). *Universal design education online.* Retrieved from http://www.udeducation.org/

Cooper, M. (1999). *Universal design of a web site.* Technology and Persons with Disabilities Conference Proceedings, California State University, Northridge.

Fichten, C. S., Asuncion, J. V., Barile, M., Genereux, C., Fossey, M., Judd, D.,... Wells, D. (2001). Technology integration for students with disabilities: Empirically based recommendations for faculty. *Educational Research and Evaluation: An International Journal on Theory and Practice, 7*(2–3), 185–221.

Hitchcock, C., & Stahl, S. (2003). Assistive technology, universal design, universal design for learning: Improved learning opportunities. *Journal of Special Education Technology, 18*(4), 45–52.

Lozada, M. (1996). Easy living: Universal design housing. *Vocational Education Journal, 71*(2), 18–21, 58.

Mace, R. (1988). Universal design: Housing for the life span of all people [Pamphlet]. Rockville, MD: U.S. Department of Housing and Urban Development.

McGuinness, K. (1997). Beyond the basics. *American School & University, 69*(11), 39–40, 42.

McGuire, J. M., Scott, S. S., & Shaw, S. F. (2003). Universal design for instruction: The paradigm, its principles and product for enhancing instructional access. *Journal on Postsecondary Education and Disability, 17*(1), 10–20.

Pisha, B., & Coyne, P. (2001). Smart from the start: The promise of universal design for learning. *Remedial and Special Education, 22*(4), 197–203.

Rose, D. H., & Meyer, A. (2002). *Teaching every student in the digital age: Universal design for learning.* Alexandria, VA: Association for Supervision and Curriculum Development.

Scott, S. S., Loewen, G., Funckes, C., & Kroeger, S. (2003). Implementing universal design in higher education: Moving beyond the built environment. *Journal on Postsecondary Education and Disability, 16*(2), 78–89.

Stahl, S. (2004). *Universal design for learning.* Unpublished manuscript.

DAVID SWEENEY
RONALD ZELLNER
Texas A&M University

See also Computers in Human Behavior; Computer Use With Students With Disabilities

UNIVERSAL NONVERBAL INTELLIGENCE TEST

The Universal Nonverbal Intelligence Test (UNIT; Bracken & McCallum, 1998) is an individually administered instrument designed for use with children and adolescents from 5-0 through 17-11 years of age. It is intended to provide a fair assessment of intelligence for those who have speech, language, or hearing impairments, different cultural or language backgrounds, those who are unable to communicate verbally, in addition to individuals with mental retardation, autism, giftedness, and learning disabilities.

The UNIT measures intelligence through six culture-reduced subtests that combine to form two Primary Scales (Reasoning [RQ] and Memory [MQ]), two Secondary Scales (Symbolic [SQ] and Nonsymbolic [NQ]), and a Full Scale [FSIQ]. Each of the subtests (Symbolic Memory, Cube Design, Spatial Memory, Analogic Reasoning, Object Memory, and Mazes) are conducted using eight reasonably universal hand and body gestures, demonstrations, scored items that do not permit examiner feedback, sample items, corrective responses, and transitional checkpoint items to explain the tasks to the examinee. The entire process is nonverbal but does require motor skills for manipulatives, paper and pencil, and pointing.

Three administrations are available for use depending on the reason for referral. These are an Abbreviated Battery containing two Subtest Scores (10 to 15 minutes), the Standard Battery containing four Subtest Scores (30 minutes), and the Extended Battery containing six Subtest Scores (45 minutes).

Standardized through a carefully generated stratified random sampling plan, the UNIT resulted in a sample that closely matched the United States population according to the 1995 census. Normative data were collected from a thorough nationwide sample of 2,100 children and adolescents, ranging from 5-0 through 17-11 years old. An additional 1,765 children and adolescents were added to the standardization sample to participate in the reliability, validity, and fairness studies. This gives a total of 3,865 participants across the variables of age, sex, race, Hispanic origin, region, community setting, classroom placement, special education services, and parental educational achievement.

Technical qualities appear to be quite strong. Reliabilities are high for both standardization and clinical samples. Validity studies show strong concurrent validity with many other measures of intelligence. The UNIT has also been acknowledged as a moderately good predictor of academic achievement. Discriminant validity evidence is cited, demonstrating that the UNIT differentiates between those with mental retardation, learning disabilities, speech-language impairments and those who are gifted. Some concern has been raised about the criterion related validity and the factor analysis for minority and clinical samples (Young & Assing, 2000) but overall this test is a theoretically and psychometrically sound measure of nonverbal intelligence.

REFERENCES

Athanasiou, M. S. (2000). Current nonverbal assessment instruments: A comparison of psychometric integrity and test fairness. *Journal of Psychoeducational Assessment, 18,* 211–229.

Bracken, B., & McCallum, R. (2009). Universal Nonverbal Intelligence Test (UNIT). *Practitioner's guide to assessing intelligence and achievement* (pp. 291–313). Hoboken, NJ: Wiley.

Bracken, B. A., & McCallum, R. S. (1998). *Universal nonverbal intelligence test, examiner's manual.* Itasca, IL: Riverside.

Caruso, J. C., & Witkiewitz, K. (2001). Memory and reasoning abilities assessed by the universal nonverbal intelligence test: A reliable component analysis (RCA) study; *Educational & Psychological Measurement, 61,* 5–22.

Drossman, E. R., & Maller, S. J. (2001). Core profiles of school-aged examinees in the national standardization sample of the Universal Nonverbal Intelligence Test. *School Psychology Review, 20,* 567–579.

Farrell, M. M., & Phelps, L. (2000). A comparison of the Leiter-R and the universal nonverbal intelligence test (UNIT) with children classified as language impaired. *Journal of Psychoeducational Assessment, 18,* 268–274.

Fives, C. J., & Flanagan, R. (2002). A review of the universal nonverbal intelligence test (UNIT): An advance for evaluating youngsters with diverse needs. *School Psychology International, 23,* 425–448.

Hooper, V., & Mee Bell, S. (2006). Concurrent validity of the universal nonverbal intelligence test and the Leiter international performance scale-revised. *Psychology in the Schools, 43*(2), 143–148.

Maller, S. J. (2000). Item invariance in four subtests of the universal nonverbal intelligence test across groups of deaf and hearing children. *Journal of Psychoeducational Assessment, 18,* 240–254.

Maller, S. J., & French B. F. (in press). UNIT factor invariance across deaf and standardization samples. *Educational and Psychological Measurement.*

McCallum, R., & Bracken, B. (2005). The Universal Nonverbal Intelligence Test: A multidimensional measure of intelligence. *Contemporary Intellectual Assessment: Theories, Tests, and Issues* (pp. 425–440). New York, NY: Guilford Press.

Pendley, J., Myers, C., & Brown, R. (2004). The universal nonverbal intelligence test with children with attention-deficit hyperactivity disorder. *Journal of Psychoeducational Assessment, 22*(2), 124–135.

Plake, B. S., & Impara, J. C. (Eds.). (2001). *The fourteenth mental measurements yearbook.* Lincoln, NE: Buros Institute of Mental Measurements.

Reed, M., & McCallum, R. (1995). Construct validity of the universal nonverbal intelligence test (UNIT). *Psychology in the Schools, 32*(4), 277–290.

Young, E. L., & Assing, R. (2000). Test review: The universal nonverbal intelligence test (*UNIT*). *Journal of Psychoeducational Assessment, 18,* 280–288.

RON DUMONT
Fairleigh Dickinson University

JOHN O. WILLIS
Rivier College

KATHLEEN VIEZEL
Fairleigh Dickinson University

JAMIE ZIBULSKY
Fairleigh Dickinson University
Fourth edition

URTICARIA PIGMENTOSA

Urticaria pigmentosa (UP) is the most common form of mastocytosis, which is a disorder characterized by mast cell proliferation (increases in cells that contain histamine and heparin) and accumulation within various organs, most commonly the skin. It is a disease that produces skin lesions, intense itching, and hive formation at the site of the lesion upon rubbing. UP is also known as systemic mastocytosis and mastocytoma.

The cause of UP is still unknown, but the suggested etiology is probably an allergy specific to the skin in susceptible individuals. Allergens may be infections such as bacterial, viral, fungal, or parasitic. Allergies to certain foods can trigger UP, such as nuts, shellfish and seafood, chocolate, and dairy products. Certain drugs, such as penicillin, sulfa drugs, and barbiturates, may cause this condition. In some individuals physical agents may trigger UP. For example, cold, local heat, or exercise can induce the disorder.

Between 0.1% and 0.8% of new patients visiting dermatology clinics have some form of mastocytosis. Most reported cases are Caucasian, and the disorder affects females and males equally. Most cases are found in children; 75% of cases occur during infancy and early childhood. There is a second peak of incidence in adults around 30 to 40 years.

Characteristics

1. Skin lesions usually appear before age 2, although this disorder can occur at any age.
2. Appearance of lesions may be tan to dark brown, and they are found more often on the trunk than on the face and extremities. The number of lesions can vary from 1 lesion to more than 1,000 lesions.
3. Welts or hives may form when lesions are rubbed or scratched.
4. In younger children, a blister may form over the lesion when it is rubbed.
5. Other symptoms less often associated with the UP form of mastocytosis are facial flushing, diarrhea, fast heart rate, headaches, and fainting (syncope).
6. In unusually severe cases, individuals may experience anaphylaxis, a severe reaction to stimuli such as insect bites and stings.

The prognosis for most patients with UP is excellent; therefore, treatment is conservative and aimed at symptom relief. It is suggested that patients avoid substances that induce mast cell mediator release such as crawfish, lobster, alcohol, spicy foods, hot beverages, and cheese. Patients should also avoid certain physical stimuli including emotional stress, temperature extremes, physical exertion, bacterial toxins, envenomation by insects to which the patient is allergic, and rubbing, scratching, or traumatizing the lesions.

Antihistamines may relieve some of the histamine-induced symptoms such as itching and flushing. Intralesional injections of small amounts of dilute corticosteroids may resolve skin lesions temporarily or indefinitely. However, this is only used in severe or persistent cases. Allergy testing may be indicated if the patient's history suggests an allergen-induced etiology.

Schoolchildren diagnosed with UP will not be eligible for special services under IDEA 1997 if they appear to be benefitting from general education. These students may be able to access educational modifications and accommodations through Section 504 of the 1974 Rehabilitation Act. School personnel should be made aware of the physical stimuli and triggering substances to avoid for this student. Additionally, school personnel should be educated about the signs and symptoms of anaphylaxis, especially for patients with severe symptoms. On average, the main problem encountered by students with UP is the extreme itchiness and possible self-consciousness about the lesions. Students need to be encouraged not to scratch the lesions, as they may form welts or hives, to use prescribed medication when necessary, and most important, to avoid certain foods and possible allergens.

The prognosis for UP depends on age of onset. Most cases exhibited before 2 years of age are associated with excellent prognosis. These cases are often resolved by puberty. The number of lesions diminishes by approximately 10% per year. If the onset of the disease is after 10 years of age, the condition may be persistent and associated with systemic disease. If this is the case, other organs may be affected (e.g., the liver, spleen, and cardiovascular system). UP as a systemic disease carries a higher risk of malignant transformation (e.g., mast cell leukemia). This outcome is rare in most cases of UP. The most common prognosis for UP is that it disappears by puberty. It is considered a self-limiting benign disease.

Although advances have been made in recent years in understanding the pathogenesis of Urticaria Pigmentosa, as yet no effective treatment has been found (Hartmann & Henz, 2001). It has long been speculated that early onset and later juvenile/adult onset UP may be based on different pathogenetic mechanisms. New genetic findings indicate that this may be so. Further research is now investigating these possible differences (Hartmann & Metcalfe, 2000). For more information contact Medlineplus Health Information, National Library of Medicine, 8600 Rockville Pike, Bethesda MD 20894; http://www.nlm.nih.gov/medlineplus/healthtopics.html.

REFERENCES

Hartmann, K., & Henz, B. M. (2001). Mastocytosis: Recent advances in defining the disease. *British Journal of Dermatology*, *144*(4), 682–695.

Hartmann, K., & Metcalfe, D. D. (2000). Pediatric mastocytosis. *Hematology/Oncology Clinics of North America*, *14*(3), 625–640.

RACHEL TOPLIS
University of Northern Colorado

USHER SYNDROME

Usher syndrome is a rare autosomal-recessive disorder manifested primarily by sensorineural hearing loss and retinitis pigmentosa. Although others described the syndrome earlier, it is named for Charles Usher, a British ophthalmologist who emphasized the role of heredity in the disorder (Usher, 1914). The degree of hearing loss in most affected individuals is severe to profound. Retinitis pigmentosa causes deterioration of the retina and progressive loss of vision, usually to blindness. Disturbances of balance occur with some types of Usher syndrome. Recent MRI evidence has indicated decreased brain and cerebellum size in a sample of Usher syndrome patients, suggesting a broader impact of the disorder than on the visual, auditory, and vestibular systems alone (Schaefer, Bodensteiner, Thompson, Kimberling, & Craft, 1998).

Usher syndrome is actually a group of conditions identified as three major types distinguished by age of onset and severity of symptoms. A fourth, X-linked type, is hypothesized. Although clinical symptoms present as three main types, gene localization studies have shown that one clinical type may be caused by any of several different genes located on different chromosomes. For example, seven different genes have been found that cause Usher syndrome Type 1 (Miner & Ciof, 2001).

Usher syndrome affects an estimated 3 to 10 per 100,000 people worldwide. It is the most common disorder that causes both hearing and vision loss, and it accounts for more than half of the estimated 16,000 cases of deaf-blind individuals in the United States. Usher syndrome Types 1 and 2 cause approximately 10% of all cases of profound deafness in children (National Organization for Rare Disorders [NORD], 2001).

Characteristics

Usher Syndrome Type 1

1. Profound deafness from birth; hearing aids usually not effective.
2. Severe balance problems.
3. Onset of retinitis pigmentosa in infancy or early childhood, progressing to blindness.

Usher Syndrome Type 2

1. Moderate to severe hearing loss from birth, especially for high frequencies.
2. Usually able to benefit from hearing aids.
3. Normal balance.
4. Onset of retinitis pigmentosa in late childhood to teenage years; legally blind by early adulthood.

Usher Syndrome Type 3

1. Normal hearing or mild hearing loss at birth.
2. Onset in teenage years of progressive hearing loss, progressing to deafness by late adulthood.
3. Mild balance disturbance.
4. Retinitis pigmentosa onset around puberty; night blindness often initial symptom, progressing to legally blind by midadulthood.

Source: Davenport, 2001; Department of Otolaryngology, Johns Hopkins University, 2001.

There is no known cure for Usher syndrome. Cochlear implants have shown significant benefits in young children (Young, Johnson, Mets, & Hain, 1995). A special form of vitamin A has been found to delay the progression of retinitis pigmentosa (NORD, 2001). Treatment of Usher syndrome primarily involves providing education and support services to optimize the functional ability of those affected by the condition. Prompt identification is important to allow initiation of treatment at the earliest opportunity.

Special education services are vital in helping individuals with Usher syndrome to cope with the often severe consequences of losing both vision and hearing. The progressive nature of the condition, coupled with onset in childhood, presents enormous challenges to successful adjustment. Treatment for the individual patient may include instruction in American Sign Language and tactile sign language; orientation and mobility training; braille education; psychological, genetic, and career counseling; assistive devices; and support groups. Opportunities for children with the disorder to interact with successful adult Usher syndrome patients can be especially helpful.

The prognosis in Usher syndrome is variable depending on type and severity. However, with appropriate intervention, Usher syndrome patients may be able to attend college or receive vocational training and work in a wide variety of occupations. Loss of vision may progress sufficiently slowly that some individuals retain functional vision well into adulthood. Research is continuing into the genetic mechanisms of the disorder, with the hope of finding methods of prevention and treatment. Improving cochlear implant technology and the possibility of retinal tissue transplants are also being studied.

REFERENCES

Davenport, S. L. H. (2001). *Usher syndrome*. Retrieved from http://www.boystown.org/btnrh/deafgene.reg/usher-sx.htm

Department of Otolaryngology, Johns Hopkins University. (2001). *What is Usher syndrome?* Retrieved from http://www.hopkins medicine.org/healthlibrary/conditions/adult/otolaryngology/us her_syndrome_85,P00474/

Miner, I., & Ciof, M. (2001). *Usher syndrome in the school setting*. Technical Assistance Center, Helen Keller National Center. Retrieved from http://nationaldb.org/library/page/2178

National Organization for Rare Disorders. (2001). *Usher syndrome*. Retrieved from http://www.rarediseases.org

Schaefer, G. B., Bodensteiner, J. B., Thompson, J. N. Jr., Kimberling, W. J., & Craft, J. M. (1998). Volumetric neuroimaging in Usher syndrome: Evidence of global involvement. *American Journal of Medical Genetics, 79*, 1–4.

Usher, C. H. (1914). On the inheritance of retinitis pigmentosa, with notes of cases. *Royal London Ophthalmic Hospital Reports, 19*, 130–138.

Young, N. M., Johnson, J. C., Mets, M. B., & Hain, T. C. (1995). Cochlear implants in young children with Usher's syndrome. *Clinical Annals of Otology, Rhinology, and Laryngology, 166*, 342–345.

DAVID R. STEINMAN
Austin Neurological Clinic Department of Psychology
University of Texas at Austin

See also Intelligence Testing

V

VAKT

VAKT is a multisensory method of instruction that uses visual, auditory, kinesthetic, and tactile senses to reinforce learning (Richek, List, & Lerner, 1983). Unlike most other teaching strategies, the VAKT method emphasizes the kinesthetic sensory input provided by tracing and the tactile sensory input provided through varying textures of stimuli. The VAKT method is based on the principle that some children learn best when redundant cues are provided through many sensory channels (Mercer & Mercer, 1985). During instruction, the student sees the stimulus, listens to the teacher pronounce the stimulus, and then traces the stimulus over some textured material (e.g., sandpaper, corduroy, Jell-O). Thorpe and Sommer-Border (1985) contend that the kinesthetic-tactile component increases students' attention to the task. Under VAKT instruction conditions, students are more likely to attend selectively to distinctive features of the target letters and words. In addition, they tend to persevere or stay on task for longer periods of time at higher rates of engagement.

Many variations in the types of sensory activities have been devised. Depending on the style of learning of individual students, emphasis may be on one sensory channel over another. Some students may need more involved sensory experiences. More potent stimulation may be provided by such activities as tracing stimuli in sand trays, cornmeal, or Jell-O. Other activities include tracing in air, tracing in air while blindfolded, and tracing over raised stimuli of varying textures. Since the activities used with the VAKT method are time consuming, it has been recommended they be used particularly in cases of severe learning deficits (Richek et al., 1983). However, VAKT activities can be used with milder deficits or even everyday learning.

Two instructional systems used for teaching word recognition that highlight the VAKT methodology are the Fernald method (Fernald, 1943) and the Gillingham method (Gillingham & Stillman, 1968). The Fernald method combines the VAKT methods with a whole-word, language experience approach; the Gillingham method combines VAKT with a synthetic phonics approach.

The Fernald method consists of four learning stages through which students must pass. Each stage has specific procedures for teaching word recognition. As the student passes through the sequential stages, instruction entails less use of the kinesthetic and tactile senses. Words are chosen by the student for study based on stories generated by the student and written down by the teacher. This language experience approach is used to maintain student interest. Stage one emphasizes tracing and writing from memory individual words selected by the student. The teacher writes down a selected word on a large card and pronounces it while writing. Next, the student traces over the word with one or two fingers while saying the word. Word tracing is repeated until the student believes that the word can be written accurately from memory. The student now writes the word without looking at it and pronounces it while writing. If the word is written correctly from memory, it is stored in a word bank. If the student cannot write the word, the tracing procedure is repeated (Richek et al., 1983).

Stage two learning is initiated when the teacher believes that the student no longer needs to trace words for learning. Instruction differs from stage one in two ways: The words are presented on smaller cards and tracing is eliminated. As in stage one, words are selected from student-generated stories. A selected word is printed on a card; the student looks at it and says the word. The student then attempts to write the word from memory (Richek et al., 1983).

During stage three, the student begins to read from textbooks. Students can read from any material that they desire. Words are selected from the text but are no longer written on cards. Instead, the student looks at the word in the text, says the word, then writes it down from memory (Richek et al., 1983).

Stage four is characterized by the student being able to read a word in context, say it, and remember it without having to write it. The student is taught to decode unknown words by associating them with known words or by using contextual cues. The student writes down for further review the words that he or she cannot figure out using these means (Richek et al., 1983).

The Gillingham method is a highly structured phonics approach that uses the VAKT methods to enhance learning. The method is based on the work of Orton (1937) dealing with the relationship between cerebral dominance and reading and language disorders. A series of associative processes are used to link the names and sounds of phonemes with their written symbols. Six fundamental associations are used in instruction: (1) visual-auditory (V-A), (2) auditory-visual (A-V), (3) auditory-kinesthetic (A-K), (4) kinesthetic-auditory (K-A), (5) visual-kinesthetic (V-K), and (6) kinesthetic-visual (K-V; Mercer & Mercer, 1985).

Instruction begins with the student learning letters and their sounds. Letter names are taught by the teacher showing the student a letter and saying the name (V-A). The student then repeats the letter name (A-K). The sounds of letters are taught next using the same procedures. The teacher prints the letter and explains its formation. The student then traces over the letter, copies the letter, and writes the letter from memory (A-K; K-A). The next stage involves reading words. The first set of words contains the vowels (V) a and i and consonants (C) b, g, h, j, k, n, p, and t. Sound blending is taught using letter patterns such as CVC, CVCe, and so on. After a basic set of words is learned, words are combined into simple sentences and stories from which the student reads. Instruction proceeds with extensive use of spelling and dictation exercises (Mercer & Mercer, 1985; Richek et al., 1983).

REFERENCES

Fernald, G. M. (1943). *Remedial techniques in basic school subjects.* New York, NY: McGraw-Hill.

Gillingham, A., & Stillman, B. (1968). *Remedial teaching for children with specific disability in reading, spelling, and penmanship.* Cambridge, MA: Educators Publishing Services.

Mercer, C. D., & Mercer, A. R. (1985). *Teaching students with learning problems* (2nd ed.). Columbus, OH: Merrill.

Orton, S. T. (1937). *Reading, writing, and speech problems in children.* New York, NY: Norton.

Richek, M. A., List, L. K., & Lerner, J. W. (1983). *Reading problems: Diagnosis and remediation.* Englewood Cliffs, NJ: Prentice Hall.

Thorpe, H. W., & Sommer-Border, K. (1985). The effect of multisensory instruction upon the on task behavior and word reading accuracy of learning disabled children. *Journal of Learning Disabilities, 18,* 279–286.

LAWRENCE J. O'SHEA
University of Florida

See also Fernald Method; Gillingham-Stillman Alphabetic Approach; Multisensory Instruction

VALETT DEVELOPMENTAL SURVEY OF BASIC LEARNING ABILITIES

The Valett Developmental Survey of Basic Learning Abilities was developed in 1966 by Robert E. Valett. The survey is designed to emphasize the use of psychoeducational diagnosis and evaluation to ascertain specific learning and behavioral problems in children ages 2 to 7 (Valett, 1967). A total of 53 learning behaviors that may appear in a deficit form have been grouped under seven major areas of learning as follows: motor integration and physical development (e.g., "Throw me the ball"); tactile discrimination (e.g., "Put your hand in the bag and find the spoon"); auditory discrimination (e.g., "Say, we are going to buy some candy for mother"); visual motor coordination (e.g., "Draw me a picture like this"); visual discrimination (e.g., "Show me one like this"); language development and verbal fluency (e.g., "What burns?"); and conceptual development (e.g., "Give me two pennies"). A graded range of one to four items for a particular age level constitutes a 233-task survey. Each of the seven major areas is operationally defined and arranged developmentally in ascending order of difficulty (Southworth, Burr, & Cox, 1980; Valett, 1967; Mann, 1972; Roger, 1972). The instrument, educational rationale for remedial programming, and remedial materials are presented in a loose-leaf workbook format that is number-keyed to the major areas and subtasks (Mann, 1972; Valett, 1966a, 1966b). Scoring is based on correct, incorrect, or partial development. The range of developmental levels and strengths and weaknesses are noted for the purpose of planning remedial programming (Southworth et al., 1980). Program suggestions that relate directly to the 53 learning behaviors are provided by Valett's (1968) *Psychological Resource Program.*

REFERENCES

Buros, O. K. (1972). *The seventh mental measurements yearbook.* Highland Park, NJ: Gryphon.

Johnson, S. K., & Marasky, R. L. (1980). *Learning disabilities* (2nd ed.). Boston, MA: Allyn & Bacon.

Mann, L. (1972). Review of the Valett Developmental Survey of Basic Learning Abilities. In O. Buros (Ed.), *The seventh mental measurements yearbook.* Highland Park, NJ: Gryphon.

Mitchell, J. V. (1983). *Tests in print III: An index to tests, test reviews and the literature on specific tests.* Lincoln: University of Nebraska Press.

Roger, R. A. (1972). Review of the Valett Developmental Survey of Basic Learning Abilities. In O. Buros (Ed.), *The seventh mental measurements yearbook.* Highland Park, NJ: Gryphon.

Southworth, L. E., Burr, R. L., & Cox, A. E. (1980). *Screening and evaluation in the young child: A handbook of instruments to use from infancy to six years.* Springfield, IL: Thomas.

Valett, R. E. (1966a). A psychoeducational profile of basic learning abilities. *Journal of School Psychology, 4,* 9–24.

Valett, R. E. (1966b). *The Valett Developmental Survey of Basic Learning Abilities.* Palo Alto, CA: Consulting Psychologist Press.

Valett, R. E. (1967). A developmental task approach to early childhood education. *Journal of School Psychology, 2,* 136–147.

Valett, R. E. (1968). *Psychological resource program*. Belmont, CA: Fearson.

FRANCES HARRINGTON
Radford University

See also Remedial Instruction

VALIDITY, TEST

Psychological and educational tests are used quite frequently in special education to help make important decisions regarding the educational and social programming of students. Scores on such tests may be used to help districts make predictions about performance on a statewide writing benchmark exam, help Student Study Teams decide if a child has serious depression that requires immediate treatment, or help administrators know if students will succeed in the workforce after graduation. The penultimate concept associated with these dimensions of testing is *validity*, which concerns the accuracy and soundness of specific *interpretations* of a test score. Fundamental to the issue of validity is the degree of empirical and theoretical support for making evaluative judgments about a person from the particular score(s) received on a test (Salvia & Ysseldyke, 2004); to wit, validity is not the property of a test but rather the *meaning* assigned to the test scores (Messick, 1995).

When special educators attempt to derive meaning about or make inferences from test scores, it should be based on (a) the balance of evidence supporting the meaning of the scores, (b) the relevance of the scores to the particular applied purpose and utility in the applied setting, (c) the credibility and value implications of score interpretation and implications for action, and (d) the evidence and arguments that make clear the functional value of testing, including its intended and unintended social consequences (Messick, 1980, 1989a, 1989b). Validity is an inductive summary of existing evidence for, and potential consequences of, score interpretation and use; although supporting evidence may come from numerous quantitative as well as qualitative sources, keep in mind that validity is a unitary concept (Messick, 1989a, 1989b) that is deeply embedded and fused within the system of science.

Measurement and Theory

Science seeks to predict and explain the world around us, and in so doing, it must engage in precise measurement and must have an explanatory framework or theory from which to attribute meaning to observed or latent variables. In order to weigh the truthfulness of those scientific explanations, scientists must start by *validating* their measurement systems and establishing rules for assigning numbers to attributes. Once measurement rules are laid down, different examiners, using the same procedures, will be more likely to arrive at the same score for a student. Formulating such procedures is critical to what is known as the *standardization* of an instrument. When instruments are standardized, the numbers assigned to attributes enables the user to report events in finer details instead of in vague generalities. Standardization, then, enables the user to communicate more clearly and opens the door for other scientists to verify or validate constructs as well. Although standardization is a key internal requirement for any measurement system to be considered useful, it is a procedural concept related to its reliability (Salvia & Ysseldyke, 2004).

It is one thing to establish the standardization and reliability of a measurement system, but the scores must also contribute to our understanding and appreciation of real-life phenomenon. High reliability does not necessarily guarantee that a test will be practical and meaningful. For example, if a score on a measure of social competence is indexed to nothing but itself, it has no meaning; for scores to be meaningful, they must be tied to other scores or variables existing within a larger network of data related to social competence. When there is a confirmatory relationship with other important dimensional variables then the validity of the instrument (or score) is established. This networked relationship among scores is at the heart of a theory, enabling scientists to explore and interpret the meaning of something.

Theory allows scientists to answer the question of "why" certain relationships exist among variables. When they unpack a theory, they will find a nomological network of constructs, hypotheses, and operational definitions or measures (Cronbach & Meehl, 1955). Constructs are related to other constructs by hypotheses. Hypotheses are the proposed interpretations of events. Constructs interconnected by one or more hypotheses provide the beginnings for a theory of the primary construct. Theories need to be translated into observable events or processes, made visible by operational definitions or measures. Once theories become more specified, they can then be tested by collecting data. When observed relationships correspond to the hypothesized relationships among the constructs, then one can be reasonably satisfied that the theory has gained utility for understanding the phenomena under study. Not only is utility gained, but so is an increased ability to infer that the operational definitions of the constructs were appropriate; that is, the measures used in this theory-building process actually represented or reflected the constructs they were designed to measure. Therefore, if a measure or test accurately captures the construct it was designed to, then *construct validity* is obtained. Tests and test validation flow through the scientific process of theory development and make convenient operational definitions of often invisible attributes of human behavior. For an excellent description of the scientific process of theory validation and constructing nomological networks, the reader is directed to the work of Gerald Patterson and colleagues from the Oregon Social Learning Center (Patterson & Bank, 1986; Patterson, Reid, & Dishion, 1992).

Types of Evidence for Validity

The preceding summary of scientific inquiry and theory development highlights the validation process whereby latent variables are given their validity. When researchers or evaluation entrepreneurs develop testing or assessment tools for public use, they must apply certain standards for ensuring their quality (American Psychological Association, American Educational Research Association, & National Council on Measurement in Education, 1999). Quality assurance can be demonstrated in several ways: by its (a) content validity, (b) criterion validity, and (c) construct validity. "Face" validity is often mentioned in assessment situations but is not an appropriate kind of validity evidence; suffice it to say that face validity is the degree to which a measure looks like it measures what it is supposed to, and it is related more to issues of social rapport or public acceptability as opposed to technical aspects of measurement (Nevo, 1985; Salvia & Ysseldyke, 2004). Measures of attention-deficit/hyperactivity disorder, for example, often have strong face validity.

Content validity deals with the appropriate degree to which test items, questions, or tasks represent the whole domain of knowledge or behaviors that constitute that trait. At its core, content validity is a sampling issue where a sample is drawn from a larger population or universe of potential items defining that trait or behavior (Gregory, 2004). Since one cannot sample all possible items, test developers hope to generalize or make inferences from the smaller to larger sample. Item sampling needs to be broad and representative before valid inferences of the construct can be made. Evidence for content validity usually comes from the subjective judgment of those designing the test or from experts who are familiar with the content area under validation and can rate the appropriateness of those items or tasks. The subjective, opinion-based portion then gives way to statistical procedures that help describe the internal homogeneity of the test's item structure, usually reported by coefficient alpha or Kuder-Richardson-Formula-20 correlational procedures. The test's item intercorrelations can then be factor analyzed to determine how many dimensions or traits are needed to explain test performance. That is, is there one general factor trait or several subfactors that best fit what the test is measuring? The process of content validation is the first step toward establishing construct validity because of how much time, consideration, and comprehensive defining goes into the construct underlying the test.

Criterion-related validity refers to whether the trait being measured by the test is related to some external behavior or measure of interest. In other words, can the measurement system predict a person's status or performance on some other criterion? For example, how well does a score on an IQ test predict future success in school as measured by grades, acceptance to college, or SAT scores? Two subtypes of criterion validity exist: (1) *predictive validity*, which examines the relationship between a score collected today and then on some future criterion score, and (2) *concurrent validity*, which examines the relationship between predictor and criterion variables collected at the same time. The primary difference between these two subtypes has to do with the timing of when predictor and criterion data are collected.

Generally speaking, criterion-related validity helps elaborate which direction and to what extent predictor and criterion variables might or might not reflect the same trait. For example, if one is evaluating an intelligence test that purportedly measures fluid and crystallized abilities, one would want a predictor variable such as a full-scale IQ to show a strong, positive relationship with criterion SAT scores. Conversely, one would not want or be particularly interested in establishing that the IQ also measures and predicts anxiety, since the construct of anxiety may not be part of the predicted underlying nomological network of one's theory of intelligence. However, if one did want to convince others that the anxiety trait is not being measured, then scores on the IQ test (the predictor) would hopefully be uncorrelated with other anxiety measures or behaviors (the criterion). Evidence for supporting criterion-related validity generally comes from mean score differences between/among groups or populations of interest, and/or from correlational data (Cronbach & Meehl, 1955). As mentioned earlier, criterion-related validity also requires demonstrating that test scores are uncorrelated with theoretically unrelated variables; that is, while one desires predictor-criterion test scores to converge and support one's theory/construct, zero or low and nonsignificant correlations between predictor-criterion variables also help support independence from other traits. If for some reason two seemingly unrelated traits do correlate, then one needs to detect if it is because the traits are being measured the same way (i.e., due to method variance) and not because the predictor and criterion variables actually measure the same trait. This complex process is known in the research literature as *convergent and discriminant validity* as validated by the *multitrait-multimethod matrix*. For a fuller discussion of this theoretical validation process, see Campbell and Fiske (1959).

Construct validity relates to whether the test or assessment system accurately measures the construct it was intended to measure. Construct validity is more than just about a correlation coefficient or saying that a test can now be used because it contains a certain *amount* of construct validity; rather, it rests on a program of research that continually seeks to gather a variety of evidence from abundant sources that lend support to a theory and its underlying nomological network of constructs, hypotheses, and operational definitions (Cronbach & Meehl, 1955; Gregory, 2004). Construct validity is regarded as the unifying concept that glues all types of validity together (Messick, 1995). Evidence such as test homogeneity, appropriate developmental changes consistent with theoretical predictions, group differences that are theory consistent, intervention effects that are theory consistent, correlations with other related and unrelated tests, logical and compelling arguments, and factor analysis of test scores are all potential evidence for supporting construct validity (Gregory, 2004; Messick, 1995).

Although all research scientists are in the business of validating constructs (i.e., construct validity), the name that is perhaps most associated with the concept is Samuel Messick (cf. Messick, 1980, 1989a, 1989b, 1995), whose writings cover the philosophy, values, ethics, social consequences, and actions of assessment. Whereas construct validity was once seen as a last resort for supporting a test (Barrett, 1992), Messick's work has moved it to the forefront, where it is now the foundational basis for all test validation because it involves doing good science in order to understand both predictor and criterion variables and their interaction. The notion of construct validity has had its fair share of critics, who describe it as a vapid utopian doctrine that is conceptually confusing and inherently difficult to translate into practical steps for research and application (Barrett, 1992; Gregory, 2004). Nevertheless, in this day and age of test proliferation and the focus on "cash validity" over good science, special educators need to be concerned about selecting measurement tools with solid construct validity because the potential social, legal, and political consequences of misusing such decision tools are enormous (Gregory, 2004; Messick, 1995). The current industry around marketing assessment tools to public education has made it all the more important for school districts to allocate as much time critically evaluating the validity of purchased assessment tools as they do evaluating students with those tools. Using poorly validated tests undermines the accuracy and soundness of test score interpretations and could potentially lead special educators away from making effective educational judgments for children. However, when special educators demand clear evidence of validity, it ultimately benefits the professional reputation of special education itself.

REFERENCES

American Psychological Association, American Educational Research Association, & National Council on Measurement in Education. (1999). *Standards for educational and psychological tests*. Washington, DC: AERA.

Barrett, G. V. (1992). Clarifying construct validity: Definitions, processes, and models. *Human Performance, 5*(1&2), 13–58.

Campbell, D. T., & Fiske, D. W. (1959). Convergent and discriminant validation by the multitrait-multimethod matrix. *Psychological Bulletin, 56*, 81–105.

Cronbach, L. J., & Meehl, P. E. (1955). Construct validity in psychological tests. *Psychological Bulletin, 52*, 281–302.

Gregory, R. J. (2004). *Psychological testing: History, principles, and applications* (4th ed.). Boston, MA: Allyn & Bacon.

Messick, S. (1980). Test validity and the ethics of assessment. *American Psychologist, 35*, 1012–1027.

Messick, S. (1989a). Meaning and values in test validation: The science and ethics of assessment. *Educational Researcher, 18*(2), 5–11.

Messick, S. (1989b). Validity. In R. L. Linn (Ed.), *Educational measurement* (3rd ed., pp. 12–103). New York, NY: Macmillan.

Messick, S. (1995). Validity of psychological assessment: Validation of inferences from persons' responses and performances as scientific inquiry into score meaning. *American Psychologist, 50*, 741–749.

Nevo, B. (1985). Face validity revisited. *Journal of Educational Measurement, 22*, 287–293.

Patterson, G. R., & Bank, L. (1986). Bootstrapping your way in the nomological thicket. *Behavioral Assessment, 8*, 49–73.

Patterson, G. R., Reid, J. B., & Dishion, T. J. (1992). *A social interactional approach, vol. 4: Antisocial boys*. Eugene, OR: Castalia Publishing.

Salvia, J., & Ysseldyke, J. E. (2004). *Assessment in special and inclusive education* (9th ed.). Boston, MA: Houghton Mifflin.

ROLLEN C. FOWLER
Eugene 4J School District,
Eugene, Oregon

See also Normal Curve Equivalent; Reliability

VALIUM

Valium (diazepam) may be used for the management of anxiety disorders or for the short-term relief of the symptoms of anxiety. Valium may be useful in the symptomatic relief of acute agitation, tremor, impending or acute delirium tremens, and hallucinosis. It also is used for the relief of skeletal muscle spasms or for spasticity caused by upper motor neuron disorders such as cerebral palsy; thus, it may be used for some children in special education classes. In some cases, it also may be used as an adjunct in status epilepticus and severe recurrent epileptic seizures. It has a central nervous system depressant effect and is thought to act on parts of the limbic system, the thalamus, and hypothalamus. Side effects may include drowsiness, fatigue, and ataxia, with less frequent reactions of confusion, depression, headache, hypoactivity, and slurred speech.

A brand name of Hoffman-LaRoche, Inc., Valium is available in tablets of 2, 5, and 10 mg and in 2 ml and 5 ml ampules for injection. Recommended dosages for children over 6 months of age is .04 to .2 mg/kg, not to exceed .6 mg/kg within an 8-hour period, with gradual increase of dosage as needed and tolerated. Oral administration to children should be at 0.12 to 0.8 mg/kg per 24 hours divided into 6- to 8-hour doses. Oral solution is 1 and 5 milligrams per ml in the injectable form, dosages of up to 5 mg for children under 5 years of age, and up to 10 mg for children over 5 years of age. The half-life varies from 20 to 80 hours.

Overdosage may produce somnolence, confusion, or coma, and withdrawal symptoms such as convulsions, cramps, and tremor may occur following abrupt discontinuance. The antidote for overdose is Romazicon. For the reversal of sedation .2 mg IV per 15 to 20 minutes is used with the maximum of 3 mg in one hour. Valium is contraindicated if patient is taking sodium oxybate.

Contraindications/Cautions: Acute angle glaucoma, alcohol intoxication, CNS depression, caution if psychosis, caution if impaired pulmonary function, caution if under 6 months old, impaired liver function, and in elderly patients.

REFERENCES

Epprocrates Rx Pro Version 7.50. (2006). Washington, DC: King Guide.

Physician's desk reference. (1984). Oradell, NJ: Medical Economics.

LAWRENCE C. HARTLAGE
Evans, Georgia
First edition

LOLETA LYNCH-GUSTAFSON
California State University,
San Bernardino
Third edition

See also Anxiety; Anxiety Disorders

VALPROIC ACID

Valproic acid is the recommended nonproprietary name for dipropylacetic acid. The common (proprietary) name for this drug is Depakene. Valproic acid is an anticonvulsant mood stabilizer. Anticonvulsant mood stabilizers are now frequently used in combination with antipsychotic drugs (APDs) in treating both schizophrenia and bipolar disorder (Ichikawa, Chung, Dai, & Meltzer, 2005). In the United States and Europe, the sodium salt of dipropylacetic acid

is used. In South America, the magnesium salt of dipropylacetic acid is also marketed. Valproic acid is effective in the treatment of absence seizures as well as epilepsy. It is considered of some use in the treatment of myoclonic seizures and in tonic-clonic seizures (Dreifuss, 1983). It is also used to treat certain forms of bipolar cyclothymia, and may be used with ADHD children who are unresponsive to or have problems with stimulant medication.

Side Effects: Weight gain, tremor, and transient hair loss are commonly reported. Importantly, valproic acid has minimal neurological adverse effects (sedation, ataxia, impairment of cognitive function) compared with other antiepileptic drugs, a finding that may be of particular relevance in many patients with epilepsy. The major side effects reported are drowsiness, gastrointestinal discomfort, and changes in appetite. The Committee on Drugs of the American Academy of Pediatrics lists valproic acid as having minimal effects on cognitive functioning. The most significant and rare side effect of valproic acid is hepatic failure.

REFERENCES

Dreifuss, F. E. (1983). How to use valproate. In P. L. Morselli, C. E. Pippenger, & J. K. Penry (Eds.), *Antiepileptic drug therapy in pediatrics* (pp. 219–227). New York, NY: Raven Press.

Ichikawa, J., Chung, Y., Dai, J., & Meltzer, H. (2005). Valproic acid potentiates both typical and atypical anti-psychotic-induced prefrontal cortical dopamine release. *Brain Research, 1052*(1), 56–62.

GRETA WILKENING
Children's Hospital
First edition

LOLETA LYNCH-GUSTAFSON
California State University,
San Bernardino
Third edition

See also Anticonvulsants; Depakene

VALUES CLARIFICATION

Values clarification, an approach to moral instruction used with students with disabilities and typically developing pupils, stems from the humanistic education movement of the 1960s. Students trained in values clarification are taught to investigate the facts pertinent to a moral issue and to examine their feelings in a systematic manner. Values clarification teaches students the process of obtaining values and encourages them to explore personally held values and examine how they affect their decision-making processes (Casteel & Stahl, 1975). Rather than defining values in terms of good or bad, students learn to see values as guiding principles that affect choices. Critics of this approach have argued that values cannot be taught from a relativist position and have questioned the appropriateness of using schools as settings for the teaching of values. As a result, values clarification started to lose its popularity as an educational force by the late 1970s (Brummer, 1984).

Raths, Harmin, and Simon (1978) outlined a seven-step process common to many values clarification curricula: (1) students are helped to examine and choose from alternative opinions; (2) they are assisted in weighing these alternatives in a thoughtful manner; (3) students are helped to see the value of making a free choice; (4) students are encouraged to prize their choices; (5) they are provided with an opportunity to publicly acclaim their chosen values; (6) students are encouraged to act on their choices; and (7) they are helped to establish behavior patterns that are consistent with their chosen values.

Students who are exposed to values-clarification training become better consumers of information by learning to ask appropriate questions. Junell (1979) states that students' involvement and identification are heightened when values are taught in the context of an emotionally charged environment. As they develop their ability to integrate factual content with emotional responses, the trained students come to understand how they assign meaning and values to problems.

Values-clarification activities might include rank ordering of preferential activities, sensitivity training, and listening skills development. Simulations are commonly employed to provide students with practice in values application. Social or philosophical dilemmas, based on real or hypothetical issues, are often presented as problems to be solved. Lockwood (1976) discusses the efficacy of using examples from other cultures when devising materials. The issues may be discussed in large or small groups, and students are encouraged to invoke their social decision-making skills in developing possible solutions.

Students receiving special education services are often faced with value decisions relating to their disabilities. For example, vocational programs for students with disabilities may rule out certain academic options. Adolescents with disabilities, limited in career opportunity, need to explore the implications of vocational choices. Values clarification can help these youngsters to pick appropriate career directions and to learn decision-making principles necessary for adequate socialization at the workplace (Miller & Schloss, 1982).

Some children with emotional disturbances or learning disabilities have been found to act without carefully considering the implications of their behaviors (Miller & Schloss, 1982). Values clarification provides a structure within which behaviorally disturbed children may find consistency. Thompson and Hudson (1982) found values clarification effective in reducing the maladaptive behavior of children with emotional disturbances. These children were also reported to be happier and less anxious.

Values clarification has also been used to help students in general education accept mainstreamed pupils with disabilities. Simpson (1980) trained students to examine the effects of social influence and group affinity and found that it eased the mainstreaming transition for both students with disabilities and typically developing students. Future research might focus on the long-range effects of values education on the attitudes of the general population toward individuals with disabilities.

REFERENCES

Brummer, J. J. (1984). Moralizing and value education. *Educational Forum, 48*(3), 263–276.

Casteel, J. D., & Stahl, R. J. (1975). *Value clarification in the classroom: A primer*. Santa Monica, CA: Goodyear.

Junell, J. S. (1979). *Matters of feeling: Values education reconsidered*. Bloomington, IN: Phi Delta Kappa Foundation.

Lockwood, A. L. (1976). *Values education and the study of other cultures*. Washington, DC: National Educational Association.

Miller, S. R., & Schloss, P. J. (1982). *Career-vocational education for handicapped youths*. Rockville, MD: Aspen Systems.

Raths, L. E., & Harmin, M., & Simon, S. B. (1978). *Values and teaching*. Columbus, OH: Merrill.

Simpson, R. L. (1980). Modifying the attitudes of regular class students toward the handicapped. *Focus on Exceptional Children, 13*(3), 1–11.

Thompson, D. G., & Hudson, G. R. (1982). Value clarification and behavioral group counseling with ninth grade boys in a residential school. *Journal of Counseling Psychology, 29,* 394–399.

GARY BERKOWITZ
Temple University

See also Conscience, Lack of in Individuals With Disabilities; Moral Reasoning

VAN DIJK, JAN (1937–   )

Jan van Dijk is world known for his work with rubella deaf-blind children. In 1958 he became a teacher of normal prelingual profoundly deaf children at the Institute for the Deaf, St. Michielsgestel, the Netherlands. His interest in the deaf-blind department led him to study at the Perkins Institute for the Blind, Watertown, Massachusetts, where he received the Inis Hall Award for his thesis. He continued his studies in education and special education at the Catholic University of Nijmegen and completed his doctoral program with the publication of *Rubella Handicapped Children* (1982), an extensive study of rubella children in Australia. Van Dijk continues his work at the institute as the director of the Deaf-Blind School and the Dyspraxic Deaf School. For his important contributions to the education of deaf-blind children, he received the Ann Sullivan Award in 1974. Van Dijk is currently with the Institute for the Deaf in St. Michielsgestel, Netherlands (van Dijk, Carlin, & Hewitt, 1991).

Educational programming begins with a differential diagnosis for each child, not only for appropriate placement within the nine schools at the institute, but also to determine the child's learning style. This diagnosis is accomplished through the clinical use of such instruments as the Test of Development of Eupraxia in Hands and Fingers in Young Children, Test for Finger Eupraxia for Intransitive Movements, Bergs-Lezine Test for Imitation of Simple Gestures, Rhythm Test of Hand and Mouth for Prelingually Deaf Preschool Children, Finger Block Test, Hiskey Nebraska Test for Learning Aptitude, Reynell-Zinkin Scales, Denver Developmental Screening Test, and an adaptation of the Rimland Diagnostic Checklist for Behavioral Disturbed Children (van Dijk, 1982).

The guiding principle of the method is that the child is in the central position. The teacher "follows" the child and "seizes," in a natural way, what the child is trying to express. In order to do this, a close attachment or bond must be developed between child and teacher so that the teacher can be sensitive to the slightest nuance of the child's expression. This guiding principle precludes the use of a teacher-developed curriculum. Rather, the curriculum develops from the child's interests and desires. As the environment responds, the child feels the sense of mastery or competency necessary to reach out into the world.

Because the deaf-blind child is deprived of the organizing senses of vision and hearing, the world appears chaotic and meaningless. Meaning is developed by ordering and structuring the child's day in place and time, and with people. At first, the activities are similar to those of normal mother-child activities. The teacher creates enjoyable situations that encourage the child to initiate activities. The child learns it is nice to do something together with someone else. Initially, he or she may need to be taken through the activities passively (resonance). Then the child begins to move together with the adult (coactive movement) until the activity is done successively rather than together (imitation).

As the child's day becomes ordered around activities of interest, ideas are formed. The child anticipates events and may express this anticipation through "signal behavior" or body language. As the teacher responds, the child realizes that these signals produce a positive reaction. They then form the child's idiosyncratic lexicon known and responded to by all adults associated with the child. Drawings and objects are also used to represent, or signal, activities (objects of reference). Gradually the drawings and objects become more and more abstract until the child is ready to use formal symbolic language systems.

The special quality of the van Dijk method is that language is not taught as a labeling process, but as a social interaction between two people having a conversation about objects, activities, and emotions of mutual interest. Results with this method may not be as immediate as with a stimulus-response program, for example. It may be several years before the child develops signal behavior. However, there is a possibility of reaching high levels of language performance. Although this method has been developed primarily for deaf children who have language potential based on a differential diagnosis, professionals working with the severely and profoundly disabled are seeing value in it for their populations as well (Sternberg, Battle, & Hill, 1980).

This entry has been informed by the sources listed below.

REFERENCES

Hammer, E. (1982). The development of language in the deaf-blind multihandicapped child: Progression of instructional methods. In D. Tweedie & E. Shroyer (Eds.), *The multihandicapped hearing impaired: Identification and instruction*. Washington, DC: Gallaudet College Press.

Sternberg, L., Battle, C., & Hill, J. (1980). Prelanguage communication programming for the severely and profoundly handicapped. *Teacher Education & Special Education, 3*, 224–233.

van Dijk, J. (1982). *Rubella handicapped children*. Lisse, The Netherlands: Swets & Zeitlinger.

van Dijk, J. (1986). An educational curriculum for deaf-blind multihandicapped persons. In D. Ellis (Ed.), *Sensory impairments in mentally handicapped people*. San Diego, CA: College Hill.

van Dijk, J., Carlin, R., & Hewitt, H. (1991). *Persons handicapped by rubella: Victors and victims—A follow-up study*. Amsterdam, The Netherlands: Swets & Zeitlinger.

van Uden, A. (1977). *A world of language for deaf children. Part I: Basic principles*. Lisse, The Netherlands: Swets & Zeitlinger.

Visser, T. (1985). A development program for deaf-blind children. *Talking Sense, 31*(3), 6–7.

PEARL E. TAIT
Florida State University

See also Rubella; Theory of Activity

VAN RIPER, CHARLES (1905–1991)

A native of Champion, Michigan, Charles Van Riper received both his BA in 1926 and MA in 1930 from the

University of Michigan, he received and his PhD in 1934 from the University of Iowa. His degrees were in speech pathology and psychology. He was a professor in the department of speech pathology and audiology of Western Michigan University. He also was the director of the Speech and Hearing Clinic at that university since 1936.

One of the premier authorities in the field of speech correction, Van Riper contributed to the theory and correction of stuttering and developed methods for understanding, evaluating, and altering speech behavior. In 1978 the sixth edition of his textbook *Speech Correction: Principles and Methods* was published.

Van Riper was concerned with involving the family in the therapy of any child with a speech problem. He believed that parents who know what they are doing are frequently better speech therapists than formally trained therapists. He began his book *Your Child's Speech Problems* (1961) with the statement that "once parents understand what the speech problem (of their child) is and what should be done, they can do great deeds" (p. xi).

A member of Phi Beta Kappa, Van Riper received the honors of the Association of the American Speech and Hearing Association. He has been included in *Leaders in Education*, *Who's Who in the South and Southwest*, and *American Men and Women of Science*.

REFERENCES

Van Riper, C. (1961). *Your child's speech problems*. New York, NY: Harper & Row.

Van Riper, C. (1978). *Speech correction: Principles and methods* (6th ed.). Englewood Cliffs, NJ: Prentice Hall.

E. Valerie Hewitt
Texas A&M University

See also Speech and Language Disabilities; Speech Disorders

VARICELLA SYNDROME, CONGENITAL

When a pregnant woman contracts chicken pox (varicella), there is a 25% incidence of transmission of the infection to the fetus. However, a very small number of these babies will show evidence at birth that they were ever infected. Their condition is called congenital varicella syndrome (CVS).

Varicella-zoster virus (VZV), the causative agent of chicken pox, has an intense affinity for rapidly developing human tissues. This proclivity explains why VZV fetal infection at certain gestational ages can have devastating consequences. The period of pregnancy between the 8th and 20th week correlates with brisk growth of the extremities and maturation of the eyes, brain, and spinal cord. These structures are most likely to show the effects of VZV infestation.

This disorder occurs in only about 2% of infants delivered to women who had varicella at 8 to 20 weeks of gestation. Only 1 to 2 in 10,000 pregnant women have chicken pox. Therefore, CVS is a very rare phenomenon.

Characteristics

1. Skin: Cicatrix (zigzag scarring patterns), decreased pigmentation
2. Eye: Cataracts, underdeveloped optic nerve, unequal pupil size, microphthalmia (small eyeball)
3. Brain: Microcephaly (small head secondary to deficient brain growth), hydrocephaly, brain calcifications, complete failure of the brain to develop
4. Spinal cord: Shortened, malformed extremities; motor and sensory losses; anal-urinary sphincter dysfunction

---

Because active fetal VZV infection resolves long before birth, treatment of CVS-affected newborns with antiviral medication (acyclovir) is neither helpful nor indicated. Pregnant women with severe cases of varicella may be given acyclovia. The effect of this practice on the fetus is unknown, and its safety has been challenged.

Varicella zoster immune globulin (VZIG), which contains high levels of antibodies against VZV, is often given to susceptible pregnant women who are exposed to chicken pox to prevent their developing varicella. The benefits to the fetus of this practice are uncertain.

Because of the microcephaly and hydrocephaly, children with CVS may exhibit a variety of difficulties including learning difficulties and developmental delays. The severity of the difficulties depends on the amount of brain damage incurred. Because the severity and type of brain injury vary from one child to another, it is difficult to determine the exact cognitive sequelae and long-term prognosis. Providing the parents with counseling and education will enable them to be advocates for their child's educational needs at an early age.

The prognosis for infants with CVS is largely dependent on gestational age at the time they acquired the infection. Infants affected from 16 to 20 weeks are most likely to have central and sensory nervous system damage, resulting in psychomotor retardation, seizure disorders, and blindness. Babies who are infected during the last few weeks of pregnancy generally have favorable outcomes.

The best strategy for eradicating CVS lies with the varicella vaccine (Varivax). Approved for use in the United States in 1995, this immunization is at least 90% to 95% effective in preventing infection when exposure to VZV occurs. The vaccine is given at 12 to 15 months of age. A booster dose is administered at 4 years of age. Ongoing studies demonstrate that this immunization scheme confers protection from VZV infection for at least two decades, with little evidence of waning immunity as vaccinated populations age.

REFERENCE

Myer, M. G., & Stanberry, L. R. (2000). Varicella-Zoster virus. In R. E. Behrman, R. M. Kleigman, & H. B. Jenson (Eds.), *Nelson's textbook of pediatrics* (16th ed., pp. 973–977). Philadelphia, PA: Saunders.

BARRY H. DAVISON
Ennis, Texas

JOAN W. MAYFIELD
Baylor Pediatric Specialty Services, Dallas, Texas

VARICELLA ZOSTER

Varicella zoster is the virus that causes chicken pox. It is a mild but highly contagious disease that is contracted by exposure to someone while in the infectious stage. It is characterized by aches and fever followed by a blister-like rash. The rash typically starts on the trunk and then spreads to other parts of the body and will break and crust over. Symptoms usually occur from 11 to 20 days after exposure to the virus (Taylor-Robinson & Caunt, 1972).

The contagious stage of varicella zoster is from 1 to 2 days before the rash appears to 5 days after it appears. Once the blisters have dried up, the contagious stage is complete.

Characteristics

1. Headache and body aches
2. Fever that persists 2 to 4 days
3. Nausea, vomiting, or loss of appetite
4. Irritability or malaise
5. Blister-like lesions appearing typically 4 to 5 days after other symptoms (the lesions cause itching and will dry up and crust over at the end of the illness)

The treatment of varicella zoster is predominantly symptomatic. Normal treatment consists of medications such as those typically used for treating cold or flu symptoms and the use of topical solutions, such as calamine lotion, to relieve itching. It is not normally a fatal disease, but it often has more serious effects on infants and adults. A varicella zoster immune globulin (VZIG) can be administered to prevent or lessen the severity of the disease if given within 96 hours of exposure to the virus.

This measure is usually reserved for high-risk patients such as those with a compromised immune system due to some other medical condition such as AIDS or leukemia or organ transplant patients. The varicella vaccine is currently available and should be administered between the ages of 12 and 18 months.

Varicella zoster is highly contagious, and those infected should be sheltered from others while in the infectious stage. School-age children should be excluded from school during this period. The prognosis for recovery in most children with a healthy immune system is good, and no special educational provisions or modifications are usually needed beyond the time of infection.

REFERENCE

Taylor-Robinson, D., & Caunt, A. E. (1972). Varicella virus. In *Virology monographs*. New York, NY: Springer-Verlag.

CAROL SCHMITT
San Diego Unified School District

VASCULITIS

Vasculitis is the inflammation of the blood vessels, which can result in damage to the vessels and is usually associated with an allergic reaction to a drug or another foreign substance. There are many different forms of vasculitis. The different forms are named according to the organ, vessels, or system affected or to the clinical pattern.

The occurrence of vasculitis in the United States is rare, and the incidence is unknown. Vasculitis occurs more often in the Caucasian population and equally in males and females. The cause of vasculitis is unknown in approximately 50% of the cases, and the remaining 50% have various causes including allergic reaction, various infections, food or food additives, and Hepatitis B and C. Vasculitis may occur at any age, but may be called Henoch-Schönlein purpura in children and acute hemorrhagic edema in infants. Henoch-Schönlein purpura is the most common form of childhood vasculitis and is the inflammation of small blood vessels.

Characteristics

1. Fever and weight loss, which may develop over weeks to months
2. Pain in the extremities
3. Headache
4. Red or purple spots that appear on the skin (petechial purpura)
5. Abdominal pain (which usually occurs about 30 minutes after eating)

---

6. Pain in the joints with the knees and the ankles being the most commonly affected

7. Blisters on the skin

8. Itching or burning of the skin

9. Involving vessels that supply blood to organs (i.e., heart, lungs, kidneys, skin, and bowel)

Treatment consists of high doses of corticosteroids to help control the fever and to heal the vascular lesions. Antibiotics are also used in the treatment of vasculitis, but care must be exercised to ensure that the antibiotic is not causing an allergic reaction.

Individuals with more involved cases of vasculitis might qualify for special education services under the Physical Disability category. Students with hypersensitivity vasculitis typically would not qualify for special education services, although counseling may be beneficial. The counseling would be beneficial if the student was singled out because of the skin lesions. Homebound services may be warranted in order to prevent exposure to unnecessary infection.

With treatment, the prognosis for this disorder is generally good, and allergic vasculitis usually resolves with time. If the vasculitis affects the major organs, there is a greater chance of mortality. If there is no treatment, the 5-year survival rate is about 20%.

This entry has been informed by the sources listed below.

REFERENCES

Magglini, S., & Francisci, G. (1990). *Dictionary of medical syndromes* (3rd ed.). Philadelphia, PA: Lippincott.

Tierney, L., McPhee, S., & Papadakis, M. (2000). *Lange current medical diagnosis and treatment* (3rd ed.). New York, NY: McGraw-Hill.

Wolff, K., & Winkelmann, R. (1980). *Vasculitis: Major problems in dermatology*. Philadelphia, PA: Saunders.

TAMMY BRANAN
University of Northern Colorado

VELO-CARDIO-FACIAL SYNDROME (SHPRINTZEN SYNDROME)

Velo-cardio-facial syndrome (VCFS) is considered to be among the most prevalent microdeletion syndromes (Pulver et al., 1994). It has a prevalence rate of 1 individual per 2,000 to 4,500 live births (Tézenas Du Montcel, Mendizabal, Aymé, Lévy, & Philip, 1996). Individuals with

VCFS are commonly described as having distinctive facial features, including a cleft palate, long face, and prominent nose; heart abnormalities; learning problems (Eliez & Feinstein, 2004; Murphy, Jones, Griffiths, Thompson, & Owen, 1998); mental retardation; hypernasal speech (Eliez & Feinstein); and an increased risk for a variety of mental illnesses, including bipolar disorder (Carlson et al., 1997) and schizophrenia (Pulver et al.).

The first published accounts of VCFS were by Sedláčková (1967), who reported finding many patients with facial abnormalities and hypernasal speech. VCFS started gaining the attention of the scientific community through the article by Shprintzen et al. (1978) reporting on the common characteristics found in 12 patients at the Center for Cranio-Facial Disorders (CCFD) of Montefiore Hospital and Medical Center (p. 56). VCFS received its name in this article.

The purpose of this article is to provide a brief overview of the current knowledge of VCFS. Discussion will begin with the physical and behavioral manifestations of VCFS. This will be followed by a discussion of its etiology, detection and assessment, and developmental course. Discussion will conclude by discussing interventions commonly used to treat VCFS.

Physical and Behavioral Manifestations of VCFS

Many physical and behavioral characteristics are associated with VCFS. Shprintzen (2000) listed over 185 clinical features of individuals diagnosed with VCFS. Although an exhaustive list of features is not feasible, this section will cover the most commonly cited traits. These traits will be grouped into seven categories: (1) physical features/medical impairments, (2) chromosomal abnormalities, (3) brain structure abnormalities, (4) cognitive impairments, (5) language difficulties, (6) motor impairments, and (7) behavioral/psychological impairments.

Eliez and Feinstein (2004) stated that over 100 physical abnormalities and medical conditions are linked to VCFS. Common physical characteristics include long a face, prominent nose, flattened cheeks, cleft secondary palate (Eliez & Feinstein), broad nasal bridge, overbite, mild fusion of the eyebrows, thick scalp hair, and narrow folds of the eyelids (Shprintzen et al., 1978). Other physical characteristics include below-average height with "slender hands and digits" (Eliez & Feinstein, p. 123). Medical conditions common to individuals with VCFS include hypothyroidism and cardiac abnormalities (Eliez & Feinstein).

Chromosomal abnormalities are generally present with VCFS. Most individuals with VCFS have a "*de novo* 3 Mb deletion at chromosome 22q11.2" (Eliez & Feinstein, 2004, p. 126). Edelmann et al. (1999) reported finding large variability in the location and deletion size. This deletion has been passed onto the children of VCFS individuals in some cases.

Several brain structure abnormalities are common in individuals with VCFS. These individuals commonly have 11% reductions in total brain volume (Eliez, Schmitt, White, & Reiss, 2000). This reduction usually consists of cerebral atrophy (E. W. C. Chow et al., 1999), with a reduction of both white and gray matter (Antshel, Kates, Roizen, Fremont, & Shprintzen, 2005; Eliez et al., 2001). Gray matter reductions are most prominent in the left hemisphere (Eliez, Schmitt, et al., 2000; Kates et al., 2001), including the left parietal lobe (Eliez, Schmitt, et al., 2000). Both temporal lobes have been found to have reduced volumes (Eliez et al., 2001). Eliez et al. (2001) found that temporal lobe volume appears to diminish with age among individuals with VCFS. Individuals with VCFS also have been found to have reduced hippocampus volumes compared to those without this disorder (Eliez et al., 2001). Individuals with VCFS have been found to have larger basal ganglia (Eliez, Barnea-Goraly, Schmitt, Liu, & Reiss, 2002), ventricles (E. W. C. Chow et al., 1999), Sylvian fissues (Bingham et al., 1997), and frontal lobes (Eliez, Schmitt, et al., 2000) than normal controls.

Several cognitive impairments are associated with VCFS. Henry et al. (2002) compared a sample of 19 adults with VCFS to a sample matched for gender, age, and IQ. They discovered deficits in planning, problem solving, visual perception, abstract thought, and social thought. Van Amelsvoort et al. (2004) found that individuals with VCFS and schizophrenia had "deficits in response inhibition, sustained attention and perceptual sensitivity" (p. 229) in comparison to participants without comorbid schizophrenia. Additionally, individuals with VCFS have been shown to have a higher prevalence of mental retardation (Eliez, Palacio-Espasa, et al., 2000; Feinstein, Eliez, Blasey, & Reiss, 2002) than those without VCFS.

A common finding among children with VCFS is a statistically significant performance over verbal IQ discrepancy (Moss et al., 1999; Swillen et al., 1999). This finding has been used as evidence of a nonverbal learning disability among many individuals with VCFS (Swillen et al., 1999). This trend, however, does not appear to hold true for individuals with comorbid schizophrenia (van Amelsvoort et al., 2004).

Individuals with VCFS commonly experience language difficulties at a greater rate than those without VCFS (Feinstein et al., 2002; Moss et al., 1999; Shprintzen et al., 1978). Individuals with VCFS typically exhibit delayed language acquisition and difficulties in social interactions (Eliez, Palacio-Espasa, et al., 2000). Eliez, Palacio-Espasa, et al. discovered that children with VCFS tend to display deficits in initiating interactions with others. These children also displayed deficits in symbolic play (Eliez, Palacio-Espasa, et al., 2000).

Several motor impairments are common to those with VCFS. Swillen et al. (1999) found that many children with VCFS displayed deficient psychomotor skills, which were more pronounced when asked to complete tasks requiring complex motor skills. Gross motor deficits were also found, with poorer performance in the left hand as opposed to the right.

Several behavioral and psychological impairments are associated with VCFS. Common behavioral problems include impulsivity, social withdrawal (Eliez, Palacio-Espasa, et al., 2000; Papolos et al., 1996), and attention problems (Eliez, Palacio-Espasa, et al.). Attention-deficit/hyperactivity disorder is commonly found among individuals diagnosed with VCFS (Papolos et al.). Impairments of thought and mood include anxiety, flat affect (Papolos et al.), high rates of obsessive-compulsive disorder, bipolar disorder (Papolos et al.), and schizophrenia (Murphy, Jones, & Owen, 1999).

Etiology of VCFS

VCFS is one of the few disorders with a relatively clear etiology; however, there is still a lot to be learned about the development of this disorder. VCFS is a congenital, dominant, autosomal condition (Eliez, Schmitt, et al., 2000). Scambler et al. (1992) discovered that the majority of patients with VCFS had a 22q11.2 chromosomal microdeletion. As a result, VCFS has more recently been termed 22q11.2 deletion syndrome (Scambler et al.). Because of this link, VCFS has been thought of as a prime disorder for studying the contribution of genetic factors to brain development across a lifespan (Eliez & Feinstein, 2004). The etiology of VCFS will be discussed in four categories: deletion, genes, enzymes, and brain structure.

Chromosomal microdeletion is thought to be a causal factor for VCFS. The genetic mutation thought to result in VCFS is linked to the 22nd chromosome. The q11.2 region of chromosome 22 is thought to be "one of the most mutable regions in the entire human genome" (Antshel et al., 2005, p. 8). The deletion occurs during gametogenesis (Edelmann et al., 1999). Then a subsequent rearrangement occurs during synapsis (Antshel et al.). A series of homologous "DNA low copy repeats (LCR)" (Antshel et al., p. 9) exist in the normal break points for the proximal and distal ends of the deletion. As a result of these homologous LCRs, these regions may misalign, causing a distal LCR of one chromatid to align with the proximal LCR of the other chromatid. Consequently, one copy ends up with two 22q11.2 segments, and the other has none. Antshel et al. stated, "this type of interchromosomal recombination event resulting in a loss of 22q11.2 in the resulting sperm or egg is by far the most common mechanism for the deletion" (p. 9).

Alternately, an interchromosomal rearrangement may occur in which there is a repetition of the proximal LCR. This causes the 22q11.2 region to loop over itself, effectively splicing out information contained between the breaking points (Antshel et al., 2005). Antshel et al. estimated that this phenomenon occurs in 10% or less of all cases. Both methods result in the loss of some genetic material due to the deletion. The discussion that follows will be on specific deleted or affected genes that may be related to the symptomology of VCFS.

Several genes are thought to contribute to VCFS. Yamagishi, Garg, Matsuoka, Thomas, and Srivastava (1999) discovered that the UFD1L gene plays a major role in the prenatal development of the brain, palate, heart, and frontonasal regions. Because of its existence on the 22q11.2 section, the absence of this gene may account for many of the abnormalities in these areas. Abnormalities in brain structure associated with VCFS may also be related to the ES2 and GSCL genes, which have been shown to be involved in the embryogenesis of mice brains (Gottlieb et al., 1997).

Saito et al. (2001) looked into the SNAP29 gene that maps onto the 22q11 chromosome. The SNAP29 gene is thought to inhibit transmission in the superior cervical ganglion regions (Li et al., 2000); therefore, it is a possible contributor to the psychopathology experienced in individuals with 22q11 deletions. Saito et al. found that all individuals with 22q11 deletions with either bipolar disorder or schizoaffective disorder had 3 Mb deletions (which included the SNAP29 gene). Only one case of VCFS with schizophrenia had a 1.5 Mb deletion. Thus, the size of the 22q11 deletion and the SNAP29 gene may be a determining factor in the development of psychopathology in individuals with VCFS.

Several enzymes contribute to the development of VCFS. Individuals diagnosed with VCFS have been found to be homozygous for the catechol-O-methyltransferase gene (COMT; Lachman et al., 1996); therefore, individuals with VCFS have the least COMT enzyme activity of any identifiable group of people. Because COMT is important for neurotransmitter function, individuals with VCFS have been prime participants for study of the genetic basis of psychopathology (Carlson et al., 1997). The association between COMT activity and psychopathology is still unclear, due to contradictory findings in the research literature (Eliez & Feinstein, 2004); therefore, the role of COMT in the etiology of various mental disorders requires further study.

Brain structure abnormalities are also thought to cause VCFS. Research into the effects of microdeletion on these disorders provides some evidence of a direct link between the deletion site and specific psychological symptoms. E. W. C. Chow et al. (1999) argued that the majority of the brain structure abnormalities in VCFS are similar to those reported in patients with schizophrenia. Bassett and Chow (1999, p. 887), for example, argued that "a 22qDS subtype could serve as a neurodevelopmental model for schizophrenia." Brain abnormalities found in adults with schizophrenia and VCFS include "T2 weighted white matter bright foci (BF), 90%; developmental midline anomalies, 45%; cerebral atrophy or ventricular enlargement, 54%; mild cerebellar atrophy, 36%; skull base abnormalities, 55%; and minor vascular abnormalities, 36%" (E. W. C. Chow

et al., 1999, p. 1436). The superior temporal gyrus abnormalities may be of particular interest in the study of schizophrenia because of its location at the auditory cortex (Pandya, 1995). Structural abnormalities in this part of the brain have been associated with reports of auditory hallucinations (Barta, Pearlson, Powers, Richards, & Tune, 1990).

Although some research shows a link between VCFS and a diagnosis of schizophrenia, other research questions if the link is direct, or if the strength of this link is misleading. Papolos et al. (1996) argued that most cases are better classified as bipolar disorder, with some cases fitting the criteria for schizoaffective disorder. Feinstein et al. (2002) argued that because of the high prevalence of psychopathology in other individuals with learning disabilities, mental retardation, or developmental language disorders, it is unclear whether the high rates of psychopathology in persons with VCFS are caused by these factors or directly from VCFS. In their prospective study of children and adolescents, Feinstein et al. (2002) compared differences in the rates of psychopathology between individuals with VCFS and individuals with developmental delays and mental retardation. They found no statistically significant differences between groups.

Detection and Assessment of VCFS

Because of the specific chromosomal deletion associated with VCFS, the presence of this disorder can be tested for at infancy (Eliez & Feinstein, 2004). One of the more common methods to determine the presence of VCFS is to look for the 22q11.2 deletion through the Fluorescent In Situ Hybridization (FISH) method (Eliez, Palacio-Espasa, et al., 2000). The FISH method has been termed "the gold standard for diagnosis of VCFS" (L. Y. Chow, Garcia-Barcelo, Wing, & Waye, 1999, p. 761). It should be noted that VCFS is just one of several phenotypes associated with 22q11 deletion syndrome.

Although the FISH method is accurate in diagnosing VCFS, it may be impractical to have every newborn undergo this scrutiny. A more practical course uses the FISH method to screen for VCFS in individuals with behavioral and physical manifestations associated with VCFS (Gothelf et al., 1999). Swillen et al. (1999) stated that speech problems and/or cardiac abnormalities typically spur professionals to look for a 22q11.2 deletion. Because of the widespread acceptance of the FISH method, some studies only include those diagnosed with this method, "to increase diagnostic certainty" (Feinstein et al., 2002, p. 313).

One way to detect VCFS is to notice developmental delay. Developmental delay is commonly associated with VCFS. Shprintzen (2000) argued that because the common facial features of individuals with VCFS are not markedly abnormal, and many of its manifestations are behavioral (not present at birth), many individuals are not diagnosed in childhood. Developmental delays have been noted to lead professionals to refer individuals for assessment for VCFS; however, developmental delays may be attributed to other health problems typical of those with VCFS, delaying the detection of VCFS (Antshel et al., 2005). Eliez, Palacio-Espasa, et al. (2000) suggest that because of the common developmental problems in language development and tendency for social withdrawal, children assessed for VCFS should also be evaluated for autism.

VCFS may be detected by observing that an individual has learning difficulties. Because of the prevalence of learning difficulties in individuals with VCFS, individuals with learning disabilities who have additional VCFS symptoms should be assessed for VCFS. At two hospitals for individuals with learning disabilities, Murphy et al. (1998) looked for patients with VCFS. They looked for individuals who also had a psychotic disorder, family history of a psychotic disorder, stereotypical facial malformations, or congenital heart disease. Out of 265 patients, they selected 74 for testing using these criteria. Of the 74 patients selected, 22 were found to have a 22q11 deletion.

A diagnosis of schizophrenia is another factor that could be used to detect VCFS. High numbers of individuals with VCFS develop schizophrenia. Some individuals with schizophrenia may have other symptoms that make them good candidates for VCFS screening. Karayiorgou et al. (1995) looked for the presence of a 22q11.2 deletion in a random sample of patients with schizophrenia. Out of that sample, they found two individuals with VCFS, representing a substantially higher prevalence than in the larger population. Gothelf et al. (1997) selected individuals with schizophrenia, palate abnormalities, and heart defects for assessment for microdeletions. Of the 20 patients with schizophrenia, they found 3 had VCFS. A similar study was conducted with 15 adults with schizophrenia who were selected for testing based on possessing two of the five qualifying criteria. Of these 15, 10 tested positive for VCFS (Bassett & Chow, 1999).

Developmental Course of VCFS

The developmental course of individuals with VCFS has been well documented. At birth, many infants with VCFS experience failure to thrive (74%), heart malformations (76%), and lower respiratory problems (65%; Shprintzen, 2000). Scherer, D'Antonio, and Kalbfleisch (1999) found that, as toddlers, developmental delays can be seen in individuals with a 22q11.2 deletion. They also stated that physical abnormalities, such as a cleft lip and palate, can also be seen at this age. Most toddlers with VCFS experience delays in receptive and expressive language, and mild delays in gross motor ability (Gerdes et al., 1999; Golding-Kushner, Weller, Shprintzen, 1985; Swillen et al., 1999). Eliez, Palacio-Espasa, et al. (2000, p. 112) studied four children with VCFS under the age of 5 and found "marked

delay in motor development, a delay in language acquisition, intellectual functioning in the mentally retarded to borderline range in three out of four subjects, and attention difficulties." They also found "deficits in initiating relationships and in symbolic play... [and] a trend toward interruption in their train of thought" (p. 112). Scherer et al. (1999) found that the IQs of toddler to preschool children with VCFS ranged from mild/moderate mentally retarded to near average range.

During middle childhood, children with VCFS experience marked improvements in some aspects of their development. They often improve in language, reading of words, spelling, and speech (Golding-Kushner et al., 1985); however, difficulties with language formulation, understanding verbal abstractions, higher-order comprehension (Golding-Kushner et al.), and vocabulary (Gerdes et al., 1999) tend to persist. Eliez and Feinstein (2004, p. 124) stated that "speech almost invariably remains hypernasal." In middle childhood, 94% of individuals with VCFS showed evidence of a learning disability or mental retardation (Cohen, Chow, Weksberg, & Bassett, 1999). In their review of literature, Eliez and Feinstein (2004) concluded that there was no prospective data on the developmental outcomes of individuals with VCFS into adulthood.

Individuals with VCFS are more likely to develop psychological impairments. The first psychological impairments associated with children known to have VCFS are separation or generalized anxiety (Shprintzen, 2000). Usiskin et al. (1999) reported that children with VCFS account for 6.4% of all cases of childhood-onset schizophrenia. Approximately 64% of children and adolescents have been found to meet the criteria for bipolar disorder (Papolos et al., 1996). This trend appears to only increase into adulthood. Shprintzen, Goldberg, Golding-Kushner, and Marion (1992) found that approximately 20–30% of individuals with VCFS over 16 years old also received a diagnosis of schizophrenia. Murphy et al. (1999) discovered that 30% of their sample of 50 adults with VCFS had a psychotic disorder.

Individuals with VCFS are more likely to develop brain structure abnormalities. Eliez and Feinstein (2004) stated that:

> A review of most of the available neuroimaging studies of children with VCFS would suggest that there is an early alteration of the parietal lobe and cerebellum, and that the decrease of temporal lobe gray matter and hippocampus can be observed only in adults. (p. 130)

Alterations of white matter are thought to "be due to delays in myelin development, disturbances in organization or density of axons within the cerebral cortex, or alterations in the cellular structure of white matter" (Antshel et al., 2005, p. 11). Glaser et al. (2002) argued that individuals with an inherited 22q11.2 microdeletion from their mothers have an accelerated loss in gray matter. This accelerated loss leads to significantly less overall gray matter volume and subsequent cognitive impairments (Glaser et al.). Because of the decrease in gray matter with age, Chow, Zipursky, Mikulis, and Bassett (2002, p. 212) stated that individuals with VCFS may follow "an abnormal or deteriorating neurodevelopmental course."

Interventions Used to Treat VCFS

Little is written on the treatment of individuals with VCFS; however, some guidelines can be drawn based on what is known about this disorder from the research literature. Compton (2004) suggested that individuals with high susceptibility for schizophrenia should be considered for preventative interventions. Gladston and Clarke (2005) suggested the use of clozapine to treat psychotic symptoms that may be a result of VCFS. Gothelf et al. (1999) discovered that a sample of individuals with VCFS who also had psychosis did not respond well to neuroleptic drugs; however, two of their patients showed a reduction of psychotic symptoms with clozapine. Based on these findings, they suggested the use of clozapine for other individuals with VCFS and psychosis. Because of the learning and speech difficulties associated with VCFS, those with this disorder may benefit from academic remediation services and speech therapy. Because of Golding-Kushner et al.'s (1985) findings that individuals with VCFS have difficulties with higher-order thinking, including the use of abstractions, these individuals may respond best to clear directions that use concrete examples.

VCFS is the most common microdeletion syndrome. This disorder has many physical and behavioral manifestations, including specific facial features, cardiac abnormalities, learning difficulties, and speech problems. VCFS is almost always caused by a 22q11.2 deletion. Because of the clear etiology of this disorder, VCFS has served as a model to understand other disorders, such as nonverbal learning disabilities and schizophrenia. VCFS can be detected through the FISH method, with priority in screening given to individuals with developmental delays, learning difficulties, or schizophrenia. Many studies have provided information on the developmental course of VCFS; however, few studies have given information on the effects of VCFS through adulthood. Because of the lack of research on treatment, more studies need to be conducted to disseminate knowledge of how to best help individuals with this disorder.

REFERENCES

Antshel, K. M., Kates, W. R., Roizen, N., Fremont, W., & Shprintzen, R. J. (2005). 22q11.2 deletion syndrome: Genetics, neuroanatomy and cognitive/behavioral features. *Child Neuropsychology, 11*, 5–19.

Barta, P. E., Pearlson, G. D., Powers, R. E., Richards, S. S., & Tune, L. E. (1990). Auditory hallucinations and smaller superior temporal gyral volume in schizophrenia. *American Journal of Psychiatry, 147*, 1457–1462.

Bassett, A. S., & Chow, E. W. C. (1999). 22q11 deletion syndrome: A genetic subtype of schizophrenia. *Biological Psychiatry, 46*, 882–891.

Bingham, P. M., Zimmerman, R. A., McDonald-McGinn, D., Driscoll, D., Emanuel, B. S., & Zackai, E. (1997). Enlarged Sylvian fissures in infants with interstitial deletion of chromosome 22q11. *American Journal of Medical Genetics (Neuropsychiatric Genetics), 74*, 538–543.

Carlson, C., Papolos, D., Pandita, R. K., Faedda, G. L., Veit, S., Goldberg, R.,... Morrow, B. (1997). Molecular analysis of velo-cardio-facial syndrome patients with psychiatric disorders. *American Journal of Human Genetics, 60*, 851–859.

Chow, E. W. C., Mikulis, D. J., Zipursky, R. B., Scutt, L. E., Weksberg, R., & Bassett, A. S. (1999). Qualitative MRI findings in adults with 22q11 deletion syndrome and schizophrenia. *Biological Psychiatry, 46*, 1436–1442.

Chow, E. W. C., Zipursky, R. B., Mikulis, D. J., & Bassett, A. S. (2002). Structural brain abnormalities in patients with schizophrenia and 22q11 deletion syndrome. *Biological Psychiatry, 51*, 208–215.

Chow, L. Y., Garcia-Barcelo, M., Wing, Y. K., & Waye, M. M. Y. (1999). Schizophrenia and hypocalcaemia: Variable phenotype of deletion at chromosome 22q11. *Australian and New Zealand Journal of Psychiatry, 33*, 760–762.

Cohen, E., Chow, E. W. C., Weksberg, R., & Bassett, A. S. (1999). Phenotype of adults with the 22q11 deletion syndrome: A review. *American Journal of Medical Genetics, 86*, 359–365.

Compton, M. T. (2004). Considering schizophrenia from a prevention perspective. *American Journal of Preventative Medicine, 26*, 178–185.

Edelmann, L., Pandita, R. K., Spiteri, E., Funke, B., Goldberg, R., Palanisamy, N.,... Morrow, B. E. (1999). A common molecular basis for rearrangement disorders on chromosome 22q11. *Human Molecular Genetics, 8*, 1157–1167.

Eliez, S., Barnea-Goraly, N., Schmitt, J. E., Liu, Y., & Reiss, A. L. (2002). Increased basal ganglia volumes in velo-cardio-facial syndrome (deletion 22q11.2). *Biological Psychiatry, 52*, 68–70.

Eliez, S., Blasely, C. M., Schmitt, E. J., White, C. D., Hu, D., & Reiss, A. L. (2001). Velocardiofacial syndrome: Are structural changes in the temporal and mesial temporal regions related to schizophrenia? *American Journal of Psychiatry, 158*, 447–453.

Eliez, S., & Feinstein, C. (2004). Velo-cardio-facial syndrome (deletion 22q11.2): A homogeneous neurodevelopmental model for schizophrenia. In M. S. Keshavan, J. L. Kennedy, & R. M. Murray (Eds.), *Neurodevelopment and schizophrenia* (pp. 121–137). New York, NY: Cambridge University Press.

Eliez, S., Palacio-Espasa, F., Spira, A., Lacroix, M., Pont, C., Luthi, F.,... Cramer, B. (2000). Young children with Velo-Cardio-Facial syndrome (CATCH-22). Psychological and language phenotypes. *European Child & Adolescent Psychology, 9*, 109–114.

Eliez, S., Schmitt, J. E., White, C. D., & Reiss, A. L. (2000). Children and adolescents with velocardiofacial syndrome: A volumetric MRI study. *American Journal of Psychiatry, 157*, 409–415.

Feinstein, C., Eliez, S., Blasey, C., & Reiss, A. L. (2002). Psychiatric disorders and behavioral problems in children with velocardiofacial syndrome: Usefulness as phenotypic indicators of schizophrenia risk. *Biological Psychiatry, 51,* 312–318.

Gerdes, M., Solot, C., Wang, P. P., Moss, E., LaRossa, D., Randall, P., ... Zackai, E. H. (1999). Cognitive and behavior profile of preschool children with chromosome 22q11.2 deletion. *American Journal of Medical Genetics, 85,* 127–133.

Gladston, S., & Clarke, D. J. (2005). Clozapine treatment of psychosis associated with velo-cardio-facial syndrome: Benefits and risks. *Journal of Intellectual Disability Research, 49,* 567–570.

Glaser, B., Mumme, D. L., Blasey, C., Morris, M. A., Dahoun, S. P., Antonarakis, S. E., ... Eliez, S. (2002). Language skills in children with velocardiofacial syndrome (deletion 22q11.2). *Journal of Pediatrics, 140,* 753–758.

Golding-Kushner, K. J., Weller, G., & Shprintzen, R. J. (1985). Velo-cardio-facial syndrome: Language and psychological profiles. *Journal of Craniofacial Genetics and Developmental Biology, 5,* 259–266.

Gothelf, D., Frisch, A., Munitz, H., Rockah, R., Aviram, A., Mozes, T., ... Frydman, M. (1997). Velocardiofacial manifestations and microdeletions in schizophrenic inpatients. *American Journal of Medical Genetics, 72,* 455–461.

Gothelf, D., Frisch, A., Munitz, H., Rockah, R., Laufer, N., Mozes, T., ... Frydman, M. (1999). Clinical characteristics of schizophrenia associated with velo-cardio-facial syndrome. *Schizophrenia Research, 35,* 105–112.

Gottlieb, S., Emanuel, B. S., Driscoll, D. A., Sellinger, B., Wang, Z., Roe, B., & Budarf, M. L. (1997). The DiGeorge syndrome minimal critical region contains a goosecoid-like (GSCL) homeobox gene that is expressed early in human development. *American Journal of Human Genetics, 60,* 1194–1201.

Henry, J. C., van Amelsvoort, T., Morris, R. G., Owen, M. J., Murphy, D. G. M., & Murphy, K. C. (2002). An investigation of the neuropsychological profile in adults with velo-cardio-facial-syndrome (VCFS). *Neuropsychologia, 40,* 471–478.

Karayiorgou, M., Morris, M. A., Morrow, B., Shprintzen, R. J., Goldberg, R., Borrow, J., ... Lasseter, V. K. (1995). Schizophrenia susceptibility associated with interstitial deletions of chromosome 22q11. *Proceedings of the National Academy of Sciences, USA, 92,* 7612–7616.

Kates, W. R., Burnette, C. P., Jabs, E. W., Rutberg, J., Murphy, A. M., Grados, M., ... Pearlson, G. D. (2001). Regional cortical white matter reductions in velocardiofacial syndrome: A volumetric MRI analysis. *Biological Psychiatry, 49,* 677–684.

Lachman, H. M., Morrow, B., Shprintzen, R., Veit, S., Parsia, S. S., Faedda, G., ... Papolos, D. F. (1996). Association of codon 108/158 catechol-O-methyltransferase gene polymorphism with the psychiatric manifestations of velo-cardio-facial syndrome. *American Journal of Medical Genetics (Neuropsychiatric Genetics), 67,* 468–472.

Li, T., Ball, D., Zhao, J., Murray, R. M., Liu, X., Sham, P. C., & Collier, D. A. (2000). Family-based linkage disequilibrium mapping using SNP marker haplotypes: Application to a potential locus for schizophrenia at chromosome 22q11. *Molecular Psychiatry, 5,* 77–84.

Moss, E. M., Batshaw, M. L., Solot, C. B., Gerdes, M., McDonald-McGinn, D. M., Driscoll, D. A., ... Wang, P. P. (1999). Psychoeducational profile of the 22q11.2 microdeletion: A complex pattern. *Journal of Pediatrics, 134,* 193–198.

Murphy, K. C., Jones, L. A., Owen, M. J. (1999). High rates of schizophrenia in adults with velo-cardio-facial syndrome. *Archives of General Psychiatry, 56,* 940–945.

Murphy, K. C., Jones, R. G., Griffiths, E., Thompson, P. W., & Owen, M. J. (1998). Chromosome 22q11 deletions: An under-recognized cause of idiopathic learning disability. *British Journal of Psychiatry, 172,* 180–183.

Pandya, D. N. (1995). Anatomy of the auditory cortex. *Revue Neurologique, 151,* 486–494.

Papolos, D. F., Faedda, G. L., Veit, S., Goldberg, R., Morrow, B., Kucherlapati, R., & Shprintzen, R. J. (1996). Bipolar spectrum disorders in patients diagnosed with velo-cardio-facial syndrome: Does a hemizygous deletion of chromosome 22q11 result in bipolar affective disorder? *American Journal of Psychiatry, 153,* 1541–1547.

Pulver, A. E., Karayiorgou, M., Wolyniec, P. S., Lasseter, V. K., Kasch, L., Nestadt, G., ... Childs, B. (1994). Sequential strategy to identify a susceptibility gene for schizophrenia: Report of potential linkage on chromosome 22q12–q13.1: Part 1. *American Journal of Medical Genetics (Neuropsychiatric Genetics), 54,* 36–43.

Saito, T., Guan, F., Papolos, D. F., Rajouria, N., Fann, C. S. J., & Lachman, H. M. (2001). Polymorphism in SNAP29 gene promoter region associated with schizophrenia. *Molecular Psychiatry, 6,* 193–201.

Scambler, P. J., Kelly, D., Lindsay, E., Williamson, R., Goldberg, R., Shprintzen, R., ... Burn, J. (1992). Velo-cardio-facial syndrome associated with chromosome 22 deletions encompassing the DiGeorge locus. *The Lancet, 339,* 1138–1139.

Scherer, N. J., D'Antonio, L. L., & Kalbfleisch, J. H. (1999). Early speech and language development in children with velocardiofacial syndrome. *American Journal of Medical Genetics (Neuropsychiatric Genetics), 88,* 714–723.

Sedláčková, E. (1967). The syndrome of the congenitally shortened velum: The dual innervation of the soft palate. *Folia Phoniatrica, 19,* 441–450.

Shprintzen, R. J. (2000). Velo-cardio-facial syndrome: A distinctive behavioral phenotype. *Mental Retardation and Developmental Disabilities, 6,* 142–147.

Shprintzen, R. J., Goldberg, R., Golding-Kushner, K. J., & Marion, R. W. (1992). Late-onset psychosis in the velo-cardio-facial syndrome. *American Journal of Medical Genetics, 42,* 141–142.

Shprintzen, R. J., Goldberg, R. B., Lewin, M. L., Sidoti, E. J., Berkman, M. D., Argamaso, R. V., & Young, D. (1978). A new syndrome involving cleft palate, cardiac anomalies, typical facies, and learning disabilities: Velo-Cardio-Facial Syndrome. *Cleft Palate Journal, 15,* 56–62.

Swillen, A., Vandeputte, L., Cracco, J., Maes, B., Ghesquière, P., Devriendt, K., & Fryns, J. P. (1999). Neuropsychological, learning and psychosocial profile of primary school aged children with the velo-cardio-facial syndrome (22q11 deletion): Evidence for a nonverbal learning disability? *Child Neuropsychology, 5,* 230–241.

Tézenas Du Montcel, S., Mendizabal, H., Aymé, S., Lévy, A., & Philip, N. (1996). Prevalence of 22q11 microdeletion. *Journal of Medical Genetics, 33*, 719.

Usiskin, S. I., Nicholson, R., Krasnewich, D. M., Yah, W., Lenane, M., Wudarsky, M.,... Rapoport, J. L. (1999). Velocardiofacial syndrome in childhood-onset schizophrenia. *Journal of the American Academy of Child & Adolescent Psychiatry, 38*, 1536–1543.

van Amelsvoort, T., Henry, J., Morris, R., Owen, M., Linszen, D., Murphy, K., & Murphy, D. (2004). Cognitive deficits associated with schizophrenia in velo-cardio-facial syndrome. *Schizophrenia Research, 70*, 223–232.

Yamagishi, H., Garg, V., Matsuoka, R., Thomas, T., & Srivastava, D. (1999). A molecular pathway revealing a genetic basis for human cardiac and craniofacial defects. *Science, 283*, 1158–1161.

Gordon D. Lamb
Texas A&M University

VELOPHARYNGEAL INADEQUACY

Velopharyngeal inadequacy (VPI) is an inclusive term that refers to deficiencies in structure or function of the velopharyngeal mechanism. Such deficiencies result in loss of control of nasal resonance in speech. This can significantly affect intelligibility and may also cause swallowing dysfunction. The velopharyngeal mechanism includes the velum (soft palate) and posterior and lateral walls of the uppermost portion of the pharynx. The role of the velopharyngeal mechanism is to perform a sphincter-like maneuver that can disconnect the upper airway (nasopharynx and nasal cavities) from the vocal tract by forming a tight seal. The sphincter can also relax to allow the free flow of air or sound into the nasal area. This action produces the differentiation of oral speech sounds such as the vowels and most consonants from nasal sounds such as *n, m*, and -*ing* in English. Another commonly used generic term is velopharyngeal dysfunction (VPD).

One problem area subsumed under VPI is anatomical structure anomalies, termed velopharyngeal insufficiency. In this case, there may be a lack of tissue in the velum, which means it is too small to make contact with the posterior pharyngeal wall, thus compromising the seal necessary for disconnecting the nasal area. Another structural problem may involve interference from or loss of tonsilar tissue. Large palatine tonsils can obstruct the movements of the velum or lateral pharyngeal walls. In addition, pharyngeal tonsils (adenoids) can temporarily reduce the distance to be covered by velar elevation and their disappearance, due to surgery or maturation, may reveal a latent velar insufficiency. Finally, oral surgery

techniques used to correct craniofacial deficiencies (e.g., maxillary advancement) may increase the diameter of the velopharyngeal portal beyond the capability of the existing velopharyngeal mechanism.

VPI also encompasses the term velopharyngeal incompetence. This term describes physiological dysfunction affecting movement of the velum or pharyngeal walls. The muscle fibers in these structures can be misdirected so that appropriate movement, such as medial motion in the lateral pharyngeal walls or elevation of the velum, is impossible. Muscle pairs may be asymmetric or asynchronous in their contraction response. Nervous supply to the muscles may be deficit, resulting in paralysis or paresis (weakness).

Velopharyngeal inadequacy can also describe the mislearning of the nasal/oral balance of specific speech sounds that occurs in the presence of hearing impairment and deafness. In addition, idiosyncratic phonological development or dialectical differences can also produce nonstandard nasal resonance patterns during speech.

Differential diagnosis of this condition involves perceptual and acoustic analysis of speech, examination of oral motor structures and functions, and visualization of the velopharyngeal mechanism using videofluoroscopy and/or endoscopy. VPI can be reduced or corrected with surgical or behavioral intervention. Determination of the best treatment options for an individual can best be made by consulting a Cleft Palate Team that includes surgical and speech-language pathology professionals.

This entry has been informed by the sources listed below.

REFERENCES

Johnson, A. F., & Jacobson, B. H. (Eds.). (1998). *Medical speech-language pathology: A practitioner's guide*. New York, NY: Thieme.

Shprintzen, R. J., & Bardach, J. (1995). *Cleft palate speech management: A multidisciplinary approach*. St. Louis, MO: Mosby.

Staff

VENEZUELA, SPECIAL EDUCATION IN

Venezuela's 25 million inhabitants, 60% of whom are younger than 29, mostly live in urban settings located in the densely populated northern coastal region. Despite its rich natural and economic resources, poverty among its people continues to increase. In 2003, 61% of its population was considered to be impoverished. In 2001, 907,694 Venezuelans, 3.7% of its population, had special educational needs, according to the last National Census data (Instituto Nacional de Estadística, 2003). In 2011 a new Census is being held which will report more current data.

Special education began in 1930 as a private philanthropic initiative. In the 1950s a medical model was employed that focused on deficiencies and provided rehabilitation services. In 1973, the Department of Exceptionality within the Education Ministry was founded. In 1975 the Special Education Office was created to assume responsibility for designing, supervising, evaluating, controlling and providing follow-up services consistent with national policy. Each of the country's 23 states has its own Department of Special Education responsible for implementing national policies. In turn local schools and agencies are responsible for implementing state policies.

In 1994, a political reorientation process began, one designed to promote the principle of equality of educational conditions and opportunities for all and to promote a comprehensive educational model for people with special needs in light of their individual needs (Cumbre Mundial de la Infancia 1990). In 1999, this process was incorporated within the National Constitution (Artículo 81, Constitución de la República Bolivariana de Venezuela, 1999) and later in 2007 by a law for individuals with discapacities (disabilities). This law is a national frame of reference and its goal is to guarantee the critical development of people with incapacities according to their capabilities and with regards to their social, family, employment, and educative integration. A national council for people with incapacities was recently created in order to guarantee the application of the law, not only for Venezuelans, but also for aliens that live in Venezuela.

Special education in Venezuela is a branch of the country's educational system (Ley Orgánica de Educación, 1980) that is guided by the principles and purposes that govern regular education while maintaining an interdependent relationship with regular education.

Special education is organized by age groups: ages 0 through 5, 6 through 15, and above 15 (Acuerdo de Santiago, 1996; Ministerio de Educación, Cultura y Deportes, 2003). In 2004 it was incorporated to higher education through a policy that refers to access, permanency, and school performance of the PcD by the Popular Power Ministry for Higher Education (PPMHE) establishing clear guidelines toward the removal of boundaries, the establishment of responsibilities in higher education, and the creation of opportunities and conditions to favor the access of this population to equal education. This is an ongoing process both in public and private universities.

Since 1997, the Educational Comprehensive Attention model has guided special education services. The needs of people with special educational needs are reviewed using a holistic model that considers an individual's strengths and weaknesses in light of biological, psychological, and social qualities. Interdisciplinary professional teams are responsible for providing special programs for persons from conception through adulthood. Strategic special-education policies are the provision of comprehensive educational attention (in schools and special education services) and the promotion of educational mainstreaming of children with special needs within the regular education system and other branches of the education system.

Attempts are made to serve persons who are classified as displaying intellectual disabilities (through institutes of special education), hearing and visual deficiencies (through special education units), physical impairments (through rehabilitation and hospital units), learning disabilities (through learning disabilities centers, psycho-educational units, and integrated classrooms), and autism (through centers for persons with autism) (Universidad Pedagógica Experimental Libertador, 1998; Ministerio de Educación, Cultura y Deportes, 2001). Various support programs exist, including prevention and early identification (through centers of child development), language (through centers for language rehabilitation), education and work (through labor educational workshops), and social integration (through of social integration programs in regular schools).

Conditions in Venezuela have prevented the attainment of its special education goals. Some examples follow. Mainstreaming and integration have not been widely implemented. Few people with special education needs are served. For example, during the 2002–2003 school year, 11% of the population with special education needs received services (101,577 out of 907,694): 0.09% of those presented with autism ($n = 888$), 0.48% with hearing deficiencies ($n = 4,432$), 0.17% with visual deficiencies ($n = 1,587$), 6.72% with learning disabilities ($n = 61,060$), 0.14% with physical impairments ($n = 1,322$), 0.12% with cerebral palsy ($n = 1,111$), 1.89% with mental retardation ($n = 17,190$), 0.33% with language disorders ($n = 2,999$), 0.03% who are talented and gifted ($n = 329$), and 1.09% considered to be at risk ($n = 9,969$) (Ministerio de Educación 2004, Memoria y Cuenta, 2002–2003). Little is known about the quality of special education services and there is a lack of reliable information to update this data. Efforts are needed to coordinate regular and special-education curriculum. Undergraduate teacher-education programs need to focus on preparing special educators (Duran & Montenegro, 2000), and other training programs are needed to prepare human-resource personnel (Moreno, 2003). Efforts to obtain a stronger commitment from society to implement prevention programs and to enable families, schools, and the community to access needed services are needed.

Venezuela is making some progress in its efforts to improve special education resources. Some examples follow. The importance of special education is receiving more public attention and support. There seems to be a growing recognition as to the importance of adapting a holistic bio-psycho-social vision of each person that considers his or her strengths and limitations (Article 81, Constitución de la

República Bolivariana de Venezuela, 1999; Article 22, Ley Orgánica para la Protección del Niño y del Adolescente, 2000). During the 1998 Social Development Summit held in Lima Peru, Venezuela reported having accomplished its beginning goals of promoting integrated education (Oficina Central de Coordinación y Planificación—Cordiplan, 1998) albeit with limited national coverage. Venezuela has participated in international summits and meetings that addressed equal opportunities and respect for diversity.

Some research projects have begun in an attempt to promote integrative, sequential, and interdisciplinary policies (León, 2003) and to collect academic research that contributes with this important theme in Venezuela (Aramayo, 2010). These projects also may help promote social integration and social and personal accomplishments in accord with the potential of each child, adolescent or adult with special educational needs. There is growing support for eliminating the duality between regular and special education national programs.

REFERENCES

Acuerdo de Santiago (1996) *Seguimiento de las metas de la infancia*. Santiago de Chile. UNICEF.

Aramayo, M. (2010). *Diversidad en la fiscapacidad*. Caracas, Venezuela: Publicaciones Universidad Monteavila.

Campagnaro, S. (1999) La integración o inclusión. Nueva modalidad educativa para eliminar el dualismo entre educación especial y educación regular. *Cuaderno de Educación* Vol. 2. 119 a 125: Caracas, Venezuela: Publicaciones UCAB.

Constitución de la República de Bolivariana de Venezuela (1999).

Duran, M.. Montenegro, L. (2000) El docente venezolano de aula regular de cara al nuevo milenio y su formación en el área de educación especial. En Ty Shea, & A. Bauer, *Educación Especial-un enfoque ecológico*. Mexico City, Mexico: McGraw-Hill.

Instituto Nacional de Estadística (INE, 2003). *Censo 2001*. Caracas, Venezuela.

Ley Orgánica de Educación (1980). Gaceta Oficial de la República de Venezuela No. 2.635. Julio 9.

Ley Orgánica para la Protección del Niño y del Adolescente (2000). Gaceta Oficial de la República Bolivariana de Venezuela No. 5.266. Octubre 2.

Ley para Personas con Discapacidad (2007). Gaceta Oficial de la República Bolivariana de Venezuela con el número 38.598, Enero 5.

León, C. (2003), *Estudio descriptivo comparativo y relacional del Desarrollo Infantil Integral en una muestra de niñas y niños de diferentes edades, niveles socioeconómicos y regiones del país*. Trabajo Doctoral No Publicado. Universidad Católica Andrés Bello. Caracas, Venezuela.

Ministerio de Educación (1997) *Jornadas de Reorientación Político Conceptual de la Modalidad de Educación Especial*. Caracas, Noviembre.

Ministerio de Educación, Cultura y Deportes (2001) *Guía técnica y pedagógica de la modalidad educación especial para el curso 2001-2002*. Dirección de Educación Especial.

Ministerio de Educación, Cultura y Deportes (2003). *El Currículum de las Personas con Necesidades Educativas Especiales*. Presentado en la Jornada de Trabajo para la organización de la discusión curricular del año escolar 2002-2003.

Ministerio de Educación, Cultura y Deportes (2004). *Memoria y Cuenta 2003*. V. CXXVIII-N°CXXIV. Caracas, Venezuela.

Ministerio del Poder Popular para la Educación Superior (MPPES) (2007) *Lineamientos sobre el Pleno Ejercicio del Derecho de las PcD a una Educación Superior de Calidad*. Gaceta Oficial Número 38731 del 23 de julio.

Moreno, Marianela (2003). *Informe de Investigación sobre Personal en Servicio de la Modalidad de Educación Especial* entregado en la Dirección de Educación Especial del Ministerio de Educación, Cultura y Deportes. Caracas, noviembre.

Nuñez, Beatriz (1999) *Conceptualización y Política de la Modalidad de Educación Especial en Venezuela. Dirección de Educación Especial*, Ministerio de Educación, Trabajo presentado en el Simposio Los Paradigmas que orientan las políticas de Educación Especial en el III Congreso Iberoamericano de Educación Especial, Foz de Iguazú (Brasil, Noviembre).

Oficina Central de Coordinación y Planificación—Cordiplan (1998). República de Venezuela: *Informe País para la Cumbre Mundial de Desarrollo Social de Lima* (Perú).

Ordenanza para la educación, el desarrollo e integración de personas con discapacidad. Gaceta Municipal. República Bolivariana de Venezuela. Estado Miranda. Municipio Baruta. 2 de Octubre de 2001.

Reglamento de la Ley Orgánica de Educación, Gaceta Oficial de la Republica Bolivariana de Venezuela N° 36.787. 15 de Septiembre de 1999.

Universidad Pedagógica Experimental Libertador (UPEL, 1998). *Conceptualización y política de la atención educativa de las personas con necesidades especiales*. Serie Publicaciones Interinstitucionales, Caracas. Fundación UPEL-IMPM. UPEL.

UNESCO (1999). *Informe Final III Reunión Regional de Directores de Educación Especial, I Reunión Regional de los Consejos Nacionales de Discapacidad. Foz de Iguazú* (Brasil), 2 al 4 de Noviembre 1999.

CARMEN LEÓN
MARIANELA MORENO
LOURDES MONTENEGRO
Andrés Bello Catholic University,
Caracas, Venezuela
Fourth edition

VENTRICULAR SEPTAL DEFECTS

Ventricular septal defects are heart defects that are present at birth. The lower two chambers of the heart (known as ventricles) are separated by the ventricular septum. Ventricular septal defects can occur in any portion of the ventricular septum. Blood returning from the lungs to the left ventricle flows to the right ventricle through the hole instead of being pumped into the aorta. The size and location of the defect determine the severity of the symptoms. This condition may be associated with other congenital heart defects or syndromes (e.g., Down syndrome). Ventricular septal defects may also be known as congenital ventricular defects and VSD. The exact cause of ventricular septal defects is not fully understood.

In the United States, the ventricular septal defect is the most common congenital heart defect in the first three decades of life. For every 1,000 live-born full-term infants, the incidence rate is 1.5 to 3.5. In premature infants, the incidence rate increases to 4.5 to 7.0 cases for every 1,000 live-born infants. Ventricular septal defect affects both male and female infants but is slightly more common in females than in males. Defects in the muscular portion of the ventricular septum are found in all ethnic groups; however, defects in the subpulmonary position are more common in the Asian population.

Characteristics

This condition is present at birth. It is most often diagnosed during a routine examination.

Symptoms include:

1. Shortness of breath
2. Paleness
3. Rapid breathing
4. Increased heart rate
5. Frequent respiratory infections

Complications include:

1. Congestive heart failure
2. Infective endocarditis (infection of the heart walls or valves)
3. Aortic insufficiency
4. Arrhythmias
5. Failure to thrive (in infancy) and delayed growth and development

---

In many children, the opening is very small and produces no symptoms. These children do not have any physical or mental limitations that prevent them from being fully active. Many small defects will close developmentally without intervention. Pediatric cardiologists often encourage children with VSD to do physical activity to keep their hearts fit; however, activity should not be encouraged without the concurrence of the managing physician. For those defects that do not spontaneously close, the outcome is good with surgical repair. Repairing a ventricular septal defect with surgery usually restores the blood circulation to normal. Surgical repair of the defect should be done between the ages of 2 and 5 years. Complications may result if the defect is not treated. Although a child with ventricular septal defect can usually get through common childhood illnesses as safely as children with normal hearts, routine medical care is important.

Most children with ventricular septal defect can benefit from regular education and do not need restrictions. Most children can participate in healthful activities (e.g., swimming, bicycling, running, etc.). In some instances, a pediatric cardiologist may advise that a child avoid strenuous activities. In rare cases, a child may have some special education needs (e.g., the school may need to limit a child's stair climbing or provide special transportation). If this is the case, the child may qualify for services under the Individuals with Disabilities Education Act (IDEA; 1997) using the physical disability category or under Section 504 of the 1974 Rehabilitation Act.

Children with small to moderately sized ventricular septal defects have an excellent prognosis. Most openings have closed by 18 years of age. Infants and children with large ventricular septal defects have a good prognosis. Appropriate timing of surgical intervention leads to the best outcome. The majority of research appears to be focusing on producing effective surgical methods to treat this condition (Hisatomi, Taira, & Moriyama, 1999; Tabuchi, Mizuno, Kuriu, & Toyama, 2001). For more information and support concerning ventricular septal defects, contact Congenital Heart Anomalies, Support, Education, and Resources, 2112 North Wilkins Road, Swanton, OH 43558, (419) 825-5575, e-mail myer106w@wonder.em.cdc.gov or chaser@compuserve.com.

REFERENCES

Hisatomi, K., Taira, A., & Moriyama, Y. (1999). Is direct closure dangerous for treatment of doubly committed subarterial ventricular septal defect? *Annals of Thoracic Surgery*, 67(3), 758–759.

Tabuchi, N., Mizuno, T., Kuriu, K., & Toyama, M. (2001). Double patch technique for repairing postinfarction ventricular septal defect. *Japanese Journal of Thoracic and Cardiovascular Surgery*, 49(4), 264–266.

RACHEL TOPLIS
University of Northern Colorado

VERBAL BEHAVIOR MILESTONES ASSESSMENT AND PLACEMENT PROGRAM VB–MAPP

The *Verbal Behavior Milestones Assessment and Placement Program (VB–MAPP) is* a criterion-referenced assessment, curriculum guide, and progress monitoring tool. The *VB-MAPP* is designed for children with autism spectrum or language disorders. The *VB-MAPP* is not a normed assessment. That is, the assessment does not compare the child's progress with the progress of groups of children. This tool is designed for parents and professionals to gain information regarding the child's current skill repertoire and to facilitate the development of learning objectives, particularly language skill objectives. The assessment can be administered by parents, teachers, or therapists through direct observation of the child's skills and though interviews with persons familiar with the child. The *VB-MAPP* was developed by Mark Sundberg, PhD, in 2008 and is based on the science of applied behavior analysis and B. F. Skinner's (1957) analysis of verbal behavior. Skinner's analysis of verbal behavior emphasizes the functional properties of language, which are derived from environmental situations. According to Skinner, expressive language can be divided into different functional categories, or operants (e.g., echoics, mands, tacts, intraverbals). The *VB-MAPP* assesses each of these verbal operants separately.

The *VB-MAPP* consists of five components: Milestones Assessment, Barriers Assessment, Transition Assessment, Task Analysis and Skills Tracking, and Placement and IEP Goals (Sundberg, 2008). The Milestones Assessment contains 170 language and learning skills that are sequenced according to their development in typically developing children. Skills relate to language, play, pre-academics, and skills needed for group or classroom settings. Skills are organized into three developmental ranges: 0–18 months, 18–30 months, and 30–48 months.

The Barriers Assessment assesses 24 barriers common in children with autism spectrum or language disorders, which prevent them from effectively participating in and benefiting from instruction (Sundberg, 2008). Such barriers pertain to challenging behaviors or specific skill deficits such as failure to attend to relevant stimuli, failure to generalize skills, and language or social skill deficits. The purpose of this assessment component is to identify barriers and plan interventions to reduce the impact of these barriers on learning.

The Transition Assessment component of the *VB-MAPP* provides an overview of the child's skills that may be required for transition to a less restrictive, or more typical, educational placement (Sundberg, 2008). This overview consists of the scores obtained on the Milestones Assessment component and the Barriers Assessment component and adaptive behaviors.

The fourth component of the *VB-MAPP* is the Task Analysis and Skills Tracking tool (Sundberg, 2008). This tool is designed to function as an individualized curriculum development guide, providing details regarding the child's performance on the skill areas assessed on the Milestones Assessment. Additionally, this tool delineates strategies and activities for promoting skill maintenance and generalization.

The last component of the *VB-MAPP* is the Placement and IEP Goals guide (Sundberg, 2008). This component assists in translating information gathered from the other four components into measurable individualized education program goals.

REFERENCES

Sundberg, M. (2008). *Verbal behavior milestones assessment and placement program*. Concord, CA: Advancements in Verbal Behavior Press.

Skinner, B. F. (1957). *Verbal behavior*. Englewood Cliffs, NJ: Prentice Hall.

MANDY J. RISPOLI
Texas A&M University
Fourth edition

VERBAL DEFICIENCY

Verbal deficiency is a term with multifaceted meaning in the field of special education. It refers to the use and understanding of language and indicates abilities that are either deficient in terms of an individual's overall level of functioning or clearly below the norm for individuals of a certain age. Frequently, verbal deficiency is diagnosed when a child's verbal IQ on an individually administered intelligence measure such as the Wechsler Intelligence Scale for Children–III, is significantly lower than performance IQ (Kaufman, 1994). Verbal deficiency is also inferred from a child's relative difficulty on those portions of group administered standardized achievement tests that rely heavily on verbal skills. Parents and educators often note that a child's verbal skills are not age appropriate. A child may exhibit difficulty in following directions given orally or comprehending information presented orally. The child also may have difficulty with verbal expression. Language arts skills such as reading, composition, and spelling may be impaired. Speech pathologists working with children may use the term verbal deficiency when referring to subnormal development of language structures, verbal fluency, and knowledge of vocabulary. A verbal deficiency may have roots and causes that are primarily medical. Hearing impairment, especially if mild, can be an undetected cause of verbal deficiency. A history of chronic otitis media (middle ear inflammation) and resulting intermittent hearing loss can be a factor as well. Neurological impairment can result in deficiencies in verbal skills while leaving other areas of functioning relatively intact. Although children with developmental disabilities often show depressed functioning in all areas, this possible cause must be considered when a child presents with verbal deficiency. It is sometimes possible to infer through evaluation and testing specific developmental difficulties that lead to verbal deficiency. These include expressive or receptive language deficiencies or a central auditory processing disorder. A learning disability (as defined by failure to learn at a normal rate despite average intellectual ability) in the language arts area also can be associated with a verbal deficiency.

Emotional factors also must be considered in understanding the concept of verbal deficiency in children. Physical or emotional abuse in the home as well as specific emotional disorders can affect the development of verbal skills. Sociocultural factors, some more readily apparent than others, may also play a role in the development of verbal deficiency. Manni, Winikur, and Keller (1984) provide discussion on this topic. English may not be the child's native language and may not be spoken in the home at all. Different dialects of the English language may be spoken at home. Educational level of the adult in the home, as well as the amount of time spent with the child on verbal tasks, may affect verbal development. Chronic school absenteeism, for medical or other reasons, can result in verbal deficiency. In conclusion, a single or combination of causes may be present when a child presents with a verbal deficiency, and Sattler (1982) and Kaufman (1979, 1994) provide a more detailed discussion of the nature and causes for such.

REFERENCES

Kaufman, A. S. (1979). WISC-R research: Implications for interpretation. *School Psychology Digest, 8*, 5–27.

Kaufman, A. S. (1994). *Intelligent testing with the WISC-III*. New York, NY: Wiley.

Manni, J. L., Winikur, D. W., & Keller, M. R. (1984). *Intelligence, mental retardation, and the culturally different child*. Springfield, IL: Thomas.

Sattler, J. M. (1982). *Assessment of children's intelligence and special abilities* (2nd ed.). Boston, MA: Allyn & Bacon.

MELANIE L. BROMLEY
*California State University,
San Bernardino*

See also Expressive Language Disorders; Receptive Language Disorders

VERBALISMS

Verbalisms is a term coined by Cutsforth (1932) to describe the use of words by individuals with visual impairments that represent terms or concepts with which they could not have had first-hand experience. Color words are one example. Children with visual impairments learn quickly that sighted individuals refer to green grass, blue sky, and a bright orange sun and use such terms freely in their own language although they never experience these colors. The development of verbalisms is important to the mastery of language and communication by individuals with visual impairments; however, the individuals should also be encouraged not to rely exclusively on verbal learning.

REFERENCE

Cutsforth, T. D. (1932). The unreality of words to the blind. *Teachers Forum, 4*, 86–89.

CECIL R. REYNOLDS
Texas A&M University

See also Blind

VERBAL SCALE IQ

The verbal scale IQ is a standard score (with mean of 100 and a standard deviation of 15) derived from a combination of six subtests that comprise the verbal scale of the Wechsler Intelligence Scales. Every subtest on the verbal scale requires that the examinee listen to an auditorily presented verbal stimulus and respond verbally. The verbal scale IQ is a measure of general verbal skills, such as verbal fluency, ability to understand and use verbal reasoning, and verbal knowledge. It is based on both formal and informal educational opportunities, and requires understanding words, drawing conceptual similarities, and knowledge of general principles and social situations. The verbal scale IQ is interpreted as a good indicator of verbal comprehension and expressive language skills and has good test-retest reliability. It is also considered to be an indicator of crystallized ability or intellectual functioning on tasks calling on previous training, education, and acculturation. Auditory attention is also reflected in the score.

Because of the verbal orientation of most American schools, the verbal scale IQ is by far the best predictor of academic achievement for students. Verbal scale alone can be used with examinees who are visually or motor impaired and examinees for whom English is a second language. Examinees from low socioeconomic backgrounds or minority cultures often earn a verbal scale IQ that is lower than their actual intellectual ability. Significant differences between verbal scale IQs and performance scale IQs are helpful in detecting and diagnosing the presence of a learning or language disability.

This entry has been informed by the sources listed below.

REFERENCES

Flanagan, D. P., & Kaufman, A. S. (2004). *Essentials of WISC-IV assessment*. Hoboken, NJ: Wiley.

Flanagan, D. P., McGrew, K. S., & Ortiz, S. O. (1999). *The Wechsler Intelligence Scales and Gf-Gc Theory: A contemporary approach to interpretation*. Boston, MA: Allyn & Bacon.

Hess, A. K. (2001). *Review of Wechsler Adult Intelligence Scale, Third Edition (WAIS-III)*. Mental Measurements Yearbook (14th ed.). (Electronic Version).

Kaufman, A. S., & Lichtenberger, E. O. (1999). *Essentials of WISC-III and WPPSI-R assessment*. New York, NY: Wiley.

The Psychological Corporation. (1997). *WAIS-III—WMS-III technical manual*. San Antonio, TX: Author.

Tulsky, D. S., & Ledbetter, M. F. (2000). Updating the WAIS-III and WMS-III: Considerations for research and clinical practice. *Psychological Assessment, 12*(3), 253–262.

KATHLEEN PELHAM-ODOR
*California State University,
San Bernardino*

VERBO-TONAL METHOD

The verbo-tonal method (VTM) is primarily an auditory method for the education of children with auditory impairments. It was developed by Petar Guberina in Zagreb, Yugoslavia (Guberina, Skaric, & Zaga, 1972) and reformulated by Asp and Guberina (1981). The term *verbo-tonal* was first coined to characterize an original audiometric technique that measured the perception of speech segments called logatomes (hence the term *verbo*) of variable main frequency spectrum (hence the word *tonal*) from the low, such as *bru-bru*, to the high, such as *si-si*.

Guberina insists on the importance of the suprasegmental, or prosodic, features of spoken language: rhythm, pitch variations, and stress. He considers that all children and adults with auditory impairments have some hearing capacities, not only inferior but also different from those of the normally hearing. Those whose cochlear function is completely lost can still perceive speech sounds through their vibro-tactile sensitivity. For every individual with auditory impairment, therefore, it is possible to determine an optimal field (OF) for speech reception, characterized by those frequencies of the speech spectrum in which residual hearing, and/or vibro-tactile perception, are most efficient. The OF can be limited to the low frequencies (including impulses of infrasound frequency perceptible by tactile sensation) or to the high frequencies. It also can be discontinuous, consisting of two restricted frequency bands, one low, one high. Having observed that better speech perception could be achieved by amplifying only the OF frequencies and eliminating the others, Guberina devised special apparatus capable of selecting distinct frequency bands.

Besides the technical equipment, specific training procedures characterize the VTM. Individual work consists of auditory and speech training. For speech correction, particular attention is given to the analysis of faults. Following this, the therapist modifies his or her own speech to counteract the erroneous perception that has led to faulty production. Several modifications of pitch, tension, duration, phonetic context, and even phonetic structure are used. The visual channel of speech reception, lip reading, is not trained specifically.

Body rhythm is based on the concept that speech is a function of the whole body and that appropriate macromotricity movements involving the body will facilitate the finer micromotricity movements of speech organs. Specific movements based on the phonetic features of the various speech sounds are executed simultaneously with their utterance. The child with auditory impairment, equipped with appropriate amplification, first watches and listens to the therapist, then is asked to reproduce the associated speech and body movements with the control of the residual hearing.

Musical rhythm aims at sensitizing the child with auditory impairments to the rhythm and changing intonation pattern of normal speech, while training him or her to perceive and reproduce every phoneme in its different positions: initial, intermediate, or terminal. This is accomplished by presenting to the child a series of rhymes, each constructed with a limited number of repetitive nonsense syllables, allowing for easy identification and reproduction.

Phonetic graphism, a later adjunct to the verbo-tonal method was developed by Gladic (1982). This technique is based on coordination between the fine hand movements of painting and writing and the subtle vocal tract motricity of the speech act.

Although devised for the education of individuals with hearing impairments, VTM has been adapted to the rehabilitation of children with a wide variety of language and personality disorders (Asp & Guberina, 1981). First developed in Zagreb in the 1950s, VTM was shortly thereafter introduced in France. In the beginning of the 1960s, it was demonstrated in several other western European countries, the United States, Canada, and some Latin American countries. It has since developed worldwide, gaining variable degrees of acceptance among oralist-oriented educators and parents of children with auditory impairments.

REFERENCES

Asp, C., & Guberina, P. (1981). *The verbo-tonal method*. New York, NY: World Rehabilitation Fund Monographs.

Gladic, V. A. (1982). *Le graphisme phonétique*. Brussels, Belgium: Labor.

Guberina, P., Skaric, I., & Zaga, B. (1972). *Case studies in the use of restricted bands of frequencies in auditory rehabilitation of the deaf*. Zagreb, Yugoslavia: Institute of Phonetics, Faculty of Arts.

OLIVIER PÉRIER
Université Libre de Bruxelles,
Centre Comprendre et Parler, Belgium

See also Deaf; Deaf Education

VERSABRAILLE

Versabraille, a device for the blind, is a computer with a braille keyboard. In lieu of a screen, there are 20 electronic braille cells, each containing the usual six dots that can be selectively raised to form braille characters. After a period of machine familiarization, reading speed on the 20-cell display is comparable to paper braille reading rates.

One of the main advantages of this system is that it can store much braille information on small floppy disks. Furthermore, it does not necessitate any printing on paper, and makes word processing and the production of tables and charts possible.

MICHEL BOURDOT
Centre d'Etude et de Reclassement,
Brussels, Belgium

See also Blind; Braille

VIDEOFLUOROSCOPY

Videofluoroscopy is a method of obtaining fluorographic/radiographic images of anatomical structure and physiological function. This procedure offers the benefits of low radiation levels, synchrony of visual and sound data for speech, and multiple viewing planes. The procedure requires an interface between common medical fluoroscopy equipment and a video recorder. The patient is observed in multiple positions to produce different views of the area of interest. A barium solution is administered to highlight soft tissue structures. The procedure is usually conducted by a team composed of a speech-language pathologist, radiologist, and an imaging technician. Two common applications of this procedure are to observe the functioning of the velopharyngeal mechanism during speech production and to track the movement of food and liquid during swallowing (Skolnick & Cohn, 1989).

Velopharyngeal inadequacy (VPI) may be suspected because an individual's speech contains inappropriate nasal resonance (i.e., hypernasality, hyponasality, assimilative nasality, cul de sac resonance). Videofluoroscopy is then used to evaluate the structure and function of the velopharyngeal mechanism while the individual produces selected speech samples that stress the valving capability of the mechanism. The information gained during this procedure aids in differential diagnosis, supports decisions regarding the efficacy of surgical or prosthetic and/or behavioral management of VPI, and can indicate the course of therapy.

Another form of the videofluoroscopy procedure, a modified barium swallow (MBS) study, can be used where neuromuscular problems have resulted in problems with swallowing. The MBS study is utilized to identify specific points of dysfunction in the upper gastrointestinal tract during eating and swallowing. The occurrence of foreign material entering the airway (aspiration) is of particular interest during the MBS study since this condition can lead to aspiration pneumonia. During this procedure, the patient is fed different consistencies and amounts of food/liquid containing a barium trace. The information gained includes how the individual is able to organize material in his or her mouth, prepare to swallow it, and how that material moves through the pharynx toward the esophagus and stomach. A treatment regimen, which can include dietary management, postural changes, and muscle stimulation, will result from an MBS study. The procedure is usually conducted by a speech-language pathologist, a radiologist, and an imaging technician, and the results are presented to a team of professionals for recommendations and follow-up.

REFERENCE

Skolnick, M. L., & Cohn, E. R. (1989). *Studies of speech in patients with cleft palate*. New York, NY: Springer-Verlag.

STAFF

VIDEOTAPING IN SPECIAL EDUCATION

Videotaping is a feedback technique that has been derived from the field of interaction analysis (Amidon & Hough, 1967; Flanders, 1970; Webb, 1981). In special education, it is often used as a training system that permits special education teachers to monitor and modify their own teaching behavior (Shea, 1974). A student teacher teaches a lesson, is critiqued, shown a videotape, and reteaches the lesson (Koetting, 1985). The interaction analysis technique allows the teacher to employ various schemes for identifying units of behavior and mapping the relationships of the behaviors in time and space.

Procedurally, an observer (special education teacher, student teacher, supervisor, or principal) sits in a classroom and views a videotape. As the observer follows the flow of events, he or she identifies specific units of behavior and makes notations of their occurrences. Identification of each unit is based on a set of descriptive categories; the resultant series of notations provides the "map," which is subject to interpretation and analysis.

The use of videotaping has improved many observation problems inherent in evaluating complex interactions of the teaching-learning process. In classrooms for the emotionally handicapped, videotaping provides a method of permanently recording and stimulating teacher-pupil interactions for professional preparation. It also provides the opportunity for immediate feedback, immediate and repetitive replay, accurate recording, and availability for analysis (Fargo, Fuchigami, & Cagauan, 1968; Haring & Fargo, 1969).

Birch (1969) demonstrated that categorizing and recording the frequency of one's own verbal behaviors may be a powerful training procedure leading to changes in recorded preservice teacher behaviors. Thomas's (1972) research supported Birch's findings that the self-monitoring procedure, viewing videotapes of one's own teaching and categorizing the behaviors observed, can have an effect on the behavior of teachers who are already teaching and who have had as many as 15 years of teaching experience.

Research also indicates that 4-minute videotape segments may provide the best, most practical diagnostic tool available to supervisors in both preservice and in-service programs (Hosford & Neuenfeldt, 1979).

Videotaping for improving target behaviors with various special education populations is reported throughout the literature. Bricker, Morgan, and Grabowski (1972) used taped recordings of cottage attendant behavior to increase the time and quality of interactions with developmentally delayed children on a ward in a residential facility. The use of commercial trading stamps as token reinforcers in combination with an on-ward training program was used. The results demonstrated increases in interaction time associated with a progressive increase in the suitability of tasks selected by the attendants across four intervention phases if training was paired with viewing the videotapes and the delivery of trading stamps.

Gilbert et al. (1982) studied the effects of a peer modeling film on anxiety reduction and skill acquisition with children with health-related disabilities who were learning to self-inject insulin. The modeling film had no effect on reducing anxiety but the girls viewing the peer modeling film showed greater skill in self-injection.

Performance training methods such as live modeling, videotaped modeling, and individual video feedback has been proven effective in altering parent-child behaviors and attitudes (O'Dell, Mahoney, Horton, & Turner, 1979; Webster-Stratton, 1981). However, these studies addressed only the short-term effectiveness of videotape training methods. Webster-Stratton (1982) studied whether changes brought about by videotape modeling are maintained over longer periods of time with 35 mothers and their 3- to 5-year-old children who exhibited inappropriate behaviors. The results of this study indicated that most of the behavioral changes noted during the short evaluation were maintained. At 1-year follow-up, mother-child interactions were significantly more positive and significantly less negative, nonaccepting, and domineering than at baseline assessment. A significant reduction in behavior problems at 1-year follow-up compared with baseline also was noted. There was a notable drop, however, in mother-child positive affect behaviors (showing lack of confidence and inability to manage problem behaviors).

The positive effects of using videotaping as a training tool for special education personnel, teachers in training, and special learners and their parents is clearly supported in the literature. The opportunity to emit behaviors and obtain feedback on performance are crucial variables of the technique.

REFERENCES

Amidon, E. J., & Hough, J. B. (Eds.). (1967). *Interaction analysis: Theory, research and application.* Reading, MA: Addison-Wesley.

Birch, D. R. (1969). *Guided self-analysis and teacher education.* Unpublished doctoral dissertation, University of California, Berkeley.

Bricker, W. A., Morgan, D. G., & Grabowski, J. G. (1972). Development and maintenance of a behavior modification repertoire of cottage attendants through TV feedback. *American Journal of Mental Deficiency, 77,* 128–136.

Fargo, C., Fuchigami, R., & Cagauan, C. A. (1968). An investigation of selected variables in the teaching of specified objectives to mentally retarded students. *Education & Training of the Mentally Retarded, 3,* 202–208.

Flanders, N. A. (1970). *Analyzing teaching behavior.* Reading, MA: Addison-Wesley.

Gilbert, B. O., Johnson, S. B., McCallum, M., Silverstein, J. H., & Rosenbloom, A. (1982). The effects of a peer-modeling film on children learning to self-inject insulin. *Behavior Therapy, 13,* 186–193.

Haring, N. G., & Fargo, G. A. (1969). Evaluating programs for preparing teachers of emotionally disturbed children. *Exceptional Children, 36,* 157–162.

Hosford, P., & Neuenfeldt, J. (1979). Teacher evaluation via videotape: Hope or heresy? *Educational Leadership, 36,* 418–422.

Koetting, J. R. (1985). *Video as a means for analyzing teaching: A process of self-reflection and critique.* Paper presented at the annual convention of the Association for Educational Communications and Technology, Anaheim, CA.

O'Dell, S. L., Mahoney, N. D., Horton, N. G., & Turner, P. E. (1979). Media assisted parent training: Alternative models. *Behavior Therapy, 10*, 103–110.

Shea, T. M. (1974). *Special education microteaching clinic: Final report* (Report No. 020533). Edwardsville: Southern Illinois University, Special Education Microteaching Clinic. (ERIC Document Reproduction Service No. ED 126 665)

Thomas, D. R. (1972). *Self-monitoring as a technique for modifying teaching behaviors.* Unpublished doctoral dissertation, University of Illinois, Urbana-Champaign.

Webb, G. (1981). An evaluation of techniques for analyzing small group work. *Programmed Learning and Educational Technology, 18*, 64–66.

Webster-Stratton, C. (1981). Videotape modeling: A method of parent education. *Journal of Clinical Child Psychology, 10*, 93–98.

Webster-Stratton, C. (1982). The long-term effects of a videotape modeling parent training program: Comparison of immediate and 1-year follow-up results. *Behavior Therapy, 13*, 702–714.

DEBORAH A. SHANLEY
Medgar Evers College,
City University of New York

See also Supervision in Special Education; Teacher Effectiveness; Teacher Training

VINELAND ADAPTIVE BEHAVIOR SCALES, SECOND EDITION

The Vineland Adaptive Behavior Scales, Second Edition (Vineland-II) is a series of forms designed to measure adaptive behavior in individuals ranging in age from birth through 90 years, 11 months. The current version of the Vineland-II includes the Survey Interview Form (2005), the Parent/Caregiver Rating Form (2005), the Expanded Interview Form (2006) and the Teacher Rating Form (2006). These forms are intended to provide assistance with diagnosis, special education qualification, treatment planning, progress monitoring, and research. The Vineland-II is particularly useful for special populations such as those with intellectual and developmental disabilities, autism spectrum disorders, attention-deficit/hyperactivity disorder (ADHD), or brain injuries or dementia.

The Parent/Caregiver Rating Form (estimated completion time: 30 to 60 minutes) and Teacher Rating Form (20 minutes), like most rating scales, are designed to be completed by a rater who knows the individual well. The respondent marks how often the individual independently completes a behavior. Conversely, the Survey Interview and the Expanded Interview are completed by the evaluator while completing a semistructured interview. The Survey Interview lasts approximately 20 to 60 minutes, whereas the more comprehensive Expanded Interview takes closer to 90 minutes. Coding responses to interview questions in this way may be a new experience for many examiners, particularly since the tester is not supposed to read items directly to the interviewee or allow the interviewee to rate individual items. Although basal and ceiling rules apply, the order of items may change depending on the flow of the interview. Regardless of the form selected, the subject obtains scores across three domains of adaptive behavior: Communication, Daily Living Skills, and Socialization. For individuals up to 6 years of age, Motor Skills are also evaluated.

The normative sample was geographically diverse and consisted of 3,695 individuals aged birth through 90 years. Because adaptive behaviors tend to have more variation with younger individuals, there were more samples of younger participants than older. Each age range included an equal number of males and females and was representative of the U.S. population in 2001 with regard to race/ethnicity, socioeconomic status, and geographic region. The standardization sample included individuals with attention-deficit/hyperactivity disorder, autism (including both verbal and nonverbal participants), emotional or behavioral disorders, and those who were deaf or hard of hearing.

Reliability was demonstrated through internal consistency (split-half), test-retest reliability, and interrater reliability. Internal consistency estimates were good, with the vast majority of coefficients having a value of 0.75 or greater. Reliabilities were generally higher for children and older adults than teenagers and younger adults, likely due to the finding that teenagers and younger adults have the highest level of adaptive functioning. Test-retest reliability coefficients were also robust, generally at or above 0.85. Because the interview forms use a flexible semistructured interview format, the consistency of scores between interviewers is also of interest. In individuals aged birth through 6 years, the inter-interviewer reliability ranged from 0.48 (Play and Leisure Time) to 0.92 (Written), with an overall Adaptive Behavior Composite reliability of 0.87. Scales that fell below 0.70 were: Receptive (0.59), Interpersonal Relationships (0.67), Play and Leisure Time, Coping Skills (0.56), Fine Motor (.63) and the Socialization composite score (0.66). In individuals aged 7–18, inter-interviewer reliability ranged from 0.55 (Play and Leisure Time) to 0.76 (Domestic), with an overall Adaptive Behavior Composite reliability of 0.74. Scales that fell below 0.70 were: Community (0.65), Coping Skills (0.66), Play and Leisure Time, and the Communication composite score (0.65). This indicates examiners should be aware that scores may vary somewhat depending on the interviewer, particularly with regards to Socialization skills. It should be noted the inter-interviewer reliabilities for adults were not calculated due to lack of variability of scores within the sample; generally because many individuals scored at or just below the ceiling.

When examining just the rating forms, interrater reliability for individuals aged birth through 6 years ranged from 0.57 (Personal) to 0.91 (Written), with an overall Adaptive Behavior Composite reliability of 0.83. The only other reliability, aside from Personal, which fell under 0.70 was the Daily Living Skills composite score, which was likely affected by the low reliability for Personal skills. For the 7- to 18-year-olds, interrater reliability ranged from 0.58 (Expressive) to 0.82 (Receptive), with an overall Adaptive Behavior Composite reliability of 0.81. Other scores under 0.70 were Personal (0.66), Play and Leisure Time (0.62) and Coping Skills (0.65). As with the interview forms, interrater reliabilities for the adult sample could not be calculated. It should be noted lower interrater reliability can be present for any rating scale measuring a child's behavior, as different individuals can have different experiences with and perceptions of the same child. It should be noted reliability studies were conducted separately for the optional Maladaptive Behavior scales and were generally high.

Evidence of validity was presented through theoretical and empirical links between test content and important constructs of adaptive behavior and evaluation of response processes and test structure. Further, the manual presents evidence of validity in using the Vineland with important diagnostic groups, including those with mental retardation, autism, attention-deficit/hyperactivity disorder, emotional/behavioral disturbance, learning disability, and visual and hearing impairments. Finally, the manual presents data relating the Vineland-II to scores on several other relevant measures.

Overall, the Vineland-II appears to be a thorough, technically sound, and useful tool to examine the adaptive behavior of a wide range of individuals. The survey interview technique provides clinicians with flexibility in administration, and the natural conversation style allotted by the semistructured interview may put clients at ease. Examiners who are unfamiliar with this process should receive training and supervision prior to independent use of the survey interview, particularly given some of the scales are subject to low inter-interviewer reliability.

This entry has been informed by the sources listed below.

REFERENCES

Stein, S. (2010). Review of the Vineland Adaptive Behavior Scales, Second Edition. In R. A. Spies, K. F. Geisinger, and J. F. Carlson (Eds.), *The eighteenth mental measurements yearbook*. Lincoln, NE: Buros Institute of Mental Measurements.

Widaman, K. F. (2010). Review of the Vineland Adaptive Behavior Scales, Second Edition. In R. A. Spies, K. F. Geisinger, and J. F. Carlson (Eds.), *The eighteenth mental measurements yearbook*. Lincoln, NE: Buros Institute of Mental Measurements.

KATHLEEN VIEZEL
JAMIE ZIBULSKY
Fairleigh Dickinson University
Fourth edition

VINELAND SOCIAL-EMOTIONAL EARLY CHILDHOOD SCALES

The Vineland Social-Emotional Early Childhood Scales (SEEC; Sparrow, Balla, & Cicchetti, 1998) is designed to measure the emotional functioning of children from birth to 5 years, 11 months. The SEEC scales were derived from the Socialization domain of the Vineland Adaptive Behavior Scales. There are three scales on the SEEC: Interpersonal Relationships, Play and Leisure Time, and Coping Skills. A Social-Emotional Composite score is also available. The types of behaviors assessed include those such as paying attention, entering social situations, understanding emotional expression, developing relationships, and developing self-regulatory behaviors. The scales are designed to help develop early intervention plans and to chart developmental progress in preschool and kindergarten programs.

Administration of the SEEC Scales is done via a semistructured interview with a child's caregiver. Items are scored based on how often a child is reported to perform a certain behavior: a score of 2 indicates that the child "usually performs," a score of 1 indicates that a child "sometimes or partially performs," and a score of 0 indicates that a child "never performs." Age-based standard scores (M = 100, SD = 15), percentile ranks, and descriptive categories are obtained from the scales. The entire SEEC Scales administration time is usually 15 to 25 minutes.

The norms of the SEEC scales were computed from the normative data of the Vineland Adaptive Behavior Scales (Sparrow et al., 1998). The standardization sample was comprised of 1,200 children from birth to age 5 years, 11 months. Median internal consistency reliability coefficients for each of the scales ranged from 0.80 for Play and Leisure Time to 0.91 for Coping Skills. The median internal consistency value for the Composite was 0.93. Interrater reliability values ranged from 0.47 to 0.60. Validity studies reported the correlation between the SEEC Scales and the Early Development Scale of the Scales of Independent Behavior to be 0.63. In addition to the convergent validity information, a number of studies have indicated that the Vineland Socialization Domain differentiates between typically developing children and children with developmental delays.

REFERENCE

Sparrow, S. S., Balla, D. A., & Cicchetti, D. V. (1998). *Vineland Social-Emotional Early Childhood Scales*. Circle Pines, MN: American Guidance Service.

ELIZABETH O. LICHTENBERGER
The Salk Institute

See also Adaptive Behavior; Vineland Adaptive Behavior Scales

VINELAND TRAINING SCHOOL

The Training School at Vineland, New Jersey, has had a long and influential role in the history of intellectual disabilities in the United States. Originally founded in 1888 by Olin S. Garrison as a private school and institution for the "feebleminded," the Training School maintained a reputation for high standards of care and for pioneering experimental and research work. Rather than being a medical setting, it was designed to provide care and research within a psychological-educational context.

In 1901 Edward R. Johnstone became director of the Training School, a position he held until 1943. The genesis of many of the institution's later activities was the establishment in 1902 of the Feebleminded Club by a group of interested professionals and financial backers (Doll, 1972). In 1904, Johnstone started the summer school, one of the first programs designed to provide training for teachers of individuals with intellectual disabilities. This program subsequently established university affiliations, and many leaders in the field were graduates of the program. In 1913 the Department of Extension was founded to publicize findings in the field. This led in 1914 to the Committee on Provisions for the Feebleminded, which undertook the first organized efforts of national scope to promote better state laws and increased institutional care for individuals with intellectual disabilities.

In 1906 the first psychological laboratory for the study of intellectual disability was established at the Training School and Henry H. Goddard was appointed director of research. It was here that Goddard did his most famous work, translating and adapting the Binet intelligence scales, helping develop World War I army tests, and conducting extensive research on intellectual disability. Goddard's (1912) study of the family history of Deborah Kallikak, a resident of the institution, became one of the

most widely read research projects of the day; it gave impetus to the eugenics movement.

The laboratory Goddard directed continued to be considered a center for research on intellectual disability for decades after his resignation in 1918. As director of research from 1925 to 1949, Edgar A. Doll made several important contributions, the most well known of his efforts being the establishment of criteria of social functioning. In the early 1960s the Training School changed its name to the American Institute for Mental Studies and in 1981 the Elwyn Institute assumed management responsibility for the facility.

REFERENCES

Doll, E. A. (1972). A historical survey of research and management of mental retardation in the United States. In E. P. Trapp & P. Himelstein (Eds.), *Readings on the exceptional child: Research and theory* (2nd ed., pp. 47–97). New York, NY: Appleton-Century-Crofts.

Goddard, H. H. (1912). *The Kallikak family*. New York, NY: Macmillan.

TIMOTHY D. LACKAYE
Hunter College,
City University of New York

See also History of Special Education; Mental Retardation

VISION TRAINING

Optometric visual training (vision therapy) is the art and science of developing visual abilities to achieve optimal vision performance and comfort. Training techniques are used in the prevention of the development of vision problems, the enhancement of visual efficiency, and the remediation and correction of existing visual problems.

Visual training encompasses orthoptics, which is a nonsurgical method of treating disorders of binocular vision. Orthoptic techniques were used as early as the seventh century by a Greek physician, Paulus Aeginaeta, who used a mask with small perforations to correct strabismus. The mask was still in use in 1583 by George Bartisch, the founder of German ophthalmology.

In the early 18th century, Buffon advocated occlusion of the good eye to improve vision in the poorer eye. This was followed by Wheatstone's mirror invention of the stereoscope, which was employed to correct postoperative divergence of the eyes. Brewster modified the stereoscope, which is still in use in visual training programs today, with lenses.

In 1864 Javal founded orthoptics and demonstrated that binocular vision could be recovered with the use of a stereoscope. Orthoptics took a step forward in 1903 when Worth established a fusion theory, classified binocular vision into three grades, developed the amblyoscope, and devised the four-dot test to detect suppression. Worth, who headed up the English orthoptic school, which stressed fusional capacity, stated that the essential cause of squint is a defect of the fusional faculty. Worth believed that the weak fusion could be reeducated.

Arneson developed optometric vision-training techniques by using the principle of peripheral stimulation with a circular disk of 30 inches in diameter. Patients were asked to fixate a rotating jewel on the Arneson rotator "to aid central fixation and fusion through motion." This was the first of many techniques that were developed by optometrists to modify visual behavior by changing the accommodative convergence relationship. In 1932 two optometrists, Crow and Fuog, published a series of visual training papers that introduced the concept of visual skills.

In addition, lens application, especially at the near point to enhance visual comfort, began to play an important role in the 1930s when Skeffington developed the analytical examination with a group of optometrists from the optometric extension program. Harmon further demonstrated that "appropriate lens for near point would reduce physiological stress." A plus lens is, therefore, prescribed as a single vision or bifocal during or after a program of optometric vision training.

The need for visual training is established with the objective and subjective findings of the visual analysis and an evaluation of the ocular motility, accommodative facility, eye teaming ability, and visual perception. The visual analysis includes a detailed ocular, medical, and genetic history followed by distance and near visual acuity determination, external evaluation of the eyes, and cover test to determine eye position. Pupillary reflexes, keratometry, objective and subjective refraction, distance and near acuity, horizontal and vertical ductions, fusional amplitudes, and accommodative tests precede any visual training therapy. Additional testing procedures evaluate suppressions, stereopsis, eye preference, macular integrity, and foveal fixation.

Visual symptoms indicating the possible need for visual training include crossed eyes, headaches, head tilt, short attention span, rubbing and constant blinking of the eyes, poor hand-eye coordination, blurring of vision, holding of books close to the eyes, double vision, word and letter reversals, covering an eye, losing the place when reading, or the avoidance of near work.

Many of the current visual training techniques developed by Brock, Nichols, Getman, MacDonald, Schrock, Kraskin, and Greenstein emphasize development of smooth eye movement skills (fixation ability). These include pursuit, the ability of the eyes to smoothly and accurately track a moving object or read a line of print, and saccadic movement, the ability to move the eyes from one object or word accurately.

Additional skills emphasized in visual training are eye-focusing skills, eye-aiming skills, eye-teaming skills (binocular fusion), eye-hand coordination, visualization, visual memory, visual imagery, and visual form perception. These techniques have been found to be effective in eliminating or reducing visual symptoms even when the visual acuity is 20/20 at distance and near on the Snellen acuity charts.

Techniques employing lenses, prisms, the steroscope, and rotator are used to align the eyes and maximize optimal visual efficiency. Visual training procedures also are used when there are overt eye turns such as those encountered in constant, intermittent, or alternating strabismus (esotropia or exotropia). Prism therapy is often used in conjunction with lens therapy in the correction of horizontal and vertical deviations of the eye.

Visual training techniques also have been used in the treatment of amblyopia, learning-related problems, and juvenile delinquency; in sports training programs; and with older adults and workers having visual difficulties on the job.

The optometrist often works on a multidisciplinary team that includes the educator, psychologist, social worker, rehabilitation specialist, orientation and mobility instructor, and child development specialist who specializes in the remediation of the child, teen, or adult with a learning disability or visual impairment. These methods are effective only if learning problems are related to vision system problems as opposed to a central processing dysfunction.

This entry has been informed by the sources listed below.

REFERENCES

American Optometric Association. (1985). *Vision therapy news backgrounder*. St. Louis, MO: Author.

Borish, I. (1970). *Clinical refraction* (3rd ed.). Chicago, IL: Professional.

Griffin, J. R. (1982). *Binocular anomalies procedures for vision therapy* (2nd ed.). Chicago, IL: Professional.

Harmon, D. B. (1945). *Lighting and child development*. Philadelphia, PA: Illuminating Engineering.

Hurtt, R. N., Rasicovici, A., & Windsor, C. (1952). *Comprehensive review of orthoptics and ocular motility*. St. Louis, MO: Mosby.

McDonald, L. W. (1970). *Optometric visual training—Its history and developments*. St. Louis, MO: American Optometric Association.

Richman, J. E., Cron, M., & Cohen, E. (1983). *Basic vision therapy: A clinical handbook*. Big Rapids, MI: Ferris State Press.

Skeffington, A. M. (1946). *Visual rehabilitation, analytical optometry*. Duncan, OK: Occupational Education Programs.

Skeffington, A. M. (1959). *The role of a convex lens.* St. Louis, MO: American Optometric Association.

Von Norden, G., & Maumenee, A. E. (1967). *Atlas of strabismus.* St. Louis, MO: Mosby.

BRUCE P. ROSENTHAL
State University of New York

See also Developmental Optometry; Optometrists; Visual Acuity; Visual Impairment

VISUAL ACUITY

Visual acuity refers to the clarity with which an individual sees, or the level of detail that can be detected at certain distances. It is dependent on both retinal function and the ability of the brain to interpret sensory information from the eyes. For students with visual impairments, both distance and near visual acuity measurements are important.

Any number of standardized tools can be used to measure distance visual acuity, though for most adults and children who can recognize letters, the most routinely used tool is the Snellen chart. For younger children or children with mild to moderate intellectual disabilities, other options include the Tumbling E chart or charts that use pictures of common objects. These charts are not considered effective for measuring the distance visual acuity of individuals with visual impairment because they do not optimize contrast, have few stimuli at certain acuity levels on which patients can demonstrate ability, and require that testing be conducted at 20 feet (Wilkinson, 2010). Wilkinson (2010) suggested that better alternatives for measuring the distance visual acuity of people with visual impairments include the Bailey-Lovie chart, the Lighthouse Distance Visual Acuity Chart, LEA symbols chart, and the Designs for Vision Distance Chart for the Partially Sighted.

Regardless of the chart used, the technique for measuring distance visual acuity involves placing the patient a specific distance from the chart, asking for the patient to identify symbols from it until they can no longer be resolved, and noting the size of the smallest symbol that was accurately identified. Distance visual acuity is recorded using a notation on which the distance is noted first, followed by a slash, and the size of the smallest row of symbols accurately identified written to the right of the slash. Most people have a distance visual acuity of 20/20, meaning that at 20 feet away, they can see the line that most other people can see from 20 feet away. If a person has a visual acuity of 20/80, he is said to see detail from 20 feet away the same as a person with normal eyesight would see it from 80 feet away.

The distance visual acuity of people with low vision is often tested at distances closer than 20 feet. In these instances, the first number of the acuity notation still specifies the distance at which the testing took place, but is a number smaller than 20. It is not unusual for these distances to be recorded in meters; for these tests, the symbols are measured in centimeters.

For very young children and children with significant cognitive disabilities, visual acuity testing often relies on observing the child's preference for viewing patterns of lines when presented with two targets of equal luminescence, but on which only one is the pattern imprinted. Typically, children will fixate on the most complex pattern that is presented to them and an estimate of acuity can be made based on their preferential viewing. For other individuals, estimates of distance visual acuity can be made based on the distance at which they react to familiar objects and comparing the size of those objects to the symbols on a distance vision chart (Wilkinson, 2010).

Near visual acuity is tested at an individual's preferred reading distance. The individual is asked to hold a test card and to read the smallest line of letters (or continuous text) possible. Both the size of these symbols and the distance at which they were read are noted. Near visual acuity may be recorded using point-size notation, Jaeger notation, or M notation. Of these, M notation is preferred by low-vision specialists (Wilkinson, 2010). A letter written in 1 M print is approximately equal to the same letter presented in 9-point font, which is the size of newsprint.

It is important to remember that visual acuity tests conducted in clinical locations may not reflect an individual's actual visual functioning within the "real" environments in which that individual spends time (Ward, 2000). Some factors, such as anxiety, can reduce clinical visual functioning, but others, such as the high quality of lighting and the contrast with which symbols are displayed, can result in visual acuity measures that are better than what is achieved in home, school, and community environments.

Visual acuity is only one measure of visual functioning and is influenced by a number of factors, including contrast and lighting. Two people with visual impairments with the same visual acuity may not function similarly. It is important, then, that a student's functional vision be evaluated to determine how that student uses vision in the environments in which that student spends time.

REFERENCES

Ward, M. E. (2000). The visual system. In M. C. Holbrook & A. J. Koenig (Eds.), *Foundations of education: Vol. 1 History and theory of teaching children and youths with visual impairments* (2nd ed., pp. 77–110). New York, NY: AFB Press.

Wilkinson, M. E. (2010). Clinical low vision services. In A. L. Corn & J. N. Erin (Eds.), *Foundations of low vision: Clinical and functional perspectives* (2nd ed., pp. 238–283). New York, NY: AFB Press.

SANDRA LEWIS
Florida State University
Fourth edition

See also Visual Impairment; Visual-Motor and Visual-Perceptual Problems; Vision Training

VISUAL ANALYSIS

With single-subject experimental designs, treatment effects are systematically examined through visual analysis of graphed data (Kazdin, 1982). In order to conduct visual analysis, specific graphing mechanisms must be utilized in order to control for distortion. Graphs should be properly proportioned, scaled, and labeled (Franklin, Gorman, Beasley, & Allison, 1996). If appropriately graphed, visual analysis of the data can be used to determine whether a meaningful change in a dependent variable (target behavior) took place and whether the change can be attributed to an independent variable (treatment or manipulation).

In order to interpret the graphs and analyze the potential change in data, the variability, trend, and level of the data are examined within and between phases or conditions of a study. Variability refers to the extent to which the data differ from one another. The more stable or consistent the data is within phases, the more confidence the viewer can have in assessing change in the data between phases (Tawney & Gast, 1984). Level describes the mean or median measurement value of the data points in each phase. Viewers look for a convergence of the data on a specific value of the vertical axis scale. Analysis of level is most useful with highly stable within-phase data. Viewers should be cautious when interpreting level and only consider level in conjunction with the trend of the data. Trend refers to the direction of the data path across time. The trend or slope can be described by the direction (increasing, decreasing, or unchanging) and by the degree (steep or gradual) of the data path. A trend line is often useful in viewing trends.

Through analysis of these data characteristics, viewers contemplate the existence of a functional relationship between the independent and dependent variables of the study. Of particular interest are the changes in the dependent variable that occur with a manipulation in the independent variable across phases. Viewers must consider the immediacy, magnitude, and consistency of the changes in the dependent variable that coincide with the application or removal of the independent variable (Jones,

Vaught, & Weinrott, 1977). There are a number of different single subject experimental designs, each with its own set of guidelines for determining a functional effect. For example, a treatment effect might be identified in a single subject reversal design if the data show: (a) low, stable rates of the dependent variable prior to implementing an intervention, (b) a steep, increasing trend and overall increase in the level of the data after the introduction of the intervention, and (c) a decreasing trend and level in the dependent variable following the removal of the intervention. With all experimental designs, the key is to determine the demonstration of a functional relationship between a change in the dependent variable and a change in the independent variable. Visual analysis is a systematic means of examining this relationship in graphically displayed data from single-subject designs.

REFERENCES

Franklin, R., Gorman, B., Beasley, T. M., Allison, D. (1996). *Design and analysis of single-case research.* Hillsdale, NJ: Erlbaum.

Jones, F., Vaught, R., & Weinrott, M. (1977). Time-series analysis in operant research. *Journal of Applied Behavior Analysis, 10,* 151–178.

Kazdin, A. E. (1982). *Single-case research designs: Methods for clinical and applied settings.* New York, NY: Oxford University Press.

Tawney, J., & Gast, D. (1984). *Single subject research in special education,* Columbus, OH: Charles E. Merill.

JESSICA H. FRANCO
University of Texas at Austin

VISUAL EFFICIENCY

Visual efficiency, as defined by Barraga (1970, 1976, 1980, 1983), relates to a variety of visual skills including eye movements, adapting to the physical environment, attending to visual stimuli, and processing information with speed and effectiveness.

In keeping with this definition is Barraga's (1983) definition of the visually impaired child as a child whose visual impairments limit his or her learning and achievement unless there are adaptations made in the way that learning experiences are presented to the child and effective learning materials are provided in appropriate learning environments.

The basic idea behind the notion of visual efficiency is that children learn to see best by actively using their visual abilities. As applied to the visually impaired (i.e., low-vision children), this means that they should be provided with such opportunities for learning and should be taught in such ways that they learn effectively to use their residual vision. Low-vision children, without proper opportunities and training, may not be able to extract much useful information from their visual environments simply by being provided with appropriate visual environments, but they can learn to use their visual information with proper opportunities and training so that they eventually can make sense out of what were previously indistinct, uncertain visual impressions. Barraga's (1983) program to develop efficiency in visual functioning, intended for the training of low-vision children, is one that emphasizes structured training for visual efficiency.

Associated with the idea of visual efficiency is the concept of functional vision. This concept is concerned with the ways that children use their vision rather than with their physical visual limitations, although the latter improves with specific training as well (Cartwright, Cartwright, & Ward, 1994).

REFERENCES

Barraga, N. C. (1970). *Teacher's guide for development of visual learning abilities and utilization of low vision*. Louisville, KY: American Printing House for the Blind.

Barraga, N. C. (1976). *Visual handicaps and learning: A developmental approach*. Belmont, CA: Wadsworth.

Barraga, N. C. (1980). *Source book on low vision*. Louisville, KY: American Printing House for the Blind.

Barraga, N. C. (1983). *Visual handicaps and learning*. Austin, TX: Exceptional Resources.

Cartwright, G. P., Cartwright, C. A., & Ward, M. J. (1994). *Educating exceptional learners* (4th ed.). Boston, MA: Wadsworth.

JANET S. BRAND
Hunter College,
City University of New York

See *also* Functional Vision

VISUAL IMPAIRMENT

A visual impairment is the condition that occurs when a disorder of the visual system results in impaired visual functioning that is uncorrectable to typical levels. The term, visual impairment, as used in the professional literature, describes both individuals who are considered blind and individuals who have low vision.

Students who have visual impairment are members of a heterogeneous group that have few characteristics other than their disordered vision in common. Even the degree of visual acuity can range from total blindness to normal, as occurs when a student experiences a significant loss of vision only in the peripheral fields. Students with visual impairments can differ on a number of other variables, including:

- *The onset of the visual disorder.* Disorders of the visual system can occur at birth, during early development, or after visual memories have been established. Because of the role that vision plays in learning about the world, children who are born with congenital visual impairments often have more challenges related to learning than do children who experience even a short period of unimpaired vision. Emotional stress related to loss of vision is more common among individuals with previously unimpaired vision whose visual functioning has diminished due to accident, disease, or expression of hereditary conditions.

- *The underlying visual disorder.* Numerous visual disorders result in visual impairment and depending on the part of the eye or brain that is affected, visual functioning will differ. Specific challenges to visual functioning can often be predicted when one knows what part of the eye is involved (Schwartz, 2010), but even with this knowledge, practitioners must expect variability in visual functioning among students diagnosed with the same disorder.

- *The presence of other exceptionalities.* Many visual disorders are related to, or caused at the same time, as disorders of the physical or cognitive systems. It is estimated that 40% of students with physical or cognitive disabilities also have visual impairment (Erin, 2006). Of the population diagnosed with visual impairment, as many as 60% have additional disabilities (Ferrell, 2000). Other students with visual impairment have exceptional gifts and talents.

- *Amount of functional vision.* Functional vision refers to how students use what vision they have in their everyday activities. Functional vision may vary depending on the task, environment, or time of day (Huebner, 2011). Much can be learned about a child's expected functional vision from the diagnosis and doctor's eye report. To understand a student's functional vision, it is crucial to assess in the natural learning environment (usually, home or school). Typically, a teacher of students with visual impairments (TVI) is responsible for conducting a functional vision assessment after a referral has been made. A functional vision assessment is based on reviewing records, parent and student interviews, observations in all environments, and direct testing. Through these methods, the evaluator records a student's visual performance on tasks that measure visual fields, eye movements, and responses to various environmental conditions, such as lighting, color, complexity, and noise. Also part of the student's performance is the level of visual fatigue, or how long attention to visual tasks can be maintained before performance declines or a break must be taken. It is also important to estimate functional visual acuity, which may differ from the doctor's eye report, which describes acuities gained under optimal conditions in a clinical environment (Huebner, 2000). Based on the functional vision report, there may be certain educational implications that need to be addressed, such as preferential seating, modified assignments, extra time, breaks, or specific lighting. Visual fatigue, ocular motor movements, visual acuity, and visual accommodation (how close the eye needs to be to see the material) are important factors to consider when describing a student's functional vision.

- *The medium in which they read.* Due to the varying degree of residual vision, students with diagnosed visual impairments may require different types of learning media. To determine a student's most efficient learning medium and reading mode (braille, print, electronic), a Learning Media Assessment (LMA) is conducted. An LMA investigates reading and writing behaviors and speed, viewing distance, visual fatigue, comprehension, and other literacy skills before a recommendation for the media in which learning is most likely to be efficient is made. For students with low vision who can access print, the effectiveness of the use of various low vision devices in increasing efficiency is an important consideration during the LMA. For students who are blind or have low vision and are not able to use print as an efficient learning medium, braille and other tactual methods of learning are often recommended.

Within the term *visual* impairment, there are classifications that are based on the doctor's eye report. *Blindness* typically refers to individuals who have little to no light perception and are, therefore, tactile learners. *Legally blind* refers to individuals with a documented central visual acuity of 20/200 or worse in the best eye with correction or a visual field less than 20 degrees (Huebner, 2000). Recently, the term *functions at the definition of blindness* has been adopted to include those students with cortical visual impairments, as their visual acuity may be normal, but the neural pathways and/or visual cortex do not properly process the visual information (Ferrell, 2011). Lastly, *low vision* refers to a level of vision that has an adverse effect on a student's ability to perform everyday tasks and cannot be corrected. However, there is no standard or legal definition of low vision (Corn & Lusk, 2010). These terms are often used on doctor's eye reports to qualify a student for certain educational or rehabilitation services and government-funded supports. It is important to note that a student identified as legally blind may be an efficient user of printed materials and that some students who self-identify as having low vision use braille for reading because of its efficiency in meeting their literacy needs.

IDEA requires that in order to qualify as for services as a student with visual impairment, a child's visual impairment must adversely affect a child's educational performance. In general, visual impairments are thought to adversely affect a child's educational performance because they interfere with incidental learning. Incidental learning refers to the spontaneous and automatic learning that occurs through observation and experience. As children observe the world around them, they imitate, receive feedback, imitate, and receive feedback until the concept or skill is learned. For students with visual impairments, it is difficult or impossible to learn from observation. In order to learn the same concepts that children with unimpaired vision learn incidentally, students with visual impairments need multiple and repeated experiences with concrete objects, learning experiences that help them to understand the whole of the object (since they only experience one part of an object at a time), and consistent language specifically describing their experiences. For most children, repetition, or practice, reinforces what is being learned or taught, and opportunities for practice are often informal. Students with visual impairments, however, may not be able to see these opportunities for practice, which results in interruptions in the learning cycle. Therefore, for students who cannot learn incidentally through observation, it is important that parents and teachers plan and create those opportunities for learning and practice (Ferrell, 2011).

A set of skills unique to the education of students with visual impairments is the expanded core curriculum (ECC). The ECC consists of nine skill areas that students with visual impairments must be taught in addition to the core curriculum that allows them to access educational material and become independently living adults (Ferrell, 2011). These nine areas are:

1. *Compensatory Skills:* Skills that students need to access and succeed in school. These skills include concept development, organizational skills, listening skills, and communications skills, such as reading or writing in print or braille.

2. *Self-Determination:* Skills that provide the foundation for students to advocate for themselves to meet their own goals and that are key to self-actualization.

3. *Sensory Efficiency:* Skills that help students to utilize all their senses (functional vision, taste, smell, hearing, and touch) efficiently and functionally. Examples may include learning to use their functional vision, optical devices, refining their listening skills, using touch to identify objects, etc.

4. *Independent Living Skills:* Skills that are needed to function in school, at home, or in the community, such as dressing, cooking, chores, shopping, and time management. Acquisition of these skills is critical to understanding much of the material that is presented within the core curriculum.

5. *Social Interaction Skills:* Skills that students need to interact with their peers and other people. These skills include eye contact, shaking hands, use of emotional expression, conversation skills, topic maintenance, and appropriate use of language.

6. *Recreation and Leisure:* Skills that students need related to their leisure and activity time. These include learning to make choices, playing games, following game and safety rules, and trying new activities. Participation in the area of recreation and leisure provides students with experiences that inform their understanding of material presented in the core curriculum and facilitates their success in social interaction skills.

7. *Orientation and Mobility (O&M):* Skills that allow the student to orient to an environment and travel independently. Typically, this area is taught by an orientation and mobility specialist and reinforced by the TVI. Among the key O&M skills are positional concepts, safely moving through space, the use of a long cane (if needed), and travel through the community.

8. *Career Education:* Knowledge and skills that teach students about careers and job options.

9. *Assistive Technology:* The development of competence in the use of various electronic devices that enable students to participate more efficiently in school, at home, and eventually, at work.

In order to ensure that students with visual impairment receive instruction in these nine areas, two primary educators with specialized knowledge and skills are involved. The first is the teacher of students with visual impairments (TVI), who has received focused preparation in the educational, functional, and developmental implications of visual impairments. TVIs are knowledgeable of learning strategies and tools and are responsible for delivering instruction in the ECC that matches each student's developmental needs. They work with the general education teacher and other team members to ensure appropriate adaptations and modifications are being made, as well as educating the team on the student's functional vision. The second instructor is the orientation and mobility specialist. This instructor is primarily responsible for teaching a student how to travel in the environment. O&M instruction often includes teaching positional concepts, school and classroom orientation, techniques for using sighted guide and the long cane, and purposeful movement and play. In the community, the orientation and mobility specialist is responsible for teaching street travel, street crossings, navigation, and transportation. Orientation and mobility specialists who have met national requirements for certification by the Academy for Certification of Vision Rehabilitation and Education Professionals (ACVREP) are designated by use of the COMS service mark.

There are many placement options for students with visual impairments, which range from the general education classroom to hospital or institution. There are several service options that can be made available in the local education agency in order to meet the needs of students as identified on their IEPs. For students who can perform similar to their peers relatively independently within the general or special education classroom, TVIs often provide itinerant TVI services, traveling from school to school to collaborate with teachers and to provide specialized instruction in ECC skills, as needed. TVIs might be assigned to a school where a group of students with visual impairment with more complex needs are placed. Working from a resource room, these TVIs provide a higher level of comprehensive academic support of students and teachers services and teach key ECC skills to facilitate both academic and functional development. Less often, TVIs who are appropriately highly qualified may be assigned a special day class to which a group of students with visual impairments and similar learning needs (e.g., preschoolers or students with concomitant visual and significant cognitive impairments), are assigned. Approximately 9% of students with visual impairments are provided services at a separate special school, such as a state school for the blind. Some students may be served at home or in a hospital or institution, but this placement is less common and usually is unrelated to the visual impairment (Lewis & Allman, 2000). It is important for IEP teams considering placement to recall that lack of access and conceptual understanding can restrict learning in environments that otherwise are considered least restrictive (Lewis, 2002). It is the needs of the student that drive placement, and the determination of the appropriate placement can be complex as the advantages and disadvantages of various placements are considered.

Students with visual impairments have unique learning needs, and the effect of the visual impairment varies student to student. Even students with the same diagnosis may use their functional vision differently, requiring different supports and materials. The TVI or other professional trained in the effects of visual impairment is responsible for assuring that students receive the individualized instructional and material support they need to access the curriculum and become independent adults.

REFERENCES

Corn, A. L., & Lusk, K. E. (2010). Perspectives on low vision. In A. L. Corn & J. N. Erin (Eds.), *Foundations of low vision: Clinical and functional perspectives* (2nd ed., pp. 3–34). New York, NY: AFB Press.

Erin, J. (2006). Children with multiple and visual impairments. In M. C. Holbrook (Ed.), *Children with visual impairments: A parents' guide* (pp. 329–362). Bethesda, MD: Woodbine House.

Ferrell, K. A. (2011). *Reach out and teach: Helping your child who is visually impaired learn and grow.* New York, NY: AFB Press.

Huebner, K. M. (2000). Visual Impairment. In M. C. Holbrook & A. J. Koenig (Eds.), *Foundations of Education: Volume 1 History and Theory of Teaching Children and Youths with Visual Impairments* (2nd ed., pp. 55–76). New York, NY: AFB Press.

Lewis, S. (2002). Some thoughts on inclusion, alienation, and meeting the need of children with visual impairments. *RE:view, 34*(3), 99–101

Lewis, S., & Allman, C. B. (2000). Educational programming. In A. J. Koenig & M. C. Holbrook (Eds.), *Foundations of education of students with visual impairments: Vol. 1: History and theory of teaching children and youths with visual impairments* (2nd ed., pp. 218–259). New York, NY: AFB Press.

Schwartz, T. L. (2010). Causes of visual impairment: Pathology and its implications. In A. L. Corn & J. N. Erin (Eds.), *Foundations of low vision: clinical and functional perspectives* (2nd ed., pp. 137–187). New York, NY: AFB Press.

KITTY GREELEY
SANDRA LEWIS
Florida State University
Fourth edition

See also Visual Perception and Discrimination; Vision Training

VISUAL-MOTOR AND VISUAL-PERCEPTUAL PROBLEMS

Many researchers have emphasized the importance of perceptual-motor skills to the development of children. Piaget and Inhelder (1956) stated that early sensory-motor experiences are basic to more advanced mental development, and Sherrington (1948) proposed that the motor system is the first neurological system to develop and the foundation for later perceptual growth. The concern for perceptual-motor development is a recurring theme in many areas of the history of special education. Although this perceptual-motor framework can be used to discuss all areas of perception that relate to motor responses—auditory, visual, haptic, olfactory, and so on—the relationships between visual-motor perception and discrimination and learning problems have received the greatest attention. The interest in visual motor perceptual problems in the United States can be traced back to the early research of Werner and Strauss (1939) and Strauss and Lehtinen (1947) with brain-damaged children. They noted that disturbances in visual perception and visual-motor perceptual functioning often accompany central nervous system damage. Their work also fostered the rapid growth and development of several visual-motor training programs by theorists such as Barsch, Frostig, Getman, and Kephart.

Although early researchers reported that visual-perceptual and visual-motor problems were evident in individuals with brain damage, a distinction between these two types of disturbances was not always made. Although Goldstein and Scheerer (1959) considered visual-motor and visual-perceptual deficits as separate entities, Bartley (1958) viewed perception as being either experiental or motor. Some of the assessment instruments used to measure visual perception are actually visual-motor copying tasks; for example, the Bender Gestalt Test, the coding subtest of the Wechsler scales of intelligence, and the developmental test of visual-motor integration, all require motor responses.

The failure to differentiate between visual-perceptual and visual-motor tasks may have far-reaching consequences. Perception is most directly tested when objects or pictures of various shapes, positions, or sizes are matched, or in some other way differentiated; it is then a task of interpreting what is seen. When the difficulty is demonstrated in a task that requires reproducing designs or spatial relationships, it is described as a visual-motor difficulty (i.e., the acts of perceiving and reproducing an object are combined). It may be possible that the child who displays a visual-motor difficulty also has a perceptual problem, although that inference cannot be made on the basis of a reproduction task. In normal development, visual perception of form precedes the visual-motor reproduction of the form (Piaget & Inhelder, 1956), and copying requires skills of an order different from perceiving (Abercrombie, 1964).

Children who have visual-motor problems have difficulty coordinating their movements with what they see. Kirk and Chalfant (1984) reported that breakdowns in three areas may occur when a child displays problems in visual-motor perception and discrimination. First, a child may have problems with laterality, or lateral dominance. This type of problem becomes apparent when both sides of the body perform the same act at the same time when that is not part of the task, or when a child uses only one side of his or her body when two sides are called for. Second, a child may have a directional disability. Directional disabilities manifest themselves when the child fails to develop an awareness of basic directions such as right from left, up from down, and front from back. Very young children will have problems in directionality; this is normal during the early stages of development, but as the child matures, this problem usually corrects itself. If these difficulties continue, the child may have problems in learning. Finally, a child is said to have a breakdown in visual-motor perception when the child's development is limited to the stage where the hand leads the eye. As visual-motor perception is refined, the eye should lead the hand.

Problems in visual-motor perception and discrimination can be seen in both academic and nonacademic tasks. In particular, visual-motor difficulties are most evident when children are involved in pencil and paper activities, play with or manipulate toys and objects, or catch or throw a ball, or when they are involved in any tasks that require good eye-hand coordination.

Many educators and psychologists have believed for years that adequate visual-motor development is directly related to academic achievement. As a result of this belief, a number of standardized tests were developed to assess children's visual-motor performance. Unfortunately, the use of these tests has not been supported by the literature. Visual-motor tests have been shown to be unreliable and theoretically or psychometrically unsound (Salvia & Ysseldyke, 1985). These inadequacies raise the question as to their usefulness and whether they should be used in planning educational programs for children.

Despite the inadequacies of visual-motor tests, they are still being used in the schools. Advocates of visual-motor testing use these assessment instruments to diagnose brain injury, to identify children with visual-motor problems so that training programs can be established to remediate learning disabilities, and to determine the degree to which visual-motor perception and discrimination problems may be interfering with academic achievement. Some of the most common assessment devices used to measure visual-motor skills include the Bender-Gestalt Test, the Developmental Test of Visual Motor Integration, and the Purdue Perceptual Motor Survey.

The methods used in visual-motor training programs are generally developmental and emphasize the importance of early motor learning and visual-spatial development in children. Although many of the advocates of visual-motor training programs have slightly different rationales for their programs, the basic perceptual-motor orientation and the recommended training activities are very similar. Barsch, Getman, Frostig, and Kephart all propose techniques for working with children with learning problems (Myers & Hammill, 1990).

One of the areas of controversy that surrounds the use of these training programs is the emphasis on training visual-motor perception processes to improve a child's skills in academic areas such as reading. Hammill and Larsen (1974) have argued that there is no evidence to support the assumption that academic learning is dependent on these types of psychological processes. However, unfortunately, both the critics and advocates of these training programs have based their arguments on highly questionable research reports (Hallahan & Kauffman, 1976). Detailed, recent meta-analyses demonstrate no real benefit to academic learning with perceptual-motor training programs (Kavale & Forness, 1999).

REFERENCES

Abercrombie, M. (1964). *Perceptual and visuo-motor disorders in cerebral palsy*. London, England: Heinemann.

Bartley, S. (1958). *Principles of perception*. New York, NY: American Orthopsychiatric Association.

Goldstein, K., & Scheerer, M. (1959). Abstract and concrete behavior: An experimental study with special tests. *Psychological Monographs, 83*, 1–155.

Hallahan, D., & Kauffman, J. (1976). *Introduction to learning disabilities*. Englewood Cliffs, NJ: Prentice Hall.

Hammill, D., & Larsen, S. (1974). The relationship of selected auditory perceptual skills and reading ability. *Journal of Learning Disabilities, 7*, 429–436.

Kavale, K., & Forness, S. (1999). The effectiveness of special education. In R. Reynolds & T. B. Gutkin (Eds.), *The handbook of school psychology* (3rd ed.). New York, NY: Wiley.

Kirk, S., & Chalfant, J. (1984). *Academic and developmental learning disabilities*. Denver, CO: Love.

Myers, P., & Hammill, D. (1990). *Methods for learning disorders*. Austin, TX: PRO-ED.

Piaget, J., & Inhelder, B. (1956). *The child's concept of space*. London: Routledge & Kegan Paul.

Salvia, J., & Ysseldyke, J. (1985). *Assessment in special and remedial education* (3rd ed.). Boston, MA: Houghton Mifflin.

Sherrington, C. (1948). *The integrative action of the nervous system*. New Haven, CT: Yale University Press.

Strauss, A., & Lehtinen, L. (1947). *Psychopathology and education of the brain injured child*. New York, NY: Grune & Stratton.

Werner, H., & Strauss, A. (1939). Types of visuo-motor activity and their relation to low and high performance ages. *Proceedings of the American Association of Mental Deficiency, 44*, 163–168.

DEBORAH C. MAY
State University of New York at Albany

DONALD S. MAROZAS
State University of New York at Geneseo

See also **Perception; Perceptual Motor Difficulties; Visual-Motor Integration**

VISUAL-MOTOR INTEGRATION

Visual-motor integration, also referred to as visual-motor association, denotes the ability to relate visual stimuli to motor responses in an accurate and appropriate manner. Historically, visual-motor problems have been associated with learning disabilities and, within a diagnostic-remedial intervention model, visual-motor skills have been taught to learning disabled pupils as a prerequisite to academic skills (Lerner, 1985). This interest in visual-motor development within the learning disabilities field can be traced to the early work of Strauss and Werner (1941), who studied the visual-motor problems of developmentally disabled students and believed that faulty visual-motor coordination was a behavioral symptom of brain damage. Werner and Strauss popularized the notion that adequate conceptual development is dependent on perceptual and motor development.

An important advocate of the magnitude of visual-motor integration to academic success is Getman. His visuomotor theory (Getman, 1965; Getman, Kane, & McKee, 1968) outlines the successive stages of visual-motor integration, including innate response, general motor systems, special motor systems, ocular motor systems, speech motor systems, visualization systems, vision or perception, and cognition. Each of these levels is conceptualized as more precise and exacting than the preceding one, with complete mastery at each stage required before completion of subsequent systems can be achieved. Therefore, within this model, academic learning must be preceded by extensive and successful motor learning. The implication is that learning-disabled children need exercise in the base levels of motor and visual-motor development before academics can be addressed.

Another proponent of the relation between learning disabilities and visual-motor integration is Kephart (1960, 1971), who theorized that breakdowns may occur at three key points in the development of visual-motor coordination. A child may fail to develop (1) an internal awareness of laterality of the left and right sides of the body and their differences; (2) left-right awareness within the body, which could lead to directionality problems; and (3) visual-motor coordination at the stage when the hand leads the eye. As Getman, Kephart believes that the education of the perceptually motor-disabled child must address motoric and visual development before conceptual skills.

Several teaching programs based on visual-motor integration theory have been designed, including Getman's Developing Learning Readiness: A Visual-Motor Tactile Skills Program. This program comprises activities in six areas: general coordination, balance, eye-hand coordination, eye movement, form recognition, and visual memory. Additionally, tests addressing visual-motor integration have been developed. One widely used measure, Beery and Buktenica's Developmental Test of Visual Motor Integration (1967), which requires examinees to reproduce geometric forms, is a norm-referenced test of the degree to which visual perception and motor behavior are integrated in young children.

Visual-motor integration assessment and remediation have been the focus of research. A test of visual-motor integration, the VMI-R, was a developmental to indicate and identify a possible learning disability involving visual perception and fine-motor development (e.g., hand-eye coordination). The VMI-R may be very helpful to professionals assessing children, because it will allow them to earlier and appropriately test a child's fine-motor and visual-perceptual development and earlier indicate a potential learning disability, but the results of such tests, which seem to elucidate etiology of or instructional procedures for learning disabilities, have failed to support the effectiveness of visual-motor training for improving academic learning (Kavale & Forness, 1999).

REFERENCES

Aylward, E. H., & Schmidt, S. (2001). An examination of three tests of visual-motor integration. *Journal of Learning Disabilities*, *19*(6), 328–330.

Beery, K. D., & Buktenica, N. A. (1967). Developmental Test of Visual-Motor Integration student test booklet. Chicago, IL: Follett.

Getman, G. N. (1965). The visuomotor complex in the acquisition of learning skills. In J. Heilmuth (Ed.), *Learning disorders* (Vol. 1, pp. 49–76). Seattle, WA: Special Child.

Getman, G. N., Kane, E. R., & McKee, G. W. (1968). *Developing learning readiness: A visual-motor tactile skills program*. Manchester, MO: Webster Division, McGraw-Hill.

Kavale, K., & Forness, S. (1999). The effectiveness of special education. In C. R. Reynolds & T. B. Gutkin (Eds.), *The handbook of school psychology* (3rd ed.). New York, NY: Wiley.

Kephart, N. C. (1960). *The slow learner in the classroom*. Columbus, OH: Merrill.

Kephart, N. C. (1971). *The slow learner in the classroom* (2nd ed.). Columbus, OH: Merrill.

Lerner, J. W. (1985). *Learning disabilities: Theories, diagnosis, and teaching strategies* (4th ed.). Boston, MA: Houghton Mifflin.

Strauss, A. A., & Werner, H. (1941). The mental organization of the brain injured mentally defective child. *American Journal of Psychiatry*, *97*, 1194–1202.

LYNN S. FUCHS
DOUGLAS FUCHS
Peabody College, Vanderbilt University
First edition

YOLANDA TENORIO
California State University, San Bernardino
Second edition

MELANIE BROMLEY
California State University, San Bernardino
Third edition

See also Diagnostic Prescriptive Teaching; Dyslexia; Visual-Motor and Visual-Perceptual Problems

VISUAL PERCEPTION AND DISCRIMINATION

Visual perception is a difficult concept that involves complex interactions between the individual and the environment. It is the ability to recognize stimuli and to differentiate among them (Frostig & Home, 1973). Visual perception is observing the surrounding physical world through our sense of sight (Sleeuwenhoek & Boter, 1995). Basically, visual perception and discrimination is the ability to physiologically interpret what is seen. There are a number of physiological factors that play a role in visual perception and discrimination, including sharpness of sight, range of vision, sense of color, adaptation to light and darkness, sensitivity to contrast, and eye movements, along with the environmental factors such as familiarity with the environment, weather conditions, the nature of the material (contrast and size), and task variables, also including a number of personality factors, including intelligence, character, age, concentration, and motivation (Sleeuwenhoek & Boter, 1995).

Visual-perceptual problems are concerned with disabilities that occur despite the fact that a child has physiologically healthy eyes. A child may have 20/20 visual acuity and adequate eye muscle control and still have visual-perceptual problems. These disabilities may include problems in form perception: discriminating the shapes of letters, numbers, pictures, or objects; position in space: discriminating the spatial orientation—left/right, top/bottom, etc.—of letters or words; visual closure: discriminating pictures or words with parts missing; and figure-ground discrimination: the ability to perceive a figure as distinct from the background (Hallahan, Kauffman, & Lloyd, 1985). A child who has problems with visual perception and discrimination may have difficulty in school because most academic activities require good visual-perceptual skills. In particular, the areas of math and reading will be difficult for the child who cannot distinguish between a multiplication and an addition sign, or who has difficulty discriminating pictures, letters, numbers, or words. During the early stages of a child's development, these problems are normal, but as a child matures, parents and teachers should become concerned if these difficulties persist.

The measurement of visual perception is complicated since it is tested by perceptual skills and motor skills. Tests such as the Visual Motor Gestalt Test, the coding subtest of the Wechsler Scales (WISC-III), and the Developmental Test of Visual-Motor Integration (VMI-3) all require motor responses and all are based on the assumption that the reproduced form is indicative of the individual's visual perception of the shape. However, Goldstein and Scheerer (1959) consider visual-perceptual and visual-motor deficits as separate entities. According to this perspective, if a child copies a figure incorrectly, a teacher cannot assume that the child has a visual-perceptual problem; additional information is needed. When a child copies a figure incorrectly, but can correctly select a picture of the figure from a group of choices, then there is an indication that the problem may be a visual-motor one. However, if the child selects an incorrect choice, then there is evidence that there may be a visual-perceptual difficulty (Hallahan et al., 1985). Some tests that measure visual perception and discrimination without requiring a drawing response include the Test of Visual-Perceptual Skills–Non-Motor (Revised), the Motor-Free Visual Perceptual Test (MVPT-R), the Visual Reception and Visual Closure subtests of the Illinois Test of Psycholinguistic Abilities (ITPA-Revised), the discrimination of forms and mutilated pictures subtests of the Stanford-Binet, and the Position in Space subtest of the Frostig Developmental Test of Visual Perception (DTVP-2).

REFERENCES

Frostig, M., & Home, D. (1973). *Frostig program for the development of visual perception*. Chicago, IL: Follett.

Goldstein, K., & Scheerer, M. (1959). Abstract and concrete behavior: An experimental study with special tests. *Psychological Monograph, 83*.

Hallahan, D., Kauffman, J., & Lloyd, J. (1985). *Introduction to learning disabilities* (2nd ed.). Englewood Cliffs, NJ: Prentice Hall.

Sleeuwenhoek, H. C., & Boter, R. D. (1995). Perceptual-motor performance and the social development of visually impaired children. *Journal of Visual Impairment & Blindness, 89*(4), 359–368.

Deborah C. May
State University of New York at Albany

Donald S. Marozas
State University of New York at Geneseo
First edition

Chaz Esparaza
California State University, San Bernardino
Third edition

See also Bender-Gestalt Test; Developmental Test of Visual Perception-2; Illinois Test of Psycholinguistic Abilities; Visual Perception and Discrimination

VISUAL TRAINING (See Vision Training.)

VISUOMOTOR COMPLEX

Visuomotor complex is a term used by Getman (1965) to describe his model of the development of the visuomotor system and its relationship to the acquisition of learning skills. This model reflects Getman's training as an optometrist by emphasizing the visual aspects of perception. It illustrates the developmental sequences that a child progresses through while acquiring visual-perceptual and motor skills, and emphasizes that each successive stage is dependent on earlier stages of development.

The six systems of learning levels in this model are (from the lowest to the highest) the innate response system, the general motor system, the special motor system, the ocular motor system, the speech-motor system, and the visualization system. These systems all contribute to vision or the perceptual event that results in cognition when many perceptions are integrated (Lerner, 1971).

This visuomotor complex requires solid learning at each level before proceeding to the next level. Getman believes that children will not succeed in educational programs if they do not have adequate experiences in the lower systems of development. A teaching program, Developing Learning Readiness: A Visual-Motor Tactile Skills Program (Getman, Kane, & McKee, 1968), is based on this model.

This visuomotor model has been criticized for simplifying learning; overemphasizing the role of vision; neglecting the role of language, speech, and feedback; and not providing empirical evidence for the theory (Lerner, 1971; Myers & Hammill, 1969).

REFERENCES

Getman, G. (1965). The visuomotor complex in the acquisition of learning skills. In J. Hellmuth (Ed.), *Learning disorders* (Vol. 1, pp. 49–76). Seattle, WA: Special Child.

Getman, G., Kane, E., & McKee, G. (1968). *Developing learning readiness: A Visual-Motor Tactile Skills Program*. Manchester, MO: Webster Division, McGraw-Hill.

Lerner, J. (1971). *Children with learning disabilities*. Boston, MA: Houghton Mifflin.

Myers, P., & Hammill, D. (1969). *Methods for learning disorders*. New York, NY: Wiley.

DEBORAH C. MAY
State University of New York at Albany

See also Visual Perception and Discrimination; Vision Training

VITAMIN E DEFICIENCY

Vitamin E is an essential nutrient for maintaining the structural and functional integrity of the developing human nervous system, skeletal muscle, and the retina (Sokol, 1990). When vitamin E deficiency does occur, it strikes people who have diseases that prevent the absorption of dietary fats and fat-soluble nutrients.

Vitamin E functions as the prevention of the natural and continual process of deterioration of all body tissues. This deterioration is provoked by a number of causes; one such cause is toxic oxygen (Olendorf, Jeryan, & Boyden, 1999). Toxic oxygen can damage the membranes that form the boundaries of every cell. Vitamin E serves the body in protecting membranes from this kind of damage. The membranes are the most sensitive to toxic oxygen damage; therefore, the main symptom of vitamin E deficiency is damage to the nervous system. Vitamin E helps maintain the integrity of the circulatory and central nervous systems; is involved in the functioning of the kidneys, lungs, liver, and genitalia; and detoxifies poisonous materials absorbed by the body (Irons-George, 2001). Vitamin E deficiency rarely occurs and has been reported in only two situations: premature infants and patients who fail to absorb fat. Because of chronic malabsorption of vitamin E, children with cystic fibrosis, chronic cholestasis (bile-flow obstruction), abetalipoproteinia, and short bowel syndrome are at risk for the development of neurological deficits caused by vitamin E deficiency. Premature infants may be at risk for vitamin E deficiency because they may be born with low tissue levels of the vitamin and because they have a poorly developed capacity for absorbing dietary sources (Olendorf et al., 1999). The best sources of vitamin E are vegetable and seed oils, sunflower seeds, nuts, whole grains, wheat germ, and leafy vegetables such as spinach.

Characteristics

1. Hemolytic anemia
2. Neurological and immunological abnormalities
3. Ataxia (poor muscle coordination with shaky movements)
4. Decreased sensation to vibration
5. Hyporeflexia
6. Limitation in upward gaze
7. Strabismus
8. Nyctalopia (night blindness)
9. Profound muscle weakness
10. Visual field constrictions
11. In severe cases, the inability to walk
12. With severe prolonged vitamin E deficiency, complete blindness, cardiac arrhythmia, and dementia

Treatment must be tailored to the underlying cause of the deficiency and may include oral or intramuscular vitamin supplementation. The treatment of vitamin E deficiency that occurs with malabsorption syndromes can be treated with weekly injections of 100 mg alpha-tocopherol that may continue for 6 months (Olendorf et al., 1999). Intramuscular administration is necessary when the deficiency occurs because of a low concentration of bile salts in the lumen of the small intestine; such patients are unable to absorb vitamin E taken orally. Vitamin E deficiency in premature infants may require treatment for only a few weeks. Patients receiving large doses of vitamin E may experience a halt in progression of the disease (Caplan & Collins, 2002).

The prognosis of vitamin E deficiency is usually reversible in the early stages, but it can have severe complications if allowed to progress. The more advanced the deficit of vitamin E, the more limited the response to therapy. Persons at risk for vitamin E deficiency should be periodically tested.

Research is being done on the absorption, transport, and tissue delivery of vitamin E in the human body. One goal is to define why vitamin E deficiency leads to neurological injury and what kind of vitamin E therapy to use with each fat malabsorption condition. Research has shown that vitamin E supplementation can significantly improve the immune response in healthy older persons. Research is being done to determine the effects of vitamin E in reducing the risk for coronary heart disease and prostate cancer and in slowing the progression of Alzheimer's disease.

REFERENCES

Caplan, G. E., & Collins, T. (2002, Jan. 2). *Vitamin E deficiency*. Retrieved from http://www.emedicine.com/med/topic2382.htm

Irons-George, T. (2001). *Magill's medical guide* (2nd rev. ed.). Pasadena, CA: Salem Press.

Olendorf, D., Jeryan, C., & Boyden, K. (1999). *The Gale encyclopedia of medicine*. Farmington Hills, MI: Gale Research.

Sokol, R. J. (1990). *Vitamin E and neurologic deficits*. Retrieved from http://www.emedicine.com/med/topic2382.htm

KAREN WILEY
University of Northern Colorado

VOCABULARY DEVELOPMENT

The knowledge of vocabulary, that is, the ability to recognize words and understand their meanings, is recognized as possibly the most important factor in being able to use and understand spoken and written language. Vocabulary knowledge is very closely associated with the ability to comprehend what is heard or read, and may be related to general intelligence and reasoning ability.

According to Harris (1970), children develop a variety of types of vocabulary knowledge in a developmental sequence. First they develop a hearing vocabulary, or the ability to respond to spoken words even before they themselves are able to use speech. For a number of years children are able to respond to more words that they hear than words that they are able to use themselves. Following the appropriate development of a hearing vocabulary,

children begin to acquire emerging reading skills and a reading vocabulary—words that they are able to recognize in print and know the meanings of in context. Gradually, the developing reader is able to recognize more words in print and is able to use more words than in the speaking and writing vocabulary. Harris has explained that a child's total vocabulary involves all the words that he or she can eventually understand and use in all the communications skills, including listening, speaking, reading, and writing.

The significance of a varied and well-developed vocabulary cannot be overemphasized, according to Johnson and Pearson (1984). They have identified and explained the reading process as a communication between an author and a reader. That communication is successful only when the reader is able to understand the author's original intent by recognizing and understanding the vocabulary that the author uses. It follows, then, that in order to be a fluent, proficient, and successful reader, it is necessary to possess a rich and varied vocabulary and word knowledge background.

General vocabulary development and the ability to recognize words either in isolation or in context have a common link in the diversity of words that the reader can both understand and use. Many of the words that the developing learner and reader uses and understands have been with him or her from early years; other words are learned and developed as they are used in the context of school-related activities. Therefore, although a rich experiential background during the preschool years is certainly a requisite for later vocabulary learning, much of the vocabulary development that the child experiences are accomplished in school. According to Smith and Johnson (1980), Stauffer (1969), and Johnson and Pearson (1984), a meaningful vocabulary is developed through reading- and writing-related activities in a variety of ways. These include the development of a basic sight vocabulary, various word identification strategies, including phonics, structural analysis, context clues, and instruction in understanding the deeper meanings of words. Through the activities outlined in basal reading programs, and occasionally through the use of content area materials, students are taught to use and understand synonyms, antonyms, homophones, and multiple meaning words. They also are taught to use the various resources such as dictionaries and thesauruses for determining word meaning.

One of the best ways to learn new words and what they mean is to become involved with reading and listening. Moffett and Wagner (1983) have stated that children need to become habitual readers. They must immerse themselves in a variety of reading and listening activities that will enable them to experience words in a variety of contexts and allow them to make generalizations about the meanings of words and how they may be used. Particularly during the elementary years, they argue, much of schooling must be involved with providing children with a variety of language-related situations that require them to be actively engaged in the production and reception of language in both oral and written forms. As the child becomes more engaged in reading and writing activities, preferably related to different content areas, not only is general vocabulary knowledge increased, but reasoning ability and conceptual development are enhanced.

The essence of reading and writing is communication, and the crucial variable in communication seems to be vocabulary knowledge. What distinguishes the fluent, successful reader from the poor reader seems to be knowledge of words and what they mean. A successful and appropriate program of vocabulary development in the school, coupled with the child's preschool experiential background, may provide that key ingredient to becoming a successful language user. Johnson and Pearson (1984) give a complete and detailed account of how to provide an appropriate program of vocabulary development in school.

REFERENCES

Harris, A. J. (1970). *How to increase reading ability* (5th ed.). New York, NY: McKay.

Johnson, D. D., & Pearson, P. D. (1984). *Teaching reading vocabulary* (2nd ed.). New York, NY: Holt, Rinehart, & Winston.

Moffett, J., & Wagner, B. J. (1983). *Student centered language arts and reading, K-13: A handbook for teachers* (3rd ed.). Boston, MA: Houghton Mifflin.

Smith, R. J., & Johnson, D. D. (1980). *Teaching children to read* (2nd ed.). Reading, MA: Addison-Wesley.

Stauffer, R. G. (1969). *Directing reading maturity as a cognitive process.* New York, NY: Harper & Row.

JOHN M. EELLS
*Souderton Area School District,
Souderton, Pennsylvania*

VOCATIONAL EDUCATION

The goal of vocational education programs is to prepare students to enter the work world. Astuto (1982) described vocational programs as focusing on the development of basic academic skills; good work habits; personally meaningful work values; self-understanding and identification of preferences, skills, and aptitudes; occupational opportunities; the ability to plan and make career decisions; and the locating and securing of employment. The basic program components for vocational education are recognized as remedial basic skills, specific job training, personal and social adjustment skills, career information, modified content in subject areas, and on-the-job training. Ondell and Hardin (1981) discussed four types of occupational activities that would be part of a vocational program: paid

work experience during the day, paid work experience after school hours, unpaid work observation, and in-school vocational laboratory.

From a historical perspective, the first piece of legislation to address the vocational educational needs of individuals with disabilities was the Vocational Education Act of 1963 (PL 88-210). The Educational Amendments of 1976 (PL 94-482) strengthened provisions for youths with disabilities in vocational education. According to Ondell and Hardin (1981) legislation promoting vocational education and the rights of individuals with disabilities has included the Smith-Hughes Act of 1917, which provided funds for vocational education in public schools; the Civilian Rehabilitation Act of 1920, which assigned responsibility for the administration of vocational rehabilitation to state boards of vocational education; the Vocational Rehabilitation Amendments of 1943, which expanded the 1920 act to include individuals with intellectual disabilities and emotional disorders; the Vocational Education Act of 1963, which provided occupational training for persons with special needs and allowed some of a state's allotment to be used in funding these programs; and the Vocational Amendments of 1968, which included more specific terminology and specified that 10% of the monies received by the state be set aside for the vocational education of individuals with disabilities. With these monies, many specifically designed programs were started, thus expanding the area of vocational education to encompass special groups (Ondell & Hardin, pp. 2–3).

In the last century, the U.S. economy has changed from being based almost solely in manufacturing and agriculture to one that, since the technology revolution, now provides mainly services and information. Computers and the Internet dictate new rules for the workplace, and thus also for vocational education. These trends have two implications for vocational education programs. It signals a shift in the type of requirements for the education and training fields to adequately prepare the upcoming U.S. workforce, and a shift in the levels of that education and training necessary to fulfill these new jobs (Shumer, 2001).

This has led to a new wave of policy reform that has put less emphasis on specific programs and more emphasis on reform and accountability. These new academic standards emerged with passage of the Carl D. Perkins Vocational and Applied Technology Education Act of 1990 (PL 101-392, also called Perkins II; Stone, Kowske, & Alfeld, 2004). This was one of "the most significant policy shifts in the history of federal involvement in vocational-technical education. For the first time, emphasis was placed on academic, as well as occupational skills" (Hayward & Benson, 1993, p. 3).

The most recent incarnation of the Carl D. Perkins Vocational and Technical Education Act (PL 105-332) was signed into law in 1998. Perkins III continues the theme of improving academic achievement while readying students for continued education and work. The law also reaffirms the commitment to serve special populations, increase accountability, and expand the use of technology (Rojewski, 2002). New initiatives include the need to negotiate core performance indicators. "Core performance indicators include things such as student attainment of identified academic and vocational proficiencies ... attainment of a high school diploma or postsecondary credential; placement in postsecondary education, the military, or employment" (Lynch, 2000).

Probably one of the most important modern acts to influence vocational education for students with special needs is the 2001 No Child Left Behind Act (NCLB). NCLB requires that all students, including students with disabilities, be held to challenging content and achievement standards—that their progress is to be measured annually by assessments aligned with those high standards, and that schools and school districts are held accountable for achieving such results (www.ed.gov). Each state must meet requirements that are directly related to achievement and instruction for the full range of students with disabilities. These core principles include: statewide participation rates for students with disabilities, for purposes of measuring "Adequate Yearly Progress (AYP), must be at or above 95%; appropriate accommodations are provided to students with disabilities who need them; alternate assessments in reading/language arts and mathematics provided to students with disabilities who are unable to participate in the regular assessment ... and results from those assessments must be reported. Each state must provide information on actions taken to raise achievement for students with disabilities or narrow the achievement gap and evidence that such efforts are improving student achievement" (PL 107-110, 2001). This means that states must raise achievement levels for students with disabilities. This emphasis on student achievement places more pressure on special education classes to find ways to increase academic performance. What this surmises is the reduced opportunity for students to take vocational classes due to the demands of more intensive academic classes. Vocational classes are trying to combat this by changing the curriculum to integrate more academics into the coursework.

REFERENCES

Astuto, T. A. (1982). *Vocational education programs and services for high school handicapped students.* Bloomington: Council of Administrators of Special Education, Indiana University.

Hayward, G. C., & Benson, C. S. (1993). *Vocational-technical education: Major reforms and debates 1917–present.* Washington, DC: U.S. Department of Education, Office of Vocational and Adult Education.

Lynch, R. L. (2000). *New directions for high school career and technical education in the 21st century* (Information Series No. 384). Columbus: The Ohio State University, ERIC Clearinghouse on Adult, Career, and Vocational Education.

No Child Left Behind Act of 2001, Public Law No. 107-110 (2001).

Ondell, J. T., & Hardin, L. (1981). *Vocational education programming for the handicapped.* Bloomington: Council of Administrators of Special Education, Indiana University.

Rojewski, J. W. (2002). Preparing the workforce of tomorrow: A conceptual framework for career and technical education. *Journal of Vocational Education Research, 27*(1), 7–35.

Shumer, R. (2001). A new, old vision of learning, working, and living: Vocational education in the 21st century. *Journal of Vocational Education Research, 26*(3), 261–272.

Spellings Announces New Special Education Guidelines, Details Workable, "Common-Sense" Policy to Help States Implement No Child Left Behind. (May 10, 2005). U.S. Department of Education. Retrieved from http://www.ed.gov

Stone, J. R., III, Kowske, B. J., & Alfeld, C. (2004). Career and technical education in the late 1990s: A descriptive study. *Journal of Vocational Education Research, 29*(3), 195–223.

Eileen McCarthy
University of Wisconsin at Madison
First edition

Michelle Evans
California State University,
San Bernardino
Third edition

See also Rehabilitation; Vocational Evaluation

VOCATIONAL EVALUATION

Vocational evaluation is a term that encompasses the processes undertaken in determining eligibility and appropriate program plans for students entering vocational education. Specific components and processes used in vocational evaluation include assessment of skills, aptitude, interests, work behaviors, social skills, and physical capabilities (Leconte, 1985; Levinson & Capps, 1985; Peterson, 1985; Rosenberg & Tesolowski, 1982). At this time, students with disabilities and students who are disadvantaged are the main targets for vocational evaluation programs (Levinson, 1994).

The area of vocational assessment is affected by the Carl Perkins Vocational Education Act of 1984, which mandates that schools provide each student with disabilities who enrolls in a vocational education program an assessment of the individual's interests, abilities, and special needs with respect to the successful completion of the vocational education program (Cobb & Larkin, 1985). During 1990 the Carl Perkins Act was amended, and it became mandatory for all states to create, and to put into practice, standards and measurements that would outline student progress. These outcomes were required to have two key measurements: (1) student progress in learning and increased aptitude, and (2) evaluating job placement, or "secondary school completion" (Association for Career & Technical Education, 1995).

It is important to note that it is the local school systems that hold the responsibility for administering and upgrading existing programs (Association for Career & Technical Education, 1995). Occasionally educational agencies will reach an agreement with vocational rehabilitation agencies to conduct vocational evaluations. This is essential for schools that don't have the necessary funds to provide a vocational evaluation program for themselves. One such agency is the Hiram G. Andrews Vocational Rehabilitation Center, which implements preparation in 26 different areas (Levinson, 1994).

The terms vocational evaluation and vocational assessment are often used interchangeably. Although Leconte (1985) indicated that the Division on Career Development (DCD) of the Council for Exceptional Children (CEC) does not discriminate between vocational evaluation and vocational assessment, he differentiated between the two terms as follows: Vocational assessment is an ongoing process carried out by professionals from many different disciplines, and information from vocational assessment is incorporated into a student's total educational program; vocational evaluation is an in-depth process conducted by a trained vocational evaluator, usually in a vocational evaluation center. There are different methods these administrators use in their evaluation. For instance, there are tests that measure individual performance, samples of individual work, written tests, and interviews that are normally employed (Levinson, 1994).

School personnel have not been able to agree on a term or title to represent the realm of student assessment in vocational education. When first introduced into school settings, programs were called vocational evaluation based on the service's origin in vocational rehabilitation. After PL 94-142, the service was aligned with services for special education, and different forms of evaluation were frequently referred to as vocational assessment. In essence, vocational evaluation has been delineated as a more intensive, time-limited service than vocational assessment. Although the term vocational evaluation represents the broad umbrella under which vocational assessment is subsumed, for our purposes the terms will be referred to as vocational evaluation assessment. The purposes and goals are well defined and agreed on throughout the literature. Vocational assessment is a process that can measure skills, attitudes, interests, and physical abilities. In addition, it can predict success in occupational placements and prescribe the necessary program plan needed to reach the necessary objectives. Furthermore, it can explore interests and match them with abilities while observing behavioral changes.

Levinson and Capps (1985) discussed vocational assessment as a process that yields critical information with which vocational programming decisions may be made.

They include the identification of appropriate goals and instructional methods in the process. Peterson (1985) suggested six guidelines for effective vocational assessment: (1) use trained personnel: (2) develop and use locally developed work samples; (3) obtain access to a vocational evaluation center; (4) plan to develop and expand vocational assessment in phases with a team; (5) ascertain that vocational assessment is instructionally relevant and useful; and (6) ensure that the vocational assessment is used for vocational guidance and the identification of appropriate career and vocational service. Peterson (1985) stated that vocational assessment can be "a powerful tool in the education of special students" since it can provide a link between special education or Chapter 1 services and vocational education. However, it has been pointed out that the current system employed for vocational evaluation is lacking (Lowman, 1993). Therefore, the challenge to fully operationalize these services with respect to students with disabilities remains firmly in place.

REFERENCES

Association for Career & Technical Education. (1995). The Test Makers. *Vocational Education Journal, 70*(3), 30.

Cobb, R. B., & Larkin, D. (1985). Assessment and placement of handicapped pupils into secondary vocational education programs. *Focus on Exceptional Children, 17*(7), 1–14.

Leconte, P. (1985, December). *Vocational assessment of the special needs learner: A vocational education perspective.* Paper presented at the meeting of the American Vocational Association Convention, Atlanta, GA.

Levinson, E. M. (1994). Current vocational assessment models for students with disabilities. *Journal of Counseling & Development, 73,* 94–101.

Levinson, F. M., & Capps, C. F. (1985). Vocational assessment and special education triennial reevaluations at the secondary school level. *Psychology in the Schools, 22,* 283–292.

Lowman, R. L. (1993). The inter-domain model of career assessment and counseling. *Journal of Counseling & Development, 71,* 549–554.

Peterson, M. (1985, December). *Vocational assessment of special students: A comprehensive developmental approach.* Paper presented at the meeting of the American Vocational Association Convention, Atlanta, GA.

Rosenberg, H., & Tesolowski, D. G. (1982). Assessment of critical vocational behaviors. *Career Development for Exceptional Individuals, 5,* 25–37.

EILEEN MCCARTHY
University of Wisconsin at Madison
First edition

CANDACE ANDREWS
California State University, San Bernardino
Third edition

See also **Vocational Rehabilitation Counseling**

VOCATIONAL REHABILITATION ACT OF 1973
(*See Rehabilitation Act of 1973*)

VOCATIONAL REHABILITATION COUNSELING

According to the 2006–2007 edition of the *Occupational Outlook Handbook* (Bureau of Labor Statistics, 2005), "Rehabilitation counselors help people deal with the personal, social, and vocational effects of disabilities. They counsel people with disabilities resulting from birth defects, illness or disease, accidents, or the stress of daily life. They evaluate the strengths and limitations of individuals, provide personal and vocational counseling, and arrange for medical care, vocational training, and job placement. Rehabilitation counselors interview both individuals with disabilities and their families, evaluate school and medical reports, and confer and plan with physicians, psychologists, occupational therapists, and employers to determine the capabilities and skills of the individual. Conferring with the client, they develop a rehabilitation program that often includes training to help the person develop job skills. Rehabilitation counselors also work toward increasing the client's capacity to live independently" (p. 6). Although this general definition is correct, the actual activities engaged in by rehabilitation counselors and the resources available to them vary considerably depending on their work setting.

Approximately 9,000 of the estimated 18,000 to 20,000 rehabilitation counselors in the United States are certified rehabilitation counselors. The prototypical rehabilitation counselor works for one of the state Department of Vocational Rehabilitation (DVR) agencies and places primary emphasis on the vocational adjustment of clients with disabilities who are adjudged to have the potential for gainful employment. Rehabilitation counselors also work in a wide variety of allied settings such as sheltered workshops, centers for individuals with developmental disabilities, rehabilitation centers, Veterans' Administration programs, employment services, alcohol and drug abuse programs, halfway houses, insurance companies, and private for-profit organizations that specialize in the rehabilitation of industrially injured clients. New developments in the rehabilitation counselor's role are seen in recent movements to provide independent living skills to individuals with severe disabilities and assistance to youth with disabilities as they make the transition from school to the world of work.

The profession of rehabilitation counseling emerged with the passage of PL 236 (Smith-Fess Act) in 1920, which established the civilian vocational rehabilitation program in the United States. However, it was not until the passage of PL 565 in 1954 that federal funds were available to encourage formal academic training for rehabilitation personnel. There are approximately 110 rehabilitation-counselor training programs accredited by the Council on Rehabilitation Education (CORE) and/or members of the National Council on Rehabilitation Education (NCRE; U.S. Congress, 1990). Today the professional identity of the rehabilitation counselor is well established, and there is consensus regarding an appropriate educational curriculum. The knowledge base and competencies for this profession are reflected in the following core subjects that are taught in most rehabilitation counselor training programs: history and philosophy of rehabilitation, vocational and personal counseling, physical disabilities, developmental disabilities, mental illness, psychosocial implications of disability, psychological testing, vocational evaluation, occupational information and employment trends, community resources, job placement, and supervised internships.

The most prominent professional organizations for rehabilitation counselors are the National Rehabilitation Association, the National Rehabilitation Counseling Association, and the American Rehabilitation Counseling Association. Within the past decade, certification procedures for rehabilitation counselors have been established through the efforts of various professional organizations. Certification is based on a combination of education, experience, and the successful completion of a national examination. Although certification procedures do guarantee minimum standards of competency, they may be criticized for restricting entrance into the profession by those who are otherwise qualified but lack formal credentials. Many rehabilitation employers expect applicants to be certified, but this is by no means universal and the eventual status of certification is unclear at present.

The high social validity of rehabilitation counseling is indicated by the continuing bipartisan congressional support that rehabilitation legislation has enjoyed for over 65 years. Additional economic benefits accrue to society from the reductions in welfare, disability, and medical assistance payments after the disabled person enters the workforce. Studies of the cost effectiveness of vocational rehabilitation programs showed that the conversion of two rehabilitative day treatment programs to supported employment programs resulted in improved vocational outcomes with no increase in costs (Clark et al., 1996). In human terms, state DVR agencies rehabilitate between 300,000 and 400,000 physically challenged people per year. The dignity and self-esteem these individuals feel when they become contributing members of society cannot be measured in dollars.

REFERENCES

Bureau of Labor Statistics. (2005). *Occupational outlook handbook: 2006–2007 edition.* Washington, DC: U.S. Department of Labor.

Clark, R. E., Bush, P. W., Becker, D. R., & Drake, R. (1996). A cost-effectiveness comparison of supported employment and rehabilitative day treatment. *Administration and Policy in Mental Health, 24,* 63–77.

U. S. Congress. (1990). *Public Law 101-476: Individuals with Disabilities Education Act*. Washington, DC: Government Printing Office.

JOHN D. SEE
University of Wisconsin at Stout
First edition

CLAUDIA CAMARILLO-DIEVENDORF
Pitzer College, Claremont
Third edition

See *also* Vocational Evaluation

VOCATIONAL VILLAGE

A vocational village is a cloistered community in which persons with and without disabilities live and work. It is often referred to as a sheltered village. There is a strong work ethic in the community. The setting is not usually designed for transition but rather as a permanent living/working arrangement for individuals with disabilities. There is usually a deep religious undertone in such villages and a majority of the time they are church sponsored. The typically developing residents of the village are often volunteer workers who have made a long-term commitment to the village. There are also some typically developing workers who are students working in practicum arrangements or in work-study activities. Baker, Seltzer, and Seltzer (1977) explain that

> Common to all sheltered villages is the segregation of the retarded person from the outside community and the implicit view that the retarded adult is better off in an environment that shelters him/her from many of the potential failures and frustrations of life in the outside community. (p. 109)

It is a delivery model that espouses the principle of separate but equal.

REFERENCE

Baker, B. L., Seltzer, G. B., & Seltzer, M. M. (1977). *As close as possible: Community residences for retarded adults*. Boston, MA: Little, Brown.

ROBERT A. SEDLAK
University of Wisconsin at Stout

See *also* Community Residential Programs; Sheltered Workshops

VOICE DISORDERS (DYSPHONIA)

Aronson (1985) says that, "A voice disorder exists when quality, pitch, loudness, or flexibility differs from the voices of others of similar age, sex, and cultural group." What constitutes an abnormal voice is a relative judgment that is made by the speaker, the listener, and professionals who may be consulted. Causes of voice disorders are usually classified as either organic (physical) or functional (behavioral). Recent studies report the incidence of voice disorders in the U.S. population of school-aged children to be between 6% and 9% (Aronson, 1985). The parameters by which a voice can be judged as abnormal are considered in context. For example, a voice that is so hoarse that it distracts the listener or interferes with intelligibility can be identified as disordered and in need of treatment. The pitch of a female voice considered to be appropriate during her school-aged years may be too high for effective function as she enters the business world. The person who cannot produce a voice loud enough to be heard in a typically noisy classroom or one whose voice is so inflexible that the speaker seems emotionless may also be identified as abnormal. In some cases, such abnormal voice symptoms indicate the presence of an underlying illness that is in need of medical diagnosis and treatment. If a hoarse voice quality exists for an extended period of time (i.e., longer than 2 weeks), it could indicate the presence of a mass lesion in the larynx (voice box) that could be benign or malignant. An inability to alter pitch or loudness to convey meaning could signal a neuromuscular problem associated with incipient neurological disease. An inappropriately high pitch, used habitually, might point to endocrine dysfunction or to psychosocial issues that require attention (Colton & Casper, 1990).

Evaluation and treatment of voice disorders requires the combined efforts of the speech-language pathologist and an otolaryngologist (ENT). These professionals will examine the physical status of the larynx, velopharyngeal mechanism, and supporting respiratory system and will analyze the voice both perceptually and acoustically to determine if a clinically significant disorder exists. They will then attempt to identify the etiological factors underlying any abnormalities and prescribe a course of treatment. Often, the first choice for treatment is behavioral modification to eliminate factors contributing to the voice disorder and to establish good vocal hygiene. Less frequently, voice problems require physical management that might include medication, for example, in allergy therapy, or a more invasive treatment, such as surgery.

REFERENCES

Aronson, A. (1985). *Clinical voice disorders*. New York, NY: Thieme.

Colton, R. H., & Casper, J. K. (1990). *Understanding voice problems*. Baltimore, MD: Williams & Wilkins.

STAFF

See *also* Speech

VOLTA REVIEW, THE

The Volta Review was founded in 1898. It is published four times a year, with a monograph issue in September. The publication is a product of the Alexander Graham Bell Association for the Deaf, a nonprofit organization founded by Alexander Graham Bell in 1890 that serves as an information center for people with hearing impairment. Bell believed that people with hearing losses could be taught to speak and, through lip reading, could learn to understand others.

Only articles devoted to the education, rehabilitation, and communicative development of individuals with hearing impairment are published by *The Volta Review*. The target audience includes teachers of the hearing impaired; professionals in the fields of education, speech, audiology, language, otology, and psychology; parents of children with hearing impairments; and adults with hearing impairments. The articles are peer-reviewed for possible publication and vary in length, and the journal includes advertisements as well as illustrations. Topics include issues related to hearing impairment such as language development, parental concerns, medical/technical and psychosocial issues, teaching, and computers.

REBECCA BAILEY
Texas A&M University
First edition

TAMARA J. MARTIN
The University of Texas of the Permian Basin
Second edition

See also Deaf; Deaf Education

VOLUNTARY AGENCIES

Voluntary agencies are organizations that use volunteers to serve on decision-making boards or to provide services for the community. Volunteers are members of a community whom, without the expectation of pay, offer their time to benefit agencies that serve particular groups in an area. Volunteers on agency governing boards make decisions on the purchase of property and capital equipment, organizational policy, specific human services that will be available in the community, allocation of funds to other agencies (United Way, foundations, etc.) or within their own agency, and fund-raising.

Approximately 84 million Americans serve as volunteers in such agencies each year (Shtulman, 1985). According to the Current Population Survey (CPS),

about 83.9 million Americans served as volunteers in 2001, resulting in an estimated $239 billion worth of work (Independent Sector, 2001). Women have provided a large portion of volunteer service, but the entry of large numbers of women into the workforce has limited their availability for volunteer service. However, an increasingly active senior citizen population is providing a pool of dependable, dedicated volunteers. Additionally, volunteering rates have increased in younger Americans from 2002–2003, with teenagers, on average, volunteering more often than other age groups (Helms, 2004). In 2005, about 38% of American high school students participated in school-based services (Haski-Leventhal et al., 2008). Youth who volunteered showed to have a positive impact on their success in school and higher self-confidence. Voluntary programs have proven to be very effective for at-risk youth by promoting social inclusion and giving the youth a place to belong (Haski-Leventhal et al., 2008). Another developing source is through the workplace. Some firms make it possible for their employees to have release time for community service; these firms say that this "loaned executive" program contributes to a better workforce through the opportunity for workers to apply or develop skills, a lower rate of absenteeism, and increased productivity (United Way, 1985).

REFERENCES

Helms, S. (2004). *Youth volunteering in the states: 2002 and 2003*. University of Maryland: The Center for Information & Research on Civic Learning & Engagement. Retrieved from http://www.civicyouth.org/PopUps/FactSheets/FS_Vol_st ate.pdf

Haski-Leventhal, D., Ronel, N., York, A. S., Ben-David, B. M. (2008). Youth volunteering for youth: Who are they serving? How are they being served? *Children and Youth Services Review 30*, 834–846.

Independent Sector. (2001). *Giving and volunteering in the United States 2001*. Retrieved from http://www.independent sector.org

Shtulman, J. (1985). *A question-and-answer session on voluntarism*. Holyoke, MA: Transcript-Telegram.

United Way. (1985). *Volunteer notes*. Alexandria, VA: Author.

DENISE M. SEDLACK
United Way of Dunn County,
  Menomonie, Wisconsin
First edition

THOMAS NEISES
California State University,
  San Bernardino
Third edition

AMANDA C. CHOW
Texas A&M University at College Station
Fourth edition

VON RECKLINGHAUSEN, FRIEDRICH (1833–1910)

Friedrich von Recklinghausen, a German pathologist, was a major contributor to the development of pathological anatomy as a branch of medicine. He is best known for his description, in 1863, of neurofibromatosis, or von Recklinghausen's disease, characterized by multiple small tumors affecting the subcutaneous nerves. The disease is hereditary and is associated with mental retardation.

This entry has been informed by the sources listed below.

REFERENCES

Talbott, J. H. (1970). *A biographical history of medicine*. Orlando, FL: Grune & Stratton.

von Recklinghausen, F. (1962). Multiple fibromas of the skin and multiple neuromas. In E. R. Long (Trans.), *Selected readings in pathology* (2nd ed.). Springfield, IL: Thomas.

PAUL IRVINE
Katonah, New York

See also Neurofibromatosis; Mental Retardation

VON WILLERBRANDS DISEASE

Von Willerbrands disease (VWD) is a common, mild type of congenital coagulopathy (bleeding disorders; Miller, Pearson, Baehner, & McMillan, 1978; Williams, Beutler, Ersler, & Rundles, 1972). VWD is thought to be associated with an X-linked autosomal dominant genetic disorder leading to a deficiency in the soluble clotting Factor VIII (antihemophilic factor) complex responsible for coagulatory responses. The prevalence of VWD has been approximated at 1% of the general population (Type I). Type III VWD, the most severe type, has an approximate prevalence of 1 in 1,000,000 births.

Characteristics

1. Uncontrollable internal or external bleeding
2. Exceptionally long or prolonged bleeding times
3. Potential joint damage
4. Psychological sequelae associated with a chronic medical illness
5. Psychosocial limitations as a result of medical condition
6. Reduced activity level

Although the disease has no direct cognitive consequences per se (except in cases of severe recurrent bleeding episodes), diseases transmitted through blood products (which are sometimes required in patients with VWD and hemophilia) has been known to cause neurocognitive impediments. The most prevalent in recent times have been the result of cognitive impairments caused by Hepatitis B or C or by horizontal transmission of HIV in VWD patients.

With regard to special education, these children are easily labeled under the Other Health Impaired label and are capable of receiving special services if they are required particularly adaptations in their curriculum involving activities that may put these children at risk.

Future research should focus on the development of cost-effective treatments (c.f. Mannuci, 1977). The development of safer homeostatic interventions particularly home-based interventions also merit attention. Similarly, future treatments should maximize the functional status and quality of life of patients.

REFERENCES

Mannuci, P. M. (1977). DDAVP: A new pharmacological approach to the management of hemophilia and von Willerbrand's disease. *Lancet, 1*, 869.

Miller, D. R., Pearson, H. A., Baehner, R. L., & McMillan, C. W. (Eds.). (1978). *Smith's blood diseases of infancy and childhood*. St. Louis, MO: Mosby.

Williams, W. J., Beutler, E., Ersler, A. J., & Rundles, R. W. (1972). *Hematology*. New York, NY: McGraw-Hill.

ANTOLIN M. LLORENTE
Baylor College of Medicine Houston, Texas

VYGOTSKY, LEV S. (1896–1934)

Lev S. Vygotsky was a Soviet psychologist and semiotician. His work had a tremendous impact on the development of psychology in the Soviet Union and is currently attracting a great deal of interest outside Russia as well (Wertsch, 1985a, 1985b).

In the West, Vygotsky is known primarily for his work on the relationship between the development of thinking and speech in ontogenesis (Vygotsky, 1962, 1978). In Vygotsky's view, the more complex forms of human thinking, memory, and attention depend on the individual's mastery of historically and culturally developed means of organizing and mediating mental activity. Vygotsky argued that words and speech are first used in social interaction to organize and mediate the mental activity of several individuals working cooperatively on a task and that these same linguistic means are later appropriated by the individual and internalized to be used in organizing and mediating his or her mental activity when working alone on similar tasks. In this sense, Vygotsky felt that certain kinds of social interaction between children and adults (or more competent peers) can create a "zone of proximal development" that raises the level of the child's cognitive functioning in the context of social interaction and helps move the child toward the next or proximal stage of independent functioning.

For Vygotsky, however, this work was only part of a much broader program of theory and research that was concerned with the relationships between historically developed modes of social behavior and the psychological development of the individual in all its aspects (Minick, 1987). In the decade following his death, the efforts of his colleagues and students to develop this broader theoretical framework led to the emergence of what is known as the theory of activity, a theoretical and research paradigm that illuminates the work of many contemporary Russian psychologists.

Vygotsky had a lifelong interest in developing theory, research, and practical intervention techniques relevant to abnormal psychological functioning and development in both children and adults. He wrote extensively on these topics (Vygotsky, 1987) and founded several institutes that continue to play an important role in Russian work in this area. Through this work and that of colleagues and students such as A. R. Luria (Luria, 1979), Vygotsky played a central role in the development of Soviet work in this domain.

REFERENCES

Luria, A. R. (1979). *The making of mind: A personal account of Soviet psychology.* Cambridge, MA: Harvard University Press.

Minick, N. (1987). The development of Vygotsky's thought. In N. Minick (Trans.), *The collected works of L. S. Vygotsky: Vol. 1. Problems of general psychology* (Introduction). New York, NY: Plenum Press.

Vygotsky, L. S. (1962). *Thought and language* (E. Hanfmann & G. Vakar, Eds. and Trans.). Cambridge, MA: MIT Press. (Original work published 1934)

Vygotsky, L. S. (1978). *Mind in society* (M. Cole, V. John-Steiner, S. Scribner, & E. Souberman, Eds.). Cambridge, MA: Harvard University Press.

Vygotsky, L. S. (1987). Thinking and speech. In R. W. Rieber & A. S. Carton (Eds.), *The collected works of L. S. Vygotsky: Vol. 1. Problems of general psychology* (pp. 3–68) [Trans. N. Minick]. New York, NY: Plenum Press. (Original work published 1934)

Wertsch, J. V. (1985a). *Vygotsky and the social formation of mind.* Cambridge, MA: Harvard University Press.

Wertsch, J. V. (Ed.). (1985b). *Culture, communication, and cognition: Vygotskian perspectives.* New York, NY: Cambridge University Press.

Norris Minick
*Center for Psychosocial Studies,
The Spencer Foundation*

See *also* Theory of Activity; Zone of Proximal Development

W

WAARDENBURG SYNDROME

Waardenburg syndrome (WS) is a hereditary, congenital disorder thought to be a variant of albinism (deficiency of pigmentation). Findings include widely spaced inner corners (canthi) of the eyes; defects in hair, skin, and iris pigmentation; and congenital sensorineural deafness. Two clinical types of WS have been identified. There is controversy regarding the existence of a Type III WS.

A mutation in the PAX3 gene on Chromosome 2 is associated with Type I WS. Type II WS is caused by a defective gene on Chromosome 3. Type III WS has also been linked to abnormalities in the PAX3 gene.

The incidence of WS is 1 to 2 per 20,000 births. Male-to-female ratio is 1:1. The mode of inheritance is autosomal dominant. The majority of new cases (nonfamilial) are closely tied to advanced paternal age.

Characteristics

1. Widely spaced inner canthi with shortening of the opening of the eyelids (palpebral fissure). This finding is a constant feature in Type I WS. It is not seen in Type II disease.

2. Broad, high bridge of the nose. Underdeveloped sides (alae) of the nose (80%).

3. Flaring of the eyebrows around the base of the nose. Eyebrows may meet in the middle of the forehead (50%).

4. Partial albinism manifests as a white clump of hair in the midfrontal scalp, hypopigmented skin lesions, and hypochromic (pale blue) iris of the eye. Heterochromia irides (one brown and one blue iris) occurs in 25% of patients. Premature graying is also common and is usually complete by age 30.

5. Congenital deafness, usually secondary to defects in inner ear or auditory nerve development, is seen in 25% of Type I disease and 50% of individuals with Type II WS.

6. Occasional associated defects include cleft lip and cleft palate, congenital heart disease, gastrointestinal anomalies, scoliosis, and malformations of the female reproductive tract.

7. Type III WS (Klein-Waardenburg syndrome) is typified by all of the aforementioned features, plus malformations of the arm and hand. These features include abnormal shortening, joint contractures, fusion of the wrist bones, syndactyly (webbing of the fingers, with or without fusion), and undeveloped muscles.

Therapy for patients with WS involves regular auditory and ophthalmological assessments. Hearing deficits may not respond to assistive devices. Early diagnosis of deafness should prompt investigation of alternative means of communication (signing), should speech development be affected. Surgical correction of specific congenital anomalies involving the mouth, heart, and gut may be necessary. Because of the hereditary nature of WS (50% chance of recurrence in familial cases), genetic counseling should be made available for affected individuals.

There are no cognitive deficits associated with WS. If the child has hearing deficits, he or she is eligible to receive special support services. An early intervention program that provides speech and language therapy will help the child reach his or her language developmental milestones.

The prognosis for children with WS is good. The syndrome has no effect on life expectancy and is not associated with any defects in mental abilities. The astute clinician should be aware of the physical findings of WS and screen all infants thought to have WS for hearing deficits because delayed diagnosis of deafness can adversely affect overall outcome for the individual patient.

REFERENCES

Darmstadt, G. L. (2000). Hypopigmented lesions. In R. E. Behrman, R. M. Kleigman, & H. B. Jenson (Eds.), *Nelson textbook of pediatrics* (16th ed., p. 1986). Philadelphia, PA: Saunders.

Jones, K. (1997). *Smith's recognizable patterns of human malformation* (5th ed.). Philadelphia, PA: Saunders.

National Organization for Rare Disorders. (2000). Waardenburg syndrome. Retrieved from http://www.rarediseases.org/

Pediatric Database. (1993). *Waardenburg syndromes*. Retrieved from http://icondata.com

Barry H. Davison
Ennis, Texas

W. Mayfield
*Baylor Pediatric Specialty Services,
Dallas, Texas*

WAGR SYNDROME

WAGR syndrome is a constellation of abnormalities that include Wilms tumor, aniridia, genitourinary anomalies or gonadoblastoma, and mental retardation (WAGR). Wilms tumor is the most common form of childhood cancer and involves the kidneys (also known as nephroblastoma). Aniridia is the absence of the colored portion of the eye (the iris). Gonadoblastoma are cancer cells that form in the testes in males and the ovaries in females. In order for a person to be diagnosed with WAGR syndrome, at least two of the conditions must be present, and in all but one case of WAGR syndrome, aniridia has been present. Therefore, the clinical representation will vary depending on the conditions present in the individual.

WAGR is a rare disorder that results from defects in Chromosome 11p and is thought to occur more often in males than in females. Currently, there is no known reason for the genetic mutations involved with this disorder. The severity of WAGR syndrome depends on the size and portion of the deletion on Chromosome 11p. There is deletion of part of Band 13 on Chromosome 11. WAGR syndrome can be diagnosed at birth. The most common physical feature associated with WAGR syndrome that is observable at birth is the absence of the colored portion of the eye. Another physical symptom that could be detected at birth is genitourinary abnormalities that may be present.

Characteristics

1. Either partial or complete absence of the colored portion of the eye
2. Presence of Wilms tumor
3. Genitourinary anomalies (i.e., renal dysplasias, horseshoe kidney, anomalies of the collecting system, pseudohermaphroditism, hypospadias, and cryptorchidism
4. Microcephaly
5. Intellectual disability
6. Delay in growth
7. Dysmorphism
8. Craniofacial dysostosis
9. Hypertension
10. Significant vision loss
11. Protruding lips

The prognosis for WAGR syndrome depends on the conditions that are present. Surgical removal of the tumor followed by both chemotherapy and radiotherapy following the surgery has been shown to be the most effective treatment. Studies have shown that patients have a better prognosis if the treatment is started when they are younger.

Individuals with WAGR syndrome would be identified for special education services under one of the following categories: physical disability, significant limited intellectual capacity, or multiple disability. The extent of the services will depend on the severity of the symptoms and on the number of conditions present.

Future research will probably revolve around the genetics involved in this syndrome. Some important goals include locating the exact location involved on Chromosome 11, looking at the way this syndrome is passed from one generation to the next, and focusing on the factors that predispose an individual to develop Wilms tumor. Currently research is being done on the effects of chemotherapy and on the risk of developing a second tumor.

This entry has been informed by the sources listed below.

REFERENCES

Pavilack, M., & Walton, D. (1993). Genetics of aniridia: The aniridia-Wilm's tumor association. *International Ophthalmology Clinics, 33*, 77–84.

Pochedly, C., & Baum, E. (1984). *Wilm's tumor: Clinical and biological manifestations*. New York, NY: Elsevier Science.

Urdang, L., & Swallow, H. (1983). *Mosby's medical and nursing dictionary*. St. Louis, MO: Mosby.

Ammy Branan
University of Northern Colorado

WALKER WARBURG SYNDROME

Walker Warburg syndrome is a type of congenital muscular dystrophy (CMD). Walker Warburg is the most severe type of CMD, affecting the muscles, eyes, and brain. It is also known as HARD ± E syndrome, which stands for hydrocephalus (an abnormal increase in the amount of cerebrospinal fluid within the cranial cavity), agyria (the condition of having a smooth cerebrum without convolutions), retina (abnormalities of the sensory membrane of the eye), dysplasia (abnormal growth or development of organs or cells in the body), and (if present) encephalocele (hernia of the brain). Walker Warburg syndrome is an autosomal recessive disorder, but at present there is no clear genetic linkage.

Walker Warburg syndrome is extremely rare. Thoene (1995) stated that only 60 cases had been reported in the medical literature. However, because of the wide range of brain and eye defects, the diagnosis is frequently not considered (Jones, 1997). There is some evidence that this syndrome affects females more than it does males.

Characteristics

1. Walker Warburg syndrome often presents with decreased fetal movement, excessive amounts of amniotic fluid (polyhydramnios), or both.
2. Severe hypotonia and weakness and mild spasticity are present at birth, along with a poor suck and cry.
3. Vision is poor, with possible ocular abnormalities (e.g., cataracts, retinal dysplasia and detachment, glaucoma).
4. Profound intellectual disability and seizures are present.
5. Lissencephaly (malformations of the cerebellum).
6. Other symptoms are sometimes associated with Walker Warburg syndrome (e.g., cleft palate, cleft lip, and encephalocele).
7. Death usually occurs within the first few years. Those individuals who live beyond 5 years of age often have less severe mental retardation. However, seizures become increasingly common with age.

There is no specific treatment for Walker Warburg syndrome. If hydrocephalus is present, a shunt procedure may be necessary. Seizures may be controlled with mediation. Other treatment is symptomatic and supportive. For example, physical therapy is necessary to preserve muscle activity and allow for maximum functioning.

A student diagnosed with Walker Warburg syndrome is likely to be severely mentally retarded and, therefore, would qualify for special services under the Individuals with Disabilities Education Act (IDEA, 1997). Educational programs need to incorporate a variety of components, including physical therapy and speech-language

pathologists, and make accommodations such as special transportation or shorter school day. Classroom arrangements will have to take into consideration mediations, special diets, and special equipment (e.g., assistive technology, augmentative-alternative communication devices). The life expectancy of a school-age individual with Walker Warburg syndrome is unknown. Therefore, the school personnel may find themselves in a death preparation or grief-counseling role.

For individuals diagnosed with Walker Warburg syndrome, death usually occurs within the first year, although rarely children will live up to 5 years. Research continues to try to identify the underlying genetic makeup of Walker Warburg syndrome (e.g., Zenker & Dorr, 2000). For more information on Walker Warburg syndrome, contact the Lissencephaly Network, Inc., 10408 Bitterroot Court, Fort Wayne, IN 46804, (219) 432-4310, home page: http://www.ninds.nih.gov/find_people/voluntary_orgs/volorg156.htm.

REFERENCES

Jones, K. L. (1997). *Smith's recognizable patterns of human malformation* (5th ed). Philadelphia, PA: Saunders.

Thoene, J. G. (Ed.). (1995). *Physicians guide to rare diseases* (2nd ed.). Montvale, NJ: Dowden.

Zenker, M., & Dorr, H. G. (2000). A case associated with Walker Warburg syndrome phenotype and homozygous pericentric inversion 9: Coincidental or aetiological factor? *Acta Paediatrica, 89*(6), 750–751.

RACHEL TOPLIS
University of Northern Colorado

WALLIN, JOHN EDWARD (J. E.) WALLACE (1876–1969)

J. E. Wallace Wallin, a pioneer in the fields of special education and clinical psychology, was born in Page County, Iowa on January 21, 1876, to Henry and Emma M. (Johnson) Wallin, originally from Sweden. Wallace was the third of nine children. He attended the public schools of Stanton, Iowa. On June 21, 1913, at the age of 37, he married Frances Geraldine Tinsley. The couple had two daughters, Geraldine Tinsley Wallin Sickler, born in 1919, and Virginia Stanton Wallin Obrinski, born in 1915, who also became a psychologist.

Wallin obtained his BA degree in 1897 from Augustana College in Rock Island, Illinois. He attended Yale and studied under Dr. Edward W. Scripture and George Trumbull Ladd. Scripture had done his own thesis under "the great

German psychologist," Wilhelm Wundt. While at Yale, Wallin completed an MA degree in 1899, and a PhD in 1901. Wallin also worked as an assistant to Dr. G. Stanley Hall at Clark University in Worcester, Massachusetts. Wallin served as head of the psychology department and vice president of the East Stroudsburg State Teachers College in Pennsylvania. While at Stroudsburg, he taught courses in physiological, child, genetic, educational, and abnormal psychology, and mental retardation. Wallin held numerous positions in the following years. He was the head of the department of psychology and education at the Normal Training School at Cleveland, Ohio, from 1909 to 1910, where he developed the field of special education, psychoclinical examinations, and one of the first group intelligence tests. By 1912, he established a psychoeducational clinic at the University of Pittsburgh, which was one of the first such clinics in the country. Wallin went on to become the director of numerous other clinics and special schools and was affiliated with more than 25 colleges and universities (Wallin, 1955).

Outspoken, argumentative, critical, and at times cantankerous, Wallin was a crusader and a pioneer for disabled children. He was a leading advocate for the use of clinical psychology in education, especially as it relates to identification, diagnosis, and prescription for children with disabilities (Irvine, 1979), and was a strong advocate for the proper training of clinicians. He worked to establish the principle that all children would benefit from an education, regardless of degree of disability, and helped to establish special classes in Western Pennsylvania, Ohio, Missouri, and Delaware. Wallin also made extensive contributions to the area of special education and the field of psychology by publishing over 30 books and 350 articles throughout his career, including psychological textbooks. He was a political activist for policies, regulations, and change to ensure appropriate education for children with special needs. He was a member of numerous professional organizations and served on many committees, such as the secretary of the committee on special education for the White House Conference on Child Health and Protection from 1929 to 1930. He continued to write into his 90s. Wallin died on August 5, 1969.

This entry has been informed by the sources listed below.

REFERENCES

Irvine, P. (1979). John Edward Wallace Wallin (1876–1969). A biographical sketch. *Journal of Special Education, 13,* 4–5.

Wallin, J. E. W. (1955). *The odyssey of a psychologist: Pioneering experiences in special education, clinical psychology, and mental hygiene with a comprehensive bibliography of the author's publications.* Wilmington, DE: Author.

KIM RYAN-ARREDONDO
Texas A&M University

WANDERING SPLEEN (CONGENITAL)

Congenital wandering spleen is a very rare birth defect in which the ligaments that hold the spleen in its usual position in the upper left abdomen (splenic peritoneal attachments) are missing or underdeveloped (Rodkey & Macknin, 1992). Congenital wandering spleen has been observed in children from 3 months to 10 years old; the disorder is most commonly found in children who are younger than 1 year old. Wandering spleen is also sometimes called displaced spleen, drifting spleen, floating spleen, splenic ptosis, splenoptosis, or systopic spleen. Wandering spleen is extremely rare, with approximately 50 recorded cases in children under 10 years of age.

Acquired wandering spleen is an adult disorder that results from the relaxation of the splenic ligaments. Acquired wandering spleen affects females at a much higher rate than it does men (in part because pregnancy can lead to such muscle relaxations).

Although congenital wandering spleen can be asymptomatic, it is usually characterized by acute and chronic abdominal pain. Characteristic signs include the presence of a mobile mass with a notched edge; this mass is usually painless in the left upper quadrant (where there is resonance on percussion) but painful in other directions. A variety of imaging techniques can be used to diagnose wandering spleen, including computer tomography, magnetic resonance imaging, nuclear scans, and ultrasonography. Kanthan and Radhi (1999) argue that ultrasonography is the least invasive and the most effective diagnostic test for wandering spleen.

Characteristics

1. May be asymptomatic.
2. Acute or chronic abdominal pain.
3. Recurrent pancreatitis (e.g., Choi et al., 1996).
4. Other symptoms include having a bulging abdominal mass or distended stomach, bloating, constipation, fatigue, fever, nausea, vomiting, weight loss, and difficulty in urination.

Wandering spleen can be treated by observing for signs of compromised spleen functioning and trying to prevent activities that might further injure the spleen. However, Dawson and Roberts (1994) recommend against such a conservative management of the disease. They recommend an early splenoplexy, a surgery that attempts to place the spleen back into its correct position in the upper left abdomen. One risk with a splenoplexy is the breakdown of the suture fixture, which can lead to a recurrence of splenic torsion. Hirose et al. (1998) report the use of a laparascopic splenoplexy to treat wandering spleen, a procedure that is less invasive.

In the case of chronic abdominal pain or blood deficiencies, a splenectomy (removal of the spleen) may be chosen. This surgery is more commonly used in emergency situations because it poses the risk of complications such as life-threatening bacterial infections. Patients who undergo splenectomies are at an increased risk for serious infection for the rest of their lives.

It is unlikely that special education services would be needed for individuals with this disorder, other than possible assistance for pain management or depression resulting from a serious illness. A child with wandering spleen may also need to miss many days of school, particularly if surgery is needed.

Research is continually being conducted on genetic disorders such as wandering spleen, ranging from the Human Genome Project to more specific studies on possible surgical treatments.

REFERENCES

Choi, Y. H., Menken, F. A., Jacobson, I. M., Lombardo, F., Kazam, E., & Barie, P. S. (1996). Recurrent acute pancreatitis: An additional manifestation of the "wandering spleen" syndrome. *American Journal of Gastroenterology, 91*(5), 1034–1038.

Dawson, J. H., & Roberts, N. G. (1994). Management of the wandering spleen. *Australian & New Zealand Journal of Surgery, 64*(6), 441–444.

Hirose, R., Kitano, S., Bando, T., Ueda, Y., Sato, K., Yoshida, T.,...Izumi, T. (1998). Laparoscopic splenoplexy for pediatric wandering spleen. *Journal of Pediatric Surgery, 33*(10), 1571–1573.

Kanthan, R., & Radhi, J. M. (1999). The "true" splenic wanderer. *Canadian Journal of Gastroenterology, 13*(2), 169–171.

Rodkey, M. L., & Macknin, M. L. (1992). Pediatric wandering spleen: Case report and review of literature. *Clinical Pediatrics, 31*(5), 289–294.

JAMES C. KAUFMAN
*Educational Testing Service Princeton,
New Jersey*

WATSON, JOHN B. (1878–1958)

John B. Watson developed and publicized the basic concepts of behaviorism, which in the 1920s became one of the major schools of psychological thought. Watson obtained his PhD at the University of Chicago and continued there as an instructor until 1908, when he accepted a professorship at Johns Hopkins University. Watson's behaviorism explained human behavior in terms of physiological responses to environmental stimuli and psychology as the study of the relationship between the two. Watson sought to make psychology "a purely objective experimental branch of natural science," with conditioning as one of its chief methods.

Watson's zealous environmentalism led him into some extreme positions, such as his assertion that he could train any healthy infant, regardless of its heredity, to become any type of person he might designate: "doctor, lawyer, artist, merchant-chief, and...even beggar-man and thief." Hyperbole aside, Watson's behaviorism was a dominant force in American psychology for decades and underlies many of today's behaviorally oriented instructional approaches. Watson eventually left the academic world, completing his career as an executive in the field of advertising.

This entry has been informed by the sources listed below.

REFERENCES

Skinner, B. F. (1959). John Broadua Watson, behaviorist. *Science, 129,* 197–198.

Watson, J. B. (1919). *Psychology from the standpoint of a behaviorist.* Philadelphia, PA: Lippincott.

PAUL IRVINE
Katonah, New York

***See also* Behavior Modification; Conditioning**

WEB ACCESSIBILITY

Web accessibility is the degree to which a web-based resource is widely usable. Resources that have a high level of accessibility will be accessible by users regardless of the device or software used to access the resource, the functional limitations or abilities of the user, or the conditions of access (e.g., low bandwidth connections, display size). Conversely, web resources that have a low level of accessibility are not usable by a majority of users because of limitations associated with platform, information format, ability/disability, or ambient conditions.

Design techniques that increase web accessibility seek to minimize these limitations, although they cannot be completely eliminated under this definition.

Since web accessibility of a specific resource is almost always situational rather than prescriptive, defining it in concrete terms is difficult. The World Wide Web Consortium (W3C), specifically the subgroup of the W3C that deals with accessibility issues (also known as the Web Accessibility Initiative, or WAI) states that "Web accessibility means that people with disabilities can perceive, understand, navigate, and interact with the web, and that they can contribute to the web. Web accessibility also benefits others, including older people with changing abilities due to aging" (W3C, 2005a). An important point to this description is that web accessibility benefits users beyond those with disabilities.

Much has been written in recent years about web accessibility, but little scholarly research has been done. Most of the available literature, much of it online, focuses on *how* to achieve web accessibility rather than *what* it is. Two well-known standards have been promulgated to this end.

Standards

The first (and most widely known) is the Web Content Accessibility Guidelines version one (WCAG1.0; W3C, 2005b). The WCAG consist of 14 guidelines that are further broken down into 65 checkpoints. These checkpoints detail design and programming rules that guide developers in how to make web-based content accessible. Each of the checkpoints is also given a priority of one, two, or three. Priority one checkpoints are those items considered to be the most critical by the W3C. Priority two checkpoints are considered important, while priority three checkpoints are considered desirable. All of the guidelines are further sorted into two overriding themes that guide accessible design: ensuring graceful transformation (of information), and making content understandable and navigable. An example of a WCAG1.0 checkpoint is given in the following.

Guideline 1. Checkpoint 1. "Provide a text equivalent for every nontext element (e.g., via 'alt,' 'longdesc,' or in element content). *This includes*: images, graphical representations of text (including symbols), image map regions, animations (e.g., animated GIFs), applets and programmatic objects, ascii art, frames, scripts, images used as list bullets, spacers, graphical buttons, sounds (played with or without user interaction), stand-alone audio files, audio tracks of video, and video" (W3C, 1999).

Taking a cue from the W3C, the federal government (specifically the Access Board) created a subset of the original WCAG1.0 guidelines in 2000 and dubbed them the Electronic and Information Technology Accessibility Standards or, as they are more commonly known, the

Section 508 standards (Access Board, 2000). These standards were based on the existing priority one checkpoints found in the WCAG1.0 standards with several minor changes. An excellent comparison of the two standards can be found online at http://www.jimthatcher.com/sidebyside.htm (Thatcher, 2005). The 508 standards apply specifically to federal agencies' websites, but the standards have been widely adopted by nonfederal institutions as they represent a succinct and demonstrable subset of the more comprehensive (and sometimes esoteric) WCAG1.0 standards. As more and more institutions, both public and private, have written institutional web accessibility policies, the 508 standards have been instructive.

Assessment

There are a variety of accessibility "checkers" available to content developers and assessment personnel. They fall into several categories of implementation:

- *Authoring Tool Checkers*: These are built-in accessibility features of software applications used to develop websites. Web authoring tools such as Dreamweaver (http://www.macromedia.com/macromedia/accessibility/) and Frontpage (http://www.microsoft.com/en-us/default.aspx) provide utilities to implement accessibility features during the development phase.
- *Stand-Alone Checkers*: These are applications that are used during the postdevelopment phase of website management. Some examples are Bobby (http://www.cast.org/bobby/) and Wave (http://webaim.org/). Stand-alone checkers are good solutions for individual web developers that have access to the website being checked.
- *Enterprise Checkers*: These are web-based applications that can check very large websites and collect/disseminate information in a web-based format. Enterprise Checkers are good for assessing large websites in a decentralized environment where the web content is located on a variety of servers. An example of an Enterprise Checker is WebXM (http://www.watchfire.com/products/webxm/default.aspx). Another example is UsableNet's LIFT (http://www.usablenet.com/).

There is a fairly comprehensive list of accessibility checkers located at http://www.webaim.org/products/evalandrepair/.

It is important to note that accessibility checkers cannot catch accessibility errors. Only about 25% of published accessibility guidelines (when using WCAG guidelines) are automatically verifiable with accessibility checking software. The other 75% may be indicated by accessibility checking software, but must be verified by the author.

REFERENCES

Access Board. (2000). *Electronic and Information Technology Accessibility Standards (Section 508)*. Retrieved from http://www.access-board.gov/

Thatcher, J. (2005). *Side by side WCAG vs. 508*. Retrieved from http://www.jimthatcher.com/sidebyside.htm

World Wide Web Consortium (W3C). (1999). *Checklist of checkpoints for web content accessibility guidelines 1.0*. Retrieved from http://www.w3.org/TR/WCAG10/full-checklist.html

World Wide Web Consortium (W3C). (2005a). *Introduction to Web accessibility*. Retrieved from http://www.w3.org/WAI/intro/accessibility.php

World Wide Web Consortium (W3C). (2005b). *WAI guidelines and techniques*. Retrieved from http://www.w3.org/WAI/guid-tech.html

DAVID SWEENEY
Texas A&M University

WECHSLER, DAVID (1896–1981)

Known primarily as the author of intelligence scales that played, and continue to play, a critical role in the lives of millions of individuals throughout the world, David Wechsler had a humanistic philosophy about testing as a part of assessment. His professional writing includes more than 60 articles and books that emphasize the importance of motivation, personality, drive, cultural opportunity, and other variables in determining an individual's functional level.

Born in Rumania, Wechsler moved with his family of nine to New York City at age 6. At 20 he completed a BA degree at City College in 1916 and an MA the following year at Columbia University under Robert S. Woodworth. The next few years were spent with the armed forces, where Wechsler helped evaluate thousands of recruits, many of whom could not read English and who had little formal schooling. Near the end of his army tour he studied with Charles Spearman and Karl Pearson in London and then, on a fellowship, with Henri Pieron and Louis Lapique in Paris. These studies provided the foundation for his continuous enthusiasm for the "nonintellective" components of intelligence.

While completing his PhD at Columbia in 1925, Wechsler worked as a psychologist in New York City's newly created Bureau of Child Study. After serving as secretary for the Psychological Corporation (1925–1927) and in private clinical practice (1927–1932), Wechsler became chief psychologist at New York's Bellevue Hospital, a post he held for 35 years. In that position he developed the tests that carried both his and the hospital's name in the early editions: the Wechsler-Bellevue Intelligence Scale I (1939) and Scale II (1942), the Wechsler Intelligence Scale for Children (1949), the Wechsler Adult Intelligence Scale (1955), and the Wechsler Preschool and Primary Scale of Intelligence (1967). He continued to help with the revision of his scales in retirement. The utility of the scales has warranted periodic updating by the publisher.

Wechsler believed his most important work to be his article "The Range of Human Capacities" (1980), the seminal work for his book by the same name that was published in 1935 and revised in 1971. A more popular contribution is the concept of a deviation quotient used for reporting adult intelligence test scores in place of mental age and ratio IQ used with the Binet tests for children and youths. Today nearly all cognitive ability tests use standard scores patterned after the deviation IQ.

The many honors Wechsler received from professional groups and universities around the world include the Distinguished Professional Contribution Award from the American Psychological Association (APA, 1973), similar awards from APA's Division of Clinical Psychology (1960) and Division of School Psychology (1973), and an honorary doctorate from the Hebrew University in Jerusalem.

JOSEPH L. FRENCH
Pennsylvania State University

See also Intelligence Testing

WECHSLER ABBREVIATED SCALE OF INTELLIGENCE

The Wechsler Abbreviated Scale of Intelligence (WASI) is an individually administered test that measures the intelligence in clinical and nonclinical populations. The test can be administered in approximately 30 minutes to individuals between the ages of 6 and 89 years of age.

The WASI consists of four subtests: Vocabulary, Similarities, Block Design, and Matrix Reasoning. All WASI items are new and parallel to their full Wechsler counterparts. Block Design consists of a set of 13 modeled or printed two-dimensional geometric patterns that the examinee replicates within a specified time limit using two-color cubes. Matrix Reasoning is similar to the WAIS-III and WISC-IV Matrix Reasoning subtest. Similarities are parallel to the WISC-IV and WAIS-III subtests and includes low-end picture items. Vocabulary has both oral and visual presentation of words and also has picture items that were designed to extend the floor of the test. The four subtests results in a Full Scale IQ score (FSIQ) and can also be divided into Verbal IQ (VIQ) scores and Performance IQ (PIQ) scores. The PIQ score consists of the performance on Matrix Reasoning, which measures nonverbal fluid ability, and Block Design, which measures visuomotor and coordination skills. The VIQ score consists of performance on the Vocabulary and Similarities subtests of the WASI. An estimate of general intellectual ability can also be obtained from just a two-subtest administration that includes Vocabulary and Matrix Reasoning and provides only the FSIQ score.

Nationally standardized with 2,245 cases, the WASI has reliability coefficients for both the children and adolescent subtests and FSIQs range from .81 to .98. The WASI subtests have significant correlations with the corresponding subtests of the WISC-III. Additionally, it has been evidenced that the WASI measures constructs similar to those measured by its WAIS-III counterparts.

Reviews of the WASI have been generally positive. However, Axelrod (2002) did note that for a clinical sample he examined, "the WASI did not consistently demonstrate desirable accuracy in predicting scores.... The results suggest that clinicians should use the WASI cautiously, if at all, especially when accurate estimates of individuals' WAIS-III results are needed."

REFERENCE

Axelrod, B. N. (2002). Validity of the Wechsler Abbreviated Scale of Intelligence and other very short forms of estimating intellectual functioning. *Assessment, 9*, 17–23.

REVIEWED IN

Canivez, G., Konold, T., Collins, J., & Wilson, G. (2009). Construct validity of the Wechsler Abbreviated Scale of Intelligence and Wide Range Intelligence Test: Convergent and structural validity. *School Psychology Quarterly, 24*(4), 252–265.

Hays, J. R., & Shaw, J. B. (2003). WASI profile variability in a sample of psychiatric inpatients. *Psychological Reports, 92*, 164–166.

Hurt, R. (2009). The Wechsler Abbreviated Scale of Intelligence: Investigating the differential subtests among populations of children and adults served by an independent private practice. *Dissertation Abstracts International, 70*.

Plake, B. S., & Impara, J. C. (Eds.). (2001). *The fourteenth mental measurements yearbook*. Lincoln, NE: Buros Institute of Mental Measurements.

Ryan, J. J., Carruthers, C. A. & Miller, L. J. (2003). Exploratory factor analysis of the Wechsler Abbreviated Scale of Intelligence (WASI) in adult standardization and clinical samples. *Applied Neuropsychology, 10*, 252–256

Saklofske, D., Caravan, G., & Schwartz, C. (2000). Concurrent validity of the Wechsler Abbreviated Scale of Intelligence (WASI) with a sample of Canadian children. *Canadian Journal of School Psychology, 16*(1), 87–94.

Stano, J. (2004). Test Review: Wechsler Abbreviated Scale of Intelligence. *Rehabilitation Counseling Bulletin, 48*(1), 56–57.

RON DUMONT
Fairleigh Dickinson University

JOHN O. WILLIS
Rivier College

KATHLEEN VEIZEL
Fairleigh Dickinson University

JAMIE ZIBULSKY
Farleigh Dickinson University
Fourth edition

WECHSLER ADULT INTELLIGENCE SCALE–FOURTH EDITION

Named for David Wechsler, the Wechsler Adult Intelligence Scale–Fourth Edition (WAIS-IV, 2008) is an individually administered measure of intellectual ability for ages 16 to 90. The WAIS-IV contains 15 subtests, which provide four indexes: Verbal Comprehension (VCI), Perceptual Organization (POI), Working Memory (WMI), and Processing Speed (PSI) and a global Full Scale IQ (FSIQ). Each of these scores is a standard score with a mean of 100 and a standard deviation of 15. On the other hand, each of the 15 subtests is a scaled score with a mean of 10 and a standard deviation of 3.

The Verbal Comprehension Index is composed of three subtests (Similarities, Vocabulary, and Information), with Comprehension acting as a supplemental subtest. The Perceptual Organization Index is composed of three subtests (Block Design, Matrix Reasoning, and Visual Puzzles) with Figure Weights and Picture Completion provided as supplemental subtests. The Working Memory Index is composed of Digit Span and Arithmetic, with Letter-Number Sequencing serving as a supplementary subtest. Finally, the Processing Speed Index is composed of Symbol Search and Coding, with Cancellation being the single supplementary subtest. Supplemental subtests are optional subtests that do not generally count toward the IQ or Index scores unless they are used to replace any spoiled subtest.

The administration time of the WAIS-IV varies according to what subtests are given and the level of ability of the examinee. Administration of the 10 core subtests required to obtain the four Index scores and the Full Scale IQ takes about 75 minutes, ranging from 60 to 90 minutes.

The WAIS-IV was standardized on a U.S. sample of 2,200 English-speaking subjects. The normative sample was stratified by age, gender, ethnicity, geographic region, and educational level, and was consistent with the 2005 U.S. Census data. This sample was divided into 13 age groups that ranged from 16 to 90 years. The sample consisted of individuals from all intellectual ability levels.

Reliability for the WAIS-IV is strong with an average split-half reliability coefficient of 0.98 for the Full Scale IQ and .90 (Processing Speed) to 0.96 (Verbal Comprehension) for Index scores. Average split-half reliabilities for the subtests ranged from 0.78 for Cancellation to 0.94 for Vocabulary. Two hundred ninety-eight individuals from the standardization sample were retested an average of 3 weeks after initial testing, and their data provided test-retest data for the WAIS-IV. The IQ and Indexes have test-retest reliability coefficients ranging from 0.87 to 0.96.

The *WAIS-IV Technical and Interpretive Manual* provides evidence, based upon several confirmatory factor analyses, to support the four-factor structure. However, Lichtenberger and Kaufman (2009) report on CFA analyses done by Keith in which he compared several models, including the four-factor model of the WAIS-IV and a five-factor model in line with Cattell-Horn-Carroll (CHC) model. These analyses suggest that a CHC model, with separate Gf and Gv constructs, fits the data well.

In contrast, Canivez and Watkins (2010) examined the factor structure of the WAIS-IV using exploratory factor analysis, multiple factor extraction criteria, and higher order exploratory factor analysis. Their results indicated that the WAIS-IV subtests were properly associated with the theoretically proposed first-order factors, but all but one factor-extraction criterion recommended extraction of one or two factors. It was concluded that the WAIS-IV provides strong measurement of general intelligence, and clinical interpretation should be primarily at that level.

Many improvements were made in the fourth edition of the WAIS. The floor of the WAIS-IV IQ scores was extended down to 40 and the ceiling was extended to 160. A number of items were modified in other subtests and the artwork was updated. Three subtests were added to the WAIS-IV: Figure Weights, Visual Puzzles, and Cancellation. Two subtests from the original Wechsler tests (Picture Arrangement and Object Assembly) have been dropped from this newest edition. The addition of Figure Weights and Visual Puzzles has enhanced the measurement of fluid reasoning and visual spatial processing.

REFERENCES

Benson, N., Hulac, D. M., & Kranzler, J. H. (2010). Independent examination of the Wechsler Adult Intelligence Scale–Fourth Edition (WAIS-IV): What does the WAIS-IV measure? *Psychological Assessment, 22*(1), 121–130.

Canivez, G. L., & Watkins, M. W. (2010). Investigation of the factor structure of the Wechsler Adult Intelligence Scale–Fourth Edition (WAIS-IV): Exploratory and higher order factor analyses. *Psychological Assessment: A Journal of Consulting and Clinical Psychology, 22*(4), 827–836.

Lichtenberger, E. O. & Kaufman, A. S. (2009). *Essentials of WAIS-IV assessment*. Hoboken, NJ: Wiley.

RON DUMONT
Fairleigh Dickinson University

JOHN O. WILLIS
Rivier College

KATHLEEN VEIZEL
Fairleigh Dickinson University

JAMIE ZIBULSKY
Fairleigh Dickinson University
Fourth edition

WECHSLER INDIVIDUAL ACHIEVEMENT TEST–THIRD EDITION

Named for David Wechsler, the Wechsler Individual Achievement Test–Third Edition (WIAT-III, 2009) is a measure of academic achievement skills and problem-solving abilities for ages 4 through 19 years, 11 months. A separate sample of adults was also included in the standardization process and allows for normative data for adults between the ages of 20 years, 0 months to 50 years, 11 months. The test allows for flexible admiration—examiners may administer a singe subtest, specific groups of subtests to obtain specific composite scores, or all 16 subtests, depending on the age or grade of the child. Administration time varies depending on the grade of the examinee and the number of subtests administered, but usually takes 45 minutes to complete for children in Kindergarten or Prekindergarten, 90 minutes for grades 1 through 3 and approximately 100 minutes for grades 4 through 12. An individual's performance is compared to others in the appropriate age range or grade level.

Materials contained in the test include the examiner's manual, a Scoring workbook, an Oral Reading Fluency booklet, three CDs (containing the technical manual, the audio for Oral Discourse Comprehension, and the Scoring Assistant), a stimulus book containing the visual stimuli for five subtests, two laminated cards used for Word Reading and Pseudoword Decoding, a student response booklet used for nine subtests, and a Response Form for scoring all subtests that also includes information regarding appropriate starting points, reversals, discontinuation rules, and appropriate prompting and querying for each of the subtests. No alternative forms are available. The examiner must provide several other materials (e.g., blank paper, CD or MP3 player, and stopwatch). The test record form's layout is very busy and crowded in places—particularly on the first two Score Summary pages. The record form itself is 50 pages long. For those using the WIAT-III with younger children (Pre-K and K), much of the record form is unused. When hand scoring and filling in the summary pages, great care must be taken to avoid error. Normative tables are provided as a PDF file, which makes looking up score conversions awkward and at times difficult to read, especially on a small laptop screen (some tables are printed in landscape mode, not portrait layout).

The WIAT-III presents one item at a time without time limits, except for four subtests (Alphabet Writing Fluency, Math Fluency, Essay Composition, and Oral Expression).

The WIAT-III has four content areas assessed using the following subtests:

Reading

Early Reading Skills: Naming letters, phonological skills (working with sounds in words), and matching written words with pictures.

Word Reading: Reading words aloud from list. Only the accuracy of the pronunciation (not comprehension) is scored.

Pseudoword Decoding: Reading nonsense words aloud from a list (phonetic word attack).

Reading Comprehension: Reading passages silently or aloud, and orally answering questions about reading passages.

Oral Reading Fluency: Reading passages aloud and answers comprehension questions. Only the speed, accuracy, and fluency of the readings (not comprehension) are scored.

Written Expression

Spelling: Written spelling of dictated letters and sounds and words that are dictated and read in sentences.

Alphabet Writing Fluency: Writing as many different letters as possible within 30 seconds.

Sentence Composition: Composed of two parts, *Sentence Combining* and *Sentence Building*: The first requires combining two or three sentences into one sentence while the second requires the writing of one sentence utilizing a target word correctly.

Essay Composition: Writing an essay within a 10-minute time limit.

Mathematics

Numerical Operations: Identifying and writing numbers, counting, and solving paper-and-pencil computation examples with only a few items for each computational skill.

Math Problem Solving: Counting, identifying shapes, and solving verbally framed "word problems" presented both orally and in writing or with illustrations. Paper and pencil are allowed and answers are given by pointing or orally.

Math Fluency (Addition, Subtraction, Multiplication): Solving written math problems within a 60-second time limit.

Oral Language

Listening Comprehension: Composed of two parts, *Receptive Vocabulary* and *Oral Discourse Comprehension.* The first uses a multiple-choice matching of pictures to spoken words while the second uses sentences and passages played from the CD after which the child orally responds to comprehension questions.

Oral Expression: Composed of three parts. *Expressive Vocabulary* has the child say the word that best describes a given picture. For *Oral Word Fluency,* the child generates lists of specific kinds of word names in 60 seconds. *Sentence Repetition* requires the verbatim repetition of sentences read to the child.

A composite score for total reading is the total of the raw scores obtained on the Word Reading, Reading Comprehension, Oral Reading Fluency (2–12), and Pseudoword Decoding subtests. A composite score for basic reading is the total of the raw scores obtained on the Word Reading and Pseudoword Decoding subtests. A composite score for reading comprehension and fluency is the total of the raw scores obtained on the Reading Comprehension and Oral Reading Fluency subtests. A composite score for written expression is the total of the raw scores obtained on Alphabet Writing Fluency (K–2), Sentence Composition (1–12), Essay Composition (3–12), and Spelling subtests. A composite score for mathematics is the total of the raw scores obtained on the Math Problem Solving and Numerical Operations subtests. A composite score for math fluency is the total of the raw scores obtained on the three math fluency subtests. Finally, a composite score for oral language is the total of the raw scores obtained on Listening Comprehension and Oral Expression subtests. Depending on the subtest, items are either scored dichotomously or assigned a score of 0, 1, or 2.

There are qualitative descriptions for the scores: very low, low, below average, average, above average, superior, very superior. The demarcation for the "average" range on the WIAT-III is a standard score from 85 (percentile rank 16) to 115 (percentile rank 84). The WIAT-III also provides scoring guidelines and additional scoring examples.

The WIAT-III provides standard scores (with a mean of 100 and a standard deviation of 15), percentiles, stanines, normal curve equivalents (NCEs), cumulative percentages, and age and grade equivalents for each of the subtests. Growth Scale Values (GSV) are also provided and allow for comparisons between performance at various periods of time. Scores are based either on the student's age (4-month intervals for ages 4 through 13, 1-year intervals for ages 14 through 16, and one interval for ages 17 through 19) or the student's grade (fall, winter, and spring norms for grades PreK through 12, and separate adult norms). Adult norms are based on three age groups (20 to 25, 26 to 35, and 36 to 50).

The samples included 1,826 students for age-based normative data, 1,400 and 1,375 students, respectively, for the fall and spring grade-based normative samples, and 225 adults for the adult normative data. The children's sample was representative of the 2005 U.S. census data with respect to grade, age, geographic region, gender, ethnicity, and parent education level. The adult sample was representative of the 2008 U.S. census data. Approximately 8% of the sample at each grade level had either a learning disability, language impairment, mild mental impairment, or ADHD. All students spoke English. A sample of 467 students was given both the WIAT-III and a Wechsler Scale (WIAT-II, WPPSI-III, WISC-IV, WAIS-IV, WNV) or the Differential Ability Scales-II (DAS-II, Elliott, 2007) so that examinees' WIAT-III scores can be compared to achievement scores predicted from their intelligence scale scores on the basis of actual test scores from the sample. Unfortunately, the only academic achievement comparison was to the WIAT-II.

The average interitem reliability coefficients range from .83 to .97 across all subtests with the single exception of Alphabet Writing Fluency (.69) and WIAT-III scores demonstrate adequate stability across time, ages, and grades. The pattern of correlations amongst the subtests provides discriminant evidence of validity. Overall, correlation coefficients among the scores suggest that, for the most part, the WIAT-III measures similar constructs to those on corresponding subtests of the WIAT-II.

Ron Dumont
Fairleigh Dickinson University

John O. Willis
Rivier College

Kathleen Veizel
Fairleigh Dickinson University

Jamie Zibulsky
Fairleigh Dickinson University
Fourth edition

WECHSLER INTELLIGENCE SCALE FOR CHILDREN–FOURTH EDITION

Named for David Wechsler, the Wechsler Intelligence Scale for Children–Fourth Edition (WISC-IV, 2003a) is an individually administered clinical instrument for assessing the cognitive ability of children of ages 6 years 0 months through 16 years 11 months. It is composed of 15 subtests, 10 of which have been retained from the WISC-III and five new subtests. Administration takes approximately 65 to 80 minutes for most children. The test provides a composite score (Full Scale IQ) that represents general intellectual ability as well as four factor index scores (Verbal Comprehension, Perceptual Reasoning, Working Memory, and Processing Speed). Each of the IQs and factor indexes are standard scores with a mean of 100 and a standard score of 15 for 33 age bands. The subtests on the WISC-IV provide scaled scores with a mean of 10 and a standard deviation of 3.

Three subtests comprise the Verbal Comprehension Index: Similarities, Vocabulary, and Comprehension. In addition, two supplementary verbal subtests, Information and Word Reasoning, are also available and may substitute for any of the other Verbal Comprehension subtests if needed. These subtests assess verbal reasoning, comprehension, and conceptualization.

Three subtests comprise the Perceptual Reasoning Index: Block Design, Picture, Concepts, and Matrix Reasoning. Picture Completion is a supplementary subtest that can be used as a substitute if necessary. These subtests measure perceptual reasoning and organization.

Two subtests comprise the Working Memory Index: Digit Span and Letter-Number Sequencing. There is also one supplementary subtest, Arithmetic, that can be used to replace either of the Working Memory subtests. These subtests measure attention, concentration, and working memory.

Two subtests comprise the Processing Speed Index: Coding and Symbol Search. Cancellation is a supplementary subtest and can be used as a substitute for either subtest of the Processing Speed Index. These subtests measure the speed of mental and graphomotor processing.

There are two manuals that accompany the WISC-IV. The Administration and Scoring Manual contains all of the information needed to administer subtests, score responses, and complete the Record Form. The Technical and Interpretive Manual (2003b) contains psychometric, technical, and basic interpretive information. During revision from the WISC-III to the WISC-IV, the Stimulus Book artwork was updated to be more attractive and engaging for children. Outdated items were revised or removed and new items were incorporated to reflect more contemporary ideas and situations. The Record Form was redesigned to reduce the occurrence of administration and scoring errors, and includes an abbreviated version of the administration and scoring rules for each subtest. Administration procedures were simplified to improve the user-friendliness of the scale. Instructions to examiners are more succinct and understandable, and similar wording is used across subtests to provide consistency and clarity. There are teaching, sample, and/or practice items along with queries and prompts incorporated within every subtest that should enhance the child's understanding and retention of the subtest task.

The standardization sample for the WISC-IV included 2,200 children divided into 11 age groups ranging from 6 to 16, with 200 participants in each age group. (Note that the Arithmetic subtest was normed on only 1100 children—100 per age). The sample was representative of the 2000 U.S. census with respect to age, sex, race, parent education level, and geographic region.

The overall internal consistency reliability for the subtests ranges from 0.79 to 0.90. For the composite scales, the internal consistency reliability ranges from 0.88 to 0.97. The test-retest reliability ranges from 0.76 to 0.92 for the subtests and from 0.86 to 0.93 for the composite scales, with a mean time interval of 32 days. Research on the Wechsler scales has provided strong evidence of validity based on the scales' internal structure. Intercorrelations among subtests provide initial evidence of both the convergent and discriminant validity of the WISC-IV. Evidence of criterion validity was also shown by moderate to high correlations between the WISC-IV and the WISC-III, WPPSI-III, WAIS-III, WASI, WIAT-II, CMS, and GRS.

This entry has been informed by the sources listed below.

REFERENCES

Brooks, B. (2010). Seeing the forest for the trees: Prevalence of low scores on the Wechsler Intelligence Scale for Children, fourth edition (WISC-IV). *Psychological Assessment, 22*(3), 650–656.

Flanagan D. P. & Kaufman A. S. (2004). *Essentials of WISC-IV Assessment.* Hoboken, NJ: Wiley.

Goldbeck, L., Daseking, M., Hellwig-Brida, S., Waldmann, H., & Petermann, F. (2010). Sex differences on the German Wechsler Intelligence Test for Children (WISC-IV). *Journal of Individual Differences, 31*(1), 22–28.

Konold, T., & Canivez, G. (2010). Differential relationships between WISC-IV and WIAT-II scales: An evaluation of potentially moderating child demographics. *Educational and Psychological Measurement, 70*(4), 613–627.

Saklofske, D., Zhu, J., Coalson, D., Raiford, S., & Weiss, L. (2010). Cognitive Proficiency Index for the Canadian edition of the Wechsler Intelligence Scale for Children–Fourth Edition. *Canadian Journal of School Psychology, 25*(3), 277–286.

Sattler, J. M., & Dumont, R. P. (2004). *Assessment of Children: WISC-IV and WPPSI-III Supplement.* San Diego, CA: Jerome Sattler.

Wechsler, D. (2003a). Wechsler Intelligence Scale for Children–Fourth Edition: Administration and Scoring Manual. San Antonio, TX: Psychological Corporation.

Wechsler, D. (2003b). Wechsler Intelligence Scale for Children–Fourth Edition: Technical and Interpretative Manual. San Antonio, TX: Psychological Corporation. http://alpha.fdu.edu/psychology/WISCIVIndex.htm

RON DUMONT
Fairleigh Dickinson University

JOHN O. WILLIS
Rivier College

KATHLEEN VEIZEL
Fairleigh Dickinson University

JAMIE ZIBULSKY
Fairleigh Dickinson University
Fourth edition

WECHSLER INTELLIGENCE SCALE FOR CHILDREN–FOURTH EDITION INTEGRATED

The Wechsler Intelligence Scale for Children–Fourth Edition Integrated (WISC-IV Integrated; Wechsler et al., 2004) enhances the Wechsler Intelligence Scale for Children–Fourth Edition (WISC-IV) by including standardized measures of test behavior, problem-solving style, and cognitive processes—many updated from the WISC-III as a Process Instrument (WISC-III PI). The Integrated subtests were designed to measure the same cognitive processes as their corresponding WISC-IV core and supplemental subtest, but with reduced demand on retrieval of information and expressive language ability.

The WISC-IV Integrated adds 16 process subtests, as well as qualitative and quantitative observations and error scores, to provide more measures of cognitive processes. The complete WISC-IV Integrated kit includes an Administration and Scoring Manual, a Technical and Interpretive Manual, three stimulus books, WISC-IV Integrated record forms, three response booklets, several scoring keys, 12 red and white blocks, a Spatial Span Board, Block Design Process Grid Overlays, and pencils. Owners of the WISC-IV can purchase an add-on kit to make it into a WISC-IV Integrated testing unit.

Initial administration involves completing the WISC-IV subtests to obtain the FSIQ and the four Index scores. Selected process subtests of the WISC-IV Integrated are then given, often in a second session, to clarify responding and to test hypotheses; process subtests take from 3 to 20 minutes to administer; nearly 3 hours could be needed if all WISC-IV and WISC-IV Integrated subtests were administered. Information about selecting process subtests for hypothesis testing is presented in the Technical and Interpretive Manual. WISC-IV Integrated subtests can never be substituted for core subtests.

The WISC-IV Integrated includes five Verbal domain process subtests: Similarities Multiple Choice, Vocabulary Multiple Choice, Picture Vocabulary Multiple Choice, Comprehension Multiple Choice, and Information Multiple Choice. The Perceptual domain includes three process subtests: Block Design Multiple Choice, Block Design Process Approach, and Elithorn Mazes. The Working Memory integrated subtests are Visual Digit Span, Spatial Span, Letter Span, Letter-Number Sequencing Process Approach, Arithmetic Process Approach, and Written Arithmetic. Finally, the Processing Speed integrated subtests include Coding Recall and Coding Copy.

Most process subtests are adaptations of the original WISC-IV subtests where additional aids, such as multiple-choice options, are used (e.g., Multiple Choice Information) or modalities are changed or supplemented (e.g., Visual Digit Span and Spatial Span).

The WISC-IV Integrated reliabilities were based on 730 examinees. Internal consistency coefficients for the 26 WISC-IV Integrated scaled process scores ranged from .67 (Letter Span Rhyming) to .91 (Block Design Multiple Choice and Block Design Multiple Choice No Time). Approximately 53% of the process and integrated reliabilities that were .90 or above came from either the Block Design or Arithmetic subtest scores. In almost all instances, the WISC-IV Integrated subtest reliability (both internal consistency and test-retest) were lower than that of their respective WISC-IV core subtest. For example, the Similarities subtest has internal consistency and test-retest reliabilities of .85 and .86, respectively, while the Similarities Multiple Choice subtest has internal consistency and test-retest reliabilities of .77 and .71, respectively.

Thirteen of the 15 validity studies presented in the manual included process subtests. For all subtests, specific patterns were detected by locating the process subtests that had the largest effect size differences between specific clinical groups' and matched controls' means. As an example, children with Expressive Language Disorders showed large effect sizes for process subtests in the Verbal and Working Memory domains. Although these findings are positive, one must note that they speak only to the differences between the scores of the clinical sample and the matched controls. They do not indicate the usefulness of the integrated subtests in adding new information over and above what is known from the original WISC-IV scores. For example, the same small sample of children with Expressive Language Disorders who are included in the clinical validity study for the integrated subtests was also the same sample used in the WISC-IV validity study. If one compares, for example, the Similarities and Similarities Multiple Choice subtest scores for the *same* sample of children with Expressive Language Disorders, one finds a mean score of 7.4 versus 7.2, which results in an effect size of only .09. The results of the validity studies, although providing initial evidence of validity, will need additional research to strengthen the empirical validity base of the WISC-IV Integrated at the process subtest level.

The record form for the WISC-IV Integrated allows space for entering subtest information (e.g., raw score, scaled score), but these additional scores result in potentially a total of 845 entries on the analysis pages (not counting the data points on the graphs) and from them there are 216 interpretive decisions.

This entry has been informed by the sources listed below.

REFERENCES

Madle, R. A., Meikamp, J., & Suppa, C. H. (2007). [Review of the Wechsler Intelligence Scale for Children–Fourth Edition Integrated]. In B. S. Plake & J. C. Impara (Eds.), *The seventeenth mental measurements yearbook* (pp. 183–187). Lincoln, NE: Buros Institute of Mental Measurements.

McCloskey, G., & Maerlender, A. (2005). The WISC-IV integrated. In A. Prifitera, D. H. Saklofske, L. G. Weiss, A. Prifitera, D. H. Saklofske, & L. G. Weiss (Eds.), *WISC-IV clinical use and interpretation: Scientist-practitioner perspectives* (pp. 101–149). San Diego, CA US: Elsevier Academic Press.

Wechsler, D., Kaplan, E., Fein, D., Kramer, J., Morris, R., Delis, D., & Maerlender, A. (2004). *Wechsler Intelligence Scale for Children–Fourth edition integrated*. San Antonio, TX: Harcourt Assessment.

RON DUMONT
Fairleigh Dickinson University

JOHN O. WILLIS
Rivier College

KATHLEEN VEIZEL
Fairleigh Dickinson University

JAMIE ZIBULSKY
Fairleigh Dickinson University
Fourth edition

WECHSLER MEMORY SCALE–FOURTH EDITION

Named for David Wechsler, the Wechsler Memory Scale–Fourth Edition (WMS-IV, 2009) is an individually administered battery designed to measure a range of memory abilities in individuals aged 16 to 90. The WMS-IV contains significant revisions from the widely used previous version, The Wechsler Memory Scale–Third Edition (WMS-III). Revision goals included updating test items and structure, improving the measure's clinical utility, improving the psychometric properties, and increasing user-friendliness, including shortened testing time for older adults. To this end, the WMS-IV is divided into two batteries: the Adult Battery for examinees aged 16–69, and the shorter Older Adult battery for individuals aged 65–90.

The WMS-IV includes five Index scores: Auditory Memory, Visual Memory, Visual Working Memory, Immediate Memory, and Delayed Memory. A Brief Cognitive Status Exam, designed to screen general cognitive ability, is also available. The WMS-IV test kit includes the Administration and Scoring Manual, the Technical and Interpretive Manual, record forms for both the adult and older adult batteries, response booklets, two Stimulus Books, a Memory Grid, Designs and Spatial Additions Cards, a Scoring Template, and an eraserless pencil. The examiner also needs to use a pencil with an eraser and a stopwatch or clock to measure elapsed time.

Auditory Memory describes the individual's ability to remember orally presented information. Subtests included in this Index are: Logical Memory I (free recall of an orally presented story) and II (delayed recall and recognition of stories presented in Logical Memory I), and Verbal Paired Associates I (verbal memory of word pairs) and II (delayed recall and recognition of word pairs). The Visual Memory Index measures the individual's memory of information presented visually. Subtests included are Designs I (using spatial memory to replicate a grid) and II (delayed recall and recognition of the gird), and Visual Reproduction I (drawing a visually presented design from memory) and II (delayed recall and recognition of the designs). The Visual Working Memory Index measures the examinee's ability to hold and manipulate visually presented material in memory. Subtests included are Spatial Addition (visual addition or subtraction of items on a grid) and Symbol Span (selecting previously presented novel visual stimuli). The Immediate Memory Index includes both visual and oral immediate memory, and includes Logical Memory I, Verbal Paired Associates I, Designs I, and Visual Reproduction I. Finally, the Delayed Memory Index measures more long-term visual and oral memory and includes scores from Logical Memory II, Verbal Paired Associates II, Designs II, and Visual Reproduction II. As with other Wechsler scales, the subtests have a mean scaled score of 10 and a standard deviation of 3, and the Index standard scores have a mean of 100 and a standard deviation of 15. Process scores and contrast scaled scores are also available to enhance clinical utility. All scores are based on age; therefore, correct calculation of the individual's test age is important.

The WMS-IV was co-normed with the Wechsler Adult Intelligence Scale–Fourth Edition (WAIS-IV); however, there was additional data collection for the WMS-IV to ensure a mean General Ability Index score of 100 in each age band. The total number of participants in the final normative sample was 1,400; 100 in each age band. Although there were generally equal numbers of males and females

in each age band, there were more women than men in the older age groups, consistent with U.S. census data. The sample was geographically diverse and the proportion of various racial/ethnic groups was based on 2005 U.S. census data. The sample was also stratified by education level. Overall, the demographics of the normative sample appear adequate and closely aligned to the U.S. population.

The manual presents a brief but helpful theoretical foundation of the reliability of memory assessment in general, including inherent limitations. Internal consistency was generally high, and there was adequate evidence of test-retest stability. There was also an impressively high degree of interscorer agreement, even for subtests for which scoring criteria is detailed and interpretive. Overall, the WMS-IV appears to be a reliable instrument.

Evidence for content validity is provided by detailing studies of the WMS-III and associated changes to the WMS-IV as well as describing the theoretical foundations and response processes of subtests. The manual utilizes research conducted on previous versions of the WMS to provide evidence of construct validity, as well as by referring to the internal consistency of the WMS-IV. Concurrent validity was evidenced by examining the relationship of the WMS-IV to a wide variety of external measures, including those measuring cognitive ability, memory, executive functioning, adaptive behavior, achievement, and some social/emotional and behavioral scales. Finally, the utility of the WMS-IV with special populations was demonstrated by clinical studies with those with Probable Dementia of the Alzheimer's Type, Mild Cognitive Impairment, Major Depressive Disorder, Traumatic Brain Injury, right and left Temporal Lobe Epilepsy, Schizophrenia, anxiety disorders, mild or moderate intellectual disabilities, Autism, Asperger's Disorder, Learning Disabilities, and Attention-Deficit/Hyperactivity Disorder. Although most studies yielded expected patterns, some were inconclusive, likely due to low sample sizes. Indeed, the sample size of many of these studies was small (as low as 8 or 10 individuals), highlighting the need for further research using the WMS-IV with clinical populations.

Overall, the WMS-IV appears to be a theoretically and psychometrically sound instrument. The manual includes good, thorough guidelines for interpretation. The Wechsler Memory Scales have a well-researched history, and this latest Fourth Edition boasts further improvements.

This entry has been informed by the sources listed below.

REFERENCES

Cassady, J., & Dacanay, A. (2010). Review of the Wechsler Memory Scale–Fourth Edition. In R. A. Spies, K. F. Geisinger, and J. F. Carlson (Eds.), *The eighteenth mental measurements yearbook*. Lincoln, NE: Buros Institute of Mental Measurements.

Chittooran, M. M. (2010). Review of the Wechsler Memory Scale–Fourth Edition. In R. A. Spies, K. F. Geisinger, & J. F.

Carlson (Eds.), *The eighteenth mental measurements yearbook.* Lincoln, NE: Buros Institute of Mental Measurements.

Hoelzle, J. B., Nelson, N. W., Smith, C. A. (2011). Comparison of Wechsler Memory Scale–Fourth Edition (WMS-IV) and Third Edition (WMS-III) dimensional structures: Improved ability to evaluate auditory and visual constructs. *Journal of Clinical and Experimental Neuropsychology, 33*(3), 283–291.

JAMIE ZIBULSKY
KATHLEEN VEIZEL
Fairleigh Dickinson University
Fourth edition

See also Memory Disorders; Tests of Memory and Learning; Wechsler, David

WECHSLER NONVERBAL SCALE OF ABILITY

The Wechsler Nonverbal Scale of Ability (WNV; Wechsler & Naglieri, 2006) was created to measure the general cognitive ability of persons ages 4-0 through 21-11. All subtests are administered using pictorial directions and require only nonverbal responses, and this instrument is, therefore, useful for assessing children whose true abilities may not be best represented by a test requiring verbal expression. Pictorial directions for each subtest are provided in the stimulus book for the measure, and examiners are instructed how to utilize nonverbal gestures in explaining each task. The test manual indicates the WNV may be particularly useful for individuals who are deaf or hard of hearing, have Autistic Disorder, are language disordered, are non-English speaking, or are from diverse backgrounds.

The WNV consists of six subtests, but no individual is administered more than four of these subtests at any given time. These subtests include:

1. *Matrices:* The examinee is required to select, from four or five similar pieces, the missing piece from a geometric pattern.
2. *Coding:* Under timed conditions, the examinee is required to copy symbols that are paired with shapes or numbers.
3. *Object Assembly:* The examinee is required to complete increasingly sophisticated puzzles under timed conditions.
4. *Recognition:* The examinee is presented with a geometric design and then asked to select that same design from four or five similar pieces.
5. *Spatial Span:* The examinee is required to tap a series of blocks in either the same or reverse order in which the examiner completed this tapping task.
6. *Picture Arrangement:* Under timed conditions, the examinee is required to put a series of pictures in a linear order.

Many of these subtests will be familiar to examiners who have used other Wechsler instruments, as several of the subtests have been included in earlier Wechsler measures or are adaptations of such measures (e.g., Spatial Span as opposed to Digit Span). In contrast to other Wechsler instruments, though, each subtest raw score is converted to a T score with a mean of 50 and a standard deviation of 10. Several optional scores can be computed after administering the Spatial Scan subtest to compare the examinee's performance on forward and backward scanning tasks. The sum of the T scores is then used to derive a Full Scale standard score with a mean to 100 and a standard deviation of 15. A Full Scale score can be derived using all versions of this measure. There are separate versions of the WNV for use with 4-0 to 7-11-year-olds, and 8-0 to 21-11-year-olds. The version for younger children includes the Matrices, Coding, Object Assembly, and Recognition subtests. If administering the two-subtest version of the measure, only the Matrices and Recognition subtests are used. The version for older children includes the Matrices, Coding, Spatial Span, and Picture Arrangement subtests. If administering the two-subtest version of the measure, the Matrices and Spatial Span subtests are used. The two-subtest version of the battery takes 15 to 20 minutes to administer, and the four-subtest version of the battery takes 45 minutes.

The test was normed concurrently in the United States and Canada. The sample in the United States included 1,350 children between the ages of 4-0 and 21-11, with 100 students comprising each age group from 4-0 to 12-11 and 75 students included in each subsequent age group. The normative group was stratified by age across the variables of geographic region, and educational level achieved by the adult participants and parents of minor participants. The Technical and Interpretive manual indicates that the sample is representative of the U.S. population with respect to these variables, but does not clearly state how closely the ethnic composition of this participant group mirrored that of the ethnic composition of the United States. Similarly, in the Canadian sample of 875 children, 100 students aged 4-0 to 4-11 and 11-0 to 11-11 were included. Fifty students were included in each group from 5-0 to 10-11 and 12-0 to 19-11. Seventy-five students were included in age group 20-0 to 21-11. The Canadian sample was also stratified according to the above variables, and the same concern about the diversity of the sample arises. The authors do note that "although the Canadian standardization sample was not stratified according to linguistic groups, great efforts were made to include examinees from all major linguistic groups" (p. 19). The Technical and Interpretive Manual provides a great deal of descriptive data about sample selection, both for norming and exploring the measure's properties within distinct populations of students, although key pieces of information are occasionally not provided (Maddux, 2010).

Internal consistency estimates for all subtests are adequate, and a confirmatory factor analysis provides additional information about the validity of the subtests. Test-retest stability was found to be adequate. Reviewers (e.g., Maddux, 2010) have raised some concerns about the criterion-related validity of the measure, as the four-subtest versions of the measure correlate 0.73–0.76 with other tests that are similar theoretically (e.g., the Wechsler Intelligence Scale for Children, Fourth Edition), reduce language loading (e.g., the Universal Nonverbal Intelligence Test), or are both theoretically similar and reduce language loading (e.g., Naglieri Nonverbal Intelligence Test). Correlations for the two-subtest version range from 0.58 to 0.71. Further information about the criterion-related validity of this measure is provided in the Technical and Interpretive Manual. Concurrent validity studies provide some evidence that this measure adequately differentiates between groups of examinees with varying levels of cognition and with other presenting problems. Notably, though, examinees with language disorders scored significantly below the mean score achieved by the control group. In sum, the authors provide detailed and thorough information regarding test development and the psychometric properties of this instrument, although "more detail is needed about how samples were obtained for many of the studies that are reported" (Maddux, 2010). This measure is regarded as a sound and appropriate screener of general cognitive ability, particularly for those examinees whose abilities would not be adequately assessed if tested verbally.

REVIEWED IN:

Maddux, C. D. (2010). Review of the Wechsler Nonverbal Scale of Ability. In R. A. Spies, J. F. Spies, & K. F. Gesinger (Eds.), *The eighteenth mental measurements yearbook*. Lincoln, NE: Buros Institute of Mental Measurements.

Tindal, G. Review of the Wechsler Nonverbal Scale of Ability. In R. A. Spies, J. F. Spies, & K. F. Gesinger (Eds.), *The eighteenth mental measurements yearbook*. Lincoln, NE: Buros Institute of Mental Measurements.

REFERENCE

Wechsler, D., & Naglieri, J. (2006). *Wechsler Nonverbal Scale of Ability*. San Antonio, TX: Pearson Clinical Assessment.

KATHLEEN VEIZEL
JAMIE ZIBULSKY
Fairleigh Dickinson University
Fourth edition

WECHSLER PRESCHOOL AND PRIMARY SCALES OF INTELLIGENCE–THIRD EDITION

Named for David Wechsler, the Wechsler Preschool and Primary Scales of Intelligence–Third Edition (WPPSI-III, 2002) is an individually administered instrument that assesses cognitive functioning and global intelligence for early childhood. The WPPSI-III is widely utilized in clinical and school settings as a means to identify potential delays or intellectual giftedness in early childhood development. It is frequently used to aid in decision making for special education preschool placement. The instrument can provide information pertaining to a child's cognitive strengths and weaknesses related to language, visual-perceptual skills, visual-motor integration, and reasoning.

The instrument covers a broad age range in which advances in development are typical for youngsters. Therefore, the instrument is divided into two separate batteries (the first for ages 2 years, 6 months through 3 years, 11 months and the second for ages 4 years through 7 years, 3 months). The test consists of 14 subtests that combine into 5 composites: Verbal IQ (VIQ), Performance IQ (PIQ), Processing Speed Quotient (PSQ) (for upper ages only), General Language Composite (GLC), and a Full Scale IQ (FSIQ).

The FSIQ is a general measure of global intelligence reflecting performance across various subtests within the VIQ and PIQ domains. In general, the VIQ contains subtests that measure general fund of information, verbal comprehension, receptive and expressive language, attention span, and degree of abstract thinking. The PIQ is comprised of subtests that collectively assess visual-motor integration, perceptual-organizational skills, concept formation, speed of mental processing, nonverbal problem solving, and graphomotor ability.

Composite scores are derived by combining scores from selected subtests as follows:

Ages 2.6–3.11

> *VIQ*: Receptive Vocabulary, and Information
> *PIQ*: Block Design and Object Assembly
> *GLC*: Receptive Vocabulary and Picture Naming
> *FSIQ*: VIQ and PIQ combined

Ages 4.0–7.3

> *VIQ*: Information, Vocabulary, and Word Reasoning (Comprehension and Similarities may be substituted)
> *PIQ*: Block Design, Matrix Reasoning, and Picture Concepts (Picture Completion and Object Assembly may be substituted)
> *PSQ*: Coding and Symbol Search

GLC: Receptive Vocabulary and Picture Naming
FSIQ: VIQ, PIQ and Coding

It is notable that there are guidelines when deciding to utilize a substitution in place of a core subtest. Only one substitution is allowed for either a core subtest from VIQ or PIQ. Overall, no more than two substitutions can be made when deriving a FSIQ.

The WPPSI-III was standardized on a sample of 1,700 children who were selected as being representative of the 2000 United States census data stratified on age, gender, geographic region ethnicity, and parental education levels. The standardization sample was divided into nine age groups; eight of the groups contained 200 children and one group (7.0–7.3-year-olds) consisted of 100 children.

There are age-specific starting points for each subtest as well as practice items to allow the child to become familiar with each task. Some subtests are scored as either pass-fail, whereas other subtests are scored based on the quality of response. The child receives full credit for all items prior to the starting point and does not receive credit for items after the discontinue rule is met. In general, the points are tabulated to formulate a raw score that is converted into standard scores. The instrument also includes reverse and discontinue rules to eliminate unnecessary fatigue or extended testing time. Reverse rules are designed to tap into items prior to the child's age-specific starting point to allow the examiner to extend the floor for children who experience difficulty with the first couple of items. The discontinue rules vary for each subtest but follow the same underlying principle, which governs the examiner to discontinue administration after the child fails to correctly respond to a set number of items.

Scores provided include scaled scores, standard scores, percentiles, and qualitative descriptors. All raw scores are converted to allow a child's performance to be compared to his or her same-aged peers from the normative sample. Scaled scores have a mean of 10 and a standard deviation of 3. The composite standard scores have a mean of 100 and a standard deviation of 15. Percentile ranks are used to describe the child's performance relative to the normative sample as being better than or equal to the calculated percentage. Descriptors include extremely low, borderline intellectual functioning, low average, average, high average, superior, and very superior range.

Internal consistency values for each subtest ranged from 0.75 to 0.96. The test-retest coefficients ranged from 0.86 to .092. The average internal consistency values and test-retest coefficients exceeded 0.80. Correlations were obtained comparing the WPPSI-III FSIQ with other global measures; when compared with alternate assessment instruments such as the Differential Ability Scales, Bayley Scales of Infant Development-II, and WPPSI-R coefficients ranged from 0.80 to 0.89.

REVIEWED IN:

Coalson, D., & Spruill, J. (2007). Cognitive assessment with the Wechsler Preschool and Primary Scale of Intelligence–Third Edition. In B. Bracken (Ed.), *The psychoeducational assessment of preschool children* (4th ed., pp. 241–265). Mahwah, NJ: Erlbaum.

Gordon, B. (2004). Review of The Wechsler Preschool and Primary Scale of Intelligence, Third Edition (WPPSI-III). *Canadian Journal of School Psychology, 19*(1–2), 205–220.

Gyurke, J., Marmor, D., & Melrose, S. (2004). The assessment of preschool children with the Wechsler Preschool and Primary Scale of Intelligence–Revised. In B. Bracken (Ed.), *The psychoeducational assessment of preschool children* (3rd ed., pp. 57–75). Mahwah, NJ: Erlbaum.

Hamilton, W., & Burns, T. (2003). WPPSI-III: Wechsler preschool and primary scale of intelligence (3rd ed.). *Applied Neuropsychology, 10*, 188–190.

Lichtenberger, E., & Kaufman, A. (2004). *Essentials of WPPSI-III Assessment.* Hoboken, NJ: Wiley.

Price, L., Raju, N., Lurie, A., Wilkins, C., & Zhu, J. (2006). Conditional Standard Errors of Measurement for Composite Scores on the Wechsler Preschool and Primary Scale of Intelligence–Third Edition. *Psychological Reports, 98*(1), 237–252.

The Psychological Corporation. (2002). *WPPSI-III technical and interpretive manual.* San Antonio, TX: Psychological Corporation.

Sattler, J. M. & Dumont, R. P. (2004). *Assessment of Children: WISC-IV and WPPSI-III Supplement.* San Diego, CA: Jerome Sattler.

Spies, R. A., & Plake, B. S. (Eds.). (2005). *The sixteenth mental measurements yearbook.* Lincoln, NE: Buros Institute of Mental Measurements.

Wechsler, D. (2002). *WPPSI-III administration and scoring manual.* San Antonio, TX: Psychological Corporation. http://alpha.fdu.edu/psychology/WPPSIII.htm

RON DUMONT
Fairleigh Dickinson University

JOHN O. WILLIS
Rivier College

KATHLEEN VEIZEL
Fairleigh Dickinson University

JAMIE ZIBULSKY
Fairleigh Dickinson University
Fourth edition

WEISMANN NETTER STUHL SYNDROME

The original name for this disorder was toxopachyosteose diaphysaire tibioperoniere. Weismann Netter Stuhl syndrome is an extremely rare skeletal disorder that occurs as the result of abnormal development of the bone. This disorder, also referred to as dwarfism, is thought to be inherited as an autosomal or X-linked dominant genetic trait (Skeletal Dysplasia, Weismann Netter Stuhl Type, 1990).

Reports are that males and females are affected in equal numbers. In dominant disorders such as this one, there is a 50% chance of the disorder's being transmitted from parent to offspring for each pregnancy, regardless of the sex of the resulting child. Age of onset is possibly prenatal, although the bowing of the legs is often not detected until the child begins to walk (Robinow & Johnson, 1988). Diagnosis may be difficult due to the lack of serious physical complications associated with the disorder (National Organization for Rare Disorders [NORD], 1996). Most adolescent or adult cases that have been documented in the literature have been discovered incidentally because the patient was admitted to the hospital for other reasons (Skeletal Dysplasia, Weismann Netter Stuhl Type, 1990). In more recent literature, diagnosis of children has been difficult due to the fact that the cases were reported primarily in the French literature (Robinow & Johnson, 1988). In 1995, Tieder, Manor, Peshin, and Alon documented the difficulty in diagnosing the disorder: Although 79 cases had been reported in the literature, only 13 were pediatric cases. Of the 13 pediatric cases, only 2 had been reported in the English literature. Tieder et al. (1995) wanted to increase the awareness of the disorder among pediatric radiologists because of the difficulty in diagnosing. There is also a possibility that some cases of Weismann Netter Stuhl syndrome have been misdiagnosed throughout the years as either syphilis or healed rickets (Robinow & Johnson, 1988).

There is very little discussion of treatment in the literature. Treatment should be symptomatic and supportive, possibly with genetic counseling for the child and the family (NORD, 1996).

Through the Individuals with Disabilities Education Act (IDEA, 1997), the child may be eligible for special-education services under the categories of orthopedic impairment, other health impaired, or physical disability. In the approximately 20% of the cases in which mental retardation is present, the child may also be eligible under the category of mental retardation, depending on the severity of the intellectual deficit. The child may require social support, occupational therapy, and other medical, social, or vocational services.

This disorder is not known to be debilitating or life threatening. Patients are expected to have a normal life span. Future research is documented in the area of surgical treatment for those who have bone disorders. The National Institutes of Health, through its Human Genome Project, is attempting to map every gene in the human body. It is hoped that such knowledge will lead to treatment of genetic and familial disorders.

REFERENCES

National Organization for Rare Disorders. (1996). *Weismann Netter Stuhl syndrome*. Retrieved from http://www.rarediseases.org

Robinow, M., & Johnson, G. F. (1988). The Weismann-Netter syndrome. *American Journal of Medical Genetics, 29*, 573–579.

Skeletal dysplasia, Weismann Netter Stuhl type. (1990). In *Birth defects encyclopedia* (p. 1540). Dover, MA: Blackwell Scientific Publications.

Tieder, M., Manor, H., Peshin, J., & Alon, U. S. (1995). The Weismann-Netter, Stuhl syndrome: A rare pediatric skeletal dysplasia. *Pediatric Radiology, 25*, 37–40.

Christine D. Cde Baca
University of Northern Colorado

Characteristics

1. Short stature and bowing of the front of the long portions of the tibia (shinbone) and of the fibula (small bone below the knee).

2. Child may also exhibit bowing of the sides of the femur (thighbone), outward curvature of the tibia, or both.

3. The child will experience a delay in the onset of walking until the age of about 18 months or older.

4. Other bones in the body may be bowed, curved, or improperly developed.

5. Mild intellectual disability has been detected in some cases.

WELSH FIGURE PREFERENCE TEST

The Welsh Figure Preference Test (FPT) was developed by George Welsh in 1949, for his doctoral thesis, as a projective assessment of psychopathology. More recently, it has been used as a measure of creativity more than as a diagnostic tool for the evaluation of psychopathology.

The Welsh FPT (Welsh, 1959) consists of a booklet containing 400 black-and-white line drawings. Welsh revised the scale in 1980. It is designed for use with individuals aged 6 years and up. It requires nearly an hour to complete and, despite being intended as a projective, provides objective scoring. Instructions to the test taker are simple. Individuals are asked to view each drawing and indicate on an answer sheet whether they like or dislike the drawing. The intent was to provide nonlanguage stimulus materials suitable for a wide range of individuals who could not be assessed with language-laden measures such as the MMPI, or projective measures such as the TAT, requiring extensive verbal expression.

The Welsh FPT can separate artists from nonartists, as can many other tests; it can also separate clinical from nonclinical populations. However, it has not been extensively researched considering its publication date. Welsh (1986) contends that the Welsh FPT is useful as a measure of creativity; it has been used in creativity research since at least 1965. Its uses in creativity research seem well established at this time, but its validity as a measure of psychopathology is questionable.

REFERENCES

Welsh, G. S. (1949). A projective figure-preference test for diagnosis of psychopathology: I. A preliminary investigation. Doctoral thesis, University of Minnesota, Minneapolis.

Welsh, G. S. (1959). *Welsh Figure Preference Test*. Palo Alto, CA: Consulting Psychologists.

Welsh, G. S. (1980). *Welsh Figure Preference Test*, revised edition. Palo Alto, CA: Consulting Psychologists.

Welsh, G. S. (1986). Positive exceptionality: The academically gifted and the creative. In R. T. Brown & C. R. Reynolds (Eds.), *Psychological perspectives on childhood exceptionality: A handbook*. New York, NY: Wiley-Interscience.

CECIL R. REYNOLDS
Texas A&M University

See also Creativity

WERDNIG-HOFFMANN DISEASE

Werdnig-Hoffmann disease (also known as infantile spinal muscular atrophy Type I, or SMA I) is a rare progressive neuromuscular degenerative disorder of infancy. SMA I is characterized by the wasting of the skeletal muscles caused by progressive deterioration of the motor nuclei within the lower brain stem and of the anterior horn cells of the spinal cord.

There are various forms of SMA with similar characteristics but different in pattern of inheritance, age of onset, severity, and prognosis. However, all forms are characterized by marked muscular weakness and hypotonia (Munsat, 1994). SMA I is the first of four main types of spinal muscle atrophy disorders, with onset occurring during fetal development (in utero) or at birth (congenital). SMA Type II (intermediate) symptoms manifest approximately between 6 and 12 months of age. SMA Type III (or Wohlfart-Kugelberg-Welander disease) can occur from 2 to 30 years of age. SMA Type IV, or Kennedy disease (bulbo-SMA) has an adult onset, from approximately 30 to 60 years of age (Beers & Berkow, 1999).

In most individuals, SMA I appears to be an inherited autosomal recessive trait, which means that both parents must be carriers of the gene for the disease for it to be expressed in the child (Heller, Alberto, Forney, & Schwartzman, 1996). SMAs are the second most common autosomal recessive disease in children (after cystic fibrosis) and the second most prevalent of the neuromuscular diseases (Heller et al., 1996). Incidence of SMAI in the United States is approximately 1 in 10,000 live births, which accounts for one fourth of all cases of SMA (Ben Hamida et al., 1994; Tsao & Armon, 2000). Incidence of SMA is higher in Saudi Arabia and Middle Eastern countries due to consanguinity (Munsat, 1994). The majority of cases of SMA occur in males (Munsat, 1994; Tsao & Arnon, 2000).

Characteristics

Werdnig-Hoffmann Disease (SMA Type I, or acute infantile form)

1. May be a lack of fetal movement in the final months of pregnancy
2. Age of onset is birth to 6 months of age
3. Severe and rapid progression of symptoms
4. Delayed milestones by 6 months of age
5. Hypotonicity (low muscle tone, feeling flabby to the touch)
6. Severe weakness and muscle atrophy
7. Unable to hold head up or sit without support
8. Frog-shaped legs and bell-shaped chest
9. Movement of extremities is limited to the hands and feet
10. Absent reflexes
11. Swallowing and feeding difficulties, with excessive drooling
12. Weak cry
13. Respiratory problems

All Types of Spinal Muscular Atrophy

1. Muscle weakness and atrophy
2. Motor function loss
3. Skeletal deformities (usually scoliosis is most common)
4. Respiratory problems

Treatment of Werdnig-Hoffmann disease is symptomatic and supportive and should include antibiotic treatment of pneumonia and other respiratory infections that are associated with the disease. It is important that respiratory infections are treated early and aggressively because respiratory failure is the leading cause of death in children with SMA I, and it is unpredictable how many children with this form of SMA will live beyond the usual limit of 2 years of age (Munsat, 1994). Also, physical therapy, orthotic supports, and rehabilitation may prove beneficial in preventing scoliosis and contractures in patients with static or slowly progressive forms of SMA.

Due to the short life expectancy of children with SMA I, the majority will not live long enough to attend school. Children with SMA I will generally appear bright and alert and will readily respond to direct stimulation. Intelligence is normal for children with any of the types of spinal muscular atrophy disorders. Children who have Type II or III often perform well in school due to more exposure to adult conversations and extra effort they expend in academics to compensate for physical limitations. However, these children will need special provisions and assistance in the classroom (see Heller et al., 1996).

The prognosis for individuals with SMA Type I is poor because the disease is invariably fatal. Death occurs in 95% of children with SMA I by age 18 months, and the majority will succumb by 2 years of age. Indeed, this form of spinal muscular atrophy is the leading cause of infant death due to inherited conditions (Heller et al., 1996). The majority of deaths in children with SMA I is usually from respiratory failure, which is caused by the rapid and progressive weakening of the muscles. However, as previously mentioned, there are rare cases of children with SMA I who exceed the usual life expectancy. Parents are urged to speak frankly with their children's physicians regarding aggressive treatment, therapeutic goals, and uncertainty as to the immediate future for children with this form of SMA (Munsat, 1994).

Genetic studies have revealed that all types of SMA are caused by defects in genes located on the long arm (q) of Chromosome 5 (Carter, 1999). Recent breakthroughs have allowed for the reliable detection of SMA I via prenatal testing (Munsat, 1994). Furthermore, current genetic research is attempting to clone the gene for SMA and identify protein composition for more direct treatment of this disease (Munsat, 1994).

REFERENCES

Beers, M. H., & Berkow, R. (Eds.). (1999). *The* Merck *manual of diagnosis and therapy* (17th ed.). Lawrenceville, NJ: Merck.

Ben Hamida, C., Soussi-Yanicostas, N., Butler-Browne, G. S., Bejaoui, K., Hentati, F., & Ben Hamida, M. (1994). Biochemical and immunocytochemical analysis in chronic proximal spinal muscular atrophy. *Muscle Nerve, 17,* 400–410.

Carter, G. (1999). Rehabilitation management in neuromuscular disease. *Journal of Neurological Rehabilitation, 11,* 69–80.

Heller, K. A., Alberto, P. A., Forney, P. E., & Schwartzman, M. N. (1996). Understanding physical, sensory, and health impairments: Characteristics and educational implications. New York, NY: Brooks/Cole.

Munsat, T. L. (1994). The spinal muscular atrophies. In S. Appel (Ed.), *Current neurology* (pp. 55–71). St. Louis, MO: Mosby-Year Books.

Tsao, B., & Armon, C. (2000, December). *Spinal muscular atrophy: Introduction.* Retrieved from http://www.emedicine.com/neuro/topic631.htm

ANDREA HOLLAND
University of Texas at Austin

WERNER, HEINZ (1890–1964)

Heinz Werner received his PhD from Vienna University in 1914 with highest honors. Perhaps the beginning of his scholarly career began when he read about the evolution of animals, man, and the cosmos. He became increasingly interested in philosophy and psychology while at the University of Vienna. His work in the field of psychological phenomena is relevant to psychologists, educators, anthropologists, students of animal behavior, and scholars investigating aesthetic phenomena.

His contributions to the field have been many. He published over 15 books and monographs and more than 150 articles within a 50-year period. His principal publications include *Comparative Psychology of Mental Development* (1940) and *Developmental Processes: Heinz Werner's Selected Writings* (1978). His selected writings include his general theory and perceptual experiences in Volume I; Volume II focuses on cognition, language, and symbolization.

Werner was a great teacher and researcher, and he inspired others to follow his example in the search for understanding of psychological phenomena. His theory was interdisciplinary because all of his developmental principles apply to all the life sciences. He founded an Institute for Human Development at Clark University in 1958. This institute made Clark an "international center directed toward the developmental analysis of phenomena in all the life sciences" (Werner, 1978). Werner's contributions to the field of developmental psychology are steadily gaining recognition.

REFERENCES

Werner, H. (1940). *Comparative psychology of mental development.* New York, NY: Harper & Brothers.

Werner, H. (1978). *Developmental processes: Heinz Werner's selected writings.* New York, NY: International Universities Press.

REBECCA BAILEY
Texas A&M University

WERNER SYNDROME

Werner syndrome (WS) is an autosomal recessive genetic disease that resembles premature aging (University of Washington, 2000). A genetic mutation on Chromosome 8, labeled WRN, is the cause of WS (National Institutes of Health [NIH], 1997). Although the disorder is not usually diagnosed until the third decade of life, the characteristic short stature and low body weight are present during childhood and adolescence (National Organization for Rare Disorders [NORD], 1999). Individuals with WS display clinical features that are similar to features of progeria. However, WS is characterized by a later age of onset, and many symptoms of WS are not manifested in progeria.

Werner syndrome is a rare disease that afflicts males and females at an equal rate (Salk, Fujiwara, & Martin, 1985). Estimates of the world prevalence of WS range between 1 and 22 cases per million people (Salk et al., 1985). Currently, the prevalence of WS in the United States is unknown. The prevalence of WS has been determined to be the highest in Japan, with an estimated 1 case per 20,000 to 40,000 people (J. Oshima, personal communication, December 14, 2000). The higher prevalence in Japan may be related to more frequent consanguineous marriages, which increases the rate for the pairing of recessive genes (Miller, 2000). Siblings of individuals with WS have approximately a 25% chance of having the disorder as well, but the likelihood of a sibling developing the disease is independent of birth order (Salk et al., 1985).

Characteristics

1. Short stature
2. Low weight relative to height
3. Premature graying and thinning of scalp hair
4. Facial abnormalities (e.g., beaked nose, unusually prominent eyes)
5. Voice changes (e.g., high-pitched, squeaky, or hoarse voice)
6. Loss of the layer of fat beneath the skin
7. Atrophy of muscle tissue
8. Degenerative skin changes (e.g., wrinkles)

Possible Characteristics

1. Juvenile cataracts (bilateral)
2. Diabetes mellitus
3. Osteoporosis
4. Arteriosclerosis
5. Hypogonadism (e.g., secondary sexual underdevelopment, diminished fertility, testicular or ovarian atrophy)

Based on information cited by the following authors: NORD (1999) and University of Washington (2000).

Due to its progressive and variable course, there is no universal treatment regimen for individuals afflicted with WS. A diversity of symptoms resembling premature aging may be displayed and increase the susceptibility to age-related diseases (NIH, 1997). A physician must treat the various medical problems that a person with WS may experience.

A diagnosis of WS may be accompanied by stress due to its degenerative nature and shortening of the life span. Reactions of sadness, anger, embarrassment, and loneliness may occur. Persons with WS may benefit from individual or family therapy. Support groups are also available; participation in such groups may decrease feelings of isolation.

Children with WS have an abnormally slow growth rate and may, therefore, become the object of teasing by their peers. This problem may lead the child to develop low self-esteem and become angry or lonely. The child's school performance could be negatively affected by these feelings, resulting in low academic achievement. If school personnel suspect that the child has a learning disability, they should consider whether the child's emotional problems better account for his or her low school achievement.

Persons diagnosed with WS have a poor prognosis. They will probably experience gradual physical deterioration and early onset of age-related disorders. Although the clinical features of WS resemble premature aging, individuals with WS are not susceptible to some medical conditions, such as Alzheimer's disease and hypertension (Yu et al., 1996). Future research should attempt to elucidate why certain age-related diseases are manifested in WS, whereas others are not. Additionally, epidemiological studies of WS should be conducted in order to determine current estimates of prevalence.

REFERENCES

Miller, R. W. (2000). *National Cancer Institute: Division of cancer epidemiology and genetics.* Retrieved from http://www-dceg.ims.nci.nih.gov/hgp/cgb/miller.html

National Institutes of Health. (1997, March 4). Statement of the director, national institute regarding aging on NIA's

FY 1998 budget. Retrieved from http://www.dceg.ims.nci.nih.gov/hgp/cgb/miller.html

National Organization for Rare Disorders. (1999). *Werner syndrome*. Retrieved from http://www.stepstn.com/cgi-win/nord.exe?proc=GetDocument&rectype=0&recNum=135

Salk, D., Fujiwara, Y., & Martin, G. M. (Eds.). (1985). *Werner syndrome and human aging*. New York, NY: Plenum Press.

University of Washington. (2000). *Werner syndrome*. Retrieved from http://www.pathology.washington.edu/werner/registry/diagnostic.html

Yu, C. E., Oshima, J., Fu, Y. H., Wijsman, E. M., Hisama, F., Alisch, R.,...Schellenberg, G. D. (1996, April 12). Positional cloning of the Werner's syndrome gene. *Science, 272*, 258–262.

EVE N. ROSENTHAL
KARLA ANHALT
Texas A&M University

WERNICKE'S APHASIA

Wernicke's aphasia is one of several subdivisions of fluent aphasia. This is the first type of aphasia described, and it is one in which the localization description still holds true in terms of the symptoms correlating with damage to a particular location in the brain. Those possessing communicative deficits consistent with Wernicke's aphasia have pathology in the dominant superior temporal gyrus. A lesion in the superior posterior temporal is obligatory for Wernicke's aphasia.

Major language characteristics of Wernicke's aphasia are defective auditory comprehension; disturbed reading and writing; defective repetition of words and sentences with speech, that is incessant at normal prosody with a rapid rate; good articulation but paraphasic speech, containing semantic and literal paraphasias and possible extra syllables added to words (Graham-Keegan & Caspari, 1997; Hegde, 1994). Other types of fluent aphasia include:

Transcortical Sensory

Here, the lesion is most frequently in the temporoparietal region but the precise Wernicke's area is spared. Damage to the posterior portion of the middle temporal gyrus is often seen; with some cases, the angular gyrus and visual and auditory association cortex are also involved.

Major language characteristics are very similar to those of Wernicke's aphasia with the difference being that in transcortical sensory aphasia repetition is intact (this skill is impaired in Wernicke's).

Conduction

This rare disorder is also called central aphasia. The neuroanatomical basis is very controversial, but consistent with the newer model of viewing the brain as a total system whose symptoms from impairment reflect impairments not only in specific locations within the brain but also in pathways and synergistic interactions. The most frequent theory of location of damage for this type of fluent aphasia is damage to the supramarginal gyrus and the arcuate fasciculus that connects Broca's area with Wernicke's area.

The major distinguishing language characteristic of conduction aphasia is severe impairment in repetition (repetitions may contain added or deleted phonemes); function words are more difficult to repeat. Individuals with conduction aphasia may comprehend problems in repeating sentences.

REFERENCES

Chapey, R. (1994). *Language intervention strategies in adult aphasia* (3rd ed.). Baltimore, MD: Williams & Wilkins.

Graham-Keegan, L., & Caspari, I. (1997). Wernicke's aphasia. In L. L. LaPointe (Ed.), *Aphasia and related neurogenic language disorders* (pp. 42–62). New York, NY: Thieme.

Hegde, M. (1994). A coursebook on aphasia and other neurogenic language disorders. San Diego, CA: Singular.

SHEELA STUART
George Washington University

See also Aphasia; Dysphasia; Language Disorders

WESTERN EUROPE, SPECIAL EDUCATION IN

Current special education practices in Europe differ from country to country and from region to region in any particular country. These practices have been strongly influenced by the affluence of particular European nations and their social welfare outlook. Although Spain and Portugal are concerned about their children and youth with disabilities, the funds and services available to them are far less than in Scandinavia.

The nature of special education funding and services also varies from country to country, depending on political structures and traditions. The degree of political-educational centralization plays an important role. In France, national authority is likely to be more strongly felt in the education of individuals with disabilities than in West Germany, where the federal government has little or no authority in public schools, and where financial support and the provision of services for special education are likely to vary from one region to another. Generally, the most comprehensive financial support for services to the handicapped, at all ages, has been in Scandinavia.

Curriculum

Special education curriculum in Western Europe has not been as narrowly academic as in the United States. Traditionally, Western European special education has been more responsive to the extra-academic aspects of special education. The graphic arts, music, and social and vocational experiences are more often woven into the disabled child's daily activities. Thus, music therapy for disabled students has received widespread support (Pratt, 1983), and the educational usefulness of toy libraries has been widely recognized (deVincentis, 1984). Theater programs for children with mental retardation, motor disabilities, and cerebral palsy have received acclaim (Cohen, 1985). Excursions and travel are considered important educational experiences. The quality of relationships between teachers and pupils is strongly emphasized.

Europeans may be becoming more Americanized in their special education outlooks in that a more instructionally directed focus appears to be emerging. American influences are also revealed in European movements toward noncategorical types of special education, often in the face of previously accepted, and often complicated, categorical models (as in the Netherlands). European attention to integration of special education with general education has also been influenced by American practices, albeit in European terms (Organisation for Economic Co-operation and Development [OECD], 1985a, 1985b). Even though Europeans have led the way in assisting the transition of handicapped youths into the world of work, American efforts in this area have influenced their practices considerably.

Early Intervention

The most pervasive and effective interventions with Western European handicapped children, prior to their enrollment in formal educational programs, are medically related. Most European nations provide mandatory health screening and reporting for young children, as well as free medical services. In Austria, a multidisciplinary team headed by a social pediatrician steps in as soon as a child has a problem. Indeed, as soon as a child is officially identified as being disabled, the child's parents begin receiving a disability pension. In France, early intervention begins with the compulsory screening of all infants at birth and again at 2 years. Interdisciplinary teams operate out of "early medico-social activity centers to provide therapies, education, and support in home and natural environments" (Zucman, 1985). However, day care of a more educational nature also can be observed. In Switzerland, a disabled child's involvement with itinerant educational services begins at an early age (even at birth) and continues, when needed, until the child's integration into school (Pahud & Besson, 1985).

Preschool

Preschool special education had its beginnings in Germany, where Froebel was the first educator to formalize it on a public basis. Current preschool special education in Western Europe varies from nation to nation. For example, different nations have different beginning ages for compulsory education, so that even the definition of preschool education varies. Also, the Europeans have traditionally favored parents as the main educators of their children, particularly when young. The social welfare underpinnings of such states as Sweden have been very supportive of parents who remain at home with their young, offering them paid leave from employment. Countries such as Italy have made remarkable advances in integrating preschoolers into regular education programs.

Least Restrictive Environment and Mainstreaming

Modern-day principles of least restrictive environment and mainstreaming originated with the Bill of Rights for the mentally retarded and the principle of normalization in Scandinavia. Both concepts strongly influenced much of Western Europe. Thus the notion of integrating students with disabilities into the main body of education was well on its way, even without American influences. Indeed, reforms in this respect were begun in Norway in 1920 (Booth, 1982). Nevertheless, the United States can take credit for institutionalizing the ideas of least restrictive environment and mainstreaming, and for offering models for the Europeans to adopt. The degree to which the principles of least restrictive environment have prevailed has differed from country to country.

In Denmark, special education is an integral part of regular education within a sophisticated range of educational services. In fact, administrative integration of services for the disabled with those for the nondisabled was passed into law on January 1, 1979, on the premise that disabled individuals should receive services in the same way as the nondisabled (Juul, 1980). Italy's Law 517/1977 has gone far beyond general recommendations for implementation of least restrictive environments to providing procedural plans for implementing the education of exceptional students within regular classrooms (Strain, 1985). On the other hand, in West Germany, where responsibility for the education of the disabled was traditionally assumed by religious and voluntary organizations, terminology for such education was originally couched in the language of segregation. Public school teachers were unfamiliar with the education of children with special needs, and it was difficult for the teachers to prepare to work with the disabled. This meant some hesitancy in certain European nations with respect to mainstreaming; however, mainstreaming has moved forward at a steady pace overall.

Transition

European efforts in transition education have been in the vanguard in many respects (Booth, 1982; OECD, 1981, 1985a, 1985b), with significant efforts being made to help exceptional youths and young adults to move into the world of work. The Netherlands has been noteworthy for providing sheltered workshops for more involved exceptional youths and adults while supervising more able ones who are actively employed in the open market. Again, the social welfare outlook in nations such as the Netherlands, which even purchases paintings from artists unable to sell their works, conditions Western European attitudes toward the handicapped. In France, the Union Nationale des Association de Parents d'Enfants Inadaptes, which operates hundreds of schools for moderately to severely handicapped children and youths, has a strong vocational emphasis in its curriculum. It also has operated the Centres d'Aide pour Travail to aid in the employment of the disabled. In Austria an organization called Jugend am Werk (Youth at Work), which originated with the idea of providing shelter and work to disadvantaged youths, went on to provide vocational training centers, sheltered workshops, and residential centers for the handicapped. Unfortunately, the employment picture in most European countries has been dismal over the past decade, with high unemployment rates for nondisabled workers. Opportunities for the handicapped to work in the normal marketplace have been significantly reduced as a consequence.

The Educateur Movement

Educateurs are special types of teacher/child-care workers who are competent to work with maladapted young people, including disabled youths. They are trained in nonacademic subjects such as sports, acting, arts and crafts, and other leisure-time activities. They teach vocational subjects, supervise vocational placements, work with families, schools, and communities, and act as advocates for their student clients. The educateur profession is well established in France, with numerous colleges providing rigorous training. The educateur movement has spread across much of Western Europe. It has also influenced Canadian services. In the United States, Project Re-Ed was a variant of the educateur model. In European nations, there have been adaptations according to national and local needs. Similar professions have emerged under different names with somewhat different identities and functions. In West Germany the educateurs are called erziehers; in the Netherlands they are identified as orthopedagogues; and in Scandinavia they are milieu therapists.

Therapeutic Communities

The Europeans have also been noted for their creation of therapeutic communities. Professionals and lay people critical of traditional government and professional roles in serving the disabled and the ill have been instrumental in fostering these.

In Great Britain, psychiatrists Laing and Cooper created a therapeutic home at Kingsley Hall, London. They viewed mentally ill individuals as victims of home and society, and saw hospitals as degrading and dehumanizing for them (1971). Laing's views of the causes of mental illness have altered over the years. Others have increasingly shared his perceptions that mental hospitals dehumanize and often harm their residents, and that relationships between professionals and their clients on a day-to-day personal basis may be the best way to help the latter.

In France the movement toward therapeutic communities following World War II began in earnest with the work of Jean Vanier (Wolfensberger, 1973) in the movement called l'Arche (place of refuge). Vanier built a small community in Trosly-Breuil, France, where mentally handicapped and nonhandicapped adults could live and work together as families. Vanier's work has inspired the creation of other similar facilities across France and elsewhere.

Most important in the therapeutic community movement has been the anthroposophic movement. Rudolf Steiner, an Austrian philosopher and educator inaugurated this at the turn of the 20th century. The inspirations of the anthroposophic movement led to the creation of the Waldorf method and Waldorf schools. The Waldorf method, although originally intended for normal children, was found also to be applicable to exceptional children. Anthroposophic education is developmental in orientation, and multifaceted. It emphasizes art, bodily movement, music, community involvement, and work. Anthroposophic schools have sought to integrate therapy with education and to engage in therapies that find their expression in art, drama, role playing, and so on. Anthroposophic schools serving the disabled are now numerous in Great Britain and on the continent. Originally oriented toward the mentally retarded and multiply handicapped, they have recently expanded to serve the emotionally disturbed as well.

Particularly noteworthy within the anthroposophic movement has been the Camphill movement, which Karl Konig began in the early 1940s. He was an Austrian-psychiatrist who came to Scotland to escape Nazi persecution. Inspired by anthroposophic philosophy, which views an individual's inner personality as remaining whole and intact despite the nature and degree of that individual's disabilities, Konig created a special village in the vicinity of Aberdeen, Scotland, in which mentally retarded villagers and normal coworkers could live and work together. The original Camphill movement has spread considerably since that time, both in Europe and the United States. Some settlements serve children, while others serve adults. The orientation of the Camphill settlements, which are self-contained communities, is contrary to modern-day notions of least restrictive environment. Nevertheless, they offer a remarkable combination of care and opportunity for self-fulfillment to many handicapped individuals.

Minority Disabled

Changed immigration policies and intensive industrialization during the postwar period saw an influx of millions of immigrants or "guest workers" from Africa, Asia, and less affluent European nations into Western Europe. Today, there are second and third generations of these minorities in most Western European nations. With some exceptions, there has been difficulty in integrating them. Decreases in employment opportunities in Western Europe have meant increased hardships and alienation for many (e.g., Turks in Germany, Arabs in France, Indians and Pakistanis in Great Britain). The children of such families constitute a large proportion of underprivileged and disadvantaged students in Western Europe. Elevated levels of handicaps and school failure are the consequence. At the same time, such students, because of their alienated status, are less likely to benefit from benign European attitudes toward the handicapped. It should be observed that the Dutch have been particularly accepting of such minority populations.

Professional Preparation

There is considerable variation in the professional preparation of special education teachers in Europe. In some countries, there appear to be few special requirements. In others, licensure or certification requirements are demanding. In certain countries, there are likely to be differences from one region to another. Germany has traditionally been interested in experimenting with different training models. In England and Wales, more systematic training was instituted as a consequence of the Warnock Report. Switzerland has a number of different teacher institutes, each of which has a special orientation to the cantons that they serve. The Institut des Science de l'Education, at Geneva, associated with the name of Piaget, has been known for its research into the cognitive processes of handicapped students; it is a national training resource. Switzerland's Zentralstelle fur Heilpadagogik coordinates the efforts of its various teacher training centers in respect to special education. In several countries, specialization in special education is entirely on the graduate level. Some countries (e.g., Scotland) require that candidates for special education training have at least 1 year of teaching in regular education. In France, theoretical studies and practicum requirements are distinguished from each other.

Voluntary Agencies

As in the United States, voluntary organizations have a significant place with respect to assisting handicapped students. They run preschool centers, schools, sheltered workshops, group homes, and hospitals. They even provide professional training. In West Germany the largest of these is the Catholic Caritas. There is also Lebenshilfe, the National Association of Parents and Friends of the Mentally Handicapped, which operates day-school nurseries, sheltered workshops, and hostels. In Switzerland, an umbrella organization called Pro Infirmis coordinates the work of other organizations serving the disabled. It provides a comprehensive educational program as well, publishes books and brochures, and offers consultations for children and adults. In Austria, the Save the Children Society assists children with special needs in homes and rehabilitation centers. It also offers help in times of crisis. In Great Britain, voluntary agencies work closely with public authorities. In Scandinavia, the Norwegian Red Cross has created special schools and vocational rehabilitation centers; after making them viable, it turns them over to the government.

Auxiliary Services

Widespread, comprehensive, and effective support services for students with disabilities are likely to be obtained in most of the nations of Western Europe. For one thing, these nations have broad-based national health insurance systems combining private and public institutions into an easily accessible network of services (Massie, 1985). Many of the medical and ancillary medical services that disabled children require are obtainable through such government-supported services.

REFERENCES

Booth, T. (1982). *Special need in education*. Stratford, England: Open University Educational Enterprises.

Cohen, H. U. (1985). "Var Teater": A Swedish model of children's theatre for participants with disabilities. *Children's Theatre Review, 34*(4), 14–16.

deVincentis, S. (1984, April). *Swedish play intervention for handicapped children*. Paper presented at the annual convention of the Council for Exceptional Children, Washington, DC.

Juul, K. D. (1979). European approaches and innovations in serving the handicapped. *Exceptional Children, 44*, 322–330.

Juul, K. D. (1980). Special education in Western Europe and Scandinavia. In L. Mann & D. A. Sabatino (Eds.), *The fourth review of special education*. New York, NY: Grune & Stratton.

Juul, K. D. (1984, April). *Toy libraries for the handicapped*. Paper presented at the annual convention of the Council for Exceptional Children, Washington, DC.

Juul, K. D., & Linton, T. E. (1978). European approaches to the treatment of behavior disordered children. *Behavior Disorders, 3*, 232–249.

Kugel, F. B., & Wolfensberger, W. (Eds.). (1968). *Changing patterns of residential services for the mentally retarded*. Washington, DC: President's Committee on Mental Retardation.

Linton, T. E. (1971). The educateur model: A theoretical monograph. *Journal of Special Education, 5,* 155–190.

Massie, R. K. (1985). The constant shadow: Reflections on the life of a chronically ill child. In N. Hobbes & J. M. Perrin (Eds.), *Issues in the care of children with chronic illness.* San Francisco: Jossey-Bass.

Organisation for Economic Co-operation and Development (OECD). (1981). *Integration in the school.* Washington, DC: Author.

Organisation for Economic Co-operation and Development (OECD). (1985a). *Handicapped youth at work: Personal experiences of school-leavers: The education of the handicapped adolescent: III.* Paris: Centre for Educational Research and Innovation.

Organisation for Economic Co-operation and Development (OECD). (1985b). *Integration of the handicapped in secondary schools: Five case studies. The education of the handicapped adolescent: II.* Washington, DC: Author.

Oyer, H. J. (1976). Communication for the hearing handicapped. An international perspective. Baltimore, MD: University Park Press.

Pahud, D., & Besson, F. (1985, Summer). Special education in Switzerland: Historical reflections and current applications. *Journal of the Division of Early Childhood, 9,* 222–229.

Pratt, R. R. (Ed.). (1983). The International Symposium on Music in Medicine, Education, and Therapy for the Handicapped. Lanham, MD: University Press of America.

Strain, P. (1985). A response to preschool handicapped in Italy: A research based developmental model. *Journal of the Division for Early Childhood, 29,* 269–271.

Tarnapol, L., & Tarnapol, M. (1976). *Reading disabilities: An international perspective.* Baltimore, MD: University Park Press.

Taylor, E. J. (1980). *Rehabilitation and world peace.* New York, NY: International Society for Rehabilitation of the Disabled.

Taylor, W. W., & Taylor, I. W. (1960). *Special education of physically handicapped children in Western Europe.* New York, NY: International Society for the Welfare of Cripples.

Wolfensberger, W. (1964). General observations on European countries. *Mental Retardation, 2,* 331–337.

Wolfensberger, W. (1973). *A selective overview of the work of Jean Vanier and the movement of L'Arche.* Toronto, Canada: National Institute of Mental Retardation.

Zucman, E. (1985). Early childhood programs for the handicapped in France. *Journal of the Division for Early Childhood, 9,* 237–245.

Don Braswell
Research Foundation,
City University of New York

See also Belgium, Special Education In; Eastern Europe, Special Education In; England, Special Education In; France, Special Education In

WHELAN, RICHARD J. (1931–   )

Born in Emmett, Kansas, Richard J. Whelan received his BA (cum laude) from Washburn University in 1955 with majors in history, political science, psychology, and education. By 1957, he completed all requirements for a MA in history, with concentrations in American, European, and Far Eastern history at the University of Kansas. In 1966, he received the EdD from the University of Kansas with concentrations in special education (emotional and behavior disorders), educational psychology and research. He is currently licensed as a social studies and psychology teacher as well as a teacher of students with emotional and behavior disorders. He also holds licenses as a special education supervisor/coordinator, director of special education, and school psychologist. The Supreme Court of the State of Kansas has certified him as a mediator and an approved trainer of mediators. He also serves as a special education administrative hearing officer and hearing officer trainer for the Kansas State Board of Education. In addition, he is a special education hearing officer for the Bureau of Indian Affairs. During the Korean War, he served as an Instructor of Electronics, Computers, and Power Control Systems at the U.S. Army Radar and Guided Missile School.

Whelan's earliest professional experiences were at the Southard School of the Menninger Clinic where he served as a recreational therapist, child-care worker, teacher, and director of education. At the University of Kansas and University of Kansas Medical Center, he has held academic appointments in psychiatry, pediatrics, and special education. His administrative posts have included chairperson of the Department of Special Education, dean of a Graduate Division, dean of the School of Education, and director of education for the University Affiliated Program at the medical center. Since 1968, he has held the chair for the Ralph L. Smith Distinguished Professor of Child Development. From 1972 to 1974, he served as director of the Division of Personnel Preparation in the Bureau of Education for the Handicapped (now Office of Special Education and Rehabilitation Services) in the Department of Health, Education, and Welfare.

Whelan has held numerous board memberships and serves as a consultant to psychiatric hospitals, universities, government agencies, schools, and other education-related organizations. During his career, Whelan has served on seven publication boards and has held offices in state and national professional organizations. He was chairperson of the Evaluation Training Consortium, a nationwide evaluation-training project funded by the U.S. Office of Education. He was a founder and officer of the Kansas Federation of the Council for Exceptional Children. He is a member of Phi Kappa Phi, and has been recognized by Leaders in Education, Who's Who in America, and Outstanding Educators of America. He has received several service awards including the Award for Leadership in Behavior Disorders from the Midwest Symposium Organization.

Whelan has contributed over 100 publications, including *Emotional and Behavioral Disorders: A 25-Year Focus* (1998) and *Educating Students with Mild Disabilities: Strategies and Methods* (Meyen, Vergason, & Whelan, 1998). His professional preparation included extensive experiences in psychoanalysis, psychoeducational and applied behavior analysis theories, and interventions. He emphasized experimental research designs and precise measurement in his own research, as well as in the classes he taught for graduate students. More importantly, he believes that the best teachers of professionals are the children they serve: "They will let you know if you are doing it correctly." Whelan put this belief into practice while teaching and while directing a psychoeducational clinic for children with disabilities and their families at the University of Kansas Medical Center.

Whelan retired from the University of Kansas, Special Education Department in 2000 after 37 years of service.

REFERENCES

Meyen, E. L., Vergason, G. A., & Whelan, R. J. (Eds.). (1998). *Educating students with mild disabilities: Strategies and methods.* Denver, CO: Love.

Whelan, R. J. (Ed.). (1998). *Emotional and behavioral disorders: A 25-year focus.* Denver, CO: Love.

STAFF

See *also* **Office of Special Education and Rehabilitative Services**

WHOLE-WORD TEACHING

The term *whole-word teaching* has been used as the label for two different approaches to beginning reading instruction. Mathews (1966) in *Teaching to Read: Historically Considered* describes the first approach as a "words-to-letters" method that was introduced into reading instruction in Germany in the 18th century and later brought to the United States.

The development of the words-to-letters method was motivated by dissatisfaction with the ABC method, the prevailing method of reading instruction since the invention of the Greek alphabet. Critics of the ABC method did not disagree with its underlying philosophy that mastery of the alphabet and syllables (combinations of vowels and consonants such as *ba, be, bu*) were prerequisite skills for learning to read. However, they took issue with the procedures used to teach those skills, namely, years of

drill, which they described as senseless, tortuous, desperately dull work. The method that eventually evolved presented beginning readers with whole words in their total form followed by an analysis of the sounds and letters. This was an analytic approach to teaching the alphabet, whereas the ABC method was a synthetic approach under which students were taught to combine syllables into words only after having mastered their pronunciation as isolated units.

Mathews (1966) refers to the second approach that has been called whole-word teaching as a "words-to-reading" method. This method, commonly called the "look-and-say" method, also had its roots in Germany and may have been used by some teachers in the United States as early as the 1830s. Horace Mann, a strong advocate of the method, is often credited with having brought about its widespread use (Betts, 1946). However, according to Mathews (1966), it was Francis Parker, the first widely known practitioner of the look-and-say method, who played a far more significant role in its initiation. Under his leadership as superintendent of schools in Quincy, Massachusetts (1875–1878), and later as principal of Cooke County Normal School, Illinois (1883–1899), students were taught to read 150 to 200 words in the context of sentences and stories before being introduced to the sounds of letters. The teaching of names of letters was delayed for at least two years so that they would not be confused with the sounds of letters. Although Parker's schools were widely acclaimed, it is doubtful that the look-and-say method would have gained the foothold it did had he not become closely associated with John Dewey, head of the departments of philosophy, psychology, and pedagogy at the University of Chicago.

When Parker was appointed director of the School of Education at the university in 1900, the two joined forces. Although Dewey was not interested in developing a methodology for teaching children to read, he thoroughly agreed with Parker's educational philosophy and adopted the look-and-say method strongly advocated by Parker. In this way, the look-and-say method came to occupy a prominent place in a new system of education (advocated by Dewey) to which the adjective progressive was applied (Mathews, 1966). As the influence of the progressive education movement grew, so did the use of the look-and-say approach to reading. During the first two decades of the 20th century, it became firmly entrenched in elementary reading programs and remained so until the mid-1950s, when Rudolf Flesch (1955) captured the growing public alarm over what was happening in the nation's elementary schools in his book *Why Johnny Can't Read*. Flesch challenged the prevailing practice in beginning reading instruction that emphasized a look-and- say approach. He advocated a return to a phonic approach using existing research as support for his position.

Flesch's book led to a great deal of public debate, which in turn spawned numerous research efforts to identify the best method(s) for beginning reading instruction. Among these were 27 U.S. Office of Education grade 1 studies and a study funded by the Carnegie Corporation of New York (Chall, 1967).

REFERENCES

Betts, E. A. (1946). *Foundations of reading instruction*. New York, NY: American Book.

Chall, J. (1967). *Learning to read: The great debate*. New York, NY: McGraw-Hill.

Flesch, R. (1955). *Why Johnny can't read and what you can do about it*. New York, NY: Harper & Brothers.

Mathews, M. M. (1966). *Teaching to read: Historically considered*. Chicago, IL: University of Chicago Press.

MARIANNE PRICE
*Montgomery County Intermediate Unit,
Norristown, Pennsylvania*

WHOOPING COUGH (PERTUSSIS)

Pertussis, also known as whooping cough, is an acute bacterial (Bordatella pertussis) infection of the cilia that line the air passages of the lower respiratory tract. Cilia are tiny, hairlike projections on cells that beat back and forth to help clear the respiratory system of mucus, bacteria, viruses, and dead cells. Bordatella pertussis interferes with the motion of the cilia. The debris accumulates and causes irritation in the respiratory tract and triggers coughing. It causes spasms (paroxysms) of uncontrollable coughing, followed by a sharp, high-pitched intake of air, which creates the characteristic whoop for which the disease is named. Pertussis is very contagious and is spread by breathing in airborne droplets expelled from the nose or throat of an infected person or by direct contact with discharges from the nose or throat of an infected person.

Before the availability of pertussis vaccine, pertussis was one of the most common childhood diseases and a major cause of death in children in the United States. After the use of the pertussis vaccine, cases decreased by 99%, but about 5,000–7,000 cases per year are still reported in the United States. Incidence of pertussis has increased steadily since the 1980s (Centers for Disease Control and Prevention, 2000). Approximately 38% of recognized cases occur in infants younger than 6 months of age, which stresses the need for early immunization. Pertussis can result in serious complications, including middle ear infections, pneumonia, convulsions (seizures), disorders of the brain, brief episodes of stopped breathing, and in 1% of the cases, death. Anyone can get pertussis, but children—especially unvaccinated or incompletely vaccinated infants under age 2—are at the most risk.

Characteristics

1. *Incubation stage*: Symptoms appear between 6 and 21 days (average 7–10) after exposure to the bacteria.
2. *Catarrhal stage*: Runny nose, low-grade fever, sneezing, and a mild cough similar to that from a common cold. Within 2 weeks, episodes of severe coughing develop.
3. *Paroxysmal stage*: Rapid spasmodic coughing followed by a characteristic intake of breath that sounds like a whoop. During such an attack, the patient may become cyanotic (turn blue) due to the lack of air. Vomiting and exhaustion commonly follow the episode. The bouts of coughing can last from 1 to 2 months. Children and young infants, especially, appear very ill and distressed. The patient usually appears normal between attacks. Diagnosis of pertussis is suspected at this stage and can be confirmed by a throat culture.
4. *Convalescent stage*: Spasms of coughing may occur, but will be less intense. This stage lasts about 3–4 weeks.
5. Infants under age 6 months, adolescents, immunized school children, and adults generally have milder symptoms without the typical whoop.

The treatment for pertussis is with the use of antibiotics (erythromycin). This treatment is limited because after the cilia are damaged, they cannot be repaired. It takes time for the cilia to grow back; until then, the patient has to wait and endure the symptoms. The antibiotics are used to prevent complicating infections and reduce the contagious period of the disease. Severe cases may require steroid treatments to reduce the severity of the disease. Hospitalization may be needed, and oxygen and mild sedation may be required to control coughing spells. Other supportive ways to help the patient to be more comfortable include monitoring liquids to prevent dehydration; resting in a quiet, dark room to decrease paroxysms; and suctioning the mucus.

The overall prognosis for a recovery is good in all age groups. Fewer than 1% of whooping cough cases end in death; this is usually in children who develop complications such as pneumonia and extreme weight loss. Special education services would probably not be needed unless long-term complications became evident.

The most effective measure to prevent the spread of pertussis is to maintain the highest level of immunization in children. Researchers are working on creating an adult vaccine to immunize adults.

REFERENCE

Centers for Disease Control and Prevention. (2000, December). *Pertussis*. Retrieved from http://www.cdc.gov/pertussis/clinical/index.html

KAREN WILEY
University of Northern Colorado

WIDE RANGE ACHIEVEMENT TEST–FOURTH EDITION

The Wide Range Achievement Test–Fourth Edition (WRAT-4; Wilkinson & Robertson, 2006) is an instrument used to measure the development of basic academic skills in the areas of reading, spelling, and arithmetic for ages 5 through 94. There are two alternate test forms, the Blue and Green versions, providing four subtests: Word Reading, which measures letter and word decoding; Sentence Comprehension, which evaluates reading comprehension through a cloze technique; Spelling, which requires examinees to write letters and words from dictation; and Math Computation, which measures basic math computations through counting, simple oral problems, and paper-and-pencil calculations. The examinee's performance on the Word Reading subtest determines the start point for Sentence Comprehension. Additionally, the Word Reading and Sentence Comprehension subtests can be considered together to form an overall Reading Composite, which is the only composite score provided by the WRAT-4.

Administration time varies depending on the age and ability of the examinee, but usually runs between 15 and 45 minutes. Materials include three protocols: the Test Form, Sentence Comprehension Test Form, and Response Forms, as well as laminated cards for administration of Word Reading, Spelling, and Sentence Comprehension. Once the examiner is familiar with the presentation of these materials, administration is relatively easy. Guidelines are found in the manual as well as on the Test Form. Examiners Scoring is also brief and relatively simple.

The WRAT-4 contains updated norms based on a sample of 3,021 individuals between 5 and 94 years of age. The sample was stratified by age, gender, ethnicity, geographic reason and educational level. Grade-based norms were based on a sample of 1,800 individuals in grades K–12. Some effort was made to include those with educational disabilities. All subtests and the Reading Composite yield standard scores (based either on examinee age or grade), confidence intervals, percentile ranks, and several optional scores, including grade equivalents, NCE, and stanine scores.

The internal consistency reliability coefficients for the four subtests and Reading Composite were generally high. Alternate form reliability (using the Blue and Green forms) ranged from 0.82 to 0.90. Although the manual presents good evidence for reliability, arguments for validity are somewhat weaker, as noted by other reviewers (i.e., Hoff, 2010). Arguments for content validity are based widely on retaining WRAT3 items. According to the test authors, changes from the WRAT3 to the WRAT4 resulted from expert review. The manual presents some evidence for internal validity by demonstrating raw scores change as predicted across development, providing correlations between subtests, and presenting differential item functioning analyses. External validity is demonstrated through correlations between the WRAT-4 and other measures of academic achievement as well as cognitive ability. Finally, a brief discussion of clinical studies using the WRAT-4 with individuals who have a learning disability, high cognitive ability, and low cognitive ability is presented in the manual, with scores following expected patterns.

Overall, the WRAT-4 may be a good choice for examiners seeking a brief and relatively simple measure of basic academic skills, particularly for screening or reevaluation. Those seeking a more comprehensive measure of academic achievement may do better with a broader measure, and further validity studies would be useful. Finally, the WRAT-4 may be most useful for those performing in the average range of ability or below, as the manual notes less precision in measurement is available for older and well-performing individuals due to the test's focus on basic skills.

This entry has been informed by the sources listed below.

REFERENCES

Dell, C., Harrold, B., & Dell, T. (2008). Test review of Wide Range Achievement Test–Fourth Edition. *Rehabilitation Counseling Bulletin, 52*(1), 57–60.

Hoff, K. E. (2010). Review of the Wide Range Achievement Test 4. In R. A. Spies, K. F. Geisinger, & J. F. Carlson (Eds.), *The eighteenth mental measurements yearbook*. Lincoln, NE: Buros Institute of Mental Measurements.

Sabers, D. L., & Olson, A. M. Review of the Wide Range Achievement Test 4. In R. A. Spies, K. F. Geisinger, & J. F. Carlson (Eds.), *The eighteenth mental measurements yearbook*. Lincoln, NE: Buros Institute of Mental Measurements.

Wilkinson, G., & Robertson, G. (2006). *The Wide Range Achievement Test–Fourth Edition*. Lutz, FL: Psychological Assessment Resources.

KATHLEEN VEIZEL
JAMIE ZIBULSKY
Fairleigh Dickinson University
Fourth edition

WIDE RANGE ASSESSMENT OF MEMORY AND LEARNING, SECOND EDITION

The Wide Range Assessment of Memory and Learning, Second Edition (WRAML-2; Adams & Sheslow, 2003) is an individually administered clinical instrument designed to measure an individual's learning and memory functions for school-age children to adults. Specifically, the test assesses an individual's ability to actively learn verbal and visual information. Moreover, the WRAML-2 allows for the acquisition of new learning, in addition to the assessment of both delayed and immediate recall.

Administration time varies depending on the age and ability of the examinee, but the Core Battery takes less than one hour to complete. A Screening Battery consisting of four subtests from the Core Battery affords a basic indication of memory functioning. This Screening Battery correlates well with the total scale and can be given in approximately 10 to 15 minutes. Several subtests are included to supplement the Core Battery, thus allowing the examiner to add supplementary indices and subtests to facilitate qualitative analyses when necessary. The test should be administered by a trained clinician under the direct supervision of a psychologist experienced in the administration of testing.

The Core Battery consists of six subtests, and each subtest yields a norm-referenced score. The WRAML-2 Core Battery is comprised of two Attention-Concentration, two Verbal, and two Visual subtests, yielding an Attention-Concentration Index, a Verbal Memory Index, and a Visual Memory Index. These subtests collectively yield a General Memory Index. In addition, a new Working Memory Index has been added and is comprised of the Symbolic Working Memory and Verbal Working Memory subtests. Also, four new recognition subtests have been added. They are the Design Recognition, Picture Recognition, Story Memory Recognition, and Verbal Recognition subtests. Since the last edition, the designs on the Design Memory cards have been changed and an additional Design Card has been added. In addition, the Picture Memory subtest includes new and contemporary full-color scenes, and the Story Memory subtest provides new stories and has been updated and lengthened to accommodate adults.

Standard scores (M = 100, SD = 15), scaled scores (M = 10, SD = 3), and percentiles can be obtained from all of the indices, which allow the examiner to make age-based comparisons of performance. Age equivalents are provided for the child and preadolescent age groups.

The WRAML-2 is normed for children and adults aged 5 to 90 years. The norm sample was formed using a national stratified sampling technique, controlling for such variables as age, education level, race, religion, and sex. A good amount of detail is included in the administration manual concerning the representativeness of the norming samples.

The administration manual also contains a good deal of information concerning the psychometric aspects of the test. Alpha reliabilities for the Core Battery Verbal Memory Index, Visual Memory Index, and Attention-Concentration Index are 0.92, 0.89, and 0.86 respectively. The Alpha Reliability for the General Index is 0.93.

This entry has been informed by the sources listed below.

REFERENCES

Adams, W., & Sheslow, D. (2003). *Wide Range Assessment of Memory and Learning–Second Edition*. Lutz, FL: Psychological Assessment Resources.

Atkinson, T. (2008). A cluster analysis of the wide range assessment of memory and learning–second edition (WRMAL-2). *Dissertation Abstracts International Section A, 68*.

Hartman, D. (2007). Test review: Wide Range Assessment of Memory and Learning–2(WRAML-2): WRedesigned and WReally improved. *Applied Neuropsychology, 14*(2), 138–140.

Lynch, P., Chen, R., & Holmes, C. (2004). Factor Structure of the Wide Range Assessment of Memory and Learning (WRAML) in Children with Insulin Dependent Diabetes Mellitus (IDDM). *Child Neuropsychology, 10*(4), 306–317.

REVIEW IN

Spies, R. A., & Plake, B. S. (Eds.). (2005). *The sixteenth mental measurements yearbook*. Lincoln, NE: Buros Institute of Mental Measurements.

RON DUMONT
Fairleigh Dickinson University

JOHN O. WILLIS
Rivier College

KATHLEEN VEIZEL
JAMIE ZIBULSKY
Fairleigh Dickinson College
Fourth edition

WIDE RANGE ASSESSMENT OF VISUAL MOTOR ABILITIES

The Wide Range Assessment of Visual Motor Abilities (WRAVMA; Adams & Sheslow, 1995) provides a Visual-Motor Integration Composite resulting from separate subtest assessments of Fine-Motor, Visual-Spatial, and Visual-Motor abilities. These three areas can be measured individually or in combination.

Administration time for each subtest of the WRAVMA takes about 4 to 10 minutes. The Fine-Motor (pegboard) test has the individual insert as many pegs as possible into a rough square, waffled pegboard. The examinee has 90 seconds to complete this task. Norms are provided for both dominant and nondominant hands. In the Visual-Spatial (matching) test, the child is asked to mark the option that "goes best" to the standard presented. Correct selection depends on visual-spatial skills such as perspective, orientation, rotation, and size discrimination. The Visual-Motor (drawing) subtest requires children to copy designs that are developmentally arranged to increase in difficulty. The Manual supplies examples of acceptable and unacceptable responses for the 24 drawing items, as well as justifications for each. The test booklets are colorful and appealing.

Performance on the subtests can be interpreted both qualitatively and quantitatively to create a more complete evaluation of visual-motor abilities. Scaled scores, standard scores, age equivalents, and percentiles may be obtained for each subtest.

The WRAVMA was normed on a representative sample of over 2,600 children, ages 3–17, stratified according to gender, geographic region, socioeconomic standing, and race/ethnic group. This sample reflected the 1990 United States Census data.

Reliability measures of the three subtests show internal consistency coefficients exceeding .90 and test-retest reliability coefficients ranging from 0.81 to 0.91. Construct validity is supported by item separations of 0.99. Concurrent validity varies from .67 for the WRAVMA Visual-Spatial test with the Motor Free Visual Perception Test, to 0.81 for the WRAVMA Fine-Motor test with the Grooved Pegboard, and 0.87 for the WRAVMA Visual-Motor test with the Beery-Buktenica Developmental Test of Visual-Motor Integration (VMI).

REFERENCE

Adams, W. & Sheslow, D. (1995). *Wide Range Assessment of Visual Motor Abilities*. Wilmington, DE: Wide Range.

REVIEWED IN

Glidden, R. (1999, August). The validity of the Wide Range Assessment of Visual Motor Abilities. *Dissertation Abstracts International, 60*.

Plake, B. S., & Impara, J. C. (Eds.). (2001). *The fourteenth mental measurements yearbook*. Lincoln, NE: Buros Institute of Mental Measurements.

RON DUMONT
Fairleigh Dickinson University

JOHN O. WILLIS
Rivier College

KATHLEEN VEIZEL
JAMIE ZIBULSKY
*Fairleigh Dickinson College
Fourth edition*

WIEACKER SYNDROME

Wieacker syndrome, also known as apraxia, involves the inability to execute familiar voluntary movements. A child with Wieacker syndrome is physically able to perform motor acts and has a desire to perform the acts, but is unable to perform the movements upon request (Merck, 1987). When motor movement does occur in a child with this syndrome, the movement is often uncontrolled, unintentional, inappropriate, and clumsy.

Selective apraxias do exist. For example, a child with constructional apraxia is unable to draw, whereas a child with oculomotor apraxia is unable to move his or her eyes (Thoene, 1992).

Apraxia results from a lesion in the neural pathways of the brain associated with the memory of learned patterns (Merck, 1987). The lesion may be due to a stroke, head injury, dementia, congenital malformation of the central nervous system, or metabolic or structural disease (Merck, 1987; Thoene, 1992).

Physical and occupational therapy is recommended to help a child with apraxia to relearn voluntary movements. If apraxia is a symptom of another disorder, treatment of the primary disorder is required (Thoene, 1992).

REFERENCES

Merck manual of diagnosis and therapy (15th ed.). (1987). Rahway, NJ: Merck.

Thoene, J. G. (Ed.). (1992). *Physician's guide to rare diseases*. Montvale, NJ: Dowden.

JOAN MAYFIELD
Baylor Pediatric Specialty Service

PATRICIA A. LOWE
University of Kansas

WIEDEMANN RAUTENSTRAUCH SYNDROME

Wiedemann Rautenstrauch syndrome, a form of progeria, is also known as neonatal progeroid syndrome. Diagnostic criteria for this disorder also include lipoatrophy, which is a deficiency in or the absence of the layer of fat under the skin. Another feature is slow growth both pre- and postnatally. The most striking feature of the syndrome is the aged appearance at birth.

This condition is thought to be autosomal recessive, which means that the baby inherited from each parent the same defective gene for the same trait. The possibility of inheriting the same defective gene increases if the parents are related by blood. If both parents are carriers for a recessive disorder, the risk of transmitting the disease to children is 25%. The risk that those children will be carriers only, without showing symptoms, is 50% (National Organization for Rare Disorders [NORD], 2001). Research literature indicates no racial predilection, with reported cases of African American, Asian, Hispanic, and Caucasian patients (Pivnick et al., 2000).

This genetic disorder appears to affect males and females equally. The literature to date includes approximately 21 cases of Wiedemann Rautenstrauch syndrome, but there are several other forms of progeria and congenital disorders that share many of this syndrome's characteristics (NORD, 2001).

Characteristics

1. Aged appearance at birth.

2. Either deficiency or absences of the layer of fat under the skin, causing the skin to be abnormally thin, fragile, and wrinkled.

3. Mild to severe intellectual disability with progressive neurological and neuromuscular abnormalities.

4. There may be neonatal incisors present that fall out during early infancy.

5. Child may have an abnormal accumulation of fatty deposits in the areas of the buttocks, genitals, and anus, as well as in the area between the ribs and hips.

6. Distinctive malformations of the head and facial area, including prominence in the forehead and sides of the skull, causing the head to appear abnormally large.

7. Small and underdeveloped bones in the face, with a beak-shaped nose that becomes more pronounced as the child ages.

Treatment should be individualized and symptom specific. Because prenatal detection of the disorder is possible through ultrasound, it is likely that pediatric specialist teams will be required immediately after birth and throughout life. The research literature documents four pairs of siblings among the 21 reported cases, suggesting that genetic counseling should be included as part of the treatment plan (NORD, 2001).

Children with this disability would be eligible for special education services under Part H of the Individuals with Disabilities Education Act (IDEA, 1997), which includes children from birth to age 2. Intervention services are possible for children in this age group who encounter delays in cognitive, physical, communication, social-emotional, or adaptive development (McLean, Bailey, & Wolery, 1996).

Infants diagnosed with Wiedemann Rautenstrauch syndrome usually die in early childhood, although there have been documented cases of survival into the early teens. The average life expectancy is somewhere between 9 and 15 months of age. Future research should be in the area of endocrine and lipid studies, as well as molecular studies of the genes that control lipid metabolism (Pivnick et al., 2000).

REFERENCES

McLean, M., Bailey, D., & Wolery, M. (1996). *Assessing infants and preschoolers with special needs*. Englewood Cliffs, NJ: Prentice Hall.

National Organization for Rare Disorders. (2001). *Wiedemann Rautenstrauch syndrome*. Retrieved from http://rarediseases.org

Pivnick, E., Angle, B., Kaufman, R., Hall, B., Pitukcheewanont, P., Hersh, J.,...Ward, J. C. (2000). Neonatal progeroid (Wiedemann-Rautenstrauch) syndrome: Report of five new cases and review. *American Journal of Medical Genetics, 90*, 131–140.

CHRISTINE D. CDE BACA
University of Northern Colorado

WILBUR, HERVEY BACKUS (1820–1883)

Hervey Backus Wilbur, physician and educator, established the first school for mentally retarded children in the United States when he took a group of retarded children into his home in Barre, Massachusetts, in 1848. With the published accounts of the educational work of Edouard Seguin to guide him, Wilbur fashioned out of his own experience a system of teaching that was successful to a degree not previously thought possible.

In 1851, the New York State legislature established an experimental residential school for mentally retarded children, the second state school for the mentally retarded in the United States, with Wilbur as superintendent. Residential schools were opened in a number of other states during the next few years, many of them patterned after the New York School. This school, over which Wilbur presided until his death, is today the Syracuse Developmental Center.

Wilbur was a founder and the first vice president (with Edouard Seguin as president) of the Association of Medical Officers of American Institutions for Idiotic and Feeble-Minded Persons, now the American Association on Mental Retardation. He produced numerous pamphlets and articles dealing with the care and treatment of mentally retarded persons.

This entry has been informed by the sources listed below.

REFERENCES

Godding, W. W. (1883). In memoriam: Hervey Backus Wilbur. *Journal of Nervous & Mental Diseases, 10,* 658–662.

Scheerenberger, R. D. (1983). *A history of mental retardation.* Baltimore, MD: Paul H. Brookes.

PAUL IRVINE
Katonah, New York

See also Adaptive Behavior Scales

WILD BOY OF AVEYRON

The Wild Boy of Aveyron—or Victor, as he later came to be known—first was noticed by a group of peasants who witnessed him fleeing through the woods of south central France. He was spotted on subsequent occasions digging up turnips and potatoes or seeking acorns. He was captured in the forest of Aveyron, France, by three hunters in July 1799. It was determined that the boy was about 11 or 12 years of age, was unable to speak, and had been living a wild existence. He was taken to the Institution of Deaf Mutes in Paris and was assigned to the care of Jean Itard.

Itard, a young French physician, believed that this wild creature was physiologically normal and that his intellectual deficiencies were due to a lack of "appropriate sensory experiences in a socialized environment" (Scheerenberger, 1983). Itard was convinced that with an adequate training program, Victor would show great intellectual development and could be transformed from a savage to a civilized being. Because Victor's intellectual deficiencies were not seen as physiologically based, but were attributed to isolation and social and educational neglect, this was viewed as an opportunity to substantiate the effectiveness of educational methods being developed at the time (Maloney & Ward, 1979).

Over the next 5 years, Itard worked intensively with Victor and established a sequence of educational activities designed to teach him speech, self-care, and manners; and to develop his intellectual functions and emotional faculties. Itard employed socialization techniques and sensory training methods much like those he had used with deaf children (Robinson & Robinson, 1965).

Victor's progress was sometimes frustratingly slow, despite Itard's affection, effort, and ingenuity. Still, the doctor made tremendous gains in his 5 years of work with the boy, later documenting this in great detail (Kirk & Gallagher, 1979). Victor accomplished a great deal: he was able to recognize objects, identify letters of the alphabet, and comprehend the meaning of many words (Maloney & Ward, 1979). However, he never learned to speak, and Itard felt his program of instruction had failed. The physician decided to terminate the program after 5 years of intensive work with Victor.

Itard's experiences with the Wild Boy of Aveyron are particularly notable since his work was the first documented, systematic attempt to teach a person with disabilities. Although his attempts to make the boy "normal" failed, Itard did make significant gains and showed that even an individual with a severe disability could make great improvements with training.

REFERENCES

Kirk, S. A., & Gallagher, J. J. (1979). *Educating exceptional children* (3rd ed.). Boston, MA: Houghton Mifflin.

Maloney, M. P., & Ward, M. P. (1979). *Mental retardation and modern society.* New York, NY: Oxford University Press.

Robinson, H. B., & Robinson, N. M. (1965). *The mentally retarded child.* New York, NY: McGraw-Hill.

Scheerenberger, R. C. (1983). *A history of mental retardation.* Baltimore, MD: Paul H. Brookes.

KATHLEEN RODDEN-NORD
GERALD TINDAL
University of Oregon

See also History of Special Education; Itard, Jean Marc

WILDERVANCK SYNDROME

Wildervanck syndrome, sometimes called cervicooculoacoustic syndrome, is a very rare disorder almost exclusively affecting females. Currently, Wilderbank syndrome is thought to be the result of random genetic mutations. According to the National Organization for Rare Disorders (NORD; 2000a), it is comprised of a triad of particular conditions: congenital deafness (caused by a malformed bone in the inner ear), Klippel-Feil syndrome (KFS), and Duane syndrome.

Klippel-Feil syndrome is characterized by a congenital fusion of at least two of the seven vertebrae in the neck area. Limited range of motion, low hairline on the back of the head, and shortened neck are typical of the disorder. Other anomalies that sometimes occur include renal, genital, respiratory, and heart malformations (National Institute of Neurological Disorders and Stroke, 2001).

The third contributor to Wildervanck syndrome is Duane syndrome. This congenital disorder limits the range of eye movement. Sometimes called Duane retraction syndrome, it affects one or both eyes, causing a retraction of the eyeball when it attempts to turn in a particular direction (NORD, 2000b).

Characteristics

1. Deafness
2. Duane syndrome (retraction of the eyeball when looking in a particular direction)
3. Klippel-Feil syndrome (fusion of at least two of the neck vertebrae)

Treatment may include physical therapy and surgery to stabilize the neck and increase mobility of the spine. It is recommended that those with Wildervanck syndrome be cautious about engaging in activities that may injure the neck because the neck is limited in its range of motion.

Within the school setting, children with Wildervanck syndrome are likely to need and qualify for a broad range of services, particularly modifications to address the hearing impairment. Preferential seating for vision impairment is in order; if vision problems are significant, a consultation with an orientation and mobility specialist may be warranted to determine the most appropriate means of working with the child. Physical activities may need to be adapted or avoided completely as per recommendation by the child's physician.

REFERENCES

National Institute of Neurological Disorders and Stroke. (2001). Klippel-Feil syndrome information page. Retrieved from http://www.ninds.nih.gov/disorders/klippel_feil/klippel_feil.htm

National Organization for Rare Disorders. (2000a). *Duane syndrome*. Retrieved from http://www.stepstn.com/cgi-win/nord.exe?proc=GetDocument&rectype=0&recnum=224

National Organization for Rare Disorders. (2000b). *Wildervanck syndrome*. Retrieved from http://www.stepstn.com/cgi-win/nord.exe?proc=GetDocument&rectype=0&recnum=1001

SHARLA FASKO
Rowan County Schools Morehead, Kentucky

WILLIAMS SYNDROME

Williams syndrome (Williams, Baratt-Boyes, & Lowe, 1961) is a rare autosomal genetic disorder that affects 1:25,000 live births. It occurs in all ethnic groups, affects males and females equally, and has been reported internationally (Pober & Dykens, 1993). The disorder is associated with facial dysmorphology, renal and cardiovascular abnormalities, statural deficiencies, characteristic dental malformation, and infantile hypercalcaemia and hyperacusis (McKusick, 1988). A microdeletion of genes on Chromosome 7q11.23 has been identified in 98% of the individuals with Williams syndrome. The missing region typically includes the ELN gene, which is thought to account for the vascular and connective tissue abnormalities (Ewart, Jin, Atkinson, Morris, & Keating, 1994). The other phenotypic characteristics are most likely linked to the adjacent 16 or more genes that are part of the standard deletion in Williams syndrome (Mervis, Morris, Bertrand, & Robinson, 1999; Tassabehji et al., 1999).

Williams syndrome belongs to a group of conditions that are not characterized by a single behavior anomaly (Flint & Yule, 1994). However, certain characteristics are sufficiently frequent to suggest that their origin lies in a common biological disorder. Characteristics may include psychiatric disorders (e.g., symptoms of anxiety, hyperactivity, and preoccupations) as well as an outgoing social nature, an exuberant enthusiasm, a sense of the dramatic, overfriendliness, inappropriate interpersonal behaviors including indiscriminate affection, a short attention span, sleep disturbance, and hyperacusis (sensitivity to noise; Einfeld, Tonge, & Florio, 1997; Williams Syndrome Association, 2002).

Since individuals with Williams syndrome often have a short attention span and tend to be highly distractible, teachers of students with Williams syndrome may want to implement the following strategies: flexibility in requirements for time spent working, frequent breaks in work time, a high-motivation curriculum, minimal distractions, rewards for attending behaviors, and, when possible, redirection around off-task behaviors, allowing some degree of choice for the child in terms of activity, and working in small groups. In addition, because individuals with Williams syndrome often have a heightened sensitivity to sounds (hyperacusis), teachers of students with Williams syndrome may want to implement these strategies: provide warning just before predictable noises when possible (e.g., fire drills, hourly bells), allow the child to view and possibly initiate the source of bothersome noises (e.g., turn the fan on and off, see where the fire alarm is turned on), make tape recordings of the sounds and encourage the child to experiment with the recording (e.g., playing it louder/softer; Williams Syndrome Association, 2002).

Persons with Williams syndrome frequently show an abnormal interest in strangers (Mervis et al., 1999). Adolescents and adults with Williams syndrome often approach strangers to engage them in conversation. Displayed photographs of unfamiliar faces were shown to young adults and their judgments were recorded about how friendly and approachable they found the faces to be (Bellugi, Adolphs, Cassady, & Chiles, 1999). Individuals with Williams syndrome offered significantly more positive ratings of faces than others of the same chronological age or mental age.

Individuals with Williams syndrome have a distinctive cognitive profile. Their IQ scores typically range between 40 and 100, with a mean of 60 (Lenoff, Wang, Greenberg, & Bellugi, 1997; Levitin & Bellugi, 1998). Although their verbal intellectual abilities are below average, they are typically higher than their visual conceptual intellectual abilities (Mervis et al., 1999). Children and adolescents with Williams syndrome generally display severely deficient spatial abilities (Bellugi, Marks, Bihrle, & Sabo, 1993; Bellugi, Poizner, & Klima, 1989; Bihrle, 1990; Mervis et al., 1999), especially on visual-motor tasks (Beery & Buktenica, 1967; Elliot, 1990). Their mathematics skills also are deficient (Pagon, Bennett, LaVeck, Stewart, & Johnson, 1987), along with difficulty performing activities that require knowledge of number, space, substance, weight, and quantity (Bellugi, Klima, & Wang, 1996).

Because individuals with Williams syndrome typically have a nonverbal learning disorder, there are several recommended learning strategies that teachers of students with Williams syndrome can implement. For example, in reading comprehension, ensure that decoding skills have been mastered first (the student must be able to read words accurately before he or she can understand meaning). Typically, a phonics-based reading curriculum is most effective. Teach reading comprehension skills directly (e.g., making inferences and deductions, understanding cause and effect). Develop self-questioning techniques to monitor comprehension. Teach students that they must interact with the text. Encourage verbalization of strategies to enable students to internalize comprehension strategies (who, what, why, where, and when). Teach the organization and structure of paragraphs and teach signal words indicating transitions. In terms of vocabulary development, make concrete associations for unknown words whenever possible. Be "child centered" (e.g., use words they encounter in their own reading, define words they want to know, work from known associations and understandings). Encourage students to verbalize and paraphrase their understandings. Work toward a depth in understanding; do not let them slide by with surface understandings. Connect words into meaningful semantic categories and teach multiple meanings. Build semantic maps or webs. Highlight morphological rules and patterns; directly teach prefixes, roots, and suffixes. Finally, in the area of writing, provide brief daily practice to improve handwriting rate and legibility. Teach the student to use verbal self-directions to guide those practices. Address posture, position of hand and paper, grasp of pencil, and directions for forming individual letters. Teach keyboarding and word-processing skills to the student at a young age. Focus on only one aspect of writing at a time (e.g., prewriting, writing, and editing). Hold expectations for rate and volume of written products based on the student's demonstrated abilities. Teach transitional words. Teach organizational patterns for writing paragraphs, then, for longer works, such as essays, provide a purpose and structure for writing (Williams Syndrome Association, 2002).

Music often holds special interest and affinity in persons with Williams syndrome. However, this interest has been recognized only recently (Reis, Schader, Milne, & Stephens, 2003). For some, music can help overcome obstacles. For example, some children have overcome acute sensitivity to loud noises in order to engage in dancing in which music is playing at levels that would otherwise bring them to tears (Williams Syndrome Association, 2002). Even though individuals with Williams syndrome have motor problems, including coordination, these problems are less apparent when playing musical instruments (Levitin & Bellugi, 1998). However, their affinity for music may be stronger than their musical ability (Williams Syndrome Association, 2002).

Williams syndrome is caused by a genetic/chromosomal defect and thus has no cure. However, early diagnosis can provide a better understanding of problems that may arise, leading to a more successful life for the child and relief and support for the parents. Medical conditions of individuals with Williams syndrome need to be monitored regularly by a physician who specializes in this disorder as well as by general practitioners and health visitors (Williams Syndrome Foundation, 2004).

REFERENCES

Beery, K. E., & Buktenica, N. A. (1967). *Developmental test of visual motor integration*. Cleveland, OH: Modern Curriculum Press.

Bellugi, U., Adolphs, R., Cassady, C., & Chiles, M. (1999). Towards the neural basis for hypersociability in a genetic syndrome. *Neuroreport, 10*, 1–5.

Bellugi, U., Klima, E. S., & Wang, P. P. (1996). Cognitive and neural development: Clues from genetically based syndromes. In D. Magnussen (Ed.), *The life-span development of individuals: Behavioral, neurobiological, and psychological perspectives* (pp. 223–243). The Nobel Symposium. New York, NY: Cambridge University Press.

Bellugi, U., Marks, S., Bihrle, A., & Sabo, H. (1993). Dissociations between language and cognitive functions in Williams syndrome. In D. Bishop & K. Mogford (Eds.), *Language development in exceptional circumstances* (pp. 177–189). Hillsdale, NJ: Erlbaum.

Bellugi, U., Poizner, H., & Klima, E. S. (1989). Language, modality and the brain. *Trends in Neurosciences, 10*, 380–388.

Bihrle, A. M. (1990). *Visuospatial processing in Williams and Down syndrome*. Unpublished doctoral dissertation, University of California and San Diego State University.

Einfield, S. L., Tonge, B., & Florio, T. (1997). Behavioral and emotional disturbance in individuals with Williams syndrome. *American Journal on Mental Retardation, 102*(1), 45–53.

Elliot, C. D. (1990). *Differential ability scale*. San Diego, CA: Harcourt, Brace, Jovanovich.

Ewart, A. K., Jin, W., Atkinson, D., Morris, C. A., & Keating, M. T. (1994). Supravalvular aortic stenosis associated with a deletion disrupting the elastin gene. *Journal of Clinical Investigation, 93*, 1071–1077.

Flint, J., & Yule, W. (1994). Behavioral phenotypes. In M. Rutter, E. Taylor, & L. Hersov (Eds.), *Child and adolescent psychiatry: Modern approaches* (3rd ed., pp. 666–689). Oxford, England: Blackwell Scientific Publications.

Lenoff, H. M., Wang, P. P., Greenberg, F., & Bellugi. (1997). Williams syndrome and the brain. *Scientific American, 277*, 68–73.

Levitin, D. J., & Bellugi, U. (1998). Musical abilities in individuals with Williams syndrome. *Music Perception, 15,* 357–389.

McKusick, V. (1988). Mendelian inheritance in man: Catalog of autosomal dominant, autosomal recessive and X-linked phenotypes. Baltimore, MD: Johns Hopkins University Press.

Mervis, C. B., Morris, C. A., Bertrand, J., & Robinson, B. F. (1999). Williams syndrome: Findings from an integrated program of research. In H. Tager-Flusberg (Ed.), *Neurodevelopmental disorders* (pp. 65–110). Boston, MA: MIT Press.

Pagon, R., Bennett, F., LaVeck, B., Stewart, K., & Johnson, J. (1987). Williams syndrome: Features in late childhood and adolescence. *Pediatrics, 80*(1), 85–91.

Pober, B. R., & Dykens, E. M. (1993). Williams syndrome: An overview of medical, cognitive, and behavioral features. *Mental Retardation, 5,* 929–943.

Reis, S., Schader, R., Milne, H., & Stephens, R. (2003). Music & minds: Using a talent development approach for young adults with Williams syndrome. *Council for Exceptional Children, 69*(3), 293–313.

Tassabehji, M., Metcalfe, K., Karmiloff-Smith, A., Carette, M. J., Grant, J., Dennis, N.,...Donnal, D. (1999). Williams syndrome: Use of chromosomal microdeletions as a tool to dissect cognitive and physical phenotypes. *American Journal of Human Genetics, 64,* 118–125.

Williams, J. C. P., Baratt-Boyes, B. G., & Lowe, J. B. (1961). Supravalvular aortic stenosis. *Circulation, 24,* 1311–1318.

Williams Syndrome Association. (2002). http://www.williams-syndrome.org/forteachers/musicandws.html

Williams Syndrome Foundation. (2004). http://www.williams-syndrome.org.uk/about_ws/treatment.htm

KRISTA SCHWENK
University of Florida

See also Infantile Hypercalcemia

WILL, MADELEINE C. (1945–   )

Madeleine C. Will obtained her BA in 1967 from Smith College and her MA in 1969 at the University of Toronto, Canada. As assistant secretary for special education and rehabilitative services in the U.S. Department of Education from 1983 to 1989, Will held the highest-ranking federal position for the advocacy of individuals with disabilities. During her tenure, she was responsible for the programs in the department's Office of Special Education, the Rehabilitation Services Administration, and the National Institute for Handicapped Research—the three units comprising the Office of Special Education and Rehabilitative Services. She supervised education department programs serving 4.5 million disabled children and 936,000 adults with disabilities. Committed to the belief that federal programs must not be administered on the basis of concepts that underestimate the potential contribution of disabled citizens, Will was responsible for the initiation of transition and supported work models that strive to direct those with disabilities toward independent living and meaningful employment.

Will has written extensively on the topic of special education, its successes, failures, and recommendations for improvements (Will, 1984, 1986, 1988). She is a strong advocate of a more cohesive, less fragmented system: what she terms a *partnership* between special education and regular education to improve service delivery to all students. For students with learning problems in regular classrooms, she proposes increased time for instruction, support systems for teachers, principal-controlled programs and resources at the building level, and new instructional approaches.

Will has advocated for individuals with disabilities in numerous ways, including her service as chair of the Government Affairs Committee of the Montgomery County Association for Retarded Citizens in 1979 and member of the Government Affairs Committee of the National Association for Retarded Citizens. Additionally, from 1974 to 1976, she assisted in the development and operation of a program integrating preschoolers with disabilities into two nursery schools in Montgomery County, Maryland.

REFERENCES

Will, M. C. (1984). Let us pause and reflect—but not too long. *Exceptional Children, 51*(1), 11–16.

Will, M. C. (1986). Educating children with learning problems: A shared responsibility. *Exceptional Children, 52*(5), 411–415.

Will, M. C. (1988). Educating students with learning problems and the changing role of the school psychologist. *School Psychology Review, 17*(3), 476–478.

TAMARA J. MARTIN
The University of Texas of the Permian Basin

See also Office of Special Education and Rehabilitative Services; National Association of Retarded Citizens

WILLOWBROOK CASE

The Willowbrook case, or *New York State Association for Retarded Children v. Carey,* was litigation tried by Judge Orrin Judd in which the conditions in the Willowbrook State School in New York State were challenged. Specific charges included widespread physical abuse, overcrowded conditions and understaffing, inhumane and destructive conditions, extended solitary confinement, and lack of therapeutic care. Brought on behalf of more than 5,000 residents of the Willowbrook State School, this class-action suit is recognized as a landmark in protection from harm litigation.

During a series of Willowbrook trials, witnesses appeared and provided court testimony documenting the inhumane conditions and the physical, mental, and emotional deterioration of residents. On April 21, 1975, the New York Civil Liberties Union, the Legal Aid Society, the Mental Health Law Project, and the U.S. Department of Justice announced that the parties to the Willowbrook litigation had agreed on a consent judgment that would resolve the suit. This consent decree, which was approved on May 5, 1975, established standards in 23 areas to secure the constitutional rights of the Willowbrook residents to protection from harm.

This consent decree, which was to be implemented within 13 months or less, identified duty ratios of direct-care staff to residents of one to four during waking hours for most residents, and required an overall ratio of one clinical staff member for every three residents. The decree prohibited seclusion, corporal punishment, degradation, medical experimentation, and routine use of restraints. It established the primary goal of Willowbrook as the preparation of residents for development and life in the community, and it mandated individual plans for the residents' education, therapy, care, and development.

Additionally, the decree required (a) 6 hours of programmed activity each weekday; (b) nutritionally adequate diets; (c) dental services; (d) 2 hours of daily recreational activities; (e) adaptive equipment as needed; (f) adequate clothing; (g) continually available physicians; (h) contracted services with an accredited hospital; (i) an immunization program; (j) compensation for voluntary labor in accordance with minimum wage laws; and (k) correction of health and safety hazards.

Another set of requirements to be implemented, but not subject to the 13-month timetable, included reduction in the number of Willowbrook beds, establishment of 200 new community placements, increased funding to Willowbrook, creation of a review panel to oversee implementation of standards of the consent decree, initiation of a consumer advisory board composed of parents and relatives of residents, community leaders, residents, and former residents, and creation of a professional advisory board.

This Willowbrook case promoted improvements in the lives of the Willowbrook residents, focused public attention on the conditions of institutionalized individuals, and, as with other landmark cases, affected many similar cases.

DOUGLAS FUCHS
LYNN S. FUCHS
Peabody College,
Vanderbilt University

See also **Deinstitutionalization; Humanism and Special Education; Mental Retardation**

WILMS TUMOR

Wilms tumor (also known as nephroblastoma) is a malignant renal tumor and is the second most common extracranial solid tumor in children. In 80% to 90% of the cases, it occurs in the renal blastoma tissue. It usually is characterized by an asymptomatic abdominal mass and abdominal swelling.

Wilms tumor comprises approximately 6% of all pediatric cancers. It is diagnosed most commonly between 1 and 5 years of age, but the peak incidence is between 3 and 4 years. Wilms tumor rarely occurs in adolescents or adults. Approximately 600 to 700 new cases are diagnosed annually in the United States (Hinkle & Schwartz, 2001). It is slightly more prevalent in Black children than it is in White children by a ratio of approximately 10:9, but boys and girls are affected equally.

The exact cause is unknown, but approximately 38% of Wilms tumors are associated with a hereditary propensity (Nathan & Orkin, 1998). Several genes have been associated with Wilms tumor. The heredity type of the disease is likely to affect both kidneys and several sites in a single kidney. If prospective parents both have the recessive disorder of Wilms tumor, they have a 25% chance of transmitting the disease to their children. Congenital anomalies occur in 12% to 15% of children with Wilms tumor (Lanzkowsky, 2000). Wilms tumor may have no symptoms initially, but the child may begin to have weight loss, lethargy, hypertension, or blood in the urine. Abdominal swelling is often the most prominent later symptom and is occasionally accompanied by pain.

Characteristics

1. Wilms tumor comprises approximately 6% of pediatric cancers and occurs in the renal tissue.
2. Wilms tumor is most often characterized as an abdominal mass and is often asymptomatic.
3. Wilms tumor is the second most common extracranial tumor in children.
4. Treatment usually consists of a combination of surgery, chemotherapy, and radiation.
5. Cure rate with the current therapeutic regimen is 85%.

Treatment of Wilms tumor usually consists of a number of interventions. Most often, surgery is used to remove the affected kidney. Surgeons must take great care not to disturb the tumor and create tumor spillage. Often during the surgery, the abdominal cavity and lymph nodes are examined for the spread of the cancer. In addition, radiotherapy and chemotherapy are often used in conjunction with surgery. Unfortunately, radiation and chemotherapy can often have short-term untoward side effects such as nausea, vomiting, and (in some cases) suppression of bone marrow. Long-term undesirable side effects can include neuropsychological deficits.

Children undergoing surgery for Wilms tumor may require supportive, short-term educational modifications in order to help the child with postsurgery complications. These children also cannot engage in physical activities such as school sports. As with other cancers treated with chemotherapy and radiotherapy, there can be cognitive and educational side effects. Therefore, children with Wilms tumor may require special education intervention in order to deal with the learning problems resulting from chemotherapy and radiotherapy. Deficits in areas such as attention, memory, and previously acquired academic skills must be thoroughly evaluated. After comprehensive neuropsychological evaluation, any deficits should be identified, and specific remedial strategies should be implemented (Powers, Vannatta, Noll, Cool, & Stehbens, 1995).

The prognosis of Wilms tumor is usually dependent on the type of tumor (histopathology) and the stage of disease at diagnosis. Obviously, if the cancer has metastasized into other organs, prognosis is much worse. The cure rate is approximately 85% with the current therapeutic regimen. Children treated for Wilms tumor are considered cured if they survive for 2 years without any indication that the disease has returned. Future research appears to be directed toward finding genetic treatments for the disorder.

REFERENCES

Hinkle, A. S., & Schwartz, C. L. (2001). Cancers in childhood. In R. A. Hoekelman (Ed.), *Primary pediatric care* (4th ed., pp. 1359–1384). St. Louis, MO: Mosby.

Lanzkowsky, P. (2000). *Manual of pediatric hematology and oncology* (3rd ed.). New York, NY: Academic Press.

Nathan, D. G., & Orkin, S. H. (1998). *Hematology of infancy and childhood* (5th ed.). Philadelphia, PA: W. B. Saunders.

Powers, S. W., Vannatta, K. V., Noll, R. B., Cool, V. A., & Stehbens, J. A. (1995). Leukemia and other childhood cancers. In M. C. Roberts (Ed.), *Handbook of pediatric psychology* (2nd ed., pp. 310–326). New York, NY: Guilford Press.

WILLIAM A. RAE
Texas A&M University

WILSON DISEASE

Wilson disease (WD), or hepatolenticular degeneration, is a rare autosomal recessive metabolic disease linked to Chromosome 13 (Schilsky & Sternlieb, 1998). It is caused by two mutant alleles of a putative copper transporter, STP7B. As a result of increased copper accumulation in the liver, brain, and corneal tissue, individuals with Wilson disease often suffer from cirrhosis of the liver, bilateral softening and degeneration of the basal ganglia, and brown pigmented rings in the periphery of the cornea, referred to as Kayser-Fleischer rings (International Hepatology Informatics Group, 1994; Sherlock & Dooley, 1993).

The disease is most commonly diagnosed in children, but symptoms can be manifested later on. In one third of all cases, the initial symptom is liver disease; however, the other two thirds present first with neurological or psychiatric symptoms (Akil & Brewer, 1995). These problems, however, are all a result of accumulated excess copper due to the liver's failure to metabolize and store the copper.

When the disease presents in young children, hepatic dysfunction is often quite severe with total organ failure being common. Most transplants for individuals with Wilson disease are performed between the ages of 10 and 15. It is less common for older individuals to have hepatic failure; most such individuals present with acute and milder symptoms of liver dysfunction (e.g., chronic hepatitis).

WD occurs at a rate of approximately 1 per 40,000 births; prevalence estimates are around 12 to 30 cases per million. All ethnic groups appear to be similarly affected by the disease (Lauterbach, 2000). On average, one fourth of full biological siblings of those with WD will also have the disease.

Characteristics

1. Hepatic manifestations include fatigue, nausea, anorexia, malnutrition, right upper quadrant pain, hepatomegaly, jaundice, edema, spontaneous bacterial peritonitis, variceal hemorrhage, endocrine abnormalities, delayed puberty, and gynecomastia.

2. Motor manifestations include dystonia, posturing, choreiform movements, resting and intention tremors, dysarthria, dysphagia, drooling, and abnormal gait.

3. Psychiatric manifestations include manic episodes, psychosis, disinhibition, emotional lability, irritability, and aggression; depression is especially common.

4. Kayer-Fleischer rings (i.e., copper deposits around the outer areas of the cornea) are common.

5. Children with a family history of chronic liver disease should be screened for Wilson disease, especially those who show cognitive abnormalities and speech slurring.

Treatment typically consists of methods to reduce the amount of copper in the liver and other tissues. Although a low-copper diet is recommended, more often than not a copper-chelating agent has to be administered (e.g., D-penicillamine). The chelating agent, however, has been shown to have serious side effects in 20% to 25% of patients (e.g., systemic lupus and a nephrotic syndrome). Trietine is an alternate treatment to D-penicillamine, and it is the drug of choice when neurological symptoms are exhibited. Zinc salt has also been used but only as a supplement. In cases of progressive liver disease such as chronic hepatitis and organ failure, liver transplants may be necessary (Shimizu, Yamaguchi, & Aoki, 1999). Prognosis is generally good after treatment is instituted; however, about 20% of patients who have to have transplants die in the first year following surgery (Schilsky & Sternlieb, 1998). Death can also occur from esophageal bleeding and infection (Sherlock & Dooley, 1993).

Children with Wilson disease may present with academic and behavioral symptoms before the diagnosis is actually made. These children may show a sudden deterioration in schoolwork, uncharacteristic and socially inappropriate behaviors, anxiety, and depression (Sternlieb & Scheinberg, 1993). Memory problems and lack of motor coordination may underlie some of these functional problems. In most cases, if accommodations are even needed, they are short term (e.g., providing the child with a homework manual or memory aide until treatment takes effect). These children should, however, be carefully evaluated by school psychologists and other ancillary staff (e.g., speech and language pathologists and occupational therapists) to determine the presence of persistent cognitive, motor, and behavior problems and to determine the need for services, including special education.

Parents and children need to be educated about the need to maintain proper diet and drugs to prevent a recurrence of symptoms. Further research is needed to facilitate early diagnosis because the delay in treatment can have devastating effects on the individual with Wilson disease. More information is also needed regarding the efficacy of certain therapies (e.g., special diets and supplements) and the potential deleterious effects of standard treatments, including D-penicillamine. Understanding the pathophysiology may also help researchers to understand such effects and to understand the development of various sequelae (in particular, behavioral and psychiatric symptoms) of Wilson disease.

REFERENCES

Akil, M., & Brewer, G. (1995). Psychiatric and behavioral abnormalities in Wilson's disease. *Advances in Neurology, 65*(11), 171–178.

International Hepatology Informatics Group. (1994). *Diseases of the liver and biliary tract*. New York, NY: Raven Press.

Lauterbach, E. C. (Ed.). (2000). Psychiatric management in neurological disease. Washington, DC: American Psychiatric Press.

Schilsky, M., & Sternlieb, I. (1998). Wilson's disease. In G. Y. Wu & J. Israel (Eds.), *Diseases of the liver and bile ducts* (pp. 285– 292). Totowa, NJ: Humana Press.

Sherlock, S., & Dooley, J. (Eds.). (1993). *Diseases of the liver and biliary system*. Cambridge, MA: Blackwell Scientific Publications.

Shimizu, N., Yamaguchi Y., & Aoki, T. (1999). Treatment and management of Wilson's disease. *Official Journal of the Japanese Pediatric Society, 41*(4), 419–422.

Sternlieb, I., & Scheinberg, I. (1993). Wilson's disease. In L. Schiff & E. Schiff (Eds.), *Diseases of the liver* (pp. 659–668). Philadelphia, PA: Lippincott.

HEATHER EDGEL
ELAINE CLARK
University of Utah

WINCHESTER SYNDROME

Winchester syndrome is thought to be a rare form of the mucopolysaccharidoses, a group of inherited metabolic disorders that are caused by a deficiency of specific lysosomal enzymes. These enzymes are needed to break down the long chains of sugar molecules (mucopolysaccharides) used to build connective tissues and organs in the body. As with mucopolysaccharidoses, some individuals with Winchester syndrome often lose oligosaccharide (a type of simple sugar) in the urine; this symptom assists in the diagnosis of this disorder (Dunger et al., 1987). Winchester syndrome is characterized by short stature and arthritis-like symptoms. Vision and skin disorders are often associated with this syndrome.

Winchester syndrome is a very rare disorder that is inherited as an autosomal recessive trait. Recessive inheritance occurs when both matching genes from the parent must be abnormal to produce the disease. If only one gene in the pair is abnormal, the disease is not manifested or is only mildly manifested; however, children can be carriers. Thoene (1995) reported only 10 identified cases. These cases occurred in individuals of Mexican, Indian, Puerto Rican, and Iranian descent. However, because the disorder is so rare, it is possible that other cases have gone undiagnosed or misdiagnosed.

Characteristics

1. Winchester syndrome usually becomes apparent at 2 years of age, when the joints swell and become stiff and painful. Shortening (contractures) of the joints can also occur.

2. The joints most often affected are fingers, elbows, knees, and feet.

3. Hypertrichosis (excessive hair growth) develops with thick leathery skin.

4. Lips and gums thicken, causing coarse facial features.

5. Short stature.

6. Loss of calcium may occur as the child grows, causing bones in ankles and feet to weaken.

7. Vision problems such as corneal opacities (opaque areas on the cornea, which block image formation on the retina) may develop.

8. Mental functioning is not usually affected.

Individuals with Winchester syndrome may benefit from physical therapy to promote the flexibility of joints and reduce immobility. Orthopedic procedures may help to reduce contractures. Individuals with Winchester syndrome may require mobility devices. Treatment may also consist of pain management and pain relief, but it tends to be symptomatic and supportive (e.g., laser surgery has had some success in reducing corneal opacities).

Students who enter school with a diagnosis of Winchester syndrome are likely to qualify for special services under the Individuals with Disabilities Education Act (IDEA, 2004) within the physical disability category. These students may need extensive modification to accommodate the physical limitations of the disorder. For example, classrooms and other areas within the school may need to be wheelchair accessible. Transportation to and from school and school functions may be required. Additionally, these students may require accommodations due to vision problems. Physical therapy may be an integral part of the student's day. Additionally, school staff may need to be cognizant of the limitations of the disability (e.g., how to use mobility and orthopedic devices). Students with Winchester syndrome may need to be educated in pain-management techniques and may require individual counseling to come to terms with how the disorder may limit their daily experiences and affect their identity development and satisfaction with their bodily image. They may also require support and education to discover how to deal with the frustration they may experience from living with this type of disorder.

There has been little research published on this syndrome; most of the published research appears to be attempting to quantify and explain Winchester syndrome and how it is recognized and diagnosed (e.g., Al Ageel et al., 2000; Dunger et al., 1987; Prapanpoch, Jorgenson, Langlais, & Nummikoski, 1992). For more information on this syndrome, contact NIH/National Arthritis and Musculoskeletal and Skin Disease Information Clearinghouse, 1 AMS Circle, Bethesda, MD 20892, (301) 495-4484.

REFERENCES

Al Ageel, A., Al Sewairi, W., Edress, B., Gorlin, R. J., Desnick, R. J., & Martignetti, J. A. (2000). Inherited multicentric osteolysis with arthritis: A variant resembling Torg syndrome in a Saudi family. *American Journal of Medical Genetics, 93*(1), 11–18.

Dunger, D. B., Dicks-Mireaux, C., O'Driscoll, P., Lake, B., Ersser, R., Shaw, D. G., & Grant, D. B. (1987). Two cases of Winchester syndrome: With increased urinary oligosaccharide excretion. *European Journal of Pediatrics, 146*(6), 615–619.

Prapanpoch, S., Jorgenson, R. J., Langlais, R. P., & Nummikoski, P. V. (1992). Winchester syndrome: A case report and literature review. *Oral Surgery, Medicine, Oral Pathology, 74*(5), 671–677.

Thoene, J. G. (1995). *Physicians' guide to rare diseases* (2nd ed.). Montvale, NJ: Dowden.

RACHEL TOPLIS
University of Northern Colorado

WITMER, LIGHTNER (1867–1956)

Lightner Witmer established the world's first psychological clinic at the University of Pennsylvania in 1896, an event that marked the beginning not only of clinical psychology but also of the diagnostic approach to teaching. Previously director of the psychological laboratory at the University of Pennsylvania, where he succeeded James McKeen Cattell, Witmer moved psychology from the theoretical concerns of the laboratory to the study of learning and behavior problems of children in the classroom. Proposing a merging of the clinical method in psychology and the diagnostic method in teaching, Witmer developed an interdisciplinary approach to education, his clinic provided training for psychologists, teachers, social workers, and physicians. He formed special classes that served as training grounds for teachers from across the nation and as models for many of the special classes that were established in the early part of the twentieth century. Anticipating special education's strong influence on mainstream education, Witmer suggested that learning-disabled children would show the way for the education of all children.

This entry has been informed by the sources listed below.

REFERENCES

Watson, R. I. (1956). Lightner Witmer: 1867–1956. *American Journal of Psychology, 69*, 680.

Witmer, L. (1911). *The special class for backward children.* Philadelphia, PA: Psychological Clinic.

PAUL IRVINE
Katonah, New York

WOLFENSBERGER, WOLF P. J. (1934–2011)

Born and raised in Germany in the period just before and during World War II, Wolf P. J. Wolfensberger studied in the United States. He earned a BA in philosophy from the now-defunct Siena College of Memphis, Tennessee. He subsequently pursued graduate training in psychology and education at St. Louis University, during which time he became a naturalized U.S. citizen in 1956, and received his MA in psychology in 1957. Wolfensberger continued his studies of psychology and special education, earning his PhD in these fields in 1962 from George Peabody College for Teachers (now Peabody College, Vanderbilt University).

Wolfensberger was mentored by two widely known psychologists while an intern: Walter Klopfer, the famous personality psychologist, at the Norfolk (Nebraska) State Hospital; and Jack Tizard, while Wolfensberger was a postdoctoral research fellow in mental retardation at Maudsley Hospital (the University of London teaching hospital) in England. Following the latter experience, Wolfensberger became a Mental Retardation research scientist at the Nebraska Psychiatric Institute (1964–1971), where he eventually rose to the rank of associate professor of medical psychology in the departments of psychiatry and pediatrics. For 2 years (1971–1973), he was a visiting scholar at the Canadian National Institute on Mental Retardation, with a joint faculty appointment at York University. From 1973 to 1992, Wolfensberger served as a professor in the Division of Special Education and Rehabilitation at Syracuse University, and from 1992 to the present, he has been a research professor in the School of Education there. At the same time, he has been the director of the Syracuse University Training Institute for Human Service Planning, Leadership and Change Agentry (Wolfensberger, personal communication, June 9, 1998).

A prolific writer and researcher, Wolfensberger devoted nearly his entire career to social advocacy for better life conditions for and high-quality services to people with disabilities. He was one of the major proponents, arguably *the* major proponent, of the principle of normalization, in 1983 designing Social Role Valorization, focusing on the relation between social roles and consequences, as the successor to this concept. His instruments (PASS and PASSING) for evaluating services in terms of normalization and Social Role Valorization criteria have been used worldwide. Additionally, Wolfensberger is the originator of the Citizen Advocacy scheme, which promotes one-to-one advocacy for people with handicaps and is used throughout the English-speaking world. Many other advocacy-related schemes have borrowed this concept (Wolfensberger, personal communication, June 9, 1998).

In 1991, Wolfensberger's work in the area of normalization was recognized by a Delphi panel of experts as the most influential work in the field of mental retardation in the United States during a 50-year period. He continued the work he began in the 1970s, conducting training workshops for human services personnel and the families of individuals with disabilities, and serves as an advocate in 11 different countries. Wolfensberger also spoke and wrote against the growing legitimization of "deathmaking" of all sorts of unwanted and devalued people (Wolfensberger, 1994).

This entry has been informed by the sources listed here.

REFERENCES

Kugel, R., & Wolfensberger, W. (Eds.). (1968). *Changing patterns in residential services for the mentally retarded.* Washington, DC: President's Committee on Mental Retardation.

Wolfensberger, W. (1972). *The principle of normalization in human services.* Toronto, Canada: National Institute on Mental Retardation.

Wolfensberger, W. (1980). Research, empiricism, and the principle of normalization. In R. J. Flynn & K. E. Witsch (Eds.), *Normalization, social integration, and community services*, Baltimore, MD: University Park Press.

Wolfensberger, W. (1994). A personal interpretation of the mental retardation scene in light of the "Signs of the Times." *Mental Retardation, 32*, 19–33.

Wolfensberger, W., & Zauha, H. (Eds.). (1973). *Citizen advocacy and protective services for the impaired and handicapped.* Toronto, Canada: National Institute on Mental Retardation.

CECIL R. REYNOLDS
Texas A&M University
First edition

TAMARA J. MARTIN
The University of Texas of the Permian Basin
Second edition

See also Normalization

WOLF-HIRSCHHORNE SYNDROME

Wolf-Hirschhorne syndrome, also known as Wolf syndrome or 4p-syndrome, is a genetic disorder resulting from a defect in Chromosome 4. The incidence rate of Wolf-Hirschhorne syndrome is 1 out of 50,000 births (Thoene, 1992). The syndrome occurs more often in females than males by a ratio of 2:1. Approximately one-third of the children who are born with the syndrome die in the first 2 years of life as a result of either cardiac failure or bronchopneumonia (O'Brien & Yule, 1995).

Primary features of the disorder include low birth weight, deficient or low muscle tone, physical and mental retardation, and a very small head. Prominent facial characteristics are also found in this syndrome, such as cleft lip, cleft palate, downturned mouth, small jaw, low-set ears, high forehead, and beaklike nose. Squinting of the eyes is another common feature. Heart and kidney problems and seizures occur in approximately 50% of the children with this disorder. In some cases, reconstructive surgery is needed to address facial abnormalities.

In schools, special education may be needed to address learning disabilities. Due to delayed psychomotor development and speech/communication abilities, physical therapy, occupational therapy, and speech services will be needed (O'Brien & Yule, 1995). Vocational services may be helpful. Genetic counseling may also be beneficial (Thoene, 1992).

REFERENCES

O'Brien, G., & Yule, W. (Eds.). (1995). *Behavioral phenotypes*. London: Mac Keith Press.

Thoene, J. G. (Ed.). (1992). *Physician's guide to rare diseases*. Montvale, NJ: Dowden.

JOAN MAYFIELD
Baylor Pediatric Specialty Service

PATRICIA A. LOWE
University of Kansas

WOLFRAM SYNDROME

Wolfram syndrome is a neurodegenerative disorder of early onset and is often referred to as the acronym DID-MOAD (diabetes insipidus, diabetes mellitus, optic atrophy, and deafness). This condition was first described by Wolfram and Wagener (1938, as cited in Inoue et al., 1998) to be the co-occurrence of diabetes mellitus and optic atrophy, which remain as the only symptoms necessary to diagnose Wolfram syndrome. Most patients, however, develop all the conditions listed previously, with many displaying additional neurological abnormalities (Rando, Horton, & Layzer, 1992). From their own magnetic resonance imaging (MRI) studies and a review of the pathological and radiological studies of persons with Wolfram syndrome, Rando et al. (1992) discovered that the degree of brain atrophy found in such patients was greater than would be predicted from clinical presentation. Neural damage to the anterior visual pathway, hypothalamic nuclei, and the vestibulocochlear nuclei appear to correlate with key symptoms of optic atrophy, diabetes insipidus, and deafness (Rando et al., 1992).

Kinsley, Swift, Dumont, and Swift (1995) describe the clinical progression of Wolfram syndrome symptomology.

In their study, diabetes mellitus was first diagnosed at a mean of 8.2 years of age and was usually the first indicator of Wolfram syndrome. Optic atrophy was determined at a mean of 13.1 years; consequently, legal blindness followed for many of the patients in a mean of 6.7 years. Although it was only present in about half of the patients, the mean age of onset for neurosensory hearing loss was 14.6, and diabetes insipidus was apparent at an average age of 15.5 years (Kinsley et al., 1995).

Genetic transmission of Wolfram syndrome is suspected to be through autosomal recessive means, although some researchers suggest that mitochondrial mutations may be implicated in some cases (Rötig et al., 1993, as cited in Polymeropoulous, Swift, & Swift, 1994). Polymeropoulous et al. (1994) linked the condition to DNA markers on the short arm of Chromosome 4. A group of researchers reported to have identified the gene WSF1 on Chromosome 4p, the mutation of which causes this disorder. This mutation results in the degeneration of insulin-secreting islet b-cells in the pancreas, causing early-onset diabetes mellitus (Inoue et al., 1998).

It is estimated that the prevalence of Wolfram syndrome is 1 in 100,000 (University of Washington School of Medicine, 1998), and the disorder appears to affect men and women equally (Kinsley et al., 1995). An estimated 1% of the United States population are thought to be heterozygous carries of the mutated gene (Swift, Perkins, Chase, Sadler, & Swift, 1991). Furthermore, Swift et al. (1991) found that carriers of the gene may be at an eightfold risk over noncarriers for psychiatric hospitalization or suicide attempts. The rate of severe mental disorders in patients with Wolfram syndrome was found to be 25% and most commonly presented as depression, aggression, or organic brain syndrome (Swift, Sadler, & Swift, 1990). Furthermore, the authors asserted that these mental conditions were not purely a response to the physical illness and that the documented diffuse neurodegenerative processes may contribute to the high rate of comorbid psychiatric illness (e.g., Gregorios, 1989, as cited in Swift et al., 1990; Rando et al., 1992).

Characteristics

1. Optic atrophy
2. Diabetes mellitus
3. Diabetes insipidus
4. Neurosensory hearing loss
5. Urinary tract disease
6. Other neurological abnormalities, including ataxia, nystagmus, mental retardation, and seizures

---

Currently, no cure exists for this neurological degenerative disorder, and treatment revolves around symptom management. The diabetes mellitus is generally treated with insulin, and Kinsley et al. (1995) report that oral hypoglycemic medications have not met with long-term treatment success. Additionally, urinary tract symptoms may require self-catheterization, and antibiotics may prevent ensuing urinary tract infections. When psychiatric disorders are present in such patients, psychopharmacological agents may improve treatment compliance (Kinsley et al., 1995).

Wolfram syndrome is associated with a high mortality rate, with the expectation that 60% of the patients presenting with this constellation of symptoms will die by age 35 (Kinsley et al., 1995). In these patients, death may result from neurological degeneration or complications from urinary tract infection. Damage to lower brain stem centers controlling motor nuclei may cause some patients to choke on food, resulting in harm or even death (Kinsley et al., 1995). There is optimism, however, that recent research findings regarding the genetic contributions of Wolfram syndrome may shed some light on the mechanisms and possible therapies for both this condition and other more common forms of diabetes (University of Washington, 1998).

Students with Wolfram syndrome will qualify for special education services under Section 504 of the Rehabilitation Act of 1973 and under the Individuals with Disabilities Act (IDEA). The individualized educational program planning team may recommend assistive technology devices to aid the student with auditory and visual impairments that interfere with learning. Furthermore, medical support for the treatment of the student's diabetes must be organized. Teachers should be sensitive to the possibility of urinary tract infections, and the school should provide appropriate accommodations. The school district may also need to consider educational supports for any associated cognitive difficulties.

REFERENCES

Gregorios, J. D. (1989). Wolfram's syndrome with schizophrenia and central hypoventilation: A neuropathological study. *Journal of Neuropathology Experimental Neurology*, 48, 308.

Inoue, H., Tanizawa, Y., Wasson, J., Behn, P., Kalidas, K., Bernal-Mizrachi, E., . . . Permutt, M. A. (1998). A gene encoding a transmembrane protein is mutated in patients with diabetes mellitus and optic atrophy (Wolfram syndrome). *Nature Genetics*, 20, 143–148.

Kinsley, B. T., Swift, M., Dumont, R. H., & Swift, R. G. (1995). Morbidity and mortality in the Wolfram syndrome. *Diabetes Care*, 18(12), 1566–1570.

Polymeropoulous, M. H., Swift, R. G., & Swift, M. (1994). Linkage of the gene for Wolfram syndrome to markers on the short arm of chromosome 4. *Nature Genetics*, 8, 95–97.

Rando, T. A., Horton, J. C., & Layzer, R. B. (1992). Wolfram syndrome: Evidence of a diffuse neurodegenerative disease by magnetic resonance imaging. *Neurology*, 42, 1220–1224.

Rötig, A., Cormier, V., Chatelain, P., Francois, R., Saudubray, J. M., Rustin, P., & Munnich, A. (1993). Deletion of mitochondrial DNA in a case of early-onset diabetes mellitus, optic atrophy, and deafness. *Journal of Clinical Investigation*, 9(3), 1095–1098.

Swift, R. G., Perkins, D. O., Chase, C. L., Sadler, D. B., & Swift, M. (1991). Psychiatric disorders in 35 families with Wolfram syndrome. *American Journal of Psychiatry*, 148, 775–779.

Swift, R. G., Sadler, D. B., & Swift, M. (1990). Psychiatric findings in Wolfram syndrome homozygotes. *Lancet (North American Edition)*, 336(8716), 667–669.

University of Washington School of Medicine. (1998). Researchers identify and isolate first gene for a form of insulin-dependent diabetes. Retrieved from http://www.sciencedaily.com/releases/1998/09/980929073115.htm

Wolfram, D. J., & Wagener, H. P. (1938). Diabetes mellitus and simple optic atrophy among siblings: Report of four cases. *Mayo Clinical Procedures*, 13, 715–718.

SARAH SCHNOEBELEN
MARGARET SEMRUD-CLIKEMAN
University of Texas at Austin

WOOD, FRANK (1929–)

Dr. Frank Wood is one of the most important figures in the development of educational programming for students with emotional and behavioral disorders (EBD). Dr. Wood received a BA degree in American History from Harvard in 1951. He worked as a high school teacher in Connecticut for a few years. He then earned his MA degree in social and technical assistance to developing nations and groups at Haverford College in 1953. In 1954 he received his BS degree in elementary education from the University of Minnesota. He taught in inner city schools and at the Seminole Indian Reservation in Florida from 1954 to 1958. In 1958 Dr. Evelyn Deno, the Special Education Director in the Minneapolis Minnesota Public Schools asked Frank if he would be interested in becoming an elementary school teacher of students with EBD. This was the first classroom for students with EBD.

Dr. Deno then encouraged Frank to continue his education at the University of Minnesota. He received his MS degree in 1962 and his PhD in 1965. He also took a position in the University of Minnesota's special education program. In this position Dr. Wood developed one of the first programs to prepare teachers to work with students with EBD. He remained at the University until he retired in 1995. Since 1995 he has been a professor emeritus.

Dr. Wood was one of the seminal figures in the formation of the International Council for Children with

Behavioral Disorders (CCBD), and the subsequent creation of the professional journal of the CCBD: *Behavioral Disorders*. He served as the president of CCBD in 1987 and was the editor of *Behavioral Disorders* from 1987 to 1993. He also has written over 120 journal articles and a number of books and book chapters on educating students with EBD.

In his career he received a number of honors for his influential work. In 1984 Dr. Wood received the J. Wallace Wallin Lifetime Achievement Award from the International Council for Exceptional Children. In 1987, he received the Outstanding Leadership Award from the Midwest Symposium for Leadership in Behavior Disorders. That same year he also was given the inaugural Dr. Frank H. Wood Award from the Minnesota Educators of the Emotionally Disturbed. The award was to be given annually for outstanding contributions to the field of emotional and behavioral disorders. In 1989 Dr. Wood also received the Outstanding Leadership Award from the CCBD.

In his career Dr. Wood has made significant contributions to improving the lives of children and adolescents with EBD, their families, and teachers. His accomplishments in this field have been so important that the CCBD Foundation created the Frank Wood Scholarship for outstanding graduate students in the area of EBD. The CCBD Foundation in announcing the Frank Wood scholarship wrote the following:

"Impressive as his professional accomplishments, Frank Wood is perhaps best known and loved for being one of the kindest, most giving, and caring mentors and colleagues the field has ever known. To a person, the people who have worked with him over the years consider him a selfless professional whose spirituality, integrity and unconditional regard for others make him one of a kind. The Board of Trustees of the CCBD Foundation is pleased to honor both the man himself and his life's work with the naming of the Dr. Frank Wood CCBD Foundation Graduate Scholarship."

MITCHELL YELL
University of South Carolina
Fourth edition

WOOD, M. MARGARET (1931–   )

M. Margaret (Peggy) Wood began in special education as an NDEA fellow at the University of Georgia where, following the awarding of her BA in elementary education in 1953 from Goucher College, she earned her MEd (special education) in 1960. Wood immediately followed the MEd with an EdD, awarded with distinction in 1963 from the University of Georgia with a major in special education and a minor in psychology. Wood then did postdoctoral study at the Hillcrest Residential Treatment Center in Washington, DC. From 1964 to 1969, Wood was director of the teacher preparation program for teachers of emotionally disturbed students in the division for exceptional children at the University of Georgia. It was during this time that her view of therapeutic approaches to children in the schools matured and she began to work in earnest toward developing a psychoeducational approach to these children's problems. This approach has become known widely as developmental therapy.

In 1970 Wood received funding for the establishment of the Rutland Center for Severely Emotionally Disturbed Children; she directed the center until 1974. Developmental therapy, as practiced at the Rutland Center under Wood's direction, became a model approach to the provision of special education services to emotionally disturbed children in the public schools. More than 250 developmental therapy centers have been established in schools worldwide, though nearly all are in North and South America. Wood has continued her active interest in developmental therapy but has focused on research and dissemination activities since 1974, when she became project director of a federally sponsored model in-service training program. Wood was promoted to the rank of professor in the division for exceptional children at the University of Georgia in 1977.

Wood has more than 50 scholarly publications to her credit, most dealing with some aspect of developmental therapy, and has authored or edited six books (Williams & Wood, 1977; Wood, 1975, 1982). Wood is best known as the originator of developmental therapy, a major innovation in public school delivery of special education services to severely emotionally disturbed children. Wood has a significant reputation as a mentor and many well-known professionals have studied with her and practiced developmental therapy at the Rutland Center.

REFERENCES

Williams, G. H., & Wood, M. M. (1977). *Developmental art therapy*. Baltimore, MD: University Park Press.

Wood, M. M. (Ed.). (1975). *Developmental therapy*. Baltimore, MD: University Park Press.

Wood, M. M. (1982). Developmental therapy: A model for therapeutic intervention in the schools. In C. R. Reynolds & T. B. Gutkin (Eds.), *The handbook of school psychology*. New York, NY: Wiley.

CECIL R. REYNOLDS
Texas A&M University

See also Developmental Therapy

WOODCOCK DIAGNOSTIC READING BATTERY

The Woodcock Diagnostic Reading Battery (WDRB; Woodcock, 1997) is a set of carefully engineered (Woodcock, 1992) tests for clinical measurement of reading achievement and important abilities related to reading. Test development, item calibration, scaling, cluster composition, and interpretation were accomplished through the Rasch single-parameter logistic test model (Rasch, 1960; Wright & Stone, 1979), and stepwise multiple regression analysis. Continuous-year norming, based on a nationally representative sample of 6,026 individuals ranging in age from 4 to 95 years, produced highly accurate normative data—10 points at each grade level and 12 points at each age level for school-aged individuals.

The WDRB consists of six tests from the WJ-R Tests of Cognitive Ability (Woodcock & Johnson, 1989b) and four tests from the WJ-R Tests of Achievement (Woodcock & Johnson, 1989a). The tests were combined into one format to be "more useful to those who are reading specialists and researchers" (Rudman, 1999). That is, one short battery of tests includes (a) tests of basic reading and reading comprehension skills, (b) important reading-related tests (phonological awareness and oral comprehension), and (c) reading aptitude tests.

The reading tests include Letter-Word Identification, Passage Comprehension, Word Attack, and Reading Vocabulary. The phonological awareness tests include Incomplete Words and Sound Blending. The oral comprehension tests are Oral Vocabulary and Listening Comprehension.

Four tests comprise the Reading Aptitude cluster: Memory for Sentences, Visual Matching, Sound Blending, and Oral Vocabulary. These tests are based on tasks that are statistically and logically associated with proficiency in reading, but are uncontaminated with reading content. The median correlation between the WDRB Reading Aptitude cluster and Broad Reading achievement clusters is 0.78.

The Reading Aptitude cluster in this battery is particularly notable in that it makes a valid aptitude measure available to a wide array of specialists who might otherwise not be trained to administer an intellectual ability test. Because the aptitude tests were conormed with the achievement tests, actual discrepancy norms are available. Use of conormed tests is the most accurate and valid method for determining the presence and severity of an aptitude/achievement discrepancy (McGrew, 1994). This is because the discrepancy norm calculation procedure fully accounts for regression to the mean (McGrew et al., 1991). (Practitioners who use separately normed instruments for aptitude/achievement discrepancy analysis do not possess actual data for both the predictor and criterion variables from the same sample of subjects.)

A reading performance model, included in the examiner's manual, helps examiners interpret the reading-related abilities. An individual's phonological awareness exerts a major influence on his or her decoding or basic reading skills. His or her oral comprehension exerts a major influence on reading comprehension. When these related tests are administered in conjunction with the reading achievement tests, examiners can obtain a better picture of why an individual has a reading problem.

Administration time is approximately 50 to 60 minutes for all 10 tests. A wide range of scores are available, notably age and grade equivalents, standard scores, percentile ranks, and instructional zones. Rudman (1999) seemed particularly impressed by the associated *Scoring and Interpretive Program for the Woodcock Diagnostic Reading Battery* (Schrank & Woodcock, 1998). He said, "The narrative reports are remarkably smooth and do not read as most computer narratives normally do" (p. 8).

The reliability and validity characteristics of the WDRB are very good and meet basic technical requirements for both individual placement and programming decisions. Repeated-measures reliability (for individuals retested 1 to 17 months after initial testing) is extremely high (McArdle & Woodcock, 1997), especially for the learned abilities, such as Letter-Word Identification (0.92) and Passage Comprehension (0.82). The median test stability over this wide range of time for all 10 tests is 0.81. Rudman (1999) described this as "a surprising picture of stability of traits." Concurrent validity evidence is established through moderate to strong correlations between the WDRB and measures of cognitive abilities, achievement, and language proficiency, including the Peabody Individual Achievement Test (Dunn & Markwardt, 1970), the Wechsler Intelligence Scale for Children–Revised (Wechsler, 1974), the Stanford-Binet Intelligence Scale–Fourth Edition (Thorndike, Hagen, & Sattler, 1986), the Kaufman Intelligence Battery for Children (Kaufman & Kaufman, 1983), the Kaufman Tests of Educational Achievement (Kaufman & Kaufman, 1985), the Basic Achievement Skills Individual Screener (Psychological Corporation, 1983), the Wide Range Achievement Tests–Revised (Jastak & Wilkinson, 1984), and the Mini-Battery of Achievement (Woodcock, McGrew, & Werder, 1994). Construct validity evidence is presented via a pattern of increasing scores with age.

REFERENCES

Dunn, L. M., & Markwardt, F. C. (1970). *Peabody Individual Achievement Test*. Circle Pines, MN: American Guidance Service.

Jastak, S. R., & Wilkinson, G. S. (1984). *Wide Range Achievement Test–Revised*. Wilmington, DE: Jastak.

Kaufman, A. S., & Kaufman, N. L. (1983). *Kaufman Assessment Battery for Children*. Circle Pines, MN: American Guidance Service.

Kaufman, A. S., & Kaufman, N. L. (1985). *Kaufman Tests of Educational Achievement*. Circle Pines, MN: American Guidance Service.

McArdle, J., & Woodcock, R. W. (1997). Modeling components of change from time-lagged test-retest data. *Psychological Methods, 2*(4), 403–435.

McGrew, K. S. (1994). Clinical interpretation of the Woodcock-Johnson Tests of Cognitive Ability–Revised. Boston, MA: Allyn & Bacon.

McGrew, K. S., Werder, J. K., & Woodcock, R. W. (1991). *WJ-R Technical Manual*. Itasca, IL: Riverside.

Psychological Corporation. (1983). *Basic Achievement Skills Individual Screener*. San Antonio, TX: Author.

Rasch, G. (1960). *Probabilistic models for some intelligence and attainment tests*. Copenhagen, Denmark: Danish Institute for Educational Research.

Rudman, H. C. (1999). Review of the Woodcock Diagnostic Reading Battery. In *The fourteenth mental measurements yearbook*. Lincoln: University of Nebraska Press.

Schrank, F. A., & Woodcock, R. W. (1998). *Scoring and interpretive program for the Woodcock Diagnostic Reading Battery*. Itasca, IL: Riverside.

Thorndike, R. L., Hagen, E. P., & Sattler, J. M. (1986). *Stanford-Binet Intelligence Scale–Fourth Edition*. Itasca, IL: Riverside.

Wechsler, D. (1974). *Wechsler Intelligence Scale for Children–Revised*. San Antonio, TX: Psychological Corporation.

Woodcock, R. W. (1992, April). *Rasch technology and test engineering*. Invited presentation to the American Educational Research Association annual conference, San Francisco.

Woodcock, R. W. (1997). *Woodcock Diagnostic Reading Battery*. Itasca, IL: Riverside.

Woodcock, R. W., & Johnson, M. B. (1989a). *Woodcock-Johnson–Revised Tests of Achievement*. Itasca, IL: Riverside.

Woodcock, R. W., & Johnson, M. B. (1989b). *Woodcock-Johnson–Revised Tests of Cognitive Ability*. Itasca, IL: Riverside.

Woodcock, R. W., McGrew, K. S., & Werder, J. K. (1994). *Mini-Battery of Achievement*. Itasca, IL: Riverside.

Wright, B. D., & Stone, M. H. (1979). *Best test design*. Chicago: MESA Press.

FREDRICK A. SCHRANK
Olympia, Washington

WOODCOCK-JOHNSON III TESTS OF ACHIEVEMENT

The Woodcock-Johnson III Tests of Achievement (WJ III; Woodcock, McGrew, & Mather, 2001) measures a great many aspects of academic achievement with a wide variety of relatively brief tests. Many of these achievement tests can be used with the WJ III Tests of Cognitive Abilities to assess a student's abilities on many specific Cattell-Horn-Carroll Gf-Gc (CHC) "cognitive factors." Examiners are permitted to select the tests they need to assess abilities in which they are interested for a particular student.

The WJ III Tests of Achievement provides interpretive information from 22 tests to measure cognitive performance.

Reading

Letter-Word Identification: Naming letters and reading words aloud from a list.

Reading Fluency: Speed of reading sentences and answering "yes" or "no" to each.

Passage Comprehension: Orally supplying the missing word removed from each sentence or very brief paragraph (e.g., "Woof," said the ____, biting the hand that fed it.).

Word Attack: Reading nonsense words (e.g., plurp, fronkett) aloud to test phonetic word attack skills.

Reading Vocabulary: Orally stating synonyms and antonyms for printed words and orally completing written analogies (e.g., elephant : big :: mouse : ____).

Written Language

Spelling: Writing letters and words from dictation.

Writing Fluency: Writing simple sentences, using three given words for each item and describing a picture, as quickly as possible for seven minutes.

Writing Samples: Writing sentences according to directions; many items include pictures; spelling does not count on most items.

Editing: Orally correcting deliberate errors in typed sentences.

Spelling of Sounds: Written spelling of dictated nonsense words.

Punctuation and Capitalization: Formal writing test of these skills.

Mathematics

Calculation: Involves arithmetic computation with paper and pencil.

Math Fluency: Speed of performing simple calculations for 3 minutes.

Applied Problems: Oral, math word problems, solved with paper and pencil.

Quantitative Concepts: Oral questions about mathematical factual information, operations signs, etc.

Oral Language

Story Recall: The student answers oral questions about stories that were dictated to the student.

Understanding Directions: The student follows oral directions to point to different parts of pictures.

Picture Vocabulary: The student points to named pictures or names pictures.

Oral Comprehension: The student provides anto- or synonyms to spoken words and completes oral analogies (e.g., elephant is to big and mouse is to ___).

Supplemental

Story Recall—Delayed: The student answers questions about the stories heard earlier.

Sound Awareness: Rhyming, deletion, substitution, and reversing of spoken sounds.

Academic Knowledge: Oral questions about factual knowledge of science, social studies, and humanities.

The WJ III provides raw scores that are converted, using age or grade-based norms, to Standard Scores, Percentile Ranks, W scores, Age and grade equivalents (AE and GE), relative proficiency index (RPI), Instructional Ranges, and Cognitive-Academic Language Proficiency (CALP) levels. All score transformation is performed through the use of the computer program (WJ III Compuscore). The program also can generate several "discrepancy" analyses: intra-ability discrepancies (intracognitive, intra-achievement, and intra-individual) and ability achievement discrepancies (predicted achievement vs. achievement, general intellectual ability versus achievement, and oral language ability versus achievement).

The WJ III was normed on 8,818 children and adults (4,783 in grades kindergarten through 12) in a well-designed, national sample. The same persons also provided norms for the WJ III tests of academic achievement, so the ability and achievement tests can be compared directly and cognitive and achievement tests can be combined to measure CHC factors. The technical manual provides extensive coverage of reliability and validity areas. The median reliability coefficient alphas for all age groups for the standard battery of the WJ III ACH for tests 1 through 12 ranged from 0.81 to 0.94. For the extended battery, median coefficients ranged from 0.76 to 0.91. The reliability scores for the WJ III meet or exceed standards. The median cluster reliabilities are mostly 0.90 or higher, and the individual test reliabilities are mostly 0.80 or higher and can be used for decision-making purposes with support from other sources. The technical manual presents a considerable amount of evidence supporting the validity of scores from the test, noting that the earlier versions of the battery have also been shown to have validity. The WJ III ACH content is similar to other achievement tests. Growth curves of cluster scores illustrate expected developmental progressions. Extensive data focus on validity evidence from confirmatory factor analyses of test scores from participants age 6 to adult. The internal correlations of the entire battery are consistent with relations between areas of achievement and between areas of achievement and ability clusters.

REFERENCE

Woodcock, R. W., McGrew, K. S., & Mather, N. (2001). *Woodcock-Johnson III Tests of Achievement*. Itasca, IL: Riverside.

REVIEWED IN:

Plake, B. S., Impara, J. C., & Spies, R. A. (Eds.). (2003). *The fifteenth mental measurements yearbook*. Lincoln, NE: Buros Institute of Mental Measurements.

Mather, N. & Jaffe, L. (2002). *Woodcock-Johnson III: Reports, recommendations, and strategies*. New York, NY: Wiley.

Mather, N., & Wendling, B. (2009). *Woodcock-Johnson III Tests of Achievement. Practitioner's guide to assessing intelligence and achievement* (pp. 503–535). Hoboken, NJ: Wiley. http://alpha.fdu.edu/psychology/woodcock_index.htm

Mather, N., Wendling, B. J., & Woodcock R. W. (2001). *The Essentials of WJ III Tests of Achievement Assessment*. New York, NY: Wiley.

RON DUMONT
Fairleigh Dickinson University

JOHN O. WILLIS
Rivier College

KATHLEEN VEIZEL
Fairleigh Dickinson College

JAMIE ZIBULSKY
Fairleigh Dickinson College
Fourth edition

WOODCOCK-JOHNSON III TESTS OF COGNITIVE ABILITIES

Unlike many individual ability tests, the Woodcock-Johnson III Tests of Cognitive Abilities (WJ III COG; Woodcock, McGrew, & Mather, 2001) are explicitly designed to assess a student's abilities on many specific Cattell-Horn-Carroll Gf-Gc (CHC) cognitive factors, not just a total score or a few factors. The General Intellectual Ability (GIA) score of the WJ III is based on a weighted combination of tests that best represents a common ability underlying all intellectual performance. Examiners can get a GIA (Std) score by administering the first 7 tests in the Tests of Cognitive Abilities or a GIA (Ext) score by administering all 14 cognitive tests. Each of the cognitive tests represents a different broad CHC factor. A Brief Intellectual Ability (BIA) score is available and takes about 10 to 15 minutes to administer and is especially useful for screenings and reevaluations. The BIA score is derived from three cognitive tests: Verbal Comprehension, Concept Formation, and Visual Matching. Examiners are permitted to select the tests they need to assess abilities in which they are interested for a particular student.

The WJ III Tests of Cognitive Abilities provides interpretive information from 20 tests to measure cognitive performance.

Comprehension-Knowledge (Gc)

Verbal Comprehension: Naming pictures, giving antonyms or synonyms for spoken words, and completing oral analogies.

General Information: Answering "where" and "what" factual questions.

Long-Term Retrieval (Glr)

Visual-Auditory Learning: The student is taught rebus symbols for words and tries to "read" sentences written with the symbols.

Retrieval Fluency: The student tries to name as many things as possible in one minute in each of three specified categories, for example, fruits.

Visual Processing (Gv)

Spatial Relations: The student tries to select by sight alone, from many choices, the fragments that could be assembled into a given geometric shape.

Picture Recognition: The student is shown one or more pictures and then tries to identify it or them on another page that includes several similar pictures

Auditory Processing (Ga)

Sound Blending: The student tries to identify words dictated broken into separate sounds.

Auditory Attention: The student tries to recognize words dictated against increasingly loud background noise.

Fluid Reasoning (Gf)

Concept Formation: For each item, the student tries to figure out the rule that divides a set of symbols into two groups.

Analysis-Synthesis: The student tries to solve logical puzzles involving color codes similar to mathematical and scientific symbolic rules.

Processing Speed (Gs)

Visual Matching: As quickly as possible for 3 minutes, the student circles two identical numbers in each row of six numbers.

Decision Speed: As quickly as possible for 3 minutes, the student tries to find the two pictures in each row that are most similar conceptually (e.g., sundial and stopwatch).

Short-Term Memory (Gsm)

Numbers Reversed: Repeating increasingly long series of dictated digits in reversed order.

Memory for Words: The student tries to repeat dictated random series of words in order.

Additional Tests

Incomplete Words: The student attempts to recognize words dictated with some sounds omitted. This is considered to be a test of Ga.

Auditory Working Memory: The student tries to repeat randomly dictated words and numbers (e.g., cow 9 up 3 5) with the words first and then the numbers in the order they were dictated. This test also measures Gsm or working memory or division of attention.

Visual-Auditory Learning–Delayed: The student tries again to "read" sentences written with the rebuses learned in Visual-Auditory Learning. There are norms from a half hour to 8 days. This is an additional measure of Glr.

Rapid Picture Naming: The student tries to name simple pictures as quickly as possible for 2 minutes. This test measures Gs and naming facility or Rapid Automatized Naming (RAN).

Planning: The student tries to trace a complex, overlapping path without lifting the pencil, retracing any part of the path, or skipping any part. Gf and Gv are involved in this test.

Pair Cancellation: The student scans rows of pictures and tries, as quickly as possible for 3 minutes to circle each instance in which a certain picture is followed by a certain other picture (e.g., each cat followed by a tree). This test also measures Gs.

The WJ III provides raw scores that are converted, using age- or grade-based norms, to Standard Scores, Percentile Ranks, W scores, Age and grade equivalents (AE and GE), relative proficiency index (RPI), Instructional Ranges, and Cognitive-Academic Language Proficiency (CALP) levels. All score transformation is performed through the use of the computer program (WJ III Compuscore). The program also can generate several "discrepancy" analyses: intra-ability discrepancies (intracognitive, intra-achievement, and intra-individual) and ability achievement discrepancies (predicted achievement vs. achievement, general intellectual ability versus achievement, and oral language ability versus achievement).

The WJ III was normed on 8,818 children and adults (4,783 in grades kindergarten through 12) in a well-designed, national sample. The same persons also provided norms for the WJ III tests of academic achievement, so the ability and achievement tests can be compared directly and cognitive and achievement tests can be combined to measure CHC factors. The technical manual provides extensive coverage of reliability and validity areas. The median reliability coefficient alphas for all age groups for the standard battery of the WJ III COG for tests 1 through 10 ranged from 0.81 to 0.94. For the extended battery, median coefficients ranged from 0.74 to 0.97. The reliability scores for the WJ III meet or exceed standards. The median cluster reliabilities are mostly 0.90 or higher, and the individual test reliabilities are mostly 0.80 or higher and can be used for decision-making purposes with support from other sources. The manual presents considerable evidence supporting the validity of scores from the test, noting that the earlier versions of the battery have also been shown to have validity. Test content on the WJ III COG has emerged from previous versions, is similar to the content found on other well-established cognitive measures, or is based on sound experimental instruments.

REFERENCE

Woodcock, R. W., McGrew, K. S., & Mather, N. (2001). *Woodcock-Johnson III Tests of Cognitive Abilities*. Itasca, IL: Riverside.

REVIEWED IN:

Grenwelge, C. (2009). Review of "Woodcock-Johnson III Tests of Achievement, Form C/Brief Battery." *Journal of Psychoeducational Assessment, 27*(4), 345–350.

Keith, T., Reynolds, M., Patel, P., & Ridley, K. (2008). Sex differences in latent cognitive abilities ages 6 to 59: Evidence from the Woodcock-Johnson III tests of cognitive abilities. *Intelligence, 36*(6), 502–525.

Plake, B. S., Impara, J. C., & Spies, R. A. (Eds.). (2003). *The fifteenth mental measurements yearbook*. Lincoln, NE: Buros Institute of Mental Measurements.

Ramos, E., Alfonso, V., & Schermerhorn, S. (2009). Graduate students' administration and scoring errors on the Woodcock-Johnson III Tests of Cognitive Abilities. *Psychology in the Schools, 46*(7), 650–657.

Rizza, M. G.; McIntosh, D. E. & McCunn, A. (2001). Profile analysis of the Woodcock-Johnson III Tests of Cognitive Abilities with gifted students. *Psychology in the Schools, 38*, Special issue: New perspectives in gifted education, 447–455.

Schrank, F. A., Flanagan D. P., Woodcock R. W., & Mascolo, J. T. (2001). *The Essentials of WJ III Cognitive Abilities Assessment*. New York, NY: Wiley.

Wendling, B., Mather, N., & Schrank, F. (2009). Woodcock-Johnson III Tests of Cognitive Abilities. *Practitioner's guide*

to assessing intelligence and achievement (pp. 191–229). Hoboken, NJ: Wiley. http://themindhub.com/.

RON DUMONT
Fairleigh Dickinson University

JOHN O. WILLIS
Rivier College

VEIZEL
Fairleigh Dickinson College

JAMIE ZIBULSKY
Fairleigh Dickinson College
Fourth edition

WOODCOCK LANGUAGE PROFICIENCY BATTERY–REVISED

The *Woodcock Language Proficiency Battery–Revised* (WLPB-R; Woodcock, 1991; Woodcock & Muñoz-Sandoval, 1995) is designed to provide an overview of a subject's language skills in English (or Spanish), to diagnose language abilities, to identify students for English as a second language instruction, and to plan broad instructional goals for developing language competencies. The instrument is appropriate for individuals aged 2 to over 90 years of age. For interpretive purposes, each WLPB-R provides cluster scores for Broad Language Ability (English or Spanish), Oral Language Ability, Reading Ability, and Written Language Ability. When the entire battery is used, the WLPB-R provides a procedure for evaluating the strengths and weaknesses among an individual's oral language, reading, and written language abilities. When both the English and Spanish forms are administered, examiners can obtain information about language dominance and relative proficiency in each language.

The WLPB-R oral language tests measure linguistic competency, semantic expression, expressive vocabulary, and verbal comprehension/reasoning. The WLPB-R reading tests measure the ability to identify sight vocabulary, to apply structural analysis skills, and comprehend single-word stimuli and short passages. The written language tests assess a broad range of writing tasks. These include tasks measuring the ability to produce simple sentences with ease, writing increasingly complex sentences to meet varied demands, and other tasks measuring punctuation, capitalization, spelling, word usage, and the ability to detect and correct errors in spelling, punctuation, capitalization, and word usage in written passages.

Administration time varies depending on the purposes of the assessment and the number of tests administered (20 minutes to over 1 hour). A wide variety of interpretive scores are available, including age and grade equivalents, instructional ranges, standard scores, and percentile ranks.

The English form was standardized on more than 6,300 individuals ranging in age from 2 to over 90. Lehmann (1995), who reviewed the WLPB-R primarily from a psychometric perspective, commented favorably on the development of continuous (gathered throughout the school year), rather than interpolated, norms. The Spanish form was standardized on more than 2,000 native Spanish-speaking subjects. The Spanish form uses equated U.S. norms for interpretive purposes.

Internal consistency reliability coefficients and standard errors of measurement (SEMs) were calculated for all tests and clusters and are reported in the *WLBP-R Examiner's Manual*. Reliabilities are generally in the high .80s and low .90s for the individual tests, and in the mid .90s for the clusters. Test-retest reliability, interrater reliability, and alternate forms reliability statistics are also reported. All provide evidence that scores from the WLPB-R are reliable. Poteat (1995) said that "the profusion of reliability data varies but generally the WLPB-R appears to have satisfactory to excellent reliability" (p. 416).

The manual also presents evidence of concurrent validity as established through moderate to strong correlations between the WLPB-R and other measures of cognitive abilities, achievement, and language proficiency. Poteat (1995) said that "it is difficult to summarize these very diverse data very succinctly, but the WLPB-R is positively correlated to measures of language development and ability" (p. 416). Intercorrelations among WLPB-R tests are also presented in the manual, providing adequate evidence of construct validity. In addition, a study by Schrank, Fletcher, and Alvarado (1996) provides evidence that the WLPB-R tests are good measures of cognitive-academic language proficiency (CALP; Cummins, 1984). The study by Schrank et al. (1996) also showed that the WLPB-R correlated highly with language performance in the classroom. This additional validity evidence was recommended in the review by Poteat (1995).

REFERENCES

Cummins, J. (1984). *Bilingualism and special education: Issues in assessment and pedagogy*. Austin, TX: PRO-ED.

Lehmann, I. J. (1995). Review of the Woodcock Language Proficiency Battery–Revised. In J. C. Conoley & J. C. Impara (Eds.), *The twelfth mental measurements yearbook* (pp. 1118–1120). Lincoln: University of Nebraska Press.

Poteat, G. M. (1995). Review of the Woodcock Language Proficiency Battery–Revised. In J. C. Conoley & J. C. Impara (Eds.), *The twelfth mental measurements yearbook* (pp. 1120–1121). Lincoln: University of Nebraska Press.

Schrank, F. A., Fletcher, T. V., & Alvarado, C. G. (1996). Comparative validity of three English oral language proficiency tests. *Bilingual Research Journal, 20*(1), 55–68.

Woodcock, R. W. (1991). *Woodcock Language Proficiency Battery–Revised, English Form*. Itasca, IL: Riverside.

Woodcock, R. W., & Muñoz-Sandoval, A. (1995). *Woodcock Language Proficiency Battery–Revised, Spanish Form*. Itasca, IL: Riverside.

FREDRICK A. SCHRANK
Olympia, Washington

See also Nondiscriminatory Assessment

WOODCOCK-MUÑOZ FOUNDATION

The Woodcock-Muñoz Foundation (WMF) is a private, nonprofit operating foundation that supports the advancement of contemporary cognitive assessment based on the Cattell-Horn-Carroll (CHC) theory of human cognitive abilities (McGrew, 2005). The foundation engages in programs of instructional support to graduate-level professional preparation programs, research concerning the abilities of individuals with diagnosed exceptionalities, and closely related educational and research projects.

The foundation promotes contemporary practices in the assessment of cognitive abilities internationally through a variety of programs that provide support for instructional materials that are important to graduate training programs in cognitive assessment, research into the cognitive profiles of individuals with diagnosed exceptionalities (learning problems, neuropsychological conditions, behavioral and psychiatric problems, and giftedness), and the advancement of effective clinical assessment practices and the dissemination of research findings through direct professional development opportunities.

The foundation's external and internal research programs facilitate a bridge between CHC theory and applied cognitive assessment practices. The foundation's external research program focuses on the investigation of profiles of cognitive abilities of individuals with diagnosed exceptionalities and the relations between subject demographic characteristics, cognitive abilities, and academic achievement. Collaborative research, particularly with early career professionals, is actively encouraged. The foundation's internal research program consists of three primary projects. The Clinical Data Base Project has as its purpose the development and analysis of a rich and evolving clinical subject cognitive ability database. The Human Cognitive Abilities Project has as its purpose the investigation of the structure and organization of human cognitive abilities via secondary analysis of historical and contemporary data sets. The International Cognitive Assessments Project has as its purpose the development of a small number of noncommercial, contemporary cognitive assessment instruments for specific populations in Eastern Europe, based on need. For more information, visit http://www.woodcock-munoz-foundation.org/.

REFERENCE

McGrew, K. S. (2005). The Cattell-Horn-Carroll Theory of Cognitive Abilities: Past, present, and future. In D. P. Flanagan & P. L. Harrison (Eds.), *Contemporary intellectual assessment* (2nd ed., pp. 136–81). New York, NY: Guilford Press.

FREDRICK A. SCHRANK
Olympia, Washington

KEVIN S. MCGREW
St. Joseph, Minnesota

WOODCOCK READING MASTERY TESTS–REVISED

Available in two forms, the Woodcock Reading Mastery Tests–Revised (WRMT-R; Woodcock, 1987) is an individually administered test designed to assess a variety of reading abilities of individuals between the ages of 4 and 75. The WRMT-R is useful in various settings, such as instructional placement, individual program planning, and progress evaluation (Cohen & Cohen, 1994). The test consists of six subtests, including Visual-Auditory Learning, Letter Identification, Word Identification, Word Attack, Word Comprehension, and Passage Comprehension. Visual-Auditory Learning involves learning several unfamiliar visual symbols representing words. Letter Identification assesses an individual's ability to identify by name or sound the letters of the alphabet. Word Identification requires the test taker to read words ranging in difficulty. Word Attack evaluates the ability to pronounce nonsense words using phonic skills. Word Comprehension is comprised of antonyms, synonyms, and analogies. Finally, Passage Comprehension is designed to evaluate reading comprehension skills. From these subtests, five cluster scores are obtained: Readiness, Basic Skills, Reading Comprehension, Total Reading–Full Scale, and Total Reading–Short Scale. Percentile ranks, grade and age equivalent scores, instructional ranges, and strengths and weaknesses can also be obtained. Depending on the form used, administration time ranges from 30 to 60 minutes.

The WRMT-R was recently renormed, and is now referred to as the Woodcock Reading Mastery Test–Revised/Normative Update (WRMT-R/NU; Woodcock, 1997). The examiner's manual for the WRMT-R/NU offers information regarding technical aspects such as norming, reliability, and validity. The WRMT-R/NU was normed using approximately 3,700 subjects; however, new norms were not collected for subjects in grades 13–16 or ages 23 and older. Subjects were randomly selected using a stratified sampling method based on variables such as geographic region, community size, sex, and so on from 1994 U.S. census data. Split-half reliability coefficients of the original WRMT-R ranged from 0.34 to 0.98, and ranged from 0.87 to 0.89 in the WRMT-R Normative Update. Content and concurrent validity were described. However, the authors do not substantiate the content validity of the WRMT-R, although they report using "outside experts" and experienced teachers. Concurrent validity was established with comparisons to such tests as Iowa Tests of Basic Skills, Peabody Individual Achievement Test–Revised, KeyMath–Revised, and Kaufman Test of Educational Achievement.

In comparing the original WRMT-R norms with those from the 1997 update, it appears that there is little change in the level of performance of students who are average to above average for their grade or age (Woodcock, 1997). However, the performance of students who are below average appears to have declined. The result of these changes is that where student performance has improved, the WRMT-R/NU standard scores and percentiles will be lower than on the original norms, and conversely, where performance has declined, WRMT-R/NU standard scores and percentiles will be higher (Woodcock, 1997).

The WRMT-R has been revised several times. An atheoretical development of this test allows for the test to be applied to many clinical and remedial settings. However, several problems with this scale exist. Cooter (1989) reported that the WRMT-R assesses reading "in fragments rather than holistically." In addition, reliability and validity data is limited. The authors report data on WRMT-R split-half reliability and establish validity in a questionable fashion (Compton, 1990). In addition, the reliability of WRMT-R individual subtests for grade 11 and above do not appear to be consistent with the reported norms of other age groups (Cohen & Cohen, 1994).

REFERENCES

Cohen, S. H., & Cohen, J. (1994). Review of the Woodcock Reading Mastery Tests–Revised. In D. J. Keyser & R. C. Sweetland (Eds.), *Test critiques: Volume X*. Austin, TX: PRO-ED.

Compton, C. (1990). *A guide to 85 tests for special education.* Belmont, CA: Fearon/Janus.

Cooter, R. (1989). Review of the Woodcock Reading Mastery Tests–Revised. In J. C. Conoley & J. J. Kramer (Eds.), *The tenth mental measurements yearbook*. Lincoln: University of Nebraska Press.

Woodcock, R. W. (1987). *Woodcock Reading Mastery Tests–Revised*. Circle Pines, MN: American Guidance Service.

Woodcock, R. W. (1997). *Woodcock Reading Mastery Tests–Revised/Normative Update*. Circle Pines, MN: American Guidance Service.

DARIELLE GREENBERG
California School of Professional Psychology

WOODS SCHOOLS

The Woods Schools, located in Langhorne, Pennsylvania, were established in 1913 to provide educational and training programs for students with development delays, intellectual disabilities, brain damage, and learning disabilities. The school is primarily a residential facility that features group home life in small cottages with an intensive staff ratio that provides for direct care and services to meet the individual needs of students. The school provides for day and residential students on a coed basis.

The schools' programs offer a wide range of educational experiences to students with severe disabilities and who require therapeutic services. Vocational training is provided. Students are trained in a wide range of vocational exploration experiences that establish appropriate work habits, basic working skills, and prevocational experiences that lead to job training. Remedial services, tutorial instruction, and therapeutic services are designed to meet the individual needs of students as they progress through the programs. For more information, visit http://www.woods.org/.

This entry has been informed by the source shown below.

REFERENCE

Sargent, J. K. (1982). *The directory for exceptional children* (9th ed.). Boston, MA: Porter Sargent.

PAUL C. RICHARDSON
Elwyn Institutes

See also Vocational Education

WORD BLINDNESS

Congenital word blindness, word blindness, dyslexia, developmental dyslexia, specific dyslexia, developmental alexia, visual aphasia, and strephosymbolia are all terms that have on some occasions been used interchangeably in the special education literature (Evans, 1982; Orton, 1937; Wallin, 1968) to indicate a child's inability to learn to read. Developmental dyslexia was defined by Critchley (1964) as a specific difficulty in learning to read, often of genetic origin, which existed in spite of good general intelligence, and without emotional problems, brain damage, or impairments of vision or hearing. Ford (1973) defined congenital word blindness or dyslexia as the inability of a child to learn the meaning of graphic symbols.

Although literature is available from as early as the 1800s (Kussmaul, 1877), there is no clear consensus on cause for this problem. Causes that have been hypothesized ranged from maternal and natal factors, ophthalmological factors, cerebral dominance issues, and minor neurological impairments, to genetic issues (Critchley, 1964). Clemesha (1915) attributed word blindness to a congenital defect or deficiency in the brain or to some pathological process. Heitmuller (1918) felt that developmental alexia or word blindness was a developmental defect of the visual memory center for the graphic symbols of language. Orton (1937) postulated that dyslexic symptoms were the result of mixed dominance, which he called motor integrating abilities. His theory attributed reading reversals to the possibility that the mirrored counterparts of words located in the dominant hemisphere were stored in the subdominant hemisphere; therefore, children without a clearly established dominant hemisphere would have confusion with learning to read words. He also believed that this difficulty in establishing dominance was inherited. DeHirsch (Hallahan & Cruickshank, 1973) postulated a central nervous system dysfunction or developmental lag as the cause of word blindness. She believed "that both delayed cerebral dominance and language disorders may reflect a maturational dysfunction" (p. 106).

Although there continues to be a lack of consensus on which terminology to use, as well as on the meaning of the terms chosen, the literature is clearly divided between the medical (those professionals who are looking for a cause) and the educational (those professionals who are more interested in determining a means to remediate the problem). The medically oriented group is more likely to see word blindness or dyslexia as an inability to learn to read owing to a central nervous system dysfunction or brain damage, while the educationally oriented group is more likely to describe this group as children who are having trouble learning to read. There are other distinctions between the medical and educational professions. Educators are more concerned with the developmental sequence of reading skills; the medical community is concerned with disabilities in language and speech, motor development, and perception. Educators differentiate between reading problems of children and adults and make a distinction between maturational lag and a central nervous system dysfunction. Educators do not see one easy way of remediating but base remediation on intensive diagnostic information related to the specific skills that individual children are missing, the child's best modality for learning, the appropriate materials, and so on. Educators are less likely to recommend individual treatment, but work within the entire school population to improve reading instruction for all children (Lerner, 1971). One final distinction between the two groups of professionals is that the medically oriented research has been conducted most often by physicians in Europe, while the educational research has been done by educators, psychologists, and reading specialists in the United States. DeHirsch, a language pathology theorist and psychiatrist (Hallahan & Cruickshank, 1973), has done extensive research in the area of dyslexia and has been greatly responsible for the integration of research from both of these groups.

Specific behavioral characteristics that may be present in children who have been diagnosed as word blind include a general clumsiness or spatial disorientation, minor sensory disorders, difficulty in eye control, defects in body image, confusion of right and left, faulty estimates of spatial and temporal categories, difficulty in interpreting the meaning of facial expressions, difficulty in arithmetic skills, difficulty with processing of complex linguistic verbalizations, difficulty with formulation, a tendency for cluttering, disorganized verbal output, hyperactivity, and difficulty with figure-group concepts (Critchley, in Franklin, 1962; DeHirsch, 1952).

Heller (1963) described screening criteria for detecting word blindness in school-aged children. These criteria include normal intelligence, normal vision and hearing, marked reduction in reading and spelling ability, discrepancy between reading and other abilities, inability to read by the sight method, ability to learn to read by auditory repetition, and evidence of dissociation of visual word image from acoustic word image. Remediation techniques traditionally have emphasized the phonetic approach (Hinshelwood, 1917; Holt, 1962; Miles, 1962; Orton, 1937), with training occurring in individualized sessions. A more individualized eclectic approach was hypothesized by Naidoo (1972) and DeHirsch (Hallahan & Cruickshank, 1973), with emphasis on evaluating each student's strengths and weaknesses and devising an individualized program based on the results. Specific remediation techniques have been well developed by Wagner (1976).

The Word Blind Centre for Dyslexic Children was established in 1962 in London, England, by the Invalid Children's Aid Association (ICAA; Naidoo, 1972). It was in operation from 1962 to 1970; its goals were both research and the treatment of dyslexic children. The ICAA has been responsible, since 1963, for the publication of the *Word Blind Bulletin*. In the United States, the National Advisory Committee on Dyslexia and Related Reading Disorders was created by the Secretary of Health, Education and Welfare (HEW) in 1968. Its purpose was to investigate, clarify, and resolve the controversial issues surrounding dyslexia. The committee determined that the term *dyslexia* served no useful educational purpose. It recommended the creation of an Office of Reading Disorders within HEW to improve reading instruction for all children who were experiencing difficulty in reading (*Report to the Secretary of the Department of Health, Education and Welfare*, 1969).

REFERENCES

Clemesha, J. C. (1915). Congenital word blindness or inability to learn to read. *Journal of Ophthalmology Oto-Laryngology, 9*(1), 1–6.

Critchley, M. (1962). In A. W. Franklin (Ed.), *Word-blindness or specific developmental dyslexia*. Proceedings of a conference called by the Invalid Children's Aid Association. London: Pitman.

Critchley, M. (1964). *Developmental dyslexia*. London, England: Heinemann Medical.

DeHirsch, K. (1952). Specific dyslexia or strephosymbolia. *Folia Phoniatrica, 4*, 231–248.

DeHirsch, K. (1973). In D. P. Hallahan & W. M. Cruickshank (Eds.), *Psychoeducational foundations of learning disabilities*. Englewood Cliffs, NJ: Prentice Hall.

Evans, M. M. (1982). Dyslexia: An annotated bibliography. *Contemporary problems of childhood #5*. Westport, CT: Greenwood.

Fisher, J. H. (1905). Case of congenital word-blindness (inability to learn to read). *Ophthalmic Review, 20*, 315–318.

Ford, F. R. (1973). Developmental word blindness and mirror writing. In *Diseases of the nervous system in infancy, childhood, and adolescence* (6th ed.). Springfield, IL: Thomas.

Franklin, A. W. (Ed.). (1962). *Word-blindness or specific developmental dyslexia*. Proceedings of a conference called by the Invalid Children's Aid Association. London, England: Pitman.

Hallahan, D. P., & Cruickshank, W. M. (1973). *Psychoeducational foundations of learning disabilities*. Englewood Cliffs, NJ: Prentice Hall.

Heitmuller, G. H. (1918). Cases of developmental alexia or congenital word blindness. *Washington Medical Annual, 17*, 124–129.

Heller, T. M. (1963). Word-blindness—A survey of the literature and a report of twenty-eight cases. *Pediatrics, 31*(4), 669–691.

Hinshelwood, J. (1917). *Congenital word-blindness*. London: H.K. Lewis.

Holt, L. M. (1962). In A. W. Franklin (Ed.), *Word-blindness or specific developmental dyslexia*. Proceedings of a conference called by the Invalid Children's Aid Association. London: Pitman.

Kussmaul, A. (1877). Word-deafness—Word blindness. In A. H. Buck & H. von Ziemssen (Eds.), *Diseases of the nervous system, and disturbances of speech. Vol. 14 of Cyclopaedia of the Practice of Medicine.* New York, NY: Wood.

Lerner, J. W. (1971). *Children with learning disabilities* (2nd ed.). Boston, MA: Houghton Mifflin.

Miles, T. R. (1962). In A.W. Franklin (Ed.), *Word-blindness or specific developmental dyslexia.* Proceedings of a conference called by the Invalid Children's Aid Association. London: Pitman.

Naidoo, S. (1972). *Specific dyslexia: The research report of the ICAA Word Blind Centre of Dyslexic Children.* London: Pitman.

Orton, S. T. (1937). *Reading, writing, and speech problems in children.* New York, NY: Norton.

Orton, S. T. (1966). *Word-blindness in school children and other papers on strephosymbolia (specific language disability—dyslexia) 1925–1946.* Pomfret, CT: Orton Society.

Report to the Secretary of the Department of Health, Education, and Welfare. (1969, August). Washington, DC: National Advisory Committee on Dyslexia and Related Disorders.

Wagner, R. F. (1976). *Helping the word blind: Effective intervention techniques for overcoming reading problems in older students.* West Nyack, NY: Center for Applied Research in Education.

Wallin, J.E.W. (1968). Congenital word blindness (dyslexia) in children. *Journal of Education, 151*(1), 36–51.

SUSANNE BLOUGH ABBOTT
*Bedford Central School District,
Mt. Kisco, New York*

See also Congenital Word Blindness, History of; Dyslexia; Reading Disorders; Reading Remediation

WORDS IN COLOR

Words in Color is a one-to-one sound-symbol approach to teaching reading that was devised in 1957 by Caleb Gattegno. Gattegno, a scientist, approached the problems of reading as he did the problems of mathematics and physics. He introduced the concept of temporal sequence into reading methodology (Gattegno, 1970) and proposed that our language is coded into a series of sounds that, when uttered in sequence, produce wholes that we call words. The timing of the sounds in sequence is essential learning for correct pronunciation (Aukerman, 1971). Words in Color is based on the premise that reading is a process of decoding printed symbols and translating them into sounds and words. Color is used in the initial stage of reading to help the learner make an association between the symbol and the sound.

In the Words in Color program, there are 21 charts of letter sounds, letters in combination, and word families. Included on these charts are the 47 distinct sounds of American English in 280 different instances of letters and letter combinations. In beginning reading instruction, the student looks at the colored charts of words, then writes the same letters or words in black and white and reads what he or she has written. The names of the letters are not used, only the sounds and colors. In Words in Color the vowels are taught as sound-symbol shapes. The learner's attention is focused on the shape of the letter and how it relates in shape to the other vowels.

Gattegno introduced his Words in Color program as a novel approach to teaching reading. He asserted that, "illiteracy can be wiped out at a far smaller cost than any wild dreamer has ever dreamed. [He is] prepared to do the computation if asked" (Gattegno, 1970). Results of research studies on the Words in Color program are mixed (Aukerman, 1971). Some studies have shown positive results (DeLacy, 1973), but Gattegno is far from reaching his goal of wiping out illiteracy with the Words in Color program.

REFERENCES

Aukerman, R. C. (1971). *Approaches to beginning reading.* New York, NY: Wiley.

DeLacy, E. (1973). Clinical reading cases—Some speculations concerning sequence in colour and look-and-say. *Slow Learning Child, 20*(3), 160–163.

Gattegno, C. (1969). *Towards a visual culture.* New York, NY: Outerbridge Dienstfrey.

Gattegno, C. (1970). The problem of reading is solved. *Harvard Educational Review, 40*(2), 283–286.

NANCY J. KAUFMAN
University of Wisconsin at Stevens Point

WORKFARE

Workfare is a term that was coined in the 1980s to describe welfare reform efforts that require able-bodied Aid to Families with Dependent Children (AFDC) parents to work in public service projects in exchange for monthly benefits. These unpaid jobs were typically at the city or county level and involved entry-level positions in clerical, human services, or park maintenance work. The majority of the participants were single females with children over the age of 6.

In 1981 the Reagan administration proposed a mandatory national workfare program, but Congress, reluctant to endorse such sweeping legislation in the absence of empirical evidence, instead passed the 1981 Omnibus Budget Reconciliation Act. This 1981 legislation encouraged, but did not require, the states to implement workfare programs as part of their welfare reform initiatives. By 1985, 37 states were experimenting with some type of workfare (Work-Not-Welfare, 1985). In most cases, workfare was but one small component in a broader employment effort that might include career planning, vocational training, high school equivalency courses, job-placement services, child-care vouchers, transportation assistance, and on-the-job training with subsidies to employers. The states were allowed to use Federal Work Incentive Program funds in these reform initiatives.

As the states began to generate their own welfare-reform models that were compatible with local philosophies and resources, it became clear that there were widely different approaches being tried across the country. This diversity provided social researchers with an unprecedented natural laboratory in which to study different systems. Manpower Demonstration Research Corporation (MDRC) of New York City conducted the most thorough research on workfare. In 1982, with financial help from the Ford Foundation, this nonprofit research group began a 4-year comparative study of welfare reform in 11 different states. The following generalizations and quotations were taken from MDRC's report on the first three study sites (Gueron, 1986): San Diego, California; Baltimore, Maryland; and two counties in Arkansas:

1. The studied states are increasing the employment of welfare recipients and, in some cases, reducing the costs of welfare.

2. The states place more emphasis on job search activities than on workfare activities and workfare "has not turned out to be either as punitive as its critics feared or as praiseworthy as its advocates claimed."

3. The findings indicate that the public service jobs are generally valued by both the participants and their supervisors, and are not considered "make work" activities.

4. In most cases, the participants already possess the necessary entry-level skills before they begin their jobs, so the workfare experience does not contribute to new vocational skills development.

5. Supervisors report that participants' productivity and attendance are as good as that of most other paid employees.

6. The majority of the participants agree that the work requirement is fair. Many feel positive about the work they do, and feel that they are making a contribution.

Undoubtedly, the most widely reported success story in work welfare reform comes from the state of Massachusetts, where 20,000 welfare recipients were placed in jobs (States Refocus, 1985). This program, which was voluntary and did not have the punitive quality often associated with workfare, reported that 86% of its first-year beneficiaries were still off welfare after 12 months. This represented savings to the state of over $60 million. This was not a controlled experiment, so it is not clear how much of Massachusetts' success was due to other variables such as general economic recovery.

In California another approach, which has the overwhelming support of both conservatives and liberals, is being tried. This approach will make participation mandatory with "strict provisions for cutting off payments to those who do not participate, and a large-scale effort to make sure that those who do will get adequate training and job-placement services" (Work for Welfare, 1985).

In conclusion, workfare is being tried in numerous settings and has wide emotional appeal because of its logical connection with such concerns as the federal deficit and the poverty cycle of AFDC families. However, a final accounting of workfare and related strategies will not be available for a number of years so it would seem prudent for policy makers to heed the advice of Manpower Demonstration Research Corporation (Gueron, 1986) when it says, no one model—including workfare—is at this point recommended for national replication.

REFERENCES

Gueron, J. (1986). *Work initiatives for welfare recipients: Lessons from a multi-state experiment.* New York, NY: Manpower Demonstration Research.

States refocus welfare, with eye on "real" jobs. (1985, October 28). *U.S. News & World Report.*

Work for welfare. (1985, October 7). *Time.*

Work-not-welfare effort encounters the deficit. (1985, July 19). *Wall Street Journal.*

JOHN D. SEE
University of Wisconsin at Stout

See also Rehabilitation; Socioeconomic Status

WORLD FEDERATION OF THE DEAF

The World Federation of the Deaf (WFD) was founded in 1951. It consists of 83 members representing the languages of English, French, and Italian. Its central office is in Rome, Italy. The WFD is a collection of associations of the deaf from various countries. These national or international organizations encompass societies and bodies acting for the deaf, health, social, and educational groups related to the aims of the federation, professionals involved with deafness or performing special assignments for the federation, and parents and friends of the deaf. Through social rehabilitation of deaf individuals, the WFD is a leader in the fight against deafness.

Among its services, the federation makes available social legislation concerning the deaf as well as statistical data. It also serves as consultant to the World Health Organization and UNESCO. The WFD sustains a library and bestows awards for merit and special achievement in education and social rehabilitation of the deaf. The federation holds commissions in the areas of communication, arts and culture, pedagogy, psychology, medicine, audiology, social and vocational rehabilitation, and spiritual care. The federation publishes a journal triannually entitled *Voices of Silence*, in addition to the *Proceedings of International Congresses and Meetings* and a dictionary.

MARY LEON PEERY
Texas A&M University

See also World Health Organization

WORLD HEALTH ORGANIZATION

The World Health Organization (WHO) is a specialized agency of the United Nations with primary responsibility for international health matters and public health. Created in 1948, it comprises delegates representing member states and is attended by representatives of intergovernmental organizations and nongovernmental organizations in official relationships with WHO. Assemblies are held annually, usually in Geneva.

The official functions of WHO are varied; they include (a) directing and coordinating authority on international health work; (b) assisting governments in strengthening health services; (c) furnishing technical assistance and emergency aid; (d) stimulating and advancing work to eradicate or control epidemic, endemic, and other diseases; (e) promoting improved nutrition, housing, sanitation, recreation, economic, and working conditions, and other aspects of environmental hygiene; (f) encouraging cooperation among scientific and professional groups that contribute to the advancement of health; (g) promoting material and child health and welfare, and fostering the ability to live harmoniously in a changing total environment; (h) fostering activities in the field of mental health; (i) working for improved standards of teaching and training in health, medical, and related professions; (j) studying and reporting on administrative and social techniques affecting public health and medical care from preventive and curative perspectives; and (k) assisting in developing informed public opinion on health matters.

Several WHO activities relate directly to diagnostic and classificatory issues in special education. First, WHO produces key writings concerning the use of health statistics and undertakes psychiatric epidemiology devoted to comparative research on mental disorders. Second, WHO compiles the International Classification of Diseases (ICD), a statistical classification of diseases; complications of pregnancy, childbirth, and the puerperium; congenital abnormalities; accidents, poisonings, and violence; and symptoms and ill-defined conditions. The ICD has been adapted for use as a nomenclature of diseases, with mental disorders constituting one major category. Subsumed in this category are classifications along with operational definitions of handicapping conditions.

Several other systems are tied to the ICD, including the *Diagnostic and Statistical Manual (DSM)* as well as the *Grossman Manuals on Terminology and Classification* of the American Association on Mental Retardation. Third, the Mental Health Unit of WHO has implemented an intensive program to acquire systematic data on variables in diagnostic practice and use of diagnostic mental disorder terms. This has resulted in a multi-axial scheme for the classification of childhood mental disorders, with three main axes: (1) clinical psychiatric syndromes; (2) individual intellectual levels of functioning regardless of etiology; and (3) associated physical, organic, and psychosocial factors in etiology.

DOUGLAS FUCHS
LYNN S. FUCHS
Peabody College,
Vanderbilt University

WORLD REHABILITATION FUND

The World Rehabilitation Fund, also known as the International Exchange of Experts and Information in Rehabilitation (IEEIR), seeks to identify, "import," disseminate, and promote the use of innovative rehabilitation and special education knowledge from other countries. Information about unique programs, practices, and research, as well as the policies of other nations, is sought for dissemination to professionals in the United States.

The IEEIR program is substantially supported by the Office of Special Education and Rehabilitation Services (OSERS) of the U.S. Department of Education. It is an outgrowth of the National Institute of Handicapped Research (NIHR, an OSERS division) mandate to facilitate the use of selected ideas and practices generated in other countries. Selection of knowledge or problem areas to guide the program staff is set jointly by OSERS, NIHR, and IEEIR staffs.

The IEEIR engages in the awarding of fellowships, the publication of monographs, and the dissemination of information. The fellowship program enables qualified U.S. experts to study and report on either special education or rehabilitation developments in other lands. This group includes rehabilitation and special education faculty, researchers, and administrators. Other specialists such as rehabilitation engineers, physicians, psychologists, independent living leaders, and consumer advocates also participate.

Overseas experts with substantial qualifications germane to the priorities set for the United States are identified and commissioned to prepare monographs for publication by the IEEIR program. Five monographs a year are commissioned.

To facilitate dissemination efforts, fellows commit themselves to reporting their observations and recommendations to their peers in relevant journals and at professional meetings. Because one of the criteria for selecting fellows is the degree to which they are centers of influence within their fields, IEEIR expects that they will influence not only students and researchers, but also practitioners and administrators. The communication skills and past record of a fellow are key considerations in awarding fellowships.

In addition to the reports they submit, fellows are expected to report their experiences and observations to professional meetings and other interested groups. Publication in professional journals is also encouraged. Both U.S. fellows and foreign monograph authors may be invited to present their findings at conferences designed for U.S. specialists to keep them abreast of innovations and new ideas.

The World Rehabilitation Fund headquarters is located at 400 East 34th Street, New York, NY 10016. Information on specific programs and monographs available may be requested from this office.

DIANE E. WOODS
World Rehabilitation Fund

See also **World Health Organization**

WRAPAROUND, POSITIVE BEHAVIOR SUPPORT

Wraparound is a philosophy of care with a defined planning process used to build constructive relationships and support networks among youth with complex emotional/behavioral needs and their families. As a team-based, collaborative process, wraparound is focused on developing and implementing individualized care plans for youth with complex mental health needs including those with or at-risk of Emotional Behavioral Disabilities (EBD) and their families. Introduced in the 1980s, wraparound was offered as an alternative to institutionalization and other restrictive placements for youth with complex emotional and behavioral needs (VanDenBerg, 1999). Now the wraparound process is being integrated into school-wide systems of PBIS as the highest level of intervention for the 1% to 3% of youth for whom lower-level behavioral supports, including complex function-based behavior plans, are not comprehensive enough to produce an effect. (Eber, Hyde, Rose, Breen, McDonald & Lewandowski, 2009). The wraparound process results in a coordinated plan that blends interagency supports and services with effective behavior, academic, and social interventions.

Emerging from the fields of mental health and child welfare, the wraparound planning process includes the development of a team that, by its membership, reflects the strengths, values, and spoken needs of the family. This uniquely constructed team, including natural support persons selected by the family and youth, develops, monitors and continuously revises the wraparound plan. The plan is focused on meeting needs defined by the family and youth at home, school, and in the community. Family and youth voice and ownership of the plan are emphasized in order to ensure interventions produce effective and timely outcomes for youth and their families and teachers. With an eye toward independence, natural support persons such as extended family, friends, a coach, a youth minister, or others with positive connections are sought for the teams. As teams problem solve how to effectively meet youths' needs, they combine supports for natural activities (e.g., child care, mentoring, making friends) with more traditional interventions (e.g., function-based behavioral interventions, specialized reading instruction, medication, etc.). Wraparound teams often have to create uniquely designed supports such as respite or in-home interventions.

The wraparound process requires a skilled facilitator to work closely with the youth and family to assemble a team based on their unique strengths and needs. The team facilitator helps engage extended family and other natural support persons to ensure that the team represents the culture and values of the family. Team members who have skills in areas of need (e.g., behavior specialist, vocational counselor, mental health clinician) or resources and credibility to support the family (e.g., family, friends and other natural supporters) collectively prioritize needs, design interventions, and plan access to needed supports and services. The focus is to ensure that those who spend the most time with the youth have full ownership of and commitment to the outcomes and are invested in the interventions used to achieve the outcomes. Under these conditions, wraparound teams can establish a context where effective interventions are likely to be developed and implemented with success.

Core Features of Wraparound

Major features of wraparound are that it is community based, culturally relevant, individualized, strength based, and family centered. The wraparound process is explicit about ensuring that the youth and their family are in lead roles in determining team membership, priorities and strategies, thus ensuring family/youth voice and ownership at every step. The logic is that by bringing together a team made up of family members, natural supports (e.g., extended family, friends, mentors), and school and community professionals, the wraparound process will produce a plan that (a) is accepted by the family, (b) addresses the family's priorities, and (c) leads to realistic and practical strategies to support the youth in his or her home, school, and community.

Wraparound plans are comprehensive and address multiple life domains across home, school, and community, including living environment; basic needs; safety; social, emotional, educational, spiritual, and cultural needs. Another defining feature of wraparound is that it is unconditional; if interventions are not achieving the desired outcomes the team rethinks the configuration of supports, services, and interventions and makes changes to ensure success in natural home, school, and community settings. In other words, youth do not fail, but plans can fail. Rather than forcing a youth to fit into existing program structures, wraparound is based on the belief that services and supports should be flexibly arranged to meet the unique needs of the youth and their families (Eber, Nelson, & Miles, 1997).

The wraparound process includes specific steps to establish ownership, and therefore investment, of people who spend the most time with the youth (i.e., family, teacher). This creates an environment in which a range of interventions, including behavioral supports, is more likely to be executed with integrity. As such, the wraparound process includes systematic assessment of the needs of the adults who support the youth and can arrange supports for these adults on behalf of the youth. For example, a wraparound team may solicit involvement from the community to assist a family with accessing stable housing and other basic living supports as parents may be better able to focus on a home-based behavior change plan for their child if stress about being evicted from an apartment is alleviated. Other examples include teams facilitating transportation, recreation opportunities, and social supports.

Wraparound is characterized by a deliberate and consistent focus on strengths and needs as defined by the youth and family (VanDenBerg, 1999). A key component in the wraparound process is the development of a rich and deep strength profile that identifies very explicit strengths across settings (e.g., home, school, community) and life domains (i.e., social, cultural, basic living skills, academics, etc.). Similar to quality of life indicators in the Person-Centered Planning (PCP) process associated with Positive Behavior Supports (Risley, 1996), "big needs" in wraparound are defined by the following criteria: (a) big enough that it will take awhile to achieve such as "James needs to feel respected at school," (b) there is more than one way to meet it. For example, "Hector needs to feel competent/able about learning" instead of "Hector will complete his assignments," (c) will motivate the family to want to participate on the team. For instance, "Maria's mother needs to feel confident that Maria will get treated fairly at school"; and (d) if met, will improve quality of life for the youth and/or those engaged with the youth on a regular basis (e.g., the family, the teacher).

Facilitating Wraparound

A team facilitator who is trained in this family-centered, strength-based philosophy and approach, leads the wraparound process. Potential wraparound facilitators in school systems include personnel who already lead intervention planning and meetings for youths with or at-risk of EBD, including school social workers, school psychologists, counselors, special education specialists, administrators, and so on (Eber, 2003).

The facilitator needs to be able to (a) engage youths, families, and teachers who have experienced failed interventions and therefore may feel frustrated, disillusioned, or angry; (b) translate youth, family and teacher "stories" into need statements and strength inventories that guide the design of interventions; (c) bring together youth, family, teacher, and natural supports to form a team; (d) ensure voice and ownership of interventions by those who are involved in implementation; and (e) organize and use multiple levels of data to guide the development and monitoring of interventions by the team on a regular basis. The role of a designated team facilitator is critical to ensure the process is adhered to and that the principles of the strength-based person/family centered approach are held fast. The wraparound facilitator guides the team through the phases of wraparound ensuring a commitment to "remain at the table," despite challenges and setbacks, until the needs of the youth and family are met and can be sustained without the wraparound team.

The Phases of the Wraparound Process

The Wraparound process is operationalized as a process with specific activities that occur across four distinct phases (Eber et al., 2009; Walker, 2008). The phases describe the steps in which a team is formed to develop, monitor, and continuously revise a plan that is focused on achieving success as defined by the youth and family.

Phase I: Engagement and Team Development lays the foundation for success by organizing relationships and support networks among youths, their families, and selected team members. During Phase I, the facilitator works closely with the family, youth, and teacher to build trust and ownership of the process. The family is encouraged to tell "their story" by articulating their perception of the strengths, needs, and experiences of their child and family. This initial contact involves a conversational discourse with the goals of: (a) developing a trusting relationship, (b) establishing an understanding of the process and what they can expect, and (c) seeking information about potential team members, strengths, and the overarching "big needs" that will guide the team's actions. During the initial conversations with the family, the facilitator assists the family to identify the natural supports, or persons who are connected to the family by relationship (e.g., relatives, friends, pastor) who may be able to participate in the wraparound process.

During *Phase II: Initial Plan Development*, the facilitator moves from engagement and assessing strengths and needs with the family and other potential team members to guiding the team through the initial wraparound meetings. Baseline data reflecting youth, family, and teacher perception of strengths and needs are shared and used to guide team consensus on and commitment to quality of life indicators, which are stated as the "big needs." These needs are prioritized and action planning begins as the facilitator guides team members to brainstorm strategies to increase strengths and meet needs. As strategies are developed, tasks and roles for all team members are clarified. A safety plan for school and/or home is developed if team members feel this to be an imminent need.

Phase III: Plan Implementation involves ongoing problem solving to effectively meet youths' needs, by combining supports for natural activities (e.g., child care, mentoring, making friends) with traditional interventions (e.g., function-based behavioral interventions, specialized reading instruction, medication). During Phase III, data-based progress monitoring is used to review initial plans and revise interventions in response to ongoing efforts. The facilitator ensures a regular meeting schedule for the team and continuous data collection and review of results so that data informs the team when things are/not working, thus sustaining objectivity among team members. Important Phase III activities including: (a) regular use of data for progress monitoring, (b) checking with the family to ensure that the plan is working, and (c) making adjustments to the wrap plan as indicated by feedback from team members. The significance of incorporating interventions across home, school, and community is highlighted.

Phase IV: Transition from Wraparound is the final phase of the wraparound process and marks the formal point of transition when frequent/regular meetings are not needed. During this phase accomplishments are reviewed and celebrated and a transition plan is developed. In Phase IV the youth/family is transitioned from the ongoing wraparound team to progress monitoring through less intensive structures, such as a parent teacher conference. Movement to Phase IV is determined by the ability to continue successful functioning with more natural supports and possibly to include continuation of one or more specific interventions that were put in place through the wraparound process (i.e., a behavior intervention plan at school, curriculum adaptations, and family connection to community-based mental health supports).

The Theory and Evidence Base for Wraparound

Burchard and his colleagues (Burchard, Bruns, & Burchard, 2002) identified ecological systems theory (Bronfenbrenner, 1979) and environmental ecology theory (Munger, 1998.) as compatible with wraparound. Both theories stress the influence of various systems (e.g., schools, health care, etc.) on the level of functioning for children and their families. Two related theories reflect the family-centered (Allen & Petr, 1998), strengths-based approach (Saleebey, 2001) of wraparound. The consistent underlying philosophy of wraparound is a change from "expert-driven" models as it places the family, not a mental health agency or the school, in the leadership role within the team process. Furthermore, the wraparound process emphasizes that services are identified and designed based on the needs of the families and youth rather than what the system has available and is experienced with providing. The ultimate goal is success for the youth within the context of their families and their home schools. These characteristics are what make wraparound a unique, family and community-based process that is often experienced differently than traditional mental health treatment planning or Individualized Educational Planning (IEP) procedures (Burchard, Bruns, & Burchard, 2002).

Wraparound has a growing evidence base yielding promising outcomes for youth with complex mental health needs. A recent meta-analysis of published, peer-reviewed, controlled research on the wraparound process (Suter & Bruns, 2009) demonstrated positive effects for youth receiving wraparound compared to youth receiving traditional services from mental health, child welfare, and juvenile justice service settings. The strongest effects were found for positive changes in the youth's living situation (e.g., successfully living at home rather than residential or hospital placements). Positive effects were also found for emotional and behavioral outcomes, reduced juvenile recidivism rates, and improved functioning at school (e.g., improved grades and attendance). Although there have been no controlled comparison studies of wraparound in schools, several researchers have examined the effectiveness of school-based wraparound, though not in conjunction with schools offering SWPBS. These studies found mixed positive results indicating that school-based wraparound can help retain youths in their local schools and communities (Eber, Osuch, & Redditt, 1996; Eber, Osuch, & Rolf, 1996), reduce behavioral problems and improve clinical functioning (Robbins, Collins, Witt, & Campbell, 2003; Vernberg, Jacobs, Nyre, Puddy, & Roberts, 2004; Vernberg, Roberts, Randall, Biggs, Nyre, Jacobs, 2006; Vernberg, Roberts, Jacobs, Randall, Biggs, & Nyre, 2008), and improved academic performance (Eber et al., 2007; Robbins, Collins, Witt, & Campbell, 2003), however findings were not consistent across all studies. Several attempts within the field of child and family services have been made to measure the fidelity of wraparound (Bruns et al., 2004; Epstein, et al., 1998) and findings from recent literature are starting to support a link between treatment fidelity and youth and family outcomes.

Wraparound in Schools

The wraparound approach offers a means for schools to succeed with the 1% to 2% of youths whose needs have become so complex that starting with an FBA/BIP process for one selected problem behavior is not efficient, effective or enough to improve quality of life issues for all those effected (Eber et al., 2009). These youths may have a range of problem behaviors with different or multiple functions across different settings. Typically, the adults in the youth's life are not getting along very well as failed interventions, which may have been too weak in dosage or intensity, can foster frustration, anxiety, and possibly fear. Blame is not uncommon; the schools may be blaming the family, the family may be blaming the school and both school and family may be blaming mental health or some other agency for not "fixing" the problems sufficiently. Wraparound allows schools the ability to shift into a more complex process that matches the intensity of problems described above. This provides the capability to partner effectively with families and community partners in a systematic process that blends home, school, and community interventions through a comprehensive yet practical plan. Through the wraparound process, lower-level interventions (school-wide instruction, small-group instruction, etc.) often begin to have an effect, thus effectively including the youth with complex needs in the daily routines and instruction provided for all youths.

Wraparound distinguishes itself from traditional service delivery in special education and mental health with its focus on connecting families, schools and community partners in effective problem-solving relationships. Unique implementation features include: (a) family and youth voice guide the design and actions of the team; (b) team composition and strategies reflect unique youth and family strengths and needs; (c) the team establishes the commitment and capacity to design and implement a comprehensive plan over time, and (d) the plan addresses outcomes across home, school, and community through one synchronized plan. Differing from IEP's and other typical school-based team processes, the wraparound process delineates specific roles for team members including natural support persons, (Eber, 2003) and detailed conditions for interventions, including specifying roles each person will play in specific circumstances.

Wraparound can be integrated into school-based planning for youths with special needs, regardless of special education label or agency involvement. The wraparound process provides a structure for schools to reposition themselves in a proactive partnership with families and community supports. The following two case studies illustrate how wraparound, as both a philosophy and a process, can effectively support youth, family, and teacher by proactively organizing and blending natural supports, interagency services, behavior supports, and academic interventions. Robert's wraparound story follows the Phase I team development into Phase III with continued wraparound planning/teaming and ongoing plan revisions to support Robert and his mother. A repeated pattern of hospitalizations was prevented through the wraparound process. Albert's story is a 2-year wraparound process that moved through Phase IV-Transition as Albert moved from a highly restrictive placement into general education placement in middle school with less intensive supports.

Robert had a history of psychiatric hospitalization prior to entering his new school in fourth grade where he had a pattern of disruptive and aggressive behaviors during the first few months. The school team put him quickly into a daily check-in-check-out (CICO) system with hourly points and added an individualized mentor (a community volunteer provided through a partnership with the school and a local church). He responded well to his mentor and began meeting daily behavior goals. However, by December, Robert was asking his mother if he could be hospitalized so "he could get better." Building upon the relationship established when the CICO and mentoring was initiated; the school social worker and mother quickly formed a wraparound team to include his teacher and his community mental health provider. During Phase I conversations, Robert stated he wanted "less yelling and more smiling" at home and he wanted "to do good at school." The stated big need that guided the team through the development of the wraparound plan was "Happiness at Home and School." Robert's mother expressed concerns about isolation in the community and identified the need for more social activities for Robert outside of school. At the first meeting (December 2009) the team, including strong participation from Robert, reviewed all the strengths and needs. Robert's mother was recognized for getting them to the mental health appointments in spite of the difficult commute with multiple buses. Robert's increase in daily points for behavioral goals achieved since the mentor was started was noted (see Figure W.1).

The team decided to continue the CICO and mentoring as well as community mental health services. They decided to complete a function-based behavior plan for school and

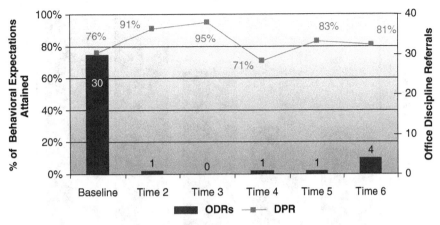

Figure W.1. Robert's daily progress report and office discipline referral data.

to assist the family in seeking YMCA membership. Robert asked to add his mentor to the team. At the second meeting (January 2010), the team noted improved behavior at home including helping with chores. No physical fights at school were also a noted improvement. The team completed the FBA/BIP to address the continued disruptive behavior at school in less structured settings where he engaged in altercations with peers. At the third meeting (March 2010), the team celebrated that he walked away from two potential fights, which he had never done before. Robert took the lead in reviewing his data noting improved daily points as well as areas "where I need to do better." Figure W.2 provides an example of the data discussed at the meeting. Engaging other community supports to assist in stabilizing their living situation in their current apartment was also discussed. The team continued to meet monthly to review progress, and make revisions to the plan.

Albert, the oldest of four siblings in a single-parent household, had been in a self-contained special education classroom for students with EBD for 2 years but his behavior problems had increased. When the wraparound process was initiated in August of 2008, his home and school

placements were considered to be at-risk as his behavior was escalating. His past relationships with his father and paternal grandmother were identified as strengths although these connections had been inconsistent during the previous 2 years. Initial needs identified during Phase I conversations with Albert and his mother included "Albert needs to feel like people care about him" and "Albert needs to feel it is possible to do well at school."

Albert's wrap team initially consisted of his mother, the school social worker who facilitated the team, a favorite teacher, and a youth counselor from a church he and his mother belonged to. During the first 6 months of the wrap team, connections with his father, paternal grandmother, and aunt were reestablished, and these extended family members also became team members. Other team members who participated over time included a coach from a summer camp, a mental health clinician from the local mental health center, and a city alderwoman who served as a community mentor for Albert. Interventions on Albert's wraparound plan (2008–2009 and 2009–2010) included:

- A CICO process with a daily progress report linked to the school-wide behavioral system

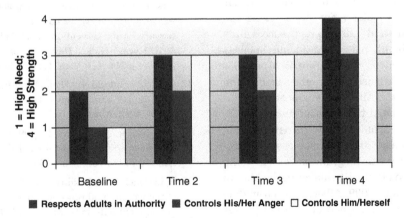

Figure W.2. Ratings of Robert's social/emotional functioning at school.

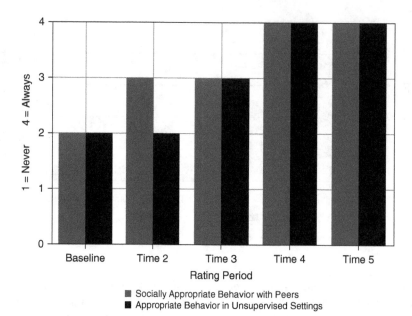

Figure W.3. Example of Albert's behavioral data.

- A function-based behavior plan to teach, prompt, and reinforce positive behaviors to replace the aggressive outburst
- Integration into general education academic classes
- Mentorship with community alderwoman
- Bike helmet, and lock
- Bus passes
- Summer programming in community
- Medical intervention for ADHD
- A community-based juvenile-diversion program

Albert experienced a significant decrease in problem behavior at school after the wraparound plan was initiated. For example, he had 19 major office discipline referrals (ODRs) and 45 days of alternative placement during the 2007–2008 school year but only 2 major ODRs during the 2008–2009 school year and only 2 major ODRs during the 2009–2010 school year. He experienced no alternative placement days during the 2009–2010 school year and participated successfully in general education for all his core academic subjects during the 2009–2010 school year. Figure W.3 provides an example of behavior data used for progress monitoring and celebrating successes at Albert's team meetings.

Other achievements noted by the team during the 2-year wraparound process included successful participation in summer camp (2009 and 2010) and successful participation in church-based youth program as well as being recognized and introduced to the city mayor in the Martin Luther King Day Parade in 2009. Albert entered middle school in the Fall of 2010 in all general education classes with behavioral supports.

REFERENCES

Allen, R. I., & Petr, C. G. (1998). Rethinking family-centered practice. *American Journal of Orthopsychiatry*, *68*, 196–204.

Bronfenbrenner, U. (1979). *The ecology of human development*. Cambridge, MA: Harvard University Press.

Bruns, E. J., Burchard, J. D., Suter, J. C., Leverentz-Brady, K., & Force, M. M. (2004). Assessing fidelity to a community based treatment for youth: The wraparound fidelity index. *Journal of Emotional and Behavioral Disorders*, *12*, 79–89.

Burchard, J. D., Bruns, E. J., & Burchard, S. N. (2002). The wraparound approach. In B. Burns & K. Hoagwood (Eds.), *Community treatment for youth: Evidence-based interventions for severe emotional and behavioral disorders*. New York, NY: Oxford University Press.

Eber, L. (2003). The art and science of wraparound: Completing the continuum of schoolwide behavioral support. Bloomington, IN: Forum on Education at Indiana University.

Eber, L., Hyde, K., Rose, J., Breen, K., McDonald, D., & Lewandowski, H. (2009). Completing the continuum of schoolwide positive behavior support: Wraparound as a tertiary-level intervention. In W. Sailor, G. Dunlap, G. Sugai, & R. Horner (Eds.), *Handbook of positive behavior support* (pp. 634–671). New York, NY: Springer.

Eber, L., Lewandoski, H., Hyde, K., & Bohanon, H. (2007). Illinois PBIS End-of-Year Progress Summaries. La Grange Park, IL: Illinois PBIS Network.

Eber, L., Nelson, M., & Miles, P. (1997). School-based wraparound for students with emotional and behavioral challenges. *Exceptional Children*, *67*(4), 539–555.

Eber, L. Osuch, R., & Redditt, C. (1996). School-based applications of the wraparound process: Early results on service provision and student outcomes. *Journal of Child and Family Studies*, *5*, 83–99.

Eber, L., Osuch, R., & Rolf, K. (1996). School-based wraparound: How implementation and evaluation can lead to system change. In C. Liberton, K. Kutash, & R. Friedman (Eds.), *The eighth annual research conference proceedings. A system of care for children's mental health: Expanding the research base* (pp. 143–147). Tampa, FL: University of South Florida, Florida Mental Health Institute, Research and Training Center for Children's Mental Health.

Epstein, M. H., Jayanthi, M., McKelvey, J., Frankenberry, E., Hardy, R., & Dennis, K. (1998). Reliability of the Wraparound Observation Form: An instrument to measure the wraparound process. *Journal of Child and Family Studies*, 7, 161–170.

Munger, R. L. (1998). *The ecology of troubled children*. Cambridge, MA: Brookline Press.

Risley, T. (1996). Get a life! Positive behavioral intervention for challenging behavior through life arrangement and life coaching. In L. K. Koegel, R. L. Koegel, & G. Dunlap (Eds.), *Positive behavior support: Including people with difficult behavior in the community*. Baltimore, MD: Paul H. Brookes.

Robbins, V., Collins, K., Witt, T., & Campbell, J. (2003). *Building bridges of support in eastern Kentucky: Promoting partnerships among families, educators, and mental health professionals*. In 14th Annual Conference Proceedings A System of Care for Children's Mental Health: Expanding the Research Base. Tampa, Florida: University of South Florida, Research and Training Center for Children's Mental Health.

Saleebey, D. (2001). *The strengths perspective in social work practice* (2nd ed.). New York, NY: Longman.

Suter, J. C., & Bruns, E. J. (2009). Effectiveness of the wraparound process for children with emotional and behavioral disorders: A meta-analysis. *Clinical Care and Family Psychology Review*, 12(4), 336–351.

VanDenBerg, J. (1999). History of the wraparound process. In B. J. Burns and S. K. Goldman (Eds.), *Promising practices in wraparound for children with serious emotional disturbance and their families* (Vol. 4, pp. 19–26). Washington, DC: Center for Effective Collaboration and Practice, American Institute for Research.

Vernberg, E. M., Jacobs, A. K., Nyre, J. E., Puddy, R. W., & Roberts, M. C. (2004). Innovative treatment for children with serious emotional disturbance: Preliminary outcomes for a school-based intensive mental health program. *Journal of Clinical Child and Adolescent Psychology*, 33, 359–365.

Vernberg, E. M., Roberts, M. C., Jacobs, A. K., Randall, C. J., Biggs, B. K., & Nyre, J. E. (2008). Outcomes and findings of program evaluation for the Intensive Mental Health Program. *Journal of Child and Family Studies*, 17(2), 178–190.

Vernberg, E. M., Roberts, M. C., Randall, C. J., Biggs, B. K., Nyre, J. E., & Jacobs, A. K. (2006). Intensive mental health services for children with serious emotional disturbances through a school-based, community-oriented program. *Clinical Child Psychology and Psychiatry*, 11, 417–430.

Walker, J. S. (2008). *How and why, does wraparound work: A theory of change*. Portland, OR: National Wraparound Initiative, Portland State University.

LUCILLE EBER
Statewide Director Illinois PBIS Network

WRAT-4 (*See* Wide Range Achievement Test–Fourth Edition)

WRITING AS EXPRESSIVE LANGUAGE

Because written expression is the most complex and the last form of language to be achieved, it can best be explained from a perspective that considers the influence of linguistic and cognitive abilities as well as the uniqueness of this expressive mode. The interrelatedness of language skills has been conceptualized by Myklebust (1965) in terms of a hierarchical construct that suggests that listening, speaking, reading, and writing develop in a progression that is ascendable and reciprocal. Implicit to this theory is the premise that competency at each rung of the language ladder is prerequisite to success at the next. Credibility for this paradigm has been provided by many researchers, including Loban (1976), who longitudinally followed a group of students from kindergarten through 12th grade and found a positive relationship of achievement among the language arts. Children who were judged to be good listeners and speakers in kindergarten were the same students who later excelled in reading and writing, retaining their status as superior language users throughout their school careers. Conversely, children who did not begin their schooling with oral language competence continued to be evaluated as below average in all language skills.

The concept that achievement in written forms is influenced by development in preceding forms has been easier to verify than the nature of the reciprocity that occurs among the linguistic functions. Wolf and Dickinson (1985) described the development of oral and written language systems as being profoundly interactive in that growth in each mode results in cognitive processing changes that exert influence in a cyclical manner. For example, these researchers noted that early phonological and metalinguistic development in oral language affects the acquisition of reading skills; in turn, achievement in the reading form influences perspectives of listening, speaking, and writing. Wolf and Dickinson further explained that written expression with its emphasis on refining alters one's cognitive orientation to speaking and reading. Thus it appears that written expression can be thought of as a shaper or enhancer of other linguistic forms.

Another complicating factor to understanding the relationship among language processes concerns the consideration that changes occur as development unfolds. Kroll (1981) has proposed a developmental model for examining the relationship between speaking and writing. This model describes four principal associations between these two expressive forms: The first phase is termed separate and involves the preparation for writing (the learning of technical skills required to produce the written symbols for speech); the second phase involves consolidation of oral and written language (the understanding that writing is similar to talk written down); the third phase focuses on differentiation of oral and written language (awareness that talking is more casually conversational than the formality of writing); and the fourth stage addresses the systematic integration of speaking and writing (the knowledge that a wide range of different forms can be used in both speaking and writing depending on the context, audience, and purpose of the communication). Although Kroll admitted that this model presents an oversimplification of the interaction that occurs, it is nonetheless helpful for explaining broad outlines of development.

For the individuals with disabilities, the acquisition of written expression is typically problematic. Difficulties that inhibit achievement in this skill can occur in each or all of the preceding forms; a child who has oral language deficits and/or reading problems will, in all likelihood, have deficiencies in written expression also. However, instruction in writing should not be postponed until competency in the other modes has been achieved. It is much more viable to simultaneously teach all language skills in a holistic manner that will encourage growth through reciprocity.

Phelps-Gunn and Phelps-Terasaki (1982) have described written expression from a multidimensional framework that considers the dynamics involved in effective writing. They have developed a Total Writing Process Model for identifying and remediating deficits. This model addresses problems with form, content, and structure; pragmatic abilities for audience and mode; and proofreading. This instructional plan appears to be extremely comprehensive and may prove to be an effective method for remediating writing deficits.

REFERENCES

Kroll, B. M. (1981). Developmental relationships between speaking and writing. In B. M. Kroll & R. J. Vann (Eds.), *Exploring speaking-writing relationships: Connections and contrasts* (pp. 32–54). Urbana, IL: National Council of Teachers of English.

Loban, W. (1976). *Language development: Kindergarten through grade twelve.* Urbana, IL: National Council of Teachers of English.

Myklebust, H. R. (1965). *Development and disorders of written language* (Vol. 1). New York, NY: Grune & Stratton.

Phelps-Gunn, T., & Phelps-Terasaki, D. (1982). *Written language instruction.* Rockville, MD: Aspen.

Wolf, M., & Dickinson, D. (1985). From oral to written language: Transition in school years. In J. B. Gleason (Ed.), *The development of language* (pp. 227–76). Columbus, OH: Merrill.

PEGGY L. ANDERSON
University of New Orleans, Lakefront

See also Writing Assessment; Writing Remediation

WRITING ASSESSMENT

Competence in writing requires the mastery and automation of a vast array of skills. To ensure that these skills develop in an efficient and efficacious manner, it is generally believed that assessment should be included as an integral part of disabled students' writing programs. This belief is primarily based on the assumption that information from the assessment process should make it possible for teachers to more readily determine a student's writing strengths and weaknesses, individualize instruction, monitor writing performance, and evaluate the effectiveness of the composition program.

The assessment of disabled students' writing should focus on both the written product and the process of writing (Graham, 1982). There are a host of procedures for evaluating the various attributes embodied in the written product; the most popular of these will be reviewed at length. Relatively few techniques, however, are available for examining the process by which students compose. The most common procedures include: (a) observing and, in some instances, timing the various activities and behaviors that the student engages in during the act of writing; (b) interviewing students about their approach to writing and questioning them about their reasons for particular composing behaviors; and (c) asking students to verbally report what they are thinking while they write. Regrettably, the reliability and validity of these procedures have not been adequately established and the results from such assessments may, as many critics have suggested, yield a distorted picture of the writing process (Humes, 1983).

Both formal and informal assessment procedures have been used to examine the relative merits and/or shortcomings of disabled students' writing. The most frequently used standardized test is the Test of Written Language (TOWL). According to the authors (Hammill & Larsen, 1983), this instrument "can be used to ascertain the general adequacy of a product written by a student and to determine specific proficiency in word usage, punctuation and capitalization (style), spelling, handwriting, vocabulary, and sentence production" (p. 5). The TOWL consists of six subtests. Scores for three of these subtests (vocabulary, thematic maturity, and handwriting) are derived from a spontaneous sample of writing. The remaining word usage, spelling, and style subtests employ a contrived format; for example, a student's proficiency in word usage is determined by a sentence completion activity. Although the TOWL appears to have a sound theoretical basis and to be reasonably valid and reliable, there is some question as to the value of the vocabulary and thematic maturity scores (Williams, 1985).

A second standardized test that has been used with disabled students is the Picture Story Language Test (PSLT; Myklebust, 1965). The PSLT has been used as a writing achievement test, a diagnostic instrument, and a research tool for studying the development and disorders of written language. In using this test, a student writes a story in response to a picture and the resulting composition is scored in terms of productivity (number of words, sentences, and words per sentence), correctness (word usage, word endings, and punctuation), and meaning (actual content conveyed). Although the PSLT has been widely used with disabled students, serious questions regarding the validity and reliability of the instrument have been raised (Anastasiow, 1972).

Informal assessment procedures have been used to assess a variety of factors ranging from story quality to writing mechanics. Not surprisingly, the quality of students' writing has proven to be the most difficult factor to define and measure. Probably the oldest measure of writing quality is the holistic method. With this method, an examiner makes a single overall judgment on the quality of a student's writing (Mishler & Hogan, 1982). Each paper is read at a fairly rapid pace and the examiner attempts to weigh the various factors (content, organization, grammar) in roughly equal proportions. The examiner's overall impression is quantified on a Likert-type scale, ranging from poor to high quality. To increase accuracy and reliability, most holistic scoring systems include representative examples of specific scores.

A more complex procedure for determining the quality of a student's writing is the analytic method. With this method, the student's paper is analyzed and scored on the basis of several different factors such as ideation, grammar, and spelling (Moran, 1982). The scores for each of these factors are then averaged to produce a single grand score. Although the analytic method may provide more useful information for instructional purposes, it is much more time-consuming than the holistic method.

A relatively recent development in the measurement of writing quality is the primary trait scoring method. With this procedure, different scoring systems are developed for different writing tasks. For a task such as writing a short story, the examiner would decide ahead of time what traits should be evaluated and what types of response will be considered appropriate and inappropriate for each trait. For example, for a short story, one of the primary traits might be the introduction and development of the protagonist (Graham & Harris, 1986). Consequently, stories that adequately present and develop the leading character would receive credit for this trait.

It must be pointed out that measures of writing quality can be influenced by a variety of factors (Graham, 1982). One prominent source of variability involves the writer. Students often evidence considerable variation in their writing quality from one assignment to the next. Writing performance also can be influenced by the popularity of the proctor, the intended audience, teacher directions, and so on. An additional source of variability resides in the examiner. There is considerable evidence that grades assigned to student's papers tend to be unreliable. Fortunately, the

consistency with which examiners score writing quality can be improved if the following guidelines and recommendations are followed: (a) examiners should receive considerable practice and training in using the intended scoring procedure; (b) the writing task should be highly structured and the assigned topic should be interesting; (c) identifying factors such as name, grade, and date should be removed from each paper; and (d) papers should not be graded for lengthy periods of time or in noisy or distracting environments.

A number of procedures have been used to evaluate the various elements embodied in the written products. Writing fluency has typically been assessed by examining total number of words written, average sentence length, and number of words written per minute. Vocabulary diversity has been measured by counting the occurrence of particular vocabulary items such as adjectives or adverbs and by computing the corrected type/token ratio (number of different words divided by the square root of twice the number of words in the sample) or the index of diversification (average number of words that appear between each occurrence of the most frequently used word in a composition). Proficiency with the mechanics of writing is generally determined by tabulating the occurrence of a particular behavior (e.g., spelling errors), while syntactic maturity is often defined in terms of the average length of T-units (main clause plus any attached or embedded subordinate clauses).

It is important to note that students' knowledge of their writing performance can be a powerful motivator and have a potent effect on learning. Nevertheless, the value of circling every misspelled word, writing "AWK" above every clumsy wording, or red-marking each deviation from standard English is questionable. Intensive evaluation may have little or no effect on writing improvement and may, in fact, make students more aware of their limitations and less willing to write (Burton & Arnold, 1963). Feedback on the positive aspects of a student's composition, in contrast, can have a facilitative effect on writing performance (Beaven, 1977). It also is desirable to dramatize a student's success through the use of charts, graphs, verbal praise, and so on.

REFERENCES

Anastasiow, N. (1972). Review of the Picture Story Language Test. In O. K. Buros (Ed.), *Seventh mental measurement yearbook*. Highland Park, NJ: Gryphon.

Beaven, M. (1977). Individualized goal setting, self-evaluation, and peer evaluation. In C. Cooper & L. Odell (Eds.), *Evaluating writing: Describing, measuring, judging* (pp. 135–156). Urbana, IL: National Council of Teachers of English.

Burton, D., & Arnold, L. (1963). The effects of frequency of writing and intensity of teacher evaluation upon high school students' performance in written composition. (Research Report No. 1523). Tallahassee, FL: USOE Cooperative.

Graham, S. (1982). Composition research and practice: A unified approach. *Focus on Exceptional Children, 14,* 1–16.

Graham, S., & Harris, K. (1986). Improving learning disabled students' compositions via story grammars: A component analysis of self-control strategy training. Paper presented at the American Educational Research Association, San Francisco.

Hammill, D., & Larsen, S. (1983). *Test of Written Language.* Austin, TX: PRO-ED.

Humes, A. (1983). Research on the composing process. *Review of Educational Research, 53,* 201–216.

Mishler, C., & Hogan, T. (1982). Holistic scoring of essays: Remedy for evaluating the third R. *Diagnostique, 8,* 4–16.

Moran, M. (1982). Analytic evaluation of formal written language skills as a diagnostic procedure. *Diagnostique, 8,* 17–31.

Myklebust, H. (1965). *Development and disorders of written language.* New York, NY: Grune & Stratton.

Williams, R. (1985). Review of Test of Written Language. In J. V. Mitchell (Ed.), *Ninth mental measurement yearbook.* Lincoln: University of Nebraska Press.

STEVE GRAHAM
University of Maryland

See also **Writing Remediation**

WRITING DISORDERS

Although research on writing disorders in context is limited, the sources of difficulty emerge when they are considered within a framework or model of writing. Writing is a complex cognitive activity (Hayes & Flower, 1980) that requires writers to coordinate and regulate the use of task-specific strategies during three overlapping and recursive writing stages (i.e., prewriting, drafting, revising). During prewriting, task-specific strategies focus on planning and organizing. Writers generate and select writing topics, decide on a purpose for writing, identify the audience, generate and gather ideas about the topic, and organize the ideas into a network or structural plan (e.g., text structure such as story narrative, compare/contrast, sequence). During drafting, task-specific strategies involve the activation of the structural plan, translation of ideas into printed sentences, fleshing out of placeholders in the plan with details, and signaling of relationships among the elements of the plan. During monitoring and revising, task-specific strategies pertain to evaluation and analysis. The writer reads the draft to see whether the objectives concerning audience, topic, purpose, and structure have been achieved, and then he or she applies correction strategies to portions of the text that fail to meet expectations.

Though these task-specific strategies are necessary, they are not sufficient for skilled writing. A second domain involves the execution of these strategies. Metacognitive knowledge is the executive or self-control mechanism that helps writers activate and orchestrate activities in each of the writing stages. Metacognitive knowledge includes the ability to self-instruct or direct oneself in the writing stages, to monitor strategy use, and to modify or correct strategy use on the basis of outcomes. Without metacognitive knowledge, writers fail to access writing strategies and monitor their use even when the strategies are in their behavioral repertoire.

A third domain includes the mechanical skills that make writing a fluent process. This domain involves writers' knowledge of rules related to spelling (orthographic knowledge), writing conventions (punctuation, capitalization), and language (syntactic knowledge). These skills are of primary importance to writers in the stage of final revision in light of the importance of legibility to the audience. In addition, for the successful strategic employment of these skills, writers must not only acquire mechanical skills, they must acquire the task-specific strategies and metacognitive knowledge governing their use. For example, writers who lack task-specific strategies may not know how to rehearse or study spelling words to improve recall, whereas writers who lack metacognitive knowledge may learn to accurately spell words for the weekly spelling test, but fail to accurately spell or monitor their spelling of the same words in written compositions. Skillful writers not only acquire the mechanical means to produce text, they acquire the cognitive tools that help them know when and how to use those means, how to monitor their use, and how to correct errors when they occur.

According to this model of writing, writing disorders may result from one of several causes (Walmsley, 1983). First, writing disorders may emanate from a lack of understanding of task-specific strategies. For example, disabled writers with task-specific strategy deficits in the use of specific organizational structures may have trouble employing a relevant text structure that can guide them in planning, organizing, drafting, and monitoring their ideas. Second, writing disabilities may result from deficiencies in metacognitive knowledge. Such writers may have learned strategies but fail to activate them in the appropriate situations. Third, impairments in related cognitive processes may affect writing performance. Specifically, inadequate or delayed development in listening, speaking, or reading may affect writing performance since these processes share a common language base and rely on similar strategic processes involving the communication and comprehension of ideas. Finally, the failure to acquire specific rule-governed principles in spelling, grammar, and writing conventions can detrimentally affect the mechanics of writing, writing fluency, and overall comprehensibility.

More is known about the specific disabilities of students in the domain of writing mechanics than is known about disabilities in the use of task-specific strategies or metacognitive knowledge. Several studies confirm that disabled learners commit more punctuation and capitalization errors than nondisabled learners (Myklebust, 1973; Poplin et al., 1980; Poteet, 1978). These deficiencies have been observed in terms of students' ability to rewrite sentences containing punctuation and capitalization errors and to generate error-free compositions. Even greater performance differences between disabled and nondisabled students have been found on measures of spelling accuracy (Myklebust, 1973; Poplin et al., 1980; Poteet, 1978). Furthermore, disabled learners have deficiencies in their ability to apply task-specific strategies involving the study of spelling words (Foster & Torgesen, 1983) and in their application of metacognitive knowledge to detect and correct spelling errors (Deshler, 1978). However, several studies suggest that strategy and metacognitive deficits may be ameliorated with training. For example, research suggests that spelling deficits can be partly overcome by the teaching of task-specific strategies involving procedures for studying spelling words (Graham & Freeman, 1985; Nulman & Gerber, 1984), and for spelling novel words by analogy to known words (Englert, Hiebert, & Stewart, 1985). Likewise, metacognitive deficiencies involving the monitoring, detection, and correction of spelling errors or mechanical errors may be remediated with self-instructional training that directs students to reread and correct errors (Schumaker et al., 1982).

Mechanical aspects involving syntactic skills also have been studied, but the results are more equivocal. On tasks that require students to produce the correct syntactic form (e.g., subject-verb agreement, plurals) in incomplete sentences, disabled writers perform significantly lower than nondisabled writers (Poplin et al., 1980). On the other hand, on measures of syntactic complexity based on the average length of sentences and clauses produced by students, several studies have reported no qualitative differences in the presence of certain syntactic structures or the complexity of sentences (Moran, 1981; Nodine, Barenbaum, & Newcomer, 1985; Poteet, 1978). At the same time, several studies have found quantitative differences in students' written productions: Disabled writers produced significantly fewer sentences and fewer total words (Myklebust, 1973; Nodine et al., 1985; Poteet, 1978). Thus, performance seems to be delimited less by students' syntactic inadequacies than by difficulties in knowing how to generate ideas and how to sustain thoughts about a topic.

Though mechanical skills are important, they are not the barrier to proficient writing once thought (Walmsley, 1983). The teaching of mechanical skills does not necessarily improve the quality of compositions, and young writers do not need to master the mechanics of writing before being introduced to writing. Instead, writers' knowledge of task-specific strategies in the actual composing process may be a more critical determinant of writing success. Of particular importance in the domain of composing strategies is students' awareness of text structures. Text structures are specific organizational schemes internalized by writers that describe the elements that should be included and how they should be ordered. There are different text structures for different writing purposes. For example, stories usually consist of five major elements: a setting (i.e., main character, time, place), a problem confronting the main character, the main character's response to the problem, the outcome of the response, and the story's conclusion. Similarly, expository materials contain structures such as compare/contrast, problem/solution, and chronological sequence. Knowledge of these structures influences the ability of writers to successfully plan, generate, organize, compose, and monitor their ideas.

Nodine et al. (1985) conducted one of the few studies examining children's use of a story structure in written compositions. A group of learning-disabled, reading-disabled, and normally achieving students were asked to write a story about three related pictures. The results suggested that learning-disabled (LD) students differed from both reading-disabled and normally achieving students in their ability to produce a tale that was storylike. Almost half of the LD students failed to generate a story that met story structure expectations. Furthermore, LD students were less aware of potential confusions caused by unrelated or inexplicable events in their compositions. Similar deficits in structural awareness have been reported in studies examining students' knowledge of expository text structures (Wong & Wilson, 1984).

The domain important to both the successful use of task-specific strategies and mechanical skills in composing is metacognitive knowledge. Metacognitive knowledge includes the abilities to self-instruct, self-monitor, self-correct, and self-regulate the writing process. Several studies suggest that disabled learners have serious deficiencies in their ability to activate previously learned strategies and to self-instruct or self-monitor during text production and comprehension (Bos & Filip, 1984; Wong, 1985). That these problems are attributable to metacognitive knowledge is suggested by two studies that indicate that the training of self-control processes improves composing and organizational abilities. Wong and Sawatsky (1984), for example, taught LD students to elaborate on or finish an initial sentence stem (e.g., The tall man helped the woman) by employing a five-step self-control procedure that helped students determine the writing purpose, draft a response, and monitor their writing. Following training, the sentence elaborations of students significantly improved. Similarly, Wong and Wilson (1984) trained LD students to organize scrambled passages by applying a five-step self-instructional procedure. The ease with which students were trained suggested that the LD children may have had some rudimentary idea about passage organization, but it was either incompletely developed or not spontaneously activated by the students. Since students readily benefited from self-control training, the results suggested that metacognitive strategies were similarly inactive or incomplete.

In summary, the literature suggests that several deficiencies may impede students' writing performance. Deficiencies in spelling, grammar, and writing conventions have been reported—though these may not be the barriers to writing success as much as students' lack of task-specific strategies and metacognitive knowledge. Research is still needed to determine the impact of other elements of the writing process (e.g., audience, prior knowledge) on performance in each of the writing stages. However, it is certain that writing competence will be associated not only with the acquisition of efficient strategies pertaining to the use of each element, but with the metacognitive knowledge that helps the writer know when and how to use the element in planning, drafting, monitoring, and revising compositions.

REFERENCES

Bos, C. S., & Filip, D. (1984). Comprehension monitoring in learning disabled and average students. *Journal of Learning Disabilities, 17*, 229–233.

Deshler, D. D. (1978). *Psychoeducational aspects of learning-disabled adolescents.* In L. M. Mann, L. Goodman, & T. L. Wiederholt (Eds.), *Teaching the learning-disabled adolescent.* Boston, MA: Houghton Mifflin.

Englert, C. S., Hiebert, E. H., & Stewart, S. R. (1985). Spelling unfamiliar words by an analogy strategy. *Journal of Special Education, 19*, 291–306.

Englert, C. S., & Thomas, C. C. (1987). Sensitivity to text structure in reading and writing: A comparison of learning disabled and nonhandicapped students. *Learning Disability Quarterly, 10*, 93–105.

Foster, K., & Torgesen, J. K. (1983). The effects of directed study on the spelling performance of two subgroups of learning disabled students. *Learning Disability Quarterly, 6*, 252–257.

Graham, S., & Freeman, S. (1985). Strategy training and teacher- vs. student-controlled study conditions: Effects on LD students' spelling performance. *Learning Disability Quarterly, 8*, 267–274.

Hayes, J. R., & Flower, L. S. (1980). Writing as problem solving. *Visible Language, 14*, 388–399.

Moran, M. R. (1981). Performance of learning disabled and low achieving secondary students on formal features of a paragraph-writing task. *Learning Disability Quarterly, 4*, 271–280.

Myklebust, H. R. (1973). Development and disorders of written language. Vol. 2. Studies of normal and exceptional children. New York, NY: Grune & Stratton.

Nodine, B. F., Barenbaum, E., & Newcomer, P. (1985). Story composition by learning disabled, reading disabled, and normal children. *Learning Disability Quarterly, 8*, 167–179.

Nulman, J.A.H., & Gerber, M. M. (1984). Improving spelling performance by imitating a child's errors. *Journal of Learning Disabilities, 17*, 328–333.

Poplin, M. S., Gray, R., Larsen, S., Barikoski, A., & Mehring, T. (1980). A comparison of components of written expression abilities in learning disabled and non-learning disabled students at three grade levels. *Learning Disability Quarterly, 3*, 46–53.

Poteet, J. A. (1978). Characteristics of written expression of learning disabled and non-learning disabled elementary school students. Muncie, IN: Ball State University. (ERIC Document Reproduction Service No. ED 1590830)

Schumaker, J. B., Deshler, D. D., Alley, G. R., Warner, M. M., Clark, F. L., & Nolan, S. (1982). Error monitoring: A learning strategy for improving adolescent academic performance. In M. W. Cruickshank & J. W. Lerner (Eds.), *Coming of age: Vol. 3. The best of ACLD.* Syracuse, NY: Syracuse University Press.

Walmsley, S. A. (1983). Writing disability. In P. Mosenthal, L. Tamor, & S. A. Walmsley (Eds.), *Research on writing: Principles and methods.* New York, NY: Longman.

Wong, B. Y. L. (1985). Metacognition and learning disabilities. In D. L. Forrest-Pressley, G. E. MacKinnon, & T. G. Waller (Eds.), *Metacognition, cognition and human performance: Vol. 2. Instructional practices* (pp. 137–80). New York, NY: Academic Press.

Wong, B. Y. L., & Sawatsky, D. (1984). Sentence elaboration and retention of good, average and poor readers. *Learning Disability Quarterly, 7*, 229–236.

Wong, B. Y. L., & Wilson, M. (1984). Investigating awareness of and teaching passage organization in learning disabled children. *Journal of Learning Disabilities, 17*, 477–482.

CAROL SUE ENGLERT
Michigan State University

See also Writing Assessment; Writing Remediation

WRITING REMEDIATION

The writing difficulties exhibited by many students with disabilities necessitate the development and use of instructional procedures aimed at improving writing competence, particularly in terms of disabled students' functional writing skills. The remediation of disabled students' writing difficulties, however, has not received much attention in either the research literature or in school settings. Leinhardt, Zigmond, and Cooley (1980) found, for example, that disabled students may spend less than 10 minutes a day generating written language. Although there are many possible reasons why writing remediation appears to receive a limited amount of time and emphasis in handicapped students' instructional programs, teacher attitudes and backgrounds may be the key factors in determining the quantity and quality of writing instruction for these students. According to Graham (1982), many teachers do not enjoy writing and are not prepared to teach composition. Furthermore, many special education teachers may feel that writing is not a critical skill for their students and may choose to spend their instructional time teaching what they consider to be more important skills (e.g., reading, arithmetic).

For the most part, writing instruction for disabled students has drawn heavily on techniques used with normally achieving youngsters. One commonly recommended instructional procedure has been to use a phase approach. This approach emphasizes the various stages of the composition process (prewriting, writing, and revising) and is designed to develop security in the use of these stages. In a phase approach described by Silverman et al. (1981), the teacher first structures the writing process with prewriting activities that involve thinking, experiencing, discussing, and interacting. The student and the teacher then develop a series of questions that are used to guide the writing process. During the revising stage, the teacher critiques the student's writing and they jointly revise the student's paper. Although empirical support for this particular model or other phase approaches is limited, this writing procedure does stress the development of two important skills: thinking as a preliminary facet of composing and revision of the initial draft of the written product. In addition, a phase approach to writing may be especially suitable for disabled students since it helps reduce cognitive strain by taking a large complex problem such as writing and breaking it down into smaller subproblems.

Another traditional approach that has been used to teach specific writing skills to disabled students is modeling. With this approach, students may be asked to imitate a specific type of sentence pattern, a well-known style of writing, a certain type of paragraph, and so on. There are two basic approaches to modeling. One approach stresses strategy explanation and model illustration; the other emphasizes problem solving. With the former, a student may be asked to mimic a specific type of paragraph (e.g., topic sentence located at the start of the paragraph) following an examination and analysis of several examples that are representative of the style to be emulated. The latter can be illustrated by examining a procedure developed by Schiff (1978). With this procedure, examples of a particular type of paragraph are selected. Sentences for each paragraph are then written on a separate strip of paper and their order randomized. Students rearrange the sentences in each paragraph and compare their arrangements with the original model. At present, it is impossible to draw any definitive conclusions on the relative effectiveness of these procedures, as there is virtually no research that examines them.

A great deal of attention has been directed at teaching disabled students information about language and writing with the aim of promoting the correct use of structure, form, and language. One of the most consistently held beliefs in the history of writing instruction is that the teaching of grammar and usage is critical to the development of writing competence. Formal grammar, however, is difficult to master and knowledge of grammatical concepts does not appear to be necessary for the skillful use of written language (Blount, 1973). This is not meant to imply that teachers should not attend to disabled students' use of structure or form in their writing or that these skills cannot be improved. Rather, improvement of usage and form "may be more effectively achieved through direct practice of desirable forms when the need arises" (Graham, 1982, p. 6).

An interesting alternative to traditional writing approaches is the use of procedures that seek to minimize or circumvent disabled students' poor writing skills. The most commonly used alternative is dictation. Traditionally, dictation has involved having a student furnish the content or ideas orally while the teacher or a peer structures the form the material takes on paper. The conventional dictation process can be adapted by using a tape recorder as an aid to organizing content (i.e., ideas are taped and later written and edited by the student). In some instances, dictation is employed as a temporary aid and its use diminishes as the student becomes more adept at the mechanics of writing. Dictation may represent a viable alternative for students with adequate oral language skills who have been unable, after years of intensive instruction, to automate and integrate basic writing skills.

A recent alternative to traditional writing instruction approaches is the cognitive-behavior modification (CBM) procedure. Typically CBM training involves teaching students to regulate task-specific and metacognitive strategies through processes such as self-instruction, self-assessment, and self-reinforcement (Harris, 1982). For example, Harris and Graham (1985) reported a CBM composition training procedure that significantly increased learning-disabled students' use of verbs, adverbs, and adjectives and resulted in higher-quality story ratings. Further, generalization and maintenance probes taken up to 14 weeks after training yielded positive results. The CBM training regimen in this study included skills training (instruction on specific task-appropriate strategies), metacognitive training (instruction in the self-regulation of those strategies), and instruction concerning the significance of such activities. In a second study, Graham and Harris (1986) found that CBM procedures also could be used to improve the overall structure of learning-disabled students' compositions through the use of a story grammar strategy. Training procedures were similar to those in the first study; however, strategy training consisted of instruction in story grammar elements: setting, goal(s), action(s), emotional responses, and ending.

Educators also have attempted to improve disabled students' writing skills by further refining or developing their reading, oral language, and thinking skills. Since reading, writing, thinking, and language skills are interrelated, it is assumed that intensive and generalized instruction in an area such as oral language, for example, will have an indirect and positive effect on a student's writing ability (Groff, 1978). Although these skills may be interrelated, they do not necessarily function in an interactive and supportive way. Generalized instruction in an area such as reading or oral language appears to be of limited value in the immediate improvement of a student's writing (Graham, 1982).

A recent development in the teaching of writing to students with disabilities has been the advent of the computer, particularly the word processor. The word processor, with its various capabilities for storing and editing texts, has the potential to both strengthen and significantly change the nature of writing instruction. The word processor and other technological advances should not, however, be viewed as a cure-all for disabled students' writing problems. MacArthur and Graham (1986), for instance, found no major differences between handwritten stories and those composed on a word processor, even though the learning-disabled students in their study had considerable experience using the computer.

Additional instructional recommendations for teaching writing to students with disabilities have been summarized by Graham (1982). These include (a) providing students with plenty of opportunities to write and exposing them to a variety of practical and imaginative assignments; (b) having writing assignments, whenever possible, serve a real purpose and be directed at an authentic audience; (c) having a pleasant and encouraging composition program; and (d) deemphasizing writing errors.

REFERENCES

Blount, N. (1973). Research on teaching literature, language, and composition. In R. Travers (Ed.), *Second handbook of research on teaching*. Chicago, IL: Rand McNally.

Graham, S. (1982). Composition research and practice: A unified approach. *Focus on Exceptional Children, 14,* 1–16.

Graham, S., & Harris, K. (1986). Improving learning disabled students' compositions via story grammars: A component analysis of self-control strategy training. Paper presented at the American Educational Research Association, San Francisco.

Groff, P. (1978). Children's oral language and their written composition. *Elementary School Journal, 78,* 181–191.

Harris, K. (1982). Cognitive behavior modification: Application with exceptional students. *Focus on Exceptional Children, 15,* 1–16.

Harris, K., & Graham, S. (1985). Improving learning disabled students' composition skills: Self-control strategy training. *Learning Disability Quarterly, 8,* 27–36.

Leinhardt, G., Zigmond, N., & Cooley, W. (1980). *Reading instruction and its effects.* Paper presented at the American Educational Research Association, Boston.

MacArthur, C., & Graham, S. (1986). *LD students' writing under three conditions: Word processing, dictation, and handwriting.* Paper presented at the American Educational Research Association, San Francisco.

Schiff, P. (1978). Problem solving and the composition model: Reorganization, manipulation, analysis. *Research in the Teaching of English, 12,* 203–210.

Silverman, R., Zigmond, N., Zimmerman, J., & Vallecorsa, A. (1981). Improving written expression in learning disabled students. *Topics in Language Disorders, 1,* 91–99.

STEVE GRAHAM
KAREN R. HARRIS
University of Maryland

See also Writing Assessment; Writing Disorders

WYATT V. STICKNEY

The case of *Wyatt v. Stickney* established constitutionally minimum standards of care; in the past two decades, *Wyatt* has been credited with establishing the legal precedent for a constitutional right to treatment for involuntarily committed mentally ill patients. Directly addressing Alabama's state institutions for the mentally ill and mentally retarded, this case represented a landmark federal judicial intervention in the mental institutions of a sovereign state and signaled dozens of *Wyatt*-type "right to treatment" lawsuits in nearly every part of the country.

As a result of the unrefuted "atrocities" documented in *Wyatt* (1972), the shocking and inhumane conditions in New York's Willowbrook State School for the Mentally Retarded (1973), and 25 other suits involving the U.S. Justice Department (1979), congressional legislation for financial assistance and a "Bill of Rights" for institutionalized persons were enacted.

Only six decisions based on the Wyatt case have ever been published in the law reports (1971–1981), although it is cited in over 200 judicial decisions and is the subject of numerous law reviews and other professional journal articles.

Ricky Wyatt was one of about 5,000 mental patients at Bryce State Hospital, Tuscaloosa, the same hospital established in 1861 through the urging of the advocate Dorothea Dix. Stonewall B. Stickney was a psychiatrist and the chief administrative officer of Alabama's Mental Health Board. The case was filed initially by 99 of 100 dismissed staff members plus Ricky Wyatt's aunt and other guardians on October 23, 1970. The plaintiff employees alleged that this reduction in staff would deprive patients at Bryce of necessary treatment and sued for reinstatement. Stickney had released over 100 of the 1,600 employees at Bryce owing to reduced state cigarette tax revenues allocated to the department, while redirecting the limited funds to community mental health services. Stickney believed in preventing institutionalization.

The employee plaintiffs withdrew their reinstatement claim prior to Judge Frank M. Johnson's initial reported decision on March 12, 1971. The court found that more than 1,500 geriatric patients and about 1,000 mentally retarded patients were involuntarily committed at Bryce for reasons other than being mentally ill and were receiving custodial care but not treatment.

Judge Johnson ordered the development and implementation of adequate treatment standards and a report within 6 months; he requested the U.S. departments of Justice and Health, Education, and Welfare, as "friends of the court," to assist in evaluating the treatment programs and standards. On August 12, 1971, the court allowed the request. All involuntary patients from Partlow State School and Hospital in Tuscaloosa, housing nearly 2,500 mental retardates with segregated facilities for blacks, and Searcy Hospital in Mount Vernon, a formerly all-black hospital for the mentally ill, were to be included in the class suit. Defendants filed the court-directed report on September 23, 1971, and Judge Johnson ruled on December 10, 1971, allowing the state 6 months to correct three basic deficiencies. He called for "a humane psychological and physical environment,... qualified staff in numbers sufficient to administer adequate treatment, and... individualized treatment plans." Following additional testimony, briefs, and standards proposed by "the foremost authorities on mental health in the United States," the parties agreed to standards that mandated a "constitutionally acceptable minimum treatment program" for the mentally ill at Bryce and Searcy as ordered by the court on April 13, 1972.

Judge Johnson also ruled, in a supplemental order issued the same day, that unrebutted evidence of the "hazardous and deplorable inadequacies in the institution's operations at Partlow was more shocking than at Bryce or Searcy." He said that "The result of almost 50 years of legislative neglect has been catastrophic; atrocities occur daily"; Judge Johnson published these findings (1972):

> A few of the atrocious incidents cited at the hearing in this case include the following: (a) a resident was scalded to death by hydrant water; (b) a resident was restrained in a straitjacket for 9 years in order to prevent hand and finger sucking; (c) a resident was inappropriately confined in seclusion for a period of years, and (d) a resident died from the insertion by another resident of a running water hose into his rectum. Each of these incidents could have been avoided had adequate staff and facilities been available.

Judge Johnson ordered the defendants to (a) implement the standards for adequate habilitation for the retarded at Partlow; (b) establish a human rights committee; (c) employ a new administrator; (d) submit a progress report to the court within 6 months; and (e) pay attorneys' fees and costs to the plaintiffs.

The defendants appealed both decisions to the Fifth Circuit Court of Appeals in May 1972. The review court, on November 8, 1974, upheld the constitutional right to treatment concept and ruled that the federal judicially determined standards did not violate the state's legislative rights.

This entry has been informed by the sources listed below.

REFERENCES

Civil rights of the institutionalized. Report of the Committee on Judiciary United States Senate on S.10 together with minority and additional views. (1979). Washington, DC: U.S. Government Printing Office.

Wyatt v. Stickney, 325 F.Supp. 781 [M.D. Ala. 1972].

LOUIS SCHWARTZ
Florida State University
First edition

KIMBERLY F. APPLEQUIST
University of Colorado at Colorado Springs
Third edition

See also History of Special Education; Philosophy of Education for Individuals with Disabilities

WYBURN-MASON SYNDROME

Wyburn-Mason syndrome, also known as Bonnet-Dechaume-Blanc syndrome, is a rare condition that is characterized by arteriovenous malformations (i.e., abnormal communication between the arteries and veins) in the central nervous system and the retina. These malformations take the form of arteriovenous aneurysms, which are widenings of the walls of an artery and a vein with abnormal blood flow between the vessels. This condition is considered to be congenital, and it is passed on via autosomal dominant inheritance, which means that an affected person has a 50% chance of passing the trait to a child. In 1937, Bonnet et al. recognized the coexistence of retinal and cerebral arteriovenous malformations (AVMs). In 1943, Wyburn-Mason recorded cases of arteriovenous malformations of the midbrain, retina, and facial nevi and found that this syndrome may also be associated with mental changes in some cases.

Prior to 1973, only 43 cases had been reported in the literature. Between then and October 1998, a further 30 cases were described. Based on the literature available so far, there does not appear to be any race predilection. Additionally, males and females are equally likely to be affected.

Characteristics

1. Wyburn-Mason syndrome is characterized by vascular malformations of the brain and of the nerve-rich, innermost membranes of the eyes

2. It typically presents with unilateral vascular abnormalities involving the facial structures, orbits, and brain; this means that the vascular (or blood vessel) abnormalities typically occur only on one side of the brain and face

3. Symptoms of lowered vision (or blindness) typically appear in the second and third decades of life but may appear in the first

4. Progressive protrusion of the eye may occur

5. Chronic intermittent headaches

6. Birthmarks or pigmented facial skin blemishes (facial nevi) may appear

7. Mental changes may occur at this time as well, in some cases

---

The discussions on the treatment and management of this particular syndrome are difficult to find in the literature. Usually the presenting symptoms are simply observed and documented. However, the National Organization for Rare Disorders (NORD) suggests contacting the National Aphasia Association (NAA, 156 Fifth Avenue, Suite 707, New York, NY 10010, 800-922-4622) for more information.

Wyburn-Mason syndrome is very rare. However, children diagnosed with this disorder would likely qualify for special education services within the visual impairment area. Depending upon the nature and impact (if any) of mental changes, the cognitive and social emotional changes would need to be addressed. Teachers and those working with affected students need to be well informed about the illness and its symptoms. School staff will need to be able to deal with the manifestation of the illness as it presents itself in class. Because this syndrome is associated with intracranial vascular malformations, concern would arise from a neuropsychological viewpoint, and frequent assessments of current functioning (cognitive, motor, and social-emotional) would be recommended.

Most of the recent publications addressing this rare syndrome focus only on the clinical and radiological findings and do not discuss treatment. Considering the fact that patients have significant intracranial vascular malformations, more attention may be given to this syndrome in future neurological literature.

This entry has been informed by the sources listed below.

REFERENCES

Bonnet, P., Dechaume, J., & Blanc, E. (1937). L'anévrysme cirsoïde de la rétine (anévrysme recémeux): ses relations avec l'anéurysme cirsoïde de la face et avec l'anévrysme cirsoïde du cerveau. *J Med Lyon, 18*: 165–78.

Muthukumar, N., Sundaralingam, M., & Prabakara, M. (1998). Retinocephalic vascular malformation: Case report. *British Journal of Neurosurgery, 12*(5), 458–460.

Patel, U., & Gupta, S. C. (1990). Wyburn-Mason syndrome. *A case report and review of the literature. Neuroradiology, 31*(6), 544–546.

Wyburn-Mason, R. (1943). Arteriovenous aneurysm of midbrain and retina, facial naevi and mental changes. *Brain, 66*: 163–203.

KATHRYN ZUPANCIC
RACHEL TOPLIS
University of Northern Colorado

X

XERODERMA PIGMENTOSUM

Xeroderma pigmentosum (XP) is an autosomal recessive disorder characterized by extreme photosensitivity of the skin and eyes (Kraemer, 1990; Worobec-Victor, Shanker, Bene-Bain, & Solomon, 1988). Even minimal sun exposure can result in blistering of the skin, freckling, or both. The disorder is due to a defect in the ability of the cell to repair DNA damaged by ultraviolet (UV) radiation. The deficiency is in endonuclease activity, and individuals can be assigned to one of nine complementation groups: A through I (Worobec-Victor et al., 1988). In addition to UV radiation, these individuals also show hypersensitivity to certain chemical carcinogens, such as those found in cigarette smoke (Kraemer, 1990).

Characteristics

1. Infantile onset.
2. Hypersensitivity of the skin to sunlight, resulting in blistering, freckling, or both with minimal exposure.
3. Photophobia and atrophic changes to the anterior portion of the eye (conjunctivitis, corneal opacities, inflammatory masses, malignancies, and ectropion and entropion of the lids).
4. Development of benign, premalignant, and malignant tumors. Of the malignancies, basal cell carcinoma, squamous cell carcinoma, and melanoma are the most common.
5. Neurological involvement is seen in some cases; these symptoms include microcephaly, intellectual impairment, ataxia, spasticity, choreoathetosis, and a progressive neurological syndrome.

Progressive atrophic changes occur in cutaneous and oculocuteneous areas exposed to sunlight. Even a single brief exposure can lead to blistering. Individuals with XP have a 2,000 times greater frequency of developing cancer—particularly, basal cell, squamous, and melanoma. Metastases are common. A small but significant increase in the incidence of internal malignancies has been reported as well (Plon & Peterson, 1997). Cancer

and secondary infection are frequent causes of death in XP individuals. Life expectancy is shortened, with death frequently occurring in childhood. There is a 70% probability of survival to age 40 years (Kraemer, 1990).

The incidence of XP is 1:250,000 in the United States and Western Europe. The incidence is higher in Japan at 1:40,000. Furthermore, in Japan there is a higher incidence of Group A, which is most often associated with severe neurological involvement. The DeSanctis-Cacchione syndrome refers to a subset of XP individuals (typically from Group A) with the most severe neurological symptoms including microcephaly, progressive mental retardation, choreoathetosis, cerebellar ataxia, diminished reflexes, spasticity, sensorineural deafness, seizures, dwarfism, and delayed sexual development (Worobec-Victor et al., 1988). Neurological involvement has also been reported in Group D, but the symptoms tend to have a later onset and are milder. The incidence of XP is equal for men and women. Incidence of XP is also typically higher in countries with a high rate of consanguinity.

Symptoms are typically evident in the newborn, and 50% of cases are diagnosed by 18 months of age; 75% are diagnosed by age 4 years (Kraemer, 1990). In addition to clinical diagnosis, XP may be diagnosed by studying fibroblasts derived from biopsy following UV radiation exposure (Worobec-Victor et al., 1988). This technique may also be used prenatally. Heterozygous carriers of XP tend to be clinically asymptomatic and cannot be consistently identified.

Treatment typically involves prevention of exposure to sunlight and other chemical carcinogens. Long hair can be helpful in shielding the neck and ears. Double layering of clothing and use of sunglasses are also helpful. Sunscreen should be used. A rather nocturnal lifestyle often develops to avoid sun exposure. As cancer or other cutaneous lesions occur, they should be treated through conventional means. Genetic counseling is difficult, as carriers are difficult to identify. For those with neurological involvement, a comprehensive neuropsychological evaluation is recommended to aid with educational and vocational planning. Specific speech, occupational, and physical therapies are often indicated in these cases. Psychological evaluation and intervention may also be indicated to help with issues of socialization due to the limitation of lifestyle and social opportunity imposed by XP. Support groups and involvement in activities such as nighttime camps may be very helpful with socialization issues (Xeroderma Pigmentosum Society, 2001). Issues of body image and longevity should also be assessed and treated as needed.

REFERENCES

Kraemer, K. H. (1990). Xeroderma pigmentosum. In M. L. Buyse (Ed.), *The birth defects encyclopedia*. Cambridge, England: Center for Birth Defects Information Services in association with Blackwell Scientific Publications.

Plon, S. E., & Peterson, L. E. (1997). Childhood cancer, heredity, and the environment. In P. A. Pizzo & D. G. Poplack (Eds.), *Principles and practice of pediatric oncology* (3rd ed.). Philadelphia, PA: Lippincott-Raven.

Worobec-Victor, S. M., Shanker, D. B., Bene-Bain, M. A., & Solomon, L. M. (1988). Genodermatoses. In L. A. Schachner & R. C. Hansen (Eds.), *Pediatric dermatology*. New York, NY: Churchill Livingstone.

Xeroderma Pigmentosum Society. (2001, May). Retrieved from http://www.xps.org

DAVID M. TUCKER
REBECCA VAURIO
Austin, Texas

X-LINKED DOMINANT INHERITANCE

The consequences of the presence of a recessive gene on one X chromosome are well known. X-linked dominant inheritance, however, follows a different pattern. First, males and females can show the trait equally, and, if a pathologic gene is concerned, patients of both sexes are affected. Second, if a male carrier of the dominant trait "A" marries a homozygous recessive female "aa," all his daughters will exhibit the trait "A" (they are heterozygous "Aa," having received one X from the "aa" mother and the paternal X with "A"), and all his sons will show the trait "a" (they have received the X chromosome from their mothers and the recessive "a" behaves like a dominant). This mode of transmission, from father to daughter, is, in fact, so characteristic that, when it is observed, the presence of an X-dominant gene is almost demonstrated. Only a few rare diseases are known to be X-linked dominants. X-linked dominant inherited diseases, though rare, result in a variety of handicapping conditions. Not all genetic disorders need result in disabilities, however. Proper care during pregnancy and throughout life can avoid many natural consequences of genetic disorders.

L. KOULISCHER
Institut de Morphologie Pathologique, Belgium

See also **Congenital Disorders; Etiology; Genetic Counseling; X-Linked Recessive Inheritance**

X-LINKED HYDROCEPHALUS SYNDROME

X-linked hydrocephalus is one type of congenital hydrocephalus that results when circulation and absorption of the cerebrospinal fluid within the ventricles are impeded or impaired. The acronym HSAS was coined because stenosis of the aqueduct of Sylvius (a narrow passageway linking the third and fourth ventricles) was originally thought to be the causative agent of the disorder (Bickers & Adams, 1949). Edwards (1961) suggested that HSAS was due to an X-linked recessive gene, with primary transmission from mother to son. Poor developmental outcome (mental retardation and severe motor impairment) for shunted HSAS infants provided further support for genetic causation (Fransen, Lemmon, Van Camp, Coucke, & Willems, 1995; Halliday, Chow, Wallace, & Danks, 1986). Recent linkage studies have suggested that X-linked hydrocephalus is associated with mutations in the gene at Xq28 (Willems et al., 1992). Further studies have identified the mutated gene as a neural cell adhesion molecule L1 (L1CAM) that is thought to impair neuronal cell migration, neurite elongation, and fasciculation of axons (see Kenwrick, Jouet, & Donnai, 1996, for a review of the literature).

Although X-linked hydrocephalus is the most common form of genetically transmitted hydrocephalus, it is a relatively rare condition, occurring in approximately 1 in 30,000 male births (Kenwrick, Jouet, & Donnai, 1996). This condition often results in stillbirth or early mortality. For example, in a study of X-linked hydrocephalus cases that occurred over a 20-year period in Victoria, Australia, 18 of the 25 study babies were stillborn or died within 1 to 2 months (Halliday et al., 1986). This study also found that three-fifths of the cases were males. There is no evidence available suggesting that specific racial or ethnic groups have a genetic predisposition for X-linked hydrocephalus.

Characteristics

1. Obviously a predominant feature of the disorder is the presence of congenital hydrocephalus and its subsequent deleterious impact on brain development. Some of the possible consequences include hypoplasia of the corpus callosum, along with reduced brain mass and disruptions of the myelination process (Fletcher, Brookshire, Bohan, Brandt, & Davidson, 1995). Larger ventricular enlargement is associated with early mortality (Kenwrick et al., 1996).

2. In the vast majority of surviving cases, significant mental deficits are present, with estimates of intellectual functioning at mental retardation ranging from severe to profound. Two studies from

the early 1960s, however, reported IQs above 70 (Kenwrick et al., 1996).

3. Flexion deformity (adducted thumbs) is present in 50% of infants with X-linked hydrocephalus (Halliday et al., 1986).

4. Spasticity of the lower limbs is common, and in more severe cases, spastic quadriplegia is often present.

5. Additional neurological abnormalities reported include nystagmus, ptosis, optical atrophy, scoliosis, torticollis, lumbar lordosis, and seizures (Kenwrick et al., 1996).

In many (but not all) cases, the presence of hydrocephalus is detected during routine ultrasound testing. For infants who survive, valve insertion is an effective treatment to relieve the cranial pressure caused by the hydrocephalus and to increase life expectancy. However, significant developmental delays (intellectual, language, and motor retardation) are usually present. Parents need to receive genetic testing and counseling because the recurrence risk in X-linked hydrocephalus is 50% for subsequent brothers (Williems, Brouwer, Dijkstra, & Wilmink, 1987).

Children with severe and profound levels of mental impairment will require individually tailored special education accommodations and services. Provision of educational services for the majority of these children will be within the confines of a special education classroom for individuals with multiple handicaps. Educational instruction—preferably with a small student-to-teacher ratio—should be multisensory and supportive with communication devices such as soundboards employed where appropriate.

Many children with X-linked hydrocephalus have motor difficulties requiring the use of mobility devices (wheelchairs, walkers) to actively participate in their school environment. To maximize the child's educational gain and overall health, it is imperative that effective communication exists between school personnel and medical care providers. For example, educational personnel (with the school nurse as team leader) should be familiar with the student's special medical needs (shunt care). It is important that school personnel be able to recognize the signs of shunt infection (low-grade fever or redness or tenderness along the shunt) in order to alert the child's family and medical care providers.

The National Institute of Neurological Disorders and Stroke (NINDS) supports research that examines brain development. This research has a long-term goal that includes the prevention of X-linked hydrocephalus (NINDS, 2000). Included on the NINDS information web page is a list of support organizations.

REFERENCES

Bickers, D. S., & Adams, R. D. (1949). Hereditary stenosis of the aqueduct of Sylvius as a cause of congenital hydrocephalus. *Brain, 72,* 246–262.

Edwards, J. H. (1961). The syndrome of sex-linked hydrocephalus. *Archives of Disease in Childhood, 36,* 486–493.

Fletcher, J. M., Brookshire, B. L., Bohan, T. P., Brandt, M. E., & Davidson, K. C. (1995). Early hydrocephalus. In B. P. Rourke (Ed.), *Syndrome of nonverbal learning disabilities* (pp. 206–238). New York, NY: Guilford Press.

Fransen, E., Lemmon, V., Van Camp, G., Coucke, P., & Willems, P. J. (1995). CRASH syndrome: Clinical spectrum of corpus callosum hypoplasia, retardation, adducted thumbs, spastic paraparesis and hydrocephalus due to mutations in one single gene, L1. *European Journal of Human Genetics, 3,* 273–284.

Halliday, J., Chow, C. W., Wallace, D., & Danks, D. M. (1986). X-linked hydrocephalus: A survey of a 20-year period in Victoria, Australia. *Journal of Medical Genetics, 23,* 23–31.

Kenwrick, S., Jouet, M., & Donnai, D. (1996). X-linked hydrocephalus and MASA syndrome. *Journal of Medical Genetics, 33,* 59–65.

National Institute of Neurological Disorders and Stroke. (2000, June). Hydrocephalus fact sheet. Retrieved from http://www.ninds.nih.gov/

Willems, P. J., Vits, L., Raeymaekers, P., Beuten, J., Coucke, P., Holden, J. J. A.,…Reicke, S. (1992). Further localization of X-linked hydrocephalus in the chromosome region Xq28. *American Journal of Human Genetics, 51,* 307–315.

Williems, P. J., Brouwer, O. F., Dijkstra, I., & Wilmink, J. (1987). X-linked hydrocephalus. *American Journal of Medical Genetics, 27,* 921–928.

Louise O'Donnell
University of Texas at Austin, University of Texas Health Science Center, San Antonio

X-LINKED LYMPHOPROLIFERATIVE SYNDROME (DUNCAN DISEASE, PURTILO SYNDROME)

X-linked lymphoproliferative syndrome (XLP) is an inherited immunodeficiency disorder characterized by one or more of three major phenotypic presentations. These presentations include a defective response to infection with the Epstein-Barr virus (EBV), acquired hypogammaglobulinemia, and malignant B-cell lymphoma (National Organization for Rare Disorders, 2001). Patients exhibit a range of symptoms, including life-threatening EBV infection, lymphoma or Hodgkins disease, suppressed bone marrow function with related immunodeficiency, aplastic anemia, and lymphohistiocytic disorder. In some cases, patients may have a proliferation of certain white blood cells (lymphocytes and histiocytes) in particular organs subsequent to an EBV infection. XLP can be associated with susceptibility to bruising and excessive bleeding because of a decrease in platelets (thrombocytopenia). The occurrence of a Burkitt type of malignant lymphoma in the ileocecal region should prompt for evaluation of XLP in the patient and family because it is a frequent finding in XLP.

Characteristics

1. Decreased immune response to Epstein-Barr virus (EBV), with susceptibility for life-threatening EBV infections
2. Acquired hypogammaglobulinemia
3. Development of malignant B-cell lymphomas
4. Normal range of intelligence
5. Decreased life span expectancy, with 50% mortality by age 10 and nearing 100% by the end of the fourth decade of life

---

An X-linked recessive genetic disorder, it is fully expressed in males only, with a mutation in gene SH2D1A, SAP (DSHP), as well as similar diagnoses appearing in maternal male relatives. Carrier females may show atypical antibody response to early antigens but are otherwise asymptomatic. More than 272 cases from 80 kindred groups are listed in the University of Nebraska Medical Center's XLP Registry. Cases are reported from Germany, the United States, Great Britain, Scandinavia, New Zealand, Australia, France, and the Middle East (Buyse, 1990).

The EBV virus is common in the general population and typically causes infectious mononucleosis without significant complications. However, in XLP patients, there is a severely inadequate immune response to the EBV infection. Onset of symptoms is typically seen sometime between 6 months to 10 years of age. About half to two thirds of those with XLP will experience a life-threatening case of mononucleosis. Phenotypic variability of XLP is considerable both across individuals and kindred groups and within kindreds and over time within an individual. A fulminant infectious mononucleosis is not necessary for the development of malignant lymphoma or hypogammaglobulinemia. There is an unclear association between genotype, phenotype, and outcome. It appears that there may be environmental or other genetic factors that contribute to the pathogenesis of XLP (Sumegi et al., 2000).

Prognosis is poor, with 50% succumbing to complications of EBV infection, especially liver failure, by age 10. Although cause of early death is typically fatal infectious mononucleosis, cause of later death is associated with complications of other infections or hemorrhage. Lymphoma or Hodgkins disease, immunodeficiency, aplastic anemia, or lymphohistiocytic disorder can follow the acute EBV infection. Although fewer than 5% of individuals with this disorder survive fulminant hepatitis, those with isolated dysgammaglobulinemia have a higher survival rate (50%). Nevertheless, survival rate nears zero by the end of the fourth decade of life.

Genetic testing is available for diagnosis in affected males; it can also identify female carriers. Treatments include antiviral agents (e.g., acyclovir and interferon-alpha), high-dose IV gamma globulin, and bone marrow transplants. Arecent promising treatment for reconstituting the immune system is umbilical cord stem cell transplantation (Ziegner et al., 2001). Those who develop the acquired hypogammaglobulinemia may benefit from prophylactic antibiotics and replacement immunoglobulin therapy. Early detection via genetic testing prior to EBV infection or other symptoms can offer the opportunity for prophylactic treatment along these lines as well. Those who develop lymphoma may receive traditional treatment with surgery, radiation, and chemotherapy. These latter patients (if not overtreated) show relatively good prognoses.

Children with XLP can be expected to display a normal range of intelligence. Special education services may be available due to other health impairments or physical disability. School accommodations will focus on the physical symptoms of the disorder (e.g., fatigue, frequent illness due to infections). The vicissitudes of hepatic functioning may be associated with fluctuations in mental status. Vigilant hygiene practices and even possible limited contact with others may help to reduce the exposure of the child to the EBV virus and other infectious agents. Home schooling may be warranted for students with severely impaired immune systems. Caution regarding physical activity is warranted, given the vulnerability to bruising and tendency for excessive bleeding (hemorrhaging). Teachers and school personnel can be educated regarding the signs and symptoms of lymphoma and hypogammaglobulinemia to aid monitoring for symptoms' possible development.

REFERENCES

Buyse, M. L. (1990). *Birth defects encyclopedia*. Oxford, England: Blackwell Scientific Publications.

National Organization for Rare Disorders. (2001, May 7). Retrieved from http://www.rarediseases.org/

Sumegi, J., Huang, D., Lanyi, A., Davis, J., Seemayer, T., Maeda, A.,...Gross, T. (2000). Correlation of mutations of the SH2D1A gene and Epstein-Barr virus infection with clinical phenotype and outcome in x-linked lymphoproliferative disease. *Blood*, *96*(9), 3118–3125.

Ziegner, U., Ochs, H., Schanen, C., Feig, S., Seyama, K., Futatani, T.,...Stiehm, E. (2001). Unrelated umbilical cord stem cell transplantation for x-linked immunodeficiencies. *Journal of Pediatrics, 138*(4), 570–573.

VICKY Y. SPRADLING
Austin State Hospital

X-LINKED RECESSIVE INHERITANCE

It is well known that the same gene may present different forms, called alleles. All alleles are located at a fixed place of a chromosome, the locus. In any person, only two alleles are present, one at each locus of the same chromosome pair. One of the two alleles originates from the father, the other from the mother. Alleles can be either dominant (usually represented by a capital letter: "A"), or recessive (represented by a small letter: "a"). As indicated by its name, the dominant form prevails over the recessive one. This means that the carrier of "Aa" (heterozygote) will show the character "A," the recessive "a" being masked. To express itself, "a" must be in the homozygote state "aa." This happens when two "Aa" heterozygotes marry: 25% of all their children will be "aa."

This general rule does not apply to the sex chromosomes. In the XX female, only one X is active in any cell, the other one being inactivated (Lyon, 1961). In a heterozygote female "Aa," the gene "A" will express itself in half of the cells, and "a" in the other half. Most often, the fact that the normal allele is active in half of the cells is enough to determine normal characteristics. For instance, if a woman is a carrier of the recessive mutation responsible for blindness for the red color (daltonism), half of the cells of her retina will be blind for red, but the others not and this will be sufficient to give almost normal color vision. The male has an XY sex chromosome set: Only one X, transmitted by the mother, is present. The Y chromosome is very small and has only a few genes.

Any boy has a 50% chance to inherit one of the two maternal Xs. If he receives the X with a normal dominant allele, there will be no problem. If he receives an X with a recessive abnormal allele from a heterozygous mother, all his cells (not half of them, as in his mother) will be affected. The gene "a" alone, although recessive, behaves like a dominant (e.g., in the case of daltonism, he will be blind to the red). In short, the mother transmits X-linked recessive gene to half her sons. If the gene determines a disease, half of the male progeny will be affected, the mother herself being apparently normal. Moreover, half her daughters will be "normal carriers" and thus will be at risk of having half their sons affected. When an affected male marries, all his children will be normal. The boys receive their X chromosome from the normal mother and the girls are heterozygous (the problem concerns their future children). Only the exceptional and seldom reported marriage of a heterozygous woman "Aa" with an affected man "a" can produce affected "aa" homozygous females.

The striking fact in this sort of X-linked recessive pedigree is that only males are affected (black squares). Inversely, when a family is found with only males presenting a disease, the transmission of an X-linked recessive gene is likely. According to McKusick (1983), there are, at present, 115 confirmed and 128 possible X-linked genes. It is not possible to cite them all in this entry. The most commonly known recessives are those associated with hemophilia, agammaglobulenemia and other immunological diseases, eye diseases including colorblindness, ocular albinism, and some forms of cataract, a few deafness syndromes, Lesch-Nyhan syndrome (mental retardation, spastic cerebral palsy, choreoathetosis, uric acid urinary stones, and self-destructive biting of fingers and lips), muscular dystrophy, myopathy, and testicular feminization.

Intellectual disabilities and X-linked recessive genes deserve special comment. It is well known that more boys than girls show intellectual disabilities. This suggests an excess of X-linked recessive diseases. Often, intellectual disability is associated with other symptoms to form a syndrome (e.g., Lesch-Nyhan syndrome). A newly discovered disease is intellectual disabiity, macroorchidism, and elongated face associated with the presence of a fragile site on the X-chromosome, known as the Xq28 fragile site, observed in 1 out of 2,000 male births. Fryns (1984) has published a review of 83 families ascertained through 83 index patients. He summarizes the problems raised by this particular chromosome anomaly: In one-third of the families, pedigree data were consistent with X-linked recessive inheritance in the other two-thirds, the presenting symptom was familial intellectual disability with a mother with intellectual disability, or mental subnormality with hyperkinetic behavior. Even the transmission through a normal asymptomatic X-fragile male carrier seemed likely in four families. Although more data are still necessary, at present the fragile Xq28 syndrome appears to be an important cause of X-linked mental retardation, with the advantage that carriers can be detected by means of relatively simply cytogenetic techniques.

From a preventive point of view, it is important first to diagnose correctly any X-linked disease with mental retardation, and to detect the normal heterozygote mothers at risk. This is not always possible, but it is a new area of research and it is hoped, with the help of biochemistry and molecular DNA analysis, to prevent in the near future the birth of affected males.

REFERENCES

Fryns, J.-P. (1984). The fragile X syndrome. A study of 83 families. *Clinical Genetics, 26,* 497–528.

Lyon, M. F. (1961). Gene action in the X-chromosome of the mouse. (Mus musculus). *Nature, 190,* 372–373.

L. KOULISCHER
*Institut de Morphologie Pathologique,
Belgium*

See also **Congenital Disorders; Genetic Counseling**

X-RAYS AND DISABILITIES

Irradiation of the developing fetus during the early stages of development as a consequence of maternal X-rays is now clearly recognized as a potential cause of later physical and cognitive abnormalities. There may be dramatic effects associated with irradiation that are clearly recognized at birth. There may be other, more subtle effects appearing at later ages, such as reduced head size.

Clinical X-rays are a major source of the radiation absorbed by the human body during any particular year. It has been estimated that people on the average absorb less than 4 rads a year and that half of this is from medical X-rays (e.g., upper gastrointestinal series, abdominal X-rays, dental and chest X-rays). This does not include treatment for cancer, during which ranges somewhere between 30 and 250 rads have been observed (Batshaw & Perrett, 1981).

Though the potential dangers to the fetus from X-ray radiation were recognized before World War II, the dangers of radiation were most dramatically brought into focus by the events of that war. It was found that there was a direct relationship between the distance of a pregnant woman from the point of impact of the atomic bombs at Hiroshima and Nagasaki and the degree of damage suffered by her unborn child. Women who survived the bomb explosion but were within a half-mile of it were found to have miscarriages, whereas there was an extremely high incidence of microcephalic children born to those who were 1 1/4 miles away (Wood, Johnson, & Omiri, 1973). Still farther away, there was no clear evidence of cognitive or physical damage to the children that were later born, but some 20 years later, as adults, they had a high incidence of leukemia (Miller, 1968).

One major study of pregnant women who were receiving cobalt treatments for cancer discovered that 20 out of 75 of the infants born to them had definitive central nervous system abnormalities. Sixteen of these were microcephalic (Copper & Cooper, 1966). The corroboration of these findings in later studies has resulted in caution and forbearance on the part of physicians with respect to the use of X-rays with pregnant women. Normally, women should not have abdominal X-rays more than 2 weeks after the last period. X-rays during the first trimester are discouraged on any but the most necessary grounds. X-rays as diagnostic tests, such as those once carried out to establish fetal size, have been replaced with less invasive procedures like ultrasound. Indeed, there has been recent evidence suggesting that some of the more subtle kinds of handicaps (e.g., those associated with learning disabilities) may be the consequences of X-ray use.

On the positive side, it should be observed that X-rays have played a role in assisting in the assessment of individuals with disabilities. Thus X-rays of the bone structures of hands and wrists have provided estimates of carpal ossification in cases where delayed maturation has been suspected. X-rays also are essential for the diagnosis of various physical problems and deformities (e.g., dislocations, fractures, internal injuries, congenital defects). Computerized axial tomography (CAT) has revolutionized medical diagnosis. Although X-rays by themselves can show only the length and width of a bodily organ, the CAT scan can also reveal depth. Significant contributions to our understanding of learning disorders have been made by CAT scans (Mann & Sabatino, 1985).

REFERENCES

Batshaw, M. L., & Perrett, Y. M. (1981). *Children with handicaps.* Baltimore, MD: Brookes.

Berg, J. M. (1968). Aetiological aspects of mental subnormality: Pathological factors. In A. M. Clarke & A. D. B. Clarke (Eds.), *Mental deficiency.* New York, NY: Free Press.

Cooper, G., & Cooper, J. B. (1966). Radiation hazards to mother and fetus. *Clinical Obstetrics & Gynecology, 9,* 11.

Mann, L., & Sabatino, D. A. (1985). *Foundations of cognitive processes in remedial and special education.* Rockville, MD: Aspen.

Miller, R. W. (1968). Effects of ionizing radiation from the atomic bomb on Japanese children. *Pediatrics, 72,* 1483.

Wood, J. W., Johnson, K. G., & Omiri, Y. (1973). In utero exposure to the Hiroshima atomic bomb. An evaluation of head size and mental retardation: Twenty years after. *Pediatrics, 39,* 385.

LESTER MANN
Hunter College, City University of New York

See also Cat Scan; Neural Efficiency Analyzer

X-RAY SCANNING TECHNIQUES

The history of X-ray scanning techniques of the brain is eloquently outlined in the text by Oldendorf (1980). Up until the advent of CAT (computed axial tomography) scanning in 1973, the image of the brain could only be grossly inferred by either bony abnormalities of the skull as seen on routine skull X-rays or by a technique (pneumoencephalography) in which air was introduced into the brain ventricles (either directly or via spinal puncture). The resultant shadowy contrast between ventricle, brain, and bone would permit some visualization of major cerebral landmarks sufficient to detect some types of gross structural pathology (e.g., hydrocephalus, tumor). However, the technique of pneumoencephalography had significant morbidity risks and was invasive. The pneumoencephalogram has been replaced by CAT scanning.

An historical predecessor of CAT scanning was the radioactive isotope scan (based on differences in rate of absorption of radioactive particles in normal and abnormal brain tissue), which began clinical use in 1947 and continued until the advent and clinical implementation of CAT scanning. The CAT and other neuroimaging techniques have essentially replaced the radioactive isotope scan. This is also the case with routine cerebral arteriography, which used to be the only way to visualize blood vessels of the neck and head; it has been replaced in large part by digital subtraction angiography (DSA). The DSA is an X-ray scanning technique that uses a computer program to "subtract" background tissue in the X-ray image that is not of the same density as blood vessels. Comparisons of these techniques, sample figures, and a more complete discussion of their diagnostic usefulness are presented in Bigler (1988).

Positron emission tomography (PET) is a technique that permits the mapping of brain metabolism by using radioactive-labeled glucose or oxygen. Based on different metabolic rates, an image of the major cerebral structures can be obtained with specific indication of which brain areas were using the most glucose or oxygen (e.g., the brain area most involved in a particular task while PET scanning was being done).

REFERENCES

Bigler, E. D. (1988). *Diagnostic clinical neuropsychology* (2nd ed.). Austin: University of Texas Press.

Oldendorf, W. H. (1980). *The quest for an image of brain.* New York, NY: Raven.

ERIN D. BIGLER
Brigham Young University

See also Cat Scan; Nuclear Magnetic Resonance

XXX SYNDROME

XXX syndrome is a disorder in which affected females have three X chromosomes. It may also be referred to as Chromosome X, Triplo-X, and Chromosome 47, XXX karyotype. XXX syndrome was first described by P. A. Jacobs in the Lancet in 1959. It is the most frequent X chromosomal anomaly in females. The incidence of XXX syndrome is 0.3–1 per 1,000 newborn females (Pedlynx, 2002).

This syndrome is very similar to XXXX syndrome, which has very similar clinical features, but it has lower incidence, with only 40 cases to date (Jones, 1997). Diagnosis for both conditions is confirmed by chromosomal analysis.

Characteristics

1. Hypertelorism
2. Tall stature (average height of 172 cm)
3. Widely spaced nipples
4. Webbed neck
5. Variable IQ, from superior to moderate-to-severe mental retardation
6. Transient gross motor delays
7. Speech and language delays
8. Fine motor delays
9. Coordination problems with awkwardness
10. Behavioral problems
11. Mild depression, conduct disorder, immature behavior, socializing problems
12. Occasional seizures

Treatment of this syndrome is multidisciplinary, utilizing professionals from pediatrics, endocrinology, neurology, and psychology. Genetic counseling is recommended, although no XXX daughter of an XXX mother has been reported.

Special education programming has been documented in 60% of cases due to frequent verbal learning and expressive language deficits. Behavior problems, including mild depression and conduct disorder, occur in 30% of cases (Jones, 1997). Due to the wide variability of symptoms with this syndrome, individualized assessment and treatment, as prescribed under special education guidelines, are quite appropriate. The prognosis for children with XXX syndrome is that they can expect to have normal life span (Pedlynx, 2002).

REFERENCES

Jones, K. L. (1997). *Smith's recognizable patterns of human malformation* (5th ed.). Philadelphia, PA: W. B. Saunders.

Pedlynx. (2002). *XXX syndrome.* Retrieved from http://icondata
.com.searchnut.com/index.php?y=10877964&r=c%3EbXOwcn
SieHFvZ3%3Au%27f%3Ebtl%3Cvt%3C33%3C2%3C2%3C219
88%3A75%3Ctuzmf2%6033%2Fdtt%3C3%3Cjoufsdptnpt%60
bggjmjbuf%60xq%60e3s%60efsq%3Cxizqbsl%3Cxizqbsl%3C8
7227%3C87227%3Ccboofe%3C%3Cbtl%3Cqbslfe%2Ftzoejdbu
jpo%2Fbtl%2Fdpn%27jqvb%60je%3E714ff%3Afe44g7eef4c1g
4c66f236c6177%27enybsht%3E8d53g56b%3A3d4d9b253g88ff
6c63ccdef&rd=3

ELAINE FLETCHER-JANZEN
The Chicago School of Professional Psychology

XXXX SYNDROME

XXXX syndrome—also called Chromosome X, poly-X—is a genetic disorder in which affected females have four X chromosomes. It was first described by Carr, Barr, and Plunkett in a medical journal in 1961. The syndrome is due to successive nondisjunctive meiotic divisions within a parent, and the diagnosis is confirmed by genetic analysis (Jones, 1997).

The incidence of XXXX syndrome is rare; there have been about 40 cases reported. The age of onset is in childhood and the phenotype is quite variable, with some patients having faces suggestive of Trisomy 21 (Pedlynx, 2002).

Characteristics

Dysmorphisms

1. Hypertelorism
2. Upward-slanting palpebral fissures
3. Epicanthal folds
4. Midfacial hypoplasia
5. Micrognathia
6. Normal to tall stature
7. Narrow shoulder girdle
8. Fifth-finger clinodactyly
9. Simian crease

Neurological Manifestations

1. IQ range from 30 to 80, with a mean of 55
2. Speech and language delays
3. Behavioral problems

Endocrine Manifestations

1. Incomplete or absent sexual development
2. Variable amenorrhea with irregular menses
3. Possible fertility problems

Other Manifestations

1. Congenital heart disease
2. Radioulnar synostosis

Treatment for XXXX syndrome is supportive and requires multidisciplinary professionals from the fields of pediatrics, endocrinology, neurology, and psychology. Genetic counseling is also prescribed for these patients and their families (Pedlynx, 2002).

The variety of sequelae for this disorder suggests that special education services would be needed for girls with XXXX syndrome. The average intellectual functioning of individuals with this disorder suggests that adaptive behavior and academic deficits would be present; it would, therefore, also identify the child for special education services under the mental retardation handicapping condition.

The prognosis for females with XXXX syndrome is dependent on appropriate and ongoing medical and educational monitoring and support.

REFERENCES

Carr, D. H., Barr, M. L., & Plunkett, E. R. (1961). An XXXX sex chromosome complex in two mentally defective females. *Canadian Medical Association Journal, 84*, 131.

Jones, K. L. (1997). *Smith's recognizable patterns of human malformation* (5th ed.). Philadelphia, PA: W. B. Saunders.

Pedlynx. (2002). *Online database: XXXX syndrome*. Retrieved from http://icondata.com.searchnut.com/index.php?y=108779 64&r=c%3EbXOwcnSieHFvZ3%3Au%27f%3Ebtl%3Cvt%3C3 3%3C2%3C2%3C21988%3A75%3Ctuzmf2%6033%2Fdtt%3C3 %3Cjoufsdptnpt%60bggjmjbuf%60xq%60e3s%60efsq%3Cxizq bsl%3Cxizqbsl%3C87227%3C87227%3Ccboofe%3C%3Cbtl%3 Cqbslfe%2Ftzoejdbujpo%2Fbtl%2Fdpn%27jqvb%60je%3E714 ff%3Afe44g7eef4c1g4c66f236c6177%27enybsht%3E8d53g56b %3A3d4d9b253g88ff6c63ccdef&rd=3

ELAINE FLETCHER-JANZEN
The Chicago School of Professional Psychology

XYY SYNDROME

XYY syndrome, or Polysomy Y, is a rare chromosomal genetic syndrome where males have an extra Y chromosome, becoming XYY instead of the normal XY sex chromosome (males) or XX (females; Cure Research, n.d.). XYY syndrome usually does not cause abnormal physical features or medical conditions. Typically XYY males are taller than average (about 6'2") and may experience severe acne (Contact a Family, 2002). Puberty occurs at the expected time; sex organs and secondary sex characteristics develop normally (Nielson, 2005). Because of the lack of distinct physical or medical features, the condition often only is detected during genetic analysis for other reasons (The Real Facts Contributions Company, n.d.).

Currently there is no known cause of the mutation that leads to the formation of the XYY syndrome (Nielson, 2005). XYY is not inherited and occurs randomly (Genetics Home Reference, 2005). The frequency of XYY is difficult to ascertain due to statistical differences between studies, as well as the fact that genetic testing is not necessarily done on all males who have the syndrome. It may be as common as 1 in 900 or as rare as 1 in 1,500, or even 1 in 2,000 (O'Neil, 2005).

Early studies of the XYY syndrome led to the erroneous conclusion that these men were genetically predisposed to antisocial, aggressive behavior, below-average intelligence, and homosexuality (O'Neil, 2005); these early myths have been disproved (Merck, 2005). Although males with XYY often have intellectual ability in the average range, their overall ability tends to be 10 to 15 points lower than their siblings (Yale New Haven Health, n.d.). Some XYY males experience learning difficulties; others experience delayed speech development and behavior problems. These difficulties can be overcome with appropriate interventions by parent, teacher, and speech language pathologist (when necessary) working together cooperatively (Nielson, 2005).

REFERENCES

Contact a Family. (2002). *XYY syndrome*. Retrieved from http://www.cafamily.org.uk/

Cure Research. (n.d.). *Introduction: Jacobs syndrome*. Retrieved from http://www.cureresearch.com/j/jacobs_syndrome/intro.htm

Genetics Home Reference. (2005). *47, XYY syndrome*. Retrieved from http://ghr.nlm.nih.gov.condition=47xyysyndrome

Merck & Co. Inc. (2005). *The Merck manual of diagnosis and therapy*. [Electronic version]. Whitehouse, NJ: Author. Retrieved from http://www.merck.com

Nielson, J. (2005). *XYY males and orientation*. Retrieved from http://www.aadk/TURNER/ENGELSK/XYY.HTM

O'Neil, D. (2005). *Sex chromosome abnormalities*. Retrieved from http://anthro.palomar.edu/abnormal/abnormal_5.htm

The Real Facts Contributions Company. (n.d.). *XYY*. Retrieved from http://www.therfcc.org/xyy-127569.html

Yale New Haven Health. (n.d.). *XYY syndrome*. Retrieved from http://yalenewhavenhealth.org/

JOSEPH D. PERRY
Kent State University
First edition

LATANYA HENRY
Texas A&M University
Third edition

See also Chromosomes, Human Anomalies, and Cytogenetic Abnormalities; Genetic Counseling

Y

YALE, CAROLINE A. (1848–1933)

Caroline A. Yale, teacher and principal at Clarke School for the Deaf in Northampton, Massachusetts, from 1870 to 1922, was a leading figure in the development of educational services for the deaf in the United States. She developed a system for teaching speech to the deaf and was a founder, with Alexander Graham Bell and others, of the American Association to Promote the Teaching of Speech to the Deaf. At Clarke School, she organized a teacher-education department that was responsible for the training of large numbers of student teachers. Through her teacher-training activities and numerous publications, Yale was a major contributor to the acceptance of instruction in speech as an essential element in the education of deaf children.

REFERENCES

Taylor, H. (1933). Caroline Ardelia Yale. *The Volta Review, 35*, 415–417.

Yale, C. A. (1931). *Years of building.* New York, NY: Longmans, Green.

PAUL IRVINE
Katonah, New York

See also Bell, Alexander Graham (1847–1922); Deaf Education

YAWS

Yaws is a chronic and contagious skin disease characterized by swollen, open sores; it primarily affects people living in rural, humid, and tropical climates. Yaws is characterized by three stages: primary, secondary, and tertiary.

Children under the age of 15 account for 75% of all new cases of yaws (Walker & Hay, 2000). The peak incidence of yaws is reported to occur between 6 and 10 years of age (Sehgal, Jain, Bhattacharya, & Thappa, 1994). Following the mass treatment programs sponsored by the World Health Organization (WHO) from 1957 to 1963, the incidence of yaws decreased dramatically from 50–100 million to fewer than 20 million cases in the 1970s. In 1997, an estimated 460,000 new cases of yaws was reported by the WHO, primarily in regions with poor hygiene and housing conditions, such as West Africa, Papua New Guinea, Indonesia, and the Solomon Islands (Nagreh, 1986). Among the reasons that yaws has yet to be completely eradicated are an underestimation of the number of untreated cases in the later stages of the disease and the prevalence of yaws in rural and remote populations (Aylward, Hennessey, Zegaria, Olive, & Cochi, 2000).

Yaws is very contagious. The most common route of transmission is when broken skin or open sores come into contact with an infected skin lesion. Three to 5 weeks after the initial infection, the first lesion, or mother yaw will appear, usually on the skin of the lower legs, which defines the primary stage of yaws. The primary lesion remains on the body, usually on the lower legs, for 2 to 9 months, by which time the lesion spontaneously disappears and scars form. Lesions marking the secondary stage are smaller and may appear as early as 1 month or as late as 24 months after the person is infected. Symptoms such as headache, fever, joint pains, and generalized lymphadenopathy may appear during the second stage of yaws. The symptoms persist for an average of 5 years, usually with interspersed latent periods. The tertiary phase is characterized by cutaneous plaque nodules, ulcers, and hyperkeratoses of the palms and soles, as well as by lesions involving the skull, sternum, tibia, or other bones. It is estimated that only 10% of those infected with yaws will ever experience the third stage (Sehgal et al., 1994).

The etiology of yaws is attributed to the treponema pertenue bacteria, which is similar in structure to the bacteria that causes syphilis to develop. However, unlike syphilis, yaws is nonvenereal and does not affect the cardiovascular or neurological systems (Sehgal et al., 1994). The mother yaw, characteristic of the primary phase, contains serous fluid with the treponemes; thus, diagnosis at this stage requires microscopic examination of the lesion for the bacteria (Nagreh, 1986). Because the treponemes are rarely present in skin lesions during the later stages, it is important to obtain an early diagnosis if possible (Chulay, 2000). In the later stages of yaws, diagnosis becomes increasingly more difficult because the skin lesions must be differentiated from lesions resulting from topical ulcers, sickle cell anemia, leprosy, tuberculosis, and so on. Yaws is not known to impair cognitive or educational functioning. Children from areas where yaws is known to exist should be forward with the teachers and nurses about their skin problems (Sehgal et al., 1994).

Characteristics

1. Infectious, chronic skin disease.
2. Primary stage symptoms include the presence of the primary skin lesion, usually on the lower legs.
3. Secondary and tertiary stage symptoms include additional lesions and ulcers on the palms and plantar surfaces. The skin, bone, and joints are also affected during these stages.

Yaws is easily treatable; however, issues of detection and eradication remain a large problem in some areas. Historically, penicillin has been the most effective treatment for curing yaws. Typically, a single dosage will cure the disease. However, in some areas, the penicillin treatment has shown to be ineffective and does not prevent the spread of yaws; thus, new treatments are needed. For example, Walker and Hay (2000) reported that penicillin treatment reportedly failed to cure yaws in areas of Papua New Guinea, possibly indicating the development of a strain of yaws resistant to penicillin. Prevention strategies can also be used to prevent the spread of yaws in the tropic areas.

REFERENCES

Aylward, B., Hennessey, K. A., Zegaria, N., Olive, J. M., & Cochi, S. (2000). When is a disease eradicable? 100 years of lessons learned. *American Journal of Public Health, 90*, 1515–1520.

Chulay, J. (2000). Treponema species (yaws, pinta, bejel). In G. L. Mandell, J. E. Bennet, & R. Dolin (Eds.), *Mandell, Douglas, and Bennett's principles and practice of infectious diseases* (5th ed., pp. 2490–2494). New York, NY: Churchill Livingstone.

Nagreh, D. S. (1986). Yaws. *Cutis, 38*, 303–305.

Sehgal, V. N., Jain, S., Bhattacharya, S. N., & Thappa, D. M. (1994). Yaws: Control eradication. *International Journal of Dermatology, 33*, 16–20.

Walker, S. L., & Hay, R. J. (2000). Yaws: A review of the last 50 years. *International Journal of Dermatology, 39*, 258–260.

JENNIFER M. GILLIS
Center for Educational Partnerships
University of California, Irvine

---

the community (Hanna, 1972). The traditional answer to the question of school responsibility was simple: Transmit the heritage, or at least that part of it considered to be important, to the educated person. The traditional school said, in effect, fit children and youths into the fixed curriculum of academic subjects. If they do not care, or in the case of many exceptional students, cannot cope with it, that is unfortunate. In the cases of many exceptional students, traditional education models forced them out or openly expelled them if attendance laws permitted. In other cases, students were tracked into vocational education or home economics. More progressive educators organized schools around a child-centered orientation in order to more effectively stimulate student interest, provide for the exploration and expression of those interests, and, therefore, assist in desirable personality growth (Olsen & Clark, 1977).

A system embracing year-round schooling is able to affirm the central values of the earlier concepts while providing programming in light of the school's basic responsibility to help improve the quality of living in the local community or region. The traditional school curriculum is still almost standard practice (Ysseldyke & Algozzine, 1983). The approach involved in year-round schools, however, provides curriculum flexibly structured about the enduring life concerns of humans everywhere. These concerns, with their attendant problems, are those of earning a living, communicating ideas and feelings, enjoying recreation, and finding some measure of self-identity.

REFERENCES

Hanna, P. (1972, May). What thwarts the community education curriculum? *Community Education Journal, 3*, 27–30.

Olsen, E. G., & Clark, P. A. (1977). *Life-centering education.* Midland, MI: Pendell.

Ysseldyke, J., & Algozzine, B. (1983). *Introduction to special education.* Boston, MA: Houghton Mifflin.

CRAIG D. SMITH
Georgia College

See also Extended School Year for Students With Disabilities; Licensing and Certification of Schools; Summer School for Individuals With Disabilities

---

YEAR-ROUND SCHOOLS

The concept and use of year-round schools for special and general education has developed, in part, as a result of changing expectations and roles of public education in

---

YOUNG CHILDREN'S ACHIEVEMENT TEST (YCAT)

The Young Children's Achievement Test (YCAT, 2000) is an individually administered measure designed to determine early academic abilities and document educational progress. Its main purpose is to help identify young children at risk for school failure. The test was designed for English speaking preschoolers, kindergarteners, and first graders (ages 4-0 through 7-11). The YCAT yields an overall Early Achievement Standard Score and individual subtest standard scores for the five subtests: General Information, Reading, Mathematics, Writing, and Spoken Language. The YCAT allows for flexibility in administration given that the subtests can be administered in any order or be given independent of each other. A variety of scores are reported for both the subtests and composite score, including standard scores (with a mean of 100 and standard deviation of 15), percentiles, and age equivalents.

The YCAT materials include an examiner's manual, picture book, examiner record booklets, and student response forms. The examiner record booklet indicates multiple examples of correct responses, which facilitates the scoring process. Items are either scored as correct (1) or incorrect (0), and there are approximately 20 items per subtest.

The YCAT was normed on 1,224 children. The sample was representative of the U.S. population as reported in the 1997 *Statistical Abstract of the United States*. Overall, the YCAT appears to be a reliable measure. Test retest reliability was calculated over a 2-week period and ranged from .97 to .99. Interrater reliability ranged from .97 to .99 for the individual subtests. Internal consistency as measured by Cronbach's coefficient alpha ranged from .74 to .92, with the majority of subtest values in the mid- to high .80s. The Early Achievement Composite Score yielded high internal consistency values of .95 to .97. With respect to validity, criterion-related validity has been demonstrated with the Comprehensive Scales of Student Abilities (1994), the Kaufman Survey of Early Academic and Language Skills (1993), the Metropolitan Readiness Tests (1995), and the Gates-MacGinitie Reading Tests (1989).

REVIEWED IN:

Plake, B. S., Impara, J. C., & Spies, R. A. (Eds.). (2003). *The fifteenth mental measurements yearbook*. Lincoln, NE: Buros Institute of Mental Measurements.

Turner, H. (2006). Review of Young Children's Achievement Test. *Journal of Psychoeducational Assessment, 24*(3), 272–277.

RON DUMONT
Fairleigh Dickinson University

JOHN WILLIS
Rivier College

KATHLEEN VEIZEL
JAMIE ZIBULSKY
Fairleigh Dickinson University
Fourth edition

YSSELDYKE, JAMES EDWARD (1944–   )

James Ysseldyle has been an active educator and researcher in the fields of psychology, school psychology, and education for over 40 years. Born in 1944 in Grand Rapids, MI, Ysseldyke began his undergraduate studies at Calvin College and earned his BA from Western Michigan University. After graduation, he returned to Grand Rapids where he taught for 2 years. He went to graduate school at the University of Illinois at Urbana-Champaign where he was awarded his MA (1968) and PhD (1971) in school psychology. In 1998, Ysseldyke was recognized as a Distinguished Alumnus (doctoral) by the College of Education of the University of Illinois. Dr. Ysseldyke currently is the Emma Birkmaier Professor of Educational Leadership in the Department of Educational Psychology at the University of Minnesota, where he has spent the majority of his professional life in higher education. He also has served as Associate Dean for Research and Director of the School Psychology program in the College of Education and Human Development at Minnesota.

Ysseldyke's research and publication efforts have influenced policies and practices in special education and school psychology at the local, state, national, and international levels. Early in his academic career he investigated the testing and data utilization in decision-making practices for special education eligibility. As part of his work as Director of the Institute for Research on Learning Disabilities (1977–1983), Ysseldyke, his colleagues, and his students helped establish the foundation for the reconceptualization of best practices for assessment of students for eligibility under the category of learning disabilities. This work was among the first to emphasize the importance of reliable and valid measurements of students' responses to their instructional experiences—now a key element of Response to Intervention (RtI) efforts under IDEA.

In 1986 Dr. Ysseldyke began a 6-year term as the editor of *Exceptional Children*, the journal of the Council of Exceptional Children. During this time, he is largely credited with turning *Exceptional Children* into perhaps the top-tier research journal in special education. His accomplishments as editor and as a researcher in special education led to Dr. Ysseldyke being awarded the J. Wallace Wallin Special Education Lifetime Achievement Award. This award, which was created by the Council of Exceptional Children, recognizes persons who have made continued and sustained contributions to the education of students with disabilities.

From 1990 to 1999, Dr. Ysseldyke was Director of the National Center on Educational Outcomes (NCEO), a research and technical assistance center for states on issues of assessment and accountability for students with disabilities. Under his leadership, NCEO researchers provided the necessary data to challenge the long-standing and common practice of excluding students with disabilities from assessments of educational outcomes. Federal and state statutes now prohibit exclusionary testing practices. Most recently, Dr. Ysseldyke has embarked on a series of projects to investigate and implement the use of emerging technologies to support better instructional outcomes for students in reading and mathematics and to improve the progress monitoring efforts of teachers.

Organizations including the School Psychology Division of the American Psychological Association, the American Educational Research Association, and the Council for Exceptional Children have recognized Dr. Ysseldyke for his research. As the author of numerous textbooks (30) and scholarly papers in professional journals (over 300), he has helped shape the theories and practices of teachers, school psychologists, educational researchers, and policy makers. Most importantly, his prolific works have provided educators of multiple generations of students with disabilities with the knowledge and practices they needed to improve the lives of their students.

JAMES G. SHRINER
University of Illinois at Urbana-Champaign
Fourth edition

See also Council for Exceptional Children; Institutes for Research on Learning Disabilities

YUNIS-VARON SYNDROME

Yunis-Varon syndrome is a rare genetic disorder caused by an autosomal recessive gene. Children with Yunis-Varon syndrome have skeletal ectodermal tissue (e.g., nails and teeth) and cardiorespiratory defects. Skeletal defects include complete or partial absence of the shoulder blades, digital abnormalities (i.e., absence of or underdeveloped thumbs, big toes, and fingertips), and abnormal growth of the bones of the cranium (i.e., the skull). These children have abnormally large hearts and respiratory difficulties, along with feeding problems, which can be life-threatening, especially in infancy (National Organization for Rare Disorders [NORD], 1997). In fact, neonatal death is a significant feature of Yunis-Varon syndrome (Lapeer & Fransman, 1992).

Other physical features of this disorder include abnormal or unusual facial characteristics. Children with this syndrome have sparse or no eyebrows and eyelashes, thin lips, and excessively small jaws. These children are also short in stature due to pre- and postnatal growth retardation (NORD, 1997).

Twelve cases of the syndrome have been reported in the literature, which suggests a rare disorder and/or a high mortality rate associated with the disorder. Children who have survived the infancy period have been reported to have additional problems, including bilateral hearing loss, spinal defects, and impacted teeth (Lapeer & Fransman, 1992). Special education support services, such as speech services, may be helpful, especially if a hearing loss is evident.

REFERENCES

Lapeer, G. L., & Fransman, S. L. (1992). Hypodontia, impacted teeth, spinal defects, and cardiomegaly in previously diagnosed case of the Yunis-Varon syndrome. *Oral Surgery, Oral Medicine, and Oral Pathology, 73*(4), 456–460.

National Organization for Rare Disorders (NORD). (1997). *Yunis-Varon syndrome.* New Fairfield, CT: Author.

PATRICIA A. LOWE
University of Kansas

JOAN W. MAYFIELD
Baylor Pediatric Specialty Service

Z

ZAR

Zar is a culture-bound syndrome found mostly in Ethiopian, Somalian, and other Middle Eastern and North African societies (American Psychiatric Association [APA], 2004). Zar syndrome is psychiatric in nature and is closely related to notions of "spiritual possession" (Besmer, 1992, p. 124). Clinical manifestations of this disorder include dissociative episodes, apathy, withdrawal, and other erratic or bizarre behaviors.

There are no known prevalence or incidence studies on zar possession. However, there are ethnographic studies pertaining to this culture-bound syndrome that link the disorder to buda, or the evil eye, and—in the Ethiopian and Hausa communities of Northern Africa—to spiritual possession. Zar is apparently geographically defined to Middle Eastern and North African populations; however, zar possession has been documented in migrant Ethiopian populations in Israel. In one ethnographic study, Ethiopian women in Israel keep their newborns indoors to shield them from the buda of others looking at them. It is believed that buda leads to spiritual or zar possession (Hodes, 1997). Among the Hausa of northern Nigeria, those with zar possession are ridiculed because of the unusual behavior associated with zar possession and because of the cultural notion that zar affects "the unenlightened people" (Besmer, 1992, p. 124). Besmer (1992, p. 124) suggests that zar possession is linked to the "marginal social categories" and members of society who maintain differential inclusion. This syndrome is not linguistically limited, but it is linked closely to spiritual possession and possession cults of both geographic areas. Zar possession is more common in adult females; however, ethnographic evidence suggests that zar possession can occur as early as infancy (Hodes, 1997).

Characteristics

1. Dissociative episodes
2. Inappropriate shouting
3. Inappropriate laughing
4. Hitting head against a wall
5. Apathy
6. Refusal to eat or carry out daily tasks
7. Withdrawal

Historically, health-care professionals have referred to zar possession as a culturally sanctioned condition, and there are no known treatments for this disorder within medical and psychiatric communities. However, within the social communities themselves, this disorder is not seen as pathological (APA, 2004). In terms of treatment, children and women are sent to the local shaman or local healers (Hodes, 1997). On many occasions, members of the community who have zar syndrome shun treatment from local healers and take membership in "spiritual cults" (Besmer, 1992, p. 126). Within these groups, ambiguous status is normalized and viewed from the perspective of "rituals of affliction" (Besmer, 1992, p. 125). Cult membership is also important in terms of family environment.

The need for differential diagnosis of this syndrome is evident in transient populations in that it is essential to determine the level of acculturation as well as family history when diagnosing zar syndrome. The overlap of this syndrome's presenting symptoms with those of other common psychiatric conditions in the United States requires cultural sensitivity on the part of the person conducting the evaluation. It is doubtful that special education services would be needed for a child exhibiting zar behaviors, but a lengthy duration would probably interfere with learning, and at some point intervention would be needed from an academic standpoint. The more unusual behaviors associated with zar would not be tolerated in most schools and would come to the attention of personnel. At this point, an acculturation assessment of the child and family would be necessary, and related services would have to be sensitive to the acculturation process of the student.

REFERENCES

American Psychiatric Association. (2004). *Diagnostic and statistical manual of mental disorders* (4th ed., text rev.). Washington, DC: Author.

Besmer, F. E. (1992). *Horses, musicians, and gods: The Hausa cult of possession-trance.* Retrieved from http://ets.umdl.umich.edu/cgi/e/ehraf/hraf-idx?type=html

Hodes, R. M. (1997). Cross-cultural medicine and diverse health beliefs: Ethiopians abroad. *Western Journal of Medicine, 166,* 29–36.

KIELY ANN FLETCHER
Ohio State University

ZEAMAN, DAVID (1921–1984)

After receiving his PhD from Columbia University in experimental psychology in 1948, David Zeaman embarked on a lifelong career developing and elaborating on an attention theory of retardate discriminative learning. In the early 1950s, he conducted pilot studies specializing in animal learning with his wife, Betty House, at the Mansfield State Training School in Connecticut. They thought that the techniques developed for studying animal behavior could be adapted for retarded children with low ability to speak or understand language. That early work proved promising, leading to funding by the National Institute of Mental Health for a project that lasted 20 years. The Mansfield State School administration provided space for a permanent laboratory that is still in existence.

The initial target behavior for Zeaman and House's research was a discriminative learning task disguised as a candy-finding game. Early results convinced them that the deficiency they observed in retarded subjects was due to attentional deficits rather than slow learning. They developed a mathematical attention model with the basic assumption that discriminative learning requires a learning chain of two responses: attending to the relevant dimension and approaching the correct cue of that dimension.

Their approach to retardation was to look for changes in parameter values of the model-related to intelligence. The parameter that was most affected by level of intelligence turned out to be the initial probability of attending to the colors and forms that were the relevant dimensions of the tasks. Later work related this finding to three factors: (1) breadth and adjustability of breadth of attention—subjects of higher intelligence can attend to more dimensions at once and can narrow attention when necessary; (2) dimensionality of the stimulus—subjects of low intelligence are likely to attend to stimuli holistically rather than analytically; and (3) fixed as well as variable components of attention such that strong dimensional preferences interfere with learning—salience of position cues in retardates slows learning about colors, forms, sizes, and other aspects of stimuli. A history of research and theory development from the first publication of the model in 1963 to 1979 can be found in Ellis's *Handbook of Mental Deficiency* (1963).

Zeaman served as editor of the *Psychological Bulletin* and as associate editor of *Intelligence*. He received many awards and honors from organizations, such as the American Psychological Association and the National Institute of Mental Health.

REFERENCE

Zeaman, D., & House, B. J. (1963). The role of attention in retardate discrimination learning. In N. R. Ellis (Ed.), *Handbook of mental deficiency: Psychological theory and research*. New York, NY: McGraw-Hill.

STAFF

See also **House, Betty; Zeaman-House Research**

ZEAMAN-HOUSE RESEARCH

David Zeaman and Betty House, along with other researchers located primarily at the University of Connecticut and the Mansfield Training School, have contributed substantial research on attention theory to the literature on intellectual disability. Though more than 100 years of psychological and educational research on attention has concluded that the process is multifactorial (Alabiso, 1972), the Zeaman-House, and later Fisher-Zeaman, focus on selective attention has provided several learning theories useful in understanding and teaching individuals with intellectual disabilities.

Using a series of simple visual discrimination tasks, Zeaman and House found that plotting of individual, rather than averaged, group responses produced learning curves that differed significantly from traditional learning curves. The former curves stayed around the chance (50%) correct level, then jumped quickly to 100% accuracy. Prior to plotting individual data with backward learning curves, the expectation would have been for a gradual, incremental curve from chance to the 100% correct level. This discontinuity caused these researchers to postulate two processes, one controlling the length of the first part of the curve, and one determining the rapid jump to correct problem solution. Individuals with intellectual disabilities in the 2- to 4-year mental-age range performed more poorly on these tasks than typically developing children at comparable mental ages. Also, Zeaman and House determined that, among subjects with intellectual disabilities, IQ was a more accurate predictor of better discrimination, independent of mental age (Robinson & Robinson, 1976).

The two-stage or two-phase discrimination learning process proposed by Zeaman and House (1963) suggests an early attention phase during which the plotted learning curve is essentially horizontal, indicating chance-level responses. During this phase, the subject has not discovered the relevant stimuli of an object and is randomly attending to various stimulus dimensions. The second phase of the discrimination process involves attention to relevant stimulus dimensions, leading to rapid improvement in learning (Mercer & Snell, 1977).

Because subjects with intellectual disabilities produced chance-level curves of longer initial duration (yet also demonstrated steeply sloped curves comparable to subjects with higher mental ages), Zeaman and House (1963) argued that the inefficient learning of individuals with intellectual disabilities was, at its core, a function of their attention. This finding was important because it suggested that the actual learning potential of individuals with intellectual disabilities was not defective and that interventions could be devised to improve attention and discrimination. The differences observed between individuals with intellectual disabilities and typically developing individuals were based more on the time it took to learn to attend to relevant stimuli than to select the relevant cue itself (Zeaman & House). The work by Zeaman and House in the area of attention and discrimination learning led to studies of other relevant variables such as transfer of training, stimulus factors (e.g., size, position, color, shape), novelty and oddity learning, and the effects of reward characteristics.

Later, their attention theory was expanded to include examinations of the relationship of retention to attention and learning. Ten years after publication of the earlier work, Fisher and Zeaman (1973) noted that although the attention deficits that affect learning in invididuals with intellectual disabilities are amenable to manipulation and improvement, the retention limitations attributable to the reduced cognitive capacity of such subjects may not be so flexible. Both the earlier and more recent work by Zeaman, House, and their colleagues have generated considerable productive research by others. These latter focuses, many of which suggest implications for education and training of individuals with intellectual disabilities, include work on the number of stimulus dimensions employed, reward and incentive conditions, and transfer and oddity learning.

REFERENCES

Alabiso, F. (1972). Inhibitory functions of attention in reducing hyperactive behavior. *American Journal of Mental Deficiency, 77,* 259–282.

Fisher, M. A., & Zeaman, D. (1973). An attention-retention theory of retardate discrimination learning. In N. R. Ellis (Ed.), *The international review of research in mental retardation* (Vol. 6, pp. 169–256). New York, NY: Academic Press.

Mercer, C. D., & Snell, M. E. (1977). *Learning theory research in mental retardation: Implications for teaching.* Columbus, OH: Merrill.

Robinson, N. M., & Robinson, H. B. (1976). *The mentally retarded child: A psychological approach.* New York, NY: McGraw-Hill.

Zeaman, D., & House, B. J. (1963). The role of attention in retardate discrimination learning. In N. R. Ellis (Ed.), *Handbook of mental deficiency* (pp. 159–223). New York, NY: McGraw-Hill.

JOHN D. WILSON
Elwyn Institutes

See also **House, Betty; Zeaman, David**

ZELLWEGER SYNDROME

Zellweger syndrome is a rare hereditary disorder characterized by decreased or missing peroxisomes in the liver, kidney, and brain cells. Manifestations include facial dysmorphology, opthamological and neurological abnormalities, hepatomegaly, and unusual problems in prenatal development.

This disease is present at birth and occurs equally between males and females. One Australian study indicated that it occurs once in 100,000 live births (United Leukodystrophy Foundation, 2000). However, more cases have occurred but have gone undiagnosed. Zellweger syndrome is inherited as an autosomal recessive trait. Both parents must be carriers, and each of their children will have a 25% chance of being affected. Carriers are completely healthy.

Characteristics

1. Infants with the disease often exhibit prenatal growth failure in spite of a normal period of gestation.
2. Syndrome can often be recognized at birth due to profound lack of muscle tone; some infants may be unable to move.
3. Other symptoms may include unusual facial characteristics, mental retardation, the inability to suck and swallow, and liver enlargement.
4. Vision problems, hearing problems, and congenital heart lesions occur less commonly.
5. Jaundice, gastrointestinal bleeding, or both due to deficiency of a coagulation factor in the blood can also occur.

Treatment of Zellweger syndrome is symptomatic and supportive. Often a multidisciplinary approach is taken in which pediatric, neurological, ophthalmological, cardiological, and other treatments are combined (Pedianet Disease Database, 2000). Genetic counseling can be of benefit to families with patients with this disorder. Infections should be guarded against carefully to avoid complications. Vitamin K may be needed to avoid abnormal bleeding. Experimental therapies with docosahexaenoic acid (DHA) are being studied. DHA is an essential fatty acid, which is deficient in patients with Zellweger syndrome. Another approach being tested is the administration of bile acids, such as cholic acid or chenodeoxycholic acid, which may be of help in respect to liver function (United Leukodystrophy Foundation, 2000). Supportive treatment may include occupational therapy, physical therapy, hearing aids, and modified nutrition intake.

If the child lives long enough to attend school, special education services for a child with Zellweger syndrome would be necessary on many levels. Because the child is likely to have some form of mental retardation, then the child would need modified education services tailored to his or her educational needs. Furthermore, the child would benefit from physical therapy and perhaps would need services outside the school setting in order to keep the child from acquiring an infection that could lead to death.

The prognosis for individuals with Zellweger syndrome is poor. Death usually occurs within 6 months after onset and may be caused by respiratory distress, gastrointestinal bleeding, or liver failure. Research is currently being done on genetic disorders, including leukodystrophies such as Zellweger syndrome. The goals of this research are to increase scientific understanding of these disorders and to find ways to prevent, treat, and cure them (National Institute of Neurological Disorders and Stroke, 2000).

REFERENCES

National Institute of Neurological Disorders and Stroke. (2000). *Zellweger syndrome.* Retrieved from http://www.ninds.nih.gov/health_and_medical/disorders/zellwege_doc.htm

Pedianet Disease Database. (2000). *Zellweger's syndrome.* Retrieved from www.rarediseases.org

United Leukodystrophy Foundation. (2000). *Zellweger syndrome.* Retrieved from http://www.ulf.org/

SARAH COMPTON
University of Texas at Austin

ZERO INFERENCE

Zero inference is a term that refers to the instructional needs of individuals with severe disabilities (Brown, Nietupski, & Hamre-Nietupski, 1976). Typically, teachers of typically developing students teach a series of core skills using a variety of materials (e.g., counting using wooden cubes). It is assumed that these students will then learn strategies, roles, and concepts necessary to the use of such core skills in other natural settings. It cannot be inferred that individuals with severe disabilities can be taught critical skills in an artificial (i.e., nonnatural) setting using artificial materials and be expected to perform the same skills in more natural settings.

Because of the nature of their mental, physical, or emotional challenges, students with severe disabilities often need educational, social, psychological, or medical services that are beyond those offered in classes for typically developing students. Educational needs are notable in that some students with severe disabilities may have severe language or perceptual-cognitive deficits. They may fail to attend to even pronounced social stimuli and may lack even the most rudimentary forms of verbal control (U.S. Office of Education, 1975). Students with severe disabilities may have the need for intensive instruction in areas including social behavior, communication skills, personal care, mobility and ambulation skills, academic and cognitive behaviors, and vocational skills (Wehman, Renzaglia, & Bates, 1985). Many of the skills required for adaptive performance in postschool environments will need to be taught to students with severe disabilities because of the nature of their performance and cognitive deficits. Such instruction is referred to as the zero-degree inference strategy.

Characteristics of the zero-degree inference strategy of instruction include the belief that no inferences can be made about training a student to perform at a skill level that he or she will be able to use in postschool settings. In order for students with severe disabilities to generalize skills taught in more natural (i.e., nonschool) settings, strategies must be used to ensure that generalization will occur (Stokes & Baer, 1977). Training across multiple settings, materials, and trainers may be included in instruction of students with severe disabilities. General case programming (Horner, Sprague, & Wilcox, 1982), in which common characteristics of several materials or settings are assessed in an effort to teach students a strategy that can be used in a variety of postschool settings, may be used. Additionally, techniques of systematic instruction, including data-based instruction and assessment of student progress, are necessary to ensure the acquisition of usable skills on the part of learners with severe disabilities (Lynch, McGuigan, & Shoemaker, 1977).

Employing training techniques including generalization or general case strategies and systematic instruction will ensure the acquisition of skills that can be used by students with severe disabilities in all necessary environments. Teachers who make zero inferences regarding student performance will be more likely to see success in student performance across situations requiring similar skills.

REFERENCES

Brown, L., Nietupski, J., & Hamre-Nietupski, S. (1976). Criterion of ultimate functioning. In M. A. Thomas (Ed.), *Hey, don't forget about me!* (pp. 2–15). Reston, VA: Council for Exceptional Children.

Horner, R. H., Sprague, J., & Wilcox, B. (1982). General case programming for community activities. In B. Wilcox & G. T. Bellamy (Eds.), *Design for high school programs for severely handicapped students* (pp. 61–68). Baltimore, MD: Brookes.

Lynch, V., McGuigan, C., & Shoemaker, S. (1977). Systematic instruction: Defining the good teacher. In N. Haring (Ed.), *An inservice program for personnel serving the severely handicapped*. Seattle, WA: Experimental Education Unit, University of Washington.

Stokes, T. F., & Baer, D. M. (1977). An implicit technology of generalization. *Journal of Applied Behavior Analysis, 10*, 349–367.

U.S. Office of Education. (1975). *Estimated number of handicapped children in the United States, 1974–75*. Washington, DC: Bureau of Education for the Handicapped.

Wehman, P., Renzaglia, A., & Bates, P. (1985). *Functional living skills for moderately and severely handicapped individuals*. Austin, TX: PRO-ED.

CORNELIA LIVELY
University of Illinois, Urbana-Champaign

See also Self-Contained Class; Self-Help Training; Transfer of Training

ZERO-REJECT

The term *zero-reject* identifies a policy of providing to all handicapped children a free, appropriate, and publicly supported education. The constitutional foundation of zero-reject is the Fourteenth Amendment, which guarantees that no state may deny any person within its "jurisdiction the equal protection of the laws." The courts have interpreted this to mean that no government may deny public services to a person because of his or her unalterable characteristics (e.g., sex, race, age, disability). Advocates of children with handicaps claimed that these children have the same rights to education as children who are not disabled. If a state treats children with disabilities differently (e.g., by denying them the opportunity to attend school, by inappropriately assigning them to a special education program), then it is denying them "equal protection of the laws" on the basis of their unalterable characteristics.

In 1975 Congress noted that over 1 million children with disabilities in the United States were being denied an appropriate public education, and passed PL 94-142, the Education of All Handicapped Children Act, which specified that no child with a handicapping condition (aged 3 to 21) could be excluded from school by recipients of federal funds for the education of children with disabilities. Zero-reject, the mandate to include all children in public schools and to provide an appropriate education for them, represented a new responsibility for public school systems at the time. The policy of zero-reject has remained strong throughout the revisions to PL 94-142, which include the 1990 passage of the Individuals with Disabilities Education Act (IDEA), and the 1997 Amendments to the IDEA.

The law promotes the zero-reject policy by requiring the schools to provide an education that would be meaningful to the child when he or she leaves school, particularly in facilitating the movement of qualified individuals with disabilities into mainstream employment. State education agencies have the responsibility of ensuring the policy of zero-reject, but the rule applies to the state, each school district, private schools, and state-operated programs such as schools for students with visual or hearing impairments.

Judicial interpretation of the zero-reject rule has included the order that students whose behavior is caused by their disability may not be expelled or suspended. The courts have also ordered, under the zero-reject policy, that students with contagious diseases may not be excluded from public education with other students unless there is a high risk that other students will be infected (Turnbull, Turnbull, Shank, & Leal, 1995).

REFERENCE

Turnbull, A. P., Turnbull, H. R., Shank, M., & Leal, D. (1995). *Exceptional lives: Special education in today's schools*. Englewood Cliffs, NJ: Prentice Hall.

CAROLE REITER GOTHELF
Hunter College, City University of New York
First edition

DONNA WALLACE
The University of Texas of the Permian Basin
Second edition

See also Equal Protection; Free Appropriate Public Education; Individuals With Disabilities Education Improvement Act of 2004 (IDEIA)

ZIGLER, EDWARD (1930–   )

Edward Zigler received his BA in history from the University of Missouri at Kansas City in 1954 and his PhD in psychology from the University of Texas, Austin in 1958. He is currently Sterling Professor of Psychology at Yale University, Director of the Bush Center in Child Development and Social Policy, and head of the psychology section of the Child Study Center.

Named by President Carter to chair the 15th anniversary Head Start Committee in 1980, Zigler was a member of the National Planning and Steering Committee for Head Start and was appointed to Head Start's first National Research Council. He was also the first director of the Office of Child Development and Chief of the U.S. Children's Bureau.

The essence of Zigler's work has been the systemic evaluation of experiential, motivational, and personality factors in the behavior of persons diagnosed with intellectual disabilities, and the demonstration of how these factors (delineated by experimental results) affect children with disabilities' performance. He also proposed a classification system for Intellectual Disabilities along two axes: one, individuals would be ordered by IQ and on the other, by organic, familial, and/or undifferentiated etiologies. Zigler believes that beyond any doubt, many of the reported differences between retarded and nonretarded persons of the same MA are a result of motivational and emotional differences that reflect variations in experiential histories (Blatt & Morris, 1984).

Zigler has authored and coauthored over 300 publications in the field including: *Familial Mental Retardation: A continuing dilemma* (1967), and, with D. Balla, *The Social Policy Implications of a Research Program on the Effects of Institutionalization on Retarded Persons* (1977).

The recipient of many awards and honors, Zigler's current research interests are cognitive and social-emotional development in children (particularly those with Intellectual Disabilities), motivational determinants of children's performance, and the applicability of developmental theory to the area of psychopathology.

REFERENCES

Blatt, B., & Morris, R. J. (1984). *Perspectives in special education personal orientations*. Glenview, IL: Scott, Foresman.

Zigler, E. (1967). Familiar mental retardation: A continuing dilemma. *Science, 155*, 292–298.

Zigler, E., & Balla, D. (1977). The social policy implications of a research program on the effects of institutionalization on retarded persons. In P. Mittler (Ed.), *Research to practice in mental retardation* (Vol. 1, pp. 267–281). Baltimore, MD: University Park Press.

ELAINE FLETCHER-JANZEN
Chicago School of Professional Psychology

See also Head Start

ZOLLINGER-ELLISON SYNDROME

Zollinger-Ellison syndrome (ZES) is a rare digestive disorder that can cause tumors in the duodenum (top of small intestine) and pancreas and can cause stomach-duodenal ulcers (Drumm et al., 1988; Kumar & Spitz, 1984). Cancerous tumors secrete serum gastrin, causing the stomach to produce excessive acid, which is responsible for peptic ulcers. The actual cause of ZES is unknown, but it may be associated with an abnormal tumor-suppressing gene.

The prevalence of ZES is unknown. Tumors are cancerous in approximately 40% to 60% of individuals with ZES. Although ZES usually has a middle-age onset, cases have been reported in adolescents and young children. With regard to cognitive effects, sequelae associated with ZES are usually the result of problems seen in individuals suffering from a chronic disease, particularly diseases associated with pancreatic illnesses, as well as side effects associated with treatment or surgery to remove tumors caused by ZES (Drumm et al., 1988; Kumar & Spitz, 1984).

Characteristics

1. Duodenal or pancreatic tumors
2. Peptic ulcers as a result of elevated levels of gastrin
3. Diarrhea, fatigue, and vomiting
4. Weakness and nausea
5. Psychomotor delays

With regard to special education, children and adolescents suffering from ZES usually qualify under an other health impaired label. Future research should focus on finding the cause of ZES and on developing successful treatment interventions.

REFERENCES

Drumm, B., Rhoades, J. M., & Stringer, D. A. (1988). Peptic ulcer disease in children: Etiology, clinical findings, and clinical course. *Pediatrics, 82*, 410.

Kumar, D., & Spitz, L. (1984). Peptic ulceration in children. *Surgery, Gynecology and Obstetrics, 159*, 163.

ANTOLIN M. LLORENTE
Baylor College of Medicine Houston, Texas

ZONE OF PROXIMAL DEVELOPMENT

Zone of proximal development (ZPD) is a concept developed by Vygotsky (1978) that refers to a range of performance that includes the child's current independent performance level as well as the level that the child could perform with the collaboration with an adult or more competent peer. The ZPD is a concept important to learning in general. If the child is approached below the zone, boredom and lessening of motivation could occur. If the child is approached above the zone, frustration can occur. Alternatively, approaching the child within the upper range of the zone facilitates participation and can maximize benefit to the child (e.g., Gray & Feldman, 2004). Maximizing the approach to the upper range of the zone of proximal development is important in extending the range. The adult must have knowledge of the child's interests, strengths, and weaknesses as well as understanding of the best methods that will move the child to more advanced levels of cognitive development (Minick, 1988).

This process of approach and guidance is referred to as scaffolding. The process by which the individual progresses from his or her initial independent learning level to being able to problem solve independently at what was previously attainable only with assistance is facilitated by scaffolding procedures. With scaffolding or assistance, the individual navigates the learning needed to be able to attain a higher level of understanding. The scaffolding process may involve joint problem solving or prompting with the adult gradually decreasing his or her support in the process (Wood, Bruner, & Ross, 1976). Although his theory and the principles associated with it originated many years ago, popularity of the concepts wax and wane along with the emphasis on the sociocultural influences of learning and development (Kozulin, 2004).

ZPD is most often considered with regard to its application to dynamic assessment as an alternative to standard psychometric testing. With dynamic assessment, the focus is not on the level of independent functioning, but rather on identifying the ZPD in which the child can function with assistance (Chaiklin, 2003). Learning potential or emergent psychological functions are seen as equally as important as what has already been mastered and a variety of techniques have been developed for assessment of ZPD (see Lidz & Gindis, 2003).

REFERENCES

Chaiklin, S. (2003). The zone of proximal development in Vygotsky's analysis of learning and instruction. In A. Kozulin, B. Gindis, V. Ageyev, & S. Miller (Eds.), *Vygotsky's educational theory in cultural context* (pp. 39–64). Cambridge, England: Cambridge University Press.

Gray, P., & Feldman, J. (2004). Playing in the zone of proximal development: Qualities of self-directed age mixing between adolescents and young children at a democratic school. *American Journal of Education, 110*(2), 108–146.

Kozulin, A. (2004). Vygotsky'z theory in the classroom: Introduction. *European Journal of Psychology of Education, XIX*, 3–7.

Lidz, C., & Gindis, B. (2003). Dynamic assessment of the evolving cognitive functions in children. In A. Kozulin, B. Gindis, V. Ageyev, & S. Miller (Eds.), *Vygotsky's educational theory in cultural context* (pp. 293–357). Cambridge, England: Cambridge University Press.

Minick, N. (1988). The zone of proximal development and dynamic assessment. In C. S. Lidz (Ed.), *Foundations of dynamic assessment*. New York, NY: Guilford Press.

Vygotsky, L. S. (1978). *Mind in society*. Cambridge, MA: Harvard University Press.

Wood, D. J., Bruner, J. S., & Ross, G. (1976). The role of tutoring in problem-solving. *Journal of Child Psychology and Psychiatry, 172*, 89–100.

CONSTANCE J. FOURNIER
CYNTHIA A. RICCIO
Texas A&M University

See also **Learning Potential; Learning Potential Assessment Device; Theory of Activity; Vygotsky, Lev S.**

Z SCORES, IN DETERMINATION OF DISCREPANCIES

Since the passage of PL 94-142 (Education for all Handicapped Children Act of 1975) several measurement discrepancy models have been recommended in the measurement and special education literature for defining a child as learning disabled (Berk, 1984; Boodoo, 1985; Reynolds et al., 1984; Willson & Reynolds, 1985). These models are all used to estimate the difference between a child's aptitude and achievement and to determine whether such a difference constitutes a severe discrepancy. The models recommended for use involve the use of standard scores. Under each model, a true discrepancy between a subject's aptitude and achievement is estimated using the subject's standard score on the respective aptitude and achievement test. Many of the standardized aptitude and achievement measures used for individualized testing are normed using the standard score scale with a mean (X) of 100 and a standard deviation (S) of 15.

An alternative scale that simplifies the statistical formulas used in the discrepancy models for assessing a severe discrepancy is the Z score scale (Hopkins & Stanley, 1981). This scale has a mean of 0 and a standard deviation of 1 and has the advantage of representing the scores directly in standard deviation units. The following illustrates its use with the simple difference model. Under this model, a difference is defined as [Aptitude (X) – Achievement (Y)] with the standard deviation of this difference, S_D, given by

$$S_D = (S_X^2 + S_Y^2 - 2r_{XY}S_X S_Y)^{1/2}$$

where r_{XY} is the correlation between X and Y. The standard error of estimate of a difference, SE, is given by

$$SE = [S_X^2(1 - r_{XX'}) + S_Y^2(1 - r_{XY'})]^{1/2}$$

where $r_{XX'}$ and $r_{YY'}$, are the reliabilities of X and Y, respectively.

Using the Z score scale, each of the aptitude and achievement scores is converted to the corresponding Z score using

$$Z_X = \frac{X - \overline{X}}{S_X}$$

and

$$Z_Y = \frac{Y - \overline{Y}}{S_Y}$$

Then, a simple difference is $(Z_X - Z_Y)$. The standard deviation of this difference is

$$S_D = (2 - 2r_{XY})^{1/2}$$

where r_{XY} is the correlation between X and Y, and the standard error of estimate is given by

$$SE = (2 - r_{XX'} - r_{YY'})^{1/2}$$

REFERENCES

Berk, R. A. (1984). *Screening and diagnosis of children with learning disabilities.* Springfield, IL: Thomas.

Boodoo, G. M. (1985). A multivariate perspective for aptitude-achievement discrepancy in learning disability assessment. *Journal of Special Education, 18,* 489–499.

Hopkins, K. D., & Stanley, J. C. (1981). *Educational and psychological measurement and evaluation* (6th ed.). Englewood Cliffs, NJ: Prentice Hall.

Reynolds, C. R., Berk, R. A., Boodoo, G. M., Cox, J., Gutkin, T. B., Mann, L., . . . Willson, V. L. (1984). Critical measurement issues in learning disabilities. Report of the USDE, SEP Work Group on Measurement Issues in the Assessment of Learning Disabilities.

Willson, V. L., & Reynolds, C. R. (1985). Another look at evaluating aptitude-achievement discrepancies in the diagnosis of learning disabilities. *Journal of Special Education, 18,* 477–488.

GWYNETH M. BOODOO
Texas A&M University

See also Discrepancy From Grade; Learning Disabilities, Severe Discrepancy Analysis in

ZYGOSITY

Merriam-Webseter defines zygosity as the makeup of characteristics of a particular zygot (zygote is the development of an individual produced from a cell). Zygosity is twinning that may result in monozygotic (MZ), or identical twins, and dizygotic (DZ), or fraternal twins. The cause of MZ twinning remains unknown while the cause of DZ twinning is largely the result of multiple ovulation (Groothuis, 1985). Placentation helps to explain zygosity of twins, where dichorionic placentas take place in all DZ pairs and in about 30% of MZ twins. Monochorionic placentas occur only with MZ twins (Siegel & Siegel, 1982). A twin birth occurs in approximately 1 in 80 pregnancies. For women who already have given birth to twins, the incidence of having a second set rises to 1 in 20. The incidence of MZ twins is 3.5 per 1,000 live births independent of race and maternal age. With maternal age DZ twinning increases. It is slightly more frequent in Blacks and most unusual in Asians (Groothuis, 1985; Siegel & Siegel, 1982).

Twinning is of relevance to special education personnel because there are increased risks for medical, psychological, developmental, and educational problems. Twin pregnancies have been associated with higher rates of such symptoms as nausea and vomiting. The greatly increased mortality of twins at birth (i.e., 15%) has been attributed to the high prematurity rate (i.e., 60%) in terms of both gestation time and birth weight. Twins also experience a higher rate of such perinatal problems as entangling of cords, prolapsed cords, hypoxia anemia, respiratory distress syndrome, and jaundice. These risks are generally higher for MZ twins and the second born of both MZ and DZ twins (Young et al., 1985). Twins also experience congenital anomalies such as heart disease, cleft lip, and cleft palate about twice as frequently as children of single births.

There is a general consensus that twins experience higher rates of developmental and behavioral problems than the general population. Like the medical difficulties, these risks are generally more severe for MZ and second-born twins. During the preschool years, problems are focused in such areas as verbal and motor development, discipline, sharing, toilet training, separation, and individual needs. Many of the problems continue for school-aged twins with classroom assignments, school avoidance, peer relations, and academic performance as special concerns. During adolescence, the identity crisis could be exacerbated for twins who have not resolved separation and individuation issues earlier. Regarding school-related abilities, the degree of impairment has been found to be dependent on birth problems and illness as antecedents (Matheny, Dolan, & Wilson, 1976). Moreover, Matheny et al. reported that twins in comparison with the general population have higher rates of learning disabilities and social immaturity. Siegel and Siegel (1982) point out that IQ deficits are questionable, especially when antecedent and environmental factors are controlled.

Typical recommendations for management and guidance follow: (a) Encourage parents to avoid emphasizing similarities; (b) separate twins at school as soon as possible but delay if problems are encountered; (c) establish individual expectations for school performance; and (d) give psychoeducation assessment to twins with early medical problems. Parents are referred to the National Mother of Twins Club for information and resources.

REFERENCES

Groothuis, J. R. (1985). Twins and twin families. A practical guide to outpatient management. *Clinics in Perinatology*, *12*, 459–474.

Matheny, A. P., Dolan, A. B., & Wilson, R. S. (1976). Twins with academic learning problems: Antecedent characteristics. *American Journal of Orthopsychiatry*, *46*, 464–469.

Merriam-Webster. (2012). *Merriam Webster Dictionary*. Retrieved from http://www.merriam-webster.com/medical/zygote

Siegel, S. J., & Siegel, M. M. (1982). Practical aspects of pediatric management of families with twins. *Pediatrics in Review*, *4*, 8–12.

Young, B. K., Suidan, J., Antoine, C., Silverman, F., Lustig, I., & Wasserman, J. (1985). Differences in twins: The importance of birth order. *American Journal of Obstetrics and Gynecology*, *151*, 915–921.

JOSEPH D. PERRY
Kent State University

See also Siblings of Individuals With Disabilities; Twins